The **Rough Guide** to

South Africa

written and researched by

Tony Pinchuck, Barbara McCrea, Donald Reid and Greg Mthembu-Salter

with additional research by

Carlos Amato, Nicci Joubert-van Doesburgh, Adam and Katrine Musgrave, Lone Mouritsen and Ross Velton

ROUGH GUIDES

NEW YORK · LONDON · DELHI

www.roughguides.com

Contents

The great outdoors
colour section
following p.352

The great indoors
colour section following
p.672

◄◄ Ndebele woman ◄ Baby elephant and mother

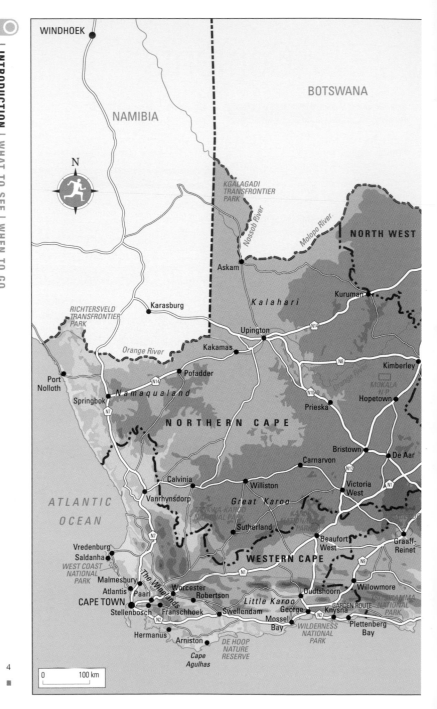

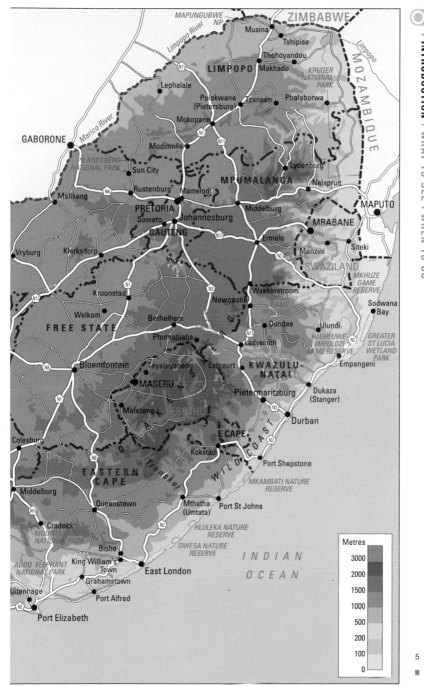

MAPUNGUBWE NP ZIMBABWE

Musina
Tshipise
Thohoyandou
Makhado

LIMPOPO

Limpopo River

KRUGER NATIONAL PARK

MOZAMBIQUE

Lephalale

Polokwane (Pietersburg) Tzaneen Phalaborwa
Mokopane

Limpopo

N1

Modimolle

Marico River

GABORONE

PILANESBERG NATIONAL PARK

Lydenburg

Sun City MPUMALANGA

Mamelodi Nelspruit

Mafikeng Rustenburg N4
PRETORIA
Soweto Johannesburg Middelburg MAPUTO
GAUTENG MBABANE
Klerksdorp Ermelo Siteki
Vryburg N17 Manzini
N3 SWAZILAND
MKHUZE GAME RESERVE

Kroonstad Wakkerstroom
Newcastle
Welkom ITALA GAME RESERVE Sodwana Bay
FREE STATE Bethlehem Dundee
Phuthatijaba Ulundi GREATER ST LUCIA WETLAND PARK
Ladysmith HLUHLUWE IMFOLOZI GAME RESERVE
N12 Estcourt Empangeni
Bloemfontein Teyateyaneng KWAZULU-NATAL
N1 MASERU
Mafeteng Pietermaritzburg Dukaza (Stanger)
N1 LESOTHO N3 Durban
DRAKENSBERG E CAPE
Colesburg Kokstad WILD COAST
Port Shepstone
N6 EASTERN CAPE Transkei
Middelburg MKAMBATI NATURE RESERVE
N10 Queenstown Mthatha (Umtata) Port St Johns
Cradock N2 HLULEKA NATURE RESERVE
MOUNTAIN ZEBRA NATIONAL PARK DWESA NATURE RESERVE
Bisho INDIAN
ADDO ELEPHANT NATIONAL PARK King William's Town OCEAN
Grahamstown East London
Uitenhage
N2 Port Alfred
Port Elizabeth

Metres	
	3000
	2000
	1500
	1000
	500
	200
	100
	0

5

Introduction to

South Africa

South Africa is a large, diverse and incredibly beautiful country. The size of France and Spain combined, and roughly twice the size of Texas, it varies from the picturesque Garden Route towns of the Western Cape to the raw subtropical coast of northern KwaZulu-Natal, with the vast Karoo semi-desert across its heart and one of Africa's premier safari destinations, Kruger National Park, in the northeast. It's also one of the great cultural meeting points of the African continent, a fact obscured by years of enforced racial segregation, but now manifest in the big cities.

Many visitors are pleasantly surprised by South Africa's excellent infrastructure, which draws favourable comparison with countries such as Australia or the United States. Good air links and bus networks, excellent roads and a growing number of first-class B&Bs and guesthouses make South Africa a perfect touring country. For those on a budget, mushrooming backpacker hostels and backpacker buses provide cost-efficient means of exploring.

Yet despite all these facilities, South Africa is also something of an enigma; after so long as an international pariah, the "rainbow nation" is still struggling to find its identity. The country was organized for the benefit of whites, so it's easy to get a very white-oriented experience of Africa. Most of the tourist industry remains white-run and, as a visitor, you'll have to make an effort to meet members of the country's African majority on equal terms. Apartheid may be dead, but its heritage still shapes South Africa in a very physical way. Nowhere is this more in evidence than in the layout of towns and cities, the African areas – often desperately poor – are usually tucked out of sight.

South Africa's **population** doesn't reduce simply to black and white. The majority are **Africans** (79.5 percent of the population); **whites** make up 9 percent, followed by **coloureds** (just under 9 percent) – the descendants

Fact file

• Covering 1,219,090 square kilometres, South Africa has a **population** of 48 million and eleven official **languages**: Zulu, Xhosa, Afrikaans, Pedi, English, Ndebele, Sotho, Setswana, siSwati, Venda and Tsonga. The country's **religions** comprise Christianity (68 percent), Islam (2 percent), Hinduism (1.5 percent) and indigenous beliefs (28.5 percent).

• South Africa is a **multiparty democracy,** the head of state being President Thabo Mbeki. Parliament sits in Cape Town, the **legislative capital,** while Pretoria is the **executive capital,** from where the President and his cabinet run the country. The **judicial capital** is Bloemfontein, where the Supreme Court of Appeal sits, though the Constitutional Court is in Johannesburg. Each of the nine provinces has its own government.

• South Africa has the most advanced **economy** in Africa, with well-developed mining, manufacturing, agricultural and financial sectors. The country also has one of the greatest disparities of wealth in the world.

• **Lesotho** covers 30,355 square kilometres and has a population of 2 million. It is a constitutional monarchy, with King Letsie III as its head. The official languages are Sesotho and English.

• The kingdom of **Swaziland**, ruled by King Mswati III, has an area of 17,363 square kilometres and a population of 1 million. The official languages are siSwati and English.

of white settlers, slaves and Africans, who speak English and Afrikaans and comprise the majority in the Western Cape. The remainder (2.5 percent) is comprised of **Indians**, who came to South Africa at the beginning of the twentieth century as indentured labourers; most of the Indian community live in KwaZulu-Natal.

Even these statistics don't tell the whole story. A better indication of South Africa's diversity is the plethora of official languages, most of which represent a distinct culture with rural roots in different parts of the country. In each region you'll see distinct styles of architecture, craftwork and sometimes dress. Perhaps more exciting still are the cities, where the whole country comes together in an alchemical blend of rural and urban, traditional and thoroughly modern.

Crime isn't the indiscriminate phenomenon that press reports suggest, but it is an issue. Really, it's a question of perspective – taking care but not becoming paranoid. Statistically, the odds of becoming a victim are highest in downtown Johannesburg, where violent crime is a daily reality. Other cities present a reduced risk – similar to, say, some parts of the United States.

▲ Beach huts, St James

Where to go

While you could circuit the whole of South Africa in a matter of weeks, a more satisfying approach is to focus your attention on one section of the country. Every one of the nine provinces (plus Lesotho and Swaziland) holds at least a couple of compelling reasons to visit, although, depending on the time of year and your interests, you'd be wise to concentrate on either the **west** or the **east**.

The **west**, best visited in the warmer months (Nov–April), has the outstanding attraction of **Cape Town**, worth experiencing for its matchless setting beneath Table Mountain, at the foot of the continent. Half a day's drive from here can take you to any other destination in the **Western Cape**, a province which owes its distinctive character to the fact that it has the longest-established colonial heritage in the country. You'll find gabled Cape Dutch architecture, historic towns and vineyard-covered mountains in the **Winelands**; forested coast along the **Garden Route**; and a dry interior punctuated by Afrikaner dorps (towns) in the **Little Karoo**.

▲ Johannesburg

House of the spirits

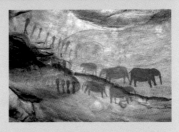

For thousands of years, San Bushman shamans in South Africa decorated rock faces with powerful religious images. These finely realized paintings, found in mountainous areas across South Africa, include animals, people, and humans changing into animals. Archeologists now regard the images as metaphors for religious experiences, one of the most significant of which is the healing trance dance, still practised by the few surviving Bushman communities. Rockfaces can be seen as portals between the human and spiritual world: when we gaze at Bushman rock art, we are looking into the house of the spirits.

If the west sounds a bit too pretty and you're after a more "African" experience, head for the **eastern** flank of the country, best visited in the cooler months (May–Oct). **Johannesburg** is likely to be your point of entry to this area: its frenetic street life, soaring office blocks and lively mix of people make it quite unlike anywhere else in the country. Half a day away by car lie **Limpopo** and **Mpumalanga** provinces, which share the mighty **Kruger National Park**. Of South Africa's roughly two dozen major parks, the Kruger attracts the largest number of first-time visitors, and is unrivalled on the continent for its cross section of mammal species.

> **Kruger National Park is unrivalled on the continent for its cross section of mammal species**

A visit to Kruger combines perfectly with KwaZulu-Natal to the south, and an excellent short cut is to drive through tiny, landlocked **Swaziland**, which has attractions all of its own: a unique Swazi culture and a number of well-managed game parks. **KwaZulu-Natal** itself offers superb game and birdlife; **Hluhluwe-Imfolozi Park** is the best place in the world to see endangered rhinos and there are several other outstanding small game reserves nearby, such as Ithala, Mkhuze and Ndumo. For hiking and nature, nothing rivals the soaring **Drakensberg** range. After Cape Town, **Durban** remains the only

◀ Penguins, Boulder's beach

9
■

city in South Africa worth visiting in its own right: a busy cultural melting pot with a bustling Indian district and lively beachfront. The long stretch of **beaches** north and south of Durban is the most developed in the country, but north towards the Mozambique border lies the wildest stretch of coast in South Africa.

Long sandy **beaches**, developed only in pockets, are characteristic of much of the 2500km of shoreline that curves from the cool Atlantic along the Northern Cape round to the subtropical Indian Ocean that foams onto KwaZulu-Natal's shores. **Jeffrey's Bay** on the **Eastern Cape** coast is reputed to be one of the world's top **surfing** spots. Much of the Eastern Cape coast is equally appealing, whether you just want to stroll, sunbathe or take in backdrops of mountains and hulking sand dunes. **Scuba diving**, especially in KwaZulu-Natal, opens up a world of coral reefs rich with colourful fish, and south of the Western Cape winelands, along the **Whale Coast**, is one of South Africa's unsung attractions – some of the best shore-based **whale-watching** in the world.

> In each region you'll see distinct styles of architecture, craftwork and sometimes dress.

The Cape Floral Kingdom

To an untrained eye much of the vegetation along South Africa's southern coastal strip is nondescript, scraggly and generally unremarkable. Closer examination reveals an enormous diversity of textures, colours and flowering plants, the most obvious and impressive of which is the **King Protea** (*Protea cynaroides*).

Aesthetics aside, scientists regard the so-called Cape Floral Kingdom as highly significant, since it harbours the third highest level of biodiversity on Earth and because over thirty percent of its plant species are found only in small localized pockets – the highest level of plant endemism on the planet.

While *fynbos* dominates, the Cape Kingdom also consists of other biomes in a relatively compact area stretching from just north of Cape Town to just west of Port Elizabeth, making it the smallest, by miles, of the world's six floral kingdoms and the only one to be restricted to a single country.

Recognizing its importance, in 2004 UNESCO listed the Cape Floral Region as a World Heritage Site, consisting of eight protected areas which include Table Mountain and Cape Town's Kirstenbosch, the first botanical garden to be so designated.

With time in hand, you might want to drive through the sparse but exhilarating **interior**, with its open horizons, switchback mountain passes, rocks, scrubby vegetation and isolated dorps. The **Northern Cape** and **North West Province** can reveal surprises. Visit the western section of the Northern Cape in August or September, and you'll be treated to a riot of colourful **wild flowers**. From the staunchly Afrikaner heartland of **Free State**, you're well poised to visit the undeveloped kingdom of **Lesotho**, set in the mountains between the Free State and KwaZulu-Natal. Lesotho has few vestiges of royalty left today, but it does offer plenty of spectacular highland scenery, best explored on a sturdy, sure-footed Basotho pony.

When to go

South Africa is a predominantly sunny country, but when it does get cold you really feel it – indoor heating is limited, and everything is geared to fine weather. You'll need to pack with the weather in mind, especially in winter. Southern hemisphere seasons are the reverse of those in the north, with **midwinter** occurring in June and July and **midsummer** over December and January, when the country shuts down for its annual holiday.

South Africa has distinct climatic zones. **Cape Town** and the **Garden Route** coastal belt have a so-called Mediterranean climate, moderated by winds blowing in from the South Atlantic. Summers tend to be warm, mild and unpredictable; rain can fall at any time of the year and winter days can be cold and wet. Many Capetonians regard March to May as the perfect season,

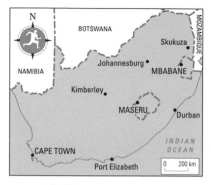

when the nagging winds drop, it's beautifully mild and the tourists have all gone home. Subtropical **KwaZulu-Natal** has warm, sunny winters, coral reefs and tepid seas; the province's Drakensberg range sees misty days in summer and mountain snow in winter. **Johannesburg** and **Pretoria** lie on the highveld plateau and have a near-perfect climate; summer days are hot, with none of the humidity of the KwaZulu-Natal coast, while the winters are dry with chilly nights. East of Johannesburg, the **lowveld**, the low-lying wedge along the Mozambique border that includes the **Kruger National Park**, is subject to similar summer and winter rainfall patterns to the highveld, but experiences far greater extremes of temperature because of its considerably lower altitude.

Average daily maximum temperatures

	Jan	Feb	Mar	Apr	May	June	July	Aug	Sept	Oct	Nov	Dec
Cape Town												
°C	27	27	26	23	20	19	17	18	19	22	24	26
°F	81	81	79	73	68	66	63	64	66	72	75	79
Durban												
°C	27	28	27	26	24	23	22	22	23	24	25	26
°F	81	82	81	79	75	73	72	72	73	75	77	79
Johannesburg												
°C	26	26	24	22	19	16	16	20	23	25	25	26
°F	79	79	75	72	66	61	61	68	73	77	77	79
Kimberley												
°C	33	31	28	25	21	19	19	22	25	28	30	32
°F	91	88	82	77	70	66	66	72	77	82	86	90
Port Elizabeth												
°C	25	26	25	23	22	20	20	20	20	21	22	24
°F	77	79	77	73	72	68	68	68	68	70	72	75
Skukuza (Kruger National Park)												
°C	31	31	30	29	27	25	25	26	29	29	30	30
°F	88	88	86	84	81	77	77	79	84	84	86	86
Maseru (Lesotho)												
°C	20	17	14	11	9	7	7	9	11	14	17	20
°F	68	63	57	52	48	45	45	48	52	57	63	68
Mbabane (Swaziland)												
°C	25	25	24	23	21	19	19	21	23	24	24	25
°F	77	77	75	73	70	66	66	70	73	75	75	77

28

things not to miss

It's not possible to see everything that South Africa has to offer in one trip – and we don't suggest you try. What follows is a selective and subjective taste of the country's highlights, including outstanding national parks, spectacular wildlife, adventure sports and beautiful architecture. They're arranged in five colour-coded categories to help you find the very best things to see, do and experience. All entries have a page reference to take you straight into the guide, where you can find out more.

01 The Drakensberg Page **499** • Hike in the mysterious "dragon mountains", which harbour South Africa's highest peaks, plus waterfalls, gorges, Bushman rock art and awesome panoramas.

02 Richtersveld Transfrontier
Page **359** • Fierce, rugged and hot, the Richtersveld offers some of the most dramatic mountainscape in the country, sparsely populated by science-fiction vegetation.

03 Indian culture Page **458** •
Durban, Africa's busiest port, boasts a large Indian population.

04 Wild flowers Page **348** • Following the winter rains, Namaqualand's normally bleak landscape explodes with colour in one of nature's most brilliant floral displays.

05 Cape Point Page **154** • The rocky promontory south of Cape Town, angry seas crashing on either side, is one of the most dramatic coastal locations on the continent.

06 **De Hoop Nature Reserve** Page **249** • Slide down mountainous dunes or watch whales from the high vantage point they provide.

07 **Whale-watching** Page **236** • Regularly visiting the southern Cape Coast, whales often approach surprisingly close to the shore.

08 **The Sani Pass** Page **773** • The most precipitous pass in southern Africa, connecting Lesotho to neighbouring KwaZulu-Natal, is also the most thrilling to drive down.

10 **Madikwe Game Reserve** Page **654** • This massive game park sees remarkably few visitors, yet boasts excellent lodges and superb wildlife-spotting opportunities, from wild dogs to lions and elephants.

09 **Robben Island** Page **129** • Just half an hour from Cape Town is the notorious offshore jail where political prisoners, including Nelson Mandela, were incarcerated.

11 **The Bulungula Lodge** Page **435** • At a beautiful river mouth on the Wild Coast, this backpacker lodge offers an all-too-rare opportunity to experience rural African life.

12 **Soweto** Page **605** • A tour around the vast, sprawling township – South Africa's largest – provides a graphic idea of how the majority of black South Africans live.

13 **Hluhluwe-Imfolozi Park** Page **514** • KwaZulu-Natal's finest game reserve offers an unsurpassed variety of wildlife-spotting activities, from night drives to self-guided walks and even donkey trails.

14 **Vernacular architecture** Page **564** • Beautifully decorative Basotho huts are characteristic of the eastern Free State's Highlands Route.

15 **Addo Elephant National Park** Page 377 • Encounter elephants and the rest of the Big Five at the eastern end of the Garden Route.

17 **Gamkaskloof** Page 222 • Go to Hell (Die Hel) down one of the spectacular passes of the Little Karoo, providing exciting drives and mountain biking.

16 **Storms River Mouth** Page 288 • The Garden Route's most spectacular coastline, where you can cross the dramatic Storms River Mouth via a suspension footbridge.

18 **Pony-trekking** Page 751 • The perfect way to experience the ruggedly beautiful "mountain kingdom" of Lesotho.

I ACTIVITIES I CONSUME I EVENTS I NATURE I SIGHTS I

20 Wine routes Page **184** • The Western Cape's wine estates combine stunning scenery, Cape Dutch architecture and some fine and affordable vintages.

19 The Wild Coast Page **425** • This part of the Eastern Cape offers peace and seclusion along a remote and spectacular subtropical coastline.

22 Live music Page **612** • Johannesburg offers the best nightlife in South Africa, attracting top musical performers from around the country and abroad.

21 Rafting Page **815** • Swaziland's Great Usutu River offers some of the most exciting whitewater rafting in southern Africa.

23 Kruger National Park Page **690** • Get spine-tinglingly close to lions and other big game at Southern Africa's ultimate wildlife destination.

24 **Game trails** Page **702** • Combine adventure with wildlife-spotting on a guided hike in the mighty Kruger National Park.

26 **The Bo-Kaap** Page **121** • The streets of Cape Town's oldest residential area are filled with colourful Cape Dutch and Georgian architecture.

28 **Kgalagadi Transfrontier Park** Page **340** • View cheetahs and other desert dwellers amid the harsh beauty of the Kalahari.

25 **Table Mountain cableway** Page **141** • The most spectacular way to ascend Cape Town's famous landmark is also the easiest – the revolving cable car.

27 **Traditional arts and crafts** Page **73** • Traditional handicrafts make useful and beautiful souvenirs in rural and urban areas alike, such as the Venda region of Limpopo.

The wildlife of Southern Africa

This field guide provides a quick reference to help you identify the mammals likely to be encountered in Southern Africa. It includes most species that are found throughout these regions, as well as a number whose range is more restricted. The photos show easily identified markings and features. The notes give clear pointers about the kinds of habitat in which you are most likely to see each mammal; its daily rhythm (usually either nocturnal or diurnal); the kind of social groups it usually forms; and general tips concerning its distribution, sighting it on safari and its relations with humans. For further details and background, see p.844.

✿ HABITAT ◖ DAILY RHYTHM ❦ SOCIAL LIFE ✓ SIGHTING TIPS

Baboon *Papio cynocephalus*

🦋 open country with trees and cliffs; adaptable, but always near water

◖ diurnal

🔆 troops led by a dominant male

✓ common (found across the whole of South Africa and can be seen in most reserves); easily becomes used to humans, frequently a nuisance and occasionally dangerous; very good chance of sightings in the Cape of Good Hope section of Table Mountain National Park

Vervet monkey

Cercopithecus aethiops

🦋 most habitats except rainforest and arid lands; arboreal and terrestrial

◖ diurnal

🔆 troops

✓ found in virtually every game reserve in North West, Limpopo, Mpumalanga and KwaZulu-Natal provinces, as well as along the coast as far west as Mossel Bay; occasionally a nuisance where used to humans

Samango monkey *Cercopithecus mitis*

🦋 forests; arboreal and occasionally terrestrial

◖ diurnal

🔆 families or small troops

✓ found in isolated pockets of forest in Eastern Cape, KwaZulu-Natal and Mpumalanga; shyer and less easily habituated to humans than the vervet

Lesser bushbaby *Galago moholi*

🦋 woodland savanna and riverine woodland

◖ nocturnal

🔆 small family groups

✓ found in Limpopo, Mpumalanga and the eastern part of North West province; generally forage in trees jumping large distances from branch to branch; at 30–40cm from head to tail, it's about half the length of the thick-tailed bushbaby (*Otolemur crassicaudatus*), found in Mpumalanga

---

🦋 HABITAT ◖ DAILY RHYTHM 🔆 SOCIAL LIFE ✓ SIGHTING TIPS

Aardvark *Orycteropus afer*

❀ open or wooded termite country; softer soil preferred

◑ nocturnal

🌱 solitary

✓ found throughout South Africa, though rarely seen; the size of a small pig; old burrows are common and often used by warthogs

Spring hare *Pedetes capensis*

❀ savanna; softer soil areas preferred

◑ nocturnal

🌱 burrows, usually with a pair and their young; often linked into a network, almost like a colony

✓ rabbit-sized rodent, found in Northern Cape, Eastern Cape, Free State, North West and Limpopo provinces; impressive and unmistakable kangaroo-like leaper

Porcupine *Hystrix africae-australis*

❀ adaptable to a wide range of habitats

◑ nocturnal and sometimes active at dusk

🌱 family groups

✓ large rodent (up to 90cm in length), rarely seen, but common away from croplands, where it's hunted as a pest; found in South Africa, Lesotho and Swaziland

Bat-eared fox *Otocyon megalotis*

❀ open country

◑ mainly nocturnal; diurnal activity increases in cooler months

🌱 monogamous pairs

✓ found in the western half of South Africa up to (but excluding) Lesotho, and in the areas bordering the Zimbabwe and Botswana borders; distribution coincides with termites, their favoured diet; they spend many hours foraging using sensitive hearing to pinpoint their underground prey

❀ HABITAT ◑ DAILY RHYTHM 🌱 SOCIAL LIFE ✓ SIGHTING TIPS

Blackbacked jackal *Canis mesomelas*

 broad range from moist mountain regions to desert, but drier areas preferred

 normally nocturnal, but diurnal in the safety of game reserves

mostly monogamous pairs; sometimes family groups

✓ common throughout Southern Africa; a bold scavenger, the size of a small dog, that steals even from lions; black saddle distinguishes it from the shyer side-striped jackal

---

Wild dog *Lycaon pictus*

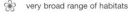 open savanna in the vicinity of grazing herds

● diurnal

nomadic packs

✓ one of the most endangered large predators in South Africa, with just a few packs surviving in the wild; found in Kruger, Hluhluwe-Imfolozi, Madikwe and Pilanesberg reserves; rarely seen, but widely noted when in the area; the size of a large dog, with distinctively rounded ears

---

Honey badger *Mellivora capensis*

very broad range of habitats

● mainly nocturnal

usually solitary, but also found in pairs

✓ widespread (though nowhere common) throughout the region except in Free State and Lesotho; omnivorous, badger-sized animal; extremely aggressive

---

Civet *Civettictis civetta*

prefers woodland and dense vegetation

● mainly nocturnal

 solitary

✓ omnivorous, medium-dog-sized, short-legged prowler; found in Limpopo, Mpumalanga and eastern North West province; not to be confused with the smaller genet

Small-spotted genet *Genetta genetta*

❀ light bush country, even arid areas; partly arboreal

◑ nocturnal, but becomes active at dusk

✿ solitary

✓ quite common, slender, cat-sized omnivore found throughout South Africa except KwaZulu-Natal; often seen at game lodges, where it easily becomes habituated to humans; has a white tail tip, in contrast to the otherwise similar, less widely distributed large-spotted genet (*G. tigrina*), which has a black tail tip

Banded mongoose *Mungos mungo*

❀ thick bush and dry forest

◑ diurnal

✿ lives in burrow colonies of up to thirty animals

✓ over a dozen mongoose species in the region, between them ranging across all of South Africa, Limpopo and Swaziland; the size of a small cat; often seen in a group, hurriedly foraging through the undergrowth

Spotted hyena *Crocuta crocuta*

❀ tolerates a wide variety of habitat, with the exception of dense forest

◑ nocturnal but also active at dusk; also diurnal in many parks

✿ highly social, usually living in extended family groups

✓ the size of a large dog with a distinctive loping gait, quite common in Kruger, Hluhluwe-Imfolozi, Kgalakgadi and Addo; carnivorous scavenger and cooperative hunter; dangerous

Caracal *Caracal caracal*

❀ open bush and plains; occasionally arboreal

◑ mostly nocturnal

✿ solitary

✓ lynx-like wild cat; rarely seen, though it is found throughout the region except in KwaZulu-Natal; most likely to be seen in the Cape of Good Hope section of Table Mountain National Park, and in Mountain Zebra, Kruger and Kgalagadi parks

❀ HABITAT ◑ DAILY RHYTHM ✿ SOCIAL LIFE ✓ SIGHTING TIPS

Cheetah *Acionyx jubatus*

 savanna, in the vicinity of plains grazers

● diurnal

 solitary or temporary nuclear family groups

✓ found in Kruger, Hluhluwe-Imfolozi and Kgalagadi reserves; much slighter build than the leopard, and distinguished from it by a small head, square snout and dark "tear mark" running from eye to jowl

Leopard *Panthera pardus*

 highly adaptable; frequently arboreal

● nocturnal; also cooler daylight hours

 solitary

✓ the size of a very large dog; not uncommon, but shy and usually infrequently seen; found in Limpopo, North West and Mpumalanga provinces (it's often seen in the Sabi Sands reserve adjoining Kruger) as well as in mountainous regions from KwaZulu-Natal to the Western Cape; rests in thick undergrowth or up trees; very dangerous

Lion *Panthera leo*

 all habitats except desert and thick forest

● nocturnal and diurnal

 prides of three to forty; more usually six to twelve

✓ found in major game reserves including Kruger, Kgalagadi, Hluhluwe-Imfolozi and Addo; commonly seen resting in shade; dangerous

Serval *Felis serval*

 reed beds or tall grassland near water

● normally nocturnal but more diurnal than most cats

 usually solitary

✓ found in KwaZulu-Natal, Limpopo, Mpumalanga and North West provinces; some resemblance to, but far smaller than, the cheetah; most likely to be seen on roadsides or water margins at dawn or dusk

Dassie or rock hyrax *Procavia capensis*

🏵 rocky areas, from mountains to isolated outcrops

◖ diurnal

🐾 colonies consisting of a territorial male with as many as thirty related females

✓ found throughout the region, except in Northern Cape and the KwaZulu-Natal coastal belt; very likely to be spotted on Table Mountain and in the Tsitsikamma National Park; rabbit-sized; often seen sunning themselves in the early morning on rocks

African elephant *Loxodonta africana*

🏵 wide range of habitats, wherever there are trees and water

◖ nocturnal and diurnal; sleeps as little as four hours a day

🐾 almost human in its complexity; cows and offspring in herds headed by a matriarch; bulls solitary or in bachelor herds

✓ found in Kruger, Pilanesberg, Hluhluwe-Imfolozi and Addo reserves; look out for fresh dung (football-sized) and recently damaged trees; frequently seen at water holes from late afternoon

Black rhinoceros *Diceros bicornis*

🏵 usually thick bush, altitudes up to 3500m

◖ active day and night, resting between periods of activity

🐾 solitary

✓ found in Kruger, Addo, Hluhluwe-Imfolozi, Ithala and Mkhuze reserves, though extremely rare and in critical danger of extinction; largely confined to parks where most individuals are known to rangers; distinctive hooked lip for browsing; small head usually held high; bad eyesight; very dangerous

White rhinoceros *Ceratotherium simum*

🏵 savanna

◖ active day and night, resting between periods of activity

🐾 mother/s and calves, or small, same-sex herds of immature animals; old males solitary

✓ rare, restricted to Kruger, Hluhluwe-Imfolozi, Ithala and Mkhuze reserves; distinctive wide mouth (hence "white" from Dutch *wijd*) for grazing; large head usually lowered; docile

🏵 HABITAT   ◖ DAILY RHYTHM   🐾 SOCIAL LIFE   ✓ SIGHTING TIPS

Burchell's zebra *Equus burchelli*

- savanna, with or without trees, up to 4500m
- active day and night, resting intermittently
- harems of several mares and foals led by a dominant stallion are usually grouped together, in herds of up to several thousand
- ✓ found in the major reserves of Mpumalanga and KwaZulu-Natal, and has been reintroduced into reserves and on farms throughout South Africa; distinguished from the far rarer Cape mountain zebra (*E. zebra zebra*) by the presence of shadow stripes in Burchell's

---

Warthog *Phacochoerus aethiopicus*

- savanna, up to an altitude of over 2000m
- diurnal
- family groups, usually of a female and her litter
- ✓ found in the northeast along the border with Botswana and in northern KwaZulu-Natal; boars are distinguishable from sows by their prominent face "warts"

Hippopotamus *Hippopotamus amphibius*

- slow-flowing rivers, dams and lakes
- principally nocturnal, leaving the water to graze
- bulls are solitary, but other animals live in family groups headed by a matriarch
- ✓ found in Kruger National Park, northern KwaZulu-Natal and in odd pockets throughout the country; usually seen by day in water, with top of head and ears breaking the surface; frequently aggressive and very dangerous when threatened or when retreat to water is blocked

---

Giraffe *Giraffa camelopardalis*

- wooded savanna and thorn country
- diurnal
- loose, non-territorial, leaderless herds
- ✓ found in the northeast of South Africa, with Kruger National Park the best place to see them

Buffalo *Syncerus caffer*

wide range of habitats, always near water, up to altitudes of 4000m

nocturnal and diurnal, but inactive during the heat of the day

found in Kruger, Hluhluwe-Imfolozi, Addo and Mountain Zebra reserves, and many conservation areas throughout the country; gregarious, with cows and calves in huge herds; young bulls often form small bachelor herds; old bulls are usually solitary

✓ very common; scent much more acute than other senses; very dangerous, old bulls especially so

Hartebeest *Alcelaphus buselaphus*

wide range of grassy habitats

diurnal

females and calves in small, wandering herds; territorial males solitary

✓ restricted to pockets of Mpumalanga and the Northern Cape; hard to confuse with any other antelope except the tsessebe

Blue wildebeest *Connochaetes taurinus*

grasslands

diurnal, occasionally also nocturnal

intensely gregarious in a wide variety of associations from small groups to sizeable herds

✓ found in Kruger National Park, KwaZulu-Natal province and in conservation areas throughout South Africa; unmistakable, nomadic grazer; long tail, mane and beard; often seen in association with zebras

Bontebok *Damaliscus dorcas dorcas*

coastal plain where Cape fynbos occurs

diurnal

rams hold territories; ewes and lamb herds numbering up to ten wander freely between territories

✓ found in two national parks, namely Bontebok and the Cape of Good Hope section of Table Mountain, and also in the De Hoop Nature Reserve (largest single population); bears resemblance to tsessebe and hartebeest, but is distinguished by its chocolate brown colouring and white facial and rump markings

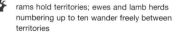

HABITAT   DAILY RHYTHM   SOCIAL LIFE   ✓ SIGHTING TIPS

Tsessebe *Damaliscus lunatus*

- 🏵 grasslands, showing a marked preference for moist savanna, near water

- ◑ diurnal

- 🐾 females and young form herds with an old male

- ✓ restricted to northern parts of South Africa bordering Botswana and Mozambique; very fast runners; male often stands sentry on an abandoned termite hill, actually marking the territory against rivals, rather than defending against predators

Springbok *Antidorcas marsupalis*

- 🏵 arid plains

- ◑ seasonally variable, but usually cooler times of day

- 🐾 highly gregarious, sometimes in thousands; various herding combinations of males, females and young

- ✓ wild in the Northern Cape, but farmed all over South Africa; medium-sized, delicately built gazelle; dark line through eye to mouth and lyre-shaped pair of horns in both sexes

Impala *Aepyceros melampus*

- 🏵 open savanna near light woodland cover

- ◑ diurnal

- 🐾 large herds of females overlap with several male territories; males highly territorial during the rut when they separate out breeding harems of up to twenty females

- ✓ common, medium-sized, no close relatives; distinctive high leaps when fleeing; the only antelope with a black tuft above the hooves; males have long, lyre-shaped horns

Reedbuck *Redunca arundinum*

- 🏵 reedbeds and tall grass near water

- ◑ nocturnal and diurnal

- 🐾 monogamous pairs or family groups in territory defended by the male

- ✓ medium-sized antelope, with a plant diet unpalatable to other herbivores; only males have horns

---

🏵 HABITAT   ◑ DAILY RHYTHM   🐾 SOCIAL LIFE   ✓ SIGHTING TIPS

Waterbuck *Kobus ellipsiprymnus*

* open woodland and savanna, near water

* nocturnal and diurnal

* territorial herds of females and young, led by dominant male, or territorial males visited by wandering female herds

✓ common, rather tame, large antelope found in Kruger National Park, the Greater St Lucia Wetland Park and along the Limpopo river; their plant diet is unpalatable to other herbivores; shaggy coat; only males have horns

---

Common duiker *Sylvicapra grimmia*

* adaptable; prefers scrub and bush

* nocturnal and diurnal

* most commonly solitary; sometimes in pairs; occasionally monogamous

✓ widespread and common small antelope with a rounded back; seen close to cover; rams have short, straight horns

---

Nyala *Tragelaphus angasi*

* dense woodland near water

* primarily nocturnal with some diurnal activity

* flexible and non-territorial; the basic unit is a female and two offspring

✓ Kruger National Park and northeastern KwaZulu-Natal province; midway in size between the lesser kudu and bushbuck, and easily mistaken for the latter; orange legs distinguish it; only males have horns

---

Bushbuck *Tragelaphus scriptus*

* thick bush and woodland close to water

* principally nocturnal, but also active during the day when cool

* solitary, but casually sociable; sometimes grazes in small groups

✓ found in KwaZulu-Natal, Limpopo, North West, Mpumalanga provinces, and also on the southern coast of South Africa; medium-sized antelope with white stripes and spots; often seen in thickets, or heard crashing through them; not to be confused with the larger nyala; the male has shortish straight horns

🌸 HABITAT   🌓 DAILY RHYTHM   ✸ SOCIAL LIFE   ✓ SIGHTING TIPS

Eland *Taurotragus oryx*

 highly adaptable; semi-desert to mountains, but prefers scrubby plains

nocturnal and diurnal

non-territorial herds of up to sixty with temporary gatherings of as many as a thousand

✓ found in the Ukhahlamba Drakensberg, Kgalagadi Transfrontier and Kruger parks; common but shy; the largest and most powerful African antelope; both sexes have straight horns with a slight spiral

Kudu *Tragelaphus strepsiceros*

semi-arid, hilly or undulating bush country; tolerant of drought

diurnal when secure; otherwise nocturnal

territorial; males usually solitary; females in small troops with young

✓ found in northern Limpopo and North West provinces, and in Mpumalanga, eastern Swaziland and northeastern Kwazulu-Natal, with isolated pockets in the Eastern and Western Cape; impressively big antelope (up to 1.5m at shoulder) with very long, spiral horns in the male; shy and not often seen

Gemsbok *Oryx gazella gazella*

 open grasslands; also waterless wastelands; tolerant of prolonged drought

nocturnal and diurnal

highly hierarchical mixed herds of up to fifteen, led by a dominant bull

✓ large antelope found in Kgalagadi Transfrontier Park, with unmistakable horns in both sexes; subspecies gazella is one of several similar forms, sometimes considered separate species

Roan antelope *Hippotragus equinus*

tall grassland near water

nocturnal and diurnal; peak afternoon feeding

small herds led by a dominant bull; herds of immature males; sometimes pairs in season

✓ large antelope found in Kruger National Park; distinguished from the sable by lighter, greyish colour, shorter horns (both sexes) and narrow, tufted ears

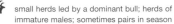

🌸 HABITAT ◖ DAILY RHYTHM 🌿 SOCIAL LIFE ✓ SIGHTING TIPS

Sable antelope *Hippotragus niger*

🏵 open woodland with medium to tall grassland near water

◐ nocturnal and diurnal

🌿 territorial; bulls divide into sub-territories, through which cows and young roam; herds of immature males; sometimes pairs in season

✓ large antelope found in Kruger National Park; upper body dark brown to black; mask-like markings on the face; both sexes have huge curved horns

Oribi *Ourebia ourebi*

🏵 open grassland

◐ diurnal

🌿 territorial harems consisting of male and one to four females

✓ small antelope localized to small pockets of KwaZulu-Natal, though not hard to see where found; only males have horns; the oribi is distinguished from the smaller grysbok and steenbok by a black tail and dark skin patch below the eye

Steenbok *Raphicerus campestris*

🏵 dry savanna

◐ nocturnal and diurnal

🌿 solitary or (less often) in pairs

✓ widespread small antelope, but shy; only males have horns

Klipspringer *Oreotragus oreotragus*

🏵 rocky country; cliffs and kopjes

◐ diurnal

🌿 territorial ram with mate or small family group; often restricted to small long-term territories

✓ small antelope inhabiting mountainous areas throughout the region; horns normally only on male; extremely agile on rocky terrain; unusually high hooves, giving the impression of walking on tiptoe

🏵 HABITAT ◐ DAILY RHYTHM 🌿 SOCIAL LIFE ✓ SIGHTING TIPS

Basics

Basics

Getting there

As sub-Saharan Africa's economic and tourism hub, South Africa is well served with flights from London and the rest of Europe. By far the majority of these touch down at Johannesburg's OR Tambo International, but there are also frequent flights into Cape Town. From North America and Australia there are only a few direct flights into Johannesburg.

Airfares always depend on the **season**, with the highest prices and greatest demand occurring in June, July, August, December and the first week of January. Prices drop during the "shoulder" season in May and September. You get the best prices during the low season in October, November and the last three weeks of January till March.

Flights from the UK and Ireland

From London there are nonstop flights with British Airways, South African Airways, Virgin Atlantic and Nationwide to Johannesburg, and all except Nationwide also fly nonstop to Cape Town. Flying time from the UK is around 11 hours to Jo'burg (about an hour longer to Cape Town) and average high/low scheduled direct fares from London are £850/650, but you can save up to £200 by flying via mainland Europe, Africa or Asia, and enduring at least one change of plane.

From the Republic of Ireland a number of European carriers fly to South Africa via their hub airports, while in high season there are direct charter flights to Cape Town operated by Slattery's Sun (see the listing under "Agents and operators" on p.41).

Flights from the US and Canada

From the US there are daily non-stop flights from **Washington** and one-stop flights from

New York via Dakar to **Johannesburg** operated by South African Airways (SAA), which take around fifteen hours. Most other flights stop off in Europe and involve a change of plane. From Canada you don't have much of a choice, with daily services from **Toronto** and **Vancouver** to **Johannesburg** operated by British Airways and by Northwest/KLM changing planes in London and Amsterdam.

On the nonstop flights from the US to Jo'burg, expect the high/low season **fare** to start from $2300/1350 for a round trip, depending on season; you might save $100–200 if you fly via Europe. Fares from Vancouver to Jo'burg start at Can$2500.

Flights from Australia and New Zealand

Southern Africa is not a cheap destination for travellers from Australia and New Zealand. **Fares** start at around Aus$2000 for a return flight from Sydney to Johannesburg, and a flight to Europe with a stopover in South Africa, or even a RTW ticket, may represent better value than a straightforward return.

There are flights from Sydney, which take 14 hours, and Perth, just under 12 hours, to Johannesburg, with onward connections to Cape Town; New Zealanders have to fly via Sydney. South African Airways (SAA) and Qantas both serve South Africa from Australia. Some Asian, African and Middle Eastern airlines fly to South Africa via their hub cities, and tend to be less expensive, but their routings often entail more stopovers.

Information relating specifically to Lesotho and Swaziland is given at the beginning of the chapters covering those countries (see p.746 & p.790).

Fly less – stay longer! Travel and climate change

Climate change is the single biggest issue facing our planet. It is caused by a build-up in the atmosphere of carbon dioxide and other greenhouse gases, which are emitted by many sources – including planes. Already, flights account for around 3–4 percent of human-induced global warming: that figure may sound small, but it is rising year on year and threatens to counteract the progress made by reducing greenhouse emissions in other areas.

Rough Guides regard travel, overall, as a global benefit, and feel strongly that the advantages to developing economies are important, as are the opportunities for greater contact and awareness among peoples. But we all have a responsibility to limit our personal "carbon footprint". That means giving thought to how often we fly and what we can do to redress the harm that our trips create.

Flying and climate change

Pretty much every form of motorized travel generates CO_2, but planes are particularly bad offenders, releasing large volumes of greenhouse gases at altitudes where their impact is far more harmful. Flying also allows us to travel much further than we would contemplate doing by road or rail, so the emissions attributable to each passenger become truly shocking. For example, one person taking a return flight between Europe and California produces the equivalent impact of 2.5 tonnes of CO_2 – similar to the yearly output of the average UK car.

Less harmful planes may evolve but it will be decades before they replace the current fleet – which could be too late for avoiding climate chaos. In the meantime, there are limited options for concerned travellers: to reduce the amount we travel by air (take fewer trips, stay longer!), to avoid night flights (when plane contrails trap heat from Earth but can't reflect sunlight back to space), and to make the trips we do take "climate neutral" via a carbon-offset scheme.

Carbon-offset schemes

Offset schemes run by **climatecare.org**, **carbonneutral.com** and others allow you to "neutralize" the greenhouse gases that you are responsible for releasing. Their websites have simple calculators that let you work out the impact of any flight. Once that's done, you can pay to fund projects that will reduce future carbon emissions by an equivalent amount (such as the distribution of low-energy light bulbs and cooking stoves in developing countries). Please take the time to visit our website and make your trip climate neutral.

ⓦ www.roughguides.com/climatechange

Airlines, agents and operators

Online booking

ⓦ www.expedia.co.uk (in UK), ⓦ www.expedia.com (in US), ⓦ www.expedia.ca (in Canada)
ⓦ www.lastminute.com (in UK)
ⓦ www.opodo.co.uk (in UK)
ⓦ www.orbitz.com (in US)
ⓦ www.travelocity.co.uk (in UK), ⓦ www.travelocity.com (in US), ⓦ www.travelocity.ca (in Canada)
ⓦ www.zuji.com.au (in Australia), ⓦ www.zuji.co.nz (in New Zealand)

Airlines

Air France US ☏ 1-800/237-2747, Canada ☏ 1-800/667-2747, UK ☏ 0870/142 4343, Australia ☏ 1300/390 190, SA ☏ 0861/340 340; ⓦ www.airfrance.com.
Air Namibia US ☏ 1-800/NAMIBIA, UK ☏ 0870/774 0965, Australia ☏ 02/9244 1841; ⓦ www.airnamibia.com.na.
British Airways US & Canada ☏ 1-800/AIRWAYS, UK ☏ 0870/850 9850, Republic of Ireland ☏ 1890/626 747, Australia ☏ 1300/767 177, New Zealand ☏ 09/966 9777, SA ☏ 114/418 600; ⓦ www.ba.com.
Cathay Pacific US ☏ 1-800/233-2742, Canada ☏ 1-800/2686-868, UK ☏ 020/8834 8888,

Australia ☎13 17 47, NZ ☎09/379 0861, SA ☎11/700 8900; ⓦwww.cathaypacific.com.

Delta Airlines US & Canada ☎1-800/221-1212, UK ☎0845/600 0950, Republic of Ireland ☎1850/882 031 or 01/407 3165, Australia ☎1300/302 849, NZ ☎09/9772232; ⓦwww.delta.com.

Emirates US & Canada ☎1-800/777-3999, UK ☎0870/243 2222, Australia ☎03/9940 7807, NZ ☎05/0836 4728, SA ☎0861/363 728; ⓦwww.emirates.com.

Gulf Air UK ☎0870/777 1717, Republic of Ireland ☎0818/272 828, Australia ☎1300/366 337, SA ☎11/268 8909; ⓦwww.gulfairco.com.

Iberia US ☎1-800/772-4642, UK ☎0870/609 0500, Republic of Ireland ☎0818/462 000, SA ☎11/884 5909; ⓦwww.iberia.com.

KLM (Royal Dutch Airlines) See Northwest/KLM. US & Canada ☎1-800/225-2525, UK ☎0870/507 4074, Republic of Ireland ☎1850/747 400, Australia ☎1300/392 192, NZ ☎09/921 6040, SA ☎11/961 6727; ⓦwww.klm.com.

Lufthansa US ☎1-800/3995-838, Canada ☎1-800/563-5954, UK ☎0870/837 7747, Republic of Ireland ☎01/844 5544, Australia ☎1300/655 727, NZ ☎0800-945 220, SA ☎0861/842 538; ⓦwww.lufthansa.com.

LTU International Airways US & Canada ☎1-866/266-5588, SA ☎0860/359 588; ⓦwww.ltu.com

Malaysia Airlines US ☎1-800/5529-264, UK ☎0870/607 9090, Republic of Ireland ☎01/6761 561, Australia ☎13 26 27, NZ ☎0800/777 747, South Africa ☎11/8809 614; ⓦwww.malaysia-airlines.com.

Northwest/KLM US ☎1-800/225-2525, UK ☎0870/507 4074, Australia ☎1-300/767-310; ⓦwww.nwa.com.

Nationwide Airlines US ☎1-866/686-6558,UK ☎0870/300 0767, SA ☎0861/737 737; ⓦwww.flynationwide.co.za.

Olympic Airways US ☎1-800/223-1226, Canada ☎1-416/964-2720, UK ☎0870/606 0460, Australia ☎02/9251 2044; ⓦwww.olympic-airways.com.

Qantas US & Canada ☎1-800/227-4500, UK ☎0845/774 7767, Republic of Ireland ☎01/407 3278, Australia ☎13 13 13, NZ ☎0800/808 767 or 09/357 8900, SA ☎11/441 8550; ⓦwww.qantas.com.

Singapore Airlines US ☎1-800/742-3333, Canada ☎1-800/663-3046, UK ☎0844/800 2380, Republic of Ireland ☎01/671 0722, Australia ☎13 10 11, NZ ☎0800/808 909, SA ☎11/880 8560 or 11/880 8566; ⓦwww.singaporeair.com.

South African Airways (SAA) US & Canada ☎1-800/722-9675, UK ☎0870/747 1111,

Australia ☎1800/221 699, NZ ☎09/977 2237, SA ☎11/978 1111; ⓦwww.flysaa.com.

Swiss International Airlines US ☎1-877/3797-947, Canada ☎1-87755-97947, UK ☎0845/601 0956, Republic of Ireland ☎1890/200 515, Australia ☎1300/724 666, NZ ☎09/977 2238, SA ☎0860/040 506; ⓦwww.swiss.com.

TAP (Air Portugal) US & Canada ☎1-800/221-7370, UK ☎0845/601 0932, Australia & NZ ☎02/9244 2344, SA ☎11/455 4907; ⓦwww.flytap.com.

Virgin Atlantic US ☎1-800/821-5438, UK ☎0870/380 2007, Australia ☎1300/727 340, SA ☎11/340 3400; ⓦwww.virgin-atlantic.com.

Agents and operators

Abercrombie & Kent UK ☎0845/0700 611, ⓦwww.abercrombiekent.co.uk, Australia ☎1300/851 800, NZ ☎0800/441 638; ⓦwww.abercrombiekent.com.au. Classy operator whose packages feature Cape Town, Johannesburg, Kruger and the luxury Rovos rail service.

Absolute Africa UK ☎020/8742 0226, ⓦwww.absoluteafrica.com. Adventure camping overland trips including ten-week epics from Nairobi to Cape Town.

Acacia Expeditions UK ☎020/7706 4700, ⓦwww.acacia-africa.com. Camping-based trips along classic South African routes, with some trips including Swaziland, Mozambique and Namibia.

Adventure Center US ☎1-800/228-8747 or 510/654-1879, ⓦwww.adventurecenter.com. Wide variety of affordable South African packages including "soft adventure" options.

Adventures Abroad US ☎1-800/665-3998, ⓦwww.adventures-abroad.com. Small-group and activity tours to South Africa and neighbouring regions, including family-friendly trips.

Africa Travel Centre UK ☎020/7387 1211, ⓦwww.africatravel.co.uk. Experienced Africa specialists with a variety of tailor-made itineraries; they act as agents for many South Africa-based overland operators.

Bales Worldwide UK ☎0870/241 3208, ⓦwww.balesworldwide.com. High-quality escorted tours that include Africa.

Classic Safari Company Australia ☎1300/130 218 or 02/9327 0666, ⓦwww.classicsafaricompany.com.au. Luxury tailor-made safaris to southern Africa.

Cox & Kings US ☎1-800/999-1758, ⓦwww.coxandkingsusa.com. Stylish operator with classic luxury journeys, including a twelve-day Cape Town to Johannesburg excursion and deluxe safaris.

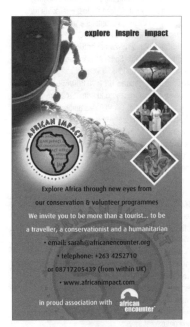
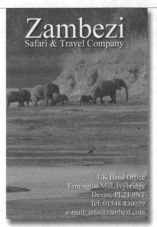

Destinations Republic of Ireland ☎ 01/855 6641, ⓦ www.destinations.ie. Specialists in long-haul destinations, including South Africa.

Dragoman UK ☎ 01728/861 133, ⓦ www .dragoman.co.uk. Extended overland journeys in purpose-built vehicles, plus shorter camping and hotel-based safaris.

ebookers UK ☎ 0800/082 3000, Republic of Ireland ☎ 01/488 3507; ⓦ www.ebookers.com, ⓦ www.ebookers.ie. Low fares on an extensive selection of scheduled flights and package deals.

Exodus UK ☎ 0870/950 0039, ⓦ www.exodus .co.uk. Small-group adventure tour operator with plenty of South Africa offerings, include trips in and around Cape Town, excursions to the country's wildlife reserves and activity packages that include horse-riding, kloofing (canyoning), mountain biking and surfing.

Expert Africa UK ☎ 020/8232 9777, ⓦ www .expertafrica.com. Small-group tours for independent travellers, as well as tailor-made trips. Specialist in good-quality accommodation/flight deals, and particularly strong on Cape Town, the Garden Route and the rest of the Western Cape.

Explore Worldwide UK ☎ 0870/3334001, ⓦ www.explore.co.uk. Good range of small-group South Africa tours, treks, expeditions and safaris, staying mostly in small local hotels.

GAP Adventures Canada ☎ 1-416/2232, ⓦ www .gapadventures.com. Canadian agent for a multitude of adventure companies, taking small groups on specialist programmes that include a 32-day safari travelling from Nairobi to Johannesburg.

Goway Travel Experiences US ☎ 1-800/387-8850, ⓦ www.goway.com. Wide range of SA packages covering all corners of the country, including rail journeys and game-viewing holidays featuring the Kruger National Park.

Guerba Expeditions UK ☎ 01373/826 611, ⓦ www.guerba.co.uk. Trans-African overland travel, plus a number of shorter packages exploring different parts of South Africa.

Joe Walsh Tours Ireland ☎ 01/676 0991, ⓦ www.joewalshtours.ie. Long-established general budget fares and holidays agent with beach and safari packages to South Africa.

Journeys International US ☎ 1-800/255-8735 or 734/665-4407, ⓦ www.journeys-intl.com. Small-group trips with a range of safaris in Southern Africa.

Journeys Worldwide Australia ☎ 1300/734 788 ⓦ www.journeysworldwide.com.au.
Escorted tours of South Africa and neighbouring countries.

Kumuka Expeditions US ☎ 1-800/517-0867, ⓦ www.kumuka.com; UK ☎ 0800 389 2328, ⓦ www.kumuka.co.uk; Australia ☎ 1800/667 277,

ⓦ www.kumuka.com.au. Five-week journeys from Nairobi to Cape Town and short tours around South Africa using local operators.

Kuoni Travel UK ☎01306/747 002, ⓦwww .kuoni.co.uk. Award-winning major tour operator running flexible package holidays to South Africa including safaris, escorted tours and golfing packages. Especially good deals for families.

Maupintour US ☎1-800/255-4266, ⓦwww .maupintour.com. A one-week Cape Town and winelands package, plus a ten-day package involving luxury travel on the Rovos train and visits to Kruger and the Victoria Falls in Zimbabwe.

North South Travel UK ☎01245/608 291, ⓦwww.northsouthtravel.co.uk. Friendly, competitive travel agency, offering discounted fares worldwide. Profits are used to support projects in the developing world, especially the promotion of sustainable tourism.

Oasis Overland UK ☎01258/471 155, ⓦwww .oasisoverland.co.uk. One of the smaller overland companies, often running budget trips through Africa.

Okavango Tours and Safaris UK ☎020/8343 3283, ⓦwww.okavango.com. Old hands with on-the-ground knowledge of sub-Saharan Africa, offering fully flexible and individual tours across South Africa.

On the Go Tours UK ☎020/7371 1113, ⓦwww .onthegotours.com. Runs group and tailor-made tours to Egypt, India, Sri Lanka, Africa, Jordan, Russia, China and Turkey.

Peregrine Adventures Australia ☎1300/791 485, ⓦwww.peregrine.net.au. Specialist small-group programmes that include a variety of wildlife packages, one of which involves tracking and monitoring animals in a private reserve in KwaZulu-Natal.

Rainbow Tours UK ☎020/7226 1004, ⓦwww.rainbowtours.co.uk. Knowledgeable and sensitive South Africa specialists whose trips emphasize eco-friendly and community-based tourism, with accommodation in good-value guesthouses, game lodges and independent hotels.

Safari Consultants UK ☎01787/888 590, ⓦwww.safari-consultants.co.uk. Individually tailored

and fairly upmarket holidays across southern Africa, with particular expertise in activity-based holidays, including walking safaris.

Slattery's Sun Republic of Ireland ☎1890/200 525, ⓦwww.slatterys.com. Cheap charter flights from Dublin to Cape Town and a vast range of South African itineraries that take in Cape Town, Kruger National Park and Zululand.

STA Travel US ☎1-800/781-4040, UK ☎0871/230 0 040, Australia ☎134 STA, NZ ☎0800/474 400, SA ☎0861/781 781; ⓦwww .statravel.com. Worldwide specialist in independent travel; also student IDs, travel insurance, car rental, rail passes and more. Good discounts for students and under-26s.

Trailfinders UK ☎0845/058 5858, Republic of Ireland ☎01/677 7888, Australia ☎1300/780 212; ⓦwww.trailfinders.com. One of the best-informed and most efficient agents for independent travellers.

Travel Bag UK ☎0800/804 8911, ⓦwww .travelbag.co.uk. Discount deals worldwide.

Tribes UK ☎01728/685 971, ⓦwww.tribes.co.uk. Unusual and off-the-beaten-track, fair-trade safaris and cultural tours in South Africa and Lesotho.

Twohigs Republic of Ireland ☎01/648 0800, ⓦwww.twohigs.com. Long-haul specialist offering South Africa packages.

USIT Republic of Ireland ☎01/602 1904, ⓦwww .usit.ie. Specialist in student, youth and independent travel, offering flights and online hostel room bookings in a number of towns in South Africa.

Wilderness Travel US ☎1-800/368-2794, ⓦwww.wildernesstravel.com. Hiking, cultural and wildlife adventures, with a sixteen-day package taking in Cape Town, the Garden Route and Kruger.

Wildlife Worldwide UK ☎0845/130 6982, ⓦwww.wildlifeworldwide.com. Tailor-made trips for wildlife and wilderness enthusiasts, including a Garden Route self-drive package and excursions taking in national parks and the winelands.

World Travel Centre Republic of Ireland ☎01/416 7007, ⓦwww.worldtravel.ie. Competitive fares to South Africa.

Getting around

Despite the large distances, travelling around most of South Africa is fairly straightforward, with a reasonably well-organized network of public transport, a good range of car rental companies, the best road system in Africa, and the continent's most comprehensive network of internal flights. The only weak point is public transport in urban areas, which is almost universally poor and often dangerous. Urban South Africans who can afford to do so tend to use private transport, and if you plan to spend much time in any one town you'd be well advised to do the same. It's virtually impossible to get to the national parks and places off the beaten track by public transport; even if you do manage, you'll most likely need a car once you're there. For information on transport in Lesotho and Swaziland, see the relevant chapters in the Guide.

Buses

South Africa's three established intercity bus companies are **Greyhound**, **Intercape** and **Translux**; between them, they reach most towns in the country. Travel on these buses (commonly called **coaches**) is safe, good value and very comfortable, and the vehicles are invariably equipped with air conditioning and toilets. Fares vary according to distances covered and the time of year, with peak fares corresponding approximately to school holidays; at other times you can expect about thirty percent off. As a rough indication you can expect to pay the following fares from Cape Town: to Paarl, R100; Mossel Bay, R150; Port Elizabeth, R250; East London, R350; Mthatha, R400; and to Durban, R475.

Translux, Greyhound and Intercape also operate the no-frills budget buslines **City to City**, **Cityliner** and **Budgetliner**, whose schedules and prices are listed on their main websites. There is also a host of small private companies about which information is thin on the ground; your best bet is to enquire at the bus station the day before you travel.

Baz Bus operates an extremely useful hop-on/hop-off system aimed at backpackers and budget travellers, with intercity buses stopping off at backpacker accommodation en route. Its services run up and down the coast in both directions between Cape Town and Port Elizabeth (1 daily), and between Port Elizabeth and Durban (5 weekly). Inland, it runs buses between Durban and Johannesburg plus Pretoria via the Drakensberg (3 weekly), between Durban and Swaziland (3 weekly) and between Swaziland and Jo'burg/Pretoria (3 weekly).

Intercity bus companies

Baz Bus ☎ 021 439 2323, ⊛ www.bazbus.com. Bookings can also be made through hostels or the Baz offices at the central tourist offices in Cape Town or Durban.
Greyhound ☎ 083 915 9000, ⊛ www.greyhound .co.za.
Intercape ☎ 0861 287 287, ⊛ www.intercape .co.za.
Translux ☎ 0861 589 282, ⊛ www.translux.co.za.

English/Afrikaans street names

Many towns have **bilingual street names** with English and Afrikaans alternatives sometimes appearing along the same road. This applies particularly in Afrikaans areas away from the large cities, where direct translations are sometimes used. Often the Afrikaans name will bear little resemblance to the English one, something it's worth being aware of when trying to map read. Some terms you may encounter on Afrikaans signage are listed in Language (see p.890).

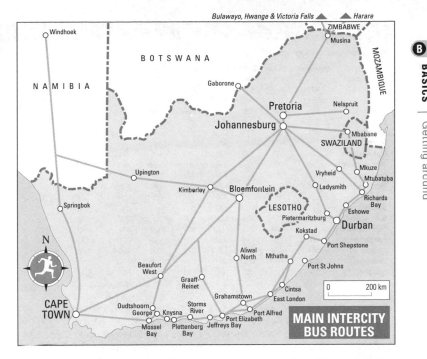

MAIN INTERCITY BUS ROUTES

0   200 km

Minibus taxis

Minibus taxis travel absolutely everywhere in South Africa, covering relatively short hops from town to town, commuter trips from township to town and back, and routes within larger towns and cities. However, the problems associated with them – unroadworthy vehicles, dangerous drivers and violent feuds between the different taxi associations competing for custom – mean that you should take local advice before using them. This is particularly true in cities, where minibus taxi ranks tend to be a magnet for petty criminals. The other problem with minibus taxis is that there is rarely much room to put luggage.

However, despite the drawbacks, don't rule out using this form of transport altogether. In 2005 the government began a seven-year programme of replacing the country's creaking taxi fleet with new vehicles, which should improve things. And short of renting a car, minibus taxis will often be your only option for getting around in remote areas, where you're unlikely to encounter trouble. You should, however, be prepared for some long waits.

Fares are very low and comparable to what you might pay on the inexpensive intercity buses. Try to have the exact change (on shorter journeys particularly), and pass your fare to the row of passengers in front of you; eventually all the fares end up with the conductor, who dishes out any change.

Trains

Travelling by **train** is just about the slowest way of getting around South Africa: the journey from Johannesburg to Cape Town, for example, takes 29 hours – compared with 19 hours by bus. Overnighting on the train, though, does at least save you the cost of accommodation elsewhere, and if you want to use your own car in both cities but can't face the long drive between them, you can actually transport your car on the train for around R2000 in December and January and around R1600 for the rest of the year. Families with children get their own private

Distance chart

Figures are given in kilometres

	Bloemfontein	Cape Town	Cradock	Durban	East London	George	Graaff-Reinet	Grahamstown	Johannesburg
Bloemfontein	–	998	384	628	546	764	422	570	396
Cape Town	998	–	811	1660	1042	436	672	873	1405
Cradock	384	811	–	806	289	481	139	175	811
Durban	628	1660	806	–	667	1240	945	796	598
East London	546	1042	289	667	–	630	388	185	992
George	764	436	481	1240	630	–	342	461	1168
Graaff-Reinet	422	672	139	945	388	342	–	274	826
Grahamstown	570	873	175	796	185	461	274	–	987
Johannesburg	396	1405	811	598	992	1168	826	987	–
Kimberley	175	960	493	842	722	734	501	654	467
Mossel Bay	808	778	547	1306	696	66	408	497	1234
Mthatha	527	1181	370	436	231	851	509	360	866
Nelspruit	754	1779	1124	689	1214	1509	1167	1242	358
Oudtshoorn	714	422	451	1244	689	63	312	479	1130
Pietermaritzburg	952	1544	733	77	594	1173	872	722	503
Port Elizabeth	676	756	251	927	300	330	251	131	1062
Pretoria	454	1324	869	656	322	1226	895	1045	58
Skukuza	880	1888	1233	809	1334	1616	1274	1349	478
Upington	576	821	669	1243	958	857	667	844	875

compartment on the train, and under-5s travel free.

Spoornet (☎086 000 8888, ⓦwww .spoornet.co.za) runs most of the intercity rail services. Its standard service, Shosholoza Meyl, offers **Sleeper Four** (first-class) and **Sleeper Six** (second-class) travel, in compartments equipped with washbasins. The principal distinction between the two classes is that, as their names suggest, one accommodates up to six people, while the other sleeps a maximum of four and tends to be quieter. **Coupés**, which take two people in Sleeper Four, are ideal if you're travelling as a couple. **Sitter** (third-class) travel is pretty crammed and uncomfortable.

The seats in the sleeper classes are comfortable and convert into bunks which offer the real possibility of getting a good night's sleep. If you don't have a sleeping bag, you can rent fresh sheets and blankets for the night, which are brought around by a bedding attendant who'll make up your bed in the evening. It's best to buy your bedding voucher when you book your train ticket.

Spoornet also runs a twice-weekly, upmarket **Premier Classe** (sic) service between Johannesburg and Cape Town, with a choice of single, double, triple and four-person compartments, with gowns and toiletries provided, and four-course lunches and five-course dinners served in a luxury dining car – all included in the fare.

Fares from Johannesburg to Cape Town in Premier Classe are around R2000 from December to mid-March, half that during November and around R1600 for most of the rest of the year, with Sleeper Four costing just under R550, and Sleeper Six tickets around R350. Tickets must be booked in advance at train stations or at Spoornet offices in the large cities.

A word of warning about **security** on trains: as thieves work the stations, especially around Gauteng, don't leave your valuables unattended in your compartment unless you have some way of locking it and, even so, make sure you close the window if leaving the carriage for a while. This may mean you won't want to eat in the dining car, so it can be worth bringing your own food and drink, although someone usually comes round selling tea or coffee once or twice during the journey.

South Africa offers a handful of **luxury** trains, worth considering if you want to travel in plush surroundings – often through wonderful scenery – and don't mind paying through the nose for the privilege. Spoornet's celebrated **Blue Train** runs between Cape Town and Pretoria, and between Cape Town and Port Elizabeth, the latter being the only

Kimberley	Mossel Bay	Mthatha	Nelspruit	Oudtshoorn	Pietermaritzburg	Port Elizabeth	Pretoria	Skukuza	Upington
175	808	527	754	714	952	676	454	880	576
960	778	1181	1779	422	1544	756	1324	1888	821
493	547	370	1124	451	733	251	869	1233	669
842	1306	436	689	1244	77	927	656	809	1243
722	696	231	1214	689	594	300	322	1334	958
734	66	851	1509	63	1173	330	1226	1616	857
501	408	509	1167	312	872	251	895	1274	667
654	497	360	1242	479	722	131	1045	1349	844
467	1234	866	358	1130	503	1062	58	478	875
–	770	779	832	676	748	763	525	952	401
770	–	857	1575	94	1226	396	1292	1695	792
779	857	–	983	839	363	490	903	1099	1178
832	1575	983	–	1472	675	1373	328	120	1144
676	94	839	1472	–	1299	358	1188	1561	698
748	1226	363	675	1299	–	854	561	727	1149
763	396	490	1373	358	854	–	1119	1459	902
525	1292	903	328	1188	561	1119	–	436	813
952	1695	1099	120	1561	727	1459	436	–	1252
401	792	1178	1144	698	1149	902	813	1252	–

passenger rail service on this route. The full Pretoria–Cape Town fare is just under R12,000 per person sharing a double berth for the 29-hour journey. Passengers must be dressed in "smart casual" clothes during the day, and appear in formal wear for the evening meal. You can reserve a seat on this popular train by booking through Blue Train's central reservations in Pretoria (☎012 334 8459, ⒲www.bluetrain.co.za) or the Cape Town reservations office (☎021 449 2672).

Another luxury rail option is offered by **Rovos Rail** (Cape Town ☎021 421 4020, Pretoria ☎012 315 8242, ⒲www.rovos.co.za), which runs trips on four routes at three levels of luxury with prices to match: from Cape Town to Pretoria (from R9000 per person sharing) and George (R5000); from Pretoria to Durban (from R10,000) and from Pretoria to Victoria Falls in Zimbabwe (from R10,000).

Domestic flights

Flying between destinations in South Africa is an attractive option if time is short. It also compares favourably with the money you'll spend covering long distances in a rental car, stopping over at places en route, and with the arrival of a clutch of competing budget airlines you can sometimes pick up good deals.

By far the biggest airline offering domestic flights is **South African Airways** (SAA), with its two associates **SA Airlink** and **SA Express** (reservations for the three go through SAA). There are several smaller airlines, of which the most significant is **British Airways Comair** and its budget subsidiary **Kulula.com**. Other no-frills airlines include **Nationwide**, **1Time** and **Mango**.

On SAA and its associates, expect to pay just under R1500 for a one-way tourist-class **fare** from Johannesburg to Cape Town, or from Cape Town to Durban. The Johannesburg–Cape Town route has become particularly cheap since the arrival of the budget operators and you'll pick up one-way fares as low as R250.

South African domestic airlines

1Time ☎0861 345 345, ⒲www.1time.co.za. Budget flights on a network that covers Johannesburg, Cape Town, East London, Durban and Bloemfontein.
British Airways Comair ☎0860 435 922 ⒲www.ba.com/travel/home/public/en_za. Flights from Johannesburg to Cape Town, Port Elizabeth and Durban; and Cape Town to Durban.
kulula.com ☎0861 585 852, ⒲www.kulula.com. Budget flights from Johannesburg to Cape Town, Durban, Port Elizabeth and George; and between Cape Town, Port Elizabeth and Durban.

Mango ☎0861 162 646, ⊛www.flymango.com.
Cheap flights from Johannesburg to Cape Town and
Durban; and from Cape Town to Jo'burg, Durban and
Bloemfontein on SAA's budget airline.
Nationwide ☎0861 737 737, ⊛www
.flynationwide.co.za. Flights from Johannesburg
to Cape Town, Nelspruit (for Kruger National Park),
Durban, Port Elizabeth and George; Cape Town to Port
Elizabeth and Durban; and between Port Elizabeth
and Durban.
South African Airways ☎0861 359 722,
⊛www.flysaa.com. Together with SA Airlink
and SA Express, they serve the major hubs of
Johannesburg, Cape Town and Durban. Among other
destinations served are Bloemfontein, East London,
George, Hoedspruit, Kimberley, Margate, Mmabatho,
Nelspruit (for Kruger), Phalaborwa, Pietermaritzburg,
Plettenberg Bay, Polokwane, Sun City, Ulundi, Mthatha
and Upington.

Driving

Short of joining a tour, the only way to get to
national parks and remoter coastal areas is
by **car**. Likewise, some of the most interesting places off the beaten track are only
accessible in your own vehicle, as buses
tend to ply just the major routes.

South Africa is ideal for driving, with a
generally well-maintained network of
highways and a high proportion of secondary
and tertiary roads which are tarred and can
be driven at speed. **Renting a vehicle** is not
prohibitively expensive and, for a small
group, it can work out a cheap option.

Filling stations are frequent on the major
routes of the country, and usually open 24
hours a day. Off the beaten track, though,
stations are less frequent, so fill up whenever
you get the chance. Stations are rarely self-
service; instead, poorly paid attendants fill
up your car, check oil, water and tyre
pressure if you ask them to, and often clean
your windscreen even if you don't. A tip of
R5 or so is always appreciated.

Rules of the road and driving tips

Foreign **driving licences** are valid in South
Africa for up to six months provided they are
printed in English. If you don't have such a
licence, you'll need to get an International
Driving Permit (available from national
motoring organizations) before arriving in
South Africa. When driving, make sure you

have your driving licence and passport on
you at all times.

You drive on the **left-hand side**; **speed
limits** range from 60kph in built-up areas
to 100kph on rural roads and 120kph on
highways and major arteries. In addition to
roundabouts, which follow the British rule
of giving way to the right, there are
four-way stops, where the rule is that the
person who got there first leaves first, and
you are not expected to give way to the
right. Note that traffic lights are called
robots in South Africa.

The only real challenge you'll face on the
roads is **other drivers**. South Africa has
among the world's worst road accident
statistics – the result of recklessness, drunken
drivers (see p.73) and unroadworthy,
overloaded vehicles. Keep your distance from
cars in front, as domino-style pile-ups are
common. Watch out also for overtaking traffic
coming towards you. Overtakers often
assume that you will head for the hard
shoulder to avoid an accident (it is legal to
drive on the hard shoulder, but be careful as
pedestrians frequently use it). If you do pull
into the hard shoulder to let a car overtake,
the other driver will probably thank you by
flashing the hazard lights. If oncoming cars
flash their headlights at you, it probably
means that there is a speed trap up ahead.

Other potential **hazards** include animals
on the road in rural areas; the problem can
be especially dangerous at night, so drive
slowly at that time. Also, the large **distances**
between major towns mean that falling
asleep at the wheel, especially when travelling through long stretches of flat landscape
in the Karoo or the Free State, is a real
danger. Plan your car journeys carefully to
include plenty of breaks and stopovers.
Finally, in urban areas, you risk the danger of
being **car-jacked**; see p.73 for safety hints.

South Africa's motoring organization, the
Automobile Association (AA; ☎083 843
22, ⊛www.aasa.co.za), provides useful
information about road conditions as well
as maps.

Car rental

Prebooking your rental car with a travel
agent before flying out is the cheapest
option, and will provide more favourable

terms and conditions (such as unlimited mileage and lower insurance excesses). Don't rely on being able to just arrive at the airport and pick up a vehicle without reserving in advance, as the rental firms do run out of cars, especially during the week.

As a rough guideline, for a one-week rental you can expect to **pay** upwards of R1650 (with a R2000 insurance excess) including about 700 free kilometres. Most companies stipulate that drivers must be a **minimum age** of 23 and must have been driving for two years at least. Note that to collect your vehicle, you will need to produce a credit (not debit) card.

The advantage of renting through major companies is that you don't have to return the car to where you hired it, but can deposit it in some other major centre instead – though rental companies usually levy a charge for this. If you're planning to drive into **Lesotho** and **Swaziland**, check that the company allows it – some don't. Insurance often doesn't cover you if you drive off the road surface, so check for this too. Local firms are almost always cheaper than chains, but usually have restrictions on how far you can take the vehicle.

Camper vans and **4WD vehicles** equipped with rooftop tents can be a good idea for getting to remote places where accommodation is scarce. Expect to pay around R1100 a day for a vehicle that sleeps two. Some companies offer standby rates that knock fifteen to twenty percent off the price if you book at short notice (one week or less ahead). Vans come fully equipped with crockery, cutlery and linen and usually a toilet. The downside of camper vans and 4WDs is that they struggle up hills and guzzle a lot of fuel (15 litres per 100km in the smaller vans), which could partly offset any savings on accommodation.

Rental agencies

Alamo US ☎1-800/462-5266, SA ☎0800 011 323; ⓦwww.alamo.com.
Auto Europe US & Canada ☎1-888/223-5555, ⓦwww.autoeurope.com.
Avis US & Canada ☎1-800/331-1212, UK ☎0870/606 0100, Republic of Ireland ☎021/428 1111, Australia ☎13 63 33 or 02/9353 9000, NZ ☎09/526 2847 or 0800/655 111, SA ☎0861 021 111; ⓦwww.avis.com.

Britz Australia ☎1800/331 454, NZ ☎0800/831 900, SA: Johannesburg ☎011 396 1860, Cape Town ☎021 982 5107; ⓦwww.britz.com. One of the biggest rental outlets for camper vans and 4WDs.
Budget US ☎1-800/527-0700, Canada ☎1-800/268-8900, UK ☎0870/156 5656, Australia ☎1300/362 848, NZ ☎0800/283 438, SA ☎0861 016 622; ⓦwww.budget.com.
Dollar US ☎1-800/800-3665, Canada ☎1-800/229 0984, UK ☎0808/234 7524, Republic of Ireland ☎1800/575 800, SA: Johannesburg ☎011 390 3454, Cape Town ☎021 936 2121; ⓦwww.dollar.com.
Drive Africa South Africa: Cape Town ☎021 447 1144, ⓦwww.driveafrica.co.za. Competitive motor-home deals and cheap car rental. If you're planning to be on the road for three months or longer, consider their rental-purchase agreement, under which you buy a car and they guarantee to buy it back for an agreed price.
Europcar US & Canada ☎1-877/940 6900, UK ☎0870/607 5000, Republic of Ireland ☎01/614 2800, Australia ☎393/306 160, SA ☎0800 011 344; ⓦwww.europcar.com.
Hertz US & Canada ☎1-800/654-3131, UK ☎020/7026 0077, Republic of Ireland ☎01/870 5777, NZ ☎0800/654 321; ⓦwww.hertz.com.
Holiday Autos US ☎866-392/9288, UK ☎0870/400 4461, Republic of Ireland ☎01/872 9366, Australia ☎299/394 433, SA ☎11/2340 597; ⓦwww.holidayautos.co.uk. Part of the lastminute.com group.
Imperial ☎0861 131 000, ⓦwww.imperialcarrental.co.za.
National US ☎1-800/CAR-RENT, UK ☎0870/400 4581, Republic of Ireland ☎0870/600 6666, NZ ☎03/366 5574, SA ☎0800 011 323; ⓦwww.nationalcar.com.
SIXT US ☎1-877/347-3227, Republic of Ireland ☎1850/206 088, UK ☎0800/4747 4227, SA ☎011 396 1080; ⓦwww.e-sixt.com.
Suncars UK ☎0870/500 5566, Republic of Ireland ☎1850/201 416; ⓦwww.suncars.com.
Tempest SA ☎0860 031 666, ⓦwww.tempestcarhire.co.za.
Thrifty US & Canada ☎1-800/847-4389, UK ☎01494/751 500, Republic of Ireland ☎01/844 1950, Australia ☎1300/367 227, NZ ☎09/256 1405; ⓦwww.thrifty.com.

Cycling

It's easy to see why **cycling** is popular in South Africa: you can get to stunning destinations on good roads unclogged by traffic, many towns have decent cycle shops for spares and equipment, and an increasing number of backpacker hostels rent out mountain bikes for reasonable rates, making it easy to do plenty of cycling without having to transport your bike into the country. You'll need to be fit though, as South Africa is a hilly place, and many roads can have punishing gradients. The weather can make life difficult, too: if it isn't raining, there is a good chance of it being very hot, so carry plenty of liquids. Cycling on the main roads is not recommended.

Hitching

Generally speaking, **hitching** in most areas of South Africa is not a good idea, particularly in large towns and cities. Even in rural areas it's risky and, while you might encounter wonderful hospitality and interesting companions, it's generally advisable not to hitch at all.

If you must hitchhike, avoid hitching alone and being dropped off in isolated areas between *dorps*. Ask drivers where they are going before you say where you want to go, and keep your bags with you: having them locked in the boot makes a hasty escape more difficult. Check the notice boards in backpacker lodges for people offering or looking to share lifts – that way, you can meet the driver in advance.

Accommodation

Relative to what's on offer in other developing countries, accommodation in South Africa may seem expensive, but standards are generally high and you get exceptional bang for your buck. Even the most modest backpacker lodge will provide a minimum of fresh sheets and clean rooms. Other than in the very cheapest rooms, a private bath or shower is almost always provided, and you'll often have the use of a garden or swimming pool. You're in luck if you're looking for something special as South Africa has some outstanding boutique hotels, luxury guesthouses, lodges and country retreats – invariably in beautiful settings – at fairly reasonable prices by developed world standards. The country's national parks and reserves themselves feature a range of accommodation, from fairly basic restcamps to incredibly slick game lodges; for more on these, see p.65. There's information on Lesotho and Swaziland accommodation in the relevant Guide chapters.

The continuing growth of **backpacker** accommodation means you'll find a hostel in most areas, and many offer excellent facilities. For **camping** and **self-catering**, you'll be spoilt for choice.

Advance booking is vital if you plan to stay in a national park or in popular areas such as Cape Town or the Garden Route, or if you're travelling in the high season. South Africa's peak season is during the midsummer **Christmas school holiday** period, which coincides with many foreign tourists piling in to catch their winter tan. The

Easter school holiday is a less intense period, when South African families migrate to the coast and inland resorts. At both Christmas and Easter, prices for budget and mid-priced accommodation (but not backpacker lodges or camping) can double, and most places get booked up months ahead. For more on the school holidays, see "Travel Essentials" on p.78.

There's a lull in the midwinter **low season** (June–Aug), during which time you should have no problem finding plenty of good-value places to stay, often with hefty

Accommodation price codes

All the accommodation listed in the Guide has been graded according to the following price codes, based on what you can expect to pay in high season (most of the summer) **per person**, and are usually based on the rate for **two sharing** a room, apartment or cottage. We've also used a price code in place of giving the rand price of **dorm beds**.

Expect rates in some areas to be significantly higher in peak season (Dec to early Jan & Easter), and look out for discounts during the winter.

- ❶ Under R100
- ❷ R101–200
- ❸ R201–300
- ❹ R301–400
- ❺ R401–500
- ❻ R501–750
- ❼ R751–1000
- ❽ R1001–2000
- ❾ Over R2000

discounts. This is the best time to go on safari in the Kruger National Park or KwaZulu-Natal, with prices at their lowest and with malarial mosquitoes dormant, temperatures moderate and the game viewing at its finest.

Hotels

Most of South Africa's budget **hotels** are throwbacks to the 1950s and 1960s. While many have degenerated into watering holes, earning most of their keep from the bar, some of the old hotels in *dorps*, where prices start at just under R200 a person, have a certain retro charm.

Mid-range hotels usually charge R300–500 per person, and you can expect decent – frequently excellent – standards, often in old and characterful refurbished buildings. Along the coastal holiday strips such as the Garden Route and southern KwaZulu-Natal and all the major seaside towns in between, these hotels are ubiquitous and frequently offer rooms right on the beachfront. Many of the mid-priced hotels – especially those on main routes in the interior – are fully booked during the week by travelling salesmen, but over the weekend, when they're often empty, you can usually negotiate reasonable discounts.

A large number of mid-range and **upmarket** establishments belong to large hotel chains, of which Protea (ⓦwww .proteahotels.com) is the largest in the country. Other groups include Southern Sun (ⓦwww.southernsun.com), Holiday Inn (ⓦwww.ichotels.com) and Three Cities (ⓦwww.threecities.co.za), all of which offer reliable but sometimes soulless accommodation.

Country lodges and boutique hotels

If you're after somewhere special to stay and have a little money to burn you can get incredible value in South Africa at small, characterful establishments – something the country really excels at. You'll find hip **boutique hotels** in the cities and *dorps* and luxurious **country lodges** in exceptional natural surroundings: eco-lodges in the middle of forests, places perched on the edge of cliffs and magical hideaways in the middle of nowhere. For a really memorable stay expect to pay from R600, but more usually from R1000. At these places you can expect to be pampered and there will often be a spa on site. There are also numerous first-rate safari camps and game lodges, which fulfil all those Out-of-Africa fantasies. For more on these, see "Parks, reserves and wilderness areas" on p.63.

B&Bs and guesthouses

The most ubiquitous form of accommodation in South Africa is in **B&Bs** and **guesthouses**, the official difference being that at a B&B the owner lives on site, and the most basic **B&B** consists of just one or two rooms in a private home, where you share washing facilities with the owners. In reality the distinction is a little hazy once you move up a notch to B&Bs and **guesthouses** that provide en-suite rooms (as is usually the case). Rates for en-suite rooms start at around R200 per person, for which you can expect somewhere clean, comfortable and relaxed, but usually away from the beach or other action. Moving up a notch, you'll be paying from R300 for a room with a bit extra, and anything from R400 upwards should offer the works: a great location, comfort and good service.

For decades the homes of black South Africans were deliberately kept hidden from tourist trails, a situation that has changed dramatically with the proliferation of township tours. Since the late 1990s, township dwellers have begun offering accommodation, opening up new possibilities for experiencing South Africa. **Township B&Bs** are still few in number, but we've tried to cover as many as possible in the Guide; expect to pay from R250 per person per night for this type of accommodation.

Along many roads in the countryside you will see signs for "Bed en Ontbyt" (Afrikaans for "bed and breakfast"), signalling **farmstay** accommodation. These offer rooms in the main homestead or in a cottage in its garden, and you can usually expect a hearty Afrikaner breakfast and prices a little below those of urban B&Bs. Some offer hiking, horse-riding, and other activities and excursions – there are some real gems dotted about, which we've listed in this Guide. Tourist offices almost always have lists of farms in the area that rent out rooms or cottages.

Caravan parks, resorts and camping

Caravanning was once the favourite way of enjoying a cheap family holiday in South Africa, and this accounts for the very large number of **caravan parks** dotted across the length and breadth of the country. However, their popularity has declined and with it the standard of many of the country's **municipal** caravan parks and campsites. Today, municipal campsites are generally pretty scruffy places, though you may find the odd pleasant one in rural areas, or near small *dorps*. Staying in a municipal campsite adjoining a city or large town is often more grief than it's worth; not only will facilities generally be run-down, but theft is a big risk. Most municipal sites charge roughly R50 per tent.

All in all, you're best off heading for the **privately owned resorts**, where for roughly the same price you get greater comfort. Although private resorts sometimes give off a holiday-camp vibe, they usually provide good washing and cooking facilities, self-catering chalets, shops selling basic goods, braai stands and swimming pools.

Virtually all **national parks** in the country – and many provincial reserves – have campsites and in some of the really remote places, such as parts of KwaZulu-Natal, camping may be your only option. Use of a campsite, is unlikely to cost more than R120. At national parks you can expect well-maintained washing facilities and there are often communal kitchen areas or at the very least a braai stand and running water, as well as decent communal shower, toilet and washing facilities (known locally as "ablutions").

Camping rough is not recommended anywhere in the country.

Backpacker lodges

Thankfully the days of **backpacker lodges** (or hostels) with ranks of grungy bunks are pretty well gone and generally you'll find well-run operations with clean linen and helpful staff. In the cities and tourist resorts you'll have a number of places to choose from and virtually any town of any significance has at least one. The cheapest beds in South Africa are in dormitories at hostels, which go for under R100 per person. Most also have a reasonable number of double rooms (around R125 per person), sometimes even with private bathrooms for which you'll pay an extra R20 or R30, and an increasing number also have family rooms that work out at around R120 per person. They usually have communal kitchens, an on-site eatery, TV, Internet access and often other facilities like bike rental. When choosing a hostel, it's worth checking out the ambience as some are party joints packed with young ravers, while others have a quieter atmosphere.

The lodges are invariably good meeting points, with a constant stream of travellers passing through, and useful notice boards filled with advertisements for hostels and backpacker facilities throughout the country. Many lodges operate reasonably priced excursions into the surrounding areas, and will pick you up from train stations or bus stops (especially Baz Bus stops) if you phone in advance.

Hostelling International (🌐www.hihostels.com) acts as an online booking agent for a growing number of South Africa's backpacker lodges.

Self-catering cottages and apartments

Away from the resorts and caravan parks, **self-catering accommodation** in cottages, apartments and small complexes provides the cheapest option apart from staying in a backpackers' lodge. One of the best things about self-catering is the wide choice of location: there are self-catering places on farms, near beaches, in forests and in wilderness areas, as well as in practically every town and city.

There's a wide range of this type of accommodation for under R250 per person per night for two people sharing. Apartments often sleep up to six, and because rates are mostly quoted for entire units, this can be very economical if you're travelling as a family or in a group. You can save a lot of money by cooking for yourself (breakfast is sometimes available for a small extra charge), and you'll get a sense of freedom and privacy missing from the nicest guesthouse or B&B. Standards are fairly high: cottages or apartments generally come fully equipped with crockery and cutlery, and even microwaves and TVs in the more modern places. Linen and towels are often provided; check before you book in.

Eating and drinking

South Africa doesn't really have a coherent indigenous cuisine, although attempts have been made to elevate Cape Cuisine to this status. The one element which seems to unite the country is a love of meat, and as a visitor you might struggle to keep in check the locals' assumption that meat – and lots of it – is the ideal choice for your meals. Having said that, South Africa is a great place to try out all kinds of interesting types of meat, from ostrich to giraffe, and good-quality steaks are inexpensive and freely available. Alternatively, it's well worth paying attention to South Africa's vast array of seafood, which includes a wide variety of fish, lobster (crayfish), oysters and mussels. Locally grown fruit and vegetables are generally of a high standard, and often available from markets and farm stalls in areas such as the Western Cape. There is no great tradition of street food and people on the move tend to pick up a pie or chicken and chips from one of the fast-food chains. Drinking is dominated by South Africa's often superb wines and by a handful of unmemorable lager beers. In the cities, and to a far lesser extent beyond them, there are numerous excellent restaurants where you can taste a spectrum of international styles.

Breakfast, lunch and dinner

South Africa's daily culinary timetable follows the British model. Most B&Bs, hotels and guesthouses serve a **breakfast** of eggs with bacon and usually some kind of sausage. Muesli, fruit, yoghurt, croissants and pastries are also becoming increasingly popular, and in the hotels you'll invariably be offered English and continental breakfasts. **Lunch** is eaten around 1pm and **dinner** in the evening around 7pm or 8pm and the two can be pretty much interchangeable as far as the menu goes, usually along the lines of meat, chicken or fish and veg; in fact, any of the dishes mentioned below. Many South Africans prefer something lighter at lunchtime, such as a sandwich, pie, salad or burger.

Styles of cooking

Traditional African food tends to focus around stiff grain porridge called **mielie pap** or pap, made of maizemeal and accompanied by meat or vegetable-based sauces. Among white South Africans, Afrikaners have evolved a style of cooking known as **boerekos**, which can be heavy-going if you're not used to it. People of British extraction favour the traditional English meat and overcooked vegetables.

Some of the best-known South African foods are mentioned below, while there's a list of South African culinary terms, including other local foods, in the Language section on p.897.

Braais

Braai (which rhymes with "dry") is an abbreviation of *braaivleis*, an Afrikaans word translated as "meat grill". More than simply the process of cooking over an outdoor fire, however, a braai is a cultural event arguably even more central to the South African identity than barbecues are to Australians. Despite its identification as part of quintessential white South Africa, braais are now popular across the races, and at any national park, nature reserve or resort you'll never be far from the distinctive odour of gently sizzling meat. A braai is an intensely social event, usually among family and friends and accompanied by gallons of beer. It's also probably the only occasion you'll catch an unreconstructed white South African man cooking.

You can braai anything, but a traditional barbecue meal consists of huge slabs of steak, lamb cutlets and **boerewors** ("farmer's sausage"), a deliciously spicy South African speciality. Potatoes and onions wrapped in aluminium foil and placed in the embers are the usual accompaniment.

Potjiekos and boerekos

A variant on the braai is **potjiekos** – pronounced "poy-key-kos"– (pot food), in which the food is cooked, preferably outdoors over an open fire, in a three-legged cast-iron cauldron (the *potjie*). In a similar vein but cooked indoors is **boerekos**, (literally "farmer's food"), a style of cooking enjoyed mainly by Afrikaners. Much of it is similar to English food, but taken to cholesterol-rich extremes, with even the vegetables prepared with butter and sugar. Should you spend the night on an Afrikaans farm, you could well find yourself waking up to a breakfast of several eggs, steak, piles of bacon and *boerewors*. *Boerekos* comes into its own in its variety of over-the-top desserts, including *koeksisters* (plaited doughnuts saturated with syrup) and *melktert* ("milk tart"), a solid, rich custard in a flan case.

Cape Cuisine

Styles of cooking brought by Asian and Madagascan slaves have evolved into **Cape Cuisine** (sometimes known as Cape Malay food – a misnomer given that few slaves came from Malaysia). Characterized by mild, semi-sweet curries with strong Indonesian influences, Cape Cuisine is worth sampling at least once, especially in Cape Town, where it developed and is associated with the Muslim community. Dishes include *bredie* (stew), of which *waterblommetjiebredie*, made using water hyacinths, is a speciality; *bobotie*, a spicy minced dish served under a savoury custard; and *sosaties*, a local version of kebab using minced meat. For dessert, dates stuffed with almonds make a light and delicious end to a meal, while *malva* pudding is a rich combination of milk, sugar, cream and apricot jam.

Although Cape Cuisine can be delicious, there isn't that much variety and few restaurants specialize in it. Despite this, most of the dishes considered as Cape Cuisine have actually crept into the South African diet, many becoming part of the Afrikaner culinary vocabulary.

Other ethnic and regional influences

Although South Africa doesn't really have distinct regional cuisines, you will find changes of emphasis and local specialities in different parts of the country. **KwaZulu-Natal**, for instance, particularly around Durban and

B

Vegetarian food

While not quite a **vegetarian** paradise, South Africa is nevertheless vegetarian-savvy and you'll find at least one concession to meatless food on most menus. Even steakhouses will have something palatable on offer and generally offer the best salad bars around – especially at the Spur chain, where you can fill up on greens for around R25. If you're self-catering in the larger cities, delicious dips and breads can be found at delis and Woolworths and Pick 'n Pay supermarkets.

Pietermaritzburg, is especially good for Indian food. The South African contribution to this great multifaceted tradition is the humble **bunny chow**, a cheap takeaway consisting of a hollowed out half-loaf of white bread originally filled with curried beans, but nowadays with anything from curried chicken to sardines.

Portuguese food made early inroads into the country because of South Africa's proximity to Mozambique. The Portuguese influence is predominantly in the use of hot and spicy *peri-peri* seasoning, which goes extremely well with braais. The best-known example of this is delicious **peri-peri chicken**, which you will find all over. **Italian food** has also been around for a while, brought over with POWs from the North Africa campaign who were incarcerated in South Africa and stayed on after World War II. You'll find some excellent Italian restaurants in the cities, from small pizzerias to smarter restaurants going the whole hog. Eastern European **Jewish food** arrived with refugees at the turn of the last century and in Jo'burg and Cape Town you'll find bagels, blinis, chopped liver and chopped herring at delis and some supermarkets.

Eating out

Restaurants in South Africa offer good value compared with Britain or North America. In every city you'll find places where you can eat a decent main course for under R75, while for R200 you can splurge on the best. All the cities and larger towns can boast some restaurants with imaginative menus. **Franschhoek**, a small town in the Winelands, has established itself as a culinary centre for the country, where you'll find some fine eating places in extremely close proximity. As a rule, restaurants are

licensed, but Muslim establishments serving Cape Cuisine don't allow alcohol at all.

An attractive phenomenon in the big cities, especially Cape Town, has been the rise of continental-style **cafés** – easy-going places where you can eat just as well as you would in a regular restaurant, but also drink coffee all night without feeling obliged to order food. Service tends to be slick and friendly, and a reasonable meal in one of these cafés is unlikely to set you back more than R60. Don't confuse this new breed of café with traditional South African cafés, found in even the tiniest country town. The equivalent of corner stores elsewhere, they commonly sell a few magazines, soft drinks, sweets, crisps and an odd collection of tins and dry goods, though no sit-down meals. Their only concession to ready-to-eat food is normally a meat pie heated in a microwave, or a leg of chicken that spent a little too long incubating in the warmer.

If popularity is the yardstick, then South Africa's real national cuisine is to be found in its **franchise restaurants**, which you'll find in every town of any size. The usual international names like KFC and Wimpy are omnipresent, but these are no match for South Africa's own American-style steakhouses, such as Spur, which projects a wholesome Wild West image and remains popular with South African families. South Africa's great contribution to the world of fast food is the Nando's Chickenland chain, which grills excellent Portuguese-style chicken, served under a variety of spicy sauces. Expect to pay around R30 for a filling burger and chips or chicken meal at any of these places and twice that for a good-sized steak.

Note that quite a few restaurants don't have well-defined hours of business, in which case we have stated in the Guide which meals they tend to open for. Phone numbers are given where booking a table might be a good idea.

Drinking

White South Africans tend to do their drinking at home, so for them pubs and bars are not the centres of social activity they are in the US or the UK, though in the African townships **shebeens** (informal bars) do occupy this role. Those **bars** that do exist in city centres have traditionally been rough, men-only places, women being corralled into stiff lounges or ladies' bars attached to hotels. The **Irish/British-style pub** is beginning to make an appearance under the invasion of a series of franchised names, as is the sports bar, but these have no deep roots in South African culture.

Beer, wines and spirits can be bought at bottle stores (the equivalent of the British off-licence), which generally keep normal shopping hours, and also at supermarkets. Licensing laws make it illegal for shops to sell liquor in the evenings or on Sundays, although you'll still be able to drink at a restaurant or pub.

There are no surprises when it comes to **soft drinks**, with all the usual names available. What does stand out is South African **fruit juice**, the range amounting to one of the most extensive selections of unsweetened juices in the world. One unusual drink you might well encounter in the country's tea rooms is locally produced **rooibos** tea, made from the leaves of an indigenous plant (see box, p.307).

Beer

Although South Africa yearns to be a major wine-producing country, **beer** is indisputably the national drink. Beer is as much an emblem of South African manhood as the braai and it cuts across all racial and class divisions. South Africans tend to be fiercely loyal to their brand of beer, though they all taste pretty much the same, given that the vast majority of beer in the country is produced by the huge South African Breweries monopoly, one of the world's largest beer makers. It's given a good run for its money by Namibian Breweries, whose Windhoek Lager is rated by cognoscenti as better than SAB's offerings. **Lager** is the predominant style, likely to taste a bit thin and bland to a British palate, though it can be wonderfully refreshing drunk ice-cold on a sweltering day.

One or two **microbreweries** have sprung up, best known of which are Mitchell's in Knysna, which produces some distinctive ales, and Birkenhead in Stanford. These can be found at some bottle stores and bars between Cape Town and Port Elizabeth. **Imported beers** are expensive compared with the local product, with the exception of the great Czech Pilsner Urquell, which has been bought by SAB as part of its global expansion.

Wine

South Africa's **wine industry** has emerged out of years of sanction-enforced doldrums, casting aside a 350-year-old tradition of trying to make French wine, and nailed its colours to the fresh, fruity style of New World wines. Production is rising all the time to meet the demands of the ever-growing export market, and a number of South African winemakers are achieving international recognition with some excellent wines at prices few visitors from overseas are likely to grumble about.

If you're looking for a truly local wine you'll find it in **pinotage**, a red unique to South Africa and made from a grape that is a hybrid of pinot noir and hermitage. South Africa produces great white wines, with a growing trend of excellent white blends. **Port** is also made, though connoisseurs of the Portuguese equivalent will struggle to recognize the over-sweet, over-sticky South African style. On the other hand, a handful of excellent **sparkling wines** are produced.

Wine is available throughout the country, although prices rise as you move out of the Western Cape. **Prices** for quaffable bottles start at R30 or below, and the vast bulk of wines cost less than R100, but you can spend R250 and up for a truly great vintage. All this means that anyone with an adventurous streak can indulge in a bacchanalia of sampling without breaking the bank.

The best way to sample wines is by visiting **wineries**, some of which charge a small tasting fee to discourage freeloading. The oldest and most rewarding wine-producing regions are the **Constantia estates** in Cape Town (see p.138) and the region known as the **Winelands** around the towns of Stellenbosch (see p.1190), Paarl (see p.197) and Franschhoek (see p.201), which all have institutionalized wine routes. Other wine-producing areas include Robertson (see p.208), the Orange River (see p.336) and Walker Bay (see p.241).

The media

South Africa lacks a strong tradition of national newspapers and instead has many regional publications of varying quality. Television delivers a mix of imported programmes and home-grown soaps heavily modelled on US fare, as well as the odd homegrown reality TV show and one or two watchable documentary slots. Radio is where South Africa is finding it easiest to meet the needs of a diverse and scattered audience. Deregulation of the airwaves has brought to life scores of small new stations.

Newspapers

Of the roughly twenty daily **newspapers**, most of which are published in English or Afrikaans, the only one that qualifies as a national is **Business Day** (Ⓦwww .businessday.co.za) which, as its name suggests, is targeted at the business community, but is a good source of serious national and international news. Each of the larger cities has its own English-language broadsheet, most of them published by South Africa's largest newspaper publisher, Independent News & Media, a subsidiary of the Irish company that owns London's *Independent* newspaper and the *Irish Independent*. In Johannesburg, **The Star** (Ⓦwww.thestar.co.za), the group's South African flagship, has a roughly equal number of black and white readers and offers somewhat uninspired Jo'burg coverage, padded out with international bits and pieces piped in from its Dublin and London counterparts. Cape Town's morning **Cape Times** (Ⓦwww.capetimes.co.za) and **Cape Argus** (Ⓦwww.capeargus.co.za), published in the afternoon, follow broadly the same tried (and tired) formula, as do the **Pretoria News** (Ⓦwww.pretorianews.co.za), the **Herald** (Ⓦwww.theherald.co.za) in Port Elizabeth and the **Daily News** (Ⓦwww.dailynews.co .za) in Durban.

In 2002, Independent Newspapers were approached by white Afrikaner journalist Deon du Plessis with the idea of a downmarket tabloid aimed at black working-class South Africans. The grandees in Dublin turned down his suggestion, for which they must still be kicking themselves, since the **Daily Sun** has turned out to be South Africa's most successful paper, selling more copies than all the Independent titles put together, and is purportedly the biggest-selling daily in sub-Saharan Africa with around four million readers. Published in Jo'burg, the *Sun* taps into the concerns of township dwellers, with a giddy cocktail of gruesome crime stories, tales of witchcraft and the supernatural, and coverage of everyday problems of ordinary people. Another tabloid published in Jo'burg and also targeted at a black Jo'burg readership is the **Sowetan** (Ⓦwww.sowetan.co.za), which has been going since the 1980s, but has so far steered a more sober course than the *Sun*. In Cape Town, a new tabloid, the studiedly sleazy **Voice**, is attempting to emulate the *Sun* in the coloured community, with a downbeat mixture of crime, the supernatural and sex advice.

Unquestionably the country's intellectual heavyweight, the **Mail & Guardian** (ⓦwww .mg.co.za) published every Friday, benefits enormously from its association with the London *Guardian* (from which it draws most of its international coverage and numerous feature articles), and frequently delivers nonpartisan and fearless investigative journalism, although at times its local reporting can tend towards the stodgy. The **Sunday Times** (ⓦwww.sundaytimes.co.za) on the other hand can attribute its sales – roughly half a million copies – to its well-calculated mix of solid investigative reporting, gossipy stories, material from Britain's *Telegraph* and rewrites of salacious scandal lifted from foreign tabloids. The **Sunday Independent** (ⓦwww.sundayindependent .co.za), from the *Independent* stable, projects a more thoughtful image but is a bit thin, with almost all its foreign news culled from its sister papers.

The easiest places to buy newspapers are corner stores and newsagents, especially the CNA chain. These outlets also sell **international publications** such as *Time*, *Newsweek*, *The Economist* and the weekly overseas editions of the British *Daily Mail*, the *Telegraph* and the *Express*.

Television

The South Africa Broadcasting Corporation's three TV channels churn out a mixed bag of domestic dramas, sport, game shows, soaps and documentaries, filled out with lashings of familiar imports. **SABC 1, 2** and **3** share the unenviable task of trying to deliver an integrated service, while having to split their time between the eleven official languages. English turns out to be most widely used, with SABC 3 (ⓦwww.sabc3 .co.za) broadcasting almost exclusively in the language and with a high proportion of British and US comedies and dramas, while SABC 2 (ⓦwww.sabc2.co.za) and SABC 1 (ⓦwww.sabc1.co.za) spread themselves thinly across all the remaining ten languages with a fair amount of English creeping in even here. SABC 1, with its high proportion of sports coverage, has the most viewers.

South Africa's first and only free-to-air independent commercial channel **e.tv** (ⓦwww.etv.co.za) won its franchise in 1998 on the promise of providing a showcase for local productions, a pledge it has signally failed to meet – its output has consisted substantially of uninspired and uninspiring imports.

There is no cable TV in South Africa, but **DSTV** (ⓦwww.dstv.co.za) offers a **satellite television** subscription service with a selection of sports, movies, news and specialist channels, some of which are piped into hotels.

Radio

Given South Africa's low literacy rate and widespread poverty, it's no surprise that **radio** is its most popular medium. The SABC operates a national radio station for each of the eleven official language groups. The English-language service, **SAfm** (ⓦwww .safm.co.za), is of a generally high standard; its best offerings are the polished evening and morning news programmes.

The SABC also runs **5FM Stereo**, a national pop station broadcasting Top 40 tracks, while its **Radio Metro** is targeted at black urban listeners.

To get a taste of what makes South Africans tick, tune into the Gauteng talk station **702** (in Jo'burg 92.7 FM and in Pretoria 106 FM, ⓦwww.702.co.za) or its Cape Town sister station **CapeTalk** (567 AM, ⓦwww.capetalk.co.za), both of which broadcast news, weather, traffic and sports reports. Apart from these, there are scores of regional, commercial and community stations, broadcasting a range of music and other material, which makes surfing the airwaves an enjoyable experience, wherever you are in the country.

Festivals

South Africa has no shortage of events – there are over eighty music festivals each year, nine of them over the Easter weekend alone. Apart from these there are umpteen small events in countless small towns – from the Uitenhage Prickly Pear Festival, to the Ficksburg Cherry Festival and the Hantam Vleisfees (an unashamed celebration of meat) in Calvinia. Diverting as these may be, you aren't going to plan your trip around them, but there are a number of more significant events (listed below) that may be worth pencilling into your holiday diary. Although Johannesburg and Cape Town tend to dominate, the country's two biggest cultural events, the National Arts Festival and the Klein Karoo Nasionale Kunstefees, both take place in small Karoo towns (Grahamstown and Oudtshoorn respectively) that, once things get humming, swell to twice their normal size.

Selected festivals and events

January

Cape Town Minstrel Carnival Cape Town. South Africa's longest and most raucous annual party, the Cape Town Minstrel Carnival (known more commonly locally by its colloquial moniker "The Coon Carnival"), brings over ten thousand spectators to Green Point stadium. It starts on January 2 for the Tweede Nuwe Jaar or "Second New Year" celebrations – an extension of New Year's Day unique to the Western Cape. Central to the festivities are the brightly decked-out minstrel troupes that vie in singing and dancing contests. Tickets (R20–50) are best reserved through Computicket – you won't get such a good view if you buy tickets at the gate on the day.

Maynardville Shakespeare Festival Cape Town ☎ 021 421 7695. A usually imaginative production of one of the Bard's plays is staged each year in the beautiful setting of the Maynardville Open Air Theatre in Wynberg.

February

Cape Town Pride Pageant ⊛www .capetownpride.co.za. Series of gay-themed events over two weeks, kicking off with a pageant at which Mr and Mrs Gay Pride are crowned and taking in a bunch of parties and a street parade.

FNB Dance Umbrella Johannesburg, Gauteng. The country's leading dance festival runs from mid-February to mid-March at several venues and showcases the diversity of forms that have developed on the subcontinent.

March

Cape Argus Pick 'n Pay Cycle Tour Cape Town (see p.171). The largest, and arguably most spectacular, individually timed bike race in the world, with over 30,000 participants on the 105-kilometre course – much of it along the ocean's edge – draws many thousands of spectators along the route. To take part you need to book early as it's heavily subscribed.

Cape Town International Jazz Festival Cape Town ⊛www.capetownjazzfest.com. Initiated in 2000 as the Cape Town counterpart of the world-famous North Sea Jazz Festival, this event, held over the last weekend of the month, has now come of age and acquired a local identity. Notable past performers have included Courtney Pine, Herbie Hancock and Randy Crawford as well as African greats such as Jimmy Dludlu, Moses Molelekwa, Youssou N'Dour, Ismael Lo and Miriam Makeba.

Klein Karoo Nasionale Kunstefees Oudtshoorn, Western Cape ⊛www.kknk.co.za. South Africa's largest Afrikaans arts and culture festival turning the otherwise dozy Karoo *dorp* of Oudtshoorn into one big jumping party. If you don't understand Afrikaans, you'll still find enough English offerings to keep you busy.

Splashy Fen Music Festival Underberg, KwaZulu-Natal ⊛www.splashyfen.co.za. Held during the second half of the month, South Africa's oldest music festival draws thousands of punters to a beautiful farm in the Drakensberg foothills, with a spread of mainstream and alternative rock and pop and a kids' programme too.

April

Two Oceans Marathon Cape Town ⓦwww
.twooceansmarathon.org.za. Another of the Western
Cape's big sporting events is in fact a 56km
ultra-marathon, with huge crowds lining the route to
cheer on the participants.

Pink Loerie Mardi Gras Knysna, Western Cape
ⓦwww.pinkloerie.com. Week-long gay pride
celebration of parties, contests, cabaret, drag shows
and performance in South Africa's oyster capital.

June

Comrades Marathon Durban/Pietermaritzburg,
KwaZulu-Natal ⓦwww.comrades.com. A national
institution, the Comrades attracts around 13,000
runners, many of them international competitors, and
is followed by a huge TV audience. The 80km route
between Durban and Pietermaritzburg passes through
the spectacular Valley of a Thousand Hills and is run
downhill towards the coast in odd years and uphill
starting from Durban in even years.

National Arts Festival Grahamstown, Eastern
Cape (see p.397). The largest arts festival in Africa,
with its own fringe festival – ten days of jazz, classical
music, dance, cabaret and theatre spanning every
conceivable type of performance.

July

Knysna Oyster Festival Knysna, Western Cape
ⓦwww.oysterfestival.co.za. A fortnight of carousing
and oyster-eating along the Garden Route, kicked
off with a road-bike race and closed with the Knysna
Marathon, with lots of wine-tasting and other satellite
events in between.

August

Oppikoppi Bushveld Festival Northam, North
West Province ⓦwww.oppikoppi.co.za. South
Africa's scaled-down answer to Woodstock, the
Oppikoppi (Afrikaans for "on the hill") Festival brings
the bushveld hills alive with the sound of music, as
some sixty local and foreign bands rock the *bundu* for
four days and nights.

Joy of Jazz Johannesburg, Gauteng ⓦwww
.joyofjazz.co.za. Jo'burg's flagship jazz festival offers
four days of varied music in the Newtown precinct
with a major focus on jazz. Past performers have
included Miriam Makeba, Jonas Gwangwa, Stanley
Clarke, George Duke and the Count Basie Orchestra.

September

Arts Alive Johannesburg, Gauteng ⓦwww
.artsalive.co.za. Jo'burg's largest arts event features
four days of dance, visual art, poetry and music

at venues in Newtown, the cultural precinct in the
inner city. A main concert, held at the Johannesburg
Stadium, has in the past boasted international
superstars such as 50 Cent and Busta Rhymes.

Cape Town International Comedy Festival
Cape Town ⓦwww.comedyfestival.co.za. Africa's
largest comedy festival showcases local and
international acts in six separate programmes that
include family-friendly mainstream performances,
street theatre and the "Danger Zone" – risqué sets
that sail close to the wind. And if your Afrikaans is up
to it, you can take in humour in the new "Bek Lash"
(tongue-lashing) programme.

Hermanus Whale Festival Hermanus, Western
Cape ⓦwww.whalefestival.co.za. To coincide with
the peak whale-watching season, the southern Cape
town of Hermanus (see p.237) stages a week-long
annual festival of arts and the environment towards
the end of the month. Activities include plays, a craft
market, a children's festival and live music.

November

Cape Town World Cinema Festival Cape Town
ⓦwww.sithengi.co.za. Exciting showcase of films
from the developing world, with an emphasis on Africa
and specifically South Africa. Material is also sourced
from Latin America, Asia and the Black Diaspora and
includes movies by independent directors from the
developed world. Screenings take place at venues all
over the Mother City.

Kirstenbosch Summer Sunset Concerts Cape
Town ⓦwww.sanbi.org/frames/whatsonfram.htm.
These popular concerts, held on the magnificent
lawns of the botanical gardens at the foot of
Table Mountain, are among the musical highlights
of the Cape Town calendar. Performances
begin at 5.30pm and cover a range of genres,
from local jazz to classical music. Come early to
find a parking place, and bring a picnic and
some Cape fizz – and enjoy. Tickets available at
the gate.

**Out in Africa South African Gay & Lesbian
Film Festival** Cape Town and Johannesburg
ⓦwww.oia.co.za. Purportedly the most popular
movie festival in the country screens gay- and
lesbian-themed international and local productions
over the first fortnight of the month.

December

Mother City Queer Projects Cape Town
(see p.169). A hugely popular party attracting
thousands of gay revellers, for which a vast venue is
chartered. Outlandish get-ups, multiple dance floors
and a mood of sustained delirium make this event
a real draw.

Carols by Candlelight at Kirstenbosch Cape Town ☎ 021 799 8783. The botanical gardens' annual carol-singing and Nativity tableaux – staged on the Thursday to Sunday before Christmas – is a Cape Town institution, drawing crowds of families with their picnic baskets. The gates open at 7pm and the singing kicks off at 8pm.

Rustler's Valley New Year's Gathering Fouriesburg, Free State ⊛ www.rustlers.co.za. Tucked away in a remote corner of the most conservative province in South Africa, Rustler's Valley is the neo-hippy capital of South Africa. Three- to four-day parties are held throughout the year, but the highlight is the New Year's Gathering, with live music, DJ sets and a veritable New Age checklist of tepees, sweat lodges, shamanic ceremonies, crystals and astrologers.

December to March

Spier Summer Festival Stellenbosch, Western Cape ⊛ www.spierarts.co.za. The amphitheatre on the Spier Estate is the venue for one of the major arts events of the Western Cape. For four months the line-up, which is increasingly taking on an African flavour, features music, opera, dance, stand-up comedy and theatre. Among the exciting productions staged here has been Brett Bailey's extraordinary take on Verdi's opera *Macbeth*, set in a central African country, and Sibongile Khumalo's interpretation of Zulu Princess Magogo's music.

Activities and outdoor pursuits

South Africa's diverse landscape of mountains, forests, rugged coast and sandy beaches, as well as kilometres of veld and game-trampled national parks, make the country supreme outdoor terrain. This fact hasn't been overlooked by South Africans themselves, who have been playing in the outdoors for decades. The result is a well-developed infrastructure for activities, an impressive national network of hiking trails and plenty of commercial operators selling adventure sports.

Hiking trails

Over the past thirty years, **hiking** has taken off in a big way in South Africa, which now has the most comprehensive system of footpaths in Africa (inspired by the US Appalachian Hiking Trail). Wherever you are – even in the middle of Johannesburg – you won't be far from some sort of trail. The best ones are in wilderness areas, where you'll find waymarked paths that vary from half-hour strolls to major hiking expeditions of two to seven days that take you right into the heart of some of the most beautiful parts of the country.

Overnight hiking trails are normally well laid out, with painted footprints or other markers to indicate the route, and campsites or huts along the way (you'll need to carry all your own equipment). Numbers are limited on most, and many trails are so popular that you may need to **book** months in advance to use them (details are given in the Guide) – although you may be lucky enough to find that there is a last-minute vacancy just when you turn up.

If you want to do a fair amount of walking but don't want to launch out on a long expedition, consider basing yourself in one of the wilderness areas such as the **Drakensberg**, where you can stay in chalets and set off on a series of day-walks, returning each night.

Characteristic of Africa are **guided wilderness trails**, where you walk in game country (such as the Kruger National Park), accompanied by an armed guide. These walks should be regarded as a way to get a feel for the wild rather than actually see any wildlife, as you'll encounter far fewer animals on foot than from a vehicle. Specialist trails include mountain biking, canoeing, horseback trails and camel trails. A handful of trails have also been set up specifically for **people with disabilities**, mostly for the visually impaired or people confined to wheelchairs.

Watersports

South Africa has some of the world's finest spots for **surfing**. The country's perfect wave at **Jeffrey's Bay** was immortalized on celluloid in the 1960s cult movie *Endless Summer*, but any surfer will tell you that there are equal, if not better, breaks all the way along the coast from the Namibian to the Mozambique border. Surfers can be a cliquey bunch, but the South African community has a reputation for being among the friendliest in the world and, provided you pay your dues, you should find yourself easily accepted. Some of the world's top shapers work here, and you can pick up an excellent board at a fraction of European or US prices. If you can face the humiliation of being regarded by the pro surfers as a "tea bag" or "doormat", boogie-boarding and body-surfing make easy alternatives to the real thing, require less skill or dedication and are great fun. **Windsurfing** (or sailboarding) is another popular sport you'll find at many resorts, where you can rent gear.

On inland waterways, South African holidaymakers are keen **speedboaters**, an activity that goes hand in hand with **waterskiing**. **Kayaking** and **canoeing** are also very popular, and you can often rent craft at resorts or national parks that lie along rivers. For the more adventurous, there's **whitewater rafting**, with some decent trips along the Tugela River in KwaZulu-Natal and on the Orange River.

Diving and snorkelling

Scuba diving is popular, and South Africa is one of the cheapest places in the world to get an internationally recognized open-water certificate. Courses start at around R2500 (including gear) and are available at all the coastal cities as well as a number of other resorts. The most rewarding diving is along the St Lucia Marine Reserve on the northern KwaZulu-Natal coast, where 100,000 dives go under every year for its coral reefs and fluorescent fish. You won't find corals and bright colours along the Cape coast, but the huge number of sunken vessels makes wreck-diving popular, and you can encounter the swaying rhythms of giant kelp forests. There are a couple of places along the southern Cape and Garden Route where you can go on **shark-cage dives** and come face to face with deadly great whites.

KwaZulu-Natal is also good for **snorkelling** and there are some underwater trails elsewhere in the country, most notable of which is in the Tsitsikamma National Park.

Other activities

Fishing is another well-developed South African activity and the coasts yield 250 species caught through rock, bay or surf angling. The confluence of the warm Indian Ocean and cooler Atlantic east of the Cape Peninsula brings one of the highest concentrations of game fish in the world, including

Beach conditions

Don't expect balmy Mediterranean seas in South Africa: of its 2500km of coastline, only the stretch along the Indian Ocean seaboard of KwaZulu-Natal and the northern section of the Eastern Cape can be considered tropical, and along the entire coast an energetic surf pounds the shore. In **Cape Town**, sea bathing is only comfortable between November and March. Generally, the further east you go from here, the warmer the water becomes and the longer the bathing season. Sea temperatures that rarely drop below 18°C make the **KwaZulu-Natal** coast warm enough for a dip at any time of year.

A word of warning: dangerous **undertows** and riptides are present along the coast and you should try to bathe where lifeguards are present. Failing that (and guards aren't that common away from main resorts out of season) you should follow local advice, never swim alone, and always treat the ocean with respect.

longfin, tunny and marlin. Inland you'll find plenty of rivers and dams stocked with freshwater fish, while trout fishing is extremely well established in Mpumalanga, the northern sections of the Eastern Cape and the KwaZulu-Natal Midlands.

There are ample opportunities for aerial activities. In the Winelands you can go **ballooning**, while **paragliding** offers a thrilling way to see Cape Town, by diving off Lion's Head and riding the thermals. More down-to-earth options include **mountaineering** and **rock climbing**, both of which have a huge following in South Africa. In a similar vein is **kloofing** (or canyoning) in which participants trace the course of a deep ravine by climbing, scrambling, jumping, abseiling or using any other means.

If you can't choose between being airborne or earthbound, you can always bounce between the two by **bungee jumping** off the Gouritz River Bridge near Mossel Bay – the world's highest commercial jump.

Horse-riding is a sport you'll find at virtually every resort, whether inland or along the coast, for two hours or two days. You can ride in the Drakensberg from the Natal parks, or go pony trekking for several days in Lesotho. Take your own hat, as not everyone provides them. **Bird-watching** is another activity you can do almost anywhere, either casually on your own, or as part of a guided trip with one of the several experts operating in South Africa. Among the very best bird-watching spots are Mkuzi and Ndumo game reserves in KwaZulu-Natal. **Golf** lovers will have a fabulous time in South Africa as courses are prolific and frequently in stunningly beautiful locations. Finally, if you decide to go **skiing** at one or two resorts in the Eastern and Western Cape, you'll be able to go home with a quirky experience of Africa.

Spectator sports

South Africa is a nation obsessed by sport, where heights of devotion are reached whenever local or international teams take to the field. Winning performances, controversial selections and scandals commonly dominate the front as well as the back pages of newspapers, and it can be hard to escape the domination of sport across radio, television and advertising media. The big spectator sports are soccer, rugby and cricket, and big matches involving the international team or big local clubs are well worth seeing live.

Soccer

Soccer is the country's most popular game, with a primarily black and coloured following, and it is now starting to attract serious money. And with the soccer World Cup due to be hosted here in 2010, the nation is in the grip of a Fifa fever that can only intensify as the big event approaches.

The professional season runs from August to May, with teams competing in the **Premier Soccer League** (PSL) and a couple of knock-out cup competitions. Unlike rugby teams, soccer teams do not own their own grounds and are forced to rent them for specific fixtures. In Gauteng, the heartland of South African soccer, all the big clubs use the same grounds, which has prevented the development of the kind of terrace fan culture found elsewhere. Nonetheless, soccer crowds are generally witty and good-spirited. The very big games, normally involving Johannesburg's big two teams, **Kaizer Chiefs** and **Orlando Pirates**, do simmer with tension, though violence is rare. Although Chiefs and Pirates are both Sowetan clubs, they have a nationwide following, and their derbies are the highlight of the PSL's fixture list.

Games are played on weekday evenings (usually at 7.30pm or 8.30pm) and at 3pm on Saturdays. Tickets cost about R25. The national squad, nicknamed **Bafana Bafana** (literally "boys boys" but connoting "our lads"), qualified for the World Cup finals in both 1998 and 2002, but in 2006 the national team bit the dust when they were brought down by a decisive 3-0 defeat to Ghana in their second match. Erratic performers, Bafana are imaginative and strong on spectacular athletic feats, but less impressive when it comes to team work and resilience. Even games the team should win have an element of unpredictability that makes for great spectator sport.

Rugby

Rugby is hugely popular with whites, especially Afrikaners, though attempts to broaden the game's appeal, particularly to a black audience, have struggled. South Africa's victory against England at the 2007 World Cup final in Paris did for a brief spell bring the whole country together, with President Thabo Mbeki flying to France to support the national team, the Springboks. The strength of emotion almost matched that shown in 1995 when South Africa hosted the event, which attracted fanatical attention nationwide, particularly when the Boks triumphed and President Nelson Mandela donned a green Springbok jersey (long associated exclusively with whites) to present the cup to the winning side. Following that, the goodwill dissipated, to be replaced by an acrimonious struggle to transform the traditionally white sports (cricket and rugby) into something more representative of all race groups, particularly following the government's policy of enforcing racial quotas in national squads.

Despite these problems, the country's two World Cup victories in twelve years testify to the fact that South Africa is extraordinarily good at rugby, and you are likely to witness high-quality play when you watch either inter-regional or international games. The main domestic competition is the **Currie Cup**, with games played on weekends from March to October; admission to one of these matches costs from R50.

More recently this has been overshadowed by the **Super 14** competition, involving regional teams from South Africa, New Zealand and Australia. Matches are staged annually from late February to the end of May in all three countries, and in South Africa you'll catch a fair bit of action in the major centres of Johannesburg, Cape Town and Durban, though smaller places such as Port Elizabeth, East London, Bloemfontein and George sometimes get a look-in.

International fixtures involving the Springboks are dominated by visiting tours by northern-hemisphere teams and by the annual **Tri-Nations** competition, in which South Africa plays home and away fixtures against Australia and New Zealand. These are normally played from June to August, and you will need to get tickets well in advance to attend.

Cricket

Cricket was for some years seen as the most progressive of the former white sports, with development programmes generating support and discovering talent among black and coloured communities. The sport was rocked to its foundations in 2000, however, when it was revealed that South African national captain, the late Hansie Cronje, had received money from betting syndicates hoping to influence the outcome of one-day matches. Cronje was banned for life, the credibility of the sport took a dive and the Proteas (formerly the Springboks), the national team, has been struggling to raise itself ever since.

The domestic season of inter-provincial games runs from October to April, and the main competitions are the four-day **Supersport Series** and the series of one-day matches, the **Standard Bank Cup**. Both contests see the eleven provincial teams slogging it out for national dominance. Games are played throughout the week, and admission is around R25 standing or sitting on the grass and R40 for a seat. In the international standings, South Africa are one of the world's top teams, and you stand a good chance of being around for an international test or one-day series if you're in the country between November and March. Expect to pay between R100 and R160 for an international.

Running and cycling

South Africa is very strong at **long-distance running**, a tradition that reached its apotheosis at the 1996 Atlanta Olympics when Josiah Thugwane won the marathon, becoming the first black South African ever to bag Olympic gold. The biggest single athletics event in South Africa, the **Comrades Marathon**, attracts nearly 15,000 participants, among them some of the world's leading international ultra-marathon runners. The ninety-kilometre course crosses the hilly country between Durban and Pietermaritzburg, with a drop of almost 800m between the town and the coast. Run annually on May 31, the race alternates direction each year and is notable for having been non-racial since 1975, although it wasn't until 1989 that a black South African, Samuel Tshabalala, won it. Since then, black athletes have begun to dominate the front rankings. Almost as famous is the **Two Oceans ultra-marathon** which attracts 10,000 competitors each April to test themselves on the 56-kilometre course that spectacularly circuits the Cape Peninsula.

Traversing a 109-kilometre route, the **Pick 'n Pay Cape Argus Cycle Tour** also includes the Cape Peninsula in its routing. The largest – and most spectacular – individually timed cycle race anywhere, it attracts 35,000 participants from around the world each year in March.

Horse racing

You'll find huge interest among rich and poor South Africans in **horse racing**, with totes and tracks in all the main cities. Its popularity is partly due to the fact that for decades this was the only form of public gambling that South Africa's Afrikaner Calvinist rulers allowed – on the pretext that it involved skill not chance. The highlight of the racing calendar is the **Durban July Handicap** held at Durban's Greyville racecourse. A flamboyant event, it attracts huge crowds, massive purses, socialites in outrageous headgear and vast amounts of media attention.

Parks, reserves and wilderness areas

No other African country has as rich a variety of parks, reserves and wilderness areas as South Africa. Literally hundreds of game reserves and state forests pepper the terrain, creating a bewildering but enticing breadth of choice. While there are dozens of unsung treasures among these, the big destinations amount to some two dozen parks geared to protecting the country's wildlife and wilderness areas.

With a few exceptions these fall under **KwaZulu-Natal Wildlife** (PO Box 13069, Cascades, Pietermaritzburg 3202; ☎033 845 1000, ⓦwww.kznwildlife.com), which controls most of the public reserves in KwaZulu-Natal, and **South African National Parks** (SAN Parks; PO Box 787, Pretoria 0001; street address 643 Leyds St, Muckleneuk, Pretoria; ☎012 428 9111, ⓦwww .sanparks.org), which covers the rest of the country. In addition to the state-run parks there are private reserves, frequently abutting onto them and sharing the same wildlife population.

It's important to realize that only some national parks are game reserves; the chart on pp.66-67 details what to expect from the major parks. While most people come for South Africa's superb **wildlife**, don't let the **Big Five** (buffalo, elephant, leopard, lion and rhino) blinker you into missing out on the marvellous **wilderness areas** that take in

Park fees, reservations and enquiries

Fees given in our park accounts are generally **conservation fees**, payable **daily**. The most expensive places are the Kruger National Park and Kgalagadi Transfrontier Park, for which foreign visitors pay a conservation fee of R132 per person. Elsewhere the conservation fee is generally between R60 and R80. As a rule of thumb, foreign visitors aged 12 and under pay half the adult rate; South African residents pay a quarter of the foreign adult fee, while citizens of the Southern Africa Development Community, to which many countries in the region belong, pay half the foreign adult fee.

If you're planning to visit several parks, you may well find it worthwhile to invest in the **Wild Card**, which provides unlimited access to SANParks-run parks for a period of a year. For foreign visitors, the pass costs R795 for an individual or R1395 for two people; there's also a family version covering two adults plus children up to the age of 18, priced at R1795. South Africans pay roughly two-thirds less for the corresponding passes, and have the additional option of buying passes specific to certain groups of parks. The pass is on sale at SANParks-run parks; for more details of the scheme, and to buy the pass online, check Ⓦ www.wildinafrica.com.

Accommodation at most of South Africa's major national parks can be **booked** in advance (to stay in high season, do so several months in advance) through South African National Parks, except at Pilanesberg, for details of which see p.652, and the KwaZulu-Natal reserves, for which you book through KZN Wildlife. Note that if you try booking for South African National Parks over the phone you could well be in for a long wait; contacting them online is recommended. For more on national parks accommodation, see opposite.

dramatic landscapes and less publicized animal life. There are parks protecting marine and coastal areas, wetlands, endangered species, forests, deserts and mountains, usually with the added attraction of assorted animals, birds, insects, reptiles or marine mammals – South Africa is one of the top destinations in the world for land-based whale watching.

If you had to choose just one of the country's top three parks, **Kruger**, stretching up the east flank of Mpumalanga and Limpopo province, would lead the pack for its sheer size (it's larger than Wales and roughly the size of Massachusetts), its range of animals, its varied lowveld habitats and unbeatable game-viewing opportunities. After Kruger, the **Tsitsikamma** in the Western Cape attracts large numbers of visitors for its ancient forests, cliff-faced oceans, the dramatic Storms River Mouth as well as its Otter Trail, South Africa's most popular **hike**. For epic mountain landscapes, nowhere in the country can touch the **Ukhahlamba Drakensberg Park**, which takes in a series of reserves on the KwaZulu-Natal border with Lesotho and offers gentle hikes along watercourses as well as ambitious mountaineering for serious climbers.

The unchallenged status of Kruger as the place for packing in elephants, lions and casts of thousands of animals tends to put the **KwaZulu-Natal parks** in the shade, quite undeservedly. As well as offering the best places in the world for seeing **rhino**, these parks feel less developed than Kruger, and often provide superior accommodation at comparable prices. Both Kruger and KwaZulu-Natal parks offer guided **wildlife trails** and **night drives**, a popular way to catch sight of the elusive denizens that creep around after dark.

Also worth a mention is the **Addo Elephant National Park** in the Eastern Cape, which is presently being expanded and has become Big Five country – the only such major game reserve in the southern half of the country. Addo has a lot more in its favour as well: it has the most diverse landscape of any reserve in the country; it is a day's drive from Cape Town; and it is the only major game reserve in the country that is malaria-free.

Park accommodation

Accommodation at national parks includes **campsites** (expect to pay about R120 per tent); **safari tents** at some of the Kruger and KwaZulu-Natal restcamps (clusters of accommodation, including chalets, safari tents and campsites, in game reserves; from R140 per person); one-room **huts** with shared washing and cooking facilities (R160 per person); one-room en-suite **bungalows** with shared cooking facilities (from R250 per person); and self-contained **cottages** with private bath or shower and cooking facilities (from R280 per person). For groups of four there are self-contained **family cottages** with private bath and kitchen, where the price of the whole unit starts at around R650. In national parks accommodation (excluding campsites) you're supplied with bedding, towels, a fridge and basic cooking utensils. In several of the KwaZulu-Natal parks restcamps, however, you aren't allowed to use the kitchen, but give your food to the camp chef and attendants who prepare and serve the meal and wash up, at no extra cost. Some restcamps have a **shop** selling supplies for picnics or braais, as well as a **restaurant**.

The ultimate wildlife accommodation is in the **private game reserves**, most of which are around the Kruger National Park. Here you pay big bucks for accommodation which is almost always **luxurious**, in large en-suite walk-in tents, or small thatched rondavels, or – in the larger and most expensive lodges – plush rooms with air conditioning. A couple of places have "bush-showers" (a hoisted bucket of hot water with a shower nozzle attached) behind reed screens but open to the sky – one of the great treats of the bush is taking a shower under the southern sky. Some chalets or tents have gaslights or lanterns in the absence of electricity. **Food** is usually good and plentiful, and vegetarians can be catered for. Expect to pay upwards of R2000, rising to several times that amount at the most fashionable spots. It's worth remembering that, high as these prices are, all your meals and game drives are

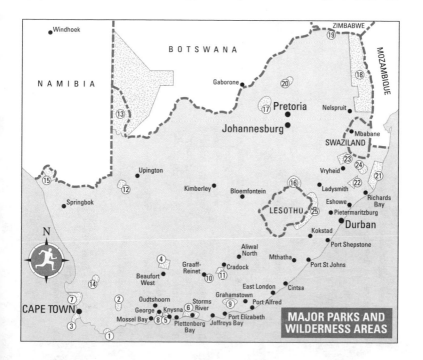

MAJOR PARKS AND WILDERNESS AREAS

Major parks and wildlife areas

Note: The key numbers correspond to those on the map on p.65

KEY	PARK	PRINCIPAL FOCUS	DESCRIPTION AND HIGHLIGHTS	DETAILS
Western Cape				
1	Agulhas NP	Marine and coastal	Rugged southernmost tip of Africa with rich plant biodiversity and significant archeological sites	p.247
2	Bontebok NP	Endangered species	At the foot of rugged mountains, it provides refuge to bontebok and Cape mountain zebra	p.243
3	Table Mountain NP (formerly Cape Peninsula NP)	The natural areas of the peninsula	Boasts extraordinarily rich and diverse flora and fauna that lives in the wild areas forming a large part of Cape Town, including Table Mountain, the Boulders Beach penguin colony and the Cape of Good Hope	p.140 p.152 & p.153
4	Karoo NP	Desert reserve	Arid mountainous landscape with ancient fossils, herbivores and wild flowers in spring	p.255
5	Knysna National Lake Area	Marine and coastal/endangered species	Focused on the Knysna Lagoon and its dramatic Heads that open to the sea, the lake area protects the endangered Knysna seahorse	p.266
6	Tsitsikamma NP	Marine and coastal	Cliffs, tidal pools, deep gorges and evergreen forests; offers snorkelling, scuba and forest trails	p.285
7	West Coast NP	Marine and coastal	Wetland wilderness with birding and watersports	p.296
8	Wilderness NP	Marine and coastal	Lakes, rivers, lagoons, forest, fynbos, beaches and the sea	p.264
Eastern Cape				
9	Addo Elephant NP	Game reserve	The only Big Five national park in the southern half of the country, known for its herd 300-strong elephant	p.377
10	Camdeboo NP	Desert reserve	Karoo semi-desert landscape in the foothills of the Sneeuberg range with 120m-high dolerite pillars rising out of a canyon, the most dramatic examples of which are found in the Valley of Desolation, plus 43 species of herbivore	p.407
11	Mountain Zebra NP	Endangered species	Dramatic hilly landscape in flat country with rare mountain zebras and other herbivores	p.402
Northern Cape				
12	Augrabies Falls NP	Desert reserve	Notable for the dramatic landmark from which the park takes its name, where the Orange River plummets down a deep ravine; also great for desert scenery, antelopes and prolific birdlife	p.345

KEY	PARK	PRINCIPAL FOCUS	DESCRIPTION AND HIGHLIGHTS	DETAILS
13	Kgalagadi Transfrontier Park	Desert/game reserve	Remote desert with rust-red dunes, desert lions, shy leopards and thousands of antelopes	p.340
Northern Cape				
14	Namaqua NP	Marine and coastal / wildflowers	Mountainous and coastal region renowned for its estimated 3500 plant varieties, among them beautiful spring wildflowers	p.353
15	Ai-Ais Richtersveld Transfrontier Park	Mountain and desert	Craggy *kloofs*, high mountains and dramatic landscapes, sweeping inland from the Orange River, which sustain a remarkable range of reptiles, birds, mammals and plant life	p.359
Free State				
16	Golden Gate	Mountain enclave	Resort at the foot of rich sandstone formations in the heart of the Maluti Mountains; trails Highlands NP	p.566
North West				
17	Pilanesberg NP	Game reserve	Mountain-encircled grassland trampled by the Big Five, accessible from Johannesburg	p.651
Limpopo province/Mpumalanga				
18	Kruger NP	Game reserve	The largest, best-stocked and most popular game reserve in the subcontinent	p.690
19	Mapungubwe NP	Archaeology /game reserve	World Heritage Site listed for its significance as the location of a highly developed Iron Age culture that produced finely crafted gold artefacts. Also noted for its landscape and biodiversity, which supports a large variety of mammals including elephants and predators	p.736
20	Marakele NP	Game reserve	Striking landscape of peaks, plateaus and cliffs stocked with lions, elephants, rhinos and a variety of other mammals	p.729
Kwazulu-Natal				
21	Isimangaliso	Coastal wetland	Vast patchwork of wetlands, wilderness, coast and game reserves	p.518
22	Huhluwe-Imfolozi GR	Game reserve	KwaZulu-Natal's hillier, smaller answer to Kruger is among the top African spots for rhinos	p.514
23	Ithala GR	Game reserve	Lesser-known small gem of a game reserve in mountainous country	p.533
24	Mkhuze GR	Game/bird reserve	Top birding venue, excellent for rhinos and other herbivores; walks in wild fig forest	p.524
25	Ukhahlamba Drakensberg Park	Mountain reserve	A series of parks covering the highest, most stirring and most dramatic peaks in South Africa	p.499

included, and as numbers are strictly limited, you get an exclusive experience of the bush in return.

Game viewing

Spotting game takes skill and experience. It's easier than you'd think to mistake a rhino for a large boulder, or to miss the king of the beasts in the tall grass – African game has after all evolved with camouflage in mind. Don't expect the volume of animals you get in wildlife documentaries: what you see is always a matter of luck, patience and skill. If you're new to the African bush and its wildlife, consider shelling out for at least two nights at one of the luxurious lodges on a private reserve (for example, those abutting Kruger); they're staffed by well-informed rangers who lead game-viewing outings in open-topped 4WDs.

The section on Kruger National Park (see p.690) gives more advice on how to go about spotting game and how to enjoy and understand what you do see – whether it's a brightly coloured lizard in a rest camp, head-butting giraffes at a waterhole or dust-kicking rhinos. For **books** that can enhance your visit to a game reserve – especially if you plan a self-drive safari – see p.881.

Self-drive safaris

The least expensive way of experiencing a game park is by renting a car and **driving** around a national park, taking advantage of the self-catering and camping facilities. You'll have the thrill of spotting game yourself and at your own pace, rather than relying on a ranger, and for people with **children**, a self-drive safari is the principal way to see a game reserve, as most of the upmarket lodges don't admit under-12s. The one real disadvantage of self-driving is that you can end up jostling with other cars to get a view, especially when it comes to lion-watching. Also, you may not know what animal signs to look for, and unless you travel in a minibus or 4WD vehicle you're unlikely to be high enough off the ground to be able to see across the veld.

The KwaZulu-Natal game reserves – foremost among them **Hluhluwe-Imfolozi**, **Mkhuze** and **Ithala** – offer rewarding opportunities for self-drive touring.

The same applies to the **Pilanesberg Game Reserve** in North West Province, while the remote **Kgalagadi Transfrontier Park** that stretches across the border into Botswana promises truly exciting wilderness driving. You might choose to cover a route that combines the substantial Kruger National Park with the more intimate reserves of KwaZulu-Natal province.

If you plan to self-drive, consider investing in good animal and bird field guides, and a decent pair of **binoculars** – one pair per person is recommended if you want to keep your relationships on a friendly footing. Finally, whether you're cooking or not, it's worth taking a thermos for tea and a cool bag to keep water cold.

Escorted safaris

It's possible to book places on a **safari excursion** – such packages are often organized by backpackers' lodges located near reserves, and occasionally by hotels and B&Bs. On the downside, these don't give you the experience of waking up in the wild, and entail spending considerably more time on the road than if you were based inside a reserve. But during South African school holidays, when Kruger, for example, is booked to capacity, you may have no other option.

Mostly, you get what you pay for as regards game-viewing packages. Be wary of any cheap deals on "safari farms" in the vicinity of Kruger. These are generally fine if you want to see animals in what are essentially huge zoos and make an acceptable overnight stop en route to Kruger, but are no substitute for a real wilderness experience – sooner or later you hit fences and gates on your game drive. Some of the better places in this category are listed in the relevant chapters.

Safaris on private reserves

If you choose well, the ultimate South African game experience has to be in a **private reserve**. You can relax while your game-viewing activities are organized, and because you spend time in a small group you get a stronger sense of the wild than you ever could at one of the big Kruger rest camps. Best of all, you get the benefit of knowledgeable rangers, who can explain the terrain and small-scale wildlife as they drive you around looking for game.

Privately run safari lodges in concessions inside Kruger and some other national parks, such as Addo, operate along similar lines. The smaller private reserves accommodate between ten and sixteen guests; larger camps often cater to two or three times as many people, and resemble hotels in the bush. Many safari lodges have their own waterholes, overlooked by the bar, from which you can watch animals drinking. Nowhere are the private reserves more developed than along the west flank of the Kruger, where you'll find the top-dollar prestigious lodges as well as some places offering more bang for fewer bucks.

A **typical day** at a private camp or lodge starts at dawn for tea or coffee followed by guided game viewing on foot, or driving. After a mid-morning brunch/breakfast, there's the chance to spend time on a viewing platform or in a hide, quietly watching the passing scene. Late-afternoon game viewing is a repeat of early morning but culminates with sundowners as the light fades, and often turns into a night drive with spotlights out looking for nocturnal creatures.

Prices, which include accommodation, meals and all game activities, vary widely. The ultra-expensive camps offer more luxury and social cachet, but not necessarily better game viewing. You might find the cheaper camps in the same areas more to your taste, their plainer and wilder atmosphere more in keeping with the bush.

Health

You can put aside most of the health fears that may be justified in some parts of Africa; run-down hospitals and bizarre tropical diseases aren't typical of South Africa. All tourist areas boast generally high standards of hygiene and safe drinking water. The only hazard you're likely to encounter, and the one the majority of visitors are most blasé about, is the sun. In some parts of the country there is a risk of malaria, and you will need to take precautions.

Public **hospitals** in South Africa are fairly well equipped, but they are facing huge pressures under which their attempts to maintain standards are unfortunately buckling. Expect long waits and frequently indifferent treatment. Private hospitals or clinics, which are well up to British or North American standards, are usually a better option for travellers. You're likely to get more personal treatment and the costs are nowhere near as high as in the US – besides which, the expense shouldn't pose a problem if you're adequately insured. Private hospitals are listed in the town and city listings throughout the Guide.

Dental care in South Africa is well up to British and North American standards, and is less expensive. You'll find **dentists** in all the cities and most smaller towns, listed after doctors at the beginning of each town in the telephone directory.

Inoculations

Although no specific **inoculations** are compulsory if you arrive from the West, it's wise to ensure that your **polio** and **tetanus** vaccinations are up to date. A **yellow fever** vaccination certificate is necessary if you've come from a country where the disease is endemic, such as Kenya, Tanzania or tropical South America.

In addition to these, the Hospital for Tropical Diseases in London recommends, depending on which parts of the country you're visiting, a course of shots against

69

typhoid and an injection against **hepatitis A**, both of which can be caught from contaminated food or water. This is a worst-case scenario, and in any case, typhoid is eminently curable and few visitors to South Africa ever catch it.

Vaccination against **hepatitis B** is essential only for people involved in health work; the disease is spread by the transfer of blood products, usually dirty needles.

If you decide to have an armful of jabs, start organizing them **six weeks** before departure. If you're going to another African country first and need the yellow fever jab, note that a yellow fever certificate only becomes valid ten days after you've had the shot.

Medical resources for travellers

UK & Ireland

Hospital for Tropical Diseases Travel Clinic ☎020/7387 4411 or 0845/155 5000, ⓦwww .thehtd.org. Reliable, up-to-date health briefing on South Africa and what precautions you should take. Also sells travellers' health products.
MASTA (Medical Advisory Service for Travellers Abroad) ☎0870/606 2782 or ⓦwww.masta.org. Online health briefs and details of UK clinics.
Travel Medicine Services ☎028/9031 5220. Travel advice before you leave.
Tropical Medical Bureau ☎1850/487 674, ⓦwww.tmb.ie. Advice on inoculations, malaria precautions and other health issues relating to South Africa.

US & Canada

Canadian Society for International Health ⓦwww.csih.org. Extensive list of travel health centres.
CDC ⓦwww.cdc.gov/travel. Official US government travel health site.
International Society for Travel Medicine wwww.istm.org. A list of travel health clinics throughout the world.

Australia & New Zealand

Travellers' Medical and Vaccination Centres ☎1300/ 658 844, ⓦwww.tmvc.com.au. Lists travel clinics in Australia and New Zealand.

Stomach upsets

Stomach upsets from food are rare. Salad and ice – the danger items in many other developing countries – are both perfectly safe. As anywhere, though, don't keep food for too long, and be sure to wash fruit and vegetables as thoroughly as possible.

If you do get a **stomach bug**, the best cure is lots of water and rest. Papayas – the flesh as well as the pips – are a good tonic to offset the runs. Otherwise, most chemists should have name-brand anti-diarrhoea remedies, such as Lomotil.

Avoid jumping for **antibiotics** at the first sign of illness. Instead keep them as a last resort – they don't work on viruses and annihilate your "gut flora" (most of which you want to keep), making you more susceptible next time round. Most tummy upsets will resolve themselves if you adopt a sensible fat-free diet for a couple of days, but if they do persist without improvement (or are accompanied by other unusual symptoms), then see a doctor as soon as possible.

The sun

The **sun** is likely to be the worst hazard you'll encounter in Southern Africa, particularly if you're fair-skinned. The dangers of overexposure to the sun, including the risk of skin cancer, are something white South Africans haven't yet caught on to, and locals still regard their tans as more important than their health.

Short-term effects of **overexposure** to the sun include burning, nausea and headaches. This usually comes from overeager tanning, which can leave you looking like a lobster. The fairer your skin, the slower you should take tanning. Start with short periods of exposure and **high protection sunscreen** (at least SPF 15), gradually increasing your time in the sun and decreasing the factor of your screen. Many people with fair skins, especially those who freckle easily, should take extra care, starting with a very high factor screen (SPF 25–30), and continue using at least SPF 15 for the rest of their stay.

Overexposure to the sun can cause sunburn to the surface of the eye, inflammation of the cornea and can result in serious short- and long-term damage. Good **sunglasses** can reduce ultraviolet (UV) light exposure to the eye by fifty percent. A **broad-brimmed hat** is also recommended.

These last measures are especially necessary for children, who should ideally be kept well covered at the seaside. Don't be lulled into complacency on cloudy days, when UV levels can still be high. UV-protective clothing is available locally, but it's best to buy before you arrive; some excellent ranges are made in Australia. If you don't come with this gear, make sure children wear T-shirts at the beach, and use SPF 30 sunscreen liberally and often.

Bilharzia

One ailment that you need to take seriously throughout sub-Saharan Africa is **bilharzia** (schistosomiasis), carried in most freshwater lakes and rivers in South Africa except in the mountains. Bilharzia is spread by tiny, parasitic worm-like flukes which leave their water-snail hosts and burrow into human skin to multiply in the bloodstream; they then work their way to the walls of the intestine or bladder, where they begin to lay eggs.

The chances are you'll avoid bilharzia even if you swim in a suspect river, but it's best to avoid swimming in dams and rivers where possible. If you go canoeing or can't avoid the water, have a test for bilharzia when you return home.

Symptoms may be no more than a feeling of lassitude and ill health. Once the infection is established, abdominal pain and blood in the urine and stools are common. Fortunately, although no vaccine is available, bilharzia is easily and effectively treatable.

Malaria

Most of South Africa is free of **malaria**, a potentially lethal disease that is widespread in tropical and subtropical Africa, where it's a major killer. However, protection against malaria is essential if you're planning to travel to any of these areas: northern and north-eastern Mpumalanga, notably the Kruger National Park; northern KwaZulu-Natal; the border regions of North West and Limpopo provinces; and low-lying areas of Swaziland. The **highest risk** is during the hot, wet months from **November to April**. The risk is reduced during the cooler, dry months from May to October, when some people decide not to take prophylactic medication.

Malaria is caused by a parasite carried in the saliva of the female anopheles mosquito. It has a variable incubation period of a few

days to several weeks, so you can become ill long after being bitten. The first **symptoms** of malaria can be mistaken for flu, starting off relatively mildly with a variable combination that includes fever, aching limbs and shivering, which come in waves, usually beginning in the early evening. Deterioration can be rapid as the parasites in the bloodstream proliferate. Malaria is not infectious, but can be fatal if not treated quickly: get **medical help** without delay if you go down with flu-like symptoms within a week of entering or three months of leaving a malarial area.

Doctors can advise on which kind of **anti-malarial tablets** to take. It's important to keep to the prescribed dose, which covers the period before and after your trip. Consult your doctor or clinic several weeks **before you travel**, as you should start taking medication a week or two before entering the affected region – depending on the particular drug you're using.

Whatever you decide to take, be aware that no antimalarial drug is totally effective – your only sure fire protection is to **avoid getting bitten**. Malaria-carrying mosquitoes are active between dusk and dawn, so try to avoid being out at this time, or at least cover yourself well. Sleep under a **mosquito net** when possible, making sure to tuck it under the mattress, and burn **mosquito coils** (which you can buy everywhere) for a peaceful, if noxious, night. Electric mosquito-destroyers which you fit with a pad every night are less pungent than mosquito coils, though note that you may not have access to a power supply at some safari lodges, or if you're camping. Mosquito "buzzers" are useless. Whenever the mosquitoes are particularly bad – and that's not often – cover your exposed parts with **insect repellent**; those containing diethyltoluamide (DEET) work well. Other locally produced repellents such as Peaceful Sleep are widely available.

Bites and stings

Bites, stings and rashes in South Africa are comparatively rare. **Snakes** are present, but hardly ever seen as they move out of the way quickly. The sluggish puff and berg adders are the most dangerous, because they often lie in paths and don't move when humans approach. The best advice if you get bitten is to note what the snake looked like and get yourself to a clinic or hospital. Most bites are not fatal and the worst thing you can do is to panic: desperate measures with razor blades and tourniquets risk doing more harm than good.

Tick-bite fever is occasionally contracted from walking in the bush, particularly in long wet grass. The offending ticks can be minute and you may not spot them. Symptoms appear a week later – swollen glands and severe aching of the bones, backache and fever. The disease will run its course in three or four days. Ticks you may find on yourself are not dangerous, just repulsive at first. Make sure you pull out the head as well as the body (it's not painful). A good way of removing small ones is to smear Vaseline or grease over them, making them release their hold.

Scorpion stings and **spider bites** are painful but almost never fatal, contrary to popular myth. Scorpions and spiders abound, but they're hardly ever seen unless you turn over logs and stones. If you're collecting wood for a campfire, knock or shake it before picking it up. Another simple precaution when camping is to shake out your shoes and clothes in the morning before you get dressed.

Rabies is present throughout southern Africa. Be wary of animals and go immediately to a clinic if bitten. Rabies can be treated effectively with a course of injections.

Sexually transmitted diseases

HIV/AIDS and venereal diseases are widespread in southern Africa among both men and women, and the danger of catching the virus through sexual contact is very real. Follow the usual precautions regarding safer sex. There's no special risk from medical treatment in the country, but if you're travelling overland and you want to play it safe, take your own needle and transfusion kit.

Crime and personal safety

Despite horror stories of sky-high crime rates, most people visit South Africa without incident; be careful, but don't be paranoid. This is not to underestimate the issue – crime is probably the most serious problem facing the country. However, once you realize that crime is disproportionately concentrated in the poor African and coloured townships, the scale becomes less terrifying. Violent crime is a particular problem not just in the townships but also in Johannesburg, where the dangers are the worst in the country.

Protecting property and "security" are major national obsessions, and it's difficult to imagine what many South Africans would discuss at their dinner parties if the problem disappeared. A substantial percentage of middle-class homes subscribe to the services of armed **private security firms**. The other obvious manifestation of this obsession is the huge number of alarms, high walls and electronically controlled gates you'll find, not just in the suburbs, but even in less deprived areas of some townships. **Guns** are openly carried by police – and often citizens.

If you fall victim to a **mugging**, you should take very seriously the usual advice not to resist and do as you're told. The chances of this happening can be greatly minimized by using common sense and following a few simple rules (see box opposite).

Drugs and drink-driving

Dagga (pronounced like "dugger" with the "gg" guttural, as in the Scottish pronunciation of "loch") is cannabis in dried leaf form, South Africa's most widely produced and widely used drug. Grown in hot regions like KwaZulu-Natal (the source of Durban Poison), Swaziland (Swazi Gold) and as a cash crop in parts of the former Transkei, it is fairly easily available and the quality is generally good – but this doesn't alter the fact that it is illegal. If you do decide to partake, you should take particular care when scoring, as visitors have run into trouble dealing with unfamiliar local conditions.

Strangely, for a country that sometimes seems to be on one massive binge, South Africa has laws that prohibit drinking in public – not that anyone pays any attention to them. The **drink-drive laws** are routinely and brazenly flouted, making the country's roads the one real danger you should be concerned about. People routinely stock up their cars with booze for long journeys, and even at filling stations you'll find places selling liquor. Levels of alcohol consumption go some way to explaining why during the Christmas holidays over a thousand people die in an annual orgy of carnage on the roads.

Safety tips

In general:
• try not to look like a tourist.
• dress down.
• don't carry a camera or video openly in cities.
• avoid wearing jewellery or expensive watches.
• leave your designer shades at home – they are sometimes pulled off people's faces.
• if you are accosted, remain calm and cooperative.

When on foot:
• grasp bags firmly under your arm.
• don't carry excessive sums of money on you.
• don't put your wallet in your back trouser pocket.
• always know where your valuables are.
• don't leave valuables exposed (on a seat or the ground) while having a meal or drink.
• develop an awareness of what people in the street around you are doing.
• don't let strangers get too close to you – especially people in groups.
• in big cities, travel around in pairs or groups.

On the road:
• lock all your car doors, especially in cities.
• keep rear windows sufficiently rolled up to keep out opportunistic hands.
• never leave anything worth stealing in view when your car is unattended.

On the beach:
• take only the bare essentials.
• don't leave valuables, especially cameras, unattended.
• safeguard car keys by pinning them to your swimming gear, or putting them in a waterproof wallet or splash box and taking them into the water with you.

At ATMs:
Cash machines are favourite hunting grounds for sophisticated con men who use cunning rather than force to steal money. Never underestimate their ability and don't get drawn into *any* interaction at an ATM, no matter how well spoken, friendly or distressed the other person appears. If they claim to have a problem with the machine, tell them to contact the bank. Don't let people crowd you or see your personal identification number (PIN) when you withdraw money; if in doubt, go to another machine. Finally, if your card gets swallowed, report it without delay.

Sexual harassment

South Africa's extremely high incidence of **rape** doesn't as a rule affect tourists. In fact women are very unlikely to need to fend off the unwanted attentions of men. However, at heart the majority of the country's males, regardless of race, hold on to fairly sexist attitudes. Sometimes your eagerness to be friendly may be taken as a sexual overture – always be sensitive to potential crossed wires and unintended signals.

Women should avoid travelling on their own, nor should they hitchhike or walk alone in deserted areas. This applies equally to cities, the countryside or anywhere after dark. Minibus taxis should be ruled out as a means of transport after dark, especially if you're not exactly sure of local geography.

The police

For many black South Africans, the **South African National Police** (SANP) still carry strong associations of collaboration with apartheid and a lot of public relations work has yet to be done to turn the police into a genuine people's law enforcement agency. Poorly paid, shot at (and frequently hit), underfunded, badly equipped, barely respected and demoralized, the police keep a low profile. If you ever get stopped, at a roadblock for example (one of the likeliest encounters), always be courteous. And if you're driving, note that under South African law you are required to carry your **driver's licence** at all times.

If you are robbed, you will need to report the incident to the police, who should give you a case reference for insurance purposes – though don't expect too much crime-cracking enthusiasm, or to get your property back.

Travel essentials

Costs

The most expensive thing about visiting South Africa is getting there. Once you've arrived, you're likely to find it a relatively inexpensive destination. How cheap you find South Africa will depend partly on exchange rates at the time of your visit – in the decade after becoming fully convertible (after the advent of democracy in South Africa) the rand has seen some massive fluctuations against sterling, the dollar and the euro.

When it comes to **daily budgets**, your biggest expense is likely to be accommodation. If you're willing to stay in backpacker lodges and self-cater, you should be able to get by on under £15/$30/€20 a day. If you stay in B&Bs and guesthouses, eat out once a day, and have a snack or two you should budget for at least double that. In luxury hotels and game lodges, expect to pay upwards of £100/US$200/€150 a day. Extras such as car rental, outdoor activities, horse-riding and safaris will add to these figures substantially. While most **museums** and **art galleries** impose an entry fee, it's usually quite low: only the most sophisticated attractions charge more than £1/$2/€1.50.

For a discussion of **costs in Lesotho and Swaziland**, see the relevant chapters in the Guide.

Disabled travellers

Facilities for **disabled travellers** in South Africa are not as sophisticated as those found in the developed world, but they're sufficient to ensure you have a satisfactory visit. By accident rather than design, you'll find pretty good accessibility to many buildings, as South Africans tend to build low (single-storey bungalows are the norm), with the result that you'll have to deal with fewer stairs than you may be accustomed to. As the car is king, you'll frequently find that you can drive to, and park right outside, your destination.

There are **organized tours** and holidays specifically for people with disabilities, and **activity-based packages** for disabled travellers to South Africa are increasingly available. These packages offer the possibility for wheelchair-bound visitors to take part in safaris, sport and a vast range of adventure activities, including whitewater rafting, horse-riding, parasailing and zip-lining. Tours can either be taken as self-drive trips or packages for large groups. The contacts below will be able to put you in touch with South Africa travel specialists.

If you want to be more independent on your travels, it's important to know where you can expect help and where you must be self-reliant, especially regarding transport and accommodation. It's also vital to know your limitations, and to make sure others know them. If you do not use a wheelchair all the time but your walking capabilities are limited, remember that you are likely to need to cover greater distances while travelling (often over rougher terrain and in hotter temperatures) than you are used to. If you use a wheelchair, have it serviced before you go and take a repair kit with you.

Titch Tours (26 Station Rd, Rondebosch 7700, Cape Town ☎021 689 4151, ⓦwww .titchtours.co.za) has a portfolio that includes programmes for physically disabled and visually impaired people. You could also visit ⓦ**www.access-able.com**, a US-based.

Emergencies

Police ☎1011, Ambulance ☎10177

Electricity

South Africa's **electricity** supply runs at 220/230V, 50Hz AC. Sockets take unique round-pinned plugs; see ⓦwww.kropla.com for details. Most hotel rooms have sockets that will take 110V electric shavers, but for other appliances US visitors will need an adaptor.

Entry requirements

Nationals of the EU, the US, Canada, Australia and New Zealand don't require a **visa** to enter South Africa. As long as you carry a passport that is valid for at least six months and with at least two empty pages

you will be granted a temporary visitor's permit, which allows you to stay in South Africa for up to 90 days. All visitors should have a valid return ticket; without one, you may be required to pay the authorities the equivalent of your fare home (the money will be refunded after you have left the country). Visitors may also need to prove that they have sufficient funds to cover their stay.

Applications for **visa extensions** must be made at one of the main offices of the Department of Home Affairs, where you will be quizzed about your intentions and your funds. In Cape Town, go to 56 Barrack St (☎021 462 4970); in Johannesburg, the office is at the corner of Plein and Harrison streets (☎011 639 4000). The Department also has offices in a number of towns – check in the telephone directory or on its website (ⓦwww.home-affairs.gov.za/regions .asp), and make sure that the office you're intending to visit is able to grant extensions.

South African diplomatic missions abroad

Australia corner State Circle and Rhodes Place, Yarralumla, Canberra, ACT 2600 ☎02/6272 7300, ⓦwww.sahc.org.au.
Canada 15 Sussex Drive, Ottawa, Ontario K1M 1M8 ☎613/744-0330, ⓦwww.southafrica-canada.ca.
Netherlands Wassenaarseweg 40, 2596 CJ, The Hague ☎070/392 4501, ⓦwww.zuidafrika.nl.
New Zealand c/o the High Commission in Australia.
UK Consular Section, 15 Whitehall, London SW1A 2DD ☎020/7925 8900, ⓦwww.southafricahouse .com.
US 3051 Massachusetts Ave NW, Washington, DC 20008 ☎202/232-4400, ⓦwww.saembassy.org. Consulates: 333 E 38th St, 9th floor, New York, NY 10016 ☎212/213-4880, ⓦwww .southafrica-newyork.net; 6300 Wilshire Blvd, Suite 600, Los Angeles, CA 90048 ☎323/651-0902, ⓦwww.link2southafrica.com.

Gay and lesbian travellers

South Africa has the world's first **gay- and lesbian-friendly** constitution, and Africa's most developed and diverse gay and lesbian scene. Not only is homosexuality legal for consenting adults of 18 or over, but the constitution outlaws any discrimination on the grounds of sexual orientation. This means that, for once, you have the law on your side. Outside the big cities, however, South Africa is a pretty conservative place where open displays of public affection by gays and lesbians are unlikely to go down well; many whites will find it un-Christian, while blacks will think it un-African.

South African Tourism, on the other hand, is well aware of the potential of pink spending power and actively woos gay travellers – an effort that is evidently paying off, with **Cape Town** ranking among the world's top gay destinations. The city is South Africa's – and indeed, the African continent's – gay capital. Like many things in the city, Cape Town's gay scene (see p.169 for more) is white dominated, though there are a few gay-friendly clubs starting to emerge in the surrounding townships. The gay scene is a lot more multiracial in **Johannesburg**, especially in the clubs. The **Pretoria** gay and lesbian scene has grown enormously over the past few years. There are also gay scenes in **Port Elizabeth** and **Durban** and you'll find a growing number of gay-run or gay-friendly establishments in small towns all over the country. Jo'burg has its own gay pride festival in September (🌐www.sapride .org), while the Out in Africa South African Gay and Lesbian Film Festival (🌐www.oia .co.za) takes place in Cape Town and Johannesburg in November. An excellent resource is the website of the lesbian travel agency **Wanderwomen** (🌐www.wanderwomen .co.za), which apart from arranging itineraries for women also has excellent links to other websites covering gay and lesbian interests.

Insurance

It's wise to take out an **insurance policy** to cover against theft, loss and illness or injury prior to visiting South Africa. A typical travel insurance policy usually provides cover for the loss of baggage, tickets and – up to a certain limit – cash or cheques, as well as cancellation or curtailment of your journey. Most of them exclude so-called **dangerous sports** unless an extra premium is paid: in South Africa this can mean scuba diving, whitewater rafting, windsurfing, horse-riding, bungee jumping and paragliding. In addition to these it's well worth checking whether you

are covered by your policy if you're hiking, kayaking, pony trekking or game viewing on safari, all activities people commonly take part in when visiting South Africa. Many policies can be chopped and changed to exclude coverage you don't need – for example, sickness and accident benefits can often be excluded or included at will. If you do take **medical coverage**, ascertain whether benefits will be paid as treatment proceeds or only after you return home, and if there is a 24-hour medical emergency number. When securing **baggage cover**, make sure that the per-article limit will cover your most valuable possession. If you need to make a claim, you should keep receipts for medicines and medical treatment, and in the event you have anything stolen, you must obtain an official statement from the police.

Rough Guides has teamed up with Columbus Direct to offer you **travel insurance** that can be tailored to suit your needs. Products include a low-cost **backpacker** option for long stays; a **short break** option for city getaways; a typical **holiday package** option; and others. There are also annual **multi-trip** policies for those who travel regularly, with variable levels of cover available. Different sports and activities (trekking, scuba diving, abseiling, etc) can usually be covered if required. See our website – 🌐www.roughguidesinsurance.com for eligibility and puchasing options. Alternatively, UK residents should call ☎0870/033-9988; for US citizens the number is ☎1-800/749-4922; Australians should call ☎1-300/669 999. All other nationalities should call ☎+44 870/890 2843.

Internet

Finding somewhere to access the **Internet** will seldom be a problem in South Africa: cybercafés are found even in relatively small towns, and most **backpacker hostels** and hotels have Internet and email facilities. If you are carrying your own computer or palm-top device you'll also be able to take advantage of the wireless hotspots at a small (but growing) number of cafés and accommodation.

Mail

The deceptively familiar feel of South African post offices can lull you into expecting an efficient British- or US-style service. In fact, **post** within the country is slow and unreliable, and money and valuables frequently disappear en route. Expect domestic delivery times from one city to another of about a week – longer if a rural town is involved at either end. **International airmail** deliveries are often quicker, especially if you're sending or receiving at Johannesburg or Cape Town – the cities with direct flights to London. A letter or package sent by surface mail can take anything up to six weeks to get from South Africa to London.

Most towns of any size have a **post office**, generally open Monday to Friday 8.30am to 4.30pm and Saturday 8am to 11.30am (closing earlier in some places). The ubiquitous private **PostNet** outlets (Ⓦwww.postnet.co.za) offer many of the same postal services as the post office and more, including courier services. Courier companies like Federal Express (☎0800 033 339, Ⓦwww.fedex.com/za) and DHL (☎0860 345 000, Ⓦwww.dhl.co.za) are more expensive and available only in the larger towns, but far more reliable than the mail.

Stamps are available at post offices and also from newsagents, such as the CNA chain as well as supermarkets. Postage is relatively inexpensive – it costs about R4 to send a postcard by airmail to anywhere in the world, while a small letter costs about R5 to send. You'll find **poste restante** facilities at the main post office in most larger centres, and in many backpackers' hostels.

Maps

Many place names in South Africa were changed after the 1994 elections – and changes are still being made – so if you buy a **map** before leaving home, make sure that it's up to date. Bartholomew produces an excellent map of **South Africa**, including Lesotho and Swaziland (1:2,000,000), as part of its World Travel Map series. The *Rough Guide Map: South Africa, Lesotho & Swaziland* covers the same turf with the advantage that it's rip-proof and waterproof. Also worth investing in are MapStudio's "Miniplan" maps of major cities such as Cape Town, Durban and Pretoria: these are a convenient size and have useful details, such as hotels, cinemas, post offices and hospitals. MapStudio also

produces good regional maps, featuring scenic routes and street maps of major towns, and a fine Natal Drakensberg map which shows hiking trails, picnic spots, campsites and places of interest.

South Africa's motoring organization, the Automobile Association (AA; see p.46), offers a wide selection of excellent regional maps, free to members, which you can pick up from its offices.

Money

South Africa's currency is the **rand** (R), often called the "buck", divided into 100 **cents**. Notes come in R10, R20, R50, R100 and R200 denominations and there are coins of 5, 10, 20 and 50 cents, as well as R1, R2 and R5. At the time of writing, the **exchange rate** was hovering at just around R14 to the pound sterling, R7 to the US dollar, R10 to the euro and R6 to the Australian dollar.

All but the tiniest settlement will have a **bank** where you can **change money** swiftly and easily. **Banking hours** are Monday to Friday 9am to 3.30pm, and Saturday 9am to 11am; the banks in smaller towns usually close for lunch. In major cities, some banks operate bureaux de change that stay open until 7pm. Outside banking hours, some hotels will change money, although this entails a fairly hefty commission. You can also change money at branches of American Express and Rennies Travel.

Cards and traveller's cheques

Credit and debit cards are the most convenient way to access your funds in South Africa. Most international cards can be used to withdraw money at **automatic teller machines** (ATMs), open 24 hours a day in the cities and elsewhere. Ask your bank which option you should choose for your card when the machine asks for the account type (cheque, savings, transmission or credit). Plastic can come in very handy for hotel bookings and for paying for more mainstream and upmarket tourist facilities, and is essential for car rental. Visa and Mastercard are the cards most widely accepted in major cities.

Traveller's cheques make a useful backup as they can be replaced if lost or stolen.

American Express, Visa and Thomas Cook are all widely recognized brands; both US dollar and sterling cheques are accepted in South Africa.

Traveller's cheques and plastic are useless if you're heading into remote areas, where you'll need to carry **cash**, preferably in a very safe place, such as a leather pouch or waist-level money belt you can keep under your clothes.

Opening hours and holidays

The working day starts and finishes early in South Africa: shops and businesses generally open on weekdays at 8.30am or 9am and close at 4.30pm or 5pm. In small towns, many places close for an hour over lunch. Many **shops** and businesses close around noon on Saturdays, and most shops are closed on Sundays. However, in every neighbourhood, you'll find small shops and supermarkets where you can buy groceries and essentials after hours.

Some establishments have summer and winter opening times. In such situations, you can take winter to mean April to August or September, while summer constitutes the rest of the year.

School holidays in South Africa can disrupt your plans, especially if you want to camp, or stay in the national parks and the cheaper end of accommodation (self-catering, cheaper B&Bs, etc), all of which are likely to be booked solid during those periods. If you do travel to South Africa over the school holidays, book your accommodation well in advance, especially for the national parks.

The longest and busiest holiday period is **Christmas (summer)**, which for schools stretches over most of December and January. Flights and train berths can be hard to get from December 16 to January 2, when many businesses and offices close for their annual break. You should book your flights – long-haul and domestic – as early as six months in advance for the Christmas period. The inland and coastal provinces stagger their school holidays, but as a general rule the remaining school holidays roughly cover the following periods: **Easter**, mid-March to mid-April; **winter**, mid-June to mid-July; and **spring**, late September to early October. Exact dates for each year are given on the government's information website: ⓦwww.info.gov.za /aboutsa/schoolcal.htm.

Phones

South Africa's telephone system, operated by the state monopoly, **Telkom**, generally works well. Public phone booths are found in every city and town, and are either coin- or card-operated. While **international calls** can be made from virtually any phone, it helps to have a phone card, as you'll be lucky to stay on the line for more than a minute or two for R20. Phone cards come in R15, R20, R50, R100 and R200 denominations, available at Telkom offices, post offices and newsagents.

Mobile phones (referred to locally as cell phones or simply cells) are extremely widely used in South Africa, with more mobile than land-line handsets now in use in the country. The competing networks – Vodacom, MTN, Cell C and VirginMobile –

South African public holidays

Many shops and tourist-related businesses remain open over public holidays, although often with shorter opening hours. Christmas Day and Good Friday, when most of the country shuts down, are the only exceptions. The main holidays are:

New Year's Day (Jan 1)
Human Rights Day (March 21)
Good Friday, Easter Monday (variable)
Freedom Day (April 27)
Workers' Day (May 1)

Youth Day (June 16)
National Women's Day (Aug 9)
Heritage Day (Sept 24)
Day of Reconciliation (Dec 16)
Christmas Day (Dec 25)
Day of Goodwill (Dec 26)

> Any South African land line has a ten-digit number incorporating the old three-digit area code at the start. Calling a land line requires you to dial all ten digits even if the number you're dialling has the same area code as yours.

cover all the main areas and the national roads connecting them.

You can use a GSM/tri-band phone from outside the country in South Africa, but you will need to arrange a **roaming agreement** with your provider at home; be warned this is likely to be expensive. A far cheaper alternative is to buy a **local SIM card** which replaces your home SIM card while you're in South Africa. (For this to work, you'll need to check that your phone hasn't been locked to your home network.) The local SIM card contains your South African phone number, and you pay for airtime with **prepaid cards**. Very inexpensive starter packs (R100 or less) containing a SIM card and some airtime can be bought from the ubiquitous mobile phone shops and a number of other outlets, including supermarkets and the CNA chain of newsagents and supermarkets.

Calling home from South Africa

To dial **out of South Africa**, the international access code is ☏00. Remember to omit any initial zero in the number of the place you're phoning.
Australia ☏61
Republic of Ireland ☏353
New Zealand ☏64
UK ☏44
US & Canada ☏1

Taxes

Value-added tax (VAT) of fourteen percent is levied on most goods and services, though it's usually already included in any quoted price. Foreign visitors can claim back VAT on any goods over R250. To do this, you must present an official tax receipt for the goods, a non-South African passport and the purchased goods themselves, at the airport just before you fly out. You need to complete a VAT refund control sheet (VAT 255) which is obtainable at international airports. For further information contact the VAT Refund Administrator (☏011 394 1117, ⓦwww .taxrefunds.co.za).

Time

There is only one **time zone** throughout the region, two hours ahead of GMT year round. If you're flying from anywhere in Europe, you shouldn't experience any jet lag.

Tipping

Ten to fifteen percent of the tab is the normal **tip** at restaurants and for taxis – but don't feel obliged to tip if service has been shoddy. Keep in mind that many of the people who'll be serving you will be black South Africans, who rely on tips to supplement a meagre wage on which they support huge extended families. Porters at hotels normally get about R5 per bag. At South African garages and filling stations, someone will always be on hand to fill your vehicle and clean your windscreen, for which you should tip around R5. It is also usual at hotels to leave some money for the person who services your room. Many establishments, especially private game lodges, take (voluntary) communal tips when you check out – by far the fairest system, which ensures that all the low-profile staff behind the scenes get their share.

Tourist information

Given South Africa's booming tourism industry, it's not surprising that you'll have no difficulty finding maps, books and brochures before you leave. **South African Tourism**, the official organization promoting the country, is reasonably efficient: if there's an office near you, it's worth visiting for its free maps and information on hotels and organized tours. Alternatively, you can check out its website ⓦwww.southafrica.net, which includes content specific to users in South Africa, the UK, the US, Canada, Germany and France.

In South Africa itself, nearly every town, even down to the sleepiest *dorp*, has some sort of **tourist office** – sometimes connected to the museum, municipal offices or library – where you can pick up local maps, lists of B&Bs and travel advice. In

Name dropping

After the victory of democracy in South Africa in 1994, the government began **changing place names**, particularly ones with apartheid associations – a process that still continues. Practically, this means you may still find inconsistencies between maps and reality, so it's worth using maps that are as up to date as you can find.

Also potentially confusing is the introduction of **metropoles** – the amalgamation for administrative purposes of the major cities with smaller surrounding ones. With the exception of the City of Cape Town (which incorporates the adjacent town of Somerset West) and the City of Johannesburg, the major metropoles have significantly different names to their main city. You will frequently find places and organizations, for example local tourism bodies, referred to by the name of their metropole. Generally, though, the name of the city itself remains in common usage. The possible exception is South Africa's administrative capital, Pretoria, which is part of the Tshwane metropole and whose correct name was still being hotly contested in 2007 (for further information on this see p.622).

The other important metropoles are:

- eThekwini (including Durban)
- Ekurhuleni (the towns adjacent to Johannesburg's east)
- Nelson Mandela Bay (including Port Elizabeth)
- Buffalo City (including East London, King William's Town and Bisho).

larger cities such as Cape Town and Durban, you'll find several branches offering everything from hotel bookings to organized safari trips. We've given precise **opening hours** of tourist offices in most cases; they generally adhere to a standard schedule of Monday to Friday 8.30am to 5pm, with many offices also open on Saturdays and Sundays. In smaller towns some close between 1pm and 2pm, while in the bigger centres some have extended hours.

In this fast-changing country the best way of finding out what's happening is often by word of mouth, and for this **backpacker hostels** are invaluable. If you're seeing South Africa on a budget, the useful notice boards, constant traveller traffic and largely helpful and friendly staff in the hostels will greatly smooth your travels.

To find out **what's on**, check out the entertainment pages of the daily newspapers or better still buy the *Mail & Guardian*, which comes out every Friday and lists the coming week's offerings in a comprehensive pullout supplement.

South Africa Tourism offices abroad

Australia Suite 301, Level 3, 117 York St, Sydney NSW 2000 ☏ 02/9261 5000.
Netherlands Jozef Isarëlskade 48A, NL-1072 SB, Amsterdam ☏ 0900/202 0433.
UK 6 Alt Grove, Wimbledon, London SW19 4DZ ☏ 0870/155 0044.
US 500 5th Ave, 20th Floor, Suite 2040, New York NY 10110 ☏ 1-800/593-1318.

Government sites

Australian Department of Foreign Affairs ⓦ www.dfat.gov.au, ⓦ www.smarttraveller.gov.au.
British Foreign & Commonwealth Office ⓦ www.fco.gov.uk.
Canadian Department of Foreign Affairs ⓦ www.dfait-maeci.gc.ca.
Irish Department of Foreign Affairs ⓦ www.foreignaffairs.gov.ie.
New Zealand Ministry of Foreign Affairs ⓦ www.mft.govt.nz.
US State Department ⓦ www.travel.state.gov.

Travelling with children

Travelling with children is straightforward in South Africa, whether you want to explore a city, relax on the beach, or find peace in the mountains. You'll find local people friendly, attentive and accepting of babies and young children. The following is aimed mainly at families with under-5s.

Although children up to 24 months only pay ten percent of the adult airfare, the illusion that this is a bargain rapidly evaporates when you realize that they get no seat or baggage allowance. Given this, you'd be well advised to secure bulkhead seats and reserve a **basinet** or sky cot, which can be attached to the bulkhead. Basinets are usually allocated to babies under six months, though some airlines use weight (under 10kg) as the criterion. When you reconfirm your flights, check that your seat and basinet are still available. A child who has a seat will usually be charged fifty percent of the adult fare and is entitled to a full baggage allowance.

For getting to and from the aircraft, and for use during your stay, take a lightweight collapsible **buggy** – not counted as part of your luggage allowance. A child-carrier backpack is another useful accessory.

Given the size of the country, you're likely to be **driving** long distances. Aim to go slowly and plan a route that allows frequent stops – or perhaps take trains or flights between centres. The Garden Route, for example, is an ideal drive, with easy stops for picnics, particularly on the section between Mossel Bay and Storms River. The route between Johannesburg and Cape Town, conversely, is tedious.

Game viewing can be boring for young children, since it too involves a lot of driving – and disappointment, should the promised beasts fail to put in an appearance. Furthermore, of course, toddlers won't particularly enjoy watching animals from afar and through a window. If they are old enough to enjoy the experience, make sure they have their own binoculars. To get in closer, some animal parks, such as Tshukudu near Kruger, have semi-tame animals, while snake and reptile parks are an old South African favourite.

Family accommodation is plentiful and hotels, guesthouses, B&Bs and a growing number of backpacker lodges have rooms with extra beds or interconnecting rooms. Kids usually stay for half-price. Self-catering options are worth considering, as most such establishments have a good deal of space to play in, and there'll often be a pool. A number of resorts are specifically aimed at families with **older children**, with suitable activities offered. The pick of the bunch is the **Forever** chain (Ⓦwww.foreversa.co.za), which has resorts in beautiful settings, including

Keurboomstrand near Plettenberg Bay, and two close to the Blyde River Canyon in Mpumalanga. Another excellent option is full-board family hotels, of which there are a number along the Wild Coast (see p.425), where not only are there playgrounds and canoes for paddling about lagoons, but also most provide nannies to look after the kids during meals or for the whole day if you want. Note that many safari camps don't allow children under 12, so you'll have to self-cater or camp at the national parks and those in KwaZulu-Natal.

Eating out with a baby or toddler is easy, particularly if you go to an outdoor venue where they can get on unhindered with their exploration of the world. Some restaurants have highchairs and offer small portions. If in doubt, there are always the ubiquitous family-oriented chains such as Spur, Nando's or Wimpy.

Breast feeding is practised by the majority of African mothers wherever they are, though you won't see many white women doing it in public. Be discreet, especially in more conservative areas – which is most of the country outside middle-class Cape Town, Johannesburg or Durban. There are relatively few **baby rooms** in public places for changing or feeding, although the situation is improving all the time and you shouldn't have a problem at shopping malls in the cities.

You can buy disposable **nappies** wherever you go (imported brands are best), as well as wipes, bottles, formula and dummies. High-street chemists and the Clicks chain are the best places to buy baby goods. If you run out of **clothes**, the Woolworths chain has good-quality stuff, while the ubiquitous Pep stores, which are present in even the smallest towns, are an excellent source of extremely cheap, functional clothes.

Malaria affects only a small part of the country, but think carefully about visiting such areas as the preventatives aren't recommended for under-2s. Avoid most of the major game reserves, particularly the Kruger National Park and those in KwaZulu-Natal, North West and Limpopo provinces and Swaziland, and opt instead for malaria-free reserves – Addo Elephant

National Park in the Eastern Cape is an excellent choice. Malarial zones carry a considerably reduced risk in winter, so if you're set on going this is the best time. For more advice on malaria, see p.71. **Tuberculosis** (TB) is widespread in South Africa, mostly (but by no means exclusively) affecting the poor, so make sure your child has had a BCG jab. For information on protection against the **sun**, see p.71.

You'll find information on child-friendly accommodation and activities at ⓦ**www .familytravelsa.co.za**.

Guide

Guide

1

Cape Town and the Cape Peninsula

CHAPTER 1 # Highlights

* **Long Street nightlife** Party till the early hours along the city centre's café, pub and nightclub strip. See p.114

* **The Bo-Kaap** One of Cape Town's oldest residential areas, its streets characterized by colourful nineteenth-century Cape Dutch and Georgian terraces. See p.121

* **Golden Lion** Highlight of the Gold of Africa Museum, a major collection of historic African works of art. See p.123

* **Robben Island** The infamous island prison that was Nelson Mandela's home for nearly two decades. See p.129

* **Kirstenbosch Gardens** Picnic in one of the world's loveliest gardens See p.135

* **Rotate up Table Mountain** Take the revolving cable car to the tabletop. See p.141

* **Chapman's Peak Drive** Enjoy spectacular views as Cape Town's most precipitous road winds along a cliffside above the pounding Atlantic. See p.146

* **Swim with penguins** Boulders Beach offers wonderful bathing and is home to a colony of African penguins. See p.152

* **Cape Point** The dramatically rocky southernmost section of the Cape Peninsula offers excellent hikes. See p.154

▲ The coastal train to Simon's Town

Cape Town and the Cape Peninsula

C APE TOWN is southern Africa's most beautiful, most romantic and most visited city. Indeed, few urban centres anywhere can match its setting along the mountainous **Cape Peninsula** spine, which slides into the Atlantic Ocean. By far the most striking – and famous – of its sights is **Table Mountain**, frequently shrouded by clouds, and rearing up from the middle of the city.

More than a scenic backdrop, Table Mountain is the solid core of Cape Town, dividing the city into distinct zones with public gardens, wilderness, forests, hiking routes, vineyards and desirable residential areas trailing down its lower slopes. Standing on the tabletop, you can look north for a giddy view of the **city centre**, its docks lined with matchbox ships. To the west, beyond the mountainous Twelve Apostles, the drop is sheer and your eye sweeps across Africa's priciest real estate, clinging to the slopes along the chilly but spectacularly beautiful **Atlantic seaboard**. To the south, the mountainsides are forested and several historic vineyards and the marvellous Botanical Gardens creep up the lower slopes. Beyond the oak-lined suburbs of Newlands and Constantia lies the warmer **False Bay seaboard**, which curves around towards **Cape Point**. Finally, relegated to the grim industrial east, are the coloured **townships** and black **ghettos**, spluttering in winter under the smoky pall of coal fires – your stark introduction to Cape Town when driving in.

To appreciate Cape Town you need to spend time **outdoors**, as Capetonians do: they hike, picnic or sunbathe, often choose mountain bikes in preference to cars, and turn **adventure activities** into an obsession. Sailboarders from around the world head for Table Bay for some of the world's best windsurfing, and the brave (or unhinged) jump off Lion's Head and paraglide down close to the Clifton beachfront. But the city offers sedate pleasures as well, along its hundreds of paths and 150km of beaches.

Cape Town's rich urban texture is immediately apparent in its diverse **architecture** (see p.136): an indigenous Cape Dutch style, rooted in the Netherlands, finds its apotheosis in the Constantia wine estates, which were themselves brought to new heights by French refugees in the seventeenth century; Muslim slaves, freed in the nineteenth century, added their minarets to the skyline; and the English, who invaded and freed these slaves, introduced Georgian and Victorian buildings. In the tightly packed terraces

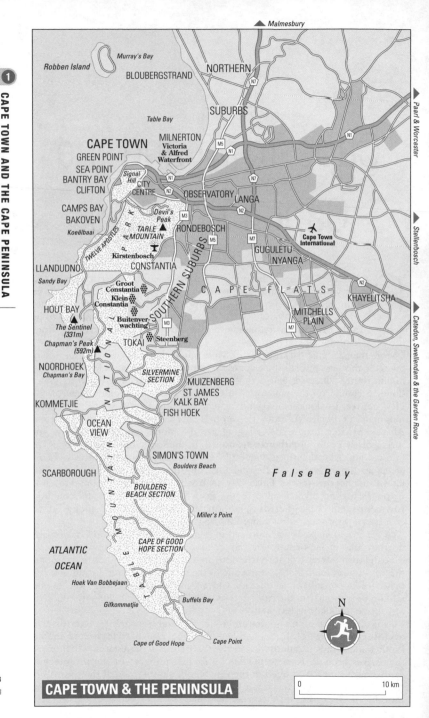

CAPE TOWN & THE PENINSULA

of twentieth-century Bo-Kaap and the tenements of District Six, coloured descendants of slaves evolved a unique, evocatively Capetonian brand of jazz, which is well worth catching live – it's still played in the Cape Flats and some city-centre clubs.

Weather is an abiding obsession of Capetonians, and no climatic feature is more dominant in the mind of the city's inhabitants than the **southeaster**, the cool summer wind that blows in across False Bay. It can singlehandedly determine what kind of day you're going to have, and when it gusts at over 60kph you won't want to be outdoors, let alone on the beach. Conversely, its gentler incarnation as the so-called **Cape Doctor** brings welcome relief on humid summer days, and lays the famous cloudy tablecloth on top of Table Mountain.

Some history

San hunter-gatherers, South Africa's first human inhabitants, moved freely through the Cape Peninsula for tens of millennia before being edged into the interior some two thousand years ago by the arrival of sheep-herding **Khoikhoi** migrants from the north. Over the next 1600 years the Khoikhoi held sway over the Cape pastures. **Portuguese** mariners, in search of a stopoff point en route to East Africa and the East Indies, first rounded the Cape in the 1480s, and named it Cabo de Boa Esperanza (Cape of Good Hope), but their attempts at trading with the Khoikhoi were short-lived, and no Europeans seriously attempted to create a permanent stopping-off point until the **Dutch East India Company** (VOC) cruised into Table Bay in 1652 and set up shop.

The VOC, the world's largest corporation at the time, planned little more at the Cape than a halfway house, to provide fresh produce to their ships travelling between Europe and the East, in search of spices, slaves and profit. Their small landing party, led by **Jan van Riebeeck**, built a mud fort where the Grand Parade now stands and established **vegetable gardens**, which they hoped to work with Khoikhoi labour.

The Khoikhoi were understandably reluctant to exchange their traditional lifestyle for the restrictions of formal employment, so Van Riebeeck began to import **slaves** in 1658. The growth of the Dutch settlement alarmed the Khoikhoi, who declared war in 1659 in an attempt to drive the Europeans out; however, they were defeated and had to cede the peninsula to the colonists.

During the early eighteenth century, Western Cape Khoikhoi society disintegrated, **German** and **French** religious refugees swelled the European population, and slavery became the economic backbone of the colony, which was now a minor colonial village of canals and low, whitewashed, flat-roofed houses. By 1750, Cape Town had become a town of over 1000 buildings, with 2500 inhabitants.

In 1795, **Britain**, deeply concerned by Napoleonic expansionism, grabbed Cape Town to secure the strategic sea route to the East. This move was not welcomed by the settlement's Calvinist Dutch burghers, but was better news for the substantially Muslim slave population, as Britain ordered the **abolition of slavery**. The British also allowed **freedom of religion**, and South Africa's first mosque was soon built by freed slaves, in Dorp Street in the Bo-Kaap.

By the turn of the nineteenth century, Cape Town had become one of the most cosmopolitan places anywhere and a sea port of major significance, growing under the influence of the British Empire. The Commercial Exchange was completed in 1819, followed by department stores, banks and insurance company buildings. In the 1860s the docks were begun, Victoria Road from the city to Sea Point was built, and the suburban railway line to Wynberg was laid. Since slavery had been abolished, Victorian Cape Town had to be built with convict labour and that of prisoners of war transported from the colonial frontier in Eastern Cape. Racial segregation wasn't far behind, and an outbreak of bubonic plague in 1901 gave the town council an excuse to establish N'dabeni, Cape Town's first black location, near Maitland.

In 1910, Cape Town was drawn into the political centre of the newly federated South Africa when it became the legislative capital of the Union. Africans and coloureds, excluded from the cosy deal between Boers and the British, had to find expression in the workplace. In 1919 they flexed their collective muscle on the docks, forming the mighty Industrial and Commercial Union, which boasted 200,000 members in its heyday.

Increasing industrialization brought an influx of black workers, who were housed in the locations of Guguletu and Nyanga, built in 1945. Three years later, the National Party came to power, promising a fearful white electorate that it would reverse the flow of Africans to the cities. In Cape Town it introduced a policy favouring coloureds for employment: among Africans, only men who had jobs were admitted (the women were excluded altogether), and the construction of family accommodation for Africans was forbidden.

Langa township became a stronghold of the Pan Africanist Congress (PAC), which organized a peaceful anti-pass demonstration in Cape Town on April 8, 1960. Police fired on the crowd, killing three people and wounding many more. As a result, the government declared a state of emergency and banned anti-apartheid opposition groups, including the PAC and ANC.

In 1966, the notorious Group Areas Act was used to uproot whole coloured communities from District Six and to move them to the desolate Cape Flats. Here, rampant gangsterism took vicious root and remains one of Cape Town's most pressing problems today. To compound the problem, the National Party stripped away coloured representation on the town council in 1972.

Eleven years later, at a huge meeting on the Cape Flats, the extra-parliamentary opposition defied government repression and re-formed as the United Democratic Front, heralding a period of intensified struggle to topple apartheid. In 1986, one of the major pillars crumbled when the government was forced to scrap influx control; blacks began pouring into Cape Town seeking work and erecting shantytowns, making Cape Town one of the fastest-growing cities in the world. On February 11, 1990, the city's history took a neat twist when, just hours after being released from prison, Nelson Mandela made his first public speech from the balcony of City Hall to a jubilant crowd spilling across the Grand Parade, the very site of the first Dutch fort. Four years later, he entered the formerly whites-only Parliament, 500m away, as South Africa's first democratically elected president.

Despite well over a decade of non-racial democracy, Cape Town remains a divided city. On the one hand, the whites still enjoy a comfortable existence in the leafy suburbs along the two coasts and the slopes of Table Mountain. On the desolate Cape Flats, while some progress has been made in bringing electricity to the shantytowns, the shacks are still there – and spreading. Despite white fears about crime, it is still blacks and coloureds who are overwhelmingly and disproportionately the victims of protracted violence, much of it gang-related.

Orientation, arrival and information

Between two mountainous flanks, reaching away from the docks, encompassing the intense city centre and up the mountain is the City Bowl

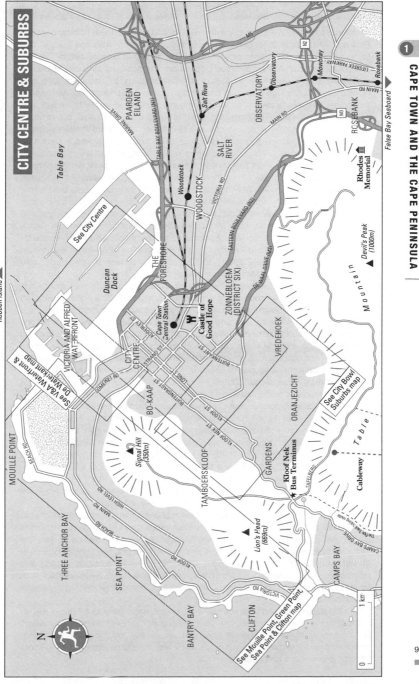

N

Robben Island ◀

Table Bay

See City Centre

Duncan Dock

VICTORIA AND ALFRED WATERFRONT

See V&A Waterfront & De Waterkant map

MOUILLE POINT

BEACH RD

THREE ANCHOR BAY

SEA POINT

MAIN RD

HIGH LEVEL RD

KLOOF RD

BANTRY BAY

CLIFTON

VICTORIA RD

See Mouille Point, Green Point, Sea Point & Clifton map

Signal Hill (350m)

BO-KAAP

BUITENGRACHT ST

CITY CENTRE

SOMERSET RD

STRAND ST

LONG ST

ADDERLEY ST

KLOOF ST

KLOOF NEK ST

TAMBOERSKLOOF

Lion's Head (669m)

GARDENS

TAFELBERG

Cableway

The free City Hop-on route

CAMPS BAY

CAMPS BAY DRIVE

Kloof Nek Bus Terminus ★

ORANJEZICHT

VREDEHOEK

See City Bowl Suburbs map

Table

MARINE DRIVE

PAARDEN EILAND

TABLE BAY BOULEVARD (N1)

THE FORESHORE

Cape Town Central Station

Castle of Good Hope ⚔

ZONNEBLOEM (DISTRICT SIX)

VICTORIA RD

WOODSTOCK

Woodstock

Salt River

SALT RIVER

EASTERN BOULEVARD (N2)

DE WAAL DRIVE (M3)

Mountain

Devil's Peak (1000m) ▲

OBSERVATORY

Observatory

MAIN RD

M5

Salt River

N2

LIESBEEK PARKWAY

Mowbray

Rosebank

MAIN RD

RONDEBOSCH

M3

Rhodes Memorial 🏛

False Bay Seaboard ▶

1 km

0

91

The language of colour

It's striking just how un-African Cape Town looks and sounds. Lying halfway between East and West, Cape Town drew its population from Africa, Asia and Europe, and traces of all three continents are found in the genes, language, culture, religion and cuisine of South Africa's coloured population. The dominant language of the city is **Afrikaans** (a close relative of Dutch), the only "European" language to evolve outside Europe. Although English is universally spoken and understood, Afrikaans is the mother tongue of a large proportion of the city's **coloured** residents, as well as a good number of whites. The term "coloured" is fraught with confusion, but in South Africa it doesn't have the same connotations as in Britain and the US; it refers to South Africans of mixed race. This comes as a surprise to most visitors, who assume that it's all black and white in South Africa, when in fact issues of ethnicity and language are extremely complex. Most brown-skinned people in Cape Town (over fifty percent of the population), and many others throughout the country, are coloureds, with slave and Khoikhoi ancestry going back to the seventeenth to early nineteenth centuries.

In the late nineteenth century, Afrikaans-speaking whites, fighting for an identity, sought to create a "racially pure" culture by driving a wedge between themselves and coloured Afrikaans-speakers. They reinvented Afrikaans as a "white man's language", eradicating the supposed stigma of its coloured ties by substituting Dutch words for those with Asian or African roots. In 1925, the white dialect of Afrikaans became an official language alongside English, and the dialects spoken by coloureds were treated as comical deviations from correct usage.

For Afrikaner nationalists this wasn't enough, and after the introduction of apartheid in 1948, they attempted to codify perceived racial differences. Under the **Population Registration Act**, all South Africans were classified as white, coloured or Bantu (the apartheid term for Africans). The underlying assumption was that these distinctions were based on objective criteria. For the apartheid authorities, it seemed fairly clear who was "Bantu" and who was white, but the coloureds posed particular problems. Firstly, they weren't homogeneous so, to accommodate this, the **Coloured Proclamation Act** of 1959 defined eight categories of coloured: Cape Coloured; Malay (Muslim); Griqua; Chinese; Indian; Other Indian; Other Asiatic; and Other Coloured. For reasons of expediency related to trade, Japanese people were defined as "honorary white".

The second difficulty surrounding coloureds was the fact that their appearance spans the entire range, from those who are indistinguishable from whites to those who look like Africans. A number of coloureds managed successfully to reinvent themselves as whites, and apartheid legislation made provision for the racial reclassification of individuals. Between 1983 and 1990, nearly five thousand "Cape Coloureds" were reclassified as "white" and over two thousand Africans were reclassified as "Cape Coloured". Notorious tests were employed – one, for example, where a pencil would be placed in a person's hair and twirled; if the hair sprang back the person would be regarded as coloured, but if it stayed twirled he or she was white.

Far more than mere semantics, these classifications became fundamental to what kind of life a person could expect. There are numerous cases of families in which one sibling was classified coloured, while another was termed white and could then live in comfortable white areas, enjoy good employment opportunities (many jobs were closed to coloureds), and have the right to send their children to better schools and universities. Many coloured professionals, on the other hand, were evicted from houses they owned in comfortable suburbs such as Claremont, which overnight were declared white.

With the demise of apartheid, the make-up of residential areas is shifting – and so is the thinking on ethnic terminology. Some people now reject the term "coloured" because of its apartheid associations, and refuse any racial definitions; others, however, proudly embrace the term, as a means of acknowledging their distinct culture, with its slave and Khoikhoi roots.

(made up of the Upper and Lower city centres and the Waterfront), where lively areas, such as Long Street, the Bo-Kaap and Gardens, rub shoulders with the wealth of suburbs such as Tamboerskloof and Oranjezicht. **Long Street** aptly runs the full length of the city centre and continues as lively **Kloof Street**, which cuts through the City Bowl suburbs to Kloof Nek, a junction that splays out to the lower cableway station, Sea Point, the Atlantic seaboard and Signal Hill. Straggling south from the centre along the eastern slope of the mountain, the predominantly white **southern suburbs** become progressively more affluent as you move from arty Observatory through the comfortably middle-class districts of Rondebosch and Newlands, culminating with the Constantia wine estates. Along the coastal belt, the **Atlantic seaboard** is drier and sunnier, with the wealthiest areas like Clifton and Camps Bay clinging to the mountainside above the sea, white sands and rocky beaches. The **False Bay** coast is wetter and greener, the sea here usually several degrees warmer than the western peninsula, making Muizenberg, Fish Hoek and Boulders Beach in Simon's Town the most popular bathing beaches in Cape Town. Curling northeast around Table Bay, the **northern suburbs**, taking in Parow, Milnerton and Bloubergstrand, are exceptionally dull, with a traditional Afrikaans flavour. South of these, and extending seemingly endlessly along the N2 into the interior, the coloured **Cape Flats townships** jostle with the desolate, litter-strewn **African ghettos** of Nyanga, Langa and Guguletu, which relentlessly overflow into kilometre after kilometre of iron, wood and cardboard shantytowns.

Arrival

Cape Town International Airport lies on the Cape Flats, 22km east of the city centre. The airport is undergoing extensive renovations so if you require a **shuttle service** you should phone Airport Shuttle (☎021 462 0272 or 082 360 9956, @airportshuttle@new.co.za) and book ahead of arrival. The fare from the airport into the city centre is R150 for the first person and R50 for each additional passenger. An alternative is the similarly priced Magic Bus (☎021 505 6300), which must be **booked** a day ahead; the bus will meet you at the airport and take you anywhere on the peninsula. Metered **taxis** operated by Touch Down Taxis, the company officially authorized by the airport, rank in reasonable numbers outside both terminals and charge about R180 per person for the trip into the city.

The major **car rental** firms have desks inside the international terminal. Pre-booking a vehicle is essential, especially during the week when there is a big demand from domestic business travellers, and over the mid-December to mid-January and Easter peak seasons. A **bureau de change** is open to coincide with international arrivals; there are also **ATMs** and a basic tourist **information desk**. There's a **hotel** at the airport, *Road Lodge* (☎021 934 7303; ❹), useful if your flight is weirdly timed; you can walk to it from the terminal buildings and it's not too pricey.

Intercity buses and trains

Greyhound, Intercape and Translux **intercity buses** and main-line **trains** terminate in the centre of town around the interlinked central complex that includes the **train station** and **Golden Acre** shopping mall, at the junction of Strand and Adderley streets. Note that Intercape and Translux arrive on the northeast side of the station, off Adderley Street, while Greyhound arrives on the northwest side in Adderley itself. The Golden Acre shopping complex can

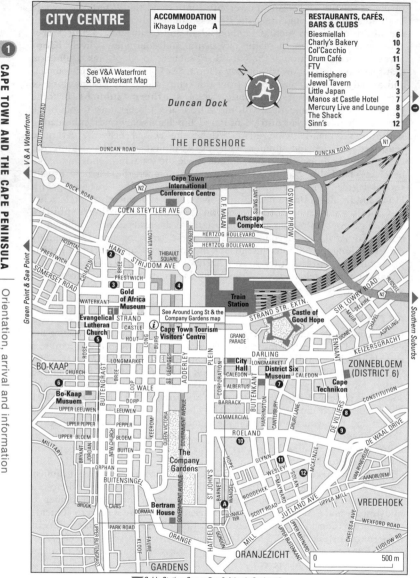

Cable Station, Camps Bay & Atlantic Seaboard

be a confusing muddle, but this is where all rail and bus transport (both intercity and from elsewhere in the city) and most minibus taxis converge – if you use public transport at all, you're bound to find yourself here at some stage. Everything you need for your next move is within two or three blocks of here, including information.

Information

The best source of information about the city is **Cape Town Tourism** (Ⓦwww .tourismcapetown.com), which has two excellent information bureaus: the city-centre visitor centre (March–Nov Mon–Fri 8am–6pm, Sat 8.30am–1pm & Sun 9am–1pm; Dec–Feb Mon–Fri 8am–7pm, Sat 8.30am–1pm & Sun 9am–1pm; Ⓣ021 426 4260), at the corner of Burg and Castle streets, a five-minute walk two blocks west of the station; and the Clocktower Precinct visitor centre (daily 9am–9pm; Ⓣ021 405 4500) in a fabulous office at the V&A Waterfront next to the Nelson Mandela Gateway to Robben Island. Both centres operate comprehensive accommodation and activity **booking services**, have a swanky coffee shop, a book shop and cybercafé as well as lots of brochures and very cheap city maps. Bookings for national parks can also be made here.

The best sources of **events listings** are the relatively unprepossessing supplements that appear in the mainstream press at the weekend. The *Top of the Times* supplement comes with Friday's *Cape Times* (Ⓦwww.capetimes .co.za), and the *Good Weekend* pullout with the Saturday *Cape Argus* (Ⓦwww .capeargus.co.za), but best of the bunch is the *Mail & Guardian*'s Friday supplement, which injects some attitude into its reviews and listings. A free two-pager, *48 Hours*, is handed out at city traffic lights on Fridays. *Cape Review*, a monthly listings magazine, gives a broad range of information on food, wine, gay venues, nightlife and sporting events. Also containing a fair amount of listings is *The Other Guide* (Ⓦwww.otherguide.co.za), a free monthly magazine aimed mainly at foreign tourists, and distributed at the airport.

If you're planning to explore beyond the confines of the city centre, you'll need to invest in one of the detailed **street atlases**, found at most bookshops, including the ubiquitous CNA chain. MapStudio's *A to Z Streetmap* is the cheapest; it's adequate for the centre and most of the suburbs, but doesn't cover Simon's Town. There are countless **guidebooks** on walks around Cape Town, hikes up Table Mountain, dive sites, fishing locations, surfing breaks and windsurfing spots. For the best-stocked shelves and nicest atmosphere, head for one of the Exclusive Books stores (see p.175). You'll also find useful books on all aspects of South Africa at the secondhand bookshops down Long Street (see p.114).

City transport

Although Cape Town's city centre is compact enough to get around on foot, many of the attractions are spread along the considerable length of the peninsula. To make the most of your visit the best option by far is to rent a car. Otherwise, **Rikkis** (see p.98) are cheaper than **taxis**, or you could take a **tour**, or make do with the pretty skeletal public transport system.

Inner-city areas west of the centre are better served by **buses** than other central suburbs, but transport north along the Atlantic coast is negligible. There is, however, a **train** service cutting through the southern suburbs and continuing all the way down to Simon's Town. It's fairly reliable and well used, though the rolling stock, which is gradually being upgraded, is looking a little battered.

Note that using public transport **after dark** is potentially risky. If you're forced to do so, take sensible precautions, such as travelling in a group (especially women) and avoiding third-class carriages on trains; otherwise, make every effort to take metered taxis at night.

Buses

The only frequent and reliable **bus** services are those from the centre to the Waterfront and Sea Point; infrequent buses also go down the Atlantic seaboard to Camps Bay and Hout Bay, and there are a couple to Kirstenbosch. Don't attempt to catch a bus to the southern suburbs: the train is much quicker and more efficient.

The principal bus station is the **Golden Acre bus terminal**, off Strand Street, wedged between Golden Acre Shopping Centre, the station and the Grand Parade. Buses depart from here to Green Point, Sea Point, Camps Bay and Hout Bay, while services for the Waterfront leave from Adderley Street outside the station. Note that the buses aren't numbered; you identify them from the destination on the front. All but the Waterfront buses are intended for use by workers, services beginning at 6.30am, and ending at 6.30pm. The Waterfront buses also start early, but continue until 10.30pm, and have the greatest frequency.

Tickets are sold by the driver: state your destination to the driver, and pay when you get on. A single ticket from the city costs around R5 to Sea Point, or about R8 to Camps Bay. Weekly and monthly tickets are also available. For **timetables**, enquire at the Golden Arrow **information booth** (toll-free ☎0800 65 64 63) at the Golden Acre bus terminal. It's advisable to check bus times and points of departure at the booth.

The open-top, hop-on, hop-off **Cape Town Sightseeing Bus** (☎021 511 6000, Ⓦwww.sightseeing.co.za), is also an extremely useful, if slightly expensive (R100 per person per day), means of negotiating the city-centre sights and the Atlantic seaboard beaches. You can get on and off, throughout the day, wherever you please along the route. **Departures** (daily: April, Sept & Oct half-hourly 9.30am–3pm; May–Aug get hourly 9.30am–2pm; Nov–March every 20min 9.30am–3.30pm & until 5pm Dec–Feb) are from the **V&A Waterfront** outside Two Oceans Aquarium. The **route** is circular and takes in the Clock Tower at the Waterfront; the Cape Town Convention Centre on the Foreshore; the city centre (buses stop at Cape Town Tourism in Strand Street, the South Africa Museum, the South Africa Jewish Museum, the Castle of Good Hope and the Gold Museum); the City Bowl suburbs; the lower cableway station (for the cable car up Table Mountain) and the Atlantic seaboard from Camps Bay to Sea Point, before returning to the Waterfront. The bus also visits Kirstenbosch National Botanical Gardens.

Useful city-bus routes

City centre to Waterfront Cape Town station–Riebeeck Street–Buitengragt Street–Waterfront (Mon–Fri every 10min, Sat & Sun every 15min).

City centre to Sea Point Golden Acre terminal–Mouille Point–Main Road Green Point–Main Road Sea Point (Mon–Sat 20 daily).

City centre to Hout Bay Golden Acre terminal–Lower Plein St–Darling Rd–Adderley Street–Green Point–Sea Point–Camps Bay–Hout Bay beach–Hout Bay harbour (Mon–Sat 6 daily, Sun 3 daily; 1hr).

City centre to Kirstenbosch Golden Acre terminal–Mowbray–Kirstenbosch at 7.30am, 12.35pm and 3.35pm, return only 9.35am and 3.30pm.

V&A Waterfront to Sea Point V&A Waterfront–Mouille Point–Green Point–Three Anchor Bay–Beach Road Sea Point (daily every 20min).

Taxis, minibus taxis and shuttle buses

The term "**taxi**" is no less ambiguous in Cape Town than elsewhere in South Africa: it's used to refer to conventional metered cars, jam-packed minibuses and their more upmarket cousins, Rikkis. **Metered taxis**, regulated by the Cape Town Municipality, don't cruise up and down looking for fares; you'll need to go to the taxi ranks around town, including the Waterfront, the train station and Greenmarket Square. Alternatively, you can phone to be picked up (see p.178). Taxis must have the driver's name and identification clearly on display and the meter clearly visible. Fares work out at around R15 per kilometre, expensive compared with other forms of transport, though definitely worth it at night, when metered taxis are the safest way of getting around.

▲ Cape Town's minibus taxis

Minibus taxis and Rikkis

Minibus taxis are cheap, frequent and bomb up and down the main routes at tearaway speeds. They can be hailed from the street – you'll recognize them from the hooting, loud music and touting – or boarded at the central taxi rank, adjacent to the train station. Once you've boarded, pay the *guardjie* (assistant), who sits near the driver, and tell him when you want to get off. Fares should be under R8 for most trips. As well as crazed driving, be prepared for pickpockets working the taxi ranks.

Rikkis are minibus taxis aimed principally at tourists (Mon–Fri 6.30am–midnight, Sat & Sun 24hr). Carrying not more than eight passengers, they are small, open-backed vehicles, covered by a canopy but open at the rear; you need to book them by telephone (℡0861 745 547). In Cape Town, Rikkis zip about the City Bowl, the Waterfront and the Atlantic seaboard as far as Camps Bay, and go to Kirstenbosch (R80 for four passengers), as well as providing the cheapest transport to the airport (R150 for a group of four).

Shuttle buses

A growth area in Cape Town is **shuttle buses**, which have to be booked, and which will pick you up from your accommodation. In some cases they run to

---

Tours

A growing number of smaller companies offer niche cultural tours; the most popular of these are townships tours, which can safely get you around the African and coloured areas that were created under apartheid. Apart from this, a number of other outfits, listed below, can help you scratch beneath Cape Town's surface. Almost all companies will pick you up from your accommodation and drop you off again at the end of the day.

Besides the companies listed below, Cape Town Tourism (see p.95) offers a city walking tour (Mon–Fri 11am & 1.30pm; R100), which covers the main sights and lasts an hour. There's a Bo-Kaap walk on Tuesdays and Thursdays at 9.30am (R75).

Tour operators

Day Trippers ℡021 511 4766, ⓦwww.daytrippers.co.za. Cycling from Scarborough into the Table Mountain National Park, with hikes down to Cape Point and a picnic, as well as tours to the usual sights such as the Winelands (all R425). The peninsula day-trip includes Hout Bay, with the option of a boat trip to Duiker Island to see the seals and Boulders Beach for the penguins.

Grassroute Tours ℡021 706 1006, ⓦwww.grassroutetours.co.za. Half-day trips (R350) include a visit to African and coloured townships, and walking tours of the Bo-Kaap, covering the *kramats* (Muslim shrines). A day tour (R525) features a visit to Robben Island, with the cost of the ferry and island tour included in the price.

Hylton Ross Tours ℡021 511 1784, ⓦwww.hyltonross.com. Offers all major guided tours in and around Cape Town including Cape Winelands, townships, whale-watching and four-day Garden Route tours.

Our Pride ℡021 531 4291 or 082 446 7974, ⓦwww.bonanitours.co.za. Highly recommended tours on which you get to meet the people of the Bo-Kaap and District Six as well as the African townships and squatter camps. A full-day Winelands or Cape Point tour will cost R500, and half-day Gospel tours are available.

Touch Africa Tours ℡021 705 3201 or 083 400 2090, ⓔatouch@iafrica.com. Offers personalized tours of all the places of interest and beauty in and around Cape Town, with trips focusing on the Winelands, townships and local culture. Also offers tours and safaris anywhere in South and Southern Africa.

a schedule, or can be chartered. They tend to be cheaper than metered taxis and take you door to door. One of the most useful services runs on demand in co-operation with Cape Town Tourism from their city centre and Waterfront visitor centres during their opening hours, going to Kirstenbosch National Botanical Gardens (R50 one-way), and also to the Table Mountain lower cableway station and other points of interest.

Reliable operators you can charter include: Sun Tours & Shuttle (⊕021 797 4646), which offers a 24-hour service between any two points on the peninsula, including the city to the airport (R250 for the first three passengers, then R60 per additional person).

Trains

Cape Town's suburban train service is run by Metrorail (timetable information ⊕0800 656 463). The only route likely to be useful to tourists is the relatively reliable if slightly run-down line going through the southern suburbs and all the way down to False Bay seaboard from Cape Town station. Three other lines run east from Cape Town to Strand (through Bellville), to the Cape Flats, and to the outlying towns of Stellenbosch and Paarl; however, the journeys aren't recommended, as they run through some less safe areas of the Flats. Even on a Simon's Town train, never board an empty carriage.

The service to the False Bay seaboard is undoubtedly one of the great urban train journeys of the world. It reaches the coast at Muizenberg and continues south to Simon's Town, sometimes so spectacularly close to the ocean that you can feel the spray and peer into rock pools. The stretch of the line to Fish Hoek is well served, with several trains an hour (Mon–Fri 5.10am–7.30pm every 15min, Sat 6.20am–6.45pm every 20min, Sun 5.50am–6.30pm roughly hourly, though more frequently during the summer). Services to Simon's Town go every 40–60 minutes.

Trains run overground, and there are no signposts to the stations on the streets. If you're staying in the southern suburbs, ask for directions at your accommodation. Tickets must be bought at the station before boarding. You're best off in the first-class carriages, which are reasonably priced (for example, Cape Town–Muizenberg is R10 one-way); curiously, there's no second class. Third class tends to be more crowded, and in the mornings can ring out with harmonies of domestic workers singing on their way to clean houses.

Driving

Cape Town has good roads and several fast freeways that, outside peak hours (7–9am & 4–6pm), can whisk you across town in next to no time. The obvious landmarks of Table Mountain and the two seaboards make orientation straightforward, particularly south of the centre, and some wonderful journeys are possible. The most notable are the drives along the Atlantic seaboard to Hout Bay and Chapman's Peak Drive, a narrow winding cliff-edge road with the Atlantic breaking hundreds of metres below; and around the Cape Point section of the Table Mountain National Park via the False Bay seaboard.

The usual precautions for defensive driving in South Africa are in order, especially since Cape Town has a few peculiarities all of its own. An unwritten rule of the road on the peninsula is that minibus taxis have the right of way – and will push in front of you without compunction. Don't mess with them: the vehicles are bigger than yours, drivers may carry handguns and will routinely run through amber lights as they change to red – as will many Capetonians.

Take care approaching a freeway: the on-ramps frequently feed directly into the fast lane, and Capetonians have no compunction in exceeding the 100kph freeway and 120kph highway speed limits. There's often little warning of branches off to the suburbs, only the final destination of the freeway being signed. Your best bet is to plan your journey, and make sure you know exactly where you're going.

Car parks are dotted all over the place in this car-friendly city. To park on the street you'll need to find a parking attendant, with a luminous yellow bib, from whom you purchase one, two or three hours' parking time. If you want to park in peace, head for one of the multistorey parking garages – there's one attached to the Golden Acre complex, and another at the north end of Lower Burg Street. Almost anywhere you park, bar the garages, you'll be expected to tip the car guards who are supposed to look after parked vehicles.

Car and motorbike rental

Given Cape Town's scant public transport, renting a vehicle is the only convenient way of exploring the Cape Peninsula, and needn't break the bank. There are dozens of competing car rental companies to choose from (see p.177). To get the best deal, either pick up one of the brochures at Cape Town Tourism office or look in the *Yellow Pages*.

For motorbike rental, Le Cap Motorcycle Hire, B9 Edgemead Business Park, on the corner of Link Way & Southdale Road, Edgemead (☎072 259 0009, ⓦwww.lecap.co.za), provides all the necessary gear and rents out serious bikes (from R400 daily, plus R1/km; weekly rental available).

One of the most popular – and hair-raising – road routes for cyclists is along the narrow hairpins of Chapman's Peak Drive (see p.146), which offer stupendous views of the Atlantic. There are also a number of dedicated mountain-biking routes in the peninsula's nature reserves. For rental outlets, see p.177.

Accommodation

Cape Town has plenty of **accommodation** to suit all budgets, but to guarantee the kind of place you want, booking ahead is recommended, especially over the Christmas holidays (mid-Dec to mid-Jan). The greatest concentration of accommodation is in the City Bowl and the Atlantic seaside strip as far as Sea Point and on to Camps Bay.

Cape Town Tourism has an efficient **accommodation booking** desk, but if you're stuck, A–Z Holiday Accommodation, 15 Winton Crescent, Woodbridge Island 7441 (☎021 551 2785, ⓦwww.a-zholidayhomes.co.za), can provide self-catering accommodation during December and January, ranging from a two-person apartment for R800 a day to a R18,000 super-luxury house.

City centre

The city centre's accommodation is highly concentrated along **Long Street**, featuring more **backpacker lodges** per square metre than on any other street in Cape Town and, in their wake, a growing number of student travel agencies, cheap car-rental outfits and adventure-activity outlets. Long Street is also the lively focus for restaurants, clubs and pubs. The heart of the city centre extends four blocks east to take in the **Company Gardens**. Accommodation in these areas is marked on the map on p.111, except for the *iKhaya Lodge*, shown on the map on p.94.

Cape Heritage Hotel 90 Bree St ☎021 424 4646, ⓦwww.capeheritage.co.za. An elegant and tastefully restored hotel located in a row of houses dating back to 1771, in Cape Heritage Square, just below the Bo-Kaap. The rooms are spacious and each is furnished according to a theme, among them African, Japanese and Dutch. Although there's no garden, there's a nice courtyard. ❼

Cape Town Hollow Hotel 88 Queen Victoria St ☎021 423 1260, ⓦwww.capetownhollow.co.za. A smart multistorey hotel with a/c rooms, cable TV, baths and showers. 2min from the South African Museum and National Gallery, an easy and pleasant walk away via the Company Gardens. ❼

Cat & Moose 305 Long St ☎021 423 7638, ⓦwww.catandmoose.co.za. The most stylish of the Long St lodges, housed in an eighteenth-century building a couple of doors from the steam baths at the south end of the city centre. Timber floors with Turkish-style rugs, exposed beams, earthy reds and ochres as well as some African masks imbue it with a warm ethnic feel. The dorms, triples and double rooms are arranged around a small leafy courtyard, with a plunge pool. Beware of the resident cat who likes to surprise guests by sneaking into their beds. Dorms ❶, rooms ❸

iKhaya Lodge Wandel St, Dunkley Square ☎021 461 8880, ⓦwww.ikhayalodge.co.za. A guesthouse three short blocks away from the Company Gardens and museums. It has eleven en-suite rooms in the main lodge building, six luxury loft suites and two self-catering apartments, all with ethnically inspired decor. You can choose between mountain or (cheaper) city views. The lodge's restaurant patio overlooks the outdoor eateries of trendy Dunkley Square and offers a stunning view of Table Mountain. There's 24hr reception, satellite TV and Wi-Fi Internet throughout. ❺

Long Street Backpackers 209 Long St ☎021 423 0615, ⓦwww.longstreetbackpackers.co.za. The oldest Long St backpacker lodge, on the top two floors of an unexceptional three-storey former apartment block arranged around a courtyard, with dorms, doubles and singles. Quieter than some of the other lodges in the vicinity, it's a well-organized place, with a laundry, Internet facilities and a travel desk; there's also a lively bar and a kitchen. ❷

Metropole Hotel 38 Long St ☎021 424 7247, ⓦwww.metropolehotel.co.za. Well-situated hotel that makes for a thoroughly urban stay. Done out in subtly contrasting oatmeal and beige shades, the rooms are comfortable if functional. The best parts are the public areas, bar and restaurant. Gay-friendly. ❻

St Paul's B&B Guest House 182 Bree St ☎021 423 4420, ⓕ021 423 1580. A charming, well-managed and inexpensive guesthouse in a Georgian building (formerly a maternity hospital) in a calm street on the city-centre fringes, within easy striking distance of the sights. The rooms are large, comfortable and light with huge windows, and sharing bathroom and kitchen facilities. ❷

Travellers' Inn 208 Long St ☎021 424 9272, ⓦwww.travellers-inn.co.za. Pleasant budget accommodation in an early twentieth-century building above a cybercafé. With no bar and no backpacker scene, this is a good bet for travellers wanting to avoid the hectic social atmosphere of the city-centre hostels. Apart from the light and spacious family rooms with twin beds and a double bunk, the rooms are small and sparsely furnished; all rooms share bathroom facilities. Weekly and monthly discounts available. ❷

Tudor Hotel 153 Longmarket St ☎021 424 1335, ⓦwww.tudorhotel.co.za. En-suite B&B rooms in a quiet, very central and reasonably priced hotel, overlooking cobbled Greenmarket Square, and handy for taxis. ❺

V&A Waterfront and De Waterkant

In keeping with the gentrified ambience of the **V&A Waterfront** (usually referred to simply as the Waterfront), accommodation here tends to be upmarket; there are, however, a couple of reasonably priced places to stay, especially in the area just south of the Waterfront and **De Waterkant**. Accommodation here is marked on the map on p.126.

Breakwater Lodge Portswood Rd, Waterfront ☎021 406 1911 (ask for Lodge Reservations), ⓦwww.breakwaterlodge.co.za. Once a nineteenth-century prison, this lodge provides the most affordable place to stay on the doorstep of the Waterfront. Some rooms are en suite, others share showers, and there are two restaurants on the premises (self-service and

waiter service), wireless hotspots throughout and ample parking. ❹

The Cape Grace West Quay, Waterfront ☎021 410 7100, ⓦwww.capegrace.com. One of South Africa's most expensive and most exclusive hotels, this was Bill and Hillary Clinton's choice when they visited Cape Town in 1998. Spectacularly sited on a slender spit overlooking the Waterfront's small

vessel marina to one side and the Alfred Basin to the other, the hotel's rooms have either harbour or Table Mountain views and are furnished in pared-back French period style. ❾
City Lodge On the corner of Alfred and Dock rds, Waterfront ☎021 419 9450, ⊛www .citylodge.co.za. A perfectly adequate if rather austere hotel, part of a national chain, less than 1km from both the Waterfront and the city centre. The rooms have TV and there's a small swimming pool. Rates are cheaper Fri–Sun nights, and you can also pick up discounts using the hotel's room-auction site ⊛www.bid2stay.co.za. ❻
De Waterkant Village and De Waterkant House Reception at 1 Loader St, De Waterkant ☎021 422 2721, ⊛www.villageandlife.com. Attractively restored historic cottages in a villagey quarter of the eighteenth-century Waterkant district of Green Point, adjacent to the Bo-Kaap

and less than 1km from the Waterfront and city centre. The luxury cottages in Waterkant, Loader, Dixon and Napier sts have up to three bedrooms; some have garages, swimming pools and roof gardens with harbour or mountain views. Also part of the district is De Waterkant House, which has nine rooms sharing a pool and terrace with views over the Waterfront. ❻
St John's Waterfront Lodge 6 Braemar Rd ☎021 439 1404, ⊛www.stjohns.co.za. The closest hostel to the Waterfront (a 15min walk away), well run by friendly and helpful staff. Accommodation is in four dorms sleeping eight to nine people, as well as thirteen doubles, three of which are en suite. There are two swimming pools, a great garden and a bar, and the restaurant serves reasonably priced light meals till midnight. There's also free Internet access, a coin-operated washing machine and a travel centre. Dorms ❷, rooms ❸

City Bowl suburbs

The **City Bowl suburbs** are popular for accommodation, and the most northerly sections are just five to ten minutes' walk from the Company Gardens and the museums. A few backpacker lodges can be found along **Kloof Street**, the continuation of trendy Long Street. The further up you go, the leafier the suburbs become, and you'll find the pricier and more comfortable B&Bs, guesthouses and hotels along the lower slopes of Table Mountain, overlooking the city centre and Duncan Dock. There's no public transport to the City Bowl suburbs, but most of the places listed below are under 3km from Cape Town centre. Accommodation here is marked on the map opposite.

Inexpensive

African Sun 3 Florida Rd, Vredehoek ☎021 461 1601, ⊜afpress@iafrica.com. A small self-catering apartment, attached to a family house a little over 1km from the city centre. Furnished with pared-back ethnic decor, it's run by friendly, well-informed owners. A five-percent discount is offered if you produce this book. Good value. ❸
Ashanti Lodge and Guest House 11 Hof St, Gardens ☎021 423 8721. King of the Cape Town lodges, this is a massive, superbly refurbished two-storey Victorian mansion. The details that give it the edge are stripped timber, chic marbling and ethnic decor, soaring ceilings, a beautifully kept front garden, cosy TV lounge and a swimming pool with sun terrace. The private rooms (with twin or double beds) and dorms (sleeping 6–8) are furnished with custom-made wrought-iron bunks and beds. Dorms ❷, rooms ❸
The Backpack 74 New Church St, Tamboerskloof ☎021 423 4530, ⊛www.backpackers.co.za. An excellent lodge in four interconnected houses, on the cusp of the City Bowl suburbs and the city

centre, and easily walkable to both. Well run and with excellent service, it's furnished with bold colours and ethnic fabrics, with plenty of outdoor space, including a pool terrace in its own garden. Accommodation is in dorms (sleeping 4–8) and private rooms (several of which are en suite); some rooms are suitable for families. There's an on-site travel centre, a 24/7 Internet café and a bar open till late. Dorms and rooms ❷
Belmont House 10 Belmont Ave, Oranjezicht ☎021 461 5417, ⊛www.capeguest.com. A tastefully restored 1920s house with seven fresh rooms, each with its own shower or bath. Either take the B&B option, or self-cater in the communal kitchen. There's a five-percent discount if you produce this book. ❹
Blencathra On the corner of De Hoop and Cambridge aves, Tamboerskloof ☎021 424 9571, ⊛www.blencathra.co.za. A large, relaxed family house with stunning views on the slopes of Lion's Head, 2km from the city centre and 4km from the Atlantic seaboard beaches. There are peaceful, spacious self-catering rooms, four of which are en

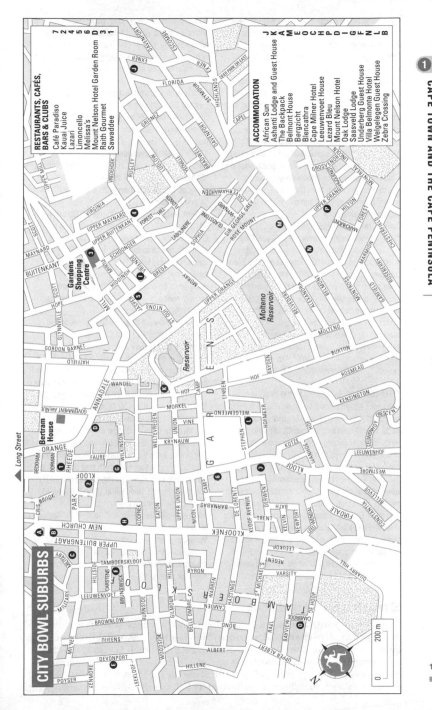

CITY BOWL SUBURBS

RESTAURANTS, CAFÉS, BARS & CLUBS

Café Paradiso	7
Kauai Juice	2
Lazari	4
Limoncello	5
Melissa's	6
Mount Nelson Hotel Garden Room	D
Raith Gourmet	3
Sawaddee	1

ACCOMMODATION

African Sun	J
Ashanti Lodge and Guest House	K
The Backpack	A
Belmont House	M
Bergzicht	E
Blencathra	O
Cape Milner Hotel	C
Leeuwenvoet House	H
Lezard Bleu	P
Mount Nelson Hotel	D
Oak Lodge	I
Saasveld Lodge	G
Underberg Guest House	F
Villa Belmonte Hotel	N
Welgelegen Guest House	L
Zebra Crossing	B

◀ Long Street

Bertram House

Gardens Shopping Centre

Reservoir

Molteno Reservoir

GARDENS

0   200 m

N

suite, attracting a young crowd who want to avoid the backpacker scene. The garden has seating and a swimming pool. ❻

Oak Lodge 21 Breda St, Gardens ⓣ021 465 6182. More an event than a lodge, this highly recommended hostel in an 1860s Victorian house has dramatic dungeons, dragon murals, and a lively atmosphere; it's also spacious and well serviced, and has an immaculate kitchen. There are four dorms and sixteen rooms, one of which is en suite. ❸

Saasveld Lodge 73 Kloof St, Tamboerskloof ⓣ021 424 6169, ⓔsaasveld@icon.co.za. A rather impersonal 1950s-style, four-storey guesthouse on a buzzing thoroughfare lined with good eating places, less than 1km from the centre. The rooms are en suite and have TV and phone. The rate excludes breakfast. ❹

Zebra Crossing 82 New Church St ⓣ021 422 1265, ⓦwww.zebra-crossing.co.za. Cape Town's only backpacker lodge that actually boasts about being quiet. On the northern edge of the City Bowl suburbs, it's an easy walk to the Kloof St restaurants and pubs as well as those in the city centre. The café-bar serves full meals and decent coffee, and there are two pleasant terraces under vines. Accommodation is in three spacious dorms (sleeping 8), eleven doubles and three singles; the best rooms are the three doubles in the annexe, from whose balcony you can take in views of the mountain. Child-friendly. Dorms ❶, ❷

Moderate to expensive

Bergzicht Guesthouse 5 Devonport Rd, Tamboerskloof ⓣ021 423 8513, ⓦwww.bergzichtguesthouse.co.za. Friendly and informal guesthouse with good views, caring hosts and a pool. Rooms are simply furnished with wicker furniture. ❺

Cape Milner Hotel 2a Milner Rd, Tamboerskloof ⓣ021 426 1101, ⓦwww.capemilner.com. A smart, reasonably priced hotel, partly incorporating an early eighteenth-century building, at the foot of Signal Hill.The airy rooms all boast views of Table Mountain and minimal decor, and the service is excellent. There's also a swimming pool, restaurant and bar on the premises. ❽

Leeuwenvoet House 8 Kloofnek Rd, Tamboerskloof ⓣ021 424 1133, ⓦwww.leeuwenvoet.co.za. A lovely, tranquil Cape Dutch gable guesthouse with a fantastic view of Table Mountain from its wide veranda. Fifteen en-suite rooms kitted out with pine and wicker and equipped with TV, phone and fan. Situated on a major thoroughfare with secure parking, it's a 15min walk from the city centre, with airport transfers available. ❺

Lezard Bleu 30 Upper Orange St, Oranjezicht ⓣ021 461 4601, ⓦwww.lezardbleu.co.za. Seven luxurious en-suite rooms, furnished with maple beds and cupboards in a spacious open-plan 1960s house. Sliding doors from each room open onto a garden. Located in a pleasant part of town, it's 1km from the centre and about half that distance to a nature reserve on the lower slopes of Table Mountain. ❻

Mount Nelson Hotel 76 Orange St, Gardens ⓣ021 483 1000, ⓦwww.mountnelson.co.za. Cape Town's *grande dame*: a fine and famous high-colonial Victorian hotel, built in 1899 (and extended in the late 1990s). Set in extensive established gardens, with arrival along a palm-lined colonnade, the hotel takes itself terribly seriously and charges accordingly; the rate excludes breakfast. ❾

Underberg Guest House 6 Tamboerskloof Rd, Tamboerskloof ⓣ021 426 2262, ⓦwww.underbergguesthouse.co.za. Located on the doorstep of the city centre, this Victorian guesthouse offers excellent value. Its high ceilings and compact size (there are only eleven rooms) create an atmosphere that is both intimate and airy. ❹

Villa Belmonte Hotel 33 Belmont Ave, Oranjezicht ⓣ021 462 1576, ⓦwww.villabelmontehotel.co.za. The Western Cape's smallest five-star hotel, on the lower slopes of Table Mountain and 1km from the city centre, feels like an elegant Italian country villa. The rooms, some of which lead onto a lovely garden, are individually decorated and rates vary according to size. Good value, given the level of comfort and style. ❽

Welgelegen Guest House 6 Stephen St, Gardens ⓣ021 426 2373, ⓦwww.welgelegen.co.za. A Victorian guesthouse with mountain views and furnished with considerable style. The mix is old classic and African chic and there is a treatment room for guests. ❻

Southern suburbs

Cape Town's **southern suburbs** are the formerly whites-only areas closest to the mountain. **Rosebank**, **Claremont**, **Newlands** and **Rondebosch** are leafy, quiet and convenient for the University and Kirstenbosch Gardens, and they're on a train line. Lush **Constantia** is one of Cape Town's poshest suburbs, only twenty minutes' drive from either coast as well as the V&A Waterfront. Sharing the same valley is the adjoining suburb of **Tokai**, worth considering if you want to be well out of the centre; it's close to forest walks and ten minutes from the beach. Inexpensive accommodation is rare in Tokai, but if money's no object and you're looking for somewhere exceptional and romantic, you might just find it here in a Cape Dutch manor house. A car is essential if you're staying in Tokai or Constantia.

Allandale Holiday Cottages 72 Zwaanswyk Rd, Tokai ☎ 021 715 3320, ⓦ www.allandale.co.za. Fifteen one-, two- and three-bedroom self-catering brick cottages on a secure smallholding adjoining Tokai Forest, on the slopes of Constantiaberg, 2min from the M3 motorway and 20min from Cape Town. Each cottage has a garden area with a braai and outdoor seating, and the site boasts a pool and tennis courts. ❹

Carmichael House 11 Wolmunster Rd, Rosebank ☎ 021 689 8350, ⓦ www.carmichaelhouse.co.za. A two-storey guesthouse in a building dating from the turn of the last century, with six big rooms equipped with phone, safe and hairdryer. There's a peaceful garden, swimming pool and secure parking, plus fax and email facilities. It's a 10min walk to Rhodes Memorial and the Contour Path, while the Rondebosch shops are 1km away. ❹

The Constantia Stables 8 Chantecler Lane, Constantia ☎&ⓕ 021 794 3653. Seven en-suite doubles, each with their own entrance and patio, in converted stables and cottages. The six-course breakfasts are excellent, and you can relax around the pool in a large garden. ❺

Constantia Uitsig Country Hotel Spaanschemat River Rd, Constantia ☎ 021 794 6500, ⓦ www .constantiauitsig.co.za. Sixteen custom-built and upmarket Cape Dutch-style cottages, in a garden setting on Constantia Uitsig wine estate, next door to Steenberg. There are a couple of excellent restaurants on site, including the *Uitsig* (see p.160). ❽

The Courtyard Liesbeek Ave, Mowbray ☎ 021 448 3929, ⓦ www.citylodge.co.za. A beautiful early nineteenth-century Cape Dutch homestead under thatch, with terracotta floors, brass chandeliers and large lawns in a semi-rural setting. There's a hotel minibus which you can pay to use. Breakfast is extra. ❼

Elephant's Eye Lodge 9 Sunwood Drive, Tokai ☎ 021 715 2432, ⓦ www.elephantseyelodge.co.za. Half a dozen rooms at a friendly B&B family home in a converted Cape Dutch farmhouse, in its own large grounds with a pool, a 10min walk from Tokai Forest. Two of the rooms are outside cottages with separate entrances and self-catering facilities. ❺

Gloucester House Bed & Breakfast 54 Weltevreden Ave, Rondebosch ☎&ⓕ 021 689 3894. A private house with two double bedrooms and a spacious lounge/dining room for self-catering. Guests may use the large garden, swimming pool and barbecue area. Breakfast can be provided for an additional R40 per person. ❸

Houtkapperspoort 1 Hout Bay Main Rd, around 7km from Hout Bay and 20km from the city centre ☎ 021 794 5216, ⓦ www.houtkapperspoort.co.za. The 26 charming one- to four-bedroom stone-and-brick self-catering cottages here are set against the Table Mountain Nature Reserve, close to Constantia Nek. You can take hiking trails up the mountain slopes, play tennis or take a dip in the solar-heated pool. Highly recommended. ❺

Ivydene Off Glebe Rd, Rondebosch ☎ 021 685 1747, ⓔ ivydene@mweb.co.za. Five flats in a delightful old house near the university, with a garden, swimming pool and friendly atmosphere. There are discounts for stays over a week or more. ❸

Kinloch Garden Apartment 3 Palm St, Newlands ☎ 021 683 5199, ⓔ marinella@mweb.co.za. Attached to a family home, this comfortably furnished self-catering apartment has a separate entrance and private garden with stunning views of Table Mountain. It's close to the university and a 20min walk to Kirstenbosch and Claremont shops. Good value. ❹

Steenberg Hotel On the corner of Steenberg and Tokai rds, Tokai ☎ 021 713 2222, ⓦ www .steenberghotel.com. A luxurious place on South Africa's oldest wine estate at the foot of the Steenberg Mountain. Accommodation is in the original manor house and three other farm buildings (now national monuments), which are perfect examples of Cape Dutch architecture, dating back to 1682. Arranged around a large formal garden, the buildings have whitewashed walls, thatched roofs, ornate gables and are furnished with seventeenth- and eighteenth-century Cape antiques. ❾

Villa Coloniale 11 Willow Rd, off Spaanschemat River Rd, Constantia ☎ 021 794 2052, ⓦ www.villacoloniale.co.za. Two pretty rooms at the home of the friendly architect owners, plus five self-catering suites set in a huge landscaped garden with willows, a stream and a saltwater pool. B&B ❻

The Vineyard On the corner of Colinton and Protea rds, Newlands ☎ 021 657 4500, ⓦ www.vineyard.co.za. An excellent, classy hotel in a restored country villa built for Lady Anne Barnard in 1799. The public spaces are decorated in elegant Cape Dutch style, with an outstanding panorama of Table Mountain from the extensive garden and with a gorgeous spa and gym at one end of the garden.

Atlantic seaboard

Down the **Atlantic seaboard** lie the seaside suburbs of Mouille (pronounced "moo-lee") Point, Green Point, Three Anchor Bay and Sea Point. Historically Cape Town's hotel and high-rise land, this is now packed with a range of accommodation, making it a good alternative to the City Bowl if you want to be close to the city centre.

South from Sea Point along Victoria Drive, the well-heeled mountainside suburb of **Camps Bay** has soaring views over the Atlantic, with the advantage of being close to the city centre, and with its own restaurants and shops. Though nearby **Llandudno** lacks shops or restaurants, it can boast similar vistas and a supremely beautiful beach with clusters of granite boulders at either end. **Hout Bay** is the main urban concentration along the lower half of the peninsula, with a harbour, pleasant waterfront development and the only public transport beyond Camps Bay. South of Hout Bay is the semi-rural settlement of **Noordhoek**, close to the Table Mountain National Park, with good horse-riding, beach walks and surfing.

Green Point

Brenda's Guest House 14 Pine Rd ☎021 434 0902 or 083 627 5583, ⊛www.pointb.co.za. Four rooms inside and another in the garden of a 1900s house, all brightly decorated, with wicker furniture. There's poolside seating on a bricked terrace. ⑤
Dale Court Guest House 1 Exhibition Terrace Rd ☎021 439 8774, ⊛www.dalecourt.co.za. Conveniently located, reasonably priced B&B directly

opposite V&A Waterfront. The guesthouse manages the eight-storey block opposite, comprising functional, self-catering apartments for families (R850–1050). ⑥
David's 12 Croxteth Rd ☎021 439 464, ⊛www.davids.co.za. An elegant, affordable and airy B&B in a quiet residential street in trendy Green Point just off the main road. It also has some self-catering apartments (R300 per unit). Gay-friendly. ③

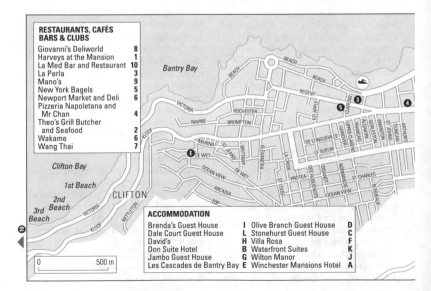

RESTAURANTS, CAFÉS BARS & CLUBS

Giovanni's Deliworld	8
Harveys at the Mansion	1
La Med Bar and Restaurant	10
La Perla	3
Mano's	9
New York Bagels	5
Newport Market and Deli	6
Pizzeria Napoletana and Mr Chan	4
Theo's Grill Butcher and Seafood	2
Wakame	6
Wang Thai	7

ACCOMMODATION

Brenda's Guest House		Olive Branch Guest House	D
Dale Court Guest House		Stonehurst Guest House	C
David's		Villa Rosa	F
Don Suite Hotel		Waterfront Suites	K
Jambo Guest House		Wilton Manor	J
Les Cascades de Bantry Bay		Winchester Mansions Hotel	A

Jambo Guest House 1 Grove Rd ☎021 439
4219, ⓦwww.jambo.co.za. Small, atmospheric
establishment with four luxury en-suite rooms and
one garden suite, in a quiet cul-de-sac off Main Rd,
just over 1km from the V&A Waterfront. The lush,
leafy exterior and enclosed garden with pond are
delightfully relaxing and the service is excellent. A
luxury suite has a large sitting area, Jacuzzi and
French doors opening onto the garden. A lavish
buffet breakfast is included. ⑥

Olive Branch Guest House 9 Richmond Rd ☎021
434 9198, ⓦwww.olivebranch.co.za. Nine
adequate en-suite rooms, reasonably priced for
Green Point with easy access to the Waterfront. ④

Waterfront Suites 153 Main Rd ☎021 439 5020.
Small four-storey block quite close to the waterfront,
with modern, impersonal but extremely comfortable
self-catering apartments. The kitchens are well
equipped, and the rooms are serviced daily. ⑤

Wilton Manor 15 Croxteth Rd ☎021 434 2572,
ⓦwww.wiltonmanor.co.za. A quiet and friendly
guesthouse with a homely atmosphere in a
Victorian house close to the city centre. Of the
seventeen B&B rooms, five are en suite; the
cheaper rooms share a bathroom, though each
room has its own hand basin. The service is good,
and there's also a small garden. ⑤

Sea Point and Bantry Bay

Don Suite Hotel 249 Beach Rd, Sea Point ☎021
434 1083, ⓦwww.don.co.za. A five-storey block of
27 self-catering apartments across the road from

the beachfront promenade and 300m from the
lively Main Rd restaurant strip. All the flats, studio
apartments and one- and two-bedroom units are
modern and well equipped; rates vary depending
on whether or not you get a view. ⑤

Les Cascades de Bantry Bay 48 De Wet Rd, Bantry
Bay ☎021 434 5209, ⓦwww.lescascades.co.za.
One of the most beautiful guesthouses in the country,
in a prime location perched above the Atlantic. It's
half the price of the much-vaunted *Ellerman's House*
in the street below, and could not be more luxurious
or relaxed. Every room has a full sea view and deck
or balcony and features Balinese-influenced decor in
warm earthy tones, and there are wonderful lounges,
verandas and swimming pools and a spa to complement the excellent services. The Belgian owners cook
up a storm. Unusually for such an upmarket place,
they do take children. ⑦

Stonehurst Guest House 3 Frere Rd, Sea Point
☎021 434 9670, ⓦwww.stonehurst.co.za. An airy
tin-roofed Victorian residence with original fittings
and Cape furniture. There's a pleasant front garden,
a kitchen and guest lounge. Most rooms are
en suite, and some rooms have balconies. ④

Villa Rosa 277 High Level Rd, Sea Point ☎021
434 2768, ⓦwww.villa-rosa.com. A friendly
eight-room guesthouse in a brick-red two-storey
Victorian house on the lower slopes of Signal Hill,
two blocks from the beachfront promenade.
Decorated with simplicity and style, all rooms have
TVs, phones and safes, but only some, on the upper
floor, have sea views. ④–⑤

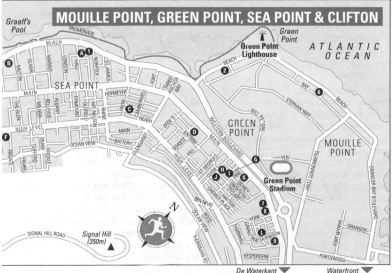

Winchester Mansions Hotel 221 Beach Rd, Sea Point ☎021 434 2351, ⓦwww.winchester.co.za. A self-consciously colonial-style 1920s hotel, in a prime spot across the road from the seashore, with an atmosphere straight from the pages of Agatha Christie. Palm trees at the front of the three-storey Cape Dutch Revival building hint at the interior: rooms have ceiling fans, and a cool Italianate courtyard restaurant is overlooked by balconies draped in luxuriant creepers. There's a good restaurant, too. ❸

Camps Bay and points south

Bay Hotel Victoria Rd, Camps Bay ☎021 438 4444, ⓦwww.thebay.co.za. Luxurious, glitzy five-star hotel on the fashionable beachfront strip. Its late 1980s construction blends neo-Cape Dutch with Mediterranean styles and cane furniture, to conjure up a laid-back colonial fantasy. ❾

Camps Bay Backpack & Budget Inn 21 Central Drive, Camps Bay ☎021 438 2691. Less than 1km from the beach is this distinctive backpacker lodge, in a contemporary white house with lots of glass and pale beech wood floors. Fluffy white duvets, towels and toiletries are provided in dorms and doubles, there's a sparkling pool, bar and gym, and

it's close to the trendy nightspots and restaurants. Dorms ❸, rooms ❹

Leeukop 25 Sedgemoor Rd, Camps Bay ☎021 438 1361, ⓔleeukopbb@hotmail.com. Near the beach and cafés, in two stylishly arty and comfortable apartments adjoining the cheerful proprietor's home. The flats are fully equipped, and you can either self-cater or stay on a B&B basis. ❺–❻

Monkey Valley Resort Mountain Rd, Noordhoek ☎021 789 1391, ⓦwww.monkeyvalleyresort.com. An attractive group of mainly wooden and thatched two-storey chalets spread over several acres of Chapman's Peak 40km south of the city centre. Overlooking the 7km of Noordhoek Beach, the site is surrounded by indigenous vegetation, with no other houses in sight, and there's an emphasis on natural products throughout. The cottages sleep six to eight people, and work out reasonably for a group. You can either eat in the restaurant, self-cater or stay on a B&B basis. ❼

Sunbird Mountain Retreat Boskykloof Rd, Hout Bay ☎021 790 7758, ⓦwww.sunbirdlodge.co.za. Three pleasant, spacious self-catering apartments and a guesthouse that includes a family unit, all nestling in a forest high up on the mountainside. All the rooms have great views and there's a secluded swimming pool. ❺

False Bay seaboard

The Metrorail line to the handsome, historic village of Simon's Town reaches the coast at **Muizenberg**, the oldest of Cape Town's seaside suburbs. To its south, en route to Simon's Town, is a series of settlements, including salubrious **St James**, **Kalk Bay** with its working harbour and great cafés, and **Fish Hoek**, which is known for the best swimming beach along the False Bay seaboard. **Simon's Town** is regarded by most Capetonians as a separate village, which it originally was, although it's now quite definitely part of the metropolis. During the day, trains arriving in Simon's Town are met by Rikkis taxis, which will take you anywhere in the vicinity.

Muizenberg to Fish Hoek

Amberley Travellers Lodge 15 Amberley Rd, Muizenberg ☎021 788 7032, ⓦwww .amberleylodge.com. A lovingly restored two-storey house with gleaming wooden floors, and spacious rooms and kitchen. ❶

Blue Oceans Backpackers 3 Church Rd, Muizenberg ☎021 788 9780. A cheerful, busy backpacker lodge in a two-storey Victorian house. Upstairs are three double rooms with their own kitchen, bathroom, and sharing a wraparound wooden deck. ❶

Chartfield Guest House 30 Gatesville Rd, Kalk Bay ☎021 788 3793, ⓦwww.chartfield.co.za. Unpretentious accommodation, 100m from Kalk

Bay station, in a well-kept rambling house halfway up the hill overlooking the harbour, with terrific sea views. The best rooms are the one in the loft with its own balcony, and the two semicircular corner ones with 180-degree views. It's a 2min walk to great restaurants. ❸

Sunny Cove Manor 72 Simon's Town Rd, Fish Hoek ☎021 782 2274, ⓦwww.sunnycovemanor .com. Near Sunny Cove station, this cheerful B&B has four suites, three of them two-bedroom affairs; all bar the back room have outstanding sea views, and there's secure on-site parking. A unique walking bridge over the commuter rail line leads you to Jager Walk and it's a short stroll to Fish Hoek Beach with its restaurants,

African township homestays

One of the best ways of getting a taste of the African townships is by spending a night there. The number of township residents offering **B&B accommodation** in their homes is still small, but growing. You'll have a chance to experience the warmth of *ubuntu* – traditional African hospitality – by staying with a family with whom you'll generally eat breakfast and dinner; they can also usually take you around their area to *shebeens*, music venues or just to meet the neighbours.

A number of the township B&Bs will send someone to meet you at the airport, while many people are dropped off at their accommodation by tour operators. If you're driving, your accommodation will give you detailed directions or arrange to meet you at a convenient landmark, such as a garage or police station.

For information about township B&Bs other than the ones listed below, contact **Cape Tourism Centre** in Guguletu (Mon–Fri 8am–5pm, Sat 8.30am–2pm; ℡021 637 8449, ⓦwww.tourismcapetown.co.za) which helps with finding township accommodation.

Kopanong Khayelitsha ℡021 361 2084 or 082 476 1278. One of the most dynamic B&B operations in the township, run by the tireless Thope Lekau, who has a mission to replace gawping tourists in their buses with guests who engage with township life. This former NGO worker will treat you to a history of the township, introduce you to local music and dish up a traditional family breakfast. A traditional dinner is available on request, as is a guided tour. B&B ❸

Majoro's Khayelitsha ℡021 361 3412 or 082 537 6882. Hosted by the charming Maria Maile in her family home, which has two rooms, sharing a bath and toilet. Dinner includes traditional fare such as *mielie pap*, and you'll be treated to an English breakfast with a difference, which may include bacon and egg with fish cakes, sausage and homemade steamed bread. B&B ❷

Malebo's Khayelitsha ℡021 361 2391. Three rooms sharing bath and toilet facilities in the welcoming home of Lydea Masoleng and her husband. In the morning you'll be served a continental breakfast; dinners, which combine Western fare with traditional African food, are available on request. You're welcome to join your hosts on outings to a *shebeen* or, on Sunday, to church. B&B ❸

Maneo Langa ℡021 694 2504. Friendly hostess Thandiwe Peter has two outside rooms and one inside the family house, in Cape Town's oldest township, and the closest to the city centre, so most guests drive here. She will take guests to some of the township highlights, including a local *shebeen* where you may see singing and dancing. B&B ❹

children's playground and ideal swimming conditions. ❹

Tranquility Guest House 25 Peak Rd, Fish Hoek ℡021 782 2060, ⓦwww.tranquil.co.za. Warm and welcoming, with panoramic views of the mountainside and ocean (the beach is within walking distance). There are four luxury B&B en-suite rooms, each with their own deck, plus a self-catering apartment with its own entrance. Guests can soak in the outdoor Jacuzzi. ❹–❺

Simon's Town and around

Boulders Beach Lodge 4 Boulders Place, Boulders Beach ℡021 786 1758, ⓦwww .bouldersbeach.co.za. Twelve B&B rooms and two self-catering flats above the Boulders Beach car park, a 2min walk from Boulders Coastal Park and

the African penguin colony, and just over 1km from Simon's Town. The self-catering units sleep two to six. Meals are available at the adjacent restaurant (daily 8am–9.30pm). ❺

British Hotel Apartments 90 St George's St ℡021 786 2214, ⓦwww.british-hotel.co.za. Three-bedroom self-catering apartments in a grand 1898 Victorian hotel that once had Cecil Rhodes and the nineteenth-century explorer, Mary Kingsley, as guests; there are also more modest doubles with baths. Part of a picturesque main street, this is an experience rather than just somewhere to stay, with Victorian colonial decor, high ceilings and huge balconies overlooking the street and the docks. ❹

Oatlands Holiday Village Froggy Pond, 3km from Simon's Town and 1km from the Boulders Beach penguin colony ℡021 786 1410,

Ⓦwww.oatlands.co.za. Across the road from the beach and near a golf course, this family resort is set in large grounds with its own pool and playground. There are over twenty self-catering chalets of various sizes, sleeping two to six people; there's also a pub and restaurant on the premises. ❹–❺

Simon's Town Backpackers 66 St George's St Ⓣ021 786 1964, Ⓦwww.capepax.co.za. Conveniently located in the heart of Simon's Town, within walking distance of the station. The renovated 1802 building offers dorms and

doubles (some en suite). There is a large balcony with a waterfront view and you can rent bicycles for a ride to Cape Point or paddle in a kayak past the penguin colony. Dorms ❶, doubles ❷–❸

Topsail House 176 St George's St Ⓣ021 786 5537. A converted old convent with more space than the average backpacker lodge, though a tad staid. It has various accommodation options including an extraordinary bedroom in a chapel, though it's the en-suite doubles upstairs that are the nicest rooms. ❸–❺

The City Centre

Strand Street marks the edge of Cape Town's original beachfront (though you'd never guess it today), and all urban development to its north stands on reclaimed land. To its south is the **Upper City Centre**, containing the remains of the city's 350-year-old historic core, which has survived the ravages of modernization and apartheid-inspired urban clearance, and emerged with enough charm to make it South Africa's most pleasing city centre. The entire area from Strand Street to the southern foot of the mountain is a collage of Georgian, Cape Dutch, Victorian and twentieth-century architecture (see p.136), as well as being the place where Europe, Asia and Africa meet in markets, alleyways and mosques. Among the substantial drawcards here are **Parliament**, the **Company Gardens** and many of Cape Town's major **museums**. North of Strand Street to the shore, the **Lower City Centre** takes in the still-functional **Duncan Dock**.

The Upper City Centre

Adderley Street, running from the train station in the north to the Gardens in the south, is the obvious orientation axis here. To its east, and close to each other just off Strand Street, are the **Castle of Good Hope**, the site of **District Six**, the **Grand Parade** and the **City Hall**. The district to the west of Adderley Street is the closest South Africa gets to a European quarter – a tight network of streets with cafés, buskers, bookstores, street stalls and antique shops congregating around the pedestrianized **St George's Mall** and **Greenmarket Square**. The **Bo-Kaap**, or Muslim district, three blocks further west across Buitengragt (which means the Outer Canal, but is actually a street), exudes a piquant contrast to this, with its minarets, spice shops and cafés selling curried snacks.

Southwest of Adderley Street, where it takes a sharp right into Wale Street, is the symbolic heart of Cape Town (and arguably South Africa), with **Parliament**, museums, archives and De Tuynhuys – the Western Cape office of the President – arranged around the **Company Gardens**.

Adderley Street

Once the place to shop in Cape Town, **Adderley Street**, lined with handsome buildings from several centuries, is still worth a stroll today. Its attractive streetscape has been wantonly blemished by a series of large 1960s shopping centres, but just minutes away from crowded malls, among the streets and alleys around Greenmarket Square, you can still find some human scale and historic texture.

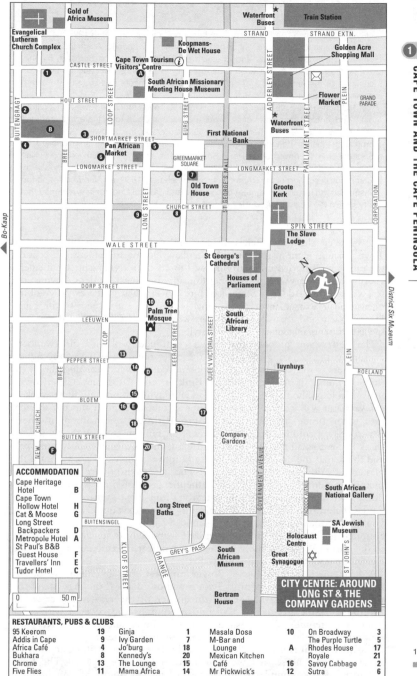

The naming of Adderley Street

Although the Dutch used Robben Island as a political prison (see p.129), the South African mainland only narrowly escaped becoming a second Australia, a **penal colony** where British felons and enemies of the state could be dumped. By the 1840s, "respectable Australians" were lobbying for a ban on the transportation of criminals to the Antipodes, and the British authorities responded by trying to divert convicts to the Cape.

In 1848, the British ship *Neptune* set sail from Bermuda for Cape Town with a cargo of 282 prisoners. When news of its departure reached Cape Town there was outrage; five thousand citizens gathered on the Grand Parade the following year to hear prominent liberals denounce the British government. When the ship docked in September 1849, governor Sir Harry Smith forbade any criminal from landing while, back in London, politician **Charles Adderley** successfully addressed the House of Commons in support of the Cape colonists. In February 1850, the *Neptune* set off for Tasmania with its full complement of convicts, and grateful Capetonians renamed the city's main thoroughfare **Adderley Street**.

Low-walled channels, ditches, bridges and sluices once ran through Cape Town, earning it the name Little Amsterdam. During the nineteenth century, the canals were buried underground, and in 1850 Heerengracht (Gentlemen's Canal), formerly a waterway that ran from the Botanical Gardens down to the sea, was renamed Adderley Street (see box above). There's little evidence of the canals today, except in name – one section of the street is still called Heerengracht and a parallel street to its west is called Buitengragt (sometimes spelled Buitengracht, after the Dutch style).

The destruction of old Cape Town continued well into the twentieth century, with the razing of many of the older buildings. One of the ugliest newcomers is the **Golden Acre** shopping complex, dominating the north (harbour) end of Adderley Street. Built in the 1970s, it's Cape Town's unavoidable public transport hub today, employing an unfriendly network of subways and walkways to draw together all the major road and rail services into town. Inside sit the **Golden Acre Ruins**, the remains of southern Africa's oldest colonial structure – a reservoir built in 1663 by the Dutch. All that's left is a small bit of wall behind glass, and you might easily walk past and think that the builders who worked on the complex forgot to finish the plastering. Although the mall itself and its environs are anything but picturesque, here you do get an authentic taste of ordinary Capetonians doing their shopping, something you won't find at the sanitized Victoria and Alfred Waterfront. On Saturday mornings, if you exit onto Adderley Street, you'll often encounter the spirited sounds of busking brass bands or choirs. Among the sidewalks and pedestrianized sections outside, which run down to the station, there's a closely packed **flea market** offering curios, crafts and electronic goods (but watch your wallet).

A little further south lies a **flower market**, run by members of the Bo-Kaap Muslim community. Two grandiose bank buildings stand on opposite sides of Adderley Street; the fussier of the two is the erstwhile **Standard Bank**, fronted by Corinthian columns and covered with a tall dome – a temple to the partnership of empire and finance. Recently renovated, at a cost of around R25m, it is now a trendy, very upmarket 220-seater **restaurant**, complete with palm trees to the ceiling, and named *Riboville* after a horse that won the Durban July race in 1974. The **First National Bank**, completed in 1913, was the last South African building designed by Sir Herbert Baker (see box, p.579). If you pop in for a quick look, still in place inside the banking hall you'll find a solid timber circular writing desk with the original inkwells, resembling an altar.

Slave Lodge

At the top corner of Adderley Street, just as it veers sharply northwest into Wale Street, you'll find **Slave Lodge** (Mon–Fri 10am–4.30pm, Sat 9am–1pm; R7, children R2), previously known as the Cultural History Museum. For nearly two centuries – more than half the city's existence as an urban settlement – Cape Town's economic and social structures were founded on slavery (see box below), and the Slave Lodge was built in 1679 for the Dutch East India Company – the largest single slaveholder at the Cape – to house its human chattels. By the 1770s, almost a thousand slaves were held at the lodge. Under VOC administration, the lodge also became the Cape Colony's main brothel, its doors thrown open to all comers for an hour each night. Following the British takeover and the auctioning of the slaves, the lodge became the Supreme Court in 1810, and remained so until 1914. From 1914, the building was used as government offices, and in 1966 became a museum.

Slave Lodge houses an eclectic collection of antiquities and artefacts from around the world, as well as good displays on the Cape and an exhibition, still evolving, about slavery. A couple of small but interesting displays can be found on the ground floor, to the left of the entrance hall. The first deals with **Khoisan hunter–gatherers**, the original inhabitants of the Cape (and South Africa), focusing on their knowledge of plants and herbs, many of which are still in use today. An adjacent room houses "**186 Years of Slavery**", centred around a model of the lodge as it was three hundred years ago. A poignant memorial plaque on one wall lists, by first name only, the slaves who endured the appalling conditions of the fortress-like structure, and a map on another wall refers to sites

Slavery at the Cape

Slavery was officially abolished at the Cape in 1838, but its legacy lives on in South Africa. The country's coloured inhabitants, who make up fifty percent of Cape Town's population, are largely descendants of slaves and indigenous Khoisan people, and some historians argue that apartheid was a natural successor to slavery. Certainly, domestic service, still widespread throughout South Africa, and certain labour practices such as the "*dop* system", in which workers on some wine farms are partially paid in rations of cheap plonk, can be traced directly back to slavery.

By the end of the eighteenth century, the almost 26,000-strong slave population of the Cape exceeded that of the free burghers. Despite the profound impact this had on the development of social relations in South Africa, it remained one of the most neglected topics of the country's history, until the publication in the 1980s of a number of studies on slavery. There's still a reluctance on the part of most coloureds to acknowledge their slave origins.

Few if any slaves were captured at the Cape for export, making the colony unique in the African trade. Paradoxically, while people were being captured elsewhere on the continent for export to the Americas, the Cape administration, forbidden by the VOC from enslaving the local indigenous population, had to look further afield. Of the 63,000 slaves imported to the Cape before 1808, most came from East Africa, Madagascar, India and Indonesia, representing one of the broadest cultural mixes of any slave society. This diversity initially worked against the establishment of a unified group identity, but eventually a **Creolized culture** emerged which, among other things, played a major role in the development of the Afrikaans language.

in the city centre with slave connections: where they worked, worshipped, were sold, punished and executed.

Behind Slave Lodge, on the traffic island in Spin Street, a simple and inconspicuous plinth marks the site of the **Old Slave Tree**, under which slaves were bought and sold.

Long Street

Parallel to Adderley Street, buzzing **Long Street** is one of Cape Town's most diverse thoroughfares, a great place for leisurely exploration, with views of Table Mountain, Signal Hill and Lion's Head, as well as glimpses of the sea. When it was first settled by Muslims some three hundred years ago, Long Street marked Cape Town's boundary; by the 1960s, it had become a sleazy alley of drinking holes and whorehouses. Miraculously, it's all still here, but with a whiff of gentrification. Mosques still coexist with bars, brothels trade above old-fashioned locksmiths, pawnbrokers function alongside porn shops, while gun shops sit next to delicatessens, antique dealers, craft shops and cafés. Also here are a number of excellent secondhand and Africana bookshops.

A Cape Town institution, established in 1906, the **Long Street Baths** (Mon–Sat 7am–8pm, Sun 8am–6pm) occupy the top of the road, where it hits Buitensingel (Outer Crescent). The steam rooms are great for relaxing on a winter's day and are open separately to women (Tues 9am–1pm, Thurs & Sat 9am–6pm) and men (Tues 1–7pm, Wed & Fri 9am–1pm, Sun 8am–noon). A four-hour session (R105) gets you a private cubicle and towel, access to the dry or wet steam rooms, the plunge pool and a short massage. Use of the pool costs R12.

Further north, an unmistakable landmark at no. 185, the **Palm Tree Mosque** (not open to the public) is fronted by a lone palm tree, its fronds caressing the upper storey. Significant as the only surviving eighteenth-century house in the street, it was erected in 1780 by Carel Lodewijk Schot as a private dwelling. The house was bought in 1807 by Frans van Bengal, a member of the local Muslim community, and a freed slave, Jan van Boughies, who became its imam, turning the upper floor into a mosque and the lower into his living quarters.

▲ Long Street

Across Wale Street is one of Cape Town's most intriguing places for African crafts, and one of the easiest to miss. The inconspicuous frontage of the **Pan African Market** (Mon–Fri 9am–5pm) at no. 76 belies the three-floor warren of passageways and rooms, which burst at the hinges with traders selling vast quantities of art and artefacts from all over the continent. Hidden among less inspiring offerings you'll find terrific masks from West Africa, brass leopards from Benin as well as contemporary South African art textiles. Also gathered here are leathersmiths, tailors, hair-braiders, a drum instructor and vendors selling CDs and musical instruments.

Further towards the harbour end of Long Street at no. 40, the **South African Missionary Meeting-House Museum** (Mon–Fri 9am–4pm; free) was the first missionary church in the country, where slaves were taught literacy and instructed in Christianity. This exceptional building, completed in 1804 by the South African Missionary Society, boasts one of the most beautiful frontages in Cape Town. Dominated by its large windows, the facade is broken into three bays by four slender Corinthian pilasters surmounted by a gabled pediment. Inside, an impressive Neoclassical timber **pulpit** perches high above the congregation on a pair of columns, framing an inlaid image of an angel in flight.

The society itself was founded in 1799 by Reverend Vos, who was alarmed that many slaveholders neglected the religious education of their property. The owners believed that once their slaves were baptized, their emancipation became obligatory – a misunderstanding of the law, which merely stated that Christian slaves couldn't be sold. Vos, himself a slaveholder, saw proselytization to those in bondage as a Christian duty, and even successfully campaigned to end the prohibition against selling Christian slaves, which he believed was "a great obstacle in this country to the progress of Christianity", because it encouraged owners to avoid baptizing their human chattels.

Greenmarket Square and around

Turning northeast from Long Street into Shortmarket Street, you'll skim the edge of **Greenmarket Square**, which is worth a little exploration to take in the cobbled streets, coffee shops and grand buildings. As its name implies, the square started as a vegetable market, though it spent many ignominious years as a car park. Human life has returned, and it's now home to a flea market, selling crafts, jewellery and hippie clobber. This is also one of the few places in Cape Town to buy from Congolese and Zimbabwean traders, selling masks and malachite carvings. On the western side are the solid limewashed walls and small shuttered windows of the **Old Town House** (Feb–Dec daily 10am–5pm; free), entered from Longmarket Street. Built in the mid-1700s, this beautiful example of Cape Dutch architecture, with its fine interior, has seen duty as a guardhouse, a police station and Cape Town's city hall. Today it houses the Michaelis collection of minor but interesting Dutch and Flemish landscape paintings. Small visiting exhibitions are also displayed, and good evening classical concerts are a regular event; pick up the town house's quarterly newsletter, which lists forthcoming events. Tickets are available at the door immediately prior to the shows.

Heading east of the square, you come to **St George's Mall**, a pedestrianized road that runs northeast from Wale Street to Thibault Square, near the train station. Coffee shops, snack bars and lots of street traders and buskers make this a more pleasant route between the station and the Company Gardens than Adderley Street, while dancers, drummers, choirs and painters add a certain buzz to the place. At the southern end of the mall, at Queen Victoria and Wale streets, **St George's Cathedral** is interesting more for its history than for its Herbert Baker Victorian Gothic design; on September 7, 1986, **Desmond Tutu** hammered on its doors symbolically demanding to be enthroned as South Africa's first black archbishop. Three years later, he heralded the last days of apartheid by leading thirty thousand people from the cathedral to the City Hall, where he coined his now famous slogan for the new order: "We are the rainbow people!" he told the crowd, "We are the new people of South Africa!"

Church Street (which crosses the mall towards its southern end) and its surrounding area abound with antique dealers, and on the pedestrianized section at its northeastern end you'll find an informal antique market. Prices are competitive and you may pick up unusual pieces of jewellery, bric-a-brac, Africana and even old sheet music.

Government Avenue and the Company Gardens

A stroll down **Government Avenue**, the southwest extension of Adderley Street, makes for one of the most serene walks in central Cape Town (all roads and paths in the Company Gardens are pedestrianized). This oak-lined boulevard runs past the rear of Parliament through the Gardens, and its benches are frequently occupied by snoring *bergies* (tramps).

Looming on your right as you enter the north end of the avenue, the **South African Library** (Mon–Fri 9am–6pm, Sat 9am–1pm; free) houses one of the country's best collections of antiquarian historical and natural history books, covering southern Africa. Built with the revenue from a tax on wine, it opened in 1822 as one of the first free libraries in the world.

Stretching from here to the South African Museum, the **Company Gardens** were the initial *raison d'être* for the Dutch settlement at the Cape. Established in 1652 to supply fresh greens to Dutch East India Company ships travelling between the Netherlands and the East, the gardens were initially worked by imported slave labour. This proved too expensive, as the slaves had to be shipped in, fed and housed, so the Company phased out its farming and granted land to free burghers, from whom it bought fresh produce. At the end of the seventeenth century, the gardens were turned over to botanical horticulture for Cape Town's growing colonial elite. Ponds, lawns, landscaping and a crisscross web of oak-shaded walkways were introduced. It was during a stroll in these gardens that Rhodes (a statue of whom you'll find here) first plotted the invasion of Matabeleland and Mashonaland (which together became Rhodesia and subsequently Zimbabwe). He also introduced an army of small, furry colonizers to the gardens – North American grey squirrels. Today the gardens are full of local plants, the result of long-standing European interest in Cape botany; experts have been sailing out since the seventeenth century to classify and name specimens. The gardens are still a pleasant place to meander, and feature an outdoor café.

Continuing along Government Avenue from the South African Library, past the rear of Parliament, you can peer through an iron gate to see the grand buildings and tended flowerbeds of **De Tuynhuys**, the office (but not residence) of the president. During Mandela's presidency, one party of tourists stood amazed as the great man, who is renowned for his common touch, strolled across the lawns for a friendly chat.

A little further along, the tree-lined walkway opens out into a formal gravel area with ponds and statues, around which are sited the National Gallery, the Jewish Museum and the Great Synagogue to the east, and the South African Museum and Planetarium to the west.

The South African National Gallery

Not far from the southern end of Government Avenue, where it's joined by the tiny Gallery Lane, the **South African National Gallery** (Tues–Sun

10am–5pm; R10, children R5, free on Sat) is an essential port of call for anyone interested in the local art scene, and includes a small but excellent permanent collection of contemporary South African art. You'll also find a fine display of traditional works from the southeast of the continent, based around a small collection donated by the German government. The exhibits, which include beadwork, carvings and craft objects, were chosen for their aesthetic qualities and rarity, and represent the gallery's policy of focusing on neglected parts of South Africa's heritage. Don't miss Jane Alexander's sculpture *Butcher Boys*, which figuratively portrays all the menace and violence inherent in South Africa, past and present. One room contains minor works by various British artists including Pre-Raphaelites, George Romney, Thomas Gainsborough and Joshua Reynolds. The gallery has a good café serving light lunches, snacks, coffees and cakes, as well as an excellent shop.

The South African Jewish Museum

Next to the National Gallery but accessed from 88 Hatfield St, the **South African Jewish Museum** (Mon–Thurs & Sun 10am–5pm, Fri 10am–2pm; R50; Ⓦ www.sajewishmuseum.co.za) is partially housed in South Africa's first synagogue, built in 1863. Officially opened by Nelson Mandela in 2000, this award-winning museum narrates the story of South African Jewry from its beginnings over 150 years ago to the present – a narrative which starts in the Old Synagogue from which visitors cross, via a gangplank, to the upper level of a new two-storey building, symbolically re-enacting the arrival by boat of the first Jewish immigrants at Table Bay harbour in the 1840s. Employing multimedia interactive displays, models and Judaica artefacts, the exhibition follows three threads: "**Memories**", looking at the roots and experiences of the immigrants; "**Reality**", covering their integration into South Africa; and "**Dreams**", examining a diversity of views about the role of Jews in South Africa, their relationship to Israel and their position in the world. Other

Jewish immigration to South Africa

Today there are around sixteen thousand Jews in Cape Town, the majority descended from **Eastern European refugees** who fled discrimination and pogroms during the late nineteenth and early twentieth centuries.

Since 1795, when the occupying British introduced freedom of worship at the Cape, Jews in South Africa have faced few legal impediments. However, there were instances of semi-official anti-Semitism during the twentieth century, the most notable being in the policy of the Nationalist Party while in opposition during the 1930s. Before World War II, elements in the party came under the influence of Nazi ideology, which was being poured into South Africa by the German foreign and propaganda offices, and began to attribute all the ills facing Afrikanerdom to a "British–Jewish capitalist" conspiracy. In 1941, the party adopted a policy of ending Jewish immigration and even repatriating "undesirable Immigrants", as well as placing stronger controls over naturalization and the introduction of a "vocational permit" system to protect "the original white population against unfair competition".

Ironically, on the eve of taking power in 1947, the party of apartheid turned its back on anti-Semitism: one of its first acts after winning the 1948 election was to recognize the newly created state of Israel, with which South Africa maintained strong links until the National Party relinquished power in 1994. The ANC government is far more sympathetic to the Palestinian cause, and far more critical of Israel than its predecessors.

displays examine anti-Semitism, apartheid and the Jews who opposed it, as well as Nelson Mandela's relationship with the Jewish community.

Drawing parallels between Judaism and the ritual practices and beliefs of South Africa's other communities, the "**Culture among Cultures**" display covers topics such as birth, marriage, circumcision and death. The **basement level** houses a walk-through reconstruction of a Lithuanian *shtetl* or village (most South African Jews have their nineteenth-century roots in Lithuania), as well as the **Discovery Centre**, an interactive computer with a genealogy bank, a searchable database on Jewish life and culture and a "glimpse into Israel". A restaurant, shop and auditorium are also housed in the museum complex.

The Holocaust Exhibition and the Great Synagogue

Opened in 1999, the **Holocaust Exhibition** (Mon–Thurs & Sun 10am–5pm, Fri 10am–1pm; free) is one of the most moving and brilliantly executed museums in Cape Town. Housed upstairs in the Holocaust Centre (in the same complex as the Jewish Museum), it resonates sharply in a country that only recently emerged from an era of racial oppression – a connection that the exhibition makes explicitly. A densely layered narrative is related through text, photographs, artefacts (such as a concentration camp uniform), film clips, soundtracks, multimedia and interactive video, while the design uses modulated lighting, cobblestones reminiscent of the ghettos and pieces of barbed wire and railway track to evoke the death camps.

Exhibits trace the history of anti-Semitism in Europe, culminating with the Nazis' Final Solution; they also look at South Africa's Greyshirts, who were motivated by Nazi propaganda during the 1930s and were later absorbed into the National Party. There are accounts of heroism, often tragic, including acts of resistance by Jews, and a touch screen portrays many individuals in Europe who risked their lives to protect or rescue the victims of Nazism. To conclude, a twenty-minute video tells the story of survivors who eventually settled in Cape Town.

The **Great Synagogue** next door is one of Cape Town's outstanding religious buildings. Designed by the Scottish architects Parker & Forsyth and completed in 1905, it features an impressive dome and two soaring towers after the style of central European Baroque churches. To see the arched interior and the alcove decorated with gilt mosaics, you need to ask at the Holocaust Centre, and may be asked to provide some form of identification.

The South African Museum and Planetarium

The nation's premier museum of natural history and human sciences, the **South African Museum** (daily 10am–5pm; R8; free on Sat; Ⓦ www.museums .org.za/sam) and **Planetarium** (daily 10am–5pm; R20, children R6) stands at 25 Queen Victoria St, west of Government Avenue. The museum's **ethnographic galleries** contain some very good displays on the traditional arts and crafts of several African groups, some exceptional examples of rock art (entire chunks of caves sitting in the display cases), and casts of the stone birds found at the archeological site of Great Zimbabwe, in Zimbabwe. Upstairs, the **natural history galleries** display mounted mammals, dioramas of prehistoric Karoo reptiles, and Table Mountain flora and fauna. The highlight is the four-storey "whale well", in which a collection of beautiful whale skeletons hang like massive mobiles, accompanied by the eerie strains of their song.

The attached **Planetarium** (shows Mon & Wed–Fri 2pm, Tues 2pm & 8pm; Sat noon, 1pm & 2.30pm) is recommended if you want to see the constellations of the southern hemisphere, accompanied by informed commentary. There's also a changing programme of shows covering topics such as San sky myths. Leaflets at the museum provide a list of forthcoming attractions, and you can buy a monthly chart of the current night sky – especially worthwhile if you're staying in an area without streetlights and can actually see the stars.

Bertram House

At the southernmost end of Government Avenue, you'll come upon **Bertram House** (Tues–Thurs 10am–4.30pm; R5, children R2), whose beautiful two-storey brick facade looks out across a fragrant herb garden. Built in the 1840s, the museum is significant as the only surviving brick Georgian-style house in Cape Town, and displays typical furniture and objects of a well-to-do colonial British family in the first half of the nineteenth century.

The site was bought in 1839 by John Barker, a Yorkshire attorney who came to the Cape in 1823. He named the house after his wife, Ann Bertram Findlay, who died in 1838, and was responsible for building it. Declared a National Monument in 1962, Bertram House was extensively restored to its current state in the 1980s: imported face brick and Welsh slate were used to recreate the original facade, while the interior walls were redecorated in their earlier dark green and ochre, based on the evidence of paint scrapings. The reception rooms are decorated in the Regency style, while the porcelain is predominantly nineteenth-century English, although there are also some very fine Chinese pieces.

Houses of Parliament

South Africa's **Houses of Parliament**, east of Government Avenue, on Parliament Street, are a complex of interlinking buildings, with labyrinthine corridors connecting hundreds of offices, debating chambers and miscellaneous other rooms. Many of these are relics of the 1980s reformist phase of apartheid when, in the interests of racial segregation, there were three distinct legislative complexes sited here to cater to different "races".

The original wing, completed in 1885, is an imposing Victorian Neoclassical building which first served as the legislative assembly of the Cape Colony. After the Boer republics and British colonies amalgamated in 1910, it became the parliament of the Union of South Africa. This is the old parliament, where over seven decades of repressive legislation, including apartheid laws, were passed. It's also where **Hendrik Verwoerd**, the arch-theorist of apartheid, met his bloody end, not at the hand of a political activist, but stabbed to death by Dimitri Tsafendas, a parliamentary messenger who inexplicably went off the rails, committing the act because, as he told police, "a tapeworm ordered me to do it." Due to his mental state, the assassin escaped the gallows to outlive apartheid – albeit in an institution. Verwoerd's portrait, depicting him as a man of vision and gravitas, used to hang over the main entrance to the dining room. In 1996 it was removed "for cleaning", along with paintings of generations of white parliamentarians.

The new chamber was built in 1983 as part of the **tricameral parliament**, P.W. Botha's attempt to avert majority rule by trying to co-opt Indians and coloureds – but in their own separate debating chambers. The "tricameral" chamber, where the three non-African "races" on occasions met together, is now the **National Assembly**, where you can watch sessions of parliament. One-hour **tours** (Mon–Fri 9am–noon on the hour; free) take in the old and new debating chambers, the library and museum, and should be booked in advance through the Tours Section (☎021 403 2201). This is also the place to contact for day tickets to the **debating sessions** – the most interesting of which is question time

(Wed from 3pm), when you can hear ministers being quizzed by MPs. To join a tour, go to the Plein Street entrance to Parliament, opposite the Receiver of Revenue (it's the more southerly of the two entrances in this street); go through a security check, where you should ask for directions to the Poorthuis entrance. From there you'll see arrows indicating the starting point for tours.

Castle of Good Hope

From the outside, South Africa's oldest building looks somewhat miserable, and its position on Darling Street, behind the train station and city-bus terminal, does nothing to dispel this. Nevertheless the **Castle of Good Hope** (daily 9am–4pm; R20; ⓦ www.castleofgoodhope.co.za) is well worth the entrance fee; inside, a meticulous ten-year restoration has returned the decor to the British Regency style introduced in 1798.

Completed in 1679, the Castle – as it's commonly known – replaced Van Riebeeck's earlier mud and timber fort, which stood on the site of the Grand Parade. The Castle was built in accordance with seventeenth-century European principles of fortification, comprising strong bastions from which the outside walls could be protected by crossfire. Construction lasted over thirteen years, with work constantly coming to a standstill because of shortages of labour or materials. The original, seaward entrance had to be moved to its present position facing landward, because the spring tide sometimes came crashing in – a remarkable thought given how far aground it is now. This newer entrance is a fine example of seventeenth-century Dutch classicism and, in the tower above, the bell cast in Amsterdam by Claude Fremy in 1697 still hangs from its original wooden beams. For 150 years, the Castle remained the symbolic heart of the Cape administration, and the centre of social and economic life, but in the late nineteenth century – when the colony had expanded far beyond its walls – there were at least three attempts by the authorities to demolish it, as it was regarded as a white elephant.

Inside the Castle are three interesting collections. The **Military Museum** has displays on the conflicts that dogged the early settlement; the **Secunde's House** has furnishings, paintings and *objets d'art* that filled the living space of the deputy governor; and the **William Fehr Collection**, one of the country's most important exhibits of decorative arts, includes paintings of the settlement, eighteenth- and nineteenth-century Dutch and Indonesian furniture, and seventeenth- and eighteenth-century Chinese and Japanese porcelain. Guided tours (daily 11am, noon & 2pm; free) are useful for orientation and cover the main features, including the prison cells and dungeons, with their centuries-old graffiti painstakingly carved by prisoners. In the elegant courtyard there is a very pleasant tea shop, with Table Mountain looming over the west wall. The Castle is also home to the Defence Force's Western Province Command; you may see armed soldiers marching through the courtyard.

The Grand Parade and the City Hall

To the west of the Castle, the **Grand Parade** is a large open area where the residents of District Six used to come to trade. On Wednesdays and Saturdays it still transforms itself into a **market**, where you can buy a whole array of bargains ranging from used clothes to spicy food.

The Grand Parade appeared on TV screens throughout the world on February 11, 1990, when 100,000 people gathered to hear **Nelson Mandela** make his first speech after being released from prison, from the balcony of **City Hall**. A slightly fussy Edwardian building dressed in Bath stone, City Hall manages, despite its drab surroundings, to look impressive against Table Mountain.

District Six

South of the Castle, in the shadow of Devil's Peak, is a vacant lot shown on maps as the suburb of **Zonnebloem**. Before being demolished by the apartheid authorities, it was an inner-city slum known as **District Six**, an impoverished but lively community of 55,000 predominantly coloured people. Once regarded as the soul of Cape Town, the district harboured a rich cultural life in its narrow alleys and crowded tenements: along the cobbled streets, hawkers rubbed shoulders with prostitutes, gangsters, drunks and gamblers, while craftsmen plied their trade in small workshops. This was a fertile place of the South African imagination, inspiring novels, poems, jazz and the blockbuster *District Six: The Musical*, by David Kramer, which in the late 1980s played to packed houses and spawned a series of hits.

In 1966 apartheid ideologues declared District Six a **White Group Area** and the bulldozers moved in, taking fifteen years to drive its presence from the skyline, leaving only the mosques and churches. But, in the wake of the demolition gangs, international and domestic outcry was so great that the area was never developed apart from a few luxury town houses on its fringes and the hefty Cape Technikon, a college that now occupies nearly a quarter of the former suburb. After years of negotiation, the original residents are moving back under a scheme to develop low-cost housing in the district.

The District Six Museum

Few places in Cape Town speak more eloquently of the effect of apartheid on the day-to-day lives of ordinary people than the compelling **District Six Museum** (Mon 9am–3pm, Tues–Sat 9am–4pm; R10; Ⓦ www.districtsix.co.za). On the northern boundary of District Six, on the corner of Buitenkant and Albertus streets, the museum occupies the former **Central Methodist Mission Church**, which offered solidarity and ministry to the victims of forced removals right up to the 1980s, and became a venue for anti-apartheid gatherings. Today, it houses a series of fascinating displays that include everyday household items and tools of trades, such as hairdressing implements, as well as documentary photographs, which evoke the lives of the individuals who once lived here. Occupying most of the floor is a huge map of District Six as it was, annotated by former residents, who describe their memories, reflections and incidents associated with places and buildings that no longer exist. There's also an almost complete collection of original street signs, secretly retrieved at the time of demolition by the man entrusted with dumping them into Table Bay.

Cape Heritage Square

Back at Long Street, if you head northwest down Shortmarket Street, you'll come to **Cape Heritage Square**, the largest restoration project ever undertaken in Cape Town. The square is home to the *Cape Heritage Hotel* as well as a conglomeration of restaurants, wine merchants, art galleries, jewellers and fashion shops, many of which are housed in a complex dating back to 1771. Set around a courtyard, in which the oldest known (and still fruit-bearing) vine in South Africa continues to flourish, the square is worth visiting for a glimpse of the superb restoration work.

The Bo-Kaap

Minutes from Parliament, on the slopes of Signal Hill, is the **Bo-Kaap**, one of Cape Town's oldest and most fascinating residential areas. Its streets are characterized by brightly coloured nineteenth-century Dutch and Georgian terraces, which conceal a network of alleyways that are the arteries of its

Muslim community. The Bo-Kaap harbours its own strong identity, made all the more unique by the destruction of District Six, with which it had much in common. A particular dialect of Afrikaans is spoken here, although it is steadily being eroded by English.

Bo-Kaap residents are descended from dissidents and slaves imported by the Dutch in the sixteenth and seventeenth centuries. They became known collectively as "**Cape Malays**", a term you'll still hear, even though it's a complete misnomer: most originated from Africa, India, Madagascar and Sri Lanka, with fewer than one percent actually from Malaysia.

The easiest way to get to the Bo-Kaap is by foot along Wale Street, which trails up from the south end of Adderley Street and across Buitengragt, to become the main drag of the Bo-Kaap. There's a deceptively quaint feel to the area: apart from Wale Street, this is not really a place to explore alone. It's better to join one of several **tours** that take in the museum and walk you around the district. The best (and cheapest, at R120 including the museum entrance fee) is run by Bo-Kaap Guided Tours (℡021 422 1554 or 082 423 6932, Ⓔshireen.narkedien@gmail.com). It lasts two hours and is operated by residents of the area, whose knowledge goes beyond the standard tour-guide script.

A good place to head for is the **Bo-Kaap Museum**, 71 Wale St (Mon–Sat 9am–4pm; R5, children R1; Ⓦwww.iziko.org.za/bokaap), near the Buitengragt end. It consists mainly of the family house and possessions of Abu Bakr Effendi, a nineteenth-century religious leader brought out from Turkey by the British in 1862 as a mediator between feuding Muslim factions. He became an important member of the community, founded an Arabic school and wrote a book in the local vernacular – now regarded as possibly the first book to be published in what can be recognized as Afrikaans. The museum also has exhibits exploring the local brand of Islam, which has its own unique traditions and nearly two dozen *kramats* (shrines) dotted about the peninsula. One block south of the museum, at Dorp Street, is the **Auwal**, South Africa's first official mosque, founded in 1795 by Tuan Guru, a Muslim activist. Ten more mosques, whose minarets give spice to the quarter's skyline, now serve its 10,000 residents.

A small Muslim shantytown, tucked away next to the old quarry below the cemetery, brings the immediacy of South Africa's housing crisis right to the edge of the city centre. Modern, low-cost developments, looking down from the heights of Signal Hill onto the photogenic Bo-Kaap townscape, have helped alleviate the community's housing shortage, but have added nothing to the architectural charm of the protected historic core bounded by Dorp and Strand streets, and Buitengragt and Pentz streets. Furthermore, many Bo-Kaap residents, tempted by the high prices their cottages can fetch, have sold them to outsiders who value the central location and picturesque quality of the area, a process which is seen to be diluting the Muslim lifestyle in the area.

Strand Street

A major artery from the N2 freeway to the central business district, **Strand Street** neatly separates the Upper from the Lower city centre. Between the mid-eighteenth and mid-nineteenth centuries, Strand Street was one of the most fashionable streets in Cape Town because of its proximity to the shore. Its former cachet is now only discernible from the handful of quietly elegant National Monuments left standing amid the roar of traffic: **Martin Melck House** (accommodating the **Gold of Africa Museum**), the **Evangelical Lutheran Church** and **Koopmans-De Wet House**.

Gold of Africa Museum

Since the discovery of gold near Johannesburg in the late nineteenth century, South Africa has been closely associated in the Western mind with the precious metal and the riches it represents. However, the outstanding **Gold of Africa Museum** at 96 Strand St (Mon–Sat 9.30am–5pm; R50; ⓦwww .goldofafrica.com), just off Buitengragt, focuses on a completely different side to gold – the exquisite **artworks** crafted by nineteenth- and twentieth-century **African goldsmiths** from Mali, Senegal, Ghana and the Cote d'Ivoire. Arguably the most important such collection in the world, acquired in 2001 from the Barbier-Mueller Museum in Geneva, it traces Africa's ancient gold routes, and includes several hundred beautiful items – precious masks, crocodiles, birds, a gold crown and human figures; the highlight is the sculpted **Golden Lion** from Ghana that is the symbol of the museum. There's also a small auditorium with a continuous **film show**; a **wine cellar**, where you can have a snack, a coffee and quaff a glass of Cape wine; a **studio** where goldsmiths practise their art; and a **shop** selling postcards, gold leaf and beautiful little souvenirs.

Evangelical Lutheran Church

Next door to the Gold of Africa Museum, at the corner of Buitengragt and Strand Street, stands the **Evangelical Lutheran Church** (Mon, Wed & Fri 9am–noon; free). Converted by Anton Anreith (see box, p.137) in 1785 from a barn, its facade includes Classical details such as a broken pediment perforated by the clock tower, as well as Gothic features such as arched windows. Inside, the magnificent **pulpit**, supported on two life-size Herculean figures, is one of Anreith's masterpieces; the white swan perched on the canopy is a symbol of Lutheranism.

The establishment of a Lutheran church in Cape Town struck a significant blow against the extreme **religious intolerance** that pervaded under VOC rule. Before 1771, when permission was granted to Lutherans to establish their own congregation, Protestantism was the only form of worship allowed and the Dutch Reformed Church held an absolute monopoly over saving people's souls. The Lutheran Church's congregation was dominated by Germans, who at the time constituted 28 percent of the colony's free burgher population.

Koopmans-De Wet House

Sandwiched between two office blocks close to Cape Town Tourism, **Koopmans–De Wet House** at 35 Strand St (Tues–Thurs 9.30am–4.30pm; R5) is an outstanding eighteenth-century pedimented Neoclassical town house and museum, accommodating a very fine collection of antique furniture and rare porcelain. An inexpensive **guide** booklet gives interesting contextual background to the house and its history, while a separate brochure describes items in the collection: both are available at the entrance.

The earliest sections of the house were built in 1701 by **Reyner Smedinga**, a well-to-do goldsmith who imported the building materials from Holland. The house changed hands more than a dozen times over the following two centuries, with minor additions made in the 1760s and a second storey added between 1774 and 1790. In 1806, it came into the hands of the De Wet family, eventually becoming the home of **Marie Koopmans–De Wet** (1834–1906), a prominent figure on the Cape social and political circuit.

The building's **facade** has been attributed to Louis Thibault and Anton Anreith (see box, p.137), but there's no proof of this. Whoever was responsible, the house represents a fine synthesis of Dutch elements (sash windows and large entrance doors) with the demands of local conditions; the huge rooms, lofty ceilings and shuttered windows reflect the high summer temperatures, while the front *stoep* has plastered masonry seats at each end. The **lantern** in the fanlight of the entrance to the house was a feature of all Cape Town houses in the eighteenth and early nineteenth centuries, its purpose to shine light onto the street and thus hinder slaves from gathering at night to plot.

The Lower City Centre

In the mid-nineteenth century, the city's middle classes viewed the **Lower City Centre** and its low-life activities with a mixture of alarm and excitement – a tension that remains today. **Lower Long Street** divides the area just inland from the docklands into two. To the east is the **Foreshore**, an ugly post-World War II wasteland of grey corporate architecture, among which is the **Artscape Centre**, Cape Town's prestige arts complex. The Foreshore is at last being redeveloped, its centrepiece being the **Cape Town International Convention Centre**, completed in 2003 and linked by a canal and pedestrian routes with the Waterfront.

The Foreshore

The Foreshore, an area of reclaimed land north of Strand Street, stretching to the docks and east of Lower Long Street, was developed in the late 1940s in a spirit of modernism – large highly planned urban spaces – that was sweeping the world. It was intended to turn Cape Town's harbour into a symbolic gateway to Africa; instead, it turned out to be a series of large concrete boxes surrounded by acres of windswept tarmac parking lots. The opening in 2004 of the prestigious International Convention Centre in the area, and its proximity to some high-rise hotels and parking garages, have opened up the area, but there is no street life at all, and no reason to explore the area.

Heerengracht, a truncated two-lane carriageway running from Adderley Street to the harbour, has massive roundabouts at each end solemnly guarded by statues of Jan van Riebeeck and Bartholomeu Dias. It was meant to be the ceremonial axis through this grand scheme, joining the city to the sea, but it never quite makes it to the water, coming to a disappointing standstill at the dock perimeter fence, before bearing east under the dismal shadow of the N1 and N2 flyovers.

The only building worth visiting here – when there's something on – is the **Artscape Complex** (previously known as the Nico Theatre Complex), Cape Town's major performance venue, in D.F. Malan Street just east of Heerengracht. Incorporating the large Main Theatre, it also houses the small Arena Theatre, the opera house and a decent coffee shop; for more on events staged here, see p.166.

Duncan Dock

North of the Foreshore, **Duncan Dock** is Cape Town's working harbour. Work started on the dock in 1938, swallowing the city beachfronts at Woodstock and Paarden Island to cater for the growing supertanker traffic that was outstripping the capacity of the Victoria and Alfred Docks. The dock today is a forbidding industrial landscape of large ships and towering cranes cut off from the city by an enormous perimeter fence.

The V&A Waterfront, De Waterkant and Robben Island

The **Victoria and Alfred Waterfront**, usually known simply as the Waterfront, adjoins the west of Duncan Dock and is Cape Town's original Victorian harbour. After two decades of stagnation, it was redeveloped in the 1990s and is now the most popular attraction on the peninsula, incorporating the city's central shopping area, its most fashionable eating and drinking venues, the site of an excellent aquarium and the Nelson Mandela Gateway – the embarkation point for trips to **Robben Island**. Authentic nineteenth-century buildings, imitation Victorian shopping malls, piers with waterside walkways and a functioning harbour complement the wide range of restaurants, outdoor cafés, pubs, clubs, cinemas, museums and outdoor entertainment, with magnificent Table Mountain rising beyond.

West of the Foreshore and rubbing up against the west side of the city centre and the V&A Waterfront to its north is Cape Town's thriving clubland, incorporating **De Waterkant** and **Somerset Road**, the city's self-proclaimed "gay village". With its high density of **nightclubs** and **pubs**, the area around Somerset Road, which heads from the city centre into Green Point, has become the best place in Cape Town to club-crawl, one of the few places you're guaranteed action seven nights a week; for more, see pp.162–165. For coverage of the coast from Mouille Point onwards, see pp.144–152.

The Waterfront

Throughout the first half of the nineteenth century, arguments raged in Cape Town over the need for a proper dock. The Cape was often known as the **Cape of Storms** because of its vicious weather, which left Table Bay littered with wrecks. Many makeshift attempts were made to ameliorate the situation, including the construction of a lighthouse in 1823, and work was begun on a jetty at the bottom of Bree Street in 1832. Clamour for a harbour grew in the 1850s, with the increase in sea traffic arriving at the Cape, reaching its peak in 1860, when the Lloyds insurance company refused the risk of covering ships dropping anchor in Table Bay.

The British colonial government dragged its heels due to the costs involved, but eventually conceded; on a suitably stormy September day in 1860, at a huge ceremony, the teenage Prince Alfred tipped the first batch of stones into Table Bay to begin the **Breakwater**, the westernmost arm of the harbour, which was subsequently completed with convict labour. In 1869, the dock – consisting of two main basins – was completed, and the sea was allowed to pour in.

The Waterfront is one of the easiest points to reach in Cape Town by **public transport**. Golden Arrow municipal buses leave for here from Adderley Street, from outside the train station and from Beach Road in Sea Point. The open-topped City Sightseeing Bus (see p.96) also stops at the Waterfront. Arriving by **car**, you'll find yourself well catered for, with several car parks and garages. If you want to leave by taxi, head for the taxi rank on Breakwater Boulevard.

The Marina and the Victoria and Alfred basins

Victoria Basin, the smaller **Alfred Basin** to its west, and the **Marina** beyond, create the northwestern half of the Waterfront's geography of piers and quays. The shopping focus of the Waterfront is **Victoria Wharf**, an enormous flashy

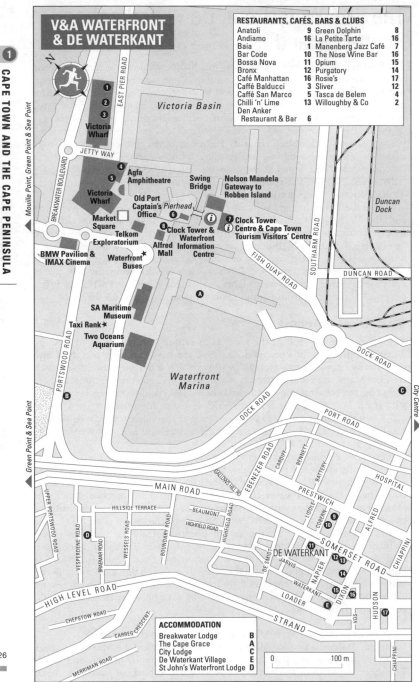

V&A WATERFRONT & DE WATERKANT

RESTAURANTS, CAFÉS, BARS & CLUBS

Anatoli	9	Green Dolphin	8
Andiamo	16	La Petite Tarte	16
Baia	1	Manenberg Jazz Café	7
Bar Code	10	The Nose Wine Bar	16
Bossa Nova	11	Opium	15
Bronx	12	Purgatory	14
Café Manhattan	16	Rosie's	17
Caffé Balducci	3	Sliver	12
Caffé San Marco	5	Tasca de Belem	4
Chilli 'n' Lime	13	Willoughby & Co	2
Den Anker Restaurant & Bar	6		

Victoria Basin

Victoria Wharf

JETTY WAY

BREAKWATER BOULEVARD

EAST PIER ROAD

Agfa Amphitheatre

Victoria Wharf

Old Port Captain's Office

Pierhead

Swing Bridge

Nelson Mandela Gateway to Robben Island

Clock Tower Centre & Cape Town Tourism Visitors' Centre

Duncan Dock

Market Square

Telkom Exploratorium

Clock Tower & Waterfront Information Centre

Alfred Mall

SOUTHARM ROAD

BMW Pavilion & IMAX Cinema

Waterfront Buses

FISH QUAY ROAD

DUNCAN ROAD

SA Maritime Museum

Taxi Rank ★

Two Oceans Aquarium

Waterfront Marina

DOCK ROAD

DOCK ROAD

PORT ROAD

City Centre

PORTSWOOD ROAD

Green Point & Sea Point

MAIN ROAD

GALLOWS HILL RD

EBENEZER ROAD

CARDIFF

BENNETT

BATTERY

PRESTWICH

LIDDLE

COBERN

ALFRED

HOSPITAL

CHIAPPINI

UPPER PORTSWOOD ROAD

HILLSIDE TERRACE

BEAUMONT

HIGHFIELD ROAD

HIGHFIELD ROAD

BOUNDARY ROAD

WESSELS ROAD

SOMERSET ROAD

DE WATERKANT

DE SMIDT

JARVIS

NAPIER

DIXON

HUDSON

VOS

VESPERDENE ROAD

BRAEMAR ROAD

HIGH LEVEL ROAD

CHEPSTOW ROAD

CARREG CRESCENT

WATERKANT

LOADER

STRAND

CHIAPPINI

MERRIMAN ROAD

Bo-Kaap ▼

ACCOMMODATION

Breakwater Lodge	B
The Cape Grace	A
City Lodge	C
De Waterkant Village	E
St John's Waterfront Lodge	D

0   100 m

Mouille Point, Green Point & Sea Point

Green Point & Sea Point

mall on two levels, extending along Quays Five and Six. It's here that most visitors to the Waterfront arrive. With outdoor seating, the restaurants and cafés on the mall's east side have fabulous views of Table Mountain across the busy harbour. On the west side of Victoria Wharf, and physically linked to it, the rather contrived **Red Shed Craft Workshop** (Mon–Sat 9am–9pm, Sun 10am–9pm) brings together craft workers such as glass-blowers, leatherworkers, township artists and jewellery-makers under one huge roof.

The outdoor action centres around **Market Square** and the **Agfa Amphitheatre**, where you can sometimes catch free rock, jazz or traditional African musical performances and occasionally hear the Cape Town Symphony Orchestra (details from the Visitor Centre).

South of here along the Alfred Basin's North Quay, **Alfred Mall Shopping Centre** is a complex of fifteen touristy curio shops, boutiques and restaurants. East of the Alfred Shopping Mall, the Pierhead is dominated by the **Old Port Captain's Office**, a gabled Arts and Crafts building erected in 1904, with an imposing presence that reflected its status as the nerve centre of the harbour in the early twentieth century. It's now the headquarters of the Victoria and Alfred Waterfront Company, which manages the Waterfront area.

Two Oceans Aquarium

One of Cape Town's highlights, the **Two Oceans Aquarium** (daily 9.30am– 6pm; adults R75, children R35; Ⓦ www.aquarium.co.za) on Dock Road at the Marina's North Wharf, showcases the Cape's unique marine environment, where the warm Indian Ocean mingles with the cold Atlantic. A designated route (which you're not obliged to follow) takes in the nine major galleries in sequence, starting on the **ground floor** with the **Indian Ocean**, where you'll see tank after tank of psychedelic fish. One of the most beautiful displays features scores of small gossamer jellyfish floating gently in their ultraviolet-lit cylindrical tank like parachutists. To the rear of the ground floor, the **Diversity Hall**, as its name implies, contains an astonishing variety of strange marine creatures, including giant spider crabs, octopuses, sea horses and the deadly devil

▲ The Two Oceans Aquarium

firefish, whose lacy beauty disguises lethal spines. Also on the ground floor, the **Agfa Auditorium** shows videos on South Africa's marine life and related topics (such as underwater photography).

The **basement** houses the **Alpha Activity Centre**, a good place to keep kids occupied, with free organized activities such as puppet shows and face painting, and computers which allow youngsters to explore marine ecology. The centre is combined with the **Diving Animals** display, where you can watch a group of resident Cape fur seals frolicking underwater.

The **top floor**, reached via a ramp, accommodates the **Story of Water**, which, in glorious reconstruction, traces the course of a river from its mouth to its source, via a salt marsh and lagoon. Not to everyone's taste, it features a small colony of African penguins (which you can see in their natural state at Boulders; see p.152), while captive sea birds fly about the rafters. In the **Kelp Forest** in an adjacent gallery a dense jungle of giant seaweed sways hypnotically with the rhythmic surge of the water; you can sit in the small amphitheatre and gaze at beautiful shoals of silvery fish shimmering through sunlit sea. From here, a ramp takes you in a gentle downward spiral through the **Predators** exhibit, for many visitors the most compelling attraction of all. A massive tank, open to the ocean, houses some large resident ragged-toothed sharks, which glide past as you walk through a glass underwater tunnel; other species confined here include rays and giant turtles.

Among the highlights of the aquarium is the **shark feeding** every Sunday at 3.30pm, when you can watch *raggies* – ragged-tooth sharks – being hand-fed by divers. Smaller sharks, stingrays and turtles get their turn on Monday, Wednesday and Friday at 3.30pm, and penguins are fed daily at noon and 3pm. If you have an Open Water 1 diving qualification, you can actually **dive** in the predators tank (book one day before on ☎021 418 3823; R450).

Fish Quay

From the Pierhead you can use the **swing bridge** to cross to **Fish Quay**, the **Clock Tower Precinct** and the **Nelson Mandela Gateway to Robben Island** (daily 7.30am–5.30pm; free). The embarkation point for ferries to Robben Island, this two-storey building also incorporates a restaurant with a great view and a small museum with hi-tech interactive displays, featuring a history of Robben Island, the voices of prisoners and resistance songs.

Rising up from Fish Quay, the **Clock Tower**, which houses a branch of the Waterfront Information Centre, is Cape Town's finest architectural folly. Built as the original Port Captain's office in 1882, this strange-looking octagonal structure with Gothic windows consists of three stacked rooms with a stairwell

---

Robben Island tours

A number of vendors at the Waterfront sell tickets for cruises, which may go close to Robben Island, but only the official ones sold at the **Nelson Mandela Gateway** will get you onto it (R150, including boat trip either on a catamaran or the historic ferry, island entry and 3hr 30min tour). Bookings must be made in advance with a credit card (☎021 419 1300, ⓦwww.robben-island.org.za) as the boats are often full, especially around December and January. Be sure to present your booking reference number and arrive at least half an hour before departure to collect your ticket. The boats operate hourly every day, except at noon and 4pm; in summer they run between 8am and 6pm, in winter between 9am and 3pm. All trips are dependent on the weather.

running through its core. The mirror room on the second floor enabled the Port Captain to survey all the activities of the harbour without leaving his office. Adjacent to the Clock Tower, the **Clock Tower Centre** is a compact two-storey shopping mall, with a substantial Cape Tourism visitor centre.

Robben Island

Lying only a few kilometres from the commerce of the Waterfront, flat and windswept **Robben Island** is suffused by a meditative, otherworldly silence. This key site of South Africa's liberation struggle was intended to silence apartheid's domestic critics, but instead became an international focus for opposition to the regime. Measuring six square kilometres and sparsely vegetated by low scrub, it was Nelson Mandela's "home" for nearly two decades.

Some history

Nelson Mandela may have been the most famous Robben Island prisoner, but he certainly wasn't the first. In the seventeenth century the island became a place of banishment for those who offended the political order (initially the Dutch, later the British and the Afrikaner Nationalists). The island's first prisoner was the indigenous Khoikhoi leader **Autshumato**, who learnt English in the early seventeenth century and became an emissary of the British. After the Dutch settlement was established, he was jailed on the island by Jan van Riebeeck in 1658. The rest of the seventeenth century saw a succession of East Indies political prisoners and Muslim holy men exiled here for opposing Dutch colonial rule.

During the nineteenth century, the **British** used Robben Island as a dumping ground for deserters, criminals and political prisoners, in much the same way as they used Australia. Captured **Xhosa leaders** who defied the British Empire during the Frontier Wars of the early to mid-nineteenth century were transported by sea from the Eastern to the Western Cape to be imprisoned, and many ended up on Robben Island. In 1846, the island's brief was extended to include a whole range of the **socially marginalized**; criminals and political detainees were now joined by vagrants, prostitutes, lunatics and the chronically ill. All were victim to a regime of brutality and maltreatment, even in hospital. In the 1890s, a leper colony existed alongside the social outcasts. Lunatics were removed in 1921 and the lepers in 1930. During World War II, the **Defence Force** took over the island to set up defensive guns against a feared Axis invasion, which never came.

Robben Island's greatest era of notoriety began in 1961, when it was taken over by the **Prisons Department**. Prisoners arriving at the island prison were greeted by a slogan on the gate that read: "Welcome to Robben Island: We Serve with Pride." By 1963, when Nelson Mandela arrived, it had become a maximum security prison, and all the warders – but none of the prisoners – were white. Prisoners were only allowed to send and receive one letter every six months, and common-law criminals and political prisoners were housed together until 1971, when they were separated in an attempt to further isolate the politicals. Harsh conditions, including routine beatings and forced hard labour, were exacerbated by geographical location: there's nothing but sea between the island and the South Pole, so icy winds routinely blow in from across the Atlantic – and inmates were made to wear shorts and flimsy jerseys. Like every other prisoner, Mandela slept on a thin mat on the floor (until 1973, when he was given a bed because he was ill) and was kept in a solitary confinement cell measuring two metres square for sixteen hours a day.

Amazingly, the prisoners found ways of **protesting**, through hunger strikes, publicizing conditions when possible (by visits from the International Committee of the Red Cross, for example) and, remarkably, by taking legal action against the prison authority to stop arbitrary punishments. They won improved conditions over the years, and the island also became a university behind bars, where people of different political views and generations met; it was not unknown for prisoners to give academic help to their warders. The last political prisoners were released from Robben Island in 1991 and the remaining common-law prisoners were transferred to the mainland in 1996. On January 1, 1997, control of Robben Island was transferred from the Department of Correctional Services to the Department of the Arts, Culture, Science and Technology, which has now established it as a museum. In December 1999 the entire island was declared a **UN World Heritage Site**.

The island

The island ferry from the Waterfront takes about half an hour to reach this potent symbol of apartheid, where ex-prisoners and ex-warders work as guides, sharing their experiences. After arrival at the tiny Murray's Bay harbour, you are taken on a **bus tour** around the island and a **tour of the prison**.

The bus tour stops off at several historical landmarks, the first of which is the **kramat**, a beautiful shrine built in memory of Tuan Guru, a Muslim cleric from present-day Indonesia who was imprisoned here by the Dutch in the eighteenth century. On his release, he helped to establish Islam among slaves in Cape Town, where it has flourished ever since. The tour also passes a **leper graveyard** and **church** designed by Sir Herbert Baker, both of which are quiet reminders that the island was a place of exile for leprosy sufferers in the early twentieth century.

Robert Sobukwe's house seems to echo with loneliness, and is perhaps the most affecting relic of incarceration on the island. It was here that Sobukwe, leader of the Pan Africanist Congress (a radical offshoot of the ANC), was held in solitary confinement for nine years. He was initially sentenced to three years, but was regarded as so dangerous by the authorities that they passed a special law – the "Sobukwe Clause" – to keep him on Robben Island for a further six years. No other political prisoners were allowed to speak to him, but he would sometimes gesture his solidarity with other sons of the African soil by letting sand trickle through his fingers as they walked past. After his release in 1969, Sobukwe was restricted to Kimberley under house arrest, until his death from cancer in 1978.

Another stopoff is the **lime quarry** where Nelson Mandela and his fellow inmates spent countless hours of hard labour. The soft, pale stone is extremely bright under the summer sun, as a result of which Mandela and others have in later years suffered eye disorders. As the years passed, the lime quarry became a place of furtive study among the prisoners, with the help of sympathetic wardens.

The bus tour also takes in a stretch of coast dotted with shipwrecks and abundant seabirds, including the elegant **Egyptian sacred ibis**. You may also spot some of a recently expanded population of **antelope**: springbok, eland and bontebok.

The Maximum Security Prison

The **Maximum Security Prison**, a forbidding complex of unadorned H-blocks on the edge of the island, is introduced with a tour through the famous **B-Section**; you'll be guided by a former inmate, after which you're free to wander. B-Section is a small compound full of tiny rooms that has become legendary in South African history; initially a place of defeat for the resistance movement, it ironically came to incubate and concentrate the energies of liberation. **Mandela's cell** has been left exactly as it was, without embellishments or display, but the rest have been left locked and empty.

In the nearby **A-Section**, the "Cell Stories" exhibition skilfully suggests the sparseness of prison life; the tiny isolation cells contain personal artefacts loaned by former prisoners (including a functional saxophone made of found objects), plus quotations, recordings and photographs.

Towards the end of the 1980s, cameras were sneaked onto the island, and inmates took snapshots of each other, which have been enlarged to almost life size and mounted as the **Smuggled Camera Exhibition** in the D-Section communal cells. The jovial demeanour of the prisoners indicates their realization that the end was within sight; moreover, the warm camaraderie that evidently connects them suggests how people endured so many years of captivity. The **Living Legacy** tour in F-Section involves ex-political prisoner guides describing their lives here and answering your questions.

The southern suburbs

Away from Table Mountain and the city centre, the bulk of Cape Town's residential sprawl extends east into South Africa's interior. It's here that the **southern suburbs**, the formerly whites-only residential areas, stretch out down the east side of Table Mountain, ending just before Muizenberg on the False Bay coast. All the main suburban attractions are concentrated in this area and, not surprisingly, the best shopping areas and cinemas.

From anywhere in the southern suburbs you can see Table Mountain rising above Cape Town. The area offers some quick escapes from the city heat into forests, gardens and vineyards, all hugging the eastern slopes of the mountain, and its extension, the Constantiaberg. The suburbs themselves are pleasant enough places to stay, eat and shop, but sights are thin on the ground.

The quickest way of reaching the southern suburbs from the city centre, Waterfront or City Bowl suburbs is the **M3 highway**. Travelling by **train**, you can get to Woodstock, Salt River, Observatory, Mowbray, Rosebank and Rondebosch.

Woodstock, Salt River and Observatory

First and oldest of the suburbs as you take an easterly exit from town is **Woodstock**, unleafy and windblown, but redeemed by some nice Victorian buildings, originally occupied by working-class coloureds, and now gentrifying. To its east, **Salt River** is a harsh, industrial, mainly coloured area, built initially for workers and artisans, while **Observatory**, abutting its southern end, is generally regarded as Cape Town's bohemian hub, a reputation fuelled by its proximity to the University of Cape Town in Rondebosch and its large student population. The refreshingly unrestored peeling arcades on Observatory's Lower Main Road, and the streets off it, have some nice cafés and lively bars, as well as a wholefood shop, an African fabrics shop, and a couple of antiques emporiums. The huge Groote Schuur Hospital, which overlooks the freeway that sweeps through Observatory, was the site of the world's first heart transplant in 1967.

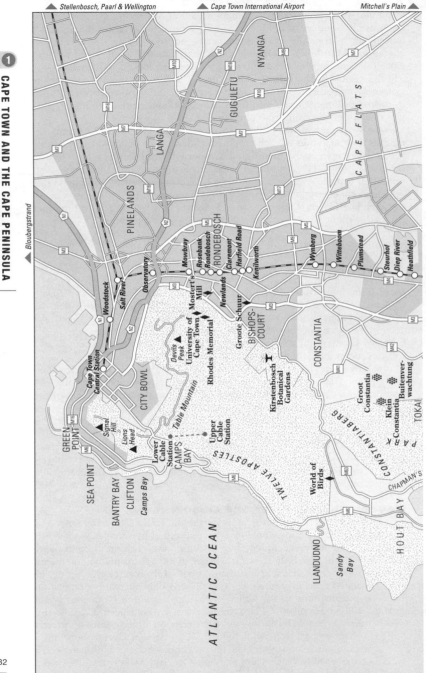

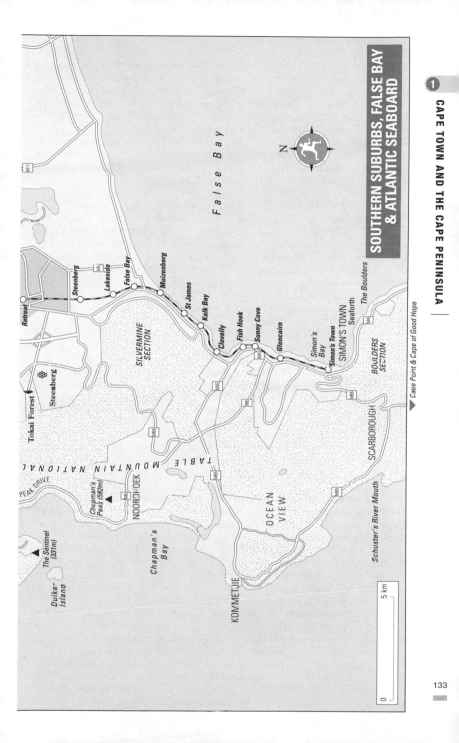

SOUTHERN SUBURBS, FALSE BAY & ATLANTIC SEABOARD

False Bay

N

Retreat
Steenberg
Lakeside
False Bay
Muizenberg
St James
Kalk Bay
Clovelly
Fish Hoek
Sunny Cove
Glencairn
Simon's Bay
Simon's Town
SIMON'S TOWN
Seaforth
The Boulders
BOULDERS SECTION

SILVERMINE SECTION

Steenberg

Tokai Forest

PEAK DRIVE

TABLE MOUNTAIN NATIONAL

Chapman's Peak (592m)

NOORDHOEK

Chapman's Bay

The Sentinel (331m)

Duiker Island

KOMMETJIE

OCEAN VIEW

SCARBOROUGH

Schuster's River Mouth

▶ *Cape Point & Cape of Good Hope*

5 km

0

133

Mowbray and Rosebank

Along Station Road, away from the mountain and south of Observatory, is **Mowbray**, originally called Drie Koppen (Three Heads), after the heads of three slaves impaled there in 1724, but its name was changed in the 1840s. In the nineteenth century this was the home of philologist Willem Bleek, who lived with a group of San convicts given up by the colonial authorities so that he could study their languages and attitudes. Bleek's pioneering work still forms the basis of much of what we know about traditional Khoisan life.

Rosebank, to Mowbray's south, has a substantial student community, some staying in the so-called Tampax Towers, the unmistakable circular residential blocks on Main Road. Just beyond them is the brown-bricked **Baxter Theatre**, one of Cape Town's premier arts complexes (see p.167).

Irma Stern Museum

Irma Stern is acknowledged as one of South Africa's pioneering artists of the twentieth century, more for the fact that she brought modern European ideas to the colonies than for any huge contribution she made to world art. The **UCT Irma Stern Museum**, Cecil Road, Rosebank (Tues–Sat 10am–5pm; R10), was the artist's home for 38 years until her death in 1966. The museum is definitely worth visiting to see Stern's collection of Iberian, African, Oriental and ancient artefacts. The whole house, in fact, reflects the artist's fascination with exoticism, starting with her own Gauguinesque paintings of "native types", the fantastic carved doors she brought back from Zanzibar, and the very untypical garden that brings a touch of the tropics to Cape Town with its exuberant bamboo thickets and palm trees.

Born in a backwater town in South Africa in 1894 to German Jewish parents, Stern studied at Germany's Weimar Academy. In reaction to the academy's conservatism, she adopted **expressionist distortion** in her paintings, some of which were included in the Neue Sezession Exhibition in Berlin in 1918. Although Stern's work was appreciated in Europe when she returned to South Africa after World War II, critics claimed that her style was simply a cover for technical incompetence. Stern went on several expeditions into Africa in the 1940s and 1950s, where she found the source for her intensely sensuous work that shocked contemporary South Africa, but which has led historians to regard her as the towering figure of her generation.

Rondebosch and the Rhodes Memorial

South of Rosebank, neighbouring **Rondebosch** is home to the **University of Cape Town** (UCT), whose nineteenth-century buildings are handsomely festooned with creepers and sit grandly on the mountainside, overlooking Main Road and the M3 highway. Next to the campus north towards the city is the **Rhodes Memorial**, built to resemble a Greek temple and conspicuous against the slopes of Devil's Peak. The monument celebrates Cecil Rhodes' energy with a sculpture of a wildly rearing horse, and the empire-builder's bust is planted at the top of a towering set of stairs. Herds of wildebeest and zebra nonchalantly graze on the slopes around the Memorial, as cars fly past on the M3. The **Tea Garden** offers terrific views of Cape Town. From the memorial you can walk to the King's Blockhouse, formerly a signalling station to Muizenberg, and onto the Contour Path which follows the eastern side of the mountain, way above the southern suburbs to Constantia Nek. Rhodes' large estate, **Groote Schuur**, bordering on Main Road, became the official prime ministerial residence of the Cape, then of South Africa, and when the country switched to a presidential system it became the home of the president, though Nelson Mandela preferred to use a nearby residence named Genadendal (his private home is in Houghton, Johannesburg). Below the Memorial, alongside the M3, is the incongruous **Mostert's Mill**, a windmill built two centuries ago when there were wheat fields here.

Newlands, Claremont, Bishopscourt and Wynberg

Continuing south from Rondebosch along the Van der Stel Freeway (the M3) or along the more congested Main Road, you pass some of Cape Town's most prestigious suburbs. **Newlands**, almost merging with Rondebosch, is home to the city's famous rugby and cricket stadiums. Worth a stopoff here at 31 Newlands Ave is **Montebello Craft and Design Centre** (Mon–Fri 9am–4.45pm, Sat & Sun 9.30am–3pm), a complex of exceptionally good craft shops and craftworkers, studios, with a restaurant under shady oaks.

The well-heeled suburb of **Claremont**, south of Newlands, is an alternative focus to the city centre for shopping and entertainment, with two cinema complexes and plenty of shops at **Cavendish Square Mall**. Alongside the high-quality shops, hawkers sell clothes, vegetables and herbs; closer to Claremont station you can buy tasty *boerewors* from women cooking them outdoors on *skottel braais* (braziers).

A little further south, beyond the signpost to Kirstenbosch Gardens, is **Bishopscourt**. As its name suggests, it's home to the Anglican bishop of Cape Town, and it was in a mansion here that Archbishop Desmond Tutu lived even in the years when blacks weren't supposed to live in whites-only suburbs. Partly because of its prime position – some plots have views of both Newlands Forest and the sea – this is one of the most prestigious areas in Cape Town; a number of consuls live here on huge properties behind high walls, which are about all you see as you pass through the area.

Further down the line, **Wynberg** is known for its Maynardville Shakespearean open-air theatre (see p.167) and its quaint row of shops and restaurants in Wolfe Street, known as **Little Chelsea**. By contrast Wynberg's Main Road offers a distinctly less genteel shopping experience, an interesting stroll past street vendors and fabric shops, as well as food outlets catering to the large number of workers travelling between Wynberg and Khayelitsha.

Kirstenbosch National Botanical Gardens

Five kilometres south of Rondebosch, in Rhodes Avenue, are the **Kirstenbosch National Botanical Gardens** (daily: April–Aug 8am–6pm; Sept–March 8am–7pm; ⊕021 799 8783; R30, children R5), the third most popular tourist attraction in Cape Town (surpassed only by the Waterfront and the cable-car trip up Table Mountain). Kirstenbosch was the first botanical garden to grow only indigenous plants, established in 1913 to promote, conserve and display the extraordinarily rich and diverse flora of southern Africa. It is internationally acclaimed as one of the world's great botanical gardens. The land was a farm, purchased by Cecil Rhodes in 1895 and left to the nation on his death in 1902. He planted the avenue of camphor and fig trees that is still here. Today, nearly 25,000 indigenous plants – and a herbarium, research unit and library – attract researchers and botanists from all over the world. There's a nursery selling local plants, while characteristic Cape plants, known as *fynbos* and found nowhere else in the world, are cultivated on the slopes above Kirstenbosch. In 2004 the gardens became South Africa's sixth UNESCO World Heritage site – the first botanical garden in the world to achieve this status, which in this instance recognizes the international significance of the *fynbos* plant kingdom (see box, p.153).

The gardens are magnificent, glorying in lush shrubs and exuberant blooms. Little signboards and paved paths guide you through the highlights of the gardens, with trees and plants identified to enhance the rambling. The most interesting route is the one created for blind visitors, with labels in Braille and an abundance of aromatic and textured plants. There is a free **walking tour** daily at 10am, and **shuttle-car tours** (R25) every hour on the hour departing from the Visitors' Centre. If you're visiting the gardens in summer, one of the undoubted delights is to bring a picnic for a Sunday-evening **open-air concert** (Dec–March 4.30–6.30pm), where you can lie back on the lawn, sip Cape wine and savour the mountain air and sunsets. There's an outdoor coffee shop, open daily for breakfast, lunch and tea, plus a restaurant with a fire going for winter days. Eating out here is more about the fabulous location than the food or service.

Cape Dutch architecture

Cape Dutch style, which developed in the Western Cape countryside from the seventeenth to the early nineteenth century, is so distinctively rooted in the Winelands that it has become an integral element of the landscape. The dazzling limewashed walls look stunning in the midst of glowing green vineyards, while the thatched roofs and elaborate curvilinear gables seem to mirror the undulations of the surrounding mountains. The style was embraced in the twentieth century as part of white South African identity, and elements appear on the facades of many **suburban homes**.

The **Posthuys** (1673) in Main Road, Muizenberg, is a rude thatch-roofed cottage consisting of a single rectangular space. Thought to be the oldest colonial dwelling in South Africa, it has tiny windows which served as a defence against feared attacks by the Khoikhoi, as well as protection from the fierce winds that lash the peninsula. One of the few surviving examples of the so-called "longhouse", it represents the primitive language from which a rich vernacular Cape Dutch architecture evolved during the first two hundred years of colonial settlement.

Although there were important developments in the internal organization of Cape houses during this period, their most obvious element is the **gable**. End-gables were common in medieval northern European and particularly Dutch buildings, but central gables set into the long side of roofs were more unusual, and became the quintessential feature of the Cape Dutch style. Large numbers of buildings in central Cape Town had gables during the eighteenth century, but they had disappeared from the urban streetscape by the 1830s, to be replaced by buildings with flush facades and flat roofs.

Arson appears to be a major reason for these developments. There was a succession of town fires believed to have been started by slaves, including one that razed Stellenbosch in 1710 and Cape Town's **great fires** of 1736 and 1798. The consequence was a series of measures that shaped the layout of central Cape Town as well as the design of its houses. Flat roofs, clad in fireproof materials, became compulsory on all VOC buildings, as exemplified by the **Old Town House** (1755) off Greenmarket Square. After the 1798 conflagration, alarmed officials studied reports from London's Great Fire of 1666 and introduced legislation based on the lessons learned. To retard the spread of flames, narrow alleys were provided between houses, there was a total ban on thatched roofs, and any protrusions on building exteriors – including shutters – were banned. This led to the flush facades and internal shutters that typify early nineteenth-century Cape town houses. With the disappearance of pitched roofs, the urban gable withered away, surviving symbolically in some instances as minimal roof decoration, one example being the **Bo-Kaap Museum** (1763–68) in Wale Street, which sports a wavy parapet.

Rural homesteads developed from the plain longhouse to become increasingly elaborate over time. As landowners became wealthier, the size of homesteads grew,

The gardens trail off into wild vegetation, covering a huge expanse of the rugged eastern slopes and wooded ravines of Table Mountain. The setting is quite breathtaking – this is a great place to have tea and stroll around gazing up the mountain, or to wander onto the paths, which meander steeply to the top with no fences cutting off the way. Two popular paths, starting from the Contour Path above Kirstenbosch, are **Nursery Ravine** and **Skeleton Gorge** (see p.144); note that there have been muggings in the isolated reaches of Kirstenbosch and on Table Mountain, and women and hikers are advised to walk in groups and avoid carrying valuables. Hikers are also advised to follow mountain safety guidelines when hiking on Table Mountain (see p.142).

If you don't have a car and don't want to take an organized tour, the best way to get to Kirstenbosch is by Rikki or one of the local taxi services, a couple of which usually rank outside the garden. Additionally, the City Sightseeing Bus

and the house plan became more complex. The spread of fire from one building to another wasn't a major consideration in the countryside, where VOC building regulations carried little weight. Consequently, the pitched roof survived here. Gables, similarly, became the hallmark of country manors, being an important element of the facade, positioned above the front door to provide a window admitting light into the loft. Because they were just above the front door, they could also provide protection for the entrance against burning thatch. From these functional origins gables evolved into important symbols of wealth, with landowners vying to erect the biggest, most elaborate and most fashionable examples.

Cape Dutch architects

Between 1750 and 1850 – the golden century of Cape architecture – three men were associated with some of the most highly regarded buildings in the colony. So elevated is their status that numerous apocryphal attributions exist, claiming their hand in various projects.

Anton Anreith (1754–1822) was born near Freiburg in Germany, where it is believed he was apprenticed to a Rococo master-sculptor. He joined the Dutch East India Company army as a private in 1776, but quickly gained employment as a carpenter, later earning the commission to reconstruct the facade of the Lutheran Church in Strand Street. In 1786 he became the VOC's master-sculptor and was probably responsible for the Kat balcony at the Castle of Good Hope.

Hermann Schutte (1761–1844), born in Bremen, was apprenticed to an architect in Germany for seven years. After joining the Dutch East India Company as a stonemason, he came to the Cape in 1790 and worked on the Robben Island quarries, where he lost an eye and a hand in a blasting accident. He was discharged from the VOC and became a private building contractor, benefiting from numerous commissions from the influential Louis Michel Thibault. Schutte designed the Groote Kerk in Adderley Street and is also believed to have been responsible for the Green Point Lighthouse, the first lighthouse erected along the South African coast.

Louis Michel Thibault (1750–1815), a highly trained architect, was born near Amiens in France. Having held the honour of premier student at l'Academie Royale d'Architecture in Paris, he joined the Dutch East India Company as Lieutenant of Engineers, effectively making him the colony's principal military engineer and government architect, in which capacity he designed most of the major public buildings in Cape Town. Examples of his work include the Good Hope Masonic Lodge, which served as the parliamentary debating chamber prior to 1884, the current facade of the Slave Lodge, and the imposing gables at Groot Constantia.

(see p.96) stops at the garden six times a day. There are municipal **bus** services (℡080 1212 111) from Cape Town's Golden Acre terminus (Mon–Fri 7.30am, 12.35pm & 3.35pm, except public holidays) and Mowbray terminus (also Mon–Fri except holidays 7am, 8am, 9am, 1pm, 2.35pm & 4pm) aimed at Kirstenbosch or Bishopscourt workers. If you're driving, take the M3 and leave it at the signposted Rhodes Drive turn-off (M63), close to Newlands.

Constantia and its winelands

South of Kirstenbosch lie the elegant suburbs of **Constantia** and the Cape's oldest **winelands**. Luxuriating on the lower slopes of Table Mountain and the Constantiaberg, with tantalizing views of False Bay, the winelands are an easy drive from town, not more than ten minutes off the Van der Stel Freeway (the M3), which runs between the centre and Muizenberg.

The winelands started cultivated life in 1685 as the farm of **Simon van der Stel**, the governor charged with opening up the fledgling Dutch colony to the interior. Thrusting himself wholeheartedly into the task, he selected for his own use an enormous tract of the choicest land set against the Constantiaberg, the section of the peninsula just south of Table Mountain. He named the estate after his daughter Constancia, and this is now (with a minor change of spelling) the name of Cape Town's oldest and most prestigious residential area. Exuding the easy ambience of landed wealth, Constantia is a green and pleasant place, shaded by oak forests and punctuated with farm stalls, stables, the Cape Dutch-style Constantia Mall and shops and, of course, the vineyards.

Constantia grapes have been making wine since Van der Stel's first output in 1705. After his death in 1712, the estate was divided up and sold off as the modern **Groot Constantia**, **Klein Constantia** and **Buitenverwachting**. In 1990, the nearby Steenberg Estate was bought up by a large Johannesburg mining conglomerate. All four estates are open to the public and offer tastings; they're definitely worth visiting if you aren't heading further afield to the Winelands proper.

There is no public **transport** to Constantia, but Groot Constantia features on most organized tours of Cape Town or the peninsula. To get to it **by car**, take the signposted Groot Constantia exit from the M3 onto Ladies Mile Extension, and follow the signs to Groot Constantia. Buitenverwachting and Klein Constantia are on Klein Constantia Road, just off Ladies Mile Extension, and are clearly signposted.

Groot Constantia

The largest estate and the one most geared to tourists is **Groot Constantia** (ⓦ www.museums.org.za/grootcon), Cape Town's fourth most visited attraction. Its big pull is that it retains the rump of Van der Stel's original estate, as well as the original buildings, though its portrayal of life in a seventeenth-century colonial chateau makes scant reference to the slave labour that underpinned its operations. The **manor house**, a quintessential Cape Dutch building, was Van der Stel's original home, modified at the end of the eighteenth century by the French architect Thibault. Walking straight through it, down the ceremonial axis, you'll come to the cellar, fronted with a carved pediment, depicting a riotous bacchanalia, which represents fertility. Otherwise, there's a pretty average **museum** full of period furniture (daily 10am–5pm; R10), a gift shop, art gallery and two **restaurants**. **Cellar tours** start every hour on the hour (daily 10am–4pm; R27 including five wines to taste; booking essential on ℡021 794 5128) and there's **wine tasting** (daily: May–Nov 10am–4.30pm; Dec–April 9am–5.30pm; R22).

Klein Constantia and Buitenverwachting

Smaller in scale than Groot Constantia, Klein Constantia and Buitenverwachting both offer free wine tasting in less regimented conditions than at the bigger estate and, although the buildings are far humbler, the settings are equally beautiful. **Klein Constantia**, Klein Constantia Road (free wine tasting & sales Mon–Fri 9am–5pm, Sat 9am–1pm; ⓦwww.kleinconstantia.com), has a friendly atmosphere and produces some fine wines. Something of a curiosity is its **Vin de Constance**, the re-creation of an eighteenth-century Constantia wine that was a favourite of Napoleon, Frederick the Great and Bismarck. It's a delicious dessert wine, packaged in a replica of the original bottle, and makes an original souvenir. There's also wildlife here: look out for the guinea fowl that roam the estate munching on beetles that attack young vine leaves; in summer, migrant steppe buzzards prey on unsuspecting starlings, which eat the grapes.

    Buitenverwachting (roughly pronounced "bay-tin-fur-vuch-ting", with the "ch" as in the Scottish rendition of loch), also on Klein Constantia Road (Mon–Fri 9am–5pm, Sat 9am–1pm; free; ⓦwww.buitenverwachting.co.za), provides its workers with some of the best living conditions of any South African farm. Unusual labour practices include the provision of two social workers, weekly visits by a doctor to the farm clinic, and worker involvement in the selection of new staff. Buitenverwachting's expensive **restaurant** of the same name (Tues–Sat lunch & dinner; ⓣ021 794 3522) is regularly voted one of South Africa's ten best. For a day out on the farm (they have cattle and horses, too), they also do luxury **picnic lunches** (Nov–April Mon–Sat 12.30–2.30pm; R100; booking essential – contact Adrienne ⓣ021 794 1012 or 082 973 8543), which you can enjoy under the oaks in their fabulous gardens.

Tokai

Effectively the southern extension of Constantia, forested **Tokai** is an excellent area for leafy recreation away from the centre, with some relaxed and child-friendly places for eating and drinking, and sheltered from the southeaster. You can also take in some wine tasting at the nearby **Steenberg Vineyards** (see p.140), which incorporates a luxury golfing resort. Across the road is Pollsmoor Prison, where numerous political prisoners did time during the apartheid era, including Nelson Mandela towards the end of his period of incarceration.

    To drive to Tokai from the centre of Cape Town, head south along the M3 and exit north onto Ladies Mile Road; continue for 100m before turning south into Spaanschemat River Road (M42), signposted Tokai, which runs through the suburb. Along the M42 before Steenberg is an outstanding, if slightly pricey, lunch stop at the *Spaanschemat River Café* (closed Sun), part of the Constantia Uitsig Wine Estate. The food is imaginative and you can eat al fresco. You can easily combine Tokai with a trip to the seaside, as the suburb is fifteen minutes' drive from the False Bay seaboard.

Tokai Forest

Most people come out to Tokai for the well-marked hiking paths and mountain-biking trails in the pine plantations of the **Tokai Forest**. You can get here from Spaanschemat River Road M42, turning west towards the mountain, into Tokai Road, which leads straight to the forest. About 500m from Spaanschemat River Road, the road passes through pine forests, equipped with picnic tables, though this isn't the nicest part of the forest or the best place to picnic. Instead, keep on till you reach the arboretum. A little further along the road from the picnic sites, you can't fail to see the imposing **Tokai Manor House** (not open to the public). Designed by Louis Michel Thibault (see p.137) and built around 1795, this National Monument is an elegant gem of Cape Dutch architecture combined with the understated elegance of French Neoclassicism.

A hundred metres to its west lies the entrance to another National Monument, the historic tree plantation that constitutes the **Tokai Arboretum** (daily dusk to dawn; R10 donation). It's the work of Joseph Storr Lister, who was a nineteenth-century Conservator of Forests for the Cape Colony. In 1885 he experimented with planting 150 species of trees from temperate countries, with oaks and eucalyptus featuring extensively as well as some beautiful California redwoods. Storr discovered that conifers were best suited to the Cape, which is why the plantation to the west of the arboretum, owned by the Safcol timber company, consists mainly of pines. The arboretum is the best place to begin rambling and an ideal place to bring **children**, with outdoor seating, plenty of shade and logs to jump on and over. There's also a car park and a thatched **café** (closed Mon) close to the entrance gate for tea and scones.

Several tracks and trails crisscross the arboretum and plantation, providing easy walks and mountain-biking trails (bring your own bike). Longer hikes include the walk from the entrance gate to **Elephant's Eye Cave** (6km there and back), which can easily be completed in well under three hours. The route passes through pine forests before opening into montane *fynbos* that covers the slopes of the Constantiaberg, eventually leading to the cave, which offers terrific panoramas. Ask for a map and directions at the entrance gate or at the adjacent café.

Steenberg Vineyards

In a fabulous location at the foot of Steenberg mountain, the **Steenberg Vineyards** (Mon–Fri 8.30am–4.30pm; Sept–Feb also Sat 9am–1pm; free; Ⓦ www.steenberg-vineyards.com) comprise a fine Cape Dutch manor house and three other farm buildings, set around a large formal garden dating from 1695. This is South Africa's oldest wine estate: the lands were granted by Governor Simon van der Stel to the five-times widowed Catherina Michelse in 1682 and sold on in 1695 to Frederik Roussouw. That year Roussouw erected the first buildings and produced the first wine here. After his death, his widow Christina Diemer turned the estate into a highly profitable business, providing hospitality to travellers and provisions to the fleet (the VOC declared Simon's Town its winter port in 1741). Steenburg now boasts a luxury country hotel, using the refurbished buildings that were declared a National Monument in 1996. Of their wines, the Merlot, Sauvignon Blanc and Semillon stand out.

Table Mountain

The icon that for hundreds of years and from hundreds of kilometres announced Cape Town to seafarers, **Table Mountain**, a 1087-metre flat-topped massif with dramatic cliffs and eroded gorges, dominates the northern end of the Peninsula. Its north face overlooks the city centre with the distinct formations of **Lion's Head** and **Signal Hill** to the west and **Devil's Peak** to the east. The west face is made up of a series of gable-like formations known as the **Twelve Apostles**; the southwest face towers over Hout Bay and the east face over the southern suburbs.

The mountain is a compelling feature in the middle of the city, a wilderness where you'll find wildlife and 1400 species of flora. Indigenous mammals include baboons, dassies (see box, p.143) and porcupines.

▲ Hikers taking a break on Table Mountain

Reckoned the most-climbed massif in the world, Table Mountain has suffered under the constant pounding of **hikers** and wanton vandalism – although the damage isn't always obvious, certainly not from the dizzying vista at the top. Every year the mountain strikes back, taking its toll of lives. One of the commonest causes of difficulties is people losing the track (often due to sudden mist falling) and becoming trapped. If you plan to tackle one of the hundreds of walks and climbs on its slopes, go properly prepared (see box, p.142). There are also **full-day guided hikes**. These guided hikes are tailored to your level of fitness and can also include rock climbing (see p.171). You may choose to come back the easy way by cable car, or partially abseil.

If you're in the city for any length of time, there are a number of hiking clubs doing day hikes you can join in with – pick up a brochure from any Cape Union Mart store.

The cable car

The least challenging, but certainly not least interesting, way up and down the mountain, is via the highly popular **cable car** at the western table, which offers dizzying views across Table Bay and the Atlantic. A state-of-the-art Swiss system was installed in 1997; the floor of the fishbowl-shaped cars is designed to complete a 360-degree rotation on the way, giving passengers a full panorama. Cars leave from the **lower cableway station** on Tafelberg Road (daily every 10–15 min: Jan & Dec 8am–9pm; Feb & March 8.30am–7.30pm; April 8.30am–5.30pm; May–Oct 8am–6pm; Nov 8am–7pm), with return **tickets** costing R130 for adults, R68 for children, while under-4s ride for free. Operations can be disrupted by bad weather or maintenance work; for information on current schedules call ☏021 424 8181, or check Ⓦ www.tablemountain.net. You can make a real outing of it by going up for breakfast, or a sunset drink and meal at the restaurant, as the upper station is an incomparable spot to watch the sun go down.

You can get to the lower cableway station by Rikki, metered taxi, or in one of the minibus taxis that ply the route here from Adderley Street. The open-topped

Table Mountain safety

Make sure you:
- Don't climb alone. As well as general mountain-safety issues, there have been a number of tourist muggings recently, so it's recommended you walk with a guide; one reliable recommendation is Ross Suter (☎082 437 5145).
- Inform someone you're going up the mountain; tell them your route, when you're leaving and when you expect to be back.
- Leave early enough to give yourself time to complete your route during daylight.
- Don't try to descend via an unknown route. If you get lost in poor weather, seek shelter, keep warm and wait for help.
- Never leave even the tiniest scrap of litter on the mountain.
- Never make fires. No cooking is allowed, even on portable stoves.

Wear:
- Good footwear. Boots or running shoes are recommended.
- A broad-rimmed hat.

Take:
- A backpack.
- A water bottle. Allow two litres per person.
- Enough food.
- A warm jersey.
- A windbreaker.
- A raincoat.
- Sunglasses.
- High-factor sunscreen.
- Plasters for blisters.
- A map (available from Cape Union Mart at the Waterfront, or Cavendish Square Shopping Centre in Claremont).

Cape Town Explorer bus also serves the cableway (p.96). If you're driving, you'll find parking along Tafelberg Road, but you may be in for a bit of a walk in peak season – the stretch of parked cars can extend several hundred metres.

Climbs and walks

Climbing the mountain will give you a greater sense of achievement than being ferried up by the cable car, but proceed with extreme caution: it may look sunny and clear when you leave, but conditions at the top could be very different. The weather is subject to rapid changes, both in general and in localized areas.

Signal Hill and Lion's Head

From the roundabout at the top of Kloofnek, a road leads all the way along **Signal Hill** to a car park and lookout, with good views over Table Bay, the docks and the city. A cannon was formerly used for sending signals to ships at anchor in the bay, and the Noon Gun, still fired from its slopes daily, sends a thunderous rumble through the Bo-Kaap and city centre below. Halfway along the road is a sacred Islamic *kramat* (shrine), one of several dotted around the peninsula which "protect" the city. You can also walk up **Lion's Head**, a non-strenuous hike that seems to bring out half the population of Cape Town every full moon.

Platteklip Gorge and Maclear's Beacon

The first recorded ascent to the summit of Table Mountain was by the Portuguese captain Antonio de Saldanha, in 1503. He wisely chose **Platteklip Gorge**, the gap visible from the front table (the north side) which, as it turned out, is the most accessible way up. A short and easy extension will get you to Maclear's Beacon which, at 1086m, is the highest point on the mountain. The Platteklip route starts out at the lower cableway station and has the added advantage of ending at the upper station, so you can descend in a car.

From the lower station, walk east along Tafelberg Road until you see a high embankment built from stone and maintained with wire netting. Just beyond and to the left of a small dam is a sign pointing to Platteklip Gorge. A steep fifteen-minute climb brings you onto the **Upper Contour Path**. About 25m east along this, take the path indicated by a sign reading "Contour Path /Platteklip Gorge". The path zigzags from here onwards and is very clear. The gorge is the biggest cleavage on the whole mountain, leading directly and safely to the top, but it's a very steep slog which will take two to three hours in total if you're reasonably fit. Once on top, turn right and ascend the last short section onto the **front table** for a breathtaking view of the city. A sign points the way to the upper cableway station – a fifteen-minute walk along a concrete path thronging with visitors.

Maclear's Beacon is about 35 minutes from the top of the Platteklip Gorge on a path leading eastward, with white squares on little yellow footsteps guiding you all the way. The path crosses the front table with Maclear's Beacon visible at all times. From the top you'll get views of False Bay and the Hottentots Holland Mountains to the east.

The Pipe Track

One of the most rewarding and easiest walks along the mountainside takes the **Pipe Track**, a service road which follows water pipes from the mountain reservoirs to Kloofnek. The track runs on the level for roughly 7km, on the west flank of Table Mountain, beneath the Twelve Apostles, following the mountain's contours and offering fantastic views of the Atlantic. The Pipe Track isn't a circular route, so you can turn back at any point; the whole walk can take up to three hours each way.

The route begins at some stone steps at Kloofnek opposite the bus terminus for the cable car, just to the west of the Tafelberg Road turn-off (if you're driving, park on Tafelberg Road). Steps lead up alongside forestry staff houses before the road levels off under some pines. The path intersects several climbs up the mountain, useful indicators as to how far you've come. The first, after about

Dassies

The outsized fluffy guinea pigs you'll encounter at the top of Table Mountain are **dassies** or hyraxes (*Procavia capensis*) which, despite their appearance, aren't rodents at all, but the closest living relatives of elephants. Their name (pronounced like "dusty" without the "t") is the Afrikaans version of *dasje*, meaning "little badger", given to them by the first Dutch settlers. Dassies are very widely distributed, having thrived in South Africa with the elimination of predators, and can be found in suitably rocky habitats all over the country. They live in colonies consisting of a dominant male and eight or more related females and their offspring.

Dassies have poor body temperature control and, like reptiles, rely on shelter against both hot sunlight and the cold. They wake up sluggish and seek out rocks where they can catch the early morning sun – this is one of the best times to look out for them. One adult stands sentry against predators and issues a low-pitched warning cry in response to a threat.

45 minutes, is indicated by a sign to Blinkwater Ravine (closed to the public due to rockfalls). A further ten to fifteen minutes brings you to the Kasteelspoort ascent (signposted under gum trees) followed by Woody Ravine and finally, roughly 25 minutes after Kasteelspoort, the signpost at Slangolie Ravine, where the path ends. The rock bed on Slangolie is unstable and to be avoided. Turn back when you see the first of the Woodhead Tunnel danger signs.

Skeleton Gorge and Nursery Ravine

You can combine a visit to the gardens at Kirstenbosch with an ascent up Table Mountain via one route and a descent down another, ending at the Kirstenbosch National Botanical Gardens' **restaurant** for tea. Starting at the restaurant, follow the **Skeleton Gorge** signs, which lead you onto the **Contour Path**. At the Contour Path, a plaque indicates that this is **Smuts' Track**, the route favoured by Jan Smuts, the Boer leader and South African prime minister. The plaque marks the start of a broad-stepped climb up Skeleton Gorge, involving wooden steps, stone steps, wooden ladders and loose boulders. Be prepared for steep ravines and difficult rock climbs – and under no circumstances stray off the path. It requires reasonable fitness, but can take as little as an hour. Skeleton Gorge can be an unpleasant way down, especially in the wet season when it gets slippery.

    Nursery Ravine is recommended for the descent. At the top of Skeleton Gorge, walk a few metres to your right to a sign indicating **Kasteelspoort**. It's just 35 minutes from the top of Skeleton along the Kasteelspoort path to the head of Nursery Ravine. The descent returns you to the 310-metre Contour Path, which leads back to Kirstenbosch. This entire walk lasts about five hours.

The Atlantic seaboard

Table Mountain's steep drop into the ocean along much of the western peninsula forces the suburbs along the **Atlantic seaboard** into a ribbon of developments clinging dramatically to the slopes. The sea washing the west side of the peninsula can be very chilly, far colder than on the False Bay seaboard. Although not ideal for bathing, the Atlantic seaboard offers mind-blowing views from some of the most incredible coastal roads in the world, particularly beyond **Sea Point**, and there are opportunities for whale-spotting (see p.148). The coast itself consists of a series of bays and white-sanded beaches edged with smoothly sculpted bleached rocks; inland, the Twelve Apostles, a series of rocky buttresses, gaze down onto the surf. The beaches are ideal for sunbathing, or sunset picnics – it's from this side of the peninsula that you can watch the sun sink into the ocean, creating fiery reflections on the sea and mountains behind as it slips away.

Mouille Point and Green Point

Just to the west of the V&A Waterfront, Mouille Point and its close neighbour, Green Point, are among the suburbs closest to the city centre. **Mouille** ("moo-lee") **Point** is known principally for its squat rectangular Victorian lighthouse, commissioned in the 1820s, and painted like a children's picture-book lighthouse, with diagonal red and white stripes.

    Mouille Point merges with the far larger suburb of **Green Point**, which continues both inland from it and west along the ragged Atlantic shore. Over the last couple of years Green Point's proximity to the Waterfront – an easy ten-or-so minutes' walk away – and its position along the coast has turned it from a sleazy district into a humming area of excellent accommodation, eating places and clubs.

Sea Point and Bantry Bay

West along Main Road, Green Point merges with **Sea Point**, a long-established place for great restaurants. Middle-class couples, pram-pushing mothers, street kids, hookers and drunks create an uneasy blend of respectability and seediness that disappears as you move into Bantry Bay and the wealthier suburbs down the Atlantic seaboard. The closest seaside to the city centre is a block down from Main Road, although it's too rocky for swimming.

Halfway along the kilometre-long beach promenade, alongside Beach Road, you'll catch views of **Graaff's Pool**, an institutionalized and exclusively male nudist spot, while at the westernmost end is the Sea Point Pool, the only place in the vicinity to swim. The unheated Olympic-sized **saltwater pool** (May–Nov 8.30am–4.30pm; Dec–April 7am–6pm; R20) is beautifully set alongside the crashing surf, with lawns for sunbathing. At the westernmost edge of Sea Point lies **Bantry Bay**, combining the density of Sea Point with the wealth of the Atlantic suburbs; here mansions are raked up on steep slopes above the Atlantic, guarded by the granite boulders of Lion's Head. The upmarket resort hotels and self-catering apartment blocks are just far enough for comfort from the sleaze of Sea Point, but close enough should you want to walk to a restaurant.

Clifton to Sandy Bay

Fashionable **Clifton**, on the next cove, along Victoria Road (the M6), sits on the most expensive real estate in Africa, studded with fabulous seaside apartments and with four sandy **beaches**, reached via steep stairways separated by clusters of granite boulders. The sea here is good for surfing and safe for swimming, but bone-chillingly cold. Hout Bay **buses** go to Clifton from the city centre several times a day (a 30min journey). Parking can be impossible along the M6 in summer, so you may be best off parking up in the residential area. Bring your own refreshments, as there's only one overpriced café. The beaches are sheltered from the wind and popular with muscular ball-players and families alike, and are especially recommended on summer evenings to enjoy the sunset and cool of the day.

A little to the south, the suburb of **Camps Bay** climbs the slopes of Table Mountain and is scooped into a small amphitheatre, bounded by the Lion's Head and the Twelve Apostles sections of the Table Mountain range. This, and the airborne views across the Atlantic, makes Camps Bay one of the most desirable places to live in Cape Town. The main drag, Victoria Road, skirts the coast and is packed with trendy restaurants, while the wide sandy beach is accessible by bus and is consequently enjoyed by families of all shapes and colours. Lined by a row of palms and some grassy verges with welcome shade for picnics, Camps Bay beach is very busy around the Christmas and Easter breaks. However, it's exposed to the southeaster, and there's the usual Atlantic chill and an occasional dangerous backwash.

There's little development between Camps Bay and the wonderful cove of **Llandudno**, 20km from Cape Town along Victoria Road (not served by public transport). Here a steep and narrow road winds down past smart homes to the shore, where the sandy beach is punctuated at either end by magnificent granite boulders and rock formations. This is a good sunbathing spot and a choice one for bring-your-own sundowners. The small car park frequently spills over into the suburban streets at peak periods.

Isolated **Sandy Bay**, Cape Town's main nudist beach, can only be reached via a twenty-minute walk from Llandudno. In the apartheid days, the South African police went to ingenious lengths to trap nudists, but nowadays the beach is relaxed, so feel free to come as undressed as feels comfortable. It's a prime gay cruising spot too. There are no facilities whatsoever – bring whatever supplies you may need. A path leads from the south end of the Llandudno car park, through *fynbos* vegetation and across some rocks, to the beach; it's a fairly easy walk, but watch out for broken glass if you're barefoot.

Hout Bay

Although no longer the quaint fishing village it once was, **Hout Bay** still has a functioning fishing harbour and is the centre of the local crayfish industry. Leopards no longer stalk its *kranse* and *koppies*, but their former presence is recalled by a bronze statue looking down from Chapman's Peak Drive. Despite ugly modern development and a growing shantytown, the natural setting is quite awesome, with the Sentinel and Chapman's Peak defining the entry to the bay. The best way to take in the landscape is on one of the short cruises just out of the bay, from the harbour to **Duiker Island**, home to a large seal colony. Nauticat (T021 790 7278) is a reliable operator with departure times approximately 9.45am, 11am, noon, 2pm and 3pm, the trip costing R50 there and back.

The sea off the long slender **beach** is no good for swimming – not only is it too cold, it's also too close to the harbour and prone to have fish scales floating in the surf – but the beach is perfect for walks. Away from the harbour, the village is just managing to hang on to a shred of its historic ambience, with the **Hout Bay Museum**, 4 St Andrews Rd (Tues–Fri 9am–4pm, Sat 8am–2pm; R5), offering good exhibits on Strandloper culture and the local fishing industry. The nearby **World of Birds**, Valley Road (daily 9am–5pm; R55, children R35), requires at least two hours to see the more than three thousand birds and animals housed in surprisingly pleasant and peaceful walk-through aviaries. From Tuesday to Thursday, and at weekends, you can watch penguins being fed at 11.30am and 3.30pm, pelicans at 12.30pm and birds of prey at 4.10pm. A large walk-in monkey jungle (daily 11.30am–1pm & 2–3.30pm) includes among its inhabitants cute squirrel monkeys; visitors can handle and play with them. There's a café serving light lunches, or you can picnic at the Flamingo Terrace. Young children are well catered for with a couple of playground areas.

Hout Bay is at a convenient junction for the rest of the peninsula. From Cape Town, it's 20km away along either the coast or inland via Constantia; at a push you can get there by bus (see p.96) or use a minibus taxi. From Simon's Town across the peninsula spine, Hout Bay is 26km away via the Glencairn Expressway. The bay has the highest concentration of **places to stay** south of Sea Point, including hotels and B&Bs. **Hout Bay Tourism** (Mon–Fri 9am–5pm, Sat 9am–1pm; T021 791 8380), adjacent to the museum, can book accommodation. Next to the harbour and car park, the little **Mariner's waterfront** development shelters the Seafood Emporium, selling fresh fish, including the Cape speciality of *snoek*, a bony but delicious fish. There's a decent fish **restaurant** upstairs with outdoor seating overlooking the beach. For straightforward fish and chips, use their downstairs takeaway facility.

Chapman's Peak Drive to Scarborough

East of Hout Bay, **Chapman's Peak Drive** is a thrilling journey. For 10km the road carves into the mountainside on the one side, dropping precipitously hundreds of metres to the ocean on the other. Unceasingly spectacular views take in the breadth of Hout Bay to the Sentinel on a curved outcrop. Chapman's Peak gets closed in very windy weather because of the danger of rock falls, and can remain so for weeks at a time. Scores of cyclists sweat their way round, making considerate driving a necessity. Chapman's Peak Drive is a toll road (R23 per vehicle) with a single toll booth at the northern (Hout Bay) end of the road.

Noordhoek, a fast-developing settlement at the southern end of the descent from Chapman's Peak Drive, consists of smallholdings and riding stables in a gentle valley planted with oaks. The Noordhoek Farm Village as you come off Chapman's Peak is a centre of sorts, with delicious fare and some decent craft shops and a children's play area. From here, a long white untamed beach stretches 6km across Chapman's Bay to Kommetjie. The sands are fantastic for walking and **horse-riding**, but can resemble a sandblaster when the southeaster blows. Swimming is hazardous, though surfers relish the rough waters around the rocks to the north. Signposted on the left if you're heading south is the excellent *Red Herring* restaurant and pub (see p.161), which has views of the beach; it's set back from the sea, about ten minutes' walk from the car park. Also signposted in the vicinity is *Monkey Valley Resort* (see p.108), which welcomes non-guests for reasonably priced meals with great views.

Although only a few kilometres south of Noordhoek along the beach, getting to **Kommetjie** by road involves a fifteen-kilometre detour inland. The beach's small inlet (*kommetjie*), which is always a few degrees above the surrounding sea temperature, is perfect for swimming. Just to the north, **Long Beach** is a favourite surfing spot, used by devotees even during the chilly winter months.

Almost 10km by road from Kommetjie, the developing village of **Scarborough** is the most far-flung suburb along the peninsula and very beautiful. A long wide beach edges temptingly to its south just beyond Schusters River Lagoon – resist its potentially treacherous sea and stick to the lagoon.

The False Bay seaboard

In summer the waters of **False Bay** are several degrees warmer than those on the Atlantic seaboard, which is why Cape Town's oldest and most popular seaside development is along this flank of the peninsula. A series of village-like suburbs, backing onto the mountains, each served by a Metrorail station, is dotted all the way south from **Muizenberg**, through **St James**, **Kalk Bay**, **Fish Hoek** and down to **Simon's Town**. Each has its own character with restaurants, shops and places to stay, while Simon's Town, one of South Africa's oldest settlements, is worth taking in as a day-trip and makes a useful base for visiting the Cape of Good Hope section of the **Table Mountain National Park** and **Cape Point** (see p.153).

Driving here from Cape Town, you can take the M3 south, or the M5 via the less salubrious Cape Flats. From Muizenberg, Main Road and the railway line spectacularly hug the shore all the way to Simon's Town; indeed, the **train** ride to Simon's Town, taking an hour from Cape Town, is reason enough to visit, and most stations are situated close to the surf.

Muizenberg and the Historical Mile

Once boasting South Africa's most fashionable beachfront, **Muizenberg** is now rather run-down, though nothing detracts from the fact that it has a long, safe and fabulous beach (though don't take any valuables onto it, and leave nothing

Cape Town's top whale spots

The commonest whales around Cape Town are southern rights, and the best **whale-watching spots** are on the warmer **False Bay** side of the peninsula, from August to November. You could also try your luck on the **Atlantic seaboard** at **Chapman's Peak** towards Hout Bay, and between **Llandudno** and **Sea Point**, where the road curves along the ocean. Whichever seaboard you're visiting, remember to have **binoculars** handy.

Along the False Bay seaboard, look out for whale signboards, indicating good places for sightings. **Boyes Drive**, running along the mountainside behind Muizenberg and Kalk Bay, provides an outstanding vantage point. To get there by car, head out on the M3 from the city centre to Muizenberg, taking a sharp right into Boyes Drive, at Lakeside, from where the road begins to climb, descending finally to join Main Road between Kalk Bay and Fish Hoek.

Alternatively, sticking close to the shore along Main Road, the stretch between **Fish Hoek** and **Simon's Town** is recommended, with a particularly nice spot above the rocks at the south end of Fish Hoek Beach, as you walk south towards Glencairn. **Boulders Beach** at the southern end of Simon's Town has a whale signboard and smooth rocky outcrops on which to sit and gaze out over the sea. Even better vantage points are further down the coast between Simon's Town and **Smitswinkelbaai**, where the road goes higher along the mountainside. Without a car, you can get the train to Fish Hoek or Simon's Town and whale-spot from the Jager's Walk beach path that runs along the coast from Fish Hoek to Sunny Cove, just below the railway line.

It's worth noting that there are more spectacular spotting opportunities further east, especially around Hermanus and Walker Bay (see p.236). Information on the locations of whale sightings in the past 24 hours is available from the MTN **Whale Route Hotline** (☎083 910 1028).

unguarded). Brightly coloured bathing boxes are reminders of a more elegant heyday, when it was visited by the likes of Agatha Christie, who enjoyed riding its waves while holidaying here in the 1920s: "Whenever we could steal time off," she wrote, "we got out our surf boards and went surfing." Muizenberg's gently shelving, sandy beach is the most popular along the peninsula for swimming; the water tends to be flat and warm, and there's good **surfing** in its breakers, with the opportunity for adults and children to take surfing lessons from Gary's Surf School on the beachfront (☎021 788 9839; R450 for two hours including gear rental). A waterslide and minigolf at the northern end of the beach help keep kids well occupied. Away from the beach, there is a thriving Congolese community, as well as pale-skinned alternative types who get their organic veggie boxes from the *Olive Station* café and deli (see p.161) off Main Road.

A short stretch of the shore, starting at Muizenberg station, is known as the **Historical Mile**, dotted with a run of notable buildings and easily explored on foot. **Muizenberg station**, an Edwardian-style edifice completed in 1913, is now a National Monument, while the **Posthuys** is a rugged whitewashed and thatched building dating from 1673 and a fine example of the Cape vernacular style. **Rhodes' Cottage Museum** (summer Mon–Sun 9.30am–4pm; winter 11am–2pm; free) was bought in 1899 by the millionaire politician, who died here in 1902 before his grander dwelling next door (closed to the public) could be completed. The cottage contains memorabilia painting a distinctly rosy portrait of the man, with photographs, a model of the Big Hole in Kimberley (where Rhodes made his fortune at the diamond diggings), and a curious diorama of World's View in Zimbabwe's Matopos Hills, where he lies buried.

Plans are in the pipeline to upgrade and restore Muizenberg's neglected beachfront, which is one of the closest beaches to the populous Cape Flats. Several decent restaurants and cafés are leading the way, though there's a dearth of beachfront hotels; to book accommodation in the area, contact **Peninsula Tourism** (Mon–Fri 8.30am–5.30pm, Sat 9am–noon; ☏ 021 787 9140), housed in the pavilion on Beach Road.

St James and Danger Beach

St James, 2km south of Muizenberg, is more upmarket, its mountainside homes accessed mostly up long stairways between Main Road and Boyes Drive. The best reason to hop off the train here is for the **sheltered tidal pool** and the twenty-minute walk along the **paved coastal path** that runs along the rocky shore to Muizenberg – one of the peninsula's easiest and most rewarding walks, with panoramas of the full sweep of False Bay. Look out for the occasional seal that makes an appearance and, in season, whales.

The compact St James beach draws considerable character from its much-photographed Victorian-style bathing boxes, whose bright, primary colours catch your eye as you pass by road or rail. The beach tends to be overcrowded at weekends and during school holidays; far fewer visitors take the trouble to stroll along the short footpath that leads south along the lawned shore from St James to the adjacent sandy stretch of **Danger Beach**, an excellent spot for sunbathing and building sand castles, and far less crowded than Muizenberg. As the name suggests, its surf should be treated with respect as there is a powerful undertow here – only go out as far as you see other bathers safely going.

▲ Power-kiting at Muizenberg Beach

Kalk Bay

One of the most southerly and smallest of Cape Town's suburbs, **Kalk Bay** centres around a lively working harbour with wooden fishing vessels, mountain views, and a tiny strip of shops packed with trendy coffee shops and antique dealers, plus a couple of places where you might catch some nightlife. Kalk Bay somehow managed to slip through the net of the Group Areas Act, making it one of the few places on the peninsula with an intact coloured community, and Kalk Bay and the larger Hout Bay are the only harbour settlements still worked by coloured fishermen.

The settlement is arranged around the small docks, where you can watch the boats come in; you can also buy fresh fish, which are flung onto the quayside and sold in spirited and noisy auctions. The harbour is busiest on Saturdays and Sundays when Capetonians descend to pick up something for a weekend braai or for lunch at *Kalky's*, an informal fish-and-chips **restaurant**. Other places to wine and dine here include *Harbour House*, the popular *Brass Bell* pub and restaurant and the *Olympia Deli* (see p.161).

Rising up behind the Kalk Bay settlement is **Silvermine Nature Reserve** (dawn–dusk; R20, children R10), which runs across the peninsula's spine, almost stretching to the west side at Chapman's Peak. Part of the Table Mountain chain, it offers walks and drives with fabulous views of False Bay, the mountains, indigenous forest and montane *fynbos*. It's most easily reached via the Ou Kaapseweg (Old Cape Road, the M64) through Tokai to Noordhoek and Simon's Town. Alongside Silvermine runs **Boyes Drive**, a high-level alternative to Main Road, with spectacular views across to the Hottentots Holland Mountains on the east side of False Bay.

Fish Hoek

Fish Hoek, south of Kalk Bay, boasts one of the peninsula's finest family **beaches** along the False Bay coast. The best and safest swimming is at its southern end, where the surf is moderately warm, tame and much enjoyed by boogie boarders. Thanks to the beach, there's a fair amount of accommodation (see p.108), but this is otherwise one of the dreariest suburbs along the entire False Bay coast. An obscure bylaw banning the sale of alcohol in supermarkets or bottle stores boosts the town's image as the Mother Grundy capital of the peninsula.

Facilities include a playground, changing rooms, toilets, fresh water, and the *Fish Hoek Galley Seafood Restaurant* right on the beach. From behind the restaurant, a picturesque concrete pathway called **Jager's Walk** skirts the rocky shoreline above the sea for 1km to Sunny Cove; from there, it continues for 6km as an unpaved track to Simon's Town. The walkway provides a good vantage point for seeing whales.

For drivers Fish Hoek is well placed for access to the Atlantic seaboard or for heading into the Constantia winelands. Just south of the suburb, you can strike west on the Glencairn Expressway (M6), or alternatively take the equally scenic Kommetjie Road (M65) about 4km further south (more convenient than the M6 if you're coming from Simon's Town). The two intersect halfway across the peninsula at Sun Valley, where Kommetjie Road continues west, veering slightly south to the coastal suburban village of Noordhoek. At Sun Valley, the M6 strikes north and splits about 1km after the intersection. The northwesterly branch hits the coast at Chapman's Point, and continues along the precipitously beautiful Chapman's Peak Drive, which eventually reaches the City Bowl along the Atlantic shore. The northeasterly branch heads along the winding tree-lined Ou Kaapseweg (M64, becoming the M42), passing through the Silvermine Nature Reserve and the winelands.

Simon's Town

The country's third-oldest European settlement, and also South Africa's principal naval base, **Simon's Town** isn't the hard-drinking, raucous place you might expect. It's exceptionally pretty, with a near perfectly preserved streetscape, slightly marred on the ocean side by the domineering **naval dockyard**, but this, and glimpses of naval squaddies square-bashing behind the high walls or strolling to the station in their crisp white uniforms, are what give the place its distinct character. Just 40km from Cape Town, roughly halfway down the coast to Cape Point, Simon's Town makes the perfect base for a mellow break along the peninsula, offering easy day-trips by train to Cape Town. A few kilometres to the south is the rock-strewn **Boulders Beach**, with its colony of nonchalant **African penguins** – reason in themselves to venture here.

Founded in 1687 as the winter anchorage of the Dutch East India Company, Simon's Town was one of several places in and around Cape Town modestly named by **Governor Simon van der Stel** after himself. Its most celebrated visitor was Lord Nelson, who convalesced here as a midshipman while returning home from the East in 1776. Nineteen years later, the British sailed into Simon's Town and occupied it as a bridgehead for their first invasion and occupation of the Cape. After just seven years they left, only to return in 1806. Simon's Town remained a British base until 1957, when it was handed over to South Africa.

There are fleeting hints, such as the occasional mosque, that the town's predominantly white appearance isn't the whole story. In fact, the first **Muslims** arrived from the East Indies in the early eighteenth century, imported as slaves to build the Dutch naval base. After the British banning of the slave trade in 1807, ships were compelled to disgorge their human cargo at Simon's Town, where one district became known as Black Town. In 1967, when Simon's Town was declared a White Group Area, there were 1200 well-established coloured families descended from these slaves. By the early 1970s, the majority had been forcibly removed under the Group Areas Act to the township of Ocean View, whose inspiring name belies its desolation. After their departure their dwellings were destroyed or allowed to rot, depriving the town of significant historic buildings. In 1973, town clerk Charles Chevalier complained that "the loss of the non-white population has had a depressing effect on the commercial life of the town".

The Town

Trains are met at Simon's Town by Rikkis (☎021 786 2136), which you can book for excursions to Boulders and on to Cape Point. A short way south of the station along St George's Street (the main drag), a signposted road to the left points to the museums. The building now housing the **Simon's Town Museum**, Court Road (Mon–Fri 9am–4pm, Sat 10am–4pm, Sun 11am–4pm; R10), was once the Old Residency built in 1772 for the Governor of the Dutch East India Company, and has also served as the slave quarters (the dungeons are in the basement) and town brothel. The museum's motley collection includes maritime material and an inordinate amount of information and exhibits on Able Seaman Just Nuisance, a much-celebrated seafaring Great Dane. He enjoyed drinking beer with the sailors he accompanied into Cape Town, and was adopted as a mascot by the Royal Navy in World War II. At the **South African Naval Museum** (daily 10am–4pm; free) next door, lively displays include the inside of a submarine, a ship's bridge that simulates rocking, and a lot of official portraits of South African Naval commanders from 1922 to the present.

In the centre of Simon's Town, a little over 1km south of the station, lies **Jubilee Square**, a palm-shaded car park just off St George's Street. Flanked by some good cafés, shops and a great fish-and-chips restaurant, the street has on its harbour-facing side a broad walkway with a statue of the ubiquitous Able Seaman Just Nuisance. A couple of sets of stairs lead down to the **Marina**, a modest development of shops and a couple of good restaurants set right on the waterfront.

Long and Seaforth beaches

Nearest to the station, **Long Beach** offers no shade and is therefore little used. However, on windless days it can be pleasant for long walks, with views of the Hottentots Holland Mountains, and its tidal pool is safe for bathing. Access is by a number of gaps in a brick wall alongside the main road and about midway along the beach (opposite Hopkirk Way), by a flight of steps. There are changing rooms and toilets nearby, and fresh water.

One of the best beaches for swimming is at **Seaforth**, where clear, deep waters lap around rocks. It's calm, protected and safe, but not pretty (bounded on one side by the looming grey mass of the naval base), but there's plenty of lawn shaded by palm trees and a good **restaurant** with outdoor seating and fresh fish on the menu.

Boulders

Two kilometres from the station towards Cape Point lies **Boulders**, the most popular local beach (R15, children R5), which offers a number of places to stay. The area takes its name from the huge rounded rocks that create a cluster of little coves with sandy beaches and clear sea pools which are gorgeous for swimming. However, the main reason people come to Boulders is for the **African penguins** (formerly known as jackass penguins), in the Boulders section of the Table Mountain National Park (open 24hr; April–Sept daily 8am–5pm; Oct–March daily 7am–7pm; R15, children R5) a fenced reserve on Boulders Beach. Passing sailors used to prey on the quirky birds and their eggs, and more recently they have fallen victim to vandals, and some locals who consider them pests; they're now protected by a guard. African penguins usually live on islands off the west side of the South African coast, the Boulders birds forming one of only two mainland colonies in the world. This is also the only place where the endangered species are actually increasing in numbers, and provides a rare opportunity to get a close look at them.

Miller's Point and Smitswinkelbaai

Almost 5km to the south is the popular **Miller's Point** resort, which has a number of small sandy beaches and a tidal pool protected from the southeaster. A **campsite** at the caravan park offers great sea views. Along Main Road, the notable *Black Marlin* seafood **restaurant** attracts busloads of tourists, while the boulders around the point attract rock agama and black zonure lizards and dassies. The last place before you get to the Cape of Good Hope Nature Reserve is **Smitswinkelbaai** (pronounced "smits-vin-cull-buy"). This little cove has a small beach safe for swimming, but feels the full blast of the southeaster. It's not accessible by car, as local property-owners fiercely guard their privacy. To get there, you must park next to the road and walk down a seemingly endless succession of stairs.

Table Mountain National Park – Cape of Good Hope

Most people come to the **Cape of Good Hope section** of the Table Mountain National Park (daily: April–Sept 7am–5pm; Oct–March 6am–6pm; R55, children R10; ℡021 780 9100, ⓦwww.tmnp.co.za) to see the southernmost tip of Africa and the place where the Indian and Atlantic oceans meet at **Cape Point**. In fact, it's the site of neither: the continent's real tip is at Cape Agulhas, some 300km southeast of here (see p.246), but Cape Point is a lot easier to get to and an awesomely dramatic spot, which should on no account be missed. The reserve sits atop massive sea cliffs with huge views, strong seas, and an even wilder wind, which whips off caps and sunglasses as visitors gaze southwards from the old lighthouse buttress.

Most people come to the Point as part of a circular trip, returning via Kommetjie and the especially scenic Chapman's Peak Drive (see p.146). Numerous tours spend a day stopping off at the peninsula highlights; Day Trippers (℡021 511 4766) runs fun tours for R425 (including a picnic lunch), some of which give you the option of cycling part of the way. For general tours that take in the reserve see p.98.

There's no public transport to the reserve, although you can charter a Simon's Town **Rikki** (℡021 786 2136) there and back. To **drive** there, take the M3 to Muizenberg, continuing on the M4 via Simon's Town to the reserve gates, where you'll be given a good **map** that marks the main driving and walking routes, as well as the tidal pools and other facilities. Go as early as you can in the day to avoid tour buses and the likelihood of the wind gusting more strongly as the day progresses. Worth a look is the **Buffelsfontein Visitors' Centre** (daily 7.30am–5pm; ℡021 780 9204), 8km from the entrance gate, which has attractive displays about the local fauna and flora as well as video screenings on the ecology of the area.

From the car park, the famous viewpoint is a short, steep walk, crawling with tourists, up to the original lighthouse. A **funicular** (R45 return) runs the less energetic to the top, where there's a curio shop. There's also a rather good **restaurant**, the *Two Oceans*, at the car park, which has outdoor seating (but it's

---

Fynbos

Early Dutch settlers were alarmed by the lack of good timber on the Cape Peninsula's hillsides, which were covered by nondescript, scrubby bush they described as *fijn bosch* (literally "fine bush") and which is now known by its Afrikaans name **fynbos** (pronounced "fayn-bos"). The settlers planted exotics, like the oaks that now shade central Cape Town, and over the ensuing centuries their descendants established pine forests on the sides of Table Mountain in an effort to create a landscape that fulfilled their European idea of the picturesque. It's only relatively recently that Capetonians have come to claim *fynbos* proudly as part of the peninsula's heritage.

Fynbos is remarkable for its astonishing variety of plants, its 8500 species making it one of the world's biodiversity hot spots. The Cape Peninsula alone, measuring less than 500 square kilometres, has 2256 plant species (nearly twice as many as Britain, which is 5000 times bigger). The four basic types of *fynbos* plants are **proteas** (South Africa's national flower); **ericas**, amounting to six hundred species of heather; **restios** (reeds); and **geophytes**, including ground orchids and the startling flaming red disas, which can be seen in flower on Table Mountain in late summer.

Cape fauna

Along with indigenous plants and flowers, you may well spot some of the animals living in the *fynbos* habitat. **Ostriches** stride through the low *fynbos*, and occasionally **African penguins** come ashore. A distinctive bird on the rocky shores is the **black oystercatcher** with a bright red beak, jabbing limpets off the rocks. You'll also see **Cape cormorants** in large flocks on the beach or rocks, often drying their outstretched wings. Running up and down the water's edge (where, as on any other beach walk in the Cape, you'll see piles of shiny brown *Ecklonia* kelp) are **white-fronted plovers** and **sanderlings**, probing for food left by the receding waves.

As for mammals, **baboons** lope along the rocky shoreline, and grazing on the heathery slopes are **bontebok**, **eland** and **red hartebeest**, as well as **Cape rhebok** and **grysbok**. If you're very lucky, you may even see some of the extremely rare **Cape mountain zebras**.

usually too windy to be pleasant) and huge picture windows taking in the drop to the sea below.

Baboons can be a menace; keep your car windows closed, as it's not unknown for them to invade vehicles, and they're adept at slyly swiping picnics. Feeding them is provocative and can incur a fine.

Cape Point and around

Cape Point is the treacherous promontory of rocks, winds and swells braved by navigators since the Portuguese first "rounded the Cape" in the fifteenth century. Plenty of wrecks lie submerged off its coast, and at **Olifantsbos** on the west side you can walk to a US ship sunk in 1942, and a South African coaster which ran aground in 1965. The **Old Lighthouse**, built in 1860, was too often dangerously shrouded in cloud, and failed to keep ships off the rocks, so another was built lower down in 1914, not always successful in averting disasters, but still the most powerful light beaming onto the sea from South Africa.

Walking and swimming

Most visitors make a beeline for Cape Point, seeing the rest of the reserve through a vehicle window, but walking is the best way to appreciate indigenous Cape **flora**. At first glance the landscape appears rocky and bleak, with short, wind-cropped plants, but the vegetation is surprisingly rich. Amazingly, many bright blooms in Britain and the US, including varieties of geraniums, freesias, gladioli, daisies, lilies and irises, are hybrids grown from indigenous Cape plants.

There are several waymarked **walks** in the Cape of Good Hope Nature Reserve. If you're planning a big hike it's best to set out early, as shade is rare and the wind can be foul, especially during summer, often increasing in intensity as the day goes on. One of the most straightforward **hiking routes** is the signposted forty-minute trek from the car park at Cape Point to the more westerly **Cape of Good Hope**. For exploring the shoreline, a clear path runs down the Atlantic side which you can join at **Gifkommetjie**, signposted off Cape Point Road. From the car park, several sandy tracks drop quite steeply down the slope across rocks, and through bushes and milkwood trees to the shore, along which you can walk in either direction. Alternatively, take a copy of the Government Printer's 1:50,000 map *3318 C.D. Cape Town* for some more intrepid exploration. Take water on any walk in the reserve, as there are no reliable fresh sources.

You'll find the **beaches** along signposted side roads branching out from the Cape Point road through the reserve. The sea is too dangerous for swimming, but there are safe tidal pools at the adjacent **Buffels Bay** and **Bordjiesrif**, midway along the east shore. Both have braai stands, but more southerly Buffels Bay is the nicer, with big lawned areas and some sheltered spots to have a picnic.

Table Bay and the northern suburbs

The **northern suburbs**, middle-class and Afrikaner-dominated, curl around the edge of Table Bay, north from Duncan Dock, and east along the N1 freeway. Few tourists see more of this area than the strip along the coast from Milnerton to Blouberg, and with good reason: the main attraction here is the much-snapped view of Table Mountain across the bay. The sea in **Table Bay** is cold, and often windy, but windsurfers and kite-fliers do well here, and the long sandy beaches are ideal for a sunset walk, when you can watch the glowing orb slip into the sea close to Robben Island. Otherwise, the northern suburbs are an unappetizing sprawl of starter homes and new developments (this is one of the few areas of Cape Town where there's room for expansion).

The N1 from the city centre follows the coast to Milnerton, Tableview, Bloubergstrand and Melkbosstrand; use the Milnerton/Paarden Island exit off the N1 to get onto Marine Drive for these suburbs. The beachfront strip at **Milnerton**, closest to central Cape Town, is a banal, neon-lit fast-food haven, offering little reason to stop, unless you're one of the surfing devotees who brave the water for the break off the lighthouse, undeterred by the debris floating across from the docks. However, those with children – or adult thrillseekers – might find themselves heading out this way to visit **Ratanga Junction** (℡ 021 550 8504, ⓦ www.ratanga.co.za; R110, children under 1.3m R55), a fantastic theme park situated just 10km from the city centre along the N1. You're advised to check the website before going as opening days and times vary.

To the west of Ratanga is **Table View**, noted for its easy access to the beach, beachside parking and its classic view of Table Mountain. Nearby **Bloubergstrand** (pronounced "blow-berg-strunt", though it's usually shortened to Blouberg), 25km from the city, is the only place to draw you out to Table Bay. Once a fishing village, this is a good place to walk and take in the views, and you can sample one of Blouberg's outdoor restaurants for meals or tea. **Big Bay** (Grootbaai), close by, draws windsurfing enthusiasts from all over the world for annual competitions.

By the time you get to **Melkbosstrand** and find yourself driving through dry, low scrub, you'll feel well and truly out of Cape Town. **Melkbos**, 30km from Cape Town, has a caravan park and one or two places to stay, but few people choose to, perhaps because the settlement is so close to Koeberg, the country's only **nuclear power station**, which generates electricity for the Western Cape. It's said that the sea around Melkbos is a few degrees warmer than elsewhere around here, heated by the water used to cool the reactor.

The Cape Flats and the townships

East of the northern and southern suburbs, among the industrial smokestacks and the windswept **Cape Flats**, reaching well beyond the airport, is Cape Town's largest residential quarter, taking in the **coloured districts**, **African**

townships and shantytown **squatter camps**. The Cape Flats are exactly that: flat, as well as being barren and windswept, with the M5 acting as a dividing line between it and the southern suburbs. Exclusively inhabited by Africans and coloureds in separate areas, the Flats can be both shocking and heartening, their abject poverty coexisting with a spirit of enterprise and stoicism.

The African townships were set up as dormitories to provide labour for white Cape Town, not as places to build a life, which is why they had no facilities and no real hub. The **men-only hostels**, another apartheid relic, are at the root of many of the area's social problems. During the 1950s, the government set out a blueprint to turn the tide of Africans flooding into Cape Town. No African was permitted to settle permanently in the Cape west of a line near the Fish River, the old frontier over 1000km from Cape Town; women were entirely banned from seeking work in Cape Town and men prohibited from bringing their wives to join them. By 1970 there were ten men for every woman in Langa.

In the end, apartheid failed to prevent the influx of work-seekers desperate to come to Cape Town. Where people couldn't find legal accommodation they set up the **squatter camps** of makeshift iron, cardboard and plastic sheeting. During the 1970s and 1980s, the government attempted to demolish these and destroy anything left inside – but no sooner had the police left than the camps reappeared, and they are now a permanent feature of the Cape Flats. One of the best known of all South Africa's squatter camps is **Crossroads**, whose inhabitants suffered campaigns of harassment that included killings by apartheid collaborators and police, and continuous attempts to bulldoze it out of existence. Through sheer determination and desperation its residents hung on, eventually winning the right to stay. Today, the government is making attempts to improve conditions in the shantytowns by introducing running water and sanitation; families and ad hoc traders are now moving in.

Langa is the oldest and most central township, lying just east of the white suburb of Pinelands and north of the N2. In this relentlessly grey place, without the tiniest patch of green relief, you'll find women selling sheep and goats' heads, alongside state-of-the-art public phone bureaus run by enterprising township businessmen from inside recycled cargo containers. Nuclear families live in smart suburban houses while, not far away, there are former men-only hostels where as many as three families share one room.

South of the African ghettos is **Mitchell's Plain**, a coloured area stretching down to the False Bay coast (you'll skirt Mitchell's Plain if you take the M5 to Muizenberg). More salubrious than any of the African townships, Mitchell's Plain reflects how, under apartheid, lighter skins meant better conditions, even if you weren't quite white. But for coloureds the forced removals were no less tragic, many being summarily forced to vacate family homes because their suburb had been declared a White Group Area. Many families were relocated here when District Six was razed (see p.121), and their communities never fully recovered – one of the symptoms of dislocation is the violent gangs that have become an everyday part of Mitchell's Plain youth culture.

Township tours and homestays

Several projects are under way to encourage tourists into the townships but, as a high proportion of Cape Town's nearly 2000 annual murders take place here, the recommended way to visit is on one of the **tours** listed in the box on p.98. All these tours are operated by residents of the Cape Flats, or in cooperation with local communities, and emphasize face-to-face encounters with ordinary people. They include visits to *shebeens*, nightclubs and a township restaurant, chats with residents of squatter camps and the Langa hostels, and meetings with traditional healers and music makers, township artists and craftworkers. Some tours also take in "sites of political struggle", where significant events in the fight against apartheid occurred. If you want really to get under the skin of the townships, there's no better way than staying in one of the **township B&Bs**; see box, p.109.

Eating

Cape Town has a large number of relaxed and convivial restaurants, which generally serve imaginative and healthy food of a high standard, with international cuisines readily available. Prices are inexpensive compared with much of the developed world, and foreign visitors can eat in upmarket restaurants with outstanding chefs creating innovative food for the kind of money they'd spend on a pizza back home. This is the city to splash out in whatever takes your fancy, and you'll find the quality of meat and fish very high, with many vegetarian options as well. As far as **prices** go, expect to pay under R50 for a main course at an inexpensive restaurant, up to R70 at a moderately priced one, more than this at an expensive place.

There are a couple of restaurants dedicated to **Cape** or **African Cuisine** (see p.52), though it's not the thing to concentrate on when you're choosing somewhere to eat. As for **seafood**, you can expect fresh fish at every good restaurant. Cape Town itself offers cold-water fish such as kingklip, hake and *snoek*; the cold waters up the West Coast yield quantities of crayfish and mussels, while fresh fish, oysters and prawns are flown in from warmer waters, including Mozambique. **Cape wines** are the obvious accompaniment to your meals. For details of where to buy seafood, wines and other provisions to **self-cater**, see p.175.

City centre

Cape Town's once down-at-heel city centre is enjoying a renaissance, and its **restaurants** are being joined by plenty of continental-style **cafés**. Most cafés here stay open till around 11pm. The establishments reviewed in the Long Street area are marked on the map on p.111; for locations of the remaining places, see the map on p.94.

Around Long Street

95 Keerom 95 Keerom St ☎021 422 0765. Flashy and fabulous for the very flush. Clean, light Italian nouvelle cuisine. Expensive. Mon–Fri lunch & dinner, Sat dinner only

Addis in Cape 41 Church St ☎021 424 5722. Delicious traditional Ethiopian dishes and yummy *injera* (flat bread) to soak up the flavours. Bring your own cutlery if required. Friendly and casual. Moderate. Mon–Sat lunch & dinner.

Africa Café 108 Shortmarket St, Cape Heritage Square ☎021 422 0221. Probably the best restaurant in Cape Town for African cuisine, with a fantastic selection from around the continent. Given that you're served a communal feast of sixteen dishes, and can have as many extra helpings as you

like, its R170 per head price tag is pretty reasonable. Booking essential. Inexpensive–moderate. Dinner daily from 6.30pm, except Sun in winter.

Bukhara 33 Church St ☎021 424 0000. A popular upmarket North Indian restaurant, with green marble floors and a show kitchen where you can watch chefs at work. The food is superb. Booking is essential to get into one of the two evening sittings (7pm & 9pm). Expensive. Mon–Sat lunch & dinner, Sun dinner only.

Five Flies 14–16 Keerom St ☎021 424 4442. Wonderfully imaginative food, with a sophisticated blend of world cuisine which really works. The presentation delights, while the feel is elegant without being formal. Expensive. Mon–Fri lunch, & dinner daily.

Ginja 121 Castle St ☏ 021 426 2368. Situated in a 160-year-old, stylishly renovated grain warehouse, this restaurant offers quality international fusion cuisine. The house speciality is the slow-roasted duck breast. Expensive. Mon–Sat dinner only.

Ivy Garden Restaurant Old Town House, Greenmarket Square. Tucked away in the sheltered courtyard of the museum, this casual place is good for salads, *bobotie*, pickled fish, *potjiekos*, or just a beer. Inexpensive. Mon–Fri 8.30am–4pm, Sat 8.30am–1pm.

Mama Africa 178 Long St ☏ 021 424 8634. Food from around the continent, including a mixed grill of springbok, impala, kudu, ostrich, even crocodile. You can also sit at the 12-metre bar – in the form of a green mamba – and listen to live African music. Moderate. Mon–Sat dinner only.

Masala Dosa 167 Long St ☏ 021 424 6772. Inexpensive and fast South Indian cuisine with a taste of Bollywood. Worth visiting just for the ginger and apple lassi. Daily noon–10pm.

Mexican Kitchen Café 13 Bloem St ☏ 021 423 1541. A casual restaurant serving good-value burritos, enchiladas, nachos and calamari fajitas, with some fine vegetarian options and deli-style takeaways. Fun atmosphere, though service is slow. Inexpensive. Daily until midnight.

Mr Pickwick's 158 Long St. The place to go for midnight munchies. Hearty and cheap "tin-plate" meals, including a challenging range of hot and cold "foot-long" sandwiches. Inexpensive. Mon & Tues 8am–2am, Wed–Sat 8am–4am.

Royale 273 Long St ☏ 021 422 4536. Gourmet burgers that pack a surprise, with unusual combinations, such as brie or roasted vegetables in the bun. Choose from lamb, beef, chicken and seven vegetarian patties including tofu. Inexpensive. Mon–Sat noon till late.

Savoy Cabbage 101 Hout St ☏ 021 424 2626. Sophisticated and innovative European-style peasant food, madly expensive but absolutely worthwhile for the best gourmet food in town. Menu changes daily. Mon–Fri lunch & dinner. Sat dinner only.

Elsewhere in the centre

Biesmiellah In the Bo-Kaap, on the corner of Upper Wales and Pentz sts ☏ 021 423 0850. One of the oldest and best-known restaurants for traditional Cape cuisine; especially recommended are the spicy stews and wickedly rich *malva* pudding. No alcohol. Moderate. Mon–Sat from 11am.

Charly's Bakery 20 Roeland St. The most spectacular cakes and pastries in Cape Town, but don't expect anything from the decor. Try the Death by Chocolate – a very rich, moist cake – or the double chocolate cheesecake. Also does breakfasts and light lunches. Inexpensive. Mon–Fri 7.30am–4pm.

Col'Cacchio Seeff House, 42 Hans Strijdom Ave. An offbeat pizza restaurant, which also serves pasta and salads, and bills itself as low-fat and heart-friendly. Has over forty different designer pizza toppings, such as smoked salmon, sour cream and caviar. No bookings. Inexpensive. Lunch Mon–Fri, dinner daily.

Jewel Tavern Off Vanguard Rd, Duncan Docks ☏ 021 448 1977. An unpretentious Taiwanese sailors' eating house, now "discovered" by Cape Town's *bon viveurs*. Located in the middle of the docks, it serves superb food, including great hot and sour soup and spring rolls, sometimes made while you watch. Moderate–expensive. Daily mid-morning till 10pm.

Little Japan 48 Riebeeck St ☏ 021 421 4360. A hole in the wall with a brilliant selection of reasonably priced Japanese food, and not just sushi. Mon–Fri lunch, dinner daily except Sun.

Manos at Castle Hotel On the corner of Canterbury and Constitution sts ☏ 021 461 4946. Mozambican Portuguese soul food. Good for steaks, seafood and *peri peri* chicken. The *Castle Bar* downstairs serves light meals. Mon–Sat lunch & dinner.

Sinn's Wembley Square, McKenzie Rd ☏ 021 465 0967. Fine dining and busy all-day cocktail bar for the hip-young Wembley Square crowd. Moderate–expensive. Daily 9am–11pm.

V&A Waterfront and De Waterkant

The **Waterfront** offers a fair bit if you want to eat well and your budget is fairly generous, though like all shopping malls in South Africa, it is full of chain eateries and unimpressive quick eats. **De Waterkant** has some nice places in a gentrified historic quarter; see the map on p.126 for locations.

The Waterfront

Baia Upper Level, Quay 6 ☏ 021 421 0935. Sit on the terraced balcony and take in the views of

Table Mountain while dining on masterfully cooked fresh fish and seafood. The spicy seafood bouillabaisse is worth a try. Expensive. Lunch & dinner daily.

Caffè Balducci Quay 6 ☎021 421 6002. An upmarket café-restaurant with a fresh feel, lovely views, and interesting Californian/Italian food with South African overtones. Expensive, but worth it. Daily 9am–midnight.

Caffè San Marco Piazza level, Victoria Wharf ☎021 418 5434. A coffee shop/bar on the piazza, offering an all-day breakfast menu, good sandwiches on Italian breads and fresh salads. The grilled calamari with garlic and chilli is delicious. There are 18 flavours of ice cream and sorbet. Moderate. Daily 8.30am–11.30pm.

Tasca de Belem Shop 154, Piazza level, Victoria Wharf ☎021 419 3009. Portuguese specialities, with funky outdoor seating in summer. The flame grilled Mozambican chicken is good, as are the *peri-peri* chicken livers. Moderate. Daily 11am–11pm.

Willoughby & Co Shop 6182, Lower Level, Victoria Wharf ☎021 418 6115. Best fish restaurant at the waterfront. Sushi and seafood, lively atmosphere. Lunch & dinner daily.

De Waterkant

Anatoli 24 Napier St ☎021 419 2501. A Turkish restaurant in an early twentieth-century warehouse buzzing with atmosphere. The excellent *meze* include exceptionally delicious *dolmades*, and there are superb desserts such as pressed dates topped with cream. Great for vegetarians. Moderate. Dinner Mon–Sat until 11pm.

Andiamo Cape Quarter piazza, Dixon St ☎021 421 3688. Italian deli with a courtyard restaurant serving salads, pastas and sandwiches. The deli itself does a great selection of meats, cheeses, salads, dips and fresh breads – phone ahead and they'll put a picnic together for you. Moderate. Daily 9am–11pm.

La Petite Tarte Cape Quarter, Dixon St ☎021 425 9077. Tiny, authentically French café whose menu includes sweet and savoury tarts, the latter including mushroom, and ham and blue cheese varieties. They also blend flavoured ceylon and herbal teas to create unusual flavours. Inexpensive. Daily 7.30am–5pm, Wed–Fri till 8pm.

The Nose Wine Bar and Restaurant Cape Quarter, Dixon St ☎021 425 2200. Tastings from a wide selection of the Cape's finest wines (there's a nominal charge for the privilege), as well as light meals, stews, fish and steaks. Moderate. Mon–Sat 11am–late.

City Bowl suburbs

The vast majority of eating places in the City Bowl suburbs lie in a continuous strip along Kloof Street – or just off it – in Gardens. See the map on p.103 for the locations of the places reviewed here.

Café Paradiso 110 Kloof St, Gardens ☎021 423 8653. Good Greek and Mediterranean dishes, including a weigh-your-plate *meze* bar. The outside terrace has views up to the mountain and down over the city and docks. Moderate. Daily lunch & dinner.

Kaual Juice 50 Kloof St, Gardens. If you're in need of something healthy, this is the place to go. They're famous for their smoothies imbued with such exotics as ginseng, wheat grass or echinacea, and they also do low-fat Thai-influenced beef, chicken and veggie sandwiches, plus delicious salads. Inexpensive. Daily 8am–10pm.

Lazari Corner of Upper Maynard St and Vredehoek Ave ☎021 461 9865. A meeting place for City Bowl habitués. Fresh, interesting breakfasts and lunches, home-baked cakes and biscuits. Moderate. Daily breakfast, lunch & dinner.

Limoncello 8 Breda St, Gardens ☎021 461 5100. Small Italian trattoria serving unfailingly excellent pastas and pizzas. Serves the best calamari in Cape Town and a great risotto of the day. Moderate. Mon–Fri lunch & dinner, Sat & Sun dinner only.

Melissa's 94 Kloof St, Gardens. Breakfasts, light meals and fine desserts in the small café, while the food emporium sells freshly made Mediterranean fare. Moderate. Mon–Fri 7.30am–9pm, Sat & Sun 8am–9pm.

Mount Nelson Hotel Garden Room 76 Orange St, Gardens. Colonial-style high tea in Cape Town's oldest and most gracious hotel is a definite culinary highlight of the city, the large tea table piled with hot and cold pastries, classic savouries like smoked salmon sandwiches, and cakes. You can skip lunch and dinner after the R135 feast you get here. Daily 1.30–5.30pm.

Raith Gourmet Gardens Centre, Mill St, Gardens. Meat-focused deli and café with an exceptional selection of foods and some marvellous sandwiches; German specialities include sauerkraut fried with strips of bacon. Inexpensive. Mon–Fri 8.30am–6pm, Sat 8.30am–1pm.

Sawaddee Orange St ☎021 422 1633. Casual, quick Thai food, close to the Labia cinema. The calamari with pepper and garlic sauce is recommended. Moderate. Closed Sun.

Southern suburbs

Woodstock to Constantia

Chandani 85 Roodebloem Rd, Woodstock ℡ 021 447 7887. Great north Indian food, with a large vegetarian menu in a tastefully restored Victorian house. Quite posh, but prices are very reasonable. Mon–Sat lunch and evenings.

Don Pedros 113 Roodebloem Rd, Woodstock ℡ 021 447 4493. Since the 1980s, when it was a regular haunt for anti-apartheid activists, *Don Pedros* has been a place for good, cheap food – curries, stews, pasta, salads – and a scruffy Capetonian ambience, somewhere to linger all evening over a beer or coffee without feeling hassled. There are smoking and non-smoking rooms; it's also a gay-friendly place where people tend to hang out after shows. Inexpensive. Daily 10am–late.

Gardener's Cottage 31 Newlands Ave, Montebello Estate, Newlands. Serves hearty English breakfasts and light lunches – quiches, salads and lasagnes – as well as tea and coffee. It's set in a complex of old farm buildings under ancient pine trees, with neighbouring arts and crafts workshops at which to browse. Moderate. Tues–Fri 8am–4.30pm, Sat & Sun 8.30am–4.30pm.

Kirstenbosch Tea Room Rhodes Drive, Newlands. The venue rather than the food is the draw here, with outdoor eating to make the most of the mountain views. There's a large self-service place, close to the main entrance, ideal for the children to romp around in while you have a coffee under the trees by the river, or another tea room under thatch and umbrellas, close to the upper entrance to the Gardens. Moderate. Daily 8.30am–5pm.

Organic Living Cafe Deli 39 Constantia Rd, Wynberg ℡ 021 797 1123. Delicious organic health-food buffet charged by weight, with fresh juices and cakes too. Sit inside or in the leafy courtyard. Good for kids. Moderate. Mon–Fri 8.30am–5pm, Sat until 3pm.

Spaanschemat River Café Constantia Uitsig Wine Estate, Spaanschemat River Rd ℡ 021 794 3010. This delightful venue, situated in the farm's old schoolhouse, serves sumptuous breakfasts, lunches and teas. Try the extravagant eggs Benedict. Booking essential in high season. Moderate–expensive. Closed Sun.

Uitsig Constantia Uitsig Country Hotel, Spaan-schemat River Rd ℡ 021 794 4480. Considered one of the finest restaurants (and one of the priciest) in South Africa for its Mediterranean-influenced cuisine. Expensive. Lunch & dinner daily. Closed July.

Wasabi Old Village Centre, Constantia Village ℡ 021 794 6546. Quality sushi bar in a stylish modern setting. The crab salad, *ramen* soups and Japanese noodles come up tops on the menu. Inexpensive–moderate. Daily lunch & dinner.

Atlantic seaboard

The places reviewed in Green Point, Mouille Point and Sea Point appear on the map on pp.106–107.

Green Point

Giovanni's Deliworld 103 Main Rd. With indoor and pavement seating, this friendly buzzing Italian deli/coffee shop is handy for coffee, excellent made-to-order sandwiches, salads and dips, as well as good pre-packaged meals. Moderate. Daily 8am–9pm.

Mano's 39 Main Rd ℡ 021 434 1090. Italian food, with exciting salads and one of the best crème brûlées in town, popular with models and beautiful people. Moderate. Mon–Fri lunch & dinner, Sat dinner only.

Theo's Grill Butcher and Seafood Beach Rd ℡ 021 439 3494. Upmarket, and right on the beachfront, *Theo's* offers superb Greek-style meat and seafood dishes. Moderate. Mon–Fri lunch & dinner, Sat dinner only.

Wang Thai 105 Main Rd ℡ 021 439 6164. Cape Town's best Thai restaurant, serving such delights as hot and spicy prawn soup, steamed fish with lemon juice and chilli, and its special – thinly sliced, seared sirloin. Moderate. Daily lunch & dinner.

Mouille Point

Newport Market and Deli 47 Beach Rd. A light, airy deli with views onto Table Bay, offering coffee, excellent sandwiches, salads and some hot dishes. Inexpensive. Mon–Fri 7.30am–8pm, Sat & Sun from 8am.

Wakame 47 Beach Rd ℡ 021 433 2377. Asian fusion food with killer desserts – try the chocolate and banana spring rolls. Every table has a view of the ocean. Booking essential. Moderate–expensive. Daily lunch & dinner.

Sea Point

Harveys at the Mansion *Winchester Mansion Hotel*, 221 Beach Rd ☎021 434 2351. The *nouvelle cuisine* menu includes combinations such as puréed peas with bone marrow, and there are great views of the sun setting over the Atlantic from the cool courtyard garden. Moderate–expensive. Daily breakfast, lunch & dinner.

La Perla On the corner of Beach and Church sts ☎021 434 2471. Classic Italian-run restaurant which has been a favourite forever, with good seafood, soup, pasta, but no pizza, at its beachfront setting. Moderate–expensive. Daily lunch & dinner.

Mr Chan 178a Main Rd ☎021 434 2239. Worthwhile Chinese restaurant with excellent Hong Kong-style beef. Moderate. Mon–Sat lunch & dinner.

New York Bagels 51 Regent Rd. A fantastic deli with a sit-down section. Choose from a dizzying array of bagels and homemade fillings, from chopped liver to herring, plus stir-fries, pasta and pastries. Inexpensive. Daily till late.

Pizzeria Napoletana 178 Main Rd ☎021 434 5386. Family-styled Italian restaurant with hearty, good-value cooking. Moderate. Mon–Sat lunch & dinner.

Camps Bay and southwards

Café Caprice 37 Victoria Rd, Camps Bay ☎021 438 8315. Directly opposite Camps Bay beach, this lively Mediterranean-style restaurant is a great place to soak up street life and sunshine. Inexpensive–moderate. Daily 9am till late.

Marika's 38 Victoria Rd, Bakhoven ☎021 438 2727. Good summer venue serving fresh Greek food. Though there are no sea views, you're close enough to the beach to explore the rocks and sand on a satisfied belly. Moderate. Tues–Sat dinner, Sun lunch only.

Paranga's Shop 1, The Promenade, Victoria Rd, Camps Bay ☎021 438 0404. Young people's hang-out at the beach, a place to see and be seen while you munch on salads, seafood, pasta or sushi. Tues–Sun 9am till late, Mon from noon.

La Cuccina Food Store Victoria Mall, Victoria Rd, Hout Bay. High-quality deli and café food in pleasant surrounds, the delicious food amply compensating for the lack of sea views. At lunchtime it has buffets of quiches, salads and lasagne. Moderate. Daily 8am–7pm.

Mariners Wharf Bistro The Harbour, Hout Bay. A relaxed, well-run place with terrace seating overlooking the harbour. Good for seafood to eat in or take away. Moderate. Daily 10am–6pm.

Red Herring On the corner of Beach and Pine rds, Noordhoek ☎021 789 1783. A country restaurant that does grilled meats including springbok and kudu, plus a good choice of vegetarian options or fresh fish. Moderate. Tues–Sun dinner only.

Theo's Grill Butcher and Seafood Promenade Building, Victoria Rd, Camps Bay ☎021 438 0410. Brilliant steaks sold by weight, plus seafood; the atmosphere is buzzy, and there's some outdoor seating. Moderate. Daily lunch & dinner.

False Bay seaboard

Muizenberg

The Olive Station Muizenberg Station, Main Rd. Bright and friendly place where you can snack on Levantine-influenced food. The olive bread, desserts and Lebanese cheese or lamb and pine-nut pies are especially good. There's a warehouse for curing olives on site, with other tasty bits on sale. Some seats overlook the station and beach. Inexpensive. Mon & Wed–Sun breakfast & lunch, Thurs only dinner till 9pm.

Wellbeing Café & Natural Medicine 37 Palmer Rd ☎021 788 9489. This Sufi-run organic food store, green-tea café and natural medicine clinic is the jewel in the crown of shabby chic Muizenberg village high street. Light meals, freshly squeezed organic juices and home-baked bread. Inexpensive. Tues–Thurs & Sat–Sun 10am–6pm, Fri 10am–noon & 4–6pm.

Kalk Bay

Brass Bell Kalk Bay station, Main Rd. Primarily an unpretentious drinking spot, *Brass Bell* has arguably the best location on the peninsula, with False Bay's waves breaking against the wall of its outdoor terrace. The views of both the peninsula mountains and the Hottentots Holland peaks are unbeatable, but the disappointing seafood meals can't match the magnificent setting. Moderate. Daily until late.

Harbour House Restaurant At the harbour ☎021 788 4133. Freshly caught seafood and Mediterranean fare, at a venue situated spectacularly on the breakwater of Kalk Bay harbour; book a table with bay views or enjoy sundowners on the deck. There's a fireplace and comfortable sofas for winter. Moderate–expensive. Daily lunch & dinner.

Kalky's At the harbour. For years, this totally unpretentious eating place has been serving the fishing community the best traditional fish and chips on the peninsula, and great-value seafood platters; fish is hauled off the boats and straight into the frying pan. You sit at benches to eat, though takeaway is available. Inexpensive. Daily.

The Olympia Café & Deli Main Rd. One of the few places that draws parochial uptown Capetonians down the False Bay seaboard, and a regular meeting spot for locals. Always buzzing, with views of the harbour, for breakfast *Olympia* offers great coffee or freshly squeezed orange juice, accompanied by freshly baked Danish pastries, filled croissants or delicious homemade biscuits. Gourmet lunch menus are chalked up on a board, with local fish often featured. Its bakery around the corner produces excellent breads and pastries every day. Moderate. Daily 7am–9pm.

Simon's Town and around

Bertha's 1 Wharf Rd ☎ 021 786 2138. Relax with views of False Bay and the harbour while enjoying a middle-of-the-road, child-friendly menu, with meat, chicken, fish and vegetarian dishes. Moderate. Daily from 7.30am until evening.

Bon Appétit 90 St George's St ☎ 021 786 2412. In the old *British Hotel*, *Bon Appetit* offers classic, beautifully presented French cuisine. Emmanuel, owner and chef, is Michelin-trained, so expect the best. Expensive. Tues–Sat lunch & dinner.

The Meeting Place 98 St George's St ☎ 021 786 1986. Enjoy Mediterranean café food while surveying harbour goings-on from the upstairs balcony. Vegetarians are well catered for, and there's a deli downstairs. Moderate. Tues–Sun lunch & dinner.

Tibetan Teahouse 2 Harrington Rd, Seaforth Beach ☎ 021 786 1544. Traditional Tibetan recipes, served up in a venue signalled by its prayer flags. It's completely vegetarian, so don't expect yak meat in the lentil Sherpa Stew. Daily 10am–5pm. Inexpensive.

Drinking, nightlife and entertainment

Cape Town has finally shaken off its reputation as a place where **nightlife** was synonymous with hitting the sack. Things have become much more lively and cosmopolitan in recent years, the scene spiced up by thousands of African and European visitors and immigrants.

Bars and clubs

The city is well populated with **bars**, ranging from the hip to the eccentric to the seedy. Traditional pubs are not a big feature: where they do exist, they're generally depressingly empty dives or cod-Irish franchises. Most liquor licences stipulate that the last round is served at 2am, but this is far from strictly followed. Expect a cover charge if live music is featured.

Mainstream house is very popular in the **clubs**, but there are also strong followings for drum 'n' bass, trance, hip-hop, dub and Latin grooves, as well as **kwaito** (see p.863). Though *kwaito* is still predominantly a black scene, coloured

---

New Year, New Year – so good they do it twice

A long-standing tradition in Cape Town is **Tweede Nuwe Jaar** (second New Year), January 2 – until recently an official public holiday. Historically this was the only day of the year when slaves were allowed off, and the day has persisted as a holiday of epic proportions. If you're in Cape Town over this period, Tweede Nuwe Jaar is the time to party, when Cape Minstrels from the coloured community dance through the streets of the city centre performing a traditional form of singing and riotous banjo playing. Expect each troupe to be dressed up in matching outfits, often featuring outrageous colour combinations. Some roads in the centre are blocked off during the day for the festivities, which process through the city and end up at Green Point Stadium.

and white youth are gradually getting into it. Many clubs have a short lifespan – and many of the best regular parties hop from venue to venue. Some of the more enduring clubs are listed here, but watch the press for up-to-the-minute information. The daily *Cape Argus* newspaper runs a club column on Tuesdays, and the monthly listings magazine *Cape Review* is also useful. Backpacker hostels are often the most up-to-date sources of party information. Cover charges vary from R40 to over R200 for big events with international DJs. And if you find yourself wandering about at night in search of a party, head for the strip of clubs along Somerset Road in Green Point, where there's always something going on well into the early hours. It's worth remembering that all drugs are illegal in South Africa, and aggressive police raids on clubs are by no means unknown.

Some of the township tours (see box, p.98) offer **music outings**, which save you the hassle of negotiating badly lit areas at night, and allow you to hear authentic sounds in township clubs. In addition, Our Pride Tours (☏ 021 531 4291) does gospel excursions to the townships. Grass Route Tours (☏ 021 706 1006) specializes in transport to venues in the Cape Flats.

City centre

Around Long Street

Chrome 6 Pepper St ☏ 083 700 6079. The Main Dance Arena caters for a younger crowd of party animals, with its own VIP area available only by reservation. The Platinum VIP Lounge offers a relaxed party vibe for the more mature punter.

Jo'burg 218 Long St ☏ 021 422 0142. A good place to schmooze to a funky soundtrack, in the company of a hip art-school and media crowd. There's a range of live music on Sun nights. Daily 5pm–4am.

Kennedy's Restaurant and Cigar Lounge 251 Long St ☏ 021 424 1212. A swanky bar offering cigars from all over the world, with brilliant Martinis and, good food, an older crowd, and live jazz every evening. Mon–Fri noon till late, Sat 7pm till late.

The Lounge 194 Long St ☏ 021 424 7636. A long-standing, trendy refuge for Cape Town's smart and glamorous. Upstairs, make for the superb balcony and grab a table overlooking vibrant Long St. House and jungle dominate the turntables. Mon–Sat 8pm–2am.

Mama Africa 178 Long St ☏ 021 424 8634. A relaxed and spacious bar-restaurant in the heart of Long St clubland, *Mama Africa* boasts a 12-metre bar in the form of a green mamba. Traditional percussion groups perform regularly, and it's popular with European and North American visitors. Music Mon–Sat 8.30pm–late.

The Purple Turtle On the corner of Shortmarket and Long sts. A cavernous, vaguely seedy bar frequented by goths, metalheads and other creatures, with bands on Sat nights. Daily 11am–late.

Rhodes House 60 Queen Victoria St ☏ 021 424 8844. A relaxed and fashion-conscious place, with a range of house sounds. Themed parties with designated dress codes also happen – call before turning up. Wed–Sat 10pm till late.

Sutra 86 Loop St ☏ 021 422 4219. Deep house and R&B sounds. Wed, Fri & Sat 9pm till late.

Elsewhere in the centre

Drum Café 84 Harrington St ☏ 021 462 1064. Every Mon & Wed at 9pm there's a facilitated drum circle lead by a South African or West African drum teacher, suitable for all levels of experience; the smaller Mon groups are better if you're a complete novice, while the Sat afternoon sessions at 3pm are for families. For those who prefer to leave things to the professionals, there are often parties at the weekends; ring for the current schedule. Light meals available, and the café is fully licensed. Mon, Wed, Fri & Sat 9pm–late.

FTV 114 Hout St ☏ 021 426 6000. *Fashiontvcafe* is a chic hangout open for coffees, lunches, cocktails and dinner. Mon–Fri open from 10am until very late, Wed, Fri & Sat open in the evenings.

Hemisphere 31st Floor, Absa Centre, 2 Riebeeck St ☏ 021 462 1064. One of the most stylish bar/lounges in a city full of style. Set at the top of one of the city's tallest buildings, providing awe-inspiring views of the city below. It's smart but relaxed and the stylish decor caters to comfort. Tues–Fri 4.30pm till late, Sat open from 9pm.

Marimbas Cape Town International Convention Centre, corner of Coen Steytler Ave and Heerengracht ☏ 021 418 3366. There's live music nightly, with an African marimba band on Thurs. Daily 10pm till late. Cover charge applies Sat & Sun.

Mercury Live and Lounge 43 De Villiers St, District Six ☏ 021 465 2106. Live music and

underground hip-hop parties at a spacious venue with minimalist decor. Mon–Sat 8pm till late.
The Shack 45b De Villiers St, District Six ☏ 021 465 2106. Comprising a restaurant, bar and pool hall, with sounds from the 1960s up to the 1980s. Under the same management is the adjoining *Blue Lizard*, which plays acid jazz, house and trip-hop. Open till late: Mon–Sat from 1pm, Sun from 6pm.

V&A Waterfront and De Waterkant

As well as upmarket restaurants, the **Waterfront** and **De Waterkant** also offer reasonably good nightlife that's largely in keeping with the area's emphatically clean-cut atmosphere.

Bossa Nova 43 Somerset Rd ☏ 021 425 0295. Upmarket lounge and dance club, where evenings start off with commercial music and gradually shift into the rhythmic sounds of Latin America. Tues–Sat; drinks and light music from 5pm and DJs from around 9.30pm.

Chilli 'n' Lime 23 Somerset Rd, De Waterkant ☏ 021 426 4469. Painfully stylish upmarket club with two dance floors and four bars, which hosts pulsing house and hip-hop parties. Frequented by a 20-something left-field student crowd. Tues–Sat 8am–4am.

Den Anker Restaurant and Bar Pierhead. One of the livelier Waterfront venues, a busy pub and Continental-style bistro, patronized by tourists and well-heeled locals. *Den Anker* specializes in imported Belgian beers, both on tap and bottled. Daily 11am–midnight.

Green Dolphin Pierhead ☏ 021 421 7471. A top-notch jazz venue (though a tad chilly in winter), hosting quality jazz bands nightly at 8.30pm. Dinner – there's excellent seafood – is served from 6pm. Daily noon–midnight.

Opium 6 Dixon St ☏ 021 425 4010. An über trendy club featuring acid jazz and funky house music. Wed–Sat 10pm–2am.

Purgatory 8b Dixon St ☏ 021 421 7464. The place to hang out with waiflike models and other good-looking people swaying to house music. Wed–Sat 11pm till late.

Southern suburbs

Boer and Brit Pub *Alphen Hotel*, Alphen Drive, off the M41, Constantia. A cosy English-style pub at a historic Cape Dutch hotel. It's gracious yet relaxed, with tables under oak trees, a warm hearth on cold nights and bar meals. Daily 10am–11pm.

Foresters' Arms 52 Newlands Ave, Newlands. Preppie students and professionals gather to quaff draught beer at the very popular and busy "Forries", in the heart of leafy Newlands. A big wood-panelled pub, it boasts a beautiful hedged-in courtyard where you can grab a bench for a drowsy afternoon pint. Mon–Sat 10am–11pm, Sun 9am–4pm.

Pedlars on the Bend Spaanschemat River Rd, Constantia. An upmarket bar at one of the posher restaurants in this ritzy suburb, with a delightful outdoor area shaded by oaks. Daily 11am–11pm.

Atlantic seaboard

Café Caprice 37 Victoria Rd, Camps Bay ☏ 021 438 8315. A lively restaurant by day, where the pace increases come evening when DJs play anything from Ella Fitzgerald to *kwaito*. Open morning till late; DJs feature nightly in summer, Fri–Sun the rest of the year.

Dizzy Jazz Café 41 Camps Bay Drive, Camps Bay ☏ 021 438 2686. A crowded and lively nightspot with a big veranda and sea views, featuring a variety of live music nightly and serving draught beer and quality seafood. R20 cover charge. Daily noon–4am (music from 8.30pm).

La Med Bar and Restaurant Glen Country Club, Victoria Rd, Clifton ☏ 021 438 5600. A great sundowner venue overlooking the rocks at Clifton Beach, drawing a sporty, mainstream crowd; it's a favourite spot for hang-gliders from Lion's Head to visit, after they've landed in the adjacent field. There's live music Wed, Fri & Sat. Daily noon till late.

Red Herring On the corner of Pine and Beach rds, Noordhoek. A pub above a smart restaurant with an outdoor deck overlooking the panoramic Noordhoek valley. Busy on warm weekend afternoons, when a clean-cut 20-something crowd gathers. Tues–Sun 11am–midnight.

Cape Flats

West End and Club Galaxy College Rd, Rylands
☎021 637 9132. Definitely the most happening
place on the Flats are these two nightclubs in one
building, the former a top jazz venue with live and
recorded sounds, the latter a straight-up dance
club playing R&B and mainstream house to a smart
young crowd. Thurs–Sat 8pm–late.

Theatre, comedy and live music

Despite scarce resources (state funds have been redirected to more pressing areas),
theatre in South Africa is making a valiant attempt to lift itself out of its
post-democracy doldrums. Protest theatre, a fertile genre in the oppressive 1970s
and 1980s, is now obsolete, and it's no longer seen as self-indulgent for plays to
deal with personal rather than political issues. As there is no real successor to
the world-renowned playwright Athol Fugard, several of whose works were first
staged here, though a steady trickle of new **plays** is being written and performed
in Cape Town, some of them innovative and hard-hitting. Writers and directors
to look out for include the brilliant Brett Bailey, Marthinus Basson, Reza de Wet,
Fiona Coyne (who also hosts the South African version of *The Weakest Link*), Roy
Sargeant and the duo of Heinrich Rosehofer and Oscar Petersen.

Comedy, too, is starting to shape up well with the annual Smirnoff International Comedy Festival, at the Baxter Theatre around October, showcasing
global and local talent. Probably South Africa's best-known stage satirist is Pieter
Dirk Uys, whose character Evita Bezuidenhout, South Africa's answer to Dame
Edna Everidge, has relentlessly roasted South African society since apartheid
days. New home-grown comedians to look out for include Marc Lottering, a
coloured Capetonian, who derives his material from his own community, and

▲ Live jazz in Cape Town

Pop music and Cape Jazz

Cape Town fosters and attracts legions of musicians, making it one of the country's most musically active cities. One of Cape Town's musical treasures is **Cape jazz**, a local derivative of the jazz genre with distinctive African flavours. Its greatest exponent is the internationally acclaimed **Abdullah Ibrahim**. Born and raised in District Six, Ibrahim is a supremely gifted pianist and composer, who has for decades produced an hypnotic fusion of African, American and Cape idioms. Some of his renowned recordings include *Mannenberg* and *African Marketplace*, combining the fluttering rhythms of *ghoema* – traditional Cape carnival music – with the call-and-answer structure of African gospel. Other Cape jazz legends include a triumvirate of distinctive saxophonists: the late Basil Coetzee, a phenomenal tenor saxophonist who played on *Mannenberg*; Robbie Jansen, alto player with a raunchy and original style; and Winston Mankunku, schooled on Coltrane, Wayne Shorter and his unique brand of African inflections. Cape jazz is growing – check the press, the Internet and local tourist offices for upcoming performances and venues, among which reliable spots include the *Green Dolphin* (p.164) and *Manenberg's* (see opposite). The Monday-night jam session at *Swingers* in Lansdowne is an institution in Cape Town and you can see some of the best local talent on show. The annual **Cape Town International Jazz Festival** (Easter) features some of the world's renowned musicians. **Ghoema** is the rhythm played on a *ghoema* drum, a sound that, for many generations, has been the basis for the popular moppies (comic songs) and *ghoemaliedjies* (picnic songs). Cape Town's colourful minstrel troops occupy the streets of the city over New Year, when the hugely popular Rio-style *nagtroepe* (literally night-time marchers) and armies of lookers-on fill the city's streets on New Year's Eve and *ghoema* troupes compete for honours in festival gatherings. Catch the Christmas Bands and Malay Choirs in this same season for **marching music** in the Mother City. Or go on personalized township tours, visiting musicians' homes and hearing it at source. Cape Town is also well stocked with charismatic **rock**, **reggae**, **ska**, **punk** and a variety of other **pop** bands, often found in the myriad nightclubs and venues lining Long and Somerset streets, and in Lower Main Road, Observatory. Check out Zula Bar, Obs Café and The Independent Armchair Theatre.

David Kau, an African, who is as caustic about Jo'burg township dwellers as he is about white South Africans.

Classical music has a relatively small but faithful following, with symphony concerts at the City Hall on Tuesdays and Thursdays. There are free lunchtime concerts, often showcasing the work of students from Cape Town University's South African College of Music, on Thursdays at 1pm during term time, and sometimes on Wednesdays at 2pm; these take place at the Baxter Theatre, or at the college itself (☎021 650 2640). Many recitals by visiting soloists and chamber ensembles are put on by an organization called Cape Town Concert Series (ⓦwww.ctconcerts.co.za). It's often a treat to catch one of the performances by Cape Town Opera (ⓦwww.capetownopera.co.za) to hear black South Africans, who are coming to dominate opera in Cape Town, injecting some African spice into a programme that still predominantly features European works. As regards **musicals**, David Kramer and the late Taliep Petersen have produced several hit shows celebrating the history and culture of Cape Town. Their *Kat and the Kings* took Broadway and London's West End by storm a few years back, bagging the 1999 Olivier Award for the best new musical.

Artscape D.F. Malan St ☎021 410 9838, ⓦwww .artscape.co.za. Once the Camelot of state-funded white performing arts, Artscape has reinvented itself as a less elitist theatre, though high-quality ballet and opera are still produced, while adventurous new dramas appear periodically. Don't be intimidated by the monumental 1970s architecture.

Baxter Theatre Centre Main Rd, Rondebosch ☎ 021 685 7880, ⓦ www.baxter.co.za. This mammoth brick theatre complex, its design inspired by Soviet Moscow's central train station, mounts an eclectic programme – innovative plays, comedy festivals, jazz and classical concerts and kids' theatre.

Little Theatre University of Cape Town, Orange St ☎ 021 480 7128, ⓦ www.uct.ac.za/about/arts /littletheatre. A showcase for innovative work from the University of Cape Town drama school; the productions range from self-indulgent to breathtaking. The drama school has a long tradition of producing fine actors, and counts Richard E. Grant among its graduates.

Manenberg's Jazz Café Clock Tower Precinct, Waterfront ☎ 021 421 5639, ⓦ www.manenbergs jazzcafe.com. One of Cape Town's premier venues for live music, specializing in Cape and African jazz and attracting some of the hottest names in South African music. Open till late: Mon & Thurs–Sun from 8.30pm, Fri & Sat from 9.30pm.

Maynardville Open Air Theatre On the corner of Church and Wolfe sts, Wynberg ⓦ www.maynardville.co.za. Under the summer stars in Maynardville Park, every year in January and February, an imaginative production of a Shakespeare play is staged by the cream of Cape Town's actors and designers. Book through Computicket (see p.178).

On Broadway 88 Shortmarket St, city centre ☎ 021 424 1194. One of the few venues committed to the city's small cabaret scene is this bar-restaurant with live performances for an ethnically mixed crowd every night. Drag shows on Tues & Sun, cabaret Wed–Sat, and satirist Pieter Dirk Uys performs Mon evenings. Daily 7pm–late.

Theatre On The Bay Link St, Camps Bay ☎ 021 438 3300, ⓦ www.theatreonthebay.co.za. An upmarket theatre catering to a mature audience, and staging accomplished – if rather predictable – productions of mainstream contemporary plays and farces, plus musical tributes and revues.

Cinemas

Despite the fact that Cape Town is booming as a film-production centre, local feature films are scarce. For an intelligent mix of art films, cult classics and new releases, try the Labia, 69 Orange St, or the Labia on Kloof, Lifestyles on Kloof Centre, Kloof Street Gardens (both on ☎ 021 424 5927, ⓦ www.labia .co.za). Mainstream cinemas most convenient for visitors are the Nu-Metro (☎ 021 419 9700, ⓦ www.numetro.co.za) and Ster-Kinekor Cinema Nouveau (☎ 021 425 8222, ⓦ www.sterkinekor.com) at the V&A Waterfront; the Ster-Kinekor Cavendish Commercial (☎ 0860 300 222) at Cavendish Square Shopping Centre, Claremont; and, at the same shopping centre, the Ster-Kinekor Cinema Nouveau (☎ 021 683 4063). The Ster-Kinekor complex at the Blue Route Mall in Tokai (☎ 021 713 1280) is convenient if you're staying along the False Bay seaboard. All the above cinemas advertise daily in the *Cape Times* and *Cape Argus*.

Cape Town for kids

Cape Town is an excellent place to travel with children. The city enjoys fine weather, and activities in its many nature reserves, gardens and historic estates let under-10s work off some energy in a safe environment. Many activities for kids are either free or inexpensive, although renting a car is pretty well essential, given the poor public transport. Where the prices in this section refer to children, they mean under-16s, unless specified.

Museums and sights

The **Two Oceans Aquarium** (see p.127) is not only one of Cape Town's most rewarding museums but also features loads of interest to kids. Apart from the excitement of just looking at the weird and wonderful sea creatures, kids can actually handle a few species in the touch pool – sometimes this includes a small shark or sea urchins – while the Alpha Activity Centre usually has puppet shows or face painting as well as computer terminals where older kids can learn about marine ecology.

The **SA Museum and Planetarium** (see p.118) is great for rainy days, especially for 5- to 12-year-olds, who'll enjoy the four-storey whale well and African animal dioramas, as well as the dinosaur displays. Its Discovery Room (Mon–Fri 10am–3pm, Sat & Sun 11am–4.30pm) features live ants, massive spiders and a crocodile display. The Planetarium has special children's shows over weekends and in school holidays.

Beaches and swimming pools

Cape Town's **beaches** are a classic and easy destination for a summer weekend family outing. This selection is particularly suitable for toddlers and smaller kids and generally also offers something for parents. Most beaches are pretty undeveloped, so it's best to take what you need in the way of food and drinks with you. Sea water and swimming pool temperatures are published each day in the weather section of the *Cape Times*. Get to the beach as early as possible so you can leave by 10–11am before the sun gets too strong, and to avoid the wind which often gusts up in the late morning.

On the False Bay seaboard, **Boulders Beach** (see p.152) is one of the few beaches to visit when the southeaster is blowing. It has safe, flat water, making it ideal for kids – and its resident penguin-breeding colony is an added attraction. **Fish Hoek** (see p.150) is one of the best peninsula beaches, with gentle waves that are warm in summer, a long stretch of sand and a playground. The paved Jager's Walk which runs along the rocky coast here is suitable for pushchairs and offers beautiful views of the Hottentots Holland Mountains. **St James** (see p.149) boasts a safe tidal pool with a small sandy beach and photogenic bathing boxes, though it is seriously overcrowded on summer weekends. From here you can walk to Muizenberg along a pushchair-friendly coastal pathway, with more views of distant mountains across the water.

The **Atlantic seaboard** is too cold for serious swimming, but does have some lovely stretches of sand, boulders and rock pools – and astonishing scenery. The beaches here are excellent for picnics, and on calm summer evenings idyllic for sundowners and sunsets. In the summer they're less windy than the False Bay beaches, but the afternoons are often baking hot. The closest stretch of coast to the centre ideal for prams – and roller-blading – is the paved **Sea Point promenade**, stretching 3km from the lighthouse in Mouille Point to Sea Point Pavilion, with the draw of playgrounds and ice-cream sellers en route. The tidal pool and small rock pools of **Camps Bay** (see p.145) make this popular beach very child-friendly, and it's easily reachable from the centre by car or bus. Finally, the six-kilometre stretch of white sand from **Noordhoek** to **Kommetjie** (see p.147) provides fine walking, kite-flying and horse-riding opportunities, with stupendous views of Chapman's Peak. If you're heading for Kommetjie you can go camel-riding at Imhoff Farm Village (see opposite).

As regards child-friendly swimming pools, **Newlands Pool** (see p.172) has a toddlers' pool and little playground in large grounds, while the marvellous **Sea Point Pool** at Sea Point Pavilion (see p.145) has two paddling pools for children, and lawns to laze on.

Outdoor and picnic spots

The Barnyard Farmstall Steenberg Rd (M42), next to Steenberg Estate, between Tokai Rd and the Ou Kaapseweg. An excellent place for an outdoor snack or cup of coffee at a small farmyard, with ducks and chickens wandering around, and an unusually good kids' playground.

Imhoff Farm Kommetjie Rd, opposite the Ocean View turn-off ⊕021 783 4545 or 083 735 5227, ⓦwww.imhofffarm.co.za. Great for camel rides (daily 11.30am–4.30pm; R25); toddlers can ride with a parent in the same saddle, while kids aged 4 and up can ride on their own. Tues–Sun 10am–5pm.

Kirstenbosch National Botanical Gardens See p.135. Top of the list for a family outing, with extensive lawns for running about, trees and rocks to climb and streams to paddle in. There's no litter, no dogs, it's extremely safe and you can push a pram all over the walkways; it's also great for picnics or to have tea outdoors at the café. For older kids there are short waymarked walks.

Newlands Forest 9km south of the centre, off the M3 to Muizenberg. Gentle walks in and around pine forests and streams on the wooded southern slopes of Table Mountain, with a flattish pathway suitable for pushchairs. It's good for picnics if you want to get out of the city and don't have time to go further afield. Safest at weekends and in the afternoons when the joggers and dog walkers are out. Use the access point off the M3 signposted "Forestry Office", where there's ample parking. Dawn–dusk; free.

Ratanga Junction See p.155. Fun-filled adventure rides for thrill-seekers young and old, with over thirty attractions.

Silvermine Nature Reserve See p.150. A good place to see *fynbos* vegetation at close quarters, stroll around the lake, paddle and picnic with small children; however, it is exposed, and not recommended in heavy winds or mist. For older children there are some mountain-top walks with relatively gentle gradients, which give spectacular views over both sides of the Peninsula.

Tokai Forest Arboretum See p.140. Walks and mountain biking, as well as a thatched tea shop with outdoor seating. It's also a great place for young children to explore, with logs to jump off and a gentle walk to a stream.

Gay Cape Town

Cape Town is South Africa's – and indeed, the African continent's – gay capital. The city has always had a vibrant gay culture, and is on its way to becoming an African Sydney, attracting gay travellers from across the country and the globe. Cape Town's **gay village**, with B&Bs, guesthouses, pubs, clubs, cruise bars and steam baths, is concentrated along the entertainment strips of Somerset Road and Main Road in the interconnected inner-city suburbs of Green Point, Sea Point and De Waterkant, adjacent to the centre. The *Pink Map*, published by A&C Maps (⊕021 685 4260, ⓦwww.capeinfo.com), lists gay-friendly and gay-owned places in Cape Town and is distributed at the visitor centre in town, the one in the Clock Tower at the V&A Waterfront, as well as the airport and hotels; they'll also send a copy free anywhere in the world on request.

Cape Town hosts a hugely popular annual **gay costume party**, organized by Mother City Queer Projects (ⓦwww.mcqp.co.za), which has turned into a ten-day festival held each December (6–16). People dress as outrageously as possible according to the official yearly theme (past ones have included "Kitchen Kitsch", "The Twinkly Sea Project" and "Farm Fresh") and the event seeks to rival Sydney's Mardi Gras. There's also an annual **gay pride festival** in February (ⓦwww.capetownpride.co.za).

Besides the South African gay **websites** and resources listed in Basics (p.76), it's worth having a look at ⓦwww.gaynetcapetown.co.za, aimed specifically at the gay traveller to Cape Town. For information on what's on, you can check out the gay section of the Western Cape listings magazine *Cape Review*, or the gay supplement published on the last Thursday of the month in the *Cape Argus*,

Cape Town's daily afternoon newspaper. While in town, be sure to tune into Bush Radio's gay programme, called "In the Pink" (Thurs 8–9pm; 89.5FM).

Clubs and bars

Bar Code 18 Cobern St, De Waterkant. A leather uniform and jeans bar that attracts an older crowd, *Bar Code* has a darkroom and hosts monthly underwear and fetish parties. Daily 9pm till late.

Bronx Somerset Rd, Green Point. A hugely popular bar with a dance floor and loads of energy. Attracts a mixed crowd. Daily 8pm till late.

Café Manhattan 74 Waterkant St, De Waterkant. A restaurant-bar which serves affordable food on an outside terrace beneath oak trees. There's live music every Thurs & Sun night. Straight-friendly. Daily 10am–late.

M-Bar and Lounge *Metropole Hotel*, 38 Long St. An upmarket gay hangout *par excellence* is this sophisticated lounge and bar in a stylishly appointed hotel. Cocktails served from midday until late. Straight-friendly.

On Broadway 88 Shortmarket St ☏021 4242 1194, Ⓦwww.onbroadway.co.za. A great restaurant-bar

with Mediterranean-style food and cabaret. One of the few venues committed to the city's small cabaret scene is this bar restaurant with live performances for an ethnically mixed crowd every night. Booking is essential. Shows nightly 7pm–late. Drag shows on Sunday nights.

Rosie's 125a Waterkant St, De Waterkant, opposite *Café Manhattan*. A small, intimate pool bar attracting bears and leather boys, with a restaurant that's a popular after-work drinking spot. Open till late: Tues–Fri from 4pm, Sat & Sun from 2pm.

Sauna

The Hothouse 18 Jarvis St, Green Point Ⓦwww.hothouse.co.za. A luxurious pleasure complex featuring Jacuzzis, sauna, a sundeck with a superb view, a full bar with a limited food menu, video room, fireplace and satellite TV. Luxury cabins R120. Entrance R60–80 depending on days and times. Mon–Fri noon–2am, Sat & Sun 24hr.

Outdoor activities and sport

One of Cape Town's most remarkable features is the fact that it melds with the Table Mountain National Park, a patchwork of mountains, forests and coastline – all on the city's doorstep. There are few, if any, cities in the world where outdoor pursuits are so easily available and affordable. You can try activities such as sea kayaking, abseiling, rock climbing and scuba diving for little more than the price of a night out back home. A notable activity locally is **abseiling**, which is not for the fainthearted. Alternatively, just let everyone else get on with it while you sink a few beers and watch the cricket, rugby or soccer.

Spectator sports

Cricket This is keenly followed by a wide range of Capetonians. The city's cricketing heart is at Newlands Cricket Ground (also known after its sponsors as Sahara Park), 61 Campground Rd, Newlands (☏021 657 2003). One of the most beautiful grounds in the world, Newlands nestles beneath venerable oaks and the elegant profile of Devil's Peak, and plays host to provincial, test and one-day international matches.

Rugby The Western Cape is one of the world's rugby heartlands, and the game is followed religiously here. Provincial, international and Super 12 contests are fought on the hallowed turf of Newlands Rugby Stadium, Boundary Rd, Newlands (☏021 659 4600).

Soccer Though soccer matches aren't as well attended as cricket or rugby, Cape Town soccer is burgeoning with talent and is likely to get a huge

boost now that South Africa is hosting the 2010 World Cup. The dusty streets of the Cape Flats have produced superb young footballers such as Benni McCarthy (Porto, Ajax Amsterdam, Celta Vigo) and Quinton Fortune (Atletico Madrid, Manchester United). The most ambitious and professional club in the city is Ajax (pronounced "I-axe") Cape Town (Ⓦwww.ajaxct.org), jointly owned by its Amsterdam namesake. The most exciting games to attend are those between a local outfit and one of the Soweto glamour teams, Orlando Pirates and Kaizer Chiefs. Matches take place at Green Point Stadium, off Beach Rd; Athlone Stadium, off Klipfontein Rd, Athlone; and Newlands Rugby Stadium (see above).

Participation sports and outdoor activities

Abseiling You can abseil off Table Mountain with Abseil Africa (☏021 424 4760) for around R395 for a half-day trip (excluding cable-car fee). They also do full-day trips (minimum group of 4) that include kloofing, hiking, abseiling, breakfast, lunch and a light supper, for R595, or a summit walk on Table Mountain for R120, which you can combine with abseiling for R495.

Bird-watching The peninsula's varied habitats attract nearly four hundred different species of birds. Good places for bird-watching include Lion's Head, Kirstenbosch Gardens and the Cape of Good Hope Nature Reserve, as well as at Kommetjie and Hout Bay; you can find out about knowledgeable guides through the Cape Bird Club (☎021 559 0726). For a more institutionalized experience, try the World of Birds in Hout Bay.

Cycling Cycling (for rental outlets see p.177) is popular all over the peninsula, and is a great way to take in the scenery. For information about the Cape Argus Pick 'n Pay Cycle Tour, the largest individually timed bike race in the world, contact Pedal Power Associates (☎021 689 8420, ⓦwww.cycletour.co.za), which also organizes fun rides from Sept–May.

Golf The Milnerton golf course, Bridge Rd, Milnerton (☎021 552 1047), is tucked in between a lagoon and Table Bay, and boasts classic views of Table Mountain. Other popular local courses are at Rondebosch Golf Club, Klipfontein Rd, Rondebosch (☎021 689 4176), and Westlake Golf Club, Westlake Ave, Lakeside (☎021 788 2020). Prices are around R190/400 for 9/18 holes; clubs can be rented for R150 and caddy fees are R130. Booking is essential.

Gyms Virgin Active clubs are upmarket, well-appointed gyms dotted around the peninsula. Contact their call centre (☎0860 200 911, ⓦwww.virginactive.co.za) to find out where the nearest one is to you and the rates.

Horse-riding Horse Trail Safaris, *Indicator Lodge*, Skaapskraal Rd, Ottery (east of Wynberg across the M5; ☎021 703 4396), offers riding through the dunes to Strandfontein and the False Bay coast as well as overnight trips; Sleepy Hollow Horse Riding, Sleepy Hollow Lane, Noordhoek (☎021 789 2341), covers the spectacular Noordhoek Beach. Both charge around R300 for 1hr 30min.

Kayaking Real Cape Adventures (☎021 790 5611 or 082 556 2520, ⓦwww.seakayak.co.za) offers a range of half- or full-day sea-kayaking packages that include trips around Cape Point, to the penguin colony at Boulders Beach and around Hout Bay. The company organizes trips of several days around the peninsula, on which you spend nights at guesthouses, and longer safaris all over South Africa and even further north. The cheapest trip costs R200 per person for two hours' kayaking.

Kite-flying At the Waterfront, the Kite Shop, Shop 110, Ground Floor, Victoria Wharf (☎021 421 6231), sells kites of all shapes, colours and sizes.

Mountain biking Day Trippers (☎021 511 4766, ⓦwww.daytrippers.co.za) offers expert mountain-bike tours, including one from Scarborough to Cape Point. Downhill Adventures, on the corner of Kloof and Orange sts in the city centre (☎021 422 0388, ⓦwww.downhilladventures.co.za), offers similar tours starting from its shop; for experienced mountain bikers it has a Tokai forest tour (R450 half day, minimum 4 people).

Paragliding Cape Town has great air thermals for paragliding. If you're tempted to leap off any of the surrounding mountains then contact Para-Pax (☎082 881 4724), which offers tandem flights for R850. A picture of your horrified face will cost R130. Dress warmly.

Rock climbing High Adventure (☎021 689 1234 or 082 437 5145) will take you to unusual and unique locations depending on your ability. Packages are tailor-made, with a minimum of two people. You can learn how to rock climb up Table Mountain's famous facade with the Cape Town School of Mountaineering (☎021 531 4290), which charges R750 for a two-day rock-climbing course, usually over weekends; it also guides experienced climbers.

Sand boarding Downhill Adventures (see under "Mountain biking") is the pioneer of this latest adventure sport. Boards, boots and bindings are provided, as well as expert instruction for beginners. Half-day (R450) and full-day (R595) trips take you to the finest slopes in the area.

Scuba diving While the Cape waters are cold, they're good for seeing wrecks, reefs and magnificent kelp forests. False Bay is invariably warmer than the Atlantic seaboard and thus preferred in winter. Short dives cost R200 from the shore, up to around R300 from a boat; expect to pay R400 to rent all the gear. An internationally recognized PADI open-water diving qualification can be completed for around R2500. To arrange scuba-diving courses and equipment rental, contact Orca Industries, corner Herschel and Bowwood rds, Claremont (☎021 671 9673); or the Scuba Shack, Shop 3, Glencairn Shopping Centre, Glencairn (☎021 782 6279).

Skydiving The ultimate way to see Table Mountain and Robben Island is from a tandem jump 3000m up; if you want an adrenaline rush contact Skydive Cape Town (☎082 800 6290, ⓦwww.skydivecapetown.za.net; R1250).

Surfing Top surfing spots include Big Bay at Bloubergstrand (competitions are held here every summer), Llandudno, Muizenberg, Kalk Bay and

Long Beach near Kommetjie and Noordhoek. For information on competitions contact Surfing South Africa (℡021 674 2972), or check out ⓦwww .wavescape.co.za, the best place on the Web for everything you want to know about surfing in SA, including what the waves are up to. To learn to surf, contact Downhill Adventures (see under "Mountain biking"; half day R350, full day R500, with all equipment provided).

Swimming In the summer there are surf lifesaver patrols on duty at Milnerton, Camps Bay, Llandudno, Muizenberg and Fish Hoek beaches. For pools, try Long Street Baths, Long St (℡021 400 3302; daily 7am–7pm), Cape Town's only public heated indoor pool; or Newlands Swimming Pool, corner of Main and San Souci rds, Newlands (℡021 674 4197; daily: April–Sept 9am–5pm; Oct–March 7am–6.30pm; R12.50, children R6.80), an Olympic-sized chlorinated pool, which isn't heated (the water temperature drops to an unappealing 15°C in winter). The excellent Sea Point Swimming Pool at Beach Rd, Sea Point (℡021 434 3341; adults R12.50, children R6.80), is an Olympic-sized chlorinated seawater pool.

Walking The best places for gentle strolls are Newlands Forest, up from Rhodes Memorial, and the beaches. For longer walks, head for anywhere on Table Mountain, Tokai Forest, Silvermine Nature

Reserve or Cape Point Nature Reserve. High Adventure (see under "Rock climbing") does guided hikes up Table Mountain, geared to your level of fitness and with experienced guides (half day R350, full day R500 including a packed lunch). If you want to go further afield, they'll arrange multi-day trips where you can opt to have your bags carried or have food prepared for you.

Windsurfing and kitesurfing While most Capetonians moan about the howling southeaster in summer, it's handy if you're into windsurfing; not much happens in the winter, as the winds just aren't as good. Langebaan, a 75min drive north of town, is one of the best spots. For further help, contact Cape Sport Centre, Langebaan (℡022 772 1114, ⓦwww.capesport.co.za), which also does kitesurfing. Prices for windsurfing start at R295 for 2hr for rigs, while instruction for beginners starts at R250; a 10hr kitesurfing package costs R1850 including gear and instruction. Otherwise, the place to go in Cape Town is Bloubergstrand. Blouberg Windsurf and Leisure (℡021 554 1663 or 082 420 2990, ⓔblouwind@mweb.co.za) rents equipment, cars with racks and has long-term accommodation at Bloubergstrand, as well as being able to offer general advice to its clients, such as information on which airlines offer free carriage of windsurfing equipment.

Shopping

The **V&A Waterfront** is the city's most popular shopping venue, with good reason: it has a vast range of shops, the setting on the harbour is lovely and there's a huge choice of places to eat and drink when you want to rest your feet – but expect to pay above the odds for everything. The city centre also offers variety and, for some people's taste, a grittier and more interesting venue for browsing, especially if you're looking for collectables, antiques and secondhand books. Cape Town's suburbanites tend to do their shopping at the upmarket Cavendish Square Mall in **Claremont** or one of many other shopping centres. If you're staying in the inner-city suburbs of Green Point and Sea Point, adjacent to the V&A Waterfront, you'll find supermarkets and other functional shops along Main Road, and the City Bowl suburbs are served by the Gardens Shopping Centre. There are other smaller shopping areas dotted about the other suburbs.

Shopping hours have traditionally been Monday to Friday 8.30am to 5pm, and Saturday until 1pm, though lots of supermarkets, bookshops and other specialist outlets are now open beyond 5pm and also on Sundays, though don't expect much to be open on Sunday afternoons, except at the Waterfront.

Malls and shopping centres

South African shopping tends to follow an American model, with **malls** where you can browse in a bookshop as well as bank, buy clothes and groceries and go to the movies. Malls always have several coffee shops and restaurants.

Blue Route Mall Tokai Rd, Tokai. A functional single-storey centre with branches of Checkers Hyper and Woolworths, handy if you're staying in Constantia or along the False Bay. Mon–Fri 9am–5.30pm, Sat 9am–5pm, Sun 9am–3pm.
Cavendish Square Claremont station, Vineyard Rd, Claremont. An upmarket multistorey complex, the major shopping focus for the southern suburbs. Mon–Thurs & Sat 9am–6pm, Fri 9am–9pm, Sun 10am–4pm.
Constantia Village Shopping Centre Main Rd, Constantia. A small exclusive mall including two large supermarkets. Mon–Fri 9am–5pm, Sat 9am–2pm.

Gardens Shopping Centre Mill St, Gardens. Small shopping mall in the City Bowl, very close to the Company Gardens and city centre, with a large supermarket, excellent deli and most of the shops you'll need. Mon–Fri 9am–6pm, Sat 9am–3pm; some shops also Sun 10am–2pm.
V&A Waterfront It would be possible to visit Cape Town and never leave the Waterfront complex, which has a vast range of upmarket shops packed into the Victoria Wharf Shopping Centre, including outlets of all the major South African chains, selling books, clothes, food and crafts. Mon–Sat 9am–9pm, Sun 10am–9pm.

Arts and crafts

Cape Town is not known for its indigenous **arts and crafts** in the way that Durban is, and many of the goods you'll buy here are from elsewhere in Africa, especially Zimbabwe and Zambia. There are several outlets in the city centre and the V&A Waterfront, but you'll often pick up the same arts and crafts for a lot less money at the pavement **markets** scattered around town. Don't expect exotic West African-style markets, however; Cape Town's markets are more like European or North American flea markets.

Craft shops

Africa Nova Cape Quarter, Dixon St, De Waterkant ℡ 021 425 5123. A better-than-average selection of ethnic crafts and curios as well as contemporary African textiles and artwork, with an emphasis on the individual and handmade. Mon–Fri 9am–5pm, Sat & Sun 10am–2pm.
African Image Branches at the corner of Church and Burg sts (℡ 021 423 8385); and Shop 6228, Victoria Wharf, V&A Waterfront (℡ 021 419 0382). One of the best places for authentic traditional and contemporary African arts and crafts, from fabrics and antique sculpture to beadwork, but goods are a little overpriced. Church & Burg branch Mon–Fri 9am–5pm, Sat 9am–1.30pm; Waterfront branch daily 9am–9pm.
Clementina Ceramics 20 Main Rd, Kalk Bay ℡ 021 788 8718. Unique contemporary South African ceramics. Tues–Sun 10am–5pm.
Ethno Bongo Mainstream Shopping Centre, Main Rd, Hout Bay ℡ 021 790 0802. A charming shop in the main shopping centre in Hout Bay, selling wonderful and well-priced crafts, jewellery and accessories made from recycled metal and wood, and also quirky kaftans and ethnic clothing – highly recommended for unique gifts and souvenirs. Mon–Fri 9.30am–5.30pm, Sat 9.30am–4pm, Sun 10am–2pm.
Kalk Bay Gallery 62 Main Rd, Kalk Bay ℡ 021 788 1674. Graphics, engravings as well as African art and artefacts – good value, with the chance of

picking up something very collectable. Mon–Fri 9am–5pm, Sat & Sun 9.30am–5pm.
Rose Korber Art Consultancy 48 Sedgemoor Rd, Camps Bay ℡ 021 438 9152. This should be the first stop for the serious collector, with an exceptional selection of contemporary art and craft, including ceramics and beadwork from around the continent. Mon–Fri 9am–5pm.
Yellow Door Upper floor, Gardens Centre, Gardens ℡ 021 465 4702. One of the largest and best selections of local crafts and design, including ceramics, fabrics, jewellery, basketry, metalwork and interior decor. Mon–Fri 9am–6pm, Sat 9am–4pm, Sun 10am–2pm.

Markets

Cape Town Station Forecourt, Adderley St. Thronging ranks of market traders selling African crafts, as well as radios and leather goods. Not principally aimed at tourists, so it's pretty authentic. Mon–Fri 8am–5pm, Sat 8am–2pm.
Constantia Craft Market Alphen Common, corner of Spaanschemat River and Ladies Mile rds, Constantia. Sizeable outdoor flea market where you can pick up good local crafts and items from around the continent, ride a camel or a pony and have a cup of tea. First & last Sat, & first Sun of the month.
Green Point Market Western Blvd, Green Point. A massive open air market displaying everything from African arts and crafts to plants, car parts, and anything home-made. Sun 9am–4pm.

▲ Man selling goods at a Cape Town market

Greenmarket Square Burg St. Open-air market where you can pick up knick-knacks, and the best place in town for colourful handmade Cape Town beachwear, from T-shirts to shorts and sandals. Mon–Fri 8am–5pm, Sat 8am–2pm.

The Pan African Market 76 Long St. A multicultural hothouse of township and contemporary art, artefacts, curios and crafts. There's music, a café specializing in African cuisine, a bookshop, a Cameroonian hairbraider and a West African tailor. Mon–Fri 9am–5pm, Sat 9am–3pm.

The Red Shed Craft Workshop Victoria Wharf, V&A Waterfront. A market where some two dozen craftworkers make and sell ceramics, textiles, candles and jewellery, and where you can see glass-blowers at work. Mon–Sat 9am–9pm, Sun 10am–9pm.

Sivuyile Craft Centre On the corner of NY1 and NY4, Gugulethu, Cape Flats. Township market attached to an information centre close to the N2 freeway, where bead-workers, wire-workers and other artists make traditional and modern crafts. Mon–Fri 8am–5pm, Sat 9am–2pm.

Victoria Rd Market Camps Bay. Carvings, beads, fabrics and baskets sold from a market spectacularly sited on a clifftop overlooking the Atlantic. Daily.

Books

South Africa produces a lot of **books** given the size of its reading population: you'll find good locally published novels and endless volumes on history, politics and natural history. For new books there are some pleasant places in the suburbs or at the Waterfront to browse for half an hour, while Upper Long Street has over half a dozen secondhand book and specialist comic shops in close proximity, interspersed with congenial cafés.

Clarke's Bookshop 211 Long St ℡021 423 5739. The best place in Cape Town for South African books, with a huge selection of local titles covering literature, history, politics, natural history and the arts, plus very well-informed staff. They also deal in collectors' editions of South African books. Mon–Fri 9am–5pm, Sat 9am–1pm.
Exclusive Books Branches at Victoria Wharf, V&A Waterfront ℡021 419 0905 (Mon–Fri 9am–10.30pm, Sat 9am–11pm, Sun 10am–9pm); Lower Mall, Cavendish Square, Claremont (℡021 674 3030; Mon–Thurs 9am–9pm, Fri & Sat 9am–10.30pm, Sun 9.30am–9pm); Constantia Village Shopping Centre, Main Rd, Constantia (℡021 794 7800; Mon–Sat 9am–8pm, Sun 9am–5pm). A friendly bookshop, ideal for browsing; the

reasonably well-stocked shelves include magazines and a wide choice of coffee-table books on Cape Town and South African topics.
Kirstenbosch Shop Kirstenbosch National Botanical Gardens ℡021 762 2510. A good selection of natural-history books, field guides and travel guides covering Southern Africa, as well as a range of titles for kids. You won't need a gardens ticket to browse. Daily 9am–7pm.
The Travellers Bookshop King's Warehouse, Victoria Wharf, V&A Waterfront ℡021 425 6880. Cape Town's only specialist travel bookshop stocks a decent range of titles, mainly about South Africa and especially the Cape, covering history, politics, natural history and the arts. Daily 9am–9pm.

Music

Look & Listen, Shop F14, Upper Level, Cavendish Square, Claremont (℡021 683 1810; daily 9am–10.30pm), is Cape Town's largest music store, with a selection of all kinds of sounds, including good local jazz and a respectable selection from all over the African continent. One of the best ranges of African music in the city is available at CD Warehouse, V&A Waterfront (next to the *V&A Hotel*; ℡021 425 6300). Also centrally located, African Music Store at 90a Long St (℡021 426 0867; Mon–Fri 9am–5pm, Sat 9am–2pm) is a small shop specializing in African music. The ubiquitous chains such as CNA and Musica tend to stock pretty unadventurous selections of mainly British and American sounds.

Food and provisions

Self-catering is the cheapest way to eat in Cape Town, and can also be good fun. **Braais** happen anywhere with any excuse, and there are countless places on beaches, in the forests or up Table Mountain where you can enjoy a terrific **picnic**. There are some excellent (if pricey) **delicatessens**, several of which are strung along Main Road, Green Point and Sea Point. You'll also find delicious food and some unusual fruit and vegetables at the more sophisticated **farm stalls**. The larger branches of the better **supermarkets** have fishmonger counters where you can buy fresh fish, though by far the most atmospheric places to buy seafood are the Hout Bay and Kalk Bay harbours (see p.146 & p.150 respectively).

Supermarkets tend to have decent **wine** at competitive prices, but for more interesting labels, there are some first-rate specialist wine merchants. Alcohol is not sold at retail outlets on a Sunday.

Supermarkets

Pick 'n Pay V&A Waterfront (daily 9am–8pm); Gardens Shopping Centre, Mill St, Gardens (Mon–Thurs 8am–7pm, Fri 8am–9pm, Sat 8am–5pm, Sun 9am–2pm); Main Rd, Camps Bay (daily 9am–7pm); Main Rd, Observatory (Mon–Thurs 7am–8.30pm, Fri & Sat 7am–10pm, Sun 8am–2pm); corner Main Rd and Campground Rd, Claremont (Mon–Thurs 8am–6pm, Fri 8am–7pm, Sat 8am–4pm, Sun 9am–2pm); Blue Route Mall, Tokai (Mon–Thurs 8.30am–6pm, Fri 8.30am–7pm, Sat 8am–6pm, Sun 9am–2pm); Constantia Village, Main Rd, Constantia (Mon–Fri 8am–8pm, Sat 8am–5pm, Sun 9am–4pm). One of the best places for groceries, considerably larger and cheaper than Woolworths, with a good deli counter and a choice of prepared meals, among which you'll find their excellent-value ready-grilled whole chickens.

Woolworths Adderley St (Mon–Fri 8.30am–5.30pm, Sat 8am–2pm); V&A Waterfront (daily 9am–9pm); Cavendish Square Mall, Claremont (Mon–Thurs 9am–6pm, Fri 8.30am–8pm, Sat 8am–6pm, Sun 9am–5pm); Blue Route Mall, Tokai (Mon–Thurs 9am–5.30pm, Fri 8.30am–7pm, Sat 8.30am–5pm, Sun 9am–2pm); Constantia Village, Main Rd, Constantia (Mon–Thurs 8.30am–7pm, Fri 8am–8pm, Sat 8.30am–6pm, Sun 9am–5pm). Excellent for quality fast-cook meals, fresh produce and cold foods, such as olives, hummus and various Mediterranean dips, but it can be pricey.

Delis and farm stalls

Andiamo Cape Quarter, Dixon St, De Waterkant. Italian Deli where you can select from meats, cheeses, salads, dips, *meze* and fresh breads to take on your mountain walk. Phone ahead and they'll put the picnic together for you. Daily 9am–11pm.

The Barnyard Farm Stall Steenberg Rd, adjacent to the well-signposted Steenberg Wine Estate, Tokai ☎ 021 712 6934. One of Cape Town's nicest farm stalls, with a selection of high-class cheeses, breads, home-baked cakes, wines, pâtés, coffee beans and many other delights. There's also the major attraction of a very good outdoor café with a children's playground attached. A good stop if you're doing the Constantia winelands. Daily 8.30am–5.30pm.

Giovanni's 103 Main Rd, Green Point. Excellent breads and delicious Italian foods to take away and – if temptation overcomes you – there's always the option of sitting down for a coffee and a snack. Daily 8.30am–9pm.

Melissa's 94 Kloof St, Gardens; and Constantia Village. Highly delectable imported and local specialities, with the option of eating in. Gardens Mon–Fri 7.30am–8pm, Sat & Sun 8am–9pm; Constantia 7.30am–7pm, Sat & Sun 8am–6pm.

New York Bagel Deli 51 Regent Rd, Sea Point. The best bagels in town with a great selection of Eastern European Jewish fillings – salt beef, gherkins, chopped liver and pickled herring – and an array of delicious pastries. Daily 7am–9pm.

Fresh fish

Fish Market Mariner's Wharf, Hout Bay Harbour. Fresh seafood from South Africa's original waterfront emporium, but slicker and less atmospheric than Kalk Bay Harbour. Mon–Fri 9am–5.30pm, Sat & Sun 9am–6pm.

Kalk Bay Harbour Harbourside, Kalk Bay. Buy fresh fish directly from the fishermen and have it gutted and scaled on the spot. Your best bet is lunchtime, especially at weekends.

Wine

Caroline's Fine Wines 15 Long St ☎ 021 419 8984; and King's Warehouse, V&A Waterfront ☎ 021 425 5701. Caroline Rillema has been in the wine business since 1979 and offers daily tastings of the Cape's finest and most exclusive wines. Mon–Fri 9am–5pm, Waterfront also Sat 9am–5pm.

Vaughan Johnson's Dock Rd, V&A Waterfront ☎ 021 419 2121. One of Cape Town's best-known wine shops, which has a huge range of labels from all over the country, though it can be a bit pricey. Mon–Fri 9am–6pm, Sat 9am–5pm, Sun 10am–5pm.

Wine Concepts 50 Kloof St; and Castle Building, on the corner of Kildare Rd and Main Rd, Newlands. An excellent selection of South African and foreign wines from a knowledgeable and helpful outfit. Mon–Thurs 9am–7pm, Fri 9am–8pm, Sat 9am–5pm.

Woolworths See above. The own-label wines of South Africa's upmarket supermarket chain have come a long way since the days when you'd sneakily decant them so no one would know their source. Cognoscenti now happily flaunt these competitively priced wines.

Holistic Cape Town

Cape Town is South Africa's **holism** capital. The Fields Health Store at 84 Kloof St, Gardens (℡021 423 9587), sells health and beauty products, with a juice bar serving a daily vegetarian lunch buffet and cakes. For homeopathic and herbal remedies try Natural Remedies, Pearce Street, Claremont (℡021 674 1692; Mon–Fri 9am–5pm, Sat 8.30am–1pm), or the central White's Chemist, 61 Plein St (℡021 465 3332; Mon–Fri 7.30am–5pm, Sat 8am–12.30pm).

The best publications for more details are *Link-Up*, a free listings magazine, and the glossier *Odyssey*, which is also the place to track down sources of southern African crystals, gemstones and essential oils – disappointingly, though, there are few oils from Cape plants except for geraniums. Both are available from health-food shops and alternative health venues.

Listings

Airlines 1Time ℡0861 345 345; British Airways ℡0860 011 747; KLM Royal Dutch Airlines ℡0860 247 747; Kulula.com ℡0861 585 852; Lufthansa ℡021 415 3535; Nationwide ℡021 936 2050; Olympic Airways ℡021 419 2502; Qantas ℡011 441 8550; SA Airlink ℡021 936 1111; South African Airways ℡021 936 1111; Virgin Atlantic ℡011 340 3400.

American Express Lost Cards ℡0800 110 0929; traveller's cheque queries ℡0800 990 123.

Banks and exchange Main branches with ATMs are easy to find in the shopping areas of the city centre, the middle-class suburbs and at the Waterfront. For foreign-exchange transactions outside normal banking hours, try one of the following: American Express, Shop 11a, Alfred Mall, Waterfront (Mon–Fri 9am–7pm, Sat 9am–5pm, Sun 9am–5pm); Rennies Foreign Exchange, Victoria Wharf, V&A Waterfront (Mon–Sat 9am–9pm, Sun 10am–9pm); or Master Currencies, Cape Town International Airport (Mon–Sun 6.30am–10pm).

Bike rental Mountain bikes are available from Rent 'n' Ride, 243 Main Rd, Three Anchor Bay (℡021 434 2382; R85 a day including helmet and lock; R1000 credit-card deposit required). Downhill Adventures (℡021 422 0388, ⓦwww.downhilladventures .co.za) has similar rentals for R100 for 24hr, and offers seven days' rental for the price of six.

Car rental Aroundaboutcars (℡0860 422 4022, ⓦwww.aroundaboutcars.com) is an independent national rental company based in Cape Town and offering great package deals and flexible pricing; the rate can be as low as R150 per day with unlimited mileage. It offers one-way rental (to drive down the Garden Route and fly back from Port Elizabeth, for example), but as with all rental agencies, there is an additional charge for this.

Another inexpensive option is Vineyard Car Hire (℡021 761 0671, ⓔvineyardcarhire@iafrica.com), which rents out vehicles for as little as R180 a day (including 200km per day free) for three to six days. Allen's Car Hire (℡021 701 8844) is reasonable, reliable and of a similar price. Staff can deliver a car to you, or meet you at the airport when you land. For details of the larger, national agencies, see Basics, p.46 To try to find the best deal, either pick up one of the brochures at Cape Town Tourism office or look in the *Yellow Pages*.

Consulates Canada, 60 St George's Mall ℡021 423 5240; Germany, St Martini Gardens, Queen Victoria St ℡021 464 3000; UK, Southern Life Centre, 8 Riebeeck St ℡021 405 2400; USA, 4th floor, Broadway Centre, Heerengracht ℡021 421 4280. The embassies for most countries are in Pretoria.

Dental care Dentists, listed in the *Yellow Pages* telephone directory, are well up to British and North American standards, and generally less expensive.

Emergencies See Basics, p.75

Hospitals and doctors The largest state hospital is Groote Schuur, Hospital Drive, Observatory (℡021 404 9111), just off the M3. Nearer the centre and convenient for the City Bowl and Atlantic seaboard is Somerset Hospital, Beach Rd, Mouille Point (℡021 402 6911); it has outpatient and emergency departments, although it's generally overcrowded, understaffed and seemingly under-equipped. If you have medical insurance you might prefer to be treated at one of the well-staffed, efficient and well-equipped private hospitals listed in the phone directory. The two largest hospital groups are the Netcare (emergency response ℡082 911) and Medi-Clinic chains, with hospitals all over the Cape Peninsula. Most central of

Netcare's hospitals is the Christiaan Barnard Memorial Hospital, 181 Longmarket St (T 021 480 6111) – you'll get to see a doctor quickly and costs are not excessive.

Laundry Most backpacker hostels have coin-operated washing machines, while guesthouses, hotels and B&Bs will usually offer a laundry service for a charge. There are laundries offering service washes in the city centre and most suburban areas.

Left luggage Virtually every backpacker hostel provides luggage storage facilities, and most other accommodation will be happy to take care of your luggage for a day or two.

Mobile phone rental Available from Cellucity, Shop 6193, V&A Waterfront (T 021 418 1306) for around R30 per day for the handset, with calls charged at R2.70/min. You'll need to provide your credit-card details. Rentals can also be done at the airport when you arrive.

Pharmacies Chemists with extended opening hours include: Hypermed Pharmacy, corner York and Main rds, Green Point (T 021 434 1414; Mon–Fri 8.30am–9pm, Sat & Sun 9am–9pm); Sunset Pharmacy, Sea Point Medical Centre, Kloof Rd, Sea

Point (T 021 434 3333; daily 8.30am–9pm); and Tamboerskloof Pharmacy, 16 Kloof Nek Rd, Tamboerskloof (T 021 424 4450; daily 9am–9pm).

Police The central station is on Caledon Square, Buitenkant St (T 021 467 8000).

Post office The main branch, on Parliament St, (Mon, Tues, Thurs & Fri 8am–4.30pm, Wed 8.30am–4.30pm, Sat 8am–noon), has a poste restante and enquiry desk.

Taxis There are a number of reliable companies, including Marine Taxi Hire (T 021 434 0434), Sea Point Radio Taxis (T 021 434 4444) and Unicab (T 021 448 1720).

Ticket agencies Computicket (T 083 915 8000, W www.computicket.co.za) books most theatre, cinema and sporting events, as well as airline and bus tickets.

Travel agents The largest travel franchise in the country is Sure Travel, which has about two dozen offices across Cape Town (call T 0800 221 656 for the nearest); try also One World Travel Centre, 309 Long St (T 021 423 0777). Cape Town Tourism can also book trips (see p.95).

Travel details

Trains

Cape Town to: Bloemfontein (1 weekly; 23hr); Durban (1 weekly; 36hr 25min); Johannesburg (1 daily; 24hr 55min); Kimberley (1 daily; 16hr 30min); Pietermaritzburg (every Mon; 34hr); Pretoria (1 daily; 26hr 20min).

Buses

Cape Town to: Bloemfontein (3 daily; 13hr); Calvinia (1 weekly; 6hr 30min); Cradock (1 daily; 10hr); Durban (3 daily; 20hr); East London (3 daily; 15hr 40min); George (4 daily; 6hr); Graaff-Reinet (1–2 daily; 9hr); Grahamstown (1 daily; 12hr 25min); Johannesburg (4 daily; 17hr); Kimberley (1 daily except Wed; 11hr 45min); Knysna (4 daily; 6hr 50min); Montagu (3 weekly; 4hr); Mossel Bay (4 daily; 5hr 15min); Oudtshoorn (3 weekly; 6hr 15min); Paarl (4 weekly; 1hr 30min); Pietermaritzburg (3 daily; 18hr 40min); Plettenberg Bay (4 daily; 7hr 30min); Port Elizabeth (4 daily; 10hr); Pretoria (4 daily; 18hr); Sedgefield (1 daily; 6hr 45min); Springbok (6 weekly; 6hr 30min); Stellenbosch (1–2 daily; 1hr); Storms River (4 daily; 10hr 10min); Umtata (1 daily; 18hr); Upington

(5 weekly; 10hr 30min); Vanrhynsdorp (1 daily; 5hr); Wilderness (4 daily; 6hr 30min); Windhoek (Namibia; 4 weekly; 16hr 30min).

Baz buses

All services below operate daily. For details of onward services from Port Elizabeth, see p.451.

Cape Town to: Bot River (1hr 30min); George (7hr; change here for shuttle bus to Oudtshoorn); Jeffrey's Bay (12hr 15min); Knysna (8hr 30min); Mossel Bay (6hr); Nature's Valley (10hr); Plettenberg Bay (9hr 30min); Port Elizabeth (13hr 30min); Storms River (10hr 30min); Swellendam (3hr); Wilderness (7hr 30min).

Domestic flights

Cape Town to: Bloemfontein (2–3 daily; 1hr 35min); Durban (10 daily; 2hr); East London (4 daily; 2hr); George (3–4 daily; 1hr); Hoedspruit (1 daily; 3hr); Johannesburg (16 daily; 2hr); Kimberley (1 daily; 2hr); Nelspruit (1 daily; 2hr 15min); Port Elizabeth (4 daily; 1hr 30min); Sun City (1 daily; 2hr); Upington (6 weekly; 1hr 50min); Walvis Bay (2 weekly; 2hr); Windhoek (5 weekly; 2hr 10min).

The Western Cape

CHAPTER 2 # Highlights

* **The Winelands** Quaff fine vintages on some of South Africa's most beautiful wine estates. See p.184

* **Route 62** This mountainous inland route takes you through dozy villages, across spectacular passes and through semi-desert. See p.202

* **De Hoop Nature Reserve** Massive dunes and edge-to-edge whales in season make this arguably the most exciting provincial nature reserve in the county. See p.249

* **Ocean safaris** Learn about whales and dolphins on an excursion around Plettenberg Bay. See p.277

* **Canopy Tour** Swing from tree to tree among the highest boughs of the Tsitsikamma Forest's arboreal giants. See p.285

* **Storms River Mouth** One of the most dramaticsections of coast, where hillside forests drop away to rocky coastline and the Storms River surges out of a gorge into the thundering ocean. See p.287

* **Seafood** Feast on endless courses of fish, lobster and whatever else the ocean yields at one of the casual beachside eating places along the West Coast. See p.290

* **Oudrif** An exceptional and remote retreat lodge on the edge of a gorge in the dry and dramatic redstone back country of the Cederberg. See p.309

▲ Dunes at De Hoop Nature Reserve

The Western Cape

The most mountainous and arguably the most beautiful of South Africa's provinces, the **Western Cape** is also the most popular area of the country for foreign tourists. Curiously, it's also the least African province. Visitors spend weeks here without exhausting its attractions, but frequently leave slightly disappointed, never having quite experienced an African beat. Of South Africa's nine provinces, only the Western Cape and the Northern Cape don't have an African majority; one person in five here is African, and the largest community, making up 55 percent of the population, are coloureds – people of mixed race descended from white settlers, indigenous Khoisan people and slaves from the East. Although the Western Cape appears to conform more closely to the developed world than any other part of the country, the impression is strictly superficial. Beneath the prosperous feel of the Winelands and the Garden Route lies a reality of developing-world poverty in **squatter camps** on the outskirts of well-to-do towns, and on some farms where nineteenth-century labour practices prevail, despite the end of apartheid.

Nevertheless, you can't fail to be moved by the sensuous physical beauty of the province's mountains, valleys and beaches. The **Winelands**, less than an hour from Cape Town, give full reign to the sybaritic pleasures of eating, drinking and visual feasting. Dutch colonial heritage reaches its peak in this region of gabled homesteads sitting among vineyards against a backdrop of slaty crags.

The best-known feature of the Western Cape is the **Garden Route**, a drive along the N2 that technically begins at **Mossel Bay**, where the freeway hits the coast, and continues east for 185km to **Storms River**. In reality it is taken as part of a journey between Cape Town and Port Elizabeth (see p.369), simply because these are the easiest places to catch flights and to pick up and drop off rental cars. The Garden Route proper can be driven in half a day, but to cover it so quickly would mean missing its essence, which can be found off the road in its coastal towns, lagoons, mountains and ancient forests, the highlight being the **Tsitsikamma National Park**, where the dark Storms River opens spectacularly into the Indian Ocean. **Public transport** along the Garden Route is better than anywhere in the country, partly because the route is a single stretch of freeway, and tour operators along the way have begun turning it into the country's most concentrated strip for packaged **adventure sports** and **outdoor activities**.

To the east of the Winelands, the **Breede River Valley** is a region usually bypassed along the N1 en route to Johannesburg, but featuring among its faceless fruit-farming towns some hideaways, such as Greyton and McGregor,

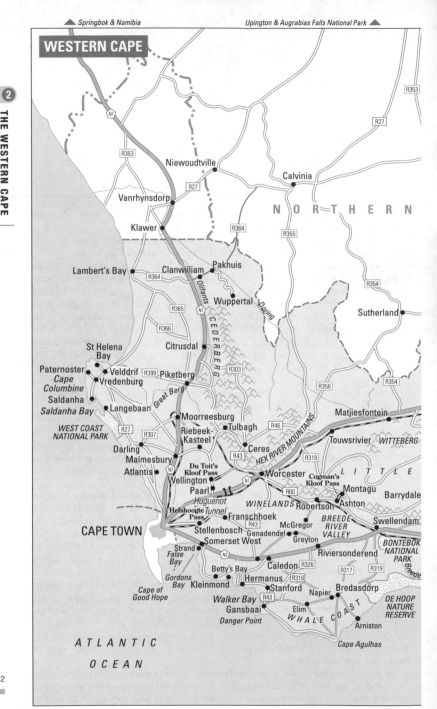

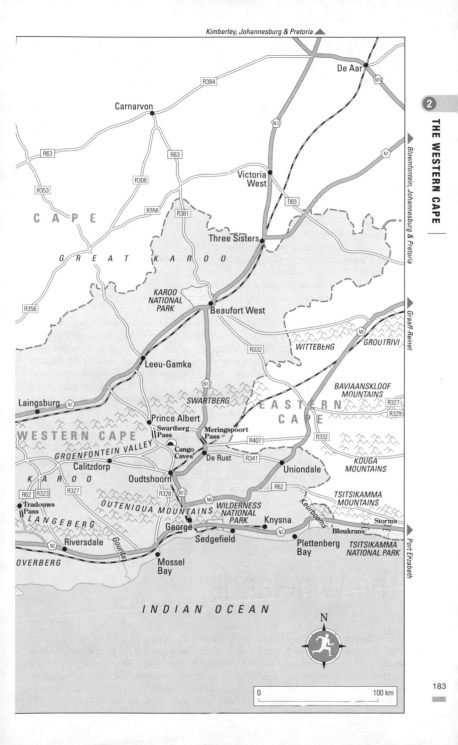

De Aar

N10

R384

Carnarvon

R63

R63

R308

R353

Victoria
West

R356   R381   R63

C A P E

G R E A T   K A R O O

Three Sisters

KAROO
NATIONAL
PARK

R356

Beaufort West

R332

WITTEBERG   GROOTRIVI

N9

Leeu-Gamka

N12

SWARTBERG

BAVIAANSKLOOF
MOUNTAINS

R327

R329

Laingsburg   N1

Prince Albert

E A S T E R N
C A P E

WESTERN CAPE

Swartberg
Pass

Meringspoort
Pass

R407

R332

GROENFONTEIN VALLEY

Cango
Caves

De Rust   R341

KOUGA
MOUNTAINS

Uniondale

K A R O O   Calitzdorp

R62   R323   R327

Oudtshoorn

R328   N12

R62

TSITSIKAMMA
MOUNTAINS

Tradouws
Pass

OUTENIQUA   MOUNTAINS

N9   WILDERNESS
NATIONAL
PARK

Keurbooms

LANGEBERG

Knysna

Storms

N2

Bloukrans

Gourits

George

Sedgefield

Plettenberg
Bay

TSITSIKAMMA
NATIONAL
PARK

N2   Riversdale

OVERBERG

Mossel
Bay

I N D I A N   O C E A N

N

0   100 km

favoured by Capetonians as weekend retreats. Though the region has been almost totally neglected by visitors in the past, some creative marketing has now literally put it on the map as the **Route 62**, most of which consists of the intriguing R62 back road tracing its way through the interior, linking **Little Karoo** towns between Cape Town and Port Elizabeth. The timeless landscapes of the Little Karoo, the curtain-raiser to the semi-desert covering one-third of South Africa's surface, is nowhere more rewarding nor more easily accessed than here. Less visited than it deserves, the Little Karoo is skirted by the N1 to the north and the N2 to the south, and offers a succession of dramatic – sometimes hair-raising – **passes** switchbacking across one mountain range after another.

The **Overberg** – roughly the area between **Arniston** and **Mossel Bay** along the coast, and as far inland as Swellendam – is another region that remains hidden behind the mountains during a hasty journey through. West of here, the **Whale Coast**, an angry stretch of Indian Ocean that has claimed hundreds of ships, is known for being the best area in the country for shore-based **whale-watching**, and there are a couple of pleasant coastal towns off the main routes along here. North of Cape Town, the less popular, remote and windswept **West Coast** is usually explored during the wild-flower months of August and September, when visitors converge on its centrepiece, the **West Coast National Park**. Its other major draw, 200km north of Cape Town on the N7, is the **Cederberg** mountain range, a rocky wilderness with hikes and hidden rock-art sites.

Apart from the annual explosion of wild flowers in the north, the Western Cape, as South Africa's **fynbos** region, really scores on wilderness and flora. The plants you'll glimpse from afar all along the coast and up every mountainside look like a nondescript grey-green blur of vegetation, but on closer examination reveal a rich kingdom of delicate flowering species rivalling the Amazon rainforest for biodiversity. Several national parks and nature reserves make excellent places to explore *fynbos*, as do all the hikes mentioned in this chapter, but you shouldn't expect to see much African wildlife here, apart from a few game sanctuaries off the Garden Route. Though most reserves have a few zebra or antelope, the big game disappeared many years ago – reflecting the fact that South Africa's longest-colonized province was also the first to taste the destructive power of firearms. By the same means, indigenous **Khoikhoi and San people** were virtually extinguished in the nineteenth century and **Africans** kept at a distance, some 1000km away on the "Eastern Frontier", which accounts for their relatively small numbers in the Western Cape.

The Winelands

South Africa has over a score of recognized wine routes extending to the Karoo and way into the Northern Cape, but the area known as the **Winelands** is restricted to the oldest wineries outside the Cape Peninsula, within a sixty-kilometre radius of Cape Town. The district contains the earliest European settlements at Stellenbosch, Paarl, Franschhoek and Somerset West, each with its own **wine route**, on which you travel from one estate to the next to taste the

Tackling the Winelands

With several hundred estates in the **Winelands**, the big question is which ones to visit. The wineries in our selection were chosen not primarily because they produce the best wine (although some are in the first rank), but for general interest – beautiful architecture or scenery – or just because they are fun. When planning your trip, bear in mind that although all the wineries offer tastings, many offer a lot more, such as restaurants, picnics and horse-riding. Choose an area to explore and don't try to visit too many wineries in a day unless you want to return home in a dizzy haze. Most estates charge a fee for a wine-tasting session (anywhere up to R25) and some only have tastings at specific times; see the individual accounts for more details.

If you plan on anything more than the briefest of tours, think about buying the annually updated *John Platter's South African Wine Guide* (®www.platteronline .com), which provides ratings of the produce of every winery in the country.

wines. On the hillsides and in the valleys around these towns you'll find a flawless blending of traditional Cape Dutch **architecture** with the landscape. The Winelands are best covered in a car, as half the pleasure is the drive through the countryside; without your own transport, you could take a day-trip to the Winelands with one of several Cape Town-based companies (see p.98).

The most satisfying of the Winelands towns is **Stellenbosch**, which enjoys an easy elegance, beautiful streetscapes, a couple of decent museums and plenty of visitor facilities. One of the region's scenic highlights is the drive along the R310 through the **Helshoogte Pass** between Stellenbosch and **Paarl**. The workaday farming town of the region, Paarl is credited as the place where Afrikaans first sprang to recognition, and has an Afrikaans language monument and a museum to honour the fact. Smallest of the Winelands towns, with a rural yet sophisticated feel, **Franschhoek** has the most magnificent setting at the head of a narrow valley, and has established itself as the culinary capital of the country. By contrast, the sprawling town of **Somerset West** has only two outstanding drawcards, **Vergelegen**, by far the most stunning of all the Winelands estates, which can be tacked onto a tour of the Stellenbosch wine route, and its neighbour **Morgenster**, which apart from producing top-notch wines also offers tastings of its award-winning olive oil and olives.

A growing number of wineries offer **lunches** or sell picnic hampers, which you can enjoy in their grounds – a great idea if you're travelling with children or simply want to drink in the mountainous views in a bucolic haze.

Stellenbosch

Dappled avenues of three-century-old oaks are the defining feature of **STELLENBOSCH**, 46km east of Cape Town – a fact reflected in its Afrikaans nickname Die Eikestad (the oak city). Street frontages of the same vintage, sidewalk cafés, water furrows and a European town layout centred on the Braak, a large village green, add up to a well-rooted urban texture that invites casual exploration. The city is the undisputed heart of the Winelands, having more urban attractions than either Paarl or Franschhoek, while at the same time being at the hub of the largest and oldest of the Cape **wine routes**.

The city is also home to Stellenbosch University, Afrikanerdom's most prestigious educational institution, which does something to enliven the atmosphere. But even the heady promise of plentiful alcohol and thousands of students haven't changed

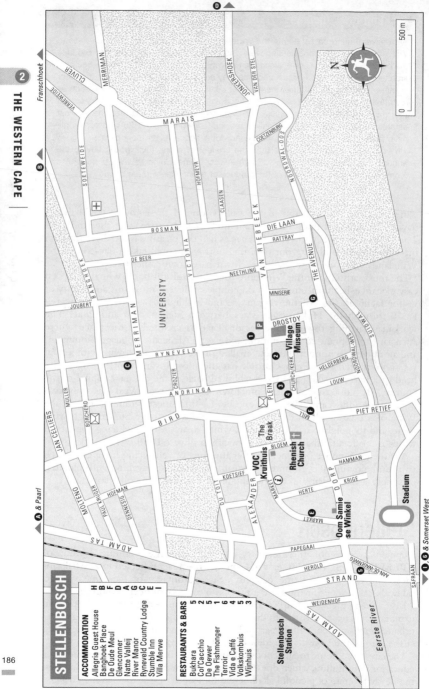

STELLENBOSCH

ACCOMMODATION

Allegria Guest House	H
Banghoek Place	B
De Oude Meul	F
Glenconner	D
Natte Vallej	A
River Manor	G
Ryneveld Country Lodge	C
Stumble Inn	E
Villa Merwe	I

RESTAURANTS & BARS

Bukhara	5
Col'Cacchio	2
De Oewer	5
The Fishmonger	1
Terroir	6
Vida e Caffé	4
Volkskombuis	5
Wijnhuis	3

0 500 m

the fact that at heart this is a conservative place, which was once the intellectual engine room of apartheid, and fostered the likes of Dr H.F. Verwoerd, the prime minister who dreamed up Grand Apartheid.

Some history

One of the first actions of **Simon van der Stel** after arriving at the Cape in November 1679 to take over as Dutch East India Company commander was to explore the area along the Eerste River (first river), where he came upon an enchanting little valley. Less than a month later it appeared on maps as Stellenbosch (Stel's bush), the first of several places dotted around the Cape which the governor was to name after himself or members of his family; another was Simonsberg overlooking the town.

Charged by the Dutch East India Company directors in the Netherlands with opening up the Cape interior, Van der Stel soon settled the first **free burghers** in Stellenbosch. Within eight years, sixty freehold grants had been made; within the next two decades, Stellenbosch had established itself as a prosperous, semi-feudal society dominated by landowners, and in 1702 the Danish traveller, Abraham Bogaert, admired how it had "grown with fine dwellings, and how great a treasure of wine and grain is grown here". By the end of the century there were over a thousand houses and some substantial burgher estates in and around Stellenbosch, many of which still exist.

Arrival and information

Metrorail **trains** (☏ 0800 65 64 63, ⓦ www.capemetrorail.co.za) travel between Cape Town and Stellenbosch roughly every two hours during the day, and take about an hour. Infrequent (and expensive) intercity buses from Cape Town and Port Elizabeth pass through Stellenbosch, calling at the train station.

The busy **tourist office**, about 1km from the station at 36 Market St (May–Aug Mon–Fri 9am–5pm, Sat 9.30am 2pm, Sun 10am–2pm; Sept–April Mon–Fri 8am–6pm, Sat 9am–5pm, Sun 10am–4pm; ☏ 021 883 3584, ⓦ www .stellenboschtourism.co.za), provides basic information on local attractions, and can supply the *Discover Stellenbosch on Foot* leaflet for R5, which describes a walking tour covering a daunting 62 sites, or direct you to another walking tour. Easy Rider Wine Tours, based at *Stumble Inn* backpacker lodge (see p.188), offers daytime packages to four wineries (R300), with cheese tasting at Fairview Estate and lunch thrown in.

Accommodation

Stellenbosch has no shortage of **places to stay**, from backpacker lodges to total luxury. Apart from a handful of out-of-town farmstays, all the accommodation is within easy walking distance of the town centre.

Allegria Guest House Cairngorm Rd, Stellenbosch ☏ 021 881 3389, ⓦ www.allegria.co.za. Small, well-run establishment on a country estate 8km west of Stellenbosch between two wine farms. Under the warm proprietorship of hospitable Dutch couple Jan and Annemarie, the guesthouse offers six rooms with three levels of luxury, a swimming pool and great views. ❷–❻

Banghoek Place 193 Banghoek Rd ☏ 021 887 0048. Slightly more upmarket sister hostel to

Stumble Inn (see p.188), with mostly en-suite double, twin and triple rooms that offer terrific value, and also three small dorms. Discount packages available that include two nights' accommodation plus a wine tour. Dorms ❶, doubles & triples ❷

De Oude Meul 10a Mill St (off Dorp St) ☏ 021 887 7085, ⓦ www.deoudemeul.snowball.co.za. Located in the middle of town on a fairly busy street, above an antique shop, these pleasing rooms are good value. ❹

Glenconner Jonkershoek Rd, 4km from centre ☎021 886 5120, ⓦwww.glenconner.co.za. Pretty cottages on a farm in a spectacular valley, tranquil and close to the walks in the Jonkershoek Nature Reserve. Breakfast can be taken under an old oak tree. Self-catering or B&B ❹

Natte Valleij On the R44, 12km north of town ☎021 875 5171, ⓦwww.nattevalleij.co.za. Guests have a choice of a large cottage sleeping six, or a smaller unit attached to an old wine cellar. There's a swimming pool, and breakfast is served on the veranda. ❸

River Manor 6–8 The Ave ☎021 887 9944, ⓦwww.rivermanor.com. Enjoy a totally romantic, if formal, stay in two historic houses with rose-petal strewn beds, oil lamps, plush dressing gowns and wicker chairs to laze on in the sun around the pool, with spa facilities on site for extra pampering. Discounts in the winter. ❻–❽

Ryneveld Country Lodge 67 Ryneveld St ☎021 887 4469, ⓦwww.ryneveldlodge.co.za. Gracious late nineteenth-century building, now a National Monument and furnished with Victorian antiques. The rooms are spotless, with the two best rooms upstairs leading onto a wooden deck. There are also three family cottages which sleep up to four, and a pool. ❹

Stumble Inn 12 Market St ☎021 887 4049, ⓦwww.stumbleinnstellenbosch.hostel.com. The town's best and oldest established hostel in two houses from the turn of the last century, with friendly, switched-on staff and a relaxed atmosphere. Just down the road from the tourist office, the hostel offers doubles, dorms and camping, and is also noted for its good-value tours (see p.187). Dorms ❶, rooms ❷

Villa Merwe 6 Cynaroides Rd, Paradyskloof ☎021 880 1185, ⓦwww.villamerwe.co.za. Three immaculate and comfortable rooms in the owner's modern house, each with its own entrance and bathroom, with a lounge, pool and garden. It's a 5min drive from the centre. ❹

The Town

Stellenbosch's attractions lie principally in its setting and streetscape; it's a lovely place to simply wander around and safe at night. The tourist office is a good place to start your explorations. Heading east up this road, you'll soon reach a whitewashed block that was the **VOC Kruithuis** (Jan–May & Sept–Dec Mon–Fri 9am–2pm), the Dutch East India Company's powder magazine, which houses a small and unprepossessing collection of four British uniforms, assorted rifles, some intriguing but unexplained laptop-sized cannons and powder kegs. From here, a right turn south down the side of the **Braak**, the large green occupying the centre of town, will take you past the **Rhenish Church** in Bloem Street, built in 1823 as a school for slaves and coloured people.

The Village Museum and Dorp Street

Head north up Ryneveld Street, and you'll encounter Stellenbosch's museum highlight, the extremely enjoyable **Village Museum** at no. 18 (Mon–Sat 9.30am–5pm, Sun 10am–5pm; R15), which cuts a cross section through the town's architectural and social heritage by means of four fortuitously adjacent historical dwellings from different periods, including the **Blettermanhuis**, an archetypal eighteenth-century Cape Dutch house. They're beautifully conserved and furnished in period style, and you'll meet the odd worker dressed in period costume. From the Village Museum, head back south into **Dorp Street**, Stellenbosch's best-preserved historic axis, well worth a slow stroll just to soak in the ambience of buildings, gables, oaks and roadside water furrows. Look out for **Krige's Cottages**, an unusual terrace of historic town houses at nos. 37–51, between Aan-de-Wagenweg and Krige Street. The houses were built as Cape Dutch cottages in the first half of the nineteenth century; Victorian features were added subsequently, resulting in an interesting hybrid, with gables housing Victorian attic windows and decorative Victorian verandas with filigree ironwork fronting the elegantly simple Cape Dutch facades.

▲ The Blettermanhuis at the Village Museum, Stellenbosch

Eating and drinking

You'll be spoilt for choices of good places to eat in Stellenbosch, both in the centre and on some of the surrounding estates. Many places have outdoor seating, and in the evenings the student presence ensures a relaxed and sometimes raucous drinking culture.

Bukhara Dorp and Bird sts ☎ 021 882 9133. Succulent North Indian dishes prepared in a kitchen behind a glass wall, in full view of diners. Prices are moderate or even steep, though portions are large. Favourites include butter chicken and tandoori lamb chops. Service is excellent and the ambience relaxed. Daily noon–3pm & 6–10.30pm.

Col'Cacchio Shop 8, Simonsplein Centre, Plein St. Better than average pizzeria, popular with students. Try the Morituri topped with bacon, chicken, feta, red pepper and avocado. Daily noon–11pm.

The Fishmonger Sanlam Building, Ryneveld St ☎ 021 887 7835. A superb seafood restaurant, reasonable value and with outdoor seating, though lacking in ambience. Mon & Tues noon–10pm, Wed noon–3.30pm & 6–10pm, Thurs–Sat noon–10pm & Sun noon–9pm.

Moyo Spier Lynedoch Rd (R310) ☎ 021 809 1133. An extravaganza of an eatery (one of four restaurants at Spier) in the gardens of one of the Western Cape's largest and most tourist-friendly wine estates. It's made to feel like a cross between an African village and a bedouin encampment, with seating for 1200 in gazebos, tents and tree houses, and the vast all-you-can-eat buffet brings together a dazzling array of flavours and dishes from across Africa. With live performance and optional face-painting thrown in, you can't help but enjoy yourself. Daily noon–4pm & 6pm till late.

Terroir Kleine Zalze Wine Estate, Strand Rd (R44) ☎ 021 880 8167. The culinary talk of the town, Terroir is some 12.5km from Stellenbosch on a wine and golf estate, with a formal but relaxed dining room and tables outside under shady oaks. French-inspired, the menu is based as far as possible on local organic produce, with a signature dish of belly of pork braised in ginger, soy and juniper berries served with smoked mash. Mon–Sat 12.30–2.30pm & 7–9.30pm, Sun lunch only.

Vida e Caffé On the corner of Bird and Kerk sts. Vibey Portuguese-style coffee shop in the middle of town. Part of a national chain, it boasts excellent service and coffee, while the clincher is the little slab of Lindt dark chocolate perched on the side of your saucer. Mon–Sat 8am–5pm & Sun 9am–4pm.

Volkskombuis and De Oewer Aan-de-Wagenweg, off Dorp St ☎ 021 887 2121. Two popular venues on the banks of the Eerste River under the same management. There's an eclectic range of dishes from North Africa and the Mediterranean at De Oewer, while platters of reasonably priced contemporary Cape Cuisine are the speciality of Volkskombuis. Mon–Sat noon–3pm & 6.30–10pm, Sun lunch only.

Wijnhuis On the corner of Church and Andringa sts ☎ 021 887 5844. At a place whose name translates as "wine house", it's no surprise that the wine list is longer than the menu. Regulars come to enjoy their tipple with Mediterranean seafood dishes, grilled meat or pastas, served in an old building with a light, contemporary feel. Wine tasting and buying wines is all part of the experience. Daily 8am–11pm.

The Stellenbosch wine estates

Stellenbosch was the first locality in the country to wake up to the marketing potential of a **wine route**. It launched its wine route in 1971, a tactic which has been hugely successful; today tens of thousands of visitors from all over the world are drawn here annually, making this the most toured area in the Winelands. Although the region accounts for only a fraction of South Africa's land under vine, its wine route is the most extensive in the country, comprising some two hundred establishments; apart from the tiny selection below (all of which are along a series of roads that radiate out from Stellenbosch) there are scores of other excellent places, which taken together would occupy months of exploration. All the wineries are clearly signposted off the main arteries.

Delaire on the Helshoogte Pass, 6km east of Stellenbosch along the R310 to Franschhoek ⓦ www.delairewinery.co.za. The restaurant here has the best views in the Winelands, looking through oaks across the Groot Drakenstein and Simonsig mountains and down into craggy valleys; the winery produces a couple of first-rate reds and whites. Mon–Fri 9am–5pm, Sat & Sun 10am–5pm; R15.

Jordan Vineyards 11.5km west of Stellenbosch off the R310 ⓦ www.jordanwines.com. A pioneer among the new-wave Cape wineries, Jordan's hi-tech cellar and modern tasting room is complemented by its friendly service. The drive

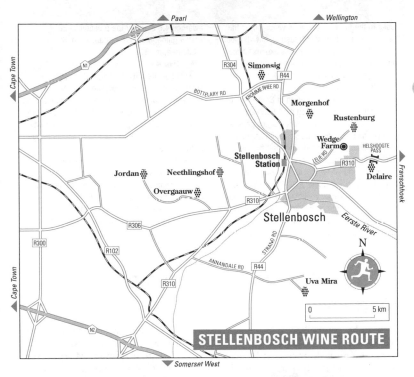

Stellenbosch
Station

Stellenbosch

STELLENBOSCH WINE ROUTE

0   5 km

there is half the fun, taking you into a *kloof*
bounded by vineyards that get a whiff of the sea
from both False Bay and Table Bay, which has
clearly done something for its output – it has a long
list of outstanding reds and whites. Mon–Fri
10am–4.30pm, Sat 9.30am–2.30pm & Sun
10am–2.30pm; R15, refundable with purchases.
Morgenhof 4km north of Stellenbosch on the
R44 ⓦ www.morgenhof.com. French-owned
château-style complex on the slopes of the
vine-covered Simonsberg, under the energetic
proprietorship of Anne Cointreau-Huchon (grand-
daughter of the founder of Remy Martin cognac).
Morgenhof has a light and airy tasting room with
a bar; among the numerous top-ranking wines
worth sampling are the Merlot, Cabernet
Sauvignon, Pinotage, Sauvignon Blanc,
Chardonnay and Chenin Blanc. Delicious light
lunches are served outside, topped off with ice
cream on the lawns. May–Oct Mon–Fri 9am–
4.30pm, Sat & Sun 10am–3pm; Nov–April Mon–
Fri 9.30am–5pm, Sat & Sun 10am–5pm; R10.
Neethlingshof 6.5km west of Stellenbosch on
Polkadraai Rd (the R306) ⓦ www.neethlingshof
.co.za. Centred around a beautifully restored Cape
Dutch manor dating back to 1814, reached down a

kilometre-long avenue of pines, Neethlingshof's
first vines were planted in 1692. The estate
produces very good wines, consistently hitting the
high notes with its stunning Weisser Riesling Noble
Late Harvest sweet dessert wines, a fine
Chardonnay and several excellent reds. Daily
9am–5pm; tasting R25.
Overgaauw 6.5km west of Stellenbosch, off the
M12. Notable for its elegant Victorian tasting room,
this pioneering estate produces reds of excellent
quality, among them Tria Corda, a claret-like wine,
and a high-flying Cabernet Sauvignon. Overgaauw
was the first winery in the country to produce
Merlots, and it's still the only one to make Sylvaner,
a well-priced, easy-drinking dry white. Mon–Fri
9am–5pm, Sat 10am–12.30pm; R10.
Rustenberg Wines Rustenberg Rd, 5km north of
Stellenbosch ⓦ www.rustenberg.co.za. One of
the closest estates to Stellenbosch, Rustenberg is
also one of the most alluring, reached after a
drive through orchards, sheep pastures and
tree-lined avenues. An unassuming working farm,
it has a romantic pastoral atmosphere, in
contrast to its architecturally stunning, hi-tech
tasting room in the former stables. The first vines
were planted here in 1692, but the viniculture

looks to the future. Most of its wines under the Rustenberg label are worth tasting, but also look out for highly drinkable and less expensive reds and whites under the Brampton brand – its second label. Mon–Fri 9am–4.30pm, Sat 10am–1.30pm; free).

Simonsig Estate 9.5km north of Stellenbosch, off Kromme Rhee Rd, which runs between the R44 and the R304 ⓦ www.simonsig.co.za. The winery has a relaxed outdoor tasting area under vine-covered pergolas, offering majestic views back to Stellenbosch of hazy stone-blue mountains and vineyards. Its vast range of first-class wines includes its cutting-edge Red Hill Pinotage, Kaapse Vonkel sparkling wine (this was the first estate in the country to produce a bottle-fermented bubbly some three decades back) and the Merindol Syrah, which was

awarded 4.5 stars by the prestigious 2007 *Platter* guide. Mon–Fri 8.30am–5pm, Sat 8.30am–4pm; R15.

🏃 **Uva Mira** about 8km south of Stellenbosch, off Annandale Rd, which spurs off the R44 ⓦ www.uvamira.co.za. Enchanting boutique winery, worth visiting just for the winding drive halfway up the Helderberg. The highly original tasting room, despite being newly built, gives the appearance of a gently decaying historic structure, and there are unsurpassed views from the deck across mountainside vineyards to False Bay some 50km away – on a clear day you can even see Robben Island. The flagship wine is a highly rated red blend, but it's the single-vineyard Chardonnay that earned Uva Mira 4.5 stars in the 2007 *Platter* guide. Mon–Fri 8am–5pm & Sat 10am–4pm; R20.

Somerset West, Vergelegen and Morgenster

The only compelling reasons to trawl out to the unpromising town of **SOMERSET WEST**, 50km east of Cape Town along the N2, are for **Vergelegen** on Lourensford Road, and its immediate neighbour **Morgenster**, which are officially part of the Helderberg wine route, but can easily be included as an extension to a visit to Stellenbosch, just 14km to the north.

Vergelegen and Morgenster

An absolute architectural treasure as well as an estate producing a stunning range of wines, **Vergelegen** (daily 9.30am–4pm; entrance R10; wine tasting R2–10 per glass; ⓦ www.vergelegen.co.za) represents a notorious episode of corruption and the arbitrary abuse of power at the Cape in the early years of Dutch East India Company rule. Built by Willem Adriaan van der Stel, who became governor in 1699 after the retirement of his father Simon, the estate formed a grand Renaissance complex in the middle of the wild backwater that was the Cape at the beginning of the eighteenth century. Van der Stel acquired the land illegally and used Dutch East India Company slaves to build Vergelegen, as well as company resources to farm vast tracts of land in the surrounding areas. At the same time he abused his power as governor to corner most of the significant markets at the Cape. When this was brought to the notice of the Dutch East India Company in the Netherlands, Van der Stel was sacked and Vergelegen was ordered to be destroyed to discourage future miscreant governors. It's believed that the destruction was never fully carried out and the current building is thought to stand on the foundations of the original.

Vergelegen was the only wine estate visited by the British queen during her 1995 state visit to South Africa – a good choice, as there's enough here to occupy even a monarch for an easy couple of hours. The **interpretive centre**, just across the courtyard from the shop at the building entrance, provides a useful history and background to the estate. Next door, the **wine-tasting centre** (open Nov–April) offers a professionally run sampling with a brief talk through each label. The **homestead**, which was restored in 1917 to its current state by Lady Florence Phillips, wife of a Johannesburg mining magnate, can also be visited. Its pale facade, reached along an axis through an octagonal garden that dances with butterflies in summer, has a classical triangular gable and pilaster-decorated doorways. Massive grounds planted with chestnuts and camphor trees and ponds around every corner make this one of the most serene places in the Cape.

Morgenster

Apart from its exquisite rustic setting, the tasting room at **Morgenster**, Vergelegen's immediate neighbour (Mon–Fri 10am–5pm, Sat & Sun 10am–4pm; R10 for wine tasting, R10 for olive tasting; ⓦ www.morgenster.co.za), has a veranda that looks onto a lovely lake with hazy mountains in the distance. Its two stellar blended reds aside, the estate offers the unusual addition of olive tasting, with three types of olive, three types of oil (including an award-winning cold-pressed extra virgin olive oil) and some delicious olive paste.

Paarl

Although **PAARL** is attractively ensconced in a fertile valley brimming with historical monuments, at heart it's a parochial *dorp*, lacking either the sophistication of Stellenbosch or the striking setting and trendiness of Franschhoek. It can claim some virtue, however, from being a prosperous farming centre that earns its keep from the agricultural light industries – grain silos, canneries and flour mills – on the north side of town, and the cornucopia of grapes, guavas, olives, oranges and maize grown on the surrounding farms. Despite its small-town feel, Paarl has the largest municipality in the Winelands, with its most exclusive areas on the vined slopes of **Paarl Mountain** overlooking the town.

Some history

In 1657, just five years after the establishment of the Dutch East India Company refreshment station on the Cape Peninsula, a party under **Abraham Gabbema** arrived in the Berg River Valley to look for trading opportunities with the Khoikhoi, and search for the legendary gold of Monomotapa. They obviously had treasure on the brain, because on waking after a rainy night to the sight of the silvery dome of granite dominating the valley, they dubbed it Peerlbergh (pearl mountain), which in its modified form, **Paarl**, became the name of the town.

Thirty years later, the commander of the Cape, Simon van der Stel, granted strips of the Khoikhoi lands on the slopes of Paarl Mountain to French Huguenot and Dutch settlers. By the time Paarl was officially granted town status in 1840, it was still an outpost at the edge of the Drakenstein Mountains, a flourishing wagon-making and last-stop provisioning centre. The town holds deep historical significance for the two competing political forces that forged modern South Africa. **Afrikanerdom** regards Paarl as the hallowed ground on which their language movement was born in 1875 (see box, p.195), while for the **ANC** (and the international community), Paarl will be remembered as the place from which Nelson Mandela made the final steps of his long walk to freedom, when he walked out of **Groot Drakenstein Prison** (then called Victor Verster) in 1990.

Arrival, information and accommodation

Metrorail and Spoornet **trains** from Cape Town pull in at Huguenot Station in Lady Grey Street at the north end of town, near to the central shops. Greyhound

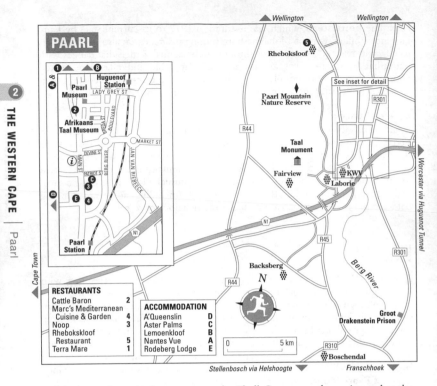

PAARL

Cape Town

RESTAURANTS
Cattle Baron	2
Marc's Mediterranean Cuisine & Garden	4
Noop	3
Rhebokskloof Restaurant	5
Terra Mare	1

ACCOMMODATION
A'Queenslin	D
Aster Palms	C
Lemoenkloof	B
Nantes Vue	A
Rodeberg Lodge	E

0   5 km

N

Stellenbosch via Helshoogte   Franschhoek

and Intercape intercity **buses** stop at the Shell Garage, on the main road at the south end of town. The garage is about 2km from the **tourist office**, 216 Main St, on the corner with Plantasie Street (Mon–Fri 8am–5pm, Sat 9am–4pm & Sun 10am–2pm; ☏021 863 4937, ⊛www.paarlonline.com), which has a selection of good **maps** and can help with finding **accommodation**.

Most places to stay in town are either along or just off Main Street, many in historic buildings, with camping and chalets just outside town for the cheapest stay.

A'Queenslin 2 Queen St ☏082 577 0635, ⊜aqueenslin@telkomsa.net. Two en-suite rooms with their own entrances and garden spaces, and three double rooms that share a bathroom, in a split-level family home set in a quiet part of town, bounded on one side by vineyards and towered over by Paarl Rock. Limited self-catering is possible – there's a fridge and microwave. Doubles ②, en suites ③

Aster Palms 3 Patriot St ☏021 872 0895, ⊛www.asterpalms.co.za. Hospitable B&B in a 1920s house a couple of blocks from the tourist office, with four airy double rooms and a lovely back garden with a solar-heated swimming pool. ④

Lemoenkloof 396a Main St ☏021 872 3782, ⊛www.lemoenkloof.co.za. A comfortable and

tranquil owner-run guesthouse in a National Monument, with 1820s Cape Dutch and Victorian features, a TV and fridge in each room, and a secluded swimming pool. ④

Nantes Vue 56 Mill St ☏021 872 7311, ⊛www.nantes-paarl.co.za. En-suite doubles and a cottage that sleeps three, decorated with artistic flair in a friendly Cape Dutch guesthouse, also a National Monument. Breakfast is served on the veranda overlooking a small garden. ④

Rodeberg Lodge 74 Main St ☏021 863 3202, ⊛www.rodeberglodge.co.za. Plain period furnishing gives the six en-suite rooms in this huge, centrally located Victorian town house a cool, spacious atmosphere. Ask for a room at the back if traffic noise bothers you. ④

The town and around

Unlike Stellenbosch and Franschhoek, which are ideal for wandering, the best preserved and oldest historical frontage in Paarl stretches for some 2km down oak-lined **Main Street**. It's here you'll find the **Paarl Museum** at no. 303 (Mon–Fri 9am–5pm, Sat 9am–1pm; R5), in a handsome, thatched Cape Dutch building. The contents don't quite match up to the exterior, but include some reasonably enlightening panels on the architecture of the town, and several eccentric glass display cases of Victorian bric-a-brac. Post-apartheid transformation has introduced some coverage of the indigenous Khoisan populations of the area and the changes that came with European colonization, including slavery.

The history of Afrikaans

Afrikaans is South Africa's third mother tongue, spoken by fifteen percent of the population and outstripped only by Zulu and Xhosa. English, by contrast, is the mother tongue of only nine percent of South Africans, and ranks fifth in the league of the eleven official languages.

Signs of the emergence of a new southern African dialect appeared as early as 1685, when H.A. Van Rheede, a Dutch East India Company official from the Netherlands, complained about a "distorted and incomprehensible" version of Dutch being spoken in the Drakenstein Valley around modern-day Paarl. By absorbing English, French, German, Malay and indigenous words and expressions, the language continued to diverge from mainstream Dutch, and by the nineteenth century was widely used in the Cape by both white and coloured speakers, but was regarded by the elite as an inferior creole, unsuitable for literary or official communication.

Ironically, it was the British defeat of the Afrikaner republics in the second Anglo-Boer War at the turn of the twentieth century that provided the catalyst for a mass white Afrikaans movement. The scorched-earth policy of the British had driven many Boers from the lands and produced a demoralized and semi-literate Boer underclass, while the official British policy of anglicizing South Africa helped to unite the white Afrikaner proletariat and elite against the common English enemy.

In 1905, **Gustav Preller**, a young journalist from a working-class Boer background, set about reinventing Afrikaans as a "white man's language". He aimed to eradicate the stigma of its "coloured" ties by substituting Dutch words for those with non-European origins. Preller began publishing the first of a series of populist magazines written in Afrikaans and glorifying Boer history and culture. Through this **Second Language Movement**, whites took spiritual control over Afrikaans and the pressure grew for its recognition as an official language, which came in 1925.

When the National Party took power in 1948, its apartheid policy went hand in hand with promoting the interests of its Afrikaans-speaking supporters and a concerted programme of the **upliftment of poor whites** began. Afrikaners were installed throughout the civil service and filled most posts in the public utilities. Despite the fact that there were more coloured than white Afrikaans speakers, the language quickly became associated with the **apartheid** establishment. This had electrifying consequences in the 1970s, when the government attempted to enforce Afrikaans as the sole medium of instruction in African schools, leading directly to the **Soweto uprising** in 1976, which marked the beginning of the end for Afrikaner hegemony in South Africa. The repressive period throughout the 1970s and 1980s and the forced removals under the Group Areas Act led many coloured Afrikaans speakers to adopt English in preference to their mother tongue, which they felt was tainted by apartheid.

There are few signs that Afrikaans will die out. Under the new constitution, existing **language rights** can't be diminished, which effectively means that Afrikaans will continue to be almost as widely used as before. It is now as much with coloured as white people that the future of the *taal* (language) rests.

South down Main Street away from the museum, a left turn into Van der Lingen Street and then a right into Pastorie Street brings you to the **Afrikaans Taal Museum** (Mon–Fri 9am–4pm; R10), which chronicles the development of the Afrikaans language (see box, p.195). The museum's displays are in Afrikaans, but a leaflet available from the reception desk gives an English summary of exhibits.

The only other sight of any interest in Paarl itself is the grandiose **Taal Monument** (daily 9am–5pm), the apartheid-era memorial to the Afrikaans language, standing just outside the centre on the top of Paarl Mountain. To get there, drive south along Main Street past the head office of the KWV, and follow the signs to your right up the slope of the mountain. The monument used to be as important a place of pilgrimage for Afrikaners as the Voortrekker Monument in Pretoria. From the coffee and curio shop you can admire a truly magnificent panorama across to the Cape Peninsula and False Bay in one direction and the Winelands ranges in the other.

Groot Drakenstein (Victor Verster) Prison

Roughly 9km south of the N1 as it cuts through Paarl, along the R301 (the southern extension of Jan van Riebeeck Street), stands the **Victor Verster Prison**. Renamed **Groot Drakenstein** in 2000, this was Nelson Mandela's last place of incarceration. It was through the gates at Victor Verster that Mandela walked to his freedom on February 11, 1990, and it was here that the first images of him in 27 years were bounced around the world – under the Prisons Act not even old pictures of him could be published throughout his incarceration. The working jail looks rather like a boys' school fronted by rugby fields beneath hazy mountains, and there's something bizarre about seeing a prison sign nonchalantly slipped in among all the vineyard and wine-route pointers.

Eating and drinking

A working town, Paarl has none of the Winelands foodie pretensions of Franschhoek, but you'll find a number of places along the main street for a decent snack and coffee or a meal, as well as a couple of outstanding places in the surrounding countryside, with great views of the vineyards and mountains.

Cattle Baron Gymnasium St ☎021 872 2000. Reliable family-oriented steakhouse that specializes in beef, chicken and fish. Mon–Fri noon–3.30pm & 6–11.30pm; Sat 6–midnight; Sun noon–3.30pm & 6–10.30pm.

Marc's Mediterranean Cuisine & Garden 129 Main St ☎021 863 3980. One of Paarl's most popular casual eateries, Marc's dishes up a simple but tasty menu that includes paella, meze, couscous, seafood and lamb, served in a converted historic house with a large outdoor area dotted with sun umbrellas and lemon trees. Mon–Sat 6.30–9.30pm; daily noon–2.30pm.

Noop 217 Main St. Supercool pavement wine bar with an impressively long list of wines by the glass and some great takes on simple favourites such as burgers, biryanis and pies, inspired, says the owner, by the old French stock pot. Mon–Fri 7.30am–11pm; Sat 7.30am–3pm.

Rhebokskloof Restaurant Rhebokskloof winery, Rhebokskloof Minor Rd ☎021 869 8386. Intimate outdoor establishment recommended for the outstanding setting as well as the food. Overlooking a lake, it has a shaded terrace for summer lunches, offering gourmet meals with thrilling combinations of flavours, both Cape and international. It's also a good place for morning or afternoon teas. Daily 9am–11.30am, noon–5pm & 6pm till late.

Terra Mare 90a Main St ☎021 863 4805. Straightforward food, such as Karoo lamb chops with spring rolls or pasta and pesto, using local ingredients and infused with considerable flair, served in a glass-and-steel restaurant with great sweeping views of the Paarl Valley. Tues–Sat 10am–2pm & 6–10pm.

Horse and quad-bike trails

Wine Valley Horse Trails (☎021 869 8687 or 083 226 8735, ⓦwww.horsetrails-sa.co
.za), based at Rhebokskloof, offers one- to four-hour equestrian trails for novices and
experts through the surrounding countryside – a choice spot for some riding. Prices
start from R250 for a one-hour trail. Longer trails are restricted to experienced riders, but
a four-hour package of a ride plus a conducted wine-tasting at the estate is available to
novices. They also do quad-bike trails which start at R250 for a one-hour trail.

The wineries

There are a couple of notable wineries in Paarl itself, but most are on farms in the
surrounding countryside. Boschendal, one of the most popular of these, is
officially on the Franschhoek wine route, but is in easy striking distance of Paarl.

▲ The goat tower at the Fairview wine estate

Backsberg Estate 22km south of Paarl on Simondium Rd (WR1) ⓦ www.backsberg.co.za. Notable as the first carbon-neutral wine estate in South Africa, Backsberg, which has been owned and run by the Back family for generations, hasn't sacrificed quality for environmental friendliness – it produces some top-ranking red blends, and a delicious Chardonnay, in its Babylons Toren and Black Label ranges. Outdoor seating, with views of the rose garden and vineyard on the slopes of the Simonsberg, makes this busy estate a nice place to while away some time. There's also a restaurant and a maze to get lost in. Mon–Fri 8am–5pm, Sat 9.30am–4.30pm, Sun 10.30am–4.30pm; R10.

Fairview Suid Agter Paarl Rd, on the southern fringes of town ⓦ www.fairview.co.za. One of the most fun of all the Paarl estates (especially for families), with a resident population of goats who clamber up the spiral tower, featured in the estate's emblem, at the entrance. A deli sells sausages and cold meats for picnics on the lawn, and you can also sample and buy the goat's, sheep's and cow's cheeses made on the estate. As far as wine tasting goes, Fairview is an innovative, family-run place, but it can get a bit hectic when the tour buses roll in. The vast array of wines includes a range of first-class Shirazes and a top-ranking Pinotage. Mon–Fri 8.30am–5pm, Sat 8.30am–4pm, Sun 9.30am–4pm; R10.

Laborie Taillefert St ⓦ www.laborie.co.za. One of the most impressive Paarl wineries, all the more remarkable for being right in town. The beautiful manor is fronted by a rose garden, acres of close-cropped lawns, historic buildings and oak trees – all towered over by the Taal Monument. There's a truly wonderful tasting room with a balcony that jetties out over the vineyards trailing up Paarl Mountain. Apart from a top-drawer Shiraz, it also produces a marvellous dry Methode Cap Classique (champagne-style) sparkler made exclusively from Chardonnay grapes, and Pineau de Laborie, a wickedly delicious Pinotage-based dessert wine. May–Sept Mon–Sat 9am–5pm, Oct–April Mon–Sun 9am–5pm; R10 for five wines.

Rhebokskloof Signposted off the R45, 11.5km northwest of Paarl ⓦ www.rhebokskloof.co.za. A highly photogenic wine estate, and popular wedding venue, Re-hebokskloof sits at the foot of sculptural granite koppies overlooking a shallow kloof that borders on the mountain nature reserve. The estate's renowned restaurant (see p.196) overlooks an artificial lake with swans. Top of its extensive range are a Cabernet Sauvignon and a Chardonnay. Horse and quad-bike trails are also operated from Rhebokskloof (see box, p.197). Daily 9am–5pm; tasting R25 which includes snacks.

Franschhoek

Between 1688 and 1700 about two hundred **French Huguenots**, desperate to escape religious persecution in France, accepted a Dutch East India Company offer of passage to the Cape and the grant of lands. They made contact with the area's earliest settlers, groups of **Khoi herders**. Conflict between the French newcomers and the Khoi followed familiar lines, with the white settlers gradually dispossessing the herdsmen, forcing them either further into the hinterland or into servitude on their farms. The establishment of white hegemony was swift and by 1713 the area was known as *de france hoek*. Though French-speaking died out within a generation because of explicit Company policy, many of the estates here are still known by their original French names. **FRANSCHHOEK** itself, 33km from Stellenbosch and 29km from Paarl, occupies parts of the original farms of La Cotte and Cabrière and is relatively young, having been established around a church built in 1833.

If sybaritic indulgence – eating, drinking and memorable lodgings – is what the Winelands is really about, then Franschhoek is the place that does it best. Despite being a fairly small *dorp*, it has managed to establish itself as the culinary capital of the Western Cape, if not the whole country. Its late Victorian and more recent Frenchified rustic architecture, the terrific setting (it's hemmed in on three sides by mountains), the vineyards down every other backstreet, and some vigorous myth-making have created a place you can really lose yourself in, a set piece that unashamedly draws its inspiration from Provence.

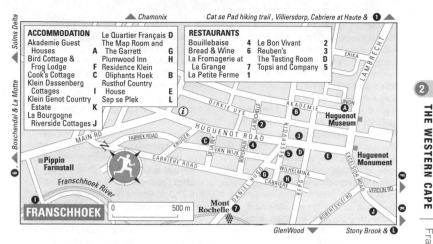

Arrival, information and accommodation

There's no public transport to Franschhoek or in the town itself. The buzzing **tourist office** is on Huguenot Road (summer Mon–Fri 9am–5pm, Sat & Sun 10am–6pm; winter Mon–Fri 9am–5pm, Sat & Sun 10am–4pm; ☏021 876 3603, ⓦ www.franschhoek.org.za), the main road through town. At no. 68, just north of the junction with Kruger Street, it can provide activities in the area and some excellent maps of the village and its winelands.

Accommodation

On the whole, guesthouse **accommodation** here is on the pricey side, but the rooms are of high quality and frequently in unparalleled settings; budget accommodation is hard to find, but there are a couple of reasonably priced self-catering cottages (listed here).

Akademie Guest Houses 5 Akademie St ☏021 876 3027, ⓔ www.aka.co.za. A beautiful room with a balcony and three characterful cottages (one of which is actually a double-storey house with a wraparound balcony and an outdoor bath) decorated with original artworks and each with its own garden and pond. Privacy is high on the agenda. There's also a huge room with a balcony. ⑥–⑧

Bird Cottage and Frog Lodge Verdun Rd, 4.5km from town ☏021 876 2136, ⓔ cindy@kingsley.co .za. Two very artistically furnished cottages surrounded by beautiful indigenous gardens close to the mountains in the midst of farmland. About as remote as you'll find this close to Franschhoek and very good value. ②

Cook's Cottage On the corner of De La Rey and Van Wyk sts ☏021 876 4229, ⓦ www .cookscottage.co.za. Spacious, beautifully decorated double-storey Victorian house in the centre of town with two bedrooms and a huge open-plan kitchen, dining room and lounge with a fireplace. Sleeps up to four people. R1300.

Klein Dassenberg Cottages off Huguenot Rd ☏021 876 2107, ⓦ www.kleindassenberg.co.za. Self-catering cottages in a peaceful and beautiful setting. Two of the cottages are ideal for a couple, while the other pair sleeps four and can accommodate families. Minimum two nights' stay over weekends. ③

Klein Genot Country Estate Green Valley Rd ☏021 876 2738, ⓦ www.kleingenot.com. Indulgent boutique lodgings in huge grounds away from the main drag, done out in *boere* baroque style – pastiche Cape Dutch architecture, thatched roofs, heavy drapes and walls dripping with original South African artwork. Rooms are arranged along the length of a koi pond, whose fishy inhabitants poke their heads out to greet guests. There's a spa on site with three therapy rooms. ⑧

La Bourgogne Riverside Cottages Excelsior Rd ☏021 876 3245, ⓦ www.labourgogne.co.za. Six converted labourers' cottages set in indigenous gardens along a river on a working fruit farm. ④

199

Le Quartier Français 16 Huguenot Rd ☎ 021 876 2151, ⓦ www.lequartier.co.za. A luxurious place with six suites (two with their own private walled garden and pool) and fifteen huge rooms decorated with sunny fabrics, all arranged around herb and flower gardens and a swimming pool. Child-friendly. Rated one of the world's top hundred hotels in 2007 by *Travel & Leisure* magazine. Also has one of the consistently best restaurants in the country (see p.202). ❽–❾

The Map Room and The Garrett 21 Cabrière St ☎ 021 876 4229, ⓦ www.cookscottage.co.za. Two adjoining and imaginatively decorated self-catering units in the centre of the village. *The Garrett* makes a cosy spot for a couple with great views and its own private garden with a pool, while the double-storey *Map Room*, which also sleeps two, has a more spacious feel with six folding doors that open onto a terrace. ❻

Plumwood Inn 11 Cabrière St ☎ 021 876 3883, ⓦ www.plumwoodinn.com. Unfailingly excellent boutique guesthouse which makes a break from Franschhoek's Francophilia with its ethnic African-inspired decor. Detail is everything – from the custom-made cotton tablecloths to the luxurious beds covered with a sea of cushions, and impeccable service from Dutch owners Roel and Lucienne Rutten. ❺

Residence Klein Oliphants Hoek 14 Akademie St ☎ 021 876 2566, ⓦ www.kleinoliphantshoek.co.za. Atmospheric eight-roomed guesthouse in a former double-storey Victorian mission station, where the massive reception room has soaring ceilings and the classrooms and missionary's quarters have been turned into bedrooms of varying size and luxury. The morning meal is taken in the breakfast room and adjoining terrace which overlooks a formal herb and rose garden. ❹–❼

Rusthof Country House 12 Huguenot St ☎ 021 876 3762, ⓦ www.rusthof.com. Modern eight-roomed guesthouse along the main drag (although it doesn't feel like it) within spitting distance of some of Franschhoek's top eateries. Rooms open onto a rose garden. Service is superb. ❻–❼

Sep se Plek Excelsior Rd ☎ 083 459 9534 or 083 444 2477 ⓔ ladboer@mweb.co.za. Possibly the only bargain you'll find in Franschhoek in the form of three fully equipped, two-bedroom cottages on the edge of a small tranquil tree-lined lake on a working fruit farm. ❷

The town and around

Away from the wining and dining, Franschhoek's attractions include hiking, horse-riding or cycling in the valley, or visiting the institutionalized Huguenot Monument and adjacent museum, which together occupy a prime position at the head of Huguenot Road, where it forms a T-junction with Lambrecht Street. The **Huguenot Monument** consists of three skinny, interlocking arches symbolizing the Holy Trinity, while the **Huguenot Memorial Museum** (Mon–Sat 9am–5pm & Sun 2–5pm; R5) gives comprehensive coverage of Huguenot history, culture and of their contribution to modern South Africa.

The best **hike** in the vicinity is the Cat se Pad (Cat's Path), which starts on your left just under 1km from the museum as you head out of town up the Franschhoek Pass. The walk leads into *fynbos* with proteas, and gives instant access to the mountains surrounding the valley, with good views. The first two-kilometre section gets you to the top of the pass, and you can keep going for another 10km in the direction of Villiersdorp (though you don't actually reach it).

A great way to take in the beauty of Franschhoek (and some wine) is in the saddle – a couple of operators offer guided **equestrian tours**, for about R100 an hour, both taking in Rickety Bridge and Mont Rochelle wineries, with more straightforward outrides or longer or purely scenic rides also available. Contact Mont Rochelle Equestrian Centre, Mont Rochelle Estate (☎ 083 300 4368), or Paradise Stables, Roberstsvlei Rd (☎ 021 876 2160 ⓦ www.paradisestables.co.za).

Museum van de Caab

Twelve kilometres north of Franschhoek along the R45, at the Solms Delta Wine Estate (see opposite), the highly recommended **Museum van de Caab** (daily 9am–5pm; free) gives a condensed and riveting slice through South African vernacular history as manifested on the farm and its surrounds. Housed alongside the atmospherically understated tasting room in the original 1740s gabled Cape Dutch cellar, the display begins with Stone Age artefacts found on the site and goes on to trace the arrival of the aboriginal Khoisan people, their colonization by Europeans, the introduction of slavery and how this eventually evolved into the apartheid system and its eventual demise.

The wineries

Franschhoek's **wineries** are small enough and sufficiently close together to make it a breeze to visit two or three in a morning. Heading north through town from the Huguenot Monument, you'll find most of the wineries signposted off Huguenot Road and its extension, Main Road; the rest are off Excelsior Road and the Franschhoek Pass Road.

Cabrière at Haute Cabrière About 2km from town along the Franschhoek Pass Rd ⓦ www .cabriere.co.za. Atmospheric winery that appears to have been tunnelled into the mountainside by Niebelungen – in fact it covers over an old quarry – with vaulted roofs that feel like they've been there forever with rough-hewn stairs winding down into the cellar. It's notable for its Pinot Noirs and colourful wine-maker Achim von Arnim, whose presence guarantees an eventful visit; try to catch him or one of his sons when they demonstrate sabrage – slicing off the upper neck of a bubbly bottle with a sabre, sending flying the neatly detached cork encased in the severed top ring of glass. Mon–Fri 9am–4.30pm, Sat 10am–4pm; R30.

GlenWood Robertsvlei Rd, signposted off the R45 ⓦ www.glenwoodvineyards.co.za. Small winery in a beautiful setting about ten-or-so minutes' drive from the village throng, which feels surprisingly remote; vineyard and cellar tours are frequently conducted by the owner. Mon–Fri 11am–4.30pm plus Sept–April Sat & Sun 11am–3pm; tasting R20, tasting and cellar tour R30.

Mont Rochelle Dassenberg Rd ⓦ www .montrochelle.co.za. Set against the Klein Dassenberg, Mont Rochelle has one of the most stunning settings in Franschhoek and an unusual cellar in a converted nineteenth-century fruit-packing shed, edged by eaves decorated with fretwork, stained-glass windows and chandeliers. A wholly black-owned winery – unusual for South Africa – its best wines are its whites. Daily 10am–6pm; R15.

Solms Delta Wine Estate & Museum 13km north of Franschhoek along the R45 ⓦ www.solms-delta.co.za. Pleasingly bucolic Solms produces unusual and consistently outstanding wines which, on a summer's day, you can taste under ancient oaks at the edge of the vineyards. You can also order a picnic basket to enjoy on the banks of the stream that traces the estate's boundary. There's a fascinating museum here too (see opposite). Half the profits from the wines produced here go into a trust that benefits residents of the farm and the Franschhoek Valley. Daily 9am–5pm; free.

Stony Brook Vineyards About 4km from Franschhoek, off Excelsior Rd ⓦ www .stonybrook.co.za. Family-run boutique winery, with just 140,000 square metres under vine, that produces first-rate wines, including its acclaimed flagship Ghost Gum Cabernet Sauvignon, which takes its name from a magnificent old tree outside the house and informal tasting room. Tastings are convivial affairs conducted by the owners. Mon–Fri 10am–3pm & Sat 10am–1pm; R20.

Eating and drinking

Eating and drinking is what Franschhoek is all about, so plan on sampling at least one or two of its excellent **restaurants**, some of which rate among the country's best. Franschhoek's cuisine is coming of age and has expanded from its French-inspired roots to incorporate Asian, South African and other influences. Restaurants in town are concentrated along Huguenot Road, but there are a number of excellent alternatives in the more rustic environment of the surrounding wine estates. **Booking** is essential.

🏊 **Bouillebaisse** 38 Huguenot St ☎ 021 876 4430. Performance cooking at its best turns great food into a wonderful evening's entertainment at this intimate bistro, where the galley kitchen, in full view, runs the length of the eatery. Although there are main courses, the strongly Asian-influenced menu is best enjoyed tapas-style – a range of flavours, served as small helpings. Ask for ringside seats – and on no account miss out on the home-made sorbets: lime-basil, orange-sweet chilli and ginger-lemongrass. Mon–Sat 10am–10pm.

Bread & Wine Môreson Farm, Happy Valley Rd, La Motte ☎ 021 876 3692. Signposted off the R45 is this genial and child-friendly venue surrounded by lemon orchards and vineyards. It serves imaginative modern Mediterranean-style country cuisine lunches (try the braised tomatoes with aubergine ravioli) accompanied by a variety of breads and the estate's own wines. Daily noon–3pm.

La Fromagerie at La Grange 13 Daniel Hugo St. Sample platters of South African cheeses accompanied by local wines in the gardens here, overlooking vineyards, or sit down for tea or lunches that include savoury tarts, terrines and soufflés. Daily for lunch and tea as well as cheese tasting noon–4pm. On summer weekends this family-friendly spot becomes a buzzing jazz venue.

La Petite Ferme Franschhoek Pass Rd ☎ 021 876 3016. A multiple award-winner rated by *Condé Nast Traveler* as one of the world's top fifteen "best value" establishments, boasting delicately flavoured, rustic contemporary cuisine and unparalleled views across a vineyard-clad valley, *La Petite Ferme* is, not surprisingly, popular. Among its specialities are home-smoked trout, roasted Karoo lamb and spiced roulade of ostrich. Meals are served with wines made in the restaurant's cellar. Daily noon–4pm.

Le Bon Vivant 22 Dirkie Uys St ☎ 021 876 2717. Well-priced and consistently excellent establishment serving two-to five-course nouvelle cuisine set meals as well as an à la carte menu with a splash of Dutch influence. Daily except Wed noon–3pm & 6.30pm till late.

Reuben's 19 Huguenot Rd ☎ 021 876 3772. Minimalist chic decor and a relaxed ambience set the tone at one of Franschhoek's top eateries, with an inspired, eclectic menu that varies from day to day. Venison features big and there's always poultry, lamb, pork, seafood and a vegetarian option, all spiced up with a touch of Indian, Japanese and other Asian accents. The starters, which have included spiced beef tartar and chilli-salted squid, are quite superb. Daily 8am till last customers leave (kitchen closes 8.30pm).

The Tasting Room at Le Quartier Français 16 Huguenot Rd ☎ 021 876 2151. The place that made Franschhoek synonymous with food remains consistently one of South Africa's best restaurants (rated among the world's Top 50 by the UK's *Restaurant* magazine), offering excellent formal evening meals with a global, contemporary flavour. There are always vegetarian options and delicious desserts. Daily 7–10pm.

Topsi & Co 7 Reservoir St West ☎ 021 876 2952. Run by one of South Africa's most eccentric and best-known chefs, Topsi Venter, this is a bag of surprises. There's no set menu, but you'll always find unlikely flavours being combined to great effect. A talking parrot called Dr Arnoldus Pannevis wanders around checking that everything is all right. Mon & Wed–Sun noon–2.30pm & 7–9pm.

Route 62
and the Little Karoo

One of the most rewarding journeys in the Western Cape is an inland counter-part to the Garden Route (see p.251) – the **mountain route** from Cape Town to Port Elizabeth, largely along the R62, and thus often referred to as **Route 62**. Nowhere near as well known as the coastal journey, this trip takes you through some of the most dramatic passes and *poorts* (valley routes) in the country and crosses a frontier of *dorps* and drylands. This "back garden" is in many respects more rewarding than the actual Garden Route, being far less developed, with spectacular landscapes, quieter roads and some great small towns to visit.

Beyond the Paarl and Stellenbosch winelands, a vast hinterland fans out away from Cape Town. Just outside Paarl, the Huguenot Tunnel on the N1 punches through the Dutoitsberg mountain range to emerge in the fruit-growing and wine-making country of the **Breede River Valley**, where mountains give way to a jigsaw of valleys, each quite distinct in character. It's here rather than in the more developed Winelands proper that so many calendar shots are taken of isolated whitewashed homesteads dwarfed by vine-covered hills.

Although the Breede River Valley is part of a through route to the Eastern Cape via Oudtshoorn, its towns also make convenient excursions from Cape Town. **Worcester**, the large functional hub of the region, is on the N1 just

Passes and poorts of the Little Karoo

The **Little Karoo** is hemmed in to the north by the Langeberg range and to the south the Outeniqua (the range separating it from the Garden Route). In between lies a gauntlet of mountains and valleys that for centuries made this area virtually impassable for wheeled transport. In the nineteenth century, the British began to tackle the problem and dozens of **passes** were built through the Cape's mountains, 34 of which were engineered by the brilliant road-builder Andrew Geddes Bain and his son Thomas. In 1878, Anthony Trollope commented that the **Outeniqua Pass**, just north of George on the way to Oudtshoorn, equalled "some of the mountain roads through the Pyrenees", a description which just as easily applies today to any number of other Little Karoo passes. In fact, whatever the Little Karoo lacks in museums and art galleries is amply compensated for by the towering drama of these Victorian masterpieces.

In **Afrikaans** there are two words for pass: *pas*, meaning "a route over the mountains", and *poort*, meaning "a valley route", often following a river. Most passes are narrow, winding and steep, and frequently untarred, so they need to be driven slowly. In any case, you won't want to rush past such fantastic views, so it's worth bringing along food and drink to enjoy at the numerous picnic spots along the way. We've listed a selection of some of the best of the passes and *poorts* below.

Bain's Kloof Pass On the R303 northeast of Paarl, with spectacular switchbacks.

Cogman's Kloof Pass Between Ashton and Montagu. A five-kilometre route that's at its most dramatic as it cuts through a rock face into the Montagu Valley (see box, p.212).

Du Toit's Kloof Pass Between Paarl and Worcester. The more exciting alternative to the Huguenot Toll Tunnel, with 1:9 gradients (see "Worcester" on p.205).

Gamkaskloof Pass Also called Die Hel (The Hell; see box, p.222), reached from the summit of the Swartberg Pass. Arguably the most awesome of all the passes leading into a dramatic and lonely valley.

Meiringspoort Just north of De Rust. A tarred road through a gorge in the Swartberg, which keeps crossing a light-brown river, while huge slabs of folded and zigzagging rock rise up on either side. There's a picnic spot at each fording place and a waterfall at Ford 17 (they're all numbered). You can walk from here for 12km into the mountains.

Prince Alfred's Pass On the R339, between the N2 just east of Knysna and Avontuur on the R62. A dramatic dirt road twisting through mountains, past a few isolated apple farms.

Swartberg Pass Between Oudtshoorn and Prince Albert. Over-the-Swartberg counterpart of Meiringspoort, with 1:7 gradients on narrow untarred roads characterized by precipitous hairpins. Not recommended in poor weather or if you suffer from vertigo.

▲ Karoo scenery

110km from Cape Town, while to its north, **Tulbagh**, a more promising destination with a perfectly restored provincial Cape Dutch street, is an easy 130km from the city. South from Worcester, the R60 shadows the groove cut by the Breede River and provides access to the rather dull little town of **Robertson**, centre of yet another wine route. Some 19km south lies **McGregor**, a small, laid-back village with a rural feel, and an excellent choice for a weekend stay. Nearby, and a similar distance from the Cape Peninsula, the pleasant historic spa town of **Montagu** is towered over by precipitous red-streaked cliffs that attract serious mountaineers from all over the country. Another 60km further east is likeable **Barrydale**, a small Karoo town, not yet on the tourist trail, with access to the hot springs at Warmwaterberg.

Continuing east from Barrydale, the R62 meanders into the Garden Route's backyard, the **Little Karoo** (or Klein Karoo), a vast and brittle khaki-coloured hinterland (the name is a Khoi word meaning "hard and dry"). The Little Karoo provides the easiest access to the semi-desert covering one-third of South Africa's surface. Open treeless plains, sporadically vegetated with low, wiry scrub, and dotted with flat-topped hills, dissolve eventually into the Great Karoo, which extends into the southern Free State and well into the Eastern and Northern Cape provinces. The Great Karoo is the harsh frontier which a succession of South Africans occupied by turns: San hunters, Khoi herders, Griqua (coloured) farmers and Afrikaner trekkers. Today Afrikaans is the dominant language, used by white and coloured speakers, the latter having absorbed what remained of the Khoi.

One unsung surprise along the way is **Calitzdorp**, a rustic little *dorp*, five to six hours' solid driving from Cape Town, down whose backstreets a few unassuming wine farms produce some of South Africa's best port. Around here you'll find neglected valleys where some of the old Karoo clings on tenuously in an almost feudal relationship between farmsteads and faded scatterings of coloured workers' cottages. By contrast, the well-trumpeted attractions of **Oudtshoorn**, half an hour further on, are the ostrich farms and the massive **Cango Caves**, one of the country's biggest tourist draws. Less than 70km from the coast, with good transport connections, Oudtshoorn marks the convergence of the mountain and coastal roads and is usually treated as a leisurely day-trip away from the Garden Route. From Oudtshoorn, over the most dramatic of all passes in the Cape – the unpaved **Swartberg Pass**, 27km of spectacular switchbacks and zigzags through the Swartberg Mountains – is **Prince Albert**, a favourite Karoo village whose spare beauty and remarkable light make it popular with artists; the village boasts a worthwhile gallery of the artists' work and some excellent accommodation.

The N1 beyond Worcester slices up through the northernmost third of the Klein Karoo, slipping past **Matjiesfontein**, a preserved Victorian railway town, and the unassuming, undervalued **Karoo National Park**, both just off the main road and definitely worth breaking a trip for. Peeling north from Matjiesfontein is **Sutherland**, a remote Karoo village with starry skies and a reputation as the coldest place in South Africa during the winter. It's here, with almost no light or pollution, where one of the largest telescopes in the southern hemisphere is housed, and scientists from all over the world have domed stations here.

Worcester to Barrydale

Heading along the back garden – the inland route from Cape Town towards Oudtshoorn – it's particularly worth breaking your journey to explore the pretty towns of **Tulbagh**, **Montagu** and **Barrydale**, while **Worcester** can safely be missed, unless you want to look at the excellent botanic gardens.

Worcester and the Karoo Botanic Gardens

The best part of the journey from Cape Town to **WORCESTER**, 100km east, is taking the **Huguenot Toll Tunnel** on the N1, burrowing through high mountains which give onto a magnificent valley. Worcester, a relatively large town for this part of the world, is an agricultural centre with a number of factories and smelly chicken farms. It's at the centre of a wine-making region, consisting mostly of cooperatives producing bulk plonk that makes up about a fifth of national output.

As you enter Worcester on the N1, signs point to the **Karoo Botanic Gardens** (daily 7am–7pm; R16; ☎023 347 0785), a sister reserve to Kirstenbosch in Cape Town (see p.135), known for its show of indigenous spring flowers and succulents. Looking out over the gardens onto an attractive mountain backdrop, the pleasant **restaurant** here (daily 9am–5pm) serves light meals.

In the town itself, there isn't any reason to dally, apart from driving down Church Street, which has attractive historical frontage, and visiting the absorbing **Kleinplasie Living Open Air Museum** (Mon–Sat 9am–4.30pm; R15), which depicts life on the Karoo frontier between 1690 and 1900. The museum is made up of about two dozen reconstructed buildings, with staff in old-style workshops engaged in crafts and home industries. Keep a lookout in particular for the corbelled shepherd's hut, which represents a vernacular style unique to the Karoo, using domed stone roofs rather than beam and lintel construction – a response to the dearth of timber in the treeless expanse. There's a **restaurant** and **café** on site, and next door a wine shop sells a good selection from the Worcester wineries. The museum is just outside the centre of town – to get there, head east along High Street and turn right onto the road to Robertson.

Those travelling with children might fancy a **stay** at *Goudini Spa* (T 023 344 3013, W www.atkv.org.za; ②–③) 10km west of Worcester on the Rawsonville Road. In a beautiful mountain setting, with three outdoor and one indoor swimming pool and a waterslide, this is a great option: thatched rondavels crowd in on each other, smoke from braais floats in the air and music blares at the poolside, but the 37°C thermal hot springs soothe adult nerves, the self-catering chalets are well kitted out, and there's a functional restaurant if you can't be bothered cooking. No-day trippers are allowed, and children have an absolute ball.

Tulbagh

Not convincingly part of the R62, you can nevertheless get to **TULBAGH** on the R43 from Worcester. Not on the way to anywhere else, the town is captured in a huge bowl of a valley, circled by the Witzenberg mountains. It's probably best visited in a day, or as a weekend getaway from Cape Town, 120km away; though if you've time, you might consider approaching via the beautiful **Bain's Kloof Pass**, on the R303 from Paarl.

You could drive into town, down Van der Stel Street and out the other end, and assume from this unexceptional main street that Tulbagh was just another humdrum *dorp*. But one block west, on **Church Street**, is the most perfectly restored eighteenth- and nineteenth-century streetscape. Only a fraction of what you see here is original (the town was flattened in 1969 by an earthquake), yet this is no Disneyland; the restoration of the buildings used salvaged materials from the ruins, following photographic and hand-drawn records.

The best way to enjoy Tulbagh is to stroll up Church Street and take in the houses, gardens and gables that are an essential element of Cape Dutch architecture. At least six different styles can be distinguished just along this short road. At no. 23, **Paddagang** (frog passage) was originally a *taphuis* (wine house); today it's a restaurant with a wine house attached (see opposite), recommended for its wonderful labels all featuring comical frogs rather than for the liquor itself. Although the gabled Old Church, built in 1743, is of some interest, you won't miss much if you don't spend long over the collection of bric-a-brac inside that constitutes the **Oude Kerk Volksmuseum**, 2 Church St (Mon–Fri 9am–5pm, Sat 10am–4pm, Sun 11am–4pm; R7). The museum has three annexes (included in entry fee) at nos. 4, 14 and 22, which won't keep you busy for too long, either. No. 4 has photographs of old houses in Tulbagh before the earthquake and traces the histories of the families who lived in them.

Just outside town, **De Oude Drostdy Museum** (Mon–Fri 10am–5pm & Sat 10am–2pm; R7), 4km to the north on the extension of Van der Stel Street, is an impressive Cape Dutch spectacle designed by the French architect Louis-Michel Thibault. Each town in the Cape, under the Dutch, had a *drostdy*, or courthouse, where justice was dispensed. These days, in Tulbagh, the dark prison quarters have become candlelit tasting rooms.

Tulbagh wineries

Several new wine farms have become established around Tulbagh, making wine tasting and buying a viable activity, though not on Sundays. The Tulbagh **wine route** (W www.tulbaghwineroute.com) has some reputable cellars, among them

Twee Jonge Gezellen (Mon–Fri 9am–4pm, Sat 10am–2pm; free) and the very contemporary Saronsberg (Mon–Fri 8.30am–5pm, Sat 10am–2pm; free). The tourist office provides an excellent map of the wine farms with opening times. In and around town, you can buy local wines at the *Paddagang Wine House* and the *Hunter's Retreat* cellar, or a few kilometres out, off the R44, at *Things I Love* on the Kloofzicht Estate, which carries a selection of local wines (Wed–Sun 10am to sunset; ☏ 023 230 1742, ⓦ www.thingsilove.co.za). If you're at Kloofzicht on the last Saturday of the month, a number of wine-merchants set up in the cellar for tasting, and excellent local cheese-makers proffer their French-style cheeses.

Practicalities

The town's **tourist office**, 4 Church St (Mon–Fri 9am–5pm, Sat & Sun 10am–4pm; ☏ 023 230 1348, ⓦ www.tulbaghtourism.org.za), can give advice on activities and accommodation in the area. There's a good range of **accommodation** in Tulbagh, from self-catering on farms to roomy guesthouses, though nothing absolutely budget in the town itself.

Accommodation

Acre Laan Farm Cottages 5km south of town, 1km off the Wolseley Rd ☏ 023 230 2991, ⓔ fanie@cfconstruksie.co.za. Two self-catering cottages with brass beds and fireplaces, sleeping four on a working farm. ②

Danie Tron 21 Church St ☏ 073 185 0507 or 082 324 4463. A designated National Monument, with three bedrooms and two bathrooms, in a quiet spot a stone's throw from the *Paddagang* restaurant where you have breakfast. The best value accommodation in town. ②

De Oude Herberg 6 Church St ☏ 023 230 0260, ⓦ www.deoudeherberg.co.za. A well-positioned inn offering country-style rooms with French doors opening onto the veranda or garden, and a pool with loungers for hot days. The grandest room, in the oldest part of the house, faces onto the street. During the summer, Tulbagh's best restaurant is open here. ④

Hunter's Retreat roughly 1.5km north of town along the main road ☏ 023 230 0582, ⓦ www.lando.co.za/HuntersRetreat. Airy B&B rooms and spacious two-storey thatched cottages with lounges, on a working farm that rears cattle, ostriches, sheep and now, more significantly, grapes for its own winery. A chapel on the farm makes this a favourite for weddings. ④

Wild Olive Farm 6km south of town, heading towards Wolseley; a signposted turn-off leads you 2km down a bumpy track ☏ 023 230 1160, ⓦ www.wildolivefarm.com. Family-oriented farm accommodation in six fully equipped, self-catering cottages with fireplaces and braai stands. Grassy campsites with spotless ablution facilities are also available. Guests receive complimentary milk and free-range eggs, and you can swim in a mountain-stream dam. ②

Eating and drinking

Boulders Bush Pub Vindoux Farm, Twee Jonge Gezellen Rd. Principally a pub, with pub meals and pizza, on a wine farm, a couple of kilometres out of town, with good views from its wooden deck.

Paddagang Restaurant and Wine House 23 Church St ☏ 023 230 0242. Tulbagh's biggest attraction, apart from its historic streetscape. Established in 1821 as one of the first taverns in the Cape, it serves moderately priced regional cooking, including *waterblommetjiebredie*, *smoersnoek* and *bobotie*, and locally produced wines. You can sit outside under vines in the lovely garden. Daily breakfast, lunch and tea, with dinner also Wed–Sat.

Pielows Restaurant at the Oude Herberg Church St ☏ 023 230 0260. Top-notch candlelit dinners with delicious fish and meat dishes. Booking essential. Dinner only Tues–Sat; closed May–Aug.

Plum 10 Church St. Cape specialities such as *bobotie* and *bredie*, as well as lighter meals of soup or quiche and salad, served in a peaceful garden with a fountain and umbrellas. Open daily for lunch.

Readers 12 Church St ☏ 023 230 0087. Small eating place in the eighteenth-century cottage once used by the church's sick comforter or "reader". The lunch and dinner menu consists of Cape country cuisine with unusual blends – so you'll find lamb cooked with citrus and served with roasted garlic, and gazpacho with avocado sorbet. Closed Tues.

Robertson

ROBERTSON, approached either from the N1 or N2 from Cape Town, is the largest town in the attractive stretch of the Breede River Valley, known locally as the Robertson Valley. The acidity level of the soil is ideal for growing grapes – indeed the Robertson Valley is responsible for some ten percent of South Africa's vineyards – but irrigation is necessary as the climate is hot and dry. The best wines here tend to be Chenin Blancs and Colombards, and some good Muscadels are conjured up too.

The only conceivable reason for visiting this fruit-picking town is to taste and buy wine, which tends to be cheaper than around the winelands closer to Cape Town, and very good.

Robertson wineries

The Robertson Valley's **wine route** extends to McGregor in the south and to Bonnievale in the east; we've picked out the best of its nearly three dozen wineries.

Bon Courage roughly 10km southeast of Roberston along the R317 ⓦ www.boncourage .co.za. Producer of some great sweet whites, especially Muscadel, with a tasting room in a beautiful old homestead along the Breede River. Its *Café Maude* (Mon–Fri 9am–4pm, Sat 9am–3pm) serves breakfast and light lunches. Mon–Fri 8am–5pm, Sat 9.30am–2pm; free.

De Wetshof about 12km southeast of town along the R317 ⓦ www.dewetshof.com Top-notch estate with photogenic mountain and vineyard views, producing several excellent whites, including its flagship Bateleur Chardonnay. Mon–Fri 8.30am–4.30pm, Sat 9.30am–12.30pm; free.

Graham Beck about 7km west of Robertson along the R60 ⓦ www.grahambeckwines.co.za. A modern, high-flying estate making an international splash, with orders from British supermarket giants for its vast range of reds and whites, many of them in the top rank. The tasting room is daringly modern. Mon–Fri 9am–5pm, Sat 10am–3pm; free.

La Verne Wine Boutique in a converted railway cottage, next to the Robertson Art Gallery as you enter town from the west on the R60

ⓦ www.lavernewines.co.za. Outlet representing fifty wine sellers from the Robertson Valley. You can taste wine here, as well as buy by the case or just the odd bottle. La Verne also has a tear-off map of the wine areas to make your ramblings easier. Mon–Thurs 9am–5.30pm, Fri 9am–6pm, Sat 9am–5pm.

Robertson Winery in town, just off the R60 ⓦ www.robertsonwinery.co.za. Producer of some good-value and highly drinkable Chardonnays and Colombards, sold cheaper here than in the shops. Mon–Thurs 8am–5pm, Fri 8am–4.30pm, Sat & Sun 9am–3pm; free

Springfield a few kilometres southeast of Robertson on the R317 ⓦ www.springfieldestate .com. Stellar estate that produces a range of really outstanding reds and whites, a number of which are among South Africa's frontrunners. Mon–Fri 8am–5pm, Sat 9am–4pm; free.

Van Loveren 15km northwest of Bonnievale along the R317 ⓦ www.vanloveren.co.za. Wine tasting in a lovely garden at a winery known for its hugely quaffable wines, including River Red, South Africa's classic plonk that offers consistently good value. Mon–Fri 8.30am–5pm, Sat 9.30am–1pm; free.

Practicalities

Robertson also has one of the best backpackers in the Western Cape, with its own reasonably priced wine tour, a fireplace for chilly winter nights and a nice garden. Situated in a spacious Victorian house, *Robertson Backpackers*, 4 Dordrecht Ave (ⓣ 023 626 1280, ⓦ www.robertsonbackpackers.co.za; ❶–❷), has doubles (some en suite) and dorms. The **tourist office** in Voortrekker Street (Mon–Fri 8am–5pm, Sat 9am–4pm, Sun 10am–2pm; ⓣ 023 626 4437, ⓦ www.robertson62 .com) does free accommodation bookings for lodgings in the area.

McGregor

If you're not stocking up on wine, press straight on from Robertson to **McGREGOR**, fifteen minutes to the south at the end of a minor road signposted off the R60, and 180km from Cape Town. Don't be tempted by an approach from the south which may look like a tempting back route – you would need a 4WD for this. McGregor is an attractive place, with thatched, whitewashed cottages glaring in the summer daylight amid the low, rusty steel-wool scrub, vines and olive trees, and a quiet, relaxed atmosphere that has attracted a small population of spiritual seekers and artists. Residents are urged to build in harmony with existing style and thus maintain the town's character. It makes a great weekend break from Cape Town with a couple of decent restaurants, plenty of well-priced accommodation, a beautiful retreat centre with reasonably priced massage and other body-work. Spending a day wine tasting around McGregor and Robertson is another drawcard, as long as it's not a Sunday when almost everything is closed.

McGregor gained modest prosperity in the nineteenth century by becoming a centre of the whipstock industry, supplying wagoners and transport riders with long bamboo sticks for goading oxen. There aren't too many ox-drawn wagons today, and tourism, though developing, is still quite limited. One main reason people come here is to walk the **Boesmanskloof Traverse** (see box, p.229), which starts 14km from McGregor and crosses to Greyton on the other side of the mountain. From McGregor you can walk a section of trail, hiking to the main waterfall and back to the trailhead, which is a three- to four-hour round hike of exceeding beauty through the river gorge, or *kloof* in Afrikaans.

Practicalities

You'll find most of what you want down Voortrekker Street, McGregor's main thoroughfare, dominated by a Dutch Reformed church. In the same street you'll also find the small, clearly signposted **tourist office** (Mon–Fri 9am–1pm & 2–4.30pm, Sat & Sun 9am–1pm; ☏023 625 1954, ⓦwww .tourismmcgregor.co.za), which can book you accommodation, and issue permits for walking the whole Boesmanskloof Traverse or simply for the waterfall section (R25). Staff will also direct you to artists' studios in town, and to complementary health practitioners, offering massage and yoga, and give you times of the daily meditation sessions at Temenos Retreat Centre. Pilates is available with Corrie van der Colff (☏023 625 1951).

Accommodation

All the central **accommodation** is in Voortrekker Street or clearly indicated off it along the town's gravel roads. The switched-on tourist office (see above) offers a free booking service and has a list of accommodation on its website.

The Barn Grewe St; book through the tourist office. Beautifully restored barn sleeping five in three rooms, with a Victorian bath, antique Cape furniture, fireplace and wood-burning stove. The barn is taken as a whole (R1000), which is a bit pricey if there are only two of you.
Green Gables Country Inn Voortrekker St ☏023 625 1626, ©grgables@telkomsa.net. Tastefully furnished rooms with doorways onto a Frenchified English country garden. There's also a street-facing pub, and restaurant on the veranda. ❸
Lady McGregor Voortrekker St; book through the tourist office. Cheapest accommodation in town, offering thoroughly decent and clean rooms and a dorm above the *Jack and Grape* pub and restaurant.

All linen provided, with good self-catering facilities, pool and satellite TV. ❷
Langewater Farm 2km outside town towards Boesmanskloof; book through the tourist office. Three no-frills, very reasonably priced self-catering cottages on a working farm. Ideal for families, with plenty of animals and space to run about. ❷
McGregor Country Cottages Voortrekker St ☏023 625 1816, ⓦwww.mcgregor.org.za /countrycottages.php. Tranquil self-catering in a complex of cottages with traditional reed ceilings and fireplaces, surrounded by gardens, orchards and vegetable patches. There's also a pool. A separate honeymoon house is available and worth the price. Wheelchair- and child-friendly. ❸

Mr Oosthuizen On the McGregor side of the Boesmanskloof Traverse ☏ 023 625 1735. Basic semi-equipped huts – bring your own sleeping bag, towels and supplies. ❶

Old Mill Lodge On the southern outskirts of town, at the end of Voortrekker St ☏ 023 625 1841, ⓦ www.oldmilllodge.co.za. A set of appealing two-bedroomed cottages at a historic country lodge, with a tranquil ambience, surrounded by vineyards and gardens. There's also a swimming pool and a good restaurant. The lovely dining area has the best views in town and log fires in winter, and the engaging wine-buff host will make sure you drink something memorable for dinner and direct you to the latest finds in the Robertson winelands. B&B ❹

Rhebokskraal Farm Cottages 2km south of town ☏ 023 625 1787, ⓔ rhebokskraal @hermann.co.za. Secluded cottages, each on a different part of this beautiful fruit, olive and grape farm, which is within easy reach of the restaurants in town. It's best to make a

reservation, though you could at a pinch just turn up at *Villagers*, the farm's shop in the main street, and ask if a cottage is available. ❷

Temenos Country Retreat On the corner of Bree and Voortrekker sts ☏ 023 625 1871, ⓦ www .temenos.org.za. Retreat centre with cottages dotted about beautiful gardens and walkways, a lap-length swimming pool, a library and meditation spaces. Safe and peaceful, it's ideal for lone women. Self-catering available, or B&B. ❸

Whipstock Farm 8km from the centre on the southerly continuation of Voortrekker St ☏ 023 625 1733, ⓦ www.whipstock.za.net. Restored cottages on an old citrus, almond and grape farm in the mountains. *Whipstock* is 5km from the McGregor side of the Boesmanskloof Traverse (see box, p.229), and the owners will pick you up from the trail for free if you're overnighting. Swimming, bikes and canoes are available free to guests. Minimum stay 2 nights. Great for kids. Full board ❹

Eating and drinking

All the establishments mentioned here are along or off Voortrekker Street. Pick of the bunch is *Tebaldi's at Temenos* (Tues–Sun 9.30am–4.30pm, dinner Thurs–Sat from 7pm), with tapas, cheeses, Italian fare and local wines served in a tranquil garden setting or at streetside tables. *Villagers* (Mon–Sat 9am–4.30pm) sells its own olives, preserves and organic fruit nectars and is good for daytime snacks and teas, with a veranda from which to watch the passing scene. Opposite, *DeliGirls and Bistro* (Mon & Wed–Sat 9.30am–4.30pm, Sun 9.30am–2.30pm) is best for picnic supplies with home-made bread, cheese, chocolate and other tempting goodies; it also serves coffee and light lunches.

At *Old Mill Lodge* you can splash out on a four-course set evening meal (though make a reservation for this by lunchtime). You can sit by the fire in the winter, or enjoy its veranda's views on summer evenings. Decidedly convivial is the *Green Gables Country Inn*, for well-priced three-course dinners, including offerings such as roast lamb with Mediterranean vegetables, plus coffee and cake during the day; there's also a friendly **pub** here. Another pub, in Voortrekker Street, is the *Jack and Grape* (Mon–Sat), which has a large TV screen for watching sport, and dishes up large steaks.

Montagu

The ultimate Breede River Valley destination, 190km from Cape Town, is **MONTAGU**. The approach from the south through Cogman's Kloof Gorge numbers among the most dramatic arrivals in the country: a five-kilometre winding road cuts through a rock face into a narrow valley dramatically opening out to Montagu. Soaring mountains rise up in vast arches of twisted strata that display reds and ochres, and from September to October the gentler tints of peach and apricot blossoms flood the valley. Montagu is certainly very pleasing, with sufficient Victorian architecture to create an historic character, and worth a night at least.

The town was named in 1851 after **John Montagu**, the visionary British Secretary of the Cape, who realized that the colony would never develop without decent communications and was responsible for commissioning the first mountain passes connecting remote areas to Cape Town. The grateful farmers of Agter Cogman's Kloof (literally: "behind Cogman's Kloof") leapt at the chance of a snappier name for their village and named it after him.

Montagu is best known for its **hot springs**, but serious **rock climbers** come for its cliff faces, which are regarded as among the country's most challenging. One of South Africa's top climbers runs *De Bos Guest Farm* (see below) which you could use as a base for climbing. You can also explore the mountains on a couple of trails or, easiest of all, on a tractor ride onto one of the peaks. Montagu is also conveniently positioned for excursions along both the Robertson and Little Karoo **wine routes** (see p.208).

Forty kilometres east of Montagu on the R62 is **Sanbona Wildlife Reserve**, the best of the Western Cape's game reserves, set on an enormous and beautiful property with free-roaming cats. A serious safari destination, with no day-trippers or elephant rides, it's ideal if you are set on seeing big game and don't have the time for Kruger, though it is very pricey and the volume of game you'll see in the semi-arid terrain can't compare with the productive bushveld of Kruger.

Arrival, information and accommodation

Buses to Montagu are restricted to a service from Belville in Cape Town via Paarl and Worcester, operated by Munniks (☎021 637 1850), departing Cape Town on Friday, Saturday and Sunday. Montagu's useful **tourist office** is at 24 Bath St (Mon–Fri 8.45am–4.45pm, Sat 9am–5pm, Sun 9.30am–noon & 3–5pm; ☎023 614 2471). Even if you're here for the springs, it is far nicer to find somewhere to **stay** in town rather than at the spa, which amounts to little more than a large crowded resort, especially at weekends and school holidays.

Accommodation

Aasvoelkrans 1 Van Riebeeck St ☎023 614 1228, ⓦwww.aasvoelkrans.co.za. Three exceptionally imaginative garden rooms at a guesthouse situated on an Arabian stud farm, in a pretty part of town. ❹

Cynthia's 3 Krom St ☎023 614 2760, ⓦwww .cynthias-cottages.co.za. Seven self catering cottages dotted around the west side of town, all in old houses, with gardens and braai areas, and near the starting point for hiking trails. Cottages go from R270–650 depending on the size of the accommodation needed.

De Bos Guest Farm 8 Brown St ☎023 614 2532, ⓦwww.debos.co.za. Camping, dorms and basic doubles on a farm at the western edge of town, run by rock climbers, where Stuart Brown can take you on guided climbs, though you need to have your own gear. You'll meet more people here and have more fun than staying at the caravan park next door. There are ponies in the paddock and you can go on hikes right from your doorstep. ❶–❷

John Montagu Victorian Guest House 30 Joubert St ☎023 614 1331, ⓦwww .johnmontagu.co.za. En-suite rooms at an elegant guesthouse with enough period furniture and

knick-knacks to create a historic ambience without being oppressive. ❺

Montagu Caravan Park At the west end of Bath St, across the Keisie River ☎023 614 2675, ⓔmontagu@telkomsa.net. A friendly municipal caravan park offering campsites and basic timber cabins sleeping four, with personal touches such as fresh flowers. The units have cooker and fridge, with the nicest cabins boasting thatched roof, TV and microwave. Ablution facilities are shared; bring your own towels. Bedding can be rented. ❷

Montagu Rose Guest House 19 Kohler St ☎023 614 2681, ⓦwww.montagurose.co.za. In a modern home, with personalized service. All rooms have baths and mountain views. Well run and good value. ❸

Montagu Springs Signposted off the R62, west of town ☎023 614 1050, ⓦwww.montagusprings .co.za. Large resort with fully equipped self-catering chalets, some more luxurious than others, sleeping four. Prices start at R425 per chalet during the week, and R650 at weekends or school holidays.

Seven Church Street 7 Church St ☎023 614 1186, ⓦwww.sevenchurchstreet.co.za. A central Victorian house, offering a very comfortable stay.

Enticements include embroidered pure cotton linen and a gorgeous garden popular for bridal photography. Friendly and well run. ❹
Squirrel's Corner On the corner of Bloem and Jouberts sts ☏023 614 1081,

Ⓦwww.squirrelscorner.co.za. B&Bs with four comfortable, spotless en-suite rooms in a friendly family house, as well as a garden suite which is two blocks from the main road. ❸

The town and around

Highly photogenic, Montagu is ideal for seeing on foot, taking in the interesting buildings or simply enjoying the setting, with its mountains, valleys and farms. There are also a couple of museums, neither of which is outstanding. The best thing about the **Montagu Museum**, 41 Long St (Mon–Fri 9am–noon & 2–4pm, Sat & Sun 9am–noon; R5), housed in a pleasant old church, is its herbal project, which traces traditional Khoisan knowledge about the medicinal properties of local plants. Work is being done in conjunction with the Pharmacology Department at the University of Cape Town and you can buy their booklet *Herbal Remedies: Montagu Museum*, which details some of the findings. The herbs themselves are also on sale, some of them grown in the gardens of the **Joubert House Museum** (Mon–Fri 9am–noon & 2–5pm, Sat 9am–noon; R5), one block west at 25 Long St. Built in 1853, this was one of the first houses standing in a vast plot which was originally a town farm, and has peach-pip floors fixed with beeswax, characteristic of the area, and period furniture on display in each of the rooms.

On Saturday mornings, don't miss the local **farmers' market** at the church, where you can get local olives and olive oil, bread, cheese, almonds and dried fruit from the surrounding farms – all exceptionally well priced.

Montagu's main draw is the **Montagu Springs Resort** (daily 8am–11pm; R50, children R30; Ⓦwww.montagusprings.co.za), about 3km northwest of town on the R318 (or reached on foot by following the Keisie River, which flows along the north edge of town). Several chlorinated open-air pools of

---

Montagu activities

Three **hikes** begin from the Old Mill at the north end of Tanner Street, where there's also a small park at the foot of cliffs; **maps** for the hikes are available from Montagu's tourist office. Shortest is the Lover's Walk, a stroll of just over 2km through Bath Kloof (or Badkloof; daily 7am–6pm) that follows the Keisie River to the hot springs. More substantial is the twelve-kilometre **Cogman's Kloof hiking trail**, which can be completed in three to six hours; only the first 2km are steep, after which it's an easy walk with nice views of Montagu, the ravines and mountains. Most ambitious is the **Bloupunt hiking trail**, at around 15.5km, which gets you up to an altitude of over 1000m and can be completed in six to nine hours; the terrain en route encompasses ravines, mountain streams, craggy cliffs and rock formations and is very strenuous. From the summit of Bloupunt you can see as far as McGregor and Robertson. Throughout the year, you will see dassies and klipspringers as well as a large variety of wild flowers because of the presence of perennial streams. The *fynbos* vegetation includes proteas, ericas, aloes, lilies, watsonias and wild orchids. Carry a waterbottle to fill up at a waterpoint about halfway up the mountain.

If you don't feel like walking up the Langeberg Mountains, you can still get to the top on a highly recommended three-hour **tractor ride** (Wed & Sat 10am & 2pm; book at the Montagu tourist office) from Protea Farm, which is 29km along the Koo/Touws River road (R318). Remember to take warm clothes. Further along the same route, on Eendracht Farm, 45km from Montagu (☏023 614 1991), you can try your hand at **paintballing** or **quad bike riding**.

different temperatures and a couple of Jacuzzis are spectacularly situated at the foot of cliffs – an effect slightly spoilt by the neon lights of a hotel complex and fast-food restaurant. It's a fabulous place to take kids, but the weekends become a mass of splashing bodies. If you want a quiet time, go first thing in the morning or last thing at night; when the outside air is cooler, the steaming waters provide a wonderfully relaxing alcohol-free nightcap. The temperatures in winter are not hot enough to be entirely comfortable, when you're better off heading to the springs at Caledon (p.226 or Warmwaterberg p.214) which are much hotter, and in many respects preferable.

Eating and drinking

Montagu has a couple of very good **restaurants** (evening meals must be reserved in advance), two farm stalls along Bath Street to pick up fresh and dried fruit, *biltong* and *boerewors*, a pleasant out-of-town tea-garden, as well as a couple of coffee shops along Bath and Long streets. Try *Sixty on Route 62*, on Long Street, for breakfasts, coffee and a big TV, or *Rambling Rose* on Bath Street, a wayside farm stall with fruit juices and local produce.

BellaMonta 4 Market St ☎023 614 2941. Reasonably priced family restaurant with pizza, burgers and a couple of fish and seafood dishes. Dinner only Mon–Sat.

Die Stal 8km out of town on the R318 ☎082 324 4318. A pleasant venue on a farm serving lunches and teas, en route to the obligatory tractor ride. Closed Mon.

Jessica's 28 Bath St ☎023 614 1805. Small and friendly, named after the proprietors' boxer dog and decorated with period dog prints. Here you'll get fairly pricey, refined, cosmopolitan bistro-style dishes and a top selection of Robertson wines; the

cajun-roasted baby chicken on wild rice with *peri-peri* cream is recommended. Daily eves, except Sun during winter.

Preston's Restaurant & Thomas Bain Pub Bath St ☎023 614 1633. Small, intimate nightspot that remains open till late and is recommended for its pub rather than its food.

Templetons@Four Oaks 46 Long St ☎023 614 2778. Pub and restaurant with meat and fish dishes, and a nice shady courtyard. Vegetarians can choose from goats' cheese ravioli or mushroom gnocchi. Lunch & dinner daily, but Sat lunch and all day Sun.

Barrydale and around

BARRYDALE, 240km from Cape Town, is perfect for a couple of days of doing very little other than experiencing small-town life in the Little Karoo, with good, reasonably priced accommodation, hot springs at **Warmwaterberg** 30km to the east, or if you're spiritually inclined, walking the **labyrinth** at Lemoenshoek, 15km east of town. West of town you'll find big game at **Sanbona Wildlife Reserve**.

Not yet on the tourist route, Barrydale nonetheless has a number of restaurants and decent places to stay, and the sixty-kilometre drive from Montagu offers spectacular mountain scenery. There's a distinct rural feel about Barrydale: vineyards line the main road, farm animals are kept on large plots of land behind dry-stone walling, and you'll find fig, peach and quince trees thriving in the dryness. A couple of wine outlets are worth a visit for tasting and buying, particularly Southern Cape Winery in Van Riebeeck (Mon–Fri 8am–5pm, Sat 9am–3pm; ☎028 572 1012).

Practicalities

The R62 swings past the village, whose entrance is marked by a tiny **visitor information centre** (Mon–Fri 8.30am–1.15pm & 2–5pm; ☎028 572 1572,). Turning off the R62 takes you along Van Riebeeck Street, the main drag, with more pedestrians than cars, dominated by the ivory church and one supermarket, which houses an ATM and post office.

The best **accommodation** along the R62 is the gay-owned *Tradouw Guest House* (℡028 572 1434, Ⓦwww.home.intekom.com/tradouwguesthouse; ❷–❸), with four rooms opening onto a courtyard shaded by vines and two onto the large garden. Rates are extremely reasonable, and the owners can pack you up a picnic lunch if you want to explore the river or, further afield, the spectacular Tradouw Pass, linking Barrydale with Swellendam. During summer, they do a garden café with soup, quiche and salad, as well as good coffee, and have their own bar for guests. For **self-catering** go for *Sandy's Place* (℡028 572 1415; ❷) – the three small hotel-style units have TV, microwave and no character, but are extremely reasonably priced.

Most of Barrydale's **eating** options are strung along the R62. Pick of the bunch are the colourful, decorative *Jam Tarts*, on whose veranda you can enjoy tapas, pizza, some health foods and divine cakes, and *Clarke of the Karoo*, for good steaks and *bobotie*, with a starter provided on the house. It's also open in the evening (weekends only), a rarity in Barrydale; otherwise at night *A Place in Time* (nightly except Wed; ℡028 572 1393) is recommended for its pizzas, game dishes, spare ribs and crème brûlée.

Sanbona Wildlife Reserve

Twenty kilometres west of Barrydale, **Sanbona Wildlife Reserve** (℡028 572 1365; Ⓦwww.sanbona.com; R2560–3350 per person per night all-inclusive), is the amalgamation of 21 farms that together create a massive wilderness area. The landscape is gorgeous – rocky outcrops, mountains and semi-desert vegetation – and there are two utterly luxurious **lodges**, *Tilney Manor*, which has a spa, and *Khanni Lodge*. The price includes two game drives a day, but, owing to the vegetation, the game is far sparser here than in the major game-viewing areas such as the Kruger National Park. Having said that, it is the only place in the Western Cape with free-roaming lions and cheetahs and there's a herd of elephants. Sanbona is worth considering only if you are set on seeing some big game and don't have time for Kruger. A two-night stay is recommended and day visitors are not allowed.

The Labyrinth and Warmwaterberg Spa

The **Labyrinth**, 15km east of Barrydale on a small farm at Lemoenhoek, (℡028 572 1643; donation), is a beautiful outdoor maze based on one at Chartres Cathedral; the circuit is demarcated by rose quartz stones and allows you to gaze at the mountains as you move through. It can be privately booked if you want a meditative walk in peace; donations go to the farm's animal rehab project.

Another 15km east, beyond *Ronnie's Sex Shop*, a pub and well-known jokey landmark in the middle of nowhere, is **Warmwaterberg Spa** (℡028 572 1609; Ⓦwww.warmwaterbergspa.co.za; ❷–❸), a Karoo farm blessed with natural hot water siphoned into two unchlorinated hot pools (closed Wed) and surrounded by lush green lawns and lofty palms. Primarily aimed at South Africans, it gets rather crowded and noisy during school holidays and over weekends. Accommodation is basic and self-catering – in wooden cabins or rooms in the main farmhouse where you rent linen, and are given your own key to an indoor spa bath. There are also some campsites, a bar and a restaurant serving dinners and breakfasts if you want a break from doing it all yourself. While day visitors from Barrydale can be accommodated, most people stay over, to make the most of the baths at night, when the steam rises into the cold, starry Karoo sky.

Oudtshoorn and around

OUDTSHOORN, 420km from Cape Town and an arid, mountainous 180km from Barrydale, has been called the "ostrich capital of the world"; the town's surrounds are indeed crammed with ostrich farms, several of which you can visit, and the local souvenir shops keep busy dreaming up 1001 tacky ways to recycle ostrich parts as comestibles and souvenirs. But Oudtshoorn has two other big draws: it's the best base for visiting the nearby **Cango Caves** (see p.217), and the town is known for its sunshine and pleasant climate. Only 63km of tar and a range of mountains separate Oudtshoorn from Wilderness on the coast, yet the weather couldn't be more different; this is especially good news in winter, when a cold downpour along the Garden Route can give the lie to the idea of "sunny South Africa". It's boiling hot in summer though, so make sure you have access to a pool, and nights in winter can freeze.

Some 50km west of Oudtshoorn, **Calitzdorp** is a delightfully unassuming Victorian village that can be seen as part of a circular excursion incorporating the scenic **Groenfontein Valley**. Its wineries and one or two tea shops offer the chance of a breather if you're travelling on the R62 through the Little Karoo. **De Rust**, a town with similar origins to Calitzdorp but 35km in the opposite direction, has benefited greatly from lying on the N12 connecting the N1 to the Garden Route, but is little more than a pleasant pit stop.

Some history

Oudtshoorn started out as a small village named in honour of Geesje Ernestina Johanna van Oudtshoorn, wife of the first civil commissioner for George. By the 1860s **ostriches**, which live in the wild in Africa, were being raised under the ideal conditions of the Oudtshoorn Valley, where the warm climate and loamy soils enabled lucerne, the favourite diet of the flightless birds, to be grown. The quirky Victorian fashion for large feathers had turned the ostriches into a source of serious wealth, and by the 1880s hundreds of thousands of kilograms of feathers were being exported, and birds were changing hands for up to £1000 a pair – an unimaginable sum in those days. On the back of this boom, sharp businessmen made their fortunes, ignorant farmers were ripped off, and labourers drew the shortest straw of all. The latter were mostly coloured descendants of the Outeniqua and Attaqua Khoikhoi and trekboers, who received derisory wages supplemented by rations of food, wine, spirits and tobacco – a practice that still continues on some farms. In the early twentieth century, the most successful farmers and traders built themselves "feather palaces", ostentatious sandstone Edwardian buildings that have become the defining feature of Oudtshoorn.

Arrival, information and accommodation

Intercity buses pull in at Queens Mall, off Voortrekker Street where you'll also find the Pick 'n Pay supermarket and Internet café. Oudtshoorn's **tourist office** (Mon–Fri 8am–5pm, Sat 9am–1pm; ☎044 279 2532, ⓦwww .oudtshoorn.com), next to the *Queens Hotel*, Baron van Reede Street, is good for information about the caves, ostrich farms and local accommodation. *Backpacker's Paradise* rents out **bikes** and also arranges spectacular **adventurous cycling trips** down the Swartberg Pass, chaperoned with motor vehicle backup.

Oudtshoorn has a number of large **hotels** catering mainly to tour buses, plus plenty of good-quality B&Bs and guesthouses, a centrally located campsite with chalets, and one of the country's best-run backpacker lodges. Some of the nicest places to stay are in the attractive countryside en route to Cango Caves.

The tourist office offers a free accommodation booking service. **Rates** fall dramatically during the winter months following the week-long **Klein Karoo Nasionale Kunstefees** (KKNK; Ⓦ www.absakknk.co.za), a major arts festival, mostly in Afrikaans, and street party in the March/April Easter holidays when people from all over the country take every bed in town.

Accommodation

141 High Street 141 High St Ⓣ 044 279 1751. Four large and reasonably priced rooms in a centrally located, handsome two-storey sandstone Dutch Reformed Church parsonage that's still in use, and has a very pleasant garden. ❸

Backpacker's Paradise 148 Baron van Reede St Ⓣ 044 272 3436, Ⓦ www.backpackersparadise .net. A friendly and well-run two-storey hostel along the main drag, which makes an effort to go the extra few centimetres with three-quarter beds, en-suite doubles and family rooms as well as three small dorms – and, in season, a portion of ostrich egg on the house for breakfast. There are nightly ostrich, or veg-friendly braais, too, and a daily shuttle from the Baz Bus drop-off in George to the hostel. The on-site adventure centre organizes cycle trips in the Swartberg Pass and there's a daily shuttle to the caves, ostrich farm and wildlife ranch. ❶–❷

Berluda on the R328, 15km from Oudtshoorn, en route to Cango Caves Ⓣ 044 272 8518, Ⓦ www .berluda.co.za. An avenue of trees leads up to a fairly modern-looking farmhouse with five bedrooms and two self-catering cottages in a well-established garden. The friendly owners can organize ostrich farm tours on their property 8km away, and there is a pool to cool off in. ❹

Buffelsdrift Game Lodge 7km from town on the road to the caves Ⓣ 044 272 0106, Ⓦ www .buffelsdrift.com. The town's top stay, in luxurious

en-suite safari tents overlooking a large dam with hippo in it, and a grand thatched dining area. Game drives or horseback rides to view rhino, buffalo, elephant, giraffe and various antelope are included in the price. No kids under 12 can be accommodated, though families can visit during the day for a meal or game activity. ❽

De Oue Werf signposted off the R328 to Cango Caves, 12km north of Oudtshoorn Ⓣ 044 272 8712, Ⓦ www.ouewerf.co.za. Luxurious and well-priced garden rooms on a working farm, run by the very welcoming sixth generation of the family. Green lawns run down to a dam which has a swinging slide and raft to play on, and lots of birdlife. Light lunches and teas can be had at the gazebo by the pool, with dinners in the candlelit dining room, presided over by family photographs. A great option if you're visiting the caves and want to stay in the country. ❹

Gum Tree Lodge 139 Church St Ⓣ 044 279 2528, Ⓦ www.gumtreelodge.co.za. Two houses opposite each other with B&B rooms, a 10min walk from the centre. There's sherry on arrival and electric blankets for the cold winter nights. ❸

Kleinplaas Holiday Resort 171 Baron van Reede St Ⓣ 044 272 5811, Ⓦ www.kleinplaas.co.za. Well-run, spick-and-span shady camping and fully equipped self-catering brick chalets, conveniently close to town, with a swimming pool and launderette. B&B is available. The owners know the town well and will show you the ropes. ❷–❸

The town and around

Oudtshoorn's town centre is a pretty straightforward place to negotiate, and has little more than a couple of museums worth checking out if you've time to kill. The town's main interest lies in its Victorian and Edwardian sandstone buildings, some of which are unusually grand and elegant for a Karoo *dorp*.

The **C.P. Nel Museum** (Mon–Sat 8am–5pm, Sat 9am–5pm; R15), on the corner of Baron van Reede Street and Voortrekker Road, is a good place to start your explorations. A handsome sandstone building, it was built in 1906 as a boys' school, but now houses an eccentric collection of items relating to ostriches. Nearby, **Le Roux Town House**, on the corner of Loop and High streets (Mon–Fri 9am–1pm & 2–5pm; R15), is a perfectly preserved family town house, and the only way to get a glimpse inside one of the much-vaunted feather palaces. The beautifully preserved furnishings were all imported from Europe between 1900 and 1920, and there is plenty to stroll around and admire.

Many people come to Oudtshoorn to see, or even ride, **ostriches**. You don't actually have to visit one of the ostrich farms to view Africa's biggest bird, as you're bound to see flocks of them as you drive past farms in the vicinity or past truckloads of them on their way to the slaughterhouse (feathers being no longer fashionable, these days ostriches are raised for their low-cholesterol flesh). A number of show farms offer **tours** (45–90min) costing around R20 a person, which include the chance to sit on an ostrich and the spectacle of jockeys racing the birds. Best of the bunch is Cango Ostrich and Butterfly Farm on the main road between Oudtshoorn and the Cango Caves, which takes only one group of visitors (or individuals) at a time.

More exciting, though less traditional for Oudtshoorn, is the opportunity to feed and touch elephants 7km out of town on the Cango Caves road at **Buffelsdrift Game Lodge** (☏044 272 0106; R120). Book ahead for a really worthwhile experience where you get to stroke elephants under the guidance of their handlers, and watch them at training and play throughout the day. From the lodge's **restaurant** on the large dam, you are likely to see hippos, and may be lucky to see other animals coming to drink.

The other "wildlife" activity around Oudtshoorn is the **Cango Wildlife Ranch** (daily 8am–6pm; R80, children R50, under 4s free; ☏044 272 5593), just outside town on the Cango Road. Guided tours lead you past white tigers and cheetahs, crocodiles and other amazing creatures from other parts of Africa, and you can pay extra to be photographed touching the animals and reptiles, and even get into the pool with the crocodiles. Don't expect it to be thrilling, though; you'll be lucky if a crocodile so much as flicks its eyes while you're in there. The ranch offers a spectacle rather than authentic wildness, but it caters well for children who can frolic in water fountains or on climbing frames while you eat lunch.

Eating and drinking

Oudtshoorn has a choice of several places to eat, mostly strung out along Baron van Reede Street and catering to the tourist trade, with the obligatory ostrich on the menu. *Kalinka's* and *Jemima's* vie for the top position with excellent and imaginative fare, and you can eat out of town on a game ranch.

Avocado Pierre 6 Baron van Reede St, opposite the museum. A central coffee shop that does nice salads, sandwiches, burgers, pitta pockets and decent coffee. Daily 8.30am–10pm, though closed Sun evenings.

Buffelsdrift Game Lodge 7km out of town towards Cango Caves ☏044 272 0106. Have a great breakfast or lunch on a wooden deck overlooking the waterhole, and do a spot of game-viewing at the same time. The lodge is open to non-guests for meals, and you could combine it with an elephant encounter or other game activity.

Godfather Restaurant 61 Voortrekker Rd ☏044 272 5404. A popular eating place with a huge menu, noted for its medium-priced pizzas, venison and ostrich steaks; also good just for a drink. It's an excellent spot in winter, when there's a roaring fire. Closed Sun.

Jemima's 94 Baron van Reede St ☏044 272

0808. An imaginative and good-value menu including *boerewors*-stuffed ravioli, butternut cheesecake, game dishes and tasty, light food. You'll have a hard time choosing, because everything is so appetizing. Open daily 6pm till late, plus 11am–2pm Tues–Fri.

Kalinka's 93 Baron van Reede St ☏044 279 2596. Sandstone house with a fountain outside specializing in game dishes, with Russian black bread at every meal, and imported vodka. Service is good and food well presented and delicious. The baked cardamom and date brandy pudding is great. Daily 6–10pm.

Paljas 109 Baron van Reede St ☏044 272 0982. One of the town's better eating places, with a contemporary South African menu that brings together Cape cuisine, Karoo cooking and African flavours from the Eastern Cape and KwaZulu-Natal. The emphasis is heavily on meat. Dinner daily.

Cango Caves

The **Cango Caves** number among South Africa's ten most popular attractions, drawing a quarter of a million visitors each year to gasp at their fantastic cavernous spaces, dripping rocks and rising columns of calcite. In the two centuries since they became known to the public, the caves have been seriously battered by human intervention, but they still represent a stunning landscape growing inside the Swartberg foothills. Don't go expecting a serene and contemplative experience, though: the only way of getting inside the caves is on a guided tour accompanied by a commentary.

Cango is a Khoi word meaning "a wet place" – accurate enough, given that the caves' awesome formations are the work of water constantly percolating through rock and dissolving limestone on the way. The solution drips from the roof of the cave and down the walls, depositing calcium carbonate which gradually builds up. Although the caves are many millions of years old, the calcite formations that you see today are geological youngsters, dating back a mere 100,000 years.

San hunter-gatherers sheltered in the entrance caves for millennia before white settlers arrived, but it's unlikely that they ever made it to the lightless underground chambers. **Jacobus van Zyl**, a Karoo farmer, was probably the first person to penetrate beneath the surface, when he slid down on a rope into the darkness in July 1780, armed with a lamp. Over the next couple of centuries the caves were visited and pillaged by growing numbers of callers, some of whom were photographed cheerfully carting off wagonloads of limestone columns.

In the 1960s and 1970s the caves were made accessible to mass consumption when a tourist complex was built, the rock-strewn floor was evened out with concrete, ladders and walkways were installed and the caverns were turned into a kitsch extravaganza with coloured lights, piped music and an indecipherable commentary that drew hundreds of thousands of visitors each year. Even apartheid put its hefty boot in: under the premiership of Dr Hendrik Verwoerd, the arch-ideologue of racial segregation, a separate "non-whites" entrance was hacked through one wall, resulting in a disastrous through-draft that began dehydrating the caves. Fortunately, the worst excesses have now ended; concerts are no longer allowed inside the chambers, and the coloured lights have been removed.

Practicalities

The **drive** here from Oudtshoorn involves heading north along Baron van Reede Street, and continuing 32km on the R328 to the caves. The visitors' complex includes an interpretive centre with quite interesting displays about geology, people and wildlife connected with the caves; the decent *Marimba* **restaurant**; and a souvenir shop. Below the complex you'll find shady picnic sites at the edge of a river that cuts its way into the mountains and along which there are hiking trails. Two **tours** leave every hour (daily 9am–4pm; ☎044 272 7410, ⓦwww .cangocaves.co.za). The one-hour Standard Tour (on the hour; R52, children R28) gets you through the first six chambers, but if you're an adrenaline junkie, the ninety-minute Adventure Tour (on the half-hour; R66) is a must; this takes you into the deepest sections open to the public, where the openings become smaller and smaller. Squeezing through tight openings with names like Lumbago Walk, Devil's Chimney and The Letterbox is not recommended for the overweight, faint-hearted or claustrophobic, and you should wear oldish clothes and shoes with a grip to negotiate the slippery floors. The caves are open every day of the year, bar Christmas Day.

The nearest **accommodation** is set beautifully on the river at *Cango Mountain Resort* (☎044 272 4506, ⓦwww.cangomountaincaravanpark.com; ❷), signposted off the R328 27km north of Oudtshoorn, and 3km off the main road. This is the best self-catering accommodation in the area, with chalets, camping and a small shop. *Wilgewandel*, a cheap place to **eat** after seeing the caves, has the draw of camel rides on the property; it's 2km from the caves on the road back to Oudtshoorn and offers burgers, steak and sandwiches.

Calitzdorp

The tiny Karoo village of **CALITZDORP** hangs in a torpor of midday stillness. After the bustle of the "ostrich capital", it comes as a welcome surprise, with its attractive, unpretentious Victorian streets and handful of wineries. There's nothing much to do here, apart from have tea, taste some wine and wander through the streets. As in many of these inland towns, you'll find Afrikaans dominating.

The low-key **tourist office** at the Shell Garage in Voortrekker Street (Mon–Fri 9am–5pm ☎044 213 3775, ⓦ www.calitzdorp.co.za) has some brochures about the village and its surroundings, as well as information about the wineries and accommodation. Some of South Africa's best ports are produced at the three modest wineries signposted down side roads, a few hundred metres from the centre. The most highly recommended is **Die Krans Estate** (Mon–Fri 8am–5pm, Sat 9am–3pm; free), where you can sample its wines and ports (its vintage reserve port is reckoned to be among the country's top three), and stretch your legs on a thirty-minute vineyard walk in lovely countryside. **Boplaas Estate** (Mon–Fri 8am–5pm, Sat 9am–3pm; free tasting; ⓦ www .boplaas.co.za) also produces some fine ports and is worth a quick look to see its massive reed-ceiling tasting room, like a cantina that fell off the set of a spaghetti western. If you've time, head for the **Calitzdorp Wine Cellar** (Mon–Fri 8am–1pm & 2–5pm, Sat 8am–noon; free), where the main attraction is the stunning view from the tasting room into the Gamka River Valley.

The best **guesthouse** in town is the very friendly *Port-Wine Guest House* (☎044 213 3131, ⓦ www.portwine.net; ❹), in a renovated early nineteenth-century homestead on the corner of Queen and Station streets and overlooking the Boplaas Estate. There's also the comfortable, country-style *Welgevonden Guest House* (☎044 213 3642, ⓦ www.welgevonguesthouse.co.za; ❷–❸), St Helena Road, on a small Chardonnay farm 300m from the main road. Airy rooms that offer exceptional value are available at *Die Dorpshuis* (☎044 213 3453, ⓦ www .diedorpshuis.co.za; B&B ❷–❸), which is centrally located at 4 Van Riebeeck St, opposite the church, and also has self-catering and mountain bikes for rent. *Die Dorpshuis* is a good place to **eat** (Mon–Sat), serving reasonably priced sandwiches, teas, light meals and heavier traditional Karoo food, such as stews and lamb.

The Groenfontein Valley

A circuitous minor route diverts just east of Calitzdorp and drops into the highly scenic **Groenfontein Valley**. The narrow dirt road twists through the Swartberg foothills, past whitewashed Karoo cottages and farms and across brooks, eventually joining the R328 to Oudtshoorn. Winding through these back roads is also an option to reach Cango Caves and Prince Albert, one of the best drives you'll ever do in South Africa. Many of the roads are unsealed but are perfectly navigable in an ordinary car if taken slowly.

An excellent reason to take this back route is to spend a couple of nights at the *Retreat at Groenfontein* (☎044 213 3880, ⓦ www.groenfontein.com; ❹–❻), 20km from Calitzdorp and 59km from Oudtshoorn. This isolated Victorian colonial farmstead borders on the 2300-square-kilometre Swartberg Nature Reserve, an outstandingly beautiful area of gorges, rivers and dirt tracks.

Accommodation is in comfortable en-suite rooms, each with its own fireplace, and rates include a very good dinner, with vegetarians well catered for. Winter rates are half those in summer.

Two good self-catering establishments are *Red Stone Hills* (℡044 213 3783, Ⓦwww.redstone.co.za) which has four lovely period-furnished Victorian cottages on a working farm 6km off the R62 (turn off 14km east of Calitzdorp), and the cheaper, homely *Kruis Rivier Guest Farm* (℡044 213 3788, Ⓦwww.kruisrivier.co.za; ❶), further along the same road as *Red Stone Hills*, which makes an excellent base for hiking, with a policy of keeping prices absolutely affordable. The owners will also do breakfast on request, and provide braai packs.

De Rust

DE RUST is a drive-through town on the N12, 415km from Cape Town, which accounts for the fact that most of the buildings along the town's small main road seem to be selling something – teas, crafts, *biltong* and ostrich products galore. You'll need to reach for your phrasebook (or consult our language glossary on p.895) in this very Afrikaans village, which has a calm atmosphere and gardens that make a bright contrast with the surrounding dry hills. De Rust is a nice enough place to stop to stretch your legs and have a drink, but there's little reason to spend the night here.

Intercity buses between Gauteng and Knysna stop opposite the **tourist office**, 2 Schoeman St (Mon–Fri 8.30am–5.30pm, Sat 8.30am–1.30pm; ℡044 241 2109), which can supply details of accommodation other than the places reviewed here. In town, the *Ashtree B&B*, 8 Church St (℡044 241 2276; ❸), has three reasonably priced en-suite **rooms** in a suburban house. To stay on a **historical farmstead**, and pay a bit more, try *Die Gat Oulap Country House*, some 15km east of town off the R341 to Uniondale (℡044 241 2250, Ⓔoulap@mweb.co.za; half board ❼), which is an unusual place to stay, a Karoo farm in the Swartberg Mountains run by Jans Rautenbach, film producer and storyteller, and his wife. Rooms are eclectically furnished with antiques, *objets d'art* and South African paintings, each of them worth a story over an excellent dinner with the host.

For outdoor **eating**, there is a good tea shop, *Herries* (daily 7am–9pm), in the main road, marked by a purple elephant outside, with pleasant seating under shady trees; it does reasonably priced meals and is licensed. For fresh bread, cakes, indoor **teas** and light meals, *Die Groen Bliktrommel*, on the same road, is recommended. For superb meals cooked by a top city chef come to live in the country, there's the *Plough* on Schoeman and Burger streets (℡044 241 2020; Tues–Sat lunch and dinner, Sun lunch only), with prior booking definitely recommended.

To see the town, take one of the **donkey carts** outside the tourist office (booking essential on ℡044 241 2109) for a slow-paced ride around this Victorian town, and in the process, support the local Donkey Awareness Programme.

Prince Albert and around

Isolation has left intact the traditional rural architecture of **PRINCE ALBERT**, an attractive little town 70km north of Oudtshoorn, and 400km from Cape Town, across the loops and razorbacks of the Swartberg Pass – one of the most dramatic drives and entries to a town imaginable. Although firmly in the thirstlands of the South African interior, on the cusp between the Little and Great Karoo, Prince Albert is all the more striking for its perennial spring, whose water trickles down furrows along its streets – a gift that propagates fruit trees and gardens. Visitors mostly come to Prince Albert for the drive through its two southerly gateways – the **Swartberg Pass** on the R328 and **Meiringspoort** on the N12 – generally driving in one way, spending the night in town, and driving out the other.

Prince Albert is small enough to explore everywhere on foot, people are friendly, and you'll find everything you want on the main road. Supremely old-fashioned displays make window-shopping as much fun as the interior of any country museum, but the essence of Prince Albert is in the fleeting impressions that give the flavour of a Karoo *dorp* like nowhere else: the silver steeple of the Dutch Reformed church puncturing a deep-blue sky, residents sauntering along or progressing slowly down the main street on squeaky bikes. The town's beauty has attracted a number of artists to live here, and you'll find the excellent **Prince Albert Gallery**, in an airy Victorian building at 57 Church St (Mon–Fri 10am–4pm, Sat & Sun 10am–1pm), where you can browse or purchase paintings, sculpture, beadwork, jewellery, ceramics and etchings by local artists. Be sure not to miss Kevin Hough's marvellous wrought-iron sculptures, created from found objects, outside the gallery.

Staying firmly in the realm of the hand-made, Prince Albert is known for its **mohair products**: rugs, socks, scarves and other garments. Browse in the *Prince of Africa* craft shop next to the *Prince Albert Hotel* on the main road or at Wolskuur Spinners, further down. *Gay's Guernsey Dairy* at the southern end of town sells fantastic, award-winning **home-made cheeses**, which you can taste before buying, yogurts and cream. If you're travelling with children, you can take them to watch the milking at sunrise, and walk around the farm looking at other farm animals and activities (daily 7am–9am & 4–6pm; free).

One of the most exciting things you can do in Prince Albert, if not in South Africa, is to watch the **night skies** with resident astronomer Hans Daehne (weekends & school holidays only; R150 for a lecture and viewing; ☎072 732 2950). The Karoo sky is heaven for astronomers with no pollution and few lights, and you get some of the Southern Hemisphere's sharpest views of the firmament from here. Since 2005 South Africa has had the biggest telescope in the Southern Hemisphere at Sutherland, deeper in the Karoo.

You can also visit **rock-art sites** with one of the country's top paleontologists and archeologists, the now retired Dr Judy Maguire (☎023 541 1713, Ⓔquestar@icon.co.za). In the studio/museum on her farm, twenty minutes' drive outside Prince Albert at the start of the Swartberg Pass, she'll run through the fundamentals and let you handle all sorts of fascinating artefacts, then walk you up a mountainside to see the paintings. It's a highly recommended way to spend an afternoon, but you'll need to book beforehand to arrange a time, and get directions to the farm, and find out her current rates. Donations to the town's museum are part of the deal.

Mountain biking and hiking trips are offered at reasonable prices (R150, plus R65 a day for bike rental) by *Dennehof Guest House*; you're driven up one of the mountains, and descend the 18km on your own two wheels.

Practicalities

Most people get to Prince Albert through the mountains by **car**, but you can get off the Cape Town–Johannesburg **train** at Prince Albert Road station,

Go to Hell

Prince Albert is one of the best places to begin a trip into **Die Hel** (also known as Hell, The Hell or Gamkaskloof), a valley that's part of the Swartberg Nature Reserve. Die Hel is not on the way to anywhere and, although it doesn't look very far on the map, you'll need to allow two and a half hours in either direction to make the spectacular but tortuous drive into it along a dirt road. A 4WD vehicle isn't needed, but you should definitely not attempt the drive in the killing heat of December or January without air conditioning. Before attempting the trip, call Nature Conservation (℡044 802 5310, Ⓔ george@cnc.org.za) for an update on the condition of the roads.

The attraction of the place is the silence, isolation and birdlife. If you don't want to go it alone, Lisa from *Onse Rus* B&B organizes tours, for a minimum of two people for R750. She'll cater for you, and you can get picked up if you want to hike a section of the road (4–12km), instead of driving it.

There's **accommodation** here in the form of two restored farm cottages (℡023 541 1737; ❷), with camping facilities also available, run by a third-generation Kloof dweller, Annetje Joubert. The valley has no electricity supply, and no shops or any other facilities, though you can order picnic baskets and cooked breakfasts and dinners from Annetje.

45km from the hamlet, and arrange to be collected by *Onse Rus* B&B (even if you don't intend to stay with them). The trains are often late, and Prince Albert Road Station has absolutely no facilities. The **tourist office** in Church Street (Mon–Fri 9am–5pm, Sat 9am–noon; ℡023 541 1366, ⓦ www.patourism.co .za) has maps with accommodation, restaurants and craft shops, and can point you to other activities in the area; at weekends, its phone calls are diverted to the Prince of Africa craft shop at the *Swartberg Hotel*, where you also go for help. For Internet access, head to the *Lazy Lizard* in Church Street which also does good light lunches at reasonable prices.

Accommodation

There's plenty of stylish accommodation in Prince Albert, mostly in historic limewashed and thatched Karoo cottages, Cape Dutch homesteads or colonial Victorian houses.

Cactus Blue Cottages behind the National Centre opposite the *Swartberg Hotel* ℡072 464 1240, ⓦ www.cactusbluecottages.co.za. Two modern, funky cottages full of space, light and pleasing colours, overlooking a small vineyard. There is a stripey day bed to loll on, a collection of DVDs to watch, and a double mattress on an outside deck if you fancy a night under the stars. ❸

Collins House 63 Church St ℡023 541 1786, ⓦ www.collinshouse.co.za. The town's top place to stay consists of three beautifully done out, a/c en-suite guest rooms in a two-storey Victorian house, with a swimming pool. The owner does evening meals and is a great cook, but you may feel rather over-directed. ❹

Dennehof Guest House Off Christina de Wit St, on the outskirts of town ℡023 541 1227,

ⓦ www.home.intekom.com/dennehof. Three self-contained cottages and suites in a homestead that is a National Monument. The owner does hiking and mountain-biking trips. B&B. ❸

Hoogenoeg Holiday Houses ℡023 541 1455. The cheapest accommodation in town is run by Tannie ("Aunt") Alta, who rents out a number of sparsely furnished but adequate, if none too clean, old houses in Prince Albert. ❶

Karoo Lodge 66 Church St ℡023 541 1467 or 082 692 7736, ⓦ www.karoolodge.com. Reasonably priced, spacious accommodation in a B&B run by keen hosts who'll show you the ropes. ❸

Onse Rus 47 Church St ℡023 541 1380, ⓦ www .onserus.co.za. Cool, thatched B&B rooms attached to a restored Cape Dutch house, with welcoming and informed owners who serve you tea and chocolate cake on arrival, and do great breakfasts too. They also run tours to Gamkaskloof and into the Swartberg range. **③–④**

Swartberg Hotel 77 Church St ☎ 023 541 1332, ⓦ www.swartberg.co.za. A Victorian two-storey National Monument, in the heart of the town, fully refurbished following a fire in 2001. Traditional Karoo dinners are served in an atmospheric dining room, though the surroundings are considerably better than the food, and there's a swimming pool. **④**

Eating

Koggelmander 61 Church St ☎ 023 541 1900. Modern Karoo food, including lamb and ostrich. Vegetarians will be happy here too, and it's a great place to have a beer on the terrace, lounge on the sofas inside, or wander about looking at the paintings on the wall. Tues–Sun 9am–4pm & daily 7pm till late. **Celestino's** next to the *Swartberg Hotel*. Steakhouse-style food every evening from 7pm. Good for families and reasonably priced.

Karoo Kombuis 18 Deurdrift St ☎ 023 541 1110. Traditional fare from this part of the country, with a home-cooked feel and meat galore. Daily evenings only, closed all day Sun.
Sampie se Plaasstal At the south end of the main road. A great place for snacks, with excellent dried fruit and rusks, as well as local olives which are among the best in South Africa. Open for breakfast, light lunches and tea.

The N1 from Worcester to Beaufort West

The **N1** is the main highway between Cape Town and Johannesburg, and with the majority of flights still arriving in Johannesburg it's common for visitors to arrive there and drive down to the coast. This account, however, assumes you'll be starting your journey in Cape Town and heading north. While this route isn't particularly inspiring, and won't take you through the diversity of the country, it does lead you into the Karoo, the huge semi-desert filling the centre-west of South Africa. The various towns along the way have a couple of interesting historic buildings and some of the flavour of the isolated Karoo in their street scenes – enough to fill an hour if you're looking for a break from the long journey. The most compelling places are undoubtedly the Victorian village of **Matjiesfontein** and the **Karoo National Park** just outside Beaufort West, as well as the tiny village of **Sutherland**, in the Karoo uplands, which is known for its crystal-clear night skies and icy winters, and is home to the **South African Large Telescope**.

Matjiesfontein

One of the quirkier manifestations of Victorian colonialism lies 250km east of Cape Town at the historic village of **MATJIESFONTEIN** (pronounced "Mikey's-fontayn"). Little more than two dusty streets beside a train track, the village resembles a film set rather than a Karoo *dorp*: every building, including the grand train station, is a classic period piece, with tin roofs, pastel walls, well-tended gardens and Victorian frills. At the eastern end of the main street is the centrepiece, the *Lord Milner*, a hotel decked out with turrets and balconies and fountains by the entrance. If you're passing by, make sure you stop at least for a look around; at less than three hours' drive from Cape Town the village is worth considering as a two-day trip in its own right.

The origins of this curious place lie in the tale of a young Scottish entrepreneur, Jimmy Logan, who came to Cape Town to work on the railways and obtained the concession to sell refreshments to passengers all the way along the line from Cape Town to Bulawayo. He built Matjiesfontein as a health resort – making much play on the clean Karoo air – and it became a gathering point for the wealthy and influential around the turn of the last century.

Today the village is doing brisk trade as a treasured relic. You can still come here in the classical manner on the main-line **train** from Cape Town to Jo'burg/Pretoria (a leisurely rather than direct journey), and **stay** at the *Lord Milner* (T 023 561 3011, W www.matjiesfontein.com; ❸–❹), either in one of the comfortable rooms in the hotel itself, or in one of the annexes in the surrounding houses; the cheapest rooms are in a separate section in the garden and don't include breakfast. The gardens themselves and the large swimming pool are delightfully restorative. Inside the hotel there are huge portraits on the wall, grand staircases, polished brass fittings and, perhaps taking the theme a touch too far, rather surly service from waitresses dressed in black and white, with doilies on their heads. For **eating and drinking**, the hotel has a dimly lit dining room and a wonderfully aged and creaking bar. Along the main street you'll find a tea room, souvenir shop and post office, all in attractive Victorian houses.

Sutherland

A detour off the N1 some 100km north of Matjiesfontein, along the R354, brings you to **SUTHERLAND**, fearfully known to South Africans as the coldest spot in the country. But it's for its clear, unpolluted skies that it's most notable, since it's one of the handful of places in the world where scientists study deep space, and you can do a tour to see a hilltop full of telescopes housed in huge silver domes where experts from all over the world spend freezing nights extending human knowledge. There are daily visits to the **Observatory** (10.30am & 2.30pm, except Tues afternoons and Sun; R10; book through the tourist office on T 023 571 1265). Even if you're not a die-hard astronomy fan, it's still interesting to call at the visitors' centre to see **SALT** (the **South African Large Telescope**), which is powerful enough, with its 91 hexagonal mirrors, to be able to see just one candle were it placed on the moon, and one of the mightiest in the Southern Hemisphere, though you don't actually get to look through it. Where you *can* get to look through a telescope is at the *Kambrokind B&B*, 19 Piet Retief St (T 023 571 1405, W www.sutherlandinfo.co.za; ❸), as owner Jurg Wagener sets one up in the garden for guests. The other thoroughly recommended place to stay is *The Ark*, 6 Church St (T 083 252 4551; ❷), a central, self-catering 1857 stone house warmed by a massive wood-fired stove, with a lady who will cook the provisions you bring in.

Beaufort West

Back on the highway, for over 100km on either side of **BEAUFORT WEST**, the scenery from the N1 is far away and hazy, so the appearance of the Nieuwveld Mountains, which rise up behind town, gives the place a certain distinction. Beyond that, however, Beaufort West is not a pretty place, with the N1 traffic trundling through its centre (watch out for speed traps and remember to stop at traffic lights), and it devotes most of its attention to servicing road-weary travellers and indeed the only compelling reason to stop off here is to break the long journey between Cape Town and Johannesburg. If you're sleeping over, it's worth thinking about spending the night in the beautiful **Karoo National Park**, just outside town.

Practicalities

Intercity **buses** pull into the Engen garage complex in Donkin Street. The town's helpful **tourist office** is at 63 Donkin St (Mon–Fri 8am–4.45pm; T 023 415 1488), one block along from the museum.

For **eating**, the best breakfasts are to be had at the *Matoppo Inn*, which is open to non-guests (7–9am). It also does four-course, set-menu Karoo-style dinners, if booked earlier in the day. On Donkin Street is the predictable but reliable *Saddles Steak House*.

Accommodation

Beaufort West has no shortage of **accommodation**, though much of it is on the busy main road. If you want to **camp**, the best option is the Karoo National Park (see below), just a few kilometres out of town, and certainly the park's accommodation is tranquil and lovely. This requires booking well in advance.

Donkin Country House 14 Donkin St ☎ 023 414 4287, ⓦ www.donkinhouse.co.za. This simple guesthouse has en-suite rooms with TV and fridge, the requisite a/c, a swimming pool and some communal space to hang out in. ❷
Matoppo Inn On the corner of Bird and Meintjies sts ☎ 023 415 1055, ⓦ www.matoppoinn .co.za. Elegant rooms with brass beds and antique furniture, as well as standard rooms in the town's

old *drostdy*, or magistrate's house. The gardens are beautiful, and there's a pool, good food and a relaxed atmosphere. ❸
Wagon Wheel Country Lodge Off the N1 on the northern fringe of town ☎ 023 414 2145, ⓦ www.info-beaufortwest.co.za/wagonwheels /index.html. En-suite motel rooms, plus camping facilities, with a splash pool for kids. Meals are extra. ❷

Karoo National Park

With an unusually mountainous setting for the generally flattish and parched Karoo, the **Karoo National Park** (gate daily 5am–10pm, reception daily 7am–7pm; ☎ 023 415 2828; R60) has emerged in recent years as a reserve with much more to offer than first meets the eye. The themes of the semi-desert are undoubtedly here, and after a night gazing at the dazzling sky, or a hot day walking on some trails and learning about the unexpectedly intricate flora of the region, you'll start to appreciate this park's special value.

Much of the experience here is in the landscape and the serene atmosphere: despite the recent introduction of some **black rhino**, big game is limited, although there are some impressive raptors, including the **black eagle**. The designated drives around a limited section of the 600-square-kilometre park aren't terribly exciting; however, there is a wider-ranging 4WD trail.

Near the main restcamp there is an environmental **education centre**, along with three **trails**: an eleven-kilometre day-walk; a short but informative tree trail; and a very imaginative fossil trail (designed to accommodate wheelchairs and incorporating Braille boards), which tells the fascinating 250-million-year geological history of the area and shows fossils of the unusual animals that lived here in the times when the Karoo was a vast inland sea. Information about these is available at camp reception.

Practicalities

The entrance gate to Karoo National Park is right on the N1, 2km south of Beaufort West. The **reception and restcamp** are 10km into the park, hidden among the appealing flat-topped mountains in a way that makes you feel as though you're a million kilometres from the town and the highway. At reception there's a shop selling basic foodstuffs and a **restaurant** (Mon–Sat 8am–8.30pm, Sun 8am–7pm), with a pool nearby. Accommodation is in thirty fully equipped **chalets** and **cottages** that sleep three people (❸), strung out on either side of the main complex; the rate is for a minimum of two people and includes breakfast in the restaurant. The **campsite** is hidden away over a rise.

The Overberg interior and the Whale Coast

East of the Winelands lies a vaguely defined region known as the **Overberg** (Afrikaans for "over the mountain"). In the seventeenth century, when Stellenbosch, Franschhoek and Paarl were remote outposts, everywhere beyond them was, to the Dutch settlers, a fuzzy hinterland drifting off into the arid sands of the Karoo. These days it extends to an imprecise point between Arniston and Mossel Bay on the coast and somewhere east of Swellendam in the interior.

Of the two main routes through the Overberg, the **N2** strikes out across the less interesting interior, a four- to five-hour stretch of undulating fields of sheep and wheat. North of the N2 is **Greyton**, a pleasant village used by Capetonians as a relaxing weekend retreat, and the starting point of the **Boesmanskloof Traverse** – a terrific two-day trail across the mountains into the Karoo. The historic Moravian mission station of **Genadendal**, ten minutes down the road from Greyton, has a strange Afro-Germanic ambience that offers a couple of hours' pleasant strolling. Along the N2 itself, the only places that justify a restorative stop are **Caledon**, for its thermal springs, and **Swellendam**, for its well-preserved streetscape as well as one of South Africa's best country museums.

The real draw of the area is the **Whale Coast**, close enough for an easy outing from Cape Town, yet surprisingly undeveloped. The exception is popular **Hermanus**, which owes its fame to its status as the whale-watching capital of South Africa. The whole of this southern Cape coast is, in fact, prime territory for land-based whale-watching. Also along this section of coast is **Cape Agulhas**, the southernmost point on the continent, where rocks peter into the ocean. Nearby, and more exclusive, is **Arniston**, one of the best-preserved fishing villages in the country, and a little to its east the **De Hoop Nature Reserve**, an exciting wilderness of bleached dunes, craggy coast and more whales.

Caledon

The first impression of **CALEDON**, some 111km east of Cape Town on the N2, is of huge, cathedral-like grain silos that dwarf its church spires. A low-key farming town, Caledon built its former prosperity on the wheat, barley and malt trade. Now the town is gambling on making its fortune through a casino and family entertainment complex, built around the town's one natural asset, its thermal springs. When the Dutch arrived here in the eighteenth century, Khoi people were already wallowing in steaming holes dug in the ground – a practice imitated by the settlers. The Victorians built a wrought-iron structure around the main rectangular pool, replaced in 2001 by a timber one that retains the feel of the original.

Today, Caledon **spa** (Tues–Sat 10am–7pm; R100; ☎028 214 5100) offers a gamut of physical indulgences – wonderfully relaxing and rejuvenating though in an artificial setting. The so-called Khoisan spa consists of a fake

▲ Caledon

waterfall tumbling down the mountainside into a series of rocky pools, getting progressively cooler as they approach the foot of the hill (the one at the top clocks 40°C). Use of the saunas, a steam room, frigidarium and gym are all included in the price; towels are provided and robes can be rented. A **treatment centre** offers a huge variety of expensive massages and beauty treatments, from aromatherapy massage to thalassotherapy (using seaweed), and there are sunbeds for chilling.

The town's **casino** forms part of a small mall with a couple of family restaurants and a few shops. If you fancy a flutter, you can try your luck at one of the scores of slot-machines lined up inside the large gambling hall, which also has a number of gaming tables.

Caledon has a couple of other decent attractions. The **House Museum** at 11 Constitution St (Mon–Fri 10am–1pm & 2–4.30pm) consists of displays of mainly domestic items in a house faithfully restored to "Victorian Caledon style" (1837–1901). A photographic display – also part of the museum – is housed with the information bureau at the old town hall. The town's outdoor attraction is the **Wildflower Garden and Nature Reserve** (10am–7pm; R25), where you can wander through *fynbos*, aloes and succulents on a lovely long amble along a rocky, wooded *kloof* into the mountains, or head out on the ten-kilometre Meiring trail, which goes deep into the nature reserve.

Practicalities

You can reach Caledon right off the N2. To get to the spa, follow the sign displaying the hotel and spa symbols which, if you're coming from Cape Town, is a little way beyond the town centre indicator.

Intercity **buses** stop off at the Spar supermarket on Market Square (corner Plein St and Prince Alfred Rd) in the centre of town. Caledon's **tourist office**, in the old town hall, 22 Plein St (Mon–Fri 8am–5pm, Sat 9am–1pm; ☎028 214 3370), has literature about the area, details of places to stay, and an attached crafts shop.

As regards **accommodation**, *Little Lotta*, 7 Disa St (☎028 212 3305; ❷), offers good-quality self-catering near the N2. *Kelkiewyn*, 22 Prince Alfred St (☎028 214 1884; ❷), is a good choice for reasonably priced rooms in a Victorian B&B on the main road, with a couple of recently built self-catering units at the back. Signposted 1km east of the centre, off the N2, *Caledon Hotel* (☎028 214 1500, ⓦwww.caledoncasino.co.za; ❺) offers the smartest accommodation and dining in town, though that's not saying much – it's a tired affair catering to weekenders and the conference market, though the hotel's front terrace, looking onto fields and hills, is shady and pleasant. The *Venster Restaurant* at the Wildflower Garden (daily 9am–10pm) serves snacks and traditional Afrikaner fare, such as *bobotie* and *bredie*. Portions are whopping – it's a challenge to finish the plate of steak and chips served here.

Greyton, Genadendal and the Boesmanskloof Traverse

Greyton, a small, peaceful village 46km north of Caledon, and 145km from Cape Town, is a favourite weekend destination for Capetonians, based around a core of Georgian and Victorian buildings, shaded by grand old oaks, and tucked away at the edge of the Riviersonderend (meaning "river with no end") Mountains. In recent years, it has changed from being a retirement village to a place where young city families come to seek a more peaceful life. It also offers good guesthouses, cafés, restaurants and places to walk, most notably the superb **Boesmanskloof Traverse** hike, which crosses the mountains to a point 14km from McGregor. South Africa's oldest mission station, **Genadendal**, a six-kilometre excursion west of Greyton, is also worth a look around.

Greyton

GREYTON is a great place to unwind, stroll and potter about in the handful of galleries, antique and tea shops. The town's **Dolls' House Museum**, at the tourist office, is filled with miniature handmade dolls' houses showing attention to the minutest details, right down to cakes and pastries.

There's no public transport to Greyton. The best route to drive here is the sealed R406 from just west of Caledon; don't attempt the untarred route from Riviersonderend, which will hammer your suspension. The **Greyton Tourism Bureau** at 29 Main St (Mon–Sat 10am–5pm, Sun 10am–3pm; ☎028 254 9414, ⓦ www.greyton.net), along the main road as you come into town, has lists of accommodation and rents out bicycles for R15 an hour.

Accommodation

It's worth staying somewhere with a fireplace if you're here in winter, as it can be cold in this mountainous terrain, and conversely look for a pool in summer. Most places charge more for a one-night stay, as it is primarily a weekend destination, not on the way to anywhere else, and there's little accommodation to be found in the lower price ranges.

The Boesmanskloof Traverse

The fourteen-kilometre **Boesmanskloof Traverse** takes you from the gentle, oak-lined streets of **Greyton** across the Riviersonderend mountain range to the glaring Karoo scrubland around the town of **McGregor** (see p.208). The stark contrast over so short a distance is staggering, made all the more so by the fact that no direct roads connect the two towns; to drive from one to the other involves a circuitous two-hour journey.

The classic way to cover the Traverse is to walk from Greyton to **Die Galg** (14km from McGregor), where people commonly spend the night, returning the same way to Greyton the following day. The Traverse rises and falls a fair bit, so you'll have to contend with a lot of uphill walking, but the route can easily be completed in a day if you're reasonably fit, and you can still have a rewarding outing venturing only part of the way and returning to Greyton for the evening. A decent day's walk takes you to **Oak Falls**, 9km from Greyton. Composed of a series of cascades, it's the highlight of the route, its most impressive feature being a large pool where you can rest and swim in cola-coloured water.

The walk takes you through numerous species of wonderful montane *fynbos*, and between July and October you can find yourself walking through magnificent groves of flowering king proteas. Mammals include small antelope, caracals, baboons and dassies, though it's unlikely you'll see many of them.

Trail practicalities

You're free to walk the first 5km of the trail and back, but to complete the whole route from Greyton to Die Galg – numbers are limited to fifty people per day – you will need a **permit** (R25 per person per day). Over weekends, the trail gets extremely full and permits must be arranged in advance through the Greyton Tourism Bureau. You get a **map** when you buy the permit, although you don't really need one as the Traverse is very clearly marked out. The walk can be strenuous, so make sure you're fit and have good shoes. It's also worth noting that this is an area of winter rainfall; summers are hot and dry.

As for **accommodation**, there's *Whipstock Farm* (see p.210) 4km beyond Die Galg (the owner can collect you free of charge from Die Galg), or the overnight dorms at Die Galg (☎023 625 1735; ask for Mr Oosthuizen), equipped with a fridge, cooker and beds (but no bedding).

Acorns On Oak 2 Oak St ☎028 254 9567, ⓦ www.acorns-on-oak.co.za. Five luxurious rooms each with underfloor heating, espresso machine, loft lounge and garden-facing patio on this riverfront property. Well-priced choice for a romantic weekend, with no children allowed. There's also a 12m heated pool and loungers in a lovely garden. ❹

Auberge Greyton corner of Oak St and Main Rd ☎028 254 9192. Simple, uncluttered farm-style rooms – if you're planning on hiking and just need a bed for the night or two, this friendly and reasonable B&B is a good bet. ❷

Barnards Boutique Hotel 16 Main Rd ☎028 254 9394, ⓦ www.barnardshotel.co.za. Modern and comfortable rooms in a new and fashionable

gay-owned establishment with a lovely pool and a great bar. ❻–❼

Guinea Fowl Ds Botha St ☎028 254 9550. Guesthouse with en-suite rooms and serving a full English breakfast. ❹

High Hopes 89 Main Rd ☎028 254 9898, ⓦ www.highhopes.co.za. One of the best B&Bs in town, in a beautiful country-style home set in magnificent gardens with a huge ornamental pond and a swimming pool. Besides three rooms, there's a self-contained unit with a kitchen, which can be taken on a B&B or self-catering basis. Afternoon tea and biscuits as well as delicious breakfasts are included in the rate, and a variety of therapies, including massage, is on offer too. ❻

Eating and drinking

The town has a short-lived Saturday **market** at the corner of Main Road and Cross Market Street (10am–noon), to which locals bring their produce: organic vegetables, fabulous and well-priced cheese, decadent cakes, breads, biscuits and preserves; also on sale are secondhand books and bric-a-brac. Otherwise, there is a limited range of food on sale at the small deli at the *Oak and Vigne Café*. The nicest place for a **drink** is at *Barnard's Boutique Hotel* on Main Road. Food at the restaurants tends to be quite sophisticated, creative, nouvelle cuisine.

254 8 Ds Botha St ☎028 254 9373. Book a candlelit veranda table for good food, fun and a welcoming atmosphere. There is always something delicious for vegetarians too.

Abbey Rose Main Rd ☎028 254 9470. Nice garden setting to enjoy salads or tea and scones. Open daily 9am–4.30pm, plus dinner Fri & Sat.

Barnard's Boutique Hotel 16 Main Rd ☎028 254 9394. Nice setting for a sundowner, with wine and tapas on the *stoep*, or by the fireplace inside. The big screen at the pub draws sports fans.

Jam Tin in the township 2km south of town ☎028 254 9075 or 076 875 8737. From her humble 200-year-old family home, Dora cooks a traditional three-course Cape Malay meal in the evening. Booking necessary and directions given to her home.

Oak and Vigne Café Ds Botha St ☎028 254 9037. Highly popular, situated in an old cottage with an oak-shaded terrace where you can savour reasonably priced Mediterranean-influenced country breakfasts, teas and gourmet lunches daily.

Genadendal

GENADENDAL, whose name means "valley of grace", was founded in 1737 by Moravians, and some of the ochre and earthy-pink architecture hints at Central European influences. Just 6km from Greyton, it's definitely worth roaming around. The village's focus is around **Church Square**, dominated by a very Germanic church building dating back to 1891. The old bell outside dates back to the eighteenth century, when it became the centre of a flaming row between the local farmers and the mission station. The scrap broke out when missionary Georg Schmidt annoyed the local white farmers by forming a small Christian congregation with impoverished Khoi – who were on the threshold of extinction – and giving refuge to maltreated labourers from local farms. What really got the farmers' goat was the fact that while they, white Christians, were illiterate, Schmidt was teaching native people, whom they considered uncivilized, to read and write. The Dutch Reformed Church, under the control of the Dutch East India Company, waded in when Schmidt began baptizing converts, and prohibited the mission from ringing the bell which called the faithful to prayer.

At one stage during the eighteenth century, Genadendal was the largest settlement in southern Africa after Cape Town. Although it never became more than a village, Genadendal experienced a golden age in the nineteenth century, with a flourishing economy based on home industries. In 1838 it established the first teacher training college in the country, which the government closed in 1926, on the grounds that coloured people didn't need tertiary education and should be employed as workers on local farms – a policy that effectively ground the community into poverty. In 1995, in recognition of the mission's role, Nelson Mandela renamed his official residence in Cape Town "Genadendal".

Today, the population of this principally coloured town numbers around four thousand people, adhering to a variety of Christian sects – no longer just Moravianism. The **Mission Museum** (Mon–Thurs 9am–1pm & 2–5pm, Fri 9am–3.30pm, Sat 9am–noon), adjacent to Church Square, is moderately interesting and provides some clues as to why Moravians came here. You should allow up to two hours to explore the museum and wander through the town, down to the rural graveyard, spiked with tombstones dating back to the early nineteenth century.

The Genadendal **tourist office** (Mon–Thurs 8.30am–5pm, Fri 8.30am–4pm, Sat 10am–2pm; ☎028 251 8291) is on Church Square in the centre of the mission. Basic budget **accommodation** aimed principally at hikers doing the strenuous, two-day, 25-kilometre Genadendal Trail (details and booking ☎028 251 8346) is available at the Hester Dorothea Conference Centre (☎028 251 8346; ❶), on the square, in dormitories and a few private rooms, sharing bathrooms and kitchen facilities. Genadendal offers few other visitor amenities, but there is a **tea room** just off Church Square, where you can get refreshments, though nothing is open on Sundays.

Swellendam and around

On the N2, 97km east of Caledon and 220km from Cape Town, **SWELLENDAM** is an attractive historic town at the foot of the Langeberg. With one of the best country museums in South Africa, it's a congenial stop along the N2 between Cape Town and the Garden Route. And because of its ample supply of good accommodation and its position – poised between the coastal De Hoop Nature Reserve and the Langeberg – it's a suitable base for spending a day or two exploring this part of the Overberg, with the Bontebok National Park, stomping ground of an attractive type of antelope, close at hand to the south.

South Africa's third-oldest white settlement, Swellendam was established in 1745 by Baron Gustav van Imhoff, a visiting Dutch East India Company bigwig. He was deeply concerned about the "moral degeneration" of burghers who were trekking further and further from Cape Town and out of Company control. Of no less concern to the Baron was the loss of revenue from these "vagabonds", who were neglecting to pay the Company for the right to hold land and were fiddling their annual tax returns. Following a brief hiccup in 1795, when burghers declared a "free republic" (quickly extinguished when Britain occupied the Cape), the town grew into a prosperous rural centre known for its wagon-making, and for being the last "civilized" port of call for trekboers heading out into the interior. The income generated from this helped build Swellendam's gracious homes, many of which went up in smoke in the fire of 1865, which razed much of the town centre.

The Town

The only building in the centre to survive the town's 1865 fire is the Cape Dutch-style **Oefeningshuis**, 36 Voortrek St, which now houses the tourist office. Built in 1838, it was first used as a place for religious activity, then as a school for freed slaves, and has surreal-looking clocks with frozen hands carved into either gable end, below which there's a real clock above the entrance. Diagonally opposite and slightly east at no. 11, the **Dutch Reformed Church**, dating from 1910, incorporates Gothic windows, a Baroque spire, Renaissance portico elements and Cape Dutch gables into a wedding cake of a building that agreeably holds its own, against the odds, and certainly still draws a good crowd on Sundays.

On the east side of town, a short way from the centre, is the excellent **Drostdy Museum**, 18 Swellegrebel St (Mon–Fri 9am–4.45pm, Sat & Sun 10am–3.45pm; R15). It's a collection of historic buildings arranged around large grounds, with a lovely nineteenth-century Cape garden. The centrepiece is the *drostdy* itself, built in 1747 as the seat of the *landdrost*, a magistrate-cum-commissioner sent out by the Dutch East India Company to control the outer reaches of its territory. The building conforms to the beautiful limewashed, thatched and shuttered Cape Dutch style of the eighteenth century, but the furnishings are of nineteenth-century vintage. From the rear garden of the *drostdy* you can stroll along a path and across Drostdy Street to **Mayville**, a middle-class Victorian homestead from the mid-nineteenth century with an old rose garden. The **Old Gaol**, with thatched roof, and thick, whitewashed walls, has been converted into the best daytime eatery in town, while the **Utamaduni Gallery** next door has good crafts for sale.

On a far flightier note, the **Sulina Faerie Sanctuary**, 33 Buitenkant St (Thurs–Sun 9am–4.30pm; R10), is the result of one Swellendam resident's obsession, housing hundreds of fairy statuettes and images. Its mystical garden has gnomes, pixies and miniature castles hidden in the undergrowth.

Practicalities

Greyhound, Intercape and Translux **buses** between Cape Town and Port Elizabeth pull in diagonally opposite the *Swellengrebel Hotel*, 91 Voortrek St, in the centre of town, while the Baz Bus will drop you off at any of the central accommodation. Swellendam has a very switched-on **tourist office** at 36 Voortrek St (Mon–Fri 9am–5pm, Sat & Sun 9am–1pm; ☏028 514 2770, ✉infoswd@swellenmun.co.za), which provides frank and helpful advice about local attractions and can book accommodation. The town is built along a very long main road with no traffic lights; it's most attractive at either end, with a mundane shopping area in the middle. The eastern end is dominated by the museum complex, and is nearest to the mountain reserve for hiking or horse-riding. This is also the area where you'll find the backpacker lodge.

The best thing to do in Swellendam is to go **horse-riding** in the forests and mountains at the eastern edge of town, securely seated in a western-style saddle. Two Feathers Horse Trails (☏082 494 8279 or 082 485 4379, ⓦwww .twofeathers.co.za) offers riding by the hour, or you can do a full-day outing with picnic lunch included. The horses are well cared for, the guide, Barry, patient and responsive, and there are mounts suitable for beginners or experienced riders.

The landscape is varied and ranges from pine forest tracks past waterfalls and mountain streams to riverside trails, meandering country roads and open grass plains.

Accommodation

Anyone who enjoys the atmosphere of historic houses will be spoilt for choice in Swellendam, where places to stay in Cape Dutch and Georgian houses are ten a penny, and rates tend to be pretty reasonable.

Augusta de Mist 3 Human St ☎ 028 514 2425, ⓦ www.augustademist.co.za. A 200-year-old homestead with three beautifully renovated cottages, two garden suites and a family unit, mostly with fireplaces and all with percale linen. A rambling terraced garden and a pool complete the picture. ⑤

Cypress Cottage 3 Voortrek St ☎ 028 514 3296, ⓦ www.cypresscottage.co.za. Five charming rooms, decorated with antiques, in the back garden of a grand house, one of the oldest in town, as well as two rooms inside the main house. Good value. ③

Eenuurkop Huisie 8km from town on the Ashton road ☎ 028 514 1447. Two self-catering cottages, one with three bedrooms, the other with one, in a stunning setting with great views and access to mountain walks. ②

Herberg Roosje Van De Kaap 5 Drostdy St ☎ 028 514 3001, ⓦ www.roosjevandekaap.com. A popular B&B in a beautiful house right near the museum, with a pool, excellent and friendly service and a good reputation for candlelit dinners, though some of the rooms are rather small. Discounts for cash payments ④

Hermitage Huisies 3km from town on R60 to Ashton ☎ 028 514 2308. Two wonderful self-catering cottages, sleeping four or five people, plus a flatlet for two, on a smallholding with a duck pond and grazing sheep. ②

Klippe Rivier Homestead Signposted off the western end of town ☎ 028 514 3341, ⓦ www.klipperivier.com. Swellendam's most formal and luxurious accommodation, in a beautiful 1825 Cape Dutch homestead with six utterly comfortable country-style bedrooms, each with a patio or veranda, a secluded cottage and saltwater swimming pool, gorgeous gardens and fabulous breakfasts. No under-10s. ⑦

Lulu's B&B 10 Voortrek St ☎ 028 514 2202 or 082 847 9523. A well-run B&B, centrally located, with two en-suite rooms and a self-catering loft apartment (sleeping up to eight) above. ②

Swellendam Backpackers 5 Lichtenstein St ☎ 028 514 2648, ⓦ www.swellendambackpackers .co.za. Swellendam's only hostel is a friendly place, well situated near the Marloth Nature Reserve and museum, with a large campsite, dorms and decent doubles; staff can also arrange activities including horse-riding, mountain biking and canoeing. Children are also welcome, as there's lots of space, and while this isn't a big party place, there is a bar conveniently near the premises. ① ③

Swellendam Country Lodge 237 Voortrek St ☎ 028 514 3629, ⓦ www.swellendamlodge.com. Six rooms with separate entrances, reed ceilings, and elegant, uncluttered decor in muted hues. ③

Eating

There's no shortage of decent places to eat in Swellendam – ranging from snack bars to formal restaurants where you can enjoy a romantic candlelit dinner – many of them in delightful old buildings. Most are on either end of the long main road.

The Old Gaol Coffee Shop Drostdy Museum, 26 Swellengrebel St ☎ 028 514 3847. Not the usual run-of-the-mill museum snack bar, this is a great place with indoor and outdoor seating where you can get fantastic coffee and cake, milk tart in a copper pan, and *roosterkoek* – traditional bread made on an open fire, with nice fillings. Open 8.30am–6pm.

The Old Mill 241–243 Voortrek St, west end ☎ 028 514 2790. Pleasant spot with daytime garden seating; satisfying, well-presented dinners, including starters such as deep-fried camembert with sesame seed coating, and main dishes of fish,

pasta and game, with the advantage of a fireplace in winter.

Roosje Van De Kaap 5 Drostdy St ☎ 028 514 3001. A highly rated restaurant offering traditional Cape food, with a great wine list – a good choice for a romantic candlelit dinner. Booking essential. Tues–Sun 7–11pm.

Woodpecker Deli Voortrek St, west end ☎ 028 514 2924. Pizzeria and cafeteria, with picnic platters with good cheeses and Italian deli fare. Good for vegetarians. Daily 9.30am–9pm, closed Sun evenings.

Bontebok National Park

Just 6km south of Swellendam along the Breede River, the **Bontebok National Park** (May–Sept 7am–6pm; Oct–April 7am–7pm; ℡028 514 2735; day visitors R20, overnight visitors free) is a compact 28-square-kilometre reserve at the foot of the Langeberg range that makes a relaxing overnight stop between Cape Town and the Garden Route. The park was established in 1931 to save the Cape's dwindling population of bontebok, an attractive antelope with distinctive cappuccino, chocolate-brown and white markings on its forehead and hindquarters. By 1930, hunting had reduced the number of animals to a mere thirty. Their survival has happily been secured and there are now three hundred of them in the park, as well as populations in other game and nature reserves in the province. There are no big cats in the park, but **mammals** you might encounter include rare Cape mountain zebra, red hartebeest and grey rhebok, and there are more than 120 **bird species**. It's also a rich environment for **fynbos**, with nearly 500 species here, including erica, gladioli and proteas. Apart from game viewing, there are opportunities to swim in the Breede River, hike a couple of short nature trails and fish.

Self-catering **accommodation** is available in ten newly built, fully equipped chalets (❸) or you can camp next to the river in your own tent. A **shop** at the park entrance sells drinks and sweets, but you'll need to bring your own food with you.

The coast from Strand to Kleinmond

The main reason you'd take the coastal route that skirts the eastern shore of False Bay is to get to Hermanus, but scenically the drive has much to recommend it, especially once you get past the commuter settlements close to Cape Town. Leaving the N2 from Cape Town at Somerset West, the first coastal settlement you hit is **Strand**, a massive industrial centre on the edge of Cape Town. Although it has a good beach, this isn't sufficient reason to stop off and the R44 quickly takes you to the ongoing commuter development of **Gordon's Bay**, your last chance for a decent sea swim for some distance. After here, the mountains bear down on the sea and the road winds its way around the folding mountainside, with the sea crashing against the rocks below – without a tree in sight, the barren landscape has a raw, dramatic quality. **Cape Hangklip**, the tip of False Bay, earned its name from the fact that Hangklip frequently fooled Portuguese mariners into thinking they were rounding the Cape of Good Hope. A dirt road takes you down to **Hangklip** itself, where a succession of dwellers have made their homes since humans left stone axes here over 20,000 years ago. In the nineteenth century, outlaws lived in Hangklip's remote caves, but were flushed out in 1852, leaving the area to its present population of baboons.

Pringle Bay, Betty's Bay and around

Cape Hangklip roughly marks the point at which the commuters become holidaymakers. Just around the corner to the east, **PRINGLE BAY**, a small collection of seaside homes, is the first of a series of rather unattractive, ever-developing settlements, with bungalows cluttering the bare mountain sides. The coast itself, though, is lovely, and the drive from Cape Town spectacular. **BETTY'S BAY**, a few kilometres further along the R44, prosaically named after Betty Youlden, daughter of the director of the first company to try to develop the area, and the focal point of the area, is rather boring. Its saving grace is that it hosts a colony of **African (jackass) penguins**, seen from a wooden boardwalk at the well-signposted Stony Point Penguin Colony (daily sunrise to sunset; R10). African penguins mate for life and return to the same nest every year, but here are suffering from interference with their turf by perlemoen (abalone) poachers. Residents urge you to tell local shopkeepers if you see poaching taking place. Betty's Bay has a classy café, the *Espresso Leopard*, at 3003 Clarence Drive, open weekends (9am–9pm), and every day bar Tuesdays in the summer, though you can **eat** year round at the Harold Porter National Botanical Garden.

Best place to eat in the entire area, and an event in itself, is the *Hook, Line and Sinker* at Pringle Bay (booking essential on ☎028 273 8688; Tues–Sun lunch & dinner), run by a husband-and-wife team in their own home. There is only seasonal fish on the menu, cooked on an open fire by larger-than-life Stephan, who has spent years deep-sea diving along the West Coast. Prices are moderate, and you won't eat better fish in the country; you can also buy the catch of the day to take home. For dessert, try the crème brûlée, caramelized at your table with an industrial blowtorch. Also in Pringle Bay the romantic and palatial modern guesthouse, *Moonstruck on Pringle Bay*, 264 Hangklip Rd (☎028 273 8162, ⓦwww.moonstruck.co.za ⑤), offers four huge rooms with sea-facing balconies. It's a short walk from the guesthouse to a bay with good swimming.

Harold Porter National Botanical Garden

Creeping up the mountains just above Betty's Bay, **Harold Porter National Botanical Garden** (Mon–Fri 8am–4pm, Sat & Sun 8am–5pm; R15) is a wild sanctuary of coastal and montane *fynbos* that makes a good stop along the R44, if only to picnic or have tea at its outdoor **café**. The relatively compact botanical garden extends over two square kilometres from the mountains, through marshland down to coastal dunes. Once here, you'll probably get lured at least some of the way up the *kloof* that runs through the reserve; as you get higher up, you're treated to sea views in one direction and rugged mountains in the other.

Although wildlife in the form of small **antelope**, **baboons** and **leopards** is present, they are rarely sighted and it's more worthwhile to look out instead for the birds and blooms. In January you can see brilliant red disas in all their glory, while the nerine lilies flower in March. Keep an eye open for colourful, nectar-loving sunbirds and scores of other bird **species** that are found here. Four **trails** of between one and three hours meander through the gardens, but you can just as easily take yourself off on an impromptu stroll, up and across the red-stained waters (the colour stems from phenols and tannins leaching from the *fynbos*) running through Disa Kloof.

Kleinmond

Because of its isolation, **KLEINMOND**, roughly 12km northeast of Betty's Bay, was an outlaws' stronghold for some two hundred years. In the twentieth century, however, relatively easy access turned the town into a holiday spot for Capetonians and for farmers from the surrounding areas. An impressive confluence of sea, dune, tidal estuary and mountain waterfalls combines with a ten-kilometre crescent **beach** curving across the Bot River Mouth to Mudge Point, a promontory that completes the vista as you look east. A strip of craft and coffee shops that includes a deli, sports bar and a visitable **abalone hatchery** is reached down the road signposted "Harbour" off the main coastal road.

Hermanus and the Whale Coast

On the edge of rocky cliffs and backed by mountains, **Hermanus**, 112km east of Cape Town, sits at the northernmost end of Walker Bay, an inlet whose protective curve attracts calving whales as it slides south to the promontory of Danger Point. From about July, southern right whales (see box below) start appearing in the warmer sheltered bays of the Western Cape, and the town trumpets itself as the **whale capital** of South Africa. To prove it, an official whale crier (purportedly the world's only one) struts around armed with a mobile phone and a dried kelp horn through which he yells the latest sightings. The hype aside, **Walker Bay** does provide some of the finest shore-based whale-watching in the world and, even if

Whale-watching

The Southern Cape, including Cape Town, provides some of the easiest and best places in the world for **whale-watching**. You don't need to rent a boat or take a pricey tour to get out to sea; if you come at the right time of year, whales are often visible from the shore, although a good pair of binoculars will come in useful for when they are far out.

All nine of the great whale species of the southern hemisphere pass by South Africa's shores, but the most commonly seen off Cape Town are **southern right whales** (their name derives from being the "right" one to kill because of their high oil and bone yields and the fact that, conveniently, they float when dead). Southern right whales are black and easily recognized from their pale, brownish **callosities**. These unappealing patches of raised, roughened skin on their snouts and heads have a distinct pattern on each animal, which helps scientists keep track of them.

Female whales come inshore to calve in sheltered bays, and stay to nurse their young for up to three months. **July to October** is the best time to see them, although they start appearing in June and some stay around until December. When the calves are big enough, the whales head off south again, to colder, stormy waters, where they feed on enormous quantities of plankton, making up for the nursing months when the females don't eat at all. Though you're most likely to see females and young, you may see **males** early in the season boisterously flopping about the females, though they neither help rear the calves nor form lasting bonds with females.

What gives away the presence of a whale is the blow or spout, a tall smoky plume which disperses after a few seconds and is actually the whale breathing out before it surfaces. If luck is on your side, you may see whales breaching – the movement when they thrust high out of the water and fall back with a great splash.

Probably the best **whale watching tour** in Hermanus is with Marine Dynamics, which operates the Dyer Island cruises (℡028 384 0406, ✉bookings@whalewatchsa.com).

The Whale Coast's hottest whale spots

In **Hermanus**, the best vantage points are the concrete cliff paths which ring the rocky shore from New Harbour to Grotto Beach. There are interpretation boards at three of the popular vantage points (Gearing's Point, Die Gang and Bientang's Cave). At their worst, the paths can be lined two or three deep with people.

Although Hermanus is best known and most geared up for whale-watching, it's also the most congested venue during the whale season and there are equally good – if not better – spots elsewhere along the Walker Bay coast. Aficionados claim that **De Kelders** (see p.244), some 39km east of Hermanus, is even better, while **De Hoop Nature Reserve** (see p.249), east of Arniston, is reckoned by some to be the ultimate place along the entire southern African coast for whale-watching, with far greater numbers of southern rights breaching here than anywhere else.

there are better spots nearby, Hermanus is the best geared-up place in the country to exploit it.

North of Hermanus are some **wineries** you can visit, while due east of Walker Bay, the inland hamlet of **Stanford** on the banks of the Klein River has managed to retain its historic village feel; it's a quieter base than Hermanus, while being near enough to the whale capital for a meal and sightseeing. Southeast down the bay from Hermanus, the unprepossessing town of **De Kelders** outshines its smarter neighbour as a whale-watching spot, but at nothing much else; and, just inland of it, the wonderful and very upmarket **Grootbos Nature Reserve** is one of the best places in the country to learn about *fynbos*. Heading further down the bay, you hit the fishing town of **Gansbaai** (Afrikaans for "goose bay"), which these days is far better known for its shark-cage diving than its waterfowl. Curving back to Hermanus, Danger Point is the promontory that indicates Walker Bay's southern extent, and marks the spot where HMS *Birkenhead* literally went down in history (see p.245).

An easy excursion from Hermanus takes you through attractive and relatively untrammelled farming country to **Bredasdorp**, a junction town on the R316 that gives you the choice of branching out to Africa's southern tip at **Cape Agulhas**; the well-preserved Moravian mission town of **Elim**; or the fishing village of **Arniston**, which is the least-developed and nicest town along the Whale Coast.

Hermanus

There is still the barest trace of a once-quiet cliff-edge fishing village around the historic harbour and in some understated seaside cottages, but for the most part **HERMANUS** has gorged itself on its whale-generated income that has produced modern shopping malls, supermarkets and craft shops. Hermanus also has good swimming and walking **beaches**, opportunities for **activities** and makes a good base for exploring the rest of the Overberg.

Arrival and information

Of the two routes here from Cape Town, taking the N2 and heading south onto the R43 at Bot River is the more direct (a 1hr 30min drive), but the winding road that hugs the coast from Strand, leaving the N2 just before Sir Lowrie's Pass, is the more scenic (2hr). Scant public transport passes through Hermanus, the exception being the **Splash bus** (℡082 658 5375, ⓔsplash@hermanus .co.za), which runs at least once daily between Cape Town train station, Cape Town International Airport and Hermanus. The **Baz Bus** drops people off at **Bot River**, 28km to the north on the N2, from where you can arrange to be collected by a shuttle operated by *Moby's Travel Lodge*, whether you're staying there or not – booking is recommended, but the Baz carries a mobile phone and can call ahead while you're en route.

There's a helpful **tourist office** (Mon–Sat 9am–5pm, plus in summer Sun 10am–3pm; ℡028 312 2629, ⓦwww.hermanus.co.za) at the old station building in Mitchell Street, with maps, useful brochures about the area and an **Internet café**. They operate a free accommodation-finding service and can take bookings for boat-based and aerial whale-watching, as well as shark-cage diving trips.

Over the last week in September the town puts on a fun show of anything that's got a whale connection, even tenuously. To find out what's on – events range from ecology talks to classical recitals – check ⓦwww .whalefestival.co.za.

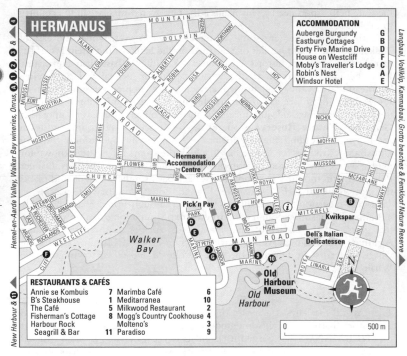

HERMANUS

MOUNTAIN • REGENT • NORTHWAY • STEENBOK

DOLPHIN • ALBERTYN • ROBIN • DISA • HOY

TALANA • FLORA • FOURIE • MPALA • BIRD • MOSSIE • NERINA • MAGNOLIA • NICHOL

MIMOSA • KORT • MUSSEL • INDUSTRIA • DUIKER • ACACIA • HARMONY • MOFFAT

HOSPITAL • MAIN ROAD • FOURIE • DE GOEDE • ALBERTYN • MUSSON • MCFARLANE

FLOWER • BIRD • MYRTLE • SPENCE • PATERSON • DIRK UYS • LORD ROBERTS • ROYAL • LUYT • STEMME • FAIRWAYS

CHURCH • PLEIN • MARINE • ABERDEEN • LONG • HOPE • BROAD • COLLEGE • MITCHELL • HILL • SEA

CANTERBURY • ORTHMANNS • ARMAGH • SMUTS • PARK • HIGH • Kwikspar

EAST • ROCHESTER • ROCKLANDS • WESTCLIFF • ST PETER • MARINE • HARBOUR • MARKET

CLIFF • MAIN ROAD • MARINE • PROTEA • LINARIA

Hermanus Accommodation Centre

Pick 'n Pay

Walker Bay

Deli's Italian Delicatessen

Old Harbour Museum

Old Harbour

N

0 ———— 500 m

ACCOMMODATION

Auberge Burgundy	G
Eastbury Cottages	B
Forty Five Marine Drive	D
House on Westcliff	F
Moby's Traveller's Lodge	C
Robin's Nest	A
Windsor Hotel	E

RESTAURANTS & CAFÉS

Annie se Kombuis		Marimba Café	6
B's Steakhouse	7	Meditarranea	10
The Café	1	Milkwood Restaurant	2
Fisherman's Cottage	5	Mogg's Country Cookhouse	4
Harbour Rock	8	Molteno's	3
Seagrill & Bar	11	Paradiso	9

Accommodation

Unsurprisingly, accommodation on the shore is in high demand and tends to be more expensive than places set back. If there are more than two of you, the best option may be to rent a whole house or apartment through Hermanus Accommodation Centre, on the corner of Church and Myrtle lanes (☎028 313 0004, ⓦ www.hermanusaccom.co.za).

Auberge Burgundy 16 Harbour Rd ☎028 313 1201, ⓦwww.auberge.co.za. A Provençal-style country house in the town centre, projecting a stylish Mediterranean feel, with imported French fabrics and a lavender garden. Breakfast is served across the road at the *Burgundy* restaurant. ❺

Eastbury Cottages 36 Luyt St ☎028 312 1258, ⓦwww.eastbury.co.za. Three very reasonably priced, fully equipped self-catering cottages close to the *Marine Hotel*. Prices are in the R350–600 range depending on how many people there are. No credit cards.

Forty Five Marine Drive 45 Marine Drive ☎028 312 3610, ⓕ028 313 1125. Cliffside self-catering luxury apartments next to the *Windsor Hotel*, with two bedrooms, two bathrooms, a kitchen and terrific views across the bay. Overflow guests may

be shunted off to its far less comely relative, the *Esplanade*. R600–900 per apartment.

House on Westcliff 96 Westcliff Rd ☎028 313 2388, ⓦwww.westcliffhouse.co.za. B&B with six bedrooms in a thatched classic Cape-style house with tranquil garden, solar-heated pool and Jacuzzi. All rooms en suite with own entrance off protected garden. ❹

Moby's Traveller's Lodge 9 Mitchell St ☎028 313 2361, ⓦwww.mobys.co.za. Centrally located hostel with doubles, dorms and a family suite as well as a lively pub and inviting relaxation areas, including a rock pool. They provide breakfast and free tea and coffee. Pre-arranged dinner is available on request, or you can self-cater. They'll organize all tours and outings, and arrange transport to and from the Baz Bus drop-off in Bot River. Dorms ❷, rooms ❹

Robin's Nest 10 Meadow Ave ☎028 316 1597, ⓦwww.hermanus.co.za/accomm/10robinsnest. Three fully equipped, self-catering studio flats in the gardens of what was once Rheezicht Farm, 4km west of the centre. Reached through the Hemel-en-Aarde shopping village, these purpose-built, two-storey flats sleep two and open onto a communal courtyard. A semi-rural alternative to staying in town. ❷

Windsor Hotel 49 Marine Drive ☎028 312 3727, ⓦwww.windsorhotel.co.za. A seafront hotel, offering a full range of accommodation on the very edge of Walker Bay. The *Windsor* is ideally situated in the centre of Hermanus and guests have sea views from the dining room, lounges and nearly half of the bedrooms. Buffet breakfast is included. ❸

The Town

Main Road, the continuation of the R43, meanders through Hermanus, briefly becoming Seventh Street. **Market Square**, just above the old harbour and to the south of Main Street, is the closest thing to a centre, and it's here you'll find the heaviest concentration of restaurants, craft shops and flea markets – the principal forms of entertainment in town when the whales are taking time out.

Just below Market Square is the **Old Harbour Museum** (Mon–Sat 9am–4.30pm, Sun noon–4pm; R3) where, among the uncompelling displays, you'll find lots of fishing tackle and some sharks' jaws. Outside, a few colourful boats, used by local fishermen from the mid-eighteenth to mid-nineteenth centuries, create a photogenic vignette in the tiny harbour.

An almost continuous five-kilometre cliff path through coastal *fynbos* hugs the rocky coastline from the old harbour to Grotto Beach in the eastern suburbs. For one short stretch the path heads away from the coast and follows Main Street before returning to the shore. East of the Old Harbour, just below the *Marine Hotel*, a beautiful tidal pool offers the only **sea swimming** around the town centre's craggy coast; it's big enough to do laps. For **beaches**, you have to head out east across the Mossel River to the suburbs, where you'll find a decent choice, starting with secluded **Langbaai**, closest to town, a cove beneath cliffs at the bottom of Sixth Avenue that has a narrow strip of beach and is excellent

---

Hermanus activities

There's more to Hermanus than whales. The surrounding Raednagael Mountains serve as a great launching pad for **paragliding**; Para-Pax offer tandem flights (☎082 881 4724; R750). The coastline, a marine reserve stretching 500m out to sea, boasts some of the best **coral reefs** in Southern Africa, viewed by flashlight because of the lack of light permeating the plankton-rich water. **Scuba Africa**, The New Harbour, Westcliff Drive, (☎028 316 2362, ⓔaron@scubaafrica.co.za), runs **diving tours** (R330 for a dive and full gear rental) for anyone who arrives with proof of certification and a log book. The water is too cold for tropical fish, but if you're lucky a whale might come over to see what you're up to. You can also see the whales from horseback; **Horse Trail Safaris** (☎082 729 7776) and **African Horse Co** (☎082 667 9232) both offer half-day beach and lagoon tours, as well as *fynbos* mountain tours and overnight trails.

After indulging in all the activities on offer, you may want to relax for a half-day at the luxury *Arabella Sheraton Western Cape Hotel & Spa* (take the R43 in the direction of Cape Town and the N2, and turn left at the Kleinmond turn-off). The **spa** here is worth a visit: for R250 you get four hours of sheer pleasure in the Turkish bathhouse with its flotation pool, Jacuzzis, steam rooms and saunas. All the regular body treatments are available at hefty prices (R430 for a one-hour Swedish massage, for instance); booking is essential (☎028 284 0000, ⓦwww.arabellasheraton.co.za).

for swimming. **Voëlklip**, at the bottom of Eighth Avenue, has grassed terraces, toilets, a nearby café for tea and is great for picnics if you prefer your sandwiches unseasoned with sand. Adjacent is **Kammabaai**, with the best surfing break around Hermanus, and 1km further east, **Grotto Beach**, which despite its name is not a rocky cove, and marks the start of a twelve-kilometre curve of dazzlingly white sand that stretches all the way to De Kelders.

Also on the east side of town, the **Fernkloof Nature Reserve** (dawn–dusk; free) encompasses fifteen square kilometres of mountainous terrain and offers sweeping views of Walker Bay. This highly recommended wilderness area is more than just another nature reserve on the edge of town – it has some 40km of **way marked footpaths**, including a 4.5-kilometre circular nature trail. Visiting is an excellent way to get close to the astonishing variety of delicate *fynbos* (over a thousand species have been identified in the reserve), much of it flowering species that attract scores of birds, including the brightly coloured sunbirds and sugarbirds endemic to the area.

A couple of kilometres west of town along Westcliff, the **New Harbour** is a working fishing harbour, dramatically surrounded by steep cliffs, projecting a gutsy counterpoint to the more manicured central area. The whales sometimes enter the harbour – and there's nowhere better to watch them than from the *Harbour Rock* (see opposite).

On the eastern edge of Hermanus, **Rotary Way** is a fantastic ten-kilometre drive that follows the mountain spine through beautiful montane *fynbos* offering sweeping views of the town, the Hemel-en-Aarde Valley and Walker Bay from Kleinmond to Danger Point. To get there from town, turn right just after the sports ground, and take a track straddled by a pair of white gateposts labelled "Rotary Way". The road is tarred for part of the way, and then becomes a dirt track, eventually petering out altogether, which means you have to return the same way.

Eating and drinking

Although **seafood** is the obvious thing to eat in Hermanus – and you'll find plenty of good restaurants serving it – there's a wide range of cuisine available here, with some gourmet **restaurants** to try.

There's no nicer way to eat on a beautiful day in Hermanus than to do a bit of self-catering or buy some fish and chips and eat out on the wall of the old harbour. *Hermanus Fish Shoppe* in Market Square does takeaway fish and chips – the best in town – as well as seafood salads and fresh seafood to cook yourself. *Ethne's*, 17B Royal Centre, Main Road, is a tiny café best known for its tasty ready-to-microwave meals (with good vegetarian options), though it also does sandwiches on home-made bread as well as takeaway coffees. Grub features large at the **market** held every Saturday morning on Market Square, where you'll find excellent home-made cheeses from Bot River as well as home-made pasta, pesto, marinated cheeses, muffins, houmous and baked goods. As for **delis**, try *Deli's Italian Delicatessen*, 181 Main Rd, a pukka Italian place selling pastas, sauces, cheeses, meats and good Italian coffee. Central **supermarkets** include Kwikspar at 247 Main Rd (daily 7am–7pm) and Pick 'n Pay at 81 Main St (Mon–Sat 8am–6pm, Sun 9am–4pm).

Restaurants and cafés

Annie se Kombuis Warrington Place, Harbour Rd. Small, simple place serving traditional South African fare, such as *bobotie* and *koeksisters*, at reasonable prices. Tues–Sat lunch & dinner, Sun lunch only.

B's Steakhouse Hemel-en-Aarde Village ☎ 028 316 3625. A friendly, buzzing steakhouse – not part of a chain – serving brilliantly prepared, reasonably priced, slabs of beef (they hasten to tell punters they don't do burgers). Its formidable wine list and child-friendliness makes it an obvious choice for families. Tues–Sun dinner, Fri & Sun also lunch.

The Café 14 Aberdeen St. Fresh salads, quiches and breads in summer, soups and stews in winter, charged by the weight of your plate. Order your coffees and drinks from the counter, and help yourself to delicious cakes and desserts. Mon–Sat 8.30am–5pm, Sun 10am–5pm.

Fisherman's Cottage Off Market Square. Housed in an old rustic cottage, with veranda seating. The menu varies, but regular specials include venison dishes and seafood curry, while the signature dish is owner/chef Garry's seafood *potjie*. All meals are reasonably priced, served in generous portions and absolutely delicious. Mon–Sat lunch 11am–2pm, then open from 4pm for drinks and dinner starts from 6pm onwards.

Harbour Rock Seagrill & Bar New Harbour ☏ 028 312 2920. Reasonably priced fish and chips and other seafood dishes; stunning views from the cliffs make it an excellent place for sundowners. Daily breakfast, lunch & dinner.

Marimba Café 9 Royal Centre, Main Rd ☏ 028 312 2148. Lively café with a constantly changing mid-priced menu from across Africa – the likes of Ethiopian roast lamb seasoned with cardamom and ginger, and *yassa* – Senegalese-style chicken. Booking essential. Also boasts a popular bar and live marimba band on Fri & Sat evenings. Daily evenings.

Meditarranea Marine Drive ☏ 028 313 1685. One of the best restaurants in town, with good views of Walker Bay. The Mediterranean-style food is expensive, but worth the treat. Tues–Sun evenings.

Milkwood Restaurant Atlantic Drive, Onrus ☏ 028 316 1516. A 15min drive west of Hermanus, *Milkwood* is especially recommended for its deck in an unsurpassed setting on a seaside lagoon, and does medium-priced steaks and excellent freshly caught fish. A good family venue. Daily noon–10.30pm.

Mogg's Country Cookhouse Hemel-en-Aarde Valley, 12km from Hermanus along the R320 to Caledon ☏ 028 312 4321. A most unlikely location for one of Hermanus's most successful restaurants – on a working farm in the back country – with superb views across the valley. *Mogg's* is an intimate, mid-priced place that's always full and unfailingly excellent, serving whatever country-cooking surprises take the fancy of chefs Jenny Mogg and her daughter Julia, but there's always a choice of three starters, main courses and desserts. Booking essential. Wed–Sun lunch, plus Fri & Sat evenings.

Molteno's Molteno St, Onrus River ☏ 028 316 2658. A 15min drive out of Hermanus, *Moltenos* is highly recommended for its ambience and its reasonably priced, family-friendly meals, including pizzas and burgers, and its heaving Sunday-lunch carvery. Special theatre nights are held once or twice a month with well-known artists invited to perform. Booking essential. Mon & Wed–Sat bar open from 3pm, food served from 6pm till late, Sun lunch only, closed Tues.

Paradiso 83 Marine Drive ☏ 028 313 1153. Situated behind the village square, this Italian restaurant offers two-for the price-of-one meals from Tues–Thurs. Tues–Sun lunch & dinner.

Listings

Emergencies Fire ☏ 028 361 0000; police (enquiries) ☏ 028 312 2626. See also p.75.
Hospital Hermanus Private Hospital, Hospital St, off Main Rd (☏ 028 313 0168), has a 24hr casualty service.
Internet access There's an Internet café at 69 Main Rd (Mon–Fri 7.30am–6pm, Sat 9am–4pm, Sun 10am–2pm).

Pharmacy Hermanus, 145 Main Rd (☏ 028 312 4039 or 312 233), is open Mon–Fri 8am–6.30pm, Sat 8am–1pm and Sun 10am–noon & 6.30–7.30pm.
Taxis Bernardus shuttle service (☏ 028 316 1093 or 083 658 7848) runs buses to and from Cape Town (R140 per person sharing one way), and can get you around town.

Hemel-en-Aarde Valley: the Walker Bay wineries

Some of South Africa's top wines come from the **Hemel-en-Aarde Valley**, about fifteen minutes by car west of Hermanus. Vineyards in the area date back to the early nineteenth century, when the Klein Hemel-en-Aarde Vineyard was part of a Moravian mission station, but winemaking has been established here for more than a decade. Four small **wineries** are dotted along a few gravel kilometres of the R320 to Caledon, which branches off the main road to Cape

Town 2km west of Hermanus, and are worth popping into for their intimate tasting rooms and first-class wines, with views of the stark scrubby mountains just inland.

Closest to town, **Whalehaven Winery** (Mon–Fri 9.30am–5pm, Sat 10.30am–1pm; free; Ⓦ www.whalehavenwines.co.za) has seen its reputation grow since its first vintage was released a decade ago; it's a couple of hundred metres after the Caledon turn-off. The longest established of the Walker Bay wineries is **Hamilton Russell** (Mon–Fri 9am–5pm, Sat 9am–1pm), which produces some of South Africa's priciest wines. Adjacent to Hamilton Russell, towards Caledon, **Bouchard Finlayson** (Mon–Fri 9am–5pm, Sat 10.30am–12.30pm; Ⓦ www .bouchardfinlayson.co.za) is another establishment with a formidable reputation, and a wider range of wines than its neighbour. Furthest from town and newest of the wineries is **Cape Bay** (Mon–Fri 9am–4pm & summer only Sun 9am–noon), just under 7km from the Hemel-en-Aarde turn-off and about half a kilometre after the tar ends.

Across the road from Whalehaven Winery, in Hemel-en-Aarde Village, is possibly the best wine shop in South Africa, the **Wine Village** (Mon–Sat 9am–6pm & Sun 10am–3pm), with a staggering selection of labels from all the country's various wine-producing districts, covering a vast price range.

Stanford

East of Hermanus the R43 takes a detour inland around the Klein River Lagoon, past the pretty riverside hamlet of **STANFORD**, fifteen minutes away. Despite its proximity to hyped-up Hermanus, this historic village, established in 1857, has become something of a refuge for arty types seeking a tranquil escape from the urban rat race. To keep visitors racing around Stanford, the hamlet's residents have created an **arts and crafts route** that takes in over a dozen artists' studios. But apart from the town's excellent microbrewery,

▲ Stanford streetscape

Stanford's principal attraction is its travel-brochure streetscape of simple **Victorian architecture** that includes limewashed houses and sandstone cottages – as well as an Anglican church – with thatched roofs that glow under the late afternoon sun.

Although the **Birkenhead Brewery** (tasting Mon–Sat 11am–4pm, free tours Mon–Fri) just across the R43 from the village (along the R326) bills itself as a "craft brewery estate", the gleaming stainless-steel pipes and equipment inside soon dispel any images of bloodshot hillbillies knocking up a bit of moonshine on the quiet. This is a very slick operation and a great place to go for a pub lunch (daily 11am–3pm) or to sample and buy beers which put those of SAB, South Africa's big brewing near-monopoly, in their place.

Two kilometres beyond the brewery is the **Klein River Cheese Farm** (Mon–Fri 9am–5pm, Sat 9am–1pm), which offers tastings of its famous Gruyère, Leiden, Colby and Dando cheeses. Buy a slab to have with a glass of wine from **Erica Vineyards** (Mon–Fri 9am–6pm), Stanford's first winery, 4km further along the R326.

Practicalities

There is no public transport to Stanford, but once there you'd have no problem getting around this tiny hamlet on foot. The **tourist office** (Mon–Fri 8am–4pm & Sat 10am–5pm; ℡028 341 0340), next to the library and opposite the Spar **mini-supermarket** in the middle of the village, has brochures about Stanford and can help with finding **accommodation**, of which Stanford has a fair selection – well-run B&Bs and self-catering cottages at reasonable prices.

Accommodation

B's Cottage 17 Morton St ℡028 341 0430, ⓔ milkwood@hermanus.co.za. A small, open-plan, self-catering thatched house, sleeping two, in an English-style country garden. ➋

Klein River Cheese Farm Cottage On the R326, 7km from Stanford ℡028 341 0693. Charming three-bedroomed/two-bathroomed Victorian cottage on the river with a fireplace for the winter. Minimum stay two nights ➋

Stanford Valley Shortmarket St ℡028 341 0574. ⓦwww.stanfordvalley.co.za. Nineteen double en-suite bedrooms each with its own private veranda, all within a walled garden. Dinner served in the *Ou Huis*, a 150-year-old restored winery. ➍

Eating

Marianne's Bistro and Home Deli Du Toit St ℡028 341 0272. In a Victorian cottage, good enough to draw Cape Town gourmands out for the day and recommended for its cream teas, home-made fare and carefully prepared and delicious lunches. Fri–Sun 9am–4pm.

Peregrine Farm Stall Queen Victoria St ℡028 341 0386. Besides selling vegetables and breads, they have a café serving breakfast and light lunches, including a traditional Sunday roast. Daily 8.30am–4pm.

Stanford Gallery Art Café Queen Victoria St. Daytime venue where you can enjoy coffee and cake surrounded by locally executed artworks by local artists.

Grootbos Private Nature Reserve

It's not hyperbole to say that the **Grootbos Private Nature Reserve** (℡028 384 8000, ⓦ www.grootbos.co.za; full board including all activities ➒; minimum stay two nights) is unique. A highlight of the area, 33km from Hermanus, this luxury reserve has superb middle-distance views of the coast, and is promoted as a "*fynbos* lodge", where experts guide you through the Western Cape's unique and richly varied plant kingdom. For the ideal family getaway, accommodation in the Garden Lodge, set in the indigenous *fynbos*, is in self-contained stone cottages with ethnic-chic furnishings, polished granite kitchen surfaces, imported fittings, temperature-controlled showers, multiple sun decks and views of the mountain from one side and the sea from the other. The rate includes a three-course dinner served in the main lodge, breakfast in your own cottage and a choice of activities, including guided horse-rides, walks or drives through the *fynbos* and conducted beach hikes. The new Forest Lodge, decked out in contemporary style, is alongside a grove of milkwood trees. If you don't want to stay, you can experience the place on one of their **day excursions** from Grootbos (R950), led by a professional guide; morning and afternoon tea and a gourmet lunch are included in the price.

De Kelders

The nearest coast is a couple of kilometres to the east at **DE KELDERS**, a haphazard and treeless hamlet that stares from bleak cliffs across Walker Bay to Hermanus. It surpasses fashionable Hermanus as a whale-watching venue and has a marvellous, long, sandy beach.

At the end of Cliff Road is a car park from which you can clamber down to the **Klipgat Strandloper Caves**, excavated in the early 1990s, when evidence was unearthed of modern human habitation from 80,000 years ago. The caves became unoccupied for a few thousand years, after which they were used again by Khoisan people 20,000 years ago. Shells, middens, tools and bones were uncovered; some of these now displayed in the South African Museum in Cape Town (see p.118). From the caves, the waymarked **Duiwelsgats hiking trail** goes east for 7km as far as Gansbaai and is a good way to explore this beautiful coastline.

Practicalities

De Kelders has few facilities, but it is gradually beginning to shake off its reputation as the backwater of the Whale Coast, with a number of decent **places to stay**. For **refreshments** the only place is *Coffee on the Rocks* (☏028 384 2017; winter Wed–Sun 9am–5pm; summer 9am–late) on Cliff Street, a small, quirky eatery that does great coffee, cakes and light meals, with a deck in an unsurpassed position for whale-watching. Booking is absolutely essential as it is very popular.

Accommodation

Ama-Krokka 28 Vyfer St ☏028 384 2776, ⓦwww.ama-krokka.co.za. B&B accommodation in two private suites in a house situated in a nature reserve with views of birdlife and *fynbos*. ❹

Cliff Lodge 6 Cliff St ☏028 384 0983, ⓦwww.clifflodge.co.za. A stylish seafront guesthouse, perched on the cliffs of De Kelders, with breathtaking views from all four luxurious bedrooms and spacious penthouse suite. You can walk to the secluded beach and swim in the ocean, frolic in the splash pool, or enjoy cappuccinos while whale-watching from the deck. This intimate place with wild, unspoilt natural surroundings is a perfect place to unwind and relax. ❻

De Kelders B&B Steyn St ☏028 384 0045, ⓦwww.dekelders.co.za. Simply furnished rooms in a house perched on the water's edge with superb views of Walker Bay from your very own viewing deck. ❺

Gansbaai and Danger Point

GANSBAAI is a workaday place, economically dependent on its fishing industry and the seafood canning factory at the harbour, which gives the place a gutsier feel than the surrounding holidaylands. The main reason people come to Gansbaai is for its **shark cage diving**. Boats set out from Gansbaai to **Dyer Island** (see box opposite), east of Danger Point, where great white sharks come to feed on the resident colony of seals. Don't miss this opportunity to go on a cruise and

Dyer Island, Shark Alley and diving for denizens

How a black American came to be living on an island off South Africa in the early nineteenth century is something of a mystery. But, according to records, **Samson Dyer** arrived here in 1806 and made a living collecting guano on the island that subsequently took his name.

Dyer Island is home to substantial **African penguin** and **seal breeding colonies**, both of which are prized morsels among great white sharks. So shark-infested is the channel between the island and the mainland at some times of year that it is known as **Shark Alley**, and these waters are used extensively by operators of great white viewing trips. In 1996, a group of West African castaways washed up here having been put out to sea by the unscrupulous skipper of a Taiwanese merchant vessel whom they had paid to take them to the Far East, where they hoped to find work. One of them drowned in the process, but the rest (amazingly) survived five days at sea, including a stint down Shark Alley, clinging to pieces of timber and barrels.

Whale-watching and shark-cage diving operators

African Wings ☎ 028 312 2701, ⓦ www.africanwings.co.za. Popular whale-watching flights as well as one-day trips to see the Big Five, charter flights and safaris throughout Southern Africa.

Great White Adventure Centre ☎ 028 384 3846. ⓦ www.adventure-centre.co.za. Trips around a series of underground caves beneath the Hermanus/Gansbaai cliffs, which, in a bid to conserve their natural beauty, are not open to the general public. An unforgettable experience.

Marine Dynamics in the Great White House, Geelbek St, Kleinbaai, between De Kelders and Gansbaai ☎ 028 384 0406, ⓦ www.whalewatchsouthafrica.com. Take an unforgettable journey into the domain of the southern right whale. Sightings guaranteed July–December.

Shark Diving Unlimited Swart St, Kleinbaai ☎ 028 384 2787, ⓦ www .sharkdivingunlimited.com. Four-hour trips, the hours depending on how long the sharks take to show up.

learn more about the marine wildlife in the area. Conservationists will show you southern right whales, Cape fur seals, great white sharks, humpback whales, African penguins and other birds too. All boat trips are dependent on the weather and there are a number of companies to choose from. For more information, contact the Gansbaai **tourist office** (Mon–Fri 9am–1pm & 2–5pm, Sat 10am–2pm; ☎ 028 384 1439, ⓦ www.gansbaaiinfo.com).

Danger Point, the southernmost point of Walker Bay, is where British naval history was purportedly made. True to its name, the Point lured the ill-fated HMS *Birkenhead* onto its hidden rocks on February 26, 1852. As was the custom, the captain of the troopship gave the order "Every man for himself". Displaying true British pluck, the soldiers are said to have lined up in their ranks on deck where they stood stock-still, knowing that if one man broke ranks it would lead to a rush that might overwhelm the lifeboats carrying women and children to safety. The precedent of "women and children first", which became known as the **Birkenhead Drill**, was thus established, even though 445 lives were lost in the disaster.

Elim

A good reason to venture along the network of dirt roads that crisscrosses the Whale Coast interior is to visit **ELIM**, a Moravian mission station 40km northwest of Agulhas, founded in 1824. The whole village is a National Monument of streets lined with thatched, whitewashed houses and fig trees. There's nothing twee about this very undeveloped and untouristy place – there isn't even a bottle store, and facilities amount to a couple of tiny shops.

The **tourist office** in Church Street (Mon–Sat 9am–12.30pm & 1.30–5pm; ☏028 482 1806) provides brochures about the area. **Tours** (R35, by arrangement) of the village start at the tourist office and take in the oldest house in the settlement, the church, the restored water mill where wheat is still ground, and the pottery studio. There's also a memorial commemorating the **emancipation of slaves** in 1834, the only such monument in South Africa; its presence reflects the fact that numerous freed slaves found refuge in mission stations like Elim.

The only **accommodation** is the community-run and very reasonably priced *Elim Guesthouse* (☏028 482 1715, ask for Christina; ❷; dinner available on request), a newly renovated 1901 thatched home. For a cup of tea or a **snack**, try the *Old Mill Tea Room* (also run by the community, and open by arrangement; contact the tourist office).

Bredasdorp

BREDASDORP, the commercial centre of the Overberg farmlands, and 193km from Cape Town, lies on the main routes to Cape Agulhas, Arniston and De Hoop Nature Reserve. The **tourism bureau** (☏028 435 7185, ⓦwww .tourismcapeagulhas.co.za) in Long Street, serves the entire region and produces an excellent booklet with all the information and maps you could desire to explore it. Although the town doesn't merit an overnight stay, it is worth calling in for a couple of good-quality craft outlets, a moderately diverting museum and a decent coffee shop and gallery. In the industrial area **Kapula Candles**, at the corner of Petterson Road and First Avenue (Mon–Fri 9am–5.30pm, Sat 9am–1pm; ☏028 424 2829, ⓦwww.kapulacandles.com), started as a cottage industry and now supplies its beautifully crafted candles to shops throughout South Africa, with outlets in Germany. The factory shop has a café where you can get a decent cup of coffee surrounded by colourful candles, or outside in the herbarium. Close to Kapula is **Bel Don**, with quality goose-down products – from duvets to African-print tea cosies.

Back in town, the **Shipwreck Museum** at 6 Independent St, diagonally opposite the town's *kerk* (Mon–Fri 9am–4.45pm, Sat & Sun 11am–3.45pm; R10), displays an interesting array of items retrieved from the many dashed vessels that have gone down off the treacherous coastline.

At 22 All Saints St (R319 to De Hoop), the earthy orange and purple *Julian's* (☏028 425 1201; Mon–Sat 9am–5pm & 6.30–8pm) serves light **lunches** such as grilled sardine fishcakes and chicken and sweetcorn soup, and impressive lemon meringue tarts with coffee, in a large sunny building which doubles as a gallery, with paintings by local artists for sale. It also houses a ceramics workshop with pieces for sale. Should you want to stay over, you'll find the most stylish rooms (❸–❹) in town here.

Cape Agulhas and around

Along the east flank of the Danger Point promontory, the rocky and shallow coastline with heavy swells and strong currents makes this one of South Africa's most treacherous stretches of coast – one that has claimed over 250 wrecks and around 2500 lives. Its rocky terrain also accounts for the lack of a coastal road from Gansbaai and Danger Point to **Cape Agulhas**, the southernmost tip of Africa.

The plain around the southern tip has been declared the **Agulhas National Park** to conserve its estimated 2000 species of indigenous plant and marine and intertidal life as well as a cultural heritage which includes shipwrecks and archeological sites – stone hearths, pottery and shell middens have been discovered. There are no facilities apart from a **tea shop and restaurant** inside the terrific **Agulhas Lighthouse** (daily 8am–5pm; R15), commissioned in 1849. At the top, reached by a series of steep ladders, there are vertiginous views and some interesting exhibits about lighthouses around South Africa and elsewhere in the world. Dinners here at the *Lighthouse Restaurant* (☎028 435 7580; daily 8am–10pm) are charming, punctuated by flashes from the lighthouse beam.

The actual tip of the continent is marked by a rock and plaque about 1km from the lighthouse, towards Suiderstrand. Following the dirt road to **Suiderstrand** itself takes you to some beautiful, undeveloped beaches with rock pools to explore, and is definitely the best part of Agulhas.

Struisbaai, about 6km east of Agulhas, has a nice harbour and long sandy beaches, but is unappealing when it's crowded in the summer. The best place to **stay** is *Cape Agulhas Backpackers* (☎082 372 3354, ⓦ www.capeagulhasbackpackers .com; ❶–❷) which has camping, dorms, doubles and self-catering cottages with a pool, garden and good bedding throughout. It's run by a couple who are big on helping you enjoy the outdoors and will organize boating, kiteboarding, riding and other activities around Struisbaai, and also arrange pick-ups from Botrivier or Swellendam.

Practicalities

L'AGULHAS, the rather windblown settlement associated with the southern tip, consists of a small collection of holiday houses and a few shops. It's reached by heading inland on the R316 to Bredasdorp, where the road splits, the more westerly branch (the R319) continuing 43km on to Agulhas, while the other fork leads to Arniston.

The smartest **accommodation** in town is the *Agulhas Country Lodge* on Main Road (☎028 435 7650, ⓦ www.agulhascountrylodge.com; ❺), in a relatively grand stone building perched halfway up a hillside. All rooms have sea views from private balconies; excellent seafood **dinners** provide another inducement to stay. Uniquely positioned on the edge of the Agulhas National Park, with kilometres of undeveloped beach to explore to the west, is the sea-facing *Pebble Beach* (☎028 435 7270 or 082 774 5008, ⓦ www .pebble-beach.co.za; ❸–❹), in Suiderstrand (follow signs to the Southern Tip of Africa and then 4km beyond for Pebble Beach), with two en-suite rooms, in a modern thatched house with white beds and wooden floors, where you can smell the *fynbos* wafting in from the dunes in front of your room. They also rent a self-catering thatched cottage right on the strand, which sleeps six people. *Southernmost* B&B on the corner of Van Breda and Lighthouse streets (☎028 435 6565, ⓦ www.southermost.co.za; closed winter months; ❸), is a well-loved and rather dilapidated historic beach cottage opposite the tidal pool with an indigenous garden sloping down to the water's edge.

Arniston

After the cool deep blues of the Atlantic to the west, the azure of the Indian Ocean at **ARNISTON** is startling, made all the more dazzling by the white dunes interspersed with rocky ledges. Reached on the R316, 24km southeast of Bredasdorp, and 220km from Cape Town, this is one of the best places to stay in the Overberg – if you want nothing more than beach life. The colours may be tropical, but the wind can howl unpredictably here, as anywhere else along the Cape coast, and when it does, there's nothing much to do. The village is known to locals by its Afrikaans name, Waenhuiskrans ("wagon-house cliff"), after a cliff containing a huge cave 1500m south of town, which trekboers reckoned was spacious enough for a wagon and span of oxen (the largest thing they could think of). The English name derives from a British ship, the *Arniston*, which hit the rocks here in 1815.

The shallow seas, so treacherous for vessels, provide Arniston with the safest swimming waters along the Whale Coast. Apart from sea bathing, the principal attraction is **Kassiesbaai**, a district of starkly beautiful limewashed cottages, now declared a National Monument and home to coloured fishing families that have for generations made their living here. Its beautifully simple dwellings invariably show up in coffee-table books whenever picturesque images of fishing villages are called for. But Kassiesbaai sits a little uneasily as a living community, as it's also a bit of a theme park for visitors stalking the streets with their cameras. More positively, all the holiday accommodation is in the adjacent new section of town where you'll find a number of exclusive holiday homes all built in the whitewashed, thatched-roof cottage style of the area. The only regular entertainment here is wandering down to the harbour at high tide to watch fishing boats being shoved down the slipway by a tractor that ends up half submerged. You can swim next to the slipway or at **Roman Beach**, the main swimming beach, just along the coast as you head south from the harbour. In season, keep your eyes open for **southern right whales**.

Heading north through Kassiesbaai at low tide, you can walk 5km along an unspoilt beach unmarred by buildings until you reach an unassuming fence – resist the temptation to climb over this, as it marks the boundary of the local testing range for military material and missiles. Heading south of the harbour for 1500m along spectacular cliffs, you'll reach the vast **cave** after which the town is named. The walk is worth doing simply for the *fynbos*-covered dunes you'll cross on the way. From the car park right by the cave, it's a short signposted walk down to the dunes and the cave, which can only be reached at low tide. The rocks can be slippery and have sharp sections, so be sure to wear shoes with tough soles and a good grip.

Practicalities

There's no public transport to Arniston. The choice for **eating** is limited. *Die Waenhuis* (Mon–Sat 8am–6.30pm) on Du Preez Street (a continuation of the national road), is decorated to resemble a fishermen's tavern and serves good fish and chips. The Arniston fishermen's wives run a small eating place in the Kassiesbaai Craft Shop (booking required on ☏028 445 9760; ask for Lilian Newman), where they'll cook up a three-course traditional fisherman's meal with the catch of the day brought in by their menfolk. The *Arniston Hotel* has outdoor seating to take in the sea views, and does fabulous, blow-out breakfasts, and pleasing fresh fish dinners; it also holds the town's only **bar**.

You can buy fresh fish from the fishermen at the slipway near the hotel. There's a small **supply store** attached to *Die Waenhuis* selling basics, but if you're self-catering it's best to stock up at the Super Spar on Church Street in Bredasdorp.

Accommodation

Accommodation is limited to one hotel, some self-catering cottages and a handful of B&Bs, which get snapped up quickly during school holidays and over weekends. The village is small and not all properties are numbered, so be sure to get directions from the main road if you're renting a house. Etna (☎028 445 9657, ⓦwww.arniston-etnas.co.za) rents out a number of cottages in the area.

Arniston Hotel ☎028 445 9000, ⓦwww .arnistonhotel.com. A luxurious and well-run hotel, dominating the seafront, with every comfort for a dreamy seaside night, including a spa with massage and beauty treatments. The best rooms have a fireplace, or a balcony. If it's way out of your budget, go during the week or in winter months when prices drop. ❼

Arniston Seaside Cottages well signposted from the national road, along the street behind the hotel ☎028 445 9772, ⓦwww.arniston-online .co.za. Limewashed self-catering cottages, fully equipped and serviced. Out-of-season rates are per person, but in season (Jan, Easter school holidays & Dec) you pay for the number of beds in the unit. ❸

Kassiesbaai Cottage Kassiesbaai ☎028 445 9760. Lilian Newman rents out her modestly furnished traditional fisherman's cottage, which contains three double rooms for self-catering. ❷

Southwinds Huxham St, just behind the *Arniston hotel* ☎028 445 9303, ⓦwww.arniston-info.co.za. Well-appointed double suites, looking onto a courtyard garden. The owners are friendly and prices drop in winter. B&B ❹

Waenhuis Caravan Park along the main road into Arniston, 300m from the centre ☎028 445 9620. Pitch your own tent or stay in one of the four- or six-bed en-suite bungalows. The cheaper, older ones don't provide linen, and you'll pay a bit more to have all the mod cons including TV. The place can get crowded and very noisy over weekends and during peak season. ❷

De Hoop Nature Reserve

De Hoop (daily 7am–6pm; R24) is the **wilderness highlight** of the Western Cape. Although the reserve could technically be done as a day-trip from Hermanus, you'll find it far more rewarding to come here for a night or more. The five-day, portered **Whale Trail** hike is one of South Africa's best walks and among the finest wildlife experiences in the world, though, inevitably, it is heavily booked out.

The breathtaking coastline is edged by bleached sand dunes standing 90m high in places, and rocky formations that at one point open to the sea in a massive craggy arch. The flora and fauna are impressive, too, encompassing 86 species of mammal, 260 different birds and 1500 varieties of plants, and it's reckoned to be the ultimate place in South Africa (surpassing even Hermanus and De Kelders) to see **southern right whales**. If you're here for a couple of days in season, you will not fail to see whales, and sometimes dozens of whales are in evidence at one time, as well as dolphins. July to October is the best time, but you stand a very good chance of a sighting from June through to November. Inland, rare **Cape mountain zebra**, **bontebok** and other **antelope** congregate on a plain near the reserve accommodation. Apart from bathing, and scrambling over rocks and sand dunes, there are mountain-biking trails (bring your own bike as there's nowhere to rent one). The huge rock pools at Koppie Allen provide hours of pleasure.

The five-day, four-night **Whale Trail** (☎028 425 5020, ⓦwww.capenature .org.za) follows a spectacularly beautiful route from the Potberg Mountains 55km along the coast to Koppie Alleen. Only moderately difficult, it's also marvellously quiet: besides your own group (and the whales) you won't see another soul and the only prints you'll come across are those of eland, baboons and ostriches. Even the porters invisibly pick up your goods and deposit them ahead of you, at huts of two or three rooms with bunk beds, idyllically located along the deserted coast. To go in whale season, though, you'll need to book a year in advance and take any date offered. Bookings are for a minimum of six and maximum of twelve people (with no children under 8), and you pay for six even if there are just two of you. You have to undertake the whole trail, not join it for a day or two. Prices are between R700 and R850 per person with R300 extra for portage.

Practicalities

De Hoop is along a signposted dirt road that spurs off the R319 as it heads out of Bredasdorp, 50km to its west. **Accommodation** (Mon-Fri 7.30am–4pm; ☎021 659 3500, ⓦwww.capenature.co.za), usually booked up at weekends, includes a **campsite** with each site shaded by a milkwood tree, and two-bedroomed **self-catering cottages** (R480) with a cooker, fridge and kitchen utensils and bedding. More expensive, but far more spacious, sleeping six, are the three thatched cottages on the lip of the estuary, also with two bedrooms, but with more privacy and a large, comfortable living room (R950); it's a twenty-minute drive from here to the coast. Best of all, if there's a group of you, at the beach itself is the newly renovated, splendidly isolated huddle of thatched cottages at Koppie Alleen. The site couldn't be more thrilling, overlooking a bay full of whales (R3750 per night for six people, and R500 per person for up to two additional people).

Overnight visitors are required to reach the reserve by 4pm. There are **no food supplies** at De Hoop, so be sure to stock up with everything before you come – the nearest shop is 15km away, in the hamlet of Ou Plaas.

If accommodation is full within De Hoop, there are some options outside the reserve. Closest to the gates, and offering full catering, is *Buchu Bushcamp* (☎028 542 1602, ⓦwww. buchu-bushcamp.com; B&B ➍) with five open-plan timber and thatch chalets, three of them sleeping four, with good linen and fittings, connected by a wooden walkway to a central dining room, lounge and bar. The whole feel is of a gracious, thatched safari-camp, set in *fynbos*. There is also a

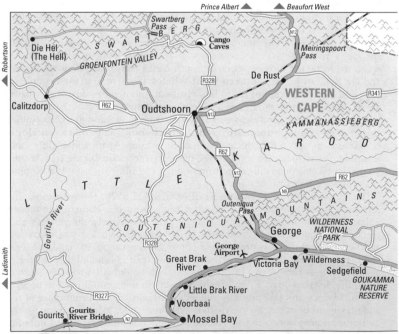

guide who can help plan your day or take you out on a nature walk. The coast itself is some 15km off. Prices, as elsewhere, are higher in summer, but surprisingly low during whale season itself. East of Buchu, and 4km beyond the hamlet of Ou Plaas towards Potberg, is *Verfheuwel Farm* (☎028 542 1038, ⓔverfheuwel@xsinet.co.za; ❸), with very reasonable self-catering or B&B rates in a cottage attached to the main farmhouse. It's run by hospitable Afrikaner farming folk who can bring dinner to your cottage if you ask in advance. The country-style cottage sleeps a couple, with beds in the living area for children. The garden is beautiful and has a swimming pool. If *Verfheuwel* is full, owner Matti can direct you to other friends and relatives in the area with farm accommodation.

The Garden Route

The **Garden Route**, a slender stretch of coastal plain between Mossel Bay and Storms River Mouth, has a legendary status as South Africa's paradise – reflected in local names such as **Garden of Eden** and **Wilderness**. This soft, green, forested swath of nearly 200km is cut by rivers from the mountains to the north, tumbling down to its southern rocky shores and sandy beaches.

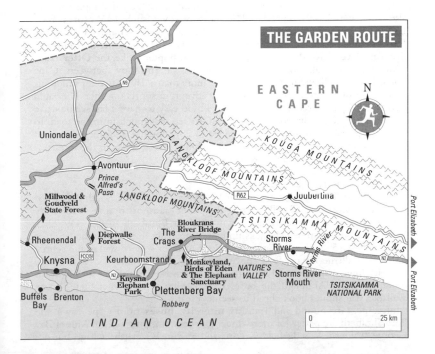

The **Khoi** herders who lived off its natural bounty considered the area a paradise, calling it Outeniqua ("the man laden with honey"). Their Eden was quickly destroyed in the eighteenth century with the arrival of Dutch **woodcutters**, who had exhausted the forests around Cape Town and set about doing the same in Outeniqua, killing or dispersing the Khoi and San in the process. Birds and animals suffered too from the encroachment of Europeans. In the 1850s, the Swedish naturalist Johan Victorin shot and feasted on the species he had come to study, some of which, including the endangered narina trogon, he noted were both "beautiful and good to eat".

Despite the dense appearance of the area, what you see today are only the remnants of one of Africa's great **forests**; much of the indigenous hardwoods have been replaced by exotic pine plantations, and the only milk and honey you'll find now is in the many shops servicing the Garden Route coastal resorts. **Conservation** has halted the wholesale destruction of the indigenous woodlands, but a huge growth in tourism and the influx of urbanites seeking a quiet life in the relatively crime-free Garden Route towns threatens to rob the area of its remaining tranquillity.

The Garden Route coast is dominated by three inlets – Mossel Bay, the Knysna lagoon and Plettenberg Bay – each with its own town. Oldest of these and closest to Cape Town is **Mossel Bay**, an industrial centre of some charm, which marks the official start of the Garden Route. **Knysna**, though younger, exudes a well-rooted urban character and is the nicest of the coastal towns, with one major drawback – unlike **Plettenberg Bay**, its eastern neighbour, it has no beach of its own. A major draw, though, is the **Knysna forest** covering some of the hilly country around Knysna, the awe-inspiring remnants of once vast ancient woodlands.

Between the coastal towns are some ugly modern holiday developments, but also some wonderful empty beaches and tiny coves, such as **Victoria Bay**, **Buffels Bay** and **Nature's Valley**. Best of all is the **Tsitsikamma National Park**, which has it all – indigenous forest, dramatic coastline, the pumping **Storms River Mouth** and South Africa's most popular hike, the **Otter trail**.

Most visitors take the Garden Route as a **journey** between Cape Town and Port Elizabeth, dallying for little more than a day or two for shopping, sightseeing or a taste of one of the many adventure sports on offer. The rapid passage cut by the excellent **N2** makes it all too easy to have a fast scenic drive – and end up disappointed because you don't see that much from the road. To make the journey worthwhile, you'll need to slow down, take some detours off the highway and explore a little to find secluded coves, walks in the forests or even mountain passes in the Karoo (see p.203).

Travel practicalities

The **Garden Route** is probably the best-served stretch of South Africa for **transport**. Most user-friendly among the public transport options is the daily **Baz Bus** service between Cape Town and Port Elizabeth (☎021 439 2323, ⓦ www.bazbus.co.za), which picks up passengers daily from accommodation at either end (7.15–8.30am). It provides a door-to-door service within the central districts of all the towns along the way, and has the advantage over the large intercity lines that buses will happily carry outdoor gear, such as surfboards or mountain bikes. Although the buses take standby passengers if there's space available, you should book ahead to secure a seat.

Intercape, Greyhound and Translux **intercity buses** from Cape Town and Port Elizabeth are better for more direct journeys, stopping only at Mossel Bay, George, Wilderness, Sedgefield, Knysna and Storms River (the village, but not

Garden Route adventure activities: the highlights

The Garden Route is fast losing its reputation as the place to go for sun-soaking idleness or to commune with nature. Adrenaline and adventure are elbowing out these passive pursuits and now thrill-junkies go expressly to throw themselves off bridges, to gape into the jaws of great white sharks and to freewheel down scary mountain passes. The choice is broad – and widely spread across the entire length of the Garden Route. To help you plan, here are some highlights.

Abseiling Drop down a cliff face at the private Featherbed Nature Reserve (box on p.271), the entrance to the Knysna lagoon, or along the Kaaimans River gorge in Wilderness (p.263).

Bungee jumping The world's highest commercial jump is at Bloukrans Bridge (see p.282); you can also try bungee swinging, a jump with a twist, at Gouritz River Bridge near Mossel Bay (see p.258).

Canopy tours and ziplining Monkey around swinging from tree to tree in an indigenous forest, 30m above the forest floor, or zing over waterfalls and across a river gorge (see box, p.288)

Hiking There's a terrific circular one-day hike along the edge of the Robberg Peninsula (p.281), with a chance of seeing whales, dolphins and seals. Otherwise, there are quite a few longer and more challenging trails to attempt; see the box on pp.254–255.

Horse-riding Sit cowboy-style in a deep saddle at *Southern Comfort Western Horse Ranch*, between Knysna and Plettenberg Bay (see p.269). Or head out with an English saddle through African countryside near Plettenberg Bay, for *fynbos* and forest trails.

Mountain biking Tear down the hair-raising Swartberg Pass, starting out from Knysna or Oudtshoorn (p.215), or pedal your way in a slightly calmer fashion round the Homtini Cycle Route in the Knysna forest (p.275).

River boat Go for a leisurely ferry ride down the spectacular Keurbooms river estuary where bird life is in abundance (p.283).

Scenic excursions The Outeniqua Choo-Tjoe steam train passes through beautiful back country between George and Mossel Bay (see below). With your own transport, try taking the old road just east of The Crags, winding your way down the fantastically scenic route to Nature's Valley (see p.285).

Whale, dolphin and shark encounters Take to the water on a well-informed eco-tour that could encounter a variety of whales and dolphins at Plettenberg Bay (pp.282–283), or enter a shark cage for a first-hand encounter with Jaws at Mossel Bay (see p.258).

Wildlife spotting There's family fun in the forest, looking for apes from around the world at Monkeyland (p.284) or avifauna at the adjacent Birds of Eden; or coming face to face with the world's largest land mammal at the Knysna Elephant Sanctuary (see p.284) and the Knysna Elephant Park (see p.276).

Ziplining See canopy tours (above).

the Mouth, which is some distance away). These buses often don't go into town, letting passengers off at filling stations on the highway instead.

More of a day out than serious transport, the **Outeniqua Choo-Tjoe** is a goods train with passenger carriages attached, running the 30km between George and Mossel Bay (Mon–Sat: summer 2 daily, less frequently at other times; 2hr 45min; R65 single, R75 return) in both directions. The route changed in 2006 after serious flooding affected the scenic route to Knysna, and the new route is not a patch on the old. You need to book your tickets a day ahead on ☎044 382 1361 or 044 801 8202. And finally, if time is tight, you may want to go by **air** to George at the west end of the Garden Route, served by scheduled flights from Cape Town, Johannesburg, Durban and Port Elizabeth.

Mossel Bay and around

MOSSEL BAY, a midsized town 397km east of Cape Town, gets a bad press from most South Africans, mainly because of the huge industrial facade it presents to the N2. Don't panic – the historic centre is a thoroughly pleasant contrast, set on a hill overlooking the small working harbour and bay, with one of the best

---

Major Garden Route hikes

If you're keen on walking and the outdoors, and want to schedule in at least one long walk somewhere in the country during your holiday, the Garden Route provides some fine possibilities. Indeed, walking is the only way to really experience the Garden Route's forests and coast and escape the clutter of holiday homes and the noisy N2.

The waymarked **hikes** listed below are two to five days long. You'll need to carry all your food, a sleeping bag for use in the communal hiking huts (mattresses are provided), lightweight cooking utensils and stove, and waterproofs. You should also wear proper worn-in hiking boots. For day-hikes and walks lasting only a couple of hours, consult Judith Hopley's *On Foot in the Garden Route*, available from Knysna's tourist office and several other outlets on the Garden Route. If you've no appetite for dried food and a heavy pack, note that the marvellous Dolphin trail is portered.

Dolphin trail
Start: Sandrif River Mouth, Tsitsikamma National Park
End: Storms River Mouth, Tsitsikamma National Park
Distance: 20km
Duration: two and a half days
Booking: ☏042 281 1607 extension 219
Cost: R3000 per person, including food, accommodation and permits
This is the Garden Route's luxury trail. Backpacks are transported to overnight stops where you're greeted with comfortable accommodation and cooked meals. The terrain through the Tsitsikamma National Park is breathtaking, covering the rugged coastal edge and the natural forest. The price includes a guide, a boat trip up the Storms River Gorge, and a 4WD drive through the Storms River Pass.

Harkerville Coast hiking trail
Start and end: Harkerville Forestry Station, 12km west of Plettenberg Bay, signposted off the N2
Distance: 26.5km
Duration: two days
Permit and booking: ☏044 302 5606
Cost: R100 per person
Closer to the roads, this circular trail doesn't feel as remote as the Otter trail (see below) but is a good second-best, taking in magnificent rocky coastline, indigenous forest and *fynbos*. Lots of rock scrambling and some traversing of exposed, narrow ledges above the sea is required, so don't attempt this if you're unfit or scared of heights. Monkeys, baboons and fish eagles are commonly seen, and you may also spot dolphins or whales.

swimming beaches along the southern Cape coast and an interesting museum. The town takes on a strong Afrikaans flavour over Christmas, when Karoo farmers and their families descend in droves to occupy its caravan parks and chalets. While Mossel Bay's modest attractions are unlikely to hold you for more than a night, it has some decent accommodation and a first-class restaurant, which make it a good place to pause before launching out along the Garden Route.

From Mossel Bay the R328 heads inland to connect with Oudtshoorn, 85km away (see p.215). A short way along this route is the **Robinson Pass** where there is a great family holidaying spot at the *Eight Bells Inn*, and the possibility of seeing game at **Botlierskop Private Game Reserve**.

Mossel Bay bears poignant historical significance as the place where indigenous Khoi cattle herders encountered the Europeans in a bloody spat that symbolically

Otter trail
Start: Storms River Mouth, Tsitsikamma National Park
End: Nature's Valley, Tsitsikamma National Park
Distance: 42km
Duration: five days
Booking: Through South African National Parks, up to twelve months in advance (☏012 426 5111). The maximum number of people on the trail is twelve.
Cost: R525 per person.
South Africa's first established hiking trail, this is a coastal walk crossing rivers, tidal pools and indigenous forest. You may see dolphins, whales and seals, and the spoor of the Cape clawless otter – although virtually impossible to spot, the creatures are certainly around. The short stretches between log-hut nightstops mean you can take things slowly, and enjoy the vegetation and birds. The Bloukrans River has to be crossed by wading or swimming: go at low tide and waterproof your backpack. Some parts of the hike are steep, so you need to be fit.

Outeniqua trail
Start: Beervlei (the old forest station – eight overnight huts); directions are given when you book
End: Harkerville Forestry Station, 12km west of Plettenberg Bay
Distance: 108km
Duration: seven days (shorter versions possible)
Permit: ☏044 302 5606
Cost: R50 per person per day
The main draw here is the indigenous forest, including giant yellowwood trees, pine plantations and gold-mining remains at Millwood in the Goudveld State Forest.

Tsitsikamma trail
Start: Nature's Valley Caravan Park, Tsitsikamma National Park
End: Storms River Bridge, Tsitsikamma National Park
Distance: 64km
Duration: five days (shorter versions possible)
Permit: ☏012 426 5111
Cost: R60 per person per night
Features: Not to be confused with the Otter trail, this is an inland walk through indigenous forest, long stretches of open *fynbos* and the Tsitsikamma mountain range. Five overnight huts accommodate thirty people. It's not a difficult hike, and you won't cover more than 17km or so per day – although after heavy rains the rivers can be hard to cross.

set the tone for five hundred years of race relations on the subcontinent. A group of Portuguese mariners under captain **Bartholomeu Dias** set sail from Portugal in August 1487 in search of a sea route to the riches of India, and months later rounded the Cape of Good Hope. In February 1488, they became the first Europeans to make landfall along the South African coast, when they pulled in for water to the safety of an inlet they called Aguado de São Bras ("watering place of St Blaize"), now Mossel Bay. The Khoikhoi were organized into distinct groups, each under its own chief and each with territorial rights over pastures and water sources. The Portuguese, who were flouting local customs, saw it as "bad manners" when the Khoikhoi tried to drive them off the spring. In a mutual babble of incomprehension the Khoi began stoning the Portuguese, who retaliated with crossbow fire that left one of the herders dead.

Arrival, information and accommodation

The N2 bypasses Mossel Bay and, of all the buses, only the **Baz Bus** comes right into town, dropping you off anywhere on request. The large **intercity buses** all stop at Shell Voorbaai Service Station, 7km from the centre, at the junction of the national highway and the road into town. The town itself is small enough to negotiate on foot, but should you need transport Jordaan runs a **taxi** service (℡082 673 7314). The busy **tourist office** (Mon–Fri 8am–6pm, Sat 9am–4pm; ℡044 691 2202, ⓦwww.visitmosselbay.co.za), bang in the centre on the corner of Church and Market streets, has shelves of brochures about Mossel Bay and the rest of the Garden Route, and a **map** of the town.

Accommodation

Mossel Bay has a broad range of **accommodation**, including a number of reasonable B&Bs that can be booked through the tourist office should our recommendations be full. There's **camping** at the municipal site, *De Bakke*, at George Road just back from the beach (℡044 691 2915, ⓦwww.mosselbaymun.co.za), which also has good self-catering chalets sleeping four (❷). *Point Caravan Park* in Point Road (℡044 690 3501; ❶), along the rocky point, is not as nice as the bay's main beach for swimming, but it's close to the start of the St Blaize hiking trail.

Edward Charles 1 Sixth Ave ℡044 691 2152 ⓦwww.edwardcharles.co.za. An upmarket guesthouse in a central location overlooking Santos Beach with a swimming pool. ❻
Green Door 49 Marsh St ℡044 691 3820, ⓦwww.greatbrakriver/greendoor. Central B&B in a charming 100-year-old sandstone building. The older family rooms, which sleep four, are less attractive than the newer doubles, but are good value if there are more than two of you. ❸
Highview Lodge 76 Rodger St ℡044 691 9038, ⓦwww.highviewlodge.co.za. Luxury self-catering and B&B rooms with exceptional views of the bay and the mountains. Self-catering ❸, B&B ❹
Huisj Te Marquette 1 Marsh St ℡044 691 3182, ⓔmarquette@pixie.co.za Twelve guest rooms in a very well-run establishment near the Point, with an adjoining backpackers with dorms and doubles. Backpackers ❶–❷, rooms ❹
Mossel Bay Guest House 61 Bruns Rd ℡044 691 2000. Comfortable rooms in an Afrikaner suburban home, not far from Santos Beach. ❸
Protea Hotel Mossel Bay Bartholomeu Dias Museum Complex, Market St ℡044 691 3738, ⓦwww.proteahotels.com/mosselbay. Opposite the tourist office, in an old Cape Dutch manor house, this quaint place has breakfast served at *Café Gannet*, Mossel Bay's nicest restaurant. ❺
Santos Express Santos Beach ℡044 691 1995. A stationary train with a great location – on the beach, just metres from the surf. Accommodation is in four-person train compartments, but you'll have one to yourself if you're a couple or a family. Morning coffee and continental breakfast are included. The restaurant is good value. ❷
Valhalla Guest House 86 Montague St ℡044 691 1075 or 082 658 2532, ⓔcranbar@yebo .co.za. An inexpensive B&B near the town centre, though a bit of a walk to the beach, with breakfast outdoors, and sea views owing to its elevation on the hillside. ❸

The Town

Mossel Bay's main urban attraction is the **Bartholomeu Dias Museum Complex**, housed in a collection of historic buildings well integrated into the small town centre, all near the tourist office and within a couple of minutes' walk of each other. The highlight is the **Maritime Museum** (Mon–Fri 8.15am–4.45pm, Sat & Sun 9am–4pm; R12), a spiral gallery with displays on the history of European, principally Portuguese, seafaring, arranged around a full-size replica of Dias' original caravel. The ship was built in Portugal and sailed from Lisbon to Mossel Bay in 1987 to celebrate the five-hundredth anniversary of Dias' historic journey. You can't fail to be awed by the idea of the original mariners setting out on the high seas into terra incognita on such a small vessel – particularly as the crew were accommodated above deck with only a sailcloth for protection against the elements.

The one Mossel Bay attraction that most South Africans have heard of is the **Post Office Tree**, just outside the Maritime Museum. Sixteenth-century mariners used to leave messages for passing ships in an old boot under a milkwood tree somewhere around here, and the plaque claims that "this may well" be the same tree. You can post mail here in a large, boot-shaped letterbox and have it stamped with a special postmark.

Of the remaining exhibitions, the **Shell Museum and Aquarium** (Mon–Fri 9am–4.45pm, Sat & Sun 10am–4pm; donation) next to the Post Office Tree is the only one worth taking time to visit. This is your chance to see some of the beautiful shells found off the South African coast, as well as specimens from around the world. The fascinating displays of living shellfish include cowries with their inhabitants still at home.

A short walk north down the hill from the Maritime Museum gets you to **Santos Beach**, the main town strand, and purportedly the only north-facing beach in South Africa – which gives it exceptionally long sunny afternoons. Adjacent to the small town harbour, the beach provides some of the finest swimming along the Garden Route, with uncharacteristically gentle surf, small waves and a depth perfect for practising your crawl.

East of the harbour, the coast bulges south towards the **Point**, which has several restaurants and a popular bar/restaurant (see opposite) with a deck at the ocean's edge, from which you may see dolphins cruising past, as well as a surreal five-hundred-metre rocky channel known as the aquarium, which is used as a natural **tidal pool**. Adjacent to this, the Department of Marine and Coastal Management has installed an **Aquarium** (Mon–Fri 9am–4pm, Sat & Sun 9am–12.30pm; donation) under *Tidals* pub, which showcases local lobsters, crabs and fish found off this coast in a handful of small tanks, as well as a pair of Amazon piranhas.

A couple of hundred metres to the south at the top of some cliffs, the **St Blaize Lighthouse**, built in 1864, is still in use as a beacon to ships. Below it, the **Cape St Blaize Cave** is both a marvellous lookout point and a significant archeological site. A boardwalk leads through the cave past three information panels describing the history of the interpretation of the cave as well as the modern understanding of it. In 1801 Sir John Barrow insisted that shells found at the site had been brought by seagulls, while others argued that they were relics of human habitation. It turned out that Barrow's opponents were right, but it wasn't till 1888 that excavations uncovered stone tools and showed that people had been using the cave for something close on 100,000 years. The path leading up to the cave continues onto the Cape St Blaize trail (see p.238).

Activities

Given that the seals of **Seal Island**, about 10km northwest of Santos Beach, are a popular delicacy for great white sharks, you'd be forgiven for wondering why scuba diving remains so popular off Mossel Bay. In 1990, the unfortunate Monique Price became the first fully kitted scuba diver to die in a great white attack – just off the island – and divers are warned to avoid its immediate environs. There are, however, several rewarding **diving and snorkelling** spots around Mossel Bay, and full facilities, including open-water certification courses (around R1900) and one-off dives, are available from Electro Dive (ⓣ&ⓕ044 698 1976 or ⓣ082 561 1259). Electro Dive rents out gear and provides shore-based and boat-based dives (R320 including kit). It also does parasailing and jetskiing. These aren't tropical seas, so don't expect clear warm waters (although temperatures tend to be warmer than at other Garden Route resorts), but with visibility usually between 4m and 10m you stand a good chance of seeing octopus, squid, sea stars, soft corals, pyjama sharks and butterfly fish.

For those who want to see **great white sharks** face to face there are a couple of outfits offering cage dives. The best months for sightings are March to November, and the worst January and February, but at no time are encounters guaranteed. One of the better operations in the country is Shark Africa, located on the corner of Church and Market streets (ⓣ044 691 3796, ⓦwww.sharkafrica .co.za), with whom you can either observe from a boat or go underwater in a cage for R800, with the assurance that if the sharks don't show you get half your money back. If you're unlucky the first time and choose to try again on another day, you'll only be charged the amount you were refunded.

Cruises around Seal Island to see the African penguin and seal colonies can be taken on the *Romonza* (hourly 10am–4pm; R70; ⓣ&ⓕ044 690 3101), a medium-sized yacht that launches from the yacht marina in the harbour. On the mainland you can check out the coast on the **St Blaize hiking trail**, an easy fifteen-kilometre walk (roughly 4hr each way; a map is available from the tourist office) along the southern shore of Mossel Bay. The route starts from the Cape St Blaize Cave, just below the lighthouse at the Point, and heads west as far as Dana Bay, taking in magnificent coastal views of cliffs, rocks, bays and coves.

If jumping off bridges is your bag, **bungee jumping** at the old Gouritz River Bridge, about 40km west of Mossel Bay along the N2, offers a considerably cheaper alternative (R180) to the Bloukrans River Bridge (see p.282) near Nature's Valley. If you're interested, just turn up and talk to Face Adrenalin at the bridge, though booking in advance will get you the time you want (ⓣ044 697 7001). Gouritz also offers the option of a **bungee swing** (again run by Face Adrenalin; R180), in which the bungee is attached to the back of the same bridge causing you to swing down and under. Prices are the same whether you go alone or in tandem, with photos included.

Eating and drinking

With the notable exception of the *Café Gannet*, the **Lighthouse Restaurant** at the *Point Hotel* is the nicest place for food and drinks, mainly because of the large stretch of sea frontage it offers, though there has been an upsurge of development here. The small Point Village shopping development at the north end has a couple of inexpensive to mid-priced family restaurants, opening daily from the morning until 11pm-ish.

Café Gannet Market St ⓣ044 691 1885. Close to the Bartholomew Dias Museum Complex is Mossel Bay's top restaurant, with moderately priced seafood lunches and dinners, served in a stylish garden with glimpses across the harbour, and a good spot for sundowners. Daily 7am–11pm.

Delfino's Espresso Bar and Pizzeria Point Village ℡ 044 690 5247. Italian food at reasonable prices, plus a view.
King Fisher Point Village ℡ 044 690 6390. A relaxed joint above *Delfino's*, specializing in seafood and offering good views.
Lighthouse Restaurant *Point Hotel*, Point Rd ℡ 044 691 3512. A wider-anging à la carte menu in a fabulous setting, with some veggie options. Daily 7am–10pm.

Santos Express Santos Beach. The restaurant attached to the train carriage on the beach, with an adjoining pub, is a lively venue with good calamari and burgers, at keen prices.
Tidals Waterfront Tavern & Pub south side of the Point. Mossel Bay's rowdiest drinking spot buzzes until the early hours on Fri & Sat, in a stunning seaside location.

Around Mossel Bay: Robinson Pass to Oudtshoorn

Heading inland towards Oudtshoorn from Mossel Bay on the R328 takes you over the forested coastal mountains over the **Robinson Pass** into the of desiccated Little Karoo. Close to the top, 35km from Mossel Bay, and a compelling stop for a meal or drink, is the *Eight Bells Mountain Inn* (℡ 044 631 0000, 🌐 www.eightbells.co.za; ⑤) a firm favourite with well-heeled families wanting a fully catered hotel-style holiday with all sorts of activities laid on for children, and rest time for adults. The atmosphere is friendly and it's superbly run with special meals and meal times for younger children, horse riding, swimming, tennis and walking. Out of school holidays it remains a restful stop-off with lovely gardens and extensive grounds.

On a nearby property, the **Botlierskop Private Game Reserve** (℡ 044 696 6055, 🌐 www.botlierskop.co.za) does game drives for day visitors at 10am and 3pm (R390, children R198) and elephant-back rides at 10am and 11am (R500, children R250) as well as horse rides (R150 an hour). Staying over in a luxury tent with meals and game drives will set you back R2500. Though it's no substitute for a safari in Kruger, and there's nothing wild about it, you will mostly (but not always) see lions in their huge enclosure, and there's a good chance of spotting elephants, rhinos, giraffes and antelope too. All activities and accommodation must be booked in advance as numbers are limited.

George, Victoria Bay and Wilderness

There's little reason to visit **GEORGE**, 66km northeast of Mossel Bay, unless you need what a big centre offers – airport, hospital and shops – and it does lie conveniently halfway between Cape Town and Port Elizabeth. Sadly, the Outeniqua Choo-Tjoe, which once lured people into George, is no longer doing its spectacular rail route to Knysna due to severe flooding, though it still runs to the less attractive destination of Mossel Bay. However, a cable car up to the top of George Peak is planned for 2010, which should be a reasonable attraction.

A large inland town, surrounded by mountains, George is a five-kilometre detour northwest off the N2, and 9km from the nearest stretch of ocean at Victoria Bay. Sadly, all that's left of the forests and quaint character that moved Anthony Trollope, during a visit in 1877, to describe it as the "prettiest village on the face of the earth", are some historic buildings, of which the beautiful **Dutch Reformed Church**, in Davidson Street at the top end of Meade Street, is the most notable. Completed in the early 1840s, the church is definitely worth a stop if you happen to be passing through, with its elegantly simple classical facade, Greek-cross plan with an impressive centrally placed pulpit and wonderful domed ceiling, panelled with glowing yellowwood. **St Mark's Cathedral**, in Cathedral Street, consecrated in 1850, is also worth seeing, but unlike the Dutch Reformed Church which is open to the public it can only be visited by appointment. Other than that, George's claim to recent fame (or notoriety) is the fact that it was the parliamentary seat of former State President

President Botha: the King Canute of apartheid

Pieter Willem Botha is credited with setting up an autocratic "Imperial Presidency" in South Africa, but in retrospect he was actually the King Canute of apartheid, closing his eyes to the incoming tide of democracy and believing that by wagging his finger (his favoured gesture of intimidation) he could turn it back.

A National Party hack from the age of 20, Botha worked his way up through the ranks, getting elected an MP in 1948 when the first apartheid government took power. He became leader of the National Party in the Cape Province and was promoted through various cabinet posts until he became **Minister of Defence**, a position he used to launch a palace coup in 1978 against his colleague, Prime Minister John Vorster. Botha immediately set about modernizing apartheid, modifying his own role from that of a British-style prime minister, answerable to parliament, to one of an executive president taking vital decisions in the secrecy of a President's Council heavily weighted with army top brass.

Informed by the army that the battle to preserve the apartheid status quo was unwinnable purely by force, Botha embarked on his **Total Strategy**, which involved reforms to peripheral aspects of apartheid and the fostering of a black middle class as a buffer against the ANC, while pumping vast sums of money into building an enormous military machine that crossed South Africa's borders to bully or crush neighbouring countries harbouring groups opposed to apartheid. South African refugees in Botswana and Zimbabwe were bombed, Angola was invaded, and arms were run to anti-government rebels in Mozambique, reducing it to ruins – a policy that has returned to haunt South Africa with those same weapons now returning across the border and finding their way into the hands of criminals. Inside South Africa, security forces enjoyed a free hand to murder, maim and torture **opponents of apartheid** on a scale that only fully emerged between 1996 and 1998, under the investigations of the Truth and Reconciliation Commission.

Botha's intransigence led to his greatest blunder in 1985, when he responded to international calls for change by hinting that he would announce significant reforms at his party congress that would irreversibly jettison apartheid. In the event, the so-called **Rubicon speech** was a disaster, as Botha proved to have insufficient steel to resist pressure from white right-wing extremists. The speech shrank away from meaningful concessions to black South Africans, the immediate result of which was a flight of capital from the country and intensified sanctions. Perhaps worst of all for the apartheid regime, the **Chase Manhattan Bank** refused to roll over its massive loan to South Africa, leaving the country an uncreditworthy pariah.

Botha blustered and wagged his finger at the opposition through the late 1980s, while his bloated military sucked the state coffers dry as it prosecuted its dirty wars. Even National Party stalwarts realized that his policies were leading to ruin, and in 1989, when he suffered a stroke, the party was quick to replace him with **F.W. de Klerk**, who immediately proceeded to announce the reforms the world had expected four years earlier from Botha's Rubicon speech.

Botha lived out his unrepentant retirement near George, declining ever to apologize for any of the brutal actions taken under his presidency to bolster apartheid. Curiously, when he died in 2006, he was given an uncritical, high-profile state funeral, broadcast on national television and attended by members of the current government, including President Thabo Mbeki.

P.W. Botha (see box opposite), the last of South Africa's apartheid hardliners. The George Museum once housed the P.W. Botha collection, an exercise in blind adulation for one of the most ruthless proponents of apartheid. The collection was regarded as unsuitable for a museum in the "New South Africa" and was removed in the 1990s.

Practicalities

The small George **airport** is 10km west of town on the N2. A Zeelie's **taxi** (☎044 874 6707) into town will set you back R50 from the airport; most tourists flying in rent a car from one of the rental companies here and set off down the Garden Route. Outeniqua Choo-Tjoe **trains** (see p.253) arrive at the Outeniqua Railway Museum, 2 Mission Rd, just off Knysna Road (☎044 801 8202). Intercape, Translux and Greyhound **intercity buses** pull in at George station, adjacent to the railway museum. The **Baz Bus** drops off at *McDonald's* on Courtenay Street. George's **tourist office**, 124 York St (Mon–Fri 8am–5pm, Sat 9am–1pm; ☎044 801 9295, ⓦ www.georgetourism.co.za), can provide town **maps** and help with accommodation bookings.

Accommodation

10 Caledon Street 10 Calendon St ☎044 873 4983, ⓦ www.10caledon.co.za. The pick of the mid-priced B&Bs, in a spotless guesthouse in a quiet street around the corner from the museum, featuring balconies with mountain views and a garden. ❸

Arbour Lodge on the corner of Davidson and Arbour rds ☎044 874 7592 or 082 412 4114, ⓦ www.ashmole.com. A modern suburban home with three large en-suite rooms with kitchenettes, close to the centre on the busy road to Oudtshoorn. It's hosted by an extremely friendly and obliging couple, who welcome children. ❸

Die Waenhuis 11 Caledon St ☎044 874 0034, ⓔ diewaenhuis@lantic.net. Mid-nineteenth-century home that has retained its period character. English breakfasts are served in a sunlit dining room. ❸

George Tourist Resort York St ☎044 874 5205. En-suite chalets (R620/R910 sleeping four/eight) and rondavels (R500 sleeping four) in well-kept pleasant gardens, with a swimming pool, children's playground, shop and laundry facilities.

Oak Tree 30 Caledon St ☎082 563 9952 or 044 874 5931, ⓦ www.oaktreebnb.co.za. This Victorian home has two comfortable rooms, with white linen and well-appointed bathrooms. Both rooms have separate entrances. ❸

Eating and drinking

Fong Ling Taiwanese corner of York and Fichat sts ☎044 884 0088. Quick mid-priced lunches or evening marathons. Daily from 11.30am–3pm & 5.30–10.30pm.

La Capannina 122 York St ☎044 874 5313. Italian restaurant with excellent pizzas. Open lunch & dinner daily, except Sat and Sun lunch.

The Old Town House corner York and Market sts ☎044 8874 3663. Lovely ambience in this original townhouse, where food is well cooked with attention to detail in an intimate setting. Open lunch & dinner daily, closed Sun.

Travel Bugs 111 York St ☎044 873 2009. Good coffee, breakfasts and light lunches in a shaded courtyard. Mon–Fri 8am–4.30pm, Sat 9am–noon.

Zanzibar Sports Pub next to the museum, in two old railway carriages. Beer and a big screen, mainly enjoyed by a younger crowd. Mon–Sat 11am till after midnight.

Victoria Bay

Some 9km south of George and 3km off the N2 lies the minuscule hamlet of **VICTORIA BAY**, on the edge of a small sandy beach wedged into a cove between cliffs, with a grassy sunbathing area, safe swimming and a tidal pool. During the December holidays, the place packs out with day-trippers, and rates as one of the top **surfing** spots in South Africa. Because of the cliffs, there's only a single row of buildings along the beachfront, with some of the most dreamily positioned guesthouses along the coast (and, therefore, some of the priciest).

There's no public **transport** to Victoria Bay, although many people hitch the few kilometres from the N2. Arriving by **car**, you'll encounter a metal barrier

▲ Beach houses at Victoria Bay

as you drop down the hill to the bay, and you'll have to try and park in a car park that's frequently full (especially in summer). If you're staying at one of the B&Bs, leave your car at the barrier and collect the key from your lodgings to gain access to the private beach road. The only places to buy **food** are a small beachside kiosk selling light refreshments and a casual restaurant where you can stroll down in flip flops and shorts. However, the resort's B&Bs are served by Mr Delivery, a service that will collect from about ten fast-food joints in George and will also fetch groceries and even videos.

Accommodation

Besides the places to stay reviewed here, there's magnificently located **camping** on the clifftop overlooking the beach, at the *Victoria Bay Caravan Park*, on the left as you approach the beach (☎044 889 0081).

Land's End Guest House The Point, Beach Rd ☎044 889 0123, ⓦ www.vicbay.com. Two self-catering studio apartments at the end of the road, sleeping two, plus two flats on a B&B basis. ➎
Pier Plesier Beach Rd ☎044 889 0051, ⓔ ianwesson@mjvn.co.za. A well-run modern brick building with upstairs and downstairs en-suite flats overlooking the sea, just 6m from the high-water mark. The flats have either one or two rooms, and can sleep four. The cheapest unit has no sea view. Self-catering ➌, B&B ➎

Sea Breeze Holiday Resort along the main road into the settlement ☎044 889 0098, ⓦ www.seabreezecabanas.co.za. A variety of budget self-catering units, including modern two-storey holiday huts and wooden chalets, sleeping two, four or eight people. The huts have no sea views, but it's an easy stroll to the beach. ➋–➍
The Waves 7 Beach Rd ☎044 889 0166, ⓦ www .gardenroute.co.za/vbay/waves. Two comfortable suites in a high-ceilinged Victorian house. ➏

Wilderness

East of Victoria Bay, across the Kaaimans River, the beach at **WILDERNESS** is so close to the N2 that you can pull over for a quick dip with barely an interruption to your journey, though African wilderness is the last thing you'll find here. Wilderness village earned its name, so the story goes, after a young man called Van den Berg bought the property in 1830 for £183 as a blind lot at a Cape Town auction. When he got engaged, his fiancée insisted that their first year of marriage should be spent out of town in the wilderness, so he romantically (or perhaps opportunistically) named his property Wilderness and built a hut on it.

If the hut still exists, you'll struggle to find it among the sprawl of retirement homes, holiday houses and thousands of beds for rent in the vicinity. The beach, which is renowned for its long stretch of sand, is backed by tall dunes, rudely blighted by holiday houses. Once in the water, stay close to the shoreline: this part of the coast is notorious for its unpredictable currents.

The main attraction of the area though, is the Wilderness National Park, whose river is lovely to paddle along, with good bird-spotting.

Practicalities

The tiny **village centre**, on the north side of the N2, has a filling station, a few shops, restaurants and a **tourist office** in *Milkwood Village Mall*, Beacon Road, off the N2 opposite the Caltex Garage (May–Sept Mon–Fri 8am–5pm, Sat 9am–1pm; Oct–April Mon–Fri 8am–6pm, Sat 8am–1pm, Sun 3–5pm; ☎044 877 0045, ⊛www.visitwilderness.co.za).

Eden Adventures (☎044 877 0179 or 083 628 8547) runs half-day **canoeing**, **cycling**, **abseiling** or **kloofing** trips along the nearby Kaaiman's River and its gorge (R250). Explore the river yourself by renting a two-seater canoe from them (R120 for 3hr including park fees). Wilderness Adventures (☎044 850 1008) runs mountain **horse-riding** tours (R150 an hour). To see it all from the air, sign up with the recommended Cloudbase Paragliding Adventures (☎044 877 1414) for a tandem **paragliding** jump that clocks in at R450. You fly for a minimum of fifteen minutes, but you'll only be taken up when the weather offers absolutely safe conditions.

When it comes to **eating**, *The Girls* on George Road (☎044 877 1648; lunch & dinner daily except Sun) in the village centre is the place to come for fusion Mediterranean food. Combining middle-European and local flavours, at moderate prices, *Palms* is the best restaurant at the Swiss-owned *Palms Wilderness Guest House*, Owen Grant Road (☎044 877 1420; dinner daily), 3km from town. For an informal meal that might include smoked salmon omelette, pizza or steak, try the *Wilderness Grill* on George Road (open daily for breakfast, lunch & dinner), with seating outside under parasols or indoors by the fire. If you're at **Milkwood Village**, there are several places to eat, one of the best being *Pomodoro*, an Italian restaurant with a pleasant ambience.

Accommodation

The Albatross Sixth Ave, take South St exit off the N2 ☎044 877 1716. Guesthouse within easy walking distance from the beach, with large balconies and perfect dolphin-watching views. ❹

Fairy Knowe Backpackers ☎044 877 1285, ⓔfairybp@mweb.co.za. The oldest home (built 1897) in the area, with a wraparound balcony and set in the quiet woodlands near the Touws River, though nowhere near the sea; to reach the site, 6km from the village, follow signs from the N2 east of Wilderness. The Baz Bus will drop off here. Dorms ❶, rooms ❷

Island Lake Holiday Resort Lakes Rd, 2km from the Hoekwil/Island Lake turn-off on the N2 ☎044 877 1194. Camping and self-catering bungalows that sleep four (R485), on one of the quietest and prettiest spots on the lakes.

Mes-Amis Homestead Buxton Close, signposted off the N2 on the coastal side of the road, directly opposite the national park turn-off ☎044 877 1928, ⊛www.mesamis.co.za. Nine double rooms, each of which has its own terrace, offering some of the best views in Wilderness. ❹–❺

The Tops Hunts Lane, on a hill about 500m from the tourist office ☎044 877 0187 or

083 631 2339. Four airy en-suite bedrooms, three of which have sea views and French doors opening onto a deck. ❸
Wilderness Bush Camp Heights Rd (follow Waterside Rd west for 1600m up the hill)

ⓣ044 877 1168, ⓦwww.boskamp.co.za. Six self-catering timber units with loft bedrooms, thatched roofs and ocean views. The camp is part of a conservation estate that you're free to roam around. ❷

Wilderness National Park

Stretching east from Wilderness village is the **Wilderness National Park** (reception open 24hr; ⓣ044 877 1197; R60), the least aptly named national park in South Africa, as it never feels very far from the rumbling N2. Although the park takes in beach frontage, it's the **forests** you should come for, as well as the 16km of inland waterways; the variety of habitats here includes coastal and montane *fynbos* and wetlands, attracting 250 species of **birds** – as well as many holidaymakers.

There are two **restcamps**, both on the west side of the park and clearly signposted off the N2. *Ebb and Flow North* (❷–❸), right on the river, is cheap, old-fashioned and away from the hustle. It offers camping, fully equipped two-person bungalows with their own showers, and slightly cheaper huts with communal washing and toilet facilities. *Ebb and Flow South* (❷–❸), signposted close by, has camping and modern accommodation in spacious log cabins on stilts and brick bungalows which, although dearer than *North* camp, represent good value if there are more than two of you (you pay for a minimum of four people) for its fully equipped, self-contained family brick bungalows or log cabins on stilts. There are also cheaper en-suite forest huts with communal kitchens for two people and, cheaper still, huts with shared ablution facilities. Seasonal discounts of twenty percent are offered on accommodation (apart from the forest huts and camping) from mid-January to mid-March and from May to November. There is a **shop** selling milk, bread and basic groceries at reception, a coin-operated **laundry**, and a small children's playground.

Activities

To take advantage of all the water, you can rent **canoes** and **pedaloes** from reception. There are also several waymarked walking trails, well worth doing to get a feeling of the indigenous vegetation and escape the N2 and holiday homes – the reception issues trail **maps**. The **Giant Kingfisher trail** is an easy seven-kilometre walk that starts at *Ebb and Flow North* camp and passes through the forest along the eastern bank of the Touws River to some rock pools teeming with little sea creatures, returning along the same route, taking three hours for the round trip. Another hike of about three hours is the six-kilometre **Cape Dune Molerat trail**, a circuit along the dunes separating Rondevlei and Swartvlei lakes, with good views onto both. It offers excellent birding opportunities and you'll see wild flowers during winter and spring. To get there, take the N2 east towards Sedgefield for 16km, take the Swartvlei turn-off and continue down a dirt road; after 2.8km turn right and continue for just over 1km to the conservation station and trail starting point.

Sedgefield, Goukamma and Buffels Bay

The drive between Wilderness and Sedgefield gives glimpses on your left of dark-coloured lakes which eventually surge out to sea, 21km later, through a wide lagoon at **SEDGEFIELD**, a lacklustre holiday village a few kilometres off the road, with a safe swimming **beach** that makes a refreshing pit stop. Until recently Sedgefield's unpromising appearance of shops, restaurants and B&Bs lining the highway hid a gloriously undeveloped beachfront. But the resort's authorities have woken up to the economic potential of development, and turned parts of the beachfront into a building site. At least accommodation prices are more reasonable here than at Knysna half an hour away (see p.266), making Sedgefield a potential base for exploring the area.

Sedgefield could be used as a base from which to explore **Goukamma Nature and Marine Reserve** and the western extent of **Groenvlei**, a freshwater lake that falls within the reserve's boundaries. An unassuming sanctuary of around 220 square kilometres, Goukamma ranges from near Sedgefield east as far as the small seaside resort of **Buffels Bay** to absorb 14km of beach frontage, some of the highest vegetated dunes in the country, and walking country covered with coastal *fynbos* and dense thickets of milkwood, yellowwood and candlewood trees.

The area has long been popular with anglers for Groenvlei's six **fish** species. Away from the water, you stand a small chance of spotting one of the area's **mammals**, including bushbuck, grysbok, mongoose, vervet monkeys, caracals and otters. Because of the diversity of coastal and wetland habitats, over 220 different kinds of **birds** have been recorded here, including fish eagles, Knysna louries, kingfishers and very rare African black oystercatchers. Offshore, southern right **whales** often make an appearance during their August to December breeding season, and bottlenose and common **dolphins** can show up at any time of year.

Apart from angling and bird-watching, the Goukamma offers a number of self-guided activities, including safe **swimming** in Groenvlei. There are several day-long hiking **trails** that enable you to explore different habitats – if you plan on hiking you should pick up the Cape Nature Conservation map from your guesthouse. A beach walk, which takes around four hours one way, traverses the 14km of crumbling cliffs and sands between the Platbank car park on the western side of the reserve and the Rowwehoek one on the eastern side. Alternatively, you can go from one end of the reserve to the other via a slightly longer inland trek across the dunes. There's also a shorter circular walk from the reserve office through a milkwood forest, as well as **horse-riding** trips run by Cherry Tree Christian Adventures (℡082 060 6751; R150/hr).

Two roads off the N2 provide **access** to the reserve. At the westernmost side, a dirt road that runs down to Platbank Beach takes you past the tiny settlement of **Lake Pleasant** on the south bank of Groenvlei, which consists of little more than a hotel and holiday resort. On the eastern side, access is via the Buffels Bay road, halfway along which is the reserve office. There are no public roads within the reserve.

Accommodation

Among the forest of holiday homes in **Sedgefield**, you'll find some decent accommodation away from the N2. Another inexpensive alternative to Knysna is **Buffels Bay**, a haphazard little development at the east of the reserve; it's 10km down a turn-off along the N2, 13km east of Sedgefield.

At Goukamma Nature Reserve (bookings ℡021 659 3500), you can choose to stay at a basic bushcamp that sleeps up to four people (**②**) or one of the thatched rondavels that sleep up to five (**①**). All have fully equipped kitchens, but you must bring your own bedding.

Coral Reef Guesthouse 28 Coral Reef Crescent, Cola Beach, Sedgefield ℡044 343 3133, ⓦwww .coralreef.co.za. Two double rooms, a triple and a family unit, all brightly decorated. There's a saltwater pool and a comfortable relaxing area. Discounts for stays of two or more nights. ❹
Lake Pleasant Chalets & Lodges Lake Pleasant, east of Sedgefield, south of the N2 ℡044 343 1985, ⓦwww.lake-pleasant.co.za. Self-catering

timber chalets and slightly smaller four-person garden lodges at a family resort with a kids' play area and a trampoline. There's also a restaurant, a pub and a store selling basics, and they rent out mountain bikes, rowing boats and canoes. ❸
Warthog Wallow 11 Begonia St, Sedgefield ℡044 343 1965, ⓦwww.arthogwallow.co.za. Peaceful timber guesthouse with views of the nearby mountains. ❸

Knysna and the Knysna forests

South Africa's 1990s tourist boom rudely shook **KNYSNA** (pronounced "Nize-nuh") from its gentle backwoods drowse, which for decades made this the hippy and craftwork capital and quiet retirement village of the country. The town, 102km east of Mossel Bay, now stands at the hub of the Garden Route, its lack of ocean beaches compensated for by its hilly setting around the **Knysna lagoon**, its handsome **forests**, good opportunities for **adventure sports**, a pleasant **waterfront development** – and some hot marketing.

Knysna's distinctive atmosphere derives from its small historic core of Georgian and Victorian buildings, which gives it a character absent from most of the Garden Route holiday towns. Coffee shops, craft galleries, street traders and a modest nightlife add to the attractions, and you may find yourself tempted to stay longer than just one night. That the town has outgrown itself is evident from the cars and tour buses which, especially in December and January, clog Main Street, the constricted artery that merges with the N2 as it enters the town.

Some history

At the beginning of the nineteenth century, the only white settlements outside Cape Town were a handful of villages that would have considered themselves lucky to have even one horse. Knysna, an undeveloped backwater hidden in the forest, was no exception. The name comes from a Khoi word meaning "hard to reach", and this remained its defining character well into the twentieth century. One important figure was not deterred by the distance – **George Rex**, a colourful colonial administrator who placed himself beyond the pale of decent colonial society by taking a coloured mistress. Shunned by his peers in Britain, he headed for Knysna at the turn of the nineteenth century in the hope of making a killing shipping out hardwood from the lagoon.

By the time of Rex's death in 1839, Knysna had become a major **timber centre**, attracting white labourers who felled trees with primitive tools for miserly payments, and looked set eventually to destroy the forest. In 1872, **Prince Alfred**, on his visit to the Cape, made his small royal contribution to this wanton destruction when he made a special detour here to come elephant hunting. The forest only narrowly escaped devastation by far-sighted and effective conservation policies introduced in the 1880s.

By the turn of the twentieth century, Knysna was still remote, and its forests were inhabited by isolated and inbred communities made up of the impoverished descendants of the woodcutters. As late as 1914, if you travelled from Knysna to George you would have to open and close 58 gates along the 75-kilometre track. Fifteen years on, the passes in the region proved too much for **George Bernard Shaw**, who did some impromptu off-road driving and

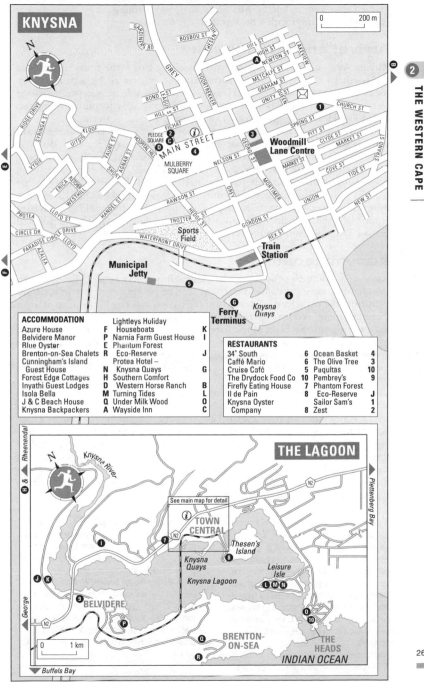

KNYSNA

0 ——— 200 m

BOSBOU ST
GARDINER'S RD
TRESEANT
GREY
LEASIDE ST
BOND
HILL ST
EAGLE ST
FICHAT
RIDGE DRIVE
SYRINGA ST
KLOOF
UITSIG
FAURE ST
HOSPITAL HILL
AGNAR ST
SHORT
VYGIE
ERICA
WESTHILL
PROTEA
BEECH
HANDEL ST
LLOYD ST
CIRCLE DR
AZALEA
PARADISE CIRCLE DRIVE
LLOYD
WATERFRONT DRIVE

VOORTREKKER
HIGH L ST
NEWTON ST
METCALFE ST
GRAHAM ST
UNITY
QUEEN
A
CHURCH ST
SPRING ST
PITT ST
CLYDE ST
MARKET ST
STRAND ST
COVE ST
TIDE ST
LAKEVIEW
B

PLEDGE SQUARE
MAIN STREET
i
MULBERRY SQUARE
NELSON ST
GEORGE ST
MORTIMER
RAWSON ST
GREY
HEDGE ST
TROTTER ST
GORDON ST
UNION
NEW ST
REX ST

Woodmill Lane Centre

Sports Field

Train Station

Municipal Jetty

Ferry Terminus

G

Knysna Quays

ACCOMMODATION

Azure House	**F**	Lightleys Holiday
Belvidere Manor	**P**	Houseboats **K**
Blue Oyster	**E**	Narnia Farm Guest House **I**
Brenton-on-Sea Chalets **R**		Phantom Forest
Cunningham's Island		Eco-Reserve **J**
Guest House	**N**	Protea Hotel –
Forest Edge Cottages	**H**	Knysna Quays **G**
Inyathi Guest Lodges	**D**	Southern Comfort
Isola Bella	**M**	Western Horse Ranch **B**
J & C Beach House	**Q**	Turning Tides **L**
Knysna Backpackers	**A**	Under Milk Wood **O**
		Wayside Inn **C**

RESTAURANTS

34° South	6	Ocean Basket	4
Caffé Mario	6	The Olive Tree	3
Cruise Café	5	Paqultas	10
The Drydock Food Co	10	Pembrey's	9
Firefly Eating House	7	Phantom Forest
Il de Pain	8	Eco-Reserve	J
Knysna Oyster		Sailor Sam's	1
Company	8	Zest	2

THE LAGOON

Knysna River

See main map for detail

i TOWN CENTRAL

Thesen's Island

Knysna Quays

Knysna Lagoon

Leisure Isle

BELVIDERE

BRENTON-ON-SEA

THE HEADS

INDIAN OCEAN

George

Rheenendal

N2

Plettenberg Bay

0 ——— 1 km

Buffels Bay

crashed into a bush, forcing Mrs Shaw to spend a couple of weeks in bed at Knysna's *Royal Hotel* with a broken leg.

Arrival and information

Knysna wraps around the lagoon, with its oldest part – the town centre – on the northern side. The lagoon's narrow mouth is guarded by a pair of steep rocky promontories called **The Heads**, the western side being a private nature reserve and the eastern one an exclusive residential area (confusingly, it's also called The Heads), along dramatic cliffs above the Indian Ocean.

Greyhound, Intercape and Translux **buses** drop passengers off at the **train station** in Remembrance Avenue opposite Knysna Quays; the **Baz Bus** will drop passengers off at any of the town's accommodation. For local transport, there are a couple of **taxi** services (see "Listings", p.272).

The **tourist office**, Knysna Tourism, at 40 Main St (Mon–Fri 8am–5pm, Sat 8.30am–1pm; slightly longer hours during the season; ☎044 382 5510, ⒲www .tourismknysna.co.za), provides maps and runs a desk for booking **activities** around Knysna – including cruises to and abseiling down The Heads and bungee jumping from the Bloukrans River Bridge.

Accommodation

Knysna has hundreds of accommodation establishments to choose from, though rates have become expensive over the years. The best places to stay in town are away from the main road, with views of the lagoon and The Heads. Out of town there are some excellent guesthouses and B&Bs as well as reasonably priced self-catering cottages right in the **forest**, where you can get well away from the town buzz. For somewhere quieter on the lagoon, make for the western edge at **Brenton-on-Sea**. It is possible to stay here or a few kilometres inland in the quaint and very upmarket settlement of **Belvidere**, through which visitors are prohibited from driving.

For something different, you can rent a **houseboat** from Lightleys, moored at the Belvidere turn-off from the N2 (☎044 386 0007, ⒲www.houseboats .co.za; R1045 for two people or R1245 for four in a four-berth Leisure Liner, R1735 for a six-berth Aqualiner). Its houseboats let you explore the lagoon's 20km of navigable water and are fully equipped, with interiors resembling those of caravans. Another option is a **township homestay**, arranged through Knysna Tourism; it runs a busy accommodation office (☎044 382 6960, Ⓔbooking@mweb.co.za) and can help you book homestays and any other type of accommodation in the vicinity.

Town centre and Knysna Quays

Knysna Backpackers 42 Queen St ☎044 382 2554, ⒲www.knysnabackpackers.co.za. Spotless, well-organized hostel in a large, rambling and centrally located Victorian house that has been declared a national monument. Totally renovated in 2007, this tranquil establishment has five rooms rented as doubles (but able to sleep up to four people) and a dorm that sleeps eight. Doubles ❷, dorms ❶

Protea Hotel – Knysna Quays Waterfront Drive ☎044 382 5005, ⒲www.proteahotels.com /protea-hotel-knysna-quays.html. A 122-room, nautically themed luxury hotel in a fabulous spot on the waterfront, within walking distance of the centre. Rooms either have views of the lagoon and the yacht basin or of the train station. ❼

Wayside Inn Pledge Square, 48 Main Rd ☎044 382 6011, ⒲www.waysideinn.co.za. A smart overnight stop right in the centre done out in sisal matting, wicker furniture and white linen on black wrought-iron bedsteads. A continental breakfast is served in your room or on the deck outside. ❹

Eastern suburbs, Leisure Isle and The Heads

Cunningham's Island Guest House 3 Kingsway, Leisure Isle ☎044 384 1319, ⓦwww.islandhouse.co.za. Purpose-built two-storey, timber-and-glass guesthouse with eight suites, decked out in dazzling white relieved by a touch of blue and some ethnic colour (stripey cushions and African baskets). Each room has its own entrance leading to the garden, which has a swimming pool shaded by giant strelitzias. Stylish and comfortable, its only drawback is the lack of views. ⑤

Isola Bella 21 Hart Lane, Leisure Isle ☎044 384 0049, ⓦwww.isolabella.co.za. You can't help but gasp at The Heads views through the huge windows of this imposing guesthouse at the lagoon's edge. You'll either love or loathe the mildly operatic decor – repro furniture, lots of oil paintings and some floral fabrics. Either way, the rooms are undeniably luxurious. Breakfast is served on the spectacularly positioned balcony overlooking the water. ⑥

Turning Tides 19 Woodbourne Drive, Leisure Isle ☎044 384 0302, ⓦwww.capetown.at/turningtides. Comfortable, simply furnished double-storey B&B run by a friendly couple – he a retired doctor, she nutritional scientist (special dietary needs catered for). Each of the three rooms in this child-friendly home has its own balcony with lagoon views. ④

Under Milk Wood George Rex Drive, The Heads ☎044 384 0745, ⓦwww.milkwood.co.za. Luxury self-catering accommodation on the lagoon at the foot of The Heads with its own private beach – safe for swimming – and terrific views of the mountains and water. The two-bedroom self-catering units, with their own sun decks, are surrounded by milkwood trees; rates vary depending on whether the unit is on the lagoon, the hillside or between. There are also two B&B rooms ⑤–⑥

West of town

Azure House 65 Circular Drive ☎044 382 1221, ⓦwww.azurehouse.com. Limewashed whites, blues and pale yellows are the signature colours in these upmarket self-catering rooms, each en suite, with a small lounge. Breakfast (optional) is served on a wicker tray on your private balcony overlooking the lagoon. ④

Blue Oyster On the corner of Rio and Stent sts ☎044 382 2265, ⓦwww.blueoyster.co.za. Hospitable three-storey, vaguely Greek-themed B&B set high on one of the hills that rise up behind Knysna, offering fabulous panoramas across the lagoon to The Heads. The four comfortable double rooms, of which the ones on the top floor have the best views, are done out in white and blue. ④–⑤

Narnia Farm Guest House signed off Welbedacht Lane, 3km west of Knysna ☎044 382 1334, ⓦwww.narnia.co.za. On a hillside with views of the lagoon, this is an immensely fun stone and rough-hewn timber farmhouse in a glorious garden, set among protea plantations. Two en-suite B&B rooms upstairs have their own balconies and swinging chairs and are decorated in a rustic-chic style, as is a comfortable semi-detached two-bedroom cottage downstairs which has a lounge, fireplace and kitchenette. The Pool House (so-called because it opens onto a gorgeous, deck-surrounded swimming pool and its spacious lounge has its own pool table) is a one-bedroom cottage not far from the house, while the Shed (R1000 for the whole unit) is a short walk from the main house and has two bedrooms. Walks on the property include one down to a small lake. Self-catering ⑤, B&B ⑥

Phantom Forest Eco-Reserve Phantom Pass Rd, west of town off the N2 ☎044 386 0046, ⓦwww.phantomforest.com. Breathtaking, tranquil forest lodge making extensive use of timber and glass, set on a hill in indigenous forest, with fabulous lagoon views. African fabrics and pure cotton linen help reinforce the sense of unbridled luxury. Timber boardwalks wind through the forest to connect the suites to the main buildings, which feature a safari-style dining room, an open-air hot tub, a massage suite and a Jacuzzi. The swimming pool teeters on the edge of the hill, cocooned by vegetation, with vervet monkeys frolicking in the forest canopy. Half board ⑧

The forest

Forest Edge Cottages Rheenendal turn-off, 16km west of Knysna on the N2 ☎082 456 1338, ⓦwww.forestedge.co.za. Ideal if you want to be close to the forest itself, these traditional tin-roofed, two-bedroomed cottages have verandas built in the vernacular tin-roofed style. Self-contained, fully equipped and serviced, the cottages sleep four. Forest walks and cycling trails start from the cottages, and you can also rent mountain bikes. ④

Southern Comfort Western Horse Ranch 3km along the Fisanthoek road, 17km east of Knysna en route to Plettenberg Bay ☎044 532 7885, ⓦwww.schranch.co.za. Very basic double rooms, dorms and a tree house, on a farm adjacent to the eastern section of the Knysna forest; staff can pick you up from the N2. Horse-riding (R140/hr, R590 for overnight forest trails) – and massages for the saddle-weary – are on offer. You can self-cater or take the meals provided. ①

Belvidere and Brenton-on-Sea

Belvidere Manor Duthie Drive, Belvidere Estate ☎044 387 1055, Ⓦwww.belvidere.co.za. A collection of tin-roofed repro Victorian cottages, nicely positioned on the water's edge. Although they're spacious and were once quite smart, the feel now is of Laura Ashley let loose in a *Holiday Inn*. However, this is the only accommodation in this unique area. ❼–❽

Brenton-on-Sea Chalets C.R. Swart Drive, Brenton beachfront ☎044 381 0081,

Ⓦwww.abalonelodges.co.za. A 15min drive from Knysna and overlooking the long curve of Brenton Beach, which swings round to Buffels Bay. The three-bedroom, self-catering chalets sleep six people, and are well equipped and comfortably furnished. R950.

J&C Beach House 116 Watsonia Ave, Brenton ☎044 381 0107, Ⓦwww.jcbeachhouse.co.za. Simple and elegant rooms, each with views of the ocean from the balcony. You can sun yourself at the pool or on nearby Brenton beach. ❺

The Town and beaches

Main Street, which used to be the hub of Knysna, lost some of its status as the heart of the town with the development of the waterfront area. But it has begun fighting back, with extensive redevelopment that has brought with it trendy coffee shops, restaurants and shops.

About 500m south of Knysna Tourism, at the end of Grey Street, lies the **Knysna Quays**, the town's waterfront complex and yacht basin. Built at the end of the 1990s, this elegant two-storey steel structure with timber boardwalks resembles a tiny version of Cape Town's V&A Waterfront – but probably owes its inspiration as much to New England or Seattle, and blows away Knysna's hippy cobwebs with a breath of upmarket supercool. Here you'll find the luxury *Protea Hotel*, some clothes and knick-knack shops and a couple of good eating places, including a stunning deli-style bistro, *34° South*, with outdoor decks, from which you can watch yachts drift past. Riding on the success of the Quays, **Thesen's Island**, reached by a causeway at the south end of Long Street, has some stylish shops and eateries, among them the Knysna Oyster Company, one of the best spots for feasting on shellfish – on the edge of the lapping lagoon.

A short way from the centre in the industrial area, **Mitchell's Brewery** offers thirty-minute tours (Mon–Fri 10.30am & 3pm) on which you get to sample its beers for next to nothing, including Foresters Draught, a Pilsner-type lager, and Bosun's Bitter, an ale modelled on Yorkshire bitter (tastings Mon–Fri 8am–5pm & Sat 9am–1pm). The brewery is in Arend Road, off George Rex Drive via Vigilance and Sandpiper roads, a twenty-minute walk away.

The main reasons to head for **Leisure Isle** off the eastern suburbs are the excellent swimming in the lagoon and the views out to sea through the gap between The Heads. The best bathing spots are along the southern shore of the island, particularly the western section along Bayswater Drive, but the swimming is only good around high tide in summer.

Continuing south along George Rex Drive brings you to the web of roads winding through the small suburban areas of The Heads and Coney Glen to the top of the **eastern Head**. Around *Paquitas* restaurant (see p.272) there are fantastic views out to sea; for an even better viewpoint head along the short walkway starting outside the restaurant, taking you along the cliff edge.

The beaches

Don't come to Knysna for a beach holiday: the closest beach is 20km from town at **Brenton-on-Sea**. A tiny settlement on the shores of Buffels Bay, it does admittedly have a quite exceptional beach. Although **Buffels Bay** (see p.265), the next beach to the west, is along the same continuous stretch of sand as

Knysna cruises and activities

One of the obligatory excursions around Knysna is a **cruise** across the lagoon to The Heads. Knysna Featherbed Company (☎044 382 1693) runs several 75-minute trips a day from Knysna Quays to The Heads (R80), a ninety-minute trip on the double-decker M/V *John Benn* (R90), as well as a dinner cruise (R295) on purportedly the only paddle-driven vessel in the country. For travel beyond The Heads, you can take a sailing trip (1hr 30min; R200) and a sunset cruise (2hr 30min; R440) with delicious food and wine. The only way to reach the private **Featherbed Nature Reserve** on the western side of the lagoon is on a four-hour Featherbed Nature Tour (R300), which includes the boat there and use of a 4WD shuttle to the top of the western Head, with the option of walking 2km back downhill to enjoy spectacular views and see flora and fauna, including Knysna louries; a buffet meal is included as well. There's a slightly shorter version (3hr 30min) which excludes the meal (R190). **Bookings** are essential, and can be made at the kiosk on the north side of Knysna Quays; **departures** are from the Waterfront Jetty and municipal jetty on Remembrance Avenue, 400m west of the quays and station.

Activities and adventure sports

Seal Adventures (☎044 382 5599, ⊛www.sealadventures.co.za) runs **abseiling** and **rap jumping** trips (the latter involving running down a mountainside while harnessed; R300) in the Featherbed Nature Reserve, **canoeing** trips on the lagoon (R180), and **quad biking** (R350) in the forests. Knysna Forest Tours and Mountain Biking Africa (see p.274) offers a range of guided forest and coastal hikes and mountain-biking trips in Knysna's forests and along the beaches as well as bird-watching and fly fishing.

    Customized tours can be arranged by Deep South (☎044 382 2010 or 083 250 9441, ⊛www.deepsoutheco.com), allowing you to combine, for example, mountain biking and a lagoon cruise (R630 per person for 2–6 people; cost includes lunch). It will also do standalone mountain biking trips or cruises.

Brenton-on-Sea, there's no direct route there; you have to return to the N2 and proceed from there. In the opposite direction from Knysna, the closest patch of sand is at **Noetzie**, a town known more for its eccentric holiday homes built to look like castles than for its seaside.

Eating, drinking and nightlife

As far as food goes, oysters are an obvious choice, with the Knysna Oyster Company here being one of the world's largest oyster farms, but you'll also find a lot of good **restaurants** catering to other palates and one or two excellent **coffee shops**. With so many forests, waterways and beaches, you may be tempted to have a **picnic**, and there's no shortage of tempting deli food in town.

    Knysna has a livelier atmosphere than you might expect from a Garden Route town. At night *Stones*, on the corner of St George's and Main roads, is where to head for local and visiting **bands** from across the country.

34° South Knysna Quays. An outstanding deli and eating place, with imported groceries, home-made fare and seafood; from here you can watch the drawbridge open to let yachts sail through. Daily 9am–1pm.

Caffé Mario Knysna Quays ☎044 382 7250. An intimate Italian waterside restaurant with outdoor seating, and *paninoteca* and *tramezzini* on its snack menu as well as great pizza and pasta. Excellent value. Daily from 9am for breakfast, lunch & dinner.

Cruise Café Featherbed Ferry Terminal, off Waterfront Drive. Relaxed eatery that fuses African and Asian flavours to bring forth starters such as *bobotie* spring rolls. Main courses include Karoo lamb with mint and cranberry reduction, and venison loin in pastry with rosemary and cranberry reduction. Afro-Asian prawn curry and grilled calamari steak with smoked oyster and sun-dried tomatoes are among the seafood offerings. The waterside deck here is one of the best places in town to sink a drink while watching the setting sun. Mon–Sat 11.30am–11pm & Sun 11.30am–4pm.

The Drydock Food Co Knysna Quays ✆ 044 382 7310. Reckoned by many to be the best place to eat in town with a great seafood menu that has coastal oysters and local salmon trout as starters and main courses of prawns, East Coast sole and meat dishes. Daily lunch & dinner.

Firefly Eating House 152a Old Cape Rd ✆ 044 382 1490. Relaxed little eatery whose fiery red decor and sparkling fairy lights match the spicy menu. Dishes draw their inspiration from Malaysia, Thailand and East and South Africa. Recommended if you like it hot. Tues–Sat 6.30–10pm.

Il de Pain Thesen Island. Trendy restaurant in a bakery, with a menu of salads, baguettes, oysters and pastas, written up on a blackboard. Try the thick crusty bread baked in a woodfired oven with butter and preserve for breakfast or settle for one of the delicious pastries with coffee. Tues–Sat 8am–3pm & Sun 9am–1.30pm.

Knysna Oyster Company Thesen Island. Run by the firm of the same name which has been in operation since 1949, this restaurant serves oysters harvested by the parent company from beds in the Knysna River Estuary. Don't worry if you're not an oyster eater – they also serve steaks, chicken and freshly caught fish. Daily 10am–9pm.

Ocean Basket Knysna Mall, corner of Main Rd and Grey St. A reliably predictable family-friendly seafood restaurant chain with everything from freshly caught fish to hake and chips, at reasonable prices. Mon–Thurs noon–10pm, Fri–Sun noon–11pm.

The Olive Tree 12 Main Rd. This local favourite offers a great buffet lunch, cooked on the day. Choice depends on the whim of the chef and the availability of ingredients. The spread can consist of spicy chick peas, chicken wings – you name it – and a range of fresh salads. Toasted sandwiches and coffee are also on offer. Daily 8am–5pm.

Paquitas Knysna Heads ✆ 044 384 0408. Burgers, ribs and pizzas in a restaurant fabulously located on the rocks beneath The Heads, where kids can run onto the beach. Daily lunch & dinner.

Pembrey's Brenton Rd, Belvidere ✆ 044 386 0005. Small, unpretentious and highly rated restaurant that fuses country cooking with haute cuisine. You'll find venison, duck confit and prawns on the menu alongside offal. Booking essential. Wed–Sun 6.30pm till the last person leaves.

Phantom Forest Eco-Reserve Phantom Pass Rd ✆ 044 386 0046. Eating is secondary to being in one of the most beautiful places in South Africa, in a forest with views of the whole estuary. The expensive Pan-African set menu ranges from ostrich medallions marinated in orange and ginger to forest mushrooms with garlic rocket and Knysna cheese, and tempting desserts such as brandy-snap baskets. Dinner daily.

Sailor Sam's Main Road, opposite the post office. A warm-hearted, old-fashioned chippy that offers incredible value, brilliant fish and chips and the cheapest oysters in town (but don't tell a soul: the delicious shellfish aren't local, they're shipped in from the West Coast). Mon–Sat 11am–8.30pm & Sun 11am–3pm.

Zest Pledge Square, Main Rd. Relaxed, stylish dining at an eatery influenced by Australian fusion food. Local seasonal produce goes into an eclectic range of dishes from Moroccan chicken to Thai-style seafood. There's always venison and ostrich and lots of daily specials. Nov–March daily 5–10pm; April–Oct Mon–Sat 5–10pm.

Listings

Car rental Avis, on the corner of Long St and Main Rd ✆ 044 382 2222; Tempest, 14 Gray St ✆ 044 382 0354.

Emergencies Tourist victim support ✆ 044 878 2139 or 082 492 3968. See also p.75.

Hospital Knysna Private Hospital, Hunters Drive (✆ 044 384 1083), is well run and has a casualty department open to visitors.

Pharmacy Marine Pharmacy, on the corner of Main and Grey sts ✆ 044 382 5614 (Mon–Fri 8am–8pm, Sat 8am–1pm & 5–8pm, Sun 9.30am–1pm & 5–8pm).

Taxis Benwill Shuttle (✆ 083 728 5181; after hours ✆ 044 384 0103) is handy for transport around town, but take care to agree the fare before getting inside.

The Knysna forests

The best reason to come to Knysna is for its **forests,** shreds of a once magnificent woodland that was home to **Khoi** clans and harboured a thrilling variety of

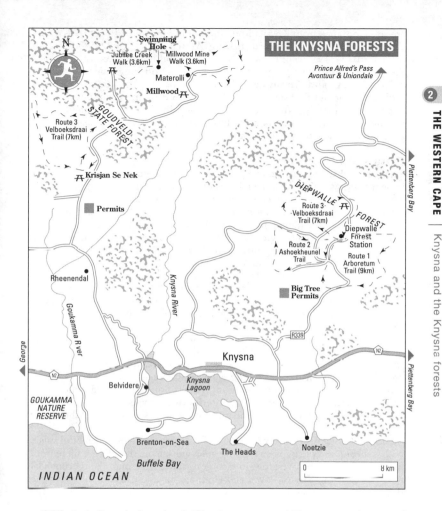

THE KNYSNA FORESTS

Swimming Hole

Jubilee Creek Walk (3.6km) — Millwood Mine Walk (3.6km)

Materolli

Millwood

Prince Alfred's Pass
Avontuur & Uniondale

GOUDVELD STATE FOREST

Route 3 Velboeksdraai Trail (7km)

Krisjan Se Nek

Permits

DIEPWALLE FOREST

Route 3 Velboeksdraai Trail (7km)

Diepwalle Forest Station

Route 2 Ashoekheunel Trail

Route 1 Arboretum Trail (9km)

Big Tree Permits

Rheenendal

Knysna River

Goukamma River

R339

Knysna

N2

George

Belvidere

Knysna Lagoon

GOUKAMMA NATURE RESERVE

Brenton-on-Sea

The Heads

Noetzie

Buffels Bay

INDIAN OCEAN

0   8 km

wildlife, including elephant herds. The forests attracted European explorers and naturalists, and in their wake woodcutters, businessmen like George Rex and gold-diggers, all bent on making their fortunes here.

The French explorer Francois Le Vaillant was one of the first **Europeans** to sample the delights of these forests. He travelled through in the eighteenth century with Khoi trackers, who shot and cooked an elephant; the explorer found the animal's feet so "delicious" that he wagered that "never can our modern epicures have such a dainty at their tables". Two hundred years later, all that's left of the Khoi people are some names of local places. The legendary Knysna elephants have hardly fared better and are teetering on certain extinction.

Eleventh-hour **conservation** has ensured that some of the hardwoods have survived to maturity in reserves of woodland that can still take your breath away. A number of walks have been laid out in several of the forests – yet the effects of the nineteenth-century timber industry mean that all these reserves are some distance from Knysna itself and require transport to get to. **Knysna Forest Tours and Mountain Biking Africa** (Tony ℡082 783 8392, or Rolf ℡073 191 5420; 🌐www.mountainbikingafrica.co.za, 🌐www.knysnaforesttours.co.za) is an adventure company offering guided forest and coastal **hikes and mountain biking trips** in the area as well as bird-watching and fly fishing. Half-day hikes and biking trips start at R350 a person including refreshments. For self-guided trips, buy the second edition of the excellent book by Judith Hopley, *On Foot in the Garden Route*, available from Knysna's tourist office.

Goudveld State Forest

The beautiful **Goudveld State Forest** (daily sunrise–sunset; R4 if attendant is present, otherwise by self-issued free permit), just over 30km northwest of Knysna, is a mixture of plantation and indigenous woodland. It takes its name from the gold boom (*goudveld* is Afrikaans for goldfields) that brought hundreds of prospectors to the mining town of **Millwood** in the 1880s. The six hundred small-time diggers who were here by 1886, scouring out the hillsides and panning Jubilee Creek for alluvial gold, were rapidly followed by larger syndicates, and a flourishing little town quickly sprang up, with six hotels, three newspapers and a music hall.

However, the singing and dancing was shortlived and bust followed boom in 1890 after most of the mining companies went to the wall. The ever-hopeful diggers took off for the newly discovered Johannesburg goldfields, and Millwood was left a deserted **ghost town**. Over the years, its buildings were demolished or relocated, leaving an old store known as Materolli as the only original building standing. Today, the old town is completely overgrown, apart from signs indicating where the old streets stood. In **Jubilee Creek**, which provides a lovely shady walk along a burbling stream, the holes scraped or blasted out of the hillside are still clearly visible. Some of the old mine works have been restored, as have the original **reduction works** around the cocopan track, used to carry the ore from the mine to the works, which is still there after a century.

The forest itself is still lovely, featuring tall, indigenous trees, a delightful valley with a stream, and plenty of swimming holes and picnic sites. To get there from Knysna, follow the N2 west toward George, turning right onto the Rheenendal road just after the Knysna River, and continue for about 25km, following the Bibby's Koep signposts until the Goudveld sign.

Hiking in the Goudveld

A number of clearly **waymarked hikes** traverse the Goudveld. The most rewarding (and easy going) is along **Jubilee Creek**, which traces the progress of a burbling brook for 3.5km through giant woodland to a gorgeous, deep rock pool – ideal for cooling off after your effort. It's also an excellent place to encounter **Knysna louries**; keep an eye focused on the branches above for the crimson flash of their flight feathers as they forage for berries, and listen out for their harsh call above the gentler chorus provided by the wide variety of other birdlife here. You can pick up a **map** directing you to the creek from the entrance gate to the reserve; note that the waymarked trail is linear, so you return via the same route. There's a pleasant **picnic site** along the banks of the stream at the start of the walk.

A more strenuous option is the circular **Woodcutter Walk**, though you can choose either the three- or the nine-kilometre version. Starting at **Krisjan se Nek**, another picnic site not far past the Goudveld entrance gate, it meanders downhill through dense forest, passing through stands of tree ferns and returns uphill to the starting point. The picnic site is also where the nineteen-kilometre **Homtini Cycle Route** starts, taking you through forest and *fynbos* and offering wonderful mountain views. Be warned though; you really have to work hard at this, with one particular section climbing over 300m in just 3km. The tourist office has maps of the area.

Diepwalle Forest

The **Diepwalle Forest** (daily 6am–6pm; small entry fee), just over 20km northeast of Knysna, is the last haunt of Knysna's almost extinct elephant population. The only elephants you can expect to see here are on the painted markers indicating the three main hikes through these woodlands. However, if you're quiet and alert, you do stand a chance of seeing vervet monkeys, bushbuck and blue duiker. To get there from Knysna, follow the N2 east towards Plettenberg Bay, after 7km turning left onto the R339, which you should take for about 16km in the direction of Avontuur and Uniondale. The **forest station** is 10.5km after the tar gives way to gravel. All trails begin at the forest station, which provides a map of them.

Diepwalle ("deep walls") is one of the highlights of the Knysna area and is renowned for its impressive density of huge trees, especially **yellowwoods**. Once the budget timber of South Africa, yellowwood was considered an inferior local substitute in place of imported pine, and found its way into the structure, floorboards, window frames and doors of thousands of often quite modest nineteenth-century houses in the Western and Eastern Cape. Today, its deep golden grain is so sought-after that it commands premium prices at the annual auctions.

The three main hiking routes cover between 7km and 9km of terrain, and pass through flat to gently undulating country covered by indigenous forest and montane *fynbos*. If you're moderately fit, the hikes should take two to two-and a-half hours. The nine-kilometre **Arboretum trail**, marked by black elephants,

---

The Knysna elephants

Traffic signs warning motorists about elephants along the N2 between Knysna and Plettenberg Bay are rather optimistic: there are few Indigenous pachyderms left and, with such an immense forest, sightings are rare. But such is the mystique attached to the **Knysna elephants** that locals tend to be a little cagey about just how few they number. By 1860, the thousands that had formerly wandered the once vast forests were down to five hundred, and by 1920 (twelve years after they were protected by law), there were only twenty animals left; the current estimate is three. Loss of habitat and consequent malnutrition, rather than full-scale hunting, seems to have been the principal cause of their decline.

An attempt was made in 1995 to create a breeding herd by introducing three young cows from the Kruger National Park, which it was hoped would breed with the forest's lone bull. The "bull" turned out also to be a cow and fled in terror when confronted with the three teenagers. In the chase that followed, one young elephant died from pneumonia, brought on by stress. By 1997, the two surviving aliens had moved east and were causing destruction to farmland near Plettenberg Bay. South African National Parks, working with local wildlife organizations, decided to relocate them to Shamwari Game Reserve (see p.380), some 300km to the east near Port Elizabeth, where they are doing well. The only elephants you're guaranteed to see near Knysna are at the **Knysna Elephant Park** (see p.276) or the **Elephant Sanctuary** (see p.284), both near Plettenberg Bay.

starts a short way back along the road you drove in on, and descends to a stream edged with tree ferns. Across the stream you'll come to the much-photographed **Big Tree**, a 600-year-old Goliath yellowwood. The easy nine-kilometre **Ashoekheuwel trail**, marked by white elephants, crosses the Gouna River, where there's a large pool allegedly used by real pachyderms. Most difficult of the three hikes is the rewarding seven-kilometre **Veldboeksdraai trail**, marked by red elephants, which passes along the foothills of the Outeniquas. Take care here to stick to the elephant markers, as they overlap with a series of painted footprints marking the Outeniqua trail, for which you need to have arranged a permit to use. Just before the Veldboeksdraai picnic site stands another mighty yellowwood regarded by some as the most beautiful in the forest.

Knysna Elephant Park

Heading east from Knysna along the N2, you come to the **Knysna Elephant Park** (daily 8.30am–5pm; ☎044 532 7732, ⓦwww.knysnaelephantpark.co.za), 9km before Plettenberg Bay. The park was established in 1994 to provide a home for abandoned, orphaned and abused young elephants, and opened to the public in 2003. The youngest of its charges are reared by park staff, who hand-feed them forty litres of baby formula a day, and sleep next to them at night. The park offers **accommodation** in upmarket self-catering units (being upgraded; rates to be announced), which, as the management points out, are "situated on the second level of the elephant *boma* and as a result the sounds of the elephants and the cleaning of their stalls in the morning will be audible".

Of the **activities** on offer, the most popular are the roughly hour-long tours which leave every half hour (daily 8.30am–4.30pm; R130, children R65, bucket of feed R25), where you'll get the chance to touch and feed one of the pachyderms. You can also take a two-hour ride on an elephant or a guided nature walk of the same duration alongside one (R495, children R275; booking essential).

▲ Handler with elephant at Knysna

Whaling and gnashing of teeth

For conservationists, the monumental 1970s eyesore of the *Beacon Island Hotel* may not be such a bad thing, especially when you consider that previously the island was the site of a whale-processing factory established in 1806 – one of some half-dozen such plants erected along the Western Cape coast that year. Whaling continued at Plettenberg Bay until 1916. Southern right whales were the favoured species, yielding more oil and **whalebone** – an essential component of Victorian corsets – than any other. In the nineteenth century, a southern right would net around three times as much as a humpback caught along the Western Cape coast, leading to a rapid decline in the southern right population by the middle of the nineteenth century.

The years between the establishment and the closing of the Plettenberg Bay factory saw worldwide whaling transformed by the inventions of the industrial revolution. In 1852, the explosive harpoon was introduced, followed by the use of steam-powered ships five years later, making them swifter and safer for the crew. In 1863, Norwegian captain Sven Foyn built the first modern whale-catching vessel, which the inventive Foyn followed up in 1868 with the **cannon-mounted harpoon**. In 1913 Plettenberg Bay was the site of one of seventeen shore-based and some dozen floating factories between West Africa and Mozambique, which that year between them took about 10,000 whales.

Inevitably, a rapid decline in humpback populations began; by 1918, all but four of the shore-based factories had closed due to lack of prey. The remaining whalers now turned their attention to fin and blue whales. When the South African fin whale population became depleted, by the mid-1960s, to twenty percent of its former size, they turned to sei and sperm whales. When these populations declined, the frustrated whalers started hunting minke whales, which at 9m in length are too small to be a viable catch. By the 1970s, the South African whaling industry was in its death throes and was finally put out of its misery in 1979, when the government harpooned it by banning all activity surrounding whaling.

Plettenberg Bay and around

Over the Christmas holidays, forty thousand residents from Johannesburg's wealthy northern suburbs decamp to **PLETTENBERG BAY** (usually called Plett), 33km east of Knysna, the flashiest of the Garden Route's seaside towns. It's wise to give it a miss during peak season, with prices doubling and accommodation impossible to find. Yet, during low season, the banal urban development on the surrounding hills somehow doesn't seem so bad because the bay views really are stupendous. Further afield, the deep-blue **Tsitsikamma Mountains** drop sharply to the inlet and its large estuary, providing a constant vista to the town and its suburbs. The bay generously curves over several kilometres of white sands separated from the mountains by forest, which makes this a green and temperate location with rainfall throughout the year.

Southern right whales appear every winter, and are a seriously underrated attraction, while **dolphins** can be seen throughout the year, hunting or riding the surf, often in substantial numbers. **Swimming** is safe, and though the waters are never tropically warm they reach a comfortable temperature between November and April. River and rock **fishing** are rewarding all year long. One of the Garden Route's best short **hikes** covers a circuit round the Robberg Peninsula – a great tongue of headland that contains the western edge of the bay.

On the east of the bay lies the seaside resort of **Keurboomstrand** and beyond that **The Crags** (both of them more or less suburbs of Plett) with its trio of

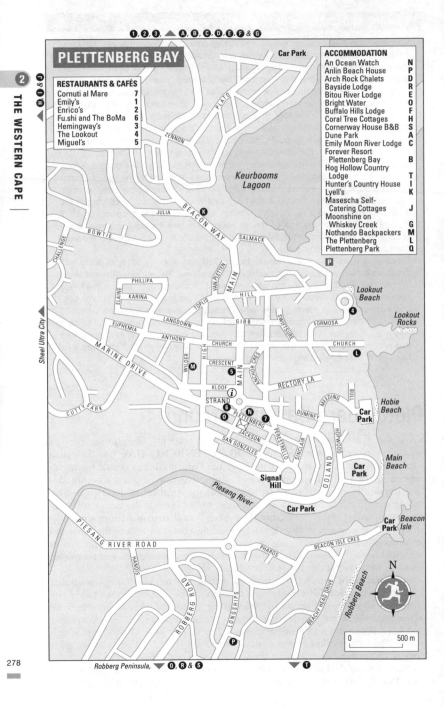

wildlife parks: **Monkeyland**, **Birds of Eden** and the **Elephant Sanctuary**, all worth a visit, especially if you're travelling with kids.

Arrival and information

Plettenberg Bay has an airport, but at the time of writing regular flights into it had been suspended. George airport, 95km away, is the closest place receiving scheduled **flights** (see p.261). Intercape, Greyhound and Translux **intercity buses** stop at the Shell Ultra City service station, just off the N2 in Marine Way, 2km from the town centre. As there's no transport around town, you'll need to arrange for your guesthouse to collect you. The **Baz Bus** drops passengers off at accommodation in town. Plett's lacklustre **tourist office**, Shop 35, Mellville Corner, Main Street (Mon–Fri 8.30am–5pm, Sat 9am–1pm; ℡044 533 4065, Ⓦwww.plettenbergbay.co.za), has photocopied maps of the town and may be able to help with finding accommodation.

Accommodation

Because of the hilly terrain, much of the **accommodation** in Plettenberg Bay has views of the sea and mountains, though you're likely to have to put up with views of holiday developments as well. Accommodation in the town has become expensive, so staying just outside has its benefits.

The town

An Ocean Watch 21 Plettenberg St ℡044 533 1700, Ⓦwww.anoceanwatchguesthouse.co.za. A beautifully decorated beach-style home in which just about everything is shimmering white or cream. Four of the six rooms have sea views Ⓖ, as does the heated swimming pool. Sea-facing Ⓖ, mountain-facing Ⓖ
Anlin Beach House 33 Roche Bonne Ave ℡044 533 3694, Ⓦwww.anlinbeachhouse.co.za. Two stylish and comfortably kitted-out garden studios with kitchenettes, and a larger family unit with three bedrooms and a kitchen, in a garden setting close to Robberg Beach. Units are serviced daily. Ⓖ
Bayside Lodge 5 Sanganer Ave ℡044 533 0601, Ⓦwww.baysidelodge.co.za. Modern two-storey brick house in a quiet suburban area about 500m from the beach with four en-suite rooms and a self-contained cottage. Ⓖ–Ⓖ
Bright Water 15 Jackson St ℡044 533 0467, Ⓦwww.brightwater.co.za. Three en-suite doubles in a centrally located, homely suburban house where you can rent the whole place or just a room, with use of the kitchen. Ⓖ–Ⓖ
Cornerway House B&B 61 Longships Drive ℡044 533 3190, Ⓦwww.cornerwayhouse.co.za. Five en-suite rooms in a comfortable bungalow decorated in English cottage style and set in a pretty garden with a swimming pool. Ⓖ
Lyell's 59 Beacon Way ℡044 533 5692. Three sparkling white en-suite B&B rooms in a suburban house, plus a budget self-catering unit. The upstairs living area has sea views. Ⓖ

Nothando Backpackers 5 Wilder St ℡044 533 0220, Ⓦwww.nothando.com. Top-notch child-friendly hostel run by a former schoolteacher. A 5min walk from Plett's main drag, the single-storey suburban house has seven double rooms (five en suite) and three dorms (two with four beds, the other with eight). Breakfast (of cereal, cheese, bread, muffins, yoghurt as well as bacon and eggs) is available for R35. Dorms Ⓞ, doubles Ⓞ
The Plettenberg 40 Church St, Lookout Rocks ℡044 533 2030, Ⓦwww.plettenberg.com. Plett's prestige hotel is a large, luxurious establishment offering unbeatable views straight onto the ocean. But despite the sky-high rates you could still end up in a room overlooking the car park. Seaview room Ⓞ, otherwise Ⓞ
🏃 **Plettenberg Park** near the end of Robberg Rd, close to the airport ℡044 533 9067, Ⓦwww.plettenbergpark.co.za. Set in a private nature reserve and perched on a cliff edge above the swirling Indian Ocean, this stupendously located boutique hotel is the obvious choice for a romantic getaway. Seven suites have sea views and the remaining three look onto a beautiful little lake surrounded by *fynbos* inhabited by small game. The supremely luxurious rooms are furnished in supercool off-whites and oaty colours, with animal-skin rugs adding a dash of Africa. The shower in one room is surrounded on four sides by glass, two of them exposed to the ocean. A set of meandering timber steps leads down from the pool deck to an isolated private beach far below with a lovely natural rock pool. Ⓞ

Robberg Beach and west of Plett

Coral Tree Cottages Off the N2, 11km west of Plettenberg Bay ℡044 532 7822, ⓦwww .coraltree.net. High-quality, spacious thatched cottages sleeping up to four, though unfortunately the roar of the N2 is never absent. ❹

Hunter's Country House Off the N2, 10km west of Plett on the way to Knysna ℡044 532 7888, ⓦwww.hunterhotels.com. Set in a woodland area, this is one of the best upmarket places to stay on the Garden Route, with an emphasis on country comfort rather than seaside glitz. Garden suite accommodation is in thatched cottages set in well-established gardens, each with an open fireplace, private patio, underfloor heating and a/c, while the forest suites are larger and more sumptuous, each with its own private pool. Garden suite ❽, forest suite ❾

Masescha Self-Catering Cottages 1km north off the N2, signposted 12km west from Plettenberg Bay ℡044 532 7647. Three plainly furnished, whitewashed cottages on a farm, with outdoor sitting areas surrounded by pleasant gardens and a forest. Good for families or couples, it has a swimming pool, and also on site are an indigenous plant nursery and natural-history bookshop. Breakfast is available as an extra. ❸–❹

Keurboomstrand and east of Plett

Arch Rock Chalets and Caravan Park Arch Rock ℡044 535 9409. A range of self-catering units and a caravan park-cum-campsite that get packed in summer with families. Self-catering units from ❸

Bitou River Lodge Bitou Valley Rd (the R340), about 4km from the N2 ℡044 535 9577, ⓦwww .bitou.co.za. Great value in a lovely spot on the banks of the Bitou River. The five bedrooms at this intimate establishment are comfortable but unfussy and rooms overlook a pretty garden with a lily pond. ❹–❺

Buffalo Hills Lodge and Safari Rietvlei Rd, Wittedrif Village ℡044 535 9739, ⓦwww .buffalohills.co.za. Farm turned game lodge on the banks of the Bitou River, a 15min drive from Plett. No substitute for seeing the big five at one of the major game reserves, it nonetheless provides a thoroughly entertaining experience. The DB&B package includes a game drive and guided walk on which you stand a chance of seeing rhino, buffalo, giraffe, zebra, bontebok and a number of other antelope. Accommodation in the main lodge, which resembles an old-style African farmhouse with animal skins thrown on a cement floor, is in four double rooms. A stone cottage a little away from the lodge sleeps four, while nine huge, luxury

walk-in tents, pitched on their own decks, have spa baths. Breakfast is served on the lawn in front of the lodge, where you can watch animals graze while you do the same. DB&B ❽

Dune Park Keurboomstrand Rd, leading off the N2 and running along the shore to Keurbooms ℡044 535 9606, ⓦwww.dunepark.co.za. Luxury hotel and self-catering cottages within spitting distance of the sea. ❼

Emily Moon River Lodge Rietvlei Rd, off the N2 (turn off at Penny Pinchers) ℡044 533 2982, ⓦwww.emilymoon.co.za. That the owner of this highly imaginative and luxurious lodge, perched on a ridge looking across the Bitou Wetlands, is a dealer in ethnic art is plain to see. The place is not only littered with Batonga sculptures and Swazi crafts, it has in places been constructed out of artworks, such as the intricate Rajasthani arched screen that is the entrance to the magnificently sited restaurant. Each of its chalets jetties out of the hillside to offer views from a private deck (and bathroom) of the oxbowing Bitou, along which small game can occasionally be seen. All chalets have fireplaces and TVs. There is a family suite that sleeps four in which kids are accommodated at a very discounted rate. ❼

Forever Resort Plettenberg Bay 6km east of Plett and signposted off the N2 near Keurboomstrand ℡044 535 9309, ⓦwww.foreversa.co.za /plettenberg. A sizeable family resort, with camping on the shady banks of the Keurbooms River, away from the sea, and a range of self-catering log cabins, some with river views. Canoes and motorboats are available to rent, and there's a swimming pool. R830 for a one-bedroom cabin.

Hog Hollow Country Lodge Askop Rd, 18km east of Plettenberg Bay (turn south off the N2 at the signpost) ℡044 534 8879, ⓦwww.hog-hollow .com. A touch of luxury on a private reserve where each of the chalets, done out in earthy colours and spiced up with African artefacts, has a bath or shower and its own wooden deck with vistas across the forest and Tsitsikamma Mountains; superb food is served as well. From here you could hike for a couple of hours through forest to Keurbooms Beach, or drive there in 15min. ❽

Moonshine on Whiskey Creek 14km east of Plettenberg Bay along the N2, signposted north of the N2 ℡044 534 8515 or 072 200 6656, ⓦwww .whiskeycreek.co.za. Fully equipped bungalows, three wooden cabins and one creatively renovated labourers' cottage, nestled in indigenous forest, with a children's play area. One of the best reasons to come here is the access to a secluded natural mountain pool and waterfall at the bottom of the nearby gorge. ❸

The town and around

Plett's town **centre**, at the top of the hill, consists of a conglomeration of supermarkets, swimwear shops, estate agents and restaurants aimed largely at the holiday trade. Visitors principally come for Plett's **beaches** – and there's a fair choice. Southeast of the town centre on a rocky promontory is **Beacon Island**, dominated by a 1970s hotel, an eyesore blighting a fabulous location. Beacon Island Beach, or **Main Beach**, right at the central shore of the bay, is where the fishing boats and seacats anchor a little out to sea. The small waves here make for calm swimming, and this is an ideal family spot. To the east is **Lookout Rocks**, attracting surfers to the break off a needle of rocks known as the Point and the predictable surf of **Lookout Beach**, to its east, which is also one of the nicest stretches of sand for bathers, body-surfers or sun lizards. Lookout Beach has the added attraction of a marvellously located restaurant (see p.283), from which you can often catch sight of **dolphins** cruising into the bay. From here you can walk several kilometres down the beach towards Keurbooms (see p.283) and the **Keurbooms Lagoon**.

Robberg Marine and Nature Reserve

One of the Garden Route's nicest walks is the four-hour, nine-kilometre circular route around the spectacular rocky peninsula of **Robberg**, 8km southeast of Plett's town centre. Here you can completely escape Plett's development and experience the coast in its wildest state, with its enormous horizons and lovely vegetation. Much of the walk takes you along high cliffs, from where you can often look down on seals surfacing near the rocks, dolphins arching through the water and, in winter, whales further out in the bay.

If you don't have time for the full circular walk, there is a shorter two-hour hike and a thirty-minute ramble. A **map** indicating these is available at the reserve gate when you pay to enter (daily: May–July 8am–6pm; rest of year 6.30am–8pm; R25). You'll need sturdy walking shoes, as the terrain is rocky and steep in parts, and the walk involves some serious rock-hopping on the west side. Bring a hat and a bottle of water, as there's no drinking water for much of the way and no tea rooms.

There's no public transport to the reserve; if you're staying at a backpacker lodge, ask about their transfers, which are generally reasonably priced. To **drive** there, take Strand Street towards Beacon Isle, turn right into Piesangs Valley Road, and 200m further on turn left into Robberg Road. Follow the airport signs, continuing for 3.5km. Look out for the Robberg turn-off to your left.

Whale- and dolphin-watching

Elevated ocean panoramas give Plettenberg Bay outstanding vantages for watching **southern right whales** during their breeding season between June and October. An especially good vantage point is the area between the wreck of the Athene at the southern end of Lookout Beach and the Keurbooms River. The Robberg Peninsula is also excellent, looming protectively over this whale nursery and giving a grandstand view of the bay. Other good town viewpoints are from Beachy Head Road at Robberg Beach; Signal Hill in San Gonzales Street past the post office and police station; the *Beacon Island Hotel* on Beacon Island; and the deck of the *Lookout* restaurant on Lookout Beach. Outside Plett, the Kranshoek viewpoint and hiking trail offers wonderful whale-watching points along the route. To get there, head for Knysna, taking the Harkerville turn-off, and continue for 7km. It's also possible to view the occasional pair (mother and calf) at Nature's Valley, 29km east of Plett on the R102, and from Storms River Mouth. For more information about whales, see the box on pp.282–283.

Whale-watching and other activities

A number of outfits run trips to see whales from the water, offering the chance of close encounters with a variety of whales and several dolphin species. Only **permitted whale watchers** are allowed to go within 50m of a whale; everyone must maintain a distance of 300m, and there are plans in the pipeline to increase this to 500m. In Plett, only Ocean Safaris and Ocean Blue (listed below) hold permits. Air-based trips have the additional attraction of spectacular aerial views of bays and river inlets.

Dolphin Adventures Central Beach ⊕083 590 3405, ⓦwww.dolphinadventures .co.za. Sea kayaking is one of the best ways to watch whales, and this outfit offers unforgettable trips with experienced and knowledgeable guides in two-person kayaks (2hr 30min; R250 including all equipment). Out of whale season it's still worth going out to see dolphins and seals.

Ocean Blue Central Beach ⊕044 533 5083 or 083 701 3583, ⓦwww.oceanblue .co.za. Sea-kayaking (R250) and boat-based whale watching (R500) are among the offerings of this licensed outfit, which also runs township tours (see below).

Ocean Safaris Shop 3, Hopwood St ⊕044 533 4963, ⓦwww.oceansafaris.co.za. Tailor-made cruises from a licensed whale watching company. Apart from southern rights, the trips run into common, bottlenose and humpback dolphins, as well as Bryde's and humpback whales – and the occasional minke and killer whale. The Close Encounter with Whales outing costs R500 per person and virtually guarantees sightings between July and November; the Discovery Cruise, which costs R300, is principally a dolphin-viewing excursion.

Other activities

Bungee jumping If you fancy swinging through the air, then pull in at Tsitsikamma Forest Village, 20km east of the turn-off for The Crags and Monkeyland along the N2, where you'll find the registration office for the world's highest commercial bungee jump. The jump takes place off the 216-metre Bloukrans River Bridge, 2km beyond the village down a signposted road that also brings you to a viewpoint. There's no need to book ahead for the jump, which costs R590 (including video) for the seven-second

Eating, drinking and nightlife

Restaurants come and go in Plett at a similar lick to the tides, but one or two long-standing establishments have managed to remain afloat. Locally caught fresh fish is the thing to look out for. And because the town is built on hills, you should generally expect terrific views.

Cornuti al Mare Seaview Properties, 1 Perestrella St ⊕044 533 1277. Terrific pizzas – the best along the Garden Route – and also great pasta dishes that won't break the bank, and endless views of sea and sky. Daily noon–11pm.

Emily's Rietvlei Rd, off the N2 (turn off at Penny Pinchers) ⊕044 533 2982. Boutique restaurant attached to *Emily Moon's Lodge* that's widely regarded as the best eatery in the area, offering stunning views of the Bitou Wetland and classical French cuisine with an edge. There's no set menu as everything is based on what seasonal ingredients are locally available on the day, but there's always a choice of five or six starters and mains with a small range of desserts. Booking is essential. Tues–Sun noon–3pm & daily 6–11pm.

Enrico's Main Beach, Keurboomstrand. Great Italian standards – thin-based pizzas, pasta and veal – to enjoy al fresco on the beach or in the stylish indoor restaurant. Daily 11.30am–10pm.

Fu.shi and The BoMa The Upper Deck, 3 Strand St. Two eateries rolled into one right in the centre, surrounded by picture windows to make the most of the elevated views. As its name suggests *Fu. shi's* menu is Asian fusion, featuring sushi and various coquettishly named dishes – Nuggets of Pleasure (wasabi prawns with cashew salad), Flights of Fantasy (sliced duck breast with pak

descent. For the not so brave there's a mesh catwalk over the jump site (R70), and a 160-metre flying fox – a zipline along which you slide while harnessed (R150, or R100 each for two people in tandem). For further information, contact Bloukrans Bungy (aka Face Adrenalin) at the bridge (℡042 281 1458, ⓦwww.faceadrenalin.com).

Canoeing If you can tear yourself away from the beach, canoeing up the Keurbooms River gives an alternative perspective on the area. Cape Nature Conservation on the east side of the Keurbooms River Bridge along the N2 (℡044 533 2125) rents out fairly basic craft (R75 per day for a two-person canoe).

Elephant encounters The Knysna Elephant Park (see p.276) and Elephant Sanctuary (see p.284) offer the opportunity of close encounters with the large mammals.

Ferry trips and motorboating Keurbooms River Ferries, signposted on the east side of the Keurbooms River Bridge (℡083 254 3551, ⓦwww.ferry.co.za), runs guided upriver boat trips (R90) with knowledgeable guides skilled at spotting rare birds, and also rents motorboats (R80/hr; minimum 2hr). Be sure to bring a picnic for any of the boat trips; the river is dotted with little beaches that are a good place to stop for a swim and walk. The indigenous forest comes right down to the river edge, and the journey gets better the higher up you go, the gorge narrowing and the pleasure boats and water-skiers now left behind. Don't be put off by the river's cola colour (which comes from harmless oxides in the water): the water is quite fresh, and wonderful to swim in during the summer. While you're here, keep an eye out for the pink-flowering keurboom trees that lend their name to the river and resort.

Skydiving If you fancy a bit of an adrenaline rush, you can go tandem skydiving (no experience required) with Skydive Plettenberg Bay (℡082 905 7440, ⓦwww .skydiveplett.com). It charges R1300 for a jump, with the option of paying extra for a DVD or video of the event.

Township tours Ocean Blue, Central Beach (℡044 533 5083 or 083 701 3583, ⓦwww.oceanadventures.co.za), arranges relaxed tours into Plett's township with a guide who is a member of the community. Outings cost R100 per person and all the takings go into a development trust which amongst other things pays teachers' salaries and funds a creche.

choi) and Cocubine's Whisper (chilli chocolate fondant with pistachio brittle). *The BoMa* is a cocktail bar cum breakfast and snack joint. Mon-Sat noon–5pm & 6pm–late; Sun 10am–5pm.
Hemingway's On the Bitou River, just off the N2 between Plettenberg Bay and Keurbooms ℡044 535 9445. Reasonably priced meals are served at this pleasant pub with outdoor seating on the edge of the calm lagoon. The fish and chips are especially recommended. Daily 11am–10pm.
The Lookout Lookout Beach. Marvellous bay views – if you're lucky, you'll see whales and

dolphins rollicking in the surf – at this casual bar-restaurant focusing on seafood, including crayfish. Daily 9.30am–late.
Miguel's Melville's Corner, corner of Main and Marine sts ℡044 533 5056. Upmarket Portuguese cuisine, in a stunning location bang in the town centre with views of the ocean and passing trade. Its speciality is *espetadas* – beef, chicken or seafood cooked with jalapeno peppers and served on a large skewer. Open daily from 8am for breakfast, lunch & dinner.

Keurboomstrand and The Crags

Some 14km east of Plettenberg Bay by road, across the Keurbooms River, is the uncluttered resort of **KEURBOOMSTRAND** (Keurbooms for short), little more than a suburb of Plett, sharing the same bay and with equally wonderful beaches, but less safe for swimming. The safest place to take the waves is at **Arch Rock**, in front of the caravan park, though **Picnic Rock Beach** is also pretty good. A calm and attractive place, Keurbooms has few facilities, and if you're intending to stay here (see "Accommodation", p.280) you should stock up in Plettenberg Bay beforehand. One of Keurbooms' highlights is **canoeing** or, if you feel less energetic, taking a ferry ride or motorboat up the Keurbooms River (see "Activities", pp.282–283).

The Crags, 2km east of Keurbooms, comprises a collection of smallholdings along the N2, a bottle store and a few other shops on the forest edge, but the reason most visitors pull in here is for the **Elephant Sanctuary**, **Monkeyland** and **Birds of Eden**. To reach them, look out for the BP filling station, then take the Monkeyland/Kurland turn-off and follow the Elephant Sanctuary /Monkeyland signs for 2km.

Elephant Sanctuary

The **Elephant Sanctuary** (daily 8am–5pm; ☎044 534 8145, ⓦwww .elephantsanctuary.co.za) offers a chance of close encounters with its half-dozen pachyderms, all of which were saved from culling in Botswana and the Kruger National Park. On the popular one-hour Trunk-in-Hand programme (daily on the hour: 8am–noon & 1.30–3.30pm; R250, children R125) you get to walk with an elephant, holding the tip of its trunk in your hand, and also to stroke, feed and interact with it. The programme includes an informative talk about elephant behaviour. Fifteen-minute elephant-back rides (R595) are among the other packages on offer.

Monkeyland

Monkeyland (daily 8.30am–5pm; free entry to viewing deck; safaris into the forest: R115; combined ticket with Birds of Eden R184; ⓦwww.monkeyland .co.za), 400m beyond the Elephant Sanctuary, brings together primates from several continents, all of them orphaned or saved from a dismal life as pets. The place is a sanctuary, so none of the animals has been taken from the wild – and most wouldn't have the skills to survive there. Life is made as comfortable as possible for them and they are free to move around the reserve, looking for food and interacting with each other and their environment in as natural a way as possible. For your own safety and that of the monkeys, you are not allowed to wander around alone. Guides take visitors on walking "**safaris**", during which you come across water holes, experience a living indigenous forest and have chance encounters with creatures such as ringtail lemurs from Madagascar and squirrel monkeys from South America. The safaris are entertaining and also feature an informed commentary covering issues such as the differences between monkeys and apes, primate communication and social systems. One of the sanctuary's highlights is crossing the Indiana Jones-esque rope bridge (at 128m, it's purportedly the longest such bridge in the southern hemisphere) spanning a canyon to pass through the upper reaches of the forest canopy, where a number of species spend their entire lives. For refreshments or meals, there's a restaurant with a forest deck at the day lodge.

Birds of Eden

Under the same management as Monkeyland and right next door, **Birds of Eden** (daily 8.30am–5pm; R115, combined ticket with Monkeyland R184) is a huge bird sanctuary which took four years to create. Great effort was taken to place netting over a substantial tract of virgin forest with as little impact as possible. The result is claimed to be the largest free-flight aviary in the world. As with Monkeyland, most of Birds of Eden's charges were already living in cages and are now free to move and fly around within the confines of the large enclosure (so large in fact that you can easily spend an hour slowly meandering along its winding, wheelchair-friendly, wooden walkway). Although it has come in for some criticism for cutting off local birds from their traditional turf and disrupting some migration routes, the result is quite remarkable, with little lakes, waterfalls and a wonderful suspension bridge along the way. Most of the birds are exotics, some impossibly brightly coloured (such as the incandescent scarlet ibis from South America and golden pheasant from China), but you'll also see a number of locals, such as the Knysna lourie and South Africa's national bird, the blue crane. Watch out for the cheeky cockatoos that may alight on your shoulder and steal buttons from your shirt or beads from round your neck. A **restaurant** by one of the lakes sells light meals and liquid refreshments.

Tsitsikamma National Park, Nature's Valley and Storms River

The **Tsitsikamma National Park**, roughly midway between Plettenberg Bay and Port Elizabeth, is the highlight of any Garden Route trip. Starting from just beyond Keurboomstrand in the west, the national park extends for 68km into the Eastern Cape along a narrow belt of coast, with dramatic foamy surges of rocky coast, deep river gorges and ancient hardwood forests clinging to the edge of tangled, green cliffs. You'd be crazy to pass up its main attraction, the **Storms River Mouth**, the most dramatic estuary on this exhilarating stretch of coast. Established in 1964, Tsitsikamma is also South Africa's oldest marine reserve, stretching 5.5km out to sea, with an **underwater trail** open to snorkellers and licensed scuba divers.

Tsitsikamma has two sections: **De Vasselot** in the west and **Storms River Mouth** in the east. Each section can only be reached down a winding tarred road from the N2 (there's no way of getting from one to the other through the park itself). De Vasselot incorporates **Nature's Valley**, the only resort in the park, and the most low-key settlement on the Garden Route, with a fabulous sandy beach stretching for 3km. South Africa's ultimate hike, the five-day **Otter trail** (see p.255), connects the two sections of the park (see box, p.254).

The nearest settlement to Storms River Mouth, some 14km to its north at the top of a steep winding road, is the confusingly named **Storms River Village**, which is outside the national park and some distance from any part of the river. While Storms River Village makes a convenient base for adventure activities in the vicinity and day-trips down to Storms River Mouth, the experience is very different to staying overnight at the coast.

Nature's Valley and De Vasselot

The **De Vasselot** section, at the western end of Tsitsikamma, extends inland into a rugged and hilly interior incised with narrow valleys and traversed by a series of footpaths. In fact De Vasselot is not a name that trips readily off South African tongues – most people know the section for **Nature's Valley**, a pleasingly old-fashioned settlement on the Groot River Lagoon with 20km of beach. Bypassed by the N2, and by intercity buses and tour parties, Nature's Valley, 29km east of Plettenberg Bay, down the lovely winding Groot River pass (along which you'll often encounter baboon troops), is the place to go if you're after a quiet time along the Garden Route.

There are plenty of good **walks** at Nature's Valley, many starting from the De Vasselot campsite, 1km north of the village, where you can pick up maps and information about birds and trees. One of the loveliest places to head for is **Salt River Mouth**, 3km west of Nature's Valley, where you can swim and picnic – though you'll need to ford the tannin-dark river at low tide. This walk starts and ends at the café at Nature's Valley. Also recommended is the circular six-kilometre **Kalanderkloof trail**, which starts at the De Vasselot campsite, ascends to a lookout point, and descends via a narrow river gorge graced with a profusion of huge Outeniqua yellowwood trees and Cape wild bananas.

Practicalities

Public transport to Nature's Valley is limited to the **Baz Bus**, which deposits passengers at their accommodation. The village centre is little more than an all-in-one restaurant, pub and small trading store that acts as an informal, but excellent, **information** bureau (☎044 531 6835, ⓦ www.natures-valley.co.za), and can help you find the limited **accommodation** available.

If you're **self-catering**, stock up on supplies before you get to Nature's Valley. The only place to buy a meal is at the **restaurant**, on the corner of Forest and St Michael streets, which serves seafood, steaks, burgers and toasted sandwiches, and provides the only nightlife apart from gazing at the stars.

Accommodation

Accommodation in Nature's Valley itself is pretty limited, which contributes to its low-key charm, but you'll find some choice options on the road leading off the N2 into the village, just before the switchbacks begin. Apart from the places listed below, self-catering accommodation can be rented through Karen van Rooyen (☎082 772 2972), who handles around eight cottages (R400–800 per cottage) in and around Nature's Valley – most of which sleep between six and eight people.

De Vasselot restcamp 1km to the north of the village. Bookings through South African National Parks (see p.63), or if you're already in Nature's Valley, the camp supervisor ☎044 531 6700. Campsites tucked into indigenous forest, and basic two-person forest huts with communal ablution facilities. ❷

Four Fields Farm Nature's Valley Rd; 3km from the N2 along the R102 and 6km from Nature's Valley. ☎044 534 8708, ⓦ http://cyberperk.co.za /fourfields. A welcoming, charmingly unpretentious former dairy farm, less than 10 mins' drive from the sea at Nature's Valley. Five en-suite bedrooms, simply furnished with beautiful old pieces, have French doors leading to their own private decks which in turn open onto a lovely garden surrounded by fields. There's also a self-catering cottage sleeping four (R600). ❺

Froggy Pond second house on the right as you enter Nature's Valley ☎044 531 6835, ⓦ www .natures-valley.co.za. Self-catering accommodation in a two-storey timber and brick cottage. Downstairs is a self-contained flatlet with a double bedroom and living area that can sleep two adults and two children; upstairs are two double rooms with en-suite showers. ❷

Lily Pond Lodge 102 Nature's Valley Rd; 3km from the N2 along the R102 and 6km from Nature's

Valley ☎044 534 8767, ⓦ www.lilypond.co.za. Probably the most memorable place to stay in the vicinity of Nature's Valley, the lodge distinguishes itself through its sharp sense of style and its commitment to luxury. Modernist in inspiration, its flowing spaces and enormous windows create a sense of supreme calm, which is echoed outdoors in the huge lily pond the lodge is named after. The four en-suite rooms have French doors opening onto private terraces, sound systems, TV and Wi-Fi access, while the two spacious luxury suites also have their own lounge, underfloor heating and king-sized beds. There are three even more luxurious garden suites and a honeymoon suite that has its own private garden. ❻–❼

Nature's Valley Guest House 411 St Patrick's Ave ☎044 531 6805, ⓦ www.naturesvalleyguesthouse .co.za. A well-located and exceptionally well-priced B&B with six doubles, three of them en suite. A snooker table, TV lounge, canoe, surfboard and windsurfer are available for guests, and you can set out from the guesthouse on two- to six-hour hikes along the beaches or through the forests. ❸

Tranquility Lodge 130 Saint Michael's St (next to the shop) ☎044 531 6663, ⓦ www.tranquilitylodge .co.za. If Nature's Valley has a centre then this comfortable lodge, next to the village's only shop, is bang in the middle of it. A two-storey brick-and-timber building set in a garden that feels like it's part of the encroaching forest, it is just 50m from the beach. Breakfast is served on an upstairs deck among the treetops. All rooms are en suite, the standard ones with a shower, the superior ones with a bath as well and satellite TV. There's also a larger honeymoon suite with a spa bath, double shower, fireplace and private deck. Standard ⑤; superior ⑥; honeymoon suite ⑦

Storms River Mouth

In contrast to the languid lagoon and long soft sands of Nature's Valley, **Storms River Mouth** (daily 7am–7pm; R80 per person; ℡042 281 1607), 55km from Plettenberg Bay, presents the elemental face of the Garden Route, with the dark Storms River surging through a gorge to battle with the surf. **Storms River Mouth Restcamp**, sited on tended lawns, is poised between a craggy shoreline of black rocks pounded by foamy white surf and steeply raking forested cliffs, and is without a doubt the ultimate location along the southern Cape coast. Don't confuse this with **Storms River Village** just off the N2, which is nowhere near the sea.

Walking is the main activity at the Mouth, and at the visitors' office at the restcamp you can get **maps** of short, waymarked coastal trails that leave from here. These include steep walks up the forested cliffs, where you can see 800-year-old yellowwood trees with views onto a wide stretch of ocean. Most rewarding is the **three-kilometre hike** west from the restcamp along the start of the Otter trail to a fantastic **waterfall** pool at the base of fifty-metre-high falls where you can swim right on the edge of the shore. Less demanding is the kilometre-long **boardwalk stroll** from the restaurant to the suspension bridge to see the river mouth. On your way to the bridge, don't miss the dank *strandloper* (beachcomber) **cave**. Hunter-gatherers frequented this area between 5000 and 2000 years ago, living off seafood in wave-cut caves near the river mouth. A modest display shows an excavated midden, with clear layers of little bones and shells.

If you're desperate to walk the **Otter trail** (see box, p.255), which begins at Storms River, and have been told that it is full, don't despair. A single person or a couple do stand a chance of getting in on the back of a last-minute cancellation, so it may be worth hanging out at the Mouth for a night or two.

Swimming at the Mouth is restricted to a safe and pristine little sandy bay below the restaurant, though conditions can be icy in summer if there are easterly winds and cold upwellings of deep water from the continental shelf. Hikes and other outdoor pursuits can be arranged through one of the local operators (see box, p.288).

Practicalities

Storms River Mouth is 18km south of **Storms River Bridge**. Most people stop at the bridge, on the N2, to gaze into the deep river gorge and fill up at the most beautifully located filling and service station in the country. Even if your time is limited and you can't spend the night at Storms River Mouth, it's still worth nipping down for a meal, a restorative walk or a swim in the summer. You'll need your own wheels, though, as there's no public transport to the Mouth. The only **eating** place is the restcamp restaurant, serving breakfasts and à la carte meals which, alas, are less memorable than the startling views.

A variety of **accommodation**, all with sea views, is available at **Storms River Mouth Restcamp** (℡042 281 1607; ❶–❸), including superb campsites just metres from where the surf breaks on the rocks; incredibly good-value two-person cabins, which provide bedding and towels, share ablutions and have communal catering facilities; comfortable one-bedroom self-catering log cottages, including breakfast; oceanette mini-apartments close to the sea, also including breakfast; and family oceanettes and cottages for a minimum of four people. All are heavily subscribed in season, so advance booking through South African National Parks is essential (see p.63).

Storms River Village

About a km south of the national road, **STORMS RIVER VILLAGE** is a tranquil place crisscrossed by a handful of dirt roads and with about forty

---

Storms River activities

Storms River Village makes a good base for numerous local adventure activities as well as those further afield. If you don't have your own transport, you can take advantage of the reasonably priced shuttle services operated for its guests by **Dijembe Backpackers** at Formosa and Assegai streets, Storms River Village (℡042 281 1842, ⓦwww.thedidge.co.za), which also acts as a central booking agency for a wide range of activities in the vicinity.

Boat trips SANParks (℡042 281 1607) runs trips (every 45min 9.30am–2.45pm; R40) about 1km up Storms River leaving from near the dive shop, just beneath the main building.

Canopy tour See Zipline (below).

Mountain biking Dijembe Backpackers rents out mountain bikes for the day (R80 for guests, R100 for others).

Quad biking Tsitsikamma Adventure Park (℡082 578 1090, ⓦwww.tsitsikamma adventure.co.za) rents out bikes for R300 an hour.

Dolphin trail A wonderful 20-kilometre trail covered in two-and-a-half days and three nights, with luxury accommodation and no carrying of backpacks. The trail starts at Storms River Mouth, and winds its way eastwards through natural *fynbos* and virgin forest, over rugged rocks at the water's edge, to end on the banks of the Sandrif River at The Fernery. The package includes all meals, two well-trained local guides, a boat trip into the Storms River Gorge and a 4WD drive through the old Storms River Pass. Book through The Fernery ℡042 280 3588, ⓦwww.dolphintrail.co.za; R3300 per person.

Horse-riding Dijembe Backpackers takes couples on guided two-and-a-half-hour hacks into the forest for R250, including lunch.

Snorkelling You can rent a wet suit, snorkel, mask and flippers for R80 from the dive shop, just below the main building at Tsitsikamma National Park (℡042 281 1607).

Woodcutters' Journey A relaxed jaunt organized by Storms River Adventures (℡042 281 1836, ⓦwww.stormsriver.com; teatime trip R90, lunch trip R175), which has its headquarters next to the Storms River village post office. The trip takes you down through the forest to the river along the old Storms River Pass in a specially designed trailer, drawn by a tractor.

Zipline Run by Storms River Adventures (see Woodcutters' Journey, above), the Canopy Tour (R420), through the treetops, gives a bird's-eye view of the forest as you travel 30m above ground along a series of interconnected cables attached to the tallest trees. The system has been constructed in such a way that not a single nail has been hammered into any tree. A faster, higher alternative, geared more to adrenaline junkies, is the zipline tour across the Kruis River at the Tsitsikamma Adventure Park (℡082 578 1090, ⓦwww.tsitsikammaadventure.co.za; R300), which at times is 50m above the ground and crisscrosses an awesome ravine, zipping over three waterfalls, with the longest slide measuring 211m.

houses, enjoying mountain vistas. It offers a number of places to stay, several of which are backpacker lodges, a couple of general dealers selling basics, a liquor store and an adventure centre which runs zip-line tours though the forest canopy (see box opposite). While Storms River Village is an excellent base for adventure activities, it is well outside the national park and if you want to be at the seaside, is no substitute for staying at the River Mouth or Nature's Valley.

As far as **eating out** goes, the choice is between the restaurant at the *Village Inn* or *Rafters* at *The Armagh* (see below).

Accommodation

The Armagh Fynbos Ave ☎042 281 1512, ⓦwww .thearmagh.com. A hospitable guesthouse in a beautiful garden that drifts off into the *fynbos*. The rooms include a rather tired-looking honeymoon suite and four standard rooms, all of which open onto the garden. There's also a decent restaurant. ❺

At the Woods Guest House 49 Formosa St, along the main drag into town ☎ 042 281 1446, ⓦwww.atthewoods.co.za. Friendly, modern guesthouse that's the nicest place in town, with traditional reed ceilings and large, comfortable rooms with king-sized beds and French doors that open onto garden verandas, or, upstairs, onto private decks with mountain views. Three-course home-cooked dinners can be arranged. ❹

Dijembe Backpackers Formosa and Assegai sts ☎042 281 1842, ⓦwww.thedidge.co.za. Chilled hostel with lots on offer, including bike rental, horse-riding and shuttles to all the local attractions as well as great-value accommodation. Dorms ❶, en-suite doubles and family room ❸

Tsitsikamma Lodge A couple of kilometres east of town along the N2, 8km east of the Storms River Bridge ☎042 280 3802, ⓦwww.tsitsikamma.com. Thirty cosy A-frame cabins with their own decks and connected by boardwalks that traverse beautifully kept gardens. Most cabins have their own Jacuzzi, and there are a number of forest walks, including the lodge's famous nudist hiking trail along the river. There's also a restaurant serving South African cuisine. ❻

Tsitsikamma Village Inn Along the road into the village and left at the T-junction ☎042 281 1711, ⓦwww.village-inn.co.za. A charmingly old-fashioned hotel – part of the huge Protea chain – in the village with 49 rooms in eleven cottages, each differently themed and surrounding a manicured garden. ❻

Tube 'n Axe On the corner of Darnell and Saffron sts ☎042 281 1757, ⓔtube-n-axe@telkomsa .net. A wacky place that works hard to compete with the bright lights of Knysna and Plett by offering backpackers drumming nights, a pool table and loads of laughs. Dorms ❶; elevated tents and double rooms ❷

The West Coast and the Cederberg

The **West Coast** of South Africa – remote, windswept and bordered by the cold Atlantic, demands a special appreciation. For many years the black sheep of Western Cape tourism (a fact borne out by the prominence of industries such as fishing, and the iron-ore terminal at Saldanha Bay), it has been set upon by developers who seem all too ready to spoil the bleached, salty emptiness which many people had just begun to value. The sandy soil and dunes harbour a distinctive **coastal fynbos** vegetation, while the coastline is almost devoid of natural inlets or safe harbours, with fierce southeasterly summer winds and dank winter fogs, though in spring **wild flowers** ever-miraculously appear in the veld. The

Bird-watching on the West Coast

The West Coast is a twitchers' dream, where you can tick off numerous wetland species. The most rewarding viewing time is just after flower season in early summer, which heralds the arrival of around 750,000 migrants on their annual pilgrimage from the northern hemisphere, many from as far off as the Arctic circle. They spend about eight months fattening up on delicacies from the tidal mudflats before their arduous journey back to their breeding grounds. **Langebaan** in the West Coast National Park is the best place in the country for such sightings and is considered the fifth most important wetland in the world, hosting over 250 bird species, more than a quarter of South Africa's total. The Berg River estuary and saltworks at **Velddrif** are another vital feeding ground for waders. The coastal lake of **Verlorenvlei**, meaning "the lost marsh", is one of the most important wetlands in South Africa; it stretches 13.5km from its mouth at Eland's Bay (25km south of Lambert's Bay) to its headwaters near Redelinghuys. Look out here for the Purple Gallinule, a colourful, shy wader, and the African Marsh Harrier, a raptor which may be declining in numbers. Here species more fond of arid conditions merge with the waders, and there have been some rare sightings including a Black Egret and a Palm-nut Vulture. At **Bird Island**, Lambert's Bay, a sunken hide makes it convenient to view the garrulous behaviour of the breeding colony of Cape gannets.

southern 200km of the region, by far the most densely populated part of the coast, has many links to Namaqualand to the north – not least the flowers.

Outside the flower months of August and September, this part of the West Coast has a wide range of attractions, particularly during summer when the lure of the sea and the cooler coast is strong. The area is well known for a wide range of activities, most popularly hiking and horse-riding along the coast or in the mountains, various types of watersports, whale-spotting and some excellent **bird-watching** (see box above).

A highlight of a number of West Coast towns is the casual but sumptuous **seafood** feast served in **open-air restaurants**, with little more than a canvas shelter held up with driftwood and lengths of fishing twine or a simple wind-cheating brush fence as props. The idea is to serve up endless courses of West Coast delicacies right by the ocean, in the style of a beach braai; you eat with your fingers and stand or perch on a rock, and you're likely to hear the waves crashing on the strand a few metres away and feel the sea air rolling in. A typical menu includes several different kinds of fish cooked in different ways – *bokkoms* (dried fish), mussels, lobster, paella, plus home-made breads with jams. Expect to pay around R150 per person for such a meal, excluding drinks. It's essential that you **book** in advance.

Immediately inland is the unusually fertile **Swartland** region; north of Swartland, the impressive **Cederberg mountain range** is an area of distinctive beauty, and a striking feature on the N7 highway, the main artery between Cape Town and Namibia. **Clanwilliam** is the attractive town at the northern end of the Cederberg, north of which the N7 connects with **Vanrhynsdorp**, within the Western Cape but for practical purposes covered with the flower routes of Namaqualand in the Northern Cape (see p.348).

Swartland

The N7 highway north from Cape Town leads quickly into the pleasing and fertile **Swartland** landscape. Swartland means "black country", but while the rolling countryside takes on some attractive hues at different times of year, it's never really black. The accepted theory is that before the area was cultivated, the predominant vegetation was a grey-coloured bush called *renosterbos* (rhinoceros bush) which, seen from the surrounding ranges of hills, gave the area a complexion sufficiently dark to justify the name.

Bordered to the west by the less fertile coastal strandveld and to the east by the tall mountain range running from Wellington to the Cederberg, Swartland is known best as a wheat-growing area, although it also supports dairy farms, horse studs, tobacco crops and vineyards famous for earthy red wines.

The N7 skirts a series of towns on its way north, including the largest in the region, **Malmesbury**. If you're travelling south towards Cape Town, look out for some unusual views of Table Mountain, and also for tortoises, which you should take care to avoid as they cross the road.

Darling and around

The small country town of **DARLING** lies caught between Swartland and the West Coast; it's famous for its rolling countryside and dairy products, and also for its displays of wild flowers in spring. Easily reached from Cape Town via the coastal R27 route, Darling boasts some handsome old buildings and has developed recently as an **artists' colony**. One of South Africa's best-loved comedians, Pieter Dirk-Uys, has established his most famous character, **Evita Bezuidenhout** (South Africa's answer to Dame Edna Everidge), as the hostess of a weekend cabaret show at *Evita se Perron*, the tiny **old train station** in the centre of town (☏022 492 2831 or ⓦwww.evita.co.za for details and reservations). Local painters are displayed at the well-cared-for **Darling Museum** (daily 9am–1pm & 2–4pm; small entry fee) on the corner of Pastorie and Hill streets, and an "Art Walk" to the homes and studios of local artists, photographers and jewellers is organized on the first weekend of every month (details from the museum).

Just under 20km to the south of Darling at **Mamre**, near the coloured commuter town of Atlantis, an old Moravian **mission station** stands on the northern edge of town. Still active (call ☏021 576 1579 for details of tours), it includes a series of old thatched mission cottages, a huge church and a working water mill, and remains one of the finest examples in the Western Cape of these pragmatic but bold early nineteenth-century outposts.

Practicalities

Darling's **tourist office** is located inside the museum (Mon–Fri 9am–1pm & 2–4pm, Sat & Sun 10am–3pm; ☏022 492 3361). Although Darling is well within the scope of a day-trip from Cape Town, it's also a good spot for a short

---

West Coast flowers

During August and September you'll find displays of **wild flowers** across the West Coast region, with significant displays starting as far south as the inland town of Darling, just 80km north of Cape Town off the main R27 coastal route. Excellent displays are also found in the West Coast National Park and the hazy coastal landscapes around Cape Columbine and Lambert's Bay, while inland Clanwilliam is the centre of some good routes. An incredible four thousand flower species are found in the region, most of them members of the daisy and mesembryanthemum groups. For up-to-date advice and guidance, contact the helpful tourist offices in Darling, Saldanha and Clanwilliam; for further tips on flower-viewing, see pp.348–349.

stay. *Trinity Guest Lodge*, 19 Long St (☎022 492 3430, Ⓦwww.trinitylodge
.co.za; ❸–❹), is a charming Victorian guesthouse set in gracious large grounds,
while *Darling Lodge*, 22 Pastorie St (☎022 492 3062, Ⓦwww.darlinglodge
.co.za; ❸–❹), a Cape cottage, has a lush garden and six en-suite rooms.

As well as *Evita se Perron* (see p.291), good **places to eat** include *Trinity
Guest Lodge* for gourmet country fare (dinners on demand, booking
essential). Light lunches and coffees are best at the *Marmelade Cat* on Main
Road, while *Hilda's Kitchen*, Groote Post Wine Estate, up on Darling Hills
(☎022 492 2825; Mon & Wed–Sun), offers highly recommended, modern
country cooking in a beautiful eighteenth-century house, complemented by
wines from the estate. Children are welcome to roam in the extensive
grounds. *Cloof Winery* (☎022 492 2839), twenty minutes' drive towards
Malmesbury, does a gourmet barbecue in the summer only. Don't expect
coils of *boerewors* here, but seared salmon on lemongrass skewers and morsels
of lamb cooked on an open wood fire.

Riebeek Kasteel and Riebeek West

To the northeast of Malmesbury and 100km from Cape Town lies an impressive
island of hills, **Kasteelberg** (castle mountain), on the far side of which lie two
small settlements, **RIEBEEK KASTEEL** and, 5km to its northwest, **RIEBEEK
WEST**. Close as they are to Cape Town, either village makes an easy weekend
break, with a couple of great guesthouses and good dining, though Riebeek
Kasteel is more arty, and has more going on. This is a **Shiraz** growing area, and
there are a couple of cellars to visit, most notably Riebeek Cellars, on Pieter
Cruythoff Avenue in Riebeek Kasteel (Mon–Fri 8am–5pm & Sat 9am–2pm;
☎022 448 1213), with great-value Shiraz, a range of other reds and whites, port
and a sparkling Cap Classique. **Olives** do well too in this sunny valley; the Olive
Boutique on Riebeek Kasteel's Church Street (Mon–Fri 9am–4pm, Sat & Sun
10am–2pm; ☎022 448 1368) is worth a stop for its home-milled olive oil
products, particularly the green olives in lime dressing and black olives in a
blueberry dressing.

Roughly 3km north of Riebeek West on the road towards Moorreesburg lies
a turning to a PPC Cement works. It's here, rather incongruously set among
rumbling conveyor belts and grey dirt heaps, that you'll find the whitewashed
cottage where **Jan Smuts**, the South African statesman and soldier, was born
in 1870. There isn't a great deal to see other than a simple old house with
wooden floors and some contemporary artefacts inside but, if you can ignore
the fact that it has been all but gobbled up by an industrial site, there are some
pleasant lawns, flowerbeds and a handful of outbuildings to wander around –
one of which displays an interesting series of storyboards about the eventful life
and times of the man (see box opposite).

Practicalities

Accommodation in Riebeek West is available in a luxurious Victorian villa,
Riebeek Valley Hotel, 4 Dennehof St (☎022 461 2672; Ⓦwww.riebeekvalleyhotel
.co.za; ❹–❺), which also has a good restaurant, beautiful garden and setting, and is
good value for what you get. Between Riebeek Kasteel and Tulbagh is *Bartholomeus
Klip* (☎022 448 1820, Ⓦwww.bartholomeus.com; full board and activities; ❻), a
historic wheat and sheep farm and nature reserve with extensive herds of antelope.
The gracious Victorian farmhouse has five en-suite rooms, elegantly decorated and
furnished with heirloom antiques. The full-board rate includes game drives and use
of the boats on the lake and bikes. There is a self-catering house on the property,

Jan Smuts

The life of **Jan Christiaan Smuts**, one of South Africa's greatest figures, perhaps embodies more than any other this country's strained relationship with itself in the first half of the twentieth century. Born to an Afrikaner farming family, Smuts spoke English with the distinctive linguistic burr of Swartland and excelled as a scholar at Stellenbosch and then Cambridge universities. During the Anglo-Boer War he waged a wide-ranging and ultimately undefeated guerrilla campaign as the leader of a Boer commando. However, he came to believe in a unified South Africa under a British flag, and was appointed commander in chief of imperial forces in East Africa during World War I, attending meetings of the British War Cabinet in the final phases of the war.

Smuts served as **prime minister** of South Africa between 1919 and 1924, and again between 1939 and 1948, when he led South Africa into World War II on the British side. Like his fellow leader and statesman Winston Churchill, he failed to hold together support at home and in 1948 lost the postwar general election to the hardline Afrikaner D.F. Malan who, coincidentally, grew up on the farm Allesvoloren, a few kilometres from Smuts' birthplace.

Smuts spent much of his career in domestic politics trying to hold together disparate political and social moralities among English and moderate Afrikaans-speaking whites. He is remembered by white South Africans as a wily, tainted politician rather than as a great humanitarian. Yet he was, like very few South Africans before or since, a man of global vision and influence who as a 76-year-old played an important role in drafting the United Nations charter in 1946. He also published a philosophical treatise and was known for his love of nature and the outdoors, in particular Table Mountain in Cape Town – one of the popular routes up the mountain carries his name.

Olive House (R935 per person), where children can be accommodated. South African Museums is using the Burchells zebra on the property to breed out the stripes in an attempt to re-create the extinct quagga – an animal which looked like a zebra, only with fewer, paler stripes – which once roamed these parts.

Riebeek Kasteel has a wonderful **place to stay**, ⚜ *The Cape Francolin Art Hotel*, 50 Church St (☎022 448 1176 or 084 314 5741, Ⓦwww. arthotel .co.za; ❸), with four double bedrooms, Irish linen sheets and breakfasts of smoked salmon and home-made walnut and fig bread with local preserves. Artist owner David Bellamy has created a guesthouse which is also a quirky conceptual art installation which looks a bit like a junk-shop or scrapyard, and instead of drawing on Tuscan/Provençal themes, so common in the Cape, he determinedly uses South African ones. There's tons of birdlife too in his garden, and metal-and wirework for sale. For self-catering, *Morewag*, 19 Fontein St (☎022 448 1710 or 072 226 7700, Ⓔbill.mare@wcaccess .co.za; ❷), has a pleasing and centrally located cottage with a swimming pool, while *Goedgedacht Rural Centre*, Riebeeksrivier Road, off the R46 (☎022 482 4466 or 083 658 3855; ❶) offers cheap, clean dorms and chalets at a development project on a working farm.

For **food**, *The Barn* (☎022 448 1377; lunch & dinner Wed–Sun) in a converted rustic barn on Church Street has one of the best settings anywhere, looking out to mountains over a field of grazing springbok, with al fresco high-quality French-style food served with a South African twist; booking is advised. *Café Oppie Square* in the centre of Riebeek Kasteel has good coffee and light meals served under a pepper tree, in front of an interesting corrugated-iron and stained-glass building (Mon–Fri 8am–5pm, Sat & Sun 9am–4pm).

Groot Winterhoek

Situated within the often hazy, fortress-like line of mountains on the eastern fringe of Swartland is the three-hundred-square-kilometre **Groot Winterhoek Wilderness Area**, an excellent place for lonely hiking and camping, with river pools and waterfalls, typical Cape mountain fauna such as klipspringer, rhebok and elusive felines, and distinctive *fynbos* vegetation. Only a couple of hours' drive north from Cape Town, these mountains are a fine option for wilderness hiking, with a couple of excellent camping and self-catering options just outside the reserve itself.

One of the most popular hikes is to De Hel, where you follow the course of a river with beautiful pools to swim in, and overnight in a cave, carrying all you need. This must be booked in advance through Nature Conservation in Cape Town (T 021 659 3500; R90). If you're doing a day hike, you can buy a permit (R35) from the office at the entrance to the reserve, and get recommendations for a route to suit your time and level of fitness. In summer, when it can be very hot, you can do a moderate walk and laze by the river.

The nearest town, 30km away, in the mundane farming valley below, is **Porterville**, where you can find accommodation via the tourist office (Mon–Fri 9am–4pm; T 022 931 3732, W www.portervilletourism.co.za). From Porterville you drive up the very steep, unpaved Dasklip Pass to the wilderness area, where you'll often see paragliders and mountain bikers.

There are two great **accommodation** options on top of the mountains, at both of which you should plan on a minimum of two nights. *Beaverlac* (T 022 931 3732; ●) is possibly the best, particularly for those with children in tow, as it's within easy reach of Cape Town, totally safe and relaxed, and it has a fabulous waterfall pool and rock to jump off, other pools to explore a little further off, and hikes. There is no electricity, and it's a rough road down to the farm from Dasklip Pass, though 4WD is not necessary. If you don't want to camp, there are a couple of secluded self-catering cottages, always with a waiting list for weekends, and some tiny wooden cabins in the campsite itself. You'll need to take all your supplies with you, though wood is available at the little kiosk, as well as a few groceries.

🦌 *Pampoenfontein Farm*, a couple of kilometres closer to the Groot Winterhoek, offers a peaceful time rather than the socializing camp life of *Beaverlac*. While there are no mountain pools on the farm, there is a lovely dam to swim in, a short hike away from the cottages. There are three reasonably priced, tasteful and well-kitted-out cottages of varying sizes, but the high demand from outdoorsy Capetonians for weekends and school holidays means you need to book as far ahead as possible. Weekdays you'll have no problem (T 022 931 3442 or 082 564 5500, W www.pampoenfontein .co.za; ●). Bring all your own supplies.

Saldanha Bay and around

To the west of rural Swartland, and immediately north of Cape Town's fast-developing northern coastal suburbs of Bloubergstrand and Table View, the West Coast of South Africa starts off much as it continues for many hundreds of kilometres north: isolated fishing settlements and windswept dune vegetation of bleak but alluring beauty. Other than river mouths, the only sea inlet and protected deep-water harbour on the entire South African Atlantic seaboard is some 100km north of Cape Town at **Saldanha Bay**. The bay is connected to Langebaan Lagoon, the attractive centrepiece to the small but precious **West Coast National Park**.

While the holiday town of **Langebaan**, just to the north of the park on the eastern shore of the lagoon, has managed to keep its focus relatively frivolous and beach-oriented, industrial development has muscled into the northern part of the bay. This has brought in its wake a 1500-metre causeway, an iron-ore railway terminal and a fast-rising steel and concrete works, which come as an ugly intrusion after the delicate simplicity of the national park. They also mean that the town of **Saldanha**, once a sturdy fishing port with historic naval and military ties, is now grim, sullied and eminently avoidable.

Langebaan

Once the home to the largest whaling station in the southern hemisphere, and for a while Cape Town's long-haul passenger flight terminus (when seaplanes from Europe touched down on the lagoon during World War II), **LANGEBAAN** now sells itself as the gateway to the West Coast National Park, though it has become depressingly overdeveloped it and if you're after a small-town west coast experience, avoid it in favour of Paternoster. The only reason to stay here is if you want to spend time in West Coast National Park itself, where there is almost zero accommodation. On the other hand, if you're into windsurfing, kitesurfing or sailing and have been wondering how to harness the big southeasterly summer winds, the excellent conditions here mean Langebaan could be just your thing. Right off the beach the water is flat, the sailing winds – as the ragged flags above the centre testify – anywhere from fresh to fearsome and, unless you catch a fast-running tide out towards the Atlantic, it's all reasonably safe.

If you want to try your hand at any of the watersports on offer, the friendly Cape Sport Centre (daily 9am–5pm, closed Sun afternoons; ☎022 772 1114, ⓦwww.capesport.co.za), on the beach on the northern edge of town, is the place to head to for gear rental and **windsurfing** and **kitesurfing** tuition; it also offers an accommodation-booking service. **Sailing** courses are offered by Ocean Sailing Academy (☎021 425 7837, ⓦwww.oceansailingacademy.co.za).

Tourist **information** is available in the municipal building in Bree Street (Mon–Fri 9am–5pm, Sat 9am–2pm, closed Sun; ☎022 772 1515, ⓦwww .laangebaaninfo.com).

Accommodation

Accommodation is plentiful – it's what the town exists on – and it's much cheaper in winter than summer. The municipal **caravan park** is a couple of blocks from the beach on Suffrens Street, and though it claims not to allow tents without permission, you probably won't need to ask when you arrive.

The Farmhouse Hotel ☎022 772 2062, ⓦwww.thefarmhouselangebaan.co.za. A luxuriously restored farmhouse set up on the hill among some new houses on the southern end of town. It has a good restaurant and impressive cellar open to non-guests if you want your fish and chips with a view of the lagoon. ❺

Friday Island Next to Cape Sport, on the beach ☎022 772 2506. Perfect for the watersports enthusiast wanting a more upmarket place to stay, the units are fresh and light with small kitchenettes, wooden decks and outdoor courtyards opening from the bathroom to hang up wet gear. There's also an in-house restaurant and pub. ❸–❹

Langebaan Beach House On the lagoon's edge ☎022 482 1101. A guesthouse with spacious,

airy rooms, and a quick stroll to restaurants and shops. B&B ❸–❹

Olifantskop Opposite the *Club Mykonos* turn-off on the coast road, halfway between Langebaan and Saldanha ☎022 772 2326, ⓦwww.oliphantskop .co.za. A guesthouse that has both rooms and self-contained cottages, plus a restaurant, bar, pool, plant nursery and tea garden, and equestrian centre where you can do outrides. ❷

Puza Moya On the corner of North and Suffern sts, Langebaan ☎022 772 1114. Cheerful en-suite rooms with a shared kitchen and courtyard for braais. A good option if you like to socialize in a relaxed environment after an active day. Self-catering or B&B. ❷

Eating

As with accommodation, there's a wide selection of **places to eat** in town. *Die Strandloper* (☏022 772 2490 or 083 227 7195; booking essential), on the beach just beyond the Cape Sport Centre on the road to Saldanha, is a good example of the West Coast's open-air seafood restaurants. On the main beach in town, *Pearly's* and *Driftwood* are crowded eating, drinking and ogling spots in a prime location. The gourmet's choice is *Froggy's*, 29 Main Rd (summer Wed–Sun lunch & dinner, plus Tues dinner; winter Tues–Sun dinner, plus Sun lunch; ☏022 772 1869), which offers delicious and unusual seafood and curries, with some vegetarian options.

West Coast National Park

The **West Coast National Park** (daily: April–Sept 7am–7pm, Oct–March 6am–8pm; R50; ☏022 772 2144) is one of the best places to savour the charm of the West Coast, which elsewhere is being devoured by housing developments. The park protects over forty percent of South Africa's remaining pristine strand-veld and 35 percent of the country's salt marshes, and incorporates both the majority of Langebaan Lagoon and a Y-shaped area of land immediately around and below it.

Much of the park's appeal lies in uplifting views over the still lagoon to an olive-coloured, rocky hillside; the sharp, saline air; the calling gulls and Atlantic mists vanishing in the harsh sunlight. This isn't a game park – a few larger antelope are located in the Postberg section of the park, an area open only during the spring flower season – but there are huge numbers of **birds**, including some 70,000 migrating waders. A number of well-organized interpretive walking trails lead through the dunes to the long, smooth, wave-beaten Atlantic coastline, offering plenty of opportunity to learn about the hardy *fynbos* vegetation which so defines the look and feel of the West Coast region. The best time to visit the park is in spring, when the sun is shining and the flowers are out, although this is, inevitably, also the busiest period. Like much of the West Coast, the national park is chilly and wet in winter, and hot and wind-blasted in summer.

On the southern tip of the lagoon is a large old farmhouse and steading called **Geelbek**. There are a number of bird hides nearby, and all the main **trails** (up to a total of 30km) start from here. If you continue from Geelbek up the peninsula on the western side of the lagoon you'll come to **Churchhaven**, a tiny village still without electricity, where there are some simple private cottages and where you can swim in the still, relatively warm water of the lagoon – though it is closed to day visitors.

A little further on is the demarcated **Postberg area**, open only during flower season (see box, p.291), but worth visiting at that time to see **zebra**, **gemsbok** and **wildebeest** wandering through fields of wild flowers. The tip of the peninsula overlooking the mouth of Saldanha Bay is owned by the South African National Defence Force and inaccessible. The reserve also includes a number of islands around the mouth of the bay, home to gannets, penguins, seals and, on one, a colony of albino rabbits.

Practicalities

There are two **entrance gates** to the park: one on the R27, roughly 10km north of the turning to Yzerfontein, and the other south of the town of Langebaan. The park isn't huge – if you're driving you'll cover the extent of the roads in a couple of hours. You can see a good chunk if you enter at one gate and come out at the other – but it's worth taking the roads slowly to enjoy the views, and a visit to

Geelbek, where there's an **information centre, booking office** and **restaurant** (☏022 772 2134; daily 9am–6pm), will allow you to appreciate a bit more of what you're seeing. Overnight **accommodation** is available here at *The Stables* (☏022 772 2798; ❶), behind the restaurant in a self-catering cottage with three bedrooms for R750 per night, and dormitories set attractively near the edge of the lagoon. One kilometre away at Duinepos (☏022 707 9900) there are seven self-catering chalets available at R550 for four people. Though the chalets are close to the lagoon, there is no access to the water because of bird breeding. Swimming possibilities are at Kraalbaai, 15km away.

One of the ultimate lagoon experiences is to sleep on a moored boat. There are two **houseboats** on the lagoon, *Larus*, sleeping four adults and two children (R1200 per night for four people), and a larger one, *Nirvana*, that can sleep up to 24 which goes for R5000 per night; for both, book through Tony and Cleo Drayton on ☏021 689 9718 or 082 258 0929, ⓦwww.houseboating.co.za.

Cape Columbine and Paternoster

The coastline north of Vredenburg is classical West Coast territory: isolated fishing settlements with small, whitewashed cottages and a salty haze over the lazy, glinting ocean. Despite the quaint image, most of the settlements possess alarmingly expanding holiday developments, offering (naturally) whitewashed cottages in classical West Coast style. Although you can still find the odd lonely coastline and some genuine character in the old villages and their coloured inhabitants, the area feels as though it has reached that sad moment of changing from "best-kept secret" to an over-subscribed building site. The best place to head for, though, is undoubtedly **Paternoster** which offers some wonderful beachside accommodation, including a budget place, *Beach Camp*, right on the sand in its own cove, which you can reach by a combination of public transport and lifts (see p.299).

Vredenburg and the West Coast Fossil Park

North of Saldanha lies a sizeable inland farming centre, **VREDENBURG**, an unremarkable town in a featureless setting. Vredenburg has well-stocked supermarkets and a **tourist office**, the West Coast Peninsula Tourism Bureau (Mon–Fri 9am–4pm; ☏022 715 1142, ⓦwww.capewestcoastpeninsula.co.za), in the Atrium Building on Main Road. The town is also a good place to buy fuel – many of the smaller towns nearby don't have filling stations.

About 10km southeast of Vredenburg, on the R45, the **West Coast Fossil Park** (Mon–Fri 8am–4pm, Sat & Sun 9am–noon; R30, children R12) was founded in 1998 on the site of a decommissioned phosphate mine. In the process of being developed, it's still a relatively small and low-key affair, but interesting and recommended nevertheless, with guided tours of the fossil site following a slide show daily at 11.30am. Displays include thousands of fossils and modern animal bones, and also information panels about the extinct species from about five million years ago found on site. Finds include fossils from sabre-toothed cats, two species of extinct elephant and *sivatheres* – long-horned, short-necked giraffe-like browsers. Perhaps strangest of all are the extinct giant bears, *Agriotherium africanum*, which weighed in at 750kg (compared to 150kg for a large lion), making them the heftiest predators – and the only known bears – to have roamed sub-Saharan Africa in the past 65 million years.

Budget **accommodation** is available on the adjacent property at *Windstone Backpackers* (☎022 766 1645 or 083 477 1756, Ⓦwww.windstone.co.za; ❶), just past the main crossroads of the R45 from Vredenburg and the R27 from Cape Town. The lodge has four- and six-bedded dorms and one room suitable for families, plus some doubles. *Windstone* makes a friendly base for exploring the region and also has a **horse-riding centre** run by owners Andy and Brenda Winder, the latter a qualified riding instructor who does outrides in the adjoining fossil park and nature reserve (R150). The lodge is on the route of the daily Elwierda bus (☎021 418 4673), between Cape Town and Saldanha; the Winders can provide mountain bikes and transport to Langebaan.

Paternoster

The best of the coast is to be found 20km northwest of Vredenburg and 145km from Cape Town, around the village of **PATERNOSTER** (whose name derives from the fact that prayers were uttered by Portuguese sailors crawling ashore from a shipwreck in the adjacent bay). Small-scale angling and crayfish netting is the principal economic activity of the village, and most of the fishermen live in the whitewashed cottages of the coloured district to the west of the hotel. When they're not out at sea, their small, brightly painted boats lie beached at the water's edge.

Unfortunately, Paternoster has become a bit of a building site of late, with lots of people building houses in this idyllic spot. Nevertheless the coast itself is beautiful, saved from development by the Cape Columbine Nature Reserve, 3km to the west, where huge waves smash against large granite rocks as smooth as whales' backs.

An adventure highlight of Paternoster is **sea kayaking** at the *Beach Camp* at Columbine Nature Reserve (☎082 926 2267, Ⓦwww.ratrace.co.za). The one-hour trips cost R150 and are as much about observing and learning about birds, whales, dolphins and seals as about paddling.

▲ Boats at Paternoster

Accommodation

One of the best areas for accommodation is on a small bay, along Sonkwas Road, before you reach the reserve. A number of fabulous guesthouses and self-catering places front the ocean, all west-facing to make the most of the afternoon sun and sunsets. There is an accommodation **booking agency** for Paternoster (☎022 752 2227), though no tourist office as yet.

Baywatch Villa 8 Ambyl Rd ☎022 752 2039, ⓦwww.baywatchvilla.co.za. Five luxurious self-catering thatched fisherman's-style cottages two minutes' walk from Long Beach, in the quiet part of town to the north. ❸

Beach Camp Signposted from Paternoster in Cape Columbine Reserve ☎082 926 2267, ⓦwww .ratrace.co.za. Right on the beach, in its own bay, *Beach Camp* has walk-in tents and small A-frames, some of which can sleep children. This is where you launch for sea-kayaking, when the swell is not too strong. There are free pick-ups from the Elwierda Bus from Vredenburg (☎021 418 4673) which departs Cape Town at 5pm Mon–Thurs. There's a bar where you can breakfast on the terrace, and fish braais are available if requested in advance. Otherwise, bring your own supplies to self-cater. ❷

Blue Dolphin 12 Warrelklip St, right on the beach ☎022 752 2001, ⓦwww.bluedolphin.co.za. Four en-suite rooms in a modern building. The owner, George, is very informative and prepares excellent breakfasts. B&B ❹

Die Opstal Sonkwasweg ☎083 988 4645. Three self-catering flats and a studio with separate entrances with handmade mosaics and paintings decorating the flats. The building is one row behind the beachside properties. ❷

Die Vissershuisie Sonkwas St ☎022 752 2048. Hardly cheap for self-catering, but a fabulous fisherman's cottage spectacularly sited on the beach between the town's top two guesthouses. You'll need to book far ahead for a weekend. ❹

Mosselbank On the corner of Trappiesklip and Mosselbank sts ☎022 752 2632, ⓦwww .weskus.com. Hospitable B&B in a suburban development, with sea views from four en-suite rooms, in the northern part of town, close to Long Beach. ❸

Oystercatchers' Haven 48 Sonkwasweg ☎022 752 2193, ⓦwww.oystercatchershaven .com. A beautiful guesthouse with three rooms, situated on the beach and the edge of Columbine Reserve. The views are wonderful, with a swimming pool and loungers close to the beach, The place has an air of the old romance of Africa, where everything you touch tells a story. ❹

The Paternoster Dunes 18 Sonkwas St ☎083 560 5600, ⓦwww .paternosterdunes.co.za. Gorgeous guesthouse with contemporary beachhouse-style rooms leading onto the sand, and everything designed to inspire and delight the senses. Breakfast is on the patio upstairs with uninterrupted Atlantic views, and the pool is protected from the wind in the central courtyard. Make sure you have a seaview room, rather than a courtyard-facing one. ❹–❺

Eating

Eating and **seafood** are virtually synonymous in Paternoster. You'll find oysters and crayfish, as well as something for vegetarians, at the informal *Noisy Oyster* (☎022 752 2196 or 079 491 5765; open Wed–Sat lunch and dinner, Sun lunch only) on the main drag. What it lacks in setting, it makes up for in ambience and good food. Spectacularly sited on the beach, the *Voorstrand* (☎022 752 2038; daily 10am–10pm), in a corrugated-iron building at the bottom of Malgas Road, serves shellfish platters, totally fresh fish of the day and a large selection of grills, though vegetarians should note that it's low on salads and vegetables. Evenings are cosy in this old fisherman's cottage, or you can sit outside and listen to the crashing waves, if it's warm enough.

Best place to sample a bit of local life is in the *Panties Bar* at the *Paternoster Hotel*, whose roof is festooned with assorted knickers and the odd trophy bra. More family orientated, next to the hotel, at *Paternoster Lodge* you can have coffee, a drink or light meal upstairs under a reed-shaded terrace to take in the views. Films are shown here too – check the billboard outside.

Columbine Nature Reserve

If you get as far as Paternoster, be sure not to miss the **Columbine Nature Reserve** (daily sunrise to sunset; R10), 3km to its west, along an unpaved road. A small area set aside to conserve the sandveld-*fynbos* heathland indigenous to the region, it makes a stunning change from the salty flats that typify the West Coast. Large vegetated dunes sweep down to a shoreline of massive pink granite boulders and little coves, with beaches that are blue-tinged, a result of mussel shells being washed up and finely crushed into the sands. Park at **Tieties Bay** where **camping** is allowed right by the ocean, in amongst the granite boulders, and you can simply follow the marked path over the rocks and along the dunes to explore the area.

Besides rambling, there are some excellent coastal **hiking trails** through these reserves, including two long day-trails (details from Vredenburg tourist office. Along the road from Paternoster to the reserve you'll pass the **Cape Columbine lighthouse** (open to the public for tours; Mon–Fri; R10), built in 1936 on Castle Rock. Usually the first lighthouse to be sighted by ships from Europe rounding Africa, it emits a single white flash every fifteen seconds. **Self-catering accommodation** (☎021 449 2400; ❷–❹) is offered in two former lighthouse keeper's cottages and a condominium, kitted out with all mod cons.

St Helena Bay

St Helena Bay was the point where **Vasco da Gama** set foot in what is now South Africa during his epic voyage around the Cape and through to India in 1497. He wasn't the first European to round the Cape of Good Hope, nor the first to land, but his voyage did open up the route to the East, which was to give the Cape its strategic importance for four centuries. Three granite lumps on the shore between the fishing villages of St Helena Bay and Stompneus Bay serve as a memorial to his landing, and a no-expenses-spared **Da Gama Museum** (daily 9am–4.30pm; free) has also been established within the largest of the new housing developments in the area at **Shelley Point**. The museum is more a rainy-day affair than a must-see, but does include some well-devised story-boards, a collection of model ships and some early navigation devices.

Throbbing away in the background of the granite memorial is a **lobster factory**, where you can usually buy fresh or frozen specimens if you enquire at reception. It's illegal to buy the lobsters if they're offered to you on the street, though in season you can obtain a permit, available from post offices, to catch them for personal consumption. Strangely enough, fishermen once regarded the lobsters that got entangled in their nets as a pest, and during the nineteenth century sold wagonloads of them to farmers to be ground up and used as fertilizer.

Velddrif

At the northern end of the R27 from Cape Town and 15km east of St Helena Bay is **VELDDRIF**, a fishing town situated at the point where the Great Berg River meets the sea. Each year the Berg River **canoe marathon** (which starts near Ceres, 49km north of Worcester) ends here at a marina development called Port Owen. During the last few years, the town has outgrown its fishing industry origins and is now dominated by a modern suburbia of brick bungalows. The town's setting on the meandering Berg River and the surrounding wetlands – as well as the vision of some locals, who have managed to stay the eager hand of the demolition crews – has resulted in Velddrif retaining a little of its historic character.

In the quieter backwaters near the Velddrif bridge, you can still see individual fishermen in small boats landing catches of mullet or horse mackerel. The fish are then dried and salted to make **bokkoms**, called by some a delicacy, but essentially a source of cheap protein for fishermen and farm workers on the West Coast. To see the rickety wooden jetties where the boats tie up, and the frames and sheds by the shore where *bokkoms* are strung up to dry, turn right at the roundabout just over the bridge coming into town on the R27, and after 1km or so take the first right-hand turn down to the riverside.

Heading straight on at the roundabout onto Church Street and then right up a dirt driveway will bring you to the **West Coast Gallery** (Mon–Fri 9am–5pm, Sat 9am–3.30pm), one of the best of its type in the area. Essentially a shop run by a local artist, it displays a wide selection of art and crafts, including some interesting driftwood collages. You can also have a cup of coffee here, explore the reed maze or have a game of petanque in the grounds. Look out for the selection of sea-salt products, including flavoured salts, seaweeds and bath salts, produced on a small pan by the coast nearby.

There is a wealth of **birdlife**, including pelicans and flamingoes along both banks of the river (see box, p.290). You can take a pleasant **boat trip** into the wetlands with well-informed birder Dan Ahlers (☎082 951 0447), who takes excursions up the Berg River. A ninety-minute trip costs R60 per person. He also leads bay cruises on which you stand a chance of seeing marine mammals, including Heaviside's dolphins, distinguished from their commoner bottlenosed cousins by their stocky bodies and short beaks.

Practicalities

The *Riviera Hotel* (☎022 783 1137, ⓦ www.eigevis.com; ❸) has ten well-equipped self-catering **chalets** near the bridge and on the water's edge. Flamingoes and many other waterbirds can be seen from the balcony. There are two pleasant and very reasonably priced self-catering cottages and rooms in the farmhouse on the historic farm of *Langrietvlei* (☎022 783 0856; ❷), halfway between Velddrif and Hopefield, which also offers walking trails. Just 5km from town on the other side of the river is *Kuifkopvisvanger* (☎022 783 0818; ❷), five charming, rustic fishermen's cottages with views of the river and marshlands.

Best of the lot, though, budget allowing, is *Kersefontein Guest Farm* (☎022 783 0850, ⓦ www.kersefontein.co.za; ❹–❺), 25km south of Velddrif on the Berg River. A definite highlight of the West Coast region, this is a working farm dating back to the eighteenth century, and boasts several handsome Cape Dutch listed buildings, some of which have been converted into stylish accommodation. All the rooms have antiques from the original homestead, and dinners are served in a chandelier-lit dining room. The atmosphere is anything but formal, though, with Julian Melck, the eighth-generation owner, treating guests to lively tales of life on a South African farm. There are delightful gardens and many kilometre of farmland to explore, the latter grazed by domestic as well as wild horses.

Velddrif has no shortage of waterside **restaurants**, one of the most charming of which is the low-key *Vishuis* (☎022 783 1183; Tues–Sat 11am–3pm & 6–9pm, Sun 9am–11am & noon–3pm), about 3km west along the atmospheric riverside dirt road from the Velddrif bridge. Housed in a restored traditional fish-drying factory, with outdoor seating offering views across the wetlands, it serves extremely well-priced English breakfasts and excellent fish-and-chips lunches, but it's best to book for dinner. Next to the bridge, the *Riviera Hotel* does good seafood and steaks, while the *Laaiplek*

Hotel is a relaxed place for a **drink** in close proximity to large boats, fish factories and cranes. At *Peroni's Ocean Deli*, at the Laaiplek harbour, you can stock up on any frozen **seafood** you like, or get good fresh **takeaways**.

Elands Bay

A lonely seventy-kilometre drive (you'll be lucky to see other cars), along a newly tarred road, joins Velddrif with **ELANDS BAY**. Until this road was built, Elands Bay was mostly frequented by surfers heading out on the dirt road for the best waves on the West Coast, provided by the unusual left break which gives exceptionally long smooth rides. Two-and-a-half hours from Cape Town, Elands (as it's usually called) is now a weekend destination in its own right, with a couple of guesthouses and restaurants, some fine bushman rock paintings on the south-side cliffs, and exceptional bird-watching in the area. It's probably a place to catch before it's developed and gentrified, though like most of the West Coast, the coastline is spare, windswept and harsh – the tide spewing mounds of kelp, shells and dried-out seal bones onto the deserted beaches. And the water, like the whole of the West Coast, is freezing.

Elands is divided into north and south sides by the **Verlorenvlei** ("lost wetland"), which supports over 200 bird species including African spoonbill, goliath herons, white pelicans and purple gallinule. The nicer side is the south, where the surfers hang out. Above here, the Bobbejaanberg ridge runs into the sea. Where the road ends under the cliffs lies the harbour, and the path up to a large cave with rock art, including some big eland and hundreds of handprints, which are thought to be connected to rites of passage – when adolescents imprinted their hands as they walked through the site. Spring flowers in this vicinity are also phenomenal.

You'll find decent self-catering **accommodation** on the south side at *Elands Bay Guest House*, 184 Kreef Rd (☎022 972 1229; ❷). On the Vlei itself, in splendid isolation, is the appealingly sited *Die Vleihuisie* (☎083 346 5394; ❷), a restored, thatched, self-catering fisherman's cottage. *Vensterklip* (☎022 972 1340, ⓦwww.vensterklip.co.za; ❷–❸), a farm also on the Vlei, 5km from Elands Bay, has variously sized self-catering cottages or very reasonable B&B accommodation. You can borrow kayaks to nose around the Vlei. On the north side, in the desultory business district, the rather deadbeat but reasonably priced and friendly *Elands Bay Hotel* (☎022 972 164, ⓦwww.elandsbayhotel.co.za; ❸) does seafood meals and has good views. The hotel also has backpackers' rooms and campsites. Across the road, try *J & J Verspreiders* for fish and chips.

Lambert's Bay

Some 27km north of Elands Bay is **LAMBERT'S BAY**, 70km due west of Clanwilliam (by tarred road), and the only settlement of any note between Velddrif and Port Nolloth, the latter almost at the Namibian border. This is an important **fishing port**, although by the sights and sounds of the harbour you soon become aware that even the fishermen have to stand aside for the impressive colony of **gannets** on **Bird Island** (R20), in the centre of the bay, where there's a visitor centre and bird hide. You can walk out to the island on the causeway which encloses the fishing-boat harbour for a closer look at the tightly packed, ear-piercing mass of petulant gannets, along with a few disapproving-looking penguins and cormorants, though viewing is not always guaranteed outside of breeding season (April–Sept). In 2005, seals attacked the colony at the height of the breeding season, killing hundreds of birds. Survivors wisely fled, but were lured back by gannet decoys, and chicks are again being safely born, though the threat is always present.

Lambert's Bay itself is rather short on charm; the fish-processing plant sits on the edge of the harbour, right in the town centre, giving you the feeling you're in a seat behind a pillar at the theatre. Nevertheless, its isolation means that there's some deserted coastline and nature nearby. During the breeding season (July–Jan), the bay plays host to a resident pod of around seven **humpback whales**. This is also the southernmost area ranged by **Heaviside's dolphins** – small, friendly mammals with wedge-shaped beaks (rather than the longer ones more commonly associated with dolphins), with a white, striped patterning reminiscent of killer whales. You may be lucky and view the cavorting mammals on trips from the fishing port.

Practicalities

The **tourist office** is on Main Road (Mon–Fri 9am–5pm, Sat 9am–12.30pm; ☎027 432 1000, ⓦwww.lambertsbay.co.za). There are a couple of **caravan parks** at either end of town, and no shortage of self-catering apartments, but nothing much by way of charm or character. In Voortrekker Street in the centre of town, the neat *Lamberts Bay Hotel* (☎027 432 1126, ⓦwww.lambertsbayhotel .co.za; ❸) offers comfortable **hotel** rooms with breakfast. *Sir Lambert's Guest House* (☎027 432 1117; ❸), 9 Donkin St, has a good reputation and is a little cheaper. Much nicer, between Lambert's Bay and Clanwilliam, is *Donkieskraal* (☎083 235 4717, ⓦwww.donkieskraal.co.za; ❷–❸), a potato and game farm with thatched chalets and a couple of safari tents on the farm, as well as a campsite. While it's self-catering, the owner, Tilla Laubscher, can do meals on request. The *Lambert's Bay Caravan Park* (☎027 432 2238) has campsites if you want to do it on the cheap.

Eating is one of Lambert's Bay's specialities. *Bosduifklip* (☎027 432 2735), an open-air restaurant set inland among some big rock formations 6km out of town along the R364, on the Graafwater Road, is a reasonable option, while the original West Coast open-air restaurant, *Muisboskerm* (☎027 432 1017), scores on location – right on the edge of the ocean, 5km south of the town towards Elands Bay. For a more conventional seafood restaurant, try *Kreefhuis* (☎027 432 2235; Mon–Sat lunch and dinner & Sun lunch) at the entrance to the harbour on Strand Street. Right on the harbour, *Isabella's Coffee Shop* does the whole gamut from light meals to prawns, but is renowned for its blowout "West Coast breakfast". Best of the lot, on the way to the harbour, *Spill the Beans* is high on fresh fruit and veg and grows its own herbs. Its French onion soup with melted mozzarella is a favourite and its chocolate cheesecake alone is worth coming to Lambert's Bay for.

The Cederberg

A bold and jagged outcrop of the Western Cape fold escarpment, the Cederberg mountain range is one of the most magical wilderness areas in the Western Cape. Rising with a striking presence on the eastern side of the Olifants river valley, around 200km north of Cape Town, these high sandstone mountains and long, dry valleys manage to combine accessibility with remote harshness, offering something for hikers, campers, naturalists and rock climbers.

The **Cederberg Wilderness Area**, flanking the N7 between Citrusdal and Clanwilliam, was created to protect the silt-free waters of the Cederberg catchment area, but also provides a recreational sanctuary with over 250km of hiking trails. In a number of places, the red-hued sandstone has been weathered into grotesque, gargoyle-like shapes and a number of memorable natural features. Throughout the area there are also numerous **San rock-art** sites, an active array of Cape mountain fauna, from baboon and small antelope to leopard, caracal and aardwolf, and some notable montane *fynbos* flora, including the gnarled and tenacious Clanwilliam cedar and the rare snow protea.

The Cederberg is easily reached from Cape Town by way of the N7: the towns of **Citrusdal** and **Clanwilliam** lie just off the highway near, respectively, the southern and northern tips of the mountain range. Both make attractive bases from which to explore the area, particularly during spring flower season, although you can find simple accommodation right in the mountains themselves. From Clanwilliam, set beside a man-made dam, there are worthwhile routes out to Lambert's Bay on the coast (see p.302) and over a spectacular mountain pass to the remote and unique mission at **Wuppertal**. **Weather conditions** are often extreme in the Cederberg, with frost and snow occasionally during winter, and blistering heat in summer. However, a number of rivers are safe for **swimming**.

Citrusdal

North of Piketberg on the N7, a long, flat plain reaches out to the line of Olifantsrivierberg Mountains, which the highway crosses by way of the impressive **Piekenierskloof Pass**, forged in 1857 by the indomitable road engineer Thomas Bain. Down the northern side of the pass, 170km from Cape Town, the humdrum town of **CITRUSDAL** appears in the rolling countryside of the Olifants River Valley, with the dramatic mountainscape of the Cederberg behind. Strange as it may seem now, early Dutch explorers saw huge herds of elephants here as they travelled north towards Namaqualand, hence the river's name.

There are no roads from Citrusdal itself into the heart of the Cederberg Wilderness Area nearby to the north, although there are various routes leading into the foothills, which are justifiably popular with mountain bikers. You can get a **map** outlining these at the town's upbeat **tourist office** at 39 Voortrekker St, the town's wide main thoroughfare (Mon–Fri 8.30am–5pm, Sat 9am–noon; ☏022 921 3210, ⓦ www.citrusdal.info). The staff here can provide useful information about self-catering cottages and guesthouses in the area.

In town, there's a pleasant **campsite** with a pool (☏022 921 3145) on the left-hand side as you come in over the bridge from the N7, and en-suite **rooms** at the reasonably priced *Cederberg Lodge* on Voortrekker Street (☏022 921 2221, ⓦ www.cederberglodge.co.za; ❸). The lodge serves Afrikaner farm-style food on a patio; a little further along the road you can get light meals in huge portions at the distinctive yellow and blue *Uitspan Coffee Shop* next to tourist information. Along the N7 between Citrusdal and Clanwilliam, there are several farm stalls where you can pull in to buy cheap fresh or dried fruit, juice and other nibbles.

Citrusdal hot springs

Surrounding Citrusdal is some attractive countryside and farmland including, as the town's name suggests, plenty of citrus groves. One of the principal attractions of this area is *The Baths* (☏022 921 8026; ❷–❸), a pleasantly old-fashioned, if rather rule-bound, mineral **spa resort** with one large hot pool (43°C), a cold pool and several large indoor spa baths. Day visitors pay R50 to use the amenities. The place is set in a beautiful wooded glen with campsites, chalets and self-catering rooms in some large old stone buildings. There's a restaurant with passable food, though most people self-cater. It's a good spot to relax, particularly if you've been hauling over mountain and rock for a few days. To get there, turn right (south) off the road leading into Citrusdal from the N7 and drive 16km down a good tarred road past the airfield – incidentally, one of the best places in the Western Cape for parachuting.

There are several **accommodation** options near Citrusdal, which can be used as a base for the springs or to do some day hikes into the nearby wilderness area. ⚘ *Petersfield Mountain Cottages*, on a working rooibos and citrus farm 4km from Citrusdal (☎022 921 3316, ⓦ www.petersfieldfarm .co.za; ❸), has some of the best self-catering cottages you'll find anywhere; each absolutely secluded cottage has its own private pool and you can hike anywhere on the farm to its rugged mountain tops and swim in a dam. For weekends, though, you'll have to book a year in advance. For bed and breakfast, try the nice rooms at *Hebron Guest House*, right on Piekenierskloof Pass before you reach Citrusdal (☎022 921 2595; ❸–❹); the Christian-run farm, of which it is a part, has strong HIV/AIDS social projects going on. Telephone in advance if you'd like to visit or know more.

The Cederberg Wilderness Area

The main route into the Cederberg, and Algeria, the forest station which serves as a focal point for the area, heads east off the N7, 28km north of Citrusdal. Although it's a rough dirt road, it's passable in an ordinary car. The 710-square-kilometre **Cederberg Wilderness Area** features many designated **trails**, including the two main peaks, **Sneeuberg** (2027m) and **Tafelberg** (1969m), and the awesome rock formations of the huge **Wolfberg Arch** in the southeast of the reserve, and a thirty-metre-high free-standing pillar shaped like (and known as) the **Maltese Cross**, to its south.

The **permit** system here allows a certain number of people to be in each of three separate parts of the wilderness area; you can hike or camp where you like within the areas you hold a permit for. The inexpensive **permits** can be bought on the day from the Cape Nature Conservation Office at at **ALGERIA**, 18km from the N7 (☎022 931 2088, ⓦ www.capenature.org.za), or from your accommodation. At Algeria, there's **camping** at a pretty riverside site and also seven unsophisticated but fully equipped **self-catering chalets** sleeping four (❷); the stone cottages are the nicest. Cheaper ones 4km away at the bottom of Uitkyk Pass are unequipped and you must bring your own bedding and cooking utensils. For all options book online or on ☎021 659 3500. Algeria, however, can get noisy and crowded at weekends and holidays, and if you want a more wilderness experience in the same area, opt for *Jamaka Organic Farm Cottages and Campsite* (☎027 482 2801, ⓔ jamaka@lando.co.za; ❶–❸) in the Grootkloof, signposted and accessed just before Algeria. The campsite on this organic citrus and mango farm has a lovely setting, and, in contrast to Algeria, strict rules about the playing of loud music and partying. If you want a roof over your head, the best of the cottages is the stone one next to the river.

To the south, there are several private places to stay on farms in the reserve, reached along the single main road passing through this section of the Cederberg. *Sanddrif* (☎027 482 2825, ⓦ www.cederbergwine.com; ❷), about 26km south of Algeria, offers fully equipped chalets with one to three rooms (bring your own bedding), on a farm where there are natural river pools and good walks. *Sanddrif* also sells permits for the classic walks on its property – the Maltese Cross and Wolfberg Arch and Cracks. Near the turn-off to the Maltese Cross there's a small **observatory** (☎021 531 5250 or 021 913 4200; donation), where, on Saturday nights, you can join star-gazing enthusiasts with powerful telescopes – though not at full moon when the stars are dim.

At *Kromrivier* (☎027 482 2807, ⑩www.namapip@netactve.co.za; ②), some 50km south of Algeria, there are thirteen fully equipped chalets, some with their own baths and cheaper ones without, sleeping four, with bedding available for a small charge. Another 12km south is the hospitable *Cederberg Oasis* (☎027 482 2819, ⑩www.cederbergoasis.co.za; ②), the only licensed B&B and restaurant in the area, serving meals of gigantic proportions. Primarily for backpackers, accommodation is in basic rooms, and there's camping. This area is great for the sandstone formations and rock art at Tanjieskraal and Stadsaal Caves, and owner Gerrit will hand-draw you a map when you plan your day's outing and sell you permits. Further south along the road on Grootrivier Farm is *Mount Ceder* (☎023 317 0113, ⑩www .mountceder.co.za; ③–④), the most luxurious place in the reserve, with B&B rooms in the lodge and six self-catering cottages. It's set along a perennial river, and there are some good horse-riding trails. If you're coming from Cape Town, it's better to approach Cederberg Oasis and Mount Ceder via Worcester on the N1, rather than along the route via the N7 to Algeria.

Clanwilliam and around

Also on the N7, 240km from Cape Town, at the northern end of the Cederberg, **CLANWILLIAM** is an attractive and assured small town. It carries off with some aplomb its various roles as a base for the majestic Cederberg Wilderness Area, as a centre for spring flowers, a service centre for surrounding farms, and the place to head for if you want to see good **rock art** within easy striking distance of Cape Town.

Established in the last years of the eighteenth century, Clanwilliam is one of the older settlements north of Cape Town, and features a number of historic buildings around town, including a tourist office (mid-Aug to mid-Sept daily 8am–5pm; rest of year Mon–Fri 8.30am–5pm, Sat 8.30am–12.30pm; ☎027 482 2024, ⑩www.clanwilliam.info) and **museum** (Mon–Sat 8am–1pm; R5) situated in the old jail at the far end of Main Road. The tourist office has good lists of accommodation, in the town itself, as well as the surrounds.

There are some genuinely interesting attractions in town, including **Kunshuis**, a good commercial art gallery on Main Street; a traditional leather **shoemaking factory** on Ou Kaapseweg; and the country's main **rooibos tea-processing factory** next door, which has a window through which you can peer in from the street, and videos of the manufacturing process (Mon–Fri 10am, 11.30am, 2pm &, 3.30pm).

Just to the south of town is **Ramskop**, a wild-flower reserve set on a hillside inside the entrance to the *Clanwilliam Dam Resort* – one of the country's top water-skiing venues – which in summer and at weekends is often monopolized by speedboat louts. Ramskop is delightful in flower season, and definitely worth a visit.

The Cederberg has something like 2500 known **rock-art sites**, some visitable on the **Sevilla bushman painting trail**, 36km north of town, on tours run by the excellent Living Landscape Project (☎027 482 1911), 18 Park St in Clanwilliam, the brainchild of John Parkington, from the University of Cape Town, whose books on rock art in the Cederberg (*The Mantis and the Moon* and *Cederberg Rock Paintings*), available at the project, are the best interpretation of the puzzling and beautiful images you'll see delicately painted on rocks and overhangs. Tours from under R100 per person can be booked everyday to

Rooibos tea

Few things in South Africa create such devotion, derision, hype and, among visitors, bemused suspicion as **rooibos** (literally, "red bush") **tea**. Still sown and harvested by hand on many farms, *rooibos* is a type of *fynbos* plant grown only in the mountainous regions around Clanwilliam and Nieuwoudtville. The caffeine-free tea brewed from its leaves has been a South African drink ever since it was developed by Asian slaves two centuries ago, but it is only in the last twenty or so years that it has broken free of health-food-shop earnestness and established some mainstream credibility. In homes and tea rooms throughout South Africa, *rooibos* is now firmly entrenched alongside regular tea and coffee. Mild in flavour, it can be drunk with milk and sugar, or just with a slice of lemon and a teaspoon of honey.

Should you want to see how the tea is grown and processed, take one of the **tours** offered by Elandsberg Eco Tours (☏027 482 2022; R50); trips start from their premises 20km west of Clanwilliam on the Lambert's Bay road. You'll need to arrange tours in advance. It also has wheelchair-friendly accommodation (❷) in two simple self-catering chalets in a beautifully secluded valley. Meals can be cooked on request. Ysterfontein Farm (☏027 482 2512), 10km further along the same road, offers accommodation in self-catering cottages under thatch next to the farmstead (❷).

Sevilla or to other sites. You'll need to set aside half a day for a tour, led by competent local guides.

Practicalities

Clanwilliam has a number of **B&Bs**, but consider going out of town to find accommodation on farms and valleys in the district, such as in the Boskloof, only 10km away. For **eating**, *Nancy's* on the main road has the best reputation in town, but for something more casual during the day, head for the café in the plant nursery opposite the tourist office. Great for a **drink** is the swanky new *Clanwilliam Lodge*, unmissable as you enter town, with reclining surfaces everywhere – by the fire in winter, or outside by the pool in summer. Otherwise, people sit just about upright at the big television in the pub on match days.

Accommodation

Clancourt B&B 2 Arnold St ☏027 482 1143, Ⓦwww.clancourt.co.za. Four en-suite rooms arranged around a swimming pool. The hosts are interesting former media personalities. ❹

Daisy Cottage ☏027 482 1603, Ⓔliciae@meb .co.za. A quaint self-catering thatched cottage in a quiet street within strolling distance of the main road. The friendly owner is a journalist with the town's newspaper. ❷

Ndedema Lodge At the end of Park St ☏027 482 1314, Ⓦwww.clanwilliam.info/ndedema. A romantic Victorian B&B with an upmarket feel, four antique-filled rooms and a charming garden with pool. ❸

Living Landscape 18 Park St ☏027 482 1911. Acceptable backpacker accommodation in the centre of Clanwilliam, with dorms and doubles in the house next door to the community project (see opposite). ❶–❷

The Boskloof

About 1km east of town along the Pakhuis Pass road, a good dirt road heads south and drops into the **Boskloof**, through which the Jan Dissels River traces its course. Although less than 10km from the town, and 290km from Cape Town, the valley feels a very long way from anywhere and is a relaxed spot where you can spend time lolling about along the riverbank, swimming in its natural pools or just walking along the dirt road which twists through the mountains. From the valley you can hike up into the Cederberg mountains, on the **Krakadouw hiking trail**, which starts at *Krakadouw Cottages* in the valley,

②

where you can buy permits. Hikes can last up to a week, though you can also do shorter day or half-day hikes along a section of the trail.

There are a number of good **places to stay** along the quiet road, which terminates in the valley. *Klein Boschkloof Chalets*, 9km from Clanwilliam (☎027 482 2441; ②), is a reasonably priced collection of 250-year-old Cape Dutch farm buildings converted into guest cottages. The thatched chalets stand in the middle of fragrant citrus groves, and are finished to a high standard, with cooking gear, bed linen and towels. Breakfast and dinner can be provided by prior arrangement. Some 4km further down the valley, *Boskloof Swemgat* (☎027 482 2522, Ⓦwww.boskloofswemgat.co.za; ②) has the advantage over Boschkloof, in its riverside setting and swimming possibilities. Accommodation is in three upgraded cottages with views opening onto the river. At the end of the road, 13km from Clanwilliam, ⚒ *Karukareb* (☎027 482 1675, Ⓦwww.karukareb.co.za; full board and activities ②) is an exceptional **luxury bushcamp** and guest lodge along the river, in one of the loveliest and wildest valleys in the Western Cape. Besides outstanding **horse-riding**, there are mountain bikes for guests, and plenty of hikes. Accommodation is either in one of five luxury safari tents along the river, or in the lodge with five rooms, close to the dining room and saltwater swimming pool. Each tent has its own section of river to swim in and wooden decks to relax on. Best of all are the baths positioned by windows, where you can relax, glass in hand, and watch the sunset reddening the mountains.

Northern Cederberg and the Pakhuis Pass

The untarred **R364** northeast from Clanwilliam winds over the **Pakhuis Pass**, a drive worth taking for its lonely roadside scenery and inspiring views. This area is said to be one of the two best places in the world for **bouldering**, so expect to see plenty of lithe climbers going to and from the graded routes, particularly in the milder winter months.

There's good-value **accommodation** at *Traveller's Rest*, situated on a farm 36km northeast from Clanwilliam on the R364 (☎027 482 1824, Ⓦwww .travellersrest.co.za; ②–③), with various self-catering cottages and the well-regarded *Khoisan Restaurant*, which serves South African farm-style home cooking. The main attraction is the four-kilometre **Sevilla bushman painting trail**, starting right beside the farm. The trail takes in nine separate rock-art sites, and provides an easy and varied introduction to rock art; if you're pushed for time, you can restrict yourself to the first six, which are the best. Enquire at the farmhouse or restaurant for **permits** (R30) and a leaflet and book covering the trail.

In a totally different league, about 1km beyond *Traveller's Rest* is *Bushman's Kloof* (☎027 482 2627, bookings ☎021 685 2598, Ⓦwww.bushmanskloof .co.za; ③), a fabulous **luxury lodge**, set in a wilderness area with game drives and rock art, with over 125 recorded sites on the property; the rangers are trained in both wildlife guiding and rock-art interpretation. The rate includes all meals, game drives and guided rock-art trails. Flying in from Cape Town will set you back R5000 return, while rates go from R2000–3500 per person a night.

Back to the realm of the ordinary, 26km north of Clanwilliam, off the R364, are two very pleasant self-catering options, both adjoining farms and popular with rock climbers. *Alpha Excelsior Guest Farm and Winery* (☎027 482 2700; Ⓦwww.alphaexcelsior.co.za; ②) has three cottages, the nicest of which, *Weaver*, is nearest to the river and sleeps two; the others sleep more, and there's an attic room in one house for dorm beds. The farm, run by friendly folk, has its own small winery too, with bottles for sale. Next door, *De Pakhuys* (☎027 482 1468, ⊛www.depakhuys.co.za; ❷) has two large garden cottages on a rooibos farm with marked hiking trails starting near the secluded campsite. *Waboomhuys*, decorated to a high standard, light and airy and with a warming fireplace, is ideal for a couple, while *De Pakhuys* sleeps six. Thys Kruger and his wife are exceptionally obliging and will ensure you have a great stay. Guests also have the use of a swimming pool and braai facilities.

Wuppertal and the Biedouw Valley

One of the best drives you'll do in the Western Cape is along the mountainous R364 dirt road, which winds through remote valleys to reach historic **WUPPERTAL**. Set deep in the tunefully named Tra-tra Valley, the Moravian mission station is one of the oldest in the Western Cape and, with a tiny collection of thatched cottages in the small centre, and along the river, it remains one of the most untouched settlements in South Africa – though these days satellite television dishes poke out of the thatched roofs. Run by the church elders and with an entirely coloured population, the mission is famous for making *velskoene* (literally "hide shoes"), the suede footwear commonly known as *vellies* and part of Afrikaner national dress. You can see the shoes being made and, of course, buy them at the little shop at die Werf – the centre which clusters around the church. Also for sale are some rooibos products, notably soap.

Aside from shoe-making, people here survive on subsistence farming, rooibos tea growing, and no alcohol, with the young generally heading off to the cities as soon as they can. There's not much going on for tourists, though the low-key *Lekkerbekkie Tearoom* (☎027 492 3410; Mon–Sat 9am–3pm) in one of the village's oldest buildings houses a small **museum** and tiny **tourist office** (☎027 492 3410, ⊛www.capewestcoast.org). Otherwise the only thing to do is to walk around taking pictures – it's highly photogenic. The road in is pretty awful and very steep in parts – while you don't need 4WD, you will need to take it slowly. While most people come for a brief visit, there are a couple of modest self-catering options in cottages (☎027 492 3410; ❶), and you can arrange in advance for meals to be cooked by *Lekkerbekkie*.

On the way to Wuppertal you can turn into the **Biedouw Valley**, which only sees traffic during the spring, when the valley floor is carpeted with flowers. The best reason to visit the valley is to **stay** at *Enjolife*, an isolated 200-year-old farmhouse 60km from Clanwilliam (☎027 482 2869; ❶–❷), run by a young German couple who offer lovely rooms at backpacker prices. It's self-catering, but you can get meals. The emphasis here is on enjoying nature, and in the hot summer you can swim in the farm dam. Due to its isolation, it's a place to spend a few days, rather than simply overnight.

Oudrif

🏕 **Oudrif** (booking essential; ☎027 482 2397, ⊛www.oudrif.co.za; full board ❺) is an exceptional retreat lodge in the Cederberg back country, 48km from Clanwilliam, some of it along rough dirt roads. It occupies inspiring countryside in the transitional zone between the foothills of the mountains and the dry Karoo, with redstone gorges and a wide valley incised by the Doring

▲ Oudrif Lodge

River. You can pick up early marine fossils on nearby hills, from the days when the area was flooded by an inland sea.

More recently, the area was once inhabited by San hunter-gatherers, who left their mark on a number of painted rock faces in the area. Although there are wonderful walks through *fynbos* to **rock art**, this is as much a place to chill out – the only rule enforced by the co-owner and manager Bill Mitchell and his wife Janine, is that there are no rules. The multi-talented Mitchell is also a qualified chef and does all the cooking at this full-board establishment. The river has beaches for sunbathing and there are some fine spots for cooling off in its flow on hot days; as a former river-rafting guide, Mitchell can take you onto the water in a boat.

Accommodation is in five straw-bale houses, built using a traditional North American method in which bales are sandwiched between solid facings – in this case concrete. The cream-coloured chalets have an uneven hewn quality that befits their isolation on the edge of the gorge that falls away to the Doring River. Each is stylishly equipped with retro furniture and has a double and a three-quarter bed; the power for lighting is provided by solar panels and showers are heated.

If you want some more sustained adrenaline, the best **whitewater rafting trips** in the Western Cape set out a short walk downstream from *Oudrif* from mid-July to mid-September, operated by River Rafters (℡021 712 5094, Ⓦwww.riverrafters.co.za; weekend trips R950 per person).

Travel details

Trains

The most useful trains in the Western Cape are the two Metrorail services connecting Cape Town with Stellenbosch and Paarl (all a 1hr journey). Outside peak morning and evening hours, trains are irregular, but run at approximately two-hour intervals; though as safety is not totally assured, they're not recommended.

Paarl to: Cape Town (18 daily; 1hr 15min).
Stellenbosch to: Cape Town (6–7 daily; 1hr 10min).

Buses

Principal routes are Cape Town–Port Elizabeth along the N2 coastal route, with an inland alternative along the Little Karoo mountain route; Cape Town–Johannesburg/Pretoria along the N1; Knysna–Johannesburg/Pretoria via Mossel Bay and the N12; and Cape Town–Windhoek via the N7.

Clanwilliam to: Cape Town (6 weekly; 3hr 45min); Citrusdal (6 weekly; 25min); Windhoek (Namibia; 6 weekly; 16hr 10min).
George to: Cape Town (6–7 daily; 6hr); Durban (1 daily; 18hr); Johannesburg (1–2 daily; 15hr); Knysna (6–7 daily; 1hr); Mossel Bay (6–7 daily; 45min); Oudtshoorn (3–4 daily; 1hr 30min); Plettenberg Bay (6–7 daily; 1hr 30min); Port Elizabeth (6–7 daily; 4hr 30min); Pretoria (1–2 daily; 16hr).
Knysna to: Cape Town (6–7 daily; 7hr); Durban (1 daily; 17hr); George (6–7 daily; 1hr); Johannesburg (1–2 daily; 16hr); Mossel Bay (6–7 daily; 1hr 15min); Oudtshoorn (1–2 daily; 2hr); Plettenberg Bay (6–7 daily; 1hr 30min); Port Elizabeth (6–7 daily; 4hr 30min); Pretoria (1–2 daily; 17hr).
Mossel Bay to: Cape Town (6–7 daily; 5hr 30min); Durban (1 daily; 18hr 30min); George (6–7 daily; 45min); Johannesburg (1–2 daily; 14hr); Knysna (6–7 daily; 1hr 15min); Oudtshoorn (1–2 daily; 1hr 15min); Plettenberg Bay (6–7 daily; 2hr 15min); Port Elizabeth (6–7 daily; 4hr 30min); Pretoria (1–2 daily; 15hr).
Oudtshoorn to: Cape Town (3 weekly; 6hr 15min); George (3–4 daily; 1hr 30min); Johannesburg (1–2 daily; 13hr 30min); Knysna (1–2 daily; 2hr); Mossel Bay (1–2 daily; 45min); Pretoria (1–2 daily; 14hr 30min).
Paarl to: Beaufort West (4–5 daily; 5hr); Cape Town (4 weekly; 1hr 30min); Durban (2 daily; 18hr); East London (daily; 11hr 30min); Johannesburg (4–5 daily; 14hr); Pretoria (4–5 daily; 15hr).
Plettenberg Bay to: Cape Town (6–7 daily; 7hr 30min); Durban (1 daily; 16hr); George (6–7 daily; 1hr 30min); Knysna (6–7 daily; 1hr 30min); Mossel Bay (6–7 daily; 2hr 15min); Port Elizabeth (6–7 daily; 2hr 30min).

Baz Bus

The Baz Bus travels once daily in both directions along the N2 between Cape Town and Port Elizabeth. You can be let off anywhere along the national road, and the bus pulls into all the major destinations along the way (with the notable exception of Storms River Mouth); see "Travel details" for Chapter 1 on p.178.

Domestic flights

George to: Cape Town (2–4 daily; 1hr); Durban (daily; 2hr 15min); Johannesburg (2 daily; 1hr 30min); Port Elizabeth (3 weekly; 1hr).

The Northern Cape

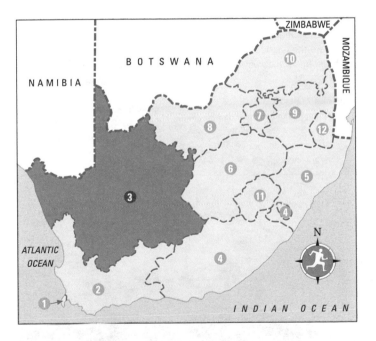

CHAPTER 3 # Highlights

＊ **The Big Hole** The vast crater that dominates Kimberley is an awesome testament to South Africa's pioneer diamond hunters. See p.323

＊ **Kgalagadi Transfrontier Park** Discover lion, gemsbok and suricate among the parched red sand dunes of the Kalahari. See p.340

＊ **Augrabies Falls** Africa's second-biggest waterfall, where the Orange River thunders into an echoing gorge. See p.345

＊ **Pella Mission** One of the country's most improbable sights, a towering yellow cathedral in the middle of a tiny, mission village. See p.347

＊ **Namaqualand flowers** In August and September the veld puts on a superb natural floral display. See p.348

＊ **Driving down the N7** The province's most scenic drive stretches south from Springbok through rocky mountains and peaceful *dorps*. See p.352

＊ **Richtersveld Transfrontier Park** South Africa's only mountain desert, a hot, dry and forbidding place which can only be explored by 4WD or by drifting down the Orange River in an inflatable canoe. See p.359

▲ Pella Mission

The Northern Cape

The vast **Northern Cape**, the largest and most dispersed of South Africa's provinces, is not an easy region to tackle as a visitor. From the lonely Atlantic coast to **Kimberley**, the provincial capital on its eastern border with the Free State, it covers over one-third of the nation's landmass, an area dominated by heat, aridity, empty spaces and huge travelling distances. The miracles of the desert are the main attraction – improbable swaths of flowers, diamonds dug from the dirt and wild animals roaming the dunes.

The most significant of these surprises is the **Orange** (or Oranje) **River**, flowing from the Lesotho Highlands to the Atlantic, where it marks South Africa's border with Namibia. The river, often with parched land stretching for hundreds of kilometres on either side, separates the **Kalahari** and **Great Karoo** – the two sparsely populated semi-desert ecosystems that fill the interior of the Northern Cape. It was by the Orange that **diamonds** were first discovered in the 1860s, although it was in the Vaal River's alluvial deposits and the nearby dry diggings around Kimberley that the story of diamonds would unfold in its most compelling detail.

Large **irrigation schemes** have created a stretch of incongruous green along the course of the Orange, principally around the isolated northern centre of **Upington**, the main town in the Kalahari region. A small but important town, Upington acts as a major gateway to the magnificent **Kgalagadi Transfrontier Park**, one of the finest game-viewing parks in South Africa, and the smaller **Augrabies Falls National Park**, where the Orange plunges dramatically into a large granite gorge.

In **Namaqualand**, on the western side of the province, the brief winter rains produce one of nature's truly glorious transformations, when in August and September the land is carpeted by a magnificent display of **wild flowers**. A similar display of blossoming succulents can be seen at the little-visited **Richtersveld Transfrontier Park**, a mountain desert tucked around a loop in the Orange River, either side of the Namibian border.

Despite these impressive natural attractions, the most traffic to the Northern Cape is in its southeastern corner, through which the two main routes between Johannesburg and Cape Town, the **N1** and the **N12**, pass. While the N12 provides a good opportunity to spend a day or so in Kimberley, neither route offers particularly inspiring scenery or sights, and so the southeast of the province isn't covered in this book. A less obvious option is to take the **N14** from Johannesburg through Upington, passing the atmospheric old mission station at **Kuruman**, and on to **Springbok** and the scenic **N7** to Cape Town. This route is around 400km longer than the N1 or N12 and, while the N14 doesn't offer respite from long, empty landscapes, the sights on the way are more

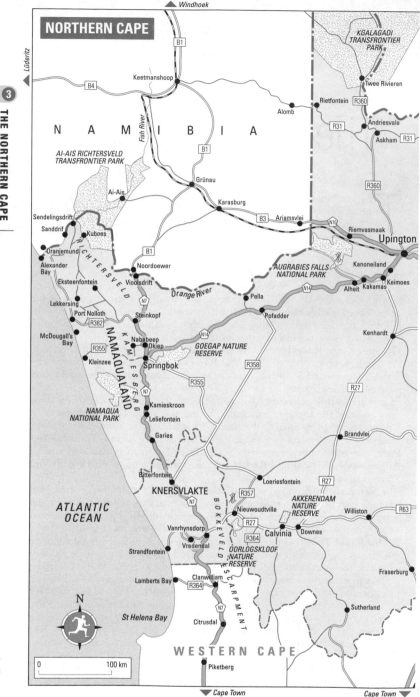

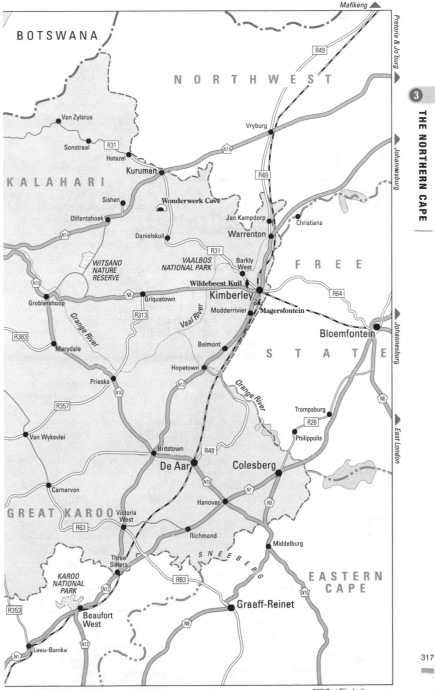

interesting; it also puts the Augrabies, Kgalagadi and Richtersveld national parks within striking distance.

Getting around by **public transport** can be a pain. While the main towns of Kimberley, Springbok and Upington lie on Intercape's bus routes (with connections to Windhoek in Namibia), many services arrive and depart at night and thus miss the scenery. Minibus taxis cover most destinations several times a day during the week, but are much reduced or nonexistent at weekends. Taxis don't serve the national parks (take an organized tour instead). As ever, early starts (6–7am) are best. Details of the most useful routes are given in the text.

Some history

The history of the Northern Cape area is intimately linked to the **San**, South Africa's first people whose hunter-gatherer lifestyle and remarkable adaptations to desert life exert a powerful fascination. Although no genuine vestiges of the San way of life can be found in South Africa (only tiny pockets remain in the Namibian and Botswanan sections of the Kalahari desert), their heritage is most visible in the countless examples of **rock art** across the province, and to a lesser extent in their ancient legends and place names. The movement of Africans from the north and east, and Europeans from the southwest, drove the San from their hunting grounds and eventually to extinction; yet for both sets of newcomers, the semi-desert of the Karoo and the Kalahari at first appeared to offer little more than hopelessness and heartbreaking horizons. What it did provide – wealth under the dusty ground – the Europeans pursued without restraint, beginning in 1685 with an expedition into Namaqualand to mine for copper, led by **Governor Simon van der Stel** soon after the Dutch first established their settlement in the Cape. The other Europeans who made an early impression on the province were **trekboers**, Dutch burghers freed from the employment of the Dutch East India Company in the Cape who wanted to farm new lands away from the authoritarian company rule, and **missionaries**, who established a framework of settlement and communication used by all who came after.

Within a few years of the discovery of **diamonds** in the area, a settlement of unprecedented size had grown up around Kimberley. The town soon boasted more trappings of civilization than most of the southern hemisphere, with public libraries, electric streetlights and tramways, as well as South Africa's first urban "location" for Africans and coloureds. The British authorities in the Cape were quick to annexe the new diamond fields – a move which didn't endear them to either the Orange Free State or the mainly coloured **Griqua** people

Diamonds are forever

Diamonds originate as carbon particles in the earth's mantle, which are subjected to such high pressure and temperature that they crystallize to form diamonds. Millions of years ago the molten rock, or magma, in the mantle burst through weak points in the earth's crust as volcanoes, and it is in the pipe of cooled magma – called **kimberlite**, after Kimberley – that diamonds are found. Finding kimberlite, however, isn't necessarily a licence to print money – in every one hundred tonnes there will be about twenty carats (4g) of diamonds.

The word "carat" derives from the carob bean – dried beans were used as a measure of weight. (Carat has a different meaning in the context of gold, where it is a measure of purity.) De Beers estimates that fifty million pieces of diamond jewellery are bought each year, which represents a lot of marriage proposals.

(see box, p.563), who both claimed this ill-defined region. It was no surprise, therefore, that at the outbreak of the **Anglo–Boer War** in 1899, rich and strategic Kimberley was one of the first towns besieged by the Boer armies, and many reminders of the war can still be seen in the area.

Kimberley and around

The **N12** highway, running from Johannesburg through **Kimberley** and then down to meet the N1 link to Cape Town, is the main reason most visitors find themselves in this area. Despite being the provincial capital, Kimberley does not really act as a gateway to the Northern Cape – it's far nearer to Bloemfontein and the Free State. For those passing through, however, there is enough in the area to justify spending a day or two here, especially if you're interested in the romantic history of South Africa's **Diamond Fields**. The biggest draw is Kimberley itself, but trips to the nearby **Anglo–Boer War battlefields** and the **alluvial diamond diggings** around the Vaal River are well worth the effort.

Kimberley

Although it's a provincial capital and the historic centre of production of one of the world's most valuable materials, **KIMBERLEY** itself is neither large nor glamorous. During the diamond rush, it was the fastest-growing city in the southern hemisphere and **Cecil Rhodes** held in his grip not only the fabulously wealthy diamond industry, but the heart and mind of the British Empire – yet status and sophistication have been draining from Kimberley ever since. Even the all-controlling **De Beers Group** (sometimes called the "grandfather" of Kimberley for the number of people it has directly and indirectly employed) closed its Kimberley mines in 2005 as part of a process to streamline the company, and the city lives in the chilly shadow of the day when the diamonds dry up altogether.

However, Kimberley's legacy gives it an historic flavour few other cities in South Africa can match. It's worth spending a few hours seeking out some of the many old buildings, not forgetting to peer into the depths of the **Big Hole**, the remarkable, hand-dug chasm taking up almost as much land area as the city's central business district (CBD).

Arrival, information and city transport

Kimberley's **airport** (℡053 861 4015) lies 7km to the west along the N8 Upington road. There's no regular transport into town, so phone for a cab (see p.322). **Intercity buses** stop outside the tourist office, which is handy when arriving on overnight Greyhound and Translux services from Cape Town, but to be avoided on daytime departures from Cape Town or Jo'burg, which arrive at night when the place is deserted. You can arrange for a hotel to pick you up, or ask to be dropped off at one of the hotels along the N12 (Bishops

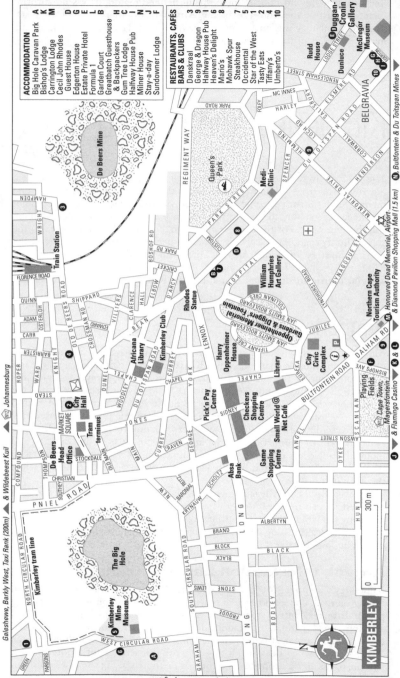

KIMBERLEY

ACCOMMODATION

Big Hole Caravan Park	A
Bishop's Lodge	K
Carrington Lodge	M
Cecil John Rhodes	
Guest House	D
Edgerton House	G
Estate Private Hotel	E
Formula 1	L
Garden Court	B
Greatbatch Guesthouse	
& Backpackers	H
Gum Tree Lodge	C
Halfway House Pub	I
Milner House	N
Stay-a-day	J
Sundowner Lodge	F

RESTAURANTS, CAFÉS BARS & CLUBS

Danskraal	3
George & Dragon	9
Halfway House Pub	6
Heaven's Delight	8
Mario's	
Mohawk Spur Steakhouse	7
Occidental	5
Star of the West	1
Tasty Eats	2
Tiffany's	4
Umberto's	10

De Beers Mine

Train Station

Kimberley tram line

The Big Hole

Kimberley Mine Museum

De Beers Head Office

City Hall

Africana Library

Kimberley Club

Rhodes Statue

Harry Oppenheimer House

Library

William Humphries Art Gallery

Oppenheimer Memorial Gardens & Diggers' Fountain

City Civic Complex

Pick 'n Pay Centre

Checkers Shopping Centre

Small World @ Net Café

Game Shopping Centre

Absa Bank

Northern Cape Tourism Authority

Flamingo Casino

Playing Fields

Medi-Clinic

Queen's Park

Rudd House

Dunluce

McGregor Museum

Duggan-Cronin Gallery

BELGRAVIA

© & Bloemfontein ▲

Ⓝ Bultfontein & Du Toitspan Mines ▶

Ⓜ Honoured Dead Memorial, Airport & Diamond Pavilion Shopping Mall (1.5 km) ▶

Ⓛ Cape Town, Magersfontein ▶

Ⓙ ▶

Galeshewe, Barkly West, Taxi Rank (200m) ▲ & Wildebeest Kuil ▲

0   300 m

Avenue) just south of the centre, or alight at the Ultra City service station 6km north of town, which is a much safer place to call a cab. The **train station** is just off Quinn Street on the northeastern edge of town; for train times, see the box on p.322.

Kimberley's helpful tourist office, the **Diamantveld Visitor Centre**, is at 121 Bultfontein Rd (Mon–Fri 8am–5pm, Sat 8am–noon; ℡053 832 7298, ℮tourism@solplaatje.org.za). The staff can provide city plans, lists of places to stay, detailed driving itineraries in the province, information on local tours (see box, p.327) and self-guided walking tours of Kimberley. For more information about the province, particularly wildlife parks and reserves, visit the **Northern Cape Tourism Authority** on Dalham Road, a few hundred metres east of the tourist office (Mon–Fri 7.30am–4pm; ℡053 832 2656, ⓦwww .northerncape.org.za).

A short history of the Diamond Fields

Once you have found your first diamond, you will never give up looking.

Digger proverb

The area now known as the Diamond Fields was once unpromising farmland, marked by occasional *koppies* inhabited by pioneer farmers and the Griquas, an independent people of mixed race (see box, p.563). In 1866 this changed forever, when a 15-year-old boy noticed a shiny white pebble on the banks of the Orange River near Hopetown, about 120km southwest of Kimberley. Just as word of that discovery was spreading, another Hopetown resident, Schalk van Niekerk, acquired from a Griqua shepherd a massive 83.5-carat diamond. These two stones became known, respectively, as "Eureka" and "The Star of South Africa"; the latter was described at the time – with some justification – by the British Colonial Secretary as the "rock on which the future success of South Africa will be built". Certainly in the short term, the discoveries provoked wild optimism: thousands of prospectors made the gruelling trek across the Karoo to sift through the alluvial deposits along the banks of the Orange and Vaal rivers, and by 1873 there were an estimated fifty thousand people living in the area.

Although plenty of diamonds were found in the rivers, prospectors also began scratching around in the dry land between them, encouraged by tales of diamonds found in farmhouse bricks made from local earth. Two of the most promising "dry diggings" were on a farm owned by two brothers, Johannes Nicolas and Diederick Arnoldus de Beer. In 1871 the brothers sold the farm, which they had bought a few years previously for £50, to prospectors for the sum of £6300. The two sites subsequently became the Kimberley Mine, or **Big Hole**, and the **De Beers Mine**, situated on either side of the centre of Kimberley. The Big Hole was the focus of the most frenetic mining activity of the early years, and the shantytown that grew up around it, New Rush, was the origin of the present city.

Kimberley in those days was a heady, rugged place to live, with little authority or structure, but with prizes rich enough to attract bold men with big ideas. Of these, two very different, if equally ambitious, men rose to prominence in the new settlement. **Barney Barnato**, a flamboyant Cockney, established his power base at the Kimberley Mine, while **Cecil Rhodes** (see p.325), a parson's son who had come out to join his brother in South Africa to improve his health, gradually took control of the De Beers Mine. The power struggle between the two men was intense, culminating in the formation in 1888 of the De Beers Consolidated Mines Limited, an agreement involving the transfer from Rhodes to Barnato of over £5 million, an astronomical sum in those days. This consolidation laid the foundation for De Beers' monopoly of the diamond industry in South Africa.

Moving on from Kimberley

South African Express and South African Airlink, both based at the airport and with the same reservations numbers (☎053 838 2120 or 053 838 3337), operate **flights** to Johannesburg and Cape Town respectively. **Trains** (station ☎053 838 2734) run daily to Cape Town (9.15pm), Mafikeng (7.30am) and Johannesburg via Klerksdorp and Potchefstroom (3.50am; with another service Fri & Sun 9.15pm). There's also a weekly service to Durban via Bloemfontein (Tues 12.03pm), and a Bloemfontein service (Mon, Thurs & Sat 4.45am; Tues noon).

Information and tickets for the three main **intercity bus** companies (Intercape, Greyhound and Translux) are available at the Tickets for Africa bureau inside the Diamantveld Visitor Centre (Mon–Fri 6am–8pm, Sat 8am–1pm; ☎053 832 6040); most buses depart from outside or from the Shell garage nearly opposite. Intercape services go to Upington (Fri & Sun 11.40am) and Bloemfontein (Thurs & Sat 12.45pm), while Greyhound has a daily service to Pretoria and Jo'burg (7am), as does Translux (6am). Big Sky (☎053 832 2007) also run a weekly bus to Bloemfontein (Sun 6.30pm) and Upington (Fri 4.15pm), and SA Roadlink (☎051 430 9061) has a daily service to Jo'burg (1am).

Minibus taxis operate from Pniel Road (the northern extension of Bultfontein Road), 1.5km from the tourist office. To be sure of a ride in daylight, arrive at 6.30am (7am winter); most destinations also have early afternoon departures, but on these you risk being dropped off at night. Except to Barkly West, fares are paid at an office on Pniel Road beside the long-distance rank.

There are a couple of reliable **metered-taxi** outfits: AA Taxis (☎053 861 4015) and Rikkis (☎053 842 1764).

When moving around town, note that many **street names** are written on the curbside rather than on signs at eyelevel.

Accommodation

The bulk of the town's hotels, guesthouses and B&Bs lie in the southern suburbs, most within a kilometre or two of the centre. The most atmospheric places – occupying historic buildings – are clustered in and around the upmarket **Belgravia** suburb. Note that rates tend to drop by anything from ten to forty percent at weekends. Most hotels have safe parking.

Hotels and guesthouses

Bishop's Lodge 9 Bishops Ave ☎053 831 7876, ⓦwww.bishopslodge.co.za. Close to the tourist office, this quiet modern affair offers spotless twin rooms and keenly priced self-catering apartments, plus a suite with wheelchair access. There's a swimming pool, but no meals. ❷

Carrington Lodge 60 Carrington Rd, at the corner with Oliver Rd ☎053 831 6448, ⓦwww.carringtonlodge.co.za. A friendly and popular guesthouse on the edge of Belgravia, with two pools and pleasant garden with braai area. The stylish rooms have Afrikaner furniture, a/c and phones, while ramps provide good wheelchair access. Book ahead on weekdays. Good value. ❸

Cecil John Rhodes Guest House 138 Du Toitspan Rd ☎053 830 2500, ⓦwww.ceciljohnrhodes.co.za. The most central of the historic guesthouses, built

in 1895, with seven airy and elegantly furnished rooms with all mod cons, and a shady tea garden (dinner on request) facing the road. ❹

Edgerton House 5 Egerton Rd ☎053 831 1150, ⓦwww.edgertonhouse.co.za. An ornate Belgravia option in an attractive black-and-white Edwardian house, now a National Monument, kitted out with crystal chandeliers and gold-plated bathroom fittings. There are thirteen rooms, plus a pool and tea room; expensive dinners on request. ❹

Estate Private Hotel 7 Lodge Rd ☎053 832 2668, ⓦwww.theestate.co.za. Seven wheelchair-friendly rooms with all mod cons in the Oppenheimers' former Belgravia home, open to visitors by day (see p.326). There's also a pool, tea garden and restaurant. ❹

Garden Court 120 Du Toitspan Rd ☎053 833 1751, ⓦwww.southernsun.com. The town's largest hotel has bright, well-appointed rooms over six floors, including one wheelchair-friendly room. Sizeable discounts at weekends. ❹

Formula 1 Memorial Drive (N12), 1500m south of the tourist office ☎053 831 2552, ⓦwww .hotelformula1.co.za. The rooms are the chain's usual diminutive prefab units, each with a double bed, bunk and TV. Prices are per room (good value for doubles and triples). Breakfast is extra. It's a safe place to be dropped at if you're arriving by bus at night. There's a *Choctaw Spur Steakhouse* adjacent. ❸

Halfway House Pub Du Toitspan Rd. at the corner with Egerton Rd ☎053 831 6324. Large and airy, if basic, en-suite rooms around a paved beer garden behind the historic boozer, handy for crashing after sampling the pub's nocturnal delights. ❷

Milner House 31 Milner St ☎053 831 6405, ⓦwww.milnerhouse.co.za. Another Belgravia guesthouse, this one more down-to-earth than the others, with six comfortable rooms and a swimming pool. ❸

Sundowner Lodge 1 Bishops Ave ☎053 831 1145, ⒺSundowner@telkomsa.net. Within shouting distance of the tourist office, this friendly family-run place has a vaguely colonial feeling (perhaps it's the boggle-eyed wildlife trophies adorning the walls), and offers fourteen huge rooms in rows of chalets. ❸

Campsites and budget lodging

Big Hole Caravan Park West Circular Rd ☎053 830 6322. The only central campsite, located among the old mine heaps over the road from the Big Hole. Lush, neat and relatively quiet, with a pool, although the shade from the trees isn't generous. The office is open daily 6am–4pm. ❶

Greatbatch Guesthouse & Backpackers 3 Egerton Rd ☎053 832 1113, ⓦwww .greatbatchguesthouse.co.za. The sole backpackers accommodation within walking distance of the centre occupies the former home of the architect of Dunluce and other notable Kimberley buildings. The dorm is a little cramped, but there is a pool and shared kitchen. Dorms ❶, rooms ❷

Gum Tree Lodge Boshof Rd (R64) ☎053 832 8577, ⓦwww.gumtreelodge.com. Large backpackers' lodge inconveniently located 5km east of town. Several spartan dorms and more comfortable self-catering units are available, while a swimming pool and "jungle playground" are popular with kids (the place gets a little hectic if there's a group in). There's an inexpensive restaurant next door. Dorms and rooms ❷

Stay-a-day 72 Lawson St ☎053 832 7239, Ⓔstayaday@lantic.net. Planned renovations should spruce up the currently rather stark rooms – some of which are en suite and wheelchair accessible – at this friendly place. There are also a couple of self-catering apartments. Run as a revenue earner by a Dutch Reformed Church orphanage, it's 1km south of the tourist office in the residential New Park district. ❷

The City

Many of Kimberley's main sights lie on or near **Du Toitspan Road**, which slices diagonally across the city centre and becomes one of the main arteries out of town to the southeast. The must-see **Big Hole** lies just west of the centre, while the more open central business district (CBD) lies to the south of Lennox Road. The fact that the Big Hole is underground doesn't make orientation immediately easy; a useful landmark is the stern-looking skyscraper, **Harry Oppenheimer House** (often referred to as HOH), near the tourist office.

The Big Hole: Kimberley Mine Museum

Although the 500-metre-wide **Big Hole**, just west of the city centre, is neither the only nor even the biggest hole in Kimberley, it remains the city's principal attraction. In 1871, with diamonds known to be in the area (see box, p.321), a group of workers known as the Red Cap Party were scratching around at the base of **Colesberg koppie**, a small hill on the De Beers brothers' farm. The story goes that they sent one of their cooks to the top of the hill as a punishment for being drunk, telling him not to return until he'd found a diamond. The unnamed servant duly came back with a peace offering, and within two years there were over fifty thousand people in the area frantically turning Colesberg *koppie* inside out. In its heyday, tens of thousands of miners swarmed over the mine to work their ten-square-metre claim, and a network of ropes and pipes crisscrossed the surface; each day saw lives lost and fortunes either discovered or squandered. Once the mining could go no further from the surface, a shaft was dug to allow further excavations beneath it to a depth of over 800m. Incredibly, the hole was dug to a depth of 240m entirely by pick and shovel, and remains one of the largest manmade excavations in the world. By 1914, when De Beers closed the mine, some 22.6 million tonnes of earth had been removed, yielding over 13.6 million carats (2722kg) of diamonds.

The only official way to see the Big Hole is from inside the **Kimberley Mine Museum** (daily 8am–6pm; R55; ⓦ www.thebighole.co.za), spread out along the western side of the hole along West Circular Road. You can take a delightfully rickety, open-sided **tram** there from the City Hall (hourly 9.15am–4.15pm, returning on the hour 9am–4pm; R7 one-way).

The museum has undergone a R52-million renovation and gives a comprehensive insight into Kimberley's main claim to fame. The Big Hole itself is viewed from a suspended platform, from which you can peer down into nothingness, where once mountains were moved in the quest for wealth. On the opposite side of the crater, the now diminutive outline of the city is almost swallowed up by the size and silence of the hollow below. An informative film puts it all into context, as do other displays, from a re-creation of a nineteenth-century mine shaft to a vault full of real diamonds – including the original "Eureka" diamond (see box, p.321). Outside the museum, the **Old Town** (which you can wander around without paying the R55 entry fee) consists of a large collection of **historic buildings**, many originating from the days of Rhodes and Barnato; they were moved here from the city centre when development and demolition threatened. With old shops, churches, a pub, banks and sundry other period institutions, including Barney Barnato's Boxing Academy and a skittle alley, there's enough here to create a fairly complete settlement, and most of the fixtures, fittings and artefacts are genuine. One of the more engaging features is an area where you can buy a bucket of alluvial river diggings (R20) and sift through it on old sorting tables, in the hope of finding one of the mock diamonds planted among the gravel. Your chances of striking lucky are about one in five – much better odds than the original miners faced.

Market Square and around

At the heart of the city centre is **Market Square**, dominated by the white, Corinthian-style **City Hall**. During the early diamond days, the square was the hub of buying and selling. It was also the scene of two occasions significant in South Africa's history: the public crushing of gold-bearing rock from the Witwatersrand that persuaded Rhodes, Barnato and others to further their investments in gold-mining; and the departure in 1890 of the Pioneer Column, which effectively established "white" Rhodesia by pursuing Rhodes' expansionist claims to the territory north of the Limpopo. Around the square, the sense of movement and commerce is perpetuated by a large taxi rank and an assortment of scruffy but colourful stalls and traders.

One block west of Market Square along the tram line, at 36 Stockdale St, lies the head office of **De Beers**, a dignified but unremarkable old building rather swallowed up by the city around it. You can read the brass plates by the door, but the building is not open to the public.

The Kimberley Club and the Africana Library

Not far southwest of Market Square, at 70–72 Du Toitspan Rd, is the two-storey **Kimberley Club**, founded in 1881 by the new settlement's movers and shakers. The club was modelled on London's gentlemen's clubs, but its colourful, enterprising members made the place dynamic rather than stuffy. It was claimed that there were more millionaires to the square metre here than any other place in the world, and acceptance into the club was allegedly a significant carrot in Rhodes' wooing of Barnato in 1888 – together with a cheque for £5 million. The present building – the third on the site – was completed in 1896 and would have been known by Rhodes, whose presence dominates even today, with countless portraits, busts and other memorabilia of the man in all parts of the building. As well as leather armchairs in the smoking lounge and marble in the hallway, there are plenty of fine antiques and a few quirky pieces, such as a weighing chair presented to the club by Lord Randolph Churchill, Winston Churchill's father. It's possible to look around or go for a drink in the **bar**, though you'll get a much less chilly welcome if you introduce yourself at the reception and respect the club's rules – which include no jeans or T-shirts, and no women in the bar.

Across the road is the small but engrossing **Africana Library** (Mon–Fri 8am–12.45pm & 1.30–4.30pm), specializing in historical material relevant to Kimberley and the Northern Cape. Opened in 1887, it retains many original features, and one of the librarians will show you around if you ask nicely. The excellent Kimberley Ghost Tour (see box, p.327) visits the library; although you don't enter the building, you'll hear about the restless spirit of its first librarian, whose presence explains why books and files keep getting mysteriously muddled.

The CBD

At the junction of Du Toitspan and Lennox roads stands a statue of **Cecil Rhodes**. He is portrayed astride a horse, and the tributes around the plinth are rich with the swagger common to most Rhodes memorials. The CBD area begins across Lennox Street, where the **Oppenheimer Memorial Gardens** contain a bust of mining magnate Sir Ernest Oppenheimer and the **Diggers' Fountain**; the latter depicts five miners holding aloft a massive sieve, and looks

---

Cecil John Rhodes

When **Cecil Rhodes** first arrived in the Kimberley Diamond Fields he was a sickly 18-year-old, sent out to join his brother for the sake of his health. Soon making money buying up claims, he returned to Britain to attend Oxford University, where his illnesses returned and he was given six months to live. He came back out to South Africa, where he was able to improve both his health and his business standing, allowing him to return to Oxford and graduate in 1881, by which time he had already founded the **De Beers Mining Company** and been elected an MP in the Cape Parliament.

Within a decade, Rhodes controlled ninety percent of the world's diamond production and was champing at the bit to expand his mining interests north into Africa, with the British Empire in tow. With much cajoling, bullying, brinkmanship and obfuscation in his dealing with imperial governments and African chiefs alike, Rhodes brought the regions north of the Limpopo under the control of his South African Company. This territory – now Zimbabwe and Zambia – became known as Rhodesia in 1895, the same year as a Rhodes-backed invasion of the Transvaal Republic, the Jameson Raid, failed humiliatingly. Rhodes was forced to resign as prime minister of the Cape Colony, a post he had assumed in 1890 at the age of 37, while the Boers and the British slid towards war. He spent the first part of the war in besieged Kimberley, trying to organize the defences and bickering publicly with the British commander. A year after the end of the war, aged only 49 and unmarried, Rhodes died at Muizenberg near Cape Town; he was buried in the Matopos Hills near Bulawayo in Zimbabwe.

▲ The Diggers' Fountain, Kimberley

particularly impressive when floodlit after dusk. The tall building overlooking the gardens is **Harry Oppenheimer House** (HOH), the offices of De Beers' DTC (Diamond Trading Company; not open to the public), on the upper floors of which all of the company's South African-mined diamonds are assessed for caratage, colour, clarity and shape. To allow this to take place in the best natural light, the building faces south, with special windows to eliminate glare; there are no windows on the other faces other than small ones along the stairwell.

On the opposite side of the gardens to HOH, in the Civic Centre, lies an unexpected gem, the **William Humphreys Art Gallery** (Mon–Fri 8am–4.45pm, Sat 10am–4.45pm, Sun & holidays 2–4.45pm; R5), South Africa's only Grade One art gallery. Although dominated by European Old Masters when it opened in 1952, the collection has always moved with the times and

Kimberley tours

While the cessation of operations at the De Beers mines has brought to an end the fascinating underground tours of a working diamond mine, Kimberley still offers a series of informative and entertaining local tours. The Diamantveld Visitor Centre maintains a list of accredited guides; alternatively, contact Diamond Tours Unlimited (℡053 861 4983 or 083 265 4795, ⊕www.diamondtours.co.za) or In-Roads Tours (℡083 398 8176), both of which are recommended.

Ghost tours

As the light fades in early evening and the city centre empties, the many restless spirits produced by over a century of surreptitious diamond wheeling and dealing begin to make their presence felt. If you're brave enough to hear the stories, or simply like the idea of poking around some of Kimberley's most interesting buildings after hours, join a **Ghost Tour** (R80) – you'll be shown scenes of strange encounters at places such as the Africana Library, the Regimental headquarters and the spooky Rudd House in Belgravia. Tours begin just before sunset at the Honoured Dead Memorial, and last three to four hours.

Township tours

Kimberley was the first settlement in South Africa to establish "locations" on its fringes to house the African and coloured labourers working in the mines. A tour of **Galeshewe**, named after a rebellious nineteenth-century chief, offers an insight into a typical modern South African township with its mix of shacks, simple government houses and the more ostentatious homes of locals-made-good. In contrast to townships attached to places like Jo'burg and Cape Town, Galeshewe has a very unintimidating atmosphere, allowing an easy introduction to township life, including *spaza* shops, African restaurants, *shebeens* and music. The tour also takes in some alternative historic sights – including the grave of Sol Plaatje (see box, p.658) and the house where Robert Sobukwe (see box, p.405), founder of the Pan-African Congress, lived under house arrest after his release from Robben Island in 1969. Most tours finish with the post-apartheid **Northern Cape Provincial Legislature** complex – an extraordinary construction combining elements of traditional African design (the conical tower is a delight) with silver polygonal slabs; it occupies part of the "buffer strip" that used to separate black and white communities.

Tours in the Kimberley area

Organized tours of the area around Kimberley include visits to the controlled area on the banks of the Vaal River, on the fringes of **Barkly West**, 35km northwest of Kimberley, where **alluvial diamond digging** takes place; **Kamfersdam**, a reservoir north along the N12 with 180 bird species to its name, including a resident flock of several thousand flamingoes; the Anglo-Boer War battlefield at **Magersfontein** (see p.331); and a series of **archeological sites**, including San rock engravings at Wildebeest Kuil (see p.330).

now houses an impressively well-balanced representation of South African art, with traditional and contemporary work, including some excellent modern sculpture. The gallery was one of the first places in the world to display San **rock paintings** as works of art rather than museum pieces. At the back of the gallery is a very pleasant **tea room**, the *Palette*, which serves breakfasts, light lunches and snacks on a terrace beside a small garden.

Just south of the CBD, in the middle of a roundabout where Dalham Road and Memorial Drive meet, is the **Honoured Dead Memorial**, a monument to the victims of the Kimberley siege during the Anglo-Boer War, and also the tomb of 27 British soldiers. Beside is the British gun known as **Long Cecil**, used in the siege; it was built in the De Beers' workshops to respond to the Boers' Long Tom cannon.

Belgravia

About 1km southeast of the CBD, along Du Toitspan Road, lies **Belgravia**, the residential suburb where most of Kimberley's wealthy families lived. A stroll around these streets is a good way to get a feel for the more refined side of the diamond age. The focus of the area is at the junction of Du Toitspan and Egerton roads, where you'll find the historic **Halfway House Pub**. Originally located on the site now occupied by the McGregor Museum, it was shifted in 1897 when the museum was built. The pub takes its name from its location halfway between the De Beers and Bultfontein mines, and gained fame as a drive-in (or, in those days, ride-in) pub, a custom started by Cecil Rhodes who liked to tipple while in the saddle. Nowadays you blow your horn to attract the bartender.

Across the road, the fabulous **McGregor Museum** (Mon–Sat 9am–5pm, Sun 2–5pm, holidays 10am–5pm; R12; ☎053 839 2700, ⓦwww.museumsnc.co.za), named after an early mayor of Kimberley, is housed in a magnificent Victorian mansion. Built in 1897 as a sanatorium, but never used as one, it saw action during the 1899 siege of Kimberley when it served as Cecil Rhodes' headquarters, and was later a hotel and a convent school. The highlight here is the extensive and imaginative **Ancestors Display**, which draws on archeological evidence to piece together an absorbing and – unusual still in South Africa – well-balanced exhibition on the various ancestral roots of today's inhabitants of the Northern Cape, going right back to evidence of the earliest hominids millions of years ago. There's also an evocative section on the siege of Kimberley, including two rooms with period furniture where Rhodes stayed during the siege, and a sensitive display tracing the implementation of apartheid and subsequent resistance to it.

Adjacent to the museum is the **Duggan-Cronin Gallery** (Mon–Fri 9am–5pm; R10), which includes over 8000 endearingly unsophisticated photographs portraying the lifestyles of the indigenous people of South Africa between the two world wars. They were taken by Alfred Duggan-Cronin, a nightwatchman for De Beers.

Still in Belgravia, you can visit a trio of restored houses, all on Lodge Road: **Rudd House** (also called "The Bungalow") at no. 5 was the mansion of mining magnate and partner of Rhodes, Charles Dunnell Rudd; at no. 10, **Dunluce** is an elegant late-Victorian home in Hollywood's favoured "haunted house" style. To see inside either house, make arrangements with the museum (weekdays only; R20). Easier to visit is the Edwardian **estate** at no. 7, birthplace of Harry Oppenheimer and the family's last Kimberley home before they moved to Johannesburg in 1915. It's now a hotel, best visited at lunchtime for its tea garden and restaurant. These and many other historic homes and points of interest are included in the **Belgravia Historical Walk**, which you can do self-guided or accompanied; details from the tourist office.

Eating, drinking and nightlife

Beyond the familiar range of franchised steakhouses, including *Mohawk Spur Steakhouse* at the *Garden Court* on Du Toitspan Road, Kimberley offers a reasonable selection of locally run, mid-priced **restaurants**, many with good **wine** lists, too. Apart from a handful of historic **pubs**, which can be entertaining for their atmosphere and clientele (use a cab at night), there's little in the way of **nightlife**. For live music, ask at the tourist office for *Destiny*, a township nightclub that hosts old-time jazz bands. Those with bursting wallets can relieve themselves at Flamingo Casino (☎053 830 2600) on Transvaal Road (the N12), 6km north of town.

THE NORTHERN CAPE | Kimberley

Restaurants, cafés, bars and clubs

Danskraal Old De Beers Rd. A popular dance hall for almost a century, particularly on Fri nights. Sat tend to be taken over by the satellite TV sports crowd, while Wed may feature drinks specials.

George & Dragon Du Toitspan Rd. Popular English theme pub and sports bar. The food – from gammon steaks to *bobotie* – tends to be rather hit or miss, but the portions are large and prices reasonable. Also features the town's best selection of draught beers.

Halfway House Pub Corner of Du Toitspan and Egerton rds. Cecil Rhodes' old refreshment stop, known as "the Half" and still a favourite for its unpretentious atmosphere. There are more tables in a paved courtyard out the back, and two pool tables. Also serves cheap and decent British pub lunches with a nicely old-fashioned twist. Closed Sun.

Heaven's Delight *Victoria Guest Lodge*, 16 West Circular Rd. Opposite the Big Hole, this handy café does good snacks, a huge and aptly named "Big Hole breakfast" (R40), and gorgeous home-made desserts, including cinnamon pancakes. Licensed. Closed Sun.

Mario's 159 Du Toitspan Rd. Bright, cheery and easy-going Italian place that's justifiably one of the most popular restaurants in town, with friendly staff and an extensive menu, ranging from light lunches and pizzas to more elaborate meals

(mains R40–70), and a good if expensive wine list. Closed Sat lunch and all day Sun.

Occidental At the Big Hole. Unlike the other museum buildings in the Old Town, this is a fully functioning bar and restaurant with a good though small menu (try the excellent Karoo lamb chops; mains around R60) and occasional live jazz. Daily 9am–10pm.

Star of the West West Circular Rd, at the corner of North Circular Rd. Kimberley's oldest pub remains a defiantly local dive, complete with characterful locals propping up the bar. It also receives its fair share of tourists, who enjoy drinking a beer or eating a decent, cheap pub meal in the beer garden. Tends to host live bands on Fri or Sat nights. Daily from 10am to way past your bedtime.

Tasty Eats Market Square, facing the tram terminus. No-frills halal meals, including dirt-cheap curries (around R15). Mon–Sat until around 5pm.

Tiffany's *The Savoy* hotel, 15 De Beers Rd. Formerly Kimberley's foremost dining experience, this formal place lacks windows and is ageing fast, though the food – mostly steaks and ribs, with a couple of vegetarian dishes loosely based on Chinese – is still good, albeit a little pricey (mains R80–100). Daily lunch & dinner.

Umberto's Du Toitspan Rd, next to *Halfway House Pub*. A regular Italian restaurant serving decent pizza and pasta – its main draw is a pleasant roof terrace. Closed Sun.

Listings

Banks Quickest for changing money is the foreign exchange counter at Absa, corner of Bultfontein Rd and Long St. Standard has branches opposite Absa on Bultfontein Rd, and on Chapel St and Old Main Rd.
Bookshops Bookbin, bottom of Jones St, has a huge selection of secondhand novels. The stationers at Game Shopping Centre sells new titles.
Car rental All the agencies are based at the airport: Avis ☎053 851 1082 or 1083; Budget ☎053 851 1183; Hertz ☎053 830 2200 or

0861 600 136; Imperial ☎053 851 1132; National ☎053 861 2508; and Tempest 053 851 1516.
Cinema Four screens at the cinema in the Pick 'n Pay Centre.
Couriers DHL is at 41 De Beers St, near Quinn St ☎011 921 3666.
Emergencies Call ☎053 831 1954 for an ambulance; for other emergency services, see p.75. The tourist office operates a 24-hr emergency and help line (☎053 861 1483).

Hospitals and doctors Best-equipped is the 24-hr Medi-Clinic, 177 Du Toitspan Rd (☏053 838 1111). There are good doctors at Medicross (☏053 833 2731), corner of Long and Stone sts.
Internet access Small World Net Café, 42 Sidney St, near the tourist office opposite the library (Mon–Fri 8am–6pm, Sat 9am–2pm). There are other Internet cafés in the Game and Pick 'n Pay centres.
Pharmacies Piet Muller Pharmacy, 52 Market Square ☏053 831 1787 (daily to 8.30pm); Medpack, 142 Du Toitspan Rd ☏053 831 1737.
Post The post office is a little east of Market Square.

Shopping For diamond jewellery, try Jewel Box, 18 West Circular Rd next to Victorian Guest Lodge or at the Big Hole, or any of the jewellers along Jones St. The best place for arts and crafts is Africa Now, 37–39 Du Toitspan Rd, close to Jones St (by appointment only; call ☏082 413 6016). There are gift shops at the Big Hole and the McGregor Museum, and antiques at Victorian Guest Lodge. For general shopping, head to the Diamond Pavilion mall, 2km south of the tourist office.
Swimming The open-air Karen Muir Pool is in Queen's Park (Sept–April); the entrance is on Park St, opposite Lyndhurst Rd.

Around Kimberley

A couple of interesting places lie on or near the **R31**, which runs northwest out of Kimberley in the direction of Kuruman: there is some fascinating San rock art at **Wildebeest Kuil**, while the area around **Barkly West** was where some of the first diamond camps sprang up in the 1860s. South of Kimberley along the N12, the mostly unremarkable landscape around **Magersfontein** was the setting for one of the most dramatic campaigns of the Anglo-Boer War.

Wildebeest Kuil

Around 15km from Kimberley along the road to Barkly West is a small *koppie* of ancient andesite rock, **Wildebeest Kuil** (Mon–Fri 9am–6pm, Sat & Sun 10am–4pm; R10, or R15 with recorded audio tour; ⓦwww .wildebeestkuil.itgo.com). This is an important **rock-art** site, unusual in that the images are engraved (rather than painted) and are found on loosely scattered rocks and small boulders, rather than cave walls or overhangs. Coming from Kimberley, you can catch one of the frequent minibus taxis to Barkly West and ask to be dropped at the signposted turning; the site is close by.

There are more than four hundred engravings here, the most recent from the 1800s, the oldest possibly dating back 1000–2000 years. They depict elephant, rhino, dancing human figures and, most commonly of all, the eland, a central shamanic metaphor in San art representing mediation between spirit realms, and also strongly associated with rain. A number of boardwalks have been built to allow access without disturbing the engravings and trained guides from the local community are on hand to show you around. The **visitor centre** at the base of the *koppie* provides an introductory display and shows a video.

Under South Africa's programme of land restitution, ownership of the site has been given to the local **!Xun** and **Khwe San communities**. Originally from Angola and Namibia, they were recruited as trackers by the South African Defence Force during the war fought in those countries in the 1970s and 1980s. When Namibia became independent in 1990, 370 of these soldiers and their families chose to relocate to South Africa. Largely ignored and forgotten thereafter, and subsisting on meagre military pensions, they established various projects to generate income. The most successful of these have been to do with **art**: some vivid and attractively designed ceramics and art work, mostly drawing on traditional San images and motifs, are on sale in the shop.

Alluvial diggings around Barkly West

The small town of **BARKLY WEST**, originally a convenient crossing point of the Vaal River known as Klipdrif, lies 20km further on from Wildebeest Kuil. It was the first important focus of the diamond rush, out of which rose the short-lived **Klipdrif Diggers' Republic**, proclaimed by militant miners when British, Boer and Griqua authorities squabbled about who was to control the area. Later, political representation came in the form of Cecil Rhodes, who was the MP for the town up to and including his time as prime minister of the Cape Colony. The alluvial beds along the river on the fringes of town are still being worked: the best way to explore is to join one of the fascinating insider **tours of the alluvial diggings** with Diamond Tours Unlimited (see box, p.333), on which you meet both the old hand-prospectors and the more modern operators.

Magersfontein

The Anglo-Boer War battlefield at **Magersfontein**, 32km south of Kimberley along the N12, provides a poignant reminder of the area's blood-spattered past. This is where Boer forces put trench warfare into effect against British troops, with devastating results (see box below). Signs point the way to the **visitor centre** (daily 8am–5pm; R5) with a small **museum**, which has some vivid exhibits, including an audiovisual re-creation of the battle. You can also hike up to various monuments situated on the western end of the line of hills. Out on the battlefield itself – now open veld with springbok grazing and the

The Kimberley campaign

At the outbreak of the **Anglo-Boer War**, the Boer forces identified diamond-rich Kimberley as an important strategic base and quickly besieged the city, trapping its residents, including Cecil Rhodes, inside. In response, the British deployed an army under **Lord Methuen** to relieve the city. The size of the army and lack of knowledge of the terrain compelled them to advance from the coast along the line of the railway so that a supply of troops, water, food and equipment could be ensured.

Methuen first encountered Boer forces at Belmont, just across the Orange River. This was followed by further battles at Graspan and the Modder River, from which the Boers made a tactical withdrawal to Magersfontein, a range of hills 30km south of Kimberley. Here the Boer generals, under the leadership of General Cronjé and the tactical direction of **Koos de la Rey**, decided to dig a line of **trenches** along the bottom of the *koppie* rather than defend the top of the ridge of hills, as was their usual tactic.

In the early hours of December 11, 1899, the British advanced on Magersfontein, fully expecting the enemy to be lined along the ridge. The British were led by the Highland Regiment fresh from campaigns in North Africa and India, and considered the elite of the British army. Just before dawn, as they fanned out into attack formation, four thousand Boers in the trenches just a few hundred metres away opened fire. The use of trenches was, at that point, a rare tactic in modern warfare, and the element of surprise caused devastation in the ranks of Highlanders. Those not killed or wounded in the first volleys were pinned down by snipers for the rest of the day, unable to move in the coverless veld and suffering appallingly under the hot sun. The next day the British withdrew to the Modder River, and the relief of Kimberley was delayed for two months. The defeat was one in a series of three the British suffered within what became known as "Black Week", news of which sent shock waves through the British public expecting their forces to overrun the "crude farmers" before Christmas.

occasional car throwing up a plume of dust along the dirt road – the lines of **trenches** can still be seen, along with other memorials, including a pair of granite crosses marking the graves of Scandinavian soldiers who fought on the Boer side. Local legend has it that at least two ghosts have lingered: a saddled but riderless horse, and a lone Scottish piper.

One of the most enjoyable ways of finding out more about the history is to book a one-day **battlefield tour** with Steve Lunderstedt (T083 732 3189) or Frank Higgo (T082 591 5327), both enthusiastic and entertaining military historians. Their tours provide a vivid picture of the campaign, with trips to battlefields, fortifications and gun positions, and walks to get a sense of the terrain and look for old shells and other evidence of the fighting. Alternatively, pick up a "Diamond Fields Battlefields Route" brochure from the tourist office in Kimberley for detailed self-drive directions.

If you want to **stay** hereabouts, *Langberg Guest Farm*, 11km towards Kimberley (T053 832 1001, W www.langberg.co.za; ❷), is a hospitable family-run game farm at the western end of the battlefield, set in several Cape Dutch horse stables and cottages. It offers activities such as hikes and trips to feed the farm's roan and sable antelopes.

The Kalahari

While the Northern Cape has no shortage of dry, endless expanses, the most emotive by far is the **Kalahari**. The very name holds a resonance of sun-bleached, faraway spaces and the unknown vastness of the African interior, both harsh and magical. The name derives from the word *kgalagadi* (saltpans, or thirsty land), and describes the semi-desert stretching north from the Orange River to the Okavango delta in northern Botswana, west into Namibia and east until the bushveld begins to dominate in the catchment areas of the Vaal and Limpopo rivers.

The Kalahari in the Northern Cape is characterized by surprisingly high, thinly vegetated red or orange sand dunes, scored with dry river beds and large, shimmering saltpans. Although this is, strictly speaking, semi-desert, temperatures are searingly hot by day in summer and numbingly cold at night in winter. North of the Orange, South Africa's largest river, the land is populated by tough, hard-working farmers and communities largely descended from the indigenous San hunter-gatherers and nomadic Khoi herders. For many land-users, there is an increasing realization that **eco-tourism** may be the only viable option on huge areas where stock farming and hunting provide at best a marginal living.

Upington, the main town in the area, stands on the northern bank of the Orange at the heart of an irrigated corridor of intensive wheat, cotton and, most prominently, grape farms. At the far end of the farming belt, about an hour's drive west, the Orange picks up speed, and froths and tumbles into a huge granite gorge at **Augrabies Falls**, the focus of one of the area's two national parks. The other is the undoubted highlight of this area, the **Kgalagadi Transfrontier Park**. A vast desert sanctuary rich in game and

Kalahari tours

To save yourself driving the vast distances of the Kalahari region – and to take advantage of specialized knowledge of the area's distinctive flora, fauna, landscapes and climate – it's worth considering joining a guided tour. Most of the tours incorporate a visit to the Augrabies Falls and the Kgalagadi Transfrontier Park, although customized itineraries are available. Prices start at R800 per person per day for a party of two, double that for upmarket trips, and include entrance fees, night game drives and guided walks. Costs can be kept to a minimum by asking to join a prebooked safari. And for a bird's eye view of the Kalahari, it's possible to go paragliding at Kuruman (see p.337) or get airborne in a microlight in Upington (see p.337). The following is a list of reliable, knowledgeable and well-organized tour operators offering a range of Kalahari-based tours:

Diamond Tours Unlimited 71 Jacobson Ave, Kimberley ℡053 861 4983, Ⓦwww .diamondtours.co.za.

Kalahari Adventure Centre *Augrabies Falls Backpackers*, Upington (see p.345) ℡054 431 1961, Ⓦwww.kalahari.co.za.

Kalahari Safaris 3 Orange St, Upington ℡054 332 5653 or 082 435 0007, Ⓦwww .kalaharisafaris.co.za.

Kalahari Tours and Travel ℡054 338 0375 or 082 493 5041, Ⓦwww.kalahari-tours .co.za.

boasting a magnificent landscape of red dunes and hardy vegetation, it's well worth the long trek to get there. If you're coming to it from Gauteng along the N14 highway, you can either turn onto the R31 (a long, bleak dirt road which should only be tackled in a sturdy vehicle) at **Kuruman**, site of a famous nineteenth-century **mission station** established by Robert and Mary Moffat, or travel on to Upington, from where the road is tarred for all but the last 45km.

Upington

As an inevitable focus of trips to Kgalagadi and Augrabies, as well as those to and from Namaqualand and Namibia, **UPINGTON**, just over 400km west of Kimberley, is a good place to stop for supplies, organize a park tour or onward accommodation, or simply draw breath. Situated on the banks of the Orange River, it can also be a mellow spot, with plenty of greenery softening the arid landscape that surrounds it – a result of the **irrigation** which allows Upington to be surrounded by vineyards – although the savage summer temperatures mean you probably won't want to linger.

Arrival and information

All **buses** stop at Intercape's office on Lutz Street, in the town centre. **Minibus taxis** use the rank north of Mark Street, between Le Roux and Park streets. The **train station** is 1km north of the centre, while the **airport**, which has no public transport, lies 7km north of town along Diedericks Road (℡054 337 7900). If you're likely to arrive at night, it's best to reserve a room and get your accommodation to pick you up when you arrive (usually R20). That said, some enterprising drivers are usually on hand to meet tourists arriving by rail or bus, or you could try ringing Shawn Scott (℡082 750 1286).

Central Upington is compact and easy to get around, with most of the activity on the three main streets running parallel to the river. Upington has two **tourist offices**. The one on Schröder Street (Mon–Fri 8am–5.30pm, Sat 9am–noon; ⓣ&ⓕ054 332 6064, ⓦwww.kharahais.gov.za) deals only with the town and its immediate surroundings, and provides brochures, an accommodation list and details of local tours. For regional information, including details of Augrabies and Kgalagadi, head to the Green Kalahari Tourist Office at the start of Swartmodder Road (Mon–Fri 7.30am–4.30pm, Sat 9–11am; ⓣ054 337 2804, ⓦwww.greenkalahari.co.za), which has even more brochures, including detailed driving itineraries.

Accommodation

Upington has accommodation for all tastes and pockets, including a quiet **backpackers lodge** within walking distance of the centre. The busiest months

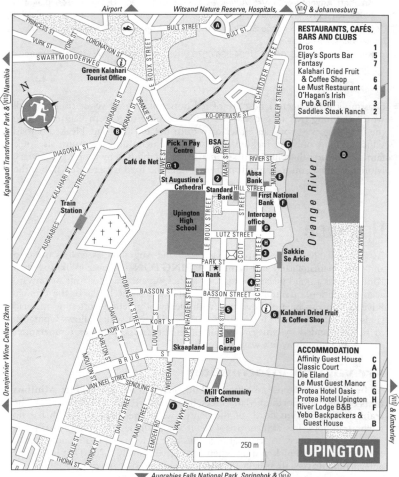

Moving on from Upington

South African Airlink (☏054 332 2161), based at the airport (☏054 337 7900), **flies** from here to Cape Town and to Johannesburg. Passenger **trains**, operated by TransNamib (✇www.transnamib.com.na) are limited to twice-weekly runs into Namibia (change at Keetmanshoop).

The only major **bus** company operating from Upington is Intercape, based at Lutz Street (Mon–Fri 6.30am–7pm, Sat 6.30am–1pm & 5.45–7pm, Sun 6.45–7.45am & 5–7pm; ☏054 332 6091). It serves Johannesburg and Pretoria (both daily 7.30am) via Kuruman, Vryburg and Klerksdorp; Cape Town (daily 7pm) via Springbok; Kimberley and Bloemfontein (Thurs & Sat 7.30am); and Windhoek in Namibia (Tues, Thurs, Fri & Sat 6.30pm). Big Sky also serves Kimberley and Bloemfontein (Sun 1pm), leaving from the Intercape office (book on ☏053 832 2006).

There are regular daily **minibus** services (fewer on Sun) to Kimberley, but only one daily to Springbok and three a week to Cape Town (via Calvinia). Bays are marked for local destinations; for long-distance runs, ask at the booking office, where you must also buy tickets.

are August and September, when Upington receives through traffic bound for Namaqualand; book ahead at this time. Particularly recommended – so long as guard dogs and a sometimes starchy neocolonial tenor don't phase you – are the **riverfront guesthouses** on Budler Street and Murray Avenue; reservations are advisable to secure a room and to ensure that someone's there when you arrive. For more options, pick up the *Upington Accommodation Collection* booklet at the tourist office. All hotels reviewed below have their own parking.

Affinity Guest House 4 Budler St ☏054 331 2101, ✇www.affinityguesthouse.co.za. The largest of the riverfront choices, offering reasonable en-suite rooms in a functional pink two-storey building, all with TV, a/c and fridge. There's a small swimming pool and braai area, and staff can arrange tours and safaris. ❸

Classic Court 26 Josling St ☏054 332 6142, ✉classiccourt@absamail.co.za. Reliable guesthouse with good-value en-suite rooms, some with wooden floors and microwaves. No river views, but there is a tiny pool. ❷

Die Eiland On an island opposite the town centre ☏054 334 0286–8. This huge, busy holiday resort has a pleasant campsite and self-catering chalets, cottages, huts and rondavels, the best of which are right by the river and sleep four. No credit cards. ❶–❸

Le Must Guest Manor 12 Murray Ave ☏054 332 3971, ✇www.lemustupington.com. Two Cape Dutch houses on the riverbank with elegant and comfortable rooms, minimalist decor and large

gardens, offering luxury and sophistication rarely encountered in the Northern Cape. ❹

Protea Hotel Upington 24 Schröder St ☏054 337 8400, ✇www.proteahotels.com/upington. Decent but mundane rooms, the main draws being a nice swimming pool and sun deck with river views, and Wi-Fi Internet access in the downstairs bar. More luxurious accommodation (❺) is offered at the *Protea Hotel Oasis* opposite. ❹

River Lodge B&B 4 Murray Ave ☏054 332 6327 or 082 399 2705. One of the most attractive places along the river, in an old Cape Dutch house guarded by particularly noisy dogs. There are just three beds in two bright rooms, plus a swimming pool, braai area, canoes and fishing equipment. ❷

Yebo Backpackers & Guest House 21 Morant St ☏054 331 2496 or 082 825 1643, ✉yebo@lantic.net. Run by a charming couple, this quiet compound has an eight-bed dorm, a kitchen, braai area and Internet access; camping is allowed. Friendly and laid-back. ❶

The Town

Upington's obvious highlight is the **Orange River**, but unless you're staying at one of the riverside guesthouses, it tends to be hidden from view. The terraces behind *O'Hagan's* (see p.336) and the *Kalahari Dried Fruit & Coffee Shop* (next to the municipal tourist office) are good places to admire the river and its swans. Better still, take a **cruise** with Sakkie se Arkie on its strange two-tier barge (daily Sept–April, by prior arrangement in winter if the river is sufficiently high; ☎082 564 5447 or 082 575 7285; R40). It's based on the riverbank at the east end of Park Street, but can also pick up clients from *Affinity Guest House* or *Die Eiland*. Upington's vineyards produce ten percent of the country's grapes – mostly table grapes and for dried fruit, though wine is also made. **Wine tasting** is offered by Oranjerivier Wine Cellars (Mon–Fri 8am–4.30pm, Sat 9–11.30am; free; ☎054 337 8800, ⓦwww.owk.co.za) in the industrial estate 3km west of the town centre off Dakota Road. Alternatively, you can sample or buy its output at *Le Must* restaurant (see below), or at the **Kalahari Dried Fruit & Coffee Shop** (Mon–Fri 8am–5pm, Sat 8am–1pm, Sun 8am–noon), which also sells other local produce, including raisins (the biggest export crop), conserves and pickles.

Consumables of another kind entirely can be found at the remarkable **Skaapland** (Sheepland; open daily), a huge modern butchery which stands testimony to the devotion locals have for red meat. Located on the corner of Brug and Le Roux streets, it's worth a visit for all but the most devout vegetarian simply to see this vast, bright and spotless emporium selling everything from whole lamb carcasses (which can be cut up and cooked to your specific requirements at a special bay) to *biltong*, which hangs in dark forests in one corner of the shop.

In early October, the *Die Eiland* resort plays host to the **Kalahari Kuierfees** (first Thursday to Saturday) combining flea markets and craft stalls with a triathlon, arts, live music and dance.

Eating, drinking and nightlife

As the only large centre for hundreds of kilometres, Upington seems like culinary heaven compared to the towns you pass through to get here. If you were ever going to appreciate a franchised **steakhouse**, it would be here and, sure enough, they are lined up in anticipation in the town centre: the best ones are *Dros* in the Pick 'n Pay Centre off Le Roux Street and *Saddles Steak Ranch* on Mark Street. For a more sophisticated dining experience, head to *Le Must Restaurant*, 11a Schröder St (book ahead on ☎054 332 6700). Formerly owned by the same people as *Le Must Guest Manor*, it remains Upington's outstanding **restaurant**, offering the likes of Kalahari lamb cutlets and rump steak with feta, which, with wine, could set you back R200.

The best place to down a **beer** is *O'Hagan's Irish Pub & Grill*, 20 Schröder St, with real Guinness and a lovely terrace at the back overlooking the river. Popular with blacks is *Eljay's Sports Bar* on Mark Street (daily mid-afternoon until 2am, closed earlier on Sun), a friendly little billiards place with a large TV screen for sports. The town's main **nightclub** is *Fantasy*, less than 1km southwest of the centre in the Lemoen Drie area, just off Lemoen Road, and good for contemporary music. Go with a local; *Eljay's* is a handy place to find volunteers.

Listings

Banks Standard, Absa and First National are all on Hill St.

Car rental You need a 4WD to visit Kgalagadi under your own steam. Recommended local rental outfits include Kalahari 4x4 Hire, Caltex garage, 66 Scott St (☎054 332 3098 or 082 490 1937, ⓦwww .kalahari4x4hire.co.za); Kgalagadi 4x4 Hire, corner Mark and Park sts, facing the taxi rank (☎054 337 7100 or 082 820 5376, ⓦwww.kgalagadi4x4 .com); and Walker's Midas, 53 Mark St (☎054 337 5200, ⓔwalkers@midas.co.za). All three can provide vehicles with camping gear. Of the international agencies, Avis is at the airport (☎054 332 4746) and Hertz on Le Roux St (☎054 337 3600).

Cinema Four screens at Ster Kalahari, Pick 'n Pay Centre (☎054 332 2107).

Courier Postnet, Mark St, opposite *Saddles Steak Ranch*.

Doctors There are several surgeries at the north end of Scott St and Mark St, especially at Medpro Arcade.

Hospitals Best is Upington Private Hospital (☎054 338 8900); the public hospital is the Gordonia (☎054 331 1580). Both are out of town off the northern continuation of Schröder St.

Internet access BSA, River St, at Le Roux; Café de Net, Pick 'n Pay Centre.

Microlight flights The long-established Upington Microlight Training Centre (☎054 331 1328, ⓦwww.microlightkalahari.co.za) offers introductory tandem flights on microlights and hang-gliders.

Pharmacies De Duine Pharmacy, Pick 'n Pay Centre (☎054 331 1458); Upington Pharmacy, 33 Schröder St (☎054 332 3071). Both Mon–Fri 9am–8pm, Sat 9am–2pm & 7–8pm, Sun 10am–1pm.

Police Corner of Schröder and Hill sts ☎054 337 3400.

Post The post office is on Mark St.

Shopping Good places for local handicrafts include the Mill Community Craft Centre along the southern extension of Mark St, where you'll also see the creators at work; and the Paper Craft and Design cooperative in Raaswater village, 16km from Upington, which makes cool papier-mâché animals.

Supermarkets Pick 'n Pay, west end of Rivier St, off Le Roux St, is open daily 8am–8pm.

Swimming pool The open-air Olympic-size municipal pool is off Borcherd St, the northern extension of Le Roux St (Sept to mid-April Mon–Sat 11am–8pm, Sun 2–6pm).

Travel agent Club Travel, Pick 'n Pay Centre (☎054 338 6420, ⓦwww.clubtravel.co.za), is clued up and efficient, handling airline ticketing and alterations, plus safari packages and trips to Botswana, Namibia and elsewhere.

Kuruman and around

Around 265km east of Upington, lying near the border between the Northern Cape and North West Province, the historic settlement of **KURUMAN** is an important landmark along the main N14 route to or from Gauteng. The settlement grew up around **The Eye**, a natural spring, which, since time immemorial and through drought and flood, has consistently delivered twenty million litres a day of crystal-clear water. The Eye was the focal point for a rather unsettled Tswana clan called the **Batlhaping**, whose chief, Mothibi, first invited missionaries to live among his people in the early nineteenth century, a decision that led to the building of the famous **Mission Station** by Robert Moffat, and the establishment of Kuruman as the "Gateway to the Interior" of darkest Africa.

Modern-day Kuruman has also gained repute in a more secular way for its **paragliding** – this is one of very few places where a 150-kilometre unpowered flight leaves your peers unimpressed. Winter is the best time, as in summer dust devils and turbulence make things dangerous. For more information, see the website of the South African Hang Gliding and Paragliding Association, ⓦwww.sahpa.co.za.

Halfway between Kuruman and Upington, reached by heading south off the N14 from Olifantshoek, is the **Witsand Nature Reserve** (☎053 313 1061–2, ⓦwww.witsandkalahari.co.za; R20 entry, R30 picnic site), famous for its pristine white "**roaring**" **dunes**: in summer a curious rumbling sound occurs when the dunes, 9km in extent, are disturbed, possibly by ground water. While the reserve isn't exactly teeming with wildlife, it does have an abundance of desert bird species, and with patience you may also be rewarded by springbok, duikers and ground squirrels. There are some superb self-catering air-conditioned **chalets** to stay in (❸), plus a campsite (R50). For organized trips, contact Kalahari Safaris in Upington (see box, p.333).

The Town

Kuruman's centre is pretty scruffy, dominated by cut-price chain stores, faceless supermarkets and litter-strewn minibus-taxi ranks. The only central sight of interest is **The Eye** ("Die Oog" in Afrikaans), next to the tourist office, but there's not much to look at: a moss-covered slab of rock dribbling water and a lily-covered pond surrounded by a high green fence (daily 8am–8pm; R5). The tourist office has details of the **Kuruman Hiking Trail**, which leads from The Eye to another natural spring, Second Eye, 11km to the east, past Anglo-Boer War forts and dolomite caves.

Some 4km north of town along Tsening Road (the R31) lies the wetland **Billy Duvenhage Nature Reserve and Bird Sanctuary** (Sat & Sun: summer 3–7pm, winter 2–6pm), a gorgeously tranquil location in which to escape the heat. Some 115 bird species have been counted here so far, mainly ducks, ibis and heron, and there's some plains game, too. Opposite is Moffat Lane and Kuruman's main attraction, **Moffat Mission Station** (daily 8am–5pm; R10). It was here that a large, often gruff, energetic Scot, **Robert Moffat**, and his demure but equally determined wife, **Mary**, established a mission station (see box below) where they lived for fifty years. During this time they produced and printed the first Tswana Bible, and saw their eldest daughter, also called Mary, married to the missionary/explorer **David Livingstone**. Charmingly overgrown and shaded by tall acacia and camelthorn trees, the old village includes the Moffat homestead, with furniture and exhibits inside, the schoolroom housing the printing press used to produce the Tswana Bible, and the large rough-stone church, with rows of pews standing on an uneven dried-dung floor, huge rafters holding up a thatched roof and shafts of sunlight angling in through the small windows and split wooden door. In front of the homestead is the furrow that carried water from The Eye, and beyond that, in Mary Moffat's garden, is the stump of the almond tree (destroyed by lightning) under which David Livingstone proposed to his future wife. Livingstone, who would go on to become one of the greatest explorers of his age, used Kuruman as an initial stepping stone for his first explorations of the interior.

Practicalities

Main Street, running east–west, is the N14 Upington–Vryburg highway. Bisecting it north–south is the R31 Kimberley–Kgalagadi Park road, which

---

The Moffats and their mission

Robert and Mary Moffat, newly married and envoys of the London Missionary Society, arrived in the Kuruman area in 1820, initially at a place rather charmingly mistranslated by early explorers as Lattakoo, about 14km from Kuruman. As a former market gardener, however, Moffat soon saw the advantages of irrigating the flow of The Eye of Kuruman, and began to build his mission on the closest land wide and flat enough to plough.

Moffat didn't clock up too many converts – by the time he had built his eight-hundred-seater "Cathedral of the Kalahari", in 1838, he had just nine – but the challenge of preaching and establishing a school inspired him not only to learn the local language, which he did by living for a period in a remote Tswana village, but also to attempt the daunting task of **translating the Bible** into Tswana, which he then published on an imported iron printing press. The mission at Kuruman, meanwhile, carried on until the passing of the Group Areas Act of 1950, which brought about the end of the school and the church as a functioning place of (multiracial) worship.

south of Main Street is called Voortrekker Street, and to the north becomes Tsening Road. The **tourist office** (Mon–Fri 8am–1pm & 2–4.30pm; ☎053 712 1001, ⓦwww.kurumankalahari.co.za) occupies the old *drostdy* (magistrate's house) at their intersection; there's a good selection of brochures and staff will phone around for accommodation if you ask nicely.

Getting to Kuruman is easiest from Upington or North West Province, with daily Intercape **buses** running to and from Jo'burg and Pretoria via Vryburg, Klerksdorp and Potchefstroom. The buses stop at Leach Toyota on Main Street, 1.5km west of the tourist office (☎053 712 3678), and tickets can be bought next door at DJ's Beads. Moving on, the Intercape bus to Upington passes through Kuruman at 2.45pm and to Jo'burg at 11.15am. To Kimberley, **minibus taxis** are the only option; in Kuruman they stop at the rank on Voortrekker Street, just south of Main Street.

To change **money**, try Absa bank at the corner of Main and Livingstone streets; other banks also have central branches. The **hospital** is on Main Street 1km east of the tourist office (☎053 712 8100 or 8101); the **post office** is on Church Street, two blocks north and one block west of the tourist office.

Accommodation and eating

The cheapest **beds** are in dorms at the Moffat Mission (☎053 712 1352; ❶), in the conference centre just behind the old homestead. There are no self-catering facilities, although meals can be arranged in advance. Closer to town, the brightly coloured *Janke Gasthaus*, 16 Chapman St (☎053 712 0949; ❸), is obvious from the road as you head out towards the mission; it has twelve en-suite rooms with air conditioning, a fish pond and a braai area. Not as characterful, but with a gorgeous swimming pool, shady gardens and restaurant, is *Riverfield Guest House*, 12 Seodin Rd (☎053 712 0003, ⓦwww .riverfield.co.za; ❸), 2km northeast of the centre: from the tourist office, walk east along Main Street, then left up Livingstone Street.

You can **camp** at *Kuruman Caravan Park* (☎053 712 1479, ⒡053 712 3581; ❶), on Voortrekker Street 500m south of the tourist office. A much more pleasant option outside weekends and school holidays (when it gets very busy) is *Red Sands Country Lodge* (☎053 712 0033 or 082 801 4414 or 4415, ⓦwww .redsands.co.za; camping ❶, rondavels & chalets ❸), set among the Kuruman Hills 15km along the N14 towards Upington. Besides camping facilities, they have a characterful thatched stone rondavel and comfy self-catering chalets sleeping up to four. There's also a good German/South African restaurant.

Almost all of Kuruman's **restaurants** lie along Main Street. Particularly recommended is *22 On Main*, 500m east of the tourist office in the Palm Gate Shopping Centre, which has lamb shank, pork chops and the like for R50–60, as well as an outside terrace. The café opposite the entrance to The Eye is a pleasant spot for breakfast or an afternoon cup of tea.

Around Kuruman

The upmarket **Tswalu Kalahari Reserve** (☎053 781 9311, reservations ☎011 274 2299, ⓦwww.tswalu.com; ❸) centres on an impeccably stylish game lodge not far from the tiny settlement of **Sonstraal**, on the R31, 100km northwest of Kuruman. Tucked under the 1500-metre Korannaberg Mountains, this is the largest privately owned game reserve in South Africa, and was created by an English businessman, the late Steven Boler. He spent R50 million bringing over nine thousand head of game to this desert setting, including some highly endangered **desert black rhino**, sable, roan antelope and cheetah. Now owned by the Oppenheimer family, it remains part rich man's dream, part dedicated wildlife protection project, and part glamorous safari experience. Along with the wide desert panoramas, serious luxury and sumptuous meals, game viewing on foot or on horseback is on offer.

Also along the R31, but in the opposite direction 43km towards Kimberley, is a major archeological site, the intriguing **Wonderwerk** (Miracle) **Cave**. It has yielded important evidence of human occupation in various eras dating back over 800,000 years, including fossils, animal teeth, San rock paintings and engraved stones. There is a small visitor centre on the site (daily 8.30am–1pm & 2–5pm), plus a **campsite** and three self-catering **chalets** sleeping four (☎082 832 7226; ❷). Sometimes there are archeologists working in the cave, but if there's no one around, you'll have to ask at the farm for the gate to be unlocked. Admission is R7.

Kgalagadi Transfrontier Park

The result of the formalization of a long-standing joint management arrangement between South Africa's Kalahari-Gemsbok National Park and Botswana's neighbouring Gemsbok National Park was the creation, in 1999, of Africa's first official transfrontier park, named **KGALAGADI TRANSFRONTIER PARK** after the ancient San name for the Kalahari (it's pronounced "kha-la-khadi", the *kh* as in the Scottish "loch"). The park is run as a single ecological unit and gate receipts are shared, although the tourist facilities in the two areas are still run autonomously. Almost all visitors to the park will, however, encounter only the South African section, where all the established tourist facilities are found.

In another development, the park entered into an agreement with the local **Mier** and **San** communities, under South Africa's programme of restitution of land rights to peoples who had lost land under apartheid. The Mier and San have in turn agreed that their land be jointly managed by themselves and South African National Parks, so the land remains part of the wildlife sanctuary. The agreement also states that tourism opportunities for the local community will be explored. While these cover obvious areas such as jobs within the park and the sale of local crafts, locals have also been employed as trackers on a lion-monitoring project and to work on dune rehabilitation and alien plant eradication.

The park covers an area of over 37,000 square kilometres – nearly twice the size of Kruger National Park – and although the South African side is by far the smaller section, it still covers a vast 9500 square kilometres, bounded on its western side by the Namibian border, and to the south by the dry Auob River and a strip of land running parallel to this. The national boundary with Botswana is along the dry Nossob river bed, along which one of the few roads in the park runs, but no fences exist along this line, allowing game to move freely along the ancient **migration routes** that are so necessary for survival in the desert.

The best time to visit the park is between **March** and **May**, when there is still some greenery left from the summer rain and the sun is not so intense. Winter can be very cold at nights, while spring, though dry, is a pleasant time before the searing heat of summer.

Practicalities

The longer approach via the **R31** is surfaced only between Kuruman and Hotazel – the remainder is a long, bleak dirt road which should only be tackled in a sturdy vehicle. From Upington, the **R360** is surfaced all the way to Andriesvale, about

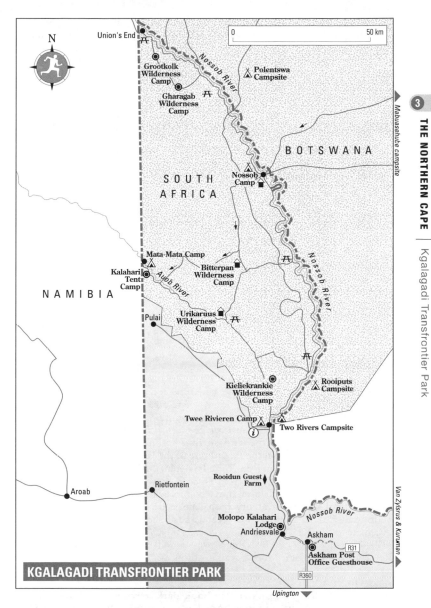

Map labels:

N

Union's End

Grootkolk Wilderness Camp

Gharagab Wilderness Camp

Polentswa Campsite

Nossob River

BOTSWANA

SOUTH AFRICA

Nossob Camp

Mata-Mata Camp

Kalahari Tents Camp

Bitterpan Wilderness Camp

Nossob River

NAMIBIA

Auob River

Pulai

Urikaruus Wilderness Camp

Kieliekrankie Wilderness Camp

Rooiputs Campsite

Twee Rivieren Camp

Two Rivers Campsite

Rooidun Guest Farm

Aroab

Rietfontein

Nossob River

Molopo Kalahari Lodge

Andriesvale

Askham

R31

Askham Post Office Guesthouse

R360

Upington

Mabuasehube campsite

Van Zylsrus & Kuruman

KGALAGADI TRANSFRONTIER PARK

0   50 km

200km, after which it becomes a sand road for the 45km to the park entrance at **Twee Rivieren**. Whichever way you travel, the journey is a hot and weary one. You'll see plenty of the classic **red dunes** of the Kalahari, and every so often a huge, crazily paved grey saltpan, but the vegetation has been largely denuded, and the landscape is filled with desolate images, such as broken windmills and rusting frames of motor cars, drowning in the desert sand.

The **park roads** are also sand. While you can travel in a normal car, bear in mind that the higher the clearance the better – a car packed with four adults might struggle. It's also a good idea to reduce the pressure in your tyres by about half a bar before setting off and to play the steering to maintain traction. You might find it's often easier to drive either side of the "road" along tracks left by other drivers. If you're in a rental car, check the small print as it may exclude cover for damaged wheels, undercarriage and paintwork. In the event of a **breakdown** you just have to sit it out until someone else passes; a park vehicle patrols most roads each day. **Fuel** is available at the restcamps at Twee Rivieren, Mata-Mata and Nossob. Entry to the **Botswana** side of Kgalagadi is only allowed by 4WD, and you must exit through the same gate you entered if you don't want to show your passport and complete immigration formalities. The Botswana section has 974km of dirt roads comprising two access routes, two self-guided 4WD trails and a game-viewing trail.

The two alternatives to making the long drive to Kgalagadi are to go on a **package tour** (see box, p.333) or to **fly** to Twee Rivieren by private charter plane (arrange this through Walker Flying Service in Upington; ☎054 337 5200), from where you can pick up a car by prior arrangement with Avis (contact its Upington office – see p.336).

Opening hours vary from month to month, roughly following first and last light. **Entrance fees** are R132 per day; if you stay longer than anticipated (unlikely, as accommodation is often fully booked), pay for the additional time when you leave. The **visitor centre** at Twee Rivieren (☎054 561 2000, ℻054 561 2005) has exhibitions and slide shows worth checking out. For safety reasons you'll be given a **permit** on arrival, and you have to sign in and out whenever you are leaving or arriving at a restcamp.

Accommodation

On the approach road to Kgalagadi there are a number of **places to stay**. However, with morning being the best time for game viewing, staying en route to the park isn't really an option if you're on a tight schedule. The closest accommodation to the entrance, 30km south of Twee Rivieren, is the **campsite** at the community-run *Rooidun Guest Farm* (☎082 589 6659; R40), which has become famous for **sand-surfing** – a bit like snow-sledging, sitting on a strip of plastic – down the face of one of the large nearby red sand dunes. A little further south, 55km from Twee Rivieren, is **ANDRIESVALE** and the *Molopo Kalahari Lodge* (☎054 511 0008, ⓦwww.molopolodge.co.za; ❸), a smart, well-run place with over thirty comfortable en-suite chalets arranged around a pool, as well as luxury bush tents, a bar and a decent **restaurant**. Andriesvale also has a **filling station** and a small shop. Alternatively, the nearby settlement of **ASKHAM** has the *Askham Post Office Guesthouse* (☎054 511 0040; ❸), which offers B&B in three spacious and clean en-suite rooms on the site of the old post office (book well in advance).

Inside the park

On the South African side, it's vital to **book park accommodation**, even for campsites, as early as you can, through South African National Parks (see p.63). The park has a choice of cottages and camping in two broad types of site: **fenced restcamps** at Twee Rivieren, Mata-Mata and Nossob, which have electricity (even in the campsites) and creature comforts such as kitchens, fans or air conditioning, braai areas and shops, and four far more basic and remote **unfenced wilderness camps**, for which you need to be completely self-sufficient. It's worth staying at least a night at a park restcamp away from Twee Rivieren to taste the raw flavour of the desert. If time is limited, the shorter distance to Mata–Mata makes more sense, but Nossob is better for atmosphere and game viewing: as well as hearing the lions roaring at night, you'll probably have your best chance of seeing them in this area. The roads to Nossob and Mata–Mata follow river beds, and so are good for spotting game. On the **Botswana side**, facilities are limited to campsites at Mabuasehube, Two Rivers, Rooiputs and Polentswa. Visitors need to be completely self-sufficient. For reservations, contact the Botswana *Parks and Reserves Reservation Office* in Gaborone (from South Africa, ☏09 267 318 0774, ✉dwnp@gov.bw).

Bitterpan Wilderness Camp Near the centre of the park on a 4WD trail between Nossob and Mata–Mata (access by 4WD only), with four unfenced reed cabins overlooking a saltpan. ❹

Gharagab Wilderness Camp Four log cabins in the remote far north (access by 4WD), giving elevated views of the dunes and thornveld. ❹

Grootkolk Wilderness Camp This unfenced desert camp near Union's End at the very northern tip of the South African section is in prime predator country; it's small, fully equipped and exclusive – and usually booked solid months in advance. ❹

Kalahari Tent Camp Guarded by an armed guide, this unfenced site has fully equipped self-catering tents built of sandbags and canvas, giving views over the Auob River. There's also a swimming pool. ❹

Kieliekrankie Wilderness Camp The closest camp to Twee Rivieren (41km), where the four cabins are sunk into a dune; accessible in ordinary vehicles. ❹

Mata–Mata Camp A fenced restcamp 120km northwest of Twee Rivieren on the (closed) Namibian border, at the end of the road that follows the course of the Auob River. Accommodation is in fully equipped family cottages (sleeping six), comfortable two-person bungalows and a campsite. Other amenities include a water hole lit up at night, a shop and fuel. ❷–❸

Nossob Camp On the Botswana border, 160km north of Twee Rivieren along the Nossob River road, this is the most remote of the three fenced restcamps. It has fifteen simple chalets, better family-size guesthouses (sleeping four), a cottage and a campsite. There's also a supply shop, fuel, plus a predator information centre (the place is famed for nocturnal visits by lions). ❷–❸

Twee Rivieren Camp The first, and most developed, of the three fenced restcamps, right by the entrance, offering over thirty pleasant self-catering chalets with thatched roofs and nice patio areas, a sizeable campsite (with or without electricity), a mediocre restaurant, pool, fuel, and a shop selling souvenirs and simple foodstuffs. ❷–❸

Urikaruus Wilderness Camp Roughly halfway between Twee Rivieren and Mata–Mata, with an attractive setting among camelthorn trees overlooking the Auob River. ❹

The park

Following the long slog to get to Twee Rivieren, be prepared to clock up even more mileage inside the park – the shortest circular game drive is over 100km long, not far short of the distance to Mata–Mata restcamp. The main roads follow the **river beds**, and this is where the game – and their predators – are most likely to be. Water flows very rarely in the two rivers, but frequent **boreholes** have been drilled to provide water for the game. Larger **trees** such as camelthorn and *witgat* (shepherd's tree) offer a degree of shade and nutrition, and desert-adapted plants, including types of melon and cucumber, are a source of moisture for the animals.

Much of the park is dominated by **red sand dunes** which, when seen from the air, lie strung out in long, wave-like bands. From a car, the perspective is different, as you are in the valley of the river bed, but this doesn't prevent the path from offering one of the finest **game-viewing** experiences in South Africa – not only for the animals, but for the setting, with its broad landscapes, the crisp light of morning and the huge open skies. The clear viewing and wonderful light are ideal for **photography**, as shown by the exhibition at the visitor centre at Twee Rivieren camp or in any number of glossy coffee-table wildlife books.

The focus in Kgalagadi Transfrontier Park is on self-guided **game drives**. **Activities** inside the park are limited to the exacting three-day Nossob 4WD

▲ Gemsbok in Kgalagadi Transfrontier Park

trail over the duneveld (book this in advance), and night game drives and day walks, which can be booked on arrival at Nossob or Twee Rivieren only. Look out for details posted at the restcamp offices about what's happening on any given day. There are no guides for hire other than for these activities.

Seeing the animals

The game-viewing highlights in Kgalagadi Transfrontier Park are, inevitably, the predators, headed by the **Kalahari lion** and, enjoying rare status alongside the Big Five, **gemsbok**, the large, lolloping antelope with classically straight, V-shaped horns. You won't find buffalo, elephant or rhino, but the other animals more than compensate. Of the remaining Big Five, the **leopards**, as elsewhere, are not uncommon, but remain elusive. Kalahari lions commonly have much darker manes than those found in the bushveld, and studies have shown their behavioural and eating patterns to be distinctively well adapted to the semi-desert conditions here. Beyond the Big Five, there are various species of **antelope**, **hyena**, **jackal**, **bat-eared fox**, **cheetah** and some extravagant **birdlife**, including vultures, eagles, the dramatic bateleur (which takes its name from the French word for an acrobatic tumbler), bustards and ostrich. There's also a good chance you'll see family groups of **suricate**, a relative of the mongoose and squirrel, striking their characteristic pose of standing tall on their hind legs, looking round nervously for signs of danger.

The best time to take your game drives is as early as possible in the **morning**, when you're more likely to see animals out in the open. Drives normally take at least four to five hours, so an early start means you can avoid the desert sun at its zenith. The last couple of hours of light in the afternoon are also a good time for game (and for taking photographs), but it's a lot more relaxing to go out for a little foray from your base than to be en route for a new camp, destined to arrive just as it's getting dark. The middle of the day, especially during summer, is a necessarily inactive time for both animals and humans, so don't plan too full a programme.

Augrabies Falls National Park

One of the undoubted highlights of any trip to the Northern Cape is **AUGRABIES FALLS NATIONAL PARK**, 120km west of Upington. Roaring out of the barren semi-desert, sending great plumes of spray up above the brown horizon, the falls are the most spectacular moment in the two-thousand-kilometre progress of the Orange River. Rafting along the eighteen-kilometres granite canyon is another draw, while the fairly inhospitable northern section of the park sustains game, including reptiles, klipspringers and springbok. The best time to visit Augrabies is from March to May, when the temperatures are slightly cooler and the river is at its maximum flow after summer rainfall up in the Lesotho catchment areas, though water levels have reduced noticeably since the diversion of some water into the Vaal River (see p.769). With your own transport, the falls are easily visited as a day-trip from Upington, although there's plenty of reasonable accommodation both in the park itself and nearby. The closest you can get to the park on public transport is **Alheit**, on the N14 at the start of the turning to the park, 28km short of the entrance; however, most of the Kalahari **tours** out of Upington and elsewhere in Northern Cape (see box, p.333) incorporate a visit to the falls.

En route to the park

The route from Upington is west along the **N14**, following the Orange River and its rich fringe of vineyards, orchards and alfalfa fields. Eighty kilometres southwest of Upington, **KAKAMAS** is the last town before the park, and a handy base for visiting Augrabies if you're driving. The settlement was founded in 1897 by the Dutch Reformed Church as a colony for livestock farmers rendered destitute by a prolonged drought; each farmer contributed manpower for a system of **irrigation** canals and tunnels, and were rewarded with a plot of irrigated land. Considered primitive by the experts of the day, their handiwork still funnels water to the land today. The inhabitants' ingenuity also saw expression in South Africa's first hydroelectric power station, modelled on an Egyptian temple and completed in 1914, and which now houses a small museum. It's at the top of Voortrekker Street as you come in along the N14.

Good **places to stay** in Kakamas include the large *Kalahari Gateway Hotel*, 19 Voortrekker St (℡054 431 0838, ⓦ www.kalaharigateway.co.za; ❸), with a swimming pool, two bars and a restaurant; and – better – *Vergelegen Guesthouse & Restaurant* (℡054 431 0976, ⓦ www.augrabiesfalls.co.za; ❸) on a farm by the main road about 3km east of Kakamas. It has sixteen neat and attractive rooms (one self-catering), a swimming pool, restaurant, coffee shop and information centre, which can arrange tours and safaris.

The *Augrabies Falls Backpackers* in **Augrabies village** (℡072 127 5400, ⓦ www.kalahari.co.za; dorms ❶, rooms ❷), 11km before the park gate, was in the process of changing ownership at the time of writing. Signs are, however, that it will continue to offer pleasant accommodation in dorms and doubles, as well as acting as the base for the Kalahari Adventure Centre (see p.333). Only a couple of kilometres from the park's main gate is *Falls Guesthouse* (℡082 928 7938; ❸), a renovated farmhouse with big, cool rooms, nice furnishings and a veranda overlooking rows of vines.

The park

The park's **reception**, a little way inside the park entrance (daily 7am–6pm; ℡054 452 9200, ⓕ054 451 5003; R60), has a shop, a self-service snack bar and

▲ Augrabies Falls

a **restaurant** with views towards the gorge. Self-catering **accommodation** is available at cottages and bungalows (both ❸) close to the gate and the falls (two of which have wheelchair access), and at a large shaded camping and caravan area. There are swimming pools at each site.

The park's mighty waterfall is still known by its Khoikhoi name, Aukoerabis, "the place of great noise". At peak flow, the huge volume of water plunging through a narrow channel at the head of a deep granite gorge actually compares with the more docile periods at Victoria Falls and Niagara, although Augrabies lacks both the height and the soul-wrenching grandeur of its larger rivals. However, it is free of rampant commercialization, and in its eerie desert setting under an azure evening sky, the falls provide a moving and absorbing experience. The sides of the canyon are shaped like a smooth parabola, and there are many tales of curious visitors going too far in their quest to peer at the falls, and sliding helplessly into the seething maelstrom below. Despite the odd miraculous survival – most famously a Scandinavian who was stripped of all his clothes by the force of the water before he was plucked out – several dozen people have died here since the national park was created in 1966.

There is now a large fence from behind which you view the falls, while a boardwalk allows wheelchair access to the viewpoint. To see more of the gorge, walk the short distance to Arrow Point or drive on the link roads round to Ararat or Echo Corner. The atmosphere is at its best near **sunset**, when the sun shines straight into the west-facing part of the gorge.

The rest of the park covers 184 square kilometres on both sides of the river. The land is dry and harsh, with sparse plants typical of arid areas, such as *kokerboom* (quiver tree), camelthorn and Namaqua fig. There are various striking rock formations, notably **potholes** scoured out by the river when it ran a different course to its present one, and **Moon Rock**, a huge dome of smooth, flaking granite rising out of the flat plains. If you drive on the (unsurfaced) roads in the park you'll probably spot some of the resident fauna, notably eland, klipspringer and other small antelope. On foot around the falls and the camp you're likely to see the smaller animals, including dassie, mongoose and lizards.

West along the N12: Pella

West of Augrabies Falls National Park, the N14 highway becomes increasingly straight, spooling across largely flat and featureless semi-desert, the flanking telegraph poles stretching off to a shimmering horizon. The scarcity of trees means that a number of poles have been adopted as hosts for huge brown **sociable weaver nests**, a distinctive feature of these arid northern regions. Roughly midway between Upington and Springbok, around 15km west of the tiny, hot and famously remote town of **Pofadder** (Afrikaans for puff adder, the highly venomous snake which is found around the country), is a turning to **PELLA**, an intriguing settlement established around a mission station founded by the London Missionary Society in 1814, then abandoned in 1872 and taken over by the Roman Catholic Church in 1878. After turning off the N14, take the right-hand fork after 3km and follow the dirt road for another 10km towards the range of mountains which follows the course of the Orange River.

Pella is a simple gathering of shacks, sandy roads and a few stone or brick buildings, in the midst of which a striking yellow **cathedral** stands in an open, dusty-white plot surrounded by stately date palms. The cathedral was built over seven years by two French missionaries in the 1880s who, lacking an experienced cathedral-builder in their group, used the *Encyclopédie des Arts et Métiers* for guidance. The surrounding mission buildings are attractive and still home to a community of nuns, and the cathedral itself is in continual use. The two small **museums** among the mission buildings are of some interest; if they're not open, ask at the mission office (Ⓣ&Ⓕ 054 971 0190).

Activities at Augrabies Falls

Various adventure activities are promoted within the park, though none really matches the adrenaline surge of the falls themselves. The half-day **3-in-1 Gariep Trail** (R140) combines a short canoeing trip in the gorge with a walk and an eleven-kilometre mountain-bike ride back to the restcamp. The **Dassie Nature Trail** is a half-day hike out from the main restcamp, while the popular three day **Klipspringer Trail** (April–September only; R130) involves two overnight stops at simple huts; advance booking is essential. **Night game drives** are also on offer (R80), and there's a 56-kilometre **self-drive tourism route** (4WD only) in the park's north-western section for viewing plains game. Reservations for all these activities must be made before 4pm the day before.

Perhaps more instantly gratifying is the **"Augrabies Rush"**, a half-day trip on small rafts down 8km of increasingly swift river immediately above the falls, run by the Kalahari Adventure Centre (see p.333; R325 per person with a minimum of four). The Adventure Centre also runs four-day rafting trails taking you deep into the empty country downriver of the falls (R2495), while another two-day trip surges down the exciting rapids of the Oneepkans Gorge near Pella (R1995).

There are no tourist facilities at Pella itself, although the excellent *Klein Pella Guest House* (℗054 972 9712, Ⓦwww.karsten.co.za; ❸), 24km away on a working farm beside the banks of the Orange River, offers both chalets and camping.

Namaqualand

NAMAQUALAND is another Northern Cape region with a name that conjures a blend of desolation and magic. According to an oft-quoted saying about the area, in Namaqualand you weep twice: once when you first arrive and once when you have to leave. This is the land of Khoikhoi herders called the **Nama**: the Little Nama, who lived south of the Orange River, and the Great Nama, who lived north of the river in what is now Namibia. Sparsely

---

Viewing the flowers of Namaqualand

The seeds of the spectacular **flowers of Namaqualand** – multicoloured daisies, mesembryanthemums (*vygies*), aloes, gladioli and lilies – lie dormant under the soil through the harshest droughts of summer, waiting for the rain that sometimes takes years to materialize. About four thousand floral species are found in the area, a quarter of which are found nowhere else on earth. With different species reacting to different conditions, the flowers in any given place will come at different times from one year to the next, and attempting to predict where the best displays will occur is fraught with uncertainty. For more or less guaranteed displays, however, head for the Skilpad section of **Namaqua National Park** (see p.352); Richtersveld Transfrontier Park (see p.359), with its ocean-mist-fed succulents, is another reliable hunting ground.

One of the clues to where the displays will occur is **winter rainfall**, unusual in semi-desert ecosystems, which is why the flowers appear only in August and September; they follow the rainfall, so early in the season they will be out near the coast, moving steadily inland. Don't expect anything in July – early rains are extremely rare, and if the rains fail or come later, displays will be below par. **Temperature** is also a factor – flowers rarely open before 10am and on cool or cloudy days the displays are muted. While most of Namaqualand's flowers are wind-pollinated, temperatures below 15°C or so indicate that the wind is likely to be too strong (usually blowing straight towards the Atlantic), so flowers stay closed to protect their pollen.

Practicalities

Flower-viewing anywhere in Namaqualand means you spend a lot of time in a **car**, simply because the distances in this region are so great and flowers can never be guaranteed – you may spend some time tracking them down. **Cycling** is an option, although it can become a frustrating exercise if the best displays turn out to be 20km away from where you're based. As for **accommodation** (which needs to be booked well in advance), you should decide whether you'd rather stay on a farm (especially viable if you don't have your own transport, as you can take a guided walk around the farm's own flower fields), or in one of the main centres, such as Springbok, from

populated, the region stretches south from the Orange to the empty **Knersvlakte** plains around Vanrhynsdorp, and from the **Atlantic coast** to the edge of the **Great Karoo**. Above all, Namaqualand is synonymous with the incredible annual display of brightly coloured **wild flowers** which carpet the landscape in August and September, one of South Africa's most compelling spectacles. Even outside flower season, swathes of orange, purple and white daisies emerge, and there is a tenacious beauty about the dry, empty landscape, with mountain deserts, mineral-bearing granite hills, and drought-defiant succulents.

The **N7** highway between Namibia and Cape Town cuts across Namaqualand, offering one of the most scenic drives in the country. At its northern end, at the junction with the dusty **N14** from Upington and the Kalahari, lies the region's capital, **Springbok**. This is the best base both for flowers – the nearby **Namaqua National Park** provides reliable displays even in years of low rainfall, when displays elsewhere may be muted – and for visiting the Province's remote northwestern corner: the **Diamond Coast**, stretching from **Port Nolloth** to the Namibian border; and, inland, the harsh but spectacular **Richtersveld Transfrontier Park**, bisected by the Orange River – rafting on which ranks high among the region's attractions.

where you can follow a wider range of routes. Tourist offices in the area can offer guidance and help organize accommodation; you can also contact the **Flower Hotline** (late July to early October; ☏083 910 1028) for updates on the best floral displays and a weather forecast. The following **tactics** are also worth keeping in mind.

- Day by day, plan your route before heading out. Your hosts will often have inside information about the best spots on a particular day. Be warned, however, that you sometimes get "gold rush" situations, with everyone flocking to certain places.
- As the flowers open up around 10am and close between 3pm and 4pm, you have plenty of time for a good breakfast and to get yourself where you want to be. Because the flowers orientate themselves to face the sun, it's best to drive westwards in the morning, eastwards in afternoon, and generally from north to south.
- Get out of your car – all the most dedicated flower-watchers have muddy patches on their knees.
- Although it goes without saying, don't pick the flowers. Take pictures, or buy a book such as the *Namaqualand: Garden of the Gods* by Freeman Patterson, or *Namaqualand: A Succulent Desert* by Richard Cowling and Shirley Pierce.
- Pack warm clothes, as it gets chilly at night.

Flower tour operators

IN CAPE TOWN

Cape Rainbow Tours Waterfront ☏021 551 5465, ⓦwww.caperainbow.com.
Landscape Tours 140 Main St, Somerset West ☏021 851 7706, ⓦwww.landscapetours.co.za.

IN NORTHERN CAPE

Diamond Tours Unlimited 71 Jacobson Ave, El Toro Park, Kimberley ☏053 861 4983 or 083 265 4765, ⓦwww.diamondtours.co.za.
Koperberg Tours & Safaris Springbok ☏083 873 3390, ⓦwww.namaqualand.net.
Virosatours Springbok ☏027 712 3650, ⓦwww.virosatours.com.

Springbok and around

The semi-arid expanse of northern Namaqualand is where the Karoo merges into the Kalahari, and both meet the ocean. If it weren't for the discovery of **copper** in the 1600s, and more recently of alluvial and offshore **diamonds** washed down from the Kimberley area by the Orange River, the region might well not have acquired any towns at all. Fresh water is scarce, and its presence here ensured the survival of **SPRINGBOK**, the region's capital, after its copper mines were exhausted.

The Town

Attractively hemmed in by hills, Springbok is the main commercial and administrative centre of Namaqualand, and an important staging post at the junction of the N7 and N14 highways. Lying 400km southwest of Upington, and just over 100km south of the border with Namibia, it makes a pleasant base for visiting northern Namaqualand's flower fields in August and September, to arrange trips to the Richtersveld Transfrontier Park (see p.359), and as a springboard for visiting the coast.

Springbok's main action is centred on the mound of granite boulders next to the taxi rank in the town centre. Called **Klipkoppie** ("rocky hill"), this was the site of a British fort blown up by General Jan Smuts' commando during the Anglo-Boer War. A few hundred metres up from Klipkoppie, at the back of town, a gash in the hillside marks the **Blue Mine**, the first commercial copper mine in South Africa, sunk in 1852. Recent activity here has been in search of gemstones – previously ignored in the search for copper ore – and zinc. A short trail wends up to a good viewpoint over town. You'll find a good selection of gemstones for sale at *Springbok Lodge*, together with an excellent display of mineralogical specimens from all over the globe.

Practicalities

Coming from Upington, the N14 eventually becomes Voortrekker Street, the town's main drag, and veers south at the **taxi rank** to rejoin the N7 for Cape Town. The helpful **tourist office**, doubling as the headquarters of the Namaqua Region Tourism Board (flower season Mon–Fri 7.30am–5pm, Sat & Sun 9am–noon; rest of year Mon–Fri 8.30am–4.15pm; ☎027 712 8035 or 8036, ⓦwww .namaqualand.com), is on Voortrekker Street 700m south of the taxi rank. Another source of local wisdom (and dour wit) is the *Springbok Lodge* on the corner or Voortrekker and Kerk streets. A hub for travellers and locals alike, it also sells an excellent selection of **books**, including plenty of titles on Namaqualand and its flowers, the history of copper mining and the Nama, the Richtersveld, and rock art.

For **Internet** access, try Something Online (Mon–Thurs 8am–4.30pm, Fri 8am–3.30pm) on Voortrekker Street next to *Melkboschkuil* restaurant. You can **change money** at the Absa bank, on Namakwa Street facing the taxi rank. Fully equipped 4WDs and camping gear can be rented from Richtersveld Challenge, facing the tourist office (☎027 718 1905, ⒺRichtersveld.challen @kingsley.co.za); other 4WD rental agencies include Tempest and Imperial (both ☎072 171 3081).

Accommodation

There's no shortage of **rooms** in Springbok, but you're still advised to book ahead in flower season. The notice board outside the tourist office has details and

Moving on from Springbok

Most **buses and minibuses** leave from the taxi rank at Klipkoppie, but will pick you up at your hotel if you ring ahead (it's recommended in any case). **Intercape buses** serving Upington, Cape Town and Windhoek leave from the Engen garage on Voortrekker Street 700m east of the taxi rank (buy tickets at Shoprite, 200m back towards town). Well-established taxi companies for **Cape Town** include Titus (☎027 712 1381), Van Wyk's (☎027 713 8559) and Carsten's (☎027 712 1847) – all operate every day except Saturdays. VIP Taxis (☎027 851 8780) has a 3pm service to Port Nolloth and Alexander Bay (Mon–Sat). For **Windhoek** in Namibia, Bailey's Reo Liner (☎+264 61 262 522) – arriving from Cape Town – runs every two days from KFC next to *Springbok Lodge*. Covering the same route three times a week is Namibian company *Econolux* (☎+264 64 205 935).

---

prices for most properties in and around town, and a map. The closest **campsite** is the plain and shadeless *Springbok Caravan Park* (☎027 718 1584; ●), 2km southeast of town along the R355 towards Goegap, with rondavels, double rooms and caravans, and a swimming pool.

In town

Annie's Cottage 4 King St, signposted from Klipkoppie ☎027 712 1451, ⓦwww .springbokinfo.com. Extremely stylish, comfortable and colourful rooms (including one that's wheelchair accessible) in a restored colonial house. There's plenty of local artwork, Internet access, a swimming pool under jacaranda trees, and hiking and biking trails in the vicinity. The gregarious owner is a good source of information about where to see the best flowers. ●

Cat Nap Voortrekker St, opposite the tourist office ☎027 718 1905, ⓔrichtersveld.challen@kingsley .co.za. Attractive African-themed rooms, two with bathrooms, and twelve rudimentary pull-down bunks in the garage, with a kitchenette – there's even room for you to park your vehicle beside your bed. Bunks ●, rooms ●

Elkoweru 1 Bree St ☎027 718 1202, ⓦwww .elkoweru.co.za. A modern two-storey guesthouse in vaguely Mediterranean style. Rooms are a bit small and ordinary, but good value (especially for single travellers), and there are also self-catering flats. ●

Masonic Hotel Van Riebeeck St ☎027 712 1505, ⓦwww.namaqualandflowers.co.za, ⓔjcb@mynet .co.za. In a building with a distinctly Art Deco feel, with well-kept if bland rooms, as well as a restaurant and bar. An annexe has some cheaper singles. ●

Mountain View Guest House 2 Overberg Ave (turn-off is 100m south of tourist office, from where it's another 1km along Overberg Ave) ☎027 712 1438,

ⓦwww.mountview.co.za. Ten tasteful, colourfully African-themed rooms (two self-catering) in this stylish guesthouse, pleasantly situated on the fringe of the town, right by a short trail offering views over Springbok and the surrounding countryside. ●

Springbok Lodge 37 Voortrekker St, entrance on Kerk St ☎027 712 1321, ⓦwww.springboklodge .com. Operates twenty guesthouses, all in distinctive white and yellow livery, and within walking distance. The rooms are plain but reasonable, and there are also some self-catering apartments. ●

Outside town

Môrewag Guest Farm 12km northwest of town – take the Kleinzee road and turn right after 8km towards Nababeep ☎084 408 0135. A pleasant working farm with plentiful flowers and succulents in season, some small game, three fully furnished guest rooms and a comfortable, old-fashioned cottage. Activities include petting farm animals, biking and walking trails. The owners are happy to pick you up from Springbok. Breakfast included. ●

Naries Namaqua Retreat 27km west of town along the Kleinzee road ☎027 712 2462, ⓦwww .naries.co.za. A homely, comfortable place to stay, this has five simple yet stylish rooms in an atmospheric Cape Dutch farmhouse, and a self-catering cottage with one double and two single beds. No under-11s allowed in the main farmhouse. The candlelight dinners are a big draw, and hiking and horse-riding can be arranged. Half board ●

Eating and drinking

There are a couple of dinner-only **restaurants**, both with mains from around R60: *Tauren Steakranch* on Hospital Street just north of the taxi rank has the usual steaks and an attractive African-style decor; *El Dago* on Voortrekker Street just south of the taxi rank is good for seafood and has a sunny street-facing balcony. Also on Voortrekker Street, halfway between the taxi rank and tourist office, is *Melkboschkuil*, once one of the province's leading restaurants but now serving burgers, pizzas and sandwiches; the attached coffee shop is a better bet, with good milkshakes and cheesecake which you can enjoy on a pleasant sundeck with views of the surrounding hills. The best place for a **drink** is *Titbits*, opposite *El Dago*, notable for its impressive cocktail selection.

Around Springbok

Following the R355 east out of Springbok for around 15km, you arrive at the entrance to **Goegap Nature Reserve** (daily 8am–6pm; R15), which proclaims itself "Namaqualand in miniature". Indeed, with close to 600 indigenous flower species, the reserve is a popular destination during flower season. You'll need your own transport to get there; or you could take a day-trip from Springbok with Virosatours (see box, p.349).

Lying 8km north of Springbok on the N7 is the slightly scruffy little town of **OKIEP** (or O'Okiep), which took over from Springbok as the copper-mining centre of Namaqualand in the 1880s. Until production ceased temporarily in 1919, it was the world's richest copper mine, and a major prize during the 1902 Anglo-Boer War, in which 900 defenders – mostly employees of the Cape Copper Company – repulsed a 53-day siege by Jan Smuts' forces. The ruins of one of the block houses built during the siege can still be seen on a hill northeast of town. Van Wyk's (see box, p.351) goes to Okiep from Springbok, leaving from Uitspan Street opposite Shoprite.

Central Namaqualand

Travelling south along the N7 from Springbok is a stimulating experience, thanks to the spectacular pink flat-topped mass of the **Matzikama Range** and the **Kamiesberg Mountains** that increasingly dominate the southern skyline. The village of **Kamieskroon** here is a good base for the flower season and is handy for visiting the Skilpad section of **Namaqua National Park**, the stage for some of Namaqualand's most reliable and spectacular floral displays.

Kamieskroon and Namaqua National Park

About 70km south of Springbok, the village of **KAMIESKROON** is set among the Kamiesberg Mountains, beneath the rocky peak – or *kroon* – from which it takes its name. There isn't much to the village other than a pretty setting, the crisp air of the mountains and, in flower season, a sense of being at the heart of the garden of the gods.

Deeper into the mountains, at places east of Kamieskroon such as **Nourivier** and the old Moravian mission station of **Leliefontein**, the land is owned and farmed as a community project by the local Nama people. In places you'll see families living in traditional *matjieshuise* (reed huts); these settlements, many of which are still based around a mission, are connected by dirt roads, and so make good flower-viewing routes.

Kamieskroon is to the left as you come off the N7, while to the right is the *Kamieskroon* (℡027 672 1614, ⓦ www.kamieskroonhotel.com; ❸), seemingly an inauspicious wayside **hotel** but in fact a vibrant and creative place. The hotel

The great outdoors

There are few countries where the great outdoors is quite as great as in South Africa. Its vast and varied landscapes provide the backdrop to a bewildering diversity of sights, activities and adventures. The Karoo semi-desert, the Mpumalanga game reserves, the peaks and passes of the Drakensberg and the mountainous dunes, deserted beaches and forested sea cliffs of the coastal plain mean you can chill out on a sun-drenched beach, pump adrenaline on a walking safari, or scare yourself witless swimming with Jaws. The choice is as wide as South Africa's open spaces.

Hyperactive South Africa

Ziplining ▲

Canoeing down the Orange River ▼

Abseiling, Table Mountain ▼

Since the arrival of democracy in South Africa in 1994 – and with it hordes of tourists – the growth of the country's **outdoor activities** has accelerated faster than a bungee jumper diving off the Bloukrans River Bridge.

Traditional activities are still there in abundance: from **scenic drives** along Cape Town's spectacular Chapman's Peak Drive, into the Northern Cape to see the veld blanketed by spring flowers, or through the breathtaking mountain passes of the Karoo; to literally hundreds of waymarked **hiking trails** that criss-cross the country – from a half-day walk around Plettenberg Bay's Robberg Peninsula to five days on the Otter Trail along the Garden Route coast. One of the great rewards of hiking in South Africa, apart from the awesome landscapes, is that there is always plentiful birdlife, and you stand a good chance of sighting small game, reptiles and insects. But it's **big game** that's the real pull, and here again you're spoilt for choice, with four major game regions to choose from (see overleaf).

For adrenaline junkies, there's a huge and ever-growing list of **extreme activities** devoted to the big rush. You can, for example, catch the surf at Jeffrey's Bay, go scooting on a sailboard across Table Bay or kayaking up the Wild Coast. You can go rafting on the frothing Great Usutu River in Swaziland, kayak down the Dusi, or spend leisurely days drifting on the Orange. If you'd rather do something completely new, try **kloofing** – basically jumping into a canyon – along the river gorges of the Western Cape. On land, there's always pony-trekking into Lesotho's

Highlands, mountain biking to Hell (Die Hel, to be precise – a pass noted for its impossibly sharp switchbacks), or 4x4 trailing in the Richtersveld. Then again, you can paraglide in the Northern Cape or skydive in Gauteng. If hair-raising descents are more your thing, there's abseiling off Table Mountain, ziplining across the Kruis River Gorge, sandboarding down the West Coast's bleached dunes, or even skiing at Tiffendell – enough to leave you breathless.

Two oceans

If South Africa's national parks offer some of Africa's best big-game experiences, its oceans provide some of the world's most rewarding encounters with marine mammals. South Africa is one of the best places anywhere to see **whales** from the shore. Although Hermanus plugs itself as the whale capital of the country, you can see large cetaceans in season (roughly July–Nov) anywhere along the coast where there's a suitable vantage point – it's not unheard of to step out of a café along Main Road, Kalk Bay, in Cape Town to see a southern right whale breaching.

With 2500km of coastline and two oceans (the warm Indian and cool Atlantic) the variety of marine and coastal life is extensive (some 2000 fish species are found in South African waters), with the possibility of eyeball-to-eyeball encounters with **great white sharks** at Gansbaai, swimming with **penguins** at Boulders Beach and tracking nesting **sea turtles** at Rocktail Bay. Among the numerous more active pursuits on offer are **sea-kayaking** from Plettenberg Bay, **snorkelling** in a kelp forest off Cape Town or **scuba diving** among bright fish in the coral reefs of Sodwana Bay.

▲ Richtersveld Transfrontier Park

▼ A southern right whale. Hermanus

Watching elephants on safari ▲

Lion, Kruger National Park ▼

The Big Four for the Big Five

The Kruger National Park is South Africa's flagship game reserve – and deservedly so. But don't rule out other outstanding reserves in other parts of the country. Apart from Kruger, South Africa has three other significant safari regions: in North West Province, KwaZulu-Natal and the Eastern Cape.

Kruger National Park in the northeast of the country is synonymous with South African safaris, with some justification: it's a huge conservation area – as large as Israel – with vast game populations, excellent infrastructure for DIY safaris and a bewildering choice of first-rate luxury safari lodges. See p.709.

Pilanesberg National Park in North West Province is the closest major game reserve to Johannesburg and Pretoria and is definitely worth thinking about if you're staying in the Gauteng region and time is tight. See p.651.

KwaZulu-Natal has a number of public and private game reserves of which Hluhluwe-Imfolozi is the most significant. This outstanding park is arguably the best place in the world for sighting endangered rhinos and feels wilder than Kruger. See p.453.

Eastern Cape is South Africa's newest Big Five region, yet has quickly become a force to be reckoned with: it's a day's drive from Cape Town, is malaria free and has the Addo Elephant National Park and some dozen private reserves, including the prestigious Shamwari, which in 2007 was named the World's Leading Safari and Game Reserve for the tenth consecutive year at the World Travel awards. See p.363.

Kamieskroon photographic workshops

Capturing on film the immensity and spectacle of the Namaqualand landscapes is no easy task. One way of improving your technique is to book a place on one of the popular photographic **workshops** at the *Kamieskroon Hotel* held during flower season. The residential courses last a week, and involve lectures, tuition and field work under the instruction of Canadian photographer Maurice Henri. You'll also learn more about the inspiring landscape and flora of Namaqualand. Although the flowers are the principal focus, workshops are also held in March and May, when fieldwork takes place around the dunes on the Atlantic coast near Hondeklip Bay. Although in semi-retirement, the internationally renowned Canadian photographer **Freeman Patterson**, whose coffee-table book on the flowers of Namaqualand, *Namaqualand: Garden of the Gods*, is a classic portrait of the region, tries to attend either the March or May session. The workshops are often fully booked, so contact the hotel as far in advance as you can. Full board with tuition starts at around R8000 per person per week for the flower season courses; the March and May field trips cost R11,000.

has become famous for running photographic workshops during the flower season (see box above), and is the centre for a growing number of activities in the surrounding Kamiesberg. Also good and informative about the region is *Randspaar Guest House*, 25 Church St (T&F027 672 1604 or 027 672 1729; self-catering ●, B&B ●), actually two guesthouses, one with en-suite bedrooms, bar and dining room, the other self-catering apartments. Other reasonable but unexciting options include *Gousblom B&B*, 95 De Waal St (T&F027 672 1004 or 082 962 3213; ●), and *Kamieskroon B&B*, Charlotte Street (T&F027 672 1652 or 082 898 2759, ●). The **campsite** at *Kamieskroon Hotel* is more pleasant than *Verbe Caravan Park*, on Kordon Street (T&F027 672 1666; R65). If everywhere is booked up in Kamieskroon for flower season, consider staying at **Garies**, 45km further south along the N7, where you'll find two satisfactory places on Main Street: *Garies Hotel* (T027 652 1042 or 072 396 1752, F027 652 1141; ●), which has a swimming pool, and *Sophie's Guesthouse* at no. 33 (T&F027 652 1069; ●), whose rooms have kitchenettes.

Namaqua National Park

A place worth going to in flower season, even if you're just passing through on the highway, is the **Skilpad section** of **Namaqua National Park** (daily 8am–6pm; T027 672 1948; R30), 17km northwest of Kamieskroon along a signposted gravel road. The displays here tend to be more reliable than elsewhere, even in years with low rainfall, with great swathes of orange colour. Butterfly fanatics and twitchers should be in for a treat, too. There's a circular five-kilometre drive around the reserve, two short walking trails and a scenic picnic site, but facilities are limited to toilets and a farm stall offering light meals.

Southern Namaqualand and the Bokkeveld

Travelling south from Kamieskroon, the mountains gradually give way to the bleaker landscape of the pebble-strewn **Knersvlakte** – the "plains of the gnashing teeth", referring to the sound made by wagon wheels toiling across the harsh terrain. Around 190km from Kamieskroon lies the small agricultural town of **Vanrhynsdorp**, the most southerly of the Namaqualand towns. Although it's officially in the Western Cape, this is the gateway to the region if you're coming from Cape Town. It marks the crossroads between the N7 Cape Town–Namibia highway and the R27, which connects via the glorious **Bokkeveld Escarpment** with Calvinia and ultimately Upington, on the northern fringe of the Great Karoo. Beyond the escarpment is the picturesque *dorp* of **Nieuwoudtville**, a great base for exploring the fertile region and its nature reserves.

Vanrhynsdorp

Set in the lee of the spectacular flat-topped Maskam mountain, **VANRHYN-SDORP** is pretty much deserted out of flower season. The town is dominated by the tall spire of its church, 500m east of the N7 highway at the end of Van Riebeeck Street. The town's **museum** is just before it (Mon–Fri 8am–1pm & 2–5pm; free), featuring a collection of old domestic and military pieces. On the same side of Van Riebeeck Street is the former **prison** (daily 9am–5pm), an attractive, low yellow building built in 1895; it now contains a small coffee shop and, making use of the old cells, various small crafts stalls displaying the woodwork and needlework of older members of the local Afrikaner population. Also in town is the quirky **Latsky Radio Museum** at the corner of Kerk and Olive streets behind the church (Mon–Sat 9am–noon & 2–5pm; free), nurturing a collection of some 200 valve radios dating back to the 1920s.

Five blocks east of the church, along Voortrekker Street, **Kokerboom Kwekery** is a nursery specializing in succulents (Mon–Fri 8am–1pm & 2–5pm; ☎027 219 1062). Around a third of the world's succulent species grow in this area, many of them endemic. Here you can obtain a permit for the three-kilometre **succulent hiking trail**, situated 25km north of town off the N7 – a worthwhile diversion if you're travelling that way.

Practicalities

Most **buses and taxis** running to and from Cape Town, Springbok or Upington stop at either the Shell or Engen garages at the start of Van Riebeck Street after turning off the highway. Onward travel to Cape Town is easiest by taxi, best at 9am when the early ones from Springbok pass through; ring ahead to be sure of a seat (see p.351). If you're going to Springbok, afternoons are better, when vehicles return from Cape Town. Note that there are no taxis in either direction on Saturdays. Intercape **buses** (tickets at Engen) run daily to Cape Town and Upington, via Springbok or Calvinia depending on which day you're travelling.

The museum also houses a simple but extremely friendly and clued-up **tourist office** (same hours as museum; ☎027 219 1552, ⊛www.tourismvanrhynsdorp .co.za). You can change **money** at Standard Bank on Voortrekker Street, close to the church. The post office is on Kerk Street; **Internet access** is available at the supermarket at the top of Van Riebeeck Street, facing the church.

Accommodation, eating and drinking

The best place to **stay** is the calm, welcoming and gay-friendly *Van Rhyn Guest House*, Van Riebeeck Street (☎027 219 1429, ⊛www.vanrhyngh.co.za; flower season full board ❺, at other times B&B ❸). The ten rooms, some in converted outhouses, have high ceilings and remain cool even during the summer heat; and excellent meals can be provided. Four hundred metres south of the church on Troe Troe Street, the friendly *Matzikamma Backpackers* (☎082 325 6564 or

082 254 0222; ❶) offers clean dorms and rooms in a quiet rural setting with a pool. Another 400m along the same road (which becomes Gifberg Road), *Vanrhynsdorp Caravan Park* (☎027 219 1287) is reasonably quiet out of season and has a cheap **campsite** and basic en-suite chalets (❷), three of them with kitchenettes. If you're planning on staying more than one night, you're probably best off looking for **farm-based accommodation** in the nearby mountains, for which you'll need a vehicle. Around 20km east of town on the road to Nieuwoudtville, the idiosyncratic *Suttridge Guest Farm* (☎027 219 1889 or 082 455 4137, ⓦwww.vanrhynsdorp.co.za; ❷) has two peaceful self-catering cottages and, unusually, an observatory from which you can gaze at the stars; 4WD trips and carriage rides through the countryside can also be arranged.

The best **restaurant** in town is *ZAR* at the caravan park (mains around R50), where well-prepared steaks are served up with snails, mussels and other interesting combinations. There are reasonable restaurants at both the Shell and Engen garages catering mainly to passing motorists, while *Phucifino*, next to Shell, is the town's liveliest **bar**.

Nieuwoudtville and around

Heading east from Vanrhynsdorp on the R27 you have a very clear impression of the sudden elevation of the land from the plains up to the Bokkeveld Escarpment, which the road tackles by way of **Van Rhyn's Pass**, complete with a couple of neck-achingly tight hairpins near the top. There's an excellent viewpoint overlooking the plains, signposted soon after you reach the plateau. You'll notice (as the early settlers did, much to their relief, after hauling their ox wagons up the escarpment) that the vegetation on top of the plateau is suddenly more fertile.

Eight kilometres on from the top of Van Rhyn's Pass, just over 50km from Vanrhynsdorp, the R27 passes just to the north of **NIEUWOUDTVILLE** ("Knee-voet-vil"), with an attractive collection of tin-roofed, honey-coloured sandstone buildings, and the sombre **ruins** of early settler homesteads on the outskirts. Founded just over a century ago, it's by far the most atmospheric place to stay at in the region, full of character and history. The soil here has the highest concentration of **bulb** species on earth, and there are several appealing nature reserves in the vicinity. Although most of the flowering species appear in August and September, a time of spectacular colourful display, you're likely to find something in flower here any time between March and October. One of the best things to do in Nieuwoudtville used to be the tours conducted by Neil MacGregor, one of the gurus of Namaqualand flowers, of his farm, **Glenlyon**. However, MacGregor has now sold his farm to the South African National Biodiversity Institute, who at the time of writing were planning to turn the site into a botanical garden. For the latest information, contact the Institute (☎012 843 5000).

Practicalities

Public transport to Nieuwoudtville is extremely limited. Buses from Upington and Vanrhynsdorp all arrive at night, while taxis are infrequent. An **information centre** (flower season daily 9am–5pm; at other times Mon, Wed & Fri 9am–5pm; ☎027 218 1336) operates out of the house in the attractively unkempt grounds of the church on Voortrekker Road – the town's only sealed road. Reliable advice is also available at the *Smidswinkel Restaurant & Information Centre* (☎027 218 1535, ⓦwww.nieuwoudtville.co.za) in a large sandstone building on Neethling Street; staff can point you to the various hiking trails in the region, and to rock-art sites.

The restaurant is also the place for booking one of the town's atmospheric *Van Zijl* **guesthouses** (➋), beautifully restored traditional sandstone buildings stuffed with characterful old furniture and located within walking distance of the restaurant. There's also the *Green Door* (July–Sept only; full board ➍), a snug loft above the restaurant. Just over 1km outside town is a pleasant **campsite**; book through the municipality office (☎027 218 8700).

Some of the farms around Nieuwoudtville offer accommodation in classic, old, thatched Karoo cottages. Particularly recommended as bases for visiting Oorlogskloof Nature Reserve (see below) are the three self-catering cottages run by the Van Wyk family. They're based at Papkuilsfontein Farm, 23km south of town off the dirt road to Clanwilliam (☎&℉027 218 1246; ➌), and are all within two hours' walk of the canyon. Activities include hikes, mountain-bike trails, birding (black and martial eagles are present) and trips to the reserve.

For somewhere to **eat**, you can't do better than the excellent *Smidswinkel Restaurant*, whose leg of lamb is famously good, especially when washed down with the local wine. For less common Afrikaner specialities like baked sheep's heads and stuffed heart, give them a day's notice.

Around Nieuwoudtville

The area receives unusually high rainfall thanks to its location at the edge of the escarpment, and consequently boasts over three hundred different floral species; flowering starts after the first rains in April or May, and peaks in August and September. The flowers are best seen at the **Nieuwoudtville Wildflower Reserve** some 3km east of town on the R27, with an unparalleled variety of bulbs, notably the orange-flowered bulbinellas.

The **Bokkeveld Nature Reserve** and its thirty-metre waterfall lie 7km north from town, towards the settlement of **Loeriesfontein**. When the Doring River is flowing between April and October, the waterfall tumbles down into an impressive gorge where large raptors can sometimes be seen soaring around the tall cliffs. A few kilometres beyond on the R357, a dirt road leading towards Gannabos will take you to another of the area's botanical oddities, an extensive **quiver tree forest**, containing some of the tallest specimens of *Aloe dichotoma* (the *kokerboom*) found in South Africa. They flower in June and July.

Worthwhile for those who have a bit of time in the area, especially out of flower season, the **Oorlogskloof Nature Reserve** encompasses a series of deep ravines and natural swimming pools carved out by the Oorlogskloof River. Perched on the edge of the escarpment, it gives breathtaking views over the Knersvlakte plain to the northwest, the surrounding mountain ranges and the river. The reserve is known for rare breeding colonies of black booted eagles, and is paradise for hikers and mountain bikers. Access is via a ten-kilometre gravel road that starts at the R27 near the top of Van Rhyn's Pass, 6km west of town. Before going, notify the Department of Nature Conservation on Goedehoop Street in Nieuwoudtville (Mon–Fri 8am–4pm; ☎ & ℉027 218 1159), which will issue you with a permit and give you the keys to the gate.

Calvinia and on to the Great Karoo

Despite its stern name, bestowed by an early dominee, **CALVINIA**, 70km east of Nieuwoudtville, has quite an appealing setting beneath the impressive Hantam Mountains. The town acts as a service centre for the western part of the Great Karoo, but it isn't a place you'll want to spend a lot of time in, unless you're here for the flowers in the surrounding area (*hantam* is Khoi for "where the red bulbs grow"). The **tourist office** on Church Street (Mon–Fri 8am–1pm & 2–5pm,

Sat 8am–noon; ℡027 341 8100, ℻027 341 8128) can provide details of **flower routes**, various 4WD trails in Hantam district, and two hiking trails in the magnificent Akkerendam Nature Reserve, just north of town in the lee of the mountains. For **accommodation**, *Hantam Huis*, 42–44 Hoop St (℡027 341 1606, Ⓦwww.calvinia.co.za; ❸), offers a characterful collection of restored old town houses, and also serves traditional Afrikaner **food** for lunch and dinner, as well as fresh bread, cakes, tea and coffee.

The Great Karoo

Strange though it may seem, the **Great Karoo**, the vast, dry, empty interior of South Africa, was an equally vast inland lake some 250 million years ago. It was populated by tiny marine creatures and, around its fringes, dinosaur-like amphibians, some of which left footprints in the mud that have been preserved as fossils. The contrast now could hardly be greater, with slow creaking windmills struggling to bring water to the surface and the baked, brown-red earth roamed only by small herds of antelope or tough merino sheep. Farmers here talk about the terrain in terms of hectares per sheep rather than sheep per hectare. The summer heat is fierce, the winter biting cold, the rain elusive, and the soil all but barren. Yet the Karoo has a special place for many South Africans, who take an almost perverse joy in the crisp air, the colours of the scattered *koppies* at sunset, the vastness of the pale sky, the depth of the darkness at night and the jostling galaxies of stars.

The west coast and the Richtersveld

North from St Helena Bay, the hook of land 100km north of Cape Town, the long, lonely **west coast** of South Africa has two simple components: the cold, grey Atlantic Ocean, and the dominant sandveld vegetation, hardy but infertile. There isn't much more to the region: between the mouth of the Olifants River near Vanrhynsdorp, and the Orange River over 400km to the north, there is just one sealed road connecting the N7 highway to the coast, which leads to the only settlement of significance, **Port Nolloth**.

Namaqualand's first **diamonds** were discovered in 1925, confirming that diamonds could be carried the length of the Orange, washed out into the ocean, and then dispersed by currents and the processes of longshore drift. Although initial prospecting was carried out along the course of the Orange and in the coastal dunes, the diamonds lying offshore on the sea bed are now more eagerly chased, mostly by boats operating with huge underwater "vacuum cleaners" and divers working in often dangerous conditions. Whereas much of Namaqualand's coast remains off-limits thanks to the presence of diamonds, the "**Diamond Coast**" from Port Nolloth to Alexander Bay, the mouth of the Orange River, is visitable, Springbok serving as a good access point.

During the flower season, the rains fall first on the coastal areas, and you can often see displays beginning about 20km inland, making the few roads down to the coast from the N7 worthwhile detours. The dirt R355 road through the **Spektakel Pass** between Springbok and Kleinzee is one of the most spectacular drives in Namaqualand, and the **Anenous Pass** on the tarred R382 between Steinkopf and Port Nolloth is also impressive. Along this road you'll also see wandering herds of goats belonging to the pastoral **Nama** people living in the area, as well as the peaks and valleys of the **Richtersveld Transfrontier Park**, the mountain desert occupying the area immediately south of the Orange River. The area surrounding the park is home to several developing **community tourism** initiatives, providing an excellent introduction to the life of the Nama.

The only public transport for Port Nolloth and Alexander Bay is the weekday **minibus**, run by VIP Taxis (℡027 851 8780), between Sanddrif on the Namibian border and Springbok. This passes through Alexander Bay at 7.45am, then Port Nolloth at 9am en route to Springbok, and turns around there at 3pm. Note that the border crossing to Oranjemund on the Namibian coast is closed; the only open border post is at Vioolsdrift.

Port Nolloth

PORT NOLLOTH, 156km northwest of Springbok, is an odd but delightful place. In the hazy sunshine the horizons are never quite in focus, while the heavy morning mists shroud the town in a quiet eeriness. Populated by an eclectic mix of races and professions, including fishermen, diamond-boat owners, fortune-seeking commercial divers, diver-seeking girls and a significant Portuguese and Nigerian community, Port Nolloth is a place with a whiff of mystery and excitement, and tales are thick about "IDB" (illegal diamond buying). You should take care when broaching the subject – paranoia and illegal firearms make a volatile combination.

Attractions are limited and the Atlantic too cold for swimming, but a stroll to the **harbour** is always interesting, and there's a small **museum** (Mon–Fri 9am–5pm) on the corner of the main road and Beach Road, where you can view an ad-hoc collection of flotsam, jetsam, photographs and newspaper articles about Port Nolloth, and find out about some of the local plant and sea life. There are no tours on the diamond boats, but the guesthouses at **McDougall's Bay**, around 5km to the south, have canoes and small boats for their guests.

The **tourist office** (Mon–Fri 8am–1pm & 1.45–4.30pm; ℡027 851 1111, ⓦwww.portnolloth.org.za) is at the museum; another good source of information is the laid-back *Bedrock Lodge* next door (℡027 851 8865, ⓦwww .bedrocklodge.co.za; ❷), a stylish old beach house with period furniture that's a great place to **stay**. There are simpler rooms in several beachfront houses at McDougall's Bay (ask locally for advice about walking there with luggage, as there have been muggings in the past), such as *McDougall's Bay Beach House Accommodation* on Haarder Street (℡027 851 8856, ⓔbeachaccom@telkomsa .net; ❷), and the similar *Port Indigo* on Kamp Street (℡027 851 8012, ⓦwww .portindigo.co.za; ❸).

For **eating**, the cosy *Anita's Tavern*, opposite the *Scotia Inn Hotel*, offers plain fish, meat and pasta dishes. The main **drinking** hole is *Diamond Hunters Pub*, on the main drag.

Alexander Bay

The most western point of South Africa is **ALEXANDER BAY**, 85km north of Port Nolloth at the mouth of the Orange River, within a stone's throw of Namibia. Alluvial **diamonds** are the town's *raison d'être*, their discovery in 1927 leading to the site's appropriation by the state, which still runs the place. The largest stone ever found here, in 1944, was the Merensky Diamond, weighing in at a cool 211.5 carats; more recently, a 111-carat stone was found by divers contracted by the state **Alexkor** mining company, which still controls most commercial activity in and around town. At the time of writing, the person who used to run the **diamond mine tours** had resigned, with no plans to replace her. For updated information on whether the tours have recommenced, call Alexkor's information centre (☎027 831 1330).

The Richtersveld

The area of northwestern Namaqualand known as the **Richtersveld** covers an area roughly bounded by the Orange River to the north, the N7 to the east, the R382 to Port Nolloth to the south and the Atlantic Ocean on its western side. Here, the starkly beautiful **AI-AIS RICHTERSVELD TRANSFRONTIER PARK** – to give it its full title – was formed in 2003 by the merger of South Africa's Richtersveld National Park (by which name the new park is still known in South Africa) and Namibia's Ai-Ais Hot Springs Game Park. Tucked along either side of a loop in the Orange, the landscape is fierce and rugged; names such as Hellskloof, Skeleton Gorge, Devil's Tooth and Gorgon's Head indicate the austerity of the inhospitable brown mountainscape, tempered only by a broad range of hardy succulents, mighty rock formations, the magnificence of the light cast at dawn and dusk, and the glittering canopy of stars at night. Annual rainfall in parts of the park is under 50mm, making this the only true desert – and mountain desert at that – in South Africa. In summer the daytime heat can be unbearable – temperatures over 50°C have been recorded – while on winter nights temperatures drop below freezing.

The best time to visit is August and September, when the area's **succulents** – representing almost one third of South Africa's species – burst into flower. There's little **fauna** in the park other than lizards and klipspringers, although

▲ Quiver trees at Ai-Ais Richtersveld Transfrontier Park

Community tourism in the Richtersveld

The Richtersveld area has several **community-based tourism initiatives**, combining basic accommodation (all in the ❶ bracket) – sometimes in the traditional *matjies* huts of the Nama – with opportunities to get to know the locals, eat traditional food and hike around the hills. **Access** – or lack thereof – is the main problem, as for most places you need your own wheels, and you'd do well to arrange things a week or so in advance by phone to be sure that places are open and food and water are available. For more information and updates (these places come and go with great regularity), contact the tourist office in Springbok.

Eksteenfontein (Xhobes) ☎027 851 7108. The oldest and most wide-ranging of the projects, this was started by local women whose husbands were away working in mines. It features the comfortable *Eksteenfontein Guesthouse*, with kitchen and shower, *matjies* huts to stay in, a coffee bar, 4WD trail, meals, and plenty of excitable kids.

Lekkersing ☎&⊕027 851 8580. Over the hills west of Eksteenfontein, this offers the modern, self-catering *Lekkersing Guesthouse*, hiking, horse-riding, donkey cart rides and even caving. The project also maintains a campsite at Koerdap.

Rooiberg ☎027 851 7108. Around 15km from Eksteenfontein at the base of a mountain, perfect for that miles-from-anywhere wilderness experience (bring water from Eksteenfontein). There's a guesthouse, campsite and hiking trails, for which you'll need a guide.

Sanddrif ☎027 831 1457 or 072 352 8137. On the Orange River off the road from Alexander Bay to Sendelingsdrift, this is the departure point for the weekday *VIP* minibus taxi to Springbok (see p.350), and is thus easily accessible.

---

leopards are present if characteristically shy. Along the Orange you'll find surprisingly rich **birdlife**, which is best enjoyed by taking a **canoeing trip** down the river – a gentle and relaxing jaunt rather than high-energy white-water rafting (by the time it reaches northern Namaqualand, the river is broad and the few rapids innocuous). Trips range from half-day tasters to full-on six- day expeditions, with camps set up by the riverbank en route; costs start at around R260 for a full day including lunch, or R500 overnight with all meals. A recommended rafting company is Bushwhacked Outdoor Adventure (☎027 761 8953, ⊛www.bushwhacked.co.za), based at the riverside *Fiddler's Creek* campsite (R45), 10km along the south bank of the river from Vioolsdrif, on the Namibian border.

Practicalities

Facilities are extremely limited – this is not the place for a casual visit, and there's no public transport either. Ordinary cars are not allowed inside the park; the only way to explore is in a 4WD or a pick-up with a high enough clearance to handle the sandy river beds and rough mountain passes between the designated campsites. Pay particular attention along the track linking the Richtersberg and De Hoop campsites, which is covered with thick sand and treacherously jagged rocks. Unless you're an experienced driver, probably the best way of seeing Richtersveld is as part of a **tour**. The most experienced operation is Richtersveld Challenge (see p.350), offering expeditions of varying lengths into the park as well as to Kgalagadi, Namibia and Botswana; also recommended are Virosatours (see p.349). Both outfits can include hiking, abseiling or rafting along the Orange in their tours.

If you are driving, it's recommended that you travel in a group of two vehicles, but note that no driving is allowed at night; fuel and limited supplies are available at the park headquarters at **Sendelingsdrift** (daily 7.30am–5.30pm; ℡027 831 1506, Ⓕ027 831 1175; R80), 94km from Alexander Bay. **Maps and guidebooks** are sold at the gate, and at *Springbok Lodge* (see p.351) in Springbok. It used to be possible to enter the park at Sendelingsdrift and exit at Helskloof Gate in the south, but because of the bad condition of the road, the Helskloof Gate exit has been closed and visitors must now enter and leave at Sendelingsdrift.

At the time of writing, the South African and Namibian sections of the park remained separated, the border closed other than for rafters camping along the Orange. However, by the time you read this, a pontoon bridge at the park headquarters should have opened to ferry vehicles across the river, and it would be reasonable to assume that tourists will be allowed to enter the Namibian side of the park so long as they return via the same route, as happens at Kgalagadi Transfrontier Park. For updated information, contact the park headquarters.

Park **accommodation** – which should be booked through South African National Parks (see p.63) – includes decent self-catering chalets (❸) at the park-run guesthouse by the gate at Sendelingsdrift, and very basic **campsites** (R55) at Kokerboomkloof, Potjiespram, Richtersberg and De Hoop inside the park; all have ablution facilities. Between April and September it's possible to **hike**, accompanied by a guide, along designated trails, and also into the park with the help of the community tourism project at Kuboes, although note that these trails are liable to closure if there are not enough qualified guides.

Travel details

Trains

Kimberley to: Beaufort West (4 weekly; 8hr); Bloemfontein (4 weekly; 2hr 45min–3hr 15min); Bloemhof (1–2 daily; 2hr 20min); Cape Town (1–2 daily; 17hr 30min–18hr); Christiana (1–2 daily; 1hr 30min); De Aar (1 daily; 4hr); Durban (Tues & Thurs; 19hr 15min); Johannesburg (1–2 daily; 8hr 30min–9hr); Klerksdorp (1–2 daily; 4hr 30min); Krugersdorp (1–2 daily; 7hr 35min–8hr); Ladysmith (Tues & Thurs; 13hr); Laingsburg (1–2 daily; 11hr 45min); Mafikeng (1–2 daily; 9hr); Pietermaritzburg (Tues & Thurs; 17hr); Potchefstroom (1–2 daily; 5hr 30min); Worcester (1–2 daily; 14hr 30min).
Upington to: Windhoek (Namibia; 2 weekly; 25hr 20min).

Buses

Kimberley to: Bloemfontein (4 weekly; 2hr 30min); Bloemhof (3 daily; 2hr); Cape Town (3–4 daily; 11hr–11hr 30min); Christiana (3 daily; 1hr 30min); George (4 weekly; 9hr 30min–9hr 55min); Johannesburg (3 daily; 6hr 30min–7hr 40min); Klerksdorp (3 daily; 3hr 45min); Mossel Bay

(4 weekly; 9hr–9hr 30min); Oudtshoorn (4 weekly; 7hr 30min); Potchefstroom (3 daily; 4hr 30min); Upington (2 weekly; 5hr).
Kuruman to: Johannesburg (1 daily; 7hr 20min); Pretoria (1 daily; 8hr 20min); Upington (1 daily; 3hr 30min); Vryburg (1 daily; 1hr 40hr).
Springbok to: Cape Town (1 daily; 6hr 30min); Upington (1 daily; 5hr); Windhoek (4 weekly; 12hr).
Upington to: Bloemfontein (3 weekly; 7hr); Cape Town (1 daily; 11hr 30min–12hr 45min); Johannesburg (1 daily; 10hr 15min); Kimberley (3 weekly; 5hr); Klerksdorp (1 daily; 7hr 20min); Kuruman (1 daily; 2hr 45min); Potchefstroom (1 daily; 8hr); Pretoria (1 daily; 11hr 15min); Springbok (1 daily; 5hr 10min); Vryburg (1 daily; 4hr 40min); Windhoek (Namibia; 4 weekly; 11hr 30min).
Vanrhynsdorp to: Cape Town (1 daily; 5hr); Springbok (1 daily; 4hr 30min); Upington (1 daily; 7hr).

Minibus taxis

Services on all routes are reduced on Saturday, and often nonexistent on Sunday. Frequencies given below refer to weekdays.

Kimberley to: Barkly West (hourly; 30min); Kuruman (1–2 daily; 2hr 30min); Upington (3–4 daily; 5hr).

Springbok to: Alexander Bay (2 daily Mon–Fri; 1hr 10min); Cape Town (5 daily except Sat; 6hr 30min); Port Nolloth (2 daily Mon–Fri; 4hr); Sanddrif (1 daily Mon–Fri; 3hr 30min); Upington (1 daily; 5hr).

Upington to: Calvinia (3 weekly; 5hr); Cape Town (3 weekly; 10hr); Johannesburg (1–2 daily; 10hr); Kimberley (2–3 daily; 5hr); Kuruman (1–2 daily; 4hr 30min); Springbok (1 daily; 5hr).

Domestic flights

Kimberley to: Cape Town (1–2 daily; 1hr 35min); Johannesburg (5–6 daily; 1hr 15min).
Upington to: Cape Town (1 daily; 1hr 50min); Johannesburg (1–2 daily; 1hr 35min).

The Eastern Cape

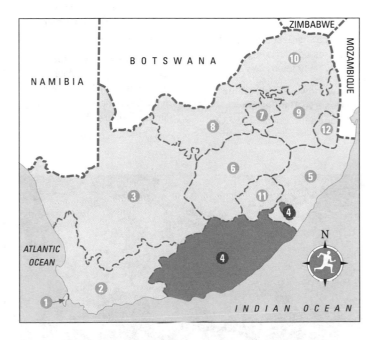

CHAPTER 4 # Highlights

* **Port Elizabeth township tour** Several guides run very accessible tours into the African areas of the province's largest city. See p.370

* **Addo Elephant National Park** See pachyderms and the rest of the Big Five in the best public game reserve in the malaria-free southern half of the country. See p.377

* **Grahamstown Festival** Africa's largest arts festival wakes up this pretty colonial university town. See p.397

* **Kwandwe Private Game Reserve** The Eastern Cape's top private Big Five destination for those with money to burn. See p.398

* **The Tuishuise** Accommodation in a street of beautifully restored and and furnished Victorian houses in the historic frontier town of Cradock. See p.402

* **Karoo farmstays** Experience the sharp light and panoramic landscape of the Karoo semi-desert that sweeps across South Africa's interior. See p.405

* **Bulungula Backpacker Lodge** In a remote Wild Coast village, this brilliant base offers a vivid experience of Xhosa life and culture. See p.435

▲ Addo Elephant National Park

The Eastern Cape

Sandwiched between the Western Cape and KwaZulu-Natal, South Africa's two most popular coastal provinces, the **Eastern Cape** tends to be bypassed by visitors – and for all the wrong reasons. The relative neglect it has suffered as a tourist destination and at the hands of the government is precisely where its charm lies. You can still find traditional African villages here, and the region's 1000km of undeveloped **coastline** alone justify a visit, sweeping back inland in immense undulations of vegetated dunefields. For anyone wanting to get off the beaten track, the province is, in fact, one of the most rewarding regions in South Africa.

Port Elizabeth is the province's commercial centre, principally used to start or end a trip along the Garden Route, though it's a useful springboard for launching out into the rest of South Africa – the city is the transport hub of the Eastern Cape, well served by flights, trains, buses and car rental companies. **Jeffrey's Bay**, 75km to the west, has a fabled reputation among surfers for its perfect waves. East of Port Elizabeth, the **R72** coastal road, a great rolling journey, provides easy access to a series of unassuming resorts, all gloriously sited on euphorbia-clad hillsides at the mouths of lazy rivers. Around an hour's drive inland are some of the province's most significant game reserves, the only places in the southern half of the country providing serious game viewing, among them **Addo Elephant National Park**, a Big Five reserve where sightings of elephants are virtually guaranteed. Addo and the private reserves nearby are among the few game reserves in South Africa that are malaria-free throughout the year. The hinterland to the north takes in areas appropriated by English immigrants shipped out in the 1820s as ballast for a new British colony. Here, **Grahamstown** glories in its twin roles as the spiritual home of English-speaking South Africa and host to Africa's biggest arts festival. Close by, the Big Five country of **Kwandwe Private Game Reserve** comprises stony hills vegetated by monumental candelabra-like succulents and a river course lined with thorn trees – the most desirable wildlife destination in the province and one of several game-viewing areas in the vicinity of Grahamstown.

The northwest is dominated by the sparse beauty of the **Karoo**, the thorny semi-desert stretching across much of central South Africa. The rugged **Mountain Zebra National Park**, 200km north of Port Elizabeth, is a terrific place to watch herbivorous game in a stirring landscape of flat-topped mountains and arid plains stretching for hundreds of kilometres. A short step to the west, **Graaff-Reinet** is the quintessential eighteenth-century Cape Dutch Karoo town, with its serene whitewashed streetscape.

The eastern part of the province, largely the former Transkei, is by far the least developed, with rural Xhosa villages predominating. **East London,**

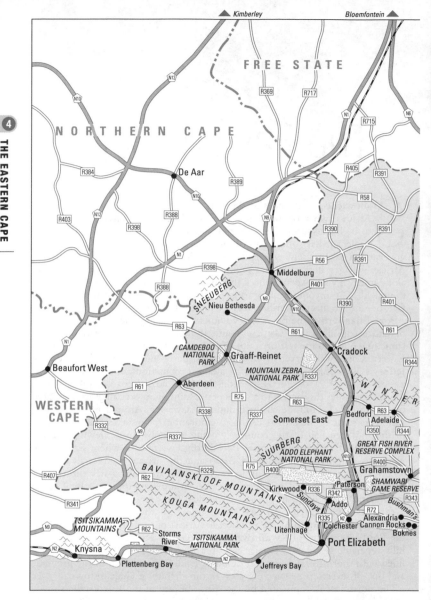

the province's only other centre of any size, sits on the cusp of the former "white" South Africa and the African "homelands", and also serves well as a springboard for heading north into the central region, where the principal interest derives from political and cultural connections. **Steve Biko** was born here, and you can visit his grave in **King William's Town** to the west. Further west is **Alice**, less well known than its university, **Fort Hare**, which educated

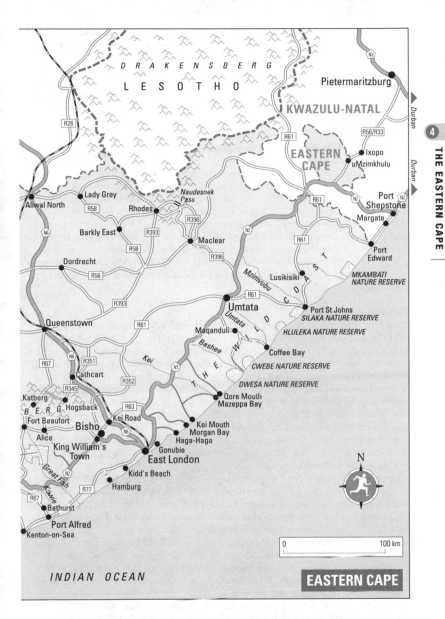

many contemporary African leaders, including Nelson Mandela. The only established resorts in this section are in the **Amatola Mountains**, where indigenous forests and mossy coolness provide relief from the dry scrublands below. Tucked into the northeastern corner of the province, the **Drakensberg range**, more commonly associated with KwaZulu-Natal, makes a steep ascent out of the Karoo and offers trout-fishing, skiing in winter and ancient San rock art. The focus of the area is the remote, lovely village of **Rhodes**, a long journey down a rough road, which rewards you with absolute tranquillity and exceptional views.

Further east, the **Wild Coast region** remains one of the least developed and most exciting regions in the country. It's also the poorest part of the poorest province, a fact reflecting its historic role as a dumping ground for black South Africans. Despite this, the region is blessed with fabulously beautiful subtropical coast. From here, all the way to the KwaZulu-Natal border, dirt roads trundle down to the coast from the N2 to dozens of remote and indolent hillside resorts, of which **Port St Johns** is the biggest and best known. West of Port St Johns, the **Wild Coast Hotel Meander**, an organized walking trail, takes in a deserted stretch of cliffs and sands with convenient stops at small family resort hotels. Along the coast to the east of town, you can explore beaches and rural villages on horseback as part of the community-run **Amadiba Trail**, which starts near the KwaZulu-Natal border. In the rugged, goat-chewed landscape inland, Xhosa-speakers live in mud-and-tin homesteads, scraping a living herding stock and growing crops. Most visitors pass as quickly as possible through **Mthatha** (formerly Umtata), the ugly former capital of the Transkei – but if you're following in the footsteps of Nelson Mandela, the **Nelson Mandela Museum** in the centre of Mthatha and **Qunu**, his birthplace southwest of the town, are obvious ports of call.

Some history

The Eastern Cape was carved up into black and white territories in a more consolidated way than anywhere else in the country. The stark contrasts between wealth and poverty were forged in the nineteenth century when the British drew the Cape colonial frontier along the **Great Fish River**, a thousand kilometres east of Cape Town, and fought over half a dozen campaigns (known as the **Frontier Wars**) to keep the **Xhosa** at bay on its east bank. In the 1820s, the British shipped in thousands of settlers to bolster white numbers and reinforce the line. West of the Kei River, which subsequently became the colonial boundary, you'll encounter fenced-off white farms, pretty historic towns and industrial development. Across the river, the scourges of imperialism and apartheid have left little but overgrazed communal lands dotted with traditional huts and skinny cattle.

Even for a country where everything is suffused with politics, the Eastern Cape's identity is excessively **political**. South Africa's black trade unions have deep roots in its soil, which also produced many anti-apartheid African leaders, including former president **Nelson Mandela**, his successor **Thabo Mbeki**, and Black Consciousness leader **Steve Biko**, who died in 1977 at the hands of Port Elizabeth security police. The Transkei or Wild Coast region, wedged between the Kei and KwaZulu-Natal, was the testing ground for grand apartheid when it became the prototype in 1963 for the Bantustan system of racial segregation. In 1976 the South African government gave it notional "independence", under the puppet leadership of the Matanzima brothers, in the hope that several million Xhosa-speaking South Africans, surplus to industry's needs, could be dumped in the territory and thereby become foreigners in "white South Africa". When the Transkei was reincorporated into South Africa in 1994 it became part of the new Eastern Cape province, which is struggling for economic survival under the weight of its apartheid-era legacy.

Port Elizabeth and the western region

A city of flyovers and sprawling townships, **Port Elizabeth** is the industrial centre of the Eastern Cape, where African shanty dwellers scrape a living on the dusty fringes of well-tended middle-class suburbs. In 1820 it was the arrival point for four thousand British settlers, who doubled the English-speaking population of South Africa. Today, their descendants risk the hellish national roads from Gauteng every Christmas to speed down to the "Friendly City" and holiday along the institutionalized beachfront, with its burger bars and performing dolphins. The port's industrial feel is mitigated by some outstanding city beaches, and should you end up killing time here (and you could certainly do worse), you'll find diversion in beautiful **coastal walks** a few kilometres from town and in the small **historical centre**. There are also a couple of excellent township tours, which offer valuable insight into apartheid and the new South Africa, and are a welcome contrast to the Garden Route's beach focus.

The main reason most people wash up here is to start or finish a tour of the **Garden Route** – or head further up the highway to **Addo Elephant National Park** (see p.377), the most significant game reserve in the southern half of the country. Also within easy striking distance are several other smaller, private and utterly luxurious game reserves such as **Shamwari, Amakhala, Lalibela and Kwandwe**.

To the east of Port Elizabeth, a handful of **resorts** are found along the **R72 East London coast road**, where the roaring surf meets enormously wide sandy beaches, backed by mountainous dunes. The inland route to East London deviates away from the coast to pass through **Grahamstown**, a handsome university town, worth at least a night (more if you're interested in English settler history and the frontier conflicts with the Xhosa). Nearby, pretty settler villages trace the spread of the 1820 settlers into the interior.

A couple of hundred kilometres north from Port Elizabeth, an area of flat-topped hills and treeless plains opens out to extend across a third of South Africa. Its name, the **Karoo**, means "hard and dry" in the tongue of the Khoikhoi pastoralists, the region's original inhabitants, who were exterminated by Dutch frontiersmen. The oldest and best known of the settlements here is the picture-postcard town of **Graaff-Reinet**, a solid fixture on bus tours. Just a few kilometres away is the awesome **Valley of Desolation**, and the village of **Nieu Bethesda**, best known for its eccentric Owl House museum. Nearly as pretty as Graaff-Reinet, though not as architecturally rich, the town of **Cradock**, to its east, has the added attractions of mineral baths and the rugged **Mountain Zebra National Park**. Some of the best places to stay in the *platteland*, or interior, are on sheep farms or in historically listed guesthouses.

Port Elizabeth

At the western end of Algoa (aka Nelson Mandela) Bay, **PORT ELIZABETH**, commonly known as **PE**, is not a place to visit if you're looking for cosmopolitan urban culture or beautiful buildings. The smokestacks along the N2 bear testimony to the fact that the Eastern Cape's largest centre has thrived on heavy industry and cheap African labour, which accounts for its deep-rooted trade unionism and strong tradition of African nationalism. So it may come as a surprise that this has long been a popular holiday destination for white Gauteng families – but then the town beachfront, stretching for several kilometres along Humewood Road, has some of the nicest, safest and cleanest **city beaches** in the country, thoroughly geared up with waterslides, performing dolphins and snakes to keep the kids occupied.

As a city, PE is pretty functional. There's enough reason to linger for a couple of days, however, and the city has some terrific accommodation and good restaurants in a relatively crime-free environment. Although the town has been ravaged by industrialization and thoughtless modernization, one or two buildings do stand out in an otherwise featureless **city centre**, and a couple of classically pretty rows of Victorian terraces still remain in the suburb of **Central**. Holidaymakers head for the beachfront suburbs of **Humewood** and **Summer-strand** where there are places to stay, bars, restaurants and clubs in abundance. There are also some excellent **tours** around PE and into the townships.

Arrival and information

Port Elizabeth's **airport** (☎041 581 2984) is conveniently situated on the edge of Walmer suburb, 4km south from the city centre. Taxis rank outside the airport and the fare to the city centre is around R35.

The **train station** (☎041 507 2662) is centrally located, with buses departing from the rank directly across the road. The **Baz Bus** will drop you off at any central location or accommodation. Arriving by **intercity bus**, you alight at Greenacres shopping mall in Newton Park suburb, 3km from the centre, served by Translux, Greyhound and Intercape. As for regional bus services, Minilux (☎043 741 3107) runs buses between East London and PE via Grahamstown four days a week.

The extremely helpful **Nelson Mandela Bay Tourism** office (Mon–Fri 8am–4.30pm, Sat & Sun 9.30am–3.30pm; ☎041 585 8884, ⓦ www.nmbt.co.za) is in the Donkin Lighthouse Building (a National Monument with a good view from the top) on the Donkin Reserve in Belmont Terrace, Central suburb.

City transport and tours

If you're staying in Central, exploring the city **on foot** is a realistic possibility – try the self-guided **Heritage Walk**, shown on a map available at the tourist office). However, for any serious exploration of PE, or for getting to and from the beachfront, **renting a car** is your best option (see "Listings", p.376), as the city's transport system leaves much to be desired. **Buses** operated by the municipal Algoa Bus Company (☎041 404 1200, ⓦ www.algoabus.co.za) are infrequent, running from the Market Square bus depot to the suburbs, the beaches and Greenacres shopping mall. PE's **minibus taxis** run from town to the beachfront on a regular basis, but are the least recommended way to travel. **Metered taxis** don't have ranks so you'll need to phone to find a taxi (see p.377); if you're going to the airport or the bus or train stations, it's advisable to book ahead.

The best way to see Port Elizabeth is on one of the excellent **bus tours**, which shed light on the culture and history of a city shaped by layers of political history. Calabash Tours (☎041 585 6162 or 084 552 4414, ⓦ www.calabashtours.co.za) operates excellent "Real City Tours" by day and *shebeen* tours by night; Tanaqua

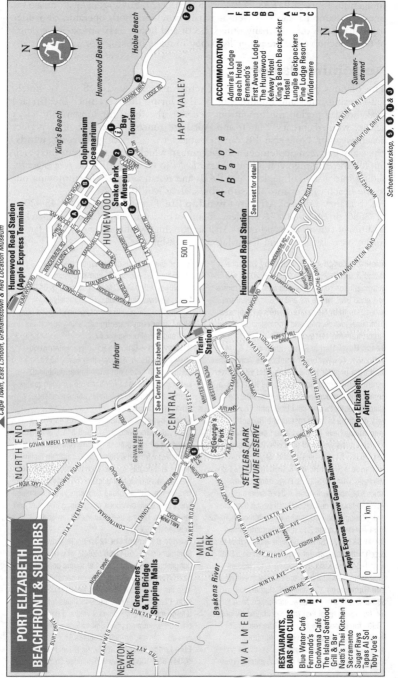

PORT ELIZABETH
BEACHFRONT & SUBURBS

◄ Cape Town, East London, Grahamstown & Red Location Museum

Humewood Road Station
(Apple Express Terminal)

ACCOMMODATION
Admiral's Lodge	I
Beach Hotel	F
Fernando's	H
First Avenue Lodge	G
The Humewood	B
Kelway Hotel	D
King's Beach Backpacker Hostel	A
Lungile Backpackers	E
Pine Lodge Resort	J
Windermere	C

N

NORTH END

LAKE VIEW

NEWTON PARK

WALMER

MILL PARK

CENTRAL

HUMEWOOD

King's Beach

Hobie Beach

Humewood Beach

HAPPY VALLEY

A l g o a   B a y

Dolphinarium
Oceanarium

Snake Park
& Museum

Bay Tourism

Harbour

Train Station

See Central Port Elizabeth map

St George's Park

SETTLERS PARK
NATURE RESERVE

Baakens River

Port Elizabeth
Airport

Humewood Road Station

See Inset for detail

Schoenmakerskop, ⑤, ⑥, ①& ① ►

Summer-
strand

Apple Express Narrow Gauge Railway

0   1 km

0   500 m

GOVAN MBEKI STREET

HARROWER ROAD

Greenacres
& The Bridge
Shopping Malls

**RESTAURANTS,
BARS AND CLUBS**
Blue Water Café	3
Fernando's	H
Gondwana Café	2
The Island Seafood Grill & Bar	5
Natti's Thai Kitchen	4
Sacramento	6
Sugar Rays	1
Tapas Al Sol	1
Toby Joe's	1

MARINE DRIVE

BRIGHTON DRIVE

WINCHESTER WAY

STRANDFONTEIN ROAD

371

Indigenous Tours (☎041 582 4304 or 083 270 9924, ⊛www.tanaquatours.co.za) offers the same packages as well as whale-watching. Both operators also offer day-trips to Addo, as do many others. B&Bs and hotels carry an extensive range of tour brochures and are generally happy to make bookings for guests.

Accommodation

The obvious place to stay is the **beachfront**, with a vast choice of hotels, self-catering suites and hundreds of B&Bs. During the December and January peak holiday period the beachfront becomes the focus for most of the city's action, while February, March and April are much quieter yet offer perfect beach weather. Note that PE can be subject to excoriatingly **strong winds**, especially between September and December, which makes going to the beach unpleasant. Although you'll find *Jikileza Lodge* in **Central PE**, the area is gently sliding into a state of neglect, and B&Bs and restaurants have been moving out to the beachfront or into the **suburbs**, such as Mill Park.

If you fancy a slice of **African township life**, *Fundani Lodge* (☎041 454 2064 or 2066 or 082 964 6563) offers an opportunity to enjoy football matches, traditional ceremonies and good African cooking, while you stay with a family in the New Brighton and KwaMagxaki townships (❷).

Admiral's Lodge 47 Admiralty Way, Summerstrand ☎041 583 1894 or 083 455 2072, ⊛www.admiralslodge.co.za. Spacious and stylish rooms at a good B&B, at the far end of Summerstrand about 7km from the centre. There's a braai area, communal lounge, pool and trampoline for the kids. Airport transfers are available. ❻

Beach Hotel Marine Drive, Humewood ☎041 583 2161, ⊛www.beachhotel.co.za. Across the road from popular Hobie Beach, and sited at the centre of the beachside action, the hotel has a great patio bar overlooking the sea, offering snacks, cocktails and cold beer, and *The Bell*, a very decent à la carte restaurant. Recent renovations have included a sun deck and pool. Ask about the weekend specials. Breakfast extra. Sea-facing ❼, non-sea-facing ❻

Fernando's Guest House & Grill 102 Cape Rd, Mill Park ☎041 373 2823. Purportedly South Africa's oldest guesthouse, in three separate Victorian houses decked out with period furniture and offering good value and a warm atmosphere. ❸

First Avenue Lodge 3 First Ave, Summerstrand ☎041 583 5173. Sixteen en-suite rooms close to the beach with their own entrances, offered on a B&B or self-catering basis, in a popular and pleasant establishment with a pool and entertainment area. ❹

The Humewood 33 Beach Rd, Humewood ☎041 585 8961, ⊛www.humewoodhotel.co.za. A large, old-fashioned hotel that reeks nostalgically of 1950s family seaside holidays. The rooms are large rooms and feature wicker furniture and summery floral prints. Service is excellent and includes laundry facilities and babysitting. There's

a good bar and sun deck. Airport transfers available. Sea-facing ❸, non-sea-facing ❹

Jikeleza Lodge 44 Cuyler St, Central ☎041 586 3721, ⊛www.highwinds.co.za. Friendly backpacker place with dorms, doubles and a family room. Its adventure centre can help you sort out tour and travel bookings. ❶

Kelway Hotel Brookes Hill Drive, Humewood ☎041 584 0638, ⊛www.thekelway.co.za. Stylish hotel kitted out with timber panelling, seagrass chairs and handcrafted wooden tables. Standard, luxury and family rooms available. Breakfast included. ❹

King's Beach Backpacker Hostel 41 Windermere Rd, Humewood ☎041 585 8113, ℮kingsb @agenet.co.za. Spotless, well-established hostel, a block away from the beach, with camping facilities, dorms and double rooms, plus an outside bar and braai area. Although principally for self-catering, it lays on tea, coffee, bread and jams in the morning. The travel desk can book township, game park and other tours. Dorms and doubles ❶, en-suite doubles ❷

Lungile Backpackers 12 La Roche Drive, Summerstrand ☎041 582 2042, ⊛www.lungilebackpackers.co.za. Large and popular beachfront hostel where you can party indoors or step out into the heart of PE's beachfront nightlife strip. Perched on a hill, it has facilities for camping, a large lawn to relax on, sea views, a pool table, bar and swimming pool. Self-catering only. Dorms and doubles ❶, en-suite doubles ❷

Pine Lodge Resort Off Marine Drive, Humewood ☎041 583 4004, ⊛www.pinelodge.co.za. Right on the beach near the wonderful historic lighthouse and next to the Cape Recife Nature Reserve, where owls, mongooses and antelope make appearances. Offers various log cabin units, some with full kitchens, sleeping from four to eight people. Besides a popular bar and restaurant, the lodge boasts a swimming pool, a gym and a games room. Cabins for four from around R350.

Windermere 35 Humewood Rd, Humewood ☎041 582 2245, ⓦwww.thewindermere.co.za. Stylish hotel with just eight suites, given an almost Zen-like feel through the subtle use of off-white to oaty colours contrasted with dark hues, such as chocolate brown, and materials that include timber and granite. ❽

The City

Port Elizabeth's **city centre** is marred by a network of freeways that cuts a swath across the south of town, blocking off the city from the harbour. The city's white population retreated to the suburbs some time ago, leaving the centre to African traders and township shoppers, who are slowly resuscitating its commercial spirit. The **suburbs** offer little to draw you away from the beachfront, unless you're a shopaholic, in which case you should make a beeline for **Newton Park**, 5km west of the centre and home to **Greenacres** and **The Bridge**, vast shopping malls to which the city-centre department stores have relocated en masse. Further afield in **New Brighton**, you'll find Port Elizabeth's most important museum, the **Red Location Museum of the People's Struggle**, housed in a building that has won several awards.

Central

The city's main street, which runs parallel to the freeway as it sweeps into town, has been renamed **Govan Mbeki Avenue** in honour of the veteran activist (father of Thabo Mbeki, South Africa's president), who died in 2001. African traders dealing a pretty standard line in crochet tat and leather goods line up

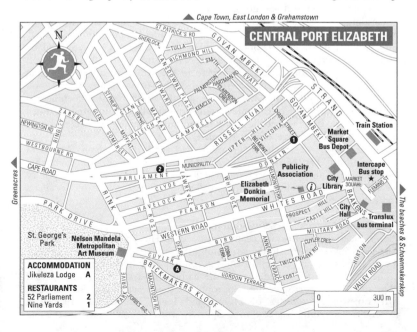

▲ Cape Town, East London & Grahamstown

CENTRAL PORT ELIZABETH

ACCOMMODATION
Jikeleza Lodge   **A**

RESTAURANTS
52 Parliament   **2**
Nine Yards   **1**

0   300 m

▲ Donkin Street, Port Elizabeth

along the pavements giving the precinct a lively feel, but it's not safe after dark. The symbolic heart of town is the **City Hall**, standing in **Market Square**, a large, empty space surrounded by some striking mid-Victorian buildings, adjacent to the train and bus stations on the edge of the harbour. But the dejection of the quarter, under the grimy shadow of a flyover, conspires against it ever pumping any real life into the district.

Heading west up hilly **Donkin Street**, you'll come upon a curious stone pyramid commemorating **Elizabeth Donkin**, after whom PE was named. Elizabeth was the young wife of the Cape's acting governor in 1820, Sir Rufane Donkin; she died of fever in India in 1818. As you stroll up Donkin Street, you could be forgiven for thinking you were in the wrong country, the wrong continent – the raked terrace of Victorian double-storey houses would look completely at home in any town on England's South Coast. The nineteen **Donkin Houses**, built in the mid-nineteenth century and declared National Monuments in 1967, reflect the desire of the English settlers to create a home from home in this strange, esiccated land.

Further west, you reach St George's Park and the **Nelson Mandela Metropolitan Art Museum**, 1 Park Drive (Mon–Fri 8.30am–5pm, Sat 9am–4.30pm, Sun 2–4.30pm; free), which has a collection of contemporary local work, visiting exhibitions and a small shop selling postcards and local arts and crafts.

The beachfront and around

PE's wonderful **beaches** are its main attraction. The protection provided by Algoa Bay makes them safe for swimming (that said, it's best to do so between the lifeguard beacons), and clean enough to make **beachcombing** a pleasure.

The beachfront strip, divided from the harbour by a large wall, starts about 2km south of the city centre. En route to the beaches, the **South End Museum** on the corner of Humewood Road and Walmer Boulevard (Mon–Fri 9am–4pm, Sat & Sun 2–5pm) is worth a visit. Based in the old

Seamen's Institute, it recalls the bygone days of the South End, a vibrant multicultural neighbourhood the growth of which had much to do with PE's then booming harbour. As a result of the Group Areas Act it was razed street by street in the 1960s, save for a handful or churches and mosques. Today, the area is full of pricey townhouses.

The first of the beaches is beautiful, wide **King's Beach**, which is somewhat marred by a jumble of coal heaps and oil tanks behind it. To the southeast lies **Humewood Beach**, across the road from which is a complex housing **Bayworld Museum, Oceanarium and Snake Park** (daily 9am–4.30pm; R35, children half-price); the Oceanarium (performing dolphin and seal shows 11am & 3pm) brings huge pleasure to hordes of excited children during the holidays. **Brookes Pavilion** next door and **Dolphin's Leap** nearby are complexes of restaurants, pubs and clubs with great views. Beyond, to the south, **Hobie Beach** and **Summerstrand** are great for walking and sunbathing, with one dive operator based at the latter (see "Listings", p.376). Summerstrand's **Boardwalk Casino Complex** has some pleasing shops, including an indigenous crafts market, cinemas and some reasonable eating places.

Marine Drive continues 15km down the coast as far as the village of **Schoenmakerskop** (Schoenies to the locals), along impressive coastline that alternates between rocky shores and sandy beaches. From here you can walk the eight-kilometre **Sacramento Trail**, a shoreline path that leads to the huge-duned **Sardinia Bay**, the wildest and most dramatic stretch of coast in the area. To get there by road, turn right at the Schoenmakerskop intersection and follow the road until Sardinia Bay is signed, on the left.

Red Location Museum of the People's Struggle

Situated in the suburb of New Brighton, 7km north of central Port Elizabeth, the **Red Location Museum of the People's Struggle**, at the corner of Olof Palme and Singaphi streets (Tues–Fri 10am–4pm, Sat & Sun 9am–3pm; R12), is dedicated to recalling the experiences of the residents of Red Location, Port Elizabeth's oldest African township, established in 1902. The settlement took its name from the rusted corrugated-iron barracks – around which New Brighton developed – that had housed troops till the end of the Anglo-Boer War. A significant site of anti-apartheid resistance, New Brighton was the stomping ground of a number of significant South Africans, including Govan Mbeki, ANC stalwart and father of South Africa's president, artist George Pemba, and internationally feted actor John Kani. Red Location was the first place in South Africa to stage a passive resistance campaign against the pass laws (see p.830) and was the birthplace of the first cell of MK (the ANC's armed wing).

The museum is housed in a striking building awarded the 2006 Royal Institute of British Architects' **Lubetkin Prize** for the most outstanding

The Apple Express

Just southeast of the harbour, on Humewood Road, **Humewood Road station** is the starting point for the **Apple Express**, a beautifully restored steam train that, during the holiday season, usually runs at 9.30am on weekends to **Thornhill** village and other destinations. En route it stops on Van Staden's River Bridge, the highest narrow-gauge railway bridge in the world. After a leisurely lunchtime break at Thornhill, the train trundles back to Humewood, arriving at 4pm. Tickets (R130 return for adults, R65 for children) can be booked through Nelson Mandela Bay Tourism Office (℡041 583 2030).

work of architecture outside the European Union. Described by the judges as a tour de force, the building wears an industrial-style saw-toothed roof that evokes the area's strong association with trade unionism. Inside, a dozen twelve-metre monumental rusted "**memory boxes**" contain exhibits exploring different themes related to the anti-apartheid struggle. The structures are inspired by the containers migrant workers used to carry their most prized possessions. Four **permanent exhibitions** trace a century of Red Location's history from 1900.

Eating, drinking and nightlife

Port Elizabeth has no great culinary reputation, but there are some decent **eating places** to suit most budgets, especially along the beachfront. Apart from the hotel bars mentioned in the accommodation section, there are a few other passable joints for a drink, and a couple of **nightclubs**.

Many of the **bars** listed below feature lively local bands playing jazz, rock and pop. The hub of the pub and club universe is Brookes Pavilion on Humewood Beach. The daily *Herald* lists the occasional **concerts** at the PE Opera House, next to the Donkin Memorial, and the odd **cabaret** event, most notably Centrestage at the Boardwalk Casino (☎041 368 3093, ⊛www.centrestage.co.za).

A reasonable range of popular **films** is screened at the Kine Park Cinema, 3 Rink St. For the usual Hollywood fare, try Nu Metro, Walmer Park Shopping Centre, Walmer; Ster Kinekor in The Bridge shopping complex; or Cinema Starz at the Boardwalk Casino Complex – check the *Herald* for programme details.

Restaurants

Blue Water Café Hobie Beach ☎041 583 4110. Great sea views, good pasta and light snacks at this pleasant eating place. Daily 8.30am–11pm.

Fernando's Guest House & Grill 102 Cape Rd, Mill Park ☎041 373 2823. The best steaks in town as well as lamb and pork loin, lamb shank and calamari, all served with home-made chips. Mon–Sat noon–2pm & 5.30–10pm.

The Island Seafood Grill & Bar *Pine Lodge Resort*, Marine Drive ☎041 583 3789. A patio bar with an indoor restaurant serving a decent range of snacks and full meals. Every dish is named after an island, though the food is in fact fairly predictable pastas, burgers and so on, all nicely presented.

Natti's Thai Kitchen 5 Park Lane ☎041 373 2763. Excellent restaurant serving authentic Thai cuisine in a relaxed atmosphere. Evenings only.

Sacramento Marine Drive. Noted for its terrific views rather than its fare, this eatery offers a range of less than exceptional pastas, steaks and toasted sandwiches along a stunning piece of coastline. Closes 5pm.

Bars and clubs

52 Parliament 52 Parliament St, Central. Late-night bar in a Victorian building decked out with interesting metal sculptures. DJs play house and other sounds, with occasional live music. Food is available. The R30–40 entrance fee deters impecunious teenagers. Wed, Fri & Sat.

Gondwana Café 2 Dolphin's Leap, Main Rd, Humewood. Relaxed, racially mixed eatery by day that doubles up as a club by night. Tues–Sun 9am–late.

Nine Yards Chapel St, Central. Cocktail and dance place with lots of drinks specials. Wed, Fri & Sat.

Sugar Rays, Tapas Al Sol & Toby Joe's Brookes Pavilion, Marine Drive. Brookes is a multilevel complex where you can dine, drink and party, the hub of late-night beachfront clubbing. The dance floors can be packed, but there are wooden decks with sea views to provide relief.

Listings

Airlines 1time ☎0861 345 345; kulula.com ☎0861 585 852; SAA ☎041 507 1111.

Car rental All at the airport: Avis ☎041 501 7200; Budget ☎041 581 4242; Hertz ☎041 508 6600;

Imperial ☎041 581 1268; Tempest ☎041 581 1256.

Diving Although the Indian Ocean around PE isn't tropically clear and warm, the diving here is good, especially for soft corals. For dive courses, try Pro Dive, at 189 Main Rd, Walmer (☏ 041 581 1144, ⓦ www.prodive.co.za), which offers a one-day scuba-diving course and refresher courses. **Emergencies** Fire ☏ 041 585 1555; see also p.75. **Hospitals** St George's (private), 40 Park Drive, Settlers Park ☏ 041 392 6111; Provincial (state), Buckingham Rd, Central ☏ 041 392 3911.

Pharmacy Mount Road Pharmacy, 559 Govan Mbeki Ave, is open daily until 11pm (☏ 041 484 3838).
Post office Brookes Pavilion, Humewood (Mon–Fri 9am–3.30pm & Sat 8.30–11am).
Taxis Hurters ☏ 041 585 5500.

The reserves around Port Elizabeth

A Big Five reserve, **Addo Elephant National Park** is just 73km north of Port Elizabeth, and should be your first choice for a relaxing few days' excursion from PE, though it is close enough to town to take in on a day-trip. If park accommodation is full, you may decide to stay at one of the nearby **private reserves** – especially if you just want to be pampered. On the N2 highway between PE and Grahamstown, alone, there are three: **Shamwari**, **Amakhala** and **Lalibela**, while **Schotia**, 1km off the N10/N2 interchange, has exciting night drives. One big attraction of Addo and these private reserves is that, unlike the country's other major game parks, they benefit from the fact that the Eastern Cape is **malaria-free**.

Addo Elephant National Park

Addo Elephant National Park (daily 7am–7pm; R100; ⓦ www .addoelephantpark.com) is undergoing an expansion programme that will see it become one of South Africa's three largest game reserves, and the only one including coastline. Its PR people are talking in terms of a "Big Seven" reserve, as the denizens of the future coastal section (adjoining the Alexandra State Forest/Woody Cape section of the park; see p.384) include whales and great white sharks. **Elephants** remain the most obvious drawcard of Addo, but with the re-introduction in 2003 of a small number of **lions**, in two prides (big cats last roamed here over a century ago), as well as the presence of the rest of the Big Five – **buffalo**, **hippos** and **leopards** – it has become a game reserve to be reckoned with. **Spotted hyenas** were also introduced in 2003 as part of a programme to re-establish predators in the local ecosystem. Other species to look out for include **cheetah**, **black rhino**, **eland**, **kudu**, **warthog**, **ostrich** and **red hartebeest**.

The Addo bush is thick, dry and prickly, making it difficult sometimes to spot any of the 450 or so elephants and other game; when you do, though, it's often thrillingly close up. The best strategy is to ask where the pachyderms and the other four of the Big Five have last been seen (enquire with staff at the park reception), and also to head for the water hole in front of the restaurant to scan the bush for large grey backs quietly moving about. It also makes sense to go on a **guided game drive** in an open vehicle with a knowledgeable national parks driver. Two-hour outings leave throughout the day and cost R160 a person for day drives, R240 for sunset trips (including snacks and drinks), and R180 for night drives; book at Main Camp. The vehicles used are higher off the ground than a normal sedan to improve viewing opportunities.

Addo also offers a couple of **activities** to spice up your visit, with more in the pipeline. Two-hour **horse rides**, suitable for the not-so-experienced (8am; R160) and three-hour rides for experienced equestrians (2pm; R210) leave from just outside the main gate and run along the exterior of the park fence (book at Main Camp). **Elephant-back safaris** are operated from a farm abutting the northern boundary of Addo (℡042 235 1400, Ⓦwww .addoelephantbacksafaris.co.za), 90km from Port Elizabeth, off the R335. Excursions last two to three hours and cost R720 per person, with air transfers possible from Port Elizabeth or nearby private lodges.

Practicalities

By far the most straighforward way of getting to Addo is via the southern gate, which is accessed off the N2 at the village of Colchester, 43km northeast of Port Elizabeth. The gate is about 5km from **Matyholweni Camp**. It's worth noting, though, that at present there is no big game in the southern section of the park, which is currently fenced off from the northern section to prevent game moving between the two parts, although humans can drive through a gated checkpoint.

To get to **Main Camp**, Addo's older and more established base, which is north of Matyholweni, you can either take a slow, scenic drive through the park, which will take at least an hour, or use the R335 road that runs outside the western flank of the park – take the N2 from Port Elizabeth east towards Grahamstown for 5km, branching off at the Addo/Motherwell/Markman signpost onto the R335 through Addo village. Narina bush camp is 22km north of Main Camp along a gravel road. The network of roads within the section of the park between Main Camp and Matyholweni is untarred, but in good condition.

Maps of the park are available at reception and indicate the location of **picnic** and braai sites. A **restaurant** (daily 6am–8pm) at Main Camp offers three meals a day, while the shop is well stocked with food and drink. Until the park is consolidated (expected to be completed by 2010), you won't be able to reach the coastal section that includes the Alexandria State Forest from inside the national park.

Accommodation

Addo's two major public restcamps, **Main** and **Matyholweni**, provide comfortable national park accommodation in a range of thatched, fully equipped self-catering units, while **Narina bush camp** has four safari tents. **Reservations** are essential in the high season, and can be made through SANParks or, less than 72 hours in advance, directly with Addo (℡042 233 8600). In addition to the national parks accommodation, there are some **luxury private lodges** inside the park – most notable of which is *Gorah Elephant Camp*.

Outside the park, but within easy striking distance, private B&Bs and guesthouses are in abundance around Addo, especially among the citrus groves of the Sundays River Valley. Many offer day and night drives in the game reserve.

Inside the park

Gorah Elephant Camp 9km west along the Addo Heights road leading from the N10 to Addo village ℡044 532 7818, Ⓦwww.gorah.com. Ultra-luxurious outfit based around a Victorian homestead decked out with the appropriate paraphernalia (mounted antelope skulls above the fireplace, evocative African landscapes, and polished tabletops you can see your reflection in) to play up those colonial-era safari fantasies. The suites are plush, there are opportunities to dine under the stars and there's a beautifully landscaped swimming pool. The steep price tag includes exclusive conducted game-viewing trips. ❾

Main Camp The oldest and largest of the National Parks camps. Besides camping facilities, there are forest cabins that share cooking facilities in communal kitchens; and more luxurious chalets with their own kitchenettes. Some of these units sleep up to four people (but the minimum charge is for two occupants). Also available are well-designed, spacious safari tents, perfect for summer, with decks right next to the perimeter fence; and for up to six people there are larger standard (R640) and luxury (R1760 for first four people, then R200 per person) family units. Two chalets have been adapted to accommodate the disabled. ❷–❹

Matyholweni Camp National Parks accommodation in a dozen fully equipped self-catering chalets with showers, and sleeping two. Set in a secluded valley surrounded by thicket that supports a wealth of birdlife, the chalets have decks from which you will be able to view game once a planned waterhole is completed. There is no restaurant, but Colchester, a 15min drive away, has shops and basic places to eat. ❹

Narina Camp Small National Parks bush camp in the mountainous Zuurberg section of Addo with four safari tents that sleep four people (R640) and share ablution and cooking facilities; bring your own provisions. Horse-riding is available.

Outside the park

Avoca River Cabins 13km northwest of Addo village on the R336 ☎ 042 234 0421 or 082 677 9920, ⓦ www.gardenroute.co.za/addo/avoca. Reasonably priced B&B and self-catering accommodation on a farm in the Sundays River Valley. There are budget cabins, more comfortable thatched huts (some on the banks of the river), and a timber chalet on stilts nestled among trees; canoes are available to rent. ❶–❸

Chrislin Africa Lodge 12km south of Addo main gate, off the R336 ☎ 042 233 0022 or 082 783 3553, ⓦ www.africanhuts-addo.co.za. Quirky B&B with thatched huts built using traditional Xhosa construction techniques, with a lovely *lapa* (courtyard) and pool, and hearty country breakfasts, as well as dinners on request. ❹–❺

🏃 **The Elephant House** 5km north of Addo village on the R335 ☎ & ⓕ 042 233 2462 or ☎ 083 799 5671, ⓦ www.elephanthouse.co.za. Just minutes from Addo is one of the Eastern Cape's top places to stay, a stunning thatch-roofed lodge filled with Persian rugs and antique furniture that perfectly balances luxury with a supremely relaxed atmosphere. The nine bedrooms, two of which are in garden cottages, open onto a lawned courtyard. Candlelit dinners available, as are massages and game drives (R550 per person) into Addo and the surrounding reserves. ❻–❽

Geelhoutboom 26 Market St, Kirkwood ☎ 042 230 1191, ⓦ www.geelhoutboom.co.za. Homely B&B with a/c rooms, a 20min drive from Addo main gate and shaded by a large yellowwood tree. Good value. ❸

Hopefield Country House 20km southwest of Addo main gate ☎ 042 234 0333, ⓦ www.hopefield.co.za. Atmospheric 1930s farmhouse set in beautiful English-style gardens on a citrus farm. The five bedrooms are imaginatively furnished with period pieces in a style the owners (a pair of classical musicians who occasionally give impromptu concerts for guests) describe as "farmhouse eclectic". ❺

Kronenhoff On the R336 as you enter Kirkwood ☎ 042 230 1448, ⓦ www.kronenhoff.co.za. In a small farming town, this is a hospitable, high-ceilinged Cape Dutch-style home, with spacious suites, polished wooden floors, large leather sofas and a sociable pub. In summer the sweet scent of orange blossom carries from the surrounding citrus groves. ❺

Orange Elephant On the R335, 8km from the National Park gate ☎ 042 233 0023, ⓦ www.addobackpackers.com. Budget accommodation at a comfortable hostel, whose management will help you organize outings into the surrounding game reserves. Dorms ❶, two-bedroom cottages (booked by the room) ❷

Woodall Country House About 1km west of Addo main gate ☎ 042 233 0128, ⓦ www.woodall-addo.co.za. Excellent luxury guesthouse on a working citrus farm with 11 self-contained suites and rooms. There's a swimming pool, gymnasium, spa and sauna (massages are available, and there's a resident beautician). A lovely sundowner deck overlooks a small lake full of swans and other waterfowl. Renowned for its outstanding country cuisine, its restaurant offers three- to six course dinners. ❼–❽

The private game reserves

Although driving through Addo can be extremely rewarding, nothing beats getting into the wild in an open vehicle with a trained guide – something the private reserves excel at. If you're strapped for cash or pushed for time a good option is one of the day or half-day safaris that start at R600 per person offered by **Schotia** and **Amakhala**. If you want the works – game drives, outstanding food, uncompromising luxury and excellent accommodation, you'll find it at **Shamwari**, with prices rising over R5000 per person a day. If you're in this league it's worth considering **Kwandwe Game Reserve** (see p.398) near Grahamstown, which is arguably the best safari destination in the Eastern Cape.

Shamwari Game Reserve

The largest and best known of the Eastern Cape's private Big Five reserves, **Shamwari Game Reserve**, 65km north of Port Elizabeth on the N2 (☎042 203 1111, ⓦwww.shamwari.com; ⑨), has cultivated an image as a jetsetter destination, hosting the rich and famous, such as Tiger Woods and John Travolta. The reserve has a diverse variety of landscapes, the requisite animals in sufficient numbers and high standards of game-viewing – which justifies its reputation as one of the leading wildlife destinations in the southern half of South Africa.

Accommodation is in the colonial-style, family-friendly *Long Lee Manor* and five other attractive lodges which don't take youngsters, dotted around the reserve and furnished with every conceivable comfort: restored Victorian homestead *Bushman's River Lodge*, overlooking a valley, the modernist stone and glass *Eagle's Crag*, ethnically decorated *Lobengula*, hotel-like *Riverdene*, and luxury tented camp *Bayethe*. Rates start at R3250 per person (May–Sept), R5250 (Oct–April).

Amakhala Game Reserve

Two kilometres north of the Shamwari turn-off, **Amakhala Game Reserve** (☎042 235 1608, ⓦwww.amakhala.co.za; ⑧) is a far more affordable option and is family-friendly too, offering children's programmes at some of the lodges. The area is stocked with the Big Five as well as cheetah, giraffe, zebra, wildebeest and many antelopes. The Bushman's River meanders through the reserve and you can go on a canoe safari, accompanied by a ranger, and sundowner cruises on a river boat. **Accommodation** comprises six independendently owned lodges that make use of the existing farmhouses on the reserve, as well as a camp where there are beds inside restored ox-wagons with private bathrooms – all with wonderful views. Rates start at R1000 per person (May–Aug), R1495 (Sept–April).

Day safaris (daily noon–6pm; booking essential) include two game drives, a river cruise and lunch and cost R720 per person.

Lalibela Game Reserve

Preferable to Shamwari if you want slightly more affordable luxury and game viewing is the **Lalibela Game Reserve**, 90km northeast of Port Elizabeth on the N2 to Grahamstown (☎041 581 8170, ⓦwww.lalibela.co.za; ⑨). It's home to the Big Five and a diversity of flora and fauna, which you can see on the morning and evening safaris that are included in the accommodation rate (R2950 per person) along with all meals and drinks. There are three fabulous **lodges** with private viewing decks, swimming pools and *bomas* to choose from: *Tree Tops* offers luxury safari tents on thatched platforms; *Lentaba Lodge* houses visitors in thatched chalets; and *Mark's Camp*, the largest of the three (it takes up to twenty people), consists of stone and thatch cottages. You can dine on terrific Eastern Cape fare and contemporary cuisine.

Schotia Private Game Reserve

Schotia Private Game Reserve (☎042 235 1436, ⓦwww.schotia.com; ⑧), on the eastern flank of Addo, is the smallest but possibly the busiest of the private reserves, on account of the excellent value it offers. While Schotia is not a Big Five reserve, it is able to offer a Big Five experience with packages that include excursions to Addo Elephant National Park. **Full-day safaris**

(R1200 per person) involve a game drive through Addo followed by lunch and an evening game drive and dinner at Schotia, after which guests are returned to their accommodation. **Overnight stays** (R1800 per person) include all this plus accommodation at Schotia in one of the three chalets or eight double rooms. If you're pushed for time or money you can opt for the **afternoon game drive** (R600 per person) in Schotia, which kicks off at 3pm and ends at 9pm. The evening excursions are full of shining eyes caught by powerful lamps, with dinner cooked on an open fire in a thatched courtyard.

Schotia's **wildlife** includes six **lions**, giraffes, rhinos, hippos, zebra and a dozen or so species of antelope. Visitors can arrange to be collected from Port Elizabeth or anywhere in the Addo vicinity; if you're driving, you're collected from a secure car park 2km up the N10 from the N2/N10 intersection.

Between Port Elizabeth and Storms River

Among the few reasons to turn off the 186-kilometre stretch of the N2 between Port Elizabeth and Storms River to the west are the resorts of **Jeffrey's Bay** and **St Francis Bay**. Of the two, Jeffrey's Bay is the more famous, at least if you happen to be a surfer; more than anywhere in the country, it has dedicated itself to having fun and making money from its pumping surf. Although St Francis Bay has some fine surfing breaks, it's thanks to its tranquil atmosphere and beauty that it's become a popular spot with upcountry South Africans. For travellers heading along the coast, both are good places to break a journey.

Jeffrey's Bay

Some 75km west of Port Elizabeth, off the N2, **JEFFREY'S BAY** (known locally as **J Bay**) is jammed during the holiday seasons, when thousands of visitors throng the beaches, surfing shops and fast-food outlets, giving the place a really tacky seaside resort feel. Mansions dot the town's hill, but there's not much by way of grace and beauty here.

For **surfing aficionados**, however, these are trifling details; J Bay is said by some to be one of the world's top three surfing spots. If you've come to surf, head for the break at **Super Tubes**, east of the main bathing beach, which produces an impressive and consistent swirling tube of whitewater, attracting surfers from all over the world throughout the year. Riding inside the vortex of a wave is considered the ultimate experience by surf buffs, but should only be attempted if you're an expert. Other key spots are at Kitchen Windows, Magna Tubes, the Point and Albatross. Surfing gear, including wet suits, can be rented from the multitude of surfing shops along Da Gama Road. **Dolphins** regularly surf the waves here, and **whales** can sometimes be seen between June and October. The main **bathing areas** are Main Beach (in town) and Kabeljous-on-Sea (a few kilometres north), with some wonderful seashells to be found between Main and Surfer's Point.

Practicalities

The **Baz Bus** stops at J Bay on its daily trek in either direction between Cape Town and Port Elizabeth. The **tourist office** (Mon–Fri 8.30am–5pm, Sat 9am–noon; ☎042 293 2588, ⊛www.jeffreysbaytourism.org), on the

▲ Surfing at Jeffrey's Bay

corner of Da Gama and Dromedaris roads, publishes a wide-ranging list of places to stay.

J Bay has the usual collection of pizza joints, burger bars and steak houses. The resort's top **restaurant** is the *Walskipper*, incongruously housed in a weather-beaten wooden shack on the beach in Marina Martinique Harbour. Here you can tuck into lovely home-made bread and pâtés and jams while the main courses – including luxurious seafood – are cooked on an outside fire.

Accommodation

With lots of **hostels** to choose from, J Bay is definitely backpacker territory – but if communal living isn't your scene, you're still in luck, as there are numerous good and inexpensive **B&Bs** and some self-catering places in town. There's also camping right near the beach at the municipal caravan parks, *Kabbeljous* (℡042 293 3330) and *Jeffrey's Bay* (℡042 200 2214) in Da Gama Road, but the price is barely cheaper than a backpacker dorm.

To stay in December, January, Easter or July it's essential to book accommodation in advance. The off-season is very quiet except during the Billabong world-championship surfing competition, usually staged in July.

A1 Knyaston 23 & 27 Chestnut Ave ℡042 296 1845, ⓦwww.a1knyaston.co.za. Friendly establishment offering rooms in two houses and a self-contained flat, with great views and mega-breakfasts. ❷–❸
Island Vibe 10 Dageraad St ℡042 293 1625, ⓦwww.islandvibe.co.za. Backpacker lodge built on a dune, with a wooden walkway onto the beach. Offers camping, dorms and doubles, with spectacular views. There's a lounge, bar, pool table and self-catering facilities. Breakfasts are available. Dorms ❶, rooms ❷

Jeffrey's Bay Backpackers 12 Jeffrey St ℡042 293 1379, ⓦwww.jeffreysbaybackpackers.co.za. Two blocks away from the beach, this functional establishment has been going for some time. The dorms and doubles have good facilities for self-catering, and guests can chill out in the bar, lounge and swimming pool. Board rental is available. Dorms and twin rooms ❶, en-suite doubles ❶
Lazee Bay 25 Mimosa St ℡042 296 2090, ⓦwww.lazeebayco.za. Light and airy B&B offering good value with panoramic views and lots of marine murals indoors. An informal place, it has a

spacious communal lounge, a kitchen, plus a pool, sun deck and airy African-inspired decor. ❷ **Super Tubes Guest House** 12 Pepper St ☏042 293 2957, ⓦ www.supertubesguesthouse.co.za. A

modest mansion in J Bay-style. Rooms are en suite, with old wooden bedsteads, and open onto a patio or garden. The Super Tubes beach is practically on the doorstep. Standard ❹, luxury ❻

St Francis Bay

A short hop south of Jeffrey's Bay, **ST FRANCIS BAY** is much more genteel than its neighbour. Part of the town is built around a network of canals leading to the river, the houses here whitewashed and thatched. The town is ringed by a series of small nature reserves, offering beautiful **walks**, some of which are trails through the *fynbos*. During the holiday season the town seethes with thousands of upcountry South Africans who own holiday homes here, but at other times peace and tranquillity reign. The commanding **lighthouse**, now a National Monument, was once described as the loneliest in Africa.

Practicalities

St Francis Bay is easily reached **by car**; turn off the N2 at Humansdorp and continue 15km south to the coast. The **tourist office** at the Village Centre on the main thoroughfare, St Francis Drive (Mon–Fri 8.30am–4.30pm & Sat 9am–12.30pm; ☏042 294 0076, ⓦ www.stfrancistourism.com) can help find accommodation. For **food**, there are lots of pubs, coffee shops and restaurants; calamari has to be pick of the menu. *Big Time Taverna*, at 10 Mayotte Circle, is recommended.

Accommodation

Accommodation in St Francis Bay ranges from modern chic resorts along the harbour to thatched rural cosiness.

The Cottage ☏042 294 0328 or 082 465 2288, ⓔ thecottage@isat.co.za. Pleasant, functional B&B with five rooms. ❸
The Sands ☏042 294 1888, ⓦ www.pehotels .co.za/the_sands. Utter luxury in a beach house where each suite comes complete with Jacuzzi and private timber deck. Breakfast is included in the rate; light meals are available on request. ❽
Thatchwoods 63 Lyme Rd, off St Francis Drive ☏042 294 0082, ⓦ www.thatchwood.com. Supremely comfy B&B where each room has its

own private garden or sun deck. It's positioned on the edge of the popular golf course, and can arrange golf rounds for guests. Good value. ❺
Waterways 37 Shore Rd ☏042 294 0282 or 083 660 8909, ⓦ www.saholidays/waterways.htm. Of the many St Francis Bay B&Bs under thatch, *Waterways* is recommended for its friendliness as well as its situation at the confluence of the canals and river, with a beautiful beach nearby. There are two en-suite bedrooms with their own outdoor living areas and spectacular views. Cruises can also be arranged. ❸

Between Port Elizabeth and Port Alfred

One of South Africa's most undeveloped stretches of coast, with wide beaches and exhilarating surf, stretches east from Port Elizabeth for a sandy 150km to **Port Alfred**. The sea temperature here is several degrees higher than around Cape Town (though not as warm as KwaZulu-Natal, and never tropically clear), and the deserted beaches are a walker's paradise, with shells, birds and rock pools. The only problem is the summer **wind**, which often affects the whole Eastern Cape coast – particularly in the afternoon, so set out as early as you can. The weather is at its calmest from April to September, and while it's not hot enough to tan, you'll certainly be comfortable picnicking or walking along the beaches. April to July is the optimum season for scuba diving, with the water at its clearest.

The resort of **Kenton-on-Sea** is one of the most arresting spots along this coast, with two rivers dotted with boats, rocky coves and fabulous beaches for swimming and walking. Most of the houses are holiday homes, unoccupied much of the year, belonging to white South Africans, but there is a fair bit of **accommodation** – good B&Bs in beautiful locations, at much lower prices than along the sometimes overrated Garden Route.

The most deserted section of the coast, once difficult to access, is now administratively part of the Addo Elephant National Park (see p.377), and includes some spectacular and enormous sand dunes, though there are no animals in this coastal section of the park. Staying at Kenton-on-Sea or Alexandria is a good way to explore this area.

Alexandria State Forest

A fifty-kilometre tract of Eastern Cape beachfront is protected by the **Alexandria State Forest**. Part of the **Woody Cape** section of the Addo Elephant National Park, it can be walked on the circular two-day **Alexandria Hiking Trail**, one of South Africa's finest coastal hikes, which winds through indigenous forest and crosses a landscape of great hulking sand dunes to the ocean.

You'll need to **book** one of the places on the trail through Addo Elephant National Park (☎041 468 0916, ✉matyholweni@sanparks.org; R70 per person per day), especially to walk it at weekends, when the trail tends to be full. The 35-kilometre trail starts at the Woody Cape office, 8km from the R72 (and not served by public transport), where you collect permits. If you're heading east, the signposted turn-off is on the right, just before you reach Alexandria, 86km from Port Elizabeth. There's an **overnight hut** at the Woody Cape office (❶), for use at the beginning or end of the trail (alternatively, stay in Alexandria or Cannons Bay nearby), and another on the coast, both with mattresses and drinking water, but no cooking facilities. The hike is quite tough going, especially along the windy dunes – the markers in the sand can get blown over, obscuring the route – but in fine weather the isolated beaches are magnificent. The **forest** can also be accessed on the seven-kilometre Tree Dassie Trail from the Woody Cape offices (R20).

Alexandria and Cannons Bay

ALEXANDRIA, a pineapple- and chicory-growing centre with a strip of shops and an imposing Dutch Reformed Church, is the closest town to Woody Cape. The best reason to stop off here is to look at the bronzework at *Quin's Sculpture Garden and B&B* at 5 Suid St (☎046 653 0121 or 082 770 8000, ⓦwww.quin-art.co.za; ❷). Animal sculptures peep through the foliage and in a section of the main house there are two bedrooms, each with their own sitting room and bathroom. Owner Maureen Quin has recently made a hundred bronze statues of Mandela, each with his signature on them, to be sold to benefit his Children's Fund. Besides *Quin's*, *Heritage Lodge*, along the main street (☎046 653 0024, ⓦwww.heritage-lodge.co.za; ❸), has reasonably priced rooms, and, although nothing special, it's a fine overnight stop. *Gordon's* **restaurant** (closed Sun & Mon eves), the only place to eat, has a good reputation. If you're in town when the restaurant is closed, *Heritage Lodge* will fix you up with a home-cooked meal from someone in the village.

From Alexandria, a good dirt road takes you 18km southeast through the State Forest and farmland to the coast at **Boknes**. This tiny resort is the start of an hour-long beach walk eastwards to the monument of **Diaz Cross**, commemorating the Portuguese adventurer and explorer Bartholomeu Diaz, who rounded the South African coast in 1487 in search of a profitable new sea route between Europe and the East. The first European to make recorded contact with the Khoikhoi, Diaz was also the first to kill one of them. The cross, on a rocky promontory, marks the spot where he was forced by his crew to turn back to Cape Town, rather than face the journey eastwards. The nicest place in the forest to stay, or just do lunch as a day visitor (book beforehand), is the very beautiful *Intsomi Forest Lodge* (☎046 653 8903, ⓦwww.intsomi.com; ❺), whose upmarket accommodation makes the most of the light and wooded area in its design.

On the coast at **CANNON ROCKS**, 2km west of Boknes and linked to Alexandria by a tarred road, is the thoroughly family-oriented *Cannon Rocks Holiday Resort* (☎046 654 0043, ⓔcannonrocks@telkomsa.net; ❷–❸), where you can pitch a tent or rent a two-bedroom chalet or luxury flat. The resort, which has a simple restaurant, is protected from the wind by trees, and is a five-minute walk to the beach. *Sandon B&B*, 187 Alice Rd (☎046 654 0217 or 082 594 4699, ⓔsandon@cybertrade.co.za; ❷–❸), a large, modern house right on the beach, has two en-suite rooms and a separate flat in the same section of the property, with two double bedrooms where you can self-cater. Although there's a small shop, you're best off buying **supplies** from Alexandria. As Cannon Rocks adjoins the boundary of Woody Cape, it is possible to walk straight into the park along the beach, and a two-hour walking trail has been laid out. This remote and undeveloped part of the Eastern Cape is set to have a couple of golf courses developed on it, so explore it while there is still access.

Kenton-on-Sea

Some 26km from Alexandria and 56km from Grahamstown, the resort of **KENTON-ON-SEA** lies along two river valleys, perfect for a short beach holiday. A conglomeration of holiday houses served by a few shops and places to eat, Kenton is a good choice if you want to be somewhere undemanding and very beautiful. There's little to do here except enjoy the surf, sandy beaches and dunes. While you can swim in the rivers, avoid getting close to the entrance to the sea, as strong **riptides** occur and drowning is a real risk. There are also a couple of good **game lodges** on the Kariega River, which can be accessed from either Kenton or Grahamstown, and a nature haven in **Kasouga**, a totally unspoilt scattering of cottages a few kilometres eastwards along the coast. The area doesn't see many foreign visitors and South Africans pack in principally during the school holidays, so the rest of the year, especially during the week, you're assured a quiet time.

If you want to spend time on Bushman's River, you can rent **canoes** from Kenton Marina (☎ & ⓕ046 648 1223; R100 per day), well signposted off the R72, 300m up the R343 to Grahamstown. You can paddle 15km upriver on the **Bushman's River Trail**, on which you pass through countryside lined with cycads and euphorbias, and filled with chattering birdlife, though motor boats are a menace. The trip takes between two and five hours depending on your fitness, the direction of the tide and weather conditions. At the end of the trail is a **hut** sleeping sixteen in bunks (book at the marina; ❶). Mattresses, cooking utensils, braai facilities and outdoor cold showers are provided, but you must bring your own sleeping bag and provisions.

The best **craft outlet** in the entire area, and a quality farm stall and café, can be found in a little strip of new shops on the R72 between Bushman's and Kenton. Juju Art and Artefacts (☎046 648 3575 or 082 711 6866;

ⓦ www.gallery@jujuart.co.za) run by Julius Bramley, a retired **African art** collector has some very affordable jewellery and African craft for sale, as well as larger, more valuable items. Next door, the Red Apple **farm stall** has a number of sophisticated goodies usually found only closer to Cape Town.

Practicalities

Kenton is a very small place, though it has a couple of restaurants, mini-supermarkets, a bank and cash machine, post office and a filling station – all along the main street, Kenton Road. Many people do their shopping fifteen minutes' drive away in Port Alfred. The **tourist office**, signposted on the main road (Jan–Nov Mon–Fri 9.30am–1pm & 2–4pm, Sat 9.30am–1pm; Dec daily 9am–5pm; ☎046 648 2418, ⓦ www.kenton.co.za), has information about most accommodation options in and around Kenton, and can certainly find you a bed. Erica McNulty, who ably runs the tourist office, also runs **Kenton township tours** and is the coordinator of various interesting sustainable community projects run by Xhosa women.

Accommodation

Kenton has reasonably priced self-catering cottages and B&Bs, most of which provide breakfast as an extra. The nicest places to stay are close to the river. You can **camp** at the well-kept *Bushman's River Caravan Park*, 2 Loerie Rd (☎046 648 3584), right in the centre of Bushman's River Mouth, a resort that's effectively an extension of Kenton. It's a few minutes' drive west of Kenton – follow the signs from the R72 turn-off to Bushman's River. Best of all, for nature lovers, is *Oribi Haven* at Kasouga (see below).

Burke's Nest 38 Van der Stel Rd ☎046 648 1894 or 082 577 2142. Garden cottage and a flatlet connected to a family home away from the beach, a short amble from the Kariega River, with B&B or self-catering. ❸

Dunwerkin 5 Park Rd ☎046 648 1173, ⓔ kariegavet@imaginet.co.za. In a fine location, a 2min walk from the beach, the most upmarket of Kenton's self-catering options, can accommodate either one or two families in a spanking new four-bedroomed house. ❸–❹

Oribi Haven Kasouga Farm, 9km from Kenton, on a gravel road off the R72 (turn right at the first cattle grid) ☎046 648 2043, ⓦ www.oribihaven .co.za. A 10min drive east of Kenton takes you to the Kasouga turn-off, where Kasouga farms sits on a hillside overlooking one of the best and least-known beaches in the country. The farm, which has been declared a natural heritage site for its large population of Oribi antelope, has two well-equipped and spacious two-bedroom cottages, which can be taken on a B&B or self-catering basis. Farm game drives can be arranged, as can sundowners on the beach, and there is the use of sandboards for the dunes, or a canoe for the river. ❷–❸

Sebumo Tude On an inland farm between Kenton and Port Alfred, off the R72 and 15km from the coast ☎072 141 2375, ⓦ www.sebumotude.co.za. The African dream of a German couple who relish the isolation and beauty of the Eastern Cape bush. The secluded thatched chalets, each with its own deck overlooking tree tops, are simply decorated yet luxurious, with magnificent bathrooms and showers outside for some romance under the stars. There's a bush restaurant serving good meals. The rate is for B&B. ❻

Wings 21 Elliot Rd ☎046 648 1834, ⓔ wings @casbusol.co.za. The bottom floor of this upmarket home overlooking the Bushman's River has three bedrooms and a kitchen with the option of B&B or self-catering. There are garden chairs and braai facilities to enjoy the view. ❸

Woodlands Country House and Tea Garden 2km from the centre along the R343 to Grahamstown ☎& ⓕ046 648 2867, ⓔ woodlands@compuscan .co.za. Acres of garden and bush leading down to the Bushman's River, with little cottages dotted along pathways cut through the vegetation. Birdlife thrives here and it's a very relaxing place to have teas or meals at the small restaurant. ❷

Eating and drinking

The best-located **eating and drinking** place in Kenton is *Homewoods* (☎046 648 2700), 1 Eastbourne Rd (closed all day Mon & Sun evenings), a restaurant and pub at the mouth of the Kariega River. It has two decks and grand views, where you can get tea or a drink, but the fare is run-of-the-mill, including steaks, fish and burgers. In the village centre, *The Local*, a pub, pizza and grill joint, is a reliable place for evening meals (closed Sunday eves), though for steaks you're best off at *La Vinia Steakhouse* (☎046 648 2662) on Kenton Road which also has a wine bar and cellar. During the day you can get breakfasts, teas and light lunches at *The Garden* on the main road, which has outdoor seating under umbrellas.

Pick of the lot, just outside town, 2km along the R67 Grahamstown Road, the homely *Woodlands Tea Garden* is the best place for teas and light lunches, serving good cheesecake, apple pie and quiches in a beautiful indigenous garden with paths leading down to the river. A kilometre further on along the same road, the child-friendly *Stanley's* (Mon–Sat lunch & dinner, Sunday lunch only; ☎046 648 1332) is an unpretentious farmhouse which offers nicely cooked English-style roasts, fish, steaks and ribs; you can eat on the deck, while taking in views of the Kariega River. Booking is essential, especially during holiday season and on Sundays. Further inland, but worth the detour, is the restaurant at *Sebumo Tude* (see opposite); you'll need to ring ahead to book and get directions.

Port Alfred

Of all the settlements between Port Elizabeth and East London, only **PORT ALFRED**, midway between the two, can make any claims to a town life outside the holiday season, when for a few weeks the small centre is transformed into a hectic bustle of cars and people. Like many other places along the coast, it is developing apace, with new mansions and housing developments sprouting along its once lonely beaches. Besides beach walking and swimming, it's an excellent place to do some **canoeing**: the Kowie Canoe Trail is an overnight jaunt up the Kowie River, or you do a day's paddle up the Lynedoch River to the east of Port Alfred. There is also an active dive school which doubles up as an adventure centre offering water-skiing, abseiling, deep-sea fishing and horse-riding, among others.

Nicknamed "Kowie" by locals, after the river, Port Alfred was named in honour of the second son of Queen Victoria, although he never actually made it here. The prince, who visited the Cape in 1870, cancelled a trip to Port Alfred at the last minute, because the prospect of an elephant hunt seemed more appealing. Although Port Alfred started life as a port for settler enterprises in the 1840s, it was never quite suitable (the river kept silting up) and it quickly faded away into a resort. No large ships navigate the river, but plenty of **fishing boats** brave its turbulent mouth every day, watched by fascinated bystanders on the end of the pier.

Arrival and information

The **Kowie River** slices through Port Alfred, creating an east and west bank, with the town and most popular swimming **beaches** to the west, and the less developed dunes stretching east. The river is traversed by two **bridges**: a concrete bowstring-arch bridge that has become Port Alfred's symbol, and an older one, which leads straight into **Main Road**, lined with banks and small shops and dominated by Heritage Mall and Pick 'n Pay supermarket. Sadly, Port Alfred's natural lagoon was blasted away in the 1980s and replaced by a marina, floating with dozens of boats and artificial islands dotted with toytown holiday homes.

The helpful **tourist office** on the riverfront at the Main Street bridge (Mon–Fri 8.30am–4.30pm, Sat 8.30am–noon; ☎046 624 1235, ⓦwww .portalfred.co.za) can guide you to adventure activities and extra accommodation, and also has the offices for Avis and Budget **car rental**.

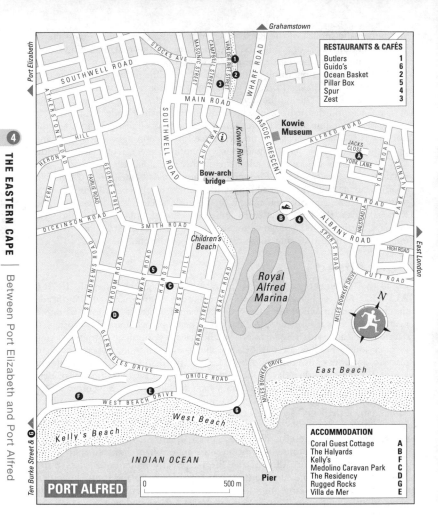

PORT ALFRED

RESTAURANTS & CAFÉS	
Butlers	1
Guido's	6
Ocean Basket	2
Pillar Box	5
Spur	4
Zest	3

ACCOMMODATION	
Coral Guest Cottage	A
The Halyards	B
Kelly's	F
Medolino Caravan Park	C
The Residency	D
Rugged Rocks	G
Villa de Mer	E

The reasonably priced SA Connection **minibus** (☎043 722 0284, ⓦwww
.saconnection.co.za) calls here on its way between Port Elizabeth and East
London (daily except Thurs), and between Cape Town and East London (Tues
& Fri). On Tuesdays and Thursdays, the Minilux **bus service** (☎043 741 3107),
connecting Port Elizabeth to East London via Grahamstown, pulls into the
Halyards Hotel, off the main coastal road on the east side of the Kowie River.
Otherwise, Wayne's Transport (☎046 624 1866 or 084 644 6060) offers a shuttle
service from Port Elizabeth's airport.

Accommodation

Outside school holidays you should have no problem finding a place to stay. The
tourist office publishes a useful accommodation list, including B&Bs and
self-catering cottages. Most B&Bs are indicated from the main roads with
official brown signs, making them relatively easy to find. If you're on a budget

and value seclusion, it's worth considering the self-catering cottages at Salt Vlei. Backpacker hostels come and go along this part of the coast, where there's no great tradition of backpacking.

Coral Guest Cottage Jack's Close ⓣ & ⓕ 046 624 2849, ⓦ www.coralcottages.co.za. Reasonably priced B&B on one of the East Bank hills, a 20min walk from East Beach. Comfortable rooms with bath in a restored corrugated-iron settler cottage, though the walls are not at all soundproof. You can expect to be pampered by the ebullient owner. ❸

Kelly's Self-Catering West Beach Drive, opposite Kelly's Beach ⓣ 082 657 0345, ⓦ www.kellys .co.za. As close to the main swimming beach as you could possibly be, these neat and clean self-catering apartments in a large face-brick house are also good value. ❸

Medolino Caravan Park Prince's Ave, Kowie West ⓣ 046 624 1651, ⓦ www.medolino.caravanparks .com. A very efficiently run place, in shady grounds behind the dunes, protected from the wind by its trees. A 10min walk from Kelly's Beach. Good camping facilities, excellent wooden self-catering chalets and swimming pool. ❷

The Residency 11 Vroom Rd ⓣ 046 624 5382, ⓦ www.theresidency.co.za. Spacious, beautifully restored Settler home with yellowwood panelling, large, comfortable beds, and breakfasts on the veranda. ❸

Rugged Rocks Salt Vlei ⓣ 046 624 3112 or 082 781 4682, ⓦ www.ruggedrocksbeachcottages.co.za. A beachside property in sizeable grounds 4km from the town centre. Fully equipped self-catering cottages, the older ones cheaper and tucked away in the coastal bush, the pricier, newer ones atop dunes with glorious views. Self-catering ❷–❹

Villa de Mer 22 West Beach Drive ⓣ & ⓕ 046 624 2315, ⓦ www.villademer.co.za. Kitsch postmodern guesthouse in the best location in town, right across the road from the beach. There are four en-suite rooms, a family unit, a courtyard swimming pool and huge windows through which to take in the views. Bella Crabtree, the friendly owner, can direct you to the best the town has to offer. ❹

The Town and beaches

Port Alfred's attractions are firmly rooted in its **beaches** and the **Kowie River**. The town itself has little else to offer. The rather expensive but obvious landmark *Halyards Hotel* and *Spur* restaurant constitute the town's ersatz caged-in waterfront; far more authentic, the river frontage on **Wharf Street**, next to the old bridge, has been revamped and the row of Victorian buildings spruced up, with the **Harbour Master and Brewery** offering its own home brew. Of passing interest is the tiny **Kowie Museum**, in Pascoe Crescent (Tues–Sat 9.30am–12.30pm; free), on the east side of the old bridge, featuring sepia photographs of Port Alfred before the marina and its mansions gobbled up the magnificent lagoon.

West Beach, where the river is sucked out to sea and the breakers pound in, makes a good start to exploring Port Alfred. From the café and stone pier you can watch the surfers and see fishing boats make dramatic entries into the river from the open ocean. Fifteen minutes' walk west along the beach lies **Kelly's Beach**, by far the most popular stretch, where you can swim safely in a gentle bay. **East Beach**, reached from the signposted road next to *Halyards Hotel*, is the nicest beach for walking, with a backdrop of hilly dunes popular for sandboarding, stretching to the horizon. For toddlers, the safest and most popular spot is **Children's Beach**, a stretch of sand close to the town centre along a shallow section of river, reached from Beach Road, a few hundred metres from the arched bridge.

When the weather is blowy (or should you want to swim laps), head for the heated indoor **swimming pool** next to *Halyards Hotel* (daily 8.30am–5pm; R10). There's a small pool for toddlers.

Eating

Port Alfred is not noted for its cuisine, though *Zest Café* (ⓣ 046 624 5783), The Courtyard, 48 Van der Riet St, serves delicious, modern and imaginative

There's a host of **adventure activities** in Port Alfred, the best being canoeing, horse-riding, diving and sandboarding. **Divers** shouldn't expect to see crystal waters and fluorescent fish around Port Alfred (the Indian Ocean isn't tropical here), though the slightly murky water contains colourful underwater denizens, as well as beautiful corals and sponges. Port Alfred is home to the reputable **Keryn's Dive School** (℡046 624 4432, @keryn@keryndiveschool.com), based next to the Children's Beach, Beach Road, on the West Bank at the Maximum Exposure Adventure Centre. You can qualify here in a week for an internationally recognized diving certificate.

Maximum Exposure also takes bookings for the **Kowie Canoe Trail**, a 21-kilometre paddle up the Kowie River, a much-sought-after trip and one of the few self-guided canoeing and hiking trails in South Africa. Much of its charm is the colourful birdlife, and the landscape – hills of dense, dry bush that slope down to the river. While the trip is almost always full at weekends, it's easy to find a place on weekdays out of school holidays, and is extremely reasonable at R125 per person per night. On the trip, you **stay overnight** in a hut in the **Horseshoe Bend Nature Reserve**, from where you can explore the forest on foot, and climb the steep escarpment to get an impressive view over the horseshoe. The biggest difficulties on this trip are the tide and the wind – Maximum Exposure will give you all the necessary advice on making your trip safe and enjoyable.

Port Alfred has two **horse-riding** establishments, outrides bookable through Maximum Exposure, or directly with the company. Three Sisters Horse Trail, signposted 14km east of Port Alfred off the R72 towards East London road (℡046 675 1269), has access to one of the loveliest stretches of the coast in the region, and is recommended for beginners and children, with beach outrides of 30–90 minutes depending on your ability. One of the best rides you'll do in South Africa is with Fish River Horse Safaris (℡046 675 1271 or 082 433 5662, @www.fishriverhorsesafaris. co.za), which has fabulous horses and tack, with Western-style trail saddles, and professional guiding through the Fort D'Acre game farm (where you can expect to see antelope, buffalo, giraffes, rhino and zebra) and onto deserted beaches and dunes at the mouth of the Fish River, 24km east of Port Alfred. Rides are 2–3 hours, and can be done by beginners, but not children, while experienced riders have a chance to put on some speed. A full-day trip can be done from Fort D'Acre, 20km down the coast.

Port Alfred's big sand dunes lend themselves to **sandboarding** – you can rent boards at Maximum Exposure and also do some other activities especially **for children**, such as Kids' Scuba, kite flying and canoeing, all bookable at Maximum Exposure.

---

lunches and coffee outdoors, from a kitchen in a wooden canteen which once stood at Grahamstown's railway station. The town's swankiest **restaurant** is *Butlers*, 25 Van der Riet St (Tues–Sat lunch & dinner, plus Sun lunch; ℡046 624 3464), which enjoys a riverside setting and is good for fish. The only place right on the beach is *Guido's* (open daily), whose pizzas and pasta dishes play second fiddle to the sundowners served on its deck. At the small boat harbour, *Spur*, accessed from *Halyards Hotel*, does as expected of this cheap steakhouse chain, but also offers a good selection of salads. *The Pillar Box* (℡046 624 3042), on the corner of Stewart Road and Princess Avenue, is an elegant choice for tea with silverware and napkins, excellent cakes, a fireplace in winter and garden seating in summer. For fish and chips, as well as sushi and a river view, head for *Ocean Basket* (℡046 624 1727), in Port Frances House on Van der Riet Street, where the service is prompt and the food spot-on.

Grahamstown

Just over 50km inland from Port Alfred, but worlds apart in terms of ambience, **GRAHAMSTOWN** projects an image of a cultured, historic town, quintessentially English, Protestant and refined. Dominated by its cathedral, university and public schools, this is a thoroughly pleasant place to wander through, with well-maintained colonial **Georgian** and **Victorian buildings** lining the streets, and pretty suburban gardens. Every July, the town hosts an **arts festival**, the largest of its kind in Africa, and purportedly the second largest in the world (after Edinburgh; see box, p.397).

As elsewhere in South Africa, there are reminders of conquest and dispossession. Climb up Gunfire Hill, where the fortress-like 1820 **Settlers Monument** celebrates the achievement of South Africa's English-speaking immigrants, and you'll be able to see Makanaskop, the hill from which the **Xhosa** made their last stand against the British invaders. Their descendants live in desperately poor ghettos here, in a town almost devoid of industry. Marking the gap are the Kowie Ditches (which you'll cross if you take the old East London Road out of town), a waterway that ran red with Xhosa blood in the 1819 battle of Grahamstown.

Despite all this, and the constant reminders of poverty, Grahamstown makes a good stopover, and is the perfect base for excursions: a number of **historic villages** are within easy reach, some **game parks** are convenient for a day or weekend visit and, best of all, kilometres of **coast** are just 45 minutes' drive away. Cupped in a valley surrounded by hills, Grahamstown itself is compact; you'll only need a car to get out of town.

Some history

Grahamstown's sedate prettiness belies its beginnings as a **military outpost** in 1811. **Colonel Graham** made his name here (and gave it to the town), driving the Xhosa out of the Zuurveld, an area between the Bushman's and Fish rivers.

▲ Grahamstown

The Fish River, 60km east of Grahamstown, marked the eastern boundary of the frontier, with Grahamstown as the capital. The ruthless expulsion of the Xhosa sparked off a series of nineteenth-century **Frontier Wars**.

A line of **forts** was built to defend the frontier, subsequently developing into the settlements, which now include Fort Beaufort, Fort Hare and Peddie, but these alone were not enough to hold the line, and the British decided to reinforce the frontier with a human barrier. With the promise of free land, they lured the dispossessed from a depressed Britain to occupy the lands west of the Fish River. In the migration mythology of English-speaking whites, these much-celebrated **1820 Settlers** came to take on a larger-than-life status as ancestors to whom many trace back their origins. However, far from discovering the hoped-for paradise, the ill-equipped settlers found themselves in a nightmare. The plots given them were unsuitable for crops and too small for cattle in the harsh Eastern Cape; drought, floods and disease were a constant problem, and the threat of Xhosa attack was never far away.

Not surprisingly, many settlers abandoned their lands and headed to Grahamstown in the early 1820s. This brought prosperity and growth to the town, which enjoyed a boom in the 1840s, when it developed into the emporium of the frontier. Xhosa traders came to barter ivory and hides for beads, buttons and brass wire, while some colonists, who had persisted with farming in the surrounding district, traded **wool** from Spanish merino sheep which thrived in the Eastern Cape.

Arrival and information

Grahamstown is on the N2, 127km inland from Port Elizabeth, roughly twelve hours by bus from Cape Town, Johannesburg or Durban. Translux, Intercape and Greyhound **buses** stop outside the *Frontier Country Hotel* on the corner of Bathurst and High streets. The Minilux **minibus**, which connects Grahamstown with the airport at Port Elizabeth daily, and goes on to Port Alfred and East London on Tuesdays and Thursdays, stops at Settler City Motors in Beaufort Street. The **train station** at the bottom of High Street sees only three trains a week, on a branch-line service connecting to the Johannesburg–Port Elizabeth line.

Grahamstown is easily covered on foot, but if you want a **taxi**, use the reliable Beeline (℡082 651 6646), the only licensed company in town. Its main trade is zipping up and down to Port Elizabeth airport. The helpful **Makana tourism office** on the High Street (Mon–Fri 8.30am–5pm, Sat 9am–1pm; ℡046 622 3241, ⓦwww.grahamstown.co.za), next to the City Hall, has information on accommodation and also takes bookings for intercity coaches.

Accommodation

Grahamstown has the distinction of hosting the country's only backpackers lodge that is housed in a historic jail, where you sleep in a former cell (though a new sister hostel, some 20min away, offers rather more comfort). Other than that, the most notable and choicest places to stay are in historic houses, and there's a good selection of hotels. If you've just arrived from the Garden Route or one of the more popular tourist areas of South Africa, accommodation rates will seem very reasonable here.

Grahamstown provides the ideal opportunity for a **township homestay** (B&B ❷) without having to traipse far – the townships are less than ten minutes' drive from the centre. The tourism office has a list of fifteen houses and can place you with a hospitable Xhosa family in Grahamstown East. Thabisa Xonxa

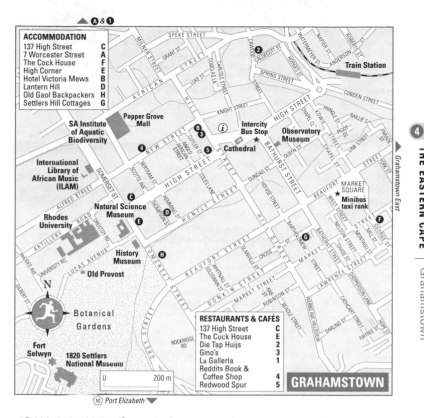

ACCOMMODATION
137 High Street	C
7 Worcester Street	A
The Cock House	F
High Corner	E
Hotel Victoria Mews	B
Lantern Hill	D
Old Gaol Backpackers	H
Settlers Hill Cottages	G

RESTAURANTS & CAFÉS
137 High Street	C
The Cock House	E
Die Tap Huijs	2
Gino's	3
La Galleria	1
Reddits Book & Coffee Shop	4
Redwood Spur	5

GRAHAMSTOWN

N2 Port Elizabeth ▼

(☎082 932 1304) offers a similar service. The rooms are mostly en suite, in proper brick houses with secure off-street parking.

The only time you may have difficulty finding accommodation is during the festival in July, for when you'd be well advised to book as early as March. Several agencies specialize in finding accommodation during this period (to look for B&B accommodation, call the Grahamstown Accommodation Office on ☎046 622 5777).

137 High Street ☎046 622 3242, ⓦwww.137highstreet.co.za. Reasonably priced rooms above and behind a central eatery, located in an 1820 house, with pure cotton linen on the beds. ❸

7 Worcester Street 7 Worcester St ☎046 622 2843, ⓦwww.worcesterstreet.co.za. Ten huge, extremely comfortable rooms furnished extravagantly with eclectic decor in a 1888 stone mansion. Good dinners on request for guests only. ❻

The Cock House 10 Market St ☎046 636 1295, ⓦwww.cockhouse.co.za. Plush rooms in a beautiful Victorian house with a good reputation for food, though not in the best location. It counts Nelson Mandela among its satisfied guests. ❺

High Corner 122 High St ☎046 622 8284, ⓦwww.highcorner.co.za. Beautiful historical home in a great location across the road from the university, with six rooms furnished with Cape antiques and original art, yellowwood stairs and Oregon pine panelling. The house last belonged to well-known South African poet Professor Guy Butler. ❹

Hotel Victoria Mews 8 New St ☎046 622 7261, ⓦwww.hotelvictoria.co.za. Decent central hotel, offering B&B or meals in its restaurant. ❸

Lantern Hill 2 Thompson St ☎046 622 8782, ⓦwww.lanternhill.co.za. Five en-suite rooms in two Victorian semi-detached houses, in a central location off High Street, modestly furnished with a

393

nice garden, and ramps for wheelchairs. Well run and efficient. ❸

Old Gaol Backpackers Somerset St ☎ 046 636 1001 or 083 982 5966, ⦿ www.daba.co.za. Dorms and doubles in the cells of an old jail built in 1824 – a genuinely atmospheric place to stay. Its sister hostel, in George St, a 20min walk away, has rooms in a spacious house. Trips are available to

Addo Elephant National Park and the Fish River, as are *shebeen* crawls and township tours. ❶–❷

Settlers Hill Cottages 8 Bartholomew St & 1 Sheblon Lane, off Cross St ☎ 046 622 9720 or 082 809 3395, ⦿ www.settlershillcottages.co.za. A couple of reasonably priced, two-person settler cottages (both National Monuments) in the old part of town, with yellowwood floors. ❸

The Town

Reminders of the **colonial past** are everywhere in central Grahamstown, not just in the architecture (the interior of the Eastern Cape quite outdoes its counterparts in Australia and New Zealand, with many buildings still in use and well preserved), but also in streets named after Cape governors and soldiers: Cradock, Meyer, Somerset, Stockenstrom and Cuyler. **High Street** is Grahamstown's major shopping axis, with terraces of nineteenth-century buildings lending it a graceful air. Running from the station at its seedier east end, High Street continues past the cathedral at the junction of Hill Street, terminating at the 150-year-old Drostdy Arch, the whitewashed entrance gate to Rhodes University, of course named after Cecil John Rhodes (see box, p.325). Hawkers on the pavements sell small bags of fruit and vegetables, and you may see young Xhosa men in new caps and jackets, with red clay on their faces, signifying that their initiation period is over. At the centre of the street is the **Cathedral of St Michael and St George**, opened in 1830 and which, like many churches in the area, became a refuge for women and children during the Frontier Wars. Inside, on the right as you come in, is a quietly ironic memorial tablet to Colonel John Graham, who commanded the frontier.

While the High Street has most of the shops you'd need, many businesses have relocated, or opened up in the **Pepper Grove mall**, five minutes' walk north of High Street, with entrances in African and Allen streets. Pepper Grove also has the town's best-stocked supermarket, a chemist, cinemas, doctor, cafés, and a natural food store selling herbal remedies.

One of Grahamstown's rewarding short walks starts at the **Old Provost** in Lucas Avenue, on the edge of the Botanical Gardens and university. Built as a prison in the nineteenth century, the whitewashed stone Provost is now a craft shop; next to it are the graves of some British soldiers killed by Xhosa warriors. The walk heads up through the gardens to the **1820 Settlers Monument**, looming on Gunfire Hill above. Built in 1974 to commemorate the British settlers, it's an ugly fortress-like building, supposedly fashioned to look like a ship. The best reason to trudge up here is for the panoramic views, or for a performance at the Monument Theatre (see p.396). Avoid wandering around the gardens alone, especially in the evenings, as there has been the occasional mugging.

Rhodes University and the museums

Strung along Somerset Street, which runs at right angles to the top (west end) of High Street, is **Rhodes University** and a succession of modest museums – all are covered by a convenient multi-entry ticket, and can take up a pleasant morning. If you've time for only one, head for the **Natural Science Museum** (Tues–Fri 9.30am–1pm & 2–5pm, Sat 9.30am–1pm; R8), just south of the university entrance on the same side of the street. The display of Eastern Cape fauna and flora from 250 million years ago is excellent, with intriguing plant fossils and the bones of dinosaurs which once roamed these parts. Also worth a look is the **gallery** of the curator who worked for 48 years at the museum, containing his personal collection of objects in beautiful old teak display cases. The **History Museum** next door houses a dusty collection of 1820 settler memorabilia, nineteenth-century paintings and antique firearms, as well as Xhosa beadwork and traditional dress.

Beyond the Drostdy Arch, tucked behind some buildings at the corner of Somerset and Prince Alfred streets, is **ILAM**, the International Library of African Music (Mon–Fri 8.30am–12.45pm & 2.15–4.45pm; free; ☎046 603 8557; Ⓦwww.ilam.ru.ac.za). The library is an absolute treasure trove of recordings of **traditional African music** from southern Africa, as well as Zaire, Rwanda, Uganda and Tanzania, and there's a collection of over two hundred traditional instruments on view (by appointment only). Reasonably priced kalimbas, handmade using high-quality timber by Hugh Tracey (Andrew's father), and many other instruments can be bought from African Musical Instruments on the corner of Cloncourt and Jarvis streets, (☎046 622 6252 or 083 404 4567, Ⓦwww .kalimba.co.za), *the* place in South Africa to buy an authentic instrument.

On the same side of the road as ILAM, the **SA Institute of Aquatic Biodiversity** (Mon–Fri 8.30am–1pm & 2–5pm; free) was originally named after J.L.B. Smith the Rhodes University scientist who shot to fame in 1939 after identifying the coelacanth, a "missing link" fish, caught off the East London coast and thought to have become extinct fifty million years ago. Plenty of coelacanths, their preferred dwelling in the pitch-dark depths of the Indian Ocean, have now been spotted by deep-sea divers; in the foyer are two huge stuffed specimens, with fins that look like budding arms and legs.

Heading back down High Street and right onto Bathurst Street brings you to the **Observatory Museum** (Mon–Fri 9am–1pm & 2–5pm; Sat 9.30am–1pm; R8), a fun display in a restored building that was the home and shop of a notable watchmaker and jeweller during the mid-1850s. Also well worth a visit is the rooftop Victorian **camera obscura**, which projects onto a wall magnified images of the streets below. It's best seen on a clear day, when the reflections are crisp and clear.

Xhosa Grahamstown

Xhosa Grahamstown starts buzzing around **Market Square**, off Beaufort Street, where you'll see hawkers by the dozen and a busy minibus-taxi rank. In the late 1820s, the square was the trading venue for ivory, hides, wool and farm produce. If you're in the area, it's worth walking west of Market Square to see the restored **1820 Settlers' cottages** in Cross and Bartholomew streets, some flat-roofed and two-storeyed, others with pitched tin roofs.

Beaufort Street, the main through road, leads up the hill towards the townships on the eastern side of town. At the top, the road cuts through a hill of white clay, where Xhosa people scratch out pigment for face markings. From this cutting, looking into the valley, well away from the squatters' shacks, you'll see some roughly made traditional huts, used during the seclusion period, when young men, **amakweta**, are initiated. All over the Eastern Cape, it's not unusual to see *amakweta* on the roadside wearing very little and smeared in white clay, which signifies they've just been circumcized and initiated into manhood (Nelson Mandela went through the same ordeal).

Township tours are recommended with guide Mbuleli Mpokela (☎082 979 5906) who can take you in your own car, which works out cheaper than using his transport. Tours usually take three hours and include a Xhosa lunch at the Umthathi self-help project, which teaches people skills such as vegetable growing.

Eating, drinking and entertainment

Eating prospects in Grahamstown include one top restaurant and a couple of decent cafés. During term time, to get a feel of arty student life, head for the Drama Café, outside the University's Drama Department, on the corner of Somerset and Prince Alfred streets for coffee and light meals. For **self-catering**, the Home Industries shop at the Pepper Grove mall is great for home-made pies, seasonal fruit and vegetables, and venison and ostrich eggs for gigantic omelettes (all produce comes from local farms).

137 High St 137 High St, close to the Drosdty Arch and university. Come here for good coffee and great cheesecake, in a Georgian building with an outdoor courtyard. Mon–Fri 7.30am–9.30pm, Sat 8am–2pm & 5–9.30pm, Sun 8am–2pm.

The Cock House Corner of Market and George sts ⊕046 636 1295. Grahamstown's best restaurant, serving country cuisine; its speciality is local lamb shank, braised and marinated. There's home-baked bread, and after-dinner rum and chocolate truffles. Breakfast, lunch & dinner daily, closed Mon lunch.

Die Tap Huijs Cawood St ⊕046 636 1356. Pub and big-screen TV with a fireplace in winter. Recommended for venison, and, surprisingly, does vegan meals too. Dinner daily, lunch Wed–Sat.

Gino's Italian Restaurant and Takeaway Corner of Hill and New sts, attached to the *Hotel Victoria Mews*. Serves pizzas (in or out), steaks and pasta, with some vegetarian options, and is a firm favourite with locals. Daily noon–11pm.

La Galleria Ristorante Italiano St Aidan's Complex, Constitution St ⊕046 622 2345. This Italian place is one of the town's top restaurants with trolleys of appetizing antipasta and desserts. It has a reputation for its home-made pasta dishes, and also excels at red meat and poultry. Mon–Sat 7pm–midnight.

Reddits Books and Coffee 29 New St ⊕046 622 6524. Enjoy light meals, salads, bagels and home-made cakes while you browse through secondhand or new books, play board games, or admire local artists' or authors' works on display. Daytime only, except the curry/biriyani evenings on Fri (bring your own wine).

Redwood Spur 97 High St, near the cathedral. Open long hours, this serves reliable American-style food, mainly burgers and beef, with generous salads and late-night bottomless coffee, served with a smile by clean-cut young waiters. Daily 8am till late.

Entertainment

Despite being the home of the country's premier **arts festival** (see box opposite), and dominated by Rhodes University, Grahamstown's nightlife and entertainment scene is far less exciting than you might expect. Outside the hectic festival fortnight in July, the town relies on the **cinema** at the Pepper Grove Mall to deliver its only regular evening entertainment. The two main venues for **live performances** are the Monument Theatre and the Rhodes University Theatre, where the Drama Department puts on productions from time to time. Well worth catching is anything staged by Andrew Buckland, a local actor with an international reputation in physical theatre.

Thanks to the university connection, the town is periodically treated to a better selection of events than you'd be likely to find in the average Karoo *dorp*. To find out what's on, check the flyposters down High Street and also look in *Grocott's Mail*, the local rag, which comes out on Tuesday and Friday afternoons.

Around Grahamstown

From Grahamstown, it's a short journey to the **coast**: Port Alfred and Kenton-on-Sea (see p.385) are both less than an hour's drive away, and each has a historic settler village en route – **Bathurst** and **Salem** respectively. A

The Grahamstown Festival

For ten days every July, Grahamstown bursts to overflowing as the town's population doubles, with visitors descending for the annual National Arts Festival – usually called the **Grahamstown Festival**, or more simply The Festival. At this time, seemingly every home is transformed into a B&B and the streets are alive with colourful food stalls. Church halls, parks and sports fields become flea markets and several hundred shows are staged, spanning every conceivable type of performance.

This is the largest arts festival in Africa, and even has its own fringe festival. The hub of the event is the 1820 Settlers Monument, which hosts not only big drama, dance and operatic productions in its theatres, but also art exhibitions and free early evening concerts. Grahamstown's festival began in 1974 when the Monument building was opened. While work by African performers and artists is well represented, and is perhaps the more interesting aspect of the festival for tourists, the festival-goers and performers are still predominantly white.

The published **programme** – spanning jazz, classical music, drama, dance, cabaret, opera, visual arts, crafts, films and a book fair – is bulky, but absolutely essential; it's worth planning your time carefully to avoid walking the potentially cold July streets without seeing much of the festival proper. If you don't feel like taking in a show, the free art exhibitions at the museums, Monument and other smaller venues are always worth a look. For more **information and bookings**, contact the Grahamstown Foundation (℡046 622 3082, ℡www.nafest.co.za).

bit further afield, you can meander down dirt roads, pausing at old settler churches, graves and Frontier War battle sites, and take in some Bushman rock art on a tour with Grahamstown's Alan Weyers, a lively historian and great storyteller (℡046 622 7896, ℡www.spiritsofthepast.co.za). On your own, these places are well-nigh impossible to find.

Grahamstown is also close to a couple of fine **wildlife reserves**, especially good for experiencing the striking, dry bush particular to this area and the animals that little over a century ago roamed the land freely. If you're on a tight budget, the only chance to see some game is at the **Great Fish River Reserve Complex** (distinct from the wetland reserve), a rambling wilderness slaked by the Great Fish and its tributary, the Kap. Its appeal lies in its backwoods feel and the beauty of its landscape, but you're not guaranteed sightings of big game as you are at the luxurious and private reserves between Grahamstown and Port Elizabeth (see p.379), or at Addo Elephant National Park (see p.377). For Eastern Cape wildlife reserves see p.399.

Bathurst and around

A significant centre in the nineteenth century, **BATHURST**, 45km south of Grahamstown, is today little more than a picturesque straggle of houses, gardens and curiosity shops. The *Pig and Whistle Hotel*, on the corner of the Grahamstown road as you drive into Bathurst, started life as a smithy in 1821, with an inn attached a few years later; they can provide maps and directions to historical sites. A pleasant two-kilometre walk from the *Pig and Whistle*, the water-powered **Bradshaw's Wool Mill** marks the spot where South Africa's wool industry started.

The setup at **Summerhill Farm** should keep kids occupied for a while, with an outsized museum of pineapples (R10) housed inside a yellow-and-green plastic pineapple, in turn plonked in the middle of a field full of the genuine article. There's also a pool, playground and mini-farm.

Accommodation, eating and drinking

Most of what happens in Bathurst is strung along the **R67**, the main road between Grahamstown and Port Alfred. New, nice and private, *Palamino Cottage*, at 387 Prince Phillip Rd, is a prettily furnished cottage on a smallholding (T072 297 3060, Wwww.palamino.co.za; ❷). The *Pig and Whistle* on the R67 (T046 625 0673, Wwww.pigandwhistle.co.za; ❸) is a colonial Victorian village inn where the old rooms upstairs, furnished with period pieces, are best. Summerhill Farm plays host to the *Protea Hotel Bathurst* (T046 625 0833, Wwww.protea-hotels.co.za; ❸), with B&B units with double beds and bunks for kids, with the use of a playground and swimming pool and a mid-priced restaurant on-site too.

The *Pig and Whistle* pub is the place to down beers on the veranda, though its food is not that great. Best for lunch is *Sanibonani*, which does cuts of venison and light meals, while in the evening there's Thai food at *Ruan Thai* (T046 625 0224) which does takeaways and buffets.

Kwandwe Private Game Reserve

Adjoining the Great Fish River complex is the Eastern Cape's top wildlife destination, the very exclusive **Kwandwe Private Game Reserve** (T011 809 4300, Wwww.kwandwereserve.com; ❾ – first week of Jan, Feb, March & Oct–Dec R5740 per person per night, last three weeks of Jan & April–Sept R2605), with 30km of Fish River frontage and the Big Five in attendance. There are four **lodges**, two of which, *Uplands Homestead*, a beautifully restored Victorian homestead which accommodates six adults, and *Melton* Manor, a modern villa with four bedrooms set back 100m from a river, are for the exclusive use of single parties, with butlers, chefs and dedicated game rangers at guests' disposal. Of the other two, the fabulous *Kwandwe Great Fish River Lodge*, close to the water, is the quintessential traditional luxury safari lodge with nine suites and thatched roofs, wooden walkways and French windows that afford panoramic views of the surrounding countryside, while the ultra-luxurious and child-friendly *Kwandwe Ecca Lodge* – a funky boutique-hotel-in-the-bush – has six chalets, ingeniously designed with glass walls that allow you to lie on your bed and feel you're totally alone in the middle of the wilderness. Each unit has its own private plunge pool set into a wooden deck.

Apart from twice-a-day game drives, Kwandwe's **safari activities** include guided river walks, canoeing on the Great Fish, and rhino tracking, in which you follow one of the large mammals on foot. It also runs cultural tours with a resident historian who looks at the fascinating social and archeological past of the area. At *Ecca Lodge* special activities are laid on for children, including family game drives, short bush walks, and frog safaris. Service at Kwandwe is superb and highly personalized.

It's easy to drive to the game reserve, which is 160km from Port Elizabeth and is reached along the R67 that runs between Grahamstown and Fort Beaufort. Road or air transfers are available from Port Elizabeth airport.

Inland to the Karoo

Travelling between Grahamstown and the towns of Cradock and Graaff-Reinet (the Eastern Cape's two most-visited Karoo towns), you'll be heading into **sheep-farming country**, with the occasional *dorp* rising against the horizon, offering the experience of archetypal Eastern Cape one-horse outposts. The roads through this vast emptiness are quiet, and lined with rhythmically spaced telephone poles. Dun-coloured sheep, angora goats and the occasional

Eastern Cape Game reserves

The Eastern Cape is fast developing as a region for game viewing. Besides Addo Elephant National Park (p.377) and the private game reserves around Port Elizabeth, as well as the upmarket Kwandwe Private Game Reserve (see opposite), new game farms are opening all the time, many of them close to Grahamstown, or between Grahamstown and the coast. What follows is a selective list.

Sibuya Game Reserve (℡046 6481040, ⓦwww.sibuya.co.za) is at the cheaper end of the spectrum since it doesn't have lions, though you could see zebra, giraffe, buffalo and rhinos on its recommended tours which collect guests by boat from Kenton-on-Sea for a meander up the Kariega River, with a game excursion and picnic or braai (R580). If you stay overnight you'll pay a reasonable R1500 for all meals, game activities and accommodation.

Pumba Private Game Reserve 22km west of Grahamstown off the N2 (℡046 603 2000, ⓦwww.pumbagamereserve.co.za), is a good bet if you also want to see lions. A 7am game drive includes breakfast at the camp, while a 4pm game drive will give you dinner, both at R720 per person. Drives are on a 10-seater Land Rover, with no children under 7 permitted. The full safari experience, with luxury accommodation, meals, drives and drinks, will set you back R4065 per person.

If you're self-driving and intrepid, the **Great Fish River Reserve Complex** on the R67, 34km north of Grahamstown (℡043 742 4450, ⓦwww.ecparksboard.co.za; office open daily 8am–5pm; R20 per vehicle plus R6 per person), is an amalgamation of three separate reserves covering 430 square kilometres situated along the banks of the Fish and Kat rivers. Stands of thorn trees afford welcome shade during the summer heat, while in the parched areas away from the rivers, the striking landscape of cliffs and dense valleys is overgrown with scrubby bush, thick with succulents, euphorbias and aloes. The catch is that although there is plenty of game, it is difficult to see, so if you want to tick off the Big Five, this reserve is not for you. In the **south-western section,** closest to Grahamstown, there's accommodation in chalets for up to four people at Mvubu (R640 per night), bookable through the Eastern Cape Parks Board (℡043 742 4450, ⓦwww.ecparksboard.co.za).

---

springbok graze on brown stubble, and you'll often see groups of charcoal-and-grey ostriches in the veld, once farmed to satisfy an Edwardian feather fetish, and now reared to cater for a fashion for lean and healthy meat.

Cradock, 240km north of Port Elizabeth, lies in the **Karoo** proper, the semi-desert heartland of South Africa, with knee-high bush, clear dry air and an enormous sense of open space. It makes a great stopover on the Port Elizabeth to Johannesburg run, not least because of the excellence of its accommodation in historical houses (a stay at the *Tuishuise* in particular is reason enough to visit Cradock), and also for its proximity to **Mountain Zebra National Park**, one of the country's most beautiful game parks.

Some 100km due west of Cradock, **Graaff-Reinet** is one of the oldest towns in South Africa, and much of its historical centre is intact. Exploring its charms takes at least a day, and many people stop over here en route between Johannesburg and the Garden Route. Surrounding the town is the **Camdeboo National Park**, and if you want to get more of a sense of the Karoo's dry timelessness, head to **Nieu Bethesda**, 50km to the north of town.

Bedford and Somerset East

In the foothills of the Kaga Mountains, on the R63 and the R350, 87km north of Grahamstown, lies **BEDFORD**, the former realm of Xhosa Chief Phato. This was one of the little "English" towns Cape governor Sir Harry Smith promised to create in the nineteenth century, and has some attractive settler buildings. In the mountainous backdrop you'll find some **farmstays**, most notably *Cavers Country Guest House*, 16km north of Bedford (T & F 046 685 0619, W www.cavers.co.za; ❹–❺), a working dairy farm tucked away in a pretty valley. It has a grand 1850 refurbished two-storey stone manor house with four, huge en-suite bedrooms, beautiful lawns and gardens and the use of a swimming pool and tennis courts; walks on the property give you the chance to see antelope and myriad birds. Reservations are required if you want to stay; the owners will give you directions.

Just under 60km west of Bedford on the R63 lies **SOMERSET EAST**, a town that gets chewing during its *biltong* festival in June, and where Afrikaans matrons with tight perms, cardigans and plump brown arms stroll the main street. The historical part of the town merits a visit; down Beaufort Street, on an axis with the white-spired Dutch Reformed Church, is the **Somerset East Museum** (Mon–Fri 8am–5pm; donation), once the home of a Victorian pastor. One block from the museum is Somerset East's second attraction, the **Walter Battiss Art Gallery** (Mon–Fri 9am–1pm & 2–4pm, Sat & Sun by arrangement through the museum), in a handsome two-storey house on the corner of Beaufort and Poulet streets. Batiss is one of South Africa's most well-known modern artists, noted for his sense of humour, which shines out even in this uneven collection of drawings and paintings (his best work hangs in galleries elsewhere).

Cradock

The silvery windmills on the surrounding sheep farms of **CRADOCK** have become an unofficial symbol of the town; Xhosa hawkers (often kids) stand along the main road around the city limits, selling intricately crafted wire model windmills, their blades spinning in the breeze. Poverty has overshadowed Cradock since the Frontier Wars of the nineteenth century and the subjugation of the Xhosa people that continued right up to the 1990s. Against this history of conquest the town has provided fertile grounds for **resistance**: some members of the ANC were based in and around the town, and almost single-handedly kept the organization alive during the 1930s. In 1985, Cradock hit the headlines when prominent anti-apartheid activist **Matthew Goniwe** and three of his colleagues were brutally murdered. It was only in 1997, during the **Truth and Reconciliation Commission** hearings, that five Port Elizabeth security policemen were named as the perpetrators, but despite the bitterness it caused the five were granted amnesty.

Political controversy is also the theme at Cradock's biggest attraction, **Schreiner House**, 9 Cross St (Mon–Fri 8am–12.45pm & 2–4.30pm; donation). The house is dedicated to the life of the writer Olive Schreiner, best known for her groundbreaking novel *The Story of an African Farm* (1883), made into a film in 2004. It was remarkable enough for a woman from the conservative backwoods of nineteenth-century Eastern Cape to write a novel (it was published under the pseudonym Ralph Iron), but even more amazing that she espoused ideas considered dangerously radical even a century later. While in London looking for a publisher, Schreiner mixed with the likes of Havelock Ellis and Eleanor Marx, returning to South Africa at the turn of the last century to campaign for universal franchise for men and women irrespective of race. After a life of campaigning, Schreiner died in Cape Town in 1921 and is buried near Cradock on the Buffelskop peak, with her one-day-old daughter and favourite dog, overlooking the Great Fish River Valley. Her **burial site** has

become something of a place of pilgrimage, and details of how to get there are available from Schreiner House, along with a photocopied Ordnance Survey map. You'll need to drive to the starting point, and should allow a good half-day for the trip, which involves a very stiff climb.

Cradock's other points of interest include the **Dutch Reformed Church** at the upper end of Church Street, based on London's St Martin-in-the-Fields and completed in 1868, and a warmish (23°C) sulphur spring-fed **swimming pool** at the Cradock Spa on Marlow Road, 4.5km from town (daily 7am–6pm; R13). It has indoor and open-air pools, though it is getting a bit run-down. Behind the town hall, the **Great Fish River Museum** (Tues–Fri 8am–4pm, Sat 8am–noon) is housed in an 1849 Dutch Reformed Church parsonage and depicts the early history of Eastern Cape pioneers.

Practicalities

Cradock is small and easily covered **on foot**, but you'll need your own transport to get to the nearby Mountain Zebra National Park. Translux and Intercape **buses** pull in daily at Shoprite Checkers on Voortrekker Street, where you can buy tickets and get information for onward travel to Cape Town, East London, Port Elizabeth and Johannesburg. Cradock is a daily stop on the Port Elizabeth–Johannesburg rail line; the station is on the west bank of the Great Fish River. The very helpful but overworked one-person **tourist office** in Stockenstroom Street (Mon–Fri 8.30am–12.30pm & 2–4.30pm;

☏048 881 2383, ⊕www.cradock.co.za) can supply maps, accommodation lists and information on farmstays and local attractions.

Accommodation

For a small town, Cradock offers some delightful accommodation; if you want to taste some Karoo country style, the *Tuishuise* is especially recommended.

Cradock Spa 4.5km north of town on the road to the signposted Mountain Zebra National Park ☏048 881 2709. The best bet for budget accommodation, with self-catering, fully equipped chalets sleeping two to four. ❷

Heritage House 45 Bree St ☏048 881 5251 or 3210. Large Victorian home with a pool landscaped into rocks in the garden and a menagerie of animals, including a tame springbok. The owner is the curator of the Olive Schreiner Museum and will pack you a picnic for an early morning hike up to the tomb. ❷

Tuishuise Market St ☏048 881 1322, ⊕www .tuishuise.co.za. Staying in this street of comfortable and very stylish one- to four-bedroomed Victorian houses for rent gives an authentic sense of colonial domestic life over a century ago. Prices are very reasonable given that you get what amounts to a mini-museum to yourself, each house kitted out with antique furniture and crockery. There's dining close at hand at the *Victoria Manor,* though you can also self-cater. ❸

Victoria Manor 36 Market St ☏048 881 1650, ⊕www.tuishuise.co.za. Effortlessly gracious, old-fashioned hotel with excellent service, bags of character and period fittings. The rooms are en suite, dining is off silverware and the breakfasts are among the best in the country. ❸–❹

Eating

The *Schreiner Tea Room* (Mon–Sat 8.30am–5pm) next to the *Victoria Manor* in Market Street is the nicest place for tea, sandwiches and hot lunches. The *Manor* itself does dinners of very tasty meat dishes and vegetables, including favourites like Karoo lamb and *malva* pudding, in a crimson Victorian dining room, and is open for teas on Sundays. The *1814* (☏048 881 5390), with a distinctive sloping red roof standing out on Main Road, is a guesthouse which also offers tasty breakfasts, lunches and teas with an Afrikaans slant. A favourite with local families is the *Black Steer*, in the Total filling station complex on Voortrekker Street (daily lunch & dinner).

Mountain Zebra National Park

When the **Mountain Zebra National Park** (daily: May–Sept 7am–6pm; Oct–April 7am–7pm; R60; ☏048 881 2427), 26km west of Cradock, was created in 1937, there were only five Cape **mountain zebras** left on its 65 square kilometres. If that wasn't bad enough, four were males. At the time, environmental issues were far from being vote-winners; indeed, one cabinet minister dismissed the threatened animals as "a lot of donkeys in football jerseys". Miraculously, conservationists managed to cobble together a breeding herd from the few survivors on surrounding farms, and the park now supports several hundred, while also translocating healthy numbers to various corners of South Africa.

For **game viewing**, the park has a couple of good part-tar, part-gravel loop roads forming a rough figure of eight. Most rewarding is the northernmost route, 14.5km long, which circuits the Rooiplaat section where the plains game tends to congregate. As well as zebra, keep an eye out for **springbok**, **blesbok** and **black wildebeest**. The introduction of **buffalo** in 1998 and plans to bring in cheetahs and rhinos adds to the wildlife interest, but means that hiking across the park isn't possible. Unlike their docile Asian water buffalo cousins, the African buffalo have a reputation for extreme aggression. There are, however, two **waymarked walks** near the camp, one of them taking you high onto rocks above the camp. Allow an hour and a half for this circular trail.

Practicalities

To reach the park, head north out of Cradock on the N10, turning west after about 6km onto the Graaff-Reinet Road. After a further 5km, you turn left at the National Park sign onto a good gravel road, which reaches the park gate after a further 16km.

The park has **accommodation** in twenty comfortable two-bedroomed cottages (❷), all of which have outstanding mountain views and their own kitchens and bathrooms. The price includes breakfast in the camp restaurant. There's also a good **campsite**, but the unrivalled highlight of the park's lodgings is the self-catering **Doornhoek Guest House** (R700 for a minimum of four people), a beautifully restored Victorian homestead set in splendid isolation, with great Karoo views across a small lake to the surrounding chain of scrubby hills. Extremely comfortable, it has three en-suite double rooms furnished with antiques. A twenty-percent discount on accommodation and camping is available from June to September, excluding school holidays (when the park is always booked out).

A small **shop** at reception sells basics, souvenirs, alcohol and soft drinks, but if you're staying for a few days you should stock up in Cradock. There's a reasonable licensed **restaurant**, a post office, a filling station and a lovely swimming pool set among huge rocks, all near reception.

Graaff-Reinet and the Camdeboo National Park

It's little wonder that tour buses pull in to **GRAAFF-REINET** in their numbers; this is a beautiful town, one of the few places in the Eastern Cape where you'd want to wander freely day and night, taking in historical buildings and the occasional little museum, and have a meal or a drink before strolling back to your accommodation.

Graaff-Reinet has a large population of Afrikaans-speaking coloured people, mostly living on the south side of town, some of slave origin, others the descendants of indigenous Khoi and San who were forced to work on frontier farms. The dry mountains surrounding the town are part of the **Camdeboo National Park** whose main attraction is the **Valley of Desolation**, a B-movie name for an impressive site. The rocky canyon, echoing bird calls and expansive skies of the valley, shouldn't be missed.

Some history

By the late eighteenth century, Dutch burghers had extended the Cape frontier northwards into the Sneeuwberg Mountains, traditionally the stomping ground of Khoi pastoralists and San hunter-gatherers. Little more than brigands, the settlers raided Khoi cattle and attacked groups of San, killing the men and abducting women and children to use as farm and domestic labourers. Friction escalated when the Khoi and San retaliated and, in 1786, the Cape authorities sent out a *landdrost* (magistrate) to **establish Graaff-Reinet**, administer the surrounding area and pacify the frontier.

Nine years later, *landdrost* Honoratus Maynier, following orders to stop vigilante rule by white settlers and to curb the maltreatment of Khoi and San servants, was forced out of town at gunpoint by a group of burghers, bandying catchphrases from the recent French revolution. Declaring South Africa's **first Boer republic**, they complained that Maynier was "protecting the Hottentots and Kafirs against the Boers".

In 1800 Maynier was again put in charge of Graaff-Reinet, and colonial control over the district was slowly consolidated, with vast tracts turned over to grazing

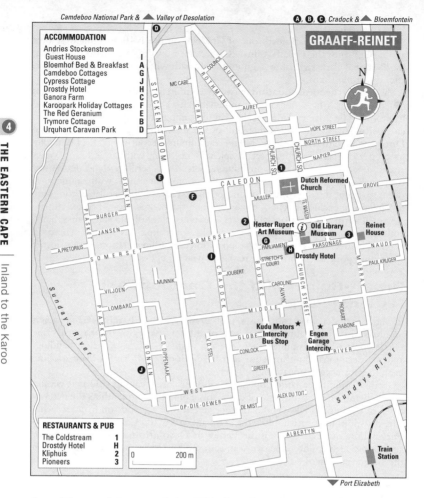

Camdeboo National Park & ▲ Valley of Desolation   Ⓐ, Ⓑ, Ⓒ, Cradock & ▲ Bloemfontein

GRAAFF-REINET

N

ACCOMMODATION

Andries Stockenstrom Guest House	I
Bloemhof Bed & Breakfast	A
Camdeboo Cottages	G
Cypress Cottage	J
Drostdy Hotel	H
Ganora Farm	C
Karoopark Holiday Cottages	F
The Red Geranium	E
Trymore Cottage	B
Urquhart Caravan Park	D

Dutch Reformed Church

Ⓔ Ⓕ CALEDON

② Hester Rupert Art Museum ⓘ Old Library Museum ③ Reinet House

Ⓖ PARLIAMENT PARSONAGE

Ⓘ STRETCH'S COURT Ⓗ Drostdy Hotel

Kudu Motors ★ Intercity Bus Stop   ★ Engen Garage Intercity

Ⓙ

RESTAURANTS & PUB

The Coldstream	1
Drostdy Hotel	H
Kliphuis	2
Pioneers	3

0   200 m

Train Station

▼ Port Elizabeth

sheep. The **wool boom** of the 1850s brought prosperity to the town and established a pattern of farming and land ownership which continues to this day.

Arrival and information

Translux **buses** between Johannesburg and Port Elizabeth, and Intercape buses connecting Jo'burg with the Garden Route towns, pull in daily at the Engen garage on Church Street. For bus tickets and timetables you need to go to the **tourist office** at 13 Church St (Mon–Fri 8am–5pm, Sat & Sun 9am–noon; ☏049 892 4248, ⓦwww.graaffreinet.co.za). This is also the place for **maps** and accommodation lists. **Umasizakhe township tours** are a recommended way to experience the other side of Graaff-Reinet; contact Xolile Speelman (see box opposite).

Accommodation

Graaff-Reinet has plenty of decent **places to stay** in the centre; the nicest are in listed historic buildings. If the Karoo landscape grabs you, you might want to head for one of the **farmstays** around here and Nieu Bethesda (see p.407), to witness some of the country's most dazzling night skies and spacious landscape. December is the busiest month, and you should definitely book well ahead if you want to stay then.

Andries Stockenstrom Guest House 100 Cradock St, a couple of streets back from the *Drostdy Hotel* ① & ⑤ 049 892 4575, ⑩ www .stockenstrom.co.za. A handsome listed house that has several times won the Automobile Association award for the best guesthouse in South Africa. It's worth staying just for the evening meals (only for guests) – outstanding French-Karoo cuisine with imaginative game and mutton dishes and scrumptious desserts. You're unlikely to eat better anywhere in the Karoo. ⑥

Camdeboo Cottages 16 Parliament St ① 049 892 3180, ⑤ 049 891 0919. Bang in the historical centre are these eight smallish, fully equipped (though rather basic) nineteenth-century self-catering cottages, built around a courtyard. Breakfast is available as an extra. ②

Cypress Cottage 80 Donkin St ① 049 892 3965 or 083 456 1795, ⑩ www.cypresscottage.co.za. A restored Karoo house with six double en-suite rooms and a communal lounge and dining room. Families are welcome and the garden makes it good for kids. ④

Drostdy Hotel 30 Church St ① 049 892 2161, ⑩ www.info@drostdy.co.za. Elegant Cape Dutch landmark in a prime location, with a dining room lit by grand chandeliers, shady gardens and fountains. The rooms, in terraced artisan cottages behind the hotel, are comfortable but small; larger rooms are pricier. ④–⑤

Karoopark Holiday Cottages 81 Caledon St ① 049 892 2557, ⑩ www.karoopark.co.za. Complex of self-catering cottages, run by the *Camdeboo Cottages* folk, set in a garden with a pool, plus dinky B&B units that are adequate for an overnight stay. ②

The Red Geranium 52 Stockenstrom St ① 049 892 2332. Three decent cottages run by a friendly owner. They're equipped for self-catering, though breakfast can be provided. ①–②

Urquhart Caravan Park On the outskirts of town, at the extension of Stockenstroom St, next to the Karoo Nature Reserve ① 049 892 2136. Large and well maintained, with campsites and good-value rondavels, chalets and bungalows, next to the Sundays River. The bungalows are more roomy than the stuffy rondavels and have linen, but you must bring your own towels. ①

Farmstays

Bloemhof Bed & Breakfast 27km north of Graaff-Reinet on the N9, and 5km down a good gravel road ① & ⑤ 049 840 0203, ⑥ murraybloemhof @ycbo.co.za. Grand homestead from the turn of the last century, built on ostrich-feather money, with enormous, yellowwood-floored rooms. It's part of a

Robert Sobukwe and the Africanists

One of Graaff-Reinet's most brilliant but often-forgotten sons is **Robert Managaliso Sobukwe**, founder of the Pan Africanist Congress (PAC). Unlike some followers of the PAC, who have not always held back from anti-white rhetoric, Sobukwe maintained that whites were capable, in time, of becoming genuine Africans. Born in 1923, Sobukwe won a scholarship to Healdtown, a boarding school near Fort Beaufort, going on to Fort Hare University (see p.418), where he joined the African National Congress Youth League. After graduating in 1947, he became a schoolteacher and then a lecturer at the University of the Witwatersrand. A charismatic member of the Africanist wing of the ANC – even the ultra-apartheid prime minister B.J. Vorster acknowledged him as "a man of magnetic personality" – Sobukwe questioned the organization's strategy of cooperating with whites, and formed the breakaway PAC in 1959. The following year he launched the nationwide **anti-pass protests**, which ended in the Sharpeville massacre and his imprisonment on Robben Island for nine years. In 1969, Sobukwe was released under a banning order to Kimberley, where he died in 1978. Five thousand people attended his funeral in Graaff-Reinet.

You can visit the Sobukwe home and grave on a **township tour** with Xolile Speelman (① 082 844 2897), who also accompanies people to traditional events, with music and the chance to meet members of Graaff-Reinet's African community.

large sheep and game farm, and serves Karoo lamb dinners. Children are welcome. ❸

Ganora Farm Off the N9, 7km east of Nieu Bethesda ☎049 841 1302 or 082 698 0029, ⓦwww.ganora.co.za. One advantage of staying on this working sheep farm is that the owners arrange trips to climb Compassberg (see p.409) and see Bushman rock shelters and Anglo-Boer War engravings. Accommodation is either half board, B&B or self-catering in a variety of units. You can also be shown how sheep farming works or view the small fossil collection. ❷–❸

Trymore Cottage Wellwood Farm, 31km north of town, on the road to Nieu Bethesda off the N9 ☎& Ⓕ049 840 0302, ⓔwellwood@wam.co.za. Self-catering, comfortable, four-bedroomed house on a long-established, beautiful farm with a merino sheep stud and an orange grove. Braai packs are available on request as are evening dinners, with Karoo lamb or venison on the menu. The well-known private collection of Karoo reptile fossils here is absolutely stunning and not open to the public, but residents may view it. Half board ❸, self-catering ❷

The Town and the national park

Graaff-Reinet centres around the imposing 1886 **Dutch Reformed Church**, with its pointy steeple and cake-icing decoration. The main thoroughfare, **Church Street**, splits at either side of the church, heading northwest to the Valley of Desolation and northeast to Nieu Bethesda, Middelburg and eventually Johannesburg. On either side of Church Street, little roads fan out, lined with whitewashed Cape Dutch, Georgian and Victorian buildings – it's in these parts that you'll find the town's museums, restaurants and most attractive buildings.

Church Street itself bustles with antique shops and businesses with Karoo-inspired names, such as Merino Pharmacy and Kudu Motors. One block south of the church is the **Old Library Museum** (Mon–Fri 8am–12.30pm & 2–5pm, Sat 9am–3pm, Sun 9am–noon & 2–4pm; R10). The only attraction here is the excellent collection of **fossil skulls** and skeletons of reptiles that populated the marshes, lakes and pools of prehistoric Karoo, some 230 million years ago. These Karoo dinosaurs were entombed in mud, and their bones became embedded in the present-day Karoo shale; the fossils were collected from the hills and river channels in the surrounding area. There's an even better collection on Wellwood Farm (see *Trymore Cottage* on above), but you'll have to stay there to see it as it is not open to the public.

Next door, in a restored 1821 mission church with Dutch gables, is the **Hester Rupert Art Museum** (Mon–Fri 9am–12.30pm & 2–5pm, Sat 9am–3pm, Sun 9am–noon; R10), which features a representative selection of work by South African artists (primarily white) active in the mid-1960s. Much of it is dreary and derivative of European art, but a few pieces stand out. Look out in particular for Cecil Skotnes's woodcuts, the strong expressionistic work of Johannes Meintjies, and Irma Stern's very appealing paintings.

Opposite the Art Museum stands the graceful, whitewashed **Drostdy Hotel**, a historical building in its own right, as the former residence of the *landdrost*. Most of the hotel guests are housed behind the main building, in Stretch's Court, a cobbled lane of nineteenth-century cottages with brightly coloured shutters. It hasn't always been so twee: Drostdy's slaves lived here, and after slavery ended in 1838 their descendants stayed on until they were kicked out under the 1950 Group Areas Act.

From the front steps of the Drostdy, you can look down Pastorie Street, lined with Cape Dutch buildings, to **Reinet House** (Mon–Fri 8am–12.30pm & 2–5pm, Sat 9am–3pm, Sun 9am–4pm; R10), Graaff-Reinet's finest museum. Formerly a parsonage, it was built in 1812 in the traditional Cape Dutch H-plan, with six gables and a spiral stairway leading to the garden. With wooden floors and airy rooms, it's essentially a period house museum, filled with covetable furniture and intriguing household objects. Strangely enough, the museum is the only place allowed to distil an illicit home-brewed spirit called "Withond" (white dog), which has an exceptionally sharp bite. Little bottles of the clear liquor, labelled with a picture of a bull terrier, are sold at the front desk.

Camdeboo National Park

The low-lying **Camdeboo National Park** (daily dawn–dusk; R40) totally surrounds the town, with its entrance 5km north of Graaff-Reinet's centre, off the Murraysburg Road. Its indisputable highlight is the strikingly deep **Valley of Desolation**, which you can gaze down into by driving the narrow tarred road from the reserve's entrance and ascending the bush-flecked mountainside; you'll pass a series of viewpoints up to the cliffs overlooking the valley. Late afternoon is the best time to enjoy the scenery, when the sun saturates the ochres and reds of the rock towers soaring from the valley floor. The views from the lip of the canyon, beyond the rocks and into the plains of Camdeboo, are truly thrilling, and even better if you tune into the echoing bird calls, especially when black eagles circle the dolomite towers, scanning the crevices for prey.

There's a 45-minute looped **walk** along the canyon lip, well marked with a lizard emblem.

Eating and drinking

You'll find only a couple of centrally located **restaurants** and **tea shops** catering for Graaff-Reinet's many visitors, and the town is pretty dead on Sundays. Lamb and beef from farms in the area is readily available as well as local venison. A local man supplies restaurants with kudu salami and venison sausage, and menus everywhere are meat oriented. If you've had your fill of lamb chops, the culinary highlight is unquestionably the *Andries Stockenstrom Guest House* (see p.405), but you need to be staying there to enjoy its cooking, which attracts gourmets from across the country.

The Coldstream 3 Church Square ℡049 8911181. Karoo lamb as well as all the local meats. Mon–Sat 9am until late.
Drostdy Hotel 30 Church St. The hotel has an unrivalled garden for drinks or tea, and a grand dining room for rather formal dinners, with a pricey English-style set menu and the odd Afrikaans speciality thrown in; better value are the buffet lunches and breakfasts. There's also an atmospheric pub here. Daily.

Kliphuis 46 Bourke St ℡049 892 2346. Come here for tea and sandwiches or a light lunch at pavement tables, and evenings for meaty dinners with one vegetarian platter thrown in. Tues–Sun 8am until late.
Pioneers Somerset St ℡049 892 6059. A local pub with good venison pie, Karoo lamb and chops, chicken, hake and a platter for vegetarians. Open from 5.30pm daily. Closed Tues, except in Dec & Jan.

Nieu Bethesda

In the mountains north of Graaff-Reinet, **NIEU BETHESDA** is drier and dustier than you might wish, especially in midsummer when it boils with harsh, bright light. There are no streetlamps, and on winter nights temperatures plummet to zero, the sky filled with icy stars. Most people who come here do so in order to marvel – or shudder – at the **Owl House** on River Street (April–Sept 9–5pm; Oct–March 8am–6pm; R16; ⓦ www.owlhouse.co.za), once the home of Helen Martins, a reclusive artist who expressed her disturbing and fascinating inner world through her work. Every corner of the house and

▲ The Owl House, Nieu Bethesda

garden has been transformed to meet her vision. The interior walls glitter with crushed glass, owls with large eyes gaze from the tin-roofed veranda, while at the back of the house, trapped by a stone wall and high chicken wire, are hundreds of glass and cement sculptures: camels, lambs, sphinxes and human figures. Martins never exhibited her work or courted publicity, though since her death in 1976 many have visited the museum and pondered on her life in this Karoo backwater. South African playwright Athol Fugard, who loves the Karoo and has a house in Nieu Bethesda, used her life and creative toil as inspiration for his celebrated play *The Road to Mecca*.

Owl House aside, the whitewashed **village** has plenty of charm. It's a tranquil place, accessible on a good gravel road, with the sound of spring water flowing down furrows into the little windmilled allotments. Once an archetypal conservative Karoo *dorp*, the town has reinvented itself as a tiny artists' colony, attracting a growing number of visitors. Nearby, a few hundred coloured residents somehow manage to eke out a living in this harsh environment. The Nieu Bethesda Community Art Group's gallery, opposite the police station, also exhibits local artwork.

The **Compassberg Mountain**, one of the highest peaks in the Eastern Cape and part of the Sneeuberg range, dominates the Nieu Bethesda skyline. You'll need local guidance to scale it; organized **hikes** up here are arranged at Ganora Farm (see p.406).

Practicalities

Nieu Bethesda is 23km off the N9 between Graaff-Reinet and Middelburg. There's a **village shop** and butcher on the main road, but if you're self-catering you should stock up elsewhere, especially for fresh fruit and vegetables, which are scarce in the Karoo. No petrol is available in Nieu Bethesda, so fill up in Graaff-Reinet; neither is there an ATM nor a tourist office.

Given how tiny Nieu Bethesda is, it's surprising to find any **restaurants** at all. The *Waenhuis Pub 'n Grub*, at the fourway stop on the main road, does a very reasonably priced buffet with *biltong* soup, kudu or eland steaks, lamb *bredie* and roast potatoes, though opening times are never guaranteed. During the day you can eat at the *Village Inn*, in New Street. along from the *Owl House* in New Street, whose cold ginger beer, cakes and home-made bread go down well. *The Brewery*, across the dry Gats River off New Street, is a first-class choice for an unhurried lunch, serving its own cold beer accompanied by home-made cheese, bread, olives and salami.

Accommodation

There's an excellent selection of cheap **places to stay**, mostly self-catering cottages, with one party per house, at around R150 per person; see ⓦwww .nieubethesda.co.za for additional recommendations. *Huis Nommer Een*, Murray Street (book through Suzette Pienaar on ⓣ049 841 1700; ❷), has three spacious rooms furnished in South African country style, a farm-style kitchen, and a handsome veranda. The only **backpacker lodge**, *Owl House*, Martin Street (ⓣ049 841 1642, ⓦwww.owlhouse.info; ❷), is friendly, laid-back and well organized, with dorm beds, B&B rooms, two self-contained cottages and a restaurant, *Outsiders*. They will collect you if you arrive in Graaff-Reinet by public transport. If you want to stay on a **farmhouse**, try the friendly *Doornberg Farm* (ⓣ & ⓕ049 841 1401, ⓦwww.nieubethesda.co.za; ❷), which has a pub and serves evening meals, or you can self-cater; there's also a trampoline, pool, riding and hiking. The nicest place to stay on the farm is in *Die Vleihuisie*, a little cottage 4km away from the farmstead.

East London and the central region

Between Port Alfred and East London lies some of the Eastern Cape's least-developed **coastline**, although it has now fallen into the hands of developers as more and more people discover the beauty of the region. **East London**, wedged uncomfortably between two ex-Bantustans, is the largest city in the central region of the province, with excellent beaches for surfing and swimming and good transport links to Johannesburg and along the coast. Inland, **Fort Hare University** near Alice has educated political leaders across the subcontinent, including Nelson Mandela, and has the country's finest collection of contemporary black South African art.

Sweeping up from Fort Hare's valley, the gentle, wooded **Amatola Mountains** yield to the dramatic landscapes of the **Eastern Cape Drakensberg**, which offer hiking, horse-riding and even skiing opportunities. Before white settlers (or even the Xhosa) arrived, these towering formations were dominated by **San hunter–gatherers**, who decorated the rock faces with thousands of ritual **paintings**, many of which remain surprisingly vivid.

The coast: Fish River Mouth to East London

Heading 30km east of Port Alfred, along the R72, you'll come to the **Great Fish River**, the boundary across which the British drove the Xhosa in the Fourth Frontier War of 1811–12. It's a major landmark, cutting through a steep-sided valley shrouded in thick prickly bush. During apartheid, the river became the frontier of the notionally independent Ciskei Bantustan, whose multi-million-rand border post on the east bank of the river stood unused until the 1990s, when it became a rather pleasant roadside tea room and Shell Ultra City Garage.

The **Great Fish River Wetland Reserve** between the R72 and the river mouth is noted for its beautiful plants and prolific birdlife. There's nowhere to stay in the reserve, but just across the Great Fish is the luxurious *Fish River Sun Hotel* (☎040 676 1102, ⓦwww.sun-international.com; ❹). Conforming to the bizarre logic of apartheid, this is where Eastern Cape whites could nip over the border to the Bantustan and the South African-owned **hotel** where they could enjoy a spot of gambling, which was banned in "White South Africa". The *Sun* has arguably the best **golf** course in the country (open to non-residents) with stunning views of the river and beach. A few kilometres further east, the *Mpekweni Beach Resort* is very comfortable, but not as glitzy (☎040 676 1026, ⓦwww.mpekweni.co.za; half board ❺). Its position couldn't be better, though, with rooms close to the beautiful lagoon and unspoilt beach, which the hotel has managed to nab for its own exclusive use.

Hamburg

One of the few resorts along the Pineapple Coast – the stretch between Port Elizabeth and East London – that feels like real Africa is **HAMBURG**, a low-key village on a good dirt road, 14km off the R72. The route passes through **Xhosa settlements** and shanties, where you'll see traditionally decorated thatch-and-mud huts. Look out for stock animals wandering perilously into your way and strolling around Hamburg itself, lending the town a truly rural feel. Hamburg is renowned for **fishing**, and the muddy-bottomed Keiskamma River is excellent for catching prawns. The sea offers a good beach break for **surfers**, but otherwise there's not much else to do here except laze on the beach, go for walks and bird-watch.

There are a couple of **places to stay**, both with views over the wide, brown Keiskamma River and high olive-green hills, but a three-kilometre walk to the beach. *Sampie's Landing* (☎040 678 1032; half board ❷) rents out rooms, and the owner takes guests fishing. There's a little shop but no restaurants. The beach itself offers nothing but a car park, broken-down toilets and kilometres of sand and sea.

East London and around

EAST LONDON, the second-largest city in the Eastern Cape, is the obvious jumping-off point for exploring the Transkei or the coast west to Port Elizabeth. It has good **connections** to the rest of the country by air, rail and bus, and you don't need a car to enjoy the beach life. The city has seen a development boom in recent years with shopping malls being upgraded and a casino and hotel complex. But without fine, warm weather, the city can be dreary. What does happen takes place along the beachfront, where there's a plethora of places to stay, eat and drink. **Nahoon Beach** is a great **surfing spot**, and the town has a dedicated and lively surfing scene. It's also gradually becoming a place for black holidaymakers – a post-apartheid phenomenon. The beaches to the east of town are very beautiful, with long stretches of sand, high dunes, estuaries and luxuriant vegetation, and good swimming. Although definitely not a fashionable city, it's small and easy to drive around, with some good restaurants and accommodation.

Before the British, and even the Xhosa, this was home to the **Khoikhoi** people, who called it Place of the Buffaloes. The Buffalo River once teemed with game, but the animals were gradually killed off with the arrival of British hunters. East London began life as a permanent British settlement during the nineteenth-century **Frontier Wars**, when it was used as a beachhead to land military supplies needed to push back the Xhosa. Taken by its strategic possibilities as a port, the British governor Sir Harry Smith optimistically called it **London** in 1848, after the capital of the empire. Later it was changed to the Port of East London, not after London's East End, but because the port was on the east side of the Buffalo River. British connections are still obvious, though: East London's main thoroughfare is called Oxford Street and there's a Fleet Street and even a Belgravia suburb.

Away from the holiday strip, East London is dominated by an industrial centre served by **Mdantsane**, a huge African township 20km from the city towards King William's Town. Apart from the active river port, there are several large factories, including a Mercedes-Benz plant, whose workers presented Nelson Mandela with a bright red, top-of-the-range Mercedes as a coming-out-of-prison present.

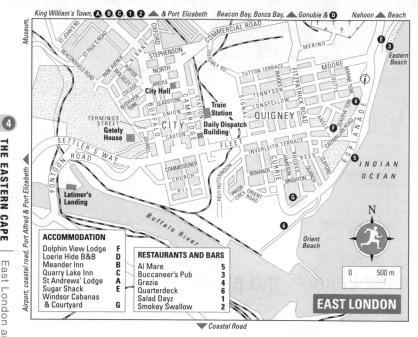

ACCOMMODATION

Dolphin View Lodge	F
Loerie Hide B&B	D
Meander Inn	B
Quarry Lake Inn	C
St Andrews' Lodge	A
Sugar Shack	E
Windsor Cabanas & Courtyard	G

RESTAURANTS AND BARS

Al Mare	5
Buccaneer's Pub	3
Grazia	4
Quarterdeck	6
Salad Dayz	1
Smokey Swallow	2

EAST LONDON

0 — 500 m

▼ Coastal Road

Arrival, information and orientation

East London's small **airport** (☏043 706 0306), a few kilometres west of the centre on the R72, connects the city to all major centres. The **airport shuttle**, the Little Red Bus (☏082 569 3599), meets all flights and drops off at the *Holiday Inn* near the beachfront (about R100 depending on your destination). The **train station** (☏0860 008 888) is on the eastern edge of East London's small business and shopping district. From here, it's a thirty-minute walk to the backpacker hostel at Eastern Beach, and a slightly shorter stroll to Orient Beach. Buses are scarce, but there are metered **taxis** outside the station.

All three of the **intercity buses** – Translux (☏0861 589 282), Intercape (☏0861 287 287) and Greyhound (☏083 915 9000) – offer a frequent, comprehensive and inexpensive service connecting East London to major centres in the coastal provinces of Northern, Western and Eastern Cape, and KwaZulu-Natal, as well as to Johannesburg and Pretoria. The buses drop off at the coach terminal at Windmill Park on Moore Street, home of the well-known Windmill Roadhouse.

Like many South African cities, central East London is gridded; with uncongested roads and easy parking, it's far more geared to **driving** than walking. **Minibus taxis** connect the townships to the centre, and buses link the **city centre** and **beachfront**. For a **taxi**, call Border Taxis (☏043 722 3946).

Maps and a comprehensive list of B&Bs are available from the helpful **tourist office** at the Esplanade on the beachfront (Mon–Fri 8am–4.30pm, Sat 9am–2pm; ☏043 722 6015, ⓦ www.visitbuffalocity.co.za). In the same building is the head office for the **Eastern Cape Tourism Board** (ⓦ www.ectourism .co.za), where you can pick up information on the rest of the province. Imonti Tours (☏043 741 3884 or 083 487 8975, ⓔ imontitours@absamail.co.za) conducts **tours** of the city centre and townships, including a visit to the Khaya La Bantu Cultural Village 30km east of town (see p.416), where there's a story-teller, Xhosa dancing and traditional food.

Accommodation

East London fills up over the Christmas period, when prices rise sharply. The **beachfront** is in the process of being developed but still sports graceless blocks of holiday apartments and functional hotels, redeemed only by their fabulous views of the Indian Ocean. The really cheap hotels are mostly filled with long-term residents, and are often rough drinking hangouts – best avoided. If the urban nature of the main beachfront doesn't appeal, your best bet is to head for the suburbs of **Nahoon Mouth** at the end of Beach Road, **Beacon Bay**, **Bonza Bay** or **Gonubie**, close to the river and sea and reached via the N2 east of the city; without your own transport, you'll need to take a taxi or arrange to be picked up. Besides a couple of old-fashioned hotels, these areas have a good selection of smart B&Bs in private houses. East London's **campsites** are out this way, too, near the water. There are also places to stay in the suburb of Selborne, 3km north of the centre off Oxford Street, near the Vincent Park Centre. For **backpackers**, the best lodge is *Sugar Shack*, at Eastern Beach, spectacularly situated in a former lifeguard's lookout.

Beachfront and northern suburbs

Dolphin View Lodge 6 Seaview Terrace ☎043 702 8600, ℮dolphin.view@mweb.co.za. Luxury guesthouse on the edge of cliffs above the beach with two budget double rooms; ten well-appointed standard rooms with limewashed furniture and crisp white linen; a suite with lounge and dining room furnished with rich dark-wood antiques and thick brocade curtains; and two self-catering family suites that sleep four (R700). ❸–❺

Meander Inn 8 Claredon Rd, Selborne ☎043 726 2310, ℮meanderinn@telkomsa.net. Five spacious, tastefully furnished rooms with white linen and ceiling fans, in a luxurious yet relaxed two-storey building. The garden is manicured and there's a swimming pool, patio and bar, and dinner on request. Often used as the starting or finishing point of the Wild Coast Hotel Meander (see box, p.428); they will do free airport transfer. ❸

Quarry Lake Inn Quartzite Drive, off Pearce St, The Quarry ☎043 707 5400, ⒲www.quarrylakeinn .co.za. Spacious, well-appointed rooms on the edge of a flooded disused quarry which has become home to an abundance of vegetation and birdlife. ❹

St Andrew's Lodge 14 St Andrew's Rd, Selborne ☎043 743 5131, ℮sandrews@iafrica.com. Four basic en-suite B&B units with separate entrances and TV inside a suburban house, as well as a garden cottage with cooking facilities. There's a swimming pool too. ❸

Sugar Shack Eastern Beach ☎ & ⒻＰ043 722 8240, ⒲www.sugarshack.co.za. Brilliantly located hostel, right on the beach, with terrific views and an outdoor relaxation area. There's transport from the hostel to the mountain resort of Hogsback (see p.420). Dorms ❶, doubles ❷

Windsor Cabanas & Courtyard George Walker Parade ☎043 743 2225, ⒲www.windsorcabanas .co.za. Spanish-style block near Orient Beach, offering great views. The *Cabanas* has comfortable one-, two- and three-bedroom self-catering apartments (❹) with breakfast available as an extra. The adjacent *Courtyard* offers B&B (❸).

Eastern suburbs and resorts

Blue Lagoon Hotel Blue Bend Place, Beacon Bay ☎043 748 4821, ℮blhotel@iafrica.com. Very pleasant accommodation surrounded by palm trees and close to the beach. Rooms are quiet and spacious, with balconies looking onto the river, which you can reach via a short path that also leads to the beach. ❹

Gonubie Resort & Caravan Park 19km east of the city off the N2 ☎043 705 9748. The best camping place in East London, well maintained and near the beach and lovely estuary, which are both safe for swimming. There are also self-catering wooden chalets, fully equipped if also a little run-down. ❷

Habitat 2 Cane St, Gonubie, one block away from Gonubie Beach ☎043 740 3703. Two basic self-catering units with private entrances, one in the garden, the other on the ground floor of the main house. No children. ❷

The Loerie Hide B&B 2B Sheerness Rd, off Beach Rd, Nahoon ☎ 043 735 3206, ⓦ www.loeriehide .co.za. Four reasonably priced en-suite rooms in the vicinity of Nahoon Beach, decorated in ethnic African and English country-cottage style, at the bottom of a garden that gives way to indigenous bushland. ❸

The City

East London's drab city centre is dominated by **Oxford Street**, once the main shopping precinct, parallel to Station Street and the train station. Although a major traffic thoroughfare, it is largely deserted at night, when you shouldn't wander around alone. The newly upgraded **Vincent Park Centre** on Devereux Avenue is a popular shopping centre with movies and restaurants. It is 5km north of the city centre (leave the centre on Oxford Street, and turn right into Devereux just beyond the museum), in the midst of the salubrious suburbs of Vincent and Stirling. This is the best place for shopping, or to find anything practical such as banks and the post office.

Apart from a couple of handsome buildings, East London's Victorian heart has progressively been demolished. From the station you can walk a few blocks north up Cambridge Street to the city centre's principal landmark, the splendid terracotta and lace-white **City Hall**, opened in 1899. Its tall, colourful clock tower amid the otherwise dreary modernish buildings is a useful orientation point. Over the road is a rather lifeless statue of martyred Black Consciousness leader **Steve Biko** (see box, p.419), a minor point of pilgrimage for visitors, unveiled by Nelson Mandela in 1997. Staying with the Biko theme, the **Daily Dispatch Building**, with a surrounding colonial-style veranda, is also worth taking in, at the corner of Caxton Street and Cambridge Road. Founded in 1879, the newspaper made national headlines in the 1970s, when the then editor, the late Donald Woods, earned the wrath of the apartheid government for being involved with Biko, who contributed to the newspaper under a pseudonym. After endless police harassment, Woods dramatically fled the country, a story told in the book and 1987 movie *Cry Freedom*.

One street north of here, Terminus Street leads to the Victorian **Gately House** (Mon & Wed–Fri 9.30am–1pm & 2–4.30pm, Sun 11am–4pm; entry by donation). This was the home of the city's first mayor, John Gately, and contains some fine period furniture. You can also enter Gately House via **Queen's Park & Zoo** (daily 9am–5pm; R17, children R10; ☎ 043 722 1171), a good spot to take children, with its farmyard, reptiles and birds, as well as a playground and refreshment kiosk. At weekends there are pony rides (10am–3pm) and a little train all day (on weekdays it operates at 11am and 2.30pm).

East of the city's train station is **Quigney**, an area of small colonial-style Victorian houses, some nicely restored with verandas and corrugated-iron roofs, others run-down. Quigney slopes downhill to the **Esplanade** and **Orient Beach**, the safest place to swim and most easily reached along Currie Street, off Fleet Street. Here you'll find the city's best curio outlet, Umzi Wethu Curio Shop, stocking handmade **African crafts**; it's at 110 Moore St, up the hill from the *Holiday Inn*. Near the station, African Culture at 46 Station St has ceramics, sculpture, drawings, batiks and tie-dyed products made on the premises. Also check out the hawkers on the esplanade selling curios, leather and woodwork.

Two kilometres uphill from the centre is **Latimer's Landing**, the working dockland waterfront on the Buffalo River. Never the success it was hoped to be, it appears a little deserted, and business is slow – but there's a pub and a couple of restaurants, and it's good for a wander around to see the boats. You can sometimes buy fresh fish when the boat comes in. To get there, head west along Fleet Street towards the airport, and just before Buffalo Bridge head steeply down Pontoon Road. **Boat trips** from here head through the Buffalo harbour out to sea and along the beachfront shore; Shemoans Boat Cruises (℡083 989 6799) offers trips by arrangement.

A few kilometres north of the city centre, the **East London Museum**, Upper Oxford Street (Mon–Fri 9am–4.30pm, Sat 10am–1pm, Sun 10am–3pm; R5), has a stunning collection of South Nguni beadwork and contemporary wire sculpture, including an inventive wire car made by Mdantsane resident Phillip Ntliziywana. The museum's pride and joy, however, is its stuffed coelacanth (see p.395), caught off the coast in the 1950s.

The beaches

East London's **Esplanade** loops from Orient Pier in a wide and beautiful sweep of rocks, beach and sand dunes to Eastern Beach, marred only by the motley assortment of holiday apartments, hotels and restaurants lining the beachfront. It's about thirty minutes' walk from the city centre; buses here are sporadic, but it's easy enough to stroll from one end to the other.

Tucked in next to Orient Pier, with dockland cranes poking their necks above the water, **Orient Beach** is a wonderful place to swim, though it looks a bit grim and industrial. The waves are gentle, the water and sandy beach clean. Red-hatted lifeguards lend a sense of security, and there are changing rooms, and a couple of little pools for kids. You pay a small fee to enter the beach area during the day, but it's free after 5pm.

From Orient Beach, the sea-walled Esplanade continues northeast, along sand and black rocks, to **Eastern Beach**, with its high, bush-capped sand dunes. Although far more attractive, Eastern Beach has had problems with muggings, though it remains a popular beach for surfers. Don't leave your belongings unattended, and give the beach a wide berth at night.

Northeast beyond Bat's Cave – a distinctive chunk of rock jutting out to sea – is popular **Nahoon Beach**, a long stretch of sand, backed by dunes. This wonderful natural setting is superb for swimming and surfing, with some of the best waves in the country. Public transport is scant, but there are three **buses** a day from the Esplanade, or you can walk the 5km from the centre if you're feeling energetic. There is a café, *The Beach Break*, right on the sand. East of the Nahoon River, 10km from the centre, the coast curves into **Bonza Bay**, with kilometres of beach walks and a lazy lagoon at the mouth of the Quinera River. Further on, **Gonubie Beach**, 18km northeast of the centre, at the Gonubie River Mouth, is still close enough to be considered part of East London, with some good accommodation, a beautiful beach and walks.

Eating, drinking and nightlife

East London has several surprisingly good restaurants and a couple of very decent places serving **fresh fish** in an outdoor setting. **Drinking** spots abound, from beachfront sleaze at lowlife hotels to lively surfers' hangouts or swanky places overlooking the ocean. Some of the pubs double up as **live music** venues, as well as offering a bite to eat.

Al Mare Esplanade ℡043 722 0287. Mediterranean-style food with good steaks, fish, pizzas and pasta, overlooking the town's aquarium and the sea. Closed Sat lunchtime & all day Sun.
Buccaneer's Pub Eastern Beach, next to *Sugar Shack*. Lively bar that buzzes till the early hours, with occasional live music (Wed, Fri & Sat). During

the day there are fantastic views of the rodeo riders of the surf. Good pub fare includes fish and chips and, best of all, chicken schnitzel. Daily lunch & dinner.
Ciao Bella 11 Chamberlain Rd, Berea ℡043 726 0554. Small coffee shop with outside seating; excellent Italian coffee as well as home-made

bagels and muffins and other light meals. Mon–Sat 7am–5pm.

Grazia Upper Esplanade ☎043 722 2009. Light and airy restaurant with stunning views of the sea, serving Italian-style food, tasty fish dishes and steaks. There's a good wine list and an outside eating area. Daily lunch & dinner.

Le Petit 54 Beach Rd Shopping Centre, Nahoon ☎043 735 3685. Highly regarded eating place serving rich Mediterranean/French-inspired food, with an emphasis on game, seafood and veal. Mon–Fri lunch & dinner, Sat dinner only, from 6pm.

Quarterdeck Orient Beach, overlooking the paddling pool ☎043 743 5312. One of the best beachside places for a quiet drink, with reasonably priced catch of the day served daily. Closed Sat lunchtime & all day Sun.

Salad Daze Balfour Rd, Vincent ☎043 726 6912. Pink and pretty wood and iron building selling lovely healthy salads, freshly squeezed juices, home-made breads and cakes and more substantial meals. Mon–Fri 8.30am–4pm, Sat morning only.

Smokey Swallows Devereux Ave, outside Vincent Park Shopping Centre ☎043 727 1349. The only restaurant in the Eastern Cape to get onto the Top 100 Restaurants in SA list, serving predominantly modern Asian cuisine. Daily 11am –midnight

Listings

Car rental Avis ☎043 736 2250, Imperial ☎043 736 2230.

Emergencies Fire ☎043 705 9000; see also p.75.

Garages Stirling Motors, 8 Old Transkei Rd (☎043 735 1580), is open 24hr.

Hospitals Frere Hospital (state), Amalinda Drive ☎043 709 1111; St Dominic's (private), 45 St Mark's Rd ☎043 743 4303.

Internet access Try Cyberlink, 58 Beach Rd, Nahoon (Mon–Sat 10am–1pm, 3–6pm & Sun 3–6pm).

Laundries There is a coin-operated launderette at the Edcott Centre, Oxford St.

Pharmacies John Forbes, 205a Oxford St (☎043 722 2062; till 10pm); Berea Pharmacy, Pearce St (☎043 721 1300; Mon–Sat 8am–10pm, Sun 9am–1pm & 2–9pm).

Travel agents Rennies Travel, 5 Surrey Rd, Vincent ☎043 705 5800; Let's Travel, Kennaway Building, Esplanade ☎043 743 2983.

Around East London

Several worthwhile excursions detailed below are within an hour's drive from East London. If you don't have your own wheels, you can cover the same ground with Imonti Tours (☎043 741 3884 or 083 487 8975, ⓦ www.imontitours.co.za).

The privately run **Inkwenkwezi Game Reserve** lies 35km from East London (book in advance for a safari; ☎043 734 3234, ⓦ www.inkwenkwezi .co.za), set in an appealing landscape, encompassing bushveld, grassland, forest and two rivers, with views of the Indian Ocean. The reserve offers luxury tented **accommodation** with full board (❻), and you can view the wildlife, including rhino, giraffe, zebra, wildebeest, various antelope and some rare birds, on early morning or afternoon/evening game drives in one of the reserve's 4WD vehicles. The centrepiece is a magnificently sited, thatched *lapa* (enclosure or corral) with spacious decks where food is served. To get there, drive north out of East London along the N2, taking the Brakfontein exit onto the East Coast Resorts Road; then travel east for about 20km, until you see the Inkwenkwezi Entrance Gate on the left.

You can do a day-trip here, without breaking the bank, particularly during the week when it is R100 cheaper than at the weekend. A full-day trip, comprising a three-hour game drive in the morning, elephant stroking and feeding followed by a three-course lunch, goes for R595 at weekends. A shorter trip, with just lunch and an afternoon game drive, costs R495.

Khaya La Buntu

KHAYA LA BUNTU, near Mooiplaas, 30km east of East London, signposted off the N2 (☎043 851 1011, ⓦ www.khayalabantu; visits by prior arrangement,

R150 including lunch), is a **Xhosa village** which sees only twenty or thirty tours a year – it's not one of the dressed-up villages deemed suitable for tourists. It's best visited for a traditional lunch, when you can watch a group doing dancing and storytelling.

The Amatola Mountains

Most visitors drive quickly through the scrubby, dry impoverished area between East London and the **Amatola Mountains** proper, to reach the cool forests and holiday lands at **Hogsback**. However, it's worth deviating en route, to see the marvellous collection of African art at **Fort Hare University**, close to the little town of Alice, and to visit apartheid martyr Steve Biko's grave in **King William's Town**, as well as take in some peeling, but intact, colonial streetscapes. King, as it's usually called, has a first-class museum, which can help you absorb some of East Cape's settler history and Xhosa culture.

King William's Town

KING WILLIAM'S TOWN, more commonly known simply as **King**, lies 56km northeast of East London. It started life as a military frontier and missionary outpost, and today has a large population drawn from the former Ciskei. There's enough historical interest here to satisfy at least half a day's visit. To get a feel for **Xhosa history**, head for the unmissable **Amatola Museum** in Alexandra Road (Mon–Fri 9am–4.30pm, Sat 9am–1pm; R5, includes the Missionary Museum; ☎043 642 4506); the Xhosa Gallery has unusually good displays, including full accounts of the British tactics and campaigns which crushed the Xhosa. Traditional culture is well represented, with contemporary exhibitions on current building styles. Don't miss Phillip Nthziywana's imaginative bus and car sculptures made from wire and discarded bits and pieces.

Two blocks north of the museum, off Albert Road, is the nineteenth-century **Edward Street Cemetery**, notable for the story it tells of the conflicts in the area. Besides a memorial to those killed in the innumerable Frontier Wars against the Xhosa, there is an open piece of ground on the far side of the cemetery which marks a mass grave where hundreds of Xhosa were buried; they died of starvation as a result of the disastrous 1857 **cattle killing**, when many Xhosa people destroyed their cattle at the behest of the false prophetess Nongqawuse (see box, p.432).

About fifteen minutes' walk north of the Amatola Museum, the **Missionary Museum** in Berkeley Street (arrange a visit through the Amatola museum) is mainly of interest for the glimpse it gives into early educational institutions in the Eastern Cape. South Africa's first black professionals were schooled here, including many of the new nation's heavyweights such as Nelson Mandela.

King's only other attraction of note is **Steve Biko's grave** in the Ginsberg Cemetery. It's a moving place, and the grave is much humbler than you'd expect for such an important figure in black politics. The polished, charcoal-coloured tombstone sits midway through the graveyard, among the large patch of paupers' graves. To get there, take Cathcart Street south out of town (towards Grahamstown), turning left onto a road signposted to the cemetery, after the bridge (just before the Alice turn-off to the right).

Rob Speirs of Speirs Tours (☎043 642 1747, ⓦwww.speirstours.co.za) offers affordable **battlefield tours** around King William's Town, visiting various forts and battle sites from the Frontier Wars and grave sites of Xhosa chiefs. Also worthwhile is the Liberation Tour which takes you through the history of the struggle against apartheid. King is also the place to set out on all or part of the **Amatola Hiking Trail**, which starts from Maiden Dam, just outside town, and continues as a five-night/six-day hike into the mountains (see box, p.421).

Practicalities

Alexandra Road is the town's main drag, where you'll find a 24-hour filling station and a few takeaway restaurants. The **minibus taxis** rank is in Cathcart Street, with connections to East London and the rest of the Eastern Cape. Best place for **shopping** is the new Stone Crescent mall off Alexandra, which has a good Pick 'n Pay supermarket.

Accommodation in King William's Town is principally geared to business travellers; at weekends, you'll find a greater choice and often discounted rates. A pleasant B&B is the *Dreamers Guest House*, 29 Gordon St (T & F 043 642 3012, W www.dreamersguesthouse.com; ③), in a centrally located Victorian building with a lovely garden, pool and real log fires in winter. The *Grosvenor Lodge*, Taylor Street, near the Amatola Museum (T 043 604 7200, W www.grosvenor.co.za; ④), is a business-class hotel with cable TV, and is much cheaper over weekends. For **eating and drinking**, the *Castle* on Queens Road serves good steaks and salads. Handy fast-food joints on Alexandra Road include *Nando's*, which offers spicy grilled chicken, *Steers* and *Spur* for steaks and burgers, and *Debonairs* for pizza.

Fort Hare University and Alice

Despite decades of deliberate neglect, and its relegation after 1959 to a "tribal" **university** under apartheid, **Fort Hare** (W www.ufh.ac.za), 64km west of King William's Town, is assured a place in South African history. Established in 1916 as a multiracial college by missionaries, it became the first institution in South Africa to deliver tertiary education to blacks, and was attended by many prominent African leaders, including Zimbabwe's president Robert Mugabe and Tanzania's former president, Julius Nyerere.

The most famous former student is **Nelson Mandela** (see box, p.442), making this an essential port of call if you're following his footsteps. Sadly, though, the Wesley Residence, from whose window the young Mandela reputedly used to climb to go ballroom dancing, has been pulled down. The spot it occupied is now the lawn just to the right as you enter through the main gate. **Freedom Square**, at the centre of the campus, was the scene of many protests at the university – this is the spot where several members of the present government cut their political teeth.

If you have even the slightest interest in African art, Fort Hare's **De Beers Art Gallery** (Mon–Fri 8am–4.30pm; free) is well worth a visit. From the outside, the cylindrical gallery resembles a high-security bank vault. Once inside, you're faced with a treasury of contemporary black southern **African art** – one of the most significant and least publicized collections anywhere. Pioneers of black painting, including Gerard Sekoto and George Pemba, are represented, and you should look out for the lively oils of Dan Rakgoate. There are some stunning sculptures: Uneas Sithole's elongated *Is My Friend the Chameleon Hiding?*, Percy Konqobe's *Ntsikana and his Cow*, and Sydney Kumalo's *Robot Man*. Also unmissable is the sequence of fifteen woodcuts by Lucky Sibiya called *Umabatha*, the Zulu adaptation of *Macbeth*. The gallery also houses Fort Hare's **ethnographic collection** – a major museum of traditional crafts and artefacts, with many rare and valuable pieces. The university library houses the **ANC's**

Steve Biko and Black Consciousness

Steve Biko's brutal interrogation and death while in police custody triggered international outrage and turned opinion further against the apartheid regime. His death was followed by the banning of the Black Consciousness organizations, and was a major factor in the imposition of a mandatory **arms embargo** against South Africa by the United Nations Security Council.

Steven Bantu Biko was born in 1946 in King William's Town. His political ascent was swift, due in no small part to his eloquence, charisma and focused vision. While still a medical student at Natal University during the late 1960s, he was elected president of the exclusively black South African Students' Organization (SASO) and started publishing articles in their journal, fiercely attacking white liberalism, which they saw as patronizing and counter-revolutionary. In an atmosphere of repression – both ANC and PAC leaders were serving hefty sentences at the time – Biko's brand of Black Consciousness immediately caught on. He called for blacks to take destiny into their own hands, to unify and rid themselves of the "shackles that bind them to perpetual servitude". He became honorary president of the Black Peoples' Convention, an umbrella organization which attracted mainly young intellectuals and professionals. From 1973 onwards, Biko suffered banning, detention and other harassment at the hands of the state. In 1974, he defended himself in court, presenting his case so brilliantly that his profile in the international press soared.

Barred from leaving King William's Town, Biko continued working and writing, frequently escaping his confinement. In 1976, black outrage burst into the open with the **Soweto riots**. The police response was brutal, and the search for "agitators" led to Biko's 101-day detention. In August the following year, he was stopped at a roadblock near Grahamstown (outside his restricted area), taken to Port Elizabeth and intensively interrogated and tortured. On September 12, 1977, he died from a brain haemorrhage, sustained at the hands of security police. No one was held accountable. Diplomats from thirteen Western countries joined the thousands of mourners at his funeral in King William's Town.

archives (Mon–Fri 8am–4.30pm; Ⓦ www.liberation.org.za), which include historic documents and photographs.

All **tours** of the university, its art gallery and ANC archives should be arranged beforehand through the curator (Mon–Thurs 8am–4.30pm, Fri 8am–3.30pm; ⓣ 040 602 2050 or 2239; free).

Alice

A handful of photogenically decaying colonial houses with peeling corrugated-iron roofs and balconies smothered in creepers constitute the main interest in **ALICE**. It's the closest town to Fort Hare University, but can in no way be called a university town. The lengthy decay of the town reflects the second-class status accorded the university under Afrikaner Nationalist rule. There's one hopelessly tiny bookshop, a depressing reflection of local poverty and the high cost of books in South Africa, which puts them beyond the reach of the majority of the population. Alice's two hotels are little more than run-down carousing joints. Of the two, the *Amatola* is favoured for drinking by university staff and students.

Just 1km east of the town centre is **Lovedale College**, older than Fort Hare, and no less significant in educating Africans. Built in 1842 as a Presbyterian mission station, it was soon educating the country's first black professionals, and became an important publishing centre. The Xhosa language was first transcribed here, and one of Lovedale's students, J. Tengo Jabavu, was the founder of South Africa's first weekly African-language paper, *Zabantsundu*. With the passing of the Bantu Education Act under the apartheid government, Lovedale was closed. Now the college is in use again as a high school, you can drive in and look at the Victorian buildings. The actual site doesn't have any displays or information – for that, visit the Missionary Museum in King William's Town (see p.417).

Practicalities

The university is a couple of kilometres east of Alice on the R63; from King William's Town there are **minibus taxis** to Alice that drop off passengers at the university gates. With the virtual absence of accommodation in Alice, you're better off making a day-trip here from Grahamstown, East London or Hogsback.

Hogsback

Made sweeter by the contrast with the hot valleys below, the village of **HOGSBACK** in the Amatola Mountains, 32km north of Alice and 145km from East London, offers cool relief after hauling through prickly, overgrazed country. The name "Hogsback" applies to the area as much as to the village, and comes from the high rocky ridge (actually three peaks) resembling a bushpig's spine, which runs above the settlement.

Hogsback represents a corner of England, a fantasy fed by mists, pine plantations and exotic trees such as oak, walnut and azaleas, and guaranteed snowfalls each winter. It's a great place to spend a relaxing couple of days, with plenty of walks and good air among the flowers, grasslands and forests, and there are many places to stay. The real attraction is the **Afro-montane cloud forest**, singing with bird calls and gauzy waterfalls, and populated by the odd troop of **samango monkeys**, which survive on the steep slopes above the pine plantations. Note that Hogsback can be wet and cold, even in summer, so bring a warm pullover, sturdy shoes and rain gear.

Winding your way up the mountains on the road from Alice, you'll have a good view of the forest, dense with yellowwood, stinkwood and Cape chestnut. The hamlet itself is strung out along 3km of gravel road, with lanes branching out on either side to hotels and cottages. The closest thing to a **centre** is the small conglomeration of a general store, post office, filling station and some nearby craft shops. Hogsback has its own **indigenous craft** found nowhere else in the country: prepare to be pestered by Xhosa kids selling the characteristic unfired clay horses and hogs with white markings.

Hogsback is prime **rambling** country, with short, relatively easy trails indicated by hogs painted onto trees. For a rewarding taste of indigenous forest, the Contour Path above the campsite makes an easy, one-hour walk. From this path, a route goes steeply up **Tor Doone**, which overlooks the settlement, and is the easiest summit to climb. One of the most rewarding waterfall trails is the one-hour steep downhill walk to the lovely **Madonna and Child Waterfall**. A number of short and long routes, including the Amatola Trail and Zingcuka Loop (see box opposite), are detailed in inexpensive **guidebooks** available at the village shops.

Practicalities

It's worth spending a couple of nights in Hogsback. A cheap shuttle (☎043 722 8240) connects *Sugar Shack* in East London (see p.413) and Cintsa (see p.430) with Hogsback five days a week; the *Away With The Fairies* hostel in Hogsback

The Amatola Trail and Zingcuka Loop

Ranked among South Africa's best forested mountain walks, the **Amatola Trail** is a tough but fabulously beautiful five-night trail, with numerous waterfalls, rivers and bathing pools en route. Starting at Maiden Dam in the Pirie Forest, some 21km north of King William's Town, it stretches 105km to end at Hogsback. There are huts with mattresses and braai facilities, some also with showers, at each designated night stop along the way.

There are a number of shortened versions of the trail, but these can only be done outside school holidays, or at short notice if the huts are not filled. Best of the shortened trails is the 36-kilometre **Zingcuka Loop** from Hogsback, which scales the Hogsback itself, and follows streams much of the way, past idyllic waterfalls and pools. Right in the forest at the base of a cliff, the overnight hut has the luxury of a primitive shower, and firewood.

To go on one of these trails, **book** through the Department of Forestry (☎043 642 2571, ⓦwww.amatola.co.za; R750 for the complete trail and R135 per day per section). You'll need well-broken-in boots, plus waterproofs and warm clothes.

can make arrangements, whether or not you intend to stay there. In the absence of a proper tourist office, you can get maps from *Nina's* (☎045 962 1326), a deli and pizza joint just off the main road. Lowestoffe (☎045 843 1716) offers **horse trails** for beginners and experienced riders alike.

Places to stay are plentiful, but the village tends to fill up during holidays and weekends, when you'll need to book ahead; the useful website ⓦwww .hogsbackinfo.co.za lists cottages. The best place for afternoon tea or lunch is *Tea Thyme at The Edge* (see "Accommodation", below), though it's off the main road and so best combined with a walk along the edge of the escarpment or around the very beautifully set labyrinth here. Hogsback has a general **shop** selling basic supplies. *Woodlands* (☎072 055 6462) on the main road does breakfasts, as well as light lunches and dinners, though you'll need to book in advance for dinner. Well-priced pub lunches are best at the *King's Lodge Hotel*, while the hotel with the top reputation for food, though a bit pricier, is *Arminel*. Both hotels have nice garden settings, and fireplaces in winter. For pizzas, pasta and deli fare, head to *Nina's* on the main road, which also has log fires going.

Accommodation

Arminel Signposted along the main road ☎045 962 1005, ⓦwww.katleisure.co.za. The best of the hotels, with a good reputation for food. All the rooms lead directly onto the well-kept hotel gardens, and some have their own wooden decks. Half board ❹

Away With The Fairies Hydrangea Lane; down the first turning on your right and signposted as you drive into Hogsback ☎045 962 1031, ⓦwww .awaywiththefairies.co.za. Unequivocally geared to the backpacker scene, this a large converted house on a sizeable property, with fabulous views of the Tyumi Valley. Small dorms sleep five to eight guests, and there are a number of twin and double rooms, some en-suite and one with its own fireplace. Horse-riding can be arranged, and the owners offer free guided hikes in the forests and mountains. One of the nicest features of the hostel is a platform in a tree for drinks and hanging out. ❶

The Edge ☎ & ⓕ045 962 1159, ⓦwww .theedge-hogsback.co.za. The best of the self-catering accommodation, nine cottages in separate locations a couple of kilometres off the main road. There are superb valley and forest views, and a herb patch from which meals are garnished – the owners grow 25 kinds of lavender on the property. There's also a labyrinth, based on the pattern of one in Chartres Cathedral in France, for meditative walks. Booking is essential for the cottages, which range in price from R375 to R850, sleeping two to four people. ❷

Granny Mouse Country House Nutwood Drive ☎045 962 1259, ⓦwww.grannymousehouse.co.za. Country-style furnishings in an old home with a beautiful garden. Self-catering as well as B&B. ❷–❸

Lowestoffe Country Lodge T & F 045 843 1716, W www.lowestoffecountrylodge.co.za. Three fairly modern cottages on a farm where you can horse-ride or fish for trout. The farm is 24km out on the unpaved road to Cathcart, so its draw is the dramatic and lonely mountain scenery, rather than the forests and gardens of central Hogsback. There are dams and mountain pools for swimming. Family-sized cottages are about R500 per night.

The Eastern Cape Drakensberg

The **Eastern Cape Drakensberg** is the most southerly section of southern Africa's highest and most extensive mountain chain, stretching east across Lesotho and up the west flank of KwaZulu-Natal into Mpumalanga. Although known misleadingly as South Africa's "little Switzerland" in tourist brochures, they are wonderful African mountains, full of **San rock paintings**, sandstone **caves** and craggy sheep farms. **Rhodes**, one of the country's best-preserved and prettiest Victorian villages, is the obvious goal in the region, a good base for riding, walking, skiing and trout fishing. While it's very cold, dry and sunny in the winter, summer is idyllically green, with river pools to swim in. There are some appealing cottages for rent on farms, and a number of **hiking trails**, many of which offer the opportunity to see rock paintings and sleep in enormous caves. Since there is no national park in the Eastern Cape Drakensberg, activities are all arranged through private farms. For **bird-watchers**, the region is especially good for raptors (notably the rare lammergeier and Cape vulture), as well as orange-breasted rock jumpers and ground woodpeckers. Very remote, Rhodes is reached from Barkly East, which itself is 130km from Aliwal North on the N6. The sixty-kilometre dirt road to Rhodes from Barkly East is tortuous and rough, taking a good ninety minutes, with sheer, unfenced drops – definitely not recommended in the dark or mist.

Rhodes and around

RHODES is almost too good to be true – a remote and beautiful village girdled by the Eastern Cape Drakensberg. Few people actually live here: like other villages in this region, Rhodes was progressively deserted as residents gravitated to the cities to make a living, leaving its Victorian tin-roofed architecture stuck in a very pleasing time warp. Today, its *raison d'être* is as a low-key holiday place for people who appreciate its isolation, wood stoves and restored cottages. Although electricity reached the village a few years ago, very few establishments have it, and paraffin lamps and candles are the norm. Given that Rhodes is not on the way to anywhere (on some maps it doesn't even appear), it is a place to dwell for a few days, rather than for an overnight stop. While nights are cool even in summer, in winter they are freezing, and there's no central heating, so pack warm clothes.

The village itself is not much more than a few crisscrossing gravel roads lined with pine trees. The trees were donated in the 1890s, so the story goes, after a group of scheming townsfolk hoped to extract a large donation from **Cecil Rhodes**, by changing the village's name in his honour. All they got from the astute entrepreneur was a sackful of seeds. At the heart of the village is the *Rhodes Hotel*, a general shop and a garage; there's also a post office and payphone, but no banking facilities and no public transport in or out of the village.

Rhodes is busiest in the winter, when **skiers** use it as a base for the Tiffendell slopes (see box opposite), an hour's 4WD drive into the highest peaks of the Eastern Cape Drakensberg. December to May are the best months for

Tiffendell Ski Resort

Tiffendell, South Africa's only ski resort, promotes itself as a little Switzerland, with Alpine ski lodges and European instructors on the slopes. However, it's essentially a venue for conspicuous South African consumers in search of a nonstop party. The resort is enormously successful, and for foreign visitors it provides, if nothing else, a quirky experience of Africa.

Skiing at Tiffendell is on **artificial snow** – despite regular winter falls, the real snow melts too quickly to provide a reliable piste. The **season** runs from May 20 to September 12. You can rent everything you need (except gloves) at the resort for about R50 per item per day. A four-hour beginner's lesson costs R230; three-night fully inclusive packages, including on-site accommodation, work out at around R2000–3600 per person, much less out of school holidays. **Rooms** at the resort's lodge are small and functional, with shared washing facilities, though the higher-priced packages provide en-suite rooms. The lodge is usually full, and many people stay at Rhodes village instead. Day visitors need to book, as there is a maximum of 180 people on the slopes per day. **Bookings** are made through the Snowscape shop in Jo'burg, at the Decor Centre, Forest Road, Fourways (☎011 787 9090, ⓦwww.snow.co.za).

Out of the ski season, Tiffendell runs as a **summer holiday** location, with trout fishing, mountain biking, grass skiing, horse-riding and hiking. Bookings for summer holidays are done locally (☎045 974 9005), and cost R280 per person per day for half board.

The shortest **route** to Tiffendell is via Rhodes, but the road is steep and needs a 4WD at all times; there are daily transfers from Rhodes (R120 return), which are a better bet.

swimming and hiking; this is one of the best places in the country for **fly-fishing**, with all the solitude and glorious landscape you could hope for and rivers jumping with rainbow and brown trout, stocked in the 1920s. The *Rhodes Hotel* can give advice about where to fish, or you could check out ⓦwww.wildtrout.co.za; better still, you can go out for a day or longer with Dave Walker of *Walkerbouts Inn* (see p.424), who can organize permits giving you access to 150km of river, but you'll need all your own gear. Dave also runs **Highlands Information** (ⓦwww.highlandsinfo.co.za), a service which can be used to book any sort of holiday in the area.

Rock-art sites

Rhodes is a good base for exploring millennia-old **San rock paintings**, the majority of which are on surrounding private farms which can be visited with the farmers' permission (some farms also take guests). The South African Heritage Resources Agency (☎021 462 4502) in Cape Town has a comprehensive list, and Rhodes locals can point you to nearby farms, such as Buttermead and Hillbury, which have their own paintings. Sue Tonkin in Maclear (☎082 686 4468) does fully guided **rock-art tours**.

Close to Rhodes, **Martin's Hoek** farm, 16km from the village, is worth a visit, not just for the well-preserved, photogenic paintings, but for the lovely, lonely valley you have to drive though to get there. Make an appointment with Russie or Lookie Schmidt to see them (☎045 974 9201). The signposted turn-off to Martin's Hoek is 8km from Rhodes on the road to Barkly East. From the turn-off it's another 8km to the site, with parking and a couple of picnic tables. The paintings are fenced off on the cliff face opposite the parking area; it's a ten-minute uphill scramble to reach them, much easier than it first appears, with views out onto the rough and streaky sandstone peaks. A second site, at **Denorben Farm**, 32km southeast of Barkly East, offers the longest

▲ San rock painting

series of San paintings in the country. It's only 1km to the farm from the main road, and the long, painted panel is behind the house, at the bottom of the garden. A nominal entry fee is charged and there's a helpful information sheet on the images, many of which are confusing. Don't miss the impressive (unpainted) cave in the farmyard – it's common practice for farmers in the area to use overhangs as cosy sheep pens and sheds.

Rock art had an essentially religious purpose, usually recording experiences of trance states (see p.506 for more); shamans' visions often included powerful animals like the eland, which you can see depicted at both Denorben and Martin's Hoek, and whose power shamans were able to access for healing. A dying eland is a metaphor for the shaman who enters a **trance** and takes on aspects of an animal. At Denorben there's a half-animal, half-human figure, an image of transformation during the trance state. Also at Denorben are painted figures dancing, clapping and singing, in the process of inducing trance.

Accommodation

Gateshead Lodges ☎045 974 9216. Several farmhouses and excellent cottages on huge properties in marvellously remote and rugged territory, all within a large radius of Rhodes. Some cater specifically for fly-fishing, river swimming, hiking, riding or bird-watching, while a few have caves and rock paintings on the property. All are clearly detailed in a brochure available from PO Box 267, Barkly East 5580. ❷

Rhodes Hotel Main Rd ☎045 974 9305. The only hotel in town, with a decorative exterior and charming Victorian furnishings. Full board ❹

Rubicon Flats ☎045 974 9268, ⓦwww .rubiconflats.co.za. The best-value, and the

warmest, place in town, this handsome old schoolhouse has been converted into self-catering rooms, each with an anthracite burner, and simple dorms. The owner, Mrs Reeders, also rents out self-catering cottages in the village and provides meals, but you need to book ahead for dinner. ❷

Walkerbouts Inn Signposted off the main road ☎045 974 9290, ⓦwww.walkerbouts.co.za. Relaxed house with six en-suite guest rooms, with room-only, B&B and half-board rates. The friendly owner, Dave Walker, knows a good deal about the area and can organize almost any activity, including fly-fishing and horse-riding. Half board ❹

Eating and drinking

For **eating**, your best choice is *Walkerbouts*, which does home-cooked meals, with two wood-burning pizza ovens on site. You can also get meals at the restaurant of the *Rubicon Flats* hotel. For **drinking**, the hotel bar is one of the most atmospheric pubs in the country. It's decorated with the horns of Wydeman, the lead ox of the supply wagon from Barkly East, who dropped dead outside the hotel in 1896. Also lining the walls are smoky relics of the days when this was a frontier town of gamblers, cattle rustlers and bar-room shoot-outs.

Naude's Nek

The most exhilarating drive out of Rhodes is on the R396 along **Naude's Nek**, the highest mountain-pass road in South Africa, connecting Rhodes with **Maclear** to the south, in a series of snaking hairpin bends and huge views. If you're chiefly looking for scenery, it's not essential to do the whole route to Maclear. Many people go from Rhodes to the top of the pass and back as a half day trip, during which you can make a call from the highest phone (with a crank handle) in the country, in a corrugated-iron booth in the middle of a sheep pen at the top of the pass.

While it's only 30km from Rhodes, the journey can take a couple of hours to the Nek because so many changing vistas en route demand stops. You don't need a 4WD, but if you feel precious about your car don't attempt this route, as the road is harsh. The surface deteriorates from the top of the pass to Maclear, with sharp stones and a hump down the centre of the road, which may scrape the bottom of your vehicle, and is definitely impassable after snow. If you're wanting to use this route into the Transkei and KwaZulu-Natal, check with the *Rhodes Hotel* as to the current state of the road, and take two spare tyres.

The Wild Coast region

The **Wild Coast region** is aptly named: this is one of South Africa's most unspoilt areas, a vast stretch of undulating hills, lush forest and spectacular beaches skirting a section of the Indian Ocean. Its undeveloped sandy beaches stretch for many kilometres, punctuated by rivers and several wonderful, reasonably priced hotels geared to family seaside holidays. The wildness goes beyond the landscape, for this is the former **Transkei** homeland, a desperately poor region that was disenfranchised during apartheid and turned into a dumping ground for Africans too old or too young for South African industry to make use of.

Few whites live in the Wild Coast region; nearly everyone is Xhosa, and those in rural areas live mostly in traditional rondavels dotting the landscape for as far as the eye can see. This neglect lives on in the negative image most white South Africans still have of the Transkei. Unless they have actually visited the area and come to appreciate it, most people have an exaggerated image of its dangers: legendary (and wildly overstated) tales of crime, hostile locals (quite untrue) and shocking roads (these are being upgraded).

Also in the Transkei's favour, this is the "Africa" completely missed by those who restrict their holiday to Cape Town and the Garden Route. One or two of the hotels – and most of the backpacker lodges – offer a chance to experience traditional **Xhosa life**, with village visits to healers or overnight stays with a Xhosa family (see the box on p.434 for some background on Xhosa traditions). In all of South Africa, this is the best and easiest place to experience authentic

uMzimkhulu ▲   ▲ Durban

R56

Port Edward
A

Mtamvuna River

Bizana

R61

Mzamba River

Kokstad

MKHAMBATHI
NATURE RESERVE

N2

Msikaba

R56

R61

Holy Cross

Mount Ayliff   Mzintlava River

INDIAN

OCEAN

Flagstaff

Lusikisiki
B

N2

Magwa Falls

River

Keneba   Mount Frere

Mzimvubu River

See Port St Johns map

Port St Johns
SILAKA NATURE RESERVE

Mount
Fletcher

R61

Umngazi Mouth
C

D

N2

Mthatha River

HLULEKA NATURE RESERVE

Libode

LUCHABA
NATURE RESERVE

E Mthatha Mouth
F Coffee Bay
G
H
I

Mthatha(Umtata)

Mthatha River

Umtata Dam

Hole in the Wall

Maclear

Jojweni/
Viedgesville

Madwaleni
Hospital

J CWEBE
NATURE
RESERVE

NDULI
NATURE
RESERVE

Qunu   Elliotdale

K

N

Z

R61

Mveso

Mbashe River

DWESA
NATURE
RESERVE

Colleywobbles

Nqabara River

Cat's Pass   Qora Mouth

L

Idutywa

M Mazeppa
Bay

Tsomo

River

N

N2

Qora River

Nxaxo
Mouth

O

Centani   Qholorha Mouth

P

Butterworth
R

Kei Mouth
Morgan Bay

S

T

Tsomo

Haga-Haga

R61

R61

Tsomo River

Cintsa
U

N2

Mooiplaas

White Kei

Kei River

Gonubie
V

N2

THE WILD COAST

0   50 km

East London

Black Kei

▼ Queenstown

ACCOMMODATION		Coffee Bay Hotel &		Hole in the Wall	**I**	Morgan Bay Hotel	**S**	Wavecrest	**O**
Anchorage	**E**	Coffee Shack	**G**	Idutywa		Ocean View	**H**	Wayside	**R**
Bomvu Paradise	**F**	Crawford's Lodge &		Kob Inn	**V**	Seagulls	**Q**	Wild Coast	
Buccaneer's	**U**	Cabins		The Kraal	**D**	Trennery's	**P**	Sun Hotel	**A**
Bulungula		Haga Haga		Mazeppa Bay	**M**	Umngazi River			
Backpackers Lodge	**J**	The Haven	**K**	Mbotyi River Lodge	**B**	Bungalows	**C**		

African rural life as a tourist. Despite the obvious hardship, it's refreshing – at least for visitors – to find that rural areas are still communally owned rather than parcelled up into private farms. Instead of the fenced-off spaces edged by squatter camps found in most of rural South Africa, here the land is unfenced and fully inhabited.

The **N2** highway runs through the middle of the region, passing through the old Transkei capital of **Mthatha** and a host of scruffy, busy little towns along the way. Northwest of the N2, towards the Lesotho border and the Drakensberg Mountains, you'll find beautiful mountainous country and endless little villages, but the lack of accommodation and poor roads make travelling here difficult.

Far more accessible is the **coastal region**, which runs from just north of East London to the mouth of the **Mtamvuna River**. With its succession of great beaches, hidden reefs, patches of subtropical forest, rural Xhosa settlements and the attractive little towns of **Coffee Bay** and **Port St Johns** (both popular with backpackers), this region, along with northern KwaZulu-Natal, offers the most deserted and undeveloped beaches in the country. The Eastern Cape Parks Board has now upgraded and renovated all accommodation in the beautiful nature reserves along the coast, facilitating access to outstanding beaches, lagoons and wildlife.

Wild Coast practicalities

The Wild Coast, unlike the Western Cape Garden Route, is not a stretch that you can easily tour by car. There has been an ongoing saga for years over a proposed toll highway between East London and Durban but this is some way off becoming a reality; for now there's no coastal road, and no direct route between one seaside resort and the next. Yet in this **remoteness** lies the region's charm. Resorts are isolated down long, winding gravel roads off the N2, which sticks to the high inland plateau. Choose one or two places, and stay put for a relaxing few days. Apart from Port St Johns, none of the places on the coast has a **bank** or ATM, so be sure to organize money in East London or Mthatha.

Although some of the southern Wild Coast roads are being surfaced as part of an upgrading programme, most in the region remain **untarred** and, while generally passable in an ordinary car, they invariably take a mechanical toll.

▲ The Wild Coast

Always carry a tool kit, a spare tyre (or two), and take the roads slowly. When you choose a resort, phone to ask for the best road route, as road conditions change. Watch out for livestock on all Wild Coast roads, including the N2, and avoid driving in rainy weather and at night. **Car theft** at night, or the removal of tyres or wheels, even in remote areas, is the biggest crime problem in the Transkei. All the hotels are surrounded by fences and lock up their gates at night to counter this problem.

Public transport in minibuses links villages throughout the region – easiest from Mthatha to Port St Johns and Coffee Bay along the tarred roads. The **Baz Bus** stops in Cintsa West, Mthatha and Port St Johns; you can arrange to be met by hostels in Port St Johns and Coffee Bay, or in Butterworth for Mazeppa. If you are flying into East London and making for a specific resort, there is a useful **shuttle service** from East London run by Ken Black (☎043 740 3060).

The **hotels** here are typically run along old-fashioned, colonial lines, with set meals – old-fangled British fare features prominently – and tea at specific times. Most of the hotels offer full board – outside Port St Johns and Mthatha, there are no restaurants besides those provided by the accommodation establishments (as for **self-catering**, you'll need to buy groceries at a big centre on the N2). Many hotels offer the services of experienced **Xhosa nannies** who can be employed for the whole day or for short stretches while you take a break to go

A walk and a gallop on the Wild Coast

Since there's no coastal road, the only way to explore stretches of the Wild Coast is **on foot** or **horseback**. Booking a package is a sensible option, not least because in most cases the tour operator takes care of transfers at the start and end of the package.

Wild Coast hiking trails

Walking packages includes transfers between East London and the Wild Coast, accommodation, all meals, picnic lunches, and the services of guides. Expect to pay around R600 per night per person for a group of four. Hotels dotted along the coast where you might stay include the *Kob Inn*, *Mazeppa Bay*, *Wavecrest*, *Trennery's*, *Seagulls* and *Morgan Bay Hotel*. All you have to carry is your day pack as porters and transport are available to take your luggage to the overnight stops. **Book** through Wild Coast Holiday Reservations (☎043 743 6181, ⊛www.wildcoastholidays.co.za).

Wild Coast Hotel Meander A 55-kilometre section of the coast from Qora Mouth to Morgan Bay, covered at an easy pace over six days (five nights). There are some modest challenges en route, such as river crossings and hiking over headlands, which will pose no problems for those of average fitness.

Wild Coast Amble Starting north of Kei River and heading south, this ends in Cintsa, covering terrain of moderate difficulty in 56km in five days (four nights). The trail includes a three-hour boat cruise up the Kei River, some canoeing and, if you don't wish to walk the whole way, horse-riding.

Wild Coast Pondo Walk Five nights based at the *Mboyti River Lodge* near Lusikisiki. Transfers aren't included, though you will be given maps and information to help you drive there and back. The hike entails two coastal walks and two inland trails that take in indigenous forest, sandy bays, escarpments and local settlements; there's also a sixteen-kilometre strenuous walk to the Magwa Falls. You might have to cover anything from 13km to 26km a day.

Hole in the Wall Walk Four nights and three days, from Presleys Bay, just north of Coffee Bay, to Hole in the Wall, with spectacular coastal scenery.

to the beach or have a meal. Some hotels even have separate meal times for children, and recommend that children stay with their nannies during adult meal times.

There are a number of good **backpacker lodges** along the coast, and plenty of campsites. Although security is no longer the worry it once was, **camping** in rural areas is not advisable, even if a beach looks idyllically deserted. If you want to stay among rural Xhosa people, the safest way to do so is with a guide.

It's wise to **book accommodation** in advance: the Mthatha-based Wild Coast Reservations (see p.440) is useful if you are planning to stay in several places on your journey. Even better is the superbly well-informed and efficient Wild Coast Holiday Reservations (☏043 743 6181, ⓦwww.wildcoastsholidays .co.za), based in East London, which, apart from being able to arrange places to stay, is unsurpassed when it comes to organizing **activities** in the region, including hiking (see box below).

The hotels themselves offer a variety of activities, from canoeing to horse-riding. To visit the region's **nature reserves** you'll need to book in advance through the Eastern Cape Parks Board (☏043 742 4450, ⓦwww .ecparks.co.za). Recently upgraded, the accommodation now ranges from luxurious lodges and Cape-style farm homesteads to wooden chalets, hikers' huts and camping sites. All are fully equipped for self-catering, but remember there are no shops nearby, so you will need to take all supplies with you.

Strandloper Hiking and Canoe Trails (☏043 841 1046, ⓦwww.strandlopertrails .org.za). Five-day, four-night hiking trail between Kei Mouth and Gonubie. Varied terrain, well-planned stages, small coastal villages and friendly pubs en route make this a popular hike. The two-day canoe trail explores the Great Kei River. Both trails are suited to family groups. If you choose the do-it-yourself option, overnight accommodation is provided in comfortable twelve-bunk self-catering cabins.

The Amadiba Horse Trail
This Wild Coast highlight is a fifty-kilometre, four- to six-day excursion from the *Wild Coast Sun* casino and hotel (served by shuttles from Durban which can be booked through the hotel) to the exquisitely beautiful Mkhambathi Nature Reserve. The package, run entirely by members of the local Pondo community, is probably the best way to spend time with Xhosa speakers and travel in unspoilt areas that you can't reach in a vehicle. Beginner riders will find the trail not unduly daunting: well-schooled horses are used, the going is easy and distances between the **tented camps** on the banks of the Kwanyana and Mtentu rivers are manageable. You while away gentle days exploring the coast, rivers and inland, sometimes visiting villages on horseback, on foot or in canoes with the guides. Fully inclusive trips cost R2320 per person for four days, R3340 for six days; the maximum group size is twelve, minimum two. To book, contact Amadiba Adventures (☏039 305 6455, ⓦwww .amadibaadventures.co.za).

Fish River Horse Safaris
A fabulous four-day trail along one of the most unspoilt stretches of coastline in the world from the *Haven Hotel* to *Bulungula Lodge,* with great horses and professional guiding. With six hours' riding per day, you need to be saddle-fit. Costs are R1500–2000 per person per day (Fish River Horse Safaris ☏046 675 1271 or 082 433 5662).

For some people, one attraction of the Wild Coast region, especially the Port St Johns area, is the ready availability of high-quality **cannabis** (*insango* in Xhosa). Be warned, though, that cannabis is illegal here as anywhere else in South Africa, and that the former Transkei police are trying to prove their worth to the national force with regular busts.

④ Cintsa and Haga-Haga

Of the smattering of resorts between East London and the Kei River, the best are at Cintsa and Morgan Bay, where endless sandy beaches back up into forested dunes sliced through by lagoons and rivers. Cintsa is actually two places with distinct characters, Cintsa East and Cintsa West, divided by a river.

CINTSA EAST, 45km from East London, is an upmarket holiday village of some two hundred houses, reached on a tarred road: turn off the N2 at the East Coast Resorts Road (30km out of East London) then, after 8km, turn left at the sign to Cefane Mouth and *Michaela's Restaurant*, from where the village is 7km away. *Crawford's Lodge & Cabins* (☎043 738 5000, ⓦ www.crawfordscabins.co.za; ④), is just a few minutes' walk from the beach and offers guesthouse accommodation with B&B and self-catering. *The Gables* (☎043 738 5353 or 083 676 0213; ④), facing inland onto a valley, is an upmarket, luxurious country lodge with five en-suite bedrooms, which also does dinner. Of the handful of **eating** places, *Michaela's* restaurant (daily except Tues 10.30am until late; ☎043 738 5139) is an excellent spot for seafood and salads, and is built spectacularly on a giant sand dune, which can be ascended on a short funicular ride. More modest fare is served at the popular and friendly *Sea Breeze* in Cintsa Drive (daily lunch & dinner).

Across the river, on the **Baz Bus** route, **CINTSA WEST** is home to *Buccaneer's* (☎043 734 3012, ⓦ www.cintsa.com; dorms ①, rooms ②), one of South Africa's most popular hostels. *Buccaneer's* has built its reputation on the excellence of its **backpacker accommodation** in ten cottages of varying sizes, with fantastic sea and lagoon views, unspoilt beaches, and a plethora of activities such as hiking, surfing (free boards) and horse-riding. You can self-cater, or eat inexpensive breakfasts and dinners in the café and pub. It also lays on trips to a local African school and township, and its adventure company will take you for surfing lessons, out kloofing, or for day-trips deeper into the Wild Coast. A three-hour game drive in neighbouring Inkwenkwezi Nature Reserve costs R495 including lunch. Finally, there's transport from here to the mountain resort of Hogsback (see p.420) and on to East London.

Just northeast of Cintsa, **HAGA-HAGA** (72km from East London, 27km of this along a dirt road off the N2) is dominated by the box-like but perfectly positioned *Haga-Haga Resort* (☎043 841 1670 or 082 659 8881, ⓦ www.hagahagahotel.co.za). It offers reasonably priced half board in hotel rooms (④), and self-catering in fourteen flatlets sleeping two or four people (③–④). A tidal swimming pool is sculpted into the rocky shoreline in front of the hotel; to reach a sandy beach, take the two-kilometre path to Pullens Bay, which is ideal for swimming among the breakers. A four-kilometre walk takes you to Bead Beach, where vendors sell beads made from carnelian, and bits of pottery.

Morgan Bay to Qora Mouth

MORGAN BAY, 90km from East London, lies magnificently in an estuary at the confluence of two rivers carving their passage through forested dunes. The friendly, well-run *Morgan Bay Hotel* (☎043 841 1062, ⓦwww.morganbay.co.za; half board ❹) overlooks a gorgeous beach and is one of the best hotels along the Wild Coast, particularly for family holidays. It offers good food and fresh, airy rooms furnished with limewashed furniture, and there's also **camping**. A hike from the hotel leads over some grassy knolls to the fifty-metre Morbay Cliffs, an excellent vantage point for spotting dolphins and, in season, whales. The bay is pounded by massive breakers, but the estuary provides a safe and tranquil place for toddlers to paddle.

Kei Mouth and Qholorha Mouth

From Morgan Bay, it's a short, rough drive to the village of **Kei Mouth** (it's not signposted, so get directions from *Morgan Bay Hotel*), with some self-catering places, a post office and small shops, though there's little point dallying. From Kei Mouth, a six-kilometre walk along the beach leads to beautiful **QHOLORHA MOUTH** (roughly pronounced "kalocha" – the "rh" in Xhosa is like the "ch" in loch). The easiest way to get here is to cross the Kei River on a small pontoon (which you can take your car on) that operates from 6am to 6pm in summer and from 7am to 5.30pm in winter; after disembarking, continue for another 17km to *Trennery's* (signposted), the marvellous family **hotel** which dominates this resort. Founded in 1928, *Trennery's* (☎047 498 0095 or 082 908 3134, ⓦwww.trennerys.co.za; full board ❹) still has its heart somewhere in the 1950s or 1960s. Uniformed nannies accompany children around the playground and the separate children's dining room, where the little darlings need neither be seen nor heard by their parents. The en-suite chalets are slightly worn, while the English-style food is wholesome and well cooked, if unrevelatory; the seamless organization and attentive service make up for these. From the hotel, it's a steep walk through luxuriant vegetation to the spectacular beach, while canoes and rowing boats are available for outings on the lagoon. They offer seven-night and weekend specials, and are a bit cheaper outside school holidays.

A recommended excursion is **Trevor's Trail**, a three-hour bush walk and boating trip to the "The Gates" – the short corridor of rock-face towering above the Qholorha River; it's run every morning 9am by local resident Trevor Wigley (☎047 498 0006, or book through your hotel; R50). Other trails run by Trevor include a visit to a local *igqirha*, or **traditional healer**; a trip to the **Gxara River**, where the prophetess Nongqawuse's disastrous visions induced the Xhosa to kill their cattle (see box, p.432); and a visit to the major **battlefields** of the last Frontier War between the Xhosa and the British in 1878. These trails involve a 4WD vehicle, so are more expensive than the daily jaunt.

Nxaxo Mouth and Wavecrest Hotel

NXAXO MOUTH, just north of Qholorha (though not drivable from there), is a tranquil location with mangrove swamps teeming with wildlife. It's an ideal place for hiking, shoreline fishing and general relaxation, as well as the more strenuous **activities** – canoeing, water-skiing and deep-sea fishing. All of this can be arranged through the resort's only **accommodation**, the *Wavecrest* (☎047 498 0022, ⓦwww.wavecrest.co.za; full board ❺), a cluster of pleasant bungalows and family rooms – arguably the most beautifully positioned of all

The great cattle killing

The 1850s were a low point for the Xhosa nation: most of their land had been seized by the British, drought had withered their crops, and cattle-sickness had decimated their precious herds. In 1856, a young woman called **Nongqawuse**, whose uncle Mhlakaza was a prophet, claimed to have seen and heard ancestral spirits in a pool on the Gxara River. The spirits told her the Xhosa must kill all their remaining cattle and destroy their remaining crops; if they did this, new cattle and crops would arise, along with new people who would drive the whites into the sea.

As news of her **prophecy** spread, opinion was sharply divided amongst the Xhosa. Those whose herds had been badly affected by cattle-sickness were most inclined to believe her. A turning point came when the Gcaleka paramount chief Sarili visited Nongqawuse, became convinced she was telling the truth and ordered his subjects to start the cull. Thousands of cattle were killed, but when the "new people" failed to materialize on the expected day, the unbelievers who had not killed their herds were blamed. By February 1857, the next date for the appearance of the new people, over 200,000 cattle had been slaughtered, their corpses left decomposing everywhere. When the new people failed once more to materialize, it was too late for many Xhosa. By July there was **widespread starvation**; 30,000 of an estimated population of 90,000 died of hunger.

The British administration saw the famine as a perfect way to force the destitute Xhosa into working on white settlers' farms. To speed up the process, the Cape governor Sir George Grey closed down the feeding stations established by missionaries and laid the blame for the disaster on the Xhosa chiefs, imprisoning many of them on Robben Island. Not surprisingly, the 1856 cattle killing is often used by whites as evidence of the folly of black superstition. The Xhosa, however, have a different interpretation: "*Intombi kaMhlakaza yathetha ubuxoke*" goes the song – "Mhlakaza's girl told lies".

---

the Wild Coast hotels. To get there, follow the 34km of tarred road to Centani from the N2 at **Butterworth**. At Centani, take the signposted road (to the left) to Nxaxo for 8km, then the dirt road to *Wavecrest* (on the right) for 24km.

Mazeppa Bay and Qora Mouth

Two good fishing and general chill-out spots on the Wild Coast, Mazeppa Bay and Qora Mouth, lie northeast of Nxaxo. **MAZEPPA BAY**, a lovely spot surrounded by dunes and coastal forest, is reached along the signposted road from Centani (34km of tarred surface from Butterworth, and about 45km further of dirt road). Since there are two routes to complete the journey, it's advisable to contact the hotel when you're about to travel for advice about road conditions. The *Mazeppa Bay* **hotel** here (☎047 498 0033, @ www.mazeppabay .co.za; ❹–❺) offers full board in comfortable cabanas or family rooms in the hotel, 39 steps up from the beach. It has the added attraction of its own island (reached along a bridge), on which there's an unexcavated Khoisan midden. Swimming in the bay is safe, and the surfing is good.

Just northeast of Mazeppa, **QORA MOUTH** is the site of the *Kob Inn* (☎047 499 0011/16, @ www.kobinn.co.za; ❺), set away from the beach on a rocky shore close to the wide Mbashe River. The hotel has well-kept thatched bungalows, a good bar with views of the sea, and a breathtaking swimming pool built into the tidal rocks. Staff can arrange a boat and fishing tackle, or equip you for canoeing, water-skiing and boardsailing. A small ferry traverses the river mouth and takes you to some good hiking trails along the coast, through grassland and into nearby forest patches. To get to Qora Mouth, take the signposted dirt road heading east for 34km from Idutywa (see below), passing through grassy rolling hills and Xhosa villages.

Butterworth and Idutywa

Butterworth, 110km from East London on the N2, and **Idutywa**, 35km further on, are places you pass through rather than visit. Both are busy centres, barely distinguishable from each other, although Butterworth is the larger. They serve the vast rural communities on either side of the N2 and each has a reasonable hotel – useful if you find yourself stranded at nightfall.

Butterworth

BUTTERWORTH, the oldest town in the Transkei, is located near the site of the Gcaleka chief Hintsa's Great Place, and was founded by Methodist missionaries in 1827. The town, known to Xhosa as Gcuwa (after the river running through it), derives its English name from the then-treasurer of the Wesleyan Mission Society, Reverend Butterworth. It was selected as the focal point of Transkeian industrial development in the 1970s, with its new industries drawing thousands of workers from the surrounding countryside. Most of the industries have now closed, but the people are still living in sprawling townships and squatter camps around the town, where unemployment is alarmingly high.

While Butterworth itself is unattractive and a bit chaotic, with tatty department stores and supermarkets, the nearby **Bawa Falls** on the Qholorha River, which have a sheer drop of nearly 100m, are spectacular and worth a visit if you're not pressed for time. The poorly maintained twenty-kilometre dirt track leading to them is just west of town past the Shell filling station, but numerous twists and turns make the falls quite hard to find, so you will need to ask directions.

The well-signposted road to Centani and the Wild Coast is at the eastern end of Butterworth, past the Gcuwa Bridge, and winds through the sprawling Zitulele Industrial Township, where the tar stops and gives way to a potholed dirt road. Butterworth's **bus station** is at the western end of town, next to the Shell garage, from which numerous buses and increasing numbers of **minibus taxis** run to East London, Mthatha and Centani. Daily Greyhound and Translux **buses** stop off the main road on Merriman Street, which is just before the Gcuwa Bridge.

The N2 highway runs through Butterworth and is lined with **takeaways**, beer halls and filling stations. The only slightly decent **accommodation** in town is the *Wayside* (℡047 491 4615, ✉elmer18za@yahoo.com; ❸), reached by turning right down King Street off the main road, and taking the first right into Sauer Street, where you'll see the hotel on your left. The rooms are comfortable and a fair bit cheaper over weekends. The hotel has safe underground parking, and a good **restaurant** serving lunchtime buffets and à la carte evening meals. The one drawback is that it's right next to a busy taxi rank swarming with people until late into the evening.

Idutywa

The small town of **IDUTYWA**, 35km north of Butterworth on the N2, is only a place to head for if you are short of fuel, or very hungry and tired. On the main road going through town you'll find a passable *KFC* and the unassuming,

Some Xhosa traditions

The Wild Coast region is largely populated by **rural Xhosa**, who still practise traditions and customs that have faded in more urban areas. Many people, for example, still believe that the sea is inhabited by strange people who do not always welcome visitors, which explains the relative scarcity of the activities you would normally find thriving among seashore-dwelling people, such as fishing and diving.

Initiation for teenage boys and young men is still common. Young men usually leave their homes to stay in "circumcision lodges", dress in distinctive white paint and costumes and learn the customs of their clan. At the circumcision ceremony the young men are expected to make no sound while their foreskin is cut off (with no anaesthetic) with a single slice of a knife. After the ceremony, they wash off the paint and wrap themselves in new blankets, and all their possessions are thrown into a hut and set alight – they must turn away from this and not look back. There follows a feast to celebrate the beginning of manhood and the start of a year-long intermediary period during which they wear ochre-coloured clay on their faces. After this, they are counted as men. Boys who have gone through the experience of initiation together are supposed to remain bonded at a deep level for the rest of their lives.

Like other African peoples, although they believe in one God, uThixo, or uNhkulukhulu (the great one), many Xhosa also believe that their **ancestors** play an active role in their lives. However, the ancestors' messages are often too obscure to be understood without the aid of specialists, or *amagqira*.

The Xhosa are patriarchal by tradition, with women's subordinate status symbolized by *lobola*, the **dowry** payment in cattle and cash that a prospective husband must make to her parents before he can marry her. If the woman is not a virgin, the man pays less. Married Xhosa women have the same right as men to smoke tobacco in **pipes**, and can often be seen doing so, the pipes' long stems designed to prevent ash falling on babies suckling at their breasts. Pipes are shared, but each person must have their own stem, not just for matters of hygiene but also to prevent witchcraft: bits of the body make the most effective poisonous medicines against people, and that includes hair, skin and spittle.

The Xhosa did not wear **cloth** until it was introduced by Europeans, when it was quickly adopted. Today, what is now seen as traditional Xhosa cloth is almost always worn by women, mostly in the form of long skirts, beautifully embroidered with horizontal black stripes placed at varying intervals, which are displayed to subtle effect when the wearer is walking. Bags in matching colours with long shoulder straps are popular accessories, especially at weddings, when people put cash gifts inside them. The breasts of unmarried women were traditionally uncovered, while those of married women were usually covered with beads or matching cloth. These days, most women wear T-shirts, though almost all women still cover their heads with scarves intricately tied to form two peaks above the forehead. The **traditional colours** of the Thembu and Bomvana clans are red or orange, while the colour of the Pondo and the Mpondomise clans is light blue. In practice, these traditions are not always observed, and married women from a number of clans often wear white instead.

old hotel *Idutywa* (℡047 489 1040; ❸), the only decent place to stay on the noisy main road between Butterworth and Mthatha. Their restaurant, the only one in town, serves a typical South African selection of steaks and grills.

A few kilometres east of town, a right-hand turn leads to **Colleywobbles**, the name given by British soldiers to a particularly tortuous and fascinating stretch of the Mbashe River about 10km down an exceedingly difficult dirt track. The river reaches the sea 50km further east, disgorging between the **Cwebe** and **Dwesa** nature reserves, but the best way for you to reach these two beautiful places is by continuing for another 60km or so along the N2 until **Jojweni** (formerly Viedgesville), and turning right down the Coffee Bay road. Another possible diversion is the open-air museum at **Mveso**, where Nelson Mandela spent the first couple of years of his life (see p.442)

Dwesa and Cwebe reserves and Nqileni

Between Qora Mouth and Coffee Bay, the **Dwesa Nature Reserve** (daily 6am–6pm) is undeveloped and remote, yet very much visitable and safe. It has well-sited self-catering (equipped with gas fridges and stoves) wooden chalets sleeping up to four people (R300) and a campsite (R145), with bush showers. Dwesa is one of the best places to stay on the coast, boasting rare animals such as tree dassies and samango monkeys, as well as red hartebeest, blesbok, blue wildebeest and buffalo, pristine forest, grassland and coastline. To stay at Dwesa you must book ahead through the Eastern Cape Parks Board (℡043 742 4450, Ⓦwww.ecparks.co.za). That said, during the week the reserve is hardly visited and there's a good chance you'll get accommodation if you just show up. Either way, make sure you have enough time to drive on to another resort if necessary. To get to the reserve, turn east off the N2 at Idutywa towards the coast and continue for 73km or so; the road forks right to *Kob Inn* and left to Dwesa.

Cwebe Nature Reserve and the Haven Hotel

North of the Mbashe River from Dwesa, the **Cwebe Nature Reserve** (daily 6am–6pm) makes up for its lack of big game with dense subtropical forest, brimming with flora and fauna. Stinkwood and samango monkeys, both of which have all but disappeared from most of southern Africa's east coast, are to be found here along a rough network of trails. Thankfully, the trail to the beautiful **Mbanyana Waterfall** is in good shape, easily walkable from the *Haven* (see below) if the ground is dry. The remainder of the reserve comprises rolling grassland and a long stretch of wonderful dune-filled shoreline lying in the shadow of the Mbashe lighthouse. The reserve was returned to the local community in 2001.

To get to **Cwebe**, take the Coffee Bay turn-off from the N2 at **Jojweni** (the town itself is not signposted but there is a Coffee Bay sign), turn right 27km later at Gogoswayo Trading Store, and follow the tarred road another 17km to the small hamlet of **Elliotdale**, the main administrative centre in the communal lands of the Bomvana people. (Avoid the route off the N2 south of Qunu to Elliotdale, as this section requires a high-clearance vehicle.) From Elliotdale it's 47km of generally good-quality dirt road to the privately owned *Haven* (℡083 996 5343, Ⓦwww.havenhotel.co.za; full board ❸–❺), a traditional family resort set inside Cwebe Forest, with **bungalows** dotted fairly close together on the fringes of a small golf course regularly grazed by wildebeest and zebra, only a short walk through milkwood groves to the sea. The swimming pool has sea views, as does the main hotel building. On offer are plenty of activities including tennis, canoeing, a children's playground, and excellent walking trails along the shore and to the lighthouse.

Nqileni and Bulungula Lodge

Idyllically located at the mouth of the Bulungula River, the spread-out village of **NQILENI** gives you the opportunity to experience rural Transkei life. The river winds its way to the sea through rolling green hills dotted with rondavels, maize fields and livestock, ending at a tranquil river mouth. The coastline is carpeted in dense forest stretching into kilometres of soft, white beach. On a walk through the village you'll invariably be invited into someone's home to have your face painted with traditional clay, to try your hand at grinding maize for the evening meal or to see traditional beer being brewed. Other possibilities include spending the day with a traditional fisherman, taking a canoe trip along the river, horse-riding across the beach or consulting a *sangoma*.

If you're looking for relaxation and an authentic cultural experience, you'll be hard pressed to find a better **place to stay** than the well-run *Bulungula Backpackers Lodge* (booking essential; ℡047 577 8900, Ⓦwww.bulungula.com; ❶), which has ten brightly painted rondavels (sleeping two or four) and camping, with shared ablutions. It's a joint venture between the community and seasoned traveller Dave Martin, who spent many of his student years involved in community development projects. The lodge buys most of its vegetables from an organic farming project run by the villagers, and is equipped with solar electricity, satellite telephone and eco-friendly toilets.

The lodge runs a **shuttle** service (R55) from the Shell Ultra City in Mthatha (arrange this when booking). To **drive** to the lodge, make for **Elliotdale** (turn off the N2 at Jojweni; see p.435), then about 500m beyond the edge of town, turn left onto a dirt road signposted for *Bulungula Lodge* and Madwaleni Hospital. Continue for another 30km until you reach the hospital, where you leave your car (secure parking costs R10 per day). Lodge staff will collect you from there. You can also reach *Bulungula* on horseback – the final destination of a fantastic four-day horse trail from *Haven Hotel* (see p.435).

Coffee Bay and around

The densely populated, gentle hills of **COFFEE BAY**, known to the Xhosa as Tshontini after a dense wood that grows there, mark the traditional boundary between the Bomvana and Pondo clans of the Xhosa nation. Coffee Bay, with its laid-back, relaxed atmosphere, draws a growing number of visitors – yet retains its feeling of idyllic obscurity. It's easily reached on a tarred road which leaves the N2 14km south of Mthatha's Shell Ultra City, and there are a number of nearby attractions such as **Hole in the Wall** village.

The **landscape** at Coffee Bay, dramatic high cliffs dropping to sandy beaches speckled with black pebbles, contrasts with the grasslands, forested sand dunes and lagoons further south. The main attraction here is the **coastal hikes**; the walk to Hole in the Wall is particularly outstanding. To start the trail, head south along the track from Coffee Bay, and turn left at a small sign just past the Telkom tower, from where it's another 5km along the coast.

The **huts** here are also very distinctive: many are thatched with a topknot made from a tyre, coloured glass or even an aloe plant – said to discourage owls, harbingers of ill-omen, from roosting on roofs. An excellent community-run **village tour** can be organized through the impressive ANC Women's League veteran, Betty Madlalisa (℡047 575 9034 or 083 339 0454; R50). Apart from visiting homesteads, the outing takes in the **Masizame Women's Project** (daily 8am–5pm), housed in a colourful building opposite the Bayview Store, 5km out of Coffee Bay on the Mthatha Road. If you're not taking the tour, it's still definitely worth visiting the project – it's one of the very few outlets in South Africa where you can buy traditional Xhosa craftwork, including beaded bags and belts, traditional clothing, baskets, mats and blankets. With advance notice, they also offer **Xhosa meals** – based mostly around meat stews, maize meal, and homegrown vegetables like spinach and pumpkin, washed down with traditional beer.

Practicalities

The smartest **accommodation** is the *Ocean View* hotel right on the sandy bay (℡047 575 2005 or 2006, Ⓦwww.oceanview.co.za; full board ❹–❺). It's an exceptionally friendly and well-run place, with bright rooms, terraced gardens, a pool area, and a trampoline and playground right next to the beach. The restaurant and bar, open to day visitors, serves good food. There is also the *Coffee Bay Hotel*, under new and reputedly improved management (℡047 575 2051, Ⓦwww.coffeebayhotel; half board ❹), at 11 Main St, just three minutes' walk from the beach, with a pool and activities on offer. Of the **backpacker lodges**, *Coffee Shack* (℡047 575 2048, Ⓦwww.coffeeshack.co.za; ❶) is the liveliest, with dorms, a double room and camping, and well located on the Bomvu River. It offers seafood suppers, day-trips and homestays with the local community, and activities such as surfing (with free lessons and boards), hiking, canoeing and abseiling. Its **shuttle bus** plies the route between Mthatha and Coffee Bay, meeting the Baz Bus on request. Also popular and on the river is *Bomvu Paradise* (℡047 575 2073 or 083 460 4155, Ⓦwww.bomvubackpackers.com) where you can attend yoga classes, make your own drum and participate in drumming sessions around an evening fire. Accommodation is in dorms and single rooms (❶), doubles (❷) and camping, and there is tasty food available from the *Ubuntu Kitchen*. One bay west of Coffee Bay, and set on a cliff high above the water, *White Clay* (℡047 575 0008; self-catering ❷–❸, half board available) has double rooms with shared bathrooms, and camping facilities. No one else lives on this bay, so you have it all to yourself, and the location couldn't be better, with gorgeous views. Whales can sometimes be seen literally a stone's throw away in the bay between August and November, and dolphins all year round.

There are no grocery shops, banks or ATMs in Coffee Bay, so make sure you come prepared. Petrol is available at the *Ocean View*, and food basics can be purchased at the expensive Bayview Trading Store, 5km out of Coffee Bay towards Port St Johns.

Hole In The Wall

The village of **HOLE IN THE WALL** has grown up on the shoreline near the large cliff that juts out of the sea a short distance from the Mpako River Mouth, from which it gets its name. The cliff has a tunnel at its base through which huge waves pound during heavy seas, making a great crashing sound that has led the Xhosa to call it esiKhaleni (the place of sound). As well as good fishing, safe swimming and snorkelling, there are several spectacular hikes, including a coastal walk northeast to Coffee Bay. A nine-kilometre gravel road – a **scenic drive** through traditional villages and along cliffs with sea views – links Coffee Bay with Hole In The Wall, a trip definitely worth making if you're based at Coffee Bay. It's a very pleasant one-kilometre walk from the village to **the hole**, a lovely spot ideal for picnics or just relaxing.

Dominating the tiny settlement, the *Hole In The Wall* **hotel** (℡047 575 0009, Ⓦwww.holeinthewall.co.za; self-catering ❷–❹) is a conglomeration of white thatched rondavels situated on a small sandy bay and surrounded by lawns, with a pool, bar and playground. The hotel doesn't have a great reputation for food, accommodation or organization, though you can self-cater (a rare option for a Wild Coast hotel; the best place for supplies is Mthatha). There are well-equipped self-catering units sleeping two to eight people. The hotel owns the quiet *Hole In The Wall Backpackers* on the same site (℡083 317 8786; dorms ❶, doubles ❷), and allows residents to use hotel facilities. There isn't the same social scene here as at the Coffee Bay hostels, but there are reasonably priced day excursions to hard-to-reach and spectacular spots along the coast, such as Umdumbi.

Mthatha River Mouth

The **Mthatha River** disgorges 6km north of Coffee Bay into another soothing lagoon. This is the site of a **hotel**, the *Anchorage* (℡047 575 9884, Ⓦwww .anchoragehotel.co.za; self-catering ❷, half board ❸), 70km from the N2, offering old-fashioned bungalow accommodation, plus camping. While it's no great shakes as a resort – there are better for the same price – it's worth considering for its setting between two rivers. The hotel is a three-kilometre walk along the beach from the Mthatha River Mouth, and also 3km from the Mdumbi River Mouth, with good fishing at both. The *Anchorage* has a **general dealer** and liquor store, where you can buy bread, milk, eggs and braai packs. An excellent way to see the surrounding area's gentle hills, coastal forest and shoreline is on **horseback**, which the hotel can arrange. The best **route** to the *Anchorage* is the tarred Coffee Bay road: around 6km before you reach Coffee Bay, there's an *Anchorage* sign where you turn left and continue 14km on a periodically graded rough dirt road.

Hluleka Nature Reserve

One of the loveliest of the Wild Coast reserves, **Hluleka Nature Reserve** (daily 6am–6pm; R5) consists of coastal forest whose coral trees flower scarlet in July and August, a strip of grassland and outstanding sandy beaches interspersed with rocky outcrops tattooed with extraordinary wind-shaped rock formations. Although Hluleka's trails are poorly maintained and frequently dead ends, the reserve is sufficiently small to make getting lost for a while no great disaster. In the grassland strip, you're likely to encounter wildebeest, zebra and blesbok.

You can reach Hluleka along the difficult coastal road from Coffee Bay. Heading towards the N2 from Coffee Bay for a short distance, take the Mdumbi turn on the right, and continue for some 30km, when signs to Hluleka appear. Alternatively – and more easily – take the Hluleka turning 30km along the R61 from Mthatha to Port St Johns, and continue for another 57km to the coast.

Accommodation (book through the Eastern Cape Parks Board ℡043 742 4450, Ⓦwww.ecparks.co.za) is in two sets of chalets which sleep up to six people, one on stilts overlooking the sea (R320), the other further up the hill in the forest (R220). Both are spacious and fully equipped for self-catering. You may be able to buy fish from local fishermen if you tell the reserve's staff, who will tip them off. **Fishing permits** should be arranged via the Eastern Cape Parks Board.

Mthatha and around

Straddling the Mthatha River and the N2 highway 235km from East London, the fractious, shambolic town of **MTHATHA** (formerly Umtata) is the erstwhile capital of the Transkei and the Wild Coast region's largest town. Unfortunately, it's a pretty ugly place, its litter-strewn streets lined with

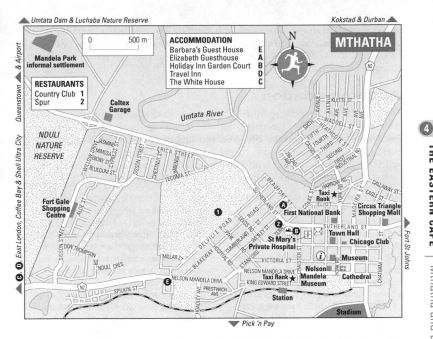

nondescript 1970s office buildings and crowded with people. However, the town is useful for stocking up and drawing money, all of which can be done at the Spar Centre or Shell Ultra City on the edge of town. The best reason to venture into the town centre is to visit the **Nelson Mandela Museum**.

The Mthatha River was traditionally the boundary between the Thembu and Pondo clans of the Xhosa nation, with the Thembu to the south and the Pondo to the north. Whites farmed by the river from the 1860s, and when Britain acquired Thembuland in 1875, Mthatha was established as the site of one of its four magistracies. From 1976 until 1994, Mthatha was the capital of the Transkei homeland, with a smattering of showcase large buildings and a reputation for some of the most corrupt officialdom in South Africa.

Arrival and information

The small Mthatha **airport** (☎047 536 0121) lies 10km west of town on the Queenstown Road. There is no public transport from the airport, but you can rent a car here (see p.443). Given the crowds, traffic and fear of crime in Mthatha, most motorists, and backpackers on the Baz Bus, orientate from **Shell Ultra City**, 6km from the centre, on the N2 towards East London. This is where the Greyhound and Translux **buses** pull in, and is served by the Baz Bus. It's a convenient place to refuel, **eat** at the reasonably pleasant *Whistle Stop Restaurant* and buy basic groceries – milk, bread, cheese, chicken and soup – from the Select Shop. There's an ATM here, and in the car park a little **Eastern Cape Tourism Board** caravan provides maps and basic information.

Mthatha's **tourist office** at 64 Owen St in the town centre (Mon–Fri 8am–4.30pm; ☎047 531 5290) has useful **maps** and knowledgeable staff. At the **Environment Office** (Fifth Floor) of the Economic Affairs Department, on the corner of York and Victoria streets (Mon–Fri 8am–4.30pm; ☎047 531 1191), you can pick up **maps** of the areas you want to visit and buy a helpful booklet about the whole coastal strip. **Wild Coast Reservations**, 3 Beaufort St (daily 8am–6pm; ☏047 532 5344), can arrange accommodation at resorts and hotels throughout the region.

Accommodation

Mthatha is not somewhere you'd choose to spend a night, but there's some decent accommodation catering mostly to people on business, predominantly on the quieter fringes of the city. Weekend nights are always less expensive and you'll find it almost impossible to get a bed on a Monday night in particular, when the place is crawling with businessmen. The cheapest B&B, half an hour out of the centre, is at the Cultural Village in Qunu (see p.442).

Barbara's Guest House 55 Nelson Mandela Drive, near the centre ☏047 531 1751, ☏barbp @cybertrade.co.za. A decent establishment with thirty mostly en-suite rooms with TV, a swimming pool, nice garden and a bar with a pool table, where you can have good pub lunches. The road is terribly noisy, though, so try to stay at the back. Half board ⑤, B&B ④

Elizabeth Guesthouse 19 Cumberland St ☏047 531 5031 or 083 755 5425. A well-run, friendly establishment in a family home in a quiet part of town. ③

Holiday Inn Garden Court Along the N2 in the town centre ☏047 537 0181, ☏www .southernsun.com. Large 1970s building with a stylish pool, slot machines, a chic cocktail bar and restaurant. The rooms are unremarkable; all the singles face the car park. ⑦

Travel Inn Adjoining Shell Ultra City ☏047 537 0761. A totally impersonal place set behind gates and fences with no public spaces or meals; it's suitable only for a stopover, but the en-suite family rooms are comfortable and clean. Very much cheaper over weekends. ④

The White House 5 Mhlobo St, South Ridge Park ☏047 537 0580 or 083 458 9810, ☏whitehouse @intekom.co.za. Seventeen rooms, eight en suite, in two adjoining suburban houses in a quiet area just off the N2, opposite the Shell Ultra City. An evening meal can be provided if booked beforehand, and there is a communal lounge and pool table. ③–④

The town and around

Central Mthatha comprises a small grid of crowded streets lined with dull office buildings, interspersed with the odd older architectural gem. One of these is the elegant **town hall** on Leeds Street, which looks down onto a war memorial and pleasant gardens. One block south, opposite the tourist office, stands the town's small and neglected **museum** (Mon–Fri 8am–4.30pm; free), which has fairly informative displays of traditional Xhosa costume, local geology and an exhibit on the ANC that stops before the 1994 elections.

Continue further south to the corner of Owen and Nelson Mandela Drive for the **Nelson Mandela Museum** (Mon–Fri 9am–4pm, Sat 9am–12.30pm; free; ☏047 532 5110, ☏www.mandelamuseum.org.za), housed in the old **parliament**, or *bungha*, built in 1927. The museum is divided into three sections, the most interesting of which is the central section, "The Long Walk to Freedom", which traces the great man's life with photos and other visual material. The other two rooms house the extraordinary number of gifts given to Mandela from all over the world. The museum also offers free guided trips to **Qunu** and **Mveso** (see opposite), Mandela's birthplace; contact the museum or the tour coordinator, Miss Tetani (☏082 483 4643).

One block east of the museum, on the corner of Alexandra and York streets, is an elegant sandstone Anglican **cathedral**, sadly permanently closed. A major taxi rank straggles along the opposite side of Alexandra Street, and behind it is the small **stadium** used by the Mthatha Bucks soccer team. If you are in town for a few days and the weather is good, head for the pleasant open-air

▲ Nelson Mandela Museum, Mthatha

swimming pool at the western end of Sutherland Street (daily 9am–12.30pm & 2–4.45pm), near the junction with Stanford Terrace.

Qunu and Mveso

Thirty kilometres south of Mthatha are the scattered dwellings of **Qunu**, where Mandela grew up (see box, p.442). The N2 thunders through it, but his large and rather plain mansion, which you may photograph but not enter, is clearly

Nelson Mandela and the Qunu connection

Nelson Rolihlahla Mandela was born near tiny **Qunu** in the even tinier village of **Mveso** on July 18, 1918. His father was a member of the Xhosa royal house and a custodian of Xhosa history – he was also chief of Mveso, until he crossed swords with the local white magistrate over a minor dispute concerning an ox. After his sacking, the family moved to a small kraal in Qunu, which Mandela remembers as consisting of several hundred poor households.

Mandela is often called **Madiba** – the name of his family's subclan of the Thembu clan. The name Nelson was given to him by a schoolteacher, and Rolihlahla means "pulling the branch of a tree" or, more colloquially, "troublemaker". Mandela has said that at home he was never allowed to ask any questions, but was expected to learn by observation. Later in life, he was shocked to visit the homes of whites and hear children firing questions at their parents and expecting replies.

Shortly after his father died, Mandela was summoned from Qunu to the royal palace at Mqhakeweni, where he sat in on disputes in court and learnt more about Xhosa culture. At 16 he was **initiated** – and burnt with shame for a long time afterwards over the cry he let slip out when circumcised. He enrolled in Clarkebury, a college for the Thembu elite, then the Wesleyan college of Healdtown at Fort Beaufort, and finally the celebrated **Fort Hare** in Alice (see p.418), which has educated generations of African leaders. Mandela was expelled from Fort Hare after clashing with the authorities, and returned to Mqhakeweni. In 1941, faced with the prospect of an arranged marriage, he ran away to Johannesburg and there immersed himself in politics.

It was only upon his released from prison in 1990 (at the age of 72) that Mandela was able to return to Qunu, visiting first the grave of his mother, who had died in his absence. He noted that the place seemed poorer than he remembered it, and that the children were now singing songs about AK47s and the armed struggle. However, he was relieved to find that none of the old spirit and warmth had left the community, and he arranged for a palace (or "country house" as he called it) to be built there. This palace has become the venue for Mandela's holidays and family reunions and has a floor plan identical to that of the house in Victor Verster prison where Mandela spent the last few years of his captivity. In his autobiography he writes:

The Victor Verster house was the first spacious and comfortable home I ever stayed in, and I liked it very much. I was familiar with its dimensions, so at Qunu I would not have to wander at night looking for the kitchen.

visible on the roadside 28km from Shell Ultra City in Mthatha (it's on the left if you're heading south), 52km from Idutywa. A tunnel under the N2 connects his house with the village, built so that visiting children especially could cross the road in safety. You can also visit the remains of Mandela's primary school, the rock he used to slide down with friends, and the graveyard where his parents, son and daughter are buried. Qunu is a village where the women still wear traditional clothing and young boys herd the family cows, and the best way to appreciate it is to take one of the **guided tours** run by the Mandela museum in Mthatha (see p.440).

Seven kilometres north of Mandela's house, the **Jonopo Cultural Village** (daily 8am–5pm; R10; ☎083 768 9904) has basic **B&B accommodation** in rondavels (❷) with a washbasin in each room and shared outside toilet. A Xhosa dinner can be cooked if ordered in advance, and there are also good crafts for sale and some exhibitions of rural life. You can also have a traditional Xhosa outfit made, which can be posted to you if you aren't able to come back to collect it.

Mandela spent his first two years at **Mveso**, on a hillside facing the Mbashe River, an hour-and-a-half south of Mthatha. The **open-air museum** here contains the remains of the rondavels where he was born and raised, and a photographic exhibition with images that include Mandela burning his pass – the infamous identity document Africans were forced to carry under apartheid. If you're approaching from Mthatha, Mveso is signed after 32km on the N2, though the route is a rough and eroded dirt road. It's better to continue 8km further down the N2, beyond Qunu, to the Elliotdale turning, on which you head 11km east on a good gravel road, until the unmarked Madondile Junction. Here you turn south for 19km to the museum, at the end of the road.

Eating

The hotel restaurants apart, there aren't many **places to eat** in Mthatha. *Spur* in Sutherland Street has a range of salads, burgers and steaks, while the *Country Club Restaurant* on Delville Road (☏047 531 0795; closed Sun) is open to non-members and has a thatch-covered deck overlooking the golf course. Mthatha has a thriving **nightlife**, with bars and *shebeens*, but exploring it without a local escort isn't recommended.

If you're self-catering, pick up **groceries** at the Spar Centre (daily 7am–9pm), 2.5km away towards town on the N2 (next to the *Wimpy* restaurant), or Pick 'n Pay (Mon–Fri 8.30am–7pm, Sat & Sun 9am–4pm) at the Southernwood Shopping Centre on Errol Spring Avenue. These supermarkets are far better stocked than the shop at the Shell Ultra City, and have an ATM.

Listings

Banks First National Bank, corner of Sutherland St and York Rd; Standard Bank, corner of York Rd and Leeds St. Expect large queues – it's better to use the ATMs at the Spar Centre or at Shell Ultra City.
Car rental Avis, at Mthatha airport ☏047 536 0066.
Emergencies Ambulance ☏10177 or 047 532 2222; see also p.75.

Garages Fort Gale Motors ☏047 501 2880 or 047 531 1555, on Queenstown Rd.
Hospital St Mary's Private Hospital, 30 Durham St ☏047 531 2911.
Pharmacy Triangle Pharmacy, Circus Triangle Centre, Port St Johns Rd ☏047 531 0215.
Travel agents Swift Travel Agents, City Centre Building, York Rd ☏047 531 1643 or 1641.

Port St Johns and around

The ninety-kilometre drive on the R61 to **PORT ST JOHNS** from Mthatha is one of the best journeys on the Wild Coast. After passing tiny **Libode**, with its small hotel and restaurant, you start the dramatic descent to the coast, past craggy ravines and epic vistas of forest and rondavel-spotted grassland. The road runs alongside the Mzimvubu River for the last few kilometres, giving you a perfect view of the Gates of St John, before reaching the town square and taxi rank. The big surprise, coming from the sparse hillsides around Mthatha, is how dramatic, hilly, lush and steamy it all is.

Port St Johns is a favoured destination for backpackers, drawn by its stunning location at the mouth of the Mzimvubu River, dominated by Mount Thesiger on the west bank and Mount Sullivan on the east. A further attraction for some visitors is the strong cannabis grown in the area, and the town's famously laid-back atmosphere may tempt you to stay for longer than you intended. Port St Johns also has good fishing and swimming beaches, a wider choice of accommodation than anywhere else on the Wild Coast, and a good tarred road all the way into town.

❹

Some history

The origins of Port St Johns' name are something of a mystery but may derive from the sixteenth-century Portuguese ship, *São João*, which was wrecked nearby, leaving around four hundred survivors to complete a seven-hundred-kilometre walk to Mozambique. Only eight survived, and one of those was shipwrecked again near the Mthatha River Mouth two years later. He reportedly died of despair, unable to face the trek to Mozambique once more.

In 1878, in an effort to reduce gun-running from the harbour, a representative of the Cape governor bought a fifteen-kilometre stretch of the river from the shore inland, and the land on the western side from the Pondo for R2000. While he was waiting for the money, an armed force arrived from Natal and annexed the eastern side of the river. A compromise was found by making Port St Johns a crown colony in its own right, though this was rescinded when the whole of Pondoland was annexed by Britain in 1895.

The area was then known for its **tobacco**, which was exported from Durban and East London. During the negotiations for the Act of Union, the Transvaal demanded the cessation of the trade to allow its white tobacco growers to expand their business without competition. The Cape Colony obliged and in 1906 stopped exporting tobacco. Local farmers responded by switching to **cannabis**, supplying the growing numbers of men from the area working in the Gauteng mines. Today, the cultivation and trade are as strong as ever, which may explain the presence of so many white South African hippies in the town.

Arrival and information

Initially the town is quite confusing – it meanders into three distinct localities, some kilometres apart. **First Beach**, where the river meets the sea, is along the main road from the post office and offers good fishing, but is unsafe for swimming. Close to First Beach is the rather run-down town centre, where you'll find shops and minibus taxis. **Second Beach**, 5km west along a tarred road off a right turn past the post office, is a fabulous swimming beach with a lagoon; it has a couple of nice places to stay close by, and a number of alternative folk living locally. The area along the river around the **Pondoland Bridge** has some accommodation popular with anglers.

The Baz Bus drops off in Port St Johns, which is also easily reached by **minibus taxi** from Mthatha: plenty run from the *Steer's* restaurant at the Circus Triangle Mall. If you're travelling from **KwaZulu-Natal** to Port St Johns by public transport, an alternative route is via Port Edward, the *Wild Coast Sun* (see p.450), Bizana and Lusikisiki on the R61. This journey is most easily done by catching the Grimboys bus from Durban, which runs daily directly to Port St Johns. This is also the route you should take if you're driving **from Durban**.

There's a **tourist office** (daily 8am–4.30pm; ☎047 564 1187) in an obvious building at the roundabout as you enter town. As well as maps, they provide information about local Xhosa homestays. Jimmy Gila from the tourist office (☎082 507 2256) runs **tours** in the area. Also in the centre you'll find a post office, a bank with an ATM and a Shoprite supermarket.

Accommodation

Port St Johns has the best selection of **accommodation** on the Wild Coast, with a healthy number of backpacker lodges, B&Bs and resort complexes.

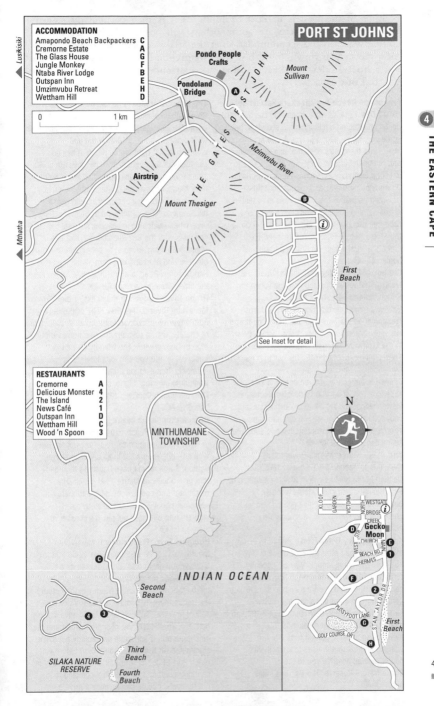

PORT ST JOHNS

See Inset for detail

ACCOMMODATION

Amapondo Beach Backpackers	**C**
Cremorne Estate	**A**
The Glass House	**G**
Jungle Monkey	**F**
Ntaba River Lodge	**B**
Outspan Inn	**E**
Umzimvubu Retreat	**H**
Wettham Hill	**D**

0 _____ 1 km

RESTAURANTS

Cremorne	**A**
Delicious Monster	**4**
The Island	**2**
News Café	**1**
Outspan Inn	**D**
Wettham Hill	**C**
Wood 'n Spoon	**3**

Pondo People Crafts

Pondoland Bridge

Mount Sullivan

Mzimvubu River

THE GATES OF ST JOHN

Airstrip

Mount Thesiger

First Beach

MNTHUMBANE TOWNSHIP

INDIAN OCEAN

Second Beach

Third Beach

Fourth Beach

SILAKA NATURE RESERVE

N

Lusikisiki

Mthatha

Gecko Moon

KLOOF
GARDEN
VICTORIA
NORTH STR
WESTGATE
BRIDGE
CREEK
CHURCH
WEST STR
MAIN
BEACH RD
HERMES
STAN TAYLOR DR
PUSSYFOOT LANE
GOLF COURSE DR
First Beach

4

THE EASTERN CAPE

Neither of the hostels in Port St Johns itself is in a particularly exciting location, although there are some other well-positioned budget options, among which is the accommodation at the Silaka reserve (see opposite). The most spectacular view is high above the Mzimvubu River, on Mount Thesiger. For a **hostel** offering a beach and rural experience, head for Mpande, some way out of town.

Amapondo Beach Backpackers Second Beach ☎047 564 1344, ⓦwww.amapondo.co.za. Lively hostel situated on a hilltop with a sea view, but some way from Second Beach. A free shuttle heads into the centre each morning, 5km away, and the hostel liaises daily with the Baz Bus to collect passengers. Accommodation comprises dorms, double rooms and permanent tents mounted on decks; Internet access is available to residents, and evening meals can be ordered. Staff can organize canoeing, hiking and trips to the Silaka Nature Reserve, or to spend the night in a rural village and meet a traditional healer. ①–②

Cremorne Estate 5km from the centre on the Mzimvubu River, signposted from the Pondoland Bridge ☎047 564 1110 or 1113, ⓦwww.cremorne.co.za. One of Port St Johns' few upmarket places, offering self-catering timber cottages on stilts set on tidy lawns running down to the Mzimvubu River, with views of Mount Thesiger's red-slabbed cliffs. The cottages have two en-suite bedrooms, making them very affordable for a party of three or four. A less expensive row of small B&B doubles shares the view; cheaper still are some tiny cabins equipped with double bunks, where you can also camp. There's a very good restaurant, bar and a relaxing swimming pool area. ①–④

The Glass House Marine Drive; follow the signs to Second Beach ☎047 564 1242. Nestled in the bushes within walking distance of First Beach, these comfortable wooden bungalows are raised to give good ocean views. Each unit has two rooms with separate entrances. ③

Jungle Monkey Berea Rd, second right off the main road after the post office ☎047 564 1517, ⓦwww.junglemonkey.co.za. Recently renovated hostel in a converted house near the centre, with camping, dorms and doubles in beautiful permanent tents and log cabins surrounded by forest. Self-catering or B&B, with a bar and live music at weekends. The owners can arrange guided trips into the villages and overnight visits to a traditional healer as well as drive you to the Silaka Nature Reserve. The Baz Bus stops here. ①–②

The Kraal Near Mpandi ☎082 871 4964, ⓦwww.thekraalbackpackers.co.za. Four traditional huts, each sleeping four people, on community land well off the beaten track. Efficiently run and wonderfully set right on the beach, it has no electricity or flushing toilets (enviroloos are used), and showers and washing facilities are in reed huts. Meals are available, often featuring crayfish, oysters and mussels; activities include beach hikes, snorkelling, surfing and dolphin-watching (also whale-watching in season). A hostel bus connects with the Baz Bus at Shell Ultra City in Mthatha (book in advance by phone); driving, turn off at Tombo Stores, 70km from Mthatha on the Port St Johns Road, and travel another 30min to the little village of Mpandi. ①–②

Ntaba River Lodge On the banks of the Mzimvubu River ☎047 564 1707 or 032 941 5320, ⓦwww.intabariverlodge.co.za. A collection of chalets, with a restaurant and a huge variety of activities on offer. The friendly service is impeccable and you can look forward to *idombolo* (home-made bread) as well as traditional dancing. Signposted on the R61 from Mthatha, just before you reach Port St Johns. Full board ⑤–⑥

Outspan Inn In the centre, past the town hall on the road to First Beach ☎047 564 1057, ⓦwww.outspaninn.co.za. Two-storey ochre B&B with en-suite rooms set in an appealing large garden. Some rooms have unusually high beds that give a view of nearby First Beach. The restaurant and pub is open daily and there's a swimming pool. Frequently used by aid workers and business people, it's cheaper at weekends. ③

Umngazi River Bungalows Umngazi river mouth, west of Port St Johns ☎047 564 1115, ⓦwww.umngazi.co.za. Unsurpassed as a Wild Coast holiday resort, *Umngazi* delivers probably the best beachside family holiday in the country. It's frequently fully booked, especially during school holidays, so reserve as far in advance as possible. The beach and pool are inviting and the lunchtime buffet spread is particularly good. It's signposted off the R61, about 10km before you reach Port St Johns from Mthatha; from the sign, continue another 11km along a potholed road. Alternatively, guests can arrange a private plane into Port St Johns and get picked up. Full board ❻–❼

Umzimvubu Retreat Follow the road to First Beach; the entrance is clearly marked after the tar road ends ☎ 047 564 1741, Ⓦ www.geocities .com/umzimvuburetreat. Homely guesthouse set in a vast natural garden with scenic views. All rooms are en suite, and there's a R300 key deposit. Book in advance for dinner at the restaurant. B&B ❹, self-catering ❸

Wettham Hill 2 Mountain Drive, signposted from the tourist office ☎ 082 453 3944, Ⓦ www .wetthamhill.co.za. Port St Johns' nicest mid-range guesthouse with panoramic views of the town and a small restaurant open to the public. The rooms are comfortable and pleasantly furnished with white linen and curtains and the odd Art Deco piece. ❹

The town and around

Although there is nothing much to see in the town, Port St Johns is still a nice place to take a leisurely stroll, particularly in the early evening, when many residents are doing the same. Most people rarely go anywhere besides First and Second beaches and Pondoland Bridge, though the rocky coastline into the **Silaka Nature Reserve** and as far as the **Umngazi River Mouth** provides wonderful walks, as do the endless stretches of pristine beach east of the Mzimvubu River. The river is muddy in summer, disgorging topsoil washed down the Drakensberg from Lesotho, but cleans up dramatically in winter, when it is clear and good for fishing.

Both the mountains of the **Gates of St John** merit a stiff climb to the top, from where you get a superb view of the lush surrounding landscape. The Gates are two sentinel-like mountainous outcrops on either side of the Mzimvubu River, marking the point where it flows out to the Indian Ocean. By car, drive up to the aircraft landing strip at the top of Mount Thesiger. Look out for the birds of prey, making use of the up draughts.

For **crafts**, check out Pondo People on the east side of the Mzimvubu River across the Pondoland Bridge, easily the best craft shop on the Wild Coast, with wooden sculptures, baskets, carved wooden animals, and immaculate bead jewellery and clothing – all at affordable prices.

Silaka Nature Reserve

Just south of town, the **Silaka Nature Reserve** (daily 6am–6pm; R10) is a small reserve with a dramatic coastline, and comprises the idyllic **Third Beach**, dense and beautiful tropical-forest areas with huge trees (through which there are good **trails**) and a handful of animals, including zebra and wildebeest. **Accommodation** is in spacious self-catering thatched family bungalows surrounded by grassland, with fully fitted kitchens and fully serviced, sleeping four (R640); book through Eastern Cape Parks Board (☎ 043 742 4450, Ⓦ www.ecparks.co.za). To get to the reserve, head down the Second Beach road from Port St Johns and then up the treacherously steep dirt road to the reserve's office. Some of the backpacker lodges can drop you in the reserve, and you can walk back along the coast.

Eating and drinking

There are a couple of decent places to **eat** and **drink** in Port St Johns. If you're self-catering, you can buy tempting local fruits which are sold by the roadside, and sometimes fresh fish is available too. In the centre, Boxer Supermarket has most foodstuffs you'll need, while Green Foods is the place for vegetables.

Cremorne Mzimvubu River; follow the signs from the Pondoland Bridge ☎047 564 1110 or 1113. Port St Johns' poshest eating place. Very good fish, steaks and puddings, a pizza oven, pub, and seating both indoors and out. Daily lunch & dinner.

Delicious Monster Near Second Beach ☎083 997 9856. A couple of tables in the owner's garden, where you can get breakfast, lunch and dinner made with fresh herbs from the garden, and home-baked goodies for tea. There's a little craft shop, too, in a caravan with nice postcards.

Gecko Moon Main Road, First Beach ☎047 564 1221. Pizzas and seafood. Daily 11am–8pm.

News Cafe On the road to First Beach, next to *Outspan Inn* ☎073 359 4281. A pub and seafood restaurant, also offering tea and cake and *koeksisters*. Daily 9am–late.

The Island Signposted off First Beach ☎047 564 1958. Funky, fun place where you sit to eat, Japanese-style, with the food anything from toasted sandwiches to Thai vegetable stir-fry,

reasonably priced, nicely cooked and well presented. You can watch videos on a giant screen in one room while large speakers blast out in another. Takeaways and deliveries possible. Daily except Tues noon–midnight.

Outspan Inn See p.446. The restaurant at this B&B is a great place for blow-out breakfasts, and has an interesting and inexpensive lunch & dinner menu. Closed Sun evenings.

Wettham Hill See p.447. A smart restaurant by Port St Johns standards, with fantastic views from its wraparound balcony. The menu changes every day, with offerings such as balsamic chicken and Mediterranean roast vegetables.

Wood 'n Spoon At Second Beach, next to the lagoon ☎083 532 8869. Operating from a red floral caravan in the German owners' garden, this serves up unusual dishes like apple and bacon macaroni cheese. Crafted chairs and tables are laid out in the garden and at night the area is lit with candles and lanterns. Breakfast, lunch & dinner daily in summer, opening erratically in winter.

The northern Wild Coast and the KwaZulu-Natal enclave

For many visitors to the northern part of the Wild Coast, the main draw is the **Wild Coast Sun**, a hotel and casino on the border of KwaZulu-Natal. However, the stretch of coast from Port St Johns to the Mzamba River by the *Sun* is outstandingly beautiful, with three of only five waterfalls in the world that fall over 100m directly into the sea, as well as countless deserted beaches and cosy bays. The best way to see it is to walk, though it's possible to drive – with some difficulty – to the **Mkhambathi Nature Reserve**, which contains a good portion of this coast.

The road from Port St Johns to the *Wild Coast Sun* via **Lusikisiki** and **Bizana** makes an interesting alternative to the N2 for getting from the Eastern Cape to KwaZulu-Natal. Inland, the road through the Eastern Cape enclave in KwaZulu-Natal takes you into the rolling hills of **Ixopo**, made famous by Alan Paton's novel, *Cry the Beloved Country*.

North to the Wild Coast Sun

The tarred road north from Port St Johns heads to the small unremarkable town of **LUSIKISIKI**, continuing on to the *Wild Coast Sun*. East of Lusikisiki lies the **Magwa Falls** and, tucked away in indigenous forest at the mouth of the **Mbotyi River**, the *Mbotyi River Lodge* (☎039 253 8822, ⊛www.mbotyi.co.za; ❺–❼). With its numerous hiking trails (it's used as the base for the Wild Coast Pondo Walk; see box, p.428), horse-riding, stretch of unblemished coastline and ideal swimming conditions, the lodge makes a good place to stop and rest for a few days. Full-board **accommodation** is in rustic thatched chalets or timber bungalows; the standard rooms have balconies and views of the forest, the luxury ones views of the sea and lagoon. The nearby *Mbotyi Campsite* (☎039 253 8295, ⓔcamping@mbotyi.co.za), run separately from the lodge as a joint venture with the local community, offers clean and comfortable self-catering rondavels (sleeping four/six R500/700), double/twin room (R290/450) with communal kitchens, ablution facilities and a dining area (you'll need to supply your own cutlery, crockery and linen). There's also ample space for **camping**, and a small **store** for basic supplies. The first 6km of the Magwa/Mbotyi road from Lusikisiki are tarred, after which it's 20km of well-maintained gravel to the lodge.

Mkhambathi Nature Reserve

Beyond Lusikisiki, the hills of Pondoland seem to stretch for kilometres, punctuated 50km later by the small village of **Flagstaff**, where you can turn east for the largest of the Wild Coast reserves, the eighty-square-kilometre **Mkhambathi Nature Reserve** (daily 6am–6pm; R20). The park consists almost entirely of grassland, flanked by the forested ravines of the Msikaba and Mtentu rivers, and a **ravishing coastline** of rocky promontories and deserted beaches. There's **plenty of game**: you're likely to see eland, hartebeest, wildebeest and blesbok, as well as Cape vultures. The highlight, though, is the Mkhambathi River itself, which cuts through the middle of the reserve down a series of striking waterfalls, of which the **Horseshoe Falls** near the sea are the most spectacular. **Horse-riding** is on offer and there's plenty of fine walking. **Swimming** is idyllic: a warm, sheltered lagoon is flanked by steep dunes down which you can slide into the water; trees offer some shade along the wide, clear river, and there's the rolling surf itself. There are no facilities at the beach, so bring whatever you need for a picnic, including drinking water.

To get to Mkhambathi, turn towards the coast at the Mkhambathi signpost at **Flagstaff** on the tarred R61. From Flagstaff, the reserve is 70km away on a dirt road, which is very variable in quality; when it has been raining hard you'll need a 4WD vehicle. From Port St Johns, count on two to three hours for the trip. Although the road to the reserve restcamp is fine, **driving** anywhere in the park except to the beach requires a high-clearance vehicle to negotiate the crumbling roads. The beach road itself is poor, and passable in an ordinary car only with considerable care in good weather and when the road is dry. Fortunately, the footpath to the beach through tropical forest is not too long.

The **accommodation** (book through Eastern Cape Parks Board – ☎043 742 4450, ⓦwww.ecparks.co.za) is fully equipped for self-catering, but bring all you need, as there are no shops. The prime place to stay, not far from the reception, is *The Main Lodge*, built as the doctor's stone house when the restcamp was a sanatorium some years ago. It has a veranda set on a hilltop overlooking the sea and its own swimming pool. Paths slither through thick vegetation, down to the lagoon, river and sea. With five en-suite double bedrooms, it's ideal for a group and costs R1950 per night. Around reception, there are five stone or pre-fab cottages each sleeping six people (minimum four people) and one cottage for two people (➊). Situated facing the Misikaba river and close to fishing spots, the *Gwe Gwe River Lodge* accommodates twenty people (R2400), ideal for groups of fishing enthusiasts, with a further six more rondavels nearby sleeping two people each (➋). All this accommodation is fully equipped with electricity. At the beach, in another dreamy location, is **The Point**, a thatched house sleeping four people (➊), the only place on the beach for many kilometres. There is no mains electricity here, just solar power and gas lamps.

Bizana and the Wild Coast Sun

Roughly 30km north of Flagstaff is a junction where you can head northwest to the N2. If you continue 20km northeast instead, through heavily populated hillsides, you reach the busy town of **BIZANA**, 60km from the coast in an area where both former ANC president **Oliver Tambo** and **Winnie Madikizela-Mandela** were born. The *Bizana Hotel* on the left side of the main road has a quiet **restaurant** serving good-value steaks and curries, but is not recommended as a place to stay.

Some 50km southeast of Bizana is the glitzy *Wild Coast Sun* (℡039 305 5111, ⊛www.suninternational.co.za; ⓞ) in a well-chosen location by the Mzamba River Mouth. The hotel marks the start of the **Amadiba Horse Trail** (see box, p.429) and is quite pleasant in parts, despite its tacky Pacific island-themed decor. Most people are here to gamble, but an impressive games arcade, ten-pin bowling, pony rides and mini-golf are also on offer. **Accommodation** is in small, well-equipped, yet very expensive, rooms, with some suites looking onto the sea. You can **eat** tasty (if overpriced) fish steaks at the *Driftwood Terrace*, which has a fantastic sea view.

Opposite the complex is the **Mzamba Crafts Market**, arranged in a circle to resemble a traditional kraal. The central shop sells authentic crafts from all over southern Africa for reasonable prices, with local ones the cheapest, particularly the grasswork. Reject goods are on sale in the outlying huts for even better prices.

There's a daily two-hour shuttle here **from Durban airport** run by Margate Mini Coach (℡039 312 1406 or 082 455 9736, ⊛www.margatecoach.co.za). **Taxis** and **buses** stop outside the market on their way to or from Bizana and **Port Edward** in KwaZulu-Natal (see p.488).

The N2 north of Mthatha

The quickest and busiest way from the Eastern Cape to KwaZulu-Natal is on the **N2**, passing by the scraggy towns of Mount Frere and Mount Ayliff, before reaching **Kokstad** and the provincial boundary. From the road you'll see hillsides dotted with densely packed dwellings. Closer inspection reveals that the hillsides are not coping well with the strain, as there are massive *dongas* (eroded gullies) creating scar-like craters in many places where huge volumes of topsoil have simply been washed away.

Mount Frere is about 100km from Mthatha, and is called kwaBhaca in Xhosa, meaning "the place of the Bhaca" – for many of those fleeing south from the Zulu king Shaka settled here, earning themselves the name *amaBhaca*, "the people who hide". Today, Mount Frere is a fairly rough town and you'd be wise to pass swiftly through.

The Eastern Cape enclave

The **Eastern Cape enclave** in KwaZulu-Natal for many years sat uncomfortably with the crass ethnic categorizations of past regimes, and the legacy of this lives on today. The people living in the enclave, whose main town is uMzimkhulu, are a mixture of Zulu, Pondo, Bhaca and Griqua, economically tied in the main to Pietermaritzburg and Durban. The apartheid regime yoked them with the Transkei, ostensibly on the grounds that most were Pondo, and thus part of the Xhosa nation, but in fact to tap them as a cheap labour reserve. Controversially, the area was included in the Eastern Cape when the boundaries were redrawn after the

1994 elections, in part because many in the area support the ANC and did not want to be part of a province ruled by the Zulu nationalist Inkatha Freedom Party.

The enclave is reached by turning off the N2 onto the R56 at the Stafford's Post junction towards **Ixopo**. It's scenic and pleasant enough to pass through, though not a good place to travel around – there's nowhere to stay or any infrastructure for tourists, and it's desperately poor. **uMzimkhulu** is a busy transport centre, with a large taxi rank by its Shell garage and plenty of fast-food outlets to feed hungry passengers, most of whom are going to and from Pietermaritzburg and Durban. After passing the remnants of a small border post just east of the town, you'll find yourself back in KwaZulu-Natal, a short distance from Ixopo.

Travel details

All major transport in the Eastern Cape runs between Port Elizabeth and East London – the two hubs of the province – or from these centres to other major cities: Johannesburg, Cape Town and Durban. Two main-line trains, the Amatola from East London, and the Algoa from Port Elizabeth, connect the Eastern Cape with Johannesburg and Pretoria, both stopping along the way. The main bus routes run from Port Elizabeth (up the N10) and East London (up the N6) to join the N1 via Bloemfontein to Johannesburg and Pretoria; and along the coast to Cape Town in the west and Durban in the east. An alternative route goes inland through the Little Karoo to Cape Town.

Trains

East London to: Bloemfontein (daily; 13hr); Johannesburg (daily; 20hr); Pretoria (daily; 21hr 30min); Queenstown (daily; 4hr 30min).
Port Elizabeth to: Bloemfontein (daily, 11hr 30min); Cradock (daily; 4hr 30min); Johannesburg (daily; 18hr); Pretoria (daily; 19hr 30min).

Buses

East London to: Alexandria (5 weekly, 3hr 15min); Aliwal North (daily; 5hr); Bloemfontein (daily; 7hr 30min); Cape Town (1–2 daily; 14hr); Durban (2 daily; 9hr); Grahamstown (2 daily; 2hr); Johannesburg (daily; 13hr); Kenton-on-Sea (5 weekly; 3hr); King William's Town (2–3 daily; 45min); Knysna (1–2 daily; 7hr 30min); Mossel Bay (1–2 daily; 9hr); Paarl (5 weekly; 14hr 30min); Plettenberg Bay (1–2 daily; 7hr); Port Alfred (3 daily; 2hr 30min); Port Elizabeth (3 daily; 4hr); Port Shepstone (2 daily; 8hr); Pretoria (daily; 14hr);

Sedgefield (1–2 daily; 8hr); Storms River (1–2 daily; 6hr); Swellendam (1–2 daily; 11hr); Mthatha (2 daily; 3hr 30min); Wilderness (1–2 daily; 8hr 30min).
Mthatha to: Cape Town (1–3 daily; 17hr 30min); Durban (3 daily; 5hr 50min); East London (1–2 daily; 3hr); Johannesburg (2 daily; 12hr 45min); Port Elizabeth (daily; 5hr 40min); Pretoria (daily; 13hr 45min).
Port Elizabeth to: Alexandria (5 weekly; 1hr); Bloemfontein (1–2 daily; 10hr); Cape Town (6–7 daily; 11hr); Durban (2 daily; 13hr 30min); East London (3 daily; 4hr); George (6–7 daily; 4hr 30min); Graaff-Reinet (5 weekly; 3hr 30min); Grahamstown (2 daily; 1hr 30min); Jeffrey's Bay (2 daily; 45min); Johannesburg (3–4 daily; 16hr); Kenton-on-Sea (5 weekly; 1hr 30min); Knysna (6–7 daily; 3hr 30min); Mossel Bay (6–7 daily; 4hr 30min); Mthatha (2 daily; 7hr 30min); Paarl (4 weekly; 10hr); Plettenberg Bay (6–7 daily; 3hr); Port Alfred (5 weekly; 1hr 45min); Port Shepstone (2 daily; 12hr); Pretoria (1–2 daily; 17hr); Sedgefield (6–7 daily; 3hr 30min); Stellenbosch (6 weekly; 10hr); Storms River (6–7 daily; 2hr); Wilderness (4 daily; 3hr 30min).

Baz Buses

The Baz Bus plies the coastal route daily between Port Elizabeth and Cape Town. It also goes all the way through to Durban five times a week.
Port Elizabeth to: Durban (5 weekly; 15hr 30min); East London (5 weekly; 2hr 30min); George (daily; 7hr 45min); Jeffrey's Bay (daily; 1hr 45min); Knysna (daily; 6hr 30min); Mossel Bay (daily; 10hr 15min); Mthatha (5 weekly; 8hr 30min); Nature's Valley (daily; 4hr 30min); Oudtshoorn (daily; 9hr); Plettenberg Bay (daily; 5hr 30min);

Port Alfred (5 weekly; 2hr 15min); Port Shepstone (5 weekly; 14hr); Wilderness (daily; 7hr 15min).

Domestic flights

East London to: Cape Town (2–3 daily; 2hr); Durban (2–4 daily; 1hr); Johannesburg (7 daily; 1hr 20min); Port Elizabeth (2–4 daily; 45min).

Mthatha to: Johannesburg (2 daily; 1hr 30min). **Port Elizabeth** to: Bloemfontein (1 daily Mon–Fri & Sun; 1hr 20min); Cape Town (3–4 daily; 1hr 15min); Durban (4 daily; 1hr 10min); East London (1–4 daily; 45min); George (1 weekly; 1hr); Johannesburg (6 daily; 1hr 30min).

THE EASTERN CAPE | Travel details

KwaZulu-Natal

CHAPTER 5 Highlights

* **Indian culture** The Hindu temples and tangy food of KwaZulu-Natal's second-largest ethnic group can be experienced in the heart of Durban. See p.470

* **Ukhahlamba Drakensberg** Towering peaks and ancient San (Bushman) rock paintings in one of KwaZulu-Natal's two World Heritage Sites. See p.499

* **Hluhluwe-Imfolozi Park** One of the best places in the world to see rhinos. See p.514

* **Isimangaliso Wetland Park** Declared a World Heritage Site in 1999, this reserve is home to five ecosystems, marine and wildlife. See p.518

* **Authentic Zulu Culture** Be a guest at a traditional Zulu wedding or coming-of-age ceremony in Eshowe. See p.537

* **Zulu baskets** The Vukani Zulu Cultural Museum in Eshowe includes some of South Africa's most beautiful woven artefacts.See p.538

* **Battlefield tours** Experience the drama of the Anglo-Zulu wars with world-renowned storytellers and guides. See p.543

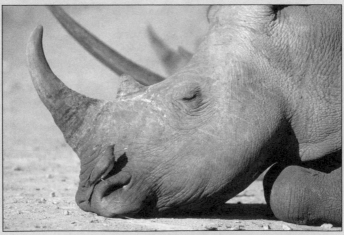

▲ Rhino and bird at Hluhluwe-Imfolozi Park

KwaZulu-Natal

K waZulu-Natal, South Africa's most African province, has everything the continent is known for – beaches, wildlife, mountains and accessible ethnic culture. South Africans are well acquainted with KwaZulu-Natal's attractions; it's the leading province for domestic tourism, although foreign visitors haven't quite cottoned on to the incredible amount packed into this compact and beautiful region.

Among white South Africans, KwaZulu-Natal is well known for its subtropical **coastline**, which offers a temperate climate even in the winter, when the Cape can be showered by an icy downpour. This is where you'll find Africa's most developed beaches, in a 250-kilometre ribbon of holiday homes stretching along the shore from the Eastern Cape border in the south to the Tugela River in the north.

At the ribbon's centre lies **Durban**, the industrial hub of the province and the country's principal harbour. Apart from Cape Town, Durban is the only major city in South Africa that warrants a visit in its own right. British in origin, it has a heady mixture of cultural flavours deriving from its Zulu, Indian and white communities. You'll find palm trees fanning Victorian buildings, African squatters living precariously under truncated flyovers, high-rise offices towering over temples and curry houses, overdeveloped beachfronts, and everywhere an irrepressible fecundity.

Paradoxically, while the coasts immediately on either side of Durban – known as the **North and South coasts** – are South Africa's busiest and least enticing, north of the Tugela River are some of the most pristine shores in the country. Here, in the **Elephant Coast**, a patchwork of wetlands, freshwater lakes,

KZN Wildlife

Most of the public game parks and wilderness areas described in this chapter fall under the auspices of **Ezemvelo KwaZulu-Natal Wildlife**, also known as Ezemvelo KZN Wildlife or KZN Wildlife (PO Box 13069, Cascades, Pietermaritzburg 3202; ℡033 845 1000, ℗www.kznwildlife.com). **Accommodation** in these areas is best booked in advance through them (exceptions or alternative ways of booking are noted in the text); if you want to do so in person, one convenient location is their head office at Tourist Junction in Durban (℡031 274 1150; see p.462). Although the areas that comprise the Isimangaliso Wetland Park are now managed by the **Isimangaliso Wetland Park Authority** (℡035 590 1633, ℗www.isimangaliso.com), almost all of the accommodation within the wetland park is still operated by KZN Wildlife, and as such reservations should still be made through them.

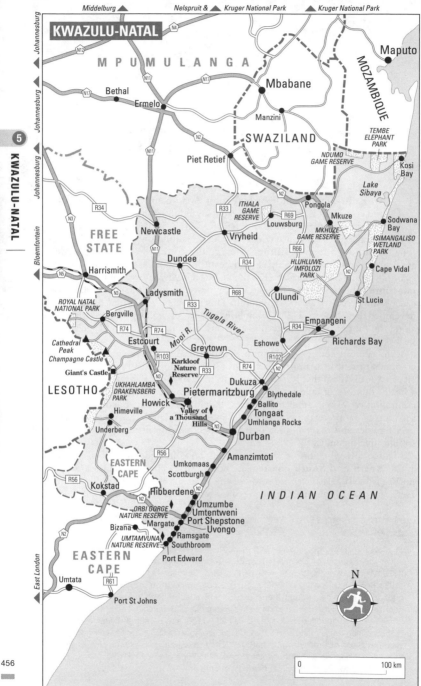

wilderness and Zulu villages meets the sea at a virtually seamless stretch of sand that begins at the St Lucia Estuary and slips across the Mozambique border at Kosi Bay. Apart from southern **Lake St Lucia**, which is fairly developed in a low-key fashion, the Elephant Coast is one of the most isolated regions in the country, though it does reward visitors with South Africa's best snorkelling and scuba diving along the coral reefs off **Sodwana Bay**.

KwaZulu-Natal's marine life is matched on land by its **game reserves**, some of which are beaten only by the Kruger National Park, and easily surpass the latter as the best place in the continent to see both black and white rhinos. Concentrated in the north, the reserves tend to be compact and feature some of the most stylish game-lodge accommodation in the country. Most famous and largest of the reserves is the **Hluhluwe–Imfolozi Park**, trampled by a respectable cross section of wildlife that includes all of the Big Five.

Since the nineteenth century, when missionaries were homing in on the region, the **Zulus** have captured the popular imagination of the West and remain one of the province's major pulls for tourists, despite the fact that you're more likely to encounter a Zulu dressed in jeans in Jo'burg than someone in traditional garb in KwaZulu-Natal. You'll find constant reminders of the old Zulu kingdom and its founder Shaka, including an excellent reconstruction of the beehive-hutted capital at **Ondini** and the more touristy **Shakaland**, near **Eshowe**. The interior north of the Tugela River was the heartland of the Zulu kingdom and saw gruesome battles between Boers and Zulus, British and Zulus, and finally Boers and British. Today, the area can be explored through **Battlefield tours**, a memorable way of taking in some of South Africa's most turbulent history.

The area south of the Tugela, designated "white man's country" in the mid-nineteenth century and consolidated a century later under apartheid, represents the most English area of South Africa. Though it is very pretty and has some fabulous accommodation in country houses, the **Midlands**' rolling green sugar estates, polo clubs and rather contrived arts-and-crafts routes pale by comparison with the drama of the rest of the province.

From the Midlands, South Africa's highest peaks sweep west into the soaring **Ukhahlamba Drakensberg** range, protected by a chain of KZN Wildlife reserves. The area's restcamps are ideal bases for walking in the mountains or heading out for ambitious hikes; with relatively little effort, you can experience crystal rivers tumbling into marbled rock pools, peaks and rock faces enriched by ancient San paintings.

KwaZulu-Natal experiences considerable variations in **climate**, from the occasional heavy winter snowstorms of the Ukhahlamba Drakensberg to the mellow, sunny days and pleasant sea temperatures a couple of hundred kilometres away along the coast. This makes the region a popular winter getaway, but in midsummer the low-lying areas, including Durban, the coastal belt and the game reserves, can experience an uncomfortably high humidity.

Some history

Despite their defeats in battles with the Boers and the British during the nineteenth century, the Zulus have remained an active force in South African politics, and are particularly strong in KwaZulu-Natal. The **Inkatha Freedom Party** (IFP), formed in 1975 by former ANC Youth League member **Mangosuthu Buthelezi** and currently the country's third-largest political party, has long been associated with Zulu nationalism and draws most of its support from Zulu-speaking people. The IFP and ANC were originally allies in the fight against apartheid, but soon the IFP's ardent nationalism was proving to be a major hassle for the ANC, who responded with attacks on opposing IFP members. A bitter and violent conflict between the two parties ensued during the 1980s and 1990s, which, according to some, claimed around 20,000 lives. Although the fighting is now restricted to isolated – and increasingly rare – incidents, the political rivalry continues. It is the ANC, however, which has gained the upper hand in KwaZulu-Natal and is currently in control of the provincial legislature. At the national level, Zulu hopes are pinned on **Jacob Zuma**, who was elected leader of the ANC in December, 2007, and is now in pole position to succeed Mbeki when he steps down as president in 2009. Zuma is from KwaZulu-Natal and, indeed, played an important role in trying to end the violence between the ANC and IFP; he often makes speeches in Zulu and has retained strong support among his people despite some recent setbacks. In 2005, Zuma's financial advisor, Schabir Shaik, was sent to prison for fifteen years for corruption, a conviction that has tainted Zuma by association and could lead to his own trial for corruption in the future. The controversial politician has already made one court appearance: in 2006, he was cleared of raping a family friend, although he was criticized heavily for having unprotected sex with his HIV-positive accuser.

Durban

Until the 1970s, **DURBAN** was regarded as white South Africa's quintessential seaside playground – a status fostered by its tropical colours, oversized vegetation and an itinerant population of surfers, hedonists and holidaying Jo'burg families. Then, in the 1980s, the collapse of apartheid population-influx controls saw a growing stream of Africans flood in from rural KwaZulu-Natal – and even from as far afield as central Africa – to stake their claims in the city centre, with shantytowns and cardboard hovels revealing the reality of one of the most unmistakably African conurbations in the country.

South Africa's third-largest city is a thriving industrial centre and the largest port in Africa. Its **beachfront** pulls thousands upon thousands of white Jo'burgers down to "Durbs" every year, while the **harbour** remains a photogenic place for meandering or eating and drinking at the dockside. Another unmistakable feature of Durban is a legacy of the city's **Indian population** (its second-largest group): mosques, bazaars and temples, festooned with wildly coloured deities, stand juxtaposed with the Victorian buildings marking out the colonial centre.

The city's main interest lies not in its seaside, but its gritty urbanity, a seemingly endless struggle to reconcile competing Indian, African and English cultures and to keep the rampant vegetation at bay. There's enough here to keep you busy for a few days, exploring the Indian area around Grey Street – newly renamed Dr Yusuf Dadoo Street as part of the country's shift towards a more culturally representative nomenclature – or experiencing some excellent restaurants and nightlife in Durban's swanky northern suburbs. However, most people come to Durban because it provides a logical springboard for the KwaZulu-Natal game parks, the Ukhahlamba Drakensberg and the Battlefields.

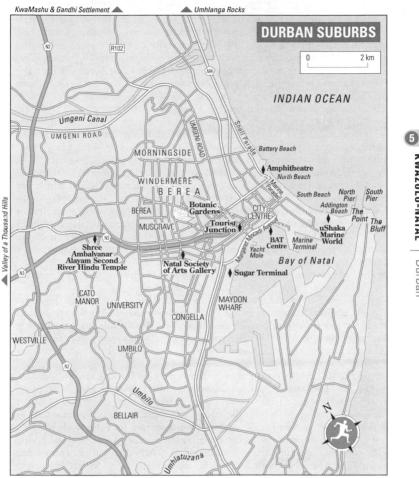

Durban is well connected to the rest of South Africa, although only one international flight (from Mauritius) currently calls here.

Some history

Less than two hundred years ago, Durban was known to Europeans as **Port Natal**, a lagoon thick with mangroves, eyed by white adventurers who saw business opportunities in its ivory and hides. In 1824, a British party led by **Francis Farewell** persuaded the Zulu king, **Shaka**, to give them some land. Not long after, the British went on to rename the settlement **Durban** after Sir Benjamin D'Urban, governor of the Cape Colony, whose support, they believed, might not go amiss later.

Britain's tenuous toehold looked threatened in 1839, when **Boers** trundled over the Ukhahlamba Drakensberg in their ox wagons and declared their Republic of Natalia nearby. The threat was compounded the following year, when a large force of now-hostile Zulus descended on the settlement and razed it, forcing the British residents to take refuge at sea in the brig *Comet*. Capitalizing on the British absence, a group of Boers annexed Durban, later laying siege to a British detachment. This provided the cue for a much-celebrated piece of Victorian melodrama, familiar until recently to every English-speaking school child in South Africa – when teenager **Dick King** heroically rode the 1000km from Durban to Grahamstown in ten days to alert the garrison there, which promptly dispatched a rescue detachment to relieve Durban.

While Cape Town was becoming a cosmopolitan centre by the 1840s, Durban's population of barely one thousand lived a basic existence in a near wilderness roamed by lions, leopards and hyenas. Things changed after Britain formally annexed the **Colony of Natal** in 1843; within ten years, a large-scale immigration of settlers from the mother country had begun. The second half of the nineteenth century was marked by the city's considerable industrial development and major influxes of other groups. Indentured **Indian labourers** arrived to work in the KwaZulu-Natal cane fields, planting the seeds for South Africa's lucrative **sugar industry** and the city's now substantial Indian community; and **Zulus** headed south after their conquest by the British, in 1879, to enter Durban's expanding economy. In 1895, the completion of the railway connecting Johannesburg and Durban accelerated the process of migrant labour. This link to South Africa's industrial heartland, and the opening of Durban's harbour mouth to large ships in 1904, ensured the city's eventual pre-eminence as South Africa's principal harbour.

In 1922, in the face of growing Indian and African populations, Durban's strongly English city council introduced **legislation** controlling the sale of land in the city to non-whites, predating Afrikaner-led apartheid by 26 years. During the boom years of World War II, Africans flooded into the city in even greater numbers, leading to calls (which were ignored) for their recognition as permanent residents.

With the strict enforcement of **apartheid** in the 1950s, Durban saw a decade of ANC-led **protests**. These started with the countrywide Defiance Campaign in 1952, and reached a peak in 1959 when *shebeen* queens – the African women who ran speakeasies – took to the streets and attacked municipal beer halls in protest at police harassment. This provided momentum for nationwide marches and protests that culminated in the government clampdown of 1961, when the authorities swamped the streets with troops, declared a state of emergency, and banned the ANC. Left with no peaceful option, the ANC formed its armed wing, with plans for a nationwide **bombing campaign** that was initiated with an explosion in Durban on December 15, 1961. Durban scored another first in 1973, when workers in the city initiated a wildcat strike, despite a total ban on black industrial action. This heralded the rebirth of South Africa's **trade unions** and reawakened anti-apartheid activity, sparking the final phase of the country's road to democracy.

Arrival and information

By the start of the 2010 World Cup, Durban should have a brand-new airport at La Mercy, 30km north of Durban (see p.490). For now, however, **Durban International airport** (☎031 451 6666) is 14km south of the centre on the Southern Freeway. The domestic and international terminals are in the same building, with arrivals on the south side and departures on the north side. Bus services leave every half hour (daily 7am–10.30pm; ☎031 465 1660; R30) for

Durban's new street names

Several of Durban's main thoroughfares will probably have **changed names** by the time you read this. At the time of writing, there had been no official rubber-stamp for the proposed changes, even though street signs were already showing the new names. On the maps for this edition, we have given the new name followed by the old name in brackets. Note, however, that people still commonly use the old names. The affected streets are:

Old name	New name
Alice Street	Johannes Nkosi Street
Commercial Street	Dr A B Xuma Street
Grey and Broad streets	Dr Yusuf Dadoo Street
NMR Avenue	Masabalala Yengwa Avenue
Northern Freeway M4	Ruth First Freeway
Point Road	Mahatma Gandhi Road
Stanger Street	Stalwart Simelane Street
Victoria Embankment	Margaret Mncadi Avenue

The *No Longer at this Address* brochure, available at the Durban Art Gallery, gives potted biographies of the newly commemorated people.

the twenty-minute journey from outside the arrivals terminal to Shell House on the corner of Aliwal and Smith streets in the city centre. A metered taxi to the city costs around R150. Julnic Tours runs a shuttle service between the airport and city accommodation (R160 one-way; ☎031 205 9119).

There's an excellent **tourist information desk** in the arrival terminal (daily 7am–9pm; ☎031 408 1000), plus several car-rental companies, including Hertz and Avis. Windermere Car Hire (see p.483) will collect you from the airport free of charge during office hours (Mon–Fri 8am–5pm, Sat 8am–noon) if you're renting one of its cars. There's an Absa Bank in the arrivals terminal (daily 7am–8pm) and a 24-hour ATM next to it.

By train

The Trans-Natal service from Johannesburg and the Trans-Oranje service from Cape Town via Free State both arrive at the grim **New Durban station** off Masabalala Yengwa Avenue (☎031 361 7609), just north of the main commercial centre. The best option from here is to take one of the metered taxis that rank in front of the motorcoach terminal that occupies the ground level of the station complex; a ride to the beachfront costs around R50.

By bus

Intercape (☎031 307 1971), Greyhound (☎031 334 9700), Translux (☎031 308 8111) and other intercity buses end their runs at the **Motorcoach Terminal** attached to the New Durban station complex. The Margate Mini Coach (☎039 312 1406) from the South Coast pulls in here, and also outside domestic departures at Durban airport. The Umhlanga Express minibus shuttle from Umhlanga Rocks (☎082 268 0651) drops off at a number of points in Durban, including the airport and opposite Tourist Junction (see p.462) in the city centre. Baz Bus (☎031 304 9099, ⓦwww.bazbus.com) stops at most of the Durban backpacker lodges.

By minibus taxi

Long-distance **minibus taxis** from Gauteng arrive opposite the Umgeni Road entrance to the train station, while those from the South Coast and

Transkei terminate at Berea Road in the Warwick Triangle area at the west of the city centre. Both are very busy points, rife with pickpockets, so take care of your baggage – and bear in mind that the city centre and beachfront accommodation are fifteen and thirty minutes' walk away respectively. If you intend to stay in the Berea, catch a Mynah bus to the main bus depot on Pine Street, from where you'll be able to get another Mynah bus connection.

Information

The obvious first port of call for information is the central **Tourist Junction** at Old Station Building, 160 Pine St (Mon–Fri 8am–5pm, Sat 9am–2pm; ℡031 304 4934, 🌐www.durbanexperience.co.za), which houses Durban Africa (the city's tourist bureau) and Tourism KwaZulu-Natal (the province's excellent tourist bureau, 🌐www.kzn.org.za). Also here are **KZN Wildlife** and **South African National Parks** booking offices, a couple of travel agents who can book intercity coaches and **tours** (including walking tours of the Dr Yusuf Dadoo Street area, city centre and historical tours; for other recommended local tour operators, see box opposite), and a **Baz Bus** office. There is another well-equipped tourist office at uShaka Marine World on the beachfront (daily 9am–9pm; ℡031 337 8099).

City transport

The easiest way to explore Durban is by **car**. The city's freeways are well signposted, and with careful map-reading getting around is straightforward. You need to plan ahead, though, as Durbanites drive fast and there's no time to dither at lane changes and junctions. **Cycling** is safe along the beachfront, but hazardous on any major road, and not really recommended. There are several car **rental companies** in Durban; we've recommended some larger operators in "Listings" (see p.483).

Buses

Durban's most useful urban transport is the cheap and regular **bus** system operated by Mynah and Aqualine, which cover the central districts, including the city centre, the beachfront, the Berea and Florida Road. For travel within the city centre, the Durban People Mover operates modern buses along two routes linking the beachfront with the centre as far east as Victoria Street Market. If you want to get to the more far-flung suburbs, Durban Transport Municipal Buses is quite functional, although slightly the worse for wear. For information about **times and routes** for all of these companies, call ☎031 309 5942, or pop into the **Pine Street bus depot**, which is adjacent to The Workshop Mall and is the starting point for most local bus services (you can also pick up bus schedules from the Tourist Junction).

Taxis and minibus taxis

There are several reputable **taxi companies** in central Durban, including Eagle (☎031 337 8333), Mozzies (☎0860 669 943) and Zippy (☎031 202 7067).

Minibus taxis can be hailed along any busy road. To get to town or the beachfront from any of the suburbs, stand along the sidewalk and signal assertively with an index finger. Minibuses follow set paths (you can get off at any point by asking the driver); once in the city centre, they follow West Street to the beachfront, then turn south into Marine Parade as far as Addington Beach.

Accommodation

Durban's high-rise **accommodation** is concentrated along the **beachfront** and in the **city centre**: both convenient locations with plenty of things going

---

Durban tours and harbour rides

One of the safest and easiest ways to get under the skin of ethnic Durban is to take a guided tour: standard three-hour tours cost around R250 per person and R400 for a full day; we have listed a few operators below. A good way to explore Durban's Indian areas is by joining the daily Oriental Walkabout tour organized by the tourist office (book at Tourist Junction; R75). You can also take a harbour ride with Ferry and Bay Services (daily on the hour 10am–5pm; R50; ☎031 301 1953).

Gailforce Tours ☎083 643 1923, ✉gailsnyman@hotmail.com. Tours of the coloured townships of Durban.

Strelitzia Tours ☎031 573 2252, ⊛www.strelitziatours.com. Daily minibus trips around the major sights, the centre and the Berea, as well as trips further afield to the game parks, the Battlefields and up Sani Pass in the Ukhahlamba Drakensberg.

Tekweni Eco Tours ☎031 332 0575 or 079 597 7643, ⊛www.tekweniecotours .co.za. Visits to Zulu villages in the Valley of a Thousand Hills for a Zulu meal and beer, traditional dancing and an encounter with a traditional healer. Also available are camping safaris into the Ukhahlamba Drakensberg.

Thuthuka Tours ☎082 264 2556. Discover the roots of resistance to apartheid by taking a township tour in the company of Langa Dube, whose late grandfather was the first president of the ANC. Langa can also take you on an overnight trip to his family homestead in a remote part of central Zululand.

Tours of Remembrance ☎031 337 7879 or 083 560 9999. A community-based tour company that can take you to the townships, the Gandhi settlement and Hindu temples.

on around, but less salubrious at night – taking taxis to your doorstep is recommended after dark. An alternative to the city centre and beachfront is the **Berea** residential area west and north of the centre. It boasts the best backpacker lodges in town, while its guesthouses and B&Bs are often housed in beautifully renovated old homes. There are plenty of restaurants and bars in the area too, in particular on Florida Road in **Morningside**.

Durban has a selection of **township homestays** where you can experience the warmth of urban Zulu hospitality. Durban Africa at Tourist Junction can arrange your accommodation as well as transport into the townships. And if you fancy basing yourself within an easy drive of the city, the most appealing option is Umhlanga Rocks.

Beachfront and city-centre establishments reviewed here appear on the map on pp.466–467; see the map on pp.474–475 for establishments in the Berea.

City centre

Banana Backpackers 61 Pine St, 1st floor, Ambassador House ☎ 031 368 4062, ✉ admin @africanroutes.co.za. Clean and simple dorms and doubles in an airy old Durban building with a congenial courtyard, very close to the beach, Tourist Junction and the Pine St bus terminal. Dorms and rooms ❶

Formula 1 Directly opposite the motorcoach terminal, near the corner of Masabalala Yengwa Ave and Jeff Taylor Crescent ☎ 031 301 1551, ⓦ www.hotelformula1.co.za. No-frills chain hotel that's tremendously convenient if you arrive late at night by train or bus. ❷

The Royal Hotel 267 Smith St ☎ 031 333 6000, ⓦ www.theroyal.co.za. Once Durban's finest hotel, but now feels a little oldfangled. Smack in the centre of town and used mainly by business visitors, it's worth considering if you can afford five-star splendour and fancy the liveried service and its legendary *Ulundi* Indian restaurant (see p.478). Discounts are often available. ❼

Beachfront

Blue Waters 175 Snell Parade ☎ 031 327 7000, ⓦ www.bluewatershotel.co.za. A delightful 1950s Durban landmark opposite Battery Beach, with mangroves on the pavement and leisure lounge with great views onto the oceanfront. ❹

Garden Court – Marine Parade 167 Marine Parade ☎ 031 337 3341, ⓦ www.southernsun .com. All the rooms face the sea (those on the top floors are best); the view from the thirtieth-floor swimming pool is fabulous. A cool through-breeze offers respite against the summer heat, and a back entrance across from Victoria Park provides handy access to the city centre. ❻

Protea Hotel Edward Marine Parade, at Seaview Rd ☎ 031 337 3681, ⓦ www.proteahotels.com. Crystal chandeliers, a colonial-style ambience, sea-view balconies and a ladies' bar leading onto a cool veranda make this Art Deco mansion the *grande dame* of the beachfront. Breakfast not included. ❻

Silversands 16 Erskine Terrace, near the Addington Hospital ☎ 031 332 1140, ⓦ www .goodersonvacations.com/silversands.html. These clean, comfortable and spacious self-catering apartments sleeping four to eight people are among the best value on the beach. Safe parking costs R32 per day. ❸

The Berea

Morningside

Goble Palms 120 Goble Rd ☎ 031 312 2598, ⓦ www.goblepalms.co.za. Exquisitely decorated home built in 1900, featuring a sunny patio with sea views, a pool and an intimate on-site English-style pub. ❹

La Bordello 47 Campbell Rd ☎ 031 309 1001, ⓦ www.beanbagbohemia.co.za. A funky Moroccan-themed B&B housed in a former brothel, hence the name; the clientele consists largely of models and film-makers. It's next to the popular *Bean Bag Bohemia* restaurant (see p.479). ❹

McAllisters on 8th 11 Eighth Ave ☎ 031 303 4991, ⓦ www.8thave.co.za. Some of the cleanest, most stylish rooms you'll find, all decked out in white linen and African artwork, and built around a courtyard pool. The recently opened *McAllisters on Madeline* (92 Madeline Rd, same phone, ⓦ www.madeline.macallisters.co.za) offers accommodation of a similar standard and price. ❹

Meg's B&B 12 Nuttall Gardens ☎ 031 312 9045, ✉ maasdyk@mweb.co.za. Home-away-from-home comforts in one of Durban's longest-established B&Bs. Recently renovated, with a pool, sauna and Jacuzzi. Meg's speciality is her lavish, beautifully presented breakfasts. Advance booking requested. Two-night minimum stay. ❹

Rosetta House 126 Rosetta Rd ☎ &ⓕ 031 303 6180, ⓦ www.rosettahouse.co.za. Just four rooms,

all warmly and tastefully decorated. There's a lush and tranquil garden to relax in, and the hosts maintain a high standard of service. ❹
Sommersby 17 Claribell Rd ☎031 312 8667 or 072 529 2594, ⓦwww.sommersby.co.za. Next to the Windermere Shopping Centre, this B&B is in a renovated Edwardian house, with wooden floors and Oregon pine furniture. ❸
Tekweni Backpackers 169 Ninth Ave ☎031 303 1433, ⓦwww.tekwenibackpackers.co.za. The cheapest accommodation around Florida Rd, with relaxing communal areas, pool table, a pool, bar and a shady veranda. The friendly staff organize braais and other social gatherings. Long-term accommodation is also available. Dorms ❶, rooms ❷

Elsewhere in the Berea

20 Palm Grove 367 Ridge Rd ☎031 240 9140, ⓦwww.20palmgrove.co.za. Well-equipped and comfortable self-catering units and B&B rooms, most with separate entrances, set in attractive gardens with two swimming pools. It's close to public transport and restaurants. ❹

🏃 **The Elephant House** 745 Ridge Rd ☎031 208 9580 or 082 4522 574, ⓦwww .elephanthousesa.com. A B&B in Durban's oldest house, built in 1850 as a hunting lodge, in the tranquil part of the ridge where the vegetation has won the day. The extremely generous hosts have a good collection of African literature and love

showing travellers around. Highly recommended for those who like to feel as though they are staying in someone's home. ❸

🏃 **Hippo Hide Lodge and Backpackers** 2 Jesmond Rd ☎031 207 4366, ⓦwww .hippohide.co.za. A stunning, imaginative and cosy lodge in a beautiful garden with a rock pool. It's clean and quiet, with a guesthouse feel, and conveniently located on the bus route to the centre (10min). Some of the doubles are en suite, and there are also log cabins. The owners have opened the new *Happy Hippo Backpackers Lodge* on Mahatma Gandhi Road near uShaka Marine World. Dorms ❶, rooms ❷
Napier House 31 Napier Rd ☎031 207 6779, ⓦwww.napierhouse.co.za. A stone's throw from the scenic Botanic Gardens, recently renovated and featuring charming rooms with flat-screen TVs and a pool. ❹
Nomad's Backpackers 70 Essenwood Rd ☎031 202 9709 or 082 920 5882, ⓦwww.nomadsbp .com. An appealing place a short walk from the Musgrave Centre, with a pool, a pool table, the *Bambooza Pub* and friendly hosts who cook up a mean Durban curry. Dorms and rooms ❶
Windmill Ridge 81 Windmill Rd ☎031 201 4972 or 082 462 2927, ⓦwww.windmill-ridge .co.za. Six comfortable rooms, all en suite, and expansive views over the city. Close to the Musgrave Centre. ❸

The City

Durban's **city centre**, confined by the Bay of Natal to the south and the beaches of the Indian Ocean to the east, grew around the arrival point of the first white settlers; the remains of the historical heart are concentrated around **Francis Farewell Square**, five minutes' walk north of the bay. Today the central business area, studded with high-rise buildings and packed with traffic, lacks views of the ocean and gives no hint you're in a seaside city.

On the western side of the city centre, around Dr Yusuf Dadoo (formerly Grey) and Victoria streets, lies Durban's most fascinating area, the **Indian district** – a pulsing warren of bazaars, alleyways and mosques. A little further west, situated in the melee of taxi ranks and bus depots, the African-dominated **Warwick Triangle** seethes with ceaseless activity; the *shebeens* do a brisk trade while the poorest of the poor spend the nights on their market stalls under plastic and cardboard.

Durban's **beachfront** on the eastern edge of the centre has one of the city's busiest concentrations of restaurants, a surfeit of tacky family entertainment, and a reputation for crime. Occupying the beachfront's southern section, the **Point** is a rather desolate peninsula which encloses the northern side of the **harbour**, the city's economic hub. Rising above the flat city centre and harbour is the **Berea**, a desirable residential district on a cooler ridge which, despite its proximity to the centre, has luxuriant gardens alive with the sounds of birds, and fashionable restaurants and shopping malls.

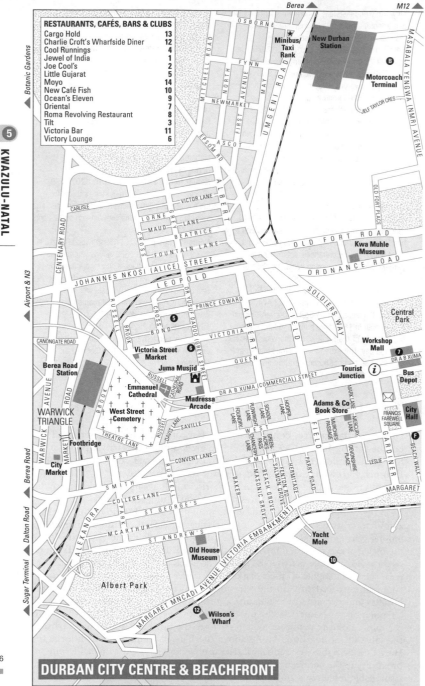

RESTAURANTS, CAFÉS, BARS & CLUBS

Cargo Hold	13
Charlie Croft's Wharfside Diner	12
Cool Runnings	4
Jewel of India	1
Joe Cool's	2
Little Gujarat	5
Moyo	14
New Café Fish	10
Ocean's Eleven	9
Oriental	7
Roma Revolving Restaurant	8
Tilt	3
Victoria Bar	11
Victory Lounge	6

DURBAN CITY CENTRE & BEACHFRONT

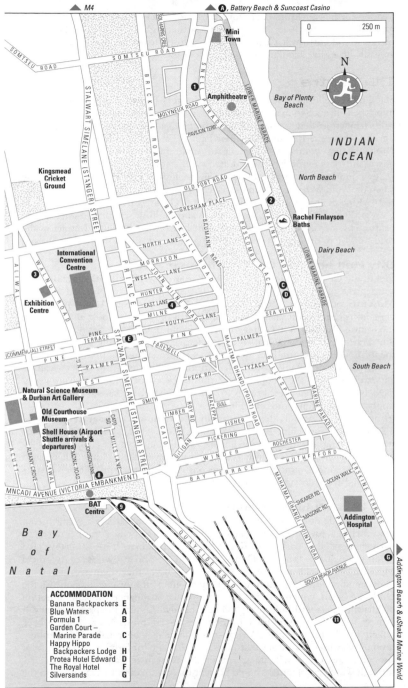

▲ M4   ▲ Ⓐ, Battery Beach & Suncoast Casino

0   250 m

Mini Town

SOL HARRIS CRES

SOMTSEU ROAD

SOMTSEU ROAD

BRICKHILL ROAD

MOLYNEUX ROAD

SNELL PARADE

LOWER MARINE PARADE

N

Bay of Plenty Beach

❶

Amphitheatre

PAVILION TERR.

INDIAN OCEAN

Kingsmead Cricket Ground

STALWART SIMELANE (STANGER) STREET

OLD FORT ROAD

North Beach

GRESHAM PLACE

BRICKHILL ROAD

BAUMANN ROAD

MARINE PARADE

BOSCOMBE PLACE

❷

Rachel Finlayson Baths

Dairy Beach

International Convention Centre

ALIWAL

WALNUT ROAD

STREET

NORTH LANE

MORRISON

PRINCE ALFRED

JOHN MILNE ROAD

WEST LANE

HUNTER

EAST LANE

MILNE

LOWER MARINE PARADE

SEA VIEW

❸

Exhibition Centre

❹

SOUTH LANE

PINE

PALMER

MAHATMA GANDHI (POINT) ROAD

South Beach

Ⓒ
Ⓓ

PINE TERRACE

Ⓔ

FAREWELL

WEST

STALWART SIMELANE (STANGER) STREET

(COMMERCIAL) STREET

PINE

PALMER

WEST

PECK RD

TYZACK

GILLESPIE

MARINE PARADE

Natural Science Museum & Durban Art Gallery

Old Courthouse Museum

Shell House (Airport Shuttle arrivals & departures)

SMITH

TIMBER

MAZEPPA

ROY RD

GULL

FISHER

PICKERING

WINDER

ROCHESTER

HUTHFRFORD

CATO

CREEK

GILLGAN

ACUTT

ALBANY GROVE

ALIWAL

MENZ ROAD

CATO SQ

MILLS LANE

JOHNSON LANE

MNCADI AVENUE (VICTORIA EMBANKMENT)

BAY TERRACE

MAHATMA GANDHI (POINT) ROAD

PRINCE

SHEARER RD

MASONIC RD

Addington Hospital

OCEAN WAY

ERSKINE TERRACE

❽

BAT Centre

❾

QUAYSIDE ROAD

B a y

o f

N a t a l

SOUTH BEACH AVENUE

Ⓖ

Addington Beach & uShaka Marine World

❶❶

ACCOMMODATION

Banana Backpackers	E
Blue Waters	A
Formula 1	B
Garden Court – Marine Parade	C
Happy Hippo Backpackers Lodge	H
Protea Hotel Edward	D
The Royal Hotel	F
Silversands	G

The Point, uShaka Marine World, ❶❸,❶❹ & Ⓗ ▼

Much further afield lie dormitory towns for blacks who commute to work every day. Among these areas are the apartheid **ghettos** of KwaMashu and Inanda to the northwest. **Cato Manor**, the closest township to the city, provides an easily accessible vignette of South Africa's growing urban contradictions.

The centre

Standing at the heart of colonial Durban, **Francis Farewell Square** is hemmed in by the centre's two main thoroughfares, West Street and Smith Street. A sultry palm-fringed garden overlooked by some fine old buildings, the square marks the site where the British adventurers Francis Farewell and Henry Fynn set up Durban's first white encampment to trade ivory with the Zulus. Today, down-and-outs enjoy its lawns, dotted with statues of city fathers, while the yellows and blues of the **Cenotaph**, a marvellous Art Deco monument to the fallen of World War I, creates an eye-catching focus for the square. North of here at 160 Pine St are the remnants of the **Natal Great Railway Station**, built in 1894 and recycled a century later as shops and the Tourist Junction information centre. The city centre's main shopping mall, Workshop Mall, is just across the road from here on the corner of Dr A B Xuma and Aliwal streets.

City Hall and the Old Courthouse Museum

East of the Cenotaph, the imposing neo-Baroque **City Hall** is the monumental centrepiece of the area. Erected in 1910, it now houses the **Natural Science Museum** on its first floor (Mon–Sat 8.30am–4pm, Sun 11am–4pm; free), containing the usual stuffed animals and worth only a brief look, and the more interesting **Durban Art Gallery** on the second floor (Mon–Sat 8.30am–4pm, Sun 11am–2pm; free), which has a few Victorian paintings, but is most notable for its pioneering vision back in the 1970s in becoming the first gallery in the country to collect **black South African art**. One room in the gallery features an exhibition on the people after whom several of Durban's main streets have been renamed (see box, p.461), explaining their careers and cultural importance through words and photographs.

Entered from Aliwal Street, the **Old Courthouse Museum** (Mon–Sat 8.30am–4pm, Sun 11am–4pm; free) east of City Hall was Durban's first two-storey building, erected in 1866 in the Natal Veranda style, characterized by wide eaves to throw off heavy subtropical downpours. Housed here in a somewhat austere atmosphere is a reconstruction of Henry Francis Fynn's wattle-and-daub cottage, Durban's first European structure.

The Kwa Muhle Museum

The north side of the city centre is dominated by **Central Park**, a large green space with a lovely mosaic water fountain as its focus. On the northern perimeter of the park, the **Kwa Muhle Museum**, 130 Ordnance Rd (Mon–Sat 8.30am–4pm, Sun 11am–4.30pm; free) – also known as the Apartheid Museum – should not be missed if you have the slightest interest in understanding modern South Africa. Permanent exhibitions include one on the Durban System, which enabled the city council to finance the administration of African affairs without ever spending a penny of white ratepayers' money. It achieved this by granting itself a monopoly on the brewing of sorghum beer, which it sold through vast, African-only municipal beer halls. The resulting revenue was used to ensure that blacks lived in an "orderly" way. The exhibit also illustrates the Pass System, one of the most hated aspects of apartheid, through which constant tabs could be kept on Africans and their influx into the urban areas. Look out, too, for photographs of life in the single-sex, artificially tribalized worker hostels, which deliberately sowed divisions among blacks by creating separations and divisions, and so played its part in much of the current violence in South Africa.

Dr Yusuf Dadoo Street and around

West of the Kwa Muhle Museum, where **Dr Yusuf Dadoo Street** draws a north–south line across the city, the pace accelerates perceptibly, and you leave behind the formal city centre for the densely packed warren of shops and

▲ Victoria Street Market, Durban

living quarters of Durban's central **Indian district**. Post-1910 Union-style architecture is well preserved here and, along with minarets and steeples, punctuates the skyline with an eclectic roofscape. Down at street level, the rich cultural blend includes African street vendors selling herbs, fruit and trinkets outside the Indian general dealers and spice merchants. If the crowds feel too intimidating, you can always explore this area on one of the reasonably priced daily **walking tours** from Tourist Junction (see box, p.463).

On the corner of Dr Yusuf Dadoo and Queen streets stands the **Juma Musjid** and its gilt-domed minarets, completed in 1927. It's the largest mosque in the southern hemisphere, and the area's focal point, although Durban's Indian population is predominantly Hindu. You're welcome to enter the mosque, but make sure you leave your shoes at the door. The colonnaded verandas give way to the alley of the bazaar-like **Madressa Arcade** next door, heaving with Indian traders peddling kerosene lamps, tailor-made outfits and beads. The arcade emerges with a start into Cathedral Street, dominated by the **Emmanuel Cathedral**, built in 1902 in Gothic Revival style.

North across Queen Street, the **Victoria Street Market** is a bright building with purple minarets, where traders sell curios and spices with labels that include "mother-in-law exterminator". The hectic fish market downstairs can provide drama, particularly on Saturdays when the stallholders compete to sell their stocks before the Sunday close-down.

A little further west, African hawkers unable to afford official stalls gather on **Russell Street**, where they scrape an existence trading *umuthi* (traditional herbal medicines), used goods or anything that might raise a few bucks. West of Russell Street and jammed between the railway tracks to the west and the N3 into town on its northern side, **West Street Cemetery** is zoned according to religion, with many of the city's colonial big names buried here, such as Durban's first mayor, George Cato, and the Victorian documentary painter, Thomas Baines. In the Muslim section some tombstones are inscribed "*hagee*" or "*hafez*", the former indicating someone who has been to Mecca and the latter an individual who managed to memorize the entire Koran.

Warwick Triangle

In an Africanized *Bladerunner* setting west of Dr Yusuf Dadoo Street, concrete freeways run overhead chaotic roadways and minibus taxi ranks; here you'll find Durban's real urban heart of hawkers, shacks and *shebeens*. You'll need to be bold to explore the **Warwick Triangle**, which lies between Berea Road, Brook Street and Cannongate Road – walk with confidence, wear nothing easily snatched, and you should be fine.

The gateway to the triangle is across Brook Street – known until 1988 as Slaughterhouse Road, because butchers slaughtered livestock here – and then through the hectic Berea station concourse full of pumping music and hawkers and across the Market Road footbridge.

Durban's major fruit, vegetable and flower **market** lies between Warwick Avenue and Market Road, extending well beyond its walls in a dense mass of vendors. The shopping is frenetic; take your own basket and load up with the cheapest produce in town, from aubergines and jackfruit to betel nut for red-stained lips and a two-minute rush.

The harbour area

Margaret Mncadi Avenue (formerly Victoria Embankment), or the Esplanade, runs the length of Durban's busy harbour, the lifeblood of the city's economic power. At the western edge of the harbour, where Margaret Mncadi Avenue joins Maydon Wharf Road, is a photogenic complex of functional industrial architecture, most notable of which are the three dramatic sugar silos at the **Sugar Terminal**, 51 Maydon Wharf Rd. The terminal, whose design has been patented and used internationally, has become something of a tourist attraction; a tour (Mon–Thurs 8.30am, 10am, 11.30am, 2pm; R13) gives you one hour of sugary history and access to half a million tons of sugar (make bookings at the SA Sugar Association Tour Centre; ☎031 365 8153).

Margaret Mncadi Avenue and the streets around it were the prime residential areas during the city's early development in the nineteenth century, and working your way back east from Maydon Wharf Road there's a reminder of the city's colonial heritage at the **Old House Museum**, one block north of Margaret Mncadi Avenue at 31 St Andrews St (Mon–Sat 8.30am–4pm, Sun 11–4pm; free). Once the home of Sir John Robinson, who became Natal's first prime minister in 1893, the two rooms of this renovated settler house are crammed full of period furniture and numerous ticking clocks.

Continuing a little further east along Margaret Mncadi Avenue brings you to the **Yacht Mole**, a slender breakwater jutting into the bay and home to the Point and Royal Natal Yacht clubs. This is also the access point for the **BAT (Bartle Arts Trust) Centre** (Ⓦ www.batcentre.co.za), an industrial-chic arts development and community venue boasting a concert hall, practical visual art workshops, classes and exhibition galleries. The *Ocean's Eleven* restaurant upstairs (see p.479) provides a magnificent lookout for watching the passing harbour scene.

Back on the Esplanade, heading east towards the Stalwart Simelane (formerly Stanger) Street intersection, enter the Harbour at Port Entrance no. 3 and follow the signs to the **Ocean Terminal Building**, which harks back to the romantic days of sea travel and is one of Durban's architectural masterpieces. Although you can't enter the building, the view from outside it at night, looking back onto the city, is spectacular.

The beachfront

Durban's **beachfront**, a high-energy holiday strip just east of the centre, is South Africa's most developed seaside, one to avoid unless you enjoy unabashed kitsch and garish amusement parks. This six-kilometre stretch from the Umgeni River in the north to the Point in the south was traditionally called the **Golden Mile**, but it's becoming known as Mugger's Mile, which is why so many middle-class Gauteng families are breaking the habit of generations and deserting the beachfront for the safer (white, middle-class) sands north and south of Durban.

Addington Beach, the southernmost swimming strand, draws Durban families to its wide expanse of sand and lawns, and is a favourite spot for apprentice surfers.

Beachfront safety

With tourists venturing onto beaches wearing expensive watches and jewellery and carrying large wads of cash, Durban's beaches are notorious hunting grounds for sharks – not of the piscean variety. Although the police presence along the beachfront has been stepped up – a trend that looks likely to continue in the lead-up to the 2010 World Cup – **muggings** here are common: to reduce the risk, stay in a group, and don't go out alone at night, no matter how enticing the seafront seems on a balmy evening. **Street children** positively thrive on the rich pickings of Durban's beachfront: no matter how small they look, many are skilful pickpockets and accomplished bag-snatchers.

The big draw here – and the only really worthwhile attraction along the beachfront – is **uShaka Marine World**. This impressive water adventure wonderland is a tropical African theme park, with palm trees, fake rock formations and thatched *bomas*. The most appealing section is **uShaka Sea World** (daily 9am–5pm; R92), designed in and around a superb mock-up of a wrecked 1920s cargo ship. The main entrance leads you down to the darkened hull with its broken wood, battered engine room, ropes and sloping floors. The walls of the hull serve as windows into the "ocean" (actually a series of large tanks) where you can see turtles, pipe fish, octopus, sharks and a host of other marine life. The complex also includes a dolphin stadium and a seal pool, where you'll see daily shows (two or three a day depending on when you visit) featuring these creatures, as well as **uShaka Wet 'n Wild**, a series of pools and water slides you'll have to pay an extra R70 to use. The **uShaka Village Walk** development and **uShaka Beach** (the southern section of Addington beach) are open from 9am until late. The Village Walk has plenty of restaurants, making it a great (and safe) night-time venue: here you can catch jazz at *Moyo* restaurant (see p.480) or have a meal with the shark tank in view at the *Cargo Hold* (see p.478).

Just north of uShaka Marine World lies **South Beach**, the busiest beach in South Africa, which nets visitors with the start of the beachfront tourist tack. Further along Marine Parade, you'll find paddling pools, stepping stones, an aerial cableway and amusement rides. Next is **Dairy Beach**, so called because of the milking factory that once stood here; now regarded as one of the country's best surfing beaches, and home to the saltwater **Rachel Finlayson Baths** (Oct–April Mon–Fri 5.30am–8.30pm, Sat 6am–5pm; May–Sept daily 6am–5pm; R5), it's a good spot for sheltered swimming and sunbathing.

Dairy Beach adjoins **North Beach** and the adjacent **Bay of Plenty**, both of which host an international professional surfing contest held every July (see p.481). Between Snell Parade and the pedestrian walkway at the Bay of Plenty is the **Amphitheatre**, the venue for Sunday flea markets (see p.483). Just north of here, near the corner of Snell Parade and Old Fort Road, **Mini Town** is a scale replica of Durban's landmarks (daily 9.30am–4.30pm; Dec, Jan, July & Sept closes at 5pm; R15), great fun for kids; walkways lead you past hotels, beaches and the airport, giving you a bird's-eye view of the city. A kilometre further north, past **Battery Beach** (a good place for swimming), is the massive **Suncoast Casino**, a mock Art Deco entertainment complex with restaurants, gambling tables, eight cinemas and a pristine private beach (R10).

The Berea

High on a north–south ridge overlooking the city centre, the **Berea** is Durban's oldest and most desirable residential district, where mansions and apartment blocks enjoy airy views to the harbour and the sea. Its palmy avenues provide an alternative to the torrid city centre and beachfront for accommodation, eating and entertainment. The term Berea actually has two meanings locally; the suburban area immediately north and west of the city centre is called the Berea, though within this is a suburb known as the Berea, as well as suburbs such as Morningside and Musgrave.

Undulating **Ridge Road** cuts a six-kilometre axis through the Berea from the Umgeni River in the north to the University of KwaZulu-Natal. South of the N3, which passes through the Berea to the city, and east of Ridge Road, in Bulwer Road, the **Natal Society of Arts Gallery** (Tues–Sun 9am–5pm; free), or NSA, adjacent to Bulwer Park, provides a breezy venue for taking in thrice-weekly exhibitions by local artists. Designed for the local climate, the

1990s building is a mass of interlinked spaces, divided by a timber screen that forms a veranda. There's a good arts and crafts shop (see p.483) and a relaxing coffee shop (same hours as the gallery).

A little way northwest of the centre and east of Musgrave, Durban's **Botanic Gardens** (daily: mid-April to mid-Sept 7.30am–5.15pm; mid-Sept to mid-April 7.30am–5.45pm) were established in 1849. They're famous for their cycad collection, which includes *Encephalartos woodii*, one of the rarest specimens in the world. The gardens also boast cool paths, excellent picnic spots, a lovely tea house and a magnificent array of orchids. A notice board just inside the main entrance on St Thomas Road advertises forthcoming events, including regular KwaZulu-Natal Philharmonic Orchestra **concerts**.

Head several blocks north from here and west into Mariott Road, and you'll find another magnificent garden at **Muckleneuk** on the corner of Essenwood Road (Mon–Fri 8am–4pm or by appointment; tours are by appointment at 11am & 2pm and cost R20; ☎031 207 3432). The Cape Dutch-revival former homestead of sugar baron Sir Marshal Campbell, it's also Durban's premier museum, with one of the finest private collections of Africana in the country, including material relating to KwaZulu-Natal's ethnic heritage. The **Killie Campbell Africana Library and Museum** at 229 Mariott Rd (Mon–Fri 8am–4pm, Sat 9am–noon) is well known for its comprehensive collection of books, manuscripts and photographs, while the **William Campbell collections** (same times) comprise artworks and excellent examples of Cape Dutch furniture. Also here is the **Mashu Museum of Ethnology** (same times), consisting of a superb collection of Zulu crafts, including tools, weapons, beadwork and pottery.

Cato Manor

A short drive west of the city centre takes you through **Cato Manor**, offering a graphic cross section of Durban's twentieth-century history, where you can see a juxtaposition of African squatter camps, Hindu temples and vegetation mingling in the heart of the city's middle-class suburbs. A large area in a valley below the Berea, Cato Manor was named after Durban's first mayor, **George Cato**, who arrived here in 1839. During the first half of the last century, the district was home to much of Durban's Indian community, who built temples on its hills. They were later joined by Africans, who were forced into crowded slums because of the shortage of housing. In 1949, an incident in which an Indian trader assaulted a Zulu man flared up into Durban's worst **riot**, with thousands of Africans attacking Indian stores and houses, leaving 142 people dead.

Because Cato Manor was right in the middle of white suburbs, the apartheid government began enforcing the Group Areas Act in the 1960s, moving Africans north to KwaMashu and Indians south to Chatsworth, leaving a derelict wasteland guarded only by the handful of Hindu temples left standing. The vacuum was filled again in the late 1980s, when Africans pouring into Durban built the closely packed tin shacks that line Bellair Road, winding its way through Cato Manor's valley.

Along this interesting, but not altogether safe, drive (carjackers are a potential hazard), it's well worth stopping to visit the **Shree Ambalvanar Alayam Second River Hindu Temple**, a National Monument in Bellair Road (something you can safely do on a tour; see box, p.463). Leave the city centre on the M13, take the Brickfield Road exit and then turn left into the M10, which becomes Bellair Road; the temple is on the right if you're coming from town, just before the Edwin Swales freeway. The building is a 1947 reconstruction of the first Hindu temple in Africa, built in 1875 on the banks of the Umbilo River and

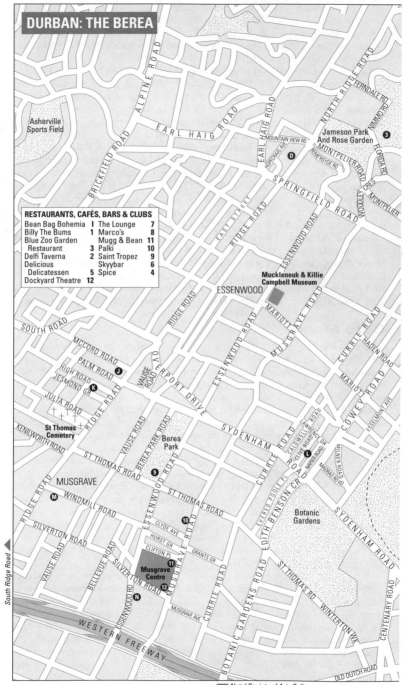

DURBAN: THE BEREA

RESTAURANTS, CAFÉS, BARS & CLUBS

Bean Bag Bohemia	**1**	The Lounge	**7**
Billy The Bums	**1**	Marco's	**8**
Blue Zoo Garden		Mugg & Bean	**11**
Restaurant	**3**	Palki	**10**
Delfi Taverna	**2**	Saint Tropez	**9**
Delicious		Skyybar	**6**
Delicatessen	**5**	Spice	**4**
Dockyard Theatre	**12**		

Asherville
Sports Field

Jameson Park
And Rose Garden

ALPINE ROAD

EARL HAIG ROAD

BRICKFIELD ROAD

EARL HAIG ROAD

NORTH RIDGE ROAD

FERNDALE RD

NIMMO RD

FLORIDA RD

MONTPELIER CRES

MONTPELIER ROAD

WOODSIDE

MONTPELIER

MOUNTAIN VIEW RD

HOPCRAIG AVE

BEMERSYDE RD

SPRINGFIELD ROAD

EAST STREET

RIDGE ROAD

ESSENWOOD ROAD

**Muckleneuk & Killie
Campbell Museum**

ESSENWOOD

MARIOTT ROAD

MUSGRAVE ROAD

CURRIE ROAD

HADEN ROAD

MARIOTT ROAD

COWEY ROAD

ESSELMONT AVE

SOUTH ROAD

MCCORD ROAD

PALM ROAD

HIGH ROAD

JESMOND GR

JULIA ROAD

RIDGE ROAD

VAUSE ROAD

DEVONPORT DRIVE

ESSENWOOD ROAD

SYDENHAM

CURRIE ROAD

LAWRENCE DR

CALDWELL ROAD

CLIVE ROAD

NAPIER ROAD

MADRAS ROAD

MILNER ROAD

St Thomas
Cemetery

KENILWORTH ROAD

ST THOMAS ROAD

VAUSE ROAD

BEREA PARK ROAD

Berea
Park

ST THOMAS ROAD

EVERED POOLE PL

EDITH BENSON CR

Botanic
Gardens

SYDENHAM ROAD

MUSGRAVE

WINDMILL ROAD

RIDGE ROAD

SILVERTON ROAD

VAUSE ROAD

ESSENWOOD ROAD

CLYDE AVE

HURST GR

GRANTS GR

ST THOMAS RD

WINTERTON WK

South Ridge Road

SILVERTON ROAD

BELLEVUE ROAD

CLIFTON PL

**Musgrave
Centre**

MUSGRAVE ROAD

MUSGRAVE AVE

CURRIE ROAD

BOTANIC GARDENS ROAD

CENTENARY ROAD

WESTERN FREEWAY

OLD DUTCH ROAD

▼ Natal Society of Arts Gallery

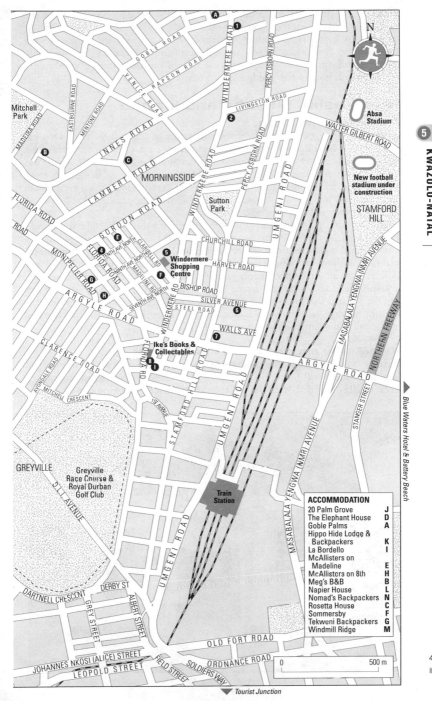

Absa Stadium

New football stadium under construction

STAMFORD HILL

Mitchell Park

MORNINGSIDE

Sutton Park

Windermere Shopping Centre

Ike's Books & Collectables

GREYVILLE

Greyville Race Course & Royal Durban Golf Club

Train Station

▶ Blue Waters Hotel & Battery Beach

ACCOMMODATION	
20 Palm Grove	J
The Elephant House	D
Goble Palms	A
Hippo Hide Lodge & Backpackers	K
La Bordello	I
McAllisters on Madeline	E
McAllisters on 8th	H
Meg's B&B	B
Napier House	L
Nomad's Backpackers	N
Rosetta House	C
Sommersby	F
Tekweni Backpackers	G
Windmill Ridge	M

0   500 m

▼ Tourist Junction

subsequently destroyed by floods. The beautifully carved entrance doors are originals salvaged from the flood, while the facade is adorned with a pantheon of wonderfully garish Hindu deities. Around Easter every year the temple hosts a **firewalking festival** in which unshod devotees walk across red-hot coals, emerging unscathed. Visitors are welcome to join the thousands of worshippers who come to honour the goddess Draudpadi.

KwaMashu, Shembe and Inanda

Even though they're not hard to reach with your own wheels, some quintessential Durban experiences rarely make it into the pages of tourist brochures. Driving, you can visit the place where Gandhi dreamed up passive resistance, witness the epic religious ceremonies of the Zulu-Christian Shembe sect and walk among the serene buildings of Inanda, a nineteenth-century seminary for Zulu girls. A word of **warning**: driving through some of the areas covered here carries a certain risk, and you're advised to go with someone familiar with the road and local customs or on an organized tour (see box, p.463).

Heading out of town towards the North Coast on the R102, take the Inanda Phoenix exit along the M25. As you leave the R102 you'll see the suburb of Duff's Road on the left; look up the hillside for Dookie Ramdaari's **Aeroplane House** and his son's **Ship House** a few metres away. An affluent Indian bus builder with a taste for the unconventional, Ramdaari was a voracious traveller, a passion reflected in his first home built in the form of a ship, sailing east out of Duff's Road Indian township. Poised for take-off, the Aeroplane House – his current abode – has wings, an undercarriage, a television room with row seats in the tail and a superb lounge in the cockpit.

KwaMashu and the Gandhi Settlement

Further on to Inanda, you'll pass the African township of **KwaMashu** on the left, established in the late 1950s to house residents of Cato Manor who had been forcibly resettled. It displays all the unimaginative planning typical of such

▲ Shree Ambalvanar Alayam Second River Hindu Temple, Cato Manor

low-cost housing schemes. The area is a sea of hills, vegetation and colour, which makes it tempting to romanticize the locality's poverty.

A well-signposted right turn off the M25 takes you to the **Gandhi Settlement** (daily 8.30am–5pm; donation expected). On the eastern edge of the vast Inanda squatter camp, it's the site of a self-help scheme established by Mohandas Gandhi soon after his arrival in Durban in 1903. It was from here that Gandhi began to forge his philosophy of passive resistance; in a sad irony, violence brought it to ruin in 1985 when squatters from the adjacent camp looted and razed the settlement. With the help of the Indian Government the settlement was rebuilt in time for its centenary celebration. A bronze bust of Gandhi now stands near the entrance to his house, **Sarvodaya** ("a place for the upliftment for all"), the building now a **museum** focusing on his time in South Africa and on Indian resistance to segregation.

Shembe

The M25 continues to **Ekupakumeni** ("the elated place"), where two "stars" laid in stone in the hilly landscape mark the spots where meteorites from the 1906 appearance of Halley's Comet struck the earth. This is also the site of the **Shembe settlement**, established by the Holy Church of Nazareth as a refuge for Africans dispossessed as a result of the Land Act of 1913. According to the founding history of the church, its prophet Isaya Shembe was "called" in 1910 to the summit of a mountain outside Durban, where he vowed before God to bring the Gospel to the Zulus. The church drew membership from rural people whose lives had been devastated by colonization and who were eager to embrace Christianity, but were unwilling to give up traditional customs. Shembe brought about a rich religious synthesis that rejected drinking, smoking and cults, while encouraging a work ethic that centred around crafts, giving rise to a sect that now has tens of thousands of adherents.

Continuing to the Inanda police station at the top of the hill, turn left to descend into the valley and cross the Umhlanga River bridge. At the next intersection, take the dirt road to the left, past the sports field, and turn left again to view **Ebuhleni**, where every July devotees of the Holy Church of Nazareth gather for a month of worship. Ignoring the dirt road turn-off, head straight on to reach the Inanda Dam. The deep gorge to your left is the **Inanda Falls**, where the Shembe have baptismal ceremonies, which visitors are welcome to attend.

The settlement resembles an emerging medieval city, replete with winding pathways negotiating the narrow spaces between buildings. Many homes are owned by believers who come to Ebuhleni only at festival times, timeshare Zulu-style. On these occasions, the men and women live on different sides of the village, and the unmarried maidens live in a separate enclosure. At the entrance gates to the settlement, rows of tables display what appear to be religious knick-knacks for sale to tourists, but which are actually religious artefacts revered by the converted of Shembe. Among the items are holographic images of Isaya Shembe, and key rings with religious icons embedded in perspex. A range of traditional outfits are sold in the village, from men's ceremonial skirts to magnificent women's headdresses.

The Inanda Seminary

It's strongly recommended that you visit Inanda in the company of a guide who knows the area well. From Ebuhleni, make your way back to the M25, and continue to the **Inanda Seminary** along a well-indicated route. The seminary, whose dignified old buildings give it an air of serenity, was established in 1869 by Daniel Lindley, an American missionary and pastor of the Voortrekkers. It's also the oldest secondary school for African girls in southern Africa, and played a pioneering role in the liberation of Zulu women. Staff members have always been drawn from all racial groups, which is why the school received no funding from the apartheid educational authorities after 1957. The story of Inanda between 1869 and 1969 is recounted in a book by Agnes Wood, *Shine Where You Are*. To return to Durban, simply turn tail and head east along the M25.

Eating

Eating out is a favourite pastime in Durban, and although all types of cooking are found here, **Indian** food is what the city excels at – hardly surprising for a place with one of the largest Indian populations outside Asia. The Indian takeaways of the city centre are good places to try *bunny chow* – Durban's big contribution to the national fast-food scene – and the not-dissimilar *rotis* (Indian bread) stuffed with curries. *Shisanyama* outlets at the African markets and around the taxi ranks offer hunks of meat cooked over an open fire. For a more refined dining experience, the **Berea** has the city's best and most diverse range of restaurants – **closing time** for most is at around 10.30pm.

City centre

Inexpensive Indian **takeaways** – all open very early and usually shut by 5pm – abound in this part of Durban. *Little Gujarat* at 107 Prince Edward St and *Victory Lounge* on the corner of Dr Yusuf Dadoo and Victoria streets are both noted for their *bunny chow; Victory Lounge* is also recommended for its traditional sweetmeats. Otherwise, the *Oriental* takeaway at the Workshop Mall does a hotchpotch of fare – delicious Lebanese *shawarmas*, plus pies and curries. If you're hankering for something much slicker in the heart of town, head to the *Ulundi* restaurant at *The Royal Hotel* (see p.464), where you'll be served light *thali* curry dishes (around R20 each; order a minimum of three) in a stylish and contemporary black-and-white dining room.

Beachfront

Restaurants

Cargo Hold uShaka Marine World. Italian-, Mexican-, North African- and Asian-influenced dishes (mains R80–100) are available here, though the best thing about this restaurant is its location next to the shark tank. Daily noon–3pm & 6–10pm.
Jewel of India *Southern Sun Elangeni*, 63 Snell Parade ☏ 031 362 1324. A plush North Indian venue with authentic Eastern decor. The food is varied and includes a superb list of vegetarian offerings. Most curries cost R40–60. Daily noon–3pm & 6–10.30pm.
Joe Cool's 137 Lower Marine Parade. A trendy eating place serving steaks, fish and pizza (generally R50–80) and pub right on the beach, with an outside terrace overlooking the sea and a rock 'n' roll band every Sun evening. Daily 10am–late.

The harbour area

Restaurants

Charlie Crofts Wharfside Diner 18 Boatsman Rd, Wilson's Wharf, west of the Yacht Mole ☏ 031 307 2935. Boasting one of the best waterfront settings in Durban, this place does delicious seafood and meat dishes at reasonable prices. The spicy calamari grill is first-class, as is the *eisbein*. Daily 11am–10pm.
New Café Fish Yacht Mole, Margaret Mncadi Ave ☏ 031 305 5062. A beautiful restaurant looking out

onto the harbour, which specializes in great seafood (mains R60–80). Ordering the catch of the day is *de rigueur*. Daily lunch & dinner.

Ocean's Eleven BAT Arts Centre, Small Craft Market, Margaret Mncadi Ave. This lively venue dishes up modern African fusion food like creamed spiced *samp* (coarse maizemeal) and beans, and ox tripe with steamed Zulu bread, all in the R40–50 range. Occasional live music and a great terrace overlooking the harbour add to the appeal.

A good place to meet the locals. Daily 10am–midnight.

Roma Revolving Restaurant John Ross House, Margaret Mncadi Ave ☎031 337 6707. No visitor to Durban should miss the view from the *Roma* as it revolves above the city. The international menu includes tasty mussel starters and Italian specialities, like gnocchi and veal dishes. You pay for the view as much as for the food; count on around R80 for main courses. Mon–Sat lunch & dinner.

The Berea

Restaurants

Bean Bag Bohemia 18 Windermere Rd, Morningside ☎031 309 6019. A trendy, gay-friendly eating place in a two-storey house, with an informal bar/bistro downstairs and a more formal restaurant above. Expect mid-priced fusion food and plenty of people-watching. The restaurant hosts art exhibitions and changes its menu to suit the art being shown. Mon–Sat till 1am, Sun till midnight.

Blue Zoo Garden Restaurant 6 Nimmo Rd, Morningside. A varied and unusual menu features delicious Moroccan chicken, lamb shank in a port wine sauce, steaks, fish, and salads with mango and chilli dressings. Beautifully located in Mitchell Park and great for kids; mains R50–80. Tues–Sat lunch & dinner, Sun & Mon lunch only.

Delfi Taverna 386 Windermere Rd, Morningside ☎031 312 7032. This cosy restaurant boasts excellent, authentic Greek dishes (mains around R40) and a wonderfully congenial atmosphere created by friendly staff and plenty of regular customers – always a good sign. Wed–Mon lunch & dinner.

Marco's 45 Windermere Rd, Morningside ☎031 303 3078. A classy, moderately priced trattoria, with fresh pasta made daily and delectable pizzas. Mon–Fri lunch & dinner, Sat dinner only.

Palki 225 Musgrave Rd, Musgrave ☎031 201 0019. The South African representative of a chain of restaurants based in the East, this has mouthwatering, authentic North and South Indian foods, created by chefs shipped in from other branches. Vegetarians are well catered for and prices decent. Daily lunch & dinner.

Spice 200 Florida Rd, Morningside ☎031 303 6375. This new Florida Road eatery already counts the likes of Bill Gates and Bill Clinton among its patrons. The excellent food is a combination of spicy curries (more aromatic than blisteringly hot) and inventive dishes such as roast duck with Amarula. Mains from R90. Tues–Sat lunch & dinner, Sun lunch only.

Cafés

Delicious Delicatessen and Coffee Shop Windermere Shopping Centre, Windermere Rd, Morningside. Delicious, healthy pasta dishes such as sweet Thai chilli, as well as salads, sandwiches and excellent coffees. Takeaways available. Mon–Fri 6.30am–6pm, Sat 6.30am–3pm, Sun 9am–1pm.

Mugg & Bean Musgrave Centre, Musgrave. A good place for endless coffee refills, inexpensive (and copious) breakfasts and light lunches, cakes and muffins. Daily 8am–10pm.

Saint Tropez Corner of Essenwood and St Thomas rds ☎031 201 9176. Housed in a former power station, this fashionable establishment has some outdoor seating and does salads, ciabatta sandwiches, pasta and a good selection of cakes. Daily 7am–11pm.

Drinking, nightlife and entertainment

Durban has a healthy nightlife scene, with a decent number of bars, clubs and music venues. For entertainment and nightlife **listings**, the *Mercury* is the better of Durban's two English-language dailies, while the *Sunday Tribune* has a thorough and comprehensive section on forthcoming events in its *SM* magazine. Durban Africa publishes a monthly events brochure available from tourist offices. The Johannesburg-based weekly *Mail & Guardian* also covers Durban nightlife in its *What's On* supplement.

Durban's **gay scene** is fairly well developed, although nothing like what you'll find in Cape Town. Among the smattering of gay or gay-friendly nightspots, the *Bean Bag Bohemia* bar-restaurant (see p.479) and *The Lounge*, 226 Stamford Hill Rd, Morningside, are two popular meeting places. For more venues, check out *The Essential Gay Guide to Durban*, available at Tourist Junction.

Bars and clubs

Billy The Bums 504 Windermere Rd, Morningside. Acrobatic barmen juggle bottles while mixing highly imaginative cocktails at this popular singles' watering hole, which also does good food. Mon–Sat noon–late.

Cool Runnings 49 Milne St, near the beachfront. An intimate, laid-back and non-threatening rasta/reggae hangout with a pool table and cheap Caribbean food. Daily noon–4am.

Skyybar 25 Silver Ave, Morningside. This flashy club on the fourth floor has a fabulous outdoor deck with views of the city, an emphasis on house music and a largely middle-class black crowd. Fri & Sat 8pm–4am; R50.

Tilt 11 Walnut Rd, opposite the *Hilton*, city centre. Central nightspot where you'll hear funky R&B and contemporary music in a sophisticated, but relaxed, atmosphere. Fri & Sat 9pm–7am; R50.

Victoria Bar Mahatma Gandhi Rd, the Point. A down-to-earth and highly popular Portuguese venue, good for boozing and watching sport on TV. *Catembe* (cola and wine) is a house speciality, as is the excellent prawn curry and *peri-peri* chicken. Mon–Thurs 10am–10pm, Fri–Sun 10am–1am.

Live music

You'll find plenty of live **indie music** on offer in Durban, much of it derivative of European or North American trends. More interesting, but less accessible, are some of the **Zulu forms** such as *iscathamiya* and *maskanda*. On the **jazz** scene, the city's most indigenous offering is a spicy combination of American mixed with township jazz and Zulu forms. The BAT Centre, next to the harbour at 42 Maritime Place (☎031 332 0451), is your best bet for live **concerts**; alternatively, *Moyo* restaurant at uShaka Marine World (☎031 332 0606) hosts a jazz band on Fridays and Saturdays at 8pm, while long-established restaurant *The Rainbow*, at 23 Stanfield Lane in Pinetown, northwest of Durban (☎031 702 9161), offers monthly Sunday-lunchtime performances ranging from Afro-fusion to jazz, and more regular Saturday sessions by up-and-coming bands.

The best place to hear **classical concerts** by the KwaZulu-Natal Philharmonic is at a sundowner concert held in the Botanical Gardens or the Kingsmead Cricket Grounds. Check for listings and adverts in the press, or on the notice board in the gardens.

Theatre and cinema

There are two major **theatres** in town: the Playhouse Drama Theatre, a mock-Tudor building at 231 Smith St (☎031 369 9555) that tends to host middle-of-the-road productions, but also sees performances by the resident progressive Playhouse Dance Company; and the Elizabeth Sneddon Theatre at the University of KwaZulu-Natal on South Ridge Road (☎031 260 2296), a modern venue for university and visiting productions. The Dockyard Theatre, at the Musgrave Centre on Musgrave Road (☎031 201 9147), puts together good-quality musicals with dinner served an hour and a half before the show begins (shows: Thurs–Sat at 8pm, Sun at 6pm). The Catalina Theatre, Wilson's Wharf (☎031 305 6889), is another supper theatre club, with performances by local actors.

The best and most convenient **cinemas** are the multiscreen complexes at the Musgrave Centre, The Workshop Mall in the city centre and the Suncoast Casino on the beachfront. The only place to see art-house movies is 15km north of town at the Gateway mall (see p.487).

Outdoor activities and spectator sports

Given Durban's seafront location, **watersports** are extremely popular, none more so than **surfing**. Night surfing competitions draw enormous crowds, as does the annual Mr Price Pro (formerly the Gunston 500), which, after the Rip Curl Pro at Bells Beach, Australia, is the world's longest-running professional surfing competition, and is held in Durban every July. The favourite spot for surfers is **North Beach**, while a good place to pick up gear is the Safari Surf Shop, 43 Brickhill Rd (☎031 337 2176), where Spider Murphy, South Africa's top board-shaper, will custom-build a world-class board for much less than a comparable order would cost in Europe or North America. Beach & Bush Adventures, 281 Florida Rd, Morningside (☎031 313 3333, ⓦwww.beachandbush.co.za), offers **surfing lessons** with experienced instructors (R150 per hour, plus R50 for board rental).

Scuba diving is an obvious and pleasurable activity in KwaZulu-Natal's subtropical waters, but is somewhat limited immediately around Durban, where the best diving sites are Vetches Pier, at the southern tip of the beachfront, and Blood Reef at the tip of the Bluff (opposite the Point). Scuba diving **courses** can be arranged through Underwater World, 251 Point Rd (☎031 332 5820); a full six-day internationally recognized NAUI or PADI course costs R1850, including use of the main gear you'll need.

An outfit called 180 Degrees Adventures (☎031 566 4955, ⓦwww.180.co.za) offers **ocean kayaking** (1hr; R150), where there's a good chance you'll see **dolphins**; the same operator also organizes dolphin-spotting boat excursions led by a knowledgeable skipper (1hr; R175).

Bird-watching

Bird-watching, a major activity in the green fringes of the city, is being aided by the Durban Metropolitan Open Space System (DMOSS), a project linking all the city parks via narrow green corridors. Promising spots include the Manor Gardens area; the Botanic Gardens; the Berea; Burman Bush, to the north of the city; Pigeon Valley, below the University of KwaZulu-Natal; the Umgeni River Mouth; Virginia Bush, on the road to Umhlanga Rocks; and the Hawaan Forest in Umhlanga, where the spotted thrush and green coucal have been seen.

Worth a visit is the **Umgeni River Bird Park**, 490 Riverside Rd, Durban North (daily 9am–5pm; R25; ⓦwww.umgeniriverbirdpark.co.za), which has a fantastic free-flight bird show (daily 11am & 2pm), with spectacular specimens as well as a vast collection of indigenous and exotic birds, including flamingos, finches, magpies and macaws.

Golf

Golf is a popular and rewarding activity in Durban. Enclosed within the tracks of the Greyville Race Course (see p.482), the Royal Durban Golf Club (☎031 309 1373; green fees R260 for eighteen holes) is notable for its unusual setting, while the Durban Country Club on Walter Gilbert Road (☎031 313 1777; green fees R425 for eighteen holes) is considered by many to be the finest course in South Africa.

Spectator sports

Not surprisingly for a city with such a British heritage, cricket and horse racing are high on the agenda when it comes to **spectator sports**. The Kingsmead Cricket Ground in the centre (☎031 335 4200) is the principal venue for local and international **cricket matches** and is home to the provincial cricket team. The **horse racing** season runs from May to August and centres around the Greyville Race Course, Avondale Road, Greyville (☎031 314 1500). The annual Vodacom Durban July (🌐www.durbanjuly .info), which, as the name suggests, takes place during July, is South Africa's premier horse-racing event, drawing bets from across the length and breadth of the country and wildly exhibitionist fashions in the spectator boxes. You'll also have plenty of opportunity to watch **rugby** in season at Absa Stadium, Walter Gilbert Road, Stamford Hill (☎031 308 8400), home to the local Sharks. The new football stadium being built next to the Absa Stadium will host matches during the 2010 World Cup.

Shopping

As one of South Africa's major cities, Durban is a good centre to pick up general supplies and local books and records. But it's for **crafts and curios** that it scores particularly highly, with a dazzling range of handmade Zulu goods (see box below). The best places to browse for crafts are in the downtown markets, the weekend flea markets and the specialist shops around the city.

Durban is littered with shopping **malls** of varying sizes, the two largest being the central Workshop Mall (see p.468) and the more upmarket Musgrave Centre in Musgrave.

Books and music

Adams & Co 341 West St, city centre 🌐www .adamsbooks.co.za. Durban's oldest bookshop has an excellent selection of books on the history of Durban and KwaZulu-Natal. There's also a branch at the Musgrave Centre. Mon–Fri 8am–5pm, Sat 8am–1pm.

Exclusive Books Lower Level, Pavilion Shopping Centre, Westville. Flashy general bookshop where browsers pore over coffee-table books. Mon–Sat 9am–6pm, Sun 9am–5pm.

Ike's Books & Collectables 48a Florida Rd, Morningside. A fascinating secondhand bookshop

---

Zulu crafts and curios

Durban's huge range of galleries, craft shops and markets makes it one of the best centres in the country to pick up **Zulu crafts**. Traditional works include functional items such as woven beer strainers and grass brooms, and basketry that can be extremely beautiful. Other traditional items are beadwork, pottery and Zulu regalia, of which *assegais* (spears), shields, leather kilts and drums are a few examples. However, the availability of cheap plastic crockery and enamelware has significantly eroded the production of traditional ceramics and woven containers for domestic use. Cheap facsimiles of these personal household items are now churned out for sale to curio hunters who are indifferent to the authenticity or quality of what they are buying.

Fortunately, the news isn't all bad. Although urbanization has stifled the production of much traditional craft, it has thrown up **creative adaptations**: the use of new materials, or new ways of using old materials. Among these are beautifully decorated black-and-white sandals made from recycled rubber tyres, wildly colourful baskets woven from telephone wire and *sjamboks* (whips) decorated with bright insulation tape. On the more frivolous side, there's a whole genre of affordable curios that break away from stereotypical tribal woodcarvings and masks, and marry industrial materials with rural life or rural materials with industrial life. Attractive tin boxes made from flattened oil cans, chickens constructed from sheet plastic, and aircraft and little 4WD vehicles carved from wood are some of the results.

with an interesting range of items covering KwaZulu-Natal's history and the fauna and flora of the area. Speciality areas include Africana and the Boer War, travel and exploration, and left-wing classics. Mon–Fri 10am–5pm, Sat 9am–2pm.
Look and Listen Lower Level, Pavilion Shopping Centre, Westville. Well-stocked music shop offering a comprehensive range of indigenous music from the whole continent, including local favourites such as Ladysmith Black Mambazo and Hugh Masekela. Mon–Sat 9am–6pm, Sun 9am–5pm.

Crafts and curios

African Art Centre 94 Florida Rd, Morningside ℡031 304 3804, Ⓦwww.afriart.org.za. A gallery and shop where many rural artists sell their work, well worth visiting for its traditional and modern Zulu and Xhosa beadwork, beaded dolls, wire sculptures, woodcuts and tapestries. Mon–Fri 8.30am–5pm, Sat 9am–3m.
The BAT Shop The BAT Centre, off Margaret Mncadi Ave. A bright and colourful venue where mainly contemporary pieces, including some

masterful wirework and attractive grass baskets, are sold. Mon–Fri 9am–4.30pm, Sat & Sun 10am–4pm.
NSA Gallery Shop NSA Gallery, Bulwer Rd, Berea ℡031 202 3686. This menagerie of contemporary hand-crafted goods includes a wonderful selection of functional art, including pewter cutlery, etchings and paintings.

Markets

Amphitheatre Fleamarket Snell Parade, beachfront. Crafts and beadwork sold both by local traders and by merchants from as far afield as Zimbabwe, Malawi and Kenya. Sun 9am–4pm.
Essenwood Craft Market Berea Park, Essenwood Rd, Musgrave. Upmarket stalls in a beautiful setting. Sat 9am–2pm.
South Plaza Fleamarket Durban Exhibition Centre, Walnut Rd, city centre. This is the largest flea market in town, where you'll find anything from handmade leather shoes to didgeridoos. Mon–Sat 8am–4pm, Sun 7.30am–5pm.

Listings

Airlines British Airways ℡031 450 7000; Kulula. com ℡861 585 852; SA Airlink ℡031 250 1111; South African Airways ℡031 250 1111.
Camera repairs Camera Clinic, Shop 4, Standard Bank Centre, 135 Musgrave Rd, Musgrave ℡031 202 5396.
Car parks The most convenient and central are those at Pine Arcade, at the west end of Pine Street, and in the Workshop Mall.
Car rental Avis ℡0861 021 111; Budget ℡0861 016 622; Europcar ℡031 469 0667; Hertz ℡031 452 1500; Imperial ℡0861 131 000; Tempest ℡031 368 5231; and Windermere ℡031 312 0339.
Consulates Canada, 27 Cypress Ave, Morningside ℡031 303 9695; Germany, 2 Devonshire Place, Smith St, city centre ℡031 305 5677; UK, 124 Davenport Rd, Glenwood ℡031 202 6823; USA, Old Mutual Centre, 31st floor, 303 West St, city centre ℡031 305 7600.
Currency exchange The First National Bank bureau de change at 306 West St, city centre, will cash Visa traveller's cheques without commission. American Express, 151 Musgrave Rd, Musgrave (Mon–Fri 8.30am–4.30pm, Sat 8.30am–noon; ℡031 202 8736) replaces lost cheques and changes money.
Emergencies AA ℡031 201 5244. See also p.75.

Hospitals and medical centres The main state hospital is the Addington, Erskine Terrace, South Beach (℡031 327 2000), which offers a 24-hr emergency ward. A better alternative is Entabeni Private Hospital, 148 South Ridge Rd, Berea (℡031 204 1300), which has a casualty unit and can also treat minor conditions, but where you'll have to pay a deposit on admission and settle up before leaving town. A convenient option, open 24hr, is South Beach Medical Centre, Rutherford St (℡031 332 3101), which has a pharmacy, doctors, an optician, a dentist, a physiotherapist, as well as aromatherapy, reflexology and homeopathy. Travel Doctor at 45 Ordnance Rd, International Convention Centre (℡031 360 1122, Ⓦwww.traveldoctor .co.za) is a clinic offering information and advice on local and international destinations, as well as on malaria and the necessary jabs for venturing into African countries to the north.
Internet access If you're staying in the Berea, both the Musgrave and Windermere centres have Internet cafés, although rates are much cheaper at the numerous Internet cafés in the city centre.
Laundries Convenient for the Berea are Musgrave Laundromat, 2nd Level, Musgrave Centre, and Econ-O-Wash, ground floor, Berea Centre, Berea Rd. South Beach Wash-Tub, 428 Point Rd, is located on the beachfront.

Left luggage Durban station has inexpensive left-luggage facilities on the first floor (Mon & Wed–Fri 6am–6pm, Tues 6am–4pm, Sat 6am–noon).

Pharmacies Sparkport, corner of Smith and Broad sts (☎031 304 9767; Mon–Sat 7.30am–9.30pm, Sun 9am–9pm), has a range of specialist treatments and all pharmaceutical travel requirements, and there's a doctor next door. Daynite Pharmacy, corner of West St and Mahatma Gandhi Rd (☎031 368 3666; Mon–Thurs 7.30am–10.30pm, Fri–Sun 7.30am–11.30pm), offers free deliveries if you order before noon.

Post The main post office, on the corner of Gardiner and West sts, has a poste restante and enquiry desk (Mon–Fri 8am–5pm, Sat 8am–1pm).

Swimming Durban's largest pool is the heated King's Park Olympic Swimming Pool on Masabalala Yengwa Ave, between Argyle and Battery Beach rds in Stamford Hill (☎031 312 0404). Convenient for the Berea are Sutton Park Baths, Stamford Hill Rd (☎031 303 1823), while the seawater Rachel Finlayson Baths, Lower Marine Parade (☎031 337 2721), are handy if you're staying near the beachfront.

Around Durban

If you're looking for quieter beaches out of the city, the **North** or **South coasts** around Durban make an obvious and easy day-trip or weekend jaunt. The coasts around Durban, with easy access to Johannesburg, the warmest waters in the country and a decidedly tropical feel, have primarily been developed for white South African families on holiday, and can seem rather bland in a country with so many spectacular landscapes. Having said that, there are kilometres of uncongested sandy beaches backed by wild banana trees, and the chance to spot dolphins, especially along the North Coast. In **March 2007** a cut-off low caused very high seas along the KwaZulu-Natal coastline. Seven-metre-high waves were recorded in some areas and considerable infrastructural damage was caused in Durban and other coastal resorts. Although Durban has recovered sufficiently for any damage to be barely noticeable, the beach areas in some of the other badly hit places, such as Amanzimtoti and parts of the Dolphin Coast, are still in a bad state of repair.

The South Coast draws diving enthusiasts to **Aliwal Shoal**, one of the country's top dive spots near Umkomaas, and is also notable for two nature reserves: **Oribi Gorge**, where you can try out some adventure sports in the gorge; and **Umtamvuna**, which offers day-walks along the Umtamvuna River. Unless you're travelling to or from the Eastern Cape, the North Coast is preferable to the South Coast – it's a lot less built-up and tacky. **Umhlanga Rocks**, an upmarket resort less than half an hour's drive from Durban, offers beach walks as well as great places to have a drink or meal.

Northwest from Durban is **Pietermaritzburg**, the provincial capital, with an excellent art gallery and some interesting red-brick Victorian architecture plus a vibrant mix of Zulu and Indian culture. Pietermaritzburg can be combined with the all-time favourite day-trip out of Durban, the scenic **Valley of a Thousand Hills**. Beyond Pietermaritzburg, and definitely more of a weekend stay than a day-trip, are the KwaZulu-Natal **Midlands**, with appealing scenery in the Ukhahlamba Drakensberg foothills, trout fishing, numerous craft shops, and a number of hotels, guesthouses and cottages catering especially for the weekend trade.

The South Coast

The South Coast, the 160-kilometre seaboard from Durban to Port Edward on the Eastern Cape border, is a ribbon of seaside suburbs linked for most of its length by the **N2** and **R102** roads, running side by side. Thousands of upcountry families have built holiday homes here along the closest stretch of sand to Johannesburg, and although in wilderness terms the area is unexciting, it does have some lovely beaches and ample accommodation. In the winter months it's much warmer and sunnier along this stretch than on any of the beaches between here and Cape Town. Away from the sea, the land is very hilly and green, dotted with sugar-cane fields, banana plantations and palm and pecan nut trees. Note that many beaches shelve steeply into the powerful surf, so only swim where it's indicated as safe.

Margate, 133km from Durban, is the transport and holiday hub of the area, with plenty of resorts lying to the east and west of it. The highlight, however, is **Oribi Gorge Nature Reserve**, just 21km inland from Port Shepstone (the South Coast's grim industrial and administrative centre), which has lovely forest hikes, breathtaking views and good-value accommodation.

Transport from Durban and Johannesburg to the South Coast is good. There are five direct **flights** a week from Johannesburg on SA Airlink (☎031 250 1111) to Margate airport (☎039 312 0560). Margate Mini Coach, Gird Mowat Building, Marine Drive, Margate (☎039 312 1406), has a daily **bus** service from Durban station (Greyhound terminal) via Durban's *Royal Hotel*, Durban airport (domestic arrivals), Amanzimtoti (prebooked only), Hibberdene (prebooked only), Hibberdene (Super Tube), Port Shepstone (LSC Motors) and Margate (Dennisons Funworld). The **Baz Bus** between Port Elizabeth and Durban pulls in at major South Coast resorts, although you can ask to be put off at intermediate destinations. **Driving**, head for the N2, which runs south from Durban as far as Port Shepstone, before heading inland to Kokstad. From Port Shepstone to Southbroom, the South Coast Toll Road is even faster and less traffic-clogged.

Aliwal Shoal

The resorts that line the first 50km of coastline south of Durban feel more like beachside suburbs than towns in their own right. Some, such as **Amanzimtoti**, 27km south of Durban, were badly affected by the high seas that ravaged parts of the KwaZulu-Natal coastline in March 2007 (see opposite) and have yet to fully recover. For diving enthusiasts, however, the faded town of **UMKOMAAS**, 20km further down the coast from Amanzimtoti, is the perfect point to set out for **Aliwal Shoal**, a scattered reef quite close to the shore and one of southern

---

The sardine run

The South Coast is witness to the extraordinary annual migration of millions of **sardines**, moving northwards along the coast in massive shoals. Around June or July, the shoals leave their feeding ground off the Southern Cape coast, and move up the coast towards Mozambique. They are followed by about 23,000 dolphins, 100,000 Cape gannets and thousands of sharks and game fish, attracting fishermen from all over the province to join in the jamboree. The shoals appear as dark patches of turbulence in the water, and when they are cornered and driven ashore by game fish, hundreds of people rush into the water either to scoop them out with their hands or to net them. For updates on shoal co-ordinates and other information of use for sardine-spotting, call the Sardine Hotline on ☎082 284 9495.

Africa's top **dive sites**. Rewards for experienced divers include sightings of whale sharks, ragged-tooth sharks, potato bass, manta rays and eels, as well as shoals of tropical fish, corals and anemones; enthusiasts can also go wreck-diving to three stunning sites. The ideal time to dive is between June and October, when visibility is at its best.

Meridian Dive Centre (☎039 973 2813, ⓦwww.scubadivesouthafrica.co.za) runs trips to Aliwal Shoal (R190, kit R185), while *Agulhas House* in the town centre (☎039 973 1640, ⓦwww.agulhashouse.com; ❸) offers B&B **accommodation** in en-suite rooms with fridges and private entrances. Amatikulu Tours (☎039 973 2534, ⓦwww.aliwalshoal.com) offers a PADI-certified four-day Open Water diving course for R1950 (includes all equipment).

South towards Oribi Gorge Nature Reserve

Continuing south, one resort after another follows the shoreline. **SCOTTBURGH**, 9km south of Umkomaas, is one of the more appealing because of its sheltered, lawn-covered beach fringes. The *Cutty Sark* on Beachfront Road (☎039 976 1230, ⓦwww.cuttysark.co.za; ❹) has rather tired, old-fashioned rooms, though discounts are available off-season. The stretch between Scottburgh and Port Shepstone is an obvious stopping point for backpackers, with the Baz Bus calling at a couple of backpacker lodges around here: in **Umzumbe** – turn off the N2 at Hibberdene and continue south along the R102 for a couple of kilometres – there's the friendly and laid-back *Mantis and Moon Backpackers*, 7/178 Station Rd (☎039 648 6256, ⓦwww.mantisandmoon.net; dorms ❶ rooms ❷); while some 15km further south along the R102 in **Umtentweni**, *The Spot Backpackers*, 23 Ambleside Rd (☎039 695 1319, ⓦwww.spotbackpackers.com; dorms and rooms ❶), is on the beach and also offers camping.

Oribi Gorge Nature Reserve

The South Coast's most compelling attraction is KZN Wildlife's **Oribi Gorge Nature Reserve** (daily 8am–4.30pm; ☎039 679 1644; R10), about 21km inland from Port Shepstone and signposted off the N2. A highly scenic area with cliffs rising from vast chasms and forest, it's traversed by the fast-flowing Umzimkulu and Umzimkulwana rivers. There are numerous idyllic picnic spots on the riverbanks (though avoid swimming here, as bilharzia parasites are present in the water) and waymarked **hikes** ranging from thirty-minute to day-long excursions, leading to dizzying lookout points or through the forest. A fine one-hour **walk** starts from the Umzimkulu car park and picnic site, crosses the river and heads immediately up some steps into the forest. You can hear the river through the dense vegetation, but you'll only see it when it opens out quite dramatically to reveal **Samango Falls** and a perfect little rock-bounded sandy beach.

Wildlife in the reserve includes bushbuck, common reedbuck, blue and grey duiker, but not oribi, which have left for the succulent shoots of the surrounding sugar-cane plantations. You're more likely to hear than to see the shy samango monkeys, hiding in the high canopy of the forest, and although leopards are present it's probable that they'll see you before you catch sight of them.

There are a few adventure activities that you can do in the reserve, all run by Wild 5 (☎039 687 0253 or 082 337 3746, ⓦwww.oribigorge.co.za), who operate from the *Oribi Gorge Hotel* (see opposite). There's an **abseil** (R210) with a tough half-hour walk out of the gorge afterwards; a **gorge swing** that requires you to leap off the top of the Lehrs Falls (R320); a Flying Fox gorge **slide** (R180), erected 160m above the gorge floor; plus horse-riding and **rafting** trips down the Umzimkulu River. The nicest **accommodation** is in the KZN Wildlife huts (❶) in the **restcamp** at the head of the Umzimkulwana Gorge, peering into the chasm of Oribi Gorge itself. There's a swimming pool here, and all crockery, cutlery and bedding is provided. Alternatively, you can stay in the colonial-style *Oribi Gorge Hotel* (☎039 687 0253, ⓦwww.oribigorge.co.za; ❻) some 16km from the restcamp, off the Oribi Flats road, which has spectacular views, including the famous overhanging rock and offers spacious rooms, meals to suit most budgets and a pleasant outdoor tea area.

The Hibiscus Coast

The 44km of coast from Port Shepstone to Port Edward has been dubbed the **Hibiscus Coast** because of its luscious, bright gardens, luxury suburbs, beachside developments and attractive caravan parks. It's also known as the **Golf Coast**: there are nine top courses on this short stretch of coastline, and many people come specifically for its golfing opportunities. Although the whole area, centred on Margate, is built up, the Hibiscus Coast gets nicer the further south you go, escaping the development.

Uvongo

Some 12km south of Port Shepstone, the Vungu River narrows into a gorge and crashes down a **waterfall** before opening out onto a broad sandy beach at **UVONGO**. The waterfall is definitely the town's biggest attraction; elsewhere, tatty clifftop developments have destroyed much of the natural vegetation. To see the falls, take the path from the bottom of the cliffs to the rear of the beach and follow the steps in the corner away from the river, following the path through some undergrowth until you reach the viewpoint on a ledge. Uvongo's pleasant beach is the site of a daily market, where Zulu women sell fruit, crafts and good-quality basketwork.

One of the most comfortable **places to stay** is *Ebenezer Palms*, 1 Emthunzi Drive (☎039 317 1128, ⓔhoatson@venturenet.co.za; ❸), with Mediterranean-style rooms, pool, and an extensive continental breakfast. The nearby *Shaka's Inhlaba Lodge*, 15 Riviera Crescent (☎039 315 5171, ⓔshakas@venturenet.co.za; ❸), is another appealing option, offering B&B and excellent, inexpensive home-cooked pub lunches and dinners. Even if you're not staying, the pub is recommended, as is the *Edelweiss* in town, which serves excellent **food** at reasonable prices. The Shelly Beach Information Centre (Mon–Fri 8am–4.30pm; ☎039 315 0265) can help you find accommodation in Uvongo itself and also all the way down to Ramsgate.

Margate and Ramsgate

The brash, built-up holiday town of **MARGATE**, 2km south of Uvongo, is as far as you'll get down the South Coast using public transport. With its high-rise apartments, fast-food outlets and ice-cream parlours, Margate offers little in the way of undiscovered coves or hidden beaches, although it (and nearby Ramsgate) does have a reasonable choice of places to stay for all budgets. The **tourist office** on the beachfront (Mon–Fri 8am–5pm, Sat 8am–1pm; ☎039 312 2322, ⓦwww.hibiscuscoast.kzn.org.za) has details of accommodation and general information for the whole South Coast area. Five minutes' drive south of Margate, across the lagoon in **RAMSGATE**, the Gaze Gallery (daily 9am–5pm; free) displays some reputable work by local artists, and serves the best waffles in the province at the attached waterside *Waffle House*.

Accommodation

Beachcomber Bay 75 Marine Drive, Ramsgate ℡039 317 4473, ⓦwww.beachcomberbay.co.za, ⓔbeachcomberbay@mweb.co.za. With views of the seafront and private access to the beach, this comfortable guesthouse has six rooms, a Jacuzzi and sauna. ❸

De Wet Caravan Park St Andrews Ave, along the beachfront, Margate ℡039 312 1022. Fully equipped four-berth caravans, park homes and grassy campsites. ❶–❷

Margate Hotel Marine Drive, Margate ℡039 312 1410. Very comfortable accommodation near the centre of town, right on the beach, with discounts offered out of season. ❺

Rock Inn Lodge and International Backpackers 835 Tegwan Rd, opposite *Waffle House* (see above), Ramsgate ℡039 314 9726. The Baz Bus stops at this hostel close to the beach, which offers a range of adventure activities from surfing to kayaking, and also has a pool. Dorms and rooms ❷

Southbroom, Palm Beach and Port Edward

Some 7km beyond Margate, **SOUTHBROOM** is known disparagingly as "Houghton-by-Sea" after Johannesburg's wealthiest suburb, which allegedly relocates here en masse in December. The town is predominantly a sumptuous development of large holiday houses set in expansive gardens; out of season, it can feel quite deserted. Huge dunes covered by lush vegetation sweep down to the sea, and there are good long walks along the shore – although heading out alone isn't advisable along this coastline for safety reasons. The best place for swimming is **Marina Beach**, 3km south of Southbroom Beach. Near Southbroom is one of the area's most upmarket **hotels**, the tranquil *Country Lodge* (℡039 316 8380, ⓦwww.thecountrylodge.co.za; ❹). Signposted off the R61 (the Port Edward road), it's a romantically secluded place surrounded by forest, away from the beachfront buzz. Champagne breakfasts and light meals are served at their marvellous *Treehouse Restaurant* on the premises. You can also eat at the *Cycad Restaurant*, adjoining the *Lodge* building, with a menu that includes delicacies like curried kudu and saffron and sweet potato gnocchi. Besides *Country Lodge*, other **places to eat** are the *Riptide Restaurant*, which is highly rated for its excellent well-priced seafood; and the *Bistro*, known for its Beef Wellington.

Heading on to Port Edward, which marks the border with the Eastern Cape, you'll soon arrive at **Palm Beach**, a rocky beach bordered with banana palms with a tidal pool for swimming, and one of the quietest spots along the South Coast. The main attraction of **PORT EDWARD**, 9km further on, is its proximity to the Umtamvuna Nature Reserve (see below), though there are some nice sandy beaches and some good **places to stay**, including the excellent *Ku-boboyi Backpackers*, Old Main Road, Leisure Bay (℡039 319 1371, ⓦwww .kuboboyi.co.za; dorms ❶, rooms ❷), a pleasant establishment on a hilltop with sweeping views of the ocean, where evening meals can be ordered.

The only public transport heading west from Port Edward is the minibus taxis that form a lively rank on the R61 just outside town, collecting passengers for the Eastern Cape, many heading across the old Transkei border to gamble at the *Wild Coast Sun* casino (see p.450).

Umtamvuna Nature Reserve

About 8km north of Port Edward, signposted off the R61 to Izingolweni, you'll find some of the best nature walks in the whole of KwaZulu-Natal at the **Umtamvuna Nature Reserve** (daily: April–Aug 6.30am–5.30pm; Sept–March 6am–6pm; R10). Extending 19km upriver along the tropical Umtamvuna River and the forested cliffs rising above it, the reserve is well known for its spring flowers, and the sunbirds and sugar birds feeding on the nectar. It's home to three hundred species of birds, including a famous colony of rare Cape **vultures**, though to see where they nest you'll have to be prepared for a whole day's walk. Waymarked paths are dotted throughout the reserve.

There are pleasant **places to stay** nearby. *Umtamvuna River Lodge*, Holiday Road (T039 311 1261; ❹), has eight rooms in tranquil forested surroundings on the banks of the river inside the reserve, and horse-riding and water-skiing are available. Within walking distance of the entrance to the reserve, *Vuna Valley Ventures*, 9/10 Michelle Rd (T039 311 3602, ❺vunavalley@telkomsa.net; dorms ❶, rooms ❷), is a family-friendly backpacker lodge on the Baz Bus route, with attractive dorms and doubles.

North of Durban: the Dolphin Coast

The **Dolphin Coast** is the appealing name given to the eighty-kilometre stretch along the coast north of Durban, from Umhlanga Rocks to the mouth of the Tugela River. The combination of a narrow continental shelf and warm, shallow waters creates ideal conditions for attracting bottle-nosed dolphins all year round to feed. Though the chances of sighting a cetacean are fairly high, you'd be unwise to base a visit solely around this possibility.

Less tacky and developed than the South Coast, the North Coast attracts an upmarket breed of holidaymaker, especially to the main resort of **Umhlanga Rocks**. With Durban less than half an hour's drive away and well served by public transport, Umhlanga Rocks is an ideal place for an easy beachside holiday close to the city; moreover, most of the infrastructural damage caused by the 2007 storm (see p.484) has been repaired, and there are good facilities for the visitor. On the other hand, the storm hit the area around **Ballito** particularly badly (damage is estimated at around R1 billion), and at the time of writing many of the beaches along this stretch of coast were still in a poor state of repair.

While the Dolphin Coast is still pretty much dominated by whites, the inland towns of **Verulam**, **Tongaat** and **Dukuza**, linked by the old **R102** road, have substantial Zulu and Indian populations, with Indian temples at Tongaat and the Shaka memorial at Duzuku. Also on the R102 is the grave of one of the ANC's best-loved leaders, Albert Luthuli, at **Groutville**.

Umhlanga Rocks

With a permanent population of around 100,000, **UMHLANGA ROCKS** is 20km from the centre of Durban and merges with the suburb of Durban North. A swish resort, the town makes a good day out from the city, with a pleasant, sandy beach dominated by a red-and-white lighthouse. The town's shopping area along Chartwell Drive has a collection of smart, well-stocked malls, while a couple of kilometres up the hill on Umhlanga Ridge, the monster **Gateway Theatre of Shopping** has four hundred shops, fourteen cinemas, a wave pool and the world's highest indoor climbing rock. To get there from Durban, follow the N2 and take the Umhlanga/Mount Edgecombe exit, then follow the signs.

Nearby, also a couple of kilometres north of Umhlanga's centre, signposted off the N2, the **KwaZulu-Natal Sharks Board**, 1a Herrwood Drive (T031 566 0400; R25), shows a multiscreen audiovisual about sharks and conducts a dissection of a recently caught shark (Tues, Wed & Thurs 9am & 2pm, Sun 2pm), which disabuses any notions of sharks as the hooligans of the oceans. It also plugs the board's work in maintaining the province's **shark nets**: although these nets protect swimmers all along the coast, they are controversial, as not just sharks but also endangered turtles and dolphins die in them, thus affecting the balance of the inshore ecosystem. The Sharks Board is investigating an electronic shark barrier that might improve the situation, while ensuring safe swimming. Without your own transport, the best way to get to the Sharks Board is by minibus taxi or shuttle; the rank is 50m west of the tourist office (see below).

A trip on a Sharks Board ski boat allows you to look out for dolphins and whales. The trips, departing at 6am, cost R200 per person (book on ☎082 403 9206), and a minimum of eleven passengers is needed for the trip to run.

Practicalities

Umhlanga Rock's **tourist office**, 14 Chartwell Drive (Mon–Fri 8.30am–5pm, Sat 9am–1pm; ☎031 561 4257, ⓦwww.umhlanga-rocks.com), is a useful source for **maps and information** about attractions up the coast. Nearby, you'll find the departure point for the Umhlanga Express minibus service (☎082 268 0651), which runs trips on request to the Musgrave Centre in Berea and to Durban city centre.

Accommodation

Anchor's Rest 14 Stanley Grace Crescent ☎031 561 7380, ⓦwww.anchorsrest.co.za. Centrally located and elegant Mediterranean-style guesthouse with spacious and well-decorated self-catering suites. ⑤

Beverly Hills Sun Lighthouse Rd ☎031 561 2211, ⓦwww.southernsun.com. The most upmarket place to stay in Umhlanga, occupying a prime location by the beach. When it reopens after renovations in 2009, the adjacent *Oyster Box* will offer a similar standard of accommodation. ⑧

Honeypot 11 Hilken Drive ☎031 561 3795, ⓦwww.honeypotguesthouse.co.za. Five B&B units decorated in rustic style with limewashed furniture and African fabric. Each room sleeps two and there's a swimming pool. ⑤

Jessica's B&B 35 Portland Drive ☎ & ⓕ031 561 3369, ⓦwww.jessicaskzn.co.za. Two self-contained garden flats with kitchens, microwaves and ovens. Good value. ③

Eating

Cottonfields 2 Lagoon Drive. A popular local bistro and bar serving up *potjiekos* and regular live music. Daily noon till late.

Ile Maurice 9 McCausland Crescent ☎031 561 7609. A gastronomic Franco-Mauritian restaurant where rabbit cooked in red wine meets octopus curry. Mains around R100. Tues–Sun 12.30–2.30pm & 6.30–10.30pm.

Olive & Oil 19 Chartwell Centre, on the 1st floor of the building opposite the tourist office. Particularly good for fish and seafood; mains in the R50–80 range. Daily lunch & dinner.

Razzmatazz *Cabana Beach Hotel*, Lagoon Drive. Enjoy springbok fillet or tamarind fish curry from the great outdoor deck with ocean views. The three-course set menu is excellent value (R85). Daily lunch & dinner.

La Mercy, Tongaat and Ballito

North of Umhlanga, the blur of development unexpectedly opens out into sugar-cane hills and subtropical coastal vegetation. Durban's new airport, the **King Shaka International Airport**, will be built at **LA MERCY**, 30km from Durban, and is expected to be finished in time for the 2010 World Cup. For the time being, however, the only reason to stop here is for a highly recommended **restaurant** – the long-established *Sea Bell*, a slightly tatty curry house under a dingy hotel, which is noted for its piquant prawns.

TONGAAT lies a few kilometres inland from here across the N2 highway, a barrier between the coastal resorts and the workings of KwaZulu-Natal's sugar industry. The town, fronted by neglected imitation Cape Dutch cottages, has long associations with South Africa's Indian community and boasts a handful of garish temples. The most distinguished of these, a National Monument, is the small **Shri Jugganath Puri Temple**, dedicated to Vishnu. A whitewashed, phallic building tipped by deities on each corner, and surrounded by mango trees, the temple was built at the turn of the last century by the Sanskrit scholar Pandit Shrikishan Maharaj, who came to KwaZulu-Natal in 1895. To get to the temple, take the R102 towards Durban, turn right into Ganie Street at the first traffic lights after the police station, then left into Planc Street and left again into Catherine Street; the temple is at the junction of Catherine and Plane. There's nothing very African about **BALLITO**, a Mediterranean-style resort a further 10km up the coast from Tongaat, with a splurge of time-shares, high-rise holiday apartments and shopping malls by the sea. Nevertheless, it's a pleasant enough place, with a beach offering safe swimming and full-time lifeguards. The swishest **place to stay** is the *Zimbali Lodge*, 1km south of Ballito (☎032 538 1007, ⍵www.sun-international.com; ❽), where accommodation is in luxury suites set in lush subtropical coastal forest in the heart of a network of wetlands. Even if you aren't staying, consider stopping here for a **meal** or, best of all, a sundowner in the bar, which is raised on stilts overlooking the fourteenth fairway of the golf course, and rewards you with soaring views across the Indian Ocean. At the other end of the price scale, *Dolphin Holiday Resort*, five minutes' walk from the beach on the corner of Compensation Beach Road and Hillary Drive (☎032 946 2187, ⍵www.dolphinholidayresort .co.za; ❷), has a well-shaded campsite and a collection of self-catering cottages.

Dukuza, Groutville and Blythedale

Heading inland from Ballito and following the R102 north for around 30km you'll come to **DUKUZA** (still widely known by its pre-1994 election name, **Stanger**), which has a special place in the cosmology of Zulu nationalists. Dukuza is the site of the Zulu king's last kraal and the place where he was treacherously stabbed to death in 1828 by his half-brother Dingane, who succeeded him. Shaka used his exceptional military talents to build up the Zulu state into the greatest power in southeast Africa by the mid-1820s – creating disquiet even among the British. The warrior-king is said to have been buried upright in a grain pit, and is commemorated by a small park and memorial in Couper Street, right in the centre of town. Near the memorial is a rock with a groove worn into it – supposedly where Shaka sharpened his spears. These days, the park is the venue for a semi-religious pilgrimage by modern-day **Zulu warriors** from all over the country – members of the fiercely Zulu nationalist Inkatha Freedom Party (IFP). Every year, on September 24, known to Zulus as Shaka's Day and now falling on a public holiday, Heritage Day, they gather here to be addressed by **Chief Mangosuthu Buthelezi**, a mercurial figure who started his political life as an ANC member but fell out with the organization. Those attending Buthelezi's speech are often colourfully clad in traditional Zulu garb and armed with traditional weapons.

At the rear of the memorial park, the **Dukuza Interpretative Centre** (daily 8.30am–4pm; free) has a small display on Shaka and a very good fifteen-minute audiovisual display; you can also see craftspeople at work and sample traditional meals in an attached café. Nearby, the lively **Dukuza Market** in Market Road, off King George Road, is where Zulu and Indian traders sell fresh spices, herbs, fruit and vegetables.

Some 8km southwest of Dukuza on the R102, just across a rusty bridge over the Mvoti River, tiny **GROUTVILLE** is remarkable mainly for the grave of **Albert Luthuli**, one of South Africa's greatest political leaders. A teacher and chief of the Zulus in Groutville, Luthuli became President General of the ANC in 1952. Advocating a non-violent struggle against apartheid, Luthuli was awarded the Nobel Peace Prize in 1960, which at home earned him a succession of banning orders restricting him to the Dukuza area. In 1967, he died in mysterious circumstances in KwaDukuza, apparently knocked down by a train. He is buried next to a whitewashed, nineteenth-century corrugated-iron mission church. Luthuli's life is recounted in the moving autobiography, *Let My People Go*.

The best **place to stay** in the vicinity is some 8km away at **BLYTHEDALE**, the closest stretch of sand to Dukuza, where a ban on high-rise construction has preserved the deserted appearance of its endless beach and kept buildings screened behind the curtain of thick coastal vegetation – indeed, this vegetation protected the beach from the high waves that hit the KwaZulu-Natal coastline in March 2007. *Palm Dune Beach Lodge*, 9 Umvoti Drive (☎032 552 1588, ⓦwww.palmdune.co.za; ⑥), is an upmarket resort where you can opt for a classy one-two, or three-bedroomed chalet, and partake in a wide range of activities, from jetskiing to beach volleyball. Also on Umvoti Drive, the cheaper *Mini Villas* (☎032 551 1277, ⓦwww.minivillas.com; ②) has well-equipped self-catering villas sleeping four to six people.

Harold Johnson Nature Reserve

Abutting the Tugela River is KZN Wildlife's **Harold Johnson Nature Reserve** (daily dawn–dusk; R10), signposted 24km north of Dukuza off the N2 (take the Zinkwazi turn-off and turn left at Darnall). With its well-preserved coastal bush, steep cliffs and gullies, this is a fine place to come for a day's visit or to camp overnight (make bookings on ☎032 486 1574) – there are no shops or facilities, so be sure to stock up before arrival. At the main picnic site and parking area you'll find a cultural museum housed in huts and featuring good displays of Zulu beadwork and aspects of Zulu society. You can follow the two-kilometre "Remedies and Rituals" **trail** from the picnic site taking you past plants whose medicinal uses you can read about. Alternatively, pick up the Tugela Trail booklet and follow a walk which highlights various historical sites in the reserve, most of them connected to the Anglo-Zulu War of 1879 and **Ultimatum Tree**. This wild fig tree, all but demolished in a cyclone in 1987, was where the British issued their ultimatum to King Cetshwayo in 1878, part of which required the Zulus to demobilize their standing army. The British used his non-compliance as an excuse to attack the Zulus and crush their independence. Also on the trail are the remains of Fort Pearson, from which the British launched their invasion of Zululand.

Valley of a Thousand Hills

The evocatively named **Valley of a Thousand Hills** (ⓦwww.1000hills.kzn .org.za), 45km from Durban on the way to Pietermaritzburg, makes for a picturesque drive along the edge of densely folded hills where Zulu people still live in traditional homesteads, and which visitors rarely venture into. The spectacular landscape goes some way to soothing any misgivings you might have about ethnographic "game viewing", but it's only worth a special effort

▲ Valley of a Thousand Hills

if you're not exploring the KwaZulu-Natal interior, where scenes like this occur in abundance. While the valley is best suited to touring in your own car, there are **daily tours** from Durban offered by Tekweni Eco Tours (see box, p.463) which take in the highlights. Alternatively, if you're in Durban on the first or the last Sunday of the month, take a **vintage train trip** with Umgeni Steam Railways (℡082 353 6003; R80), which boasts one of the largest collections of historic locomotives and coaches in the southern hemisphere. There are two trips, at 8.30am and 12.30pm, from the Kloof station, Stockers Arms, Old Main Road.

The trip to the valley and back can be done in half a day, but there are sufficient attractions laid on along the route to extend it to a full day's outing. If you're driving, head inland from Durban along the N3, following the Pinetown signs. At the Hillcrest/Old Main Road turn-off, turn right over the freeway onto the Old Main Road (M13) and continue along here following the Thousand Hills Experience Route sign. Within 1km you'll pass the thriving Victorian-styled **Heritage Market**, with craft shops, restaurants and jewellery stores. Continue for several kilometres, past the Fainting Goat, a small shopping centre, and turn left to the appealing *Pot & Kettle* restaurant and gallery, which offers unparalleled views of the Thousand Hills. Just around the bend is **Phezulu Safari Park** (daily 8.30am–4.30pm; ℡031 777 1000), which brings you close to deadly serpents – tucked away in cramped little glass boxes – plus crocodiles and other penned animals. There's also a reconstruction of a pre-colonial Zulu village, where you can watch tourist-geared – but nonetheless spirited – displays of **Zulu dancing**, set against the dramatic horizon of the valley (daily 10am, 11.30am, 2pm & 3.30pm). Prices depend on what you intend to see in the park: the snake and crocodile farms cost R25; add another R20 for the Zulu dancing.

One of the nicest places to stop is *The View* **restaurant** at 330 Old Main Rd (daily 9am–4.30pm), with magnificent views over the valley (into which you can walk from here) and a shaded patio. It's a good stop for tea or lunch, with savoury and sweet pancakes on offer. Attached is a Zulu women's weaving project selling brightly coloured handwoven crafts, though not traditionally styled.

Pietermaritzburg

Although **PIETERMARITZBURG** (often called Maritzburg), the provincial capital of KwaZulu-Natal, sells itself as the best-preserved Victorian city in South Africa, with strong British connections, little of its colonial heritage remains, and it's actually a very South African city. Zulus make up the largest community, with people of Indian descent coming second, and those of British extraction a minority – albeit a high-profile one. This multiculturalism, together with a substantial student population, adds up to a fairly lively city that's also relatively safe and small enough to explore on foot. Only 80km inland from Durban along the fast N3 freeway, Pietermaritzburg is an easy day's outing from the coastal city, and one you can combine with visiting the Valley of a Thousand Hills (see p.492) along the Old Main Road (R103). The city is also well positioned for an overnight stop on your way to the Ukhahlamba Drakensberg (see p.499) or the Battlefields in the vicinity of Ladysmith (see p.546).

Pietermaritzburg's Afrikaner origins are reflected in its name; after slaughtering three thousand Zulus at the Battle of Blood River, the Voortrekkers established the fledgling Republic of Natalia in 1839, naming their capital in honour of the Boer leaders **Piet Retief** and **Gerrit Maritz**. The republic's independence was short-lived; only four years later, Britain annexed it; and by the closing decade of the nineteenth century Maritzburg was the most important centre in the colony of Natal, with a population of nearly 10,000 (more than Durban at that time).

Indians arrived at the turn of the last century, mostly as indentured labourers, but also as traders. Among their number was a young, little-known lawyer called Mohandas Gandhi, who went on to change the history of India. He later traced the embryo of his devastatingly successful tactic of passive resistance to an incident in 1893, when as a non-white he was thrown out of a first-class train compartment at Pietermaritzburg station.

Arrival and information

Flights from Johannesburg, used mainly by business travellers, arrive at the city's **Oribi airport** (☎033 386 9577), about 6km south of the centre. The only means of getting to town from here is by taxi. All intercity **buses** pull in at the *McDonalds* on the corner of Burger and Chief Albert Luthuli (formerly Commercial) streets. Translux (☎011 774 3333), Intercape (☎033 342 3287) and SA Roadlink (☎033 345 6890) have their own offices here, while Greyhound tickets can be bought at African Link Travel on Burger Street opposite *McDonalds's* (☎033 345 3175). The **Baz Bus** drops off at either of the two backpacker lodges in town.

The **train station** (☎033 897 2350) lies at the unsavoury southwest end of Langalibalele (formerly Longmarket) Street, one of the main city thoroughfares, from where it's advisable to arrange beforehand to be collected, particularly at night. The hectic **minibus taxi rank** lies outside the tourist office and stretches right down the block (bays are clearly marked with destinations). Metered taxis should be booked in advance (see "Listings", p.498), and in this compact city are unlikely to break the bank.

The **tourist office** at Publicity House, on the corner of Langalibalele and Chief Albert Luthuli streets (Mon–Fri 8am–5pm, Sat 8am–1pm; ☎033 345 1348, ⓦwww.pmbtourism.co.za), stocks an excellent selection of books and accommodation leaflets, and also has information on the Ukhahlamba Drakensberg and other nearby attractions.

Accommodation

Maritzburg has a good selection of reasonably priced accommodation. There are some excellent B&Bs, but note that the majority of them lie a few kilometres from the town centre. The tourist office or Pietermaritzburg B&B Network (☎073 154 4444) can help book accommodation.

Africa's Eden 30 Taunton Rd, Wembley, 2km from centre ☎ & ⓕ033 394 5141, ⓦwww.africaseden .co.za. One mini-suite and one cottage sleeping six rented on a self-catering or B&B basis. Guests have use of the garden, tennis court and swimming pool. ❷

Brevisbrook 28 Waverleydale Rd, Boughton, 5km from centre ☎033 344 1402 or 072 244 9766, ⓦwww.brevisbrook.co.za. Old-fashioned hospitality and attention to detail make a stay here memorable. All five rooms have a private entrance and bathtubs, and there's a wonderful woodsy braii area and a swimming pool. ❸

Briar Ghyll Lodge George MacFarlane Lane, off Howick Rd, Town Hill, 5km from centre ☎033 342 2664, ⓦwww.bglodge.co.za. A magnificent Victorian homestead on rolling lawns, with a tennis court and swimming pool. You can choose between spacious suites within the main homestead or two self-contained cottages. Pick-ups from the airport or bus station. ❹

City Royal Hotel 301 Burger St, city centre ☎033 394 7072, ⓦwww.cityroyalhotel.co.za. A modernized 1930s building catering mainly to African business travellers. Less impersonal than you'd expect, and boasting a good central location. Discounts available at weekends. ❻

Prince Alfred St Backpackers 312 Prince Alfred St, city centre ☎033 345 7045, ⓦwww.chauncey.co.za. A notch above your average backpacker lodge, here there are no dorms, but just five attractive rooms (some en suite) which cost the same whether you're travelling alone or with someone. Calm, clean, gay-friendly and highly recommended. ❶

Redlands Hotel & Lodge 1 George MacFarlane Lane, Wembley, 3km from centre ☎033 394 3333, ⓔredlands@mweb.co.za. This upmarket boutique hotel has luxury finishes, a swimming pool and tennis court. Besides rooms, they offer self-catering one- and two-bed apartments. ❹

The City

Most places of interest in Pietermaritzburg are within easy walking distance of the centre's heart, which is crossed by the junction of Chief Albert Luthuli and Langalibalele streets. The imposing **City Hall**, on the corner of Chief Albert Luthuli and Church streets, is a great example of late Victorian red-brick civic architecture, self-assuredly holding the prime spot in town, with wonderful detailing and an impressive fifteen-metre clock tower. Across Chief Albert Luthuli Street, the **Tatham Art Gallery** (Tues–Sun 10am–6pm; free), another fine brick edifice that was previously the Supreme Court of the Colony of Natal, is the highlight of Pietermaritzburg's formal attractions. It houses one of the country's best collections of international and local art, exhibiting pieces by black South Africans such as Zwelethu Mthethwa and Sam Nhlengethwa alongside those by Pablo Picasso, Edgar Degas and Henri Matisse. A good way to enjoy the art is by attending the free **classical music concerts** that take place at the gallery every Wednesday afternoon.

Adjacent to the Tatham, the **Old Natal Parliament Building** represents a typical piece of imperial architecture, complete with a statue of Queen Victoria standing amid the formal front gardens. From here, heading down Langalibalele

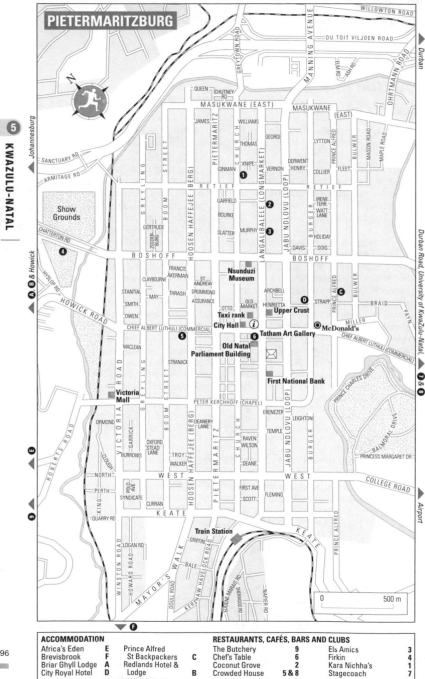

PIETERMARITZBURG

Street as far as Peter Kerchhoff (formerly Chapel) Street, you'll pass a series of attractive period buildings. Most notable of these, and considered a daringly tall skyscraper in its day, is the **First National Bank**, which dates from 1903 and had its facade chosen from an Edwardian catalogue and shipped out from the mother country. Between this section of Langalibalele and Peter Kerchhoff streets is the tightly gridded warren of alleyways known as **the Lanes**, a mostly pedestrianized quarter of lawyers' offices, takeaways, shops and an inordinate number of hairdressers. The area, which was the financial hub of Natal from 1888 to 1931 and housed four separate stock exchanges, is enjoyable to explore during the day, but is a notorious stamping ground of pickpockets, so stay alert and don't come here after dark.

The town has a few ordinary **museums**, the best of which is the **Nsunduzi** (formerly the Voortrekker) **Museum** on Boshoff Street, a couple of blocks north of the City Hall (Mon–Fri 9am–4pm, Sat 9am–1pm; R5), which centres on the original Church of the Vow, built in 1838 by Boers in honour of their victory over the Zulus three years earlier at the Battle of Blood River. The church was their part of a bargain allegedly struck with God (see p.546). The museum connects with the Voortrekker roots of Pietermaritzburg and is worth a fleeting visit to gain some insight into life on trek. The most interesting items are the home-made children's toys and beautifully embroidered *kappies* (hats) which the women used to shield themselves from the sun. Across the lovely courtyard garden is the reconstructed house of **Andries Pretorius**, leader of the Voortrekkers at Blood River and the driving force behind the establishment of the Boer Republic of Natalia. The thatched house, originally built in 1846, is appealing for its sheer simplicity, which stands in contrast to fussy Victorian fashion.

Pietermaritzburg's inevitable old apartheid divisions are marked out by roads and railways, with the African majority crammed into townships south of the train station, as they used to be excluded from the city centre. By contrast, Indians were allowed to bring their business into the city fringes, but only as far as Boshoff Street. Around here, and in the nearby Asian suburbs of Woodlands, Mountain Rise and Willowton, you'll find the greatest concentration of shops selling cheap spicy snacks like *rotis* and *bunny chows*, as well as the city centre's mosques and Hindu temples.

Alan Paton

Writer, teacher and politician **Alan Paton** was born in Pietermaritzburg in 1903. His visionary first novel, *Cry, the Beloved Country*, focused international attention on the plight of black South Africans and sold millions of copies worldwide. The book was published in 1948 – the same year the National Party assumed power and began to establish apartheid – and Paton subsequently entered politics to become a founder-member of the non-racial and fiercely anti-apartheid Liberal Party. He was president of the party from 1960 until 1968, when it was forced to disband by repressive legislation forbidding multiracial political organizations.

Paton died in Durban in 1988, having published a number of works, including two biographies and his own autobiography. The following year, the Alan Paton Centre was established at the University of KwaZulu-Natal's archives building at 165 King Edward Ave (visits by appointment; ☏033 260 5926). The Centre includes a re-creation of Paton's study, as well as personal memorabilia and documents.

Eating, drinking, nightlife and entertainment

Pietermaritzburg has a fairly good choice of **restaurants**, as well as a handful of decent nightclubs and pubs, particularly along Chief Albert Luthuli Street. If you want to self-cater, you'll find home-baked pastries and pies, and a good range of breads at Upper Crust, a **delicatessen** on Langalibalele Street opposite the taxi rank (daily 7.30am–7.30pm).

The three **cinema** complexes – the Nu Metro, in the Cascades Centre, McCarthy Drive; the Cine Centre at the Liberty Midlands Mall, Chatterton Road (both of these in the northern suburbs); and Ster-Kinekor, 50 Durban Road, in Scottsville – show mainstream releases. Also in Scottsville, the University of KwaZulu-Natal's Hexagon Theatre hosts occasional **drama** productions (bookings on ☎033 260 5537); check the *Witness* newspaper for details.

Restaurants and cafés

The Butchery 101 Roberts Rd, Wembley ☎033 342 5239. A good place not just for steaks, ribs and chicken, but also for salads and vegetarian dishes. There's also a good-value Italian restaurant, *Pesto Deli & Trattoria*, at the same address. Both daily from noon.

Chef's Table Tatham Art Gallery, Chief Albert Luthuli St. The best place in town for coffee and light lunches. Closed Sun & Mon.

Coconut Grove 426 Langalibalele St. Popular with Indian families, serving cheap curries (under R40) as well as an extensive range of burgers.

Els Amics 380 Langalibalele St ☎033 345 6524. Set in a colonial house a bit back from the main road, Maritzburg's oldest restaurant is a popular place with a pleasant atmosphere, good prices and varied menu. Tues–Fri lunch & dinner, Sat dinner only.

Kara Nichha's 470 Church St. An excellent, very cheap Indian takeaway, particularly good for filled *rotis* and Indian sweets.

Bars and clubs

Crowded House Chief Albert Luthuli St. Centrally located nightclub with pleasant indoor and outdoor bars attracting a young crowd. Wed, Fri & Sat; R25.

Firkin Show Grounds, Chatterton Rd. A restaurant and pub serving fifteen types of draught beer. It's a popular watering hole with office workers, and has a large outdoor deck. Daily from noon until late.

Stagecoach 44 Durban Rd. Close to the university, this lively student hangout has bands playing mainly rock music and good pub food.

Listings

Emergencies AA ☎082 16111; see also p.75.
Hospital For medical emergencies, contact the Med 24 hospital, Payn St ☎033 342 7023 or 033 342 7024.
Internet access Cyber World Internet Café, Victoria Inn Arcade, Langalibalele St (daily 8am–5pm).

Laundry The Wash Tub, Shop 2, Park Lane Centre, 12 Commercial Rd (daily 7am–6pm, Sat 8am–4pm, Sun 8am–3pm).
Pharmacy Medpharm, Victoria Mall, 157 Victoria Rd (24hr).
Taxis Junior Taxi Service ☎033 394 5454; Yellow Cabs ☎033 397 1910.

The Midlands

For most travellers, the verdant farmland that makes up the **Midlands** is picture-postcard terrain, to be whizzed through on the two-hour journey from Durban or Pietermaritzburg to the Ukhahlamba Drakensberg. There's little reason to dally here, unless you fancy taking in the region's quaint, English-style country inns, tea shops and craft shops, several of which are on the so-called **Midlands Meander**, a route that weaves its way around the N3 on back roads between Pietermaritzburg and the **Mooi River** 60km to the northwest.

As you head north out of Pietermaritzburg on the N3 through the Midlands, you're roughly tracing the last journey of **Nelson Mandela** as a free man before his arrest in 1962. On the run from the police, Mandela had been continuing his political activities, often travelling in disguise – a practice that earned him the nickname of the "Black Pimpernel". **Howick**, 18km northwest of Pietermaritzburg, is recorded as the place where his historic detention began; the actual spot is on the R103, 2km north of a side road heading to the Tweedie junction. On this occasion, he was masquerading as the chauffeur of a white friend, when their car was stopped on the old Howick road, apparently because of a tip-off. A memorial unveiled by Mandela himself in 1996 marks the unassuming spot, along farmland between a railway line and the road.

The Midlands offers a couple of adventure activities, both of which involve dangling from cables and ropes. In Howick, Over The Top Adventures organizes a 107-metre **abseil** down the Howick Falls (☎082 736 3651, Ⓦwww.overthetop .co.za; R280 per person with a minimum charge of R840 per group). North of Howick at the Karkloof Nature Reserve, you can undertake a **canopy tour** with Karkloof Canopy Tours (☎033 330 3415, Ⓦwww.karkloofcanopytour .co.za; R395 including lunch), on which you're strapped into a harness and glide along steel cables that link platforms erected high above the forest floor.

Practicalities

A free **map** outlining the attractions on the Midlands Meander is available from most tourist offices in the vicinity, and there's a range of **accommodation** in the Midlands, including some upmarket country hotels; we review a selection below. For lists of self-catering accommodation hereabouts, contact KZN Wildlife or the Midlands Meander Association (☎033 330 7260, Ⓦwww .midlandsmeander.co.za), which can make bookings on your behalf.

Granny Mouse Country House Old Main Rd, Balgowan, 28km northwest of Howick on the R103 ☎033 234 4071, Ⓦwww.grannymouse.co.za. Stylishly renovated and offering sixteen rooms in thatched cottages decorated with rich textured fabrics. There's a swimming pool, health spa, restaurant and loads of small lounges with large comfortable chairs to relax in. Midweek discounts are available. ❶

Loxley House South off the Lonteni/Sani Pass Rd in the hamlet of Nottingham Rd, 30km northwest of Howick on the R103 ☎033 266 6362, Ⓦwww.loxleyhouse.com. Six comfortable rooms in a small B&B with its own restaurant; electric blankets on request. ❸

Rawdon's Old Main Rd, Nottingham Rd ☎033 266 6044, Ⓦwww.rawdons.co.za. Set in a gracious country estate looking onto its own trout lake, with welcoming log fires for cool misty days and airy verandas for hot summers. It has an atmospheric pub with its own brewery on site. ❺

The Ukhahlamba Drakensberg

Hugging the border with Lesotho, South Africa's premier mountain wilderness is mostly a vast national park, officially known as the **Ukhahlamba Drakensberg Park**. The tallest range in southern Africa, the "Dragon Mountains" (or, in Zulu,

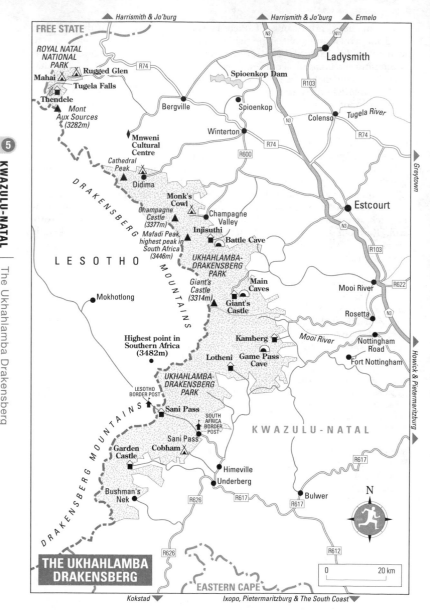

the "barrier of spears") reach their highest peaks along the border with Lesotho. The range is actually an escarpment separating a high interior plateau from the coastal lowlands of KwaZulu-Natal, and is the source of many streams and rivers which flow out to the Indian and Atlantic oceans. Although this is a continuation of the same escarpment that divides the Mpumalanga highveld from the game-rich lowveld of the Kruger National Park, and continues into the northern section of the Eastern Cape, when people talk of the Berg, they invariably mean the range in KwaZulu-Natal.

For elating scenery – massive spires, rock buttresses, wide grasslands, glorious waterfalls, rivers, pools and fern-carpeted forests – the Ukhahlamba Drakensberg is unrivalled. Wild and unpopulated, it's a paradise for **hiking**. While the southern section of the Ukhahlamba Drakensberg lacks the drama and varied landscape found further north, it does have an outstanding highlight in the hair-raising **Sani Pass**, a precipitous series of hairpins that twist to the top of the escarpment, up to the highest point in southern Africa reachable on wheels. One of the richest **San rock-art** repositories in the world, the Ukhahlamba Drakensberg is also a World Heritage Site. There are more than six hundred recorded sites hidden all over the mountains (three easily accessible ones are at **Giant's Castle**, **Injisuthi** and **Kamberg**), featuring more than 22,000 individual paintings by the original inhabitants of the area.

Visitors to the Ukhahlamba Drakensberg can **stay** either in the self-catering and camping options provided by KZN Wildlife, or in hotels or backpacker lodges outside the park, which are the most feasible option if you don't have your own transport. The highest concentration of hotels and resorts is in the Central Berg, midway between Johannesburg and Durban. As for the **weather**, summers are warm but wet, and see dramatic thunderstorms, with lightning flashing across huge charcoal skies, as well as misty days that block out the views. Winters tend to be dry, sunny and chilly, and you can expect freezing nights and, on the high peaks, occasional snow. The best times for hiking are spring and autumn. As the weather can change rapidly at any time of year, always take sufficient clothing and food, and don't forget a hat – the sun is fierce and bright, even in winter.

There are no towns close to the mountains. Instead the park is hemmed in by rural African areas – former "homeland" territory, unsignposted and unnamed on many maps, but interesting to drive through and take in a slice of traditional **Zulu life**, complete with beehive-shaped huts.

Getting there

You can **reach** the Southern Drakensberg using the **R626** or **R612/R617**, both routes putting you within striking distance of Sani Pass. For the Central and Northern Drakensberg, most roads to the mountains branch off westwards from the **N3** between Pietermaritzburg and the Ladysmith area, and come to a halt at various KZN Wildlife camps. With no connecting road system through the Ukhahlamba Drakensberg, it's not possible to drive from one end to the other. Public transport serving the Ukhahlamba Drakensberg is limited. Many hotels offer transfers from the Greyhound or Translux **intercity bus terminals** in Estcourt, a commercial centre 88km north of Pietermaritzburg on the N3, or Ladysmith. **Sani Pass Carriers'** shuttle service (see p.503) connects Pietermaritzburg at least daily with Underberg and, further south, Kokstad, while the **Baz Bus** Durban–Jo'burg service goes via Winterton for the Central Drakensberg or the *Amphitheatre Backpackers* (see p.511) for the Northern Drakensberg.

The Southern Drakensberg

From Pietermaritzburg and the N3, the main access to the Southern Berg is along the R617 (take the Bulwer/Underberg exit west off the N3). **UNDERBERG** 150km west of Pietermaritzburg on the R617 is the main

Hiking and other activities

Whether you choose to take your time on easy walks or embark on a challenging three- or four-day trip into the mountains, **hiking** in the Ukhahlamba Drakensberg remains one of South Africa's top wilderness experiences. The marvel of setting out on foot in these mountains is that you're unlikely to encounter vehicles, settlements, or even other people, and the scenery is sublime.

The Ukhahlamba Drakensberg is divided into the High Berg and Little Berg, according to altitude. In the **High Berg**, you're in the land of spires and great rock buttresses, where the only places to sleep are in caves or, in some areas, huts. You'll need to be totally self-sufficient and obey wilderness rules, taking a trowel and toilet paper with you and not fouling natural water with anything – which means carrying water away from the streams to wash in. Both mountaineers' huts and caves must be booked with the KZN Wildlife office you start out from, and you'll also need to write down your route details in the mountain register. Slogging up the passes to the top of the mountains requires a high degree of fitness, some hiking experience and a companion or guide who knows the terrain.

The **Little Berg**, with its gentler summits, rivers, rock paintings, valleys and forests, is equally remote and beautiful. It's also safer, and easy enough to explore if you're of average fitness. If you don't want to carry a backpack and sleep in caves or huts, it's feasible to base yourself at one of the KZN Wildlife camps and set out on day hikes, of which there are endless choices. It's also possible to do a two-day walk from one of the camps, spending one night in a cave. Two highly recommended bases for walking are **Injisuthi** in the Giant's Castle Game Reserve (see p.507), or **Thendele** in the Royal KwaZulu-Natal National Park (see p.511). If you want the luxury of spending the nights in a hotel, base yourself in the **Cathedral Peak** area at the *Cathedral Peak Hotel* (see p.509). With extensive grasslands, the Southern Berg is the terrain of the highly recommended **Giant's Cup Hiking Trail**, an exhilarating introduction to the mountains (see opposite).

KZN Wildlife offices sell books on Ukhahlamba Drakensberg walks, as well as *Slingsby* **maps** (1:150,000), though note that some of the paths you'll find indicated are no longer in existence. If you don't feel confident tackling the terrain, or are alone, you could contact Stef Steyn (☎033 330 4293, ⓦ www.kzntours.co.za), who specializes in **guided hikes** across the Ukhahlamba Drakensberg, as well as scenic tours all over the province.

As for other activities, **angling** at Lotheni, Kamberg, Cobham Garden Castle or Giant's Castle costs R35–60 per day by permit only from KZN Wildlife, with a bag limit of ten trout per day. You'll need to bring all your own gear.

---

gateway to the Southern Drakensberg, with a good supermarket for stocking up on supplies, as well as a pharmacy and the River Manor **private hospital** (☎033 701 1911). At the *Underberg Inn* a few metres from the supermarket is the Major Adventures office (☎033 701 1628, ⓦ www.majoradventures.com), where you can book two-day **tours to Lesotho** (R960).

HIMEVILLE, 4km north of Underberg, is the last village you'll find before heading up Sani Pass. At the centre of the village, Sani Saunter Publicity (Mon–Fri 8am–4pm; ☎033 701 1471, ⓦ www.sanisaunter.com) is the best place to get **information** about the region. Opposite is the decent *Himeville Arms* (☎033 702 1305, ⓦ www.himevillehotel.co.za; ❸), a country **inn** which makes a good stopover before the final haul to the mountains. It organizes 4WD trips, horse-riding, tennis and golf, and also has dorm accommodation (R110) for backpackers. There's a plethora of **B&Bs** along this road, one of the nicest being *Yellowwood Cottage* (☎ & ⓕ033 702 1065; ❸); set in a spectacular garden with wonderful Berg views, it has three en-suite rooms and a fully equipped kitchenette.

Sani Pass

Sani Pass is the only place in the KwaZulu-Natal Ukhahlamba Drakensberg range where you can actually drive up the mountains, using the only road from KwaZulu-Natal into Lesotho, connecting to the tiny highland outpost of **Mokhotlong** (see p.772). It's the pass itself, zigzagging into the clouds, that draws increasing numbers into the High Berg.

For all its isolation, Sani Pass is fairly straightforward to get to. Sani Pass Carriers, based in Underberg (☏033 701 1017, ✉spc@y.co.za), operates a Pietermaritzburg–Underberg **bus** service (Mon–Fri 2 daily, Sat 1 daily; R125 one-way, R230 return) timed to connect with intercity buses. It also runs a service between Underberg and Kokstad (Mon & Thurs). Hostels in the Sani Pass area will pick you up from **Baz Bus** stops in Pietermaritzburg for an additional fee.

If you intend to **drive** up to Sani Pass, it's preferable to use a 4WD vehicle, and you'll need your passport. The South African and Lesotho border posts are both open daily from 8am to 4pm. As for **organized trips**, Thaba Tours in Underberg (☏033 701 2888, ⊛www.thabatours.co.za) does a daily jaunt into Lesotho, taking you by 4WD to the highest point on the Sani–Mokhotlong Road to visit shepherds and learn about their lifestyle; it also organizes horse-riding trails and walking trips to see rock art. It's also possible to do Sani Pass as a worthwhile, though very long, day-trip from Durban, with Strelitzia Tours (see box, p.463), which includes a visit to a Lesotho village.

Accommodation

Most accommodation is at the foot of the mountains, just before the pass hairpins its way up to the top. Closest to the start of the pass is *Mkomazana Lodge*, while the highest up is *Sani Top Chalets*.

Giant's Cup Hiking Trail

The sixty-kilometre, five-day **Giant's Cup Hiking Trail** (R60 per person per night, includes entrance fee to the reserve), part of which traverses a depression which explains the trail's name, is the only laid-out trail in the Ukhahlamba Drakensberg. It starts at the Sani Pass road, then leads through the foothills of the southern Ukhahlamba Drakensberg and winds past eroded sandstone formations, overhangs with San paintings, grassy plains, and beautiful valleys with river pools to swim in. No single day's hike is longer than 14km and, although there are some steep sections, this is not a difficult trail – you need to be fit to enjoy it, but not an athlete.

The **mountain huts** at the five overnight stops have running water, toilets, tables and benches, and bunks with mattresses. It's essential to bring a camping stove, food and a sleeping bag. The trail can be shortened by missing the first day and starting out at Pholela Hut, an old farmhouse where you spend the night, then terminating one day earlier at Swiman Hut, close to the KZN Wildlife office at Garden Castle. You can also lengthen the trail by spending an extra night at Bushmen's Nek Hut, in an area with numerous caves and rock-art sites.

The trail is restricted to thirty people per day and tends to get booked out during holiday periods; **bookings** should be made through KZN Wildlife, where you can also get a map and a trail booklet. **Transport** at the end of the hike to get back to where you started should be arranged through Sani Pass Carriers (see above), who can pick you up at Himeville or Underberg, or move and store your car if you're driving.

Mkomazana Lodge 25km northwest of Underberg along the Sani Pass road ☎ 033 702 0340, ⓔ wendy@mkomazana.co.za. Self-catering in five cottages sleeping two to six people. The lodge is near the start of Giant's Cup Hiking Trail, and you can safely leave your car here before setting out on the trek. Less ambitious walks into the mountains begin on the property, which has its own river and waterfall, and a private dam with trout. ❸

Sani Lodge 19km northwest of Underberg along the Sani Pass road ☎ 033 702 0330, ⓦ www .sanilodge.co.za. Dorms, doubles and self-catering cottages at this backpacker lodge with pleasant verandas and lawns where meals are served all day, and a mean reputation for chocolate cake. It's a good base for walking to waterfalls and rock

paintings – packed lunches can be supplied – and there's also horse-riding and tours up Sani Pass and into Lesotho on offer. Dorms ❶, rooms ❷

Sani Pass Hotel A little beyond *Sani Lodge* ☎ 033 702 1320, ⓦ www.sanipasshotel.co.za. A comfortable hotel offering full board and plenty of extras, including horse-riding, tennis facilities and free golf at the hotel's nine-hole course. ❻

Sani Top Chalets At the top of Sani Pass, just inside Lesotho ☎ 082 715 1131, ⓦ www .sanitopchalet.co.za. Recommended if you're after a serious hiking vibe, but with a relaxed atmosphere, spectacular views and the highest pub in Africa. En-suite rondavels and chalets with shared toilets come with full board, or there are dorm beds for backpackers. Dorms ❷, rooms ❺

Lotheni and Kamberg

Well off the beaten track, along dirt roads and seldom explored by foreign visitors, the two **KZN Wildlife camps** at Lotheni and Kamberg (both daily: April–Sept 6am–6pm; Oct–March 5am–7pm; R20) are worth venturing into for their isolated wilderness, good trout fishing and, at Kamberg, some exquisite San rock paintings.

In a valley in the foothills of the Berg, **LOTHENI** is tranquil and beautiful, with waterfalls, grasslands and the lure of fishing in the Lotheni River, which flows through the reserve and is stocked with brown trout. The **Settler Museum** is worth a quick look (Mon–Fri 9am–4pm, Sat 9am–noon; R10); it's housed in the original stone buildings belonging to the Root family who left Britain in the nineteenth century and farmed here for two generations before the area was proclaimed a reserve, and Arnold Root became the first warden. Displays include wagons, farm tools and period furniture, re-creating early settler life.

It's possible to get to Lotheni by car either via Nottingham Road to the northeast or from Himeville to the southeast. Lotheni offers a small campsite and twelve comfortable self-catering **chalets** (❷), all with three beds as well as their own well-equipped kitchen and bathroom. Best of all here is *Simes Cottage* (❺), a stone farmhouse with a majestic outlook, its own trout lake and grounds traversed by bushbuck and eland. The cottage sleeps ten, and there's a minimum charge for six people. You'll need to bring all your own supplies; there's a trading store about 10km before you reach the restcamp.

The best reason to visit **KAMBERG**, 42km west of **Rosetta**, apart from the superb fishing, is for the rock art. At **Game Pass Cave** (one of the three caves in the Ukhahlamba Drakensberg open to the public, also known as Shelter Cave), images of stylized figures in trance states and large, polychrome eland dance across the wall. The paintings can only be visited with a guide; arrange this beforehand, or join one of the guided tours departing daily from the restcamp (R50) at 9am. The walk there and back takes around three hours, following a contour path through grasslands. There are other less distinct paintings (free), which you can visit at will, near the waterfall. There's also a **rock-art centre** at the restcamp that's worth a visit. **Walks** from Kamberg are undemanding and very scenic, and include a four-kilometre trail with handrails for wheelchair-users and the visually impaired.

Kamberg's **restcamp** consists of chalets, huts and a rustic cottage (❷–❸); there's a communal kitchen but no campsite. The nearest major supplies are at

Rosetta, so it's best to bring all your own food and drink, though there's a basic supply store just before you reach the reserve.

The Central Drakensberg

The **Central Drakensberg** incorporates four distinct areas, all clearly signposted from the N3. **Giant's Castle**, the site of a beautiful game reserve, is where you'll find the popular Lammergeie bird hide and access to important San rock paintings. More San art is at **Injisuthi** to the north, principally a hiking destination and the place to head for if you're after complete wilderness. Far more accessible and tourist-trammelled is **Champagne Valley**, which offers a healthy number of hotels with ample sporting facilities, while to the north, and out on a limb, the hotel at **Cathedral Peak** is the best place to base yourself for some serious walking.

There's not much to detain you en route to the Central Drakensberg, although the tiny hamlet of **WINTERTON**, some 90km north of Pietermaritzburg along the R74 as it deviates west off the N3, does have some pleasant **places to stay**, such as *Lilac Lodge*, 8 Springfield Rd (☏036 488 1025; ❷) – the main drag as you drive into the town – with accommodation in small cottages and its own coffee and arts and crafts shop. Another appealing choice is *Rolling M Ranch* (☏083 489 7834, Ⓦwww.rollingmranch.co.za; ❷), a working farm outside town on the banks of the Tugela River – to get there, head 2km north from Winterton on the R600, then turn right at the signposted Skietdrift road; the camp is around 15km down this route and has self-catering cabins and cottages as well as a bush camp. Since the farm is on the Battlefields route, there are trails from here to Spioenkop and Buller's Cross monuments. If you fancy **whitewater rafting**, the Tugela River east of the Drakensberg can be accessed from Winterton on trips run by Four Rivers Rafting and Adventures (☏083 785 1693, Ⓦfourriversadventures.co.za); its inflatable-raft forays into the river gorge last from one to three days and cost from R430.

Giant's Castle Game Reserve

Giant's Castle Game Reserve (daily: April–Sept 6am–6pm; Oct–March 5am–7pm; R20) was created to protect the dwindling numbers of **eland**, which occurred in great numbers in the Ukhahlamba Drakensberg before the arrival of colonialists. Antelope of the montane zone are also found here – oribi, grey rhebok, mountain reedbuck and bushbuck – as well as four dozen other mammal species and around 160 bird species. The reserve is bordered to the west by three of the four highest peaks in South Africa: Mafadi (the highest at 3410m), Popple Peak (3325m) and the bulky ramparts of Giant's Castle itself (3314m).

This is not a traditional game park – there are no roads inside the reserve apart from access routes, which terminate at the two main KZN Wildlife accommodation areas, **Giant's Castle** and **Injisuthi**; the way to see the wildlife here is by walking or hiking through the terrain. One of the big attractions at the Giant's Head peak is the thrilling **lammergeier hide** (May–Sept), where you may see the rare lammergeier, a giant, black and golden bird with massive wings and a diamond-shaped tail. A scavenger, the lammergeier is an evolutionary link between eagles and vultures and was thought extinct in southern Africa until only a couple of decades ago. The bird is found only in mountainous areas such as the Himalayan foothills, and in South Africa only in the Ukhahlamba Drakensberg and Maloti mountains. In the locality you may also spot Cape

The San and their rock paintings

Southern Africa's earliest inhabitants and the most direct descendants of the late Stone Age, the **San**, or Bushmen, lived in the caves and shelters of the Ukhahlamba Drakensberg for thousands of years before the arrival of the Nguni people and later the white farmers. There is still some disagreement over what to call these early hunter-gatherers. Many liberal writers use the word "Bushmen" in a strictly non-pejorative sense – though the word was originally deeply insulting. Several historians and anthropologists have plumped for "San" but, as the term refers to a language group and not a culture, this isn't strictly accurate either. Since there is no agreed term, you'll find both words used in this book.

The San hunted and gathered on the subcontinent for a considerable period – paintings in Namibia date back 25,000 years. In the last two thousand years, the southward migration of Bantu-speaking farmers forced change on the San, but there is evidence that the two groups were able to live side by side. However, serious tensions arose when the white settlers began to annex lands for hunting and farming. As the San started to take cattle from farmers, whites came to regard these people as vermin, and felt free to hunt them in genocidal campaigns in the Cape, and later in other areas, including the Ukhahlamba Drakensberg, until they were wiped off the South African map.

San artists were also **shamans**, and their paintings of hunting, dancing and animals mostly depict their religious beliefs rather than realistic narratives of everyday life in the Ukhahlamba Drakensberg. It's difficult to **date** the paintings with accuracy, but the oldest are likely to be at least 800 years old (although Bushmen lived in the area for thousands of years before that) and the most recent are believed to have been painted after the arrival of the whites towards the end of the nineteenth century. However, it's easy and rewarding to pick out some of the most significant elements in San paintings. The **medicine** or **trance dance** – journeying into the spiritual world in order to harness healing power – was the Bushmen's most important religious ritual and is depicted in much of their art. Look out for the postures which the shamans adopted during the dance, including arms outstretched behind them, bending forward, kneeling, or pointing fingers. Dots along the spine often relate to the sensation of energy boiling upwards, while lines on faces or coming out of the nose usually depict nosebleeds – a common side effect of the trance state. Other feelings experienced in trance, such as that of elongation, attenuation or the sensation of flight, are expressed by feathers or streamers. The depictions of horses, cattle and white settlers, particularly in the Southern Berg, mark the end of the traditional way of life for the Ukhahlamba Drakensberg Bushmen, and it is possible that the settlers were painted by shamans as a supernatural technique to try to ward off their all-too-real bullets.

To enter the spirit world, shamans often tapped into the spiritual power of certain animals. You'll see the spiral-horned **eland** depicted in every cave – not because these antelope were prolific in the Berg, but because they were considered to have more power than any other animal. Sometimes the elands are painted in layers to increase their spiritual potency. In the caves open to the public, you can see depictions of human-like figures in the process of transforming into their power animal. Besides antelope, other animals associated with trance are honeybees, felines, snakes and sometimes elephants and rhinos.

Paintings weather and fade, and many have been vandalized. Well-meaning people dabbing water on them to make them clearer, or touching them, has also caused them to disappear – so never be tempted. One of the best and most up-to-date introductions to rock art is the slim **booklet** by David Lewis-Williams, *Rock Paintings of the Natal Ukhahlamba Drakensberg*, published by the University of KwaZulu-Natal Press and available from most decent bookshops.

vulture, black eagle, jackal buzzard and lanner falcon, attracted by the carcasses of animals put out by rangers during the winter. To visit the hide (R170 per person, minimum three people), you'll have to **book** as much as a year in advance through KZN Wildlife.

Giant's Castle has one of the three major **rock-art sites** open to the public in the Ukhahlamba Drakensberg, with more than five hundred paintings at **Main Caves**, about a half-hour's easy walk up the Bushman's River Valley. There's a R25 entry fee to the caves, which are fenced in (the gates are opened on the hour from 9am–3pm), and self-guided tours with some interpretative materials on site.

KZN Wildlife's Giant's Castle **camp** has comfortable self-contained two-, four- and six-bed chalets (❸–❻), some with wonderful picture windows looking out to the peaks, and cosy fireplaces. For food, there's the pleasant *Izimbali* buffet-style **restaurant**, and you can buy frozen meat for braais and some tinned food at the curio shop in the reception area, though it's preferable to stock up before getting here. The reserve's only **filling station** is at the main entrance. There are fabulous **hiking trails** from the camp, with some of the Berg's best-located, though basic, hiking **huts** – Meander Hut, Giant's Hut and Bannerman's Hut (all ❶).

If the KZN Wildlife accommodation is full, you'll have to head for the one **hotel** that gives access to the reserve: *White Mountain Lodge* (℡&℻036 353 3437, Ⓦwww.whitemountain.co.za; ❷), along the road to Giant's Castle hutted camp, 34km on a tarred road from Estcourt and 32km from the reserve. The hotel offers full board as well as self-catering cottages, and is in the foothills and close to Zulu villages and farmlands, so while the area is pretty, it's neither grand nor remote.

Injisuthi

In the northern section of the Giant's Castle Game Reserve, some 50km from both Winterton and Estcourt, **INJISUTHI** (April–Sept 6am–6pm; Oct–March 5am–7pm; R20) is a hiker's dream. You can walk straight out into the mountains (there are ten different day hikes, lasting 1–10hr), swim in the rivers or take in rock art. One of the best day walks, albeit a tough one, is up Van Heyningen's Pass to the viewpoint – the friendly staff at reception will direct you. To get there, take the indicated turning off the R615, which takes you along 30km of dirt road, passing through **Zulu villages** with traditional beehive huts along roads frequently blocked by groups of Nguni cattle.

If you have even a passing interest in rock art, don't miss the paintings at **Battle Cave**, so-named because of a series of paintings that apparently depict an armed conflict between two groups of Bushmen. San art authority David Lewis-Williams has argued that these paintings are unlikely to depict a conflict over territory because there is no evidence that such conflicts took place in a society that was very loosely organized and unterritorial. Instead, he claims, the paintings are about the San spiritual experience and shamanic trance, the battles taking place in the spiritual realm where marauding evil shamans shoot arrows of "sickness", while good shamans attempt to fight them off.

There are more than 750 beautifully painted people and animals in this extensive cave, though many are faded. The paintings are fenced off, and can be visited only in the company of a KZN Wildlife guide, who sets out most days at 8.30am on the five-hour walk (bookings a day in advance through the Injisuthi office on ℡036 431 7848; R50 per person; minimum four people).

KZN Wildlife **accommodation** at Injisuthi includes comfortable self-catering chalets (❷) as well as campsites. Most people come here with the express purpose of taking to the hills and camping in one of the designated **caves**, which have absolutely no facilities and must be booked at reception.

Champagne Castle and Champagne Valley

Champagne Castle, the second-highest peak in South Africa, provides the most popular view in the Ukhahlamba Drakensberg, with scores of resorts in the valley cashing in on the soaring backdrop. The name, so the story goes, derives from an incident in 1861, when a Major Grantham made the first recorded ascent of the peak accompanied by his batman, who inadvertently dropped the bottle of bubbly and christened the mountainside.

These days, champagne tends to be enjoyed within the confines of the hotels down in **Champagne Valley**, by cityslickers who refuse to follow in the major's footsteps. The valley is an easy 32km from Winterton, and has shops, restaurants and facilities absent in other parts of the Ukhahlamba Drakensberg, all indicated along the route. This overcivilized but extremely pretty area, which lies outside the KZN Wildlife reserve, is best avoided if you want to hike from your doorstep – you'll have to drive west along the R600 through the valley to **Monk's Cowl** (entrance fee R25, overnight hiking R30; campsite can be booked on ☏036 468 1103), from where plenty of hikes set off into the mountains.

The **Ardmore Ceramic Art Studio**, 20km from Winterton off the R600 (daily 9am–4.30pm; ⓦwww.ardmoreceramics.co.za) and signposted between the *Nest Hotel* and the *Drakensberg Sun*, is one of the area's highlights. The studio was started in the 1980s by fine-arts graduate **Fée Halsted–Berning** with trainee **Bonnie Ntshalintshali**, a young Zulu girl suffering from polio. By 1990 they had collected a clutch of awards for their distinctive ceramic works, and the studio now has around forty people creating beautiful sculpture and crockery with wildly colourful and often impossibly irrational motifs that have included rhinos dressed as preachers, administering the sacrament to a congregation of wild animals. Bonnie died of AIDS, as have at least eight other artists at the studio, but the distinctive style she pioneered has been continued here, and the works are well worth seeing and buying. There's also a less pricey local **curio shop** on the premises, selling works by other local artists.

Accommodation

You shouldn't have any problem finding a **place to stay** in Champagne Valley, as numerous hotels, family resorts and B&Bs are signposted off the R600. There are no KZN Wildlife chalets, only a campsite at **Monk's Cowl** (☏036 468 1103).

Ardmore Guest Farm Signposted off the R600, midway between Winterton and Monk's Cowl ☏036 468 1314, ⓦwww.ardmore.co.za. A thoroughly hospitable farmstay, with accommodation in en-suite rondavels or inside the main house, attached to the Ardmore Ceramic Art Studio. Guests eat together from marvellous hand-crafted crockery made on the farm. Staff can arrange horse trails into Spioenkop Game Reserve through the Battlefields. ❸
Champagne Castle Along the R600 ☏036 468 1063, ⓦwww.champagnecastle.co.za. This old-fashioned hotel, the closest accommodation to the hiking trails beginning at Monk's Cowl, has comfortable en-suite rooms and self-catering chalets sleeping six set in lovely gardens with a swimming pool. Full board ❻
Graceland Cottage Signposted off the R600 ☏036 468 1091, ⓦwww.gracelandsa.com. A four-bedroomed self-catering cottage with TV and fireplace as well as a smaller, two-bedroomed cottage, the Homestead, perched right on the edge of a mountain with spectacular views. ❺–❻

Inkosana Lodge and Trekking Along the R600, midway between Winterton and Monk's Cowl ⓣ & ⓕ036 468 1202, ⓦwww .inkosana.co.za. Backpacker and B&B accommodation in unpretentious, ethnic-style rooms, with beautiful indigenous gardens and a retreat-centre feel. Self-catering and camping are available, and the lodge can provide free transfers from the Baz Bus stop in Winterton and up to the Berg trailheads. Dorms and rooms ❶

Cathedral Peak

North of Monk's Cowl and the Champagne Valley resorts are the Mlambonja River Valley and **Cathedral Peak**, a freestanding pinnacle sticking out of the five-kilometre-long basalt Cathedral Ridge. The peak looks nothing like a cathedral (its Zulu name, Mponjwane, means "the horn on a heifer's head").

The only **hotel** here is the excellent *Cathedral Peak* (ⓣ036 488 1888, ⓦwww.cathedralpeak.co.za; full board ❺), the closest hotel in the Ukhahlamba Drakensberg to the mountains, and within the KZN Wildlife protected area. The views are perfect and the rooms in thatched two-storey wings are comfortably furnished with pine and country-style floral fabrics. The hotel is well signposted, 44km from either Winterton or Bergville.

There are **hiking trails** starting right from the hotel, which can provide maps and books. One of the most popular day walks is to the beautiful **Rainbow Gorge**, an eleven-kilometre round trip (4–5hr) following the Ndumeni River, with pools, rapids, falls, lichens, mosses and ferns to detain you. The hike can be wet, so wear proper walking boots. The hotel also operates guided trips up to Cathedral Peak, taking nine hours, which includes plenty of time at the top to revel in the views. It's a very steep climb, and the final section beyond Orange Peel Gap should only be tackled by experienced climbers – you'll probably be quite satisfied to stop at this point.

The only other places to stay are the small KZN Wildlife **campsite** (ⓣ036 488 1880), opposite the Mike's Pass guardhouse, about 4km before the hotel, or at **Didima** (ⓣ036 488 8000), one of the newer KZN Wildlife camps, offering self-catering chalets (❹) with satellite TV and fireplaces. Here you'll also find the Didima San Art Centre (R40), which has displays on San rock art and shows a short film.

The guardhouse itself is the place to buy a permit to drive up **Mike's Pass** (R25 per person, R35 per vehicle), a ten-kilometre twisting forestry road which takes you to a car park from where, on a clear day, you'll get outstanding views of the entire region. There's a scale model on top to help identify the peaks. An ordinary car will make the journey when the weather is dry and the road is hard, but you'll need a 4WD when it's wet.

The Northern Drakensberg

The dramatically beautiful **Northern Drakensberg** consists mainly of the **Royal Natal National Park** with a few resorts scattered around the fringes. The Tugela River and its bouldered gorge offer some of the most awe-inspiring scenery in the area, its most striking geographical feature being the **Amphitheatre**, the crescent-shaped five-kilometre rock wall over which the Tugela plunges. With a complete cross section of accommodation, the Northern Berg is a very desirable area to visit. The best place to get a real feeling of these pristine mountains and valleys is at **Thendele**, the main KZN Wildlife camp, with chalets but oddly enough no camping.

▲ The Mnweni Valley, Northern Drakensberg

The small and rather ugly village of **BERGVILLE**, 23km north of Winterton, is the last place to stock up before heading on to the Royal KwaZulu-Natal National Park. Apart from the helpful **Ukhahlamba Drakensberg Tourism Association** (Mon–Fri 8am–4.30pm, Sat 8am–noon; ☏036 448 1557, ⓦwww.drakensberg.org.za) at the Sunbird Nursery on Winterton Road, there's not much to keep you here. More worthwhile is the **Mnweni Cultural Centre** (☏072 712 2401; R20), in the Mnweni Valley 30km west of Bergville along the Woodstock Dam/Rookdale roads, which is home to the amaNgwane community, who own the land of this breathtaking valley and have opened it up to tourism. The centre has **accommodation** in a simple four-bed thatched cottage and rondavel (both ❷) with shared ablutions and kitchen facilities. Aside from hiking in the mountains (R35 per night), there are craft stalls, horse-riding and some San rock paintings to keep you busy for a few days.

Royal Natal National Park

The **Royal Natal National Park** (daily 24hr; R25), 46km west of Bergville, is famed for its views of the Amphitheatre, which probably appears on more posters and postcards and in more books than any other single feature of the Ukhahlamba Drakensberg. Almost everyone does the **Tugela Gorge walk**, a fabulous six-hour round trip from Thendele, which gives close-up views of the **Amphitheatre** and the **Tugela Falls** plummeting over the 947-metre rock wall.

Established in 1916, the park only earned its royal sobriquet in 1947, when the Windsors paid a visit. The park is at the northern end of the Ukhahlamba Drakensberg, tucked in between Lesotho to the west and Free State province to the north. The three defining peaks are the Sentinel (3165m), the Eastern Buttress (3048m) and the Mont Aux Sources (3282m), which is also where five rivers rise – hence its name, given by French missionaries in 1878. **Routes** to the park are surfaced all the way. Coming from the south along the N3, take the Winterton/Berg resorts turn-off and follow the clear signposts through Bergville to the park entrance, some 46km away. Several of the resorts offer transfers from Bergville or the N3 if you book ahead and notify them, but they tend to be expensive.

Accommodation

KZN Wildlife accommodation consists of two campsites and the *Thendele Hutted Camp* (see below). The huge *Mahai Campsite* (☏036 438 6303, ℻036 438 6231) is set along the river adjacent to the national park, and caters for up to four hundred campers, attracting hordes of South Africans over school holidays and weekends. From here you can strike straight into the mountains for some of the best walks in the Berg. Smaller and quieter – and often only open at busy times, such as school holidays – the *Rugged Glen Campsite* is signposted 4km from Mahai (☏036 438 6303, ℻036 438 6231). The views and walks here aren't as good, though conveniently the *Orion Mont-Aux Sources Hotel* is an easy walk away – handy if you want a substantial meal. While you can book the KZN Wildlife chalets through their usual reservation system (see box, p.455), use of campsites here is best arranged by calling the sites concerned.

Outside the park, a well-signposted dirt road heading north, just before you reach the entry gate from Bergville, is the location for the handful of resort-style hotels in the area, including all the places listed below except the *Amphitheatre* backpacker lodge and *The Cavern*.

Amphitheatre Backpackers On the R74, 21km west of Bergville ☏036 438 6675, ⓦwww .amphibackpackers.co.za. On the Baz Bus route, this place is convenient for those without their own transport who want to explore the Northern Drakensberg. Accommodation is in en-suite dorms, with a good range of private rooms also on offer. There's a bar and restaurant, and organized hiking trips and other activities such as horse-riding and mountain biking are available. Dorms and rooms ①

The Cavern Off the R74, about 20km from the Royal Natal National Park ☏036 438 6270, ⓦwww.cavernberg.co.za. The most tucked-away of the hotels, the *Cavern* is family-run and has an old-fashioned feel, with adequate rooms. It's very much a South African weekend getaway with a swimming pool, horse-riding, Saturday-night dances and a TV room. Full board ③

Hlalanathi Berg Resort About 10km from the Royal Natal National Park ☏036 438 6308, ⓦwww.hlalanathi.co.za. This family resort offers camping and self-catering thatched chalets, which sleep two to six people. There's also a swimming pool, trampolines, a TV room as well as a sit-down and takeaway restaurant serving cheap burgers, sandwiches and more substantial meals. ②

Orion Mont-Aux-Sources Hotel About 4km from the Royal Natal National Park ☏036 438 6230, ⓦwww.oriongroup.co.za. A smart but impersonal hotel with views of the Amphitheatre behind scrawny villages and cattle-chewed hillsides. ⑥

Thendele Hutted Camp At the end of the road into the Royal Natal National Park

☎ 033 845 1000, 🖷 033 845 1001. Right in the mountains, this is one of the most sought-after places to stay in South Africa, with splendid views of the Amphitheatre and excellent walks right from your front door. Accommodation is in comfortable two-, four- or six-bed en-suite units, the cheapest of which have hotplates, fridges, kettles, toasters and eating utensils. If you opt for the more luxurious cottages or lodge, chefs are on hand to cook, though you need to bring the ingredients. There's a good curio and supply shop. ❸–❼

The Elephant Coast and Zululand game reserves

In startling contrast to the intensely developed 250-kilometre ribbon of coastline which runs north and south of Durban, the seaboard to the north of the Dolphin Coast drifts off into some of the wildest and most breathtaking sea frontage in South Africa – an area known as the **Elephant Coast**.

If you've travelled along the Garden Route and wondered where stereotypical Africa was, the answer is right here, in the northern reaches of the Elephant Coast – traditionally known as **Maputaland** – with its tight patchwork of wilderness and **ancestral African lands**. The figures speak for themselves: the area, hemmed in by Swaziland and Mozambique, has more *nyangas* and *sangomas* (traditional healers and spirit mediums) than anywhere else in the country. With one traditional healer for every 550 people – compared with one Western-style doctor to 18,000 people – **traditional life** continues in this forgotten corner of sub-Saharan Africa's most industrialized country. There's only one tarred road leading all the way from the N2 up the Elephant Coast's 200km of virtually uninterrupted beachfront, most of which is still only accessible with a 4WD vehicle – although this will probably change in the next few years.

Further south, less than three hours' drive north on the N2 from Durban, is the big game country of **Hluhluwe–Imfolozi**, which rivals even the Kruger National Park in beauty and a sense of the wild. Drive the same distance, but turn right instead of left at the Mtubatuba junction, and you'll hit the southernmost extent of South Africa's most satisfyingly "tropical" coast, protected all the way up to Mozambique by wetland reserve and marine sanctuaries – Lake St Lucia, Cape Vidal, Charter's Creek, False Bay Park, Mkhuze Game Reserve, Sodwana Bay, Lake Sibaya, Kosi Bay and other interlinked areas, with few roads linking one area to another. All the reserves fall under the umbrella of South Africa's third-largest protected area, the **Isimangaliso Wetland Park** (formerly the Greater St Lucia Wetland Park), a 2750-square-kilometre patchwork encompassing five distinct ecosystems and a UNESCO World Heritage Site. Vastly popular here for its outstanding scuba diving and fishing opportunities is **Sodwana Bay**. The coast gets remoter and more exhilarating the further north you head, with two of South Africa's best upmarket beachside stays near Mozambique at **Rocktail Bay** and **Kosi Bay**.

The **Baz Bus** service between Durban and Swaziland along the N2 stops in Kwambonambi, Mtubatuba, St Lucia and at the *Isinkwe Backpackers Bush Camp* (see p.514) just south of Hluhluwe. Note that the northern KwaZulu-Natal coastal region is **malarial**.

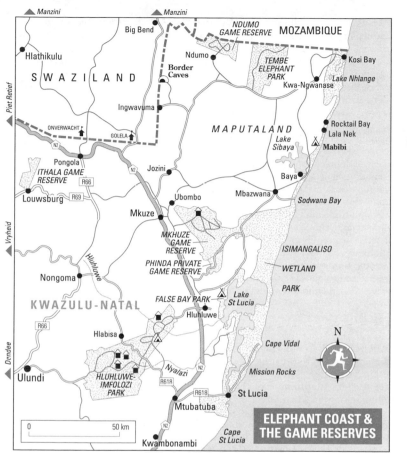

En route to Hluhluwe-Imfolozi Park

Travelling north on the N2 from Durban and the main town in these parts, **Richards Bay**, a large industrial port 185km from Durban that's completely at odds with the remote and pristine coast to the north, you'll pass a few, predominantly African villages that make adequate bases for exploring the Hluhluwe-Imfolozi Park.

Some 26km north of Richards Bay, the safe and friendly village of **KWAMBONAMBI** (known locally as Kwambo) has a small supermarket, a bottle store, post office and filling station, and an excellent **backpacker lodge**, the congenial *Cuckoo's Nest*, 28 Alibizia St (☎035 580 1001, ⓦwww .cuck-nest.co.za; dorms and rooms ❶), which has A-frame doubles, camping, dorms, plus a great tree-house. The lodge can organize game drives to the Hluhluwe-Imfolozi Park, boat tours on the St Lucia estuary and visits to a traditional Zulu village.

Another 25km further north, **MTUBATUBA** (often shortened to Mtuba) features lots of herbalists, traditional healers and a Zulu market. It's also a thriving centre for the local sugar-cane industry – both large commercial farms and small-scale African growers. Situated where the R618 intersects the N2, it's just twenty minutes from both the southern section of the Hluhluwe-Imfolozi Park and St Lucia. Among its facilities are some banks, pharmacies, supermarkets and filling stations. There are also a couple of good **places to stay**: *Wendy's Country Lodge*, 3 Riverview Drive (☎035 550 0407 or 083 628 1601, ⓦwww.wendybnb .co.za; ❸), has eight luxurious rooms in a house set in tropical gardens, with a swimming pool. *The Circle*, 92 Umkuhla Crescent (☎035 550 0660, ⓦwww .circlebedandbreakfast.co.za; ❸), is a tranquil place with one self-catering cottage and one double room. From here you can go on forest walks and experience an array of wildlife activities.

Some 40km north of Mtubatuba, the **Baz Bus** stops at *Isinkwe Backpackers Bushcamp* (☎035 562 2258, ⓦwww.isinkwe.co.za; dorms and rooms ❷), a well-run rustic hostel offering camping, wooden cabins for four and a traditional Zulu-style beehive hut dorm, as well as more comfortable doubles in the lodge. It serves reasonably priced meals (or you can self-cater), and arranges tours to Hluhluwe-Imfolozi Park and St Lucia. To get there with your own transport, take the Bushlands turn-off on the east side of the N2; from here turn left, then immediately right over the motorway bridge and continue until you reach the gravel road, then follow the signs for another 2km.

Hluhluwe

Just off the N2 nearly 60km north of Mtuba is the straggling village of **HLUHLUWE** (rendered "shla-shloo-wee"), which is handy for accessing the northern section of the Hluhluwe-Imfolozi Park, although it's the least attractive of the villages en route to the park. Hluhluwe has a few shops and the friendly **Elephant Coast Tourism Association** office at the Engen filling station on Main Street (Mon–Fri 8am–5pm, Sat 9am–1pm; ☎035 562 0353, ⓦwww.elephantcoast.kzn.org.za), providing details of numerous lodges and game farms in the vicinity. The most interesting **place to stay** is a Zulu **homestay** organized by Mbonise Cultural Concepts and Safaris (☎035 562 1329 or 082 953 5601, ⓦwww.mbonise.com; ❹). Staying with the Mdaka family in their homestead, you'll also be taken to visit the Nompondo Community adjacent to the Hluhluwe-Imfolozi Park; the price includes meals, walking tours and the services of a Zulu guide. Otherwise, there's comfy, en-suite **B&B** accommodation at the *Hluhluwe Guest House* in the residential area behind the Engen garage (☎035 562 0838 or 079 477 9520; ❸), with a pool and small bar, and meals on request. The guesthouse can arrange trips into the Hluhluwe-Imfolozi Park. Five minutes' drive from Hluhluwe, *Ilala Weavers and Savanna Restaurant* is a hub of community projects selling well-priced traditional **crafts** in a cheerful atmosphere, with a **restaurant** serving decent breakfasts, lunches and dinners, and cold beers.

Hluhluwe-Imfolozi Park

Hluhluwe-Imfolozi (daily: April–Sept 6am–6pm; Oct–March 5am–7pm; R80 per person per day) is KwaZulu-Natal's most outstanding game reserve, considered by some even better than the Kruger. While it certainly can't match Kruger's sheer scale (Hluhluwe is a twentieth of the size) or its teeming game populations, its relatively compact 960 square kilometres have a wilder feel. This has something to do with the fact that, apart from **Hilltop**, an elegant hotel-style restcamp in the northern half of the park, none of the other restcamps is fenced off, and wild animals are free to wander through. The vegetation, with subtropical forest in places, adds to the sense of adventure. The park also offers the best **trails** in the country.

The park used to be two distinct entities – hence its tongue-twisting double-barrelled name (pronounced something like "shla-shloo-wee-oom-fa-low-zcc") – and the two sections retain their separate characters, reinforced by a public road slicing between them. The southern **Imfolozi section** takes its name from a corruption of *mfulawozi*, a Zulu word that refers to the fibrous bushes that grow along its rivers. The topography here is characterized by wide, deep valleys incised by the Black and White Imfolozi rivers, with altitudes varying between 60 and 650 metres. Luxuriant riverine vegetation gives way in drier areas to a variety of woodland, savanna, thickets and grassy plains. The notable feature of the northern **Hluhluwe section** is the river of the same name, so-called because of the dangling monkey ropes that hang from the riverside forest canopy. A slender, slithering waterway, punctuated by elongated pools, the Hluhluwe rises in the mountains north of the park and passes along sandbanks, rock beds and steep cliffs in the game reserve before seeping away into Lake St Lucia to the east.

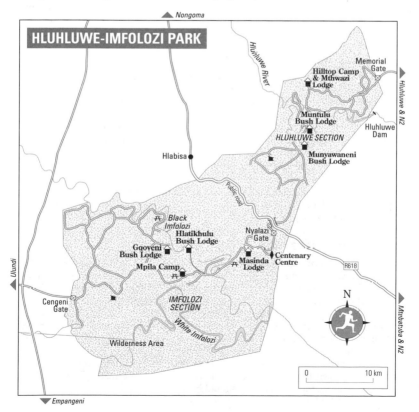

The higher ground is covered by veld and dense thicket, while the well-watered ridges support the softer cover of ferns, lichens, mosses and orchid.

Some history

Despite Hluhluwe-Imfolozi being the oldest proclaimed national park in Africa (it was created in 1895), its future as a game refuge has hung by a thread on several occasions in the last two hundred years. In the nineteenth century, the park lay at the very centre of the **Zulu kingdom** and Imfolozi was the private hunting preserve of the Zulu king, Shaka. During Shaka's reign between 1818 and 1828 the area saw the most sustained campaign of hunting in Zulu history, but this was nothing compared to the destruction caused by white men in the twentieth century, when the park was twice de-gazetted under pressure from neighbouring farmers whose cattle were being infected by **nagana**, a disease transmitted by tsetse flies from wild to domestic stock. Between 1929 and 1950, a crusade of game **extermination** was launched to wipe out the disease and saw 100,000 head of game from sixteen species fall to the gun, with rhinos alone spared.

It was only in 1952, when the park was handed over to the newly formed organization now known as **KZN Wildlife**, that the slow process of resuscitating the threadbare game reserve began. The sense of pristine wilderness you now get at Hluhluwe-Imfolozi is the result of careful management, crowned by the brilliant success of re-establishing its white rhino population from twenty animals at the start of the twentieth century to 2500 today. In 1994, the **white rhino** became the first species to be removed from the World Conservation Union's endangered list, their survival down mostly to conservationists in the Hluhluwe-Imfolozi Park, which has become the world's breeding bank for these animals.

Arrival and information

There is no public transport to Hluhluwe-Imfolozi. Without your own car, you can choose from any of the day-trips offered by accommodation within an hour's drive of the park, or from the tours operated by the Durban firms listed in the box on p.463.

Access to the park is via three gates. Just north of Mtubatuba, the R618 to Hlabisa and Nongoma reaches **Nyalazi Gate** after 21km, providing access to the southern section of the park. Further north, on the N3, an unclassified but signposted and tarred road near the turning for Hluhluwe takes you via **Memorial Gate** into the northernmost section of the park. A third gate, **Cengeni**, is accessible along a thirty-kilometre tarred road from Ulundi to the west. Maps and **information**, including details of guided walks, night drives and boat trips, are available at the receptions of the *Hilltop* and *Mpila* camps.

Accommodation

Accommodation is available in both the Imfolozi and Hluhluwe sections of the game reserve; Imfolozi is the less developed of the two. Hluhluwe's *Hilltop* camp has a pleasant **restaurant**, the *Mpunyane*, and a bar lounge, the *Uzavolo*, both attached to the central block. Some of the lodges include the services of a cook to prepare your meals, although you'll have to provide the ingredients. *Hilltop* also has a small store selling basics, but it's best to stock up before you enter the park. Hluhluwe village and Mtubatuba have well-stocked supermarkets. In Imfolozi you'll find the Centenary Centre (daily 8am–4pm), with a small takeaway restaurant, a craft centre, and *bomas* which house animals brought from other parks to be introduced here. **Bookings** for accommodation are made through KZN Wildlife as usual, though camping should be arranged locally.

Hluhluwe section

Hilltop Camp Probably the best publicly run safari camp in South Africa, set high on the edge of a slope, with sweeping views across the park's hills and valleys. The camp has modern, comfortable and varied accommodation: budget two-bed rondavels that share communal ablutions and kitchen facilities; en-suite chalets with bar-fridges, tea- and coffee-making facilities, and some kitchenettes; and en-suite chalets without kitchens. *Hilltop* is surrounded by an electric fence, which keeps out most animals. You may, however, come across nyala, zebra and other herbivores grazing around the chalets – remember that all wild animals are potentially dangerous and should be treated with respect. ❸–❻

Mthwazi Lodge Near *Hilltop*. Four luxurious en-suite rooms at this lodge set attractively in a secluded private garden. A chef is available to prepare meals. Minimum charge for four people. ❽

Muntulu and Munyawaneni bush lodges Four bedrooms with private verandas at each of two upmarket bush lodges overlooking the Hluhluwe River. A cook is on hand to cater and a field ranger is available to take guests on walks. Minimum charge for six people. ❽

Imfolozi section

There are no fences around the Imfolozi camps, so take care when walking around, particularly at night.

Gqoyeni and Hlatikhulu bush lodges Each of these lodges has four two-bed units which are elevated above the Black Imfolozi River and linked to the living area by wooden walkways. Their field ranger can conduct walks in the area, and they have a chef to cook meals. Minimum charge for six people. ❽

Masinda Lodge Near the Nyalazi Gate, this renovated upmarket lodge has three en-suite bedrooms decorated with Zulu art, plus the services of a cook. Minimum charge for three people. ❼

Mpila Camp This camp in the centre of Imfolozi has excellent views of the surrounding wilderness from twelve one-roomed huts with four beds each and communal ablutions; two self-contained three-bedroom cottages for seven people (minimum charge for four people); and six self-catering chalets that accommodate five people (minimum charge for three people). There is also a safari camp with seven tents with two beds, and two with four. ❸–❻

Game viewing and activities

Despite its compact size, Hluhluwe-Imfolozi is home to 84 mammal species and close on 350 varieties of birds. The Big Five are all here, and it's no exaggeration to say that this is the best place in the world to see **rhinos**, both black and white. **Lions** had become extinct in Imfolozi until 1958, when a black-maned male made an appearance, apparently having traversed the 400km from Mozambique. Females were later introduced, and today there are around seventy of the big cats in the reserve, although they're not easy to see and their future hangs in the balance. Other **predators** present are cheetah, leopard, spotted hyena and wild dog. **Herbivores** include blue wildebeest, buffalo, giraffe, hippo, impala, kudu, nyala and zebra. When it comes to **birds**, there are over a dozen species of **eagle**, as well as other **raptors** including hawks, goshawks and honey buzzards. Other larger birds include ground hornbills, vultures, owls and herons, and there are hundreds of other beautiful species to look out for. **Reptile** species number in the sixties, including crocodiles and several types of venomous snake, none of which you're likely to see. Along the Hluhluwe River, keep an eye open for the harmless monitor lizards.

Where Hluhluwe-Imfolozi really scores over the Kruger is in the variety of activities on offer. Apart from **self-driving** around the park, there are also **self-guided walks** near several of the restcamps, **guided trails** in the company of an armed field ranger, guided **night drives**, and a **boat trip** on the Hluhluwe Dam. South Africa's first **wilderness trail** started in Imfolozi, and the reserve has remained the best place in South Africa for these. The three-night **Base Camp Trail** (mid-March to mid-Nov; R2800 per person) involves day walks in the Wilderness Area, with nights spent at the Mndindini Trails camp not far from Mpila; the three-night **Primitive Trail** (March to mid-Nov; R2050 per person) departs from Mpila and requires you to carry your own gear and sleep under the stars, wherever the ranger chooses; and the **Short Wilderness Trail** (mid-Feb to mid-Nov; R1700 per person) starts from Mpila at noon on Friday and ends on Sunday, also at Mpila. On all of these trails, which must be booked through the KZN Wildlife, you'll be accompanied by an armed ranger; and all gear – including linen and food – is included in the price.

Lake St Lucia

The most striking feature of the **Isimangaliso Wetland Park** is the 360-square-kilometre **Lake St Lucia**, South Africa's largest inland body of water, formed 25,000 years ago when the oceans receded. The lake is flanked by mountainous **dunes** covered by forest and grassland, whose peaks soar to an astonishing 200m above the beach to form a slender rampart against the Indian Ocean. Aside from the lake and dune ecosystems, the reserve protects a **marine zone** of warm tropical seas, coral reefs and endless sandy beaches; the **papyrus and reed wetland** of the Mkhuze swamps, on the north of the lake; and, on the western shore, dry **savanna** and **thornveld**. Any one of these would justify conservation, but their confluence around the lake makes this a world-class wilderness.

Since 2002, low rainfall has put the park under severe strain, and the estuary through which the lake drains into the ocean has been closed off by sand. The lake's low water level has meant that the number of visitors to areas like Charter's Creek and Fanies Island has had to be limited, and unless there is exceptional rainfall the lake could be gone altogether in the next fifteen or twenty years.

St Lucia and Cape Vidal

Once a rough and out-of-the-way anglers' hangout, **ST LUCIA**, which lies at the mouth of the **St Lucia Estuary** in the extreme south of the park, is in the process of reinventing itself as a well-organized eco-destination. At the end of the R618, 32km east of Mtubatuba, the town can become pretty hectic in midsummer when the **angling** fanatics descend on the town for the school holidays. The real prize of the area, however, is **Cape Vidal** inside the wetland park, though the limited accommodation there may necessitate your making a day-trip from St Lucia town.

The Town

St Lucia's best feature is the **estuary**, whose mouth was reached by Portuguese explorers in 1576, and which they named Santa Lucia. During the second half of the eighteenth century, landlocked Boers made attempts to claim the mouth as a port, but were pipped at the post by the British, who sent HMS *Goshawk* in 1884 to annex the whole area, which then developed as a fishing resort. In the 1920s the town got its first hotel, and in the 1950s it was connected to the mainland by a bridge. The estuary is hidden behind the buildings along the main drag, and easy to miss if you drive quickly through.

There's not much to do in St Lucia itself, but it does provide an excellent base for a number of activities (see box, pp.520–521), as well as having a good choice of accommodation. Fishing aside, the main way of killing time is at the **St Lucia Crocodile Centre** (Mon–Fri 7.30am–4.30pm, Sat 8.30am–5pm, Sun 9am–4pm; crocodile feeding Sat 3pm; R35), at the park gate about 2km north of town on the road to Cape Vidal. This isn't another of the exploitative wildlife freak-shows common throughout South Africa, but a serious educative spin-off of KZN Wildlife's crocodile conservation campaign. Up until the end of the 1960s, "flat dogs" or "travelling handbags" were regarded as pests, and this led to a hunting free-for-all that saw them facing extinction in the area. Just in time, it was realized that crocs have an important role in the ecological cycle, and KZN Wildlife began a successful **breeding programme**, returning the crocs to the wild to bolster numbers. The Crocodile Centre aims to rehabilitate the reputation of these maligned creatures, with informative displays and an astonishing cross section of species lounging around enclosed pools (only the Nile crocodile occurs in the wild in South Africa). There's also an impressive collection of snakes and a very good **bookshop** at the centre, with items on natural history and cheap, informative booklets about the local coastal and wetland ecology, as well as the *Crocodile Bites* tea garden.

Practicalities

The **Baz Bus** comes into town three times a week and drops off and picks up passengers at *Bib's International Backpackers* (see below). The main drag is McKenzie Street, which runs parallel to the estuary. For **information**, the most helpful place is St Lucia Tours & Charters at the Dolphin Centre on the corner of McKenzie Street and the R618 as you enter the village (Mon–Fri 7.15am–4pm, Sat & Sun 7.15am–3pm; ☎035 590 1259 or 035 590 1180), which is also where you'll find the **taxi rank** for Mtubatuba. **KZN Wildlife** has an office at the south end of Pelican Road (daily 8am–4pm; ☎035 590 1340), which is two blocks east of and parallel to McKenzie. *Bib's International Backpackers* has an **Internet café**.

The local black village of **Khula**, 7km west of St Lucia on the Mtuba road, has an excellent **tourist office** specializing in responsible eco-tourism on the Elephant Coast. Facilities in St Lucia include filling stations, a couple of well-stocked supermarkets, self-service laundries, an ATM and three banks.

Accommodation

Out of season, accommodation across a range of budgets isn't hard to find in St Lucia. KZN Wildlife has two excellent **campsites**: *Eden Park*, on the banks of the estuary, across the road from the KZN Wildlife office; and *Sugarloaf*, a sizeable camp on the best site in St Lucia, also along the estuary and a few hundred metres north of Eden Park on the same road.

For a chance to experience warm Zulu hospitality, there's a worthwhile **homestay** in Khula village (❷). Accommodation is with *Mngo B&B* (☎082 711 9444; ask for Jane) or *Igugulamandlovu B&B* (☎083 437 8089; Mr Nkosi).

Bib's International Backpackers 310 McKenzie St ☎035 590 1056, ⓦwww.bibs.co.za. Firmly on the Baz Bus route, this thatched lodge offers camping, dorms, doubles and self-catering en-suite private rooms, and facilities such as Internet access, microwaves, laundry and pool tables. It also offers a range of excursions, including boat trips, cultural visits and overnight trails and drives. Dorms and rooms ❶

iGwalagwala Guest House 91 Pelican St ☎035 590 1069, ⓦwww.igwala.co.za. Spacious en-suite rooms in a quiet part of town, with a large garden and a small swimming pool. ❸

Jo-a-Lize 116 McKenzie St ☎035 590 1224, ⓔjoalizelodge@futurenet.co.za. One of the cheaper places, offering self-contained, self-catering flats and tiny en-suite units on a B&B basis. ❷

Small as it is, St Lucia is the biggest settlement around the Isimangaliso Wetland Park, and the best place to organize activities. Other than booking through the activity operators themselves, you can make reservations through St Lucia Tours & Charters on McKenzie Street (☎035 590 1259). If you are using St Lucia as a base from which to visit the Hluhluwe-Imfolozi Park, informative half- and full-day game drives (R450–550) are conducted by St Lucia-based Extreme Nature Tours (☎035 590 1624 or 076 485 5366, ⓦwww.extremenaturetours.co.za), which also organizes other tours in and around St Lucia.

Biking

Birders on Bikes is the best-value cycling package in town, and one of the most interesting tours available. A two- to three-hour gentle cycle leads you through the southern part of the estuary, along the beach and into the Cape Vidal reserve. Knowledgeable Zulu guides teach you about flora and fauna and the use of plants in Zulu culture and medicine. Book through Shaka Barker Tours (43 Hornbill St; ☎035 590 1162, ⓦwww.shakabarker.com; R85 including bike rental).

Fishing

Deep sea fishing trips for novices and seasoned anglers with a skipper, guide, experienced fisherman, bait and tackle supplied. Either tag and release your game fish or take it home to cook. The approximately six-hour trip run by St Lucia Tours & Charters (☎035 590 1259) costs from R550. Bring your own lunch and refreshments.

Hiking

There are a number of rewarding short and longer hikes in the St Lucia/Cape Vidal area. At the time of writing, the one-day Wetland Walk and the five-day/four-night Emoyeni Trail, previously organized by KZN Wildlife, were about to be taken over by a private tour operator (for more information, contact the KZN Wildlife office in St Lucia); KZN Wildlife still organizes the three-day/two-night Mziki Trail (R50 per person per night) and the excellent, fully catered and portered four-night Wilderness Trail (R1500 per person).

Horse-riding

Bhangzi Horse Safaris (☎035 550 4898 or 083 668 7693) offers rides through bushland, forests and lakes where you can view wildlife. The half-day trip costs R460.

Kingfisher Lodge 187 McKenzie St ☎035 590 1015, ⓔstluciakingfisherlodge@mweb.co.za. One of the most comfortable B&Bs in town, with seven stylish chalets and views of the estuary. ④

Protea Hotel 3 Mullet St ☎035 590 1001, ⓦwww.proteahotels.com. St Lucia's only hotel, offering all the comforts associated with this chain, as well as a pool, a fantastic deck for evening drinks and good views of the estuary. ⑥

Seasands Lodge 135 Hornbill St ☎035 590 1082, ⓦwww.seasands.co.za. Comfortable suites with patios and balconies overlooking shaded gardens. Each unit has a fully equipped kitchen, and there's also a small restaurant. ④

St Lucia Wetlands Guest House 20 Kingfisher St ☎035 590 1098, ⓦwww.stluciawetlands.com. With six large en-suite rooms fitted out in elegant wooden furnishings, exceptional service, friendly hosts and extras such as Internet access and a car-washing service, this is one of the best places to stay in St Lucia. ④

Sunset Lodge 154 McKenzie St ☎035 590 1197, ⓔinfo@sunsetstlucia.co.za. Attractive self-catering log cabins, sleeping two or four, with balconies and views of the estuary. Hippos occasionally feed on the grasslands in front of the wooden pool deck. Good value. ②

Kayaking

Kayaking in the lake system gives an unparalleled experience of the wetland. St Lucia Kayak Safaris (☎ 035 590 1233 or 083 463 3253) runs half- and full-day outings which cost R225–375 including all gear, transfers to the launch site, a light lunch and refreshments.

Khula Village tours

Trips operated by Veyane Cultural Tours (☎ 035 550 4325 or 072 588 8290) depart St Lucia for nearby **Khula village**, where you can visit the local school, a *shebeen*, a *sangoma* and witness a Zulu dance. Tours cost around R100 per person, though you can visit independently.

Lake cruises

If you spend any time in St Lucia, it's well worth going on a lake cruise with St Lucia Tours & Charters (☎ 035 590 1259; R130; 2hr), departing from the eastern shore at the jetty next to *Für Elize* (see below) or with KZN Wildlife on its vessel *Santa Lucia* (☎ 035 590 1340; R110; 1hr 30min), departing from the west side of the estuary next to the bridge. You stand a good chance of seeing crocodiles and hippos, as well as pelicans, fish eagles, kingfishers and storks.

Wetland wildlife tours

An outstanding range of tours in the wetland is led by Kian Barker, a qualified zoologist and marine biologist, including the full-day St Lucia World Heritage Tour (R395) and the interesting and unusual Chameleon Night Drive (R250), which goes out in search of the sixteen chameleon species of the St Lucia region (a staggering fourteen of which are endemic). Also recommended is the one-night, two-day Turtle Tour (Nov–Feb; R1750) to watch the annual turtle egg-laying migration at Kosi Bay. Book through Shaka Barker Tours (see opposite).

Whale-watching

Humpback and southern right whales cruise along the wetland's shore, and in season (June–Nov) you can join a boat excursion to look for them. Book through Advantage Tours & Charters (☎ 035 590 1180, ⓦ www.advantagetours.co.za; R600; 2hr; 40-percent refund if you don't see a whale); the trips leave from its office on McKenzie St. There's no jetty down at the beach and launching the boat into the waves is an adventure in itself; if the ocean is choppy, expect to get soaked.

Eating

The freshest **seafood** in town can be had at *Fishy Pete's*, 61 McKenzie St, next to the Engen garage, a friendly and inexpensive place covered with fishing memorabilia that's also good for a drink. *Für Elize* on McKenzie Street near the boat jetty also does seafood, as well as crocodile curries (mains around R60). The *Boat House Gallery Fish Grill*, at the ski-boat club at the end of Pelican Street, has pleasant views of the estuary, but don't expect too much from the food. The town's main **bar**, and the place that you're most likely to find open when everywhere else has closed for the night, is *Monkey Lounge* on McKenzie Street near *Bib's International Backpackers*.

Cape Vidal

Another popular fishing spot, **Cape Vidal** (daily: April–Sept 6am–6pm; Oct–March 5am–7pm; R30 per vehicle, R25 per person) can only be reached via St Lucia, from where you take a tarred road north (the extension of

McKenzie St) for 32km, navigating a narrow land bridge between the lake and the Indian Ocean. En route you'll pass through grassland and wetlands populated by small game, rhino, birdlife and the occasional leopard.

There's enough stunning wilderness at Cape Vidal to keep you chilling out for several days, even if you aren't a keen angler. The sea is only minutes from the KZN Wildlife accommodation, and an offshore reef shelters the coast from the high seas, making it safe for **swimming**. If you're keen on **snorkelling**, an underwater extravaganza of hard and soft corals and colourful fish awaits. Go gazing into the tiny **rock pools** and you'll be rewarded with sightings of seaweeds, snails, crabs, sea cucumbers, anemones, urchins and small fish, though burly anglers who use the rocks for casting their lines into the wide ocean may look on you in disbelief.

Large mammals and fish move just offshore in the open seas beyond the reef. Cape Vidal is an excellent place for shore sightings of **humpback whales**, which breed off Mozambique, not far to the north, in winter. In October they move south, drifting on the warm Agulhas current with their calves. If you're lucky you may see these and other whales from the dunes, but without binoculars they'll just look like specks on the horizon. A **whale-watching tower**, reached through the dune forest south of the restcamp, provides an even higher viewpoint. Eighteen-metre plankton-feeding whale sharks, the largest and gentlest of the sharks, have been sighted off this coast in schools of up to seventy at a time, and manta rays and dolphins are also common in these waters.

Practicalities

There's no public transport to Cape Vidal. If you're planning to stay overnight (highly recommended), book **accommodation** in advance. There are eighteen five-bed and eleven eight-bed Swiss-style log cabins, all of which are en suite and provided with linen and cooking utensils (❷–❹). The Bhangazi complex has cabins ranging from eight to twenty beds in dormitory rooms which are let out to groups (❷–❺), and there's also a campsite with space for fifty tents in the dune forest near the beach, with ablution facilities.

▲ Fishing at Cape Vidal

Reservations for cabins and chalets should be made through KZN Wildlife. Bookings for the campsite in particular are vital during school holidays and over long weekends. There's a small store selling basics and a petrol pump at the beach. St Lucia is close enough to stock up on anything else you should need.

The western shore

Accessible only with your own transport, the **western shore** of Lake St Lucia marks the old seashore, harking back aeons to a time when the ocean level was 2m higher than it is today. Decayed matter from marine animals has created a rich soil that once supported an extensive array of animal life, and although the Big Five were shot out ages ago, **birdlife** and over a hundred species of **butterfly** still flit about. Among the **herbivores** are suni – Africa's smallest antelope – as well as nyala and red duiker. With no dangerous predators apart from **crocodiles** (take care along the shore), the inland bushveld and woodlands are safe for walking without a guide.

Drought in recent years has limited the number of visitors permitted in certain areas along the western shore. At the time of writing, both **Charter's Creek**, at the southern end of the lake, and **Fanies Island**, 20km north of Charter's Creek, were closed completely. The situation can change quickly depending on how much rain the area receives – for instance, Charter's Creek is sporadically open for day visitors only – so contact the KZN Wildlife office in St Lucia for updated information.

False Bay Park

About 20km north of Fanies Island, **False Bay Park** (daily: April–Sept 6am–8pm; Oct–March 5am–8pm; R25) perches on the west shore of a small, lozenge-shaped waterway which is connected to Lake St Lucia by a narrow, steep-sided channel known colourfully as "Hell's Gates". The park gives an excellent, low-key experience of the lake, although the low water level means that it is currently not possible to launch boats. You can, however, get out into the bush: the eight-kilometre **Dugandlovu Trail** and the ten-kilometre circular **Mpophomeni Trail** are clearly waymarked, pass through a variety of terrain and offer the opportunity of seeing birds and a decent variety of antelope and other small mammals such as jackals, mongooses, servals, genets, warthogs and vervet monkeys. If you're not feeling so energetic, there's the shorter six-kilometre **Ingwe Trail** alongside the lake.

You reach the park **via Hluhluwe** (see p.514); continue east through the village to a T-junction at the end of the road and follow the signposts for 15km to the False Bay Gate. There's a **campsite** at Lister's Point about midway down the west shore of False Bay, which has communal ablutions, but you must supply everything else. About 8km to the south, *Dugandlovu* **hutted camp** has four basic four-bed chalets (**②**) with cold showers (you can heat water over the fire in pots provided), toilets, gas cookers and paraffin lamps. You must bring all your own gear, including linen and sleeping bags. To make **bookings**, call ☏035 562 0425.

A couple of places to stay lie just outside False Bay Park and are signposted from Hluhluwe. The *Sand Forest Lodge* (☏035 562 2509, ⓦwww.sandforest.co.za; **③**) has more campsites plus self-catering cottages. The lodge is located on a small reserve with antelope, zebra and wildebeest, and meals are available on request. For a touch of luxury, the *Falaza Game Park* (☏035 562 2319, ⓦwww.falaza.co.za; **⑥**) has slick tented accommodation in another small reserve, and also boasts a reasonably priced health spa and a pool which the rhino enjoy lounging around. Activities such as guided walks and boat trips, or game drives into Hluhluwe-Imfolozi Park, can be arranged.

Mkhuze and Phinda game reserves

Reached across the Lebombo Mountains, 28km east of **Mkuze** village on the N2, **Mkhuze Game Reserve** has a rich cross section of mammals covering 78 species, though it's for its varied and highly beautiful countryside and its birdlife that the reserve really rates. The reserve is a major part of the Isimangaliso Wetland Park, connected to the coastal plain by a slender corridor through which the Mkuze River flows before emptying itself in Lake St Lucia.

At Mkuze's southern end is the **Phinda Private Game Reserve**, open only to resident guests. Not one of the great South African game-viewing destinations, it makes up for this abundantly by the sheer panache with which it provides fine-tuned hospitality to the upmarket clientele.

Mkhuze Game Reserve

Defined to the west by the Lebombo Mountains, **Mkhuze Game Reserve** (daily: April–Sept 6am–6pm; Oct–March 5am–7pm; R35 per vehicle, R30 per person) marks the final haul of the coastal plain stretching down the east of the continent from Kenya. The landscape varies from the **Muzi Pans**, wetlands consisting of seasonal flood plains floating with waterlilies, reed beds and swamps, to savanna. Elsewhere you'll come across stands of acacias, and in the south across the Mkuzi River you can wander through the cathedral-like fig forest that echoes to the shriek of trumpeter hornbills.

If you're **driving**, the easiest way to get to the reserve is to leave the N2 at **MKUZE** village and follow the signs along a good dirt road to **Emshopi Gate**. An alternative route, which leaves the N2 further south, 35km north of Hluhluwe, involves a lot more driving on dirt and doesn't knock much off the distance. Another entry point has recently opened providing quick access from Sodwana Bay via the new **Ophansi Bridge** which crosses the Mkuze River on the eastern side of the reserve. From Sodwana Bay, travel south on the R22 and turn down the D820 access road upon which the bridge is built; it's about a forty-minute drive from Sodwana Bay to the reserve. There's no public transport into Mkhuze, and if you don't have your own vehicle you'll need to join one of the daytime or night-time **excursions** into the park from Mkuze village. The village has a few shops for supplies, a garage and the excellent *Ghost Mountain Inn* (T035 573 1025, Wwww.ghostmountaininn.co.za; ❺) signposted off the N2, which is great for a drink or meal and a dunk in their pool, even if you aren't staying. The hotel organizes four-hour daytime **game drives** in Mkhuze (from R265 per person; minimum four people). If you have time to climb **Ghost Mountain**, which overlooks Mkuze, you can combine the experience with tales of the battles associated with the peak, as told by local guides (hikes 3–4hr; R100 per person; minimum two people; book through *Ghost Mountain Inn*).

For navigating your way around the park, the **reception office** (T035 573 9004) provides a clear **map** that shows all routes and distances and gives general information about the park. You can buy fuel at the entrance gate, and there is a **shop** selling basic supplies and books at reception, but you should stock up on provisions in Mkuze village before heading out here.

A **campsite** is situated right at Emshopi Gate, while **Mantuma**, the main public restcamp, 9km into the park in the northern section, has a range of

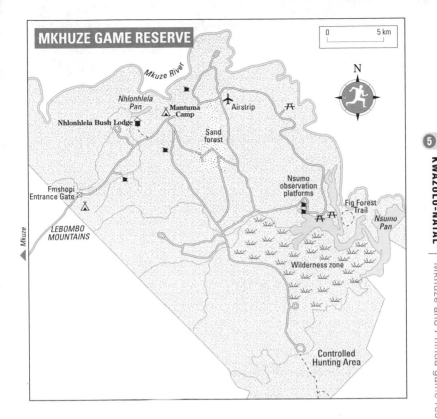

MKHUZE GAME RESERVE

0   5 km

N

Mkuze River

Nhlonhlela Pan

Mantuma Camp

Nhlonhlela Bush Lodge

Airstrip

Sand forest

Emshopi Entrance Gate

LEBOMBO MOUNTAINS

Mkuze

Nsumo observation platforms

Fig Forest Trail

Nsumo Pan

Wilderness zone

Controlled Hunting Area

accommodation. Cheapest are the two-bed rest huts with shared ablution facilities and a kitchen (❷). There are also larger chalets that sleep two, four or six (❸–❺). The most enticing units are the large two- or four-person safari tents, each with its own roof and ablutions (❸). *Nhlonhlela Bush Lodge* overlooking Nhlonhlela Pan between Mantuma and Emshopi Gate has four two-bed rooms (❻; minimum charge for six people) connected by wooden walkways to a communal kitchen and living area. A cook (you bring the ingredients) and a field ranger are included in the price. **Reservations** should be made through KZN Wildlife.

Game viewing and activities

Some 84km of road traverse Mkhuze, but one of the best ways to see game is to stay put and wait for the animals to come to you. Several **hides** have been erected at artificial waterholes and on the edge of pans. All animals have to drink at some time, particularly in the drier months when naturally occurring water is scarcer, so you're bound to have a relaxed and interesting time at a hide if you chill out with a pair of binoculars and a good field guide.

Mkhuze is among the top spots for **bird-watching** in the country, with an impressive 430 species on record. Some of the prizes include Pels fishing owl and Rudd's apalis, a small insect-eating bird with a very restricted distribution. Even if you know nothing about birds, you're likely to appreciate one of Africa's most colourful here – the lilac-breasted roller. The two hides at **Nsumo Pan**, in the southern section of the park, apart from overlooking a very beautiful natural waterway, are superbly placed for observing **waterfowl**. Between July and September, if conditions are right, you can catch up to five hundred birds on the water at one time. Flocks of pelicans and flamingos make their appearance, as do kingfishers, fish eagles, waders, ducks, geese and countless other species. To arrange a specialist birding guide, contact the Zululand Birding Route (⌾035 753 5644, ⓦ www.zbr.co.za; R250 half day, R350 full day). Nsumo's picnic site is one of the few places in the game reserve where you may leave your car, and it makes a great place to stop and eat.

Of the predators, there are no lions, while **cheetah** and **leopard** are present but rarely glimpsed; you stand a better chance of seeing fox-like black-backed **jackals**. The obvious draw of Mkhuze, however, is its black and white **rhinos**. The **impala** antelope will also be hard to miss, and you should catch sight of the large, spiral-horned **eland** and **kudu**. **Baboons** and **vervet monkeys** are generally found rustling around in the trees and making a nuisance of themselves on the ground, while at night you could be treated to the eerie call of the thick-tailed **bushbaby** from the canopy.

KZN Wildlife offers a number of activities, including recommended **night drives** from Mantuma (R100). During the day, you can explore Mkhuze on foot with a field ranger on a two-hour conducted **walk** (R60) that concentrates on game, and a three-hour walk (R70) that focuses on trees and birds and ventures into the Muzi Pans. Many of the older rangers speak very little English, and their main function is to protect you. Current KZN Wildlife policy, however, is to employ younger guides who speak English well and have a knowledge of the environment, so check out the situation when you book your walk at the restcamp reception. One of the areas you can explore with a guide is the three-kilometre **Mkhuze Fig Forest Trail** – another highlight of the reserve. Sycamore fig forest is one of the rarest types of woodland in South Africa, and the stands of massive trees give the forest a gentle green glow. Look out for the flashing red flight feathers of fruit-eating **birds** like the purple-crested lourie or green pigeons, and listen for the tap-tap of golden-tailed woodpeckers on the trees. Monkeys and baboons, which pass through from time to time, pose no threat though they might steal your food, but you should keep alert to the possibility of encountering black rhinos or hippos.

Phinda Private Game Reserve

On a 150-square-kilometre ranch, **Phinda Private Game Reserve** offers a good chance of seeing **lion**, **cheetah** and both varieties of **rhino** on game drives, but it's hard not to feel that it's all a bit too well managed. At the moment the property is too small to sustain a self-regulating wildlife ecology, but if, as is hoped, it becomes integrated with surrounding parks (as has happened around the Kruger National Park) this could change dramatically.

Accommodation is at six lodges (**❾** including all meals and game activities): *Mountain Lodge* offers vistas of the Lebombo range and the nearby St Lucia coastal plain; *Rock Lodge* embraces a more intimate experience, with just six stone chalets chiselled into rock; *Forest Lodge* consists of stunning Afro–Japanese-style timber houses on stilts, each tucked away discreetly among bush and trees; *Vlei Lodge*, in a sand forest on the edge of a pan system, features highly polished thatched chalets; and both *Zuka Lodge* and *Getty House* in the western part of the reserve are rented out to groups and come with a ranger, butler, cook and 4WD safari vehicle. The **food**, described as "eclectic pan-African", is excellent.

All game drives or walks are accompanied by well-informed expert guides, who are as good as any you'll find in South Africa.

Bookings should be made through Conservation Corporation Africa (☎011 809 4300 or 021 532 5800, ⓦwww.ccafrica.com), or through one of the specialist travel agents listed in Basics. Detailed instructions on how to get there are provided when you make your booking.

The far north of the Elephant Coast

Also known as **Maputaland**, the extreme northeast section of the Elephant Coast is the remotest tract of South Africa, mostly accessible only along dirt roads that work their tortuous way to the coast. The quickest way of reaching this area is from **Hluhluwe** village, where a tarred road, the **R22**, strikes north for some 150km, passing **Sodwana Bay** and terminating near **Kosi Bay** and the Mozambique border. Another road, 11km north of **Mkuze** village, snakes north and then east for 133km, eventually connecting with the R22 about 40km south of Kosi Bay. This road gives access to the border village of **Ingwavuma**, home to a fascinating women's crafts project, a Zulu festival and the base for some excellent hikes, as well as the **Ndumo Game Reserve** and **Tembe Elephant Park** (ⓦwww.tembe.co.za), both reserves reaching down from the Mozambique border. The elephant park is not described here, as it's a very underdeveloped conservation area to which only the dedicated go in 4WD vehicles.

For much of this area, a **4WD** vehicle is essential and it's best to travel in two vehicles as there's nowhere to get repairs done and facilities are poor. It's also essential to carry an inflated spare tyre, jack and wheel spanner and spare water. Watch out for unattended stray animals and school children wandering onto the roads; never resort to speeding on dirt roads to make up time, and watch out for potholes on all roads.

Sodwana Bay

A tiny scoop in the Zululand Coast, **SODWANA BAY** (daily 24hr; R20), around 80km northeast of Hluhluwe village, is the only breach in an almost flawless strand extending 170km from St Lucia to Kosi Bay. It's the tortuitous convergence of the bay (which makes it easy to launch boats) with the world's southernmost coral reefs that makes Sodwana the most popular base in the country for **scuba diving** and the most popular KZN Wildlife resort. Because the continental shelf comes extremely close to shore (near-vertical drops are less than 1km away), it offers very deep waters, much loved by anglers who gather here for some of South Africa's best deep-sea **game fishing**, mostly tag and release. The abundance of game fish also makes for some of the best surf fly-fishing in the country.

When there's no one around, Sodwana Bay is paradise, with tepid waters, terrific sandy beaches, relaxed diving or snorkelling and plenty of basic accommodation. Over weekends and during school holidays, however, fashion-conscious Jo'burgers tear down in their 4WDs, while thick-set anglers from Gauteng, Free State and Mpumalanga come here and drink themselves into a stupor. Thankfully, government regulations now limit the number of 4WDs using the beach as a car park. A gentler presence from mid-November to February are the leatherback and loggerhead **turtles**, who make their way onto Sodwana's beaches to reproduce, as they've been doing for the last 60,000 years (see box, p.531).

There is no public transport to Sodwana Bay other than the **Baz Bus**, which can arrange for you to connect with a shuttle service to *Coral Divers* (see below) from the Baz Bus drop-off point in Bushlands off the N2. Some of the dive outfits provide transport from Hluhluwe to Sodwana. **Hitching** is possible, but even if you succeed in thumbing a lift here, the place is so spread out that getting around on foot is a major hassle.

The national park takes in the bay itself, while the desultory collection of shops and an upmarket lodge that pass for the **town** are 8km to the west, back along the Mbazwana road. The KZN Wildlife office, park entry gate, campsites, chalets and two of the dive lodges are up the hill past the town. Here you'll also find a small shop selling **food** and other camping basics (Mon–Sat 8am–5pm, Sun 8am–1pm; no liquor available), and a clinic (daily 8–9am and 4–5pm; for emergencies call ☎035 571 0283 or 083 777 3455). **Petrol** is available at the entry gate from 6am till 6pm. There is no ATM, but the shop may allow you to draw cash on your credit card.

For **eating**, the reasonably priced *Leatherback's Seafood and Grill* at *Sodwana Bay Lodge* (see below) offers decent food, including the best pizzas around and carvery fare most evenings. *Jabu Takeaways*, located in an old caravan parked next to the craft market, is a regular hangout for divers and dishes out cheap, filling half-loaves of bread stuffed with fried potatoes, fried egg or curry.

Accommodation

Most **accommodation** at Sodwana Bay lies inside the KZN Wildlife conservation area along the bay's beaches. Rates tend to be on the high side because of the lack of competition in the area.

Staggeringly, there are more than four hundred KZN Wildlife **campsites** here (☎035 571 0051, ℻035 571 0115), with a minimum fee of R140 per site during public and school holidays as well as on Friday and Saturday nights. The seasonal population explosion allegedly makes Sodwana Bay the largest campsite in the southern hemisphere. There are also twenty KZN Wildlife **chalets**, fully equipped log cabins with either five beds (❸) or eight (❺; minimum charge for four people).

If you're staying inside the park at the privately run *Coral Divers* or *Mseni*, you must pay a R50 daily camping fee to KZN Wildlife. *Mseni* includes the fee in its rate; to stay at *Coral Divers*, pay the fee at the KZN Wildlife office.

Coral Divers ☎035 571 0290, ⊛www.coraldiver .co.za. The largest dive outfit at Sodwana Bay is a basic, rather tired, backpacker haunt with a variety of two-bed safari tents, two-bed cabins with shared ablutions, and two-bed en-suite cabins. You can self-cater or pay for half board, and takeaways are available throughout the day. It lays on transport to and from the beach to coincide with dives and meal times. ❷–❹

Mseni Lodge ☎035 571 0284, ⊛www.mseni .co.za. The only establishment to have direct access to the beach, this is a comfortable lodge of twenty en-suite log cabins spread out amid thick coastal forest. There's a restaurant, bar, satellite TV and swimming pool. Half board ❻

Sodwana Bay Lodge In the village ☎035 571 6000, ⊛www.sodwanadiving.co.za. Simple yet comfortable reed and thatched en-suite two-bed B&B chalets (insist on getting a renovated one). A groovers' bar downstairs has pool tables, music, a swimming pool and a sun deck that attracts both visitors and locals. Half board ❻

Visagie Lodge 500m beyond *Sodwana Bay Lodge*, towards the bay ☎035 571 0104, ℮visa1234 @iafrica.com. Basic accommodation in cabins sleeping from two to six people, with a restaurant and bar on site. ❷

Diving and snorkelling

Unless you're a keen angler, the principal reason to come to Sodwana Bay is for the diving off its **coral reefs** which, along with bright tropical fish, thrive here in the warm waters carried down the coast by the Agulhas current. Delicate convolutions of both soft and hard corals cover the rocks with a range of textures, shades and colours. The waters are clear, silt-free and perfect for spotting some of the 1200 varieties of **fish** that inhabit the waters off northern KwaZulu-Natal, making it second only to the Great Barrier Reef in its richness.

The closest reef to the bay, and consequently the most visited, is **Two Mile Reef**, 2km long and 900m wide, offering excellent dives. Among the others is **Five Mile Reef**, which is further north and is known for its miniature staghorn corals, while beyond that, **Seven Mile Reef** is inhabited by large anemone communities and offers protection to turtles and rays, which may be found resting here.

There's excellent **snorkelling** at Jesser Point, a tiny promontory at the southern end of the bay. Just off here is **Quarter Mile Reef**, which attracts a wide variety of fish, including moray eels and rays. Low tide is the best time to venture out – a sign on the beach indicates daily tide times. You can buy competitively priced snorkels and masks (or rent them for R25 per day) from the dive shop at *Sodwana Bay Lodge*. Here you'll also find a **dive operation** offering various diving courses, diving packages and scuba equipment rental. There are also dive operators providing similar services at *Coral Divers* and *Mseni Lodge*.

The Mngobolezeni Trail

The five-kilometre circular **Mngobolezeni Trail** winds its way from just across from the park reception through a variety of habitats, including woodland, to the coastal lake that gives the hike its name. Arrows and signs indicate the way – but take care not to get sidetracked down one of the many game paths that crisscross it. The walk takes around three hours and there's no drinkable water along the way, so you should bring refreshment. **Crocodiles** live in the lake, as do hippos, who leave the water to feed, usually at dusk. If you encounter a hippo on land, treat it with the utmost respect: hippos are responsible for more human deaths than any other African mammal. Avoid getting between a hippo and its line of retreat, which will generally be the most direct route to the safety of the water. If you do disturb one, find a tree to hide behind or, even better, to climb.

Apart from hippos, you may be lucky enough to see some of the other animals that inhabit the dune forest and its surrounds, among them bushbuck, duiker (red and common), reedbuck and Tonga squirrels. A trail **booklet** available from the park reception interprets points of interest along the way.

Other activities

There's more to do in Sodwana Bay than diving. Exodus Adventures, whose office is opposite the park reception (℡083 349 8575), has a number of **horse-riding** trails that take you through forest (1hr) and beach (1hr) and cost from R220. Guided **quad bike-rides** are available from a nearby outlet called Off-Road Fun (℡082 785 7704; R150 per hr), either within the bay area or, more ambitiously, on a three-hour jaunt to Lake Sibaya (R300). It's also possible to go **microlighting** over the pristine beaches and wilderness (book on ℡072 211 6662; R200 for 12min).

During December and January, when loggerhead and leatherback turtles (see box, p.531) come to nest and lay their eggs on the beach, you can join one of the guided **turtle tours** from Sodwana Bay. As a limited number of licences are issued each year for these, the operators change from year to year, so enquire locally.

Lake Sibaya and Mabibi

Lake Sibaya (free entrance), South Africa's largest natural freshwater lake, covers 77 square kilometres, and is fringed by white sandy beaches disappearing into dense forest. On a windless day the lake, 10km due north of Sodwana Bay, appears glassy, azure and flat; the waters are so transparent that when KZN Wildlife take a hippo census they just fly over and count the dark blobs clearly visible from the air. From the margins, timid crocodiles cut the lake surface, exchanging the warmth of the sun for the safety of the water. This is not an unpopulated wilderness: the lake fringes are dotted with traditional African lands and villages. There's an exceptionally easy-going three-kilometre **circular walk** that starts from the viewing platform behind KZN Wildlife's now closed *Baya Camp*. **Bird-watching** can be rewarding (there are two hides) with close on three hundred species present. Needless to say, with crocs and hippos lolling about, swimming in the lake is most unwise.

Around 10km further up the coast, **MABIBI** is probably the most remote and idyllic campsite in South Africa (daily: April–Sept 6am–8pm; Oct–March 5am–8pm; R20 per person, R15 per vehicle). Situated in luxuriant subtropical forest, the ten **campsites** (❶) perch on a plateau at the top of monumental dunes that descend sharply to the sea. The camp is protected from the winds by the dune forest and a boardwalk leads down the duneside to the **sea** – a walk that takes about ten minutes. This is one of the most undisturbed sections of coast in KwaZulu-Natal, and outside school holidays you stand a fair chance of having a perfect tropical beach all to yourself. You won't get the frenetic activity of outboard motors and 4WD vehicles found at Sodwana Bay and other spots to the south – they're banned within the Maputaland Coastal Forest Reserve, which Mabibi falls under. The coast here offers **surf angling** and **snorkelling** matching that at Sodwana Bay, with rich tropical marine life thriving on the coral reefs offshore. A number of mammals live in the forest, but most of them – bushbabies, large-spotted genets and porcupines – only come out after dark.

The campsites should be booked through Isibindi Africa (☎035 474 1473, ⓦwww.isibindi.co.za), which also runs the luxury Robinson Crusoe-style *Thonga Beach Lodge* (full board ❾), its thatched suites secluded in the coastal dune forest. The lodge has a wellness centre, dive operation, turtle tracking tours, and sundowners at Lake Sibaya.

One approach to Mabibi is the tarred Kwa-Ngwanase (also called Manguzi) road from the N2, some 11km north of Mkuze. At the Manzengwenya intersection, turn right and follow the (poorly marked) signboards to Mabibi. Because this final 45km from the junction is along gravel and thick sand tracks, a 4WD vehicle, or at least one with high clearance such as a *bakkie* (pick-up truck), and competent driving are essential. You can also reach Mabibi on the coastal forest link road (also called Coastal Cashews road) from Mbazwana; turn right at the Manzengwenya road and follow the signs. If you're staying at *Thonga Beach Lodge*, you'll be collected at the end of the tarred road, beyond the Manzengwenya intersection.

Rocktail Bay

South Africa's most sublime beachstay lies about 20km north of Mabibi along the coast at **ROCKTAIL BAY**, a stretch of sand and sea that is restricted to guests who are prepared to pay for the privilege of staying at the *Rocktail Bay*

Lodge (book through Wilderness Safaris; ℡011 807 1800 or 021 702 7500, Ⓦwww.wilderness-safaris.com or Ⓦwww.rocktailbay.com; full board ❾). **Accommodation** is in eleven en-suite reed-and-thatch chalets raised on stilts into the forest canopy, each with its own wooden deck. This is the ideal place to get away: there's no phone, limited solar electricity, and the last few kilometres are so heavy-going that you leave your vehicle at the Coastal Cashews Farm on the dirt road from Mabibi, and get ferried in by 4WD (included in the rate).

Few parts of the South African coastline are as unspoilt as the beaches around here, and although there's no big game to pull in the punters, there's excellent **scuba diving** offshore – one of the highlights is diving with pregnant ragged-tooth sharks as they migrate north up the KwaZulu-Natal coast from around late September to May – and a dive centre with a qualified PADI instructor, a boat and skipper. You can also go **snorkelling** in the bay at low tide (fins and snorkels are available to guests). The **bird-watching** here is excellent; among a number of rare species are the green twinspot, green coucal, grey waxbill, purple-crested and Livingstone's louries as well as the Natal robin, emerald cuckoo and – particularly prized – the palmnut vulture.

Supreme idleness is one of the big attractions of the place, but you can walk in the coastal forest, join an excursion to a fossilized dune called Black Rock and watch turtles during the summer egg-laying season. **Surf fishing** for shad, springer, kingfish, bonefish, stumpnose, barracuda and blacktail is another possibility.

Ingwavuma

A small village high up in the Lebomba Mountains, on the border with Swaziland, **INGWAVUMA** is home to the **Ingwavuma Women's Centre**, a

---

Turtles

Sea turtles from as far afield as Malindi in Kenya (3500km to the north) and Cape Agulhas (2000km west along the South African coastline) come ashore on the beaches of the northern Elephant Coast every year between October and February to lay their eggs. The turtles have survived virtually unchanged for almost a hundred million years and it's reckoned that loggerhead turtles have been using Maputaland's beaches to lay their eggs for 60,000 years.

It is believed that the turtles are lured onto the beach by a hormone that oozes from the beach, a scent that they follow and which is thought to have been programmed into their subconscious while they were themselves in their eggs. The myopic turtle, whose eyes are adapted to underwater vision, pulls herself along the beach in the dark until she encounters an obstruction such as a bank or a log, where she begins digging a pit using her front flippers until she has scooped out a nest big enough to hold her own volume. She then digs a flask-shaped hole about 50cm deep and lays her eggs into this, a process which takes about ten minutes. The turtle fills the hole with sand using her front flippers, disguising the place where the eggs are stored, and returns to the sea. After about two months the eggs hatch, and the entire clutch of hatched turtles will simultaneously race down the beach. Once in the ocean, the hatchlings swim out to sea where they are either carried away by the Agulhas current into the Atlantic or along the Indian Ocean coast. Only one in five hundred will survive to return.

The whole of the northern Elephant Coast is excellent for spotting loggerhead and leatherback turtles, with **Rocktail Bay** probably the best spot of all. As the turtles are easily disturbed, only a few licensed operators are allowed to escort visitors to watch the turtles at night.

poverty alleviation project started in 2001. The project (arrange a visit through Beni Williams on ☎035 591 0135) employs nearly three hundred women to undertake basket weaving, embroidery, wire work and beading, and you can get informal instruction in these traditional Zulu art forms. The most fascinating craft to learn is sisal-basket weaving, which requires you to know how to collect the correct grass. The centre offers simple B&B **accommodation** in three en-suite rooms (booking is essential; ☎035 591 0133 or 082 296 0942, Ⓔstembenivw@xsinet.co.za; ❷).

The area offers a rich mix of Zulu and Swazi culture, where you can experience the foods and dances of both nations. The Zulu King has a palace in Ingwavuma and a **Reed Dance** (see box, p.538) takes place here during the last week of September. Guides are available to take you on mountain **nature walks** and to visit **caves** spectacularly overlooking a five-hundred-metre drop into Swaziland (daily 9am–4pm; free).

Ndumo Game Reserve

One of the most beautiful of the KwaZulu-Natal reserves, **Ndumo** (daily: April–Sept 6am–6pm; Oct–March 5am–7pm; R40 per person, R35 per vehicle) looks across the flood plain into Mozambique to the north and up to the Lebombo Mountains in the south. Its northern extent hugs the **Usutu River**, which rises in Swaziland and defines South Africa's border with Mozambique. The turn-off to the reserve is 56km north of Jozini, with the final 15km along a rough gravel track.

No great volume of animals trammel the reserve, but the beauty, solitude and prolific birdlife here make this a good place to head for if you're not simply into ticking off your checklist of **mammals**. That's not to underplay the 62 species here (including buffalo, jackal, wildebeest, giraffe, hippo, hyena, zebra and both species of rhino), but they may be more difficult to see than elsewhere. For twitchers, however, Ndumo ranks among the country's top **bird-watching** spots. The staggering 430 different varieties recorded here include the African broadbill, pink-throated twinspot, Pels fishing owl, gorgeous bushshrike, cuckoo hawk, southern banded snake eagle and the palmnut vulture.

You can **drive** around some areas, one of the highlights being the trip to **Redcliffs**, where there's a picnic site with a towering vantage point offering soaring views across the Usutu River into both Swaziland and Mozambique. KZN Wildlife offers open-topped 4WD outings in the mornings and evenings to the lovely **Inyamiti pan**, which is inhabited by hippos and crocodiles and receives visits from an array of waterfowl; guided **walking trails** are also available.

The small KZN Wildlife **restcamp** (☎035 591 0058) is sited on a hill and has a number of campsites and seven well-maintained, two-bed **huts** (❸), each with a fridge and shared ablutions. A shop near the entrance gate sells basic **supplies**, but you're better off stocking up en route in Mkuze village. Just outside the park, the *Ndumu River Lodge* (☎035 591 0011, Ⓦwww.ndumu.com; ❷) is a pleasant place to stay, offering en-suite rooms or self-catering chalets; directions are given when you book.

Kosi Bay

The northernmost place along the KwaZulu-Natal coast, **KOSI BAY** (daily: April–Sept 6am–8pm; Oct–March 5am–8pm; R15 per vehicle, R20 per person) is at the centre of an enthralling area of waterways fringed by forest. Despite the name, this is not a bay at all, but a system of four lakes connected by narrow reed channels which eventually empty into the sea at Kosi Mouth.

One of the most striking images of Kosi Bay is of mazes of reed fences in the estuary and other parts of the lake system. These are **fish kraals**, or traps, built by local Tonga people, a practice that has been going on for hundreds of years. Custom has made the method of harvesting sustainable, because trap numbers are strictly controlled; the traps are passed down from father to son and capture only a small fraction of the fish that pass through.

Staying at Kosi Bay, you're likely to feel frustratingly landlocked – you won't so much as glimpse the coast unless you sign up for the four-day **Amanzimnyama Trail**. This circular hike begins at the base camp on the west shore of Nhlange, the largest lake in the area, and passes through beautiful coastal forest, along the beach, through groves of cycad and giant raffia palm. In summer, there's the chance of seeing turtles on the beach. Beds, pots, cookers, ablution facilities and limited water are available at night stops along the route, but there's no electricity or refrigeration, and you must bring your own utensils, food, bedding, torches and snorkelling gear. Mosquito repellent is recommended, and this is one of the few parts of the country where it's advisable to use water purification tablets. **Bookings** for the trail, which costs R2500 per person, should be made through KZN Wildlife central office.

A highly recommended alternative way to explore the area is on a **tour** guided by members of the local community, who can show you the lakes and the fish traps. The frequency of the trips depends on the number of guides available at the time, and they start just outside the restcamp from the reserve **office** (T035 592 0236), where you can gather more **information**.

Accommodation

The KZN Wildlife **restcamp** (❷–❹) is inside the reserve, on the west shore of Nhlange, the largest of the lakes, and offers two-bed, five-bed (minimum charge for three people) and six-bed (minimum charge for four people) cabins, with a small campsite nearby. A number of locally owned and operated restcamps have opened in recent times, the proprietors all enthusiastic hosts and knowledgeable guides. Directions to the camps are given when you book, and 4WD transfers from Kwa-Ngwanase can be arranged for an additional charge.

Hlalanathi Forest Camp T072 345 6260. Campsites, bungalows and tented accommodation, with a communal kitchen (bring your own provisions) and dining area. It's uniquely positioned in the sand forest at Bhanga Nek. ❷

Kosi Forest Lodge Inside the reserve T035 474 1473, Wwww.isibindiafrica.co.za. Arguably the most dreamy place to stay in KwaZulu-Natal, featuring eight reed-and-thatch suites in a remote landscape of palms, lakes, sand forest and bleached white beaches. There is no electricity, and you have to be collected by 4WD from the Total garage in Kwa-Ngwanase and taken along sandy tracks to the lodge. Activities include guided canoeing trips, reef snorkelling and forest walks; there's a good chance you'll see hippos, crocodiles and marine turtles. The rate is inclusive of all meals and activities. ❽

Victor's Camp T073 150 9350. Six well-run chalets sleeping two, with shared ablution facilities, a communal kitchen and good views. There's also a campsite. ❷

Ithala Game Reserve

West of Maputaland and close to the Swaziland border, the small **Ithala Game Reserve** (daily: April–Sept 6am–6pm; Oct–March 5am–7pm; R35 per person, R30 per vehicle) is little known, despite being one of the country's most uncrowded and spectacularly scenic places to watch wildlife. The reserve's relative youth (it was only proclaimed in 1972) may be one reason why it is frequently bypassed by visitors. This could soon change, especially as Ithala's main camp, **Ntshondwe**, is one of the best game-reserve restcamps in South Africa. Ithala is largely mountainous, and the terrain extremely varied, with numerous cliffs and rock-faces contained within a protective basin.

Like the rest of the KwaZulu-Natal game reserves, Ithala is excellent for white **rhinos** and there's plenty of **plains game**, including zebras and giraffes. Of the **predators**, you could, if you're very lucky, encounter brown hyenas, cheetahs and leopards. If you're obsessed with seeing the Big Five, however, Ithala is not the place to visit – the king of the beasts is notably absent here, even though the other four make periodic appearances. But the best idea is to throw away your mammal checklist and take a slow drive around the mountains into the valleys and along the watercourses. As there are no lions, the game is relaxed, and on a quiet weekday watching **animal behaviour** can be fascinating. Slow down, keep your eyes open, and you may see a rhino male defending his territory, or two young giraffes testing their strength with neck wrestling. One of the most rewarding **drives** is along Ngubhu Loop, with a detour to Ngubhu picnic site.

There are some **self-guided trails** into the wooded mountainside above *Ntshondwe Camp*, which give the chance to stretch your legs if you've spent a morning driving around. **Day and night drives** in open vehicles can be booked through the restcamp's reception at a cost of R150 per person.

Practicalities

There's no public **transport** to the park or near it, so driving here is your only option. All accommodation here is run by KZN Wildlife. The main restcamp, **Ntshondwe**, 7km beyond the entrance gate, is ingeniously camouflaged against a high plateau with views at the foot of huge cliffs. The camp's reception can provide **information** and **maps**.

Ntshondwe has a **restaurant** serving a surprisingly varied range of foods from *escargot* to steaks – though meat-free meals aren't always on the menu – and a cosy **bar** whose sundeck looks out over the waterhole and across the valleys. If you want to self-cater, you'll need to get **supplies** before you come – the camp shop specializes in beer and frozen meat and hasn't much by way of fresh food. **Louwsburg**, signed from the surfaced road along the southern section of the reserve, has a very small general store that's a little better and, further afield, Vryheid, Pongola or Mkuze are better still.

Accommodation

Mbizo Bush Camp If you want an extremely pared-down bush experience, you can't beat this marvellous bush camp with space for just sixteen people, shaded by thorn trees and ilala palms, on the banks of the Mbizo River. Expect no frills here – it's cold showers in reed enclosures and cooking over wood fires, the only concession to civilization being a flushing toilet. Minimum charge for four people. ❻

Mhlangeni and Thalu bush camps A wonderful choice for something a bit wilder, these camps are both in beautiful secluded settings and have four (Thalu; minimum charge for two people) or ten (Mhlangeni; minimum charge for five people) beds. Both are staffed by an attendant and you can make arrangements to have a field ranger to take you on walks. ❹–❼

Ntshondwe Camp Offers extremely comfortable two- and four-bed self-catering chalets with fully equipped kitchens, lounge areas and verandas, as well as two-bed non-self-catering units. Each chalet is surrounded by indigenous bush through which paved walkways weave their way around granite rocks and trees to the main reception area. ❸

Ntshondwe Lodge Next to the restcamp, yet completely secluded, this luxury lodge has three beautifully decorated rooms, a restaurant and a small plunge pool overlooking the reserve. Minimum charge for three people. ❻

Central Zululand and the Battlefields

Central Zululand – the Zulu heartland – radiates out from the unlovely modern town of **Ulundi**, some 30km west of the Hluhluwe-Imfolozi Park. At the height of its influence in the 1820s and 1830s, under King Shaka, the core of the Zulu state lay between the **Black Imfolozi River** in the north, and, in the south, the **Tugela**, which discharges into the Indian Ocean roughly 100km north of Durban.

Despite being a beautiful area of dry thornveld, large hills and impressive views, Central Zululand tends to be visited as a series of routes taking in museums and **Battlefield sites**. The Zulu heartland, where you'll find **museums** relating to local history and culture, is concentrated just to the west of the Hluhluwe-Imfolozi Park, King Shaka's personal hunting preserve. The heartland can be taken as a side trip from a visit to Hluhluwe-Imfolozi or Ithala Game Reserve, which lies about 150km north of Ulundi.

Contained in a relatively small area to the west of the heartland is a series of sites of nineteenth-century battles, first between Zulus and Boers, then Zulus and the British, and finally between the Boers and Brits. Don't attempt to visit this area on your own: all you'll see is empty veld with a few memorials. Far better is to join a tour with one of the several excellent guides who make it their business to bring the region's dramatic history alive (see box, p.543).

The Zulu heartland

Don't expect to see "tribal" people who conform to the Zulu myth outside theme parks such as Shakaland, near Eshowe. Traditional dress and the **traditional lifestyle** are largely a nineteenth-century phenomenon, deliberately smashed by the British a century ago, when they imposed a poll tax that had to be paid in cash – thus ending Zulu self-sufficiency, generating urbanization and forcing the Africans into the modern industrial economy, where they were needed as workers.

You will find beautiful Zulu crafts in this part of the country, the best examples being in museums such as the little-known but outstanding **Vukani Zulu Cultural Museum** in Eshowe. Also worth checking out is the reconstructed royal enclosure of Cetshwayo, the last king of the independent Zulu, at **Ondini**, near Ulundi.

Some history

The truth behind the Zulus is difficult to separate from the mythology, which was fed by both the Zulus themselves as well as white settlers. Accounts of the Zulu kingdom in the 1820s rely heavily on the diaries of the two adventurers, **Henry Fynn** and **Nathaniel Isaacs**, who portrayed King Shaka as a mercurial and bloodthirsty tyrant who killed his subjects willy-nilly for a bit of fun. Despite their attempts to cover up their profligate disregard for the truth, a letter from Isaacs to Fynn was uncovered in the 1940s. In it he encourages his friend,

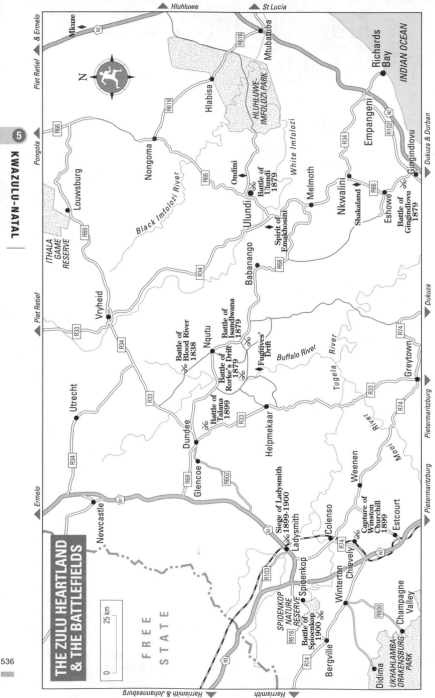

5

536

THE ZULU HEARTLAND & THE BATTLEFIELDS

0   25 km

N

FREE STATE

INDIAN OCEAN

Hluhluwe   St Lucia

Mkuze

Piet Retief & Ermelo

Pongola

R66

Louwsburg

ITHALA GAME RESERVE

R69

Nongoma

Black Imfolozi River

R66

Ulundi

Ondini
Battle of Ulundi 1879

Spirit of Emakhosini

Babanango

R68

Melmoth

Nkwalini

Shakaland

R66

Eshowe
Battle of Gingindlovu 1879

Empangeni

R34

Richards Bay

Mtubatuba

R618

Hlabisa

HLUHLUWE-IMFOLOZI PARK

White Imfolozi

Gingindlovu

R102 N2

Dukwa & Durban

Dukuza

Vryheid

R34

Nqutu

Battle of Blood River 1838

Battle of Isandhlwana 1879

Fugitives' Drift

Battle of Rorke's Drift 1879

Buffalo River

Tugela River

Greytown

R74

R33

Dukuza

Pietermaritzburg

Utrecht

R33

R34

Dundee

Battle of Talana 1899

Helpmekaar

Mooi River

Weenen

Capture of Winston Churchill 1899

Estcourt

Pietermaritzburg

R33

Glencoe

R68

R602

Newcastle

N11

Siege of Ladysmith 1899-1900
Ladysmith

Colenso

Chievely

R74

N2

Ermelo

R103

Spioenkop

SPIOENKOP NATURE RESERVE

Winterton

R616

Bergville

Battle of Spioenkop 1900

Champagne Valley

R600

Didima

UKHAHLAMBA-DRAKENSBURG PARK

Harrismith & Johannesburg

Harrismith

Pietermaritzburg

N3

R74

N2

R618

Piet Retief

who was en route to London to publish his memoirs, to depict the Zulu kings as "bloodthirsty as you can, and describe frivolous crimes people lose their lives for. It all tends to swell up the work and make it interesting."

A current debate divides historians about the real extent of the **Zulu empire** during the nineteenth century. Some now question the conventional wisdom that Shaka was the "African Napoleon", a military genius who transformed the politics of nineteenth-century South Africa. What we do know is that in the 1820s Shaka consolidated a state that was one of the most powerful political forces in the subcontinent, and that internal dissent to his rule culminated in his assassination by his half-brothers **Dingane and Mhlangana** in 1828.

In the 1830s, pressure from whites exacerbated internal tensions in the Zulu state and reached a climax when a relatively small party of Boers defeated Dingane's army at **Blood River**, leading to a split in the Zulu state, with one half following **King Mpande**. Collapse threatened when Mpande's sons Mbuyazi and Cetshwayo led opposing forces in a pitched battle for the succession. **Cetshwayo** emerged victorious and successfully set about rebuilding the state, but too late. Britain had already determined that its own interest would best be served by a confederated South Africa under its own control and a powerful Zulu state wasn't going to be allowed to stand in the way. On the banks of the Tugela River, the high commissioner, Sir Bartle Frere, delivered a Hobson's choice of an **ultimatum** that Cetshwayo should dismantle his polity or face invasion.

In January 1879, the British army crossed the Tugela, and suffered a humiliating disaster at **Isandlwana** – the British army's worst defeat ever at the hands of native armies. However, the tide turned against the Zulus after just over a hundred British soldiers repulsed a force of between 3000 and 4000 Zulus at Rorke's Drift. By the end of July, Zulu independence had been snuffed, when the British lured the reluctant (and effectively already broken) Zulus, who were now eager for peace, into battle at Ulundi. The British set alight Cetshwayo's capital at Ondini – a fire which blazed for four days – and the king was taken prisoner and held in the Castle in Cape Town.

Gingindlovu

There's nothing much to see in **GINGINDLOVU** (shortened to Ging by local whites), 50km north of Dukuza along the R102, although the town did play a significant role in the Anglo-Zulu War. It was here that the Zulus attacked a British relief column on April 2, 1879, as it was marching on Eshowe to relieve a siege. In one of the decisive battles of the Anglo-Zulu War, the colonial invaders delivered a crushing defeat to the Zulus that destroyed their morale, with the loss of only thirteen British lives. The following day, the British column continued its advance, and successfully raised the Eshowe siege.

Eshowe

The name **ESHOWE** has an onomatopoeic Zulu derivation, evoking the sound of the wind blowing through the trees. Though visitors generally give the town a miss on the way to the more obvious drama of Ondini and the Battlefields, the place deserves more than a passing glance, as it offers a gentle introduction to the Zulu heartland. Apart from its attractive setting 22km inland from Gingindlovu, interlacing with the **Dlinza Forest**, the town is home to one of the world's finest collections of Zulu crafts and has a tour operator offering excellent excursions that take you out to experience some authentic Zulu culture, as well as other aspects of life in Zululand that you would otherwise most likely miss.

Zulu festivals

In September and October KwaZulu-Natal is host to three significant Zulu **festivals** that until recently were only attended by the actual participants, though it's now possible to witness these with the Eshowe-based Zululand Eco-Adventures (ⓦ www .eshowe.com). If you're not around in September or October, Zululand Eco-Adventures can arrange for you to attend several lower-key Zulu ceremonies that give an authentic, non-touristy insight into various aspects of Zulu life. These range from *sangoma* healing ceremonies (Wed & Sun), Zulu weddings (Sat & Sun), coming-of-age ceremonies (Sat & Sun) and a visit to a Zulu gospel church (Sun). All take place within a radius of about 20km of Eshowe and at each one you're likely to be the only white people present.

The Royal Reed Dance

In the second week of September, the Zulu King hosts a four-day celebration at his royal residence at **Nongoma**. The event is both a rite of passage to womanhood for the young maidens of the Zulu nation, and a chance for them to show off their singing and dancing talents. The festival, known as **Umkhosi woMhlanga** in Zulu, takes its name from the riverbed reeds that play a significant role in Zulu life. Young women carry the reed sticks, which symbolize the power of nature, to the king. According to Zulu mythology, only virgins should take part, and if a woman participant is not a virgin, this will be revealed by her reed stick breaking. A second Reed Dance takes place in the last week of September at the king's other residence in Ingwavuma (see p.531).

King Shaka Day

In honour of King Shaka, a celebration is held yearly on September 24 in **Dukuza** (see p.491), Shaka's original homestead and the place where he was murdered in 1828 by his brothers Dingane and Mhlangana. It was Shaka who brought together smaller tribes and formed them into the greatest warrior nation in Southern Africa. Today, the celebration is attended by a who's who of South African Zulu society, and there are speeches, music and fantastic displays of warrior dancing, the men decked out in full ceremonial gear.

Shembe Festival

Held in mid- to late October in **Judea**, near Eshowe, the Shembe Festival is the culmination of weeks of endless rituals, dancing and prayers held throughout KwaZulu-Natal. Some thirty thousand members of the Shembe church (see p.477) return here every year to meet their leader and celebrate their religion, with prayer dances and displays of drumming.

The Town

Containing more than 3000 examples of traditional Zulu arts and crafts, the brilliant **Vukani Zulu Cultural Museum** is housed in a purpose-built structure in the grounds of Fort Nongqayi on Nongqayi Road, a few minutes' walk from the city centre (Mon–Sat 9am–4pm, Sun 10am–4pm; R20, includes everything in the Fort Nongqayi complex; ☎035 474 5274). The best way to see the museum is to arrange a 45-minute guided tour, which is included in the price. On display is a huge range of **baskets**, something Zulu culture excels at (and examples of which are held in many major international art collections), each made for a specific purpose, the finest of which are the ones by **Reuben Ndwandwe**, arguably the greatest Zulu basket weaver, who died in 2007. There are also carvings, beadwork, tapestries and some outstanding ceramics, including works by **Nesta Nala**, one of the leading proponents of the form, who died in 2005. The benchmark examples here allow you to form an idea of the quality of basketry and crafts you'll see for sale as you work your way around Zululand.

Also inside Fort Nongqayi is the **Zululand Historical Museum** (Mon–Fri 7.30am–4pm, Sat & Sun 9am–4pm), a collection that is eccentric and informative by turns, but never dull. Among the displays is furniture belonging to **John Dunn**, the only white man to become a Zulu chief and, incidentally, also to take 49 wives, so becoming the progenitor of Eshowe's coloured community, many of whom still carry his last name. You can also see Zulu household artefacts and displays on Zulu history. One of these covers the **Bambatha Rebellion**, in which Fort Nongqayi saw action, when Natal's colonial forces put down the last armed resistance by Africans till the formation of the ANC's armed wing in the 1960s. Also in the Fort Nongqayi complex are the **Zululand Missionary Museum** (same hours as the Zululand Historical Museum) in a replica of the fort's chapel, which contains exhibits relating to the Norwegian missionaries who came to this part of South Africa in the nineteenth century; a working **paper mill** where you can see boxes, photo frames, notepads and the like being made from sugar-cane fibre and even elephant dung; and the very touching **Phoenix Gallery** (same hours as the Vukani Zulu Cultural Museum), where drawings and paintings by the male (overwhelmingly black) inmates of Eshowe prison are stark and sometimes shocking expressions of their feelings of alienation and anger. There's also a crafts shop and the *Adams' Outpost* restaurant (see p.540) on site.

Dlinza Forest and aerial boardwalk

A must for bird-watchers, **Dlinza Forest** is also a great place for picnics or strolling along the impressive **Dlinza Forest Aerial Boardwalk** off Kangella Street (May–Aug 7am–5pm; Sept–April 6am–6pm; R25), on the southwestern side of Eshowe (it's accessed from the museums complex at Fort Nongqayi). Wheelchair-friendly, the boardwalk spans 125m and is raised 10m into the air just under the forest canopy, giving visitors a chance to experience a section of

▲ Zulu crafts being made at Eshowe

the woodland normally restricted to birds. The boardwalk leads to a twenty-metre-high stainless-steel **observation tower**, offering stunning panoramas across the treetops to the Indian Ocean shimmering in the distance. A **visitor information centre** at the foot of the boardwalk provides information about forest ecology. Among the birds you might see here are black sparrowhawks, crowned eagles and green coucals, while eighty species of butterfly have also been recorded in the forest.

Practicalities

The Durban–Swaziland **Baz Bus** passes through town, dropping off and picking up passengers at *Zululand Backpackers* at the *George Hotel*. The **Vukani shop** on Main Street, near the *George Hotel*, sells examples of contemporary Zulu craftwork. There's **Internet access** at Kils-Tec on Main Street opposite the Shell garage.

Based at the *George Hotel*, Zululand Eco-Adventures (☎035 474 4919, Ⓦwww.eshowe.com) offers **tours** giving an authentic experience of local Zulu life. It can take you to rural Zulu communities where you'll have the opportunity to attend a variety of Zulu ceremonies (see box, p.538), and see markets and *shebeens* without feeling as if you're in a theme park. The company takes an active role in the local community and one of the best things that you can do in Eshowe is to have it take you out to a school or an orphanage in the morning, where you'll spend an unhurried day with the kids before being picked up again in the afternoon – a rewarding experience for both you and the children, and one that involves only a negligible charge for the transport. Occasionally, **volunteers** are needed to work in various upliftment projects in the Eshowe area; if interested, contact Zululand Eco-Adventures.

Accommodation

Amble Inn 116 Main St ☎035 474 1300, Ⓔambleinn@corpdial.co.za. Simple rooms, half of them en suite, a large pool and meals on request. ❸

The Chase About 1km along John Ross Highway from the KFC on Main St ☎035 474 5491, Ⓦwww.thechase.co.za. This lovely, peaceful farm has two large en-suite rooms and endless views of the surrounding sugar-cane fields. There's also a small cottage sleeping five, with the option of B&B or self-catering. A pool, tennis court, Internet access and charming hosts add to the appeal. ❸

Chennells Guesthouse 36 Pearson Ave ☎035 479 4919, Ⓦwww.eshowe.com. A beautiful colonial home built over a century ago, with a large garden and very comfortable rooms. It's run by Graham Chennells and his son, Richard, who also own Zululand Eco-Adventures, the *George Hotel* and *Zululand Backpackers*. ❹

George Hotel 36 Main St ☎035 474 4919, Ⓦwww.eshowe.com. Compact and functional en-suite hotel rooms (some of them renovated) with TVs, but you'll probably come here more for the hotel's bar and restaurant (see below) than to stay. ❸

Zululand Backpackers behind *George Hotel* ☎035 474 4919, Ⓦwww.eshowe.com. The cheapest beds in town, with dorm rooms, doubles and camping. Dorms ❶, rooms ❷

Eating and drinking

The most popular place to **eat** in Eshowe is the restaurant at the *George Hotel* (daily breakfast, lunch & dinner), where you can get a filling lamb shank or steak dinner for around R80. Elsewhere, your best bet is *Adams' Outpost* in the museum complex at Fort Nongqayi (daily breakfast & lunch only), which serves healthy soups, lasagnes and home-made bread (mains around R50) as well as a good-value lunch buffet (R65) every Saturday. For drinking, head to the **bar** at the *George Hotel*, a newly renovated and quite stylish space which, if you're lucky, will be serving a beer or two brewed at the on-site **Zululand Brewery**.

Shakaland and Simunye

North of Eshowe, the winding R66 leaves behind the softer vistas of the Dlinza Forest, the citrus groves and green seas of cane plantations and looks across huge views of the valleys that figure in the creation mythology of the Zulu nation. In no time you're into thornveld (acacias, rocky *koppies* and aloes) and **theme park** country. Most accessible of these "Zulu-village hotels" is **Shakaland**, 14km north of Eshowe off the R68 at Norman Hurst Farm, Nkwalini (☎035 460 0912, ⓦwww.shakaland.com).

Built in 1984 as the set for the wildly romanticized TV series *Shaka Zulu*, Shakaland was taken over in 1988 by the Protea hotel chain. What the brochures don't tell you is that the village is a reconstruction of a nineteenth-century Zulu kraal and quite unrepresentative of how people live today. However, Shakaland just about manages to remain on the acceptable side of exploiting ethnic culture, and does offer the chance to sample **Zulu food** in a spectacular dining area. **Tours** for day visitors (daily 11am & 12.30pm; R210) begin with an audiovisual presentation about the origin of the Zulus, followed by a guided walk around the huts, an explanation of traditional social organization, a beer-drinking ceremony and a buffet lunch with traditional food (including vegetarian fare). The finale is probably one of the best choreographed Zulu **dancing** shows in the country, with the dramatic landscape as the backdrop; it's worthwhile putting up with all the other stuff just to see it. You also get to see a Zulu courting ritual, stick fighting and spear throwing, all of which are included in the price. **Accommodation** is available in comfortable traditional beehive huts (ⓞ), with untraditional luxuries such as electricity and en-suite bathrooms.

In a different league, **Simunye Zulu Lodge**, along the D256, off the R34, and 6km north of Melmoth, offers a far more authentic experience of Zulu culture, introducing guests to contemporary ways of life as well as traditional customs. Visitors are conveyed to the camp by horse, ox wagon or 4WD, and get to see dancing, visit a working kraal and meet local people. There's **accommodation** here (☎035 450 3111, ⓦwww.protea-hotels.co.za; full board ⓞ), encompassing stone-and-thatch cottages carved into the cliffside overlooking the Mfule River, as well as a beehive hut or rondavels at a kraal – all options have electricity.

Ulundi and Ondini

Some 83km north of Eshowe on the R66, **ULUNDI** is the former capital of the KwaZulu Bantustan and lies at the centre of the **Emakhosini Valley** (Valley of the Kings). The latter holds a semi-mythical status among Zulu nationalists as the birthplace of the Zulu state and the area where several of its founding fathers lived and are now buried. A memorial to them was erected in 2003, the Spirit of Emakhosini, on a hill 3km up the R34, beyond the junction with the R66 for Ulundi. The circular memorial is surrounded by seven large aluminum horns representing the kings that came before Shaka, while in the centre is an impressive six-hundred-litre bronze traditional beer pot. A local guide is available to explain the significance of the site (daily 8am–4pm; donation expected).

Now that KwaZulu has been reintegrated with Natal, this rather unattractive modern town has been tussling with Pietermaritzburg for pre-eminence in the province. Until recently it was the joint capital of the province with Pietermaritzburg, but when the ANC took control of the KwaZulu-Natal legislature in 2004, Maritzburg was named as the sole capital.

The **Battle of Ulundi Memorial**, just outside town on the tarred road to the Cengeni Gate of the Hluhluwe-Imfolozi Park, is the poignant spot marking the final defeat of the Zulus. An understated small stone structure with a silver dome houses a series of plaques listing all the regiments on both sides involved in the last stand of the Zulus on July 4, 1879. The rectangular park around the memorial marks the site of the hollow square formation adopted by the British infantry and supported to devastating effect by seven- and nine-pounder guns.

By far the most interesting sight around here is the **Ondini Historical Reserve**, a few kilometres further along the road (daily 9am–4pm; R15), which houses the reconstruction of the royal residence of **King Cetshwayo**, a site museum and a cultural museum. After the decisive Battle of Ulundi, the royal residence at Ondini was razed to the ground and Cetshwayo was captured. Still puzzled by Britain's actions, Cetshwayo wrote to the British governor in 1881 from his exile at the Castle in Cape Town: "I have done you no wrong, therefore you must have some other object in view in invading my land." The *isigodlo*, or **royal enclosure**, has been partially reconstructed with traditional Zulu beehive huts, which you can wander round, while the site museum has a model showing the full original arrangement. Among the items in the **Cultural Museum** is a major bead collection.

A **picnic site** has been provided in the extensive grounds of the reserve and there's **accommodation** at the well-run *uMuzi Bushcamp*. Here you can stay in a traditional Zulu hut, the choice ranging from beehives to grass and reed rondavels and more modern concrete huts, some en suite (❷–❸). All the huts are located in a traditional *umuzi* (homestead) with a central fire area for night-time gatherings. The camp offers tours to Emakhosini Valley, the surrounding battlefields, and Hluhluwe-Imfolozi Game Park, booked through Tinta Safaris (ⓣ035 870 2500, ⓦwww.tintasafaris.co.za).

The Battlefields

Most of the major KwaZulu-Natal Battlefields lie in the northwestern corner of the province, where first the Boers came out of the mountains from the northeast into Zulu territory and inflicted a severe defeat on the Zulus at **Blood River** in 1838, 13km southeast of the tiny town of Utrecht. Some four decades later, the British spoiled for war and marched north to fight a series of battles against the Zulus, the most notable being at **Isandlwana** and **Rorke's Drift**, southeast of Dundee. If you're only planning to take in one battlefield site, then Isandlwana should be the one, and you really should take in Rorke's Drift as well to complete the day; both sites are eerily beautiful.

Twenty years on, Britain again provoked war, this time against the **Boers** of the South African Republic and the Orange Free State to the north and west. The Second Anglo-Boer War (also known as the South African War) was fought over control of the Gauteng **goldfields**. British troops were landed at Durban, in the British colony of Natal, and boldly marched north. Britain believed the campaign would be quick, cheap and over by Christmas. But in the early stages of the war, the huge, lumbering British machine proved no match for the mobile Boers who fought a guerrilla campaign that checked the British advance in northern KwaZulu-Natal.

At **Ladysmith**, the British endured months of an embarrassing siege, while nearby, at **Spioenkop**, bungling British leadership snatched defeat from the jaws of victory. Although the empire successfully struck back, it took three years

Visiting the **Battlefields** with a qualified guide will infinitely enhance the experience. The guides below specialize in different battle sites, usually those closest to their base. Most guides have negotiable fees; expect to pay in the region of R350–800 for a day-trip, and to have your own transport.

The next best thing to hiring a guide is buying an **audio tour** to listen to in your car; these are available from reception at the Talana Museum (see p.545). The late David Rattray's excellent set of tapes/CDs *The Day of the Dead Moon*, covering Rorke's Drift and Isandlwana, is available from Exclusive Books in Durban (see p.482) or directly from *Fugitive's Drift Lodge* (see p.545/below). As for reading matter, one of the most authoritative **books** about the Anglo-Boer War is the highly entertaining *Boer War* by Thomas Pakenham (see p.878).

Recommended guides

Elisabeth Durham 39 Tatham St, Dundee ☏034 212 1014, ⓦwww.cheznousbb .com. Informative tours in English and French (R600–1000) of Rorke's Drift, Isandlwana and the route followed by the French Prince Imperial, who fell at Nqutu.

Ron Gold KwaZulu-Natal Tours ☏033 263 1908 or 083 557 4068, ⓦwww .kwazulu-nataltours.com. Gold specializes in the battles of Spioenkop, Willow Grange and Colenso, and the site of Churchill's arrest, offering half- and full-day tours (R600–800).

Fugitive's Drift Lodge ☏034 642 1843, ⓦwww.fugitives-drift-lodge.com. David Rattray, the doyen of battlefield guides, was based at this lodge (reviewed on p.545) near Rorke's Drift until his untimely murder during a botched robbery. The baton has now been passed to the lodge's other excellent guides, Rob Caskie, Joseph Ndima and George Irwin, who, like Rattray, are great storytellers. Their Isandlwana and Rorke's Drift tours leave the lodge at 7.30am and 2.30pm, respectively; each trip costs R790 per person.

Evan Jones ☏ & ⓕ034 212 4040, ⓦwww.battleguide.co.za. Extensive tours of the Battlefields (from R650) by a guide with a vast repository of knowledge, who breathes life into the battles.

Pat Rundgren ☏034 212 4560 or 082 690 7812, ⓔgunners@trsutnet.co.za. A large, burly man of Scandinavian/Irish descent, Pat provides an alternative perspective on the battles around the Dundee area. Tours cost R350 per day.

Foy Vermaak PO Box 1358, Dundee 3000 ☏ & ⓕ034 642 1925, ⓦwww.pennyf .co.za. Based close to Isandlwana and Rorke's Drift sites, in which he specializes; he also covers Helpmekaar and Fugitive's Drift. Tour rates are R650 per day for up to four people.

to subdue the South African Republic and the Orange Free State, two of the smallest states in the world, after committing half a million troops to the field in an operation that was the costliest campaign since the Napoleonic Wars nearly a century earlier.

Isandlwana and Rorke's Drift

On January 22, 1879, the British suffered the most humiliating defeat in their colonial history when virtually their entire force of 1200 men at Isandlwana was obliterated by warriors armed with spears. Dominated by an eerie hill, the **Isandlwana Battlefield**, off the R68 just over 130km northwest of Eshowe and 70km southeast of Dundee (daily 9am–4pm; R15), remains unspoilt and unchanged apart from some small homesteads and the graves of those who fell. A small **interpretation centre** houses artefacts and mementos.

The monumental bungling and the scale of the Zulu victory over the British sent shock waves back to London. Following the British ultimatum to the Zulus, three colonial columns were sent to invade Zululand. King Cetshwayo responded by sending a force against each of these. On January 21, 1879, Zulu troops encamped 6km from Isandlwana Hill, where one of the British columns had set up camp. Unaware of the Zulus over the brow, the British commander took a large detachment to support another British force, leaving the men at Isandlwana undefended and unfortified.

Meanwhile, a British scouting party rode to the brow of a hill and was stunned to find the valley filled with some 25,000 Zulu warriors sitting in utter silence. Because of a superstition surrounding the phase of the moon, the Zulus were waiting for a more propitious moment to attack. On being discovered, they rose up and converged on the British encampment using the classic Zulu "horns of the bull" formation to outflank the unprotected British, whom they completely overran.

The British press at the time demonized the Zulus for disembowelling the dead. In fact, the practice had a religious significance for the Zulus, who believed that it released the spirit of the dead. The custom also had a less spiritual significance; a Zulu warrior was required to "wash his spear" (ie kill an enemy) before he was allowed to marry.

Rorke's Drift

The same evening as the Isandlwana battle, tattered British honour was restored when a group of British veterans and sick successfully defended the field hospital at **Rorke's Drift**, just across the Buffalo River from the site of the earlier disaster, against four advancing Zulu regiments. Despite Cetshwayo's express orders not to attack Rorke's Drift, 3000–4000 hot-headed young Zulu men were so fired up by the Isandlwana victory and so eager to "wash their spears" – they were part of a reserve force and had not yet seen action – that they launched the assault. For twelve hours spanning January 22 and 23, 1879,

▲ The Isandlwana Battlefield

just over a hundred British soldiers (many of whom were ill) repulsed repeated attacks by the Zulus and so earned eleven Victoria Crosses – the largest number ever awarded in one battle.

Connected by the D30 road with Isandlwana, 15km to the east, Rorke's Drift is the most rewarding Battlefield to visit on your own, thanks to its excellent **field museum** and interpretation centre (daily 9am–4pm; R15). While you're here, it's also worth taking in the **Rorke's Drift ELC Craft Centre** (Mon–Fri 9am–4pm, Sat 10am–3pm), known for its hand-printed fabrics and tapestries depicting rural scenes.

Practicalities

For somewhere to stay in the vicinity, you could do worse than the blink-and-you've-missed-it village of **BABANANGO**, 92km northwest of Eshowe, which consists of a shop or two and not much else. The only decent option here is *Babanango Valley Lodge*, signposted 4km west of Babanango on the R68 (☎035 835 0062, ⊛www.babanangovalley.co.za; half board R990). It's situated on a Natural Heritage Site deep in a beautiful valley, where you can be taken on walks to explore the veld, rocks and river. **Accommodation** is in pleasant en-suite rooms, and there's a swimming pool. Under the same ownership is the luxury tented *Rockpools Bush Camp*, which consists of nine units along the edge of a stream, each with its own private patio and rock pool (❺). With a degree in animal behaviour, the proprietor John Turner combines tours of Hluhluwe-Imfolozi Park and ecological topics, including birding and basic tree identification, with Zulu historical sites and the Anglo-Zulu Battlefield.

Near the minuscule settlement of **HELPMEKAAR**, along the R33 south of the Rorke's Drift Battlefield and 30km south of Dundee, *Penny Farthing* (☎& ⒻÐ034 642 1925, ⊛www.pennyf.co.za; ❹) is a historic pioneer farm still furnished with a lot of original objects and generations of hunting trophies, set in an area of big open grasslands and hills, crisscrossed with hiking trails. The host Foy Vermaak is a Battlefields guide (see box, p.543) who enjoys fireside chats on the subject, and has a personal collection of memorabilia.

The ultimate Battlefields place to stay, however, is *Fugitives' Drift Lodge* (☎034 642 1843, ⊛www.fugitives-drift-lodge.com; full board ❾) 9km north of Rorke's Drift along the D31 dirt road. Located on a huge game farm, this luxury lodge overlooks the drift where the few British survivors of Isandlwana fled across the Buffalo River. The colonial-style rooms are in individual cottages that open onto lawns and gardens, and guests eat together in a central dining room among the world's largest Zulu battlefield memorabilia collection. Owned by the Rattray family, the lodge used to be the base of eminent Battlefields historian David Rattray until his death (see box, p.543). His several protégés now conduct the tours for which Rattray was famous, each proving to be accomplished raconteurs in their own right indeed, the Battlefields tours offered here remain among the best available (if the *Lodge* is beyond your budget, you can always stay in Dundee and book one of the tours).

Dundee and the Talana Museum

Some 32km west of the Rorke's Drift turn-off, along the R68, **DUNDEE** has little to offer except shops, supermarkets and pharmacies, catering to a population suffering from the effects of large industries who have left the area in recent years. Dundee does, however, serve as a good base to explore the surrounding areas, and features the excellent **Talana Museum** (Mon–Fri 8am–4.30pm, Sat & Sun 10am–4.30pm; R15), 2km outside town on the R33 to Vryheid.

Under shady blue gums, the museum consists of ten historic whitewashed buildings from the time of the Battle of Talana Hill, the first engagement of the Anglo-Boer War, in 1899. The most interesting of these is **Talana House**, which gives information about northern KwaZulu-Natal conflicts, including Anglo-Zulu, Zulu-Boer and Anglo-Boer wars. The displays include weapons and uniforms, but most evocative are the photographs, which really personalize the wars and provide fascinating details such as the POW camps Boers were exiled to in far-flung parts of the British Empire, including St Helena and the Far East. Often-neglected aspects of the Anglo-Boer War, including the roles of Africans and Indians, also get some coverage. In a photograph of Indian stretcher-bearers, you may be able to spot the youthful Mohandas Gandhi, who carried wounded British soldiers off the Spioenkop and Colenso Battlefields. Arrangements can be made with the curator for guided tours of the museum and surrounding Battlefields (T034 212 2654). The museum also has the lovely *Miners Rest Tea Shop*.

There's backpacker **accommodation** in the vicinity at *Battlefields Backpackers International*, 90 Victoria St (T034 212 4040, Wwww.bbibackpackers.co.za; dorms ❶, rooms ❷), a small lodge with two doubles, two dorms and camping, which also offers worthwhile Battlefield tours conducted by owner Evan Jones (see box, p.543). Advance booking is essential at the unpretentious and comfortable *Lennox Guest Cottage* 3km east of town on the R68 (T&F034 218 2201, Wwww.lennox.co.za; ❹), run by former rugby Springbok Dirk Froneman and his wife, Salome. Be sure to sample Salome's four-course **dinner** (R170) – which rivals the fare at any sophisticated city restaurant. You can also stay in a cottage on a B&B or self-catering basis at *Chez Nous*, 39 Tatham St (T034 212 1014; ❹), run by charming French hostess and Battlefields guide Elisabeth Durham (see box, p.543).

Ncome Blood River

You can't fail to be amazed by the monument at the **Blood River Battlefield** (daily 8am–4.30pm; R15), 48km from Dundee on the way to Vryheid off the R33. Of all the Afrikaner quasi-religious shrines across the country, this definitely takes the biscuit, comprising a replica laager of 64 life-size bronze wagons on the site where the Boers defeated a Zulu army on December 16, 1838. During the apartheid years, this date was celebrated by Afrikaners as the **Day of the Vow**, a public holiday honouring a supposed covenant made by the Boers with God himself that if he granted them victory, they would hold the day sacred. Afrikaners still visit the monument on this day, but under the new government the public holiday has been recycled as the **Day of Reconciliation**, with Blood River also referred to by its Zulu name, Ncome. On the eastern side of the river, the **Ncome Monument and Museum Complex** (daily 8am–4pm; free) contains a display about the Zulu martial pincer formation, and a reed garden relating the importance of river reeds in Zulu life.

Ladysmith and around

LADYSMITH, 61km south of Dundee on the N11, owes its modest fame to one of the worst sieges in British military history nearly a century ago – the best reason to linger is to learn about the Anglo-Boer War at the Ladysmith Siege Museum – and more recently to **Ladysmith Black Mambazo**, the local vocal group that helped Paul Simon revive a flagging career in the mid-1980s.

"[Ladysmith] is famous to the uttermost ends of the earth: centre of the world's attention, the scene of famous deeds," wrote Winston Churchill as a young, gung-ho journalist covering the Anglo-Boer War for the *London Morning*

The unknown soldiers

Africans are rarely mentioned in the context of the Anglo-Boer war, a confrontation fought in a theatre where eighty percent of the population was black. Although both sides denied that Africans served on their side, the British employed around 100,000 blacks both as labourers and under arms, while the Boers had at least 10,000 blacks on their side – often press-ganged into service. After the war, the British denied recognition to Africans who had seen service with them, to the extent that Sir George Leuchars, Natal Minister for Native Affairs, blocked them from receiving their campaign medals on the grounds that it would "irritate" the Boers – to whom the British were now nuzzling up.

Post. Some 40km south of Ladysmith, near **Chievely**, is the spot where an armoured train carrying Churchill was blown up by Boers.

It's easy enough to walk around Ladysmith's small centre; Murchison Street is the main artery running through town, where you'll find banks, the post office and shops. Adjacent to the Town Hall, on the corner of Queen and Murchison streets, the **Ladysmith Siege Museum** (Mon–Fri 9am–4pm, Sat 9am–1pm; R10) is the obvious starting point for any tour of the Anglo-Boer Battlefields. The siege began on November 2, 1899, and lasted 118 days, with 12,000 British troops suffering the indignity of being pinned down by undisciplined farmers. This compelling little museum tells the story of the war through text and photographs, conveying the appalling conditions during the siege as well as key points in a war that helped shape twentieth-century South Africa, paving the way for its unification. The museum is also a good place to browse books about the war, written from both the British and Boer points of view.

Practicalities

Greyhound Johannesburg–Durban **buses** pull into Ladysmith at *BJ's Restaurant*. The **train station** (☎036 637 7273) is 500m east of the town hall, but arrival and departure times during the night make the train an unrealistic option. The **tourist office** at the Town Hall (Mon–Fri 9am–4pm, Sat 9am–1pm; ☎036 637 2992) has a good selection of literature on the Battlefields. Local battlefields tour guide Liz Spiret (☎036 637 7702 or 072 262 9669, ✉lizs@telkom.net) charges R650 for up to four people (you need to have your own transport).

As for dining, the **restaurant** at the *Royal Hotel*, patronized in former times by the more privileged of the besieged, including Frank Rhodes (brother of the more famous Cecil), is still the best place to eat in town (count on around R80 for dinner). Less formal are the *Robin Hood Steakhouse* on Alfred Street, noted for its spare ribs; and *Spur*, Oval Shopping Centre, Murchison Street (next to the Ladysmith Siege Museum), which does a wide selection of burgers, steaks, chicken and a salad buffet (daily 11am–11pm).

Accommodation

There are plenty of **places to stay** in Ladysmith, some of them plugging right into the Battlefields scene, with proprietors offering themselves as "Battlefields hosts".

Budleigh House 12 Berea Rd ☎036 635 7700, ✉slabb12@telkomsa.net. Rooms at this guesthouse are pleasantly decorated, featuring wooden floors and a subtle African feel. There's also a pool and sunny patio. ❸

Bullers Rest Lodge 59/61 Cove Crescent ☎036 637 6154, ✉info@bullersrestlodge.co.za. A smart thatched establishment with a large wooden deck overlooking town. The pub is filled with original battlefield artefacts. ❸

Hunters' Lodge 6 Hunter St ☎036 637 2359 or 083 627 8480, ✉jem@futurenet.co.za. This lovely old home is located in a peaceful neighbourhood and has eleven en-suite rooms surrounded by a well-manicured garden. ❹
Royal Hotel 140 Murchison St ☎ & ℗036 637 2176, ⓦwww.royalhotel.co.za. In the heart of town, this is the hotel that harboured the upper classes during the siege – and was regularly shelled by the Boers. Now a three-star establishment catering mainly to travelling reps, it's full during the week, which makes booking essential at any time of year. It can be noisy due to traffic. ❹

Spioenkop

Spioenkop Battlefield (daily 9am–5pm; R15) lies 35km west of Ladysmith and is set in the **Spioenkop Nature Reserve** (daily: April–Sept 6am–6pm; Oct–March 6am–7pm; R15). The bloodiest of all the Anglo-Boer War battles, Spioenkop took more British lives than any other and taught the British command that wars fought by means of set-piece battles were no longer viable. After this, the guerrilla-style tactics of modern warfare were increasingly adopted.

Some 1700 British troops took the hill under cover of a mist without firing a shot, but were able to dig only shallow trenches because the surface was so hard. When the mist lifted they discovered that they had misjudged the crest of the hill, but their real failure was one of flawed command and desperately poor intelligence. Had the British reconnoitred properly, they might have discovered that they were facing a motley collection of fewer than 500 Boers with only seven pieces of artillery, and they could have called in their 1600 reserves to relieve them. Despite holding lower ground, the Boers were able to keep the British, crammed eight men per metre into their trenches, pinned down for an entire sweltering midsummer day. Around six hundred British troops perished and were buried where they fell on the so-called "acre of massacre".

Meanwhile the Boers, who were aware of the British reinforcements at the base of the hill, had gradually been drifting off and, by the end of the day, unbeknownst to the British, there were only 350 Boers left. In the evening the British withdrew, leaving the hill to the enemy.

On the slopes of Spioenkop Mountain, the KZN Wildlife Ipika **bush camp** has two-bed safari tents with shared toilets, six-bed en-suite self-catering chalets (R120–175) and camping. Tours of the battlefield and outdoor activities, including wildlife-spotting, can be arranged at the colonially stylish *Three Tree Hill Lodge* adjoining the reserve (☎036 448 1171, ⓦwww.threetreehill.co.za; full board ❽).

Travel details

Trains

Durban to: Cape Town (2 weekly; 36hr); Bloemfontein (2 weekly; 17hr); Johannesburg (daily except Tues; 15hr); Pietermaritzburg (daily except Tues; 2hr 10min).

Buses

Durban to: Ballito (1 daily; 35min); Bloemfontein (2 daily; 10–12hr); Cape Town (3–4 daily; 20hr); Dukuza (1 daily; 1hr); East London (1–3 daily; 9hr); Grahamstown (2 daily; 12hr); Harrismith (5–6 daily; 4hr 30min); Johannesburg (11 daily; 11hr 30min); Knysna (1–3 daily; 15hr); Ladysmith (2 daily; 3hr 30min); Margate (2 daily; 2hr); Melmoth (1 daily; 4hr); Pietermaritzburg (12 daily; 2hr 15min); Plettenberg Bay (2 daily; 14hr 30min); Port Elizabeth (2 daily; 13hr 30min); Port Shepstone (2 daily; 1hr 30min); Pretoria (9 daily; 9hr); Richards Bay (1 daily; 2hr 30min); Sedgefield (2 daily; 15hr); Umhlanga Rocks (1 daily; 15min); Umtata (3–4 daily; 6hr); Vryheid (1 daily; 6hr).
Margate to: Durban (2 daily; 2hr); Johannesburg (4 daily; 8hr 30min); Pretoria (2 daily; 10hr).
Pietermaritzburg to: Bloemfontein (2 daily; 8hr 30min); Cape Town (1 daily; 19hr); Durban (12 daily; 2hr 15min); Johannesburg (16 daily; 7hr); Ladysmith (1 daily; 2hr); Pretoria (12 daily; 8hr).
Richards Bay to: Durban (1 daily; 2hr 30min); Johannesburg (1 daily; 9hr 30min); Pretoria (1 daily; 10hr).

Baz Buses

Baz Buses north from Durban to Johannesburg and Pretoria travel either via the Drakensberg or via Swaziland, the latter being an overnight journey. For more about Baz Bus routes, see p.42.

Durban to: Amphitheatre (3 weekly; 5hr); Ballito (3 weekly; 45min); Bushlands (3 weekly; 6hr); Cintsa (5 weekly; 6hr 30min); Coffee Bay (5 weekly; 8hr); East London (5 weekly; 9hr 45min); Eshowe (3 weekly; 2hr); Gingindlovu (3 weekly; 1hr 30min); Johannesburg (3 weekly via the Drakensberg; 10hr); Kwambonambi (3 weekly; 4hr); Malkerns (Swaziland; 3 weekly; 10hr); Margate (5 weekly; 2hr 30min); Mtubatuba (3 weekly; 6hr 15min); Pietermaritzburg (3 weekly; 2hr); Port Alfred (5 weekly; 11hr 45 min); Port Elizabeth (5 weekly; 13hr 30min); Port Shepstone (5 weekly; 1hr 30min); Pretoria (3 weekly; 11hr); St Lucia (3 weekly; 5hr); Umtata (5 weekly; 5hr 45min); Warner Beach (5 weekly; 30min); Winterton (3 weekly; 4hr).
Pietermaritzburg to: Amphitheatre (3 weekly; 3hr); Durban (3 weekly; 2hr); Johannesburg (3 weekly; 8hr); Pretoria (3 weekly; 9hr); Winterton (3 weekly; 2hr).

Domestic flights

Durban to: Bloemfontein (5–6 weekly; 1hr 05min); Cape Town (2–7 daily; 2hr 15min); George (1 daily; 1hr 50min); Johannesburg (at least 33 daily; 1hr 10min); Nelspruit (1–2 daily; 1hr 20min); Port Elizabeth (3–6 daily; 1hr 20min); Pretoria (2–3 daily; 1hr 10min).
Margate to: Johannesburg (5 weekly; 1hr 30min).
Pietermaritzburg to: Johannesburg (4–7 daily; 1hr 30min).
Richards Bay to: Johannesburg (2–4 daily; 1hr 20min).

Free State

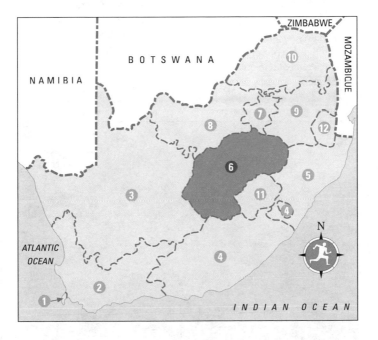

CHAPTER 6

Highlights

* **Highlands Route** A scenic drive past massive rock formations, cherry orchards and sandstone farming towns. See p.563

* **Basotho vernacular architecture** See the decorative adobe huts typical of the Eastern Free State and Lesotho at the Basotho Cultural Village. See p.564

* **Drakensberg Escarpment** Catch some of South Africa's most spectacular mountain views by climbing to the highest point on the escarpment via a chain ladder. See p.566

* **Golden Gate Highlands National Park** A stunning reserve dominated by the beautiful Maluti Mountains with their stripy red sandstone outcrops. See p.566

* **Street Café Restaurant** Sample one of 107 varieties of beer, sitting outdoors in the delightful town of Clarens. See p.569

▲ Basotho Cultural Village

6

Free State

The Highlands Route, one of South Africa's most scenic drives, skirts the mountainous eastern flank of the **Free State**, the traditional heartland of conservative **Afrikanerdom**, which lies landlocked at the centre of the country. If you're driving from Johannesburg to Port Elizabeth or Cape Town, the **Eastern Highlands**, which sweep up to the subcontinent's highest peaks in the Lesotho Drakensberg, are worth the detour off the more humdrum N6. The eastern Free State is also the **gateway to Lesotho**, with border posts close to each of the small towns on the South African side. **Bloemfontein**, the capital, is only worth visiting if you are driving on the N6 to reach the Western or Eastern Cape, rather than taking the Highlands Route, but once there you'll find very good guesthouses, restaurants and museums.

The highlight of the Eastern Highlands is the **Golden Gate National Park**, designated a national park not for its wildlife, but because of the beauty of the Maluti Mountains with their stripy red sandstone outcrops. It's an easy three- to four-hour drive from Johannesburg, and from here it's possible to do a round trip of the Highlands, taking in Lesotho as well. Southeast of Golden Gate you can drive to the Sentinel car park — access point for hikes up to the highest plateaus of the **Drakensberg** — via the interesting **Basotho Cultural Village** and **Phuthadijhaba**. West of Golden Gate is **Clarens**, by far the nicest of the string of towns running along the Lesotho border, with a distinctly arty feel, good guesthouses and outdoor cafés, and some of the country's best horse-riding. For young travellers, partygoers and ageing hippies, the real focus of the region is **Rustler's Valley**, west of Clarens, where you can ride, hike in the hills, party or simply hang out on a truly magnificent farm.

In the rest of the province, flat farmlands roll away into kilometres of bright-yellow sunflowers and mauve- and pink-petalled cosmos, with maize and wheat fields glowing under immense blue skies. Nelson Mandela described this area as gladdening his heart, "no matter what my mood. When I am here I feel that nothing can shut me in, that my thoughts can roam as far as the horizons."

Some history

Intriguing though it sounds, the name "Free State" applies to former redneck country. For nearly 150 years, the only free people in the Free State were its **white settlers**, who in 1854 were granted independence from Britain in a territory between the Orange and Vaal rivers, where they created a Boer Republic called the **Orange Free State**. The "Orange" part of the name came from the Orange River, which in its turn was named in 1777 by Colonel Robert Gordon, commander of the British garrison at the Cape, after the royal Dutch House of Orange. The system of government in the

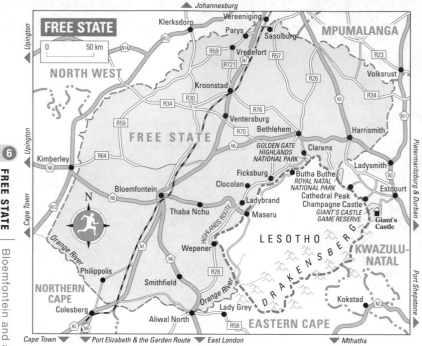

republic, inspired by the US Constitution, was highly democratic – if you were white and male. Women couldn't vote, while Africans had no rights at all, and were even forbidden from owning land. In 1912 the ANC was formed in the Manguang township of Batho, while the Nationalist Party was founded in Bloemfontien. In 1914, the Orange Free State became a bastion of apartheid, being the only province to ban anyone of Asian descent from remaining within its borders for longer than 24 hours. Africans fared little better; in 1970, under the grand apartheid scheme, a tiny barren enclave wedged between Lesotho, KwaZulu-Natal and the Free State became **QwaQwa**, a "homeland" for Southern Sotho people – a result of forced clearances from white-designated areas. The Bantustans have since been reincorporated into South Africa and, after an ANC landslide in Free State province in the 1994 elections, the "Orange" part of the name, with its Dutch Calvinist associations, was dropped.

Bloemfontein and around

BLOEMFONTEIN is located at the crossroads of South Africa, which means that many travellers break their journey across the country here. There's enough diversion for a day or two in Bloemfontein's surprisingly fine **Oliewenhuis Art Gallery**, set in beautiful gardens, and in the unmistakably provincial **President Brand Street**, lined with handsome, sandstone public buildings.

As an overnight stop, the city offers good accommodation at reasonable prices, upmarket shopping centres and a couple of nightlife opportunities.

People home in from all over the Free State for hospital treatment, for the university and boarding schools. As Free State's heavyweight city, Bloem (as it is usually called) is also the seat of the provincial parliament and South Africa's Court of Appeal. It's also a thriving international centre for **gliding**, the flatness of the local terrain and the hot summer weather producing some of the world's finest thermals.

If you're around in September, try to catch the ten-day **Manguang African Cultural Festival**, which fills the city with storytelling, poetry, art, music and dance and attracts people from all over the country (Ⓦwww.macufe.co.za). Otherwise, on April 28, there's the popular **Granaat Music Festival**.

Arrival and information

Translux, Intercape, S A Roadlink and Greyhound **buses** pull in at the central bus terminal in the tourist complex on Park Road, next to the swimming pool. There's also a **tourist office** here (Mon–Fri 8am–4.15pm, Sat 8am–noon; ℡051 405 8489, Ⓦwww.mangaung.co.za), which provides maps of the city.

Many travellers fly into the small **Bloemfontein airport** (℡051 4072240), 10km east of town on the N8. Although there are SAA scheduled flights between here and the major cities, they are very expensive, though there is one low-cost airline, Mango (Ⓦwww.flymango.com). There are no regular shuttle buses from the airport into town, so your only choice is to phone for a **minibus taxi service** (℡072 630 6210) or rent a car (see "Listings" on p.561 for details of both). By **train**, you arrive at Bloemfontein station (℡051 408 2262 or 086 000 8888) on Harvey Road at the east end of Maitland Street. One block west of the station on Hanger Street lies the **minibus taxi rank**. The area around the station and the minibus taxi rank is regarded by some residents as the dodgiest in the city centre, but there have been few actual incidents; stay alert, and avoid the area at night. Fortunately, metered taxis usually gather outside the train and bus stations; alternatively, you can phone for one (see "Listings" on p.562).

Accommodation

Bloemfontein's excellent *Hobbit Boutique Hotel* has won several awards over the last decade. The city also boasts some of the cheapest overnight **accommodation** in South Africa, mainly concentrated around the hospitals,

Gauteng to Bloemfontein: some route tips

Taking the **N1** from Johannesburg to Bloemfontein is the fastest way of covering the distance – and there's a lot to be said for getting the journey over with as quickly as possible. This is no scenic route, especially the Gauteng section and the northern Free State area, which is full of ugly little towns. Toll booths are strategically positioned at intervals along the N1, but the charge hardly makes it worth taking free detours. **Kroonstad**, 207km south of Johannesburg, is the biggest town along the N1 before you get to Bloemfontein. The Kroon Park, a large and popular resort beside a river, with a swimming pool, offers a pit stop if you want to cool off or get something to eat.

The alternative route from just south of the provincial border to Kroonstad goes via **Parys**, first along the R59 and turning onto the R721 at Vredefort, 13km south of Parys. But while Parys is quite green and pleasant, you're likely to get stuck behind slow traffic, whereas the N1 at this point is still straight, smooth and wide. The further south you go, the flatter the Free State becomes. There's an exceptionally long, dull stretch with no services between **Ventersburg** and Bloemfontein.

National Women's Monument & War Memorial

in Universitas suburb to the west of the city centre, and around Fichardt Park to its south. However, you're far better off heading for the more central suburbs of **Westdene** and **Waverley**, both just north of the centre and easily reached on foot.

Bohemian Guest House 16 Connor St, Westdene ☎051 448 0820, ⓦwww.bohemianguesthouse .co.za. A small, friendly guesthouse with large comfortable rooms in an unusual 1930s home. ❷

Canada House 19 Waverley Rd, Waverley ☎0514334592 or 082 486 8376, ⓦwww .wheretostay.co.za/canadahouse. A reasonably priced self-catering option, offering four units with separate entrances, all with good-quality beds and linen. Pet-friendly. Breakfast on request. ❸

Cherry Tree Cottage 12A Peter Crescent, Waverley ☎051 436 4334 or 072 291 0336. ⓦwww.sa-venues.com/fs/cherrytree.htm. A peaceful, a/c B&B set in a beautifully landscaped garden and bordering a reserve with resident giraffe. Four bedrooms under thatch and a family unit with separate entrances. ❸

City Lodge On the corner of Nelson Mandela Drive and Parfitt Ave, Westdene, and well situated for lively Second St ☎051 444 2974, ⓦwww .citylodge.co.za. A fully revamped hotel in a fairly characterless chain offering good value, with cheaper rates at weekends. Serves excellent breakfasts. ❹

Hobbit Boutique Hotel 19 President Steyn Ave, Westdene ☎051 447 0663, ⓦwww.hobbit.co.za. Inspired by Tolkien's *The Hobbit*, this is the best place to stay in Bloemfontein, a luxurious establishment filled with beautiful and comfort-able antique furniture, with teddy bears tucked into every bed under handmade quilts. Excellent three-course dinners are available for guests (phone by lunchtime). Book well in advance. ❹

Hotel Formula One 200 Nelson Mandela Drive ℡051 444 3523. No frills, thrills or surprises at this basic but predictably clean and reliable budget chain hotel. ❷

Kleine Eden Guest House 2 Moffett St, Fichardt Park ℡051 525 2633, ⓦwww.kleine-eden.co.za. Well-maintained guesthouse with B&B, self-catering and family unit options. Rooms all have their own entrance and private garden. ❷–❸

De Oude Kraal Country Lodge 35km south of Bloemfontein on the N1, off the Riversford exit ℡051 564 0636, ⓦwww.oudekraal.co.za. A restored original farmhouse furnished with family heirlooms, famed for its splendid Afrikaner meals. The en-suite rooms have their own fireplace. ❹

Southern Sun Bloemfontein On the corner of Nelson Mandela Drive and Melville St, Brandwag ℡051 444 1253, ⓦwww.southernsun .co.za. The best of the large hotels, with sizeable rooms, a nice swimming pool, and weekend discounts. ❹

The City

For a city with a countrywide reputation as the bumpkin capital of South Africa, Bloemfontein is actually quite agreeable, with a high standard of living for its middle-class residents. The slightly unreal character results from many of its late nineteenth- and early twentieth-century **public buildings** paying a pick'n'mix homage to Mediterranean, British, Renaissance and Classical influences. The lack of public transport is no obstacle to getting around, as the central area can easily be crossed on foot in ten minutes.

In common with other South African cities, the white population has deserted the city centre. Instead, the suburb of **Westdene**, just to the north of the city centre, has become the place to shop and hang out; the large four-storied Mimosa Mall in Kellner Street provides all you'd need, from coffee shops and chain restaurants to banks and bookshops. Westdene's Second Avenue has burgeoned with restaurants and nightspots, and is safe to stroll about at night, as is the **Waterfront** on Loch Logan, three blocks west of the City Hall – all conveniently near most of the accommodation. The city centre is nevertheless well worth exploring for its architecture.

City Hall and around

For a rewarding stroll in the centre, head down **President Brand Street**, starting at the **City Hall** at the north end on the corner of Charles Street. Built in 1934, the hall was designed in the "new tradition style" by Gordon Leith, a former employee of Sir Herbert Baker. On the opposite side of President Brand Street, **Hertzog Square** honours the dubious achievements of the Boer general, high court judge and Afrikaner nationalist **J.B.M. Hertzog**, who founded the National Party in 1914 and went on to become prime minister of the Union of South Africa in 1924. Across the square at 36 Aliwal St, the **National Museum** (Mon–Sat 10am–5pm, Sun noon–5.30pm; R5; ⓦwww.nasmus.co.za) is worth visiting for its rather good dinosaur fossil collection, an actual beehive, cut away to reveal the workings within, and an outstanding reconstruction of a turn-of-the-twentieth century Bloemfontein street. The museum also has a tearoom.

Returning to President Brand Street, south of the City Hall stands the Roman-style **Court of Appeal of South Africa** built in 1929. Staring at it from across the road is the **Fourth Raadsaal**, the last parliament building of the independent Orange Free State republic (it's now the provincial legislature). Built in 1890 – and still regarded as the province's "architectural jewel" – the Raadsaal is an imposing sandstone and red-brick construction, typical of Free State buildings of the period, and brilliantly merging Greek, Roman and Renaissance elements.

J.R.R. Tolkien

Bloemfontein's biggest surprise is that it's the birthplace of **John Ronald Reuel Tolkien**, author of *Lord of the Rings* and *The Hobbit*, a fact the city seems curiously reluctant to publicize.

Tolkien's father, Arthur, left his native Birmingham to work in the colonies, eventually becoming manager of the Bank of Africa in Bloemfontein. J.R.R. was born in 1892, in a house standing on the corner of West Burger and Maitland streets, a couple of blocks east of President Brand Street. When Arthur Tolkien died in 1895, his wife returned to England with her two infant sons; their house was later torn down to make way for a Bradlow's showroom, part of a nationwide cheap furniture chain. Despite wild claims that Tolkien's experience of the South African landscape inspired him to create the world of Bilbo Baggins, in fact, the flatness of the Free State and the down-to-earth Calvinism of its farming community could hardly be further from *The Hobbit*'s fantastical realm of mountains, forests and supernatural beings. Some accounts claim Tolkien was inspired by the Natal Drakensberg, or the Amatola Mountains around Hogsback. While both these areas do seem to possess an otherworldly magic, it should also be noted that Tolkien left South Africa for good when he was 3 years old, never having set foot outside Bloemfontein prior to his departure.

National Afrikaans Literary Museum

One block south of the Appeal Court in the Old Government Building, on the corner of President Brand and Maitland streets is the **National Afrikaans Literary Museum** (Mon–Fri 8am–noon & 1–3.45pm; free). Inside, a corridor of offices has been reconstructed as the studies of luminaries of Afrikaans writing; nameplates on the doors make you feel rude for not knocking before entering. Look out for the display on **Eugene Marais**, a remarkable polymath active around the turn of the twentieth century. A lawyer, poet and journalist, Marais contributed articles to the *Observer* and *The Times* in London and to the Reuter news agency – his works also include a couple of trail-blazing natural histories on termites and baboons. Also represented are the "Sestigers" (generation of the Sixties), including novelist **André Brink**, a vociferous critic of apartheid, and poet **Breyten Breytenbach**, who went into exile in Paris in 1961. Breytenbach returned to South Africa under cover in 1975 to gain support for Okhela, a largely white section of the ANC, and was captured by the South African authorities and imprisoned for seven years, leading to the publication after his release of *The True Confessions of an Albino Terrorist*.

Towards the end of the museum, a couple of rooms are devoted to displays of Afrikaans as a language of oppression. One of the leading lights of coloured Afrikaans (which has its own distinct flavour) is the poet **Adam Small**; in one display, he describes the predicament of being a member of an oppressed community, while at the same time being a speaker of Afrikaans – regarded as the language of white persecutors during the uprisings of the 1970s. "I grew up with Afrikaans. Afrikaans is part of my culture," he is quoted as saying, "and when people said to you that Afrikaans was the language of the oppressor it was very painful, because it was also the language you got from your parents, it was your mother tongue and it was beautiful and full of humanity."

The Waterfront and Zoo

Following the huge success of the Victoria and Alfred Waterfront in Cape Town, every city in the country, landlocked or not, seems eager to jump on the bandwagon. Bloemfontein is no exception; its **Waterfront**, opened in 1998 on

Loch Logan in King's Park, is a couple of blocks west of the National Afrikaans Literary Museum, and boasts movie houses, pubs and restaurants. Also in King's Park, **Bloemfontein Zoo** (daily: summer 8am–6pm; winter 8am–5pm) is a reasonable place to catch African wildlife. As well as the "Big Five", the zoo provides sanctuary for several antelope species, tigers, panthers, hippos and apes, and has a large variety of birds. Its most unusual inhabitant is the liger, a cross between a lion and a tiger.

The Supreme Court, Old Presidency and First Raadsaal

Carrying on south down President Brand Street to the corner of Selborne Street, opposite the Fire Station, is the **Supreme Court**, completed in 1906. It stands on the site of the home of the Fischers, a prominent Orange Free State Afrikaner family, whose heir, lawyer Bram Fischer, defended Nelson Mandela during the 1963 Rivonia Trial. After Mandela was found guilty and handed a life sentence, it was discovered that all the time Fischer had secretly been the leader of the proscribed Communist Party, and he too was jailed for life, later being released to die at home of cancer.

The **Old Presidency**, on the opposite side, was built on the site of the home of Major Henry Warden, the founder of Bloemfontein. It was built in 1861 in "Scottish baronial style" as the official seat of the head of the republic.

National Women's Monument and War Museum

Just over 2km south of the centre, along Monument Street, across the train tracks in an ugly industrial part of town, a sandstone needle pointing skywards marks the **National Women's Monument and War Museum** (Mon–Fri 8am–4.30pm, Sat 10am–5pm, Sun 2–5pm; R5). This stands as a memorial to the 26,370 Afrikaner women and children who died in British concentration camps during the second Anglo-Boer War. At the foot of the monument lies buried **Emily Hobhouse**, a British woman who energetically campaigned on behalf of the Boer internees, calling off her own engagement so she could dedicate herself to improving the appalling conditions in the concentration camps.

The interest of the adjacent **museum** lies principally in its status as a record of apartheid propaganda. The suffering depicted isn't an exaggeration, but it's a little heavy-handed in its unrelenting dioramas of dignified Boers suffering at the hands of faceless British brutes. Two cursory panels on concentration camps for Africans (never widely publicized in South Africa in the old days) are a post-apartheid afterthought that at least provides a partial record of the more than 14,000 black South Africans who died incarcerated.

Oliewenhuis Art Gallery and Freshford House Museum

The best of Bloemfontein's museums is the **Oliewenhuis Art Gallery** on Harry Smith Street (Mon–Fri 8am–5pm, Sat 10am–5pm, Sun 1–5pm; free), 2km north of the centre off Aliwal Street. The collection – which includes a surprisingly good range of **South African sculpture** and **painting** – is housed in the former residency of South African presidents, a beautifully light neo-Cape Dutch manor set in large, attractive gardens, surrounded by wild bush traversed by short walking trails. Particularly satisfying is the landscape collection, which includes a Van Gogh-esque interpretation of one of the city churches by **Bertha Everard**, and a **Thomas Baines** painting of Bloemfontein as a tiny settlement in 1850. Even if you're not interested in the gallery, it's still worth having tea at the **café** on the lawn – its trees and fountain make it the most harmonious location in town.

▲ National Women's Monument, Bloemfontein

Also to the north of the city centre, just across Nelson Mandela Drive, the **Freshford House Museum** at 31 Kellner St (Mon–Fri 10am–1pm, Sat & Sun 2–5pm; R3) makes a lightweight but enjoyable visit. This is especially true if you're interested in **interiors**, as it has been refurbished impeccably in Victorian and Edwardian style. One highlight is a room authentically decorated in daring lime green, with three distinct William Morris wallpapers.

Eating and drinking

While Bloemfontein is no culinary capital and there are no regional specialities to sample, you can still have a good and inexpensive **meal** here, with the best places mainly concentrated around Second Avenue. You'll also find the usual steakhouse chains scattered around the centre and in the shopping malls. For gluttonous **breakfasts**, the *City Lodge* and *Southern Sun Bloemfontein* hotels are always good bets.

Barbas Café Second Ave, near the university ℡051 430 2542. *Barbas* serves good Greek food, a range of cocktails and the best coffee in town. Its starkly fashionable decor also helps attract the young and trendy, with parties every Sat night. Mon–Sat 8am–midnight.

Beef Baron 22 Second Ave ℡051 447 4290. This high-quality restaurant specializes in rump steaks and tempting seafood dishes, and boasts an excellent and recently improved wine cellar. Open Mon–Fri for lunch & dinner, Sat dinner only.

Café Euro Mimosa Mall, Kellner St ℡051 444 6222. Gourmet sandwiches, salads and baked potatoes in relaxing surroundings. A handy stop if you're doing a bit of mall shopping. Daily 8.30am–11.30pm.

De Oude Kraal 35km south of town on the N1 ℡051 564 0636, ⊛www.deoudekraal.com. Five-course blow-out evening meals of rich, fattening Afrikaner-style food in lovely surroundings on a historic farm. Booking essential.

Fishpaste 31 President Steyn St, Westdene ℡051 430 2662. The trendiest restaurant in town, *Fishpaste* offers fusion cuisine from a well-planned menu. The artwork on display is part of the owner's gallery. Mon–Fri & Sun 11am–11pm, Sat 6pm–late.

Jazz Time Waterfront ℡051 430 5727. Live jazz once a month (usually last Fri & Sat), otherwise background music and a lively atmosphere; there's also a wooden deck from which you can survey passing pedestrians. Good cocktail menu, burgers and Middle Eastern food. Mon–Fri 8am–11pm, Fri & Sat until midnight.

Mystic Boer 84 Kellner St. Good choice for a drink, with a reasonable pub menu featuring pizzas and vegetarian meals.

The Terrace Harry Smith St, signposted off the R700. Tables in the formal gardens at the back of the gallery, leading onto a nature reserve, make this Bloemfontein's nicest place for a relaxing outdoor tea or lunch. Though the food itself is generally nothing to write home about, this is definitely *the* place for Sunday-afternoon tea and cake.

Nightlife and entertainment

Finding out what's going on in Bloemfontein can be a problem for visitors, as there's no English-language newspaper. A handful of bars down Second Avenue are worth checking out, including *Barbas Café* (see above), which is a lively place for a drink. The excellent *Moods and Flavours* (℡051 432 4399) in Heidedal – the coloured quarter – has live jazz from all over the country, though only on two to four nights a month; people dress up for a really good time here. There's monthly live jazz at *Jazz Time* (see above).

Bloemfontein's handful of **theatres** include the Observatory, inside a real observatory north of the centre on the crest of Naval Hill. It's situated in the city's nature reserve, which supports a few giraffe and some antelope. The most prestigious theatre is the Sand du Plessis, on the corner of Markgraaff and St Andrew streets, with the smaller André Huguenot Theatre in the same complex. Bloemfontein has several **cinemas**, mostly in suburban shopping malls and all showing mainstream movies; the Mimosa Mall in Westdene and the Waterfront are among the largest.

Listings

Airlines South African Airways, St Andrew's St ℡051 408 4800; Mango ⊛www.flymango.com.
Car rental Avis ℡051 433 2331, Budget ℡051 433 1178, Hertz ℡051 400 2100 and Imperial ℡051 433 3511 – all at the airport.
Emergencies Fire ℡10178; see also p.75.
Hospitals The main state hospital is Universitas, offering a free 24-hr emergency ward, but you may

wait hours and the level of care is variable. Far better, if you can afford it or have travel insurance, is one of the private hospitals: Mediclinic, Kellner St ℡051 404 6666; and Rosepark, Fichmed Centre, Gustav Crescent ℡051 505 5111.
Pharmacies Medirex Pharmacy, Southern Life Building, Maitland St ℡051 447 5822 (daily 8am–9pm).

Post office Main branch, corner of East Burger
and Maitland sts (Mon, Tues, Thurs & Fri 8am–
4.30pm, Wed 8.30am–4.30pm, Sat 8am–noon).

Taxis GG Taxis ☎051 522 6969; Bloem Taxis
☎051 433 3776.
Train information Spoornet ☎0860 008888.

South from Bloemfontein

Two major routes splay out and head south from Bloemfontein, the **N6** to the
Eastern Cape via Aliwal North and the **N1** to the Western Cape via Colesberg.
There's nothing much along either route apart from a couple of quirky small
towns. **SMITHFIELD**, a tiny *dorp* 145km south of Bloemfontein, makes a
good place to break a journey along the N6, if only to stay at the pleasant *Artists
Colony Guest House* (☎051 683 1138, ⊛www.artistscolony.co.za; ❸), or the
more luxurious *Smithfield House* in Brand Street (☎051 683 0071, ⊛www
.wheretostay.co.za; ❹), a restored Victorian house on the outskirts of town with
three en-suite rooms, its own pool and tennis court, and a seven-acre garden
where kids are welcome to run about. *Luigi's* (☎051 683 0021; daily
10am–10pm), along the N6, off Juana Square, is the place to **eat**, with good
Italian fare, steaks and homemade chilli-chocolate ice cream.

PHILIPPOLIS, 168km south of Bloemfontein along a slight detour (tarred)
off the N1 between Trompsberg and Colesberg, was one of the first settlements
north of the Orange River, established in the 1830s and named in honour of
Dr John Philip, a British cleric who set up a mission station here. Way ahead
of his time, Philip actively campaigned for the full integration of former slaves,
Africans and coloured people into the white economic and social system.

Today the village is mainly known for being the place where Sir **Laurens
van der Post** (see box) grew up. Laurens, the thirteenth of fifteen children,
was born on a farm outside the centre in 1906 and moved here when he was
still very young. The old Van der Post family home, on Colin Fraser Street, is
privately owned, but if you contact the owners you may be allowed to look
around it. Van der Post's ashes are in the Sir Laurens van der Post Memorial
Centre and Gardens, unmissable as you drive into Philippolis from Bloemfontein. The Centre includes Van der Post's large library, while the Gardens have
been built round the old pathway linking the white side of town with the
black township. *The Artist's Retreat* (☎051 773 0203, ⊛ww.phillipolis.org.za
/post.htm; ❷) is a small two-bedroomed guesthouse adjoining the centre, and

Laurens van der Post

Laurens van der Post achieved world renown as an explorer, writer, soldier and
philosopher. He became fascinated by the stories and legends of the "Bushmen", the
San people dispossessed of their traditional homes by the advance of African and
European settlers and forced into the northern deserts. "What drew me so strongly to
the Bushman was that he appeared to belong to my native land as no other human
being has ever belonged," wrote Van der Post, referring to the Bushman's self-sufficient
yet intensely spiritual and aesthetic way of life. It prompted him to take a famous journey
in search of the last remnants of the San, one he recorded in his book (later a film) *The
Lost World of the Kalahari*. This narrative, along with its sequel *The Heart of the Hunter*,
was one of the first literary works to prick the Western conscience with the idea that
such a primitive "tribe" had anything to teach us.

Van der Post was also a Japanese prisoner of war during World War II. His book
about these experiences, *The Seed and the Sower*, was made into the film *Merry
Christmas, Mr Lawrence*. He lived in both London and South Africa, and died in
1996, aged 90.

The Griquas

In the early nineteenth century, roving bands of cattle-herders and raiders with a reputation for horsemanship and fierce independence appeared on the eastern edge of the Cape Colony around the Orange River. They called themselves, with some pride, "Bastaards", being mixed descendants of European, Khoikhoi, Asian and African people. Missionaries persuaded them to establish settlements at places such as Griquatown, Campbell and Philippolis, but took exception to their name, which was changed to **Griqua**. Though Griqualand West was still theoretically independent, clashes with the Boers and squabbles over land ownership when diamonds were found in their territory saw the Griquas turning to the British for protection, faith which was all too hastily swallowed up by the gorging Cape Colony.

In 1861, three thousand Griquas from Philippolis under their leader Adam Kok III trekked across the Drakensberg to southern Natal to found a pocket of land known as **Griqualand East**. The settlement failed, and slowly the Griquas dispersed and became assimilated into the wider coloured community, although there are still odd pockets of their descendants living in various places around the Northern, Western and Eastern Cape provinces.

there are plans to create a Van der Post museum and writers' retreat in the little house next door.

Besides the Van der Post connection, there isn't much to the village, although it's a good place to see the mighty **Orange River** – it's easier to stop and contemplate the river on a quiet country road than flashing over it at 120kph as you do on the highway. Many of the tourists passing through Philippolis are disaffected city people in search of a rural idyll. Seventy-five of the village's houses have been declared National Heritage sites – a mixture of simple, flat-roofed Karoo and Cape Dutch gabled houses and Victorian buildings with characteristic wrought-iron decorative flourishes. Among the attractive old buildings lining the few streets is the house of **Adam Kok III**, leader of the Griqua. This small, white, flat-roofed house lies just before the post office on Voortrekker Street, the main thoroughfare running through the village. At the end of Voortrekker Street stands the large **Dutch Reformed Church**, built on the site of the original Griqua mission station. It's worth visiting on Sundays to sample local Afrikaans culture.

Signposted along the main road, the Van der Post Information Bureau (℡051 773 0203) can direct you to **accommodation** and informal tours of the village and provides a booking service. For self-catering, the *Philippolis Old Gaol* on Justisie Street (℡082 550 4421; ❷), two streets off the main road, is cheap, clean and more attractive than it sounds, with two beds to a cell. *Groenhuis Guest House and Restaurant* on Koksfontein Street (℡051 773 0073; ❷) is a very reasonable option with a warm and rustic charm, and home-cooked meals as extra, or try the inexpensive *Philipollis Lodge* on Kok Street (℡051 773 0203; ❷), a guesthouse with a restaurant (closed Sun). There's also *The Artist's Retreat* at the Van der Post Centre (see p.opposite). For **eating**, apart from *Philipollis Lodge* and *Groenhuis*, the central *Kokkewiet Café* is the village's meeting place; on Sundays, churchgoers sit at plastic tables and chairs to gossip and drink tea.

The Highlands Route

Hugging the Lesotho border for 280km from **Phuthadijhaba** (Witsieshoek) in the north to Wepener, beyond Ladybrand, in the south, the tarred

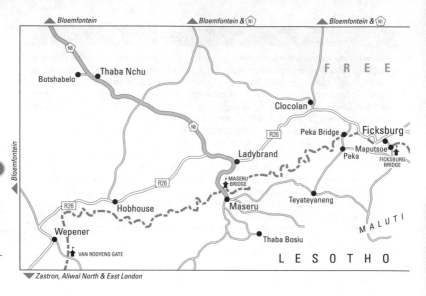

Bloemfontein

Bloemfontein & N1

Bloemfontein & N1

F R E E

Botshabelo
Thaba Nchu

Clocolan

Peka Bridge
Ficksburg

Ladybrand
R26
Peka
Maputsoe
FICKSBURG
BRIDGE

R26
MASERU
BRIDGE

Hobhouse
Maseru
Teyateyaneng

Wepener
Thaba Bosiu
M A L U T I

VAN ROOYENS GATE
L E S O T H O

Zastron, Aliwal North & East London

Highlands Route offers one of South Africa's most scenic drives, taking you past massive rock formations streaked with red and ochre, cherry orchards and sandstone farming towns. Wedged into a corner between Lesotho and northern KwaZulu-Natal, Phuthadijhaba is the gateway to **the Sentinel**, the easiest route onto the **Drakensberg Escarpment**, the roof of southern Africa. Not far to the west is the highlight of the region, the **Golden Gate Highlands National Park**, encompassing wide-open mountain country. The park is an easy three- to four-hour drive from Johannesburg, which means you could easily use it as a first- or last-night stop if you're arriving or leaving from Johannesburg and don't want to spend the night in the city. Nearby, the **Basotho Cultural Village** is worth visiting to gain some insight into Basotho traditions. The closest village to the Golden Gate is **Clarens**, a centre for arts and crafts and the most attractive of all the villages along the route, while to its west is the mountain retreat of **Rustler's Valley**, South Africa's New Age honeypot, which attracted young ravers and ageing hippies to its regular music festivals until it burned down in September 2007.

Basotho Cultural Village

The **Basotho Cultural Village** (Mon–Fri 8am–4pm, Sat & Sun 8.30am–4.30pm; entrance and half-hour guided tour R20; ☎058 721 0300, ⓔbasotho @sac.fs.gov.za) is 20km east of Golden Gate National Park and signposted from the main road, in the QwaQwa Nature Park. It offers a sanitized view of the traditional lives of the **Basotho** people, who have lived in the vicinity for centuries and have a close affinity to the people living just across the border in Lesotho. The main display in the village is a courtyard of beautiful **Basotho huts**, from organic circular sixteenth-century constructions to square huts with tin roofs and bright interior decor. In the courtyard are people in traditional dress; visitors get to meet the chief and sample traditional beer, hear musicians play and see a traditional healer. Also interesting is the *litema*, or external decoration on houses, put on by women and still visible in rural Basotho

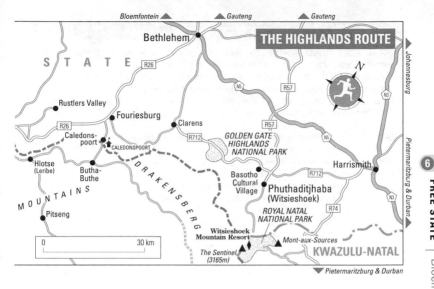

Bloemfontein ▲   ▲ Gauteng   ▲ Gauteng

Bethlehem ●

S T A T E

R26

N
Johannesburg

Rustlers Valley ●
Fouriesburg ●
Clarens ●
R26
Caledons-
poort ● CALEDONSPOORT
GOLDEN GATE
HIGHLANDS
NATIONAL PARK
R712
R57
R57
N5

●Hlotse
(Leribe)   Butha-
Buthe ●
Basotho
Cultural
Village ● Phuthaditjhaba
(Witsieshoek)
Harrismith ●
R712
N3

M O U N T A I N S
D R A K E N S B E R G
● Pitseng
ROYAL NATAL
NATIONAL PARK
R74

0   30 km
Witsieshoek
Mountain Resort
● Mont-aux-Sources
The Sentinel
(3165m)
KWAZULU-NATAL

Pietermaritzburg & Durban

FREE STATE   Bloemfontein and around

6

▼ Pietermaritzburg & Durban

settlements. The decoration varies from repeat patterns scratched into the mud-coloured plasterwork to vivid, modern motifs.

The views across the QwaQwa Nature Park are awesome, and this is a great place to visit, with an endless choice of walks. A **curio shop** sells some quality local crafts (look out for raffia mats and baskets and the conical hats unique to this area), and an open-air **tea garden** serves teas and traditional food.

Phuthadijhaba and around

The only reason you're likely to drive through **PHUTHADIJHABA** (sometimes called Witsieshoek), roughly 2km off the R712 and east of Golden Gate, is to reach the *Witsieshoek Mountain Resort* and the Sentinel car park, the easiest hiking access onto the High Drakensberg Escarpment. Phuthadijhaba itself is rather bleak and functional, home to light industry and brick matchbox houses. In contrast to the emptiness of the landscape around Golden Gate, in Phuthadijhaba you'll see minibus taxis zipping around, and people and animals walking on the roadsides past shacks, their tin roofs weighted down against the wind with stones. Phuthadijhaba was the artificially created capital of the former **QwaQwa** Bantustan, and references to that miserable episode are still found in road signs and around town.

The *Witsieshoek Mountain Resort* is reached along the R720 and is clearly signposted from Phuthadijhaba. About 15km from Phuthadijhaba the road comes to a fork, one branch of which ends at the inn and the other at the **Sentinel car park**. The road is tarred until the final few kilometres. On maps, it looks as if the Royal Natal National Park and *Witsieshoek Mountain Resort* are adjoining. They are, but only via footpaths up and down mountains – by road, the journey from the Royal Natal National Park to the Sentinel car park is about 100km, into KwaZulu-Natal and around the high peaks.

The *Witsieshoek Mountain Resort* (☎058 713 6361 or 6362, Ⓕ058 789 4984; ❸) is one of the great lost opportunities of South African architecture; it has the most spectacular setting of any mountain resort in the country, but possibly the worst planning. **Accommodation** has been placed just below the brow of a plateau,

Hiking up the Drakensberg Escarpment

South Africa's most spectacular mountain views are from the **Drakensberg Escarpment**, the broad area right at the top of the major peaks, and from the top of the Amphitheatre, the grand sweep of mountains dominating the Royal Natal National Park. Both of these require a high level of fitness to reach if approached from KwaZulu-Natal (see p.502). However, they can be achieved relatively easily via the Free State from the Sentinel car park. A tough ten-hour climb from the *Mahai* campsite in the Royal Natal National Park (see p.511), or a 2.5-hour, three-kilometre walk from the Sentinel car park brings you to the foot of a thirty-metre-high **chain ladder** leading up an almost vertical face; from the top, you can make the final short onslaught to the summit of **Mont aux Sources**, the highest peak on the escarpment (3278m). The downside of this shortcut is the litter around the ladder, although no more than 100 people are allowed up per day (book via the Basotho Cultural Village, p.564). Don't be lulled by your apparently easy conquest: it's the Berg's prerogative to have the last word. Always tackle the magic ladder with enough food, water, clothes and a tent in which to sit out violent storms, and set out early so you have the whole day for the excursion.

For those bitten by the mountain bug, some serious **hikes** are available, including a two-week trek along the escarpment plateau to Sani Pass in the southern Drakensberg. You can also take in the most dramatic parts of the Berg on a five-day, 62-kilometre escarpment traverse, sleeping in caves, from the Sentinel car park to Cathedral Peak in the Natal Drakensberg Park, roughly 40km to the southwest. For any hikes of this nature you'll need a map and the excellent *Drakensberg Walks* by David Bristow (see p.880), available in most bookshops.

---

thus denying guests one of the best views in the entire Drakensberg. Still, you can always walk in the mountains to take in the views, and the functionality of the rooms is made up for by friendly service. The more expensive rooms have excellent views of the Sentinel Mountain. There is an overnight hikers' hostel in the hotel grounds (①), which sleeps twelve and has electricity and hot water – but you need your own sleeping bag.

Golden Gate Highlands National Park

Roughly 300km northeast of Bloemfontein on the R712, **Golden Gate Highlands National Park** (open daily; R60 per person per day; ☎058 255 0012, ⊛www.sanparks.org/parks/golden_gate) is Free State's only national park. It was designated for its outstanding beauty rather than its wildlife; although **eland**, **zebra**, **mountain reedbuck** and **black wildebeest** roam the hillsides, the real attraction here is the unfettered space, eroded sandstone bastions and seamless blue skies. These rocks, grassy plateaus and incised valleys belong to the Drakensberg range, characterized here by spectacular yellow and red cliffs and overhangs.

A number of hour-long **rambles** into the sandstone ravines start from a direction board near the footbridge at the *Glen Reenen* campsite. There aren't many medium-length hikes in the park, the only exception being a physically challenging half-day walk up **Wodehouse Kop**, which offers great views. The most strenuous hike is the demanding two-day circular **Rhebok Trail**, which reaches the highest and lowest points of the park. You'll need to make an early start from the *Glen Reenen* campsite, where the trail begins; the Rhebok mountain hut on the trail provides basic overnight accommodation for hikers – bookings for the trail and hut must be made through South African National Parks. **Horse-riding** is also on offer, and can be booked, along with all activities, through the campsite (☎058 255 0012). In the summer you can **swim** in a natural waterfall pool close to the campsite, as well as in a regular pool; other activities at Golden Gate include fossil tours, scenic drives and hiking trails.

Practicalities

Golden Gate is almost equidistant from Bloemfontein and Johannesburg (320km to the north on good, tarred roads), and is easily reached from either city. There are no entry gates to the park, which is open 24 hours.

For **accommodation** on the day, call ☎058 255 0075, but for advance bookings call South African National Parks in Pretoria (☎012 428 9111, Ⓦwww.sanparks.org). **Glen Reenen Restcamp** has a swimming pool, a provisions store selling basics as well as frozen braai packs, firewood and alcohol, picnic sites and a filling station. The **Glen Reenen Chalets** have been upgraded with semi-luxury (❸) and economy family cottages (❷) and basic self-catering units (❷). The smartest place to stay, *The Brandwag Hotel* (☎058 255 1000 or 012 428 9111, Ⓦwww.sanparks.org), has well-equipped self-catering chalets (❸) and comfortable B&B rooms (❹), with breakfast and dinner available on request. Away from the crowds, and beautifully located, the **Highlands Mountain Retreat** offers luxury family log cabins (❸) and double rooms (❸). If the accommodation is full at Golden Gate, or you want somewhere cheaper to stay, head to nearby Clarens (see below) for a wider range of guesthouse options.

Your only choice for **eating and drinking** out here is at the *Brandwag Hotel*, which has a bar, coffee shop and restaurant – otherwise, once again, drive to Clarens.

Clarens

Some 20km west of Golden Gate Highlands National Park lies the tree-fringed village of **CLARENS**, the most appealing of the settlements along the Highlands Route. Founded in 1912, Clarens is especially remarkable for its dressed stone architecture, which glows under the sandstone massif of the

▲ Golden Gate Highlands National Park

Rooiberge (Red Mountains) and the **Malutis** to the southeast. The best time to see the village is spring, when the fruit trees blossom, or in autumn, when the poplar leaves turn golden russet. But at any time of year, Clarens's relaxed air makes it a rare phenomenon in the Free State – a *dorp* you'd actually want to explore, or sip a sidewalk lager and simply hang out in. All year round, but especially during autumn, when the leaves turn gold, the scenery is a magnet for artists and photographers.

Clarens is an **arts and crafts centre**, with a number of studios and shops peppering the streets. If you arrive around lunchtime on a weekend, there's a chance you'll catch some local live music at one of the streetside cafés on **President Square**, effectively the town centre in the middle of Main Street.

The several **galleries** along Main Street and around President Square are worth a visit if you're after gifts or souvenirs, though they're all quite similar in style; look out for the local Basotho tapestries, baskets and traditional hats. A real treat is the Di Mezza & De Jager Trading Store; to get there, follow the main road northwest to Bethlehem, before taking the *Maluti Lodge* turn-off. This is one of the few places in South Africa outside a museum where you're likely to catch an old-time general dealer's. The shop is crammed with provisions, lamps, bicycle parts, sweets and colourful blankets. These last are traditionally worn like cloaks by Basotho people, and make outstanding souvenirs.

Farmstays and horse-riding around Clarens

Horse-riding is big along the Eastern Highlands. A couple of **farms** near Clarens – both excellent family destinations – provide outstanding riding onto the Drakensberg Escarpment, from where you can gaze across into Lesotho and view southern Africa's highest peaks.

Friendly and very Afrikaans **Bokpoort** (℡058 256 1181, ⓦwww.bokpoort.co.za; ➊–➍) has a range of accommodation, from upmarket en-suite chalets, with fireplaces and kitchenettes, to self-contained, en-suite "mountain" huts, and dorms in an old sandstone barn (for which you'll need your own bedding). If you're camping, there's a good communal cooking and eating place. Reasonably priced meals, including dinner, can be ordered from the farmhouse kitchen, while a small shop sells basics. Bokpoort's big draw is the memorable **Western-style riding** in deep, comfortable cowboy saddles on sure-footed horses. Short rides from the farmhouse (R250 for 2hr) take in San rock paintings and swimmable river-pools, with the chance of seeing eland, zebra and springbok on the adjoining game farm. One-day riding trails into the mountains on the Lesotho border cost R550 per person (including picnic basket), R1000 or R1800 respectively for two- or three-day trails (including meals and overnight stay); a 4WD vehicle brings the food and bedding (you sleep on mattresses in a remote mountain hut), and you ride about six hours a day.

High-quality horses and riding are also available at **Schaaplaats Cottage & Ashgar Connemara Stud** (℡058 256 1176 or ℡083 630 3713, ⓦwww.ashgarhorses.co.za), in the mountains 6km south of Clarens off the R711 to Fouriesburg. An establishment with a more English flavour, this turn-of-the-twentieth century farm has four sandstone cottages sleeping two to eight people. (➋) From here you can go on terrific mountain hikes, visit Boer War graves and San rock paintings and, of course, ride horses (R150 per person for 2hr). There's also a chance to brush up your equestrian skills, as the owner is a qualified riding teacher. Moreover, there is some game on the farm (zebra and antelope), which adds zest to any ride.

Other activities in Clarens include bird-watching, fly-fishing, abseiling, whitewater rafting, swimming and tennis: contact the Adventure Info Service at Clarence Inn (℡058 256 1358).

Accommodation

There's plenty of **accommodation**, both in the village (all signposted off Main Street and easily walkable) and on surrounding farms. A useful **website** for booking accommodation and general information on the town is Clarens Destinations (☎058 256 1189 or 1542 or 082 921 8611, ⓦwww .goclarens.co.za).

Clarens Inn Van Reenen St ☎058 256 1480 or 082 377 3621, ⓔschwim@netactive.co.za. The cheapest place to stay, with the choice between a functional dorm, camping, two teepees and a range of self-catering units sleeping up to six people. ❶–❷

Cottage Pie 89 Malherbe St ☎058 256 1214 or 082 853 5947, ⓦwww. cottagep.co.za. One of the town's best B&Bs, with a garden chalet and two rooms inside the main house, offering breakfast on the patio and views onto a stream. ❸

Maluti Mountain Lodge Signposted just off the R712 on the edge of town ☎058 256 1422, ⓦwww.malutilodge.co.za. The most expensive place to stay, in pleasant rondavels in the garden or rooms in the lodge, the best of which are mountain-facing. ❹–❺

Red Mountain House ☎ & ⓕ058 256 1456 or 082 777 4755, ⓦwww.wheretostay.co.za. Centrally situated B&B which has rooms on the upper floor opening onto balconies with views onto Market Square's gardens and the Maluti Mountains. Rooms have fireplaces and are luxuriously furnished with Persian rugs and Victorian antiques. There is one large self-catering unit for families, and a restaurant and bar on the premises. ❹

Eating and drinking

Of the half-dozen or so **eating and drinking** places in Clarens, the *Street Café Restaurant* on Main Street is the busiest, due to its reasonably priced pizzas, snacks, steaks and salads, and the 107 (at last count) varieties of local and imported beers on offer. *The Highland Brasserie* (Tues–Sun daytime, Wed & Fri nights) on the town square offers similar prices, with an indoor fire in winter and outdoor tables and chairs when the weather is fine; it's especially recommended for breakfasts and cheesecake and coffee. *Red Mountain House*, 325 Market Square, offers specialized game and traditional dishes from an extensive menu, and has a good wine selection and a well-stocked pub. For an excellent meal try *Clementines Restaurant*, one block from the main square, opposite the post office (☎058 256 1616; lunch and dinner Tues–Sun), with good steak, salads, fish and pasta.

Fouriesburg and around

The funny little town of **FOURIESBURG**, 36km southeast from Clarens on the R711, earned its name from the high density of people named Fourie who farmed in the district. The hamlet hit the big time briefly in 1900; when Bloemfontein fell to the British in the Anglo-Boer War, Fouriesburg was proclaimed capital of the Orange Free State. Nothing much seems to have happened since, and a century later they still haven't got round to rescinding the proclamation – so technically it's still the provincial capital.

Overshadowed by the Maluti Mountains and the Witteberge (White Mountains), Fouriesburg serves as a decent overnight stop. There's some good **accommodation**, with the nicest place to stay being the *Fouriesburg*, 17 Reitz St (☎058 223 0207, ⓦwww.fouriesburgcountryinn.co.za; ❸). This small, wonderfully antiquated hotel has a green, low-slung corrugated-iron roof and comfortable rooms leading off the street-facing veranda. Lunch and dinner are served (the dining room is open to non-guests too), and the owners even let you rummage through the wine cellar to pick a bottle to accompany your meal. Just under 2km out of town, and signposted from the centre, the **Meiringskloof Nature Reserve** (☎ & ⓕ058 223 0067, ⓦwww.meiringskloof.co.za; ❷) offers one of the few places worth **camping** along the Highlands Route, and also a few self-catering stone chalets. Set in a sandstone *kloof* with plenty of trees, a swimming pool and a small grocery shop, the reserve is best avoided during holidays, when it gets packed. It's the starting point for a number of short **hikes**.

Rustler's Valley

In contrast to the conservatism of Fouriesburg, **Rustler's Valley**, 23km to the south and well signposted off the R26, set itself up as the **New Age epicentre** of South Africa. Located in a very beautiful valley in the foothills of the Maluti Mountains, this "mountain retreat" brought together a mixture of rave culture, Gaia philosophy, organic food production and environmentally friendly practices, plus plain old-fashioned hippiedom, with music festivals and parties drawing huge crowds.

Unfortunately, Rustler's Valley burned down in September 2007. For progress on its restoration call ☎051 933 3939 or check ⓦ www.rustlers.co.za.

Ficksburg

FICKSBURG, 48km south of Fouriesburg, is the closest town to Rustler's Valley. It's also the centre of South Africa's cherry and asparagus farming. The town's sandstone architecture gives it a pleasant ambience, and it's a good place to make a stop halfway down the Highlands Route. An annual **Cherry Festival** in the third week of November is the highlight of Ficksburg's calendar; it features a marathon, floats, stalls, a "cherry queen" competition and a popular beer festival.

The cheapest way to stay here is **camping** at *Thom Park* (☎051 9332905 or 083 592 1267; ❶), a caravan park bang in the centre of town, on the corner of Bloem and Piet Retief streets. Nearby, *Bella Rosa*, 21 Bloem St (☎ & ⓕ051 933 2623; ❹–❺), is a hugely popular and well-priced pair of Victorian sandstone houses with twelve nicely furnished **rooms**, all with baths, telephones and TVs. Dinner is available but must be booked, and tea is served on the very pleasant veranda. An alternative is *Green Acorn*, 7 Fontein St (☎051 933 2746; ❸), which has decent rooms with baths inside the house and in the garden. The best options for **eating** are the *Bella Rosa* (Mon–Fri till 9pm), which is licensed and serves above-average English-style food, and the family-oriented *Bottling Co*, at the corner of Piet Retief and Erwee streets (closed Sun), which also serves booze and does steaks, pastas, chicken, fish and a good lobster bisque.

Clocolan and around

CLOCOLAN, 33km west of Ficksburg, is a tiny farming town dominated by enormous grain silos. The town itself has little to offer travellers apart from a visit to the **Lethoteng Weavers**, in a house on the main road. The weavers are Southern Sotho women who use mohair and wool to produce lively tapestries based on traditional geometric motifs and imaginative illustrations of everyday life. To get to the main point of interest around here, you need to head some 9km out of town to the **Tandjiesberg rock paintings** at Tripolatania Farm (☎051 924 2475). Here you'll find some of the best San art in the Free State, with panel after panel of rock paintings overpainted with animal, human and supernatural motifs. These are also interpreted in an excellent monograph available from Bloemfontein's National Museum (see p.557) and sometimes from the farmer, from whom you have to collect keys and pay a small fee to get to the paintings.

If you're simply passing through, look for Clocolan's best overnight **accommodation** at *Makoadi B&B* (☎ & ℉051 943 0273; ❸) on Makoadi Farm, clearly signposted 1km northeast of town along the R708. Its spacious rooms off a veranda are furnished with antique farm items and ball-and-claw baths, and have original mud-and-dung floors. Rooms are available for the same price on a B&B or self-catering basis. There is a well-stocked shop on the premises, and on the farm Basotho women spin and knit most beautiful garments for sale. For longer stays, try the outstanding *Evening Star Cottage* (☎083 305 0658; ❷), which accommodates two people. *Evening Star* is 13km west from Clocolan on the R703. This romantically secluded self-catering thatched cottage is tucked into a rocky outcrop, its French doors opening onto a balcony with views of farmlands and mountains. Cooking is done on a fire outside in a beautiful rocky sitting area, with breakfast, lunch or dinner baskets sent up to the cottage so you needn't move. Near the cottage, there's a converted monastery with an overgrown garden, where the owner sells her own pottery and other crafts, and there's also a good hiking trail.

Ladybrand

LADYBRAND lies on the main route into Lesotho, just over 40km south of Clocolan. It's one of the only towns in the Free State which is booming economically, owing to its proximity to the Lesotho border, 12km away. Most people working on projects in Lesotho stay in Ladybrand rather than in Maseru, as it's pleasanter. As a consequence, **accommodation** is in very high demand, and doesn't come cheap. One of the best, and most popular, options is *Cranberry Cottage*, 37 Beeton St (☎051 924 2290 or 082 921 1575, Ⓦwww .cranberrycottage.co.za; ❹–❺), which offers 25 comfortable country-style B&B rooms (including five self-catering units), and excellent dinners, with vegetarians well catered for; guests also have use of a gym and health spa. The owners act as an unofficial tourist information centre and are able to give guests **information** on restaurants and rock-art sites.

The area is certainly fine **horse-riding** country, and Greenock Riding (☎051 924 2961, wwww.africanhorses.com/greenock; ❷), in a beautiful valley just north of town, offers superlative guided riding in isolated mountains. Accommodation is in self-catering log cabins, although you can take plain, well-cooked meals with the friendly hosts (and their pets) for a very reasonable amount.

When it comes to **eating**, there's pasta and pizza on offer at *Spizzy Pizzas* (closed Sun), a small café and bar on Church Street. For light meals, teas and coffees, *Cuppa Java* on the same street (Mon–Sat 8am–5pm) is the best daytime place in town. It serves sandwiches made with bread baked on the premises in clay ovens – and its delicious cakes are recommended. The best restaurant for dinner is the *Greedy Goose*, 32 Erasmus St (☎051 924 5124), open daily for steaks, salads and pasta.

Travel details

Trains

Bloemfontein to: Cape Town (Wed; 20hr 45min); Durban (Mon; 16hr); East London (daily except Wed & Sat; 14hr 15min); Johannesburg (Wed, Fri & Sun; 13hr); Port Elizabeth (daily except Tues & Sat; 12hr 15min); Pretoria (daily; 15hr 45min).

Buses

Bloemfontein to: Cape Town (4 daily; 11hr); Durban (2–3 daily; 9hr); East London (daily; 7hr 10min); Graaff-Reinet (5 weekly; 7hr); Grahamstown (daily; 7hr 30min); Johannesburg (4–5 daily; 6hr); Knysna (5 weekly; 11hr); Mossel Bay (5 weekly; 9hr 30min); Oudtshoorn (5 weekly; 8hr); Pietermaritzburg (2–3 daily; 8hr); Port Elizabeth (1–2 daily; 9hr); Pretoria (4–5 daily; 7hr).

Domestic flights

Bloemfontein to: Cape Town (2 daily; 1hr 20min); Durban (2 daily; 1hr 15min); Johannesburg (6 daily Mon–Fri, 2 daily Sat & Sun; 1hr 10min); Port Elizabeth (1 daily; 1hr 20min).

Gauteng

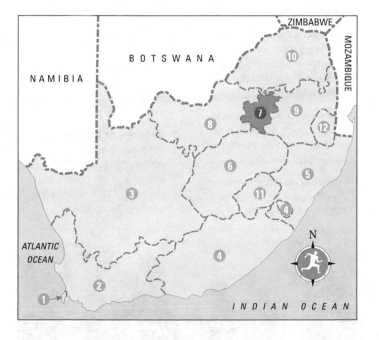

CHAPTER 7

Highlights

✳ **Downtown Johannesburg**
Experience a truly pan-African urban buzz at the heart of the continent's richest city.
See p.588

✳ **Melville** Hang out with Jo'burg's hipsters in one of the city's few places where bars, cafés and decent restaurants line the street.
See p.598

✳ **The Apartheid Museum, Jo'burg** A powerful, inspiring journey through the South African struggle for freedom.
See p.602

✳ **Soweto tours** Experience the vibrancy of South Africa's most historically significant township. See p.605

✳ **The big match** Whether it's Chiefs v Pirates or the Springboks v All Blacks, sport in Jo'burg is always big news.
See p.611

✳ **Live music** Make the effort and you'll find that Jo'burg has the best scene in the country. See p.612

✳ **Cradle of Humankind** A series of caves on the fringe of Johannesburg provides vital fossil evidence of human ancestry. See p.617

✳ **Church Square, Pretoria**
Sip an espresso at the century-old *Café Riche* or sit in the shade of Paul Kruger's statue and admire the grand architecture. See p.626

✳ **Voortrekker Monument, Pretoria** This icon of Afrikanerdom offers an insight into the people who dominated South Africa for a century. See p.629

▲ Township life

Gauteng

Gauteng means "Place of Gold" in Sotho, and no wonder: South Africa's smallest region comprises less than five percent of its landmass, yet contributes around forty percent of the GDP. Home to nearly ten million people, Gauteng is almost entirely urban. While the province encompasses a section of the Magaliesberg Mountains to the east and the gold-rich Witwatersrand to the south and west, the area is dominated by the huge conurbation incorporating Johannesburg, Pretoria and a host of industrial towns and townships which surround them.

Although lacking the spectacular natural attractions of the Cape Province or Mpumalanga, Gauteng has a subtle physical power. Startling outcrops of rock known as *koppies*, with intriguing and often lucrative geology, are found in the sprawling suburbs and grassy plains of deep-red earth that fringe the cities. The older parts of Johannesburg and Pretoria are gloriously green in summer: both are among the most tree-rich cities on earth, and Johannesburg, home to ten million of them, is proudly described by locals as the world's largest man-made forest. (When the ubiquitous jacaranda trees blossom in late spring, satellite images of the province take on a purple tint.)

Much of Gauteng's beauty lies in its glorious climate: days are mild, dry and nearly always clear in winter, but the long, balmy summer is especially addictive. On many hot summer afternoons, a sudden, thrilling thunderstorm gathers, sheds a mighty blast of warm rain, and then departs as quickly as it arrived, leaving behind a luminous, fragrant dusk. The region's **light**, particularly at dawn and dusk, is a photographer's dream, rendering serene even the starkest of industrial landscapes.

Gauteng is dominated by **Johannesburg**, whose origins lie in the exploitation of **gold**. Although it has grown rapidly in just over a century to become the richest metropolis in Africa, it is a hectic, sometimes dangerous city, home to extreme contrasts of wealth and poverty. It has a reputation among both visitors and South Africans as a place to avoid, but those who acquire a taste for Jo'burg – something you can do in just a few days – are seduced by its energy and vibrancy, unmatched by any other city in South Africa. A highly cosmopolitan city, and the most Africanized in the country, Jo'burg boasts South Africa's most famous townships, its most active and diverse cultural life, some of its best restaurants and the most progressive nightlife.

Some 50km north lies dignified **Pretoria**, the country's administrative capital. Historically an Afrikaner stronghold, today it is a fast-changing place full of civil servants and students from South Africa and around the world. Smaller and more relaxed than Johannesburg, Pretoria is an important and

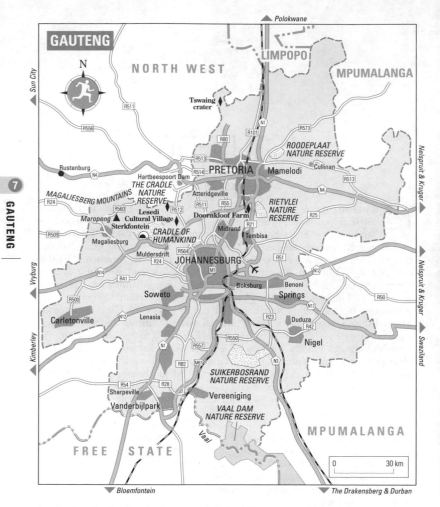

intriguing destination in its own right, with a range of interesting museums and historic buildings. Many visitors, however, see it simply as a safer and less intimidating alternative to its larger neighbour.

Less than an hour's travel from the centre of Jo'burg, the section of the **Magaliesberg Mountains** which extends into Gauteng is a magnet for Johannesburgers desperate to escape the city's hectic tempo. Although the hills can hardly be described as remote and untamed, you'll find ample opportunities for nature trailing and hiking. As in much of Gauteng, however, the important part lies underground, with a series of caves, underground passages and archeological sites making up the **Cradle of Humankind** World Heritage Site. Most famous of these sites are the **Sterkfontein Caves**, where some of the world's most important discoveries of pre-human primate fossils have been made.

Johannesburg and around

Frenetic, electrifying **JOHANNESBURG** has had a reputation for striving, greed and violence ever since its first plot auction in December 1886. Despite its status as the largest and wealthiest city in the country, it has never been the seat of government or national political power, allowing it to concentrate fully on what it has always done best: make money and get ahead.

Back in October 1886, when gold was discovered, what is now Johannesburg was an expanse of sleepy veld. Now it is the economic engine of Africa: a sprawling, infuriating, invigorating home to eight million people. Money remains Johannesburg's *raison d'être*, but its compulsive materialism has perversely made it a place of vision, possibility and openness. Ever since the first seam of gold was opened, the city has invited ambition. Radical politicians, inspired entrepreneurs, groundbreaking writers and hard-living entertainers have always been drawn to "Jozi", as it's affectionately known, from across South Africa and beyond.

During the apartheid era, Johannesburg was the city in which black resistance and urban culture was most strident: Nelson Mandela and Walter Sisulu formed the country's first black law firm here in 1952, before helping to sow the seeds of liberation. The township of Sophiatown, or "Kofifi", was a creative whirlpool of jazz, literature and journalism until the state erased it from the map with forced removals in 1955. In the democratic era, Johannesburg has been the vanguard of the gradual deracialization of South African society. The fast-growing **black elite** and **middle class** are concentrated here, and the city is a giant soup of ethnicities: Zulu and Sotho-speaking blacks, Afrikaners and English-speaking whites predominate, but Jozi culture is also enriched by immigrants from across Africa, as well as sizeable Indian, coloured, Chinese, Greek, Jewish, Portuguese and Lebanese communities. Jo'burg is an unpretentious, loud, ballsy city. Outsiders are quickly accepted, and the city's frantic materialism is leavened by a pervasive social warmth that keeps many of its more relaxed citizens – who you'd expect to prefer Cape Town – from leaving.

There are still astonishing extremes of wealth and poverty here and the inequity of the old South Africa remains apparent, but it is not as starkly racial as it once was: about one million black Jo'burgers have become middle class or rich since liberation, and there are many poor whites. That does not make the contrasts any less surreal: mansions in verdant **suburbs** are protected by high walls and electrified fences, only a kilometre or two from sprawling **shanty towns**. More township dwellers are moving to the suburbs than ever before – but jobseekers from the provinces are always arriving in even greater numbers.

A long spell of strong economic growth has sparked the construction of countless new malls – including the gobsmackingly lavish Maponya Mall in Soweto – and fantastically ugly townhouse complexes across the city, with property values rocketing. But growing pains abound: new low-income housing is not being built fast enough due to land costs, energy supply is wobbling as demand surges, and traffic is often hellish in the absence of a quality public transport network.

The central business district, which in the 1990s was all but abandoned by big business fleeing crime and grime, is undergoing a slow rebirth, with crime rates dropping and bolder property investors moving in. In the nearby inner-city flatlands of Hillbrow and Yeoville, hundreds of thousands of immigrants, mostly from Zimbabwe, have formed a teeming ghetto economy, since the formal job market cannot absorb most of them. As the centre readjusts, so the fringes expand: the city is reaching northwards every day, and soon there will be a continuous ribbon of development between Johannesburg and Pretoria, originally 50km apart.

The bewildering size of Jo'burg can be daunting for all but the most determined traveller. Some visitors fall into the trap of being too intimidated by the city's reputation to explore, venturing out only to the bland, safe, covered shopping malls and restaurants of the northern suburbs while making hasty plans to move on. However, once you've found a convenient way of getting around, either by car or in the company of a tour guide, the history, diversity and crackling energy of the city can quickly become compelling. Johannesburg offers fascinating **museums**, most notably the Apartheid Museum in Gold Reef City and the Museum Africa in Newtown, as well as excellent art galleries. Several suburbs have a thriving **café culture**, which by the evening transforms into a lively restaurant scene.

Shopping is Jo'burg's biggest addiction, and the city offers an abundance of superb contemporary African art, fashion and design. And then there are the **townships**, most easily explored on a tour but, in some cases, possible to get to under your own steam.

Jo'burg is also a great place to watch **sport**, with soccer, rugby and cricket teams commanding feverish support. Attending a soccer match between any of the three giants – Orlando Pirates, Kaizer Chiefs and Pretoria's Mamelodi Sundowns – is an exhilarating experience. And of course, the 2010 Soccer World Cup will be headquartered in Johannesburg and the final held at the spectacularly refurbished Soccer City stadium, near Soweto, which will seat almost 95,000 fans.

Some history

Johannesburg dates back to 1886, when Australian prospector **George Harrison** found the main Witwatersrand gold-bearing reef. Almost immediately, this quiet area of the Transvaal became swamped with diggers from near and far, and a tented city sprang up around the site. The Pretoria authorities were forced to proclaim a township nearby: they chose a useless triangle of land called the Randjeslaagte, which had been left unclaimed by local farmers. **Johan Rissik**, the surveyor, called it Johannesburg, either after himself or Christiaan Johannes Joubert, the chief of mining, or the president of the South African Republic (ZAR), Paul Johannes Kruger.

Mining magnates such as Cecil Rhodes and Barney Barnato possessed the capital necessary to exploit the world's richest gold reef, and their **Chamber of Mines** (a self-regulatory body for mine owners, founded in 1889), attempted to bring some order to the digging frenzy, with common policies on recruitment, wages and working conditions. In 1893, due partly to pressure from white workers, and with the approval of the ZAR government, the chamber introduced the **colour bar**, which excluded black workers from all but manual labour.

By 1895, Johannesburg's population had soared to over 100,000, many of whom were not Boers and had no interest in the ZAR's independence. Kruger and the burghers regarded these *uitlanders* (foreigners) as a potential threat to their political supremacy, and denied them the vote despite the income they generated for the state's coffers. Legislation was also passed to control the influx of blacks to Johannesburg, and Indians were forcibly moved out of the city into a western location. Before long, large shantytowns filled with blacks and Indians were springing up on the outskirts of Johannesburg.

In 1900, during the Anglo-Boer War, Johannesburg fell to the British, who had been attempting to annex the gold-rich area for some time. The High Commissioner, Sir Alfred Milner, imported whizz kids fresh out of Oxford and Cambridge to modernize the city. They lived in Parktown, and commissioned their houses from the celebrated English architect, **Sir Herbert Baker** (see p.597). At the same time, more black townships were established, including **Sophiatown** (1903) in an area previously used for dumping sewage, and **Alexandra** (1905). Bubonic plague erupted on the northern fringes of the city in 1904, providing justification for the authorities to burn several Indian and African locations, including **Newtown**, just west of the centre.

Meanwhile, white mine workers were becoming unionized, and outbreaks of fighting over pay and working hours were a frequent occurrence. Their poorly paid black counterparts were also mobilizing; their main grievance was the ruling that skilled jobs were the preserve of white workers. Resentments came to a head in the **Rand Revolt** of 1922, after the Chamber of Mines, anxious to cut costs, decided to allow blacks into the skilled jobs previously held only by whites. White workers were furious: street battles broke out and lasted for four days. Government troops were called in to restore order and over two hundred men were killed. Alarmed at the scale of white discontent, Prime Minister Jan Smuts ruled that the colour bar be maintained, and throughout the 1920s the government passed laws restricting the movement of blacks.

During the 1930s, the township of **Orlando** became established southwest of the city, with accommodation for 80,000 blacks; this was the nucleus around which **Soweto** evolved. By 1945, 400,000 blacks were living in and around Johannesburg – an increase of 100 percent in a decade. In August 1946, 70,000 African Mineworkers Union members went on strike over working conditions. The government sent police in, and twelve miners were killed and over 1000 injured. In the same year, informal settlers on municipal land attempted a rent boycott, proclaiming "Asinamali!" ("We have no money!"). They were ignored, and non-rent-payers were evicted.

Forced removals of black residents from Johannesburg's inner suburbs, particularly from Sophiatown, began in 1955. Thousands were dumped far from the city centre, in the new township of Meadowlands, next to Orlando, and Sophiatown was crassly renamed Triomf (triumph). The **ANC** (see p.829) established itself as the most important black protest organization during this period, proclaiming the **Freedom Charter** in Kliptown, Soweto, that year.

During the 1950s, a vigorous black urban culture began to emerge in the townships, and the new *marabi* jazz and its offspring, the jubilant *kwela* pennywhistle style, were played in illegal drinking houses called *shebeens*. This was also the era of *Drum Magazine*, which celebrated a glamorous, sophisticated township zeitgeist, and introduced a host of talented journalists, such as Can Temba and Casey "Kid" Motsisi, to the city and the world. *Mbaqanga* music emerged later, with its heavy basslines and sensuous melodies capturing the bittersweet essence of life in the townships.

The formation in 1972 of the **Black Consciousness Movement** (BCM) rekindled political activism, particularly among Soweto students. On June 16, 1976, student riots erupted in the township, and the unrest spread nationwide (see p.606). The youth's war against the State escalated in the 1980s, resulting in regular "**states of emergency**", during which the armed forces had permission to do anything they liked to contain revolt. Towards the end of the decade, the government relaxed "petty" apartheid, turning a blind eye to the growth of "grey" areas like Hillbrow – white suburbs where blacks were moving in.

The three years after **Nelson Mandela**'s release in 1990 saw widespread political violence in Gauteng right up until the day before elections. However, as elsewhere in South Africa, the election on April 27, 1994, went off peacefully. The ANC won comfortably in Gauteng then, and retained their hold in 1999 and 2004.

Just as new faces populate the corridors of political power, so blacks are also making steady inroads into positions of influence in business, finance and industry, where the true power of the province lies. Signs of such change can be seen almost daily on the pages of the country's business newspapers, and public–private partnerships are now initiating some bold plans for the province, notably the Gautrain Rapid Rail Link, a high-speed train system that will eventually link Johannesburg airport, the city centre, Rosebank, Sandton, Midrand and Pretoria. By 2010, the first phase of the network will be complete, connecting OR Tambo airport with Rosebank and Sandton.

Orientation, arrival and information

Johannesburg is large, sprawling and poorly planned, with few conventional sights and a bewildering number of districts. The **central business district (CBD)** is the Manhattan of Africa, a forest of huge office blocks looming over a bustling daytime street life. Nearby, the **Newtown Cultural Precinct** is the place to head for jazz bars, theatre and the highly informative Museum Africa. The inner-city suburbs of **Berea** and **Hillbrow** are packed with migrants from all over the continent, and are generally no-go areas for visitors. Some now apply the same label to **Yeoville**, once the city's trendiest and most integrated suburb. For a map of central Johannesburg, see pp.590–591.

The city's seemingly endless **northern suburbs**, the preserve of affluent, predominantly white Johannesburg, do offer a few pleasant surprises, notably **Parktown**, the original home of Johannesburg's richest residents, leafy **Melville**, with its trendy street cafés and agreeably unpretentious nightlife, and **Rosebank**, an easy-going area with some decent galleries and craft markets. Further north, opulent **Sandton** is the archetypal northern suburb, full of brand-new offices and mind-boggling shopping malls. Strangely enough, only the highway separates Sandton from one of Jo'burg's poorest areas, **Alexandra** township to the east. Southwest of the centre lies the city's most famous township, **Soweto**, the single most popular tourist destination in Johannesburg. Soweto is so vast it's arguably a city in its own right. Increasingly wealthy and forward-looking, it remains suffused with evocative memories of the struggle against apartheid.

Arrival

Johannesburg's **OR Tambo International Airport** (flight information ℡086 727 7888), once known as Jan Smuts, but renamed in 2006 after the ANC's greatest leader in exile, lies 20km east of the city. The international arrivals hall has an easily located **tourist information desk** (daily 7am–9pm; ℡0113903614) set in the middle of the terminal, offering a full range of brochures on Johannesburg and other parts of South Africa, including lists of places to stay, though it doesn't offer a booking service. There are 24-hour facilities for changing money and ATMs at various points in the terminal.

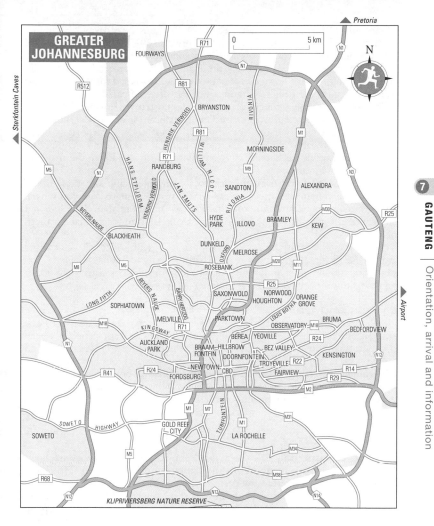

GREATER
JOHANNESBURG

▲ Pretoria

▲ Sterkfontein Caves

0   5 km

N

FOURWAYS

R71

R512

R81

BRYANSTON

RIVONIA

R81

HENDRIK VERWOERD

WILLIAM NICOL

MORNINGSIDE

R71

RANDBURG

HANS STRIJDOM

HENDRIK VERWOERD

JAN SMUTS

M9

M1

M5

N1

SANDTON

RIVONIA

ALEXANDRA

N3

R25

M30

HYDE PARK

ILLOVO

BRAMLEY

KEW

BEYERS NAUDE

BLACKHEATH

DUNKELD

OXFORD

MELROSE

M8

M5

M5

ROSEBANK

M20

M11

BEYERS NAUDE

BARRY HERTZOG

R25

SAXONWOLD

NORWOOD

HOUGHTON

ORANGE GROVE

LONG FIFTH

SOPHIATOWN

MELVILLE

R71

PARKTOWN

LOUIS BOTHA

OBSERVATORY

M18

BRUMA

M18

KINGSWAY

BEREA

YEOVILLE

R24

BEDFORDVIEW

N1

AUCKLAND PARK

BRAAM-FONTEIN

HILLBROW

BEZ VALLEY

KENSINGTON

N12

R41

R24

DOORNFONTEIN

R22

NEWTOWN

TROYEVILLE

R14

FORDSBURG

CBD

FAIRVIEW

R29

M2

M1

M7

TURFFONTEIN

M1

M31

SOWETO

HIGHWAY

GOLD REEF CITY

LA ROCHELLE

M34

SOWETO

M5

M38

R68

R12

KLIPRIVIERSBERG NATURE RESERVE

R12

N14

▲ Airport

7

GAUTENG | Orientation, arrival and information

There's a range of options for getting from the airport into the city or suburbs, which you can get advice on from the **public transport desk** in the arrivals terminal (daily 6am–10pm), where you can also book a taxi.

The **Airport Shuttle** (☎0861 748 8853; R210–290, R50 extra between 9pm and 5.30am) is another option, offering a round-the-clock pick-up and drop-off service, but bookings should be made a day in advance.

Another good bet is the **Magic Bus** service, which offers door-to-door transfers throughout Jo'burg (R220–350 depending on destination, R30–40 extra per additional passenger). By day, the Magic Bus also offers shuttles to major Sandton hotels (8am, 10am, noon, 2pm, 4pm & 6pm); 30min; R110). Get tickets at the company's kiosk (☎011 394 6902) on the ground floor of the Parkade building, just outside the domestic arrivals foyer.

Stanford Hlatshwayo (☎084 857 4967) runs **Aeroway**, a highly recommended taxi service from the airport (R150–250 for most parts of Johannesburg). He also offers township and general sightseeing tours, collecting and dropping off in-transit visitors at the airport. **KDR Tours** (☎011 3261700) also offers an in-transit Soweto cultural tour, charging R350 for the round-trip from the airport. For details of transport to Pretoria, see p.622.

The more expensive hotels often provide **courtesy buses**, while most backpackers hostels and some smaller guesthouses or B&Bs offer free **pick-ups** (but may charge for the trip back to the airport) or can recommend a reliable transport service. Touting at the airport by competing backpackers hostels has been very aggressive recently – sidestep the mayhem by booking in advance.

Taking a metered **taxi** from the airport is convenient and safe, though you should make certain the driver knows where you're going before you set off, and get a quote beforehand. You should pay no more than R250 to get anywhere in central Jo'burg, and no more than R350 to reach a far northern or western suburb.

If you want to prearrange a taxi, Airport Link (☎011 792 2017) charges around R275 for the first person and R50 for each additional passenger. You can also consult your hotel for more recommendations: there are many reputable tour operators who offer transfers at set prices.

By bus and train

Greyhound, Intercape and Translux **buses**, and **intercity trains**, arrive at **Park station** in the centre of town. Once notoriously unsafe, Park station has been significantly improved in recent years, and the main concourse is big, open and secure, with information desks for all the bus companies. From here, you're best off – and safest – taking a taxi to your final destination or arranging a pick-up with your accommodation. While buses and minibuses run from the station to virtually everywhere, finding out about them can be confusing, and waiting around outside the station – especially surrounded by luggage – can be risky.

Information

Gauteng Tourism (daily 8.30am–5pm; ☎011 327 2000, ⓦwww.gauteng.net) runs the show in Johannesburg; its most useful outlet is a **kiosk** (Tues–Sun 8.30am–4.30pm) attached to the African Craft Market in Rosebank.

Various free **maps** are available from tourist offices, but normally these cover only the CBD and parts of the northern suburbs. To get around other parts, particularly if you're driving around the city, you'll need a detailed street guide; the hefty *Witwatersrand Street Guide* is best, available from CNA newsagents or Exclusive Books bookshops.

A very useful website for information on events in Jo'burg is ⓦ**www .joburg.org.za**. It includes accounts of all the suburbs, and has lots of downloadable maps.

City transport

Johannesburg's **public transport system** leaves much to be desired: it's slow and unreliable, and practically nonexistent after commuting hours. **Driving** is very much the order of the day, though with patience and a bit of stamina it's possible to negotiate your way around the city by **bus**, and some areas are easily

With Johannesburg's extremes of poverty and wealth, its brash, get-ahead culture and the presence of illegal firearms, it's hardly surprising that the city can be a dangerous place. Despite the city's unenviable reputation, it's important to retain a sense of proportion about potential risks and not to let paranoia ruin your stay. Remember that all but a tiny minority of Jo'burgers have no intention of doing you any harm at all. The sensible course is to do as they do: juggle your fear and your bravado, without letting one swamp the other. As in all major cities, taking precautions – see Basics, p.73, and below – is likely to see you through safely.

If you're wandering around **on foot**, the crime you are most at risk from is **mugging** (sometimes violent). Although significant effort has gone into making the riskiest areas safer, remain alert when exploring the central business district (CBD), Braamfontein and Newtown, and only walk the streets here during office hours.

Security cameras monitoring the city centre have had a dramatic effect on cutting crime rates, but Jo'burg's CBD should not be considered as safe as Cape Town's, particularly at night, when it is deserted. A general rule of thumb, throughout Jo'burg, is to stick to the busy parts of town, and never be complacent.

Joubert Park, Hillbrow and Berea are regarded at present as no-go zones, and although Yeoville and Observatory are a little safer, these are places for those who are particularly confident or have someone to show them around. You're very unlikely to be mugged on the streets in Melville, Parktown or Rosebank. If you want to walk around one of the riskier areas, study maps beforehand (not on street corners), avoid asking for directions from passers-by, and don't walk around with luggage. Observe crowds coming your way to see if there are any young men (the main offenders) moving as a block. If you're carrying valuables, make a portion of them easily available, so that muggers are likely to be quickly satisfied. Never resist muggers; running like hell can work, but some have guns, which you won't know about until it's too late. You're unlikely to be mugged on public transport but, as always, it's wise to stay alert, especially around busy spots such as Park station and bus stations or taxi ranks. Waiting for buses in the northern suburbs is generally safe.

If you're **driving** around, note that there is a small risk of carjacking, particularly of German cars, and thieves have also been known to reach into open windows or break side windows to snatch valuables left on passenger seats. It's a good idea to keep all car doors locked and windows up – never wait in an unlocked car while a friend goes into a shop. Leaving or returning to your car are the most risky times, so keep a good lookout, don't dawdle, and seek out secure – preferably guarded – parking. Although local urban legends suggest you should only slow down at traffic lights at night, statistics show that more people get injured in car accidents than become victims of crime. When stopping at traffic lights in areas regarded as risky, keep a good distance behind the car in front and be aware of anyone moving around the car.

Don't expect too much from the **police**. Police on the street are rare, and normally have priorities other than keeping an eye out for tourists. In the city centre and Rosebank you can make use of **City Ambassadors**, people hired by a partnership between local government and local shops and businesses to provide an anti-crime presence on the street. Identifiable by their yellow caps and bibs, they're worth approaching for directions or if you think you're being followed.

explored **on foot**. Avoid the city's **train** system, which has a poor reputation and very limited services.

For short journeys around the city, consider using **private taxis**, which should be booked in advance by telephone (see "Listings" on p.617). This is an expensive option, however, as a simple journey to the CBD from the northern suburbs will cost at least R170.

Driving

By far the best way to explore Johannesburg is in your own car. The city is relatively well served as regards **car rental** agencies (see "Listings" on p.616), and you'll often find that backpacker lodges and some guesthouses can arrange the best deals. While the risk of carjacking is minimal, be aware that the cars most often targeted by criminals are German models, particularly luxury ones, as these are coveted both in South Africa and in neighbouring countries where they are smuggled by syndicates. The safest bet is to rent a French, Korean, Italian, Swedish or American car.

Although road signs can be poor and the local drivers pushy, familiarity with a few **key roads** and careful map reading before you set out makes driving around relatively straightforward. In the city centre, the grid system does make navigation reasonably logical, though it's beset by one-way streets and pedestrian precincts. The **M1** connects the centre to the northern suburbs, crossing above Newtown on a flyover, through Braamfontein and Parktown, and heading into Houghton and Sandton, eventually turning into the N1 for Pretoria. South of the centre, the M1 is one of the best routes to Soweto. The next artery west of the M1, also useful for heading north, is **Oxford Road**, which starts off in Parktown, and becomes Rivonia Road once it enters Sandton. Rosebank's Gautrain station construction site enforces a brief detour from Oxford Road, for northbound traffic, until 2010. West again is **Jan Smuts Avenue**, which passes through Rosebank and Dunkeld before hitting Sandton.

Buses

Johannesburg's **buses**, many of which are double-deckers, offer the safest and cheapest public transport during weekdays. Most bus routes start and end at the main terminus (℡011 403 4300) in Gandhi Square, off Eloff Street in the city centre; this is also where you can pick up timetables and route maps.

Buses only run between the suburbs and the centre, so are useless for getting from one suburb to another, unless they both lie on the same route to town. Most buses stop by 6.30pm, though a small number keep going until 9.30pm. At weekends very few routes have services and there are waits of at least an hour between buses. Fares (typically in the R4–10 range depending on distance) should be paid to the driver; ensure you get a ticket as you may need to show it to a ticket inspector.

Minibus taxis

Even cheaper than buses, **minibus taxis** cover a far wider area, and can be picked up at ranks, or hailed mid-route by either raising your forefinger (if you're heading into town), pointing downwards (if you want to go uptown) or pointing towards yourself (if you want Park station). The drawbacks, however, are worth bearing in mind; cramped cars, hair-raising driving, frequent accidents and petty criminals working the major taxi ranks have combined to deter most affluent Jo'burgers from using this mode of transport. If you do want to try one out, you'd be wise to wait at a smaller taxi rank, or wave one down en route – but never with bulky baggage. Most backpacker lodges know nearby useful routes and pick-up points and can give you a few tips.

Accommodation

Accommodation in Johannesburg is fairly easy to find. As a basic rule of thumb, the further from the city centre you stay, the safer but more soulless the suburb. There's little prospect of staying in the **CBD**, most hotels and hostels having joined the exodus to the northern suburbs when inner-city crime rocketed in the early 1990s. If you do want to be close to town, there are a couple of pleasant options in the central suburbs around the CBD: in **Braamfontein** just to the north, and in **Observatory**, just to the east. Points further east are only worth considering if you need easy access to the airport: **Eastgate** and **Bruma Lake** are self-contained around their vast eponymous shopping centres, while plain and suburban **Bedfordview** is easily reached from the motorway.

There's plenty of accommodation to be found in the **northern suburbs**, which, along with various artery roads leading out from the centre, are the easiest places to stay if you have to rely on public transport. **Melville** and its neighbour **Auckland Park** offer something many visitors don't expect to find in Johannesburg: a characterful, tight-knit community with hip cafés, restaurants and bars within walking distance of most of the guesthouses. **Rosebank** is well located at the heart of the northern suburbs, and has a number of popular shopping malls with a decent selection of places to eat out or shop. In **Sandton** there is a wealth of pricey chain hotels aimed at business executives, as well as some lovely large private homes with huge gardens which offer bed and breakfast. West of Sandton, **Randburg** is less expensive, but a bit isolated from the best parts of the city.

It is possible to stay in the **townships**, where a few guesthouses have been starting up. The most rewarding option is to stay with locals, something best arranged through an experienced tour operator (see p.605).

Some of the places reviewed in the central suburbs appear on the map on pp.590–591. The maps of Melville (p.599) and the northern suburbs from Rosebank to Sandown (p.596) also show the locations of many of the places reviewed.

Backpacker and budget accommodation

Jo'burg's **backpacker hostels** are less numerous and more changeable than the backpacker lodges in Cape Town or Durban. Most lodges offer free pick-ups from the airport, and although there are a couple close to the airport, the more attractive options are located at least twenty minutes' drive from the airport. Most hostels offer basic singles and doubles as well as dorms.

Central suburbs

Brown Sugar 75 Observatory Ave, Observatory Extension ☎011 648 7397, ✉brownsugar2000 @hotmail.com. A notorious backpackers hostel on Observatory Ridge, located in a mansion formerly owned by a drug baron and the only hostel left near Yeoville's Rockey St. Come here for a fast-track introduction to Jo'burg's hedonistic nightlife rather than comfort or chilled-out vibes. Free airport pick-up. ❶–❷

Diamond Diggers Backpackers 36 Doris St, Kensington ☎011 624 1676, Boasting a dramatic view of the inner-city skyline, this cheap but clean and organized lodge is not too far from the airport, but spiritually and geographically close to the pulse of the real Jo'burg. One of the best budget deals in town. ❶

Northern suburbs

Backpackers' Ritz 1A North Rd (off Jan Smuts Ave), Dunkeld West ☎011 325 7125, ⓦwww.backpackers-ritz.co.za. A well-known, busy lodge in a large suburban house halfway between Rosebank and Sandton (see map, p.596), with a pool, gardens, travel centre and a good bar. It's popular with overlanders, and camping is allowed in the grounds. ❷

Pension iDube 11 Walton Ave, Auckland Park ☎011 482 4055 or 082 682 3799, ✉idube@mail .com. Not so much a backpacker lodge as (in its own words) an "economy-class" B&B, with tastefully decorated doubles, a pool and a friendly, easy-going atmosphere, only a few blocks from Melville's cafés and nightlife (see map, p.577). Breakfast is included in the price, though you have to prepare it yourself. ❷

Sleek Backpackers 447 Jan Smuts Ave, Randburg ☎011 787 8070, ⓦwww.sleek.co.za. Relatively new to the backpacker circuit, this family-operated establishment is basic and clean with a pool, pool table and Internet access. It also offers a 24-hr minibus service, for a nominal price. ❷

Eastern suburbs

Airport En Route 97 Boden Rd, Benoni Small Farms, Benoni ☎011 963 1089, ⓦwww.sa-venues.com/ga/airportenroute.htm. Ten minutes from OR Tambo airport, this is a tidy, congenial lodge in the famously dozy suburb of Benoni, where film star Charlize Theron grew up. Free daytime airport pick-up. ❷

Gemini Backpackers Lodge 1 Van Gelder St, Crystal Gardens ☎ 011882 6845. ⓦwww.geminibackpackers.co.za. Rambling suburban property near Kew in the northeast of the city. There are dorms, double rooms and all kinds of extras such as a full-sized snooker table, tennis court, free Internet access, a pool and a rudimentary gym tucked away in an assortment of outbuildings. You'll need a car or the local bus service to get to decent shops and bars, although meals are served here daily. Free airport pick-up. ❷

Purple Palms 1 Boompeiper Ave, Birch Acres, Kempton Park ☎011 393 4393, ⓦwww.purplepalms.co.za. Cheerful, organized backpacker lodge, not far from OR Tambo Airport. Offers pool, ADSL Internet and book exchanges, plus a pick-up service for Kruger National Park safaris. ❷

Shoestrings Africa Airport Lodge 85 Gladiator St, Kempton Park ☎011 975 0474, ⓦwww.shoestringsafrica.com. This backpacker lodge occupies a large plot within sight of the airport, yet is surprisingly quiet, with decent dorm beds and private rooms available. Campers can pitch their tents in the spacious back yard. ❷

Hotels, guesthouses and B&Bs

While most of Jo'burg's hotels are tailored for the business traveller, it's possible to find some very comfortable and characterful **guesthouses** and **bed and breakfast** establishments, particularly in the northern suburbs. There are also some wonderfully opulent upmarket **hotels**, as well as large multinational **chain hotels** operated by Holiday Inn/Southern Sun (☎086 144 7744, ⓦwww.southernsun.com), Protea Hotels (☎086 111 9000, ⓦwww.proteahotels.com), City Lodge (☎086 156 3437, ⓦwww.citylodge.co.za) and Formula 1 (☎011 8070750 ⓦwww.formule1.co.za). All of these offer reasonable – if predictably characterless – rooms and are often well located; many can offer good deals. Also available are short-stay **self-catering apartments**: Don Apartments (☎011 709 1900, ⓦwww.don.co.za; ❹) has various apartment blocks around the city, including some in Rosebank and Sandton; all are secure, tastefully furnished and well equipped.

Central suburbs

The Cottages 30 Gill St, Observatory ☎011 487 2829, ⓔinfo@thecottages.co.za. Thirteen comfortable, characterful cottages perched on the Observatory ridge, with a large rock pool and paths through the lush plot opening out to great views from the top of the *koppie*. Self-catering or B&B accommodation is offered, with evening meals available on request. A safe, relaxing and welcoming place. ❹

Devonshire Hotel On the corner of Melle and Jorissen sts, Braamfontein ☎011 339 5611, ⓦwww.oriongroup.co.za. A decent choice if you have to be near the downtown area, this smart, business-oriented hotel offers the best views in the area, and features several bars and restaurants. ❺

The Westcliff 67 Jan Smuts Ave, Westcliff ☎011 481 6000, ⓦwww.westcliff.co.za. The *grande dame* of Jo'burg's upmarket hotels, and the preferred choice of visiting movie stars. *The Westcliff* is the size of a small village, painted pink and built on a high east-facing ridge. A main attraction is the hilariously affected Polo Lounge bar, which overlooks the lush green expanse of the northern suburbs – you can even watch the elephants in the nearby zoo. The cocktails are fantastic. ❾

Northern suburbs

Coopers' Croft 26 Cross St, Randburg ☎011 787 2679, ⓦwww.cooperscroft.co.za. A homely, no-frills B&B located on a suburban street near the Waterfront lakeside development, and with a gentle, friendly atmosphere. There's also a pool and tennis courts. ❸

Die Agterplaas 66 Sixth Ave, Melville ☎011 726 8452 or 082 410 4046, ⓦwww.agterplaas.co.za. Just a short walk from Melville's restaurants and cafés, this neat, tasteful seven-room guesthouse provides views over the Melville *koppies* from pleasant balconies. **❹**

The Grace in Rosebank 54 Bath Ave, Rosebank ☎011 280 7200, ⓦwww.thegrace.co.za. One of the most luxurious hotels in town, in a convenient central location used mainly by upmarket business travellers. **❾**

Melrose Place 12A North St, Melrose ☎011 442 5231 or 083 4574021, ⓦwww.melroseplace.co.za. A friendly, well-run family guesthouse with a stunning pool and garden, and spacious self-catering cottages and double rooms filled with African artefacts. It's close to Melrose Arch shopping and nightlife development, and the Wanderers cricket stadium. **❻**

The Melville House 59 Fourth Ave, Melville ☎011 726 3503, ⓦwww.themelvillehouse.com. One of the best Melville guesthouses, only a few hundred metres from Melville's cafés and restaurants. It's a lively, sociable place, genuinely plugged into what's going on in Jo'burg. The main building has a pleasant little garden and tastefully decorated rooms. **❹**

🏃 **The Melville Manor** 80 Second Ave, Melville ☎011 7268765, ⓦwww.melvillemanor.co.za. In an elegantly restored Victorian house, managed superbly and managed guesthouse is less than a minute's walk from the Melville restaurant strip. Pool, airport transfers and Internet in rooms. **❸–❹**

Melville Turret Guesthouse 118 Second Ave, Melville ☎011 482 7197 or 083 612 9632, ⓦwww.melvilleturret.co.za. This pleasant guesthouse, two blocks away from the trendy Melville main road, has designer decor, an airy patio and a tranquil atmosphere. **❸–❹**

A Room with a View 1 Tolip St, Melville ☎011 482 5435 or 082 567 9328, ⓦwww.aroomwithaview.co.za. A grand and charmingly surreal two-storey Italian-style villa, laid out and decorated in exuberant style, with seven double rooms and efficient service. Balconies and skylights make it light and bright, and provide something of a relief given the opulence of some of the antique furniture and artwork. **❹–❻**

Saffron House 84 Fourth Ave, Melville ☎011 726 6646, ⓦwww.saffronguesthouse.co.za. Located on a rather small plot just a few metres from the heart of Melville. The rooms use an inspired mix of Moroccan and Mexican decor that offers a unique sense of comfort. **❹**

Ten Bompas 10 Bompas Rd, Dunkeld West ☎011 341 0282, ⓦwww.tenbompas.com. One of Jo'burg's most stylish small hotels, each of its ten rooms decorated by a different interior designer. Quiet and intimate. **❽**

Eastern suburbs

Ah Ha Guest House 17a Talisman Ave, Bedfordview ☎011 616 3702 or 073 274 4917, ⓦwww.ahhalux.co.za. A pleasant if unglamorous family-run guesthouse, located near various shopping malls halfway between the airport and city centre, offering comfortable double rooms, self-catering suites and a decent swimming pool. **❺**

The Bedford View 26 Douglas Rd, Bedfordview ☎011 455 1055, ⓔbview@global.co.za. A fairly typical, neat suburban guesthouse with five rooms (two of which are in self-catering units), a nice garden and pool, within easy reach of various local shopping centres. **❺**

Dove's Nest 78 Gladiator St, Kempton Park ☎011 975 1746, ⓔdovesnest@hotmail.com. Only minutes away from the airport, this guesthouse has simple, clean, comfortable rooms. A free shuttle is operated to and from the airport and the nearby Caesar's casino complex, which has numerous restaurants and shops. **❸**

Jo'burg – French Guest House 16 Meintjies St, Rhodesfield, Kempton Park ☎011 394 5245, ⓦwww.joburg-frenchguesthouse.com. French-owned guesthouse offering a pool and free Internet access, conveniently located not far from the airport. **❸**

Soweto

Botle's Guest House 6648 Monyane St, Dube Village ☎011 762 6634. A block away from *Wandie's* restaurant, *Botle's* is an unprepossessing brick house, but it's very comfortable, secure and a short trip from Mandela's house, Desmond Tutu's house and the Hector Peterson Memorial. **❸**

Lolo's Guest House 1320 Diepkloof Extension, Diepkloof ☎011 762 6634. Smart, award-winning guesthouse in the historic Diepkloof district. Conference facilities, laundry services and tailor-made tours available. **❸**

Vhavenda Hills Bed & Breakfast 11479 Mampuru St, Orlando West ☎011 936 4275. This well-groomed, colourful inn is close to the Soweto tourism district. Satellite TV, laundry service and struggle stories are part of the deal. **❸**

Wandie's Place 618 Makhalamele St, Dube ☎011 982 2796. Situated next to the restaurant of the same name, these en-suite rooms are in a thriving neighbourhood. **❸**

Zizwe Guesthouse 8108 Ngakane St, Orlando West ☎011 942 2685 or 011 936 8983, ⓔzizwe@telkomsa.net. Close to Mandela's original home in the heart of Soweto, this guesthouse occupies one of the unadorned, flat-roofed buildings typical of the area. Rooms are simply furnished and have their own private bathroom, with use of a shared kitchen. **❷**

The City

For a decade and more, downtown Johannesburg has been battling urban decay and crime, but much is being done to inject vitality back into the city centre. The task of making the streets safe again has been taken up by the **Central Johannesburg Partnership** (CJP; Ⓦwww.cjp.co.za), who deployed the first yellow-bibbed City Ambassadors (see p.583). Real investment has followed: streets are being pedestrianized and adorned with public works of art, Vanderbijl bus station was redeveloped into Gandhi Square, and Mary Fitzgerald Square in Newtown upgraded.

It's now relatively safe to walk downtown, boutique hotels are being established and property prices have skyrocketed. Post-democracy landmarks such as the constitutional court at Constitution Hill, in Braamfontein just outside the CBD, and the spectacular Nelson Mandela Bridge from Braamfontein to Newtown have lent the area a touch of sophistication. The hope is that, before long, downtown Jo'burg will be transformed from a no-go into a must-go area for locals and tourists.

The central business district (CBD)

Johannesburg's **CBD**, the grid of streets and tightly packed skyscrapers just to the south of the Witwatersrand ridge, is the most recognizable part of the city. For a century after the first mining camp was built, on what is today Commissioner Street, the CBD was the core of Jo'burg's buzzing commercial and financial life. Then, in the 1980s and 1990s it became riddled with crime, precipitating a mass evacuation by businesses, shoppers, restaurants and tourists. When the Jo'burg Stock Exchange moved out in 1999 in favour of Sandton, the city centre was all but written off. However, with determined efforts over the last few years to regenerate the area precinct by precinct, many parts of the CBD are now not only safe, but are drawing businesses and tourists back. A visit offers the chance to see buildings and institutions with a fascinating history and get a taste of the bustle, sounds and thrills of a genuinely African city.

If you're coming into the city centre by car, **park** either underneath Gandhi Square or in the Carlton Centre nearby. Scheduled city **buses** from the northern suburbs terminate at Gandhi Square. Another good way to see the city centre is in the company of a **guide**: Dumela Africa (☎073 255 8780, Ⓔsayabona@gmail.com) offers expert walking tours of the downtown area as well as Jo'burg as a whole.

The Carlton Centre and around

The **Carlton Centre**, roughly halfway down Commissioner Street, is a good place to start explorations. There's a tourist office on the ground floor, and lots of shops and fast-food outlets, but the main attraction of this fifty-storey building is its top-floor **Top of Africa** lookout point (daily 9am–7pm; R10), which offers breathtaking views of the centre of Johannesburg, and how the mine dumps, reef and city concrete exist cheek by jowl.

From the Carlton Centre, head west for about three blocks along Commissioner or pedestrianized Fox Street, then turn south to **Gandhi Square**. A good example of the city's regeneration, this was formerly Vanderbijl Square, full of grim bus shelters and gangsters. As the former location of the Magistrate's Court where Gandhi spent so much of his time working in the city, the square was named in his honour and spruced up with some attractive brickwork. Still the main station for city buses, it's now a safe place to orientate yourself.

Gandhi in Johannesburg

Although **Mohandas Gandhi** has many strong links with Durban, the South African city he arrived at in 1893, it was the ten years he spent in Johannesburg between 1903 and 1913 that first tested the philosophies for which he is famous. As an advocate, he frequently appeared in the Transvaal Law Courts (now demolished), which stood in what has since been renamed Gandhi Square in downtown Jo'burg. Defending mainly South African Indians accused of breaking the restrictive and racist registration laws, Gandhi began to see practical applications for his concept of **Satyagraha**, soul force, or passive resistance, as a means of defying immoral state oppression.

Gandhi himself was twice imprisoned along with other passive resisters in the fort in Braamfontein, on what is now Constitution Hill. On one of these occasions he was taken from his cell to the office of General Jan Smuts to negotiate the prisoners' release, but finding himself at liberty had to borrow the railway fare home from the general's secretary.

Gandhi's ideas found resonance in the non-violent ideals of those who established the **African National Congress** in 1912. Forty years later, only a few years after Gandhi's successful use of Satyagraha to end the British Raj in India, the start of the ANC's Defiance Campaign against the pass laws in 1952 owed much to Gandhi's principles. Museum Africa (see p.592) contains displays on Gandhi's time in Johannesburg.

A couple of blocks to the northwest, on Loveday Street, the grandiose **Rand Club** (visits by prior arrangement only; ☎011 834 8311) is where mining magnates have come to dine and unwind for nearly a century. Completed in 1904, the building is actually the fourth to occupy the site, as each successive club was replaced to reflect the owners' growing wealth.

Four blocks south on Frederick Street lies the superb **Standard Bank Art Gallery** (Mon–Fri 8am–4.30pm, Sat 9am–1pm; free), a large and imposing round building with sweeping staircases, where changing exhibitions consistently show off some the best contemporary African art in South Africa. Just across the road in Standard Bank's head office at 5 Simmonds St, you can take a lift from the main concourse down to **Ferreira's Stope** (Mon–Fri 8.30am–5pm; free), an old mine tunnel discovered when the building was being constructed in 1986. The plain rock face you see still bears pick-axe scars, and there's a simple though fascinating display putting the history of Johannesburg in context; look out for the old sepia photographs of the mine and early Jo'burg.

Among the city's skyscrapers, imperious mining halls and boarded-up office blocks stand numerous interesting buildings, quirky facades and architectural features. North of Commissioner Street, look out for the recently revamped **Gauteng Legislature**, formerly the City Hall, on the corner of Harrison Street, while the former **post office** is one block east on the corner of Rissik Street. When this was completed in 1897 it was the tallest building in the city, and is still impressive, despite being dwarfed by later additions to the skyline. Neo-Baroque in style, it has quirky Dutch touches, primarily in its gabling. The fourth floor and clock tower are later additions, timed to coincide with the accession of the British king, Edward VII, in 1902. Elsewhere, on Pritchard Street stands **Cuthberts**, a department store which opened as a shoe shop in 1904, and **Markham's**, another department store, built in 1886. Two blocks further east on Pritchard Street is the **Johannesburg High Court**, a hated symbol of oppression when it used to be the Rand Supreme Court.

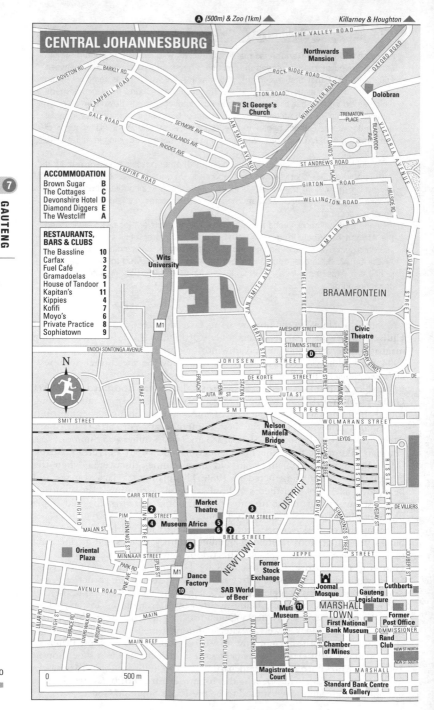

CENTRAL JOHANNESBURG

THE VALLEY ROAD

Northwards Mansion

DOVETON RD | BARKLY RD.

ROCK RIDGE ROAD

ETON ROAD

Dolobran

CAMPBELL ROAD

St George's Church

TREMATON PLACE

GALE ROAD

SEYMORE AVE

FALKLANDS AVE

RHODES AVE

ST ANDREWS ROAD

EMPIRE ROAD

GIRTON ROAD

WELLINGTON ROAD

ACCOMMODATION

Brown Sugar	B
The Cottages	C
Devonshire Hotel	D
Diamond Diggers	E
The Westcliff	A

RESTAURANTS, BARS & CLUBS

The Bassline	10
Carfax	3
Fuel Café	2
Gramadoelas	5
House of Tandoor	1
Kapitan's	11
Kippies	4
Kofifi	7
Moyo's	6
Private Practice	8
Sophiatown	9

Wits University

EMPIRE ROAD

BRAAMFONTEIN

Civic Theatre

N

M1

ENOCH SONTONGA AVENUE

AMESHOFF STREET

STEIMENS STREET

JORISSEN STREET

DE KORTE STREET

JUTA ST

SMIT STREET

SMIT STREET

WOLMARANS STREET

Nelson Mandela Bridge

LEYDS ST

DISTRICT

CARR STREET

Market Theatre

PIM STREET

Museum Africa

BREE STREET

JEPPE STREET

Oriental Plaza

MINNAAR STREET

NEWTOWN

Former Stock Exchange

Dance Factory

SAB World of Beer

Joomal Mosque

Gauteng Legislature

Cuthberts

AVENUE ROAD

Muti Museum

MARSHALL TOWN

First National Bank Museum

Former Post Office

MAIN

Chamber of Mines

Rand Club

MAIN REEF

Magistrates' Court

MARSHALL

Standard Bank Centre & Gallery

0   500 m

▲ Killarney, Houghton & Norwood

The Wilds

QUEENS

ST PATRICK ROAD
ST MARK ROAD
ST DAVID ROAD
ELM STREET

Emoyeni

JUBILEE ROAD

YORK ROAD

HOUGHTON DRIVE

PRINCESS OF WALES TERRACE

ST DAVID ROAD
ST JOHN ROAD

PARKTOWN

CARSE O'GOWRIE ROAD

Holiday Inn
RIDGE ROAD

BOUNDARY ROAD

ST ANDREW ROAD
ST JOHN ROAD

FIFE AVE
ST ANDREW RD
ST JOHN RD

LOUIS BOTHA AVENUE

JOHNSTON ST

FRANCES ST
HUNTER ST

QUARTZ RD

The View
Hazeldene Hall

JUNCTION AVE
JUNCTION AVE

WILLIE ST

MITCHELL

STREET

YORK AVE

LILY AVENUE

RALEIGH ROAD

FORTESQUE RD

PRINCESS PL

PARK LANE

CLARENDON PLACE

BEREA

TONEY STREET

HIGH STREET

HILLBROW STREET

HOPKINS ST
YEO ST
BECKER ST
PAGE ST

YEOVILLE

EMPIRE ROAD

QUEENS

JAGER ST
PAUL NEL ST

PARK LANE
YETTAH ST

FIFE AVENUE

BEATRICE LA

LUDHOPE AVE

DORIS ST

YORK ST

WEBB ST

HARROW ROAD

RALEIGH RD

GRAFTON RD

SAM HANCOCK STREET

BRUCE ST
CAROLINE ST

BANKET STREET

CLAIM STREET

BARNATO ST

SAUNDERS ST
MINORS
HARLEY ST

CONSTITUTION HILL

GOLDREICH ST
VAN DER MERWE ST

CATHERINE AVENUE

ALEXANDRA STREET

JOEL RD

JOEL RD

OLIVIA RD

HENDON ST
PERCY ST
HIGHLANDS RD

HILLBROW

PRETORIA ST

CAVELL ST
TWIST STREET

FREE AVENUE

ABEL ROAD

LILY AVE

Medical Research Institute and Adler Museum

KOTZE STREET

ESSELEN STREET

SOPAR ROAD

O'REILLY ROAD

HIGHLANDS

KORTE

HOSPITAL ST

KLEIN STREET

KAPTEIJN ST

PIETERSEN ST

TWIST STREET

CLAIM STREET

PRIMROSE TERR

SARATOGA AVENUE

Ponte Tower

GORDON TERRACE
CHARLTON TERRACE

Windybrow Theatre

SMIT STREET

WOLMARANS STREET

SHERWEL ST

Alhambra Theatre

Johannesburg Stadium

VAN BEEK ST

Park Station

JOUBERT PARK

WANDERERS ST
KING GEORGE ST

LEYDS ST
BOK ST
KOCH ST
HANCOCK ST

BANKET ST
CLAIM STREET

NUGGET STREET

BEIT ST
NIND ST

DOORNFONTEIN

DAVIES ST

CURREY ST

DORA STREET

BERTHA STREET

NORTH PARK LANE

ERNEST STREET

St Mary's Cathedral

KING GEORGE STREET

Johannesburg Art Gallery

PLEIN ST
BREE STREET

GOOD ST

NEW DOORNFONTEIN

Ellis Park Stadium

UPPER RAILWAY RD

MILLER ST
5TH STREET
8TH ST
ST ANDREW ST
BEAUFORT ST

PLEIN STREET

JEPPE ST

END STREET

ROCKEY ST
SHERWELL ST

BUXTON ST

SIEMERT ROAD

LOWER RAILWAY RD

7TH ST
6TH
VOORHOUT ST
GOLD ST

ELOFF ST

High Court

VON WIELLIGH STREET
DEVERS ST
TROYE STREET

CLAIM ST

MOSELEY ST
DAVIES ST

VAN BEEK ST
STAIB ST

BEACON RD

ANGLE ST

VERWEY

PRITCHARD STREET
PRESIDENT STREET

VON BRANDIS ST
SMALL ST

MARKET STREET

BEZUIDENHOUT AVENUE

OP DE BERGEN ST

Carlton Centre & Top of Africa

MARKET ST

GANDHI SQUARE

FOX STREET

COMMISSIONER STREET

FOX ST
KRUGER ST
ALBRECHT ST

JANE ST

JOHN PAGE DRIVE

Bus Station

MAIN ST

MAIN ST

PHILIP ST

GREENE ST

BETTY ST
AUFET ST

MARZBURG STREET

GUS ST

MACHINTYRE ST

MADISON ST

ANDERSON STREET

FREDERICK STREET

ALBERT STREET

7

GAUTENG

① Norwood & Orange Grove

⑥, ⑦ (1.2km) Observatory & Cyrildene

Bezuidenhout Valley (1.5km)

⑥ & Kensington

591

Diagonal Street

Moving west from Simmonds Street in the vicinity of Pritchard and Jeppe streets, look out for the rather forbidding **Bank City**, home of a number of banks, but also with the kind of arcades and plazas found in a continental European capital. West of this is **Diagonal Street**, heart of one of the most fascinating areas in the CBD. In the shadow of various concrete and glass behemoths, including the former Johannesburg Stock Exchange, are streets of old two-storey buildings, some of which date back to the 1890s; the lines of washing on the upstairs balconies show that they are still residential. On the streets is a jumble of traders and shops, peddling traditional medicines (*umuthi*), Sotho blankets and paraffin stoves alongside mobile phones. Though it might not feel it at first, the area is fairly safe, and with businessmen mingling with hawkers it has a very urban-African buzz.

If you're feeling brave, take a look at the rather spooky **KwaZulu Muti Museum of Man and Science** at 14 Diagonal St, a shop selling all kinds of traditional medicines, often manufactured from the dried animal skins hanging from the ceiling. You might also find yourself brushing against dangling ostrich feet or a pair of monkey skulls.

Newtown

On the western edge of the CBD between Diagonal Street and the M1 motorway flyover, **Newtown** is an area of redevelopment where some of Johannesburg's most vibrant cultural hot spots are found alongside derelict factories and areas of wasteland. The construction of the striking **Nelson Mandela Bridge** in 2004 provided a swift link to the district from the northern suburbs. Newtown's main draw is its **Cultural Precinct**, where a lot of money has been spent to ensure it's a safe place to visit, not just by day but also at night, when the various music and theatre venues are in full swing.

At its heart is the excellent **Museum Africa** at 121 Bree St (Tues–Sun 9am–5pm; R7), overlooking Mary Fitzgerald Square. The sheer size of the museum, which occupies the city's former fruit and vegetable market, can make it seem

▲ The Nelson Mandela Bridge, Johannesburg

a bit sparse and empty, but in fact the four permanent exhibitions and numerous temporary displays are well worth seeing. Most successful is **Johannesburg Transformations**, which tells the story of the city from early days of gold prospecting to the 1994 elections. Among the imaginative exhibits are re-creations of shacks and *shebeens* playing well-selected soundtracks from musical giants of the past, such as *kwela* maestro Spokes Mashiane. In a side room, look out for **Tried for Treason**, an exhibition dedicated to the Treason Trial of the 1950s, when 156 people, including Nelson Mandela and many well-known ANC activists of all races, were accused of plotting against the state.

On the upper floor, and rather less engaging, is the **Bensusan Museum of Photography**, which grandly aspires to be a "newseum of the present and future" but adds up to little more than a collection of cameras, holograms and CD-ROMs.

At the eastern end of the same building is the entrance to the famous **Market Theatre** (see p.614), a reliable source of stimulating and often ground-breaking dramatic output over the last thirty years or so. Outside, there's a worthwhile collection of shops, places to eat and drink, and *Kippies*, a former public toilet which is now South Africa's most famous jazz venue (see p.613). The cultural centre continues south of Jeppe Street, with Jo'burg's best live music venue, **The Bassline**, and a dance rehearsal and performing space called the **Dance Factory**, which is used for the annual Arts Alive Festival (see box, p.614). One of the city's better **flea markets** takes place every Saturday outside the theatre and on Mary Fitzgerald Square (see "Shopping" on p.615).

On the corner of President and Bezuidenhout streets is the **South African Breweries (SAB) World of Beer** (Tues–Sat 10am–6pm; R10). Its ninety-minute tour takes you through six thousand years of brewing history, which begs the question why SAB's ubiquitous end product, the anaemic, fizzy Castle lager, is so disappointing. Still, the reconstructed gold-rush pubs and Sixties *shebeen* are fun, along with the greenhouse where sample crops of barley and hops grow, and from the balcony of the *Tap Room* bar you can watch the city rush by.

Moving southwest, over President and Main streets, you'll come to the infamous **John Vorster Square**, site of the Johannesburg police headquarters, where anti-apartheid activists were detained and tortured, and some fell to their deaths having "jumped" from the tenth floor. After this, it's a pleasant relief to find the remains of the old Indian neighbourhood just further west, where Jeppe Street turns into Minnaar Street. A busy commercial street ends up at the **Oriental Plaza**, a hugely popular, Indian-owned shopping complex, selling everything from suitcases and bric-a-brac to fabrics and spices. This is just about all that remains of Newtown's once-thriving Indian community, most of whom were forcibly removed in 1904 to make way for whites.

Joubert Park

On the eastern side of Park Station, **Joubert Park**, named after General Piet Joubert (who lost the South African Republic general election to Paul Kruger in 1893), is the only inner-city green space but largely regarded as a no-go area. The one sight you can visit here is the **Johannesburg Art Gallery** (Tues–Sun 10am–5pm; free), an elegant, predominantly nineteenth-century building and one of the most progressive galleries in the country. If you're planning to walk there, it's probably best to find a City Ambassador willing to escort you; otherwise get a taxi to drop you off at the main entrance on Klein Street or make use of the gallery's secure parking.

The regular exhibits include vast wooden sculptures by the visionary Venda artist Jackson Hlungwani that tower up to the gallery's ceilings. Elsewhere, the gallery shows a very South African mixture of African artworks and artefacts from the ceremonial to the purely decorative, and a range of European paintings, including some minor Dutch Masters. The special exhibitions are usually excellent, too; consult the *Mail & Guardian* newspaper for details.

The central suburbs

Grouped around the CBD are various suburbs which, given Johannesburg's itinerant population and fast-changing demography, seem to be in a state of constant change. Some, particularly Hillbrow, Berea and Yeoville, were once the "grey areas" of Johannesburg, where apartheid first started to break down in the 1980s. The police turned a blind eye as large numbers of blacks started moving from the townships into these previously all-white areas. **Yeoville**, east across Harrow Road from Berea, and in particular its main drag Rockey Street, was long a melting pot where bohemian whites and progressive blacks mixed in Johannesburg's most vibrant and decadent area. But in recent years the crime and drug-dealing of Hillbrow have moved in too. Today, most whites have left these areas – though they still reside in leafy, residential **Observatory**, just east of Yeoville – while migrants from all over Africa have flooded in. The hectic street life of Yeoville, Berea and Hillbrow can be very exciting, but you should not venture into these areas at night or without a street-smart local guide.

Braamfontein

It's not just for the transport facilities at **Park Station** that you might have cause to visit **Braamfontein**, which starts at the main train station and extends north as far as Empire Road.

The area features one of the newest additions to the tourist circuit, **Constitution Hill**, on the corner of Joubert and Sam Hancock streets (daily 9am–5pm; R15). This has been the home since 2003 of the Constitutional Court, South Africa's highest court. Its hearings are fascinating for those interested in law or political science: the court must tread a difficult path between the decade-old constitution's array of popular rights and the frustrating realities of a state that is struggling to guarantee them. The Court is decorated with over 200 mostly excellent modern and contemporary South African paintings and sculptures, worth seeing in themselves.

Near the Court is the **Old Fort prison complex**, which includes the spine-chilling **Number Four** prison building, where black men were incarcerated and tortured during apartheid for breaking racist laws or fighting for their repeal. Gandhi and Pan-Africanist Congress leader Robert Sobukwe were both held here. At the exit to Number Four is a **Memory and Response Room**, where you can listen to the audio responses and memories of other visitors and record your own, in a booth using a microphone and a touch-screen computer. The recordings are archived in the Constitution Hill Oral History Database, which will offer a rich historical resource in decades to come.

Nearby is the **Women's Jail**, built in 1910, a grand Edwardian building which held black and white women prisoners in separate sections. The notorious serial poisoner Daisy de Melker was held here when she was on death row, but major political leaders such as Winnie Madikizela-Mandela, Albertina Sisulu, Helen Joseph and Ruth First also became familiar with its cells. From the 1950s onward, most of the prison's inmates were pass-law offenders, until that grotesquely petty form of repression (the systematic restriction of the movement of black people) was repealed in 1986.

A **Visitor Centre** (☎011 274 5300) outside Number Four, housed in an old police stable, provides information and bookings for tours of the Hill and the Court itself. Rich in symbolism, the Court and the prison complex provide a subtle but arresting testimony to the country's ongoing transformation, eloquently expressing the pride South Africans have in their new constitution and the democratic principles enshrined therein.

Other attractions worth a visit are the **Civic Theatre** between Simmons and Loveday streets, which hosts some of Johannesburg's best theatrical, musical and dance productions (see p.614), and the **University of the Witwatersrand**, otherwise known as "Wits", which lies in Braamfontein's northwest corner. The university has played an important role in the country's history, educating many future leaders, and acting as a site of major intellectual and political struggles. The large, attractive campus contains a number of impressive Neoclassical buildings and some lovely terraced gardens, a far cry from the bustling streets nearby. On the ground floor of Senate House (best accessed from Jorissen Street) is the **Gertrude Posel Gallery** (Mon–Fri 10am–4pm; free), which houses an extensive collection of traditional and contemporary African art.

Hillbrow

Smit Street, to the north of Joubert Park, marks the boundary with infamous and densely populated **Hillbrow**, dominated by high-rise apartment buildings all crammed with people. Hillbrow has always attracted Jo'burg's new immigrants. Immediately after World War II, the typical immigrant was English, Italian or East European Jewish. These days, Africans from all over the continent are arriving in numbers, giving Hillbrow a uniquely pan-African atmosphere, with music from Lagos to Kinshasa to Harare pumping from the bars and clubs. Along the many side streets, the scene is distinctly seedy, with drug pushers loitering outside lurid strip joints. The main thoroughfares, with their markets, clubs and bars, teem with activity, but the suburb is widely regarded as a **no-go area** for tourists; your best chance to experience it is to visit one of the better-known nightclubs or bars in a group, accompanied by a knowledgeable local.

If you're in the area, keep an eye out for nearby **Berea**'s most famous apartment building, **Ponte Tower** or "le petit Kinshasa", the 173-metre round tower visible from many kilometres around that is home to many Congolese immigrants. Like the Carlton Centre (see p.588), Ponte is a concrete legacy of apartheid South Africa's gold-fuelled boom years of the early 1970s – and its future is a matter of endless debate. Also worth a look is the lovely mock-Tudor **Windybrow Theatre** on Nugget Street.

The northern suburbs

Safe, prosperous and packed with shops and restaurants, the **northern suburbs** seem a world apart from the CBD and its surrounds. The name is actually a catch-all term for the seemingly endless urban sprawl running over 30km from Parktown, beyond the N1 ring road and into an area known as Midrand, which is itself creeping toward the southern edge of Pretoria. With the notable exception of Alexandra, this is a moneyed area, where plush shopping malls and well-tended parks are often the only communal meeting points, and the majority of homes use high walls, iron gates and electric fences to advertise how security-conscious a life the owners lead. Despite the often numbing sheen of affluence, however, interesting pockets do exist, such as the centres of the

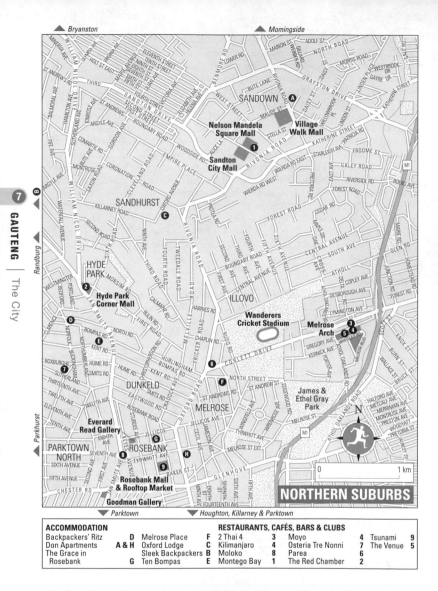

Bryanston ▲   Momingside ▲

SANDOWN Ⓐ

Nelson Mandela
Square Mall

Village
Walk Mall

Sandton
City Mall

SANDHURST Ⓒ

HYDE
PARK

Hyde Park
Corner Mall

ILLOVO

Wanderers
Cricket Stadium

Melrose
Arch

DUNKELD

James &
Ethel Gray
Park

MELROSE

Everard
Read Gallery

PARKTOWN
NORTH

ROSEBANK

Rosebank Mall
& Rooftop Market

Goodman Gallery

N

0   1 km

NORTHERN SUBURBS

▼ Parktown   ▼ Houghton, Killarney & Parktown

ACCOMMODATION			RESTAURANTS, CAFÉS, BARS & CLUBS			
Backpackers' Ritz	**D**	Melrose Place	**F**	2 Thai 4	**3**	Moyo	**4**	Tsunami	**9**
Don Apartments	**A & H**	Oxford Lodge	**C**	Kilimanjaro	**4**	Osteria Tre Nonni	**7**	The Venue	**5**
The Grace in		Sleek Backpackers	**B**	Moloko	**8**	Parea	**6**		
Rosebank	**G**	Ten Bompas	**E**	Montego Bay	**1**	The Red Chamber	**2**		

suburbs of Melville, Rosebank and Parkhurst. Most of the suburbs are close to
major arterial roads and best explored by car.

Parktown

The first elite residential area in Johannesburg, **Parktown** has retained its
upmarket status despite its proximity to Hillbrow, which lies just southeast on
the other side of Empire Road. The first people to settle in Parktown were Sir
Lionel Philips, president of the Chamber of Mines, and his wife Lady Florence.
In 1892, seeking a residence that looked onto the Magaliesberg rather than the

South Africa's most famous architect, **Sir Herbert Baker** was born in Kent, England, in 1862. Apprenticed to his architect uncle in London at the age of 17, Baker attended classes at the Royal Academy and Architectural Association, where he took care to make the contacts he would use so skilfully in later life. By the time he left for the Cape in 1892, Baker was already a convert to the new so-called Free Style, which advocated an often bizarre, but roughly historical eclecticism. The young architect's favourite influences, which would crop up again and again in his work, were Renaissance Italian and medieval Kentish.

Once in the Cape, Baker met **Cecil Rhodes**, and this connection, assiduously cultivated, established him as a major architectural player. The second Anglo-Boer War began in 1899 and Rhodes, assuming eventual British victory, sent Baker off to study the Classical architecture of Italy and Greece, hoping that he would return fully equipped to create a British imperial architecture in South Africa. Baker returned to South Africa deeply influenced by what he had seen, and was summoned by **Lord Alfred Milner**, the administrator of the defeated Transvaal, to fulfil Rhodes' hopes.

Baker took up the challenge enthusiastically, beginning with the homes of the so-called "kindergarten", the young men, mostly Oxford- and Cambridge-educated, whom Milner had imported to bring British-style "good governance" to the defeated territory. The result was the **Parktown mansions**, the opulent houses lining the roads of Johannesburg's wealthiest suburb. In adherence to the architectural creeds he had learnt in England, Baker trained local craftsmen and used local materials for these mansions. He also pioneered the use of local *koppie* stone, lending a dramatic aspect even to unadventurous designs.

Baker's major public commissions were the **St George's Cathedral** in Cape Town, the **South African Institute for Medical Research** in Johannesburg, and the sober, assertive **Union Buildings** in Pretoria, which more than any other building express the British imperial dream – obsessed with Classical precedent, and in a location chosen because of its similarity to the site of the Acropolis in Athens. Baker left South Africa in 1913 to design the Secretariat in New Delhi, India, returning to England on its completion, where he worked on South Africa House in Trafalgar Square, London. He was knighted in 1923; he died in 1946, and is buried in Westminster Abbey.

mine dumps, they had a house built on what was then the Braamfontein farm. The rest of the farm was planted with eucalyptus trees and became known as the Sachsenwald Forest, some of which was given over to the Johannesburg Zoo a few years later. The remaining land was cleared in 1925 to make way for more residential developments.

Parktown's main attraction lies in its distinctive **architecture**, largely the legacy of Sir Herbert Baker (see box above). Baker's arrival in 1902 heralded a style particular to this district, still evident today in the opulent mansions lining the streets. Parktown & Westcliff Heritage Trust (office open Mon–Fri 9am–1pm; ⓣ011 482 3349, ⓦwww.parktownheritage.co.za) runs **walking or bus tours** most Saturday afternoons. These follow themes such as "Johannesburg Gold" or "Edwardian Elegance" and often involve knowledgeable guides decked out in full Edwardian costume, who show you through some of the lavish mansions and their grounds. Tours cost R40–80, and can be booked directly through Computicket (see p.610). The Trust also publishes an inexpensive walking-tour guide, so you can walk or drive the routes covered by the tours unguided, but without access to the houses.

A good place to start an independent visit is **Ridge Road**, just north of the Randjeslaagte beacon, which marks the northern point of old Johannesburg.

The *Holiday Inn* here is a massive complex which Lord Alfred Milner used as his governor's residence from 1900. The best of the houses nearby are **Hazeldene Hall**, built in 1902 and featuring cast-iron verandas imported from Glasgow, and **The View**, built in 1897, with carved wooden verandas and an elegant red-brick exterior. To the north of Ridge Road, York Road curves to the left into Jubilee Road, with several palaces on its northern side; the neo-Queen Anne-style **Emoyeni**, at no. 15, built in 1905, is especially striking. At the corner of Jubilee Road and Victoria Avenue stands **Dolobran**, a weird and impressive house, also built in 1905, with a perfect veranda, wonderful red-brick chimneys, red Marseilles roof tiles and hallucinatory stained glass.

Crossing the busy M1 onto **Rock Ridge Road**, you'll reach the **Northwards Mansion**, built by Sir Herbert Baker in 1904 and home of the Parktown Trust. Unfortunately, there's no access along the road to Baker's own residence at no. 5. On parallel Sherborne Road you can see Baker's attractive **St George's Church** and its rectory, which mix Kentish and Italian features and were built in local rock.

Johannesburg Zoo and Houghton

Roughly 2km north of Parktown, off Jan Smuts Avenue, **Johannesburg Zoo** (daily 8.30am–5.30pm; R36; Ⓦwww.jhbzoo.org.za) is home to over three thousand species, including polar bears, tigers and lions. Despite recent attempts at revitalization, a sad air pervades the place. A few years ago, it hit the headlines when a criminal tried to avoid pursuing policemen by hopping over the wall into the zoo. Unfortunately, he jumped straight into the cage of Max the gorilla; the indignant Max suffered a gunshot wound from the encounter, while the criminal was hospitalized with serious bites.

Next door, and of greater interest, is the **National Museum of Military History** (daily 9.30am–4.30pm; R10), where among the tanks, guns and uniforms you'll find a display on **Umkhonto we Sizwe (MK)**, the armed wing of the ANC, although the other liberation armies are conspicuous by their absence. The display focuses on the wing's commander, Joe Modise, who became Minister of Defence in the ANC government.

Opposite the zoo, on the west side of Jan Smuts Avenue, is the artificial but pleasant **Zoo Lake**. The park here is a popular and safe walking and picnic spot and occasionally hosts outdoor performances, including an all-day music event every September during the Arts Alive festival (see box, p.614). You can rent a rowing boat and pootle around the lake, or sample some excellent African cuisine at the lakeside restaurant, *Moyo*, which has outdoor and indoor tables, live a cappella singers and plenty of peaceful, shady nooks in which to eat.

A couple of kilometres east of the zoo is the suburb of **Houghton**, one of Johannesburg's wealthiest and greenest suburbs. This is where Nelson Mandela lives, in a large white mansion dubbed Casa Graça after his third wife, Graça Machel. Interestingly, between 1961 and 1974 it was the country's only constituency to return an anti-apartheid MP, Helen Suzman.

Melville

The most relaxed and appealing of the northern suburbs, **Melville** lies west of Parktown between the two main road arteries of Barry Hertzog and Beyers Naude (formerly D.F. Malan). The suburb's villagey atmosphere has proved highly attractive to the stressed ranks of Johannesburg's upwardly mobile, who are steadily buying up property here. When so many shops and restaurants in Jo'burg are tucked away in soulless malls, it's refreshing to find streets with busy shops and pavement cafés. The suburb's most interesting shops lie around the

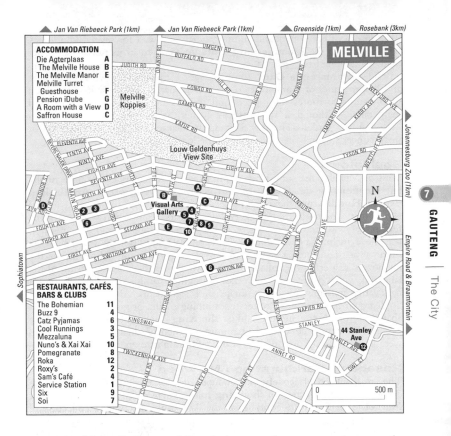

ACCOMMODATION

Die Agterplaas	A
The Melville House	B
The Melville Manor	E
Melville Turret Guesthouse	F
Pension iDube	G
A Room with a View	D
Saffron House	C

Melville Koppies

Louw Geldenhuys View Site

Visual Arts Gallery

N

Sophiatown

Johannesburg Zoo (1km)

Empire Road & Braamfontein

RESTAURANTS, CAFÉS, BARS & CLUBS

The Bohemian	11
Buzz 9	4
Catz Pyjamas	6
Cool Runnings	3
Mezzaluna	5
Nuno's & Xai Xai	10
Pomegranate	8
Roka	12
Roxy's	2
Sam's Café	4
Service Station	1
Six	9
Soi	7

44 Stanley Ave

0   500 m

junction of Seventh Street and Fourth Avenue, where you can linger in the inviting coffee shops, trendy restaurants, secondhand bookshops, galleries and quirky antique dealers. There's plenty going on in Melville at night, too, when it's still safe to walk the main streets.

Clustered around Melville are the tiny neighbourhoods of **Richmond**, **Westdene** and **Milpark**, which boast a couple of interesting nightclubs and cafés. **Auckland Park**, an old suburb west and south of Melville, is the home of the South African Broadcasting Corporation. Its programming is beamed from the nearby **Brixton Tower**, a spectacularly phallic monstrosity atop a ridge overlooking northern Jo'burg. **Brixton**, west of the tower, is a seedy but charismatic neighbourhood, featuring some beautiful corrugated-iron gold-rush houses dating back to the 1880s, and west of Melville is **Westdene**: both suburbs boast a couple of interesting cafés and nightclubs.

The **Melville Koppies Nature Reserve** (☎011 482 4797) to the north of the suburb is a pleasant hillside reserve containing hundreds of species of indigenous flora and fauna, as well as archeological remains of both Stone and Iron-Age settlements. There are two parts to the reserve. The **Louw Geldenhuys View Site**, reached from Zambesi Road, offers great views over Jo'burg and has open access at all times; to the west, the larger **central section** has a number of good walking trails, but is open only on the first three Sundays of each month. On the northern side of the reserve lies **Jan van Riebeeck Park**, a large spread of green parkland running north and west for several kilometres, which contains the **Johannesburg Botanic Garden** in its northeast corner (daily 8am–5pm; free).

Besides **Emmarentia Dam**, a popular spot for paddling, rowing, picnicking and boozy games of tennis-ball cricket, the garden is noted for its wide-open spaces and safe routes for joggers and walkers rather than for its botanical exuberance – although in the northeast corner there are some attractive formal herb and rose gardens. The tiny Shakespeare Garden is often used for plays or small concerts, which are advertised in the local press.

Sophiatown

West of Melville, the suburb of **Sophiatown** is unremarkable architecturally but significant in the history of apartheid – it was here that **Archbishop Trevor Huddleston**, the English cleric who established the Anti-Apartheid Movement, worked in the 1950s. For many years, Sophiatown was one of the few places within the city where blacks owned property, and as a result it became a melting pot of culture and political radicalism. In the 1960s the suburb was designated a white area by the government, who sent in the bulldozers, scattering the inhabitants to Soweto regardless of their claim to the land and, with a degree of irony, if not foresight, renaming the suburb Triomf, a name that remains on many maps and signboards. Although the name Sophiatown has now been reinstated, nothing of the original suburb remains apart from one house and the **Christ the King** Anglican church, from where Trevor Huddleston conducted his ministry. When he died in 1998, his ashes were brought from London to be scattered in Sophiatown.

Rosebank, Parkhurst and Norwood

The small suburb of **Rosebank**, a couple of kilometres north of the zoo, is dominated by a collection of **shopping malls**. There is also the **African Craft Market** (Tues–Sun 9am–5pm) above the Rosebank Mall, with a collection of stalls selling reasonable-quality African arts and crafts. It's not the cheapest place to buy crafts in the city, but prices are still much lower than the upmarket galleries nearby, and you are able to bargain. Sundays are the busiest day for crafts, when a large **flea market** selling everything from drums to cheese takes over a floor of the car park adjoining the Rosebank Mall.

Also in and around Rosebank are a number of galleries where you can view (and often purchase) traditional and contemporary African art, often of a very high standard. The **Everard Read Gallery** (Mon–Fri 9am–6pm, Sat 9am–5pm; free; Ⓦwww.everardread.co.za) at 6 Jellicoe Ave has varied exhibitions, often featuring South Africa's leading painters and sculptors. Smaller and more avant-garde is the **Goodman Art Gallery** (Tues–Fri 9.30am–5.30pm, Sat 9.30am–4pm; Ⓦwww.goodman-gallery.com) at 163 Jan Smuts Ave, while along the same road, at no. 153, the **Kim Sacks Art Gallery** specializes in traditional arts and crafts from around Africa, with most items on display for sale.

North of Rosebank are **Hyde Park** and **Melrose**, swanky suburbs notable for their giant, plush malls (Hyde Park Mall and Melrose Arch respectively).

Not far to the west of Rosebank and the gracious but sleepy old suburb of Parktown North lies **Parkhurst** which, along with Melville, is one of the few northern suburbs to boast decent street life – particularly on and around Fourth Avenue, which is well populated with upmarket cafés, restaurants, antique and interior design shops. West of Parkhurst is **Greenside**, another hip neighbourhood worth eating in.

To the east of Rosebank is **Norwood**, a chic suburb centred around Grant Avenue, a lively restaurant and clubbing strip on weekend nights. To the south of Norwood, huddled around the bottom end of the furiously busy Louis Botha Avenue, is **Orange Grove**, an old neighbourhood featuring intriguing second hand furniture stores and a couple of agreeably seedy bars.

Sandton, Randburg, Honeydew, Morningside, Bryanston and Fourways

Some 20km north of the CBD, **Sandton** is the archetypal northern suburb. It is outrageously rich, with plush shopping centres and endless rows of lavish houses. In the 1980s and 1990s, it became the retreat of choice for banks and large corporations fleeing the CBD. A stroll through the linked **Sandton City** and **Nelson Mandela Square** shopping centres, complete with a pseudo-Italian piazza crammed with restaurants and cafés, may make you shudder at the ostentation, but if you have some cash to burn yourself you'll have fun.

At one end of Nelson Mandela Square is a large bronze statue of the man himself: sadly, it's a mediocre work, achieving neither a compelling likeness nor any originality of approach.

North of Sandton, the suburbs roll on for 15km and more. Here you'll find large domestic plots interspersed with lush country clubs, shopping centres and, increasingly, the new phenomenon of "clusters", little developments of upmarket, newly built houses behind an imposing perimeter wall and equipped with every available security device. Whether such defences are altogether necessary in keeping crime at bay – or whether they invite criminals to defeat them – is not a subject you'll find open to debate among locals.

West of Sandton is **Randburg**, a large but deeply uninteresting area, whose only attraction is The Brightwater Commons on Republic Road, a faintly shabby mall set around an artificial lake. Randburg extends northwest into **Honeydew**, beyond the N1 freeway, where the tedium of vast townhouse complexes reaches mind-numbing levels. North of Randburg is the swankier expanse of **Bryanston** and **Morningside**, where many of Jo'burg's wealthiest citizens live. Further north again is **Fourways**, where the mammoth **Monte Casino** shopping and entertainment complex looks from the outside like a mutant mock-Italian palazzo; on the inside it's a monstrous replica of a Tuscan village, filled with cobbled streets, cast-iron street lamps and red-tiled buildings housing chain shops such as Diesel and Next. Alongside are restaurants, cinemas, a theatre, a casino and banks of gaming machines. Monte Casino is a preposterous place, but if you fancy a bout of roulette and/or some intensive retail therapy, it will do the job.

Alexandra

The contrast between desperately poor **Alexandra**, just east of the M1, and the surrounding suburbs could hardly be greater. When it was founded, this black township was one of the few places where blacks could own property. The sense of ownership and independence helped Alex, as it is commonly known, to avoid the forced removals of former governments. Despite the simple grid design its map suggests, the township is actually a bewildering maze of smashed-up streets, filled to bursting point with people, with overcrowded housing and a woeful lack of basic services such as sewerage and water. Half a million people live here in an area of less than eight square kilometres.

"Exhilarating and precarious" was how Nelson Mandela described Alex when he lived here in the early 1940s after running away from the Eastern Cape to find work in Jo'burg as an articled law clerk. In those days, the township was well known for its gangsters as well as its developing political militancy, which saw **bus boycotts** preventing bus companies from raising their fares, one of the first examples of mass action by blacks achieving political results. Alexandra has long been an ANC stronghold, and paid dearly for it until the collapse of apartheid, with ongoing warfare between Inkatha vigilantes and the ANC in the 1980s leading to one section of Alex being dubbed "Beirut".

While the old spirit of Alex lives on in the bustling streets on the western side of the polluted Jukskei River, the eastern bank is now lined with **new houses**, some built by government funding and others by middle-class blacks looking to improve their quality of life but wanting to remain in the township. Here you can also see the athletes' village built when the 1999 All African Games were held in Johannesburg; named "Tsutsumane" (Shangaan for "runner"), it has been turned into housing for locals. Not far from here a patch of land has been turned into a **cricket oval**; it's surreal to watch this most colonial of games being played against a backdrop of densely packed township shacks, with the skyscrapers of opulent Sandton peeking over the horizon beyond.

As part of Alex's renewal programme (for more on which, see Ⓦwww .alexandra.co.za), guided **tours** of the township are available. Much less formalized and certainly less touristy than Soweto tours, these trips are a great way to get close to the raw energy and spontaneity of township life. Abbey Sechoaro of Bosele Township Experience (Ⓣ076 366 6089) runs excellent tours, and others can be booked at Ⓦwww.alextourism.co.za.

The eastern suburbs

Among the oldest of the city's suburbs, and for years home to Johannesburg's Jewish and Portuguese communities, the eastern suburb of **Bezuidenhout Valley** (better known as Bez Valley) has also changed dramatically in recent years, with whites moving out of much of the old housing to make way for township and immigrant blacks. Southeast of Bez Valley is **Kensington**, a relaxed, multiracial suburb boasting a range of decent restaurants on Queen Street. **Cyrildene**, to the east of Observatory, has become the city's new Chinatown, with a fascinating collection of Chinese supermarkets, businesses and authentic restaurants along Derrick Avenue near its junction with Marcia Street.

Most visitors to this area, however, come to **Bruma Lake**, an artificial stretch of water which has proved a disappointing attraction save for its popular and lively **flea market** (Tues–Sun 9am–5pm), one of the best places in Johannesburg to find inexpensive curios – as long as you don't mind pseudo-traditional dance troupes entertaining you while you browse. Nearby, and safe for walkers, joggers and picnickers, is one of central Johannesburg's more accessible green spaces, **Gillooly's Farm**, a park set around a dam. The park is overlooked by a dramatic *koppie* which can be climbed in twenty minutes.

East of the M2 freeway is a vast expanse of featureless, soporific suburbs: **Edenvale**, **Kempton Park**, **Germiston** and **Benoni** (whose chief claim to fame is that it gave the world actress Charlize Theron).

Gold Reef City and the Apartheid Museum

The suburbs immediately south of the city centre were traditionally the preserve of the white working class. After the repeal of the Group Areas Act in 1990, blacks started moving in; unusually in contemporary South Africa, many are wealthier than the original residents. Besides Gold Reef City and the adjoining Apartheid Museum, the only other attraction south of the city is the sizeable **Klipriviersberg Nature Reserve**, in Winchester Hills just beyond the N12. Few Jo'burgers know about this undeveloped, unspoilt parkland, which provides wonderful views of the city to the north. To get there, take the N1 heading south, turn left into Columbine Avenue (the M68), and then right a kilometre or two further, at Ormonde Street.

Gold Reef City

Gold Reef City (Tues–Sun 9.30am–5pm; R110, R60 children shorter than 120cm; ⓦ www.goldreefcity.co.za), 15km south of the city centre, is where old Johannesburg meets Disneyland: a large, gaudy entertainment complex built around the old no. 14 shaft of the Crown Mines. If you can take the tackiness and piped ragtime music, there are some points of interest at what is essentially a theme park, notably the **old gold mine** itself, into which you can descend 200m and get an inkling of how it is to work underground. Keep an eye out, too, for the tribal dancing that happens five times a day; the dancers are excellent, even if their routines bear little resemblance to the real thing.

You can wander round the streets filled with period houses, shops and museums, though most are generally disappointing, with the possible exception of those dedicated to early Johannesburg, such as Olthaver and Nourse House. Otherwise, the most enjoyable thing to do in Gold Reef City is to go on one of the **thrill rides** (all included in the entrance ticket), which include the Raging Rapids water ride and the terrifying Anaconda roller coaster. In the unlikely event that you want to stay the night, the *Gold Reef City Protea Hotel* (☏011 248 5700; ❼) offers Victorian-themed decor, complete with a saloon, mock oil lamps and four-poster beds. Various restaurants serve decent though pricey food, but the main focus of this section of Gold Reef City is the vast **casino**, complete with hundreds of slot machines and various gaming tables.

To get to Gold Reef City, take the M1 south, and turn off at the Xavier Street exit. Otherwise, join one of the many tours that go there, advertised in nearly every hotel lobby.

The Apartheid Museum

Just to the left of the main entrance to the Gold Reef complex is the recently built **Apartheid Museum** (Tues–Sun 10am–5pm, R25; ⓦ www.apartheidmuseum .org). Featuring separate entrances for "whites" and "non-whites" (your race is randomly assigned), this is truly a world-class museum, delivering a sophisticated visual history that is at once distressing, inspiring and illuminating. Give yourself plenty of time to view the permanent exhibition of photographs of the 1976 Soweto uprising, by Peter Magubane. Nor should you miss an exhilarating short documentary on the State of Emergency during the mid-1980s, when a wave of mass demonstrations and riots, though violently suppressed, shook the resolve of the regime.

The museum offers a nuanced insight into the deep social damage wrought by apartheid – and by colonial policies that long preceded it – and helps to explain the persistence of poverty and racial tension in the new South Africa. On the other hand, the museum's visual account of the jubilant advent of democracy serves to remind us how miraculous the transition was.

Soweto

South Africa's most famous township, **Soweto** (short for South West Townships), is a place of surreal contrasts. The area has the only street in the world where two Nobel Peace Prize winners once lived, yet suffers one of the highest rates

▲ Soweto street art

of murder and rape in the world; it is the richest township in South Africa, home to a growing number of millionaires, but has some of the most desperate poverty; it is the most political township, yet has the most nihilistic youth.

Southwest of the city centre, Soweto is huge, stretching as far as the eye can see, with a population estimated at between three and four million. Like any city of that size, it is divided into a number of different **suburbs**, with middle- and upper-class neighbourhoods among them. At first sight, it appears an endless jumble of houses and shacks, overshadowed by palls of smoke, though parts of it have a villagey feel. Apart from the Hector Peterson Memorial and Museum, most of Soweto's **tourist highlights** are physically unimpressive, their fame stemming from historical associations. That history and the people of Soweto, however, are enthralling, not least because here it is told with a perspective and context rarely found in the rest of South Africa. For visitors it means an insight not just into a place much mentioned in 1980s news bulletins for funerals and fighting, but into a way of life most Westerners rarely encounter.

A visit to Soweto with one of the many **tours** (see box opposite) is the single most popular attraction in Johannesburg. Where once these had a whiff of daring and originality, a well-trodden tourist trail has developed, and unless you're content to follow the herds of minibuses and coaches around the conventional sights, it's well worth using an operator who mixes the highlights with lesser-known sights.

At one time, taking yourself to Soweto would have meant a display of bravado bordering on foolhardiness, but it's now possible to visit the main sights independently; your time will be your own, and you'll be able to check out the growing number of bars and eating places catering to tourists. In Soweto, residents will stop to greet you or to chat, regardless of your colour. There are surprisingly few criminal incidents affecting tourists, though as ever it pays to remain vigilant on a visit; exploring less-visited areas by yourself, or going after dark, isn't recommended for safety reasons. If you want to **drive** to Soweto, you'll need good navigational skills – the lack of obvious landmarks amid kilometre upon kilometre of boxy little houses can be highly confusing. Taking a **minibus taxi** to Soweto is more confusing than dangerous, as it isn't always easy to ascertain which part of the township it's heading for, for which reason it's not recommended. Forming a cross with two fingers is the recognized minibus signal indicating that you want to go to "crossroads", which will bring you to the centre of Soweto. From here you can pick up another taxi to whichever sight you want to visit, though even in a taxi you may be let out on one of the main roads and have to walk a little way to reach your target. For information, the township has a **Soweto Tourism Centre**, on Madhlala Street on Walter Sisulu Square in Kliptown – next to the colourful giant chimneys of the power station. There's also some useful information about Soweto's sights and tourist infrastructure at ⓦ www.soweto.co.za, run by a local tour operator.

Perhaps the most exciting way to discover Soweto, if you have some time on your hands and fancy learning some Zulu or Sotho, is to be hosted by a Soweto family for a few days or a couple of weeks. You can do this through the **TALK Tourism** project (ⓣ011 487 1798, ⓦ www.phaphama.org) run by an NGO called Phaphama. It's a flexible programme: anyone can be hosted, and bookings can be made at short notice. The host families all work closely with Phaphama: they guide guests around Soweto, feed and entertain them, and teach them their mother tongue. The cost is R2200 per night for a single visitor, but much less per person if you come in a group.

Orlando West and Dube

Set in the northern part of Soweto, **Orlando West** and **Dube** qualify as two of its more affluent suburbs, with a number of sights and the greatest concentration of places to eat and drink. Orlando East, across Klipspruit Valley from Orlando

---

Soweto tours

The most common – and safest – way to visit Soweto is with a **tour operator**. By far the oldest, biggest and slickest operation is Jimmy's Face to Face Tours (ⓣ011 331 6109). Jimmy pioneered tours into the township, and his operation has grown steadily over the years. Imbizo Tours (ⓣ011 838 2667 or 083 700 9098), run by the irrepressible Mandy Mankazana, provides stiff competition. Mandy is a mine of information and contacts, and her three-hour day tours and four-hour night tours of Soweto are excellent. Tours can be customized, and Imbizo also organizes evening *shebeen* crawls lasting up to five hours, depending on your stamina. Indicate what kind of company you would like to keep, from politicians to sports fanatics, and Mandy will select an appropriate venue.

As well as the well-established operators, smaller, more flexible outfits offer imaginative **alternative tours** such as jazz outings, walks around Orlando West and Diepkloof, visits to Sowetan artists or local churches, and homestays with locals. Try Max Maximum (ⓣ082 770 0247), African Prime Tours (ⓣ011 794 5708 or 083 758 4288) or Stanford Hlatshwayo (ⓣ084 857 4967); alternatively, your accommodation may well have links to a reliable tour company.

Before you go to Soweto on any kind of tour, it's worth preparing yourself for the fact that as a tourist you will stand out, and that there's a good chance you'll run into other groups of tourists. Most outfits are keen for you to "meet the people", though they all tend to visit the same shantytowns and *shebeens*, and you'll find that resulting conversations sometimes lead to your leaving a donation, tipping casual guides or buying local craftwork. While this gets a few tourist dollars directly into the townships, it often leaves visitors feeling pressurized and vulnerable. Ask your guide about the best way to deal with this.

West, was the first part of Soweto to be established in 1932, and the area is fairly easily accessible off the Soweto Highway (M70).

On Old Potchefstroom Road, Soweto's main arterial road running between Orlando West and Pimville, is the **Maponya Mall**, a vast, spectacular shopping complex serving Soweto's rapidly growing bourgeoisie. Opened in 2007, the mall packs 65,000 square metres of retail space, an eight-screen cinema complex and hundreds of stores and restaurants. It's well worth visiting, being both a dramatic illustration of Soweto's economic rise and a convenient place to peruse designer goods of almost every description.

On Plea Street in the heart of Orlando West, the **Hector Petersen Memorial and Museum** (daily 10am–5pm; R10), opened in 2002, was named after the first student to be killed in the Soweto uprising (see box below). Dedicated to

The Soweto uprising of 1976

The **student uprising** that began in Soweto in June 1976 was a defining moment in South African history. The revolt was sparked off by a government ruling that **Afrikaans** should be used on an equal basis with English in black secondary schools. While this was feasible in some rural areas, it was quite impossible in the townships, where neither pupils nor teachers knew the language.

On June 16, student delegates from every Soweto school launched their long-planned mass protest march through the township and a rally at the Orlando football stadium. Incredibly, details of the plan were kept secret from the omnipresent *impimpis* (informers). Soon after the march started, however, the police attacked, throwing tear gas and then firing. The crowd panicked, and demonstrators started throwing stones at the police. The police fired again. Out of this bedlam came the famous photograph of the first student to die, Hector Petersen, bleeding at the mouth, being carried by a friend, while a young girl looks on in anguished horror.

The police retreated to Orlando East, and students rushed to collect the injured and dead, erect barricades, and destroy everything they could belonging to the municipal authority, including beer halls. The attacks heightened the antagonism between the youth and many older people who thought that class boycotts were irresponsible, given the students' already dismal employment prospects. Students responded angrily, accusing their elders of apathy in the face of oppression, which they attributed in part to drunkenness. In a society that has traditionally regarded respect for the old as sacrosanct, this was a historic departure and its effects still reverberate throughout South Africa's townships.

In the days following June 16, all Soweto schools were closed indefinitely, thousands of police were stationed throughout the township, and police brutality continued unabated. In the face of worldwide condemnation, the government insisted that there was no real problem, ascribing the violence to Communist agitation. As evidence, it cited the clenched-fist salutes of the students, though this was really an indication of their support for South Africa's **Black Consciousness Movement**, founded by Steve Biko (see p.419). Meanwhile, rebellion spread to other townships, particularly in Cape Town. In Soweto, schools did not reopen until 1978, by which time many students had abandoned any hope of formal education. Some had left the country to join the military wings of the ANC and PAC, while others stayed at home, forming "street committees" to politicize and police the communities. Others drifted into unemployment.

Now the armed struggle is over, the problems that face the former students of 1976 are manifold. As their parents warned, their lack of qualifications count against them in the job market, even if June 16 is now a national holiday, during which they are praised for their role in the struggle. The street committees have dissolved, but the guns remain.

Petersen and the other students who died, the museum focuses specifically on the events surrounding and leading up to the Soweto uprising. The startling brutality used in the repression of student activists is depicted in video and pictures, including images from well-known black photographers such as Peter Magubane and Sam Nzima.

Vilakazi Street, a few hundred metres to the southwest, was once home to Nelson Mandela and Desmond Tutu. Mandela's bungalow is where he lived with Winnie in the late 1950s and early 1960s, before his imprisonment on Robben Island, and where Winnie lived until exiled to the Free State (from which she returned to an imposing brick house with high walls and security cameras, just down the road). On his release, Nelson insisted on returning to his old home, but its smallness and lack of security proved too much of a strain, and he moved out of Soweto. Tours of the old bungalow, **The Mandela Family Museum** (daily 10am–4.30pm; R20), mix fascinatingly mundane memorabilia and large amounts of pro-Winnie propaganda; it was she who turned the house into a museum. Rather spoiling the scene is a coffee shop and restaurant crudely tacked onto the outside of the house.

About 1500m away, near the junction of Klipsruit Valley (the M10) and Potchefstroom (the M68) roads, is **Regina Mundi Church**, Soweto's largest Catholic church and the focus of numerous gatherings in the struggle years. Again, its impact owes more to historical aura than aesthetic appeal, although with so few large buildings in the township it has a certain presence. Inside, look out for the **art gallery** displaying and selling the work of various Sowetan artists. Church services here, as in all townships, are friendly affairs, with liberal doses of fantastic music and, depending on the denomination, religious ecstasy too. If you attend, be prepared to give at least a small testimony – a brief rundown of your spiritual life to date. Services last several hours, but no one will think it a crime if you leave before the end.

Other tourist attractions will undoubtedly develop, such as **Freedom Square** – currently a combination of wasteland and taxi rank – in **Dube**, where the ANC's Freedom Charter was proclaimed to thousands in 1955. In the meantime many visitors enjoy paying a visit to the various **shebeens**, restaurants and coffee shops that are making a big effort to attract outsiders as well as locals. We've listed the best in "Eating", below.

Eating

The wealth, diversity and fast-paced social life of Johannesburg means that the city has a huge range of places to **eat out**, from chic fusion cafés to formica-tabled Chinese eating dens without English menus, and from meat-guzzling steakhouses to wonderfully graceful Thai restaurants. Cultural interaction was obstructed for so long that a cuisine unique to the city has never emerged, but such is the cosmopolitan nature of Jo'burg that authentic French, Italian, Chinese, Greek and Portuguese restaurants are all found here, and there are increasing numbers of African restaurants, not just township South African but also Congolese, Moroccan, Ethiopian and Cape Malay. **Prices** are inevitably a bit higher than elsewhere in the country outside Cape Town and the Winelands, and you can blow out in spectacular style, but an average meal out is still good value.

All of Jo'burg's **shopping malls** are well stocked with takeaways and restaurants, frequently unadventurous, bland chains, though some very top-notch venues do exist in malls. If you don't fancy heading out even for a takeaway meal, you can make use of a service called Mr Delivery, which picks up and delivers meals from a range of reasonable mid-market eating places: contact them on ⓦwww .mrdelivery.com or by phone on ☎011 482 4748 (Melville), ☎011 442 4411 (Rosebank) or ☎011 784 6000 (Sandton).

CBD and central suburbs

There are one or two truly original lunch options in downtown Jo'burg, but at night **Newtown** is the only area to eat out. Expect some inventive riffs on traditional African food.

Gramadoelas at the Market Theatre Wolhuter St, Newtown ☎011 838 6960. One of the best-known spots for excellent Cape and African dishes like *sosaties*, *mopane* worms and *melktert*. The visitors' book is star-studded. Not cheap. Closed Sun & Mon lunch.

Kapitan's 11a Kort St ☎011 834 8048. Located upstairs in a decrepit-looking building near Diagonal St, and gloomy and kitsch inside, this Jo'burg classic serves delicious South African curries. It was Mandela's favourite eating place in the 1950s when he worked as a lawyer nearby – his letter from prison holds pride of place. Mon–Sat lunchtime only.

Kofifi Newtown Cultural Precinct. Lively bar and restaurant directly opposite the Market Theatre, serving inexpensive burgers and simple African dishes, occasionally with live music.

Moyo's @ the Market Wolhuter St, Newtown ☎011 838-1715, ⓦwww.moyoafrica.co.za. The decor – carved wood and welded metal – creates a distinct South African ambience; a great variety of African food and music by local artists complete the experience. There' are more spectacular branches at Melrose Arch and Zoo Lake (see p.598).

🏃 **Sophiatown 1** Central Place, at the corner of Jeppe and Henry Nxumalo sts, Newtown Cultural Precinct ☎011 836 5999. A recent township-retro addition to Newtown nightlife, and already a favourite among chic black Jo'burgers. The excellent food includes crocodile, kudu and ostrich, all served to a soundtrack of old- and nu-school Afrojazz and Afropop. Smart but relaxed, it's a perfect place to begin a balmy summer night out.

The northern suburbs

A number of suburbs have small, interesting eating places; the key places to try are Seventh Street in **Melville**, the junction of Greenway and Gleneagles in **Greenside** (sandwiched between Jan van Riebeeck Park and Parktown North), Grant Avenue in **Norwood** (to the east of Houghton) and, to a lesser extent, Fourth Avenue in **Parkhurst** (west of Parktown North).

Rosebank, Hyde Park, Melrose and Sandton

See the map on p.596 for the locations of the places below.

2 Thai 4 On the corner of Cross St and Corlett Drive, very near Melrose Arch ☎011 440 3000. A quality, mainstream Thai restaurant, easy-going and with decent prices.

Montego Bay Sandton Square, Sandton ☎011 883 6407. Pricey but lip-smackingly good seafood (including fresh oysters) together with slick service.

Moyo Melrose Arch ☎011 684 1477, ⓦwww .moyoafrica.co.za. In the very upmarket Melrose Arch complex, this stylish venue occupying five floors offers an excellent variety of African dishes, from chicken with Ethiopian spices to ostrich steaks, along with performances of dance and music, often by established local or international acts.

Osteria Tre Nonni 9 Grafton Ave ☎011 327 0096. This is one of Jo'burg's best Italian restaurants, with a range of food from northern Italy, and a comfortable ambience. Great home-made *grappa* liqueurs round off the evening. Book ahead. Closed Mon & Sun.

Parea 3 Corlett Drive, Melrose North ☎011 788 8777. A long-established, unpretentious spot with no shortage of local Greek customers delighted to sample the real thing.

The Red Chamber Upper Mall, Hyde Park Corner, Hyde Park ☎011 325 6048. A good spot for medium-priced Chinese food in rather plusher surroundings than you tend to get in Chinatown.

Tsunami Rosebank Mall, Rosebank ☎011 880 8409. Disastrous name, but this swanky eatery serves very decent sushi. The service can be sluggish, but it's worth the wait if you're not in a rush.

Greenside, Houghton and Parkhurst

Circle 141 Greenway, Greenside ☎ 011 646 3744. The fusion menu introduces all sorts of interesting flavours, and trendy Jo'burgers flock here. Don't be discouraged when your bread arrives in a brown paper bag – they do want you to hang around. Closed Sun & Mon.

Doppio Zero corner of Barry Herzog and Mowbray rds, Greenside ☎ 011 646 8740. Unpretentious and hugely popular Italian place with an eclectic menu. Breakfast is a big draw: the omelettes are exceptional.

Karma Gleneagles Rd, Greenside ☎ 011 646 8555. A small but stylish modern Indian restaurant specializing in tandooris, with a few fusion dishes thrown in for good measure.

La Rustica 103 Houghton Drive, Houghton. Hidden away in a leafy area close to Observatory, this cosy restaurant serves up delicious, moderately priced Italian fare.

Ruby Grapefruit 24 Fourth Ave, Parkhurst. A fun and funky little sushi bar, open during the daytime only, with healthy snacks and drinks also on offer.

Melville

The places reviewed here are shown on the map on p.599.

Mezzaluna 9a Seventh St ☎ 011 4822477. It's not cheap by Jo'burg standards, but *Mezzaluna*'s eclectic and ungimmicky food is fantastic, with the lamb, oxtail and salmon especially delicious. Quiet and secluded, it's also a good place to eat if you want to talk.

Nuno's Seventh St ☎ 011 482 6990. This moderately priced, popular restaurant offers very decent Portuguese food and a relaxed bohemian atmosphere. The Sunday fish specials are cheap and scrumptious.

Pomegranate 79 Third Ave ☎ 011 482 2366. Set in a typically charming Melville house, *Pomegranate* offers a high-quality, innovative

international menu with a Thai touch. Closed Sat lunchtime & Sun.

Sam's Café 11 Seventh St ☎ 011 726 8142. Smarter than its name implies, and comfortably sophisticated, *Sam's* serves mostly Mediterranean dishes which are reliably tasty, at moderate prices (particularly the specials). Closed Sat lunchtime & Sun.

Service Station corner of Ninth St and Rustenburg Rd. A superbly stylish café/deli housed in a converted garage, it serves inventive, classy food including breakfasts, tasty sandwiches and great cakes. Daytime only.

Soi corner of Seventh St and Third Ave ☎ 011 726 5775. With exquisitely understated bamboo and dark wood decor, this smart and popular Thai/Vietnamese restaurant serves authentic food at reasonable prices.

Bryanston, Morningside and Randburg

Bistro 277 Cramerview Centre, 277 Main Rd, Bryanston ☎ 011 706 2837. Deep in the northern suburbs but away from the glitzy malls, this long-standing favourite serves excellent – if expensive – traditional French provincial cooking in pleasant, spacious surroundings. Closed Sun night.

The Codfather 1 First Ave, on the corner of Rivonia Rd, Morningside ☎ 011 803 2077. Select fresh fish from the vast displays, then watch as it's scaled, filleted and cooked to order. Hugely popular, with a sushi bar alongside. Daily noon–10pm.

Fruits and Roots Hobart Corner Shopping Centre, Grosvenor Rd, Bryanston. One of the city's top organic, health and wholefood shops, with a great sandwich bar/café alongside. Mon–Wed daytime only, Thurs–Sat till 8.30pm.

Jimmy's Killer Prawns Piazza Centre, corner of Jan Smuts Ave and Republic Rd, Randburg. A big, noisy restaurant, with a long menu offering large helpings of seafood. The expansive views of the city lights are entirely appropriate. Closed Sat lunchtime & Sun evening.

East of the centre

The key area for dining in the eastern part of the city is **Norwood** (east of Houghton), where Grant Avenue offers little else but wall-to-wall cafés and restaurants. The more adventurous can explore **Kensington** with its homely feel and **Cyrildene**, home of the city's new Chinatown, between Observatory and Bruma.

The Fisherman's Plate 18 Derrick Ave, Cyrildene ☎011 622 0480. Loud and unfussy, with Formica-topped tables and no-nonsense lighting, this cult favourite serves fearsomely flavourful Chinese cuisine. Try the crab if you're feeling brave.

Kutya 38 Grant Ave, Norwood ☎011 728 2257. Smart but unfussy restaurant which reinvents traditional South African dishes with a bistro-cuisine touch: *morogo* and *mealie pap* have never been so fancy. Design is low-key Afro-kitsch.

Singing Fig 44 The Avenue, Norwood ☎011 728 2434. One of the most acclaimed restaurants in town, the *Singing Fig* does French provincial with a New World twist.

Soweto

Soweto **tours** all stop off for a meal in a local restaurant, bar or *shebeen*, and so long as you're not part of a huge group of tourists, it's not a bad way to meet some locals. If you're heading to Soweto under your own steam or with a local contact, any of the places below are worth checking out and will give you a warm welcome. Commonly, some kind of meat and pap is the main dish on offer, often with local favourites such as tripe or ox shin as an alternative.

Kwa-thabeng 9138 Zone 6 Extension, Pimville ☎011 938 3337. A friendly restaurant serving typical South African dishes with à la carte selections as well as a buffet. There's a pleasant outdoor seating area.

The Rock 1987 Vundla Drive, Rockville ☎011 986 8182. A massively popular upmarket venue for eating, drinking and dancing, with DJs or live jazz on offer most nights. The roof deck is a wonderful spot to unwind, get an overview of Soweto, and enjoy a sundowner.

Sakhumzi 6980 Vilakazi St, Orlando West. Situated in the heart of Soweto, next to Desmond Tutu's old house, it features typical Sowetan food in its buffet.

Shana's Place 9138 Zone 6 Extension, Pimville ☎072 127 1619. Located on Enoch Sontoga Hill overlooking Orlando, this classy bar-café has the Soweto yuppies flocking. Cappuccino, cocktails and food available.

Vardo's Place 2525 Ngalela St, Mapetla ☎083 260 3970. One of the most upwardly mobile *shebeens* in Soweto, a burgeoning open-plan bar and club under one of the township's few thatched roofs. Come to shoot pool, watch sport or admire the water features.

Wandie's Place 618 Makhalamele St, Dube ☎011 982 2796. Once Soweto's archetypal tourist-friendly *shebeen*, now the area's smartest eating spot, though it retains its popularity with locals. Local African food predominates.

Drinking, nightlife and entertainment

Johannesburg has always offered the best **entertainment** and **nightlife** in South Africa: the city draws top performers from all over the world, and its well-integrated audiences are the most sophisticated around. Though newspapers offer some event pointers, the best way to find out what's on is to listen to the local radio stations (see box, p.613) and keep your eyes peeled for roadside posters and leaflets. The *Mail & Guardian* newspaper, published on Fridays, carries decent listings and articles on the main events, while the daily *Star* newspaper tracks mainstream cinema and theatre. For information on **spectator sport** in Johannesburg, see opposite. Tickets for most events can be booked through Computicket (☎011 445 8000 or 083 915 8000, ⓦwww.computicket.com).

Clubs and bars

Jo'burgers tend to stay home on weeknights, unless they're students, but they compensate spectacularly on weekends – an uproarious night out offers a precious antidote to the city's hectic workday stress. Jo'burg has the country's most racially mixed nightlife, particularly in places such as **Melville** and **Newtown**, where the hippest citizens congregate. The problem for visitors is that the best clubs are far-flung, and there's only one proper nightlife strip, Melville's Seventh Avenue, which is great fun for drinking but can't compete with Cape Town's Long Street if your intention is to dance. In many parts of the city, particularly the **northern suburbs**, old-school pubs and bars have been replaced by combination café/bar/restaurants, open most hours and commonly located in malls and shopping centres. "Cigar bars", where smoking and posing are encouraged, tend to be pretentious and are best avoided, while Irish theme pubs and sports bars are often packed and jovial, if not exactly cutting-edge. The adventurous can enjoy some excellent nightlife in the **CBD** and **central suburbs**, though to sample the clubs of Hillbrow and Yeoville you'll need to go with a knowledgeable local. For Soweto *shebeens* you can visit during the day, see "Eating" on opposite; at night, only head to the townships in the company of a guide.

CBD and central suburbs

Carfax 39 Pim St, Newtown ☏011 834 9187. A hip, cavernous venue catering to students and hard-partying media types. *Carfax* regularly hosts top foreign DJs and local rock, hip-hop and reggae bands.

Fuel Café Corner of Quinn and Carr sts, Newtown ☏011 838 9277. A small, popular, exquisitely hip dance bar that hosts funk, indie and electro DJs. Critical mass is reached at 2am on weekend nights.

House of Tandoor 26 Rockey St, Yeoville. This legendary nightclub, once the heart of Jo'burg counterculture in the 1980s, is still trundling on, though live music has given way to ragga, hip-hop and reggae DJs. Bear in mind that Yeoville is not for the nervous – only come here if you're in a group and confident about being in the area at night.

Spectator sport in Jo'burg

Sport is huge anywhere you go in South Africa, but in Johannesburg it's an obsession. Here you'll find the biggest stadiums and the biggest teams, and the usually fantastic weather makes going to a match a deeply agreeable experience. The major **cricket** games, including five-day test matches, are played at the **Wanderers Stadium**, off Corlett Drive, Illovo (☏011 788 1008), though if you look carefully at the touring programme for any visiting international teams you may find fixtures scheduled to be played in Soweto or Alexandra.

The towering **Ellis Park** in downtown Jo'burg (☏011 402 8644) is a South African **rugby** shrine, particularly since the triumph there of the Springboks in the 1995 World Cup. As well as hosting international fixtures it's also home ground to the provincial Gauteng Lions team. The best way to get there is to make use of the park-and-ride system which operates for big games, with buses shuttling in from car parks outside the centre.

The biggest sport in town is **soccer**, and there's a passionate rivalry between Jo'burg's two biggest teams, fuelled by scandal, intrigue and mutual loathing, which keeps armies of sports reporters in work. In Jo'burg (and, more particularly, Soweto), you're either a fan of **Kaizer Chiefs** or **Orlando Pirates**, and for decades local derbies have pulled mammoth crowds of 70,000 to FNB Stadium, on the NASREC road on the outskirts of Soweto. However, the stadium is currently being expanded and revamped ahead of the 2010 World Cup; in the interim matches are being played at smaller grounds such as Ellis Park, the scene of a tragic crush at a Chiefs-Pirates game in 2001 in which over fifty fans died. You should try to go to a home game of either team, especially one against Pretoria giants Mamelodi Sundowns. Tickets are cheap, the football can be exciting – if a little chaotic – and the atmosphere is often exhilarating. Crowd violence is very rare, and there is secure parking. Tickets for big games can be bought from Computicket (☏011 445 8000 or 083 915 8000, ⓦwww.computicket.com).

Private Practice 18th Floor, Lister Medical Building, 195 Jeppe St, CBD. A deliciously hip new art and events venue, presenting live music on weekend nights. Exhilarating views of the Jo'burg skyscraper district – from its heart. Underground parking is available on Bree St, parallel north of Jeppe.

Northern suburbs

Rosebank, Melrose, Sandton, Randburg

Kilimanjaro Melrose Arch, Melrose. One of the more upmarket "afro-chic" nightclubs with DJs spinning hip-hop, R&B and *kwaito* until the early hours. Dress codes are strictly enforced at the door, and you have to be at least 25 to get in.

Moloko Corner of Jan Smuts and Seventh aves, Rosebank ☏011 447 0479. Roomy and snazzy soul and hip-hop club that's a favoured haunt of young black hipsters.

The Red Room corner of Juice and Beyers Naude sts, Honeydew ☏011 463 8901. Hugely popular rock and indie club, attracting a varied crowd of Goths, yuppies and hipsters.

Sublime 130 Eleventh St, Parkmore, Sandton ☏011 884 1649. A short way northwest of Sandton is this smart dance venue with big-name DJs playing house and hip-hop.

Melville, Auckland Park, Westdene, Richmond

The Bohemian 5 Park Rd, Richmond ☏011 482 1725. A pleasantly seedy pool hall hosting punk,

folk and rockabilly bands on weekend nights. As its name would suggest, *The Bohemian* is a refuge for many of Jo'burg's crustier citizens.

Buzz 9 On the corner of Seventh St and Third Ave, Melville. A cramped but groovy all-night bar, with innovative cocktails, hearty food and agreeable staff.

Catz Pyjamas Main Rd, Melville. A 24hr bar and food stop; it's nothing special during daylight hours, but gets more interesting when the clubs spill out in the wee small hours.

Cool Runnings Fourth Ave, Melville. A hugely popular Jamaican-themed bar, with drumming sessions and comedy, decent food and lots of Red Stripe beer and rum.

Roka 44 Stanley Ave, Auckland Park ☏011 482 2038. Stylish, relaxed bar that hosts excellent house and indie DJs, attracting a mixed crowd. Quality live jazz on Wed nights.

Six Seventh Ave, Melville. One of the vibiest bars in Jo'burg, *Six* pulls a funky, left-of-centre crowd. Music is supplied by a jukebox, but the punters don't care – they come to sit, drink and talk till the break of dawn.

Xai Xai Seventh Ave, Melville. Terminally relaxed bar, named after the Mozambican resort town. Much loved by Jo'burg's small but committed hippie crowd. Delicious Mozambican beers are a big draw.

Live music

Johannesburg dominates the South African music scene, offering a much wider spectrum of sounds than Cape Town or Durban. Friday and Saturday nights are the busiest times for gigs. Large concerts tend to happen at the Dome in Northgate, northwest of the city, or at Mary Fitzgerald Square in Newtown.

The Newtown Cultural Precinct and a couple of venues in the northern suburbs are your best bets for live **jazz**. Jo'burg is always discovering superb new jazz talent, but established artists to look out for include the scorchingly gifted vocalist Simphiwe Dana, pianist Andile Yenana, bassist Carlo Mombelli and trumpeter Marcus Wyatt. Zimbabwean folk maestro Oliver Mtukudzi often comes to town, as do jazz–pop merchants Freshlyground and captivating singer–songwriter Vusi Mahlasela.

Jo'burg's **burgeoning indie rock scene** has an eager young audience in Melville, Norwood and the northern suburbs. Notable acts include the brilliant Mozambican ska outfit 340ml, indie-pop hot-shots Desmond and the Tutus and instrumental noise rockers Kid of Doom.

Kwaito, the hugely popular township-house genre, is rarely performed live except at major concerts. Look out for gigs with the excellent Hip-Hop Pantsula (HHP), Teargas, Skwatta Kamp or Pitch Black Afro on the bill.

A number of bars and clubs have occasional live acts, but normally feature DJs – some of these are listed in "Clubs and bars" above. As for **classical music**,

South Africa's National Symphony Orchestra performs regularly at Linder Auditorium in Parktown (☎011 714 4501).

The *Mail & Guardian* newspaper, which hits the streets on Fridays, carries the best live-music listings in town. A useful online gig guide is provided by ⓦ www.jhblive.co.za.

CBD and central suburbs

Kippies corner of Quinn and Carr sts, Newtown ☎011 836 1805, ⓦ www.kippies.co.za. Probably the country's finest jazz venue, *Kippies* earned its fame in a converted municipal toilet next to the Market Theatre, but moved to Carr Street when the old building was condemned. The cream of jazz acts from Jo'burg and beyond play Fri and Sat nights.

The Bassline 10 Henry Nxumalo St, Newtown Music Centre ☎011 836 9145. The city's leading live venue by some distance. The hottest local artists across the genres play here, and world-class acts from west and central Africa also stop by.

Northern and eastern suburbs

The Blues Room Village Walk Mall, Sandton ☎011 784 5527, ⓦ www.bluesroom.co.za. Quite smart (as you'd expect for Sandton), but also refreshingly mixed and lively, and featuring some of the best blues sounds in town.

The Radium 282 Louis Botha Ave, Orange Grove ☎011 728 3866. A charmingly shabby Victorian pub – the oldest in town – with live music four nights a week. On the first Sun of every month, don't miss the entertaining eighteen-piece band playing juicy jazz and swing.

Roxy's Rhythm Bar 20 Main Rd, Melville ☎011 726 6019. A large, veteran establishment hosting local indie bands, and a raucous student favourite. The rooftop bar is great on summer nights.

The 88 Lounge 114 William Rd, Norwood ☎011 728 8417. A consistently debauched live venue with a huge open-air deck that buzzes on summer nights. Top rock and reggae acts, off-centre dance DJs and comedy are all on the menu.

The Venue Melrose Arch Shopping Centre Melrose. Intimidatingly swanky conference hall that relaxes with decent rock acts on weekend nights.

Theatre, opera, dance and film

The Civic Theatre in Braamfontein and the Market Theatre in Newtown are Johannesburg's premier venues for **theatre** and **opera** productions, but there

Local radio

Given that Jo'burgers spend so much time in their cars, radio is huge in Gauteng. If you're in town for a few days it's worth flicking around the airwaves to sample some of the local stations, which will give you a flavour of the city. Not all are in English, of course, but don't let that put you off; the following is a selection of the current favourites.

YFM 99.2FM. *The* station for under-21s. A blistering introduction to the upwardly mobile young black culture of Johannesburg, with wall-to-wall hip-hop and *kwaito*.

JoziFM 105.8FM. Ballsy talk station that broadcasts to Soweto and surrounding areas. A fairly recent addition to the radio fray, it has won close to a million listeners.

Highveld Stereo 94.7FM. Endless classic mainstream tracks, soft rock and Celine Dion for the northern suburbs.

Khaya 96.9FM. For listeners who are too old for YFM, Khaya has a mellower mix of mainstream Afro-pop and smooth jazz, with good information on who's playing live in Johannesburg. Audible citywide.

Radio 702 702MW. A well-established local talk-radio station famed for its lively discussion programmes, excellent presenters and news coverage.

SAfm 104–107FM. A national SABC news and talk station, featuring some very skilled presenters and robust political debate. A fascinating gauge of the political dynamics of the country, though many callers are infuriating or waffly or both.

are several other good venues, and the city is blessed with some innovative arts companies, including the Johannesburg Youth Theatre. Johannesburg **dance** is undergoing a revival: key players are the Moving into Dance Academy, which is rearing new generations of South African choreographers, and the Dance Factory in the Newtown Cultural Precinct.

Civic Theatre Loveday St, Braamfontein ☎ 011 877 6800, ⓦ www.showbusiness.co.za. A good mix of both mainstream and more adventurous productions at this impressive, four-stage venue.

The Dance Factory Newtown Cultural Precinct ☎ 011 833 1347. An interesting but irregular programme – check local papers for details.

Liberty Life Theatre on the Square Nelson Mandela Square, Sandton ☎ 011 883 8606. One of the few theatres in the northern suburbs, featuring lightweight drama and a handful of mainstream music or cultural acts.

Market Theatre Newtown Cultural Precinct ☎ 011 832 1641, ⓦ www.markettheatre.co.za. The venue for some of Johannesburg's finest stage productions and top-grade visiting music acts; also celebrated for its innovative community theatre, and the odd costly epic.

Pieter Toerien Theatre Montecasino, Fourways ☎ 011 511 1818. Stages heavyweight productions as well as comedies, musicals and touring shows.

Cinemas

The multiscreen Nu-Metro and Ster-Kinekor cinemas control the movie market and can be found all over the city, especially in shopping malls. The *Mail & Guardian* newspaper contains good cinema listings. The venues below feature independent and foreign films.

Barnyard Theatre Broadacres Shopping Centre, Fourways ☎ 011 467 6983. A massively popular theatre staging musical tribute shows and cabarets. Scorned by the highbrow theatre crowd, who fail to put anything like as many bums on seats.

Hyde Park IMAX Theatre Hyde Park Mall ☎ 011 325 6182. Impressive short films on the vast IMAX screens, mostly on natural history themes.

Northcliff corner of Weltevreden and Arbor sts, Blackheath ☎ 011 782 6816. In the northwest of the city, off Beyers Naude Drive, this shows a good selection of art-house movies.

Rosebank Cinema Nouveau Mall of Rosebank, Rosebank ☎ 011 880 2866. The best art-house cinema in town, offering a decent selection of eight art flicks at a time.

Johannesburg arts festivals

Johannesburg hosts regular festivals in nearly every artistic field. These include:

Arts Alive Festival ☎ 011 673 9272, ⓦ www.artsalive.co.za. Every September. The city's major festival for the performing arts takes place over three weeks at various venues, mainly in the Newtown Cultural Precinct, but also in some townships. Live music dominates, but dance, cabaret and theatre are also well represented. "Jazz on the Lake", on Zoo Lake, is a mainstay of the festival, and always features major South African artists in front of big crowds.

FNB Vita Dance Umbrella Wits Theatre, Braamfontein ☎ 011 482 4140, ⓦ www .at.artslink.co.za/~arts. Three weeks during February and March. Africa's largest festival of dance and choreography hosts international companies but also acts as the major national platform for work by South African talent such as Robyn Orlin and Boyzie Cekwana.

Heritage Weekend Run by Parktown & Westcliff Heritage Trust (office open Mon–Fri 9am–1pm; ☎ 011 482 3349). On the second weekend in September there are tours and special events around the magnificent Parktown mansions of the Randlords.

Joy of Jazz Festival Newtown Cultural Precinct ☎ 011 726 2610, ⓦ www.joyofjazz .co.za. Late August/early September. A weekend festival which draws the cream of South African jazz, including the likes of Pops Mohamed and Hugh Masekela, along with international guest stars.

Village Walk Nu-Metro Village Walk Mall, Rivonia Rd, Sandton ☎ 011 883 9558. One art-house venue squeezed between action-movie screens, in a rather nondescript uptown mall.

Shopping

Johannesburg is a magnet for consumers from all over the subcontinent, who zoom down the city's highways to burn some currency before heading back the same day. For visitors, the city is the best place in South Africa to find **arts and crafts**, with excellent flea markets and galleries offering a plethora of goods, some of very high quality. As the queen of **mall culture**, Johannesburg is also home to over twenty major malls (typically open daily 8am–6pm), most of which are depressingly anonymous, though the handful listed below are so plush and enormous that they arguably merit visiting in their own right.

Malls

Eastgate Shopping Centre Bradford Rd, Bedfordview. A teeming monster mall, home to 250 stores. There are few consumer goods you can't buy here, and most of those can be bought across the road at Park Meadows Shopping Centre.

Hyde Park Mall Jan Smuts Ave, Hyde Park. Trendy and upmarket, awash with swanky cafés and *haute couture* outlets. The excellent Exclusive Books chain has a huge branch here, arguably the best single bookshop in South Africa.

Maponya Mall Old Potchefstroom Rd, Kliptown, Soweto. A fabulously swanky mall, opened in 2007, catering to Soweto's rapidly growing economic elite. It has hundreds of stores and restaurants, and its glitzy, hypermodern architecture is a big advance on the brutalist or faux-Tuscan traditions of Jo'burg mall design.

Randburg Waterfront Republic Rd, Randburg. Built around an artificial lake, this popular if slightly downmarket centre offers restaurants, a flea market and a cinema alongside the clothes shops and chain stores.

Rosebank Mall On the corner of Baker and Cradock sts, Rosebank. One of the city's coolest and least soulless malls, with exclusive boutiques, craft shops and – unusually – outdoor cafés, restaurants and walkways. It adjoins The Zone shopping centre, which is home to some of the best independent clothing stores in town.

Sandton City Shopping Centre corner of Sandton Drive and Rivonia Rd, Sandton. Linked to the astonishingly opulent Nelson Mandela Square mall, this enormous complex has a mind-boggling abundance of shops (including some good bookshops), plus cinemas and African art galleries.

Craft shops, markets and private art galleries

44 Stanley Avenue Auckland Park. A deeply hip design and art complex with cafés, restaurants, galleries and antique shops. Great for a Sun browse.

Art Africa 62 Tyrone Ave, Parkview ☎ 011 486 2052. West of the zoo, this has a good selection of innovative and more familiar crafts, many ingeniously created out of recycled material.

Bright House Bamboo Centre corner of Ninth St and Rustenburg Rd, Melville ☎ 011 726 5657. Inspiringly stylish contemporary interior design shop, with an impressive selection of South African products, most items made locally yet devoid of "ethnic" gimmickry.

Bruma Lake Flea Market Bruma Lake, east of the centre. A huge, permanent market of mostly

African crafts and souvenirs, mainstream and fairly inexpensive.

Everard Read Gallery 6 Jellicoe Ave, Rosebank. Not an especially innovative gallery, and much of the work shown caters to the less tasteful end of the corporate art market. But some fine contemporary artists can be seen here regularly, so it's worth a visit.

Goodman Art Gallery 163 Jan Smuts Ave, Rosebank ⊛ www.goodman-gallery.com. The city's leading contemporary gallery, regularly hosting shows by globally renowned South African artists such as William Kentridge, David Goldblatt and Moshekwa Langa.

Kim Sacks Art Gallery 153 Jan Smuts Ave, Rosebank. A trove of magnificent craft and traditional

615

art from across Africa. The prices can be hefty, but the quality is consistently exceptional.

M2 Highway CBD. An informal market stretching underneath this major artery, a few blocks south of Anderson St. Most stalls specialize in *umuthi* folk medicine, but there are plenty of local crafts as well.

Market Africa Newtown. The city's liveliest flea market, next to the Market Theatre; rifle through colourful blankets from Mali, Congolese masks and statues, and more. Sat 9am–4pm.

Michael Mount Organic Market Culross Rd, off Main Rd, Bryanston ☎011 706 3671. Right-on collection of stalls selling lovely organic food, unusual home crafts and handmade clothes. Hosted by Michael Mount Waldorf School. Thurs & Sat mornings.

Rosebank Rooftop Market Rosebank Mall, 50 Bath Ave, Rosebank. An entertaining place with an impressive array of cottage-industry crafts and clothes. Sun 9am–5pm.

Rural Craft Shop 42E, Mutual Gardens, Rosebank ☎011 788 5821. This non-profit-making city outlet for various craft co-operatives around South Africa makes a refreshing alternative to hard-sell pavement hawkers. Mon–Fri 10am–4pm, Sat 9am–1pm.

Bookshops

Books Galore Shop 2B on Main Rd, Melville (☎011 726 6502) and 66 Tyrone Ave, Parkview (☎011 486 4198). These friendly shops offer a good selection of secondhand books.

Exclusive Books South Africa's biggest and best bookshop chain, with all the latest titles. There are branches in many malls, but the best shops are in: Hyde Park Mall, Jan Smuts Ave, Hyde Park (☎011 325 4298); Sandton Square (☎011 748 5416); Killarney Mall, Houghton (☎011 646 0931); and The Mall of Rosebank (☎011 447 3028).

Out of Print 78 Fourth Ave, Melville ☎011 482 6516. A great little antiquarian and secondhand bookseller, open till 9pm every day of the week during summer, with a tiny Internet café at the back of the shop.

Music shops

The Musica chain of shops, found in most malls, concentrates on soul and rock import CDs, with small selections of local music. In the CBD there are dozens of small shops selling cassettes of South African as well as American sounds.

CD Wherehouse Mutual Square, Rosebank and Sandton City, Sandton. Best selection of CDs in Johannesburg, with all the latest local and international sounds, good deals and helpful staff.

Kohinoor 54 Market St, CBD. Excellent vinyl selection, as well as a range of tapes and CDs. The focus is on jazz, but you'll find all manner of South African styles here, ranging from gospel to *maskanda* and *mbaqanga*.

Plum CD Rosebank Mall, Rosebank ☎011 788 5588. Specialist jazz and world music store. A bit pricey, but offers obscurities unavailable elsewhere.

Rhythmic Beat Park Meadows Shopping Centre, Kensington (opposite Eastgate). Well-stocked and well-run music store, staffed by civil and knowledgeable sales assistants.

Listings

Airlines Air France/KLM, Illovo First floor, International Departures, OR Tambo International Airport ☎011 523 8001; British Airways/Comair, First floor, International Departures, OR Tambo International Airport ☎011 441 8600; Lufthansa, First floor, International Departures, OR Tambo International Airport ☎0861 842 538; Qantas, 195 Jan Smuts Ave ☎011 441 8550; South African Airways, Airlink, & SA Express, at the airport ☎0861 359 722; Virgin Atlantic, 50 Sixth Rd, Hyde Park ☎011 340 3400.

American Express The Zone, 177 Oxford Rd, Rosebank (☎011 880 8382); Sandton City Shopping Centre, Sandton Drive (☎011 883 9009).

Banks and exchange All the main shopping malls have banks where you can change money.

Car rental Standard deals are available from the main companies such as Avis (☎0861 021 111); Budget (☎0861 016 622); EuropCar/Imperial (☎0800 011 344); and Tempest (toll-free ☎0860 031 666). For cheaper, local deals try Apex (☎011 402 5150) and Comet (☎011 974 9618). It's also always worth asking at your accommodation if they have any discount arrangements.

Hospitals and ambulance services In any medical emergency, your best bet is to call the private Netcare 911 ambulance service on ☏082 911. Patients are taken to a Netcare private hospital, which will be expensive but more dependable than a public hospital. State-run hospitals with 24hr casualty departments include Johannesburg General Hospital, Parktown (☏011 488 3334/5); Helen Joseph, Auckland Park (☏011 489 1011); and Baragwanath, Zone 6, Diepkloof, Soweto (☏011 933 8000). Private hospitals include Milpark Hospital, Guild St, Parktown (☏011 480 5600), and Morning-side Medi-Clinic, off Rivonia Rd in Morningside (☏011 282 5000). Private hospitals are always the best option, but without proof of medical insurance, a hefty payment will be needed on admission.

Internet access It's very easy to get online in Jo'burg – most malls have at least one Internet café.

Post offices Most major suburbs have a centrally located post office. The main poste restante post office is on Jeppe St.

Swimming & gyms Public swimming pools around Johannesburg are not always kept in great repair, one exception being the superb, outdoor, Olympic-sized Ellis Park pool (Sept–March Mon–Fri 6.30am–9pm, Sat & Sun 6.30am–6pm). As for gyms, try the chain of Virgin Active gyms around the city (☏0860 200 911, ⊛www.virginactive .co.za); some hotels can give you a voucher valid for one visit to the gyms, otherwise you can pay the single-visit fee of R50.

Taxis Maxi Taxis (☏011 648 1212) are the most reliable for almost all parts of town. Otherwise Rose Radio (☏011 403 9625 or 011 403 0000) is cheap and covers most of the city. Taxis often also wait outside the large hotels.

Around Johannesburg

Johannesburgers wanting to get away from it all tend to head northwest in the direction of the **Magaliesberg mountains**, stretching from Pretoria in the east to Rustenberg in the west. Don't expect to see a horizon of impressive peaks: much of the area is private farmland running across rolling countryside, although there are some impressive *kloofs*, as well as refreshingly wide vistas after the crowded roads and high walls of the big city.

Unprepossessing as the mountain range might be, a series of caves on their southeastern (Johannesburg) side holds some of the world's most important information about human evolution stretching back some three and a half million years. These caves, including the renowned Sterkfontein Caves, are now protected as part of the **Cradle of Humankind**, one of South Africa's first World Heritage Sites.

The Cradle of Humankind

Covering some 47,000 hectares, the **Cradle of Humankind** is the name given to the area in which a series of dolomitic caves have in the last fifty years or so produced nearly two-fifths of the world's hominid fossil discoveries. Given its accessibility and the richness of the finds, it has now arguably overtaken Tanzania's Olduvai Gorge as Africa's (and therefore the world's) most important paleontological site.

As yet, the tourist facilities are few: many of the caves are fragile, and jealously protected by the scientists working on them. However, you can see inside the famous **Sterkfontein Caves**, and there are excellent specialized paleontological tours available (see box, p.619). Elsewhere within the Cradle are the **Maropeng Museum**, as well as largely unrelated attractions, such as the **Rhino and Lion Nature Reserve** and the **Kromdraai Wonder Cave**.

To reach the Cradle of Humankind by **car**, head west out of Johannesburg on the R47 (Hendrik Potgieter Road) or M5 (Beyers Naude Drive), then follow the N14 until the R563 junction. A few kilometres northwest along the R563 is a right turn which will take you to the Sterkfontein Caves turn-off.

Sterkfontein Caves

The best-known of the Cradle of Humankind sites are the **Sterkfontein Caves**
(Tues–Sun 9am–5pm; ☎011 956 6342; R25, ⓦwww.sterkfontein-caves.co.za),
believed to have been inhabited by pre-human primates who lived here up to
3.5 million years ago. They first came to European attention in 1896, when an
Italian lime prospector, Gulgimo Martinaglia, stumbled upon them. Martinaglia
was only interested in the bat droppings, and promptly stripped them out, thus
destroying the caves' dolomite formation. Archeologist Dr Robert Broom
excavated the caves between 1936 and 1951; in 1947, he found the skull of a
female hominid (nicknamed "Mrs Ples") that was over 2.5 million years old. In
1995, another archeologist, Ronald Clarke, found "Little Foot", the bones of a 3
million-year-old walking hominid, with big toes that functioned like our thumbs
do today. In 1998 an *Australopithecus* skeleton discovered here was the oldest
complete specimen known, reckoned to be 3.3 million years old.

Fairly well-informed, if rather short, **guided tours** of the cave leave every
hour (departing on the half-hour) and take you around the main features.

Kromdraai Wonder Cave and the Rhino and Lion Nature Reserve

The only other cave with open public access is the **Kromdraai Wonder Cave**
(daily 8am–5pm; R25), located on the edge of the Rhino and Lion Nature
Reserve to the northeast of Sterkfontein. Also mined for lime in the 1890s, this
cave hasn't revealed any paleontological finds, and the main focus of attention
is the extraordinary stalactites, stalagmites and rimstone pools to be found in a
huge underground chamber. Once you've descended into the cave by a lift,
carefully placed lighting and marked trails make the experience theatrical and
unashamedly commercial. For a few more thrills, you can **abseil** into the cave
rather than use the lift – make arrangements with Wild Cave Adventures (☎011
956 6197 or 082 632 1718). The easier route to the cave is through the Rhino
and Lion Nature Reserve, although you'll have to pay the entrance charge to

▲ Dr Broom meets Mrs Ples, the Cradle of Humankind

Mrs Ples and friends

Embedded in the dolomitic rock within a dozen caves in the area now called the Cradle of Humankind are the fossilized remains of **hominids** which lived in South Africa up to 3.3 million years ago. Samples of fossilized pollen, plant material and animal bones also found in the caves indicate that the area was once a tropical rainforest inhabited by giant monkeys, long-legged hunting hyenas and sabre-toothed cats.

Quite when hominids arrived on the scene isn't certain, but scientists now believe that the human lineage split from apes in Africa around five to six million years ago. The oldest identified group of hominids is *Australopithecus*, a bipedal, small-brained form of man. The first *Australopithecus* discovery in South Africa was in 1924, when Professor Raymond Dart discovered the **Taung child** in what is now North West Province. In 1936, australopithecine fossils were first found in the Sterkfontein Caves, and in 1947 Dr Robert Broom excavated a nearly complete skull which he first called *Plesianthropus transvaalensis* ("near-man" of the Transvaal), later confirmed as a 2.6 million-year-old *Australopithecus africanus*. Identified as a female, she was nicknamed **"Mrs Ples"**, and for many years she was the closest thing the world had to what is rather confusingly dubbed **"the missing link"**.

A number of even older fossils have since been discovered at Sterkfontein and nearby caves, along with evidence of several other genus and species, including *Australopithecus robustus*, dating from between one and two million years ago, and *Homo ergaster*, possibly the immediate predecesor of *Homo sapiens*, who used stone tools and fire.

If you're keen to learn more about this fascinating topic and want to visit some of the caves and dig sites not open to the general public, you could try one of the excellent **tours** offered by Palaeo-Tours (☎011 726 8788 or 082 804 2899, ⓦwww .palaeotours.com), run by Colin Menter, a paleo-anthropologist working at the University of the Witwatersrand.

the reserve; the alternative route is on a longer, rough dirt road on the left before you get to the nature reserve.

The fourteen-square-kilometre **Rhino and Lion Nature Reserve** (daily 8am–5pm; R60) is really more a safari park than anything resembling a wilderness game reserve as found in other parts of South Africa, but it is Gauteng's best site for seeing large mammals. The main section of the reserve has white rhino, wildebeest, hartebeest and giraffe roaming free, while the Lion and Predator Camp has several large enclosures containing lions, cheetahs and wild dogs. Elsewhere, there's a Cape vulture hide, a series of hippo pools and a breeding centre. Game drives, horse trails and mountain-bike trails are also all available – contact the Booking and Information Office ☎011 957 0109. They can also organize a visit to the nearby **Old Kromdraai Gold Mine**, the second-oldest mine on the Witwatersrand, where you can follow the original mining tunnel 150m into the hillside.

Maropeng

The recently built **Maropeng** museum (daily 9am–5pm; R80, children R45; ☎014 577 9000, ⓦwww.maropeng.co.za) is situated a little way down the R400 turn-off from the R563, northwest of the Sterkfontein Caves. Housed in a striking building, The Tumulus, half clad in grassy earth to simulate a burial mound, Maropeng ("returning to the place of our ancestors" in SeTswana) is an impressive museum dedicated to human origins and evolution. Visitors can take a dramatic underground boat ride into the mists of time, and then browse through some very nifty interactive displays occupying 2500 square metres of exhibition space. A changing exhibit of original hominid, plant and animal fossils, loaned from various institutions across South Africa, provides the centrepiece. Attached to the museum are a four-star boutique hotel and the swanky *Tumulus* restaurant.

Accommodation and eating

Not far from the Sterkfontein Caves, on Kromdraai Road towards Lanseria Airport, northwest of Johannesburg, is the Cradle Nature Reserve, a small but peaceful patch of wilderness. Here, the *Cradle Forest Camp* (ⓉO11 659 1622, Ⓦwww.thecradle.co.za; ❷–❸) offers cheap but perfectly decent self-catering A-frame chalets, just big enough for a couple, while the Cradle restaurant nearby is renowned for its fine food, modern, minimalist decor and exhilarating views, as well as regular jazz evenings.

More upmarket is *Toadbury Hall* (ⓉO11 659 0335, Ⓦwww.toadburyhall.co.za; ❺), a colonial-style country lodge, while the rather old-fashioned *Aloe Ridge Hotel* (ⓉO11 957 2070, Ⓦwww.aloeridgehotel.com; ❹) has the unique attraction of a 25-inch telescope and a resident astronomer. You can come here simply for a meal, or stay in a specially erected Zulu village of grass huts (❷). The *Maropeng Hotel* (ⓉO14 577 9100; ❻), alongside the Maropeng Museum, is not cheap, but each of its rooms has a patio commanding a dramatic Magaliesberg view. The design approach is earth-toned southern African chic, and if you're after a bit of innovative, low-kitsch luxury, it's worth it. Other accommodation options include the self-catering chalet sleeping four in the Rhino and Lion Nature Reserve (❹) and the many hotels and guesthouses which are part of the Magalies Meander (Ⓦwww.magaliesmeander.co.za) and the Crocodile Ramble (Ⓦwww.theramble.co.za). These two fairly humdrum tourism routes are aimed mainly at Jo'burgers needing a quick weekend break; the committed traveller is better off hitting some real backwoods further afield.

Pretoria and around

Gauteng's two major cities are just 50km apart, but could hardly be more different. With its graceful government buildings, wide avenues of purple flowering jacarandas, and stolid Boer farming origins, **PRETORIA** – or **TSHWANE** as the metropolitan area has now been officially renamed (see p.622) – has always been a staid, sleepy city. Yet although South Africa's administrative capital was long regarded as a bastion of **Afrikaner nationalism**, home to the notorious supreme court and a massive prison, things are changing fast. Ever since democracy arrived, Pretoria has become increasingly cosmopolitan, with a substantial diplomatic community living in Arcadia and Hatfield, east of the city centre. Furthermore, most Pretorians are not Afrikaans, but Pedi and Tswana, and the change of government has brought many more middle-class blacks into the ranks of civil servants living in the capital. The city's Afrikaans community is hardly monolithic, either: alongside the old-school khaki-shorted types, there are thousands of students, a progressive art scene and a thriving Afrikaans gay and lesbian community.

Pretoria is close enough to Johannesburg's airport to provide a practical alternative base in Gauteng. It feels safer and less spread out than Johannesburg (though don't make the blithe assumption that Pretoria is crime-free), there are more conventional sights, and the **nightlife** is energetic and fun.

Some history

Unlike Johannesburg, Pretoria developed at a leisurely pace from its humble origins as a **Boer farming community** on the fertile land around the Apies River. When the city was founded in 1855 by **Marthinus Wessel Pretorius**, who named it after his father, Andries Pretorius, it was intended to be the capital around which the new South African Republic (ZAR) would prosper. Embodying the Afrikaners' conviction that the land they took was God-given, Pretoria's first building was a church. The town was then laid out in a grid of streets wide enough for teams of oxen brought in by farmers to make U-turns.

In 1860, the city was proclaimed the capital of the new ZAR, the result of tireless efforts by Stephanus Schoeman to unite the squabbling statelets of the Transvaal. From this base, the settlers continued their campaigns against local African peoples, bringing thousands into service, particularly on farms. Infighting also continued among the settlers, and violent skirmishes between faction leaders were common. These leaders bought most of the best land, resulting in the dispossession and embitterment of many white trekkers, and also in the massacre of most of the wild animals of the region, particularly its elephants.

The British annexed Pretoria in 1877, and investment followed in their wake. Although the town prospered and grew, farmer **Paul Kruger**, who was determined not to be subjugated by the British again, mobilized commandos of Afrikaner farmers to drive them out. This resulted in the first Anglo-Boer War (1877–81). After defeat at Majuba on the Natal border, the colonial government abandoned the war and ceded **independence** in 1884. Paul Kruger became ZAR president, and ruled until 1903. However, his mission to keep the ZAR Boer was confounded by the discovery of **gold** in the Witwatersrand, which precipitated an unstoppable flood of foreigners. Kruger's policy of taxing the newcomers, while retaining the Boer monopoly on political power, worked for a while. Most of the elegant buildings of Church Square were built with mining revenues, while the Raadsaal (parliament) remained firmly in Boer hands. At the same time, the ZAR's military arsenal grew, largely thanks to imported German weapons.

ZAR independence ended with the second Anglo-Boer War (1899–1902), but, despite the brutality of the conflict, Pretoria remained unscathed. With the creation of the **Union of South Africa** in 1910, the city became the administrative capital of the entire country. In 1913, Sir Herbert Baker built the epic Union Buildings to house the civil service, and some ministries, including the office of the president, are still there today.

In 1928, the government laid the foundations of Pretoria's industry by establishing the **Iron and Steel Industrial Corporation** (Iscor), which rapidly generated a whole series of related and service industries. These, together with the civil service, ensured white Pretoria's quiet, insular prosperity. Meanwhile, increasing landlessness among blacks drove many of them into the city's burgeoning **townships**. Marabastad and Atteridgeville are the oldest, and Mamelodi is the biggest and poorest.

After the introduction of apartheid by the National Party in 1948, Pretoria acquired a hated reputation among the country's black population. Its supreme court and central prison were notorious as the source of the laws and regulations that made their lives a nightmare.

Mandela's inauguration at the Union Buildings in 1994 was the symbolic new beginning for Pretoria's political redemption. Through the 1990s, the stages of South Africa's revolution could be seen as clearly in Pretoria as anywhere else: the gradual replacement of the diehards from institutions like the army and civil service, new faces in almost all the old government offices, the return of foreign diplomats, aid agencies and NGOs, the influx of students and the change in demographics of the city-centre suburbs. While the newcomers have absorbed a good deal of the sense of decorum which was always a hallmark of Pretoria, even in the apartheid years, they have also imparted creativity and vibrancy to the capital city.

Pretoria's metropolitan area was renamed Tshwane in 2005 by the city council, after a Tswana-Ndebele chief who ruled in the area before Boer settlers arrived. The central business district remains Pretoria, but the compromise is awkward, with most media, and indeed most citizens, still calling the whole city Pretoria. Many Afrikaners resent what they see as a spiteful and costly attempt to erase the city's Afrikaans origins from public memory, while many black Pretorians don't see why a post-apartheid, mainly black city should still bear a name deeply associated with racial oppression. It seems likely that the city will lug two names around for years to come.

Arrival, information and city transport

The nearest airport to Pretoria is **OR Tambo International Airport**, some 50km away to the southeast (see p.580), from where driver and tour guide Stanford Hlatshwayo (☎084 857 4967; R270) runs a highly recommended **taxi service** to the city. The Airport Shuttle (☎0861 748 8853; R270–290) is another option. Alternatively, and probably less expensively, you could arrange with your accommodation to be collected from the airport.

If you're arriving by **train** you'll alight at Pretoria station, designed by Sir Herbert Baker, to the south of the city centre; **intercity buses** stop beside the station building. The main point of **information** for Pretoria is the Tourist Information Centre, in the Old Nederlandsche Bank building on Church Square (Mon–Fri 7.30am–4pm; ☎012 358 1430)

Pretoria's city centre is easily explored on foot, but for journeys to the suburbs, you'll need the municipal **bus** services, which start in Church Square. You buy tickets – which are never more than a few rand – when you get on; timetables are available from Church Square, where there's a bus information office (☎012 358 0839), as well as on the buses themselves and from pharmacies.

The best place to catch **minibus taxis** is from the corner of Jacob Maré and Bosman streets, just north of the railway station, though you can hail them from anywhere. As in Johannesburg, you can't generally hail metered **taxis**, though you'll usually find one on or near Church Square; alternatively, cabs can be booked ahead by phone (see "Listings" on p.634).

Accommodation

With plenty of government custom, Pretoria has no shortage of soulless modern **hotel** complexes, most run by multinational chains. A much nicer option is to stay at one of the few hotels and guesthouses with genuine character. Unlike in Johannesburg, you can feel reasonably comfortable staying close to the centre, although there isn't much nightlife here – for that, you might prefer to base yourself in Hatfield or Brooklyn, where there are a number of excellent guesthouses.

Backpackers can choose from a good selection of **hostels**, most of which are in the Sunnyside, Arcadia and Hatfield districts. Most offer transfers from the airport, which are among the cheapest you'll find. As with Jo'burg, it's worth booking your first night before you arrive.

Backpacker lodges

North South Backpackers 355 Glyn St, Hatfield ☎012 362 0989, ⓦwww .northsouthbackpackers.com. Now established as one of Pretoria's best backpacker hostels, this neat, well-run establishment is in a good location close to Hatfield's buzzing nightlife. On offer are dorms and plenty of doubles in a large, quiet suburban house with a great garden and pool. The owners also run a convenient travel centre.❷

Pretoria Backpackers 425 Farenden St, Clydesdale ☎012 343 9754 or 083 302 1976, ⓦwww.pretoriabackpackers.net. A more upmarket backpacker place with plenty of doubles as well as smallish dorms spread over two lovely old houses with wooden floors, original features and a relaxing garden *stoep*. Massages and beauty treatment are available, while the knowledgeable owner, François, is a great Pretoria enthusiast and runs a useful travel centre for local tours and onward travel.❷

Word of Mouth 430 Reitz St, Sunnyside ☎012 343 7499, ⓦwww.travelinafrica.co.za. A colourful, welcoming but slightly downmarket hostel not far from the centre, with some wooden Wendy houses in the garden serving as doubles. ❶–❷

Hotels, guesthouses and B&Bs

Arcadia Hotel 515 Proes St ☎012 326 9311, ⓦwww.arcadiahotel.co.za. This central, business-oriented hotel has no pool, but the rooms are comfortable and the restaurant reliable. ❸

Battiss-Zeederberg Guesthouse 3 Fook Island, 92 Twentieth St, Menlo Park ☎012 460 7318 or 083 271 0819, ⓦwww.battiss.co.za. Very comfortable B&B accommodation in the original home of eccentric Walter Battiss, one of South Africa's greatest twentieth-century artists. Brightly painted floors, unusual decorations and a distinctly Greek feel. ❸

Brooks Cottage 283 Brooks St, Brooklyn ☎012 362 3150 or 082 448 3902, ⓦwww .brookscottage.co.za. An elegant Cape Dutch-style home – a national monument – with five rooms. Smartly done, with cable TV and a pool. ❸

Hotel 224 corner of Leyds and Schoeman sts ☎012 440 5281, ⓦwww.hotel224.com. Single and double rooms in a dated-looking but fairly characterful budget hotel near the Union Buildings, with a restaurant and bar attached and safe parking. ❸

La Maison 235 Hilda St, Hatfield ☎012 430 4341, ⓦwww.lamaison.co.za. A very pleasant guesthouse with lovely gardens, six Victorian-styled rooms full of antiques, and an outstanding restaurant. ❹

Osborne House 82 Anderson St, Brooklyn ☎012 362 2334 or 083 302 1049, ⓦwww .osborneguesthouse.com. A wonderfully elegant guesthouse set in a restored Edwardian manor house with lovely furniture, big windows, wooden floors and a pleasant, secluded pool. ❹

Sheraton Pretoria 643 Church St, Arcadia ☎012 429 9999, ⓦwww.sheraton.com/pretoria. This fine five-star hotel boasts all the usual upmarket Sheraton touches, but most importantly has the best views of the Union Buildings. If you can't afford a room with a view, head to the *Union Gardens Lounge* beside *Tiffens Bar & Lounge* for high tea. ❼

Ted's Place 961 Wagon Wheel Ave, Wapadrand ☎012 807 2803 or 083 452 5546, ⓦwww .teds-place.za.net. One of the nicest places to stay on the outskirts of Pretoria, this large, elegant hilltop house offers friendly B&B with great views over the city and the Magaliesberg. ❸

That's It Guest Home 5 Brecher St, Clydesdale ☎012 344 3404, ⓦwww.thatsit.co.za. A neat, unelaborate, reasonably priced B&B in a family home with four rooms and a relaxing garden and pool. ❸

Victoria Hotel corner of Scheiding and Paul Kruger sts ☎012 323 6054, ✉hvic@freemail .absa.co.za. This historic building opposite the train station was once the railway workers' bar; now it offers plush accommodation and is often filled with affluent travellers taking luxury trains to Cape Town. ❹

Whistletree Lodge 1267 Whistletree Drive, Queenswood ☎012 333 9915 or 082 446 8858, ⓦwww.whistletreelodge.com. Roughly 10km northeast of the centre is this small luxury boutique hotel, with beautiful antiques, eclectic artwork and stylish furniture. Facilities include a pool, sauna and private balconies. ❻

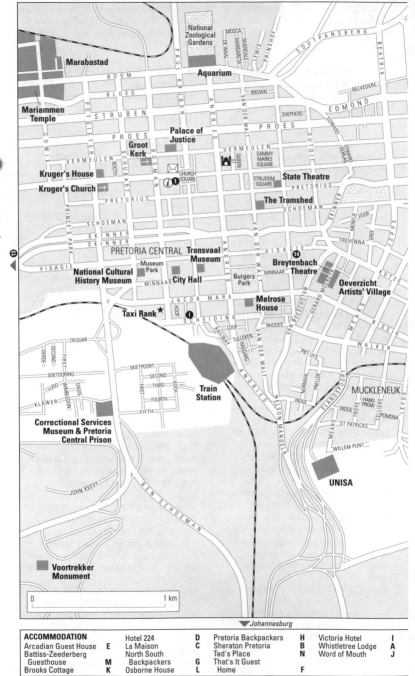

National
Zoological
Gardens

MOSCA
RIVERDALE
MARGARETA
DE WAAL
LEWIS
PRINSHOF
SOUTPANSBERG

BEATRIX

Marabastad

BOOM

Aquarium

BROWN

BELVEDERE

Mariammen
Temple

BLOED

STRUBEN

EDMOND

SHEPHERD

EDWARD

PROES

PROES

DUTOIT

EDWARD
JOUBAS

Palace of
Justice

Groot
Kerk

VERMEULEN

VERMEULEN

SAMMY
MARKS

Kruger's House

BOOTH

CHURCH
SQUARE

QUEEN

STRIJDOM
SQUARE

State Theatre

Kruger's Church

PRETORIUS

PRETORIUS

The Tramshed

SCHOEMAN

SCHOEMAN

SKINNER

MENLYE

VOOR

GREE

SKINNER

TREVENNA

JEPPE

PRETORIA CENTRAL

Transvaal
Museum

VISAGIE

VISAGIE

Breytenbach
Theatre

KOTZE

RISSIK

National Cultural
History Museum

Museum
Park

MINNAAR

City Hall

Burgers
Park

MINNAAR

Oeverzicht
Artists' Village

MEARS

Melrose
House

JACOB MARE

Taxi Rank ★

SCHEIDING

RHODES

WALKER

LOOP

PIET UYS

Train
Station

RAILWAY

TULLEKEN

HAGGARD

MUCKLENEUK

HANS
PROW

DEQUAR

SECOND
THIRD

SKIETPOORT

SECOND

FIRST

THIRD

KOCH

RIDGE

ST PATRICKS

CELLIERS

LEYDS

SOETDORING

LUDO

FOURTH

WIMBLEDON

OASIS

FIFTH

WILLEM PUNT

KLAWER

Correctional Services
Museum & Pretoria
Central Prison

UNISA

JOHN KEEVY

BEN SCHOEMAN

Voortrekker
Monument

0   1 km

▼ Johannesburg

ACCOMMODATION							
Arcadian Guest House	E	Hotel 224	D	Pretoria Backpackers	H	Victoria Hotel	I
Battiss-Zeederberg		La Maison	C	Sheraton Pretoria	B	Whistletree Lodge	A
Guesthouse	M	North South		Ted's Place	N	Word of Mouth	J
Brooks Cottage	K	Backpackers	G	That's It Guest			
		Osborne House	L	Home	F		

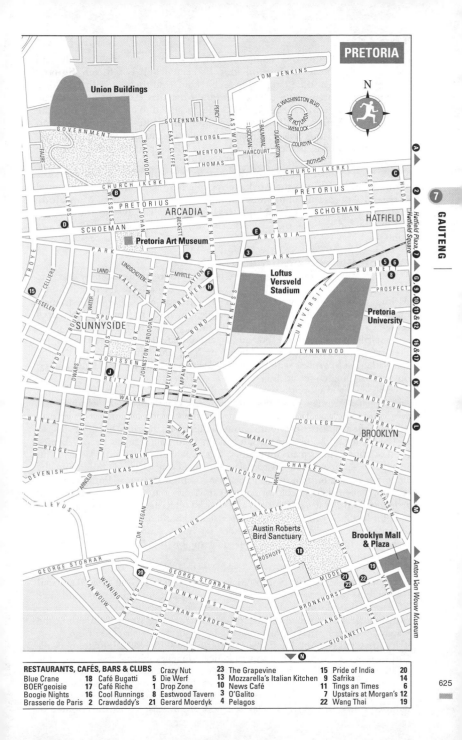

Union Buildings

■ **Pretoria Art Museum**

Loftus Versveld Stadium

Pretoria University

ARCADIA

HATFIELD

BURNET

PROSPECT

SUNNYSIDE

LYNNWOOD

BROOKS

ANDERSON

MURRAY

BROOKLYN

COLLEGE

MARAIS

MARAIS

MACKENZIE

CHARLES

NICOLSON

Austin Roberts Bird Sanctuary

Brooklyn Mall & Plaza

GEORGE STORRAR

BRONKHORST

BRONKHORST

GIOVANETTI

N

↑ Hatfield Plaza
↑ Hatfield Square
→ Anton van Wouw Museum

RESTAURANTS, CAFÉS, BARS & CLUBS			
Blue Crane	18	Café Bugatti	17
BOER'geoisie	17	Café Riche	1
Boogie Nights	16	Cool Runnings	8
Brasserie de Paris	2	Crawdaddy's	21
Crazy Nut	23	The Grapevine	15
Die Werf	5	Mozzarella's Italian Kitchen	13
Drop Zone	10	News Café	11
Eastwood Tavern	3	O'Galito	7
Gerard Moerdyk	4	Pelagos	22
Pride of India	20
Safrika	14
Tings an Times	6
Upstairs at Morgan's	12
Wang Thai	19

The City

Pretoria's city centre is a compact grid of wide, busy streets, easily and comparatively safe to explore on foot. Its central hub is **Church Square**, where you can see some fascinating architecture, and there are other historic buildings and museums close by around the **Museum Park**. To the north lie the vast **Zoological Gardens**, while the Arcadia district is the site of the city's famous **Union Buildings**. Away from the centre, **Hatfield**, close to Pretoria University, is where students and yuppies throng the latest bars and restaurants, as well as being the home of Pretoria's diplomats, who live in the swankiest houses in town.

On the southern fringes of the city is the remarkable **Voortrekker Monument**, as close as the Afrikaner people have to a sacred site. You need to travel 15km east out of town to find the sprawling township of **Mamelodi**; Pretoria's other major township, **Atteridgeville**, is equally far out of town to the west, off the N4, or R104, on the way to the Hartbeesport Dam and Sun City.

Church Square and the city centre

The heart of Pretoria is undoubtedly **Church Square**, surrounded by dramatic and important buildings, and a place where you can at least try to put South Africa's complex history into perspective. It was here that Boer farmers outspanned their oxen when they came into town for the quarterly Nagmaal (Holy Communion) of the Dutch Reformed Church, turning the square temporarily into a campsite. Today this spot continues to be a meeting point for Pretorians of all races, many of whom you'll see lounging on the grass in the sun, gathering to protest with placards and singing, or simply watching it all go on while sipping coffee at the cultured *Café Riche*.

Nearly every important white meeting, protest or takeover the city has known happened in Church Square; the ZAR Vierkleur ("four colours") flag was lowered here in 1877 to make way for the Union Jack, only to rise again in 1881, after the British eviction from the republic; the British flag flew again in 1900 but was lowered for the last time in 1910; Paul Kruger was proclaimed head of state in the square four times, and 30,000 crammed it in 1904 for his memorial service. Such historical resonances are viewed differently by Pretoria's black community, and the square's central **statue of Paul Kruger** – the work of Afrikaner sculptor Anton Van Wouw – is for many an unwanted relic of a dismal past. Van Wouw had to work fast: Kruger hated posing and the sculptor had little time with him. Nevertheless he still managed to produce this frighteningly miserable representation, set above four rugged Voortrekker archetypes; today, the pigeons that squat on his top hat provide a suitably subversive touch.

The Continental-style square is surrounded on all sides by some of the most impressive buildings in South Africa. Look out for the old **Raadsaal** (parliament) on the southwest corner of the square, built in neo-Renaissance style in 1891, and still exuding the bourgeois respectability yearned for by the parliamentarians of the ZAR. Across the narrow side street from this is the Capitol Theatre, rarely used now as a performance space but home to Tshwane Craft Market. Next door to this is the **Old Nederlandsche Bank Building**, now home of the tourist office. Unbelievably, it took a gathering of 10,000 people in 1975 and five years of deliberation to reverse a decision to demolish this building and its two neighbours. The Art Nouveau **Café Riche** (see p.633), on the corner of Church Square, adds a sophisticated and cultured touch to the day-to-day business of the area; it's a handy source of information, and here you can buy a booklet or rent a cassette player explaining the history and architecture of the square.

On the opposite side of Church Street is the imposing **General Post Office**, beside which is a **Stamp Museum** (Mon–Fri 7.30am–4pm; free) displaying over half a million stamps, including a rare Cape Triangle of 1853. The grandiose **Palace of Justice**, on the northwest side of the square, was started in 1897 and, half completed, was used as a hospital for British troops during the second Anglo-Boer War. After its completion in 1902, the building was home to the Transvaal Supreme Court for many years and was the location of the Rivonia Trial in 1963–64, which saw Nelson Mandela and other leaders of the ANC sentenced to life imprisonment. Recent restoration work has revealed and repaired the splendid facade and balconies, although the new court is an ugly box sitting squatly in a street behind the Palace. Next to this is the **Reserve Bank** building, designed in distinctive style by Sir Herbert Baker (see box, p.597). Other buildings of note around the eastern and northern side of the square include the **Tudor Chambers**, built in neo-Tudor style in 1904, and the Neoclassical **Standard Bank** building on the site of the old *Grand Hotel*.

Sammy Marks Square and around

East of Church Square, Church Street takes you towards Sammy Marks Square. Just before you get there, a left turn into Queen Street and a further left turn along a passageway halfway down the block reveals the unexpected site of a bright white **mosque**, oriented at an angle to the city grid so as to face Mecca. Pretoria's Muslims, who reportedly got on well with Kruger, acquired the site in 1896, and the current building was constructed in 1927 by Cape artisans. The mosque is now hemmed in by ugly tower blocks, but is somehow all the more indomitable for that.

Garish **Sammy Marks Square** itself, dominated by modern shopping malls filled with chain stores, is named after the founder of South African Breweries (SAB), who was a patron of the city. The only thing worth checking out here is the excellent **library** (Mon–Fri 8am–5.50pm, Sat 8am–12.50pm; ☎012 313 8956), geared to adult education, with every available space decked out in Pretoria's trademark purple.

Across Church Street is **Strijdom Square**, so named because it was the location of a vast and horrific bust of the man himself, encased in a modernist arch. Prime minister from 1954 to 1958, Strijdom began the wave of apartheid legislation that peaked under his successor, Hendrik Verwoerd, and was a firm believer in "white supremacy". Dramatically, on May 31, 2001, forty years to the day after the statue was completed, a structural fault (or divine intervention, depending on your point of view) caused it to collapse. While many would like to see it remain a symbolic pile of rubble, others say it's high time the statue was replaced by a memorial to the seven victims of the random shooting at minibus taxis here by a right-wing maniac namesake, Barend Strijdom, in 1993.

Paul Kruger's House and around

To find **Paul Kruger's House** (Mon–Fri 9am–4.30pm, Sat, Sun & public holidays 8.30am–5pm; R16), head west along Church Street from Church Square, crossing Bosman and Schubart streets. Kruger's House was built in 1884 by the English-speaking Charles Clark, described by Kruger as one of his "tame Englishmen", who mixed his cement with milk instead of water. Inside, the museum is rather dull, though you may find some interest in Kruger's effects, such as his large collection of spittoons. The *stoep* is the most famous feature of the house, for here the old president would sit and chat to any white person who chose to join him. Out at the back is Kruger's private railway coach, built in 1898, which he used during the second Anglo-Boer War.

Opposite is a characteristically grim Reformed church known as **Kruger's Church**. The **Groot Kerk** (**Great Church**), on the corner of Vermeulen and Bosman streets, is more impressive; its strikingly ornate tower is one of the finest in the country.

Burgers Park and the Museum Park

South from Church Square lies a precinct of museums and open spaces that has drawn favourable comparisons with Washington DC's Smithsonian Institute. On Jacob Maré Street between Andries and Van der Walt streets is the restful **Burgers Park** (daily 8am–6pm; free), named after ineffective ZAR president Thomas Burgers, who was in office between 1873 and 1877. The park has a good botanical garden, a quirkily designed curator's house and a pavilion at its centre, once the preserve of brass bands and all-white tea parties, but now multiracial and a good place to relax.

Opposite the park's southern border, **Melrose House**, 275 Jacob Maré St (Tues–Sun 10am–5pm; R5; ⓦ www.melrosehouse.co.za), is an overdecorated Victorian domicile with a wonderful conservatory, interesting exhibitions and a great African arts and crafts shop. The house was built in 1884 for local businessman George Heys, who made his money running mailcoach services. Lord Kitchener used the house during the second Anglo-Boer War, and the treaty of Vereeniging that ended hostilities was signed inside. Outside, a sumptuous tea garden serves cakes and scones, light meals and, on certain days, hearty South African lunches such as *bobotie* and savoury rice.

Head west of Burger Park along Minnaar Street, and then turn right into Paul Kruger Street and past a huge whale skeleton for the grand **Transvaal Museum** (daily 8am–5pm; R10), Pretoria's oldest museum and centrepiece of the Northern Flagship Institution (ⓦ www.nfi.org.za), the collective name for Pretoria's main museums. Dedicated to natural history, the museum has plenty of stuffed animals, models of dinosaurs and wonderful fossil remains, some over a million years old. This is a good place to come if your interest in man's origins has been stirred by the discoveries of the nearby Cradle of Humankind (see p.617): alongside a bronze bust of Robert Broom staring into the three-million-year-old eye sockets of Mrs Ples is an assortment of fossilized discoveries and various models and reconstructions of early hominid life. Nearby is a selection of stuffed animals, never particularly inspiring when many of the animals can be seen alive and kicking in game reserves not too far away. In the Austin Roberts Bird Hall, you'll find an informative exhibit on South Africa's many species of birds, while the Geoscience Museum showcases another Gauteng speciality, rocks and minerals.

Opposite the museum at the far end of a series of fountains and well-tended flowerbeds is the **City Hall**, with its mix of Greek and Roman architectural styles, and two rather good statues of Andries and Marthinus Pretorius immediately outside. The next large block to the west is taken up by the **National Cultural History Museum** (daily 8am–4pm; R8), formerly known as the **African Window**, accessed from Visagie Street. This large, airy exhibition space is, like many public collections, gradually feeling its way in the new South Africa. Generous room is given to temporary displays, although this tends to give the museum a rather tentative air. The permanent exhibitions are interesting in themselves but seem a bit unconnected. They include "Access to Power", which displays and explains San rock art, and "People's Choice", where groups of local people, including township women's groups and schoolchildren, have been invited to select objects from the museum's vast collection of some three million pieces. Also here is a room showing work by J.H. Pierneef (1886–1957), one of the country's most famous artists, who is known for his dramatically stylized bushveld landscapes.

The zoo and the Mariammen Temple

North of Church Square, busy Proes and Struben streets are filled with cut-price stores, black shoppers and minibus taxis heading for the townships. While other parts of central Pretoria are fairly safe to walk around if you take the normal precautions, take extra care if you're wandering in this direction, as gangs have been known to work these streets, and a number of tourists have been mugged here.

Head across Bloed and Boom streets for the **National Zoological Gardens** (daily 8am–6pm; R36, children R22; ☏012 328 3265), which are spacious and surprisingly good, housing rare species of antelope, a white rhinoceros, and a wide selection of South American as well as African animals. A cableway (R10) carries you right over the zoo on both sides of the Apies River, and you can even rent golf cars if you're feeling lazy (R70 per hour). It's well worth trying to book one of the **night tours** (R50; ☏012 328 3265), starting at 6pm on Wednesdays, Fridays and Saturdays, when you'll see some of the zoo's freakiest creatures at their most active. Next door, the **Pretoria Aquarium and Reptile Park** (entrance included with zoo entry charge) is less impressive, but nonetheless has plenty of beasts, some very weird and highly poisonous.

West of here lie the scruffy streets of **Marabastad**, the city's first "non-white" area which, while fascinating, can feel quite intimidating; you may feel more comfortable exploring them with a guide. Don't miss the intricately decorated Hindu **Mariammen Temple**, right next to the market.

The Correctional Services Museum

The chilling **Correctional Services Museum** (Mon–Fri 9am–3pm; free) at Pretoria Central Prison is well worth a visit. Make for Potgieter Street, which runs north–south three blocks west of Church Square, and stay on it while it becomes the R101 to Johannesburg. You'll see the notorious prison, where many famous political prisoners were held (and many executed), on your right. Be prepared to walk past depressed-looking visiting relatives on your way in. Inside the museum you can see artworks made by prisoners, including a life-size statue of an inmate crawling towards an expressionless prison warder, who has his arms outstretched, ready to correct him. There are also exhibits of knives concealed in Bibles and shoes, files in cakes and so forth. Most alarming by far are the group photos of various forbidding-looking prison warders through the ages, which seem a strange sort of propaganda for the prison service.

The Voortrekker Monument

Continuing on the R101, follow the signs to view the famous **Voortrekker Monument and Museum** (daily 8am–6pm; R30; ☏www.voortrekkermon .org.za). For many years an ominous symbol of Afrikaner domination, the monument is now generally accepted as one of South Africa's many cultural waypoints, and a visit does allow you some penetrating insights into the Afrikaner mindset. The striking, austere block of granite was built in 1940 to commemorate the Boer victory over the Zulu army at Blood River on December 16, 1838 (see p.546), and its symbolism is crushingly heavy-handed. The monument is enclosed by reliefs of ox wagons, with a large statue of a woman standing outside, shaking her fist at imaginary oppressors. Inside, a series of moving reliefs depicts scenes from the Great Trek. Outside, hidden by some trees, are two pint-sized replicas of the huts of Zulu kings Dingane and Cetshwayo.

The monument is set within a small **nature reserve** which has various hiking and mountain-bike trails, leading to lookout points over Pretoria and the surrounding countryside. You can also explore the reserve on a pony trek (book in advance on ☏012 323 0682).

Arcadia and the Union Buildings

Head east along Vermeulen or Church streets, and you'll soon reach the **Arcadia** district, where Pretoria's **Union Buildings**, the headquarters of the South African government, perch majestically on the main hill. Designed by Herbert Baker (see box, p.597) in 1910, allegedly to symbolize the union of Briton and Boer, the lashings of colonnades and lavish amphitheatre seem instead to glorify British imperial self-confidence. Nelson Mandela had an office inside, and the buildings were famously the site of his inauguration in 1994. This was perhaps the first time their imperialist symbols were transformed, not least by the African praise-singers who delivered their odes from the amphitheatre, proclaiming Mandela as the latest in a long line of African heroes from Shaka to Hintsa, and beyond. You can walk around the buildings and their gardens, and, if you're a particular enthusiast of Baker's work and the Union Buildings in particular, take one of the **tours** called The Baker's Dozen, run by the talkative Leone Jackson (around R50; ☏012 344 3197).

South of the Union Buildings, the **Pretoria Art Museum**, corner of Schoeman and Wessels streets (Tues–Sun 10am–4.30pm; R5), houses an excellent selection of South African art and Dutch Masters, as well as some black artists, including Ephraim Ngatane and Gerard Sekoto. There is a small gallery (same hours; free) just beyond the main entrance which is worth popping into for its contemporary exhibitions and small café.

Sunnyside

Southeast of the centre, desegregated **Sunnyside** is the central suburb with the strongest African feel, with a busy street life, distinctive old houses and a multitude of cafés. **Esselen Street** is the busiest thoroughfare, brimming with bars and street hawkers. A little way to the west, **Oeverzicht Artists' Village**, on the corner of Kotze and Gerard Moerdyk streets, was once a lively little node of old cottages with interesting craft shops and restaurants, though there's now quite a rapid turnover of business and fewer of the venues which gave the place some spark. The **Breytenbach Theatre** at 137 Gerard Moerdyk St – said to be haunted by the ghosts of those who died there when it was a hospital for Germans – hosts mainly student productions.

Loftus Versveld Stadium and Pretoria University

East of Sunnyside is the huge **Loftus Versveld Stadium**, home to Pretoria's hugely popular sporting giants: the Bulls rugby team and the Mamelodi Sundowns soccer team. On the other side of the railway line from here, **Pretoria University** has some excellent gallery and museum space, including an exhibition in the Ou Lettere (Old Arts) building (Tues–Fri 10am–4pm; free) dedicated to the remarkable archeological finds at Mapungubwe (see p.736), a hilltop fort near the Limpopo River which was the ancient capital of a major southern African kingdom. Among the artefacts on display are a rhinoceros made from thin gold foil, figurines, jewellery and decorated pots, all at least 700 years old. Also in the same building is an art gallery with changing exhibits; the

▲ Union Buildings, Pretoria

university has a fantastic permanent collection, including Dutch Masters and Chinese ceramics dating back to the Han dynasty (206 BC–221 AD), but this is viewable by appointment only (☎012 420 3100).

Hatfield and Brooklyn

Beyond Pretoria University is **Hatfield**, which has developed in the last few years into Pretoria's liveliest area, with the trendiest hangouts and nightlife around Park, Burnett and Hilda streets, where you'll find a plethora of studenty cafés, bars and restaurants.

To visit the elegant house and museum of acclaimed Afrikaner sculptor **Anton van Wouw**, 299 Clark St (Mon–Fri 10am–4pm; free), you'll need to head southeast of the university to the wealthy suburb of **Brooklyn**. Van Wouw was responsible for most of the brooding effigies of Afrikaner public figures from the 1890s to the 1930s scattered around the country, including the Kruger statue in Pretoria's Church Square (see p.626). His most famous work is at the Voortrekker Monument (see p.629). The museum, designed by the celebrated architect Norman Eaton in 1938, houses a collection of his smaller pieces. Van Wouw's figures tend to be placed in rural settings, but here you'll find two striking, non-rural pieces, one of a mine worker, the other an accused man standing in the dock. Keep an eye out, too, for *The Guitar Player*, a feisty-looking woman strumming away with a trace of a smile on her face.

UNISA

Travelling south towards Johannesburg on Elandspoort Road, you can't miss the enormous and head-shakingly ugly **UNISA**, South Africa's largest university, which lurches over the freeway to Jo'burg like a renegade ocean liner. Over 200,000 students are enrolled here – though most of them study by correspondence. Inside, on the fifth floor, a very good **art gallery** (Tues–Fri 10am–4pm; ☎012 429 6255; free) hosts some of Pretoria's most innovative exhibitions, as well as a permanent collection exhibiting young South African talent of all races. UNISA's library (☎012 429 2361; R35 for a day pass) is vast, peaceful and superbly run: it's the finest academic library in the country, with astoundingly rich collections on South African history, art and biology; special memberships with borrowing rights can easily be arranged if you're in town for a while.

Eating and drinking

Pretoria has plenty of good **restaurants**, particularly around the Hatfield and Brooklyn areas, where they tend to congregate around a handful of popular upmarket shopping centres. If you're prepared to explore a bit further there are some very interesting places serving South African food. **Cafés** are numerous and varied; again, Hatfield is the more stylish area, although you can still find a place to sip espresso right in the city centre.

Restaurants

Alla Turka Shop 10, Garsfontein Village Centre, Serene St (off General Louis Botha), Garsfontein ☎012 993 0286. Welcoming, radiantly colourful eatery owned by a Turkish-Lebanese couple. The menu features a medley of Mediterranean flavours, and belly dancers perform on Fri & Sat nights, for a R15 per person performance fee.

Blue Crane 156 Melk St, New Muckleneuk ☎012 460 7615. A fairly traditional and smart restaurant in a unique location, overlooking the dam and the Austin Roberts Bird Sanctuary. Open daily for breakfast, afternoon tea and hearty, moderately priced main meals.

BOER'geoisie Greenlyn Village, Thirteenth St, Menlo Park ☎012 460 0264. The name says it all – hearty, traditional *boerekos* jazzed up with bistro-cuisine flourishes. The *potjies* (stews) are the house speciality; options include lamb with dumplings and

tripe and trotters with onions. Vegans beware. Closed Sun evenings.

Brasserie de Paris 525 Duncan St, Hatfield ☎012 362 2247. This faithful reproduction of the classic Parisian café has a pleasant terrace, spacious and classy interior, smart service and a great menu. Twice voted among the country's top ten restaurants, it's quite expensive. Closed Sat lunchtime & Sun.

Crawdaddy's Brooklyn Plaza, corner Middel and Dey sts, Brooklyn ☎012 460 0889. A popular and congenial Cajun-themed restaurant, serving tasty steaks and a range of decent seafood dishes.

Crazy Nut corner of Day and Bronkhorst sts, Brooklyn. A surprisingly large setup incorporating a vegetarian café-restaurant and well-stocked health-food store.

Die Werf Plot 66, Olympus Rd, Pretoria East ☎021 991 1809. Serves up a hearty and reasonably priced selection of home-cooked *boerekos* classics, including *kerrie skaapafval* (curried tripe and trotters) and *melktert* (milk tart). Closed Sun evening & Mon.

Gerard Moerdyk 752 Park St, Arcadia ☎012 344 4856. Beautifully prepared South African cuisine served at a price amid lavish surroundings; choose from ostrich, springbok pie and other intriguing dishes. Closed Sat lunchtime & Sun.

Mozzarella's Italian Kitchen Hatfield Square, Burnett St, Hatfield ☎012 362 6464. Set among a range of bars and restaurants in a lively location, this offers decent and reasonably priced Italian fare as well as good steaks and seafood.

O'Galito Shop 30, Woodlands Blvd, corner of De Villebois Mareuil and Garfontein rds, Pretoria East ☎012 997 4164. Excellent Mozambican-Portuguese food, with giant Maputo prawns, oysters and chicken *peri-peri* topping the bill. A snazzy venue, with a sushi bar attached.

Pride of India Groenkloof Plaza, George Storrar Drive, Groenkloof ☎012 346 3684. Filled with exquisite, imported Indian artefacts and oozing class and confidence, this is the place in town for beautifully prepared North Indian and Goan curries. Closed Sat lunch & Sun evening.

Safrika Kutlwanong Democracy Centre, 357 Visagie St. The best African restaurant in Pretoria, a small, friendly place frequented by high-powered NGO officials and civil servants. The decor is fairly plain, but the food is tasty, authentic and inexpensive. Closed Sun.

Wang Thai 281 Middel St, Brooklyn ☎012 346 6230. An elegant, authentic Thai restaurant in the heart of Brooklyn, complete with noble stone carvings and calm, friendly staff. A favourite among Pretoria's horde of fine-dining diplomats.

Bars and cafés

Café Bugatti Hatfield Galleries, Burnett St, Hatfield. A popular spot for breakfasts among the Hatfield smart set. Portions are generous.

Café Riche 2 Church Square West. It opened in 1905, and it remains one of the finest cafés in the country, boasting a Continental atmosphere and a quirky events programme, including late-night philosophical discussions. Thabo Mbeki has been a regular visitor. Great for Sunday brunch on Church Square. Daily 6am–midnight.

Cool Runnings 1071 Burnett St. A massively successful reggae bar where booze is cheap and there always seems to be a party going on; it also serves hearty food.

Eastwood Tavern 391 Eastwood Rd, Arcadia. A popular, often raucous pub near Loftus Versveld stadium, serving huge, inexpensive steak dishes. There's a DIY barbecue area, with raw meat provided, if you fancy.

The Grapevine 204 Sunnyside Galleries, Esselen St, Sunnyside. A long-established French-style café-patisserie, with generally mellow and cheerful regulars. It's also a great bakery if you want a quick takeout.

News Café Hatfield Square, Burnett St, Hatfield. Deservedly popular establishment serving breakfasts and brunches from 9.30am at weekends, and decent food well into the night all week. It mutates into a fully fledged nightclub after dark on weekends.

Tings and Times Hatfield Galleries, Burnett St, Hatfield ☎012 362 5537. One of Pretoria's funkiest bars; usually crawling with arty students, it also draws a wider clientele who come for the easy-going style and eclectic soundtrack.

Nightlife and entertainment

Pretoria lacks the dynamism and breadth of Johannesburg's **arts and music** scene, but there's still a fair amount going on. Sunnyside was once the city's most dynamic area for nightlife, but it's now a bit sleazy in places. Much of the scene is now in the Hatfield and Brooklyn areas, where stylish yuppies and richer students tend to hang out. Things are very different in the township areas of Mamelodi and Atteridgeville, where plenty of small clubs play South African and soul sounds.

The city's main venue for **theatre**, **opera** and **classical concerts** is the State Theatre, Church Street (☎012 392 4000, ⊛www.statetheatre.co.za). Under the leadership of Hugh Masekela and then Aubrey Sekhabi, it has put on an interesting programme of jazz and black theatre. For lively student theatre, head for the Breytenbach, 137 Gerard Moerdyk St (☎012 440 4834).

Pretoria's **cinemas** carry the typical selection of Hollywood fare, and the city is among the first to receive new releases. For big blockbusters, the Nu-Metro in Menlyn Park east of the centre (☎012 368 1301) is the biggest and best; there's also an IMAX screen here (☎012 368 1186). You'll find branches of the Ster-Kinekor chain at Beatrix Street in Arcadia (☎012 341 7568), and the New Brooklyn Mall in Brooklyn (☎012 346 7683). Back in the centre, on the corner of Schoeman and Van der Walt streets, the cinema in The Tramshed (☎012 320 4300) screens decent non-mainstream films. Also recommended for art-house films is the Cinema Nouveau in the New Brooklyn Mall (☎012 346 3435). The *Pretoria News* is good for theatre and cinema **listings**, while the national *Mail & Guardian* covers the visual arts, theatre and major musical events. Computicket (☎083 915 8000, ⓦ www.computicket.com) is the big central ticket outlet for most arts and sports events, with outlets in malls and department stores.

Live music and clubs

Boogie Nights 297 Lynnwood Rd, Lynnwood. A popular, busy club with student nights and various DJs through the week.

Drop Zone Hatfield Square, Hatfield. For rap and R&B sounds, and a mass of grooving students, this venue is the place. Wed, Thurs & Sat.

Upstairs at Morgan's Burnett St, Hatfield ☎012 362 6610. Live music Mon–Sat, though it's worth phoning to check what's on, as the acts range from South Africa's hottest bands to fairly run-of-the-mill fare. There are frequent party nights and promotions, and it's popular with students.

Listings

American Express 306 Brooklyn Mall, Bronkhorst St, Brooklyn (travel section: Mon–Fri 8.30am–5pm; foreign exchange: Mon–Fri 9am–4.30pm; ☎012 346 3580, after hours ☎082 901 5910).

Banks Most banks are around Church Square and along Church St.

Bookshops Exclusive Books at the Centurion Centre in Centurion (☎012 663 3204) is the best in the city. Protea Book House, 1067 Burnett St, Hatfield (☎012 362 5683), claims to be the largest bookshop in South Africa, with a huge range of new and secondhand books.

Camping/hiking Trappers Trading, Atterbury Value Mart, Atterbury Rd ☎012 991 5585; Cape Union Mart, Brooklyn Mall, Bronkhorst St, Brooklyn ☎012 460 5511.

Car rental Avis ☎012 301 0700; Budget ☎0465086 101 66 22 ; Imperial/Europcar ☎012 322 2538; Tempest, 1117 Church St ☎0861 836 7378.

Embassies and consulates Australia, 292 Orient St, Arcadia ☎012 342 3740; Canada, 1103 Arcadia St, Hatfield ☎012 422 3000; Germany, 180 Blackwood St, Arcadia ☎012 427 8900; Ireland, Southern Life Plaza, 1059 Schoemann St, Arcadia ☎012 342 5062; Lesotho, 391 Anderson St, Menlo Park ☎012 460 7648, ⓔ lesothoh@global.co.za; Malawi, 770 Government Ave, Arcadia ☎012 342 0146; Mozambique, 199 Beckett St, Arcadia ☎012 401 0300; Netherlands, 210 Queen Wilhelmina Ave (corner Muckleneuk St), New Muckleneuk ☎012 425 4500; Swaziland, 715 Government Ave,

Arcadia ☎012 344 1917; UK, 256 Glen St, Hatfield ☎012 421 7802; US, 1 River St, Killarney ☎011 644 8000; Zambia, 570 Ziervogel St, Arcadia ☎012 326 1854; Zimbabwe, 798 Merton St, Arcadia ☎012 342 5125.

Emergencies Private ambulance (Netcare 911) ☎082 911; ambulance ☎10177; fire ☎012 310 6300; police ☎10111.

Flea markets Hatfield Flea Market, Hatfield Plaza (every Sun), is Pretoria's best flea market, with crafts, bric-a-brac and lively banter.

Hospitals Those with 24hr casualty services include Pretoria Academic Hospital, Doctor Savage Rd ☎012 354 1000; and Pretoria West, Trans Oranje Rd ☎012 386 5111.

Intercity buses Intercape (☎0861 287 287), Greyhound (☎083 915 9000) and Translux (☎0861 589 282) have their terminal and office beside the train station.

Internet cafés It's easy to find places to get online in malls and elsewhere in the city. Places you could try include: Net Café, Hatfield Square, Burnett St, Hatfield (Mon–Sat 10am–3am; Sun 10am–2am); Odyssey, Hatfield Galleries, Burnett St, Hatfield (daily 9am–11.30pm); May Vision, Shop 11, Pavilion Center, 92 Jeppe St, Sunnyside (daily 8am–2am).

Pharmacies Crest, Duncan Walk, Hatfield ☎012 362 0304; Station, 509 Paul Kruger St ☎012 323 1239; and in every shopping mall.

Taxis The best local firm is Rixi Mini Cabs (☎012 325 8072). An alternative is Hatfield Shuttles (☎012 333 7973).

Tours Leopard Tours (☎ 012 998 0075, ⓦ www .leopardtourssa.co.za) organizes local and regional tours; for township tours, try Moshito wa Tshwane (☎ 012 358 1430).

Trains Besides the usual Spoornet trains, Pretoria is served by the luxury Blue Train and Rovos Rail services. For details of all three, see Basics, p.44.

Around Pretoria

The most absorbing sight in the immediate vicinity of Pretoria is **Doornkloof Farm**, the former home of Prime Minister Jan Smuts. Further out, to the east of Pretoria, the mining town of **Cullinan** harks back to the pioneering days of diamond prospecting a century ago, while north of the city the **Tswaing meteorite crater** and nearby **Mapoch Ndebele Village** are efforts by disadvantaged communities to create a worthwhile tourist attraction in their area. To the west, on the other hand, the **Hartbeespoort Dam** and nearby **Lesedi Cultural Village** have become victims of their own popularity, and most visitors happily bypass them on their way to less crowded and more genuine attractions in the provinces beyond.

Doornkloof Farm and Rietvlei Nature Reserve

Doornkloof Farm in **IRENE**, just south of Pretoria, was the home of **Jan Smuts** for much of his life, including his periods as prime minister of South Africa. His fairly simple wood-and-corrugated iron house is now a museum (Mon–Fri 9.30am–4.30pm, Sat & Sun 9.30am–5pm; R5), which does tend toward hagiography but still manages to shed light on one of South Africa's most enigmatic politicians (see box, p.293). To get to the museum, head south from Pretoria towards Irene on the M18 or R21 for about 20km, and follow the signs to Smuts House.

The massive library on the site reflects Smuts' intellectual range, while numerous mementos confirm his internationalism. Other displays focus on Smuts' role as one of the most successful commanders of Boer forces during the Anglo-Boer wars. The surrounding farm is part of the museum, and features the pleasant 2.5-kilometre **Oubaas Trail** leading from the house to the top of a nearby *koppie*, a walk the nature-loving Smuts took every day. Scattered near the house are various pieces of military hardware such as cannon and armoured vehicles – a little incongruously, given the declarations of peace and tranquillity posted along the trail and elsewhere. For refreshment, there's a **tea room** next to the house.

The **Rietvlei Nature Reserve** (Mon–Fri 7am–6pm, Sat & Sun 6am–6pm; R15), on the other side of the R21, is unspectacular but is home to Burchell's zebra, rhino and antelope, and plenty of birdlife.

Cullinan

Popular with tourist coaches, **Cullinan** lies 50km east of Pretoria. It was in the town's Premier Mine, still worked today, that the world's largest diamond, the 3106-carat Star of Africa, was discovered in 1905. The De Beers mine dominates the small town, but the oldest buildings, many from the turn of the last century, are being used to cater to the swarms of tourists. Unless you take a **surface tour** of the mine (Mon–Fri 10am & 2.30pm, Sat & Sun 10am; R30), there isn't much to do other than wander around, though there are a couple of pleasant places to **eat**, including the *Station Restaurant* in the old train station and the *Lemon Tree* tea garden on Oak Avenue. You can **stay** here at *The Oak House* (☎ 012 305 2364; ➍), Cullinan's second-oldest building, attractively set on Oak Avenue leading up to the mine.

⑦

GAUTENG | Around Pretoria

Tswaing Crater and Mapoch Ndebele Village

Some 40km north of Pretoria, off the M35, **Tswaing Crater** (daily 7.30am–4pm; R15 unguided, R80 for a guided group tour) is one of the youngest and best-preserved meteorite craters in the world, a 500-metre-wide depression created around 220,000 years ago. Tswaing means "place of salt" in Tswana, and the rich deposits of salt and soda around the edge of the shallow crater lake have attracted people since ancient times; artefacts up to 150,000 years old have been discovered here. A simple visitors' centre marks the start of a seven-kilometre trail to the crater and back, while a shorter walk, which you can do alone or in the company of a local guide, goes to a viewpoint on the crater rim.

Around 20km west of Tswaing is **Mapoch Ndebele Village** (daily 10am–4pm; R15), where the houses and enclosures are painted with the colourful geometric patterns for which the Ndebele are famous, often incorporating modern aspects such as telephones and the South African flag. These, and the equally colourful beadwork, both among South Africa's most distinctive art forms, are always done by women. Unlike other Ndebele villages, Mapoch is relatively uncommercialized, and little attempt is made to cover up the less traditional parts of the village. Visitors are expected to pay for a guide (R10–20) in addition to the admission charge.

Hartbeespoort Dam, Lesedi Cultural Village and the De Wildt Cheetah Centre

In the Magaliesberg Mountains west of Pretoria, the man-made **Hartbeespoort Dam** has the potential to be a pleasant escape from the urban sprawl of Gauteng. Unfortunately, large numbers of Gauteng's inhabitants have already had the idea, and the dam and its surrounds have been thoroughly mauled by camping and picnic sites, animal parks, cableways, mini-resorts and endless ranks of arts-and-craft emporiums. The midweek jams of Sandton and Randburg are simply transferred to the countryside at weekends, and petrol-heads scream up and down the dam on jet skis in much the same way as they do the M1 in urban 4WDs.

▲ Lesedi Cultural Village

Slightly more interesting, though hardly more inspiring, **Lesedi Cultural Village** (tours daily at 11.30am & 4.30pm; R260 for the tour plus a meal and dance performance, R170 tour only; Ⓦwww.lesedi.com), off the R512 south of Hartbeespoort, crams four cultural villages into one bewildering experience, with the Zulu, Pedi, Xhosa, Ndebele and Basotho all represented. Twice a day, tourists are escorted round the fairly authentic kraals, entertained by a lively display of colourful costumes, singing and dancing, then fed heartily with a **traditional African feast** in the vividly decorated restaurant. You can also **stay** the night in a grass hut with a Lesedi family (Ⓣ012 205 1394; half board ❼ including a full tour).

North of Hartbeespoort Dam, off the R513, is the **De Wildt Cheetah Centre**, a world-renowned conservation project (cheetah tours available Tues, Thurs, Sat & Sun at 8.30am & 1.30pm; R150; book in advance; Ⓣ012 504 1921, Ⓦwww.dewildt.org.za). The centre's mission is to protect the cheetah by developing predator management policies with farmers, breeding cubs in captivity (700 have been raised to date) and releasing them into the wild (150 adults have been released into reserves so far). Other endangered animals bred and/or cared for at the centre include African wild dogs, vultures and brown hyenas.

Visitors can get up close and personal with the centre's senior cheetahs, who are utterly relaxed in human company. The opportunity to photograph cheetahs on the run is a big drawcard, and there's also a cheetah adoption programme if you get passionate about the centre's cause.

Travel details

Trains

Johannesburg to: Bloemfontein (1 daily; 12hr); Cape Town (1 daily; 26hr 15min); Durban (1 daily; 11hr 40min); East London (1 daily; 20hr); Kimberley (1 daily; 8hr 15min); Musina (1 daily; 15hr); Nelspruit (1 daily; 9hr 45min); Port Elizabeth (1 daily; 18hr); Pretoria (32 daily; 1hr 30min).
Pretoria to: Bloemfontein (1 daily; 14hr 50min); Cape Town (1 daily; 29hr); Johannesburg (32 daily; 1hr 30min); Kimberley (1 daily; 10hr 35min); Musina (1 daily; 15hr); Nelspruit (1 daily; 8hr 20min).

Buses

Johannesburg to: Beitbridge (2 daily; 8–10hr); Bloemfontein (3 daily; 5–6hr); Cape Town (3–5 daily; 16–18hr); Durban (3 daily; 8–11hr); East London (1 daily; 11hr 30min); Kimberley (3–4 daily; 6–8hr); King William's Town (2 daily; 12hr 15min); Klerksdorp (3–5 daily; 2–4hr); Knysna (1 daily; 14–16hr); Kuruman (daily; 8hr 15min); Ladysmith (daily; 6hr 30min); Louis Trichardt (daily; 4hr 15min); Mossel Bay (2 daily; 14hr 30min); Nelspruit (2 daily; 5hr); Newcastle (1 daily; 4hr 45min); Oudtshoorn (1 daily; 13hr);

Pietermaritzburg (6–7 daily; 7hr); Pietersburg (3 daily; 3hr 45min); Plettenberg Bay (daily; 15hr 30min); Port Elizabeth (3–4 daily; 16hr); Potchefstroom (1–2 daily; 1hr 30min); Pretoria (over 70 daily; 1hr); Queenstown (2 daily; 10hr); Rustenburg (daily; 2hr); Umtata (4 weekly; 12hr 45min).
Pretoria to: Aliwal North (1 daily; 9hr); Beaufort West (3 daily; 12–13hr); Bloemfontein (6 daily; 6–7hr); Cape Town (3 daily; 17hr); Durban (6 daily; 9hr); East London (1 daily; 12hr 30min); Ermelo (1 daily; 4hr 20min); George (1–2 daily; 16hr); Graaff-Reinet (daily; 11hr 45min); Harrismith (daily; 4hr 45min); Johannesburg (over 70 daily; 1hr); Kimberley (3–4 daily; 7hr); King William's Town (2 daily; 13hr 25min); Klerksdorp (1–2 daily; 3hr–4hr 30min); Knysna (2–3 daily; 16hr); Kuruman (daily; 9hr 15min); Ladysmith (daily; 7hr 30min); Louis Trichardt (daily; 5hr 15min); Mossel Bay (1–2 daily; 15hr 35min); Nelspruit (2 daily; 4hr); Newcastle (1 daily; 4hr 45min); Oudtshoorn (daily; 14hr); Pietermaritzburg (7 daily; 7hr 15min); Pietersburg (3 daily; 3hr); Plettenberg Bay (daily; 16hr 30min); Port Elizabeth (2–4 daily; 16hr); Potchefstroom (1–2 daily; 2hr 30min); Queenstown (2 daily;

10–11hr); Umtata (1 Mon, Wed, Fri & Sun; 13hr 45min).

Baz Buses

From Jo'burg, Baz Bus operates services to Durban, either via the Drakensberg (3 weekly) or via Nelspruit and then Swaziland (3 weekly), where they overnight in Manzini. For details of services from Manzini on to Durban via the Elephant Coast, see Travel details for Chapter 12.

Johannesburg to: Durban (via the Drakensberg; 9hr); Manzini (Swaziland; 9hr); Malkerns Valley (Swaziland; 8hr 45min); Mbabane (Swaziland; 8hr); Mooi River (6hr); Nelspruit (5hr); Pietermaritzburg (8hr); Pretoria (separate shuttle; 30min–1hr); Winterton (4hr 30min).

Domestic flights

Johannesburg to: Bloemfontein (8 daily Mon–Fri, 3 daily Sat & Sun; 1hr 10min); Cape Town (more than 20 daily; 2hr); Durban (16 daily; 1hr); East London (7 daily; 1hr 25min); Hoedspruit (1 daily; 1hr); Kimberley (5 daily; 1hr 15min); Manzini (3–4 daily; 1hr); Nelspruit (7 daily; 1hr 50min); Polokwane (3 daily Mon–Fri, 1 daily Sat & Sun; 50min); Port Elizabeth (6 daily; 1hr 40min); Upington (1 daily; 1hr 50min).

North West Province

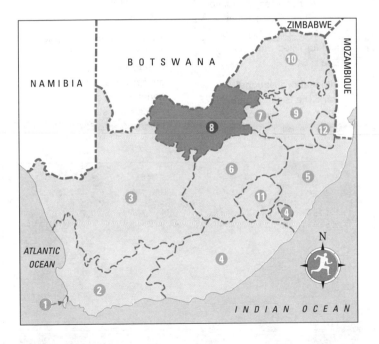

CHAPTER 8 # Highlights

✳ **Kgaswane Mountain Reserve** Rolling hills, rocky *kloofs* and sparkling streams in the Magaliesberg mountains – ideal hiking territory. See p.648

✳ **Sun City** A unique fantasyland of hotels, slot machines, stage shows and lush golf courses, complete with a Lost City, opulent palace, explorable jungle and fun-filled water park. See p.649

✳ **Pilanesberg National Park** The Big Five park most accessible from Johannesburg and Pretoria, with beautiful landscapes and terrific game viewing. See p.651

✳ **Groot Marico** One of the most characterful of South Africa's tiny *dorps*, or small farming towns, famed for its literary connections and the potency of the local fruit spirit, *mampoer*. See p.653

✳ **Madikwe Game Reserve** An often-overlooked Big Five reserve in the corner of the Province; prepare to be pampered in some of South Africa's classiest wildlife lodges. See p.654

▲ Herd of wildebeest, Pilanesberg National Park

8

North West Province

S outh Africa's **North West Province** is one of the country's least-understood regions – renowned, among tourists at least, for the stunning **Sun City** resort and Big Five **Pilanesberg National Park**, but not much else. Few people venture beyond these attractions to explore this area in greater depth; consequently, it can be curiously rewarding to do so. The old-fashioned hospitality of the myriad little *dorps* scattered throughout the region, and the tranquillity of the endless stretches of grassland and fields of *mielies* (sweetcorn) make a refreshing change after hectic Johannesburg and Pretoria.

North West Province extends west from Gauteng to the Botswana border and the Kalahari Desert. Along the Province's eastern flank, essentially separating it from Gauteng, loom the **Magaliesberg mountains**, one hundred times older than the Himalayas and these days dotted with holiday resorts for nature-starved Jo'burgers. The **N4** from Pretoria cuts through the mountains to the main town of the northeastern part of the Province, **Rustenburg**, gateway to the windswept **Kgaswane Mountain Reserve** where you can hike high enough to gaze down onto the shimmering plains beneath. **Groot Marico**, further west along the N4, is a friendly *dorp* with powerful home-brews and laid-back people to share them with. Further on lies the provincial capital of **Mafikeng** – famed for its siege during the second Anglo-Boer War – whilst towards the Botswanan capital, Gaborone, **Madikwe Game Reserve** is one of South Africa's undiscovered wildlife gems, a massive Big Five park which sees remarkably few visitors and boasts some superb game lodges.

Relentless sun alleviated only by torrential rain makes summer in North West Province something of an endurance test: aim to come here in spring or autumn. For the more adventurous, **camping** in the quiet and timeless veld is especially rewarding in this part of South Africa. **Tourist information** for the Province is provided by the **North West Parks & Tourism Board** (☎018 397 1500, call centre 082 232 7500, Ⓦ www.tourismnorthwest.co.za), which will mail brochures and other information on request. Its website has information or links to all of the region's parks. Malaria is absent throughout the Province.

Some history

San hunter-gatherers were the Province's first inhabitants: they were displaced 500–1000 years ago by cattle-herding Iron-Age peoples from the north, who pitched their first settlements on low ground near watercourses. By the sixteenth century, these settlements had developed into stone-walled towns on hilltops; the largest, Karechuenya (near Madikwe), was estimated by

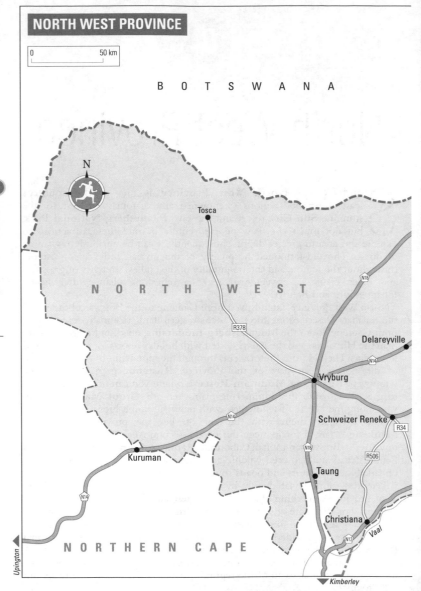

NORTH WEST PROVINCE

0   50 km

B O T S W A N A

N

Tosca

N O R T H   W E S T

N18

R378

Delareyville

N14

Vryburg

N14

Schweizer Reneke

R34

N18

R506

Kuruman

Taung

Christiana

Vaal

N12

N O R T H E R N   C A P E

Upington

Kimberley

a Scottish observer in 1820 to have at least 20,000 inhabitants – more than Cape Town had at that time. By the nineteenth century, the dominance of the Rolong, Taung, Tlhaping and Tlokwa clans was established. European observers classified them all as **Tswana**, but it's unclear whether these people regarded themselves as very different from people further east classified as "Sotho".

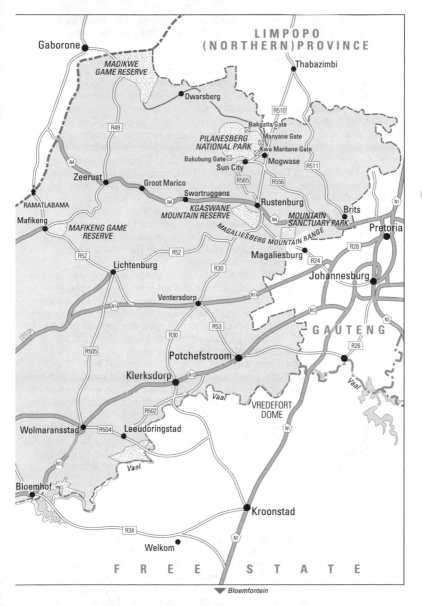

▼ *Bloemfontein*

The outbreak of intense **inter-clan violence** in the early 1800s was due to displacements caused by the expansion of white *trekboers*, and the growing availability of firearms. Victory went to those who made alliances with the new arrivals, whether **Griqua** from the Northern Cape or **Afrikaners** from further south. The Tlhaping were soon driven out, eventually finding their way to Zambia. Mzilikazi's Ndebele ruled the region in the 1820s and 1830s, but they too were forced out, this time to modern Zimbabwe. The victories of the remaining clans were short-lived: their Griqua and Afrikaner allies soon evicted them from their land and forced them into service.

Potchefstroom and Klerksdorp were the first towns established here by the Afrikaners, and more followed, each forming the nucleus for a quarrelsome mini-state. In 1860 these mini-states amalgamated to form the **South African Republic** (ZAR), with Pretoria as its capital. The first Anglo-Boer War lasted from 1877 until British defeat in 1881, with most of the Province unaffected. In 1885, the British successfully fought the Afrikaners of the Goshen Republic near Mmabatho (Mafikeng) and established the protectorate of north and south Bechuanaland – the north later became Botswana, while the south was annexed to the Cape Colony by Cecil Rhodes in 1895. British intervention meant that some land remaining in Tswana hands stayed that way, but by then the clans had lost almost everything. When **gold** was discovered on the Witwatersrand and around Klerksdorp, Tswana men left in droves to work in the mines.

Of far greater impact was the **second Anglo–Boer War** (1899–1902). As well as the celebrated **siege of Mafikeng**, where British and Tswana forces held out for 217 days against Afrikaner troops, there were protracted skirmishes up and down the Vaal River. Both Afrikaner and Tswana had their lands torched, and many were thrown into concentration camps.

The Union Treaty of 1910 left the Province, as the western part of the Transvaal, firmly in Afrikaner hands. Its smaller *dorps* soon became synonymous with rural racism, epitomized in the 1980s by the fascistic AWB led by **Eugene Terreblanche**, whose power base was here. The migration of so many Tswana men and the lack of industrial development impeded the growth of a black working class in the Province, which is why North West Province played a relatively minor role in the national struggle against apartheid.

The **Bophuthatswana** Bantustan – or "Bop" – was created in 1977 out of the old "native reserves", the poor-quality land into which Tswana had been forced. Far from being a long-awaited "homeland" for blacks, Bop proved to be a confusing amalgamation of enclaves, ruled by the corrupt **Lucas Mangope**, who grew rich on the revenues from **Sol Kerzner**'s casinos in Sun City and Mmabatho and the discovery of platinum. Bophuthatswana's short life came to an end in March 1994, a month before South Africa's elections, when its army mutinied. Mangope called in hundreds of armed AWB neo-fascists to help quell the uprising, but the AWB – and Mangope – were ingloriously defeated.

Bojanala Region

Bordering Gauteng, **Bojanala Region** lies in North West Province's northeastern bushveld, and is a popular weekend destination for Jo'burgers. Given that large parts of the province are empty and flat, one of the region's more distinctive assets is the **Magaliesberg mountain range**, which gets its name from the Tswana chief **Mogale** of the Kwena clan. Kwena people lived here from the seventeenth century until 1825, when most of them were forced out by the Ndebele chief **Mzilikazi**. Afrikaner farmers continued the process of eviction, and today the dispossession of the Kwena in the Magaliesberg is complete. The Magaliesberg's great asset is that it's easily reached from Johannesburg and Pretoria, with the result that great chunks have been fenced off and turned into time-shares or resorts. Nevertheless, there are oases of unspoilt nature, notably **Kgaswane Mountain Reserve** – accessed from the region's main town, **Rustenburg** – and the **Mountain Sanctuary Park**, both preserved in something like their previous natural state and well stocked with wildlife. The southeastern Magaliesberg mountains, which are even easier to get to from Gauteng, are covered in Chapter 7.

Further north, occupying an ancient volcanic crater, is the outstanding **Pilanesberg National Park** – the "Big Five" mainstay of Gauteng-based safari operators. If you're in the mood for a fun-in-the-sun waterpark and some surreal tourist opulence, **Sun City** is worth checking out, if only as a stopover on your way in to Pilanesberg.

Rustenburg and around

Some 120km northwest of Johannesburg lies the platinum-mining town of **RUSTENBURG**, the oldest town in the former Western Transvaal. With its grid of prefabricated chain stores and shopping malls, the place is a pretty dreary hymn to misguided town planning. Still, you'll probably end up staying if you're visiting the glorious **Kgaswane Mountain Reserve**, 7km south of town. The town is currently experiencing a boom with the recent development of new platinum reserves, and the new wealth has brought with it an increase in **crime** – be mindful of this when walking around town, especially at night.

Arrival, information and accommodation

Intercape's daily **bus** from Pretoria and Johannesburg drops you at the Engen garage 3km east of the centre on the road to the Waterfall Mall. Long-distance **minibus taxis** arrive in the town centre at the terminal at the western end of Nelson Mandela Drive by Bethlehem Drive. When leaving the terminal, avoid its northern section around the KFC and the raucous *Castle Tavern*: muggings are common in this area.

Rustenburg's **tourist office** (Mon–Fri 8am–4.30pm; ☎014 597 0904–6, ✉tidcrust@mweb.co.za) is unhelpfully located 2km east of the bus terminal along the N4; head out of town along Nelson Mandela Drive or Fatima Bhayat Street, and ignore signposts to the contrary, which are out of date.

You'll get the most out of the area by **staying** out of town. You can **camp** at Kgaswane Mountain Reserve (see p.648) and Mountain Sanctuary Park (see p.649), while for drivers there are dozens of rural (and sometimes quite flashy) B&Bs and resorts in the surrounding countryside – you'll find a selection online at ⓦ www.rustenburgaccommodation.co.za. There's safe parking at all the following town-centre recommendations.

Town centre
Cashane Hotel 66 Steen St ☎014 592 8541–3, ⒻF 014 592 3016. An ageing but well-kept business-class hotel on six floors (lift access), with comfortable, well-equipped rooms and views over town. There's also a good bar and dull restaurant. ❸
Palm Lodge 99 Beyers Naude Drive ☎ & Ⓕ014 597 2520. A large thatch-roofed complex appearing swankier than it is, with dozens of small, dark rooms with TVs and phones, a swimming pool, two bars and a restaurant. ❷
Travellers Inn 99 Leyds St ☎014 592 7658, ✉travinn@mweb.co.za. The friendliest in town, with good modern rooms and adjacent parking bays. There's a swimming pool, a

lovely rustic bar and superb food. Gay and lesbian couples welcome. Camping possible. ❷

Out of town
Kedar Country Hotel (Kruger Country House) 20km northwest of town in Boshoek, 500m off the R565 to Sun City ☎014 573 3218, ⓦwww.rali.co.za. Set amidst plentiful game and birdlife, this lovingly restored farmhouse once belonged to President Kruger, who's honoured by a small museum. The simple if luxurious Afrikaner-style decor makes for a refreshingly tranquil rural getaway, and there's also a swimming pool (and two suites with private plunge pools). Half board ❺

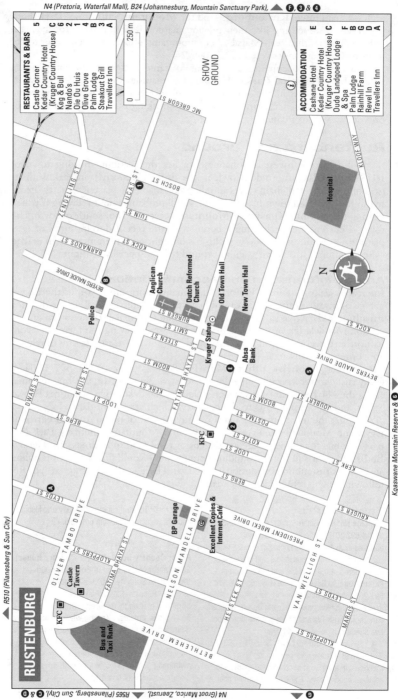

RUSTENBURG

8 NORTH WEST PROVINCE

RESTAURANTS & BARS

Castle Corner	5
Kedar Country Hotel (Kruger Country House)	C
Keg & Bull	6
Nando's	2
Ole Ou Huis	1
Olive Grove	4
Palm Lodge	B
Steakout Grill	3
Travellers Inn	A

ACCOMMODATION

Cashane Hotel	E
Kedar Country Hotel (Kruger Country House)	C
Oude Landgoed Lodge & Spa	F
Palm Lodge	B
Rainhill Farm	G
Revel In	D
Travellers Inn	A

N4 (Pretoria, Waterfall Mall), B24 (Johannesburg, Mountain Sanctuary Park), ▲ **F**, **3** & **4**

0 _____ 250 m

SHOW GROUND

R510 (Pilanesberg & Sun City)

Kgaswane Mountain Reserve & **6**

N4 (Groot Marico, Zeerust), ▲ R565 (Pilanesberg, Sun City), **C** & **D**

MC GREGOR ST
ZENDELING ST
LUCAS ST
BOSCH ST
TUIN ST
BARNADOS ST
KOCK ST
BEYERS NAUDE DRIVE
Police
B
Anglican Church
Dutch Reformed Church
Old Town Hall
New Town Hall
BURGER ST
SMIT ST
STEEN ST
Kruger Statue
BOOM ST
FATIMA BHAYAT ST
Absa Bank
E
KERK ST
KOCK ST
BEYERS NAUDE DRIVE
JOUBERT ST
DWARS ST
KRUIS ST
LOOP ST
BERG ST
BOOM ST
POSMA ST
KOTZE ST
KFC
2
LOOP ST
BERG ST
KERK ST
KRUGER ST
LEVDS ST
OLIVER TAMBO DRIVE
KLOPPERS ST
FATIMA BHAYAT ST
NELSON MANDELA DRIVE
BP Garage
Excellent Copies & Internet Café
G
PRESIDENT MBEKI DRIVE
HEYSTEK ST
VAN WIELLIGH ST
LEYDS ST
MARAIS ST
KLOPPERS ST
A
Castle Tavern
KFC
Bus and Taxi Rank
BETHLEHEM DRIVE

Hospital
KLOOF WAY

N

i

Kedar Country Hotel
(Kruger Country House)

5

Oude Landgoed Lodge & Spa 8km along the R24 towards Johannesburg ☎014 537 2369, ⓦwww .oudelandgoed.co.za. It's not the rooms but the health spa (☎083 365 2519; Mon–Fri 8am–5pm; R90 membership includes sauna, steam room, swimming pool and Jacuzzi) that makes this place special, with a welter of treatments on the menu, including aromatherapy, massage and hot stones. ❸

Rainhill Farm 4km southwest of town; follow Bethlehem Drive south from the bus terminal to its end, right along Brink St, left along Watsonia Rd, right at the end ☎014 592 8911, ⓦwww.rainhill .co.za. Four charming rooms in 1940s chalets decked out with antiques, perfect for families or honeymooners. Catch a minibus taxi to Rustenburg Kloof. ❸

Revel In 40km west along the Swartruggens road, then right at Bokfontein for 6.5km ☎072 225 7182, ⓦwww.revelin.co.za. A recommended backpackers on a farm, with dorms, bungalows and tree cabins, plus meals, a good bar, hiking trails and pool. ❶

The Town

Rustenburg's historic centre is limited to two blocks of Burger Street, from Nelson Mandela Drive to Oliver Tambo Drive. Here you'll find two churches: the old **Anglican church**, dating from 1871, and the 1850 **Dutch Reformed Church**. Facing the latter is the graceful 1935 town hall and a **statue of Paul Kruger** by French sculptor Jean Georges Achard, showing the president in his last days in exile in France sitting grumpily in an armchair.

There's not much else to do in Rustenburg itself. The gleaming **Waterfall Mall**, 5km east of town (follow Nelson Mandela Drive) offers the province's best shopping, while **stock-car races** take place once a month (usually on Saturdays) at the Show Ground, on the north side of Fatima Bhayat Street opposite the tourist office.

Eating, drinking and nightlife

Rustenburg is dominated by **fast-food** joints: Nelson Mandela Drive and Fatima Bhayat Street have plenty, including a Nando's, while the more appealing places, such as *Steakout Grill* and *Olive Grove*, are located at Waterfall Mall. Infinitely more interesting for a daytime snack though are the **street food** stands in and around the bus terminal (for maize, grilled chicken legs, and *pap* with stew) – although exercise caution in this area where thefts are common. For fresh dairy produce, go to Smith's Dairy at 15 Heystek St; fresh juices are sold at the Cottage Bakery supermarket at the west end of Oliver Tambo Drive. Rustenburg's several **pubs** also serve food; and some have live music.

Town centre

Castle Corner Heystek St. Posh English-style pub with lots of beer on tap, reasonable grub and satellite sports, that gets busy whenever there's rugby on the TV.

Oie Ou Huis Corner of Bosch and Luxcas sts. Notable for its pleasant beer garden and live music (Fri–Sun). One of Rustenburg's more gay-friendly watering holes.

Travellers Inn 99 Leyds St. Offering well-balanced and excellently prepared food (R80 for a buffet dinner), this small and cosy nook is the closest Rustenburg gets to a backpackers' bar. Mon–Sat till at least 11pm.

Out of town

Hartley's *Rainhill Farm*, see "Accommodation", above ☎014 594 1992. Tranquil country-style pub and family restaurant. The pub area is called *The Milk Shed*, while *The Pack House* is the more formal, non-smoking restaurant. The food at both ranges from ribs and steaks to prawns and seafood platters – don't miss trying the farm's famous orange marmalade. Most mains R50–75.

Kedar Country Hotel See "Accommodation", p.645 ☎014 573 3218. Enjoy some seriously good Afrikaner and Cape Malay cuisine at this restaurant housed in a Victorian-style house.

Keg & Bull Safari Gardens shopping centre, 3km south of the centre. A popular pub catering to residents of the town's expanding southern and eastern suburbs. There's karaoke on Tues nights and a live band on Thurs.

Listings

Banks Absa at Waterfall Mall has a bureau de change.
Car rental Avis, 45 Nelson Mandela Drive ☎014 592 1328.
Health Doctors and dentists are available at the Medicross Medical Centre on the corner of

President Mbeki Drive and Van Wielligh St ☎014 592 8562.
Internet Excellent Copies & Internet Café, Nelson Mandela Drive, opposite the BP garage.
Police Corner of Beyers Naude Drive and Kruis Street ☎014 590 3232.

Kgaswane Mountain Reserve

Soaring up behind Rustenburg's southern suburbs, the **KGASWANE MOUNTAIN RESERVE** (daily April–Aug 6am–6pm; Sept–March 5.30am–7pm; ☎014 533 2050, Ⓦwww.tourismnorthwest.co.za/parks/kgaswane.html; R10, plus R10 per vehicle or R5 per bicycle) spans a spectacular forty-square-kilometre portion of the Magaliesberg, and offers sweeping views and great hikes. The terrain is dotted with rock formations created by millennia of erosion. You'll find dry veld too, and streams coursing through the valleys that have generated a lush flora all of their own. Scattered around the reserve are aloes indigenous to the Magaliesberg, and the discreet *frithiapulchra*, a succulent with only its leaf tips exposed, flowering between November and March. The many crags are perfect for **predatory birds**; keep a lookout for the rare black eagle, Martial eagle and Cape vulture, as well as parrots and paradise flycatchers. Kgaswane is also home to eight hundred **antelopes**, representing most of South Africa's species, and also zebras. **Predators** are few in number and limited to caracal, aardwolf, black-backed jackals and elusive leopard.

The reserve can be explored on a day or two-night hike, or by bicycle (bring your own). There are two short trails for **day hikes**. The three-hour, five-kilometre Peglarae Trail goes over fairly steep and rocky terrain but takes in most of the reserve's best features, and the visitors' centre provides a good booklet to go with it. Shorter and easier is the two-kilometre Vleiramble to a viewing hut on the *vlei*, popular with birders. **Overnight hikes** follow the Rustenburg Hiking Trail (19.5km or 23.5km) and last two days and two nights. Accommodation is in huts which provide firewood and cooking utensils, but you must bring food, and enough clothing in winter – nights get bitterly cold. It's best to book ahead for the overnight trails, though you may strike lucky midweek.

The reserve entrance is 7km from Rustenburg and there's no public transport: head south along Beyers Naudè Drive for 2km until it becomes Helen Joseph Street, then continue for another 5km until you reach the gate. From here, the road winds dramatically up to the mountaintop, where you'll find the **visitors' centre**, with useful maps and information on hikes and trails, as well as camping (R20) and braai facilities.

Moving on from Rustenburg

The daily **Intercape bus** between Pretoria/Johannesburg and Gaborone stops in Rustenburg. In addition, an ageing fleet of rickety buses is operated by **Bojanala Bus** (☎014 565 6550) – its most useful service is a daily run to Mafikeng (although note that this takes a circuitous route that bypasses Groot Marico). Bojanala Bus and long-distance **minibus taxis** (which cover most of the Province – including Groot Marico and Mafikeng – and also go to Lesotho) leave run from the chaotic terminal at the western end of Nelson Mandela Drive by Bethlehem Drive. Bays are clearly marked with destinations but there are no ticket offices; it's best to check your options the day before you travel.

Mountain Sanctuary Park

Smaller than Kgaswane but a gem nonetheless, the privately owned **Mountain Sanctuary Park** (daily: March–April & Sept–Feb 8am–6.30pm; May–Aug 8am–5pm; ☎014 534 0114, ⓦwww.mountain-sanctuary.co.za; R25, plus R10 per vehicle) lies about 15km east of Rustenburg and is only accessible by private vehicle. The park is dotted with bilharzia-free streams safe for swimming, and spectacular *kloofs* and gullies. Klipspringer, rhebok and duiker wander freely, and the area supports abundant birdlife.

Chalets, log cabins with fireplaces and campsites are available for **overnight stays** (minimum charge two nights and two people at weekends; R95–225), but you'll need to bring your own bedding or rent it on site. There's an extraordinary **swimming pool** by the campsite, which gives the impression that you're on the edge of a precipice as you look out into the valley below. The simplest way to **get to the park** is to take the N4 as far as the Marikana turn-off, turn right, then take the second dirt track on your left and continue for about 3km. Phone ahead before you go, as visitor numbers are limited.

Sun City

A surreal pocket of high-rise hotels and tinkling gaming machines in the endless bushveld, **SUN CITY** consists of four hotel/resorts tightly packed together with golf courses, a water park and various other attractions. When entrepreneur Sol Kerzner began building the vast complex in the 1970s, the area was part of the Bophuthatswana Bantustan and therefore one of the few places in the country where you could **gamble** legally. Thousands visited from "across the border" to sample Kerzner's blend of gaming, topless shows and over-the-top hotels. However, now that gambling is legal in South Africa, Sun City has altered its focus, promoting itself these days as a family destination – indeed, if you have kids to entertain, this is an excellent place to bring them. The resort also makes a good base for exploring Pilanesberg National Park.

Arrival and information

Minibus taxis from Rustenburg to Mogwase pass by the Sun City entrance, and daily **shuttle buses** operated by Ingelosi Tours (☎014 557 4488) drive from Johannesburg and Pretoria. If you're **driving** from Pretoria or Johannesburg, follow the N4 past the Brits turn-off, and turn right onto the R556, from where it's roughly 70km. A popular option is to join a **day tour** from Pretoria or Johannesburg; a large number of operators based in those cities offer trips, with prices depending on the target market; expect to pay at least R350–500, plus R200–300 if combined with a short safari at Pilanesberg.

Entrance costs R70, R30 of which you get back in Sunbucks, the Sun City currency, used to pay for most things inside, including restaurant meals; rand is also accepted everywhere. From the vast car park by the main gate, hop on one of the free **shuttle buses** that go to all of the hotels as well as the **Welcome Centre** (information: Mon–Thurs & Sun 8am–7pm, Fri & Sat 8am–10pm; ☎014 557 1544). This is a good starting point for an exploration of Sun City (which, though it looks huge, is easily explored on foot), and provides plenty of maps, leaflets and details of special offers. You can also book **game drives** into Pilanesberg from here; and there's an information centre for the North West Parks & Tourism Board (Mon–Fri 8am–4.30pm, Sat & Sun 9am–2pm; ☎014 557 1907).

Accommodation

Rooms can be booked through Sun City Reservations (☎014 557 1000, ⓦwww.suninternational.co.za), but will be considerably cheaper if arranged through a tour company as part of a package, or over the Internet. All hotels are enormous – *Cascades*, the smallest, has a mere 243 rooms.

Cabanas The cheapest accommodation in Sun City, and close to most of the kids' activities. A relaxed atmosphere, moderately priced restaurants and good indoor pool complete the picture. ❽

Cascades After the *Palace*, this is the resort's most comfortable place to stay. Next door to the Entertainment Centre, it's a stylish high-rise, with "designer-tropical" decor, a mini rainforest and aviary, and outside lifts offering splendid views of Sun City and the surrounding hills. The inviting pool and bar are for residents only. ❾

Palace of the Lost City Like something out of an Indiana Jones movie, the enormous *Palace* is a fantastically opulent and imaginative hotel, designed as a soaring African jungle palace with towers, domes, extravagant carvings and sculptures. A stay here is bank-breakingly expensive, but unforgettable. ❾

Sun City Hotel The resort's original hotel houses the main casino, so is a good choice if gambling is your main reason for visiting Sun City. The refurbished rooms are well furnished, and there are four decent restaurants. ❾

The Resort

The resort is divided into three distinct areas: Cabanas (which includes Waterworld), the Entertainment Centre, and the showpiece **Lost City**, separated from the rest of the complex by a R70 entrance fee (free if you're staying at one of the hotels) and the vibrating Bridge of Time. On entering it, you'll encounter the **Valley of the Waves**, a gigantic pool area designed to look like a beach, complete with sand, palm trees, four waterslides and a machine producing two-metre-high breakers suitable for surfing. Deeper into the acres of specially planted rainforest above the valley, you'll find waterfalls, trickling streams and a network of explorable paths, all interspersed with "remains" of the lost city. Overlooking the whole scene is the staggering *Palace of the Lost City* hotel; you can pop in for a drink if you're not staying, or join a **Palace tour** (8 daily: 11.30am–4pm from the Welcome Centre; R60) for a more thorough look.

The **Entertainment Centre** next to the towering triangle of *Cascades* hotel is the focal point of the rest of Sun City, with rows of bleeping slot machines

▲ Palace of the Lost City, Sun City

and arcade games, a **cinema**, upmarket shops, and the Superbowl **concert hall**, which hosts various musical acts and other events. Next to the Entertainment Centre you'll find an aviary, tennis courts, health spa and the renowned **Gary Player Golf Course** (book well in advance – a waiting list of several months is not uncommon).

Cabanas, close to the entrance, is the area that young kids will enjoy most: it has a small zoo, horse-riding, a crèche, another aviary with summer flying displays by hawks, falcons and owls, and a crocodile sanctuary, where you can feed the hungry denizens at 4.30pm. Behind it is **Waterworld**, a large artificial lake used for watersports from parasailing to water-skiing.

Eating, drinking and nightlife

The Entertainment Centre has lots of moderately priced **restaurants**, snack bars and cafés. Of the more upscale places, the one that stands out is *Santorini*, serving good Mediterranean food beside the lovely pool at *Cascades* hotel. The sumptuous breakfast buffet at the *Palace* is another recommended dining experience. For drinking and dancing, the main **bar** and **nightclub** is on the upper level of the Entertainment Centre, which is where you'll also find an alcohol-free nightclub for teenagers only.

Pilanesberg National Park

Adjacent to Sun City and home to a huge variety of animals, the **PILANESBERG NATIONAL PARK** is North West Province's biggest tourist draw. The artificially created reserve was, until 1979, occupied by farmers and the **Tswana** people, who were unceremoniously evicted when **Operation Genesis** saw over six thousand animals shipped in from all over the country to fill the park. Just two hours' drive from Pretoria and Jo'burg, Pilanesberg is definitely the place to come to see some game if you're based in Gauteng and have only limited time in South Africa. Don't let the crowds or the managed nature of the place put you off: the park offers game-viewing thrills aplenty, with a good chance of seeing all of the **Big Five**, along with hippo, brown hyena, giraffe and zebra. The majority of antelope species are here, too, and there's a vast array of **birdlife** – over 365 species recorded so far. At night, some fantastic creatures emerge, including civet, porcupine and caracal, though you'll be lucky to spot them.

Covering some 650 square kilometres, and with 200km of good-quality tar and gravel roads, you'll need at least a day to do Pilanesberg justice. The reserve is easily explored by sedan car, especially with the official map. The park's many beautiful hills – the result of an unusual volcanic eruption that occurred 1200–1300 years ago – are in some ways Pilanesberg's finest feature, though they are often ignored by visitors more interested in scouring their slopes for wildlife. Pilanesberg's natural focus, for visitors and wildlife alike, is the alkaline **Lake Mankwe** ("place of the leopard"), whose goings-on are best observed from several walk-in hides. The various picnic spots and hides dotted around are ideal for breaking the drive – the hides in particular aren't used by many visitors and as a result can be cool, peaceful places to appreciate the natural surroundings.

Practicalities

There are four **entrance gates** (daily: March, April, Sept & Oct 6am–6.30pm; May–Aug 6.30am–6pm; Nov–Feb 5.30am–7pm; R15 per person, R20 per car) to the reserve; the most commonly used are Manyane (or Mogwase), on the eastern side of the reserve, and Bakubung to the south, just to the west of Sun

City off the R565. The **park headquarters** are at Mogwase (℡014 555 1600, Ⓦwww.pilanesberg-game-reserve.co.za). An excellent **map** and **guidebook** explaining the various habitats are available at the gates, enabling you to plan your journey around what you most want to see. Bear in mind that other drivers have this map too, so the areas recommended for popular animals can become congested during daytime; the traffic disappears after dark, when only tour buses on **night-game drives** are allowed in, making this one of the optimum times to visit the park (although be sure to bring some warm clothes on winter nights). At the time of writing, the **Pilanesberg Centre**, an old Cape Dutch building located in the centre of the park, was closed for repairs after a fire, but should again be functioning as a café, gift shop and open-air restaurant when this edition is published. It also has a notice board for wildlife sightings, useful for tracking down any outstanding quarries on your checklist.

If you don't have a vehicle, you can rent one from Avis in Sun City (℡014 557 1584), or arrange things through a tour operator as the park itself does not provide any services. Apart from **organized safaris** (mostly from Sun City, Pretoria and Johannesburg), the park's *concessionaires* offer a range of **alternative activities** (see box below). Whilst all these activities can be booked on arrival, it's best to reserve them in advance either directly or through your lodge to avoid missing out. There are frequent **minibus taxis** running the 54km from Rustenburg to Manyane Gate (ask for Mogwase).

Accommodation

Pilanesberg has large numbers of day visitors – many from Sun City – but like any other decent game park you'll get most from it if you're able to stay a little bit longer and put yourself in pole position for the best game-viewing time, at dawn, before the day visitors arrive. Pilanesberg's **accommodation** ranges from upmarket lodges where game drives are included in the prices, to large, resort-style complexes on the fringes of the park, and cheaper and more basic camps outside the boundaries. **Bookings** for *Bakgatla*, *Bosele* and *Manyane* must be made through Golden Leopard Resorts (℡014 555 1000, Ⓦwww.goldenleopard.co.za),

Pilanesberg tour operators

Rates for normal safaris depend on group size (larger groups are cheaper), and whether the tour is scheduled or private. On a scheduled tour, you may be sharing a minibus with up to fifteen other visitors; check also whether lunch and entry fees are included. The special activities organized by Gametrackers and Mankwe (see below) can usually be incorporated into trips run by other operators, particularly if you have the flexibility of a private tour. Prices for day trips from Gauteng average R500–800 per person on a scheduled tour; private tours start at around R1000 for the day. Rates for overnight trips vary according to where you stay; budget on upwards of R3000.

Gametrackers Outdoor Adventures Sun City ℡014 552 5020, Ⓦwww.gametrac .co.za. Two big crowd-pullers here: balloon flights (R2700) and elephant-back safaris (R1090). The five trusty mounts were orphaned in 1980s Zimbabwe and subsequently domesticated; rides take place early in the morning and late afternoon. Day and night game drives (from R295) are also available.

Mankwe Safaris Manyane Gate ℡014 555 7056, Ⓦwww.mankwesafaris.co.za. A *concessionaire* offering day and night game drives (from R230) plus "Heritage Tours", blending nearby cultural attractions with the Big Five.

Ulysses Tours & Safaris *Protea Waterfront Hotel*, Centurion, Pretoria ℡012 663 4941, Ⓦwww.ulysses.co.za. A well-regarded and professionally run upmarket outfit with day-trips to Pilanesberg from R800.

and those for *Bakubung*, *Kwa Maritane* and *Tshukudu* through Legacy Hotels (℡011 806 6888, Ⓦ www.legacyhotels.co.za). For *Ivory Tree*, book direct with the lodge. **Camping** (R100) is possible at Golden Leopard's places. *Bakubung* and *Kwa Maritane* have shuttle buses every other hour to and from Sun City, while all lodges can arrange game drives and guided walks if not included in the rates. Some may insist on two-night stays at weekends.

Bakgatla Resort Near Bakgatla Gate at the foot of Garamoga Hills. Large collection of reasonable self-catering chalets and safari tents with attached bathrooms and shady verandas, a caravan park and several campsites. Rates are cheaper per person if you share between four or five. Meals available. ❺–❻

Bakubung Bush Lodge On the southern edge of the park, just west of Sun City. The highlight at this large, modern lodge is the hippo pool, a stone's throw from the restaurant. The hotel rooms and chalets are pleasant if bland. ❽

Bosele Bush Camp By Manyane Gate. Intended primarily for large groups, though you may be able to get an inexpensive dorm bed here if it's not full. Kitchen facilities are shared, and you can use the pool, shop and restaurant at neighbouring *Manyane Resort*. ❷

Ivory Tree Lodge Near Bakgatla Gate ℡014 556 8100 or 011 781 1661, Ⓦ www.ivorytreegamelodge .com. Luxurious lodge with stylish rooms, a health spa, conference centre and a rather hotel-like feel. Full board ❽

Kwa Maritane Bush Lodge In the park's southeast corner near Pilanesberg airport. This vast, upmarket lodge feels detached from its fabulous surroundings – no surprise really, with 90 rooms, 28 cabanas and 25 chalets. There's a game hide at the end of a 130-metre tunnel. ❼

Manyane Resort Just outside Manyane Gate. Low cost and convenience compensate for the distinctly un-bushlike atmosphere of the park's main camp. Stay in thatched chalets with TVs and kitchen, or bring a tent or caravan; there's also a bar and restaurant, pool, mini-golf and walking trails. ❺

Tshukudu Bush Lodge 8km from Bakubung Gate. Gaze out at big game at the waterhole from your veranda at Pilanesberg's most upmarket and exclusive lodge, attractively located on a hilltop with sweeping views in the southwest. Six picturesque thatched cottages offer luxury accommodation with sunken baths and roaring log fires; there's also a swimming pool. No children under 12. Full board ❾

The Central Region

Thanks to its scrawny and desolate dryness, North West Province's **Central Region** feels especially remote, and there are not all that many towns worth visiting. **Mmabatho**, once the capital of Bophuthatswana and now incorporated into neighbouring **Mafikeng**, the provincial capital, forces reluctant bureaucratic pilgrimages on people from all over. The region's appeal lies elsewhere, in the brooding plains and lush river valleys of Marico and the rarely visited game reserves, including **Madikwe** on the Botswana border. Then there are the remains of the rich but depressing history of the region, centring on the relentless dispossession of the Tswana, but also including the famed **siege of Mafikeng** during the second Anglo Boer War and the incredible **Lichtenburg diamond rush** of 1926. Lastly, there are the people themselves: local Tswana and Afrikaners are both short on English but long on hospitality, at least to visitors, a trait best experienced at the village of **Groot Marico**, famed nationwide for its *mampoer* peach brandy and quintessentially laid-back spirit.

Groot Marico

GROOT MARICO, a tiny and dusty but characterful *dorp* resting contentedly by the banks of the Marico River, just south of the N4 and 90km west of Rustenburg, gained fame through **Herman Charles Bosman**'s short stories based on his time as a teacher here (see box opposite). In mid-October, Groot Marico hosts the literary Bosman Weekend, drawing fans of one of South Africa's best-loved authors from far and wide. The town's handful of attractions include the **Art Factory** on Paul Kruger Street (daily 9am–5pm), where you can pick up news about what's going on, as well as Tswana cultural artefacts and locally made Afrikaner crafts such as wooden pipes, whips and clocks.

Although prone to stultifying heat, particularly in summer, the hills of the Marico district are good for hiking, and when it all gets too much you can make for the river for cool relief. The water of the **Marico Oog** ("Marico Eye"), a spring 20km south of town, is particularly clear and refreshing: festooned with water lilies and surrounded by beautiful dolomitic rocks, it makes a tranquil place for a picnic, and can be paradise for bird-watchers, with over four hundred species recorded here. It's also a favoured spot for **scuba divers**; contact the town's information centre for more information.

Practicalities

Minibus taxis travelling along the N4 from Pretoria or Rustenburg to Mafikeng or Botswana will stop at the Groot Marico turn-off, a twenty-minute walk north of the village. The first place to head for is the town's friendly **tourist office** (daily 8am–6pm; ☎014 503 0085 or 083 272 2958, ⓦwww .marico.co.za), marked by a small signpost along Paul Kruger Street next to First National Bank, in an enclosure built by Italian POWs in World War II. As well as providing a welter of information on the town and its activities, it also handles bookings for a wide range of accommodation (including farm stays) and affordable *mampoer* tours, which can include a visit to Marico Oog spring, or to Iron-Age and Anglo-Boer War sites. The *Bosman Hotel* along the same street has the pick of Groot Marico's three **bars**, where white locals, inspired by beer, brandy and their own good humour, have been known to dance traditional Afrikaans two-steps.

The best way of experiencing Groot Marico is to **stay** on a farm or in a cottage (❷–❸): the tourist office provides details and handles bookings, or there's a good selection at ⓦwww.marico.co.za/FarmAccommodation.htm. Particularly recommended are a couple of small self-catering cottages by the river, 3–4km west of town: *Casper's Kaya* (❷) and *David's Cottage* (❷), both in a secluded and heavily forested valley, just perfect for birders; swimming in the river is possible, and there are also canoes for rent and drumming workshops. Should you prefer a more central location, the friendly *Angela's Guest House* (☎014 503 0085, ⓔangela_s@telkomsa.net; ❸), between the village and the N4 highway, has four comfortable en-suite rooms and a self-catering cottage set in a lovely garden and orchard, and can organize massage and beauty treatments as well as meals. The nicest **camping** spots are on the Mafikeng Road, 1km from the centre of the village (details from the tourist office), and *Sallileni Camping Site*, 6km out beside a dam, where there are also five rondavels (bring bedding; ❶), a kitchen and thatched braai area, hot water, electricity and swimming in the reservoir.

Madikwe Game Reserve

Tucked up in the very north of the Province near the Botswana border lies the 765-square-kilometre **MADIKWE GAME RESERVE** (☎018 350 9931, ⓦwww.madikwe-game-reserve.co.za), one of South Africa's largest wildlife areas. The reserve was established in 1991 from reclaimed farmland, and thanks to **Operation Phoenix**, which saw the reintroduction of over eight thousand

Mampoer

It is said that it was a Pedi chief by the name of Mampuru who introduced the art of distilling peach brandy to the Boers. Named **mampoer** in his honour, the fearsomely strong spirit has inspired locals and visitors alike ever since. Any fruit can be used to make *mampoer*, but peach is the most traditional: until 1878, much of North West Province's farmland grew peach trees solely devoted to this purpose. Things changed with the ZAR government's distilling tax, and the new licensing system introduced in 1894, and thousands of *mampoer* stills were destroyed. A few, however, escaped detection. One farmer, according to a local story, cleaned out his entire drainage system but made no attempt to conceal his fifteen barrels of *mampoer*. The inspectors found the barrels, split them open and poured the entire contents down the drain. Meanwhile, the canny farmer had his family stationed in the field where the pipe ended up with every container the household possessed, and managed to recover fourteen of the fifteen barrels.

The drink is celebrated in Herman Charles Bosman's **short story**, *Willem Prinsloo's Peach Brandy*, set in the 1920s:

"We arrived at Willem Prinsloo's house. There were so many ox-waggons drawn up on the veld that the place looked like a laager [circle of wagons]. Prinsloo met us at the door.

'Go right through, kerels,' he said. 'The dancing is in the voorhuis [barn]. The peach brandy is in the kitchen.'

Although the voorhuis was big, it was so crowded as to make it almost impossible to dance. But it was not as crowded as the kitchen. Nor was the music in the voorhuis – which was provided by a number of men with guitars and concertinas – as loud as the music in the kitchen, where there was no band, but each man sang for himself.

We knew from these signs that the party was a success.

When I had been in the kitchen for about half an hour I decided to go into the voorhuis. It seemed a long way, now, from the kitchen to the voorhuis, and I had to lean against the wall several times to think. I passed a number of men who were also leaning against the wall like that, thinking. One man even found that he could think best by sitting on the floor with his head in his arms.

You could see that Willem Prinsloo made a pretty good peach brandy."

If you want to sample *mampoer*, either head for Pieter Roets's **Vergenoeg Farm** (open most days, closed evenings) a few kilometres south of Marico along the untarred main road, where you can cautiously pick up a bottle of barbed-wire-entwined, eighty-percent-proof *Doringdraad*, or to Tienie Zwart's **Driefontein Farm**, 2.5km beyond the Groot Marico turn-off on the N4, where you can see the stuff being made. In the old days the alcohol content was measured by throwing a chunk of lard into a sample: if it floated halfway, the *mampoer* was perfect. Nowadays, you just hold a match over it – the higher and cleaner the blue flame, the better the brew. Groot Marico's tourist office organizes a *mampoer* tour every Saturday for R130 per person.

animals, Madikwe's largely low-lying plains of woodland and grassland are now amply stocked with the Big Five (including black and white rhino and a stable population of 250 elephants) and dozens of other mammals, including cheetah, wild dogs, spotted hyena, and most of southern Africa's flavours of plains antelopes. Twitchers won't be disappointed, with some 350 species recorded so far; the Marico River, on the eastern border, and the *koppies* scattered all around, are particularly rewarding birding areas.

Long promoted as South Africa's "bijoux reserve", the low tourist density so liberally vaunted in the brochures no longer quite rings true given that around

20 lodges now vie for your trade, although Madikwe does remain one of the least known of South Africa's large wildlife areas. Access is reserved to guests of its lodges and **day visitors** who must book a package through one of the lodges that includes a **game drive** and lunch; independent day visits are not allowed.

Practicalities

Road access to Madikwe is normally through Tau Gate, 12km off the R49 although, depending on where you're staying, the reserve can also be approached from the east via Dwarsberg by way of gravel roads. Whichever approach you take, you'll need to inform your lodge prior to arrival. It's also possible to **fly in** on regular light aircraft from Johannesburg; fares are R1365 one-way, R2730 return; tickets can be reserved through the lodges or directly with Madikwe Air (☎011 805 4888, ⊛www.madikwecharter.com). **Accommodation** rates at all lodges include full board, day and night game drives, and guided bush walks. There is no budget accommodation or camping.

Jaci's Safari Lodge & Tree Lodge ☎014 778 9900, ⊛www.madikwe.com. Two exceptional lodges whose sense of style, comfort and laid-back luxury are hard to beat. The *Safari Lodge* overlooks a natural waterhole on the Marico River and has a natural rock swimming pool nearby, while the *Tree Lodge's* rooms are built around trees several metres off the ground. Children welcome. ❾

Madikwe Hills Private Game Lodge ☎018 365 9904; reservations ☎013 737 6626 or 6627, ⊛www.madikwehills.com. Another gem, this one built around a *koppie* close to the riverbank. Rooms are modern and have views over the veld. There are even better views from the sundowner terrace and its small swimming pool, plus there's a gym, health spa, childcare facilities, and some excellent cooks. ❾

Mateya Safari Lodge ☎014 778 9200, ⊛www .mateyasafari.com. Experience the ultimate in bush chic at these five luxurious suites, each boasting their own swimming pool, as well as both indoor and outdoor showers. There's a beauty therapist on hand, Jacuzzi and gym, and the lodge's culinary sorcery is best sampled on the terrace overlooking the veld. No children under 16. ❾

Mosetlha Bush Camp ☎011 444 9345, ⊛www .thebushcamp.com. Madikwe's only "budget" accommodation, also offering the reserve's most

▲ The Royal Madikwe Luxury Game Lodge

intense wilderness experience: located in the reserve's centre, there's no perimeter fence and accommodation is in very simple open-sided log cabins, with no electricity, and hot outdoor showers delivered by an ingenious donkey boiler and bucket system. What it lacks in luxury it makes up in atmosphere and expertise, with the emphasis placed on game walks as much as drives. ❼

Royal Madikwe Luxury Game Lodge
☎082 568 8867, ⓦwww.royalmadikwe.co.za. A sumptuous blend of colonial and "ethnic" styles, perfect for pampering, amidst an area of *marula* and red ivory trees. The five luxurious chalets each have a terrace from where you'll see plenty of wildlife. Good food, and there's a pool. ❾

Mafikeng and Mmabatho

The twin towns of Mafikeng and Mmabatho offer a unique portrait of the vision of apartheid and its deep contradictions. **MAFIKENG**, which acts as a shopping and transport hub for the wide area of farmland that surrounds it, is most famous for Baden-Powell and the Boer **siege** of 1899–1900 (see box, p.658). Less than 5km away, but a world apart in appearance, values and atmosphere, is **MMABATHO**, designated capital of the former homeland of Bophuthatswana, and a showcase for the grandiose visions of Bop dictator **Lucas Mangope** – it's worth a visit, even if the wiser course for finding somewhere to stay or eat and drink is to retreat to the Mafikeng side.

Arrival, information and accommodation

Mafikeng lies 25km south of the Ramatlabama border post with Botswana. None of the major intercity bus companies comes here, so you'll have to rely on **minibus taxis** (or buses operated by Atamelung or Bojanala Bus), which pull in at the hassle-free terminal between Hatchard and Victoria streets on the northern side of town. The **train station** is on the western edge at Station Street. Arriving by **plane**, you land at Mmabatho International Airport, 17km west along the Disaneng road (☎018 385 1140). There are no taxis or buses into town, but mid- and upmarket hotels will pick up guests, and the airport also has a branch of Avis (see "Listings" on p.660).

The municipal **tourist office** (Mon–Fri 8am–4.30pm; ☎018 381 3155 or 3156, ⓕ018 381 6058) is awkwardly placed 1.5km south of the centre along Nelson Mandela Drive, next to Mafikeng Game Reserve. Apart from the usual brochures, hotel lists and city plans (R5), it also sells books. For questions about the Province's parks and nature reserves, visit the **North West Parks & Tourism Board** headquarters at Heritage House next to Cooke's Lake, 500m closer to town (Mon–Fri 7.30am–4.30pm; ☎018 397 1500, call centre ☎082 232 7500, ⓦwww.tourismnorthwest.co.za).

Most **accommodation** rates include breakfast.

Boga Legaba Guest House 6 Interlaken Ave, Riviera Park, 2km east of the centre ☎018 381 6808, ⓦwww.bogalegaba.co.za. Characterful place decorated with African artwork, and with a spacious garden and pool. ❸
Buffalo Park Lodge 59 Molopo Rd, at the corner with Botha Rd ☎018 381 2159, ⓦwww .buffalolodge.co.za. Family-run place with small, cool and well-kept twin-bed rooms with TVs, though it's the excellent bar and restaurant that recommend it. There's also a Lilliputian swimming pool. ❸
Cooke's Lake Chalets Cooke's Lake, access beside the tourist office on Nelson Mandela Drive

☎018 381 6020. Next to the lake, these beautiful two-storey wood-and-thatch chalets are the most attractive places to stay in Mafikeng. ❹
Garden View Guest Lodge Corner of North and Havenga sts ☎018 381 3110, ⓦwww .travellodge.co.za. Comfortable B&B rooms in a colonial-era building with a pleasant patio area, secure parking, and attached restaurant (closed weekends) and ladies' bar. ❸
Getaway Guest Lodge 39 Tillard St, at the corner with Baden-Powell St ☎018 381 1150. Under the same management as the *Garden View* and priced identically, with 31 good en-suite rooms, safe parking and a nice pool. ❸

Surrey 32 Shippard St ☎018 381 0420, ℱ018 381 1353. The only cheap accommodation in town, with large if run-down rooms, most with bathrooms (and bathtubs). Can be noisy to around midnight thanks to the adjacent ladies' bar. Good value. ❷

Mafikeng

The town's main attraction is **Mafikeng Museum** on Martin Street (Mon–Fri 8am–4pm, Sat 10am–1pm; donation), housed in the impressive former town hall, built in 1902, two years after the siege ended. You can't miss it, as there's a restored steam locomotive outside, in use from 1901 until 1971 when it pulled the Kimberley–Bulawayo Express. The museum has some intriguing exhibits on the **San**, including photos of the hand signals they use when hunting in their customary silence, as well as a range of hunting weapons and poisons. Tswana exhibits include a life-size re-creation of a traditional hut, complete with its trademark enclosed porch, and samples of pottery and beadwork. The **siege of Mafikeng** is given a room of its own, filled with classic British imperial memorabilia, including a tattered flag, weaponry, diaries and a wonderful collection of photos. Keep an eye out too for the fascinating exhibit on Mafikeng and the **railways**, which provides evidence of the connection between their spread from Cape Town and Rhodes' mission to colonize Africa. The museum sells an excellent visitor guide (R30), and a glossy but very informative publication about North West Province (R90).

If you're looking for something else to do, the **Mafikeng Game Reserve**, which starts on the eastern edge of town (daily: May–Aug 7am–6pm, Sept–April 6.30am–7pm; ☎018 381 5611, ⓦwww.tourismnorthwest.co.za/mafikeng_reserve/index.html; R15, plus R5 per car), covers some 46 square kilometres of

---

The siege of Mafikeng

Mafikeng was besieged within three days of the start of the second Anglo-Boer War (1899–1902) by generals Snyman and Cronje. **Colonel Robert Baden-Powell** (founder of the Boy Scouts) had the task of defending the town. This he did for 217 days, from October 16, 1899, until May 17, 1900, when relief arrived from Rhodesia and from the south. In the process, Baden-Powell became a British household name and hero, and the exuberant scenes of jubilation in London that greeted news of the relief gave rise to a new word in the English language: *maffick*, which meant to celebrate unduly.

Strategically, Mafikeng was irrelevant to the war; Baden-Powell's real achievement was to distract the six thousand Afrikaners besieging the town from fighting elsewhere. He relied heavily on the **Barolong** people for defence, labour and reconnaissance, but failed to record this either in his dispatches to London or in his memoirs, despite the fact that four hundred Barolong lost their lives during the siege – twice as many as British (look for some of the British casualties of the siege in the town's cemetery on Carrington Street, next to the railway sidings; they're marked by white iron crosses). Until the 1980s this was a whites-only cemetery, and today it still commemorates only the Europeans who died during the siege. The Barolong also received far fewer rations, and over one thousand subsequently died of starvation; they received none of the £29,000 raised in Britain for the rehabilitation of Mafikeng. To add insult to injury, not one Barolong was decorated for bravery, in contrast to the plentiful medals dished out to the British regiments, and none of the promises Baden-Powell made about land grants to them was ever kept. An important legacy of the involvement of the black population was the diary of the siege kept by **Sol Plaatje**, one of the first black writers to make an impact on English literature, who was later to become a founder member of the South African Native Congress, forerunner to the ANC.

MAFIKENG

Baden-Powell Scouts Hall

Standard Bank **A**

Victoria Hospital

Prison

St Joseph's Convent

@ Cybernet Computers **B**

Taxi Rank

Game Shopping Centre

Mafikeng Museum

St John's Anglican Church

Police

Absa Bank

Train station **3**

Northwest Mall

Methodist Church

Library

Standard Bank

Mafikeng Market Square

Mr. Food Grocery

Caltex **C**

First National Bank **E**

Cooke's Lake **F**

North West Parks & Tourism Board

Mafikeng Game Reserve, R27 & Zeerust

8

NORTH WEST PROVINCE | The Central Region

Airport, Disaneng & R27 Vryburg

ACCOMMODATION
Boga Legaba Guest House	D
Buffalo Park Lodge	C
Cooke's Lake Chalets	F
Garden View Lodge	A
Getaway Guest Lodge	B
Surrey	E

RESTAURANTS, BARS & CLUBS
Buffalo Park Lodge	C
Captain DoRego's	5
Ebony and Ivory Jazz Bar	3
Graceland	2
Ivory Pot	4
Tony's Corner	1

0   500 m

rather drab Kalahari grassland and thornscrub and is well stocked with primarily herbivorous plains game, including **white rhino** and **buffalo**. The principal circuit around the reserve takes two hours and offers rewarding game viewing, particularly around waterholes. **Cooke's Lake**, in the reserve's western corner next to town, is reasonably good for waterfowl and mongooses (and the snakes they prey on). There are two **entrances**: one 10km east of Mafikeng along the R49 towards Zeerust, the other just 3km from the town centre – go down Shippard Street and turn right after the railway bridge (2km) onto Jacaranda Street. Aslaagte Gate is straight ahead.

Mmabatho

Four kilometres north of Mafikeng along Nelson Mandela Drive (catch a minibus taxi from next to the Boxer Superstore on Station St) is **Mmabatho**, created in 1977 as capital of the new "independent homeland" of Bophuthatswana, but now subsumed into Mafikeng. The city prospered fast, both from the discovery of platinum and the revenue from Sol Kerzner's gambling resorts. Under the direction of Bop president Lucas Mangope, the capital became an ostentatious attempt to show off what a prosperous independent African state could become, though in practice it was a bloated and surreal quasi-state, riddled with corruption and egocentricity. Huge buildings were constructed for the burgeoning civil service, and brand-new casino-hotels catered to the new black elite, as well as South Africans chasing the illicit thrills denied them across the border. Money was poured into bizarre enterprises, including an Israeli-built sports stadium with 75,000 seats but scarcely any shade and a state-of-the-art **recording studio**, which has been seeing more use since the end of apartheid: the sound track for *The Lion King* was recorded here.

659

There's not, to be honest, all that much to do in Mmabatho other than get a sense of the scale of Mangope's ambitions, or indulge in a spot of window- shopping at the modern **Mega City Shopping Mall**. That said, one place definitely worth visiting if you happen to be here at the right time is the highly regarded **North West Arts Complex** (☎018 384 4890) on Sekama Street opposite Mega City. Home to dance and theatre companies, and the National Chamber Orchestra, the complex hosts occasional performances and festivals; ring ahead for the schedule.

Eating, drinking and nightlife

Apart from its smattering of **restaurants** – including one of South Africa's few truly African eateries – Mafikeng has the usual fast-food places (there's a branch of *Captain DoRego's* in Mafikeng Market Square on Shippard Street), a large Superspar **supermarket** at Game Shopping Centre between Nelson Mandela Drive and the taxi terminal, and the Mr Food grocery on Shippard Street (daily 6.30am–9pm), which sells a wide selection of hot take-outs, including stews, and cheap breakfasts.

Walking around at night is not recommended, and as Mafikeng still lacks a telephone taxi service, unless you have wheels or can find a local to accompany you, **nightlife** is limited to within a block or two of your hotel.

Buffalo Park Lodge See "Accommodation", p.657. The best restaurant in town, with a menu including seafood, vegetarian pub lunches and unusual Afrikaner specialities such as "steak carpetbagger" (stuffed with cheese and mussels, topped with mushroom sauce). Mains R50–80. The attached *Waterhole* pub is a pleasant place for a drink while watching sports on the TV. Daily to 11pm or later; last food orders 10pm.

Ebony and Ivory Jazz Bar Corner of Martin and Station sts. Recently renovated and sporting a plush modern interior, this is one of the better local dives, with an unintimidating atmosphere and playing nicely mellow music.

Graceland Main St, near Nelson Mandela Drive. The town's only central nightclub, positively heaving weekend nights. Go with a local. Wed, Fri & Sat 9pm–5am.

Ivory Pot 11 Shippard St. A small but highly recommended restaurant serving only African food. Choose from various delicious stews, washed down with tangy home-made ginger beer. Meals R22. Daily 8am–5pm.

Tony's Corner Corner of Gemsbok and Tillard sts, 1km northeast of the centre. This casual and welcoming pub is the town's main upmarket drinking hole, with several beers on tap, and reliably good grub. The new management was considering a name change at the time of writing.

Listings

Banks Money exchange at First National Bank, Robinson St.
Car rental Avis, Mmabatho International Airport ☎018 385 1114.
Hospitals Best is the private Victoria Hospital, Victoria St ☎018 381 2043. The state hospital is Mafikeng Provincial Hospital, south of the tourist office in Danville ☎018 383 2005.

Internet access Cybernet Computers, Nelson Mandela Drive, opposite Game Shopping Centre.
Pharmacies and doctors There are several at Game Shopping Centre and Mega City Shopping Mall in Mmabatho.
Police Corner ofT illard and Carrington sts.
Post The post office is on Carrington St.

Lichtenburg and Potchefstroom

The deeply conservative *dorp* of **LICHTENBURG** lies some 65km southeast of Mafikeng on the R52, close to the N14 highway connecting Northern Cape to Gauteng. The town became famous when **diamonds** were discovered here in 1926; barely a year later a shantytown of 150,000 people had sprung up, supporting 25,000 diggers and sporting over 200 diamond-buying offices. The

Protours' daily **bus** to Johannesburg starts at the Mega City Shopping Mall in Mmabatho and stops at Mafikeng Market Square on Shippard Street (purchase tickets from the driver). Atamelang (T018 381 2680) has a daily service to Johannesburg, while Bojanala Bus (T014 565 6550) runs once a day to Rustenburg; buses start at the minibus taxi terminal between Victoria and Hatchard streets. **Minibus taxis** cover most destinations within the Province, as well as Kimberley in Northern Cape (these leave from in front of the train station on Station St). An alternative approach to Northern Cape is the daily 7.30am train to Kimberley (9hr). There's also an 11.20pm service on Sundays to Johannesburg, arriving the following morning at 5am. The station entrance (tickets 6am–7.30pm) isn't obvious; it's opposite Tillard Street between the Boxer Superstore and the mobile phone mast, next to a footbridge. South African Airlink (T011 978 1111, Wwww.saairlink.co.za) **flies** to Johannesburg twice daily from Monday to Friday.

quantity of diamonds discovered in Lichtenburg threatened the diamond market, but De Beers bought nearly every one – including the world's largest flawless red diamond – to maintain its monopoly and the diamonds' worth. The **Diggings Museum** on Melville Street (Mon–Fri 10am–1pm & 2–4pm; free) offers some background to the 1926 rush with assorted artefacts and some lively stories from Lichtenburg's heady days as a diamond town. The best **accommodation** is at the Georgian *Scott's Manor*, 21 Bree St, on the northern edge of town and well signposted from the Mafikeng and Zeerust roads (T018 632 0255, Wwww.scottsmanor.com; ❸); amenities include a swimming pool, restaurant and cocktail bar.

Located on the **N12** highway, 140km southeast of Lichtenburg, **POTCHEFSTROOM** is the largest town in North West Province's **Southern Region**, not generally a part of the province with much to detain the visitor for too long. The town was once the capital of the ZAR, but today is best known for its university. Although there's not much to do here, the presence of a large student population does give parts of town a youthful and energetic vibe, and it's a pleasant enough place to **spend the night** if you're travelling along the N12 between Johannesburg and Kimberley: *Cosy Cottage B&B*, 38 Parys Ave (T018 290 5710, Wwww.cosy-cottage.co.za; ❷), has self-catering cottages and rondavels next to the Mooi River – a good spot for bird-watching.

Travel details

Trains

Mafikeng to: Johannesburg (1 daily; 6hr); Kimberley (1 daily; 9hr).
Potchefstroom to: Bloemhof (1 daily; 3hr 10min); Cape Town (1–2 daily; 24hr); Johannesburg (1–2 daily; 3hr); Kimberley (1–2 daily; 6hr 20min).

Buses

Mafikeng to: Johannesburg (2 daily; 3hr); Rustenburg (1 daily; 3hr).
Potchefstroom to: George (1 daily; 13hr 30min); Johannesburg (4–9 daily; 1hr 30min); Kimberley (4–5 daily; 4hr 30min); Oudtshoorn (4–5 weekly; 11hr 30min); Pretoria (4–9 daily; 2hr 30min).
Rustenburg to: Johannesburg (1 daily; 2hr); Mafikeng (1 daily; 3hr); Pretoria (1 daily; 3hr).

Taxis

Minibus taxis follow more or less the same routes as buses, taking a little less time, but you may need to add several hours' initial waiting time before the taxi leaves. The main route covered by minibus taxis but not by bus is Mafikeng to Kimberley (2–3 daily; 5hr); taxis are also useful for short legs between towns.

Domestic flights

Madikwe to: Johannesburg (1 daily; 45min).
Mafikeng to: Johannesburg (2 daily Mon–Fri only; 1hr).

Mpumalanga

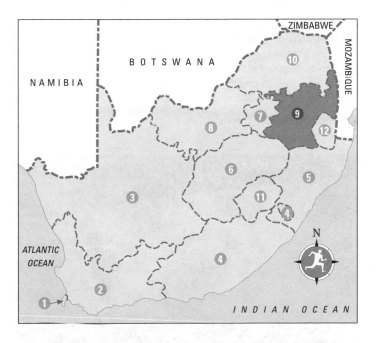

CHAPTER 9 # Highlights

* **Aerial Cable Trail** Glide over tree tops on a 1.2-kilometre trail near Hazyview. See p.685

* **African meals at the Shangana Cultural Village** Here you can sample crocodile or mopane worms – as well as more conventional fare such as beef pot roast. See p.685

* **Brushing an elephant** Enjoy a close encounter with an elephant at the Hazyview Elephant Sanctuary. See p.685

* **Bush breakfasts** There's no more satisfying way to round off a couple of hours of game-viewing than with a cooked breakfast in the wilds of Kruger. See box, p.692

* **Walking safaris in Kruger** It's worth leaving behind the security of a vehicle for the thrill of potential close encounters with animals. See p.702

* **Leopard-spotting** The luxury camps in the Sabi Sands Game Reserve offer excellent opportunities to observe leopards. See p.707

▲ Lion meets tourist at Kruger National Park

Mpumalanga

Mpumalanga, "the land of the rising sun" to its Siswati- and Zulu-speaking residents, extends east from Gauteng to Mozambique and Swaziland. To many visitors the province is synonymous with the **Kruger National Park**, the real draw of South Africa's east flank, and one of Africa's best game parks. Kruger occupies most of Mpumalanga's and Limpopo Province's borders with Mozambique, and covers over 20,000 square kilometres – an area the size of Wales or Massachusetts. Unashamedly populist, Kruger is the easiest African game park to drive around in on your own, with many well-run restcamps for accommodation. On its western border lie a number of **private reserves**, offering the chance – at a price – to escape the Kruger crush, with well-informed rangers conducting safaris in open vehicles.

Apart from the irresistible magnet of big-game country, Mpumalanga also has some spectacular scenery in the mountainous area known as the **Escarpment**, usually passed through en route to Kruger. The most famous viewpoints – **God's Window**, **Bourke's Luck Potholes** and **Three Rondavels** – are along the lip of the Escarpment, which can be seen on a 150-kilometre drive from the lowveld known as the **Panorama Route**. The views of **Blyde River Canyon** are most famous of all and, while you can't drive into the canyon, there are some fabulous hiking and river-rafting opportunities in this area. None of the Escarpment towns merits exploration, but they are fine as night stops.

Jammed between the mountains and Kruger are the former African **bantustans**, created under apartheid: Lebowa for Sotho speakers and Gazankulu for Shangaan- and Tsonga-speaking people. The poverty of these artificial statelets was exacerbated in the 1980s, when hundreds of thousands of Mozambicans fled into Gazankulu to escape the civil war in their home country. Even today, with the war over, Mozambicans attempt to cross illegally into South Africa, braving lions, National Parks officials and anti-poaching units in Kruger in a quest to reach the "golden city" of Johannesburg.

For overseas visitors, the **route** is usually the other way round, starting from Johannesburg and heading through the unattractive industrial corridor traversed by the N4 as it races to **Nelspruit**, the modern capital of Mpumalanga. From here the N4 continues to the **Mozambique border**, a route which also gives access to the southernmost part of Kruger. Nelspruit also connects with the road south through **Barberton** to Swaziland.

Descending the Escarpment on one of four mountain passes takes you into the tropical-fruit-growing and bushveld country of the **lowveld**, with impressive views back towards the towering massif of the Escarpment. A number of places close to the **Blydepoort Dam** at the foot of the Blyde River Canyon can be taken in as bushveld breaks on the way to or from Kruger.

Closest to this area is the small but growing centre of **Hoedspruit** (actually in Limpopo Province, but covered here because of its proximity to Kruger) with its own airport, a jumping-off point for safaris in the central and northern section of the park, and yielding access to the Manyeleti and Timbabavati private game reserves. Note that **malaria** (see p.71) is a potential hazard in the lowveld and Kruger, particularly in summer.

Johannesburg is the nearest city to Mpumalanga and is five or six hours' drive from Kruger; the city also has the best transport connections with the province. There's a daily **train** service between Johannesburg and Nelspruit and a daily Greyhound or Translux **bus** between the two cities. The Baz Bus travels between Johannesburg and Durban via Nelspruit and Swaziland. **Flights** link Jo'burg with Nelspruit, Hoedspruit and Phalaborwa; from Cape Town, you can fly into Nelspruit or Hoedspruit, both via Johannesburg, and cheapest on Nationwide Airline, while Nelspruit also has flights from Durban. Backpacker lodges do transfers from Nelspruit and all have their own tours to Kruger and the Escarpment. To get anywhere else in the province by public transport, you need to use Nelspruit as a springboard and take **minibus taxis**.

The Escarpment

Four hours' drive east of Johannesburg International Airport is one of the city's favoured mountain retreats: the waving grasslands and luxury guesthouses of the Mpumalanga Drakensberg, generally known as the **Escarpment**. While most travellers visit the region purely because of its proximity to the Kruger National Park, it provides some of the most dramatic views in the country, which can be enjoyed with little effort. Unlike the range in KwaZulu-Natal, this section of the Drakensberg is one you can tour in your own car, stopping at one of the tourist towns for lunch and retiring to comfortable lodgings at the end of the day. This tour, known as the **Panorama Route**, can also be taken as a day-trip by numerous tour operators and lodgings closer to Kruger, and is worth it for the landscape.

The main draw of the Escarpment is the **Blyde River Canyon**, whose dizzying views into one of the world's great gorges appear in countless South African tourist brochures. In addition to a number of viewpoints along the Escarpment lip, the canyon can also be experienced on a hiking trail which gives access to the flora and (if you're quiet and lucky) fauna of the reserve, which include zebra, hippo, kudu and the entire range of South African primates – baboons, vervet and samango monkeys and bushbabies.

The little forestry towns of **Sabie** and **Graskop** have ample accommodation for all budgets and are convenient bases for exploring the area, with the added pull of a plethora of **adventure activities**. **Dullstroom** has established itself as an upmarket fly-fishing resort, while **Pilgrim's Rest**, a reconstructed mining settlement from the gold-rush days at the turn of the last century, is designed to draw in the tour buses, but like all the towns above can be safely given a miss if what you're really after is the game in Kruger Park, in the lowveld below these mountains.

Dullstroom and Lydenburg

Some 209km east of Johannesburg, the R540 branches off the N4 at nondescript **Belfast** and heads into the hills, where the highveld countryside is covered by grasslands, waving tall and green in summer, but turning russet in winter.

Unless your passion is fly-fishing, chances are you'll find the small crossroads settlement of **DULLSTROOM**, 35km north of Belfast on the R540, as unexciting as its name suggests, though the *Birds of Prey Rehabilitation Centre*, 1km outside Dullstroom on the R540 (daily 9am–4pm; R30, with demonstrations at 10.30am & 2pm; ☎013 254 0777, ⓦwww.birdsofprey .co.za), makes a worthwhile visit, exclusively devoted to the housing, nourishment and rehabilitation of raptors, with very good flying demonstrations daily. The centre is run by two extremely knowledgeable and witty Englishmen, both called Mark and passionate about the birds they care for.

Dullstroom can be a useful place to stop over for a night on your way to Kruger National Park; the Dullstroom Information office, at Auldstone House on Hugenoten Street (Mon–Thurs 8.30am–5pm, Fri 8.30am–6pm, Sat 9am–5pm, Sun 9am–2pm; ☎013 254 0254, ⓦwww.dullstroom.biz), can help with finding accommodation, with over ninety establishments on its books, covering all budgets.

The town certainly caters to the weekend trade of Johannesburg escapees looking for a rest and fine **food** – most of the accommodation doubles up as restaurants. One of Dullstroom's best-known restaurants, *Pickles & Things*, on the main street (☎013 254 0115), is a popular, busy, largely daytime place with big breakfasts, home-made bread, and an inviting garden, with dinners on Friday and Saturday nights only. The deli at the front of the restaurant stocks smoked trout and other delicacies like nougat. The *Dullstroom Inn*, signposted just off the main street, is open from breakfast to dinner and has a welcoming fireplace in the busy pub, with chalked-up dishes of the day, including vegetarian fare and lots of trout.

Accommodation

Critchley Hackle Lodge Teding van Berkhout St ☎013 254 0149, ⓦwww.critchleyhackle.co.za. A gracious country-style hotel with stone and brick cottages, each with a fireplace. Its restaurant is recommended, and has a bar for after-dinner cognac, whiskey and cigars; there's also a patio for tea and scones. ❻–❼

Dullstroom Inn Teding van Berkhout St ☎013 254 0071, ⓦwww.dullstroom.info/dullstroominn. A pleasantly cool Victorian country inn. Its pub serves draught beer and gets packed at weekends. ❹

Old Transvaal Inn 117 Hugenote St ☎013 254 0222, ⒺGGG@worldonline.co.za. A quiet and friendly B&B offering good food, a fine location and cultivated quaintness of style. ❸

The Poacher 66 Hugenote St ☎013 254 0108, Ⓔinfo@poacher.co.za. A small, friendly lodge with four rooms, river frontage and a tackle shop. Best of all is its restaurant, serving sophisticated country fare and pub grub, with Guinness on tap in the pub. ❷

Lydenburg and Long Tom Pass

Some 58km north of Dullstroom, humdrum **LYDENBURG** is the site of one of South Africa's major archeological finds, replicas of which are on display at the **Lydenburg Museum** (Mon–Fri 9am–noon & 2–4.15pm, Sat & Sun 10am–4pm; small entry fee) in the Gustav Klingbiel Nature Reserve, 3km out of town along the R37 to Sabie. The **Lydenburg Heads**, seven beautiful ceramic masks (probably ceremonial) dating back to the fifth century, are some of the first figurative sculptures in southern Africa. As well as replicas of these heads (the originals are in the South African Museum in Cape Town), there are excellent displays on human activity in the vicinity over the past million years or so.

Striking east from Lydenburg, the R37 twists its way up **Long Tom Pass**, which takes its name from the Scheider siege guns used here by the Boers during the 1899–1902 Second Anglo-Boer War against the British. Known as Long Toms because of their elongated necks, the artillery pieces were able to throw a 43kg shell a distance of 10km. You can still see the holes blasted by retreating Boers into the series of switchbacks cutting up the pass, known as the Staircase.

Sabie, Pilgrim's Rest and Graskop

Sabie, the largest of the three towns occupying the heights of the Escarpment, has its personality split between serving the surrounding agroforestry industry and trying to please the tourists who use it as a base. Of the other two,

Pilgrim's Rest unashamedly plays to the tour buses, pushing hard with its restored gold-rush buildings and themed museums, while the relatively uninteresting timber centre of **Graskop** is trying to develop its potential in an attempt to secure those elusive tourist bucks. Though they all advertise themselves as bases for Kruger, they most definitely are not, since it takes a good couple of hours of twisting down mountain passes to get to Kruger, and once you are in the park, all you do is drive anyway. If you want a Kruger base outside the park, stay as close to an entry gate as possible.

Sabie and around

Lying on the R37 beyond Long Tom Pass, **SABIE** (pronounced "Saabie", like the car) is the centre of Mpumalanga's agroforestry industry. It holds the dubious distinction of lying at the heart of South Africa's largest artificial forests, with 450 square kilometres under active cultivation. The extensive pine plantations look monotonous compared to the rich, jungly variety of the remaining pockets of indigenous woodland.

Before the foresters arrived, Sabie made its name as a gold centre, with a lucky strike in 1895 at the Klein Sabie Falls. Mining stopped halfway through the twentieth century, and today the gold prospectors have been replaced by escapees from hectic Johannesburg, who make a living here running restaurants, B&Bs or craft shops.

Sabie's compact size, slow pace, mildly arty ambience and gentle climate make it a congenial base for exploring the Escarpment. If you don't have your own transport, you can still take advantage of its well-organized backpacker lodge, and a raft of adventure activities.

Arrival, information and accommodation

Public **transport** to Sabie is limited to minibus taxis plying the routes from neighbouring towns; otherwise *Sabie Backpackers* does have a reasonably priced **shuttle** between Nelspruit and Sabie. The centrally located *Trips SA*, 90 Main Rd opposite St Peter's church (Mon–Fri 8am–5pm, Sat 9am–1pm; ☏013 764 1177, ⓦ www.sabie.co.za), is the better of the two **information** offices in the village.

Sabie offers a good supply of reasonably priced **accommodation**, though prices can rise dramatically during South African school holidays. Avoid the rock-bottom B&Bs which the information bureaus list: most of them offer no privacy.

Hillwatering Country House 50 Marula St ☏013 764 1421, ⓦ www.hillwatering.8m.com. Renovated 1950s home with four large bedrooms, each with their own veranda, overlooking the Bridal Veil Falls. The reception is warm and breakfast excellent. ❸

Merry Pebbles Holiday Resort 2km west from the centre on the Old Lydenburg Rd ☏013 764 2266, ⓦ www.merrypebbles.co.za. Go for the newer, nicely renovated units at this resort which also offers camping, self-catering and en-suite chalets. The facilities include a heated pool and children's playground. Mercifully no quad bikes or motorbikes are allowed. ❷–❸

Misty Mountain Lodge 24km southwest of Sabie on Long Tom Pass ☏013 764 3377, ⓦ www .mistymountain.co.za. Pleasant, B&B units, some

with splendid views across pine plantations into the valleys. There's trout fishing on the property, with rods and flies for rent at a nominal rate; the lodge is also well placed for walks into indigenous forest. You can self-cater or take advantage of the restaurant and pub on the premises. Rates are the same whether you take breakfast or not. ❹

Sabie Backpackers Lodge 185 Main Rd ☏013 764 2118, ⓦ www.sabiextreme.co.za. A well-run, fun hostel, with camping, dorms and doubles, featuring sturdy beds and warm bedding. There's also accommodation for two in a tree house. Xtreme Adventures, based here, organizes a host of adventure activities (see box, p.671), and the lodge has good weekend packages with wall-to-wall adventure activities. Dorms ❶, rooms ❷

Villa Ticino On the corner of Louis Trichardt and Second sts ℡013 764 2598, Ⓦwww.villaticino.co.za. Hospitable, and often full, Swiss-owned B&B with a terrace looking onto the hills, and a lounge with a pool table. Winter discounts are available. ❸–❹

The town and around

Sabie is segmented by **Main Street** (the R37 from Lydenburg and the Long Tom Pass), which meanders into the town centre where it hits **Main Road** at right angles. At the junction of the two, the compact **St Peter's**, an English-style country church designed in 1912 by Sir Herbert Baker, hides in a verdant garden dominated by a gigantic jacaranda tree, which in early summer covers the lawn with mauve petals like confetti. Nearby at the corner of Tenth and Seventh streets, the **Komatiland Forest and Industry Museum** (Mon–Fri 8am–4pm, Sat & Sun 8am–noon; R10) has a small, worthwhile display on the history of forestry and the timber industry in South Africa, plus a section on papermaking.

A large number of **waterfalls** drop down the slopes outside Sabie. Just 7km from town, down the Old Lydenburg Road, you can visit three of the most impressive: **Bridal Veil**, **Horseshoe** and, appropriately at the end of the road, **Lone Creek Falls**. The loveliest and most accessible of the three, it's conveniently reached down a paved, circular path that crosses a river and works its way back to the car park, though if you're pressed for time, the waterfalls can safely be missed. The most visited of them lies 13km north of Sabie along the Graskop road. Here you'll find the more spectacular 65-metre **Mac Mac Falls** (R10 entry) – named after the many people of Scottish descent who died looking for gold in the area and whose names appear on dozens of tombstones in the vicinity. Unfortunately, views here are restricted by a mesh fence around the viewing platform. Local craftworkers have set up a **market** in the car park. While you can't swim in the inviting waterfall pool at the base of the falls, there is a river pool at the Mac Mac Pools, 2km before you reach the falls themselves, where there's also a picnic and braai area (R10 entry) and the three-kilometre **Secretary Bird Walking Trail**. Less popular, but surpassing the Mac Mac Falls, are the **Berlin** and **Lisbon** falls, both signposted and easily accessible off the R532 (close to God's Window). The vertiginous drops are unfenced, allowing you to get close enough to feel the spray.

Eating and drinking

Sabie has a couple of memorable and relaxed places for light meals or drinks.

The Wild Fig Tree On the corner of Main and Louis Trichardt sts. South African dishes are the speciality at this family restaurant set in an attractive, lush garden. Open daily 8am–10pm.
Woodsman Restaurant On the corner of Main and Mac Mac rds. A licensed restaurant with a beer garden, serving Cypriot Greek food, including vegetarian *meze*, plus local specialities such as ostrich and trout, and delicious slow-cooked lamb. Also good for coffee and snacks on the terrace, or at the cosy fire. Open daily 8am–10pm.

Pilgrim's Rest

Hiding in a valley 35km north of Sabie, **PILGRIM'S REST**, an almost too-perfectly restored gold-mining town, is an irresistible port of call for the scores of tour buses meandering daily through the Escarpment's passes. A collection of red-roofed, corrugated-iron buildings, including a period bank, a filling station with pre-1920 fuel pumps and the characterful *Royal Hotel* brimming with Victoriana, the place is undeniably photogenic. But you can't help feeling there's little substance behind the romanticized gold-rush image, especially when the village nods off after 5pm once the day-trippers have been spirited away, and everything is designed to fleece the tourist.

Adventure activities in Sabie

With its forest, massive gorge and mountains, the Escarpment offers good opportunities for adventure activities. Among the operators running a range of these is Sabie Xtreme Adventures, based at *Sabie Backpackers Lodge* (see p.669). The activities on offer include **Bunji Swing**, with a 69-metre drop into the Graskop Gorge, **horse trails**, **caving** by candlelight in the Lone Creek Caves, waterfall abseiling at the Sabie Falls, mountain **biking** and **whitewater tubing** and **canyoning**.

For **river rafting** in the Blyde River Canyon, one of the largest in the world, Induna Adventures is recommended (℡013 737 8308, 🌐www.indunaadventures.com). Its half-day trip (R245) goes either in the morning or afternoon and takes three hours.

The best activities here are **gold panning** and **horse-riding**. The SA Gold Panning Association (℡013 768 1471 or 1472, 🌐www.sagoldpanning.co.za) hosts the annual SA Gold Panning Championships here as well as daily sessions where you get to learn how to do it yourself. For horse-riding, Ponieskrantz is a charming stable 1km outside Pilgrim's Rest on the Graskop road (℡013 768 1465, 🌐www .pilgrimsreststables.co.za). The riding country is breathtaking, the horses healthy and well schooled, while the manager and guide Colleen is very knowledgeable about the animals and the region. She takes catered trails of up to three days across the mountains where you can also see wild horses (R1500 per person). There are also two bungalows you can rent if you want to stay longer (see p.672).

Pilgrim's Rest owes its origins to South Africa's first **gold rush**, which predates the uncovering of the great Gauteng seams. In 1873, Alex "Wheelbarrow" Patterson discovered gold in the creek. His attempts to keep his discovery secret were a total failure, and by the end of the year Patterson had been joined by 1500 diggers frantically working 4000 claims. Far from the pristine little village of today, the **Pilgrim's Rest diggings** were the site of gruelling labour and unhygienic conditions. Many diggers arrived malnourished, suffering from dysentery and malaria after punishing treks through the lowveld. Those who survived could expect drab lives in tents or, if they struck lucky, more permanent wattle-and-daub huts. In 1896, the diggings were bought up by the Transvaal Gold Mining Estates (TGME), which closed its Beta Mine in 1972, handing Pilgrim's Rest over to the provincial administration.

The whole settlement was declared a historic monument in the 1980s. But mining continues behind the hill to the southwest of town, away from tourist eyes, with functional buildings, cyanide-filled slime dams and great red scars hacked into the hillside, the indigenous forest having been bulldozed out of existence.

Arrival and information

Pilgrim's Rest stretches along its one main road and is divided into Uptown and Downtown. Commercialized **Uptown**, to the east, has the greatest concentration of shops and restaurants and consequently draws the bulk of tourists; the area centres around the *Royal Hotel* and the **tourist office** (daily 8.30am–4.30pm; ℡013 768 1060, 🌐www.pilgrimsrest.co.za) which can provide details of accommodation. **Downtown**, just 1km to the west, has a more down-to-earth atmosphere, and its restaurants are a little cheaper – though many visitors slip in and out of Pilgrim's Rest without realizing the area even exists.

Accommodation

Though Pilgrim's Rest is by far the prettiest of the Escarpment towns, there's very little accommodation in the town itself.

Crystal Springs Mountain Lodge 10km out of town on the R533 to Lydenburg ☏013 768 5000, ⓦwww.grc-resorts.co.za. A large time-share resort which couldn't be better planned, better organized or situated, or boast better facilities; this is a pure slice of suburban South Africa on holiday. The thatched cottages each have a deck and escarpment views, and there's a restaurant and bar on site, plus trampolines, a heated pool, playground, a games room and, for adults, a Jacuzzi, sauna and steambath. From the cottages there are well-marked walking trails into a ravine. Rates fall during the week, and out of school holidays. ❸

District Six Miners' Cottages Downtown ☏013 768 1211 or 083 271 8262. Self-catering accommodation, run by the Public Works Department, in authentic two-bedroomed 1920s workers' houses, sleeping two to four, with verandas overlooking the town and mountains. These are among the best places to stay on the Escarpment. You'll need to book ahead (Mon–Fri 8.30am–4pm), as there's no on-site office. If you do arrive over the weekend, or after hours, use the mobile number. ❷

Ponieskranz Cottages 1km out of town on the Graskop Rd ☏013 768 1465, ⓦwww .pilgrimsreststables.co.za. Self-catering cottage on a farm with a riding stable, sleeping four, while a bigger wooden trail cabin can take up to twelve people. The early morning sun streams into both cottages which have great views and no neighbours. ❷

Pilgrim's Rest Caravan Park Downtown ☏013 768 1309, ⓔnormane@webmail.co.za. Grassy campsite with a river running through it. Accommodation comprises seven tents sleeping six people, rooms sleeping four, some cheap doubles and a backpackers' dorm. Not recommended unless you're stuck and need a cheap place to stay. ❶–❷

The Royal Hotel Main St, Uptown ☏013 768 1100, ⓦwww.royal-hotel.co.za. Atmospheric hotel that dates back to the gold-rush days and brims with luxurious Victoriana, with guests mostly accommodated in restored houses on the main road. ❺

The Town

Apart from souvenir hunting and lingering in the cafés and tea shops, the main activity in Pilgrim's Rest is visiting its handful of **museums**. Tickets for all these must be bought in advance at the tourist office. You can whip through the three modest town "museums" in a matter of minutes, as they amount to little more than rooms reconstructed as they were in the gold-rush days. More interesting are those out of the centre. To get a really authentic impression of the gold-mining days, head for the open-air **Diggings Site Museum** on the eastern edge of town on the Graskop Road (guided tours only, daily at 10am, 11am, noon, 2pm & 3pm; R10), where you can see demonstrations of alluvial gold-panning and get a guided tour around the bleak diggers' huts, remnants of workings and machinery from the early mining days. By contrast, if you want to see how those at the top lived, visit **Alanglade**, just west of the Downtown area (guided tours only, Mon–Sat 11am & 2pm; R20), the reconstructed home of the former general manager of the mine. The house has a wonderful collection of early twentieth-century British fashion and decorative arts and reveals a sheltered way of life far removed from either Africa or mining.

Eating and drinking

Pilgrim's Rest has plenty of restaurants and tea shops to provide for the daily influx of visitors using Graskop or Sabie as their base, but the choice of food is a big yawn, with endless pancakes and burgers. Of the **places to eat** in Uptown, *Mona's* (daytime only), on the right above the hotel, has an elevated coffee terrace fronting a shop selling curios and prints, with some gold-mining memorabilia to keep you browsing. There are a couple more daytime places along the Downtown section of the main drag, all of which have outdoor seating: *Scott's Café* (daily 9am–6pm) serves pancakes, sandwiches, salads and other light meals, and has a pleasant bar, while *Jubilee Potters & Coffee Shop* (daily 9am–7pm) does steaks, sandwiches and burgers.

The great indoors

If there's one thing the tourist brochures put across it's that South Africa is a country of big, beautiful landscapes. What you don't often hear about is its abundant architectural heritage, apart perhaps for the odd mention of Cape Dutch buildings. Yet Africans have been developing a wide range of vernacular styles in the countryside for millennia and the country's urban fabric is a richly textured collage of three centuries of colonial – and modern – buildings.

Donkin Street, Port Elizabeth ▲

The Cape Dutch Tokai Manor House ▼

Interior, Sandton hotel, Johannesburg ▼

Mud huts to modernism

The wealth of South African architecture lies in its plethora of traditions, spread across all nine provinces, with as many styles as there are spoken tongues (and remember, this country has eleven official languages – and many others besides).

Take **African vernacular construction**. If you thought this consisted of round mud huts with thatched roofs, you'd only be partially right. Yes, along the Eastern Cape's Wild Coast, the **Xhosa rondavels** that dot the landscape *are* frequently round and made of mud, but at Ondini in rural KwaZulu-Natal, the historic **Zulu beehive huts** are woven – essentially enormous upside-down baskets made from timber interlaced with reeds or grass. Elsewhere, the beautiful **Basotho homes** of Lesotho and the eastern Free State are rectangular, with spectacular earth-coloured wall decorations. Most striking of all are the rectangular **Ndebele houses** of Mpumalanga with their distinctive, brightly coloured geometric motifs, which have entered mainstream graphic design – Ndebele mural artist **Esther Mahlangu** has exhibited worldwide and was commissioned by BMW to decorate one of its art cars.

When it comes to European influences, the sheer diversity of colonial styles is astounding, and no city in southern Africa offers the abundance and variety of **Cape Town**. Stroll down Long Street and you'll be greeted by a collage of frontages spanning three centuries of Dutch and British architecture: the eighteenth-century Palm Tree Mosque rubs shoulders with backpacker lodges housed in two- and three-storey **Victorian** buildings, while the magnificent early-nineteenth-century

Dutch Reformed Mission Church abuts an **Art Nouveau** office.

In the Eastern Cape's oldest city, Port Elizabeth, intact **Country Georgian** terraces from the 1820s could pass for pockets of English South Coast towns, while further east in KwaZulu-Natal, the cities of **Durban** and **Pietermaritzburg** have a touch of the Raj about them – an effect amplified by the subtropical climate, large Indian community, **Hindu temples** and colonial **veranda houses** – large mansions with wraparound porches – built for the local sugar barons.

Inland, the city centre of the Free State capital, **Bloemfontein**, glows when the evening light catches its golden sandstone public buildings. Mostly **late Victorian** and **Edwardian**, these are modest compared to Gauteng's offerings from the same period. The **Union Buildings** in **Pretoria**, for example, are a grand and immensely symbolic pile built in 1912 as the seat of government of the newly federated South Africa – and still used for that purpose, while in **Johannesburg**, the chatter of architecture feels as caffeine-charged as its residents. Here old money (anyone who's had it for more than 50 years) occupies the Edwardian mansions built for the randlords (mining magnates), while new money just builds big. If you're looking for **modern South African architecture**, this is where you'll find it, whether in the ostentatious houses and hotels of Sandton, the extraordinary inverted cone of the Grand Central Water Tower in Midrand, the monolithic BankCity downtown, or South Africa's most ubiquitous contemporary style – the **corrugated iron shacks** of the informal rust and polychrome settlements that are springing up everywhere.

▲ Victorian clock tower, Pietermaritzburg

▼ Ndebele house, Mpumalanga

Historic feather palace, Oudtshoorn ▲

Crossroads township, Cape Town ▼

Colonial architecture, Cape Town ▼

Backcountry buildings

Some of South Africa's most rewarding historic architecture is away from the big cities – off the beaten track, along back roads and in the dorps. In the Western Cape, all over the place you'll encounter picturesque limewashed dwellings that were – and often still are – farmworkers' cottages.

Many of the small country towns take their character from their buildings and the Western and Eastern Cape provinces are particularly rewarding for exploring **Cape Dutch** and **Colonial Victorian** architecture. The settlement of **Matjiesfontein** in the Western Cape is a set piece of Victorian architecture with its castellated *Hotel Milner*, street lanterns imported from England and the period interior decor.

All along the inland R62, which passes through the mountains of the Little Karoo, you'll encounter dorp after dorp with **historic streetscapes**, among them Montagu, Barrydale and Calitzdorp, while Oudtshoorn is striking for its unique sandstone Victorian Gothic "**feather palaces**", built during the ostrich-feather boom.

In the Eastern Cape, Graaff-Reinet, the eighteenth-century frontier town, is particularly well endowed with streets lined with Cape Dutch buildings, while Grahamstown takes its character from its wonderful **Country Georgian** frontages and a number of fortified buildings that testify to the presence of military engineers in this frontier town during the early nineteenth century. From a different era, Pilgrim's Rest in Mpumalanga is an almost perfectly preserved **mining village**, noted for its prefabricated corrugated-iron buildings.

Equally fascinating are the myriad historic **mission stations**, such as Genadendal in the Western Cape with its German-influenced buildings and surreal Pella in the middle of the Northern Cape desert, whose cathedral was erected by French missionaries in the 1880s.

The only place for an evening meal, apart from the hotel, is *Divine*, on the main road Downtown, open daily from 9am until late.

Graskop

Some 15km east of Pilgrim's Rest, **GRASKOP** owes its place on the tourist map to *Harrie's Pancake Shop*, which serves much-imitated but rarely rivalled crepes, and attracts all the tour buses doing the Escarpment viewpoints. The town itself is very ordinary, with timber trucks rumbling heavily through, and nothing much to see in the centre apart from the shops eyeing the tourist trade. Its location, however, as the closest town to the Blyde River Canyon to the north, goes some way towards compensating, and the growing number of artists here, together with a small gay community, are helping to shift Graskop's lumberjack image. One notable village industry is its **wild African silk** factory and showroom, a couple of doors down from the tourist office, which manufactures and sells a range of clothes, soft furnishing, silk-filled duvets and even teddy bears from the silk of mopane silkworms (indigenous to Botswana). Also on the main street is Curio D'Afrique, which sells collectors' items and old African art from French African countries. For adrenaline junkies Graskop's **Big Swing** (℡013 737 8191; R285) is the best of all the big swings on the escarpment – a 68-metre free fall done in under three seconds, on one of the world's highest cable gorge swings. After the drop, you "fly free" across the gorge on a 135-metre highwire "*foefie* slide", 130m above ground, to glimpse the Graskop falls.

Practicalities

Panorama Information & Central Reservations (daily 8am–5pm; ℡013 767 1377, ⓦwww.panoramainfo.co.za), on Louis Trichardt Street, is the official **tourist office**. For **eating**, the legendary and well-signposted *Harrie's* on Louis Trichardt Street serves sweet or savoury pancakes and has a nice outdoor terrace, and an inside dining room with a roaring log fire in winter. *The Silver Spoon*, on the corner of Louis Trichardt and Kerk streets, works hard to compete, with pancakes and waffles from 7am onward. For excellent Portuguese and Mozambican cuisine, try *Canimambo*, on the corner of Hoof and Louis Trichardt streets (daily 9am–9pm; ℡013 767 1868).

Accommodation

Given its diminutive size and lack of excitement, Graskop has a decent spread of accommodation including the delightful, stylish and reasonably priced *Graskop Hotel*.

Graskop Hotel On the corner of High and Louis Trichardt sts ℡013 767 1244, ⓦwww.graskophotel.co.za. One of the nicest places to stay on the Escarpment, with a personal and relaxed atmosphere. Though unprepossessing from the outside, it actually has a very stylish interior of retro furniture, African baskets, fabrics and sculptures. The rooms, some of which are in garden wings, are airy and decorated with considerable flair. ❹

Graskop Log Cabin Village Oorwinning St ℡013 767 1974, ⓦwww.logcabin.co.za. A resort right in the centre of town, with a swimming pool, but no views. Cheaper during the week and for longer stays. There are also now some pretty corrugated iron "settlers' huts" (ⓦwww.settlersvillage.co.za) with verandas, decorated in line with the Pilgrim's Rest theme. ❸

Westlodge B&B 12 Hugenoten St ℡013 767 1390 or 1869, ⓦwww.westlodge .co.za. Bright, spacious rooms and a warm welcome, with a lounge and balcony for guests' exclusive use. ❹

Blyde River Canyon and Blydepoort Dam

There are few places in South Africa where you can enjoy such easily accessible and dramatic scenery than the colossal **Blyde River Canyon**, weathered out of strata of red rock and dropping sharply away from the Escarpment into the lowveld. The **Blyde River Canyon Nature Reserve** (also known as Blyderivierspoort Nature Reserve) stretches from a narrow tail near Graskop in the south, and broadens into a great amphitheatre partially flooded by the **Blydepoort Dam** about 60km to the north.

The views of the canyon are wonderful from both above and below, but the nicest way to take in the vistas is on an easy half-day's drive along the canyon lip. Some 3km north of Graskop, the road branches, the easterly route being a fifteen-kilometre loop (the R534) past a series of superb **viewpoints** (R22 entry fee). The road winds through pine plantations until it comes to the turn-off to the **Pinnacle**, a gigantic quartzite column topped with trees, rising out of a ferny gorge. After another 4km the road reaches the sheer drop and lowveld views of **God's Window**, one of the most famous of the viewpoints; it's also one of the most developed, with toilets and specially constructed stalls for curio sellers. The looping road returns to rejoin the R532, which continues north for 28km beyond the turn-off to reach **Bourke's Luck Potholes** at the confluence of the Treur and Blyde rivers – a collection of strange, smoothly scooped formations carved into the rocks by water-driven pebbles. The best view of all lies 14km beyond, at the **Three Rondavels**. The name describes only one small feature of this cinemascope vista: three cylinders in the shape of huts with the meandering Blyde River twisting its way hundreds of metres below. No photograph does justice to the sheer enormity of the view, punctuated by one series of cliffs after another buttressing into the valley.

▲ Blyde River Canyon

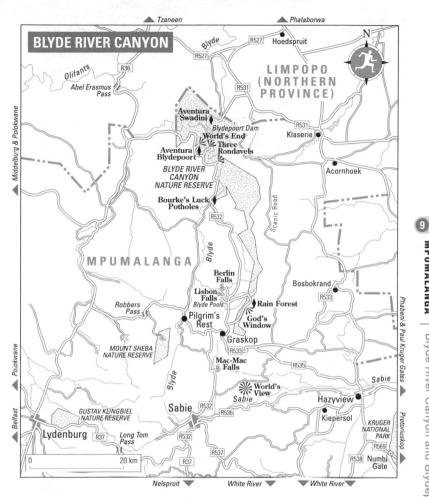

BLYDE RIVER CANYON

The only **place to stay** in the nature reserve is *Aventura Blydepoort* (☎013 769 8005, ⓦwww.foreversa.co.za; ❸), 5km north of the turn-off to the Three Rondavels lookout. The resort has comfortable, self-contained and fully equipped cottages, a swimming pool, supermarket, bottle store and filling station; the atmosphere can feel a little institutionalized, but it's a good place for children.

A guided three-day **Prime Canyon Route** is available with *Hike Africa* (☎084 775 8831, ⓦwww.hikeafrica.co.za), taking in shaded *kloofs*, impressive waterfalls and relaxing pools. You sleep in overnight huts equipped with braai facilities; bring your own hiking gear, including a sleeping bag. The trail costs approximately R100 per day.

Three Rondavels to Blydepoort Dam

The ninety-kilometre **drive** from the Three Rondavels viewpoint to the base of the canyon provides spectacular views of the Escarpment cliffs rising out of the lowveld and is easily incorporated into your itinerary if you're heading to or from Kruger. The drive winds west to join with the R36 and heads north to begin its descent through the Abel Erasmus Pass and then the J.G. Strijdom Tunnel through the mountain, with the wide lowveld plains opening out on the other side. The road takes a wide arching trajectory to circumnavigate the canyon. Apart from near the dam itself, there is some excellent accommodation in the area between the base of the mountains and Hoedspruit, covered in the lowveld section on p.578.

To reach the **Blydepoort Dam**, take the R527 once the road splits when you're out of the tunnel, and follow the signposts to a dead end where you'll find the **Blyde River Canyon Adventure Centre** (daily 7am–5pm; small entry fee; ☎015 795 5961) which has interesting displays on local ecology and a useful model of the canyon that helps you get orientated. Most people come here to take a recommended boat trip on the dam (daily at 9am, 11am & 3pm; R75, children under 12 R45) which has great views of the mountain ravines above and of the formations created by calcium deposits from natural springs. You may catch sight of hippos or crocs, and the spectacular ravines of the Drakensberg. If you want to stay close by, the best place is *Aventura Swadini* (☎015 795 5141, ⓦwww .foreversa.co.za/swadini; ❸) which has **chalets** for up to six and a **campsite** with stunning scenic surrounds; it's great for kids, and cheap for a group, but has a similar institutional feel to its sister resort on the mountain. A number of short trails start from here if you want to explore the environs.

The lowveld

South Africa's **lowveld**, wedged between the Mpumalanga section of the Drakensberg and Mozambique, is part of a vast subtropical region of savanna that stretches north through Zimbabwe and Zambia, as far north as Central Africa. Closely associated at the turn of the last century with fortune-seekers, hunters, gold-diggers and adventurers, these days the South African lowveld's claim to fame is its proximity to the Kruger National Park and the adjacent private game reserves. Although several of the towns on the game park fringes are pleasant enough, most people come here to get into big-game country.

Largest of the lowveld towns, and the capital of Mpumalanga, is **Nelspruit**, accessible by air and bus (including buses from Maputo). East of Nelspruit, the N4 runs close to the southern border of the Kruger, providing easy access to its Malelane and Crocodile Bridge gates; the latter is just 12km north of **Komatipoort**, a humid frontier town on the border with **Mozambique**. From Nelspruit, you can also head 32km south to **Barberton**, an attractive settlement in the hills with strong mining connections, or continue another 41km to **Swaziland**. With your own transport, Barberton makes a more relaxed staging post than Nelspruit for journeys between the south of the Kruger National Park and Swaziland.

The R40 north of the provincial capital passes through **White River, Hazyview, Klaserie, Hoedspruit** and **Phalaborwa**, a series of small towns which act as bases for exploring Kruger. Each town is well supplied with accommodation, and has a Kruger entrance gate nearby; tours are available from some. The closest to Nelspruit and an entry point into the Park, Hazyview is now leader of the pack. Hoedspruit and Phalaborwa actually fall within Limpopo Province, but for the sake of continuity have been included in this chapter.

The lowveld area is **malarial**; for details on necessary precautions, see p.71.

Nelspruit and around

Fast-growing **NELSPRUIT**, 358km east of Johannesburg on the N4, grew in the 1890s as a base for traders, farmers and prospectors, but there is little evidence left of these origins. Most of the old buildings have been ripped out and replaced by shopping malls and freeways, and the town has a bustling and prosperous feel. It's a major commercial centre, not only for the lowveld but also for shoppers from Swaziland and Mozambique.

The town also has the best transport connections in the province, including air links with Johannesburg, Cape Town, Durban and Maputo, with flights to further-flung destinations in the pipeline. Unfortunately, flights to Nelspruit are among the most expensive in the country, and it may work out cheaper to fly into Johannesburg and continue here by car. Nelspruit also has an excellent hospital and all the facilities and shops you might need.

A worthwhile trip, just fifteen minutes out of Nelspruit on the R40 to Barberton, is **Chimpanzee Eden**, where you can see rescued chimps in the trees of their new home.

Arrival and information

Flights on SA Airlink (☎013 750 2531) and Nationwide (☎013 750 2640) arrive at the **Kruger Mpumalanga International Airport** (KMIA; ☎013 753 7500), 20km north of town off the R40 to White River, where you'll find various car-rental companies (see "Listings", p.680). Tina Bohm of Malachite

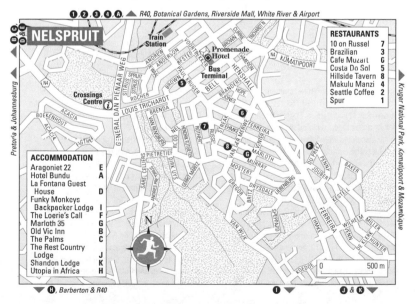

Tours and Transfers (☎083 459 4150, ⓦwww.malachitetours.co.za) meets flights and does reliable and reasonably priced transfers into Nelspruit (or into Kruger and the private reserves, to Hazyview, and onwards from Nelspruit to Mozambique).

Intercity buses stop in the *Promenade* hotel's parking area in Louis Trichardt Street. Greyhound has its offices opposite the hotel (☎013 753 2100). The **Baz Bus** drops off at the town lodges on its trips from Mbabane (Swaziland) and Jo'burg. Citybug **shuttle buses** (☎013 753 3392, ⓦwww.citybug.co.za), which operate daily from Jo'burg and Pretoria, and weekly from Durban, pull into the BP garage in the Sonpark Centre, Piet Retief Street, just south of the city centre. **Minibus taxis** generally rank in Bester Street North, just east of the **train station** (☎013 752 9203), off Andrew Street at the north end of the town centre.

Lowveld Info, signposted as you hit town from Johannesburg, is the town's main **tourist office**. At the Crossings Centre, corner of the N4 and General Dan Pienaar Street (Mon–Fri 8am–5pm, Sat 8am–1pm; ☎013 755 1988/1989, ⓦwww.lcbt.co.za), it provides **maps** and basic information, and arranges accommodation, including bookings for Kruger's restcamps, as well as day-trips with various tour operators. Lowveld Info also has a kiosk at the upmarket **Riverside Mall**, just north of the city centre on the R40. Adjacent to the casino and provincial parliament, the mall has the best collection of shops in the province, and is a good place to stock up if you're planning to self-cater in the Kruger Park.

Nelspruit is also the jumping-off point to **Maputo** in Mozambique. The Cheetah Express (☎013 75 335 71, ⓔdananip@galileo.co.za; R160 one way) is a **shuttle service** between the two cities – it leaves Nelspruit at 4pm (Mon–Sat), a journey of two and a half hours. Tickets can be purchased from the Dana Agency at the Crossings Centre.

Accommodation

Nelspruit's **accommodation** is largely geared to business travellers. Most places have swimming pools to beat the summer heat, outdoor eating areas and tropical gardens.

Aragoniet 22 22 Aragoniet St ☎083 631 2136. Spotless, spacious and cheap self-catering in two garden flats and some log cabins overlooking the river. ❷

Hotel Bundu 11km from Nelspruit off the R40 towards White River ☎013 758 1221, ⓦwww.bundulodge.co.za. Popular, good-value family accommodation in an old-fashioned country hotel, decorated with animal hides and hunting trophies. There are two swimming pools; the hotel also offers horse-riding and hikes to caves with rock paintings. ❷

La Fontana Guest House Corner of John Vorster and Besembos rds ☎013 741 3138, ⓦwww.lafontana.co.za. Mid-range B&B with seven rooms, a relaxed feel and a large pool and garden. ❸

Funky Monkeys Backpacker Lodge 102 Van Wijk St ☎013 744 1310, ⓦwww.funkymonkeys.co.za. Popular hostel with a licensed bar, pool table, shady veranda, swimming pool and broadband Internet. It offers 1to 3-day tours into Kruger, reasonable car rental and can arrange visas in one day for Mozambique. ❶–❷

The Loerie's Call 2 Du Preez St ☎013 744 1251 or 083 283 6190, ⓦwww.loeriescall.co.za. A modern place with a pool, offering upmarket en-suite rooms with private verandas overlooking the Crocodile River Valley. As it's often fully booked, reserve well ahead. ❹

Marloth 35 35 Marloth St ☎013 752 4529, ⓔggink@lantic.net. A simply furnished B&B with ceramic-tiled rooms and breakfast served outdoors. There's a swimming pool and braai facilities. ❷

Old Vic Inn 12 Impala St, 3km from town ☎013 744 0993 or 082 340 1508, ⓦwww.krugerandmore.co.za. Six clean, comfortable doubles and a dorm in a quiet backpacker hostel, with a pool, garden and walks in the adjoining nature reserve. There's also a unit suitable for a family. The owners can arrange transport from the centre of town and from the airport, and can organize tours, including Kruger packages. Other

perks include free breakfasts and good Internet access. Dorms ❶, rooms ❷
The Palms 25 Van Wyk St ☎013 755 4374, ✉thepalmsnelspruit@absamail.co.za. British couple running a good setup with a lovely garden and sunny breakfast room. Three rooms overlook the pool and palm trees, while two back onto the nature reserve. ❸
The Rest Country Lodge Uitkyk Rd, 10km from Nelspruit ☎013 744 9991 or 013 744 9992, ⓦwww.therest.co.za. Each luxury suite in this modern, purpose-built lodge has its own balcony with beautiful views over the lowveld. ❻

Shandon Lodge 1 Saturn St ☎013 744 9934, ⓦwww.shandon.co.za. Rooms with private entrances arranged around a swimming pool and tropical garden, in a well-established colonial-style home. The hosts are friendly and engaged and provide good food – including picnic hampers for a day out in Kruger – as well as loads of information. ❹
Utopia in Africa 6 Daleen St, Sonheuwel Extension ☎013 745 7714, ⓦwww.utopiainafrica .com. Airy rooms under thatch, full of colourful and stylish African artefacts, in a hilly location, 4km from the centre. ❹

The Town

The town centre, roughly six streets crisscrossed by another half dozen, could hardly be easier to get around. The N4 from Johannesburg to Komatipoort sweeps through town, briefly pausing to become **Louis Trichardt**, Nelspruit's main street, before reassuming its identity as the national highway.

Snazziest of the malls is the **Riverside Mall** complex, some 5km north of the city centre, which feels as if it could have been lifted straight out of affluent northern Jo'burg suburbs, with all the same shops, including a well-stocked supermarket, some excellent coffee shops and a better-than-average bookshop. Next to the mall is a casino and, perhaps aptly, the controversial **provincial legislature**, which cost around R600m to build. The massive price tag attached to its towering beehive domes and Queen-of-Sheba-style architecture caused a scandal in 1999 when it turned out that the legislature would have to slash its departmental budgets to pay the construction costs.

Over the road from the Riverside Mall is Nelspruit's major attraction, the **Lowveld National Botanical Garden** (daily: May–Sept 8am–5.15pm; Oct–April 8am–6pm; R10). Set on the banks of the Crocodile River, the garden comes a close second to Cape Town's Kirstenbosch Gardens. Natural waterfalls and walks through rainforest make a pleasant break from the boiling midday heat. If you've been to Kruger, you'll have a chance to look at some of the same **trees** here, grouped according to habitat and helpfully identified with labels. The garden specializes in **cycads** from around the world, and there's also a grove of baobabs from South Africa and other African countries. A useful brochure sold at the entrance gate has a map showing the highlights of the garden and the paths through it. Don't miss the **Makulu Manzi Restaurant**, which has a wooden deck and an outlook over the waterfalls.

Eating and drinking

Most of Nelspruit's **restaurants** are buried in shopping malls, where you'll find all the usual steakhouses and fast-food chains. In the Riverside Mall, *Spur* is good for salads, while *Seattle Coffee* and the *Brazilian* are both excellent for coffee and sandwiches. For a more expensive and imaginative meal, head for *Costa Do Sol* (☎013 752 6382; Mon–Fri noon until late, Sat from 6pm), in Absa Square Building, on the corner of Kruger and Louis Trichardt streets, serving good Portuguese and Italian dishes. Best of all is *Makulu Manzi* (☎013 757 0396; daily 8am–10pm; closed Sun eves) in the Botanical Gardens. The food, including unusual specialities such as ostrich with blue cheese and fig preserve, is beautifully presented, and there's plenty for vegetarians too. For a gourmet dinner, *10 on Russel* (☏013 755 2376; Mon–Sat 10am–10pm) is recommended.

Listings

Car rental Major companies like Avis (☏013 741 1087) and National (☏013 750 2538) have rental desks at the airport, while local firm Abba (☏013 752 7925) is cheaper. The backpacker establishments such as *Funky Monkeys* (see p.678) are able to offer good deals too.
Embassies Mozambique, Brown St ☏013 752 7396.
Emergencies Ambulance ☏013 10177; see also p.75.

Hospitals Nelspruit Private Hospital ☏013 759 0500.
Internet access There is an Internet café in the *Mugg & Bean* restaurant at the Crossings Centre.
Pharmacy Chemist Mopani, Crossings Centre (☏013 755 5500, out of hours ☏082 761 1603).
Post office The main post office, in Voortrekker St, is open 8.30am–4pm. Each shopping centre has a Postnet.

Chimpanzee Eden

Just fifteen minutes out of Nelspruit on the R40 to Barberton is the Jane Goodall-sponsored **Chimpanzee Eden**, dedicated to the rescue and rehabilitation of chimpanzees. The sanctuary is situated on a massive forested conservancy with spectacular views of the nearby De Kaap River mountains, and run by the dynamic and visionary Eugene Cussons, who struggled for more than eight years to secure the required permits and licences. Here you may see chimpanzees, rescued from terrible conditions in places like Angola and Somalia, re-learning to climb trees, foraging for food in the leaves, carefully grooming each other and establishing troop relationships, though you don't get to touch or interact with them in any way. There is a visitors' complex, offering guided tours – geared around feeding times when you'll see all the chimps (daily 10am & 2pm.; R250, children R50; ☏013 745 7406, ⓦwww.janegoodall.co.za). If you want to stay overnight, the five-star *Umhloti Lodge* (☏013 745 7406, ⓦwww .umhloti.co.za; ❽), walkable from the centre, offers luxurious accommodation which includes dinner, breakfast and a guided tour.

East from Nelspruit: Kruger's southern fringe

The N4 east of Nelspruit roughly follows the progress of the **Crocodile River**, which traces the southern boundary of Kruger National Park. For 58km to the tiny settlement of **Malelane**, the road travels within view of the Crocodile's riverine forest, passing lush, subtropical farmlands and the Dali-esque grey formations of granite *koppies*. Some 4km further on, the road turns off to Kruger's **Malelane Gate**, the most convenient entry point for *Berg-en-Dal* restcamp (see p.698). A signpost 12km east of Malelane indicates *Buhala Game Lodge* (☏013 792 4372 or 4817, ⓦwww.buhala.co.za; ❼), a fabulous **guesthouse** on a mango, sugar-cane and papaya farm set high on the banks of the Crocodile, with views across the slow water into Kruger. Trips into the Kruger Park can be arranged from here for around R600 per person, as well as walks in Kruger Park for R450. Even pricier, but good for the soul, is *Serenity Luxury Mountain and Forest Lodge* (ⓦwww.mpumalanga.lodgeguide .co.za; ❼), its nine enormous log cabins set in deep forest. You drive down a bumpy twelve-kilometre track from Malelane to get there, but you're rewarded with butterflies, clear streams and tranquillity. Close by is the Malelane golf course, and the *Lodge* offers golf packages. Two kilometres from Malelane Gate are self-catering garden cottages at *Selati 103* (℡013 790 0978 or 083 305 4479, Ⓦwww.selati103.co.za; ❹–❼), with breakfast or dinner available with notice. While there is no restaurant on site, the Park does have a pool, and there are two well-stocked supermarkets, restaurants and takeaway places 5km away at Malelane village.

Barberton

BARBERTON, 36km south of Nelspruit, began its urban existence after Auguste Robert ("French Bob") discovered **gold** in 1883 on a nearby farm. Despite his attempts to keep the news to himself, other diggers realized something was up when French Bob began building a canal to his claims. The following year, **Graham Barber** discovered another incredibly rich gold reef and got his name hitched to the town at a riotous christening using a bottle of gin. An influx of shopkeepers, hoteliers, barmen, prostitutes, even ministers of religion, soon joined the diggers in the growing frontier town, which consisted of tents, tin, thatch and mud, with nearly every second building functioning as a boozing joint. During the fabulous boom of the 1880s the mines slipped out of the grasp of the small-time prospectors and came under the control of the large corporations that still own them today. This is the best place in the country to take a **gold-mining tour**, or watch gold panning being done. This attraction aside, Barberton also has a colonial backwater charm, reasonably priced accommodation, a handful of historical sights, tropical vegetation and an attractive setting in a basin surrounded by mountains.

The closest and most beautiful route **into Swaziland** from Barberton is through the border crossing at Bulembu (8am–4pm), but the road is poor and should be avoided in the summer unless you're in a 4WD vehicle, though an ordinary car can make it in the dry season. A more practical option which takes the same time, though it's a longer way round, is to enter Swaziland via the border posts of Ngwenya/Oshoek (7am–10pm) or Jeppe's Reef/Matsamo (7am–8pm), the latter route requiring you to pass through the Kaapmuiden toll gate on the N4.

Arrival, information and accommodation

No scheduled public **transport** comes into Barberton, though from Nelspruit you can find a minibus taxi for Barberton. The outstanding **tourist office**, Crown Street (Mon–Fri 8am–4.30pm, Sat & Sun 9am–4pm; ℡013 712 2880, Ⓦwww.barberton.co.za), can help find accommodation in the area, or point you to local walks, as well as supply you with reams of brochures and maps covering the whole province. It can also book **mining tours**, **horse-riding** or **microlight** flights.

Barberton's **accommodation** is cheaper than in its uppity cousins like Hazyview, and just as good.

Barberton Manor 81 Sheba Rd ℡013 712 4826, Ⓦwww.barbertonmanor.com. The town's most upmarket stay is this large mansion, where everything is beautiful and just so. ❹–❺

Fountain Baths Guest House 48 Pilgrim St ℡013 712 2707, @suehicks@icon.co.za. Pleasant B&B rooms and self-catering mini-apartments for two to four people, in a tropical garden edging onto Saddleback Hill. ❸

Old Coach Road Guest House and Restaurant 13km north of Barberton on the R38 to Kaapmuiden ☏013 719 9755, ⓦwww .oldcoachroad.co.za. Comfortable twin and double en-suite rooms, as well as two family units, at a friendly establishment set in its own peaceful grounds, with a pool, big lawn and monkeys in the trees. The licensed restaurant (eves only) has a terrace looking onto spectacular mountains. ❸–❹ Oppikoppi 27 Henry Nettman St ☏013 752 6551 ⓔoppikoppi@promattron.com. Thatched accommodation ranging from bush huts to honeymoon cottages, on a *koppie* with balconies and great views. All self-catering, they're kitted out with everything from irons to microwaves, and there's a pool and *lapa* as well. ❸ The Phoenix 20 Pilgrim St ☏013 712 4211, ⓔphoenix@soft.co.za. Barberton's only hotel, an old-fashioned place renovated by a British hotelier, has a long corridor of comfortable en-suite rooms, and a decent restaurant. ❸

The Town

There are seven working **mines** around Barberton, each with its own entertainment venues, which means you won't find miners packing out public bars as in the wild days of old. You can explore the mining history of the town at the **Barberton Museum**, 36 Pilgrim St (Mon–Fri 9am–4pm, Sat & Sun 9am–1pm & 2–4pm; free), three blocks east of the tourist office. In a well-designed, modern building, the museum has good displays on the gold-rush era. More thrilling is watching young black students working gold from Agnes Mine at the **Umjindi Jewellery Project** (Mon–Fri 8am–5pm, Sat 8am–2pm) next to the museum. The project trains people in the area to become jewellery designers and makers over three years. Some of the work produced is on sale, and there's a good coffee shop doing espressos and lattes – rather adventurous for Barberton.

The museum can provide a map of the town's **Heritage Walk**, on which green and white signposts direct you to some historical houses and monuments. Built for a wealthy middle-class family and restored to its 1904 grandeur, **Belhaven House** at 18 Lee Rd (daily 9am–4pm, with tours on the hour 10am–3pm; R10) is a five-minute walk north from the museum. To the east is the most interesting of the historical houses, **Stopforth House** at 18 Bowness St (daily 9am–4pm; tour times as for Belhaven). The original wood-and-iron

Barberton mining tours and trails

Unlike at Pilgrim's Rest, where you'll have to be content with merely watching how panning was done, at Barberton you can try it yourself. One mine, **Agnes**, offers a two-hour **hike** to Mamba Creek (daily; R120; ☏083 482 1803) where you learn how to pan for gold – swilling water and sand in a big dish to watch for the telltale thread of gold appearing in the dark sand. Agnes is 9km out of town, along the extension of Crown Street, where there is also a restaurant. You need to book for the hike beforehand, and no children under 12 are allowed.

Another fascinating trip is along a disused ox-wagon track, focusing on the geology of the area and showing you meteorite deposits. The trip finishes at **Eureka City**, an 1880s mining settlement that died after forty years. Eureka hasn't been reconstructed like Pilgrim's Rest – you'll only see walls and foundations, after driving through a real mine to get there. To get a sense of what the old mines were like, the two-kilometre circular **Fortuna Mine Hiking Trail**, just south of town, takes you through a disused tunnel built to transport gold-bearing ore to the Fortuna Mine. The trail, which starts at the car park off Crown Street to the south of town, goes through an attractive area of indigenous trees before entering the six-hundred-metre tunnel (bring a torch), and once you're through you get good views of Barberton and the De Kaap Valley. Maps are available from the tourist office.

house and outbuildings were built by James Stopforth, a local baker and general dealer. The entry fee is covered by the visit to Belhaven.

Eating and drinking

Barberton's best place to **eat** is the cheap and friendly *Co-Co Pan* in Crown Street (daily 8am–9pm) which serves straightforward hamburgers, steaks and omelettes. Your best chance to meet locals is to head downstairs to the lively John Henry **pub** below the restaurant. Next to the tourist office on Crown Street is the pleasant *Victorian Tea Garden* (Mon–Fri 8am–5pm, Sat 8am–1pm), with a white gazebo straight out of a London park, and good tea and light snacks served outdoors. The *Old Coach Guest House*, 9km out of town on the R38, is recommended for its beautiful surroundings; it's open only in the evening for three-course meals.

North from Nelspruit: Kruger's western flank

The **R40** heads north from Nelspruit along the western border of the Kruger National Park, passing through prosperous tropical-fruit-growing farmlands and poverty-stricken former black "homeland" areas. The only reason you're likely to find yourself heading north along this road from **Hazyview** is to access the private game reserves – **Sabi Sands**, **Manyeleti** or **Timbavati** – that join up with the western flank of Kruger (see p.708), or to reach the **Orpen Gate**, for the rewarding central section of Kruger National Park. Guesthouses, many of them fairly upmarket, pop up all along the way to Hazyview until you reach the densely populated former Bantustan areas around **Bosbokrand**. Though marked prominently on maps, **Klaserie**, which lies on the border of Mpumalanga and Limpopo Province, is little more than an easily missed petrol station and shop, surrounded by a number of private game farms – poor cousins to the pricier lodges inside the game reserves to the east.

North of the Mpumalanga border you'll pass little towns en route to the central section of Kruger National Park and the Manyeleti and Timbavati private game reserves. Coming down the Escarpment along the R36/R527 from the Blyde River viewpoints, you'll encounter a fork in the road after about 75km. The more northerly road leads to the towns of **Hoedspruit**, which has some good accommodation option in its environs, particularly in the area at the foot of the Escarpment, and Klaserie. Much further north and generally reached from Polokwane on the N1, the mining town of **Phalaborwa** is conveniently 2km from the Phalaborwa Gate into central Kruger and the rewarding camps of Letaba and Olifants.

Hazyview

HAZYVIEW, 43km north of Nelspruit, used to be little more than a couple of large, well-stocked shopping centres buzzing with minibus taxis and small market stalls selling fruit and goods to the surrounding African community. But with the opening of the **Phabeni Gate** into Kruger Park, a mere 10km from town, Hazyview is perfectly positioned for access to the game-rich southern section of the game reserve. The town is one of the best bases for visitors who want to stay outside the park, and do some adventure activities and tours, as well as view game. Best of the activities include encounters with three rehabilitated African elephants at the Elephant Sanctuary and an exhilarating aerial tree-top cable way.

Practicalities

The shortest and quickest route here from Johannesburg, 421km away, is via the N4 and Nelspruit. No public **transport** apart from minibus taxis comes into Hazyview, but if you're staying at one of the local backpacker lodges you can arrange to be collected from Nelspruit. Hazyview is spread out, but **Perry's Bridge**, on the corner of the R536 and R40, is a central stop-off with a small complex of luxury shops, craft outlets and restaurants. **Big 5 Country Tourism** (Mon–Sat 8am–5pm, Sun 10am–1pm; ☎013 737 8191, ⓦwww .big5country.com) is the best information office in Mpumalanga, and can book accommodation, safaris into Kruger Park, adventure activities and transfers. It has created the clearest map of the region and has its own activity booklets, all available at the office. It covers the Escarpment as well. Conveniently, the Paper Chain Internet Café is here too, though is closed on Sundays.

Accommodation

Hazyview has a wide range of **accommodation**, most of it in farmland strung along the roads radiating out to the neighbouring towns of Sabie (the R536), Graskop (the R535) and White River (the R538), as well as to Kruger's Paul Kruger Gate (the R40).

Bohms Zeederberg Country House 17km from Hazyview, on the R536 ☎013 737 8101, ⓦwww.bohms.co.za. Ten individually decorated chalets, set in subtropical gardens around a swimming pool, with magnificent views and walking trails to the river below. Wheelchair-friendly. ❻

Bushpackers at Gecko Lodge 3km from Hazyview on the R536 ☎013 737 8140 or 082 342 6598; ⓦwww.gecko-bushpackers.co.za. Situated next to *Gecko Lodge* (see below), with a swimming pool, camping, dorms and doubles, plus transfers to and from Nelspruit, and trips of a day or longer into Kruger Park. ❶–❷

Eagle's Nest Chalets 5km from Hazyview on the R536 road to Sabie ☎013 737 8434, ⓦwww .eagles-nest.co.za. Twelve well-run self-catering chalets perched on top of a hill, in tropical gardens, with a swimming pool and mini golf. From the R536 take the Kiepersol road and wind up 2.2km of dirt road. ❸

Gecko Lodge 3km from Hazyview on the R536 ☎013 737 8374 or 082 556 6458, ⓦwww .geckolodge.net. Probably the nicest setting in Hazyview, with lush riverine vegetation and a stream running through the grounds. Rooms are decent and well priced, and there is a pub as well as restaurant. The lodge is also the starting point of the aerial cable trails. ❹

Hotel Numbi Main Rd ☎013 737 7301, ⓦwww .hotelnumbi.co.za. An old-fashioned, comfortable

place, right in the centre, offering camping, garden suites and hotel rooms. The grounds are shady and the hotel's restaurant serves good steaks. ❹

Idle and Wild 6km from Hazyview, on the R536 ☎013 737 8173 or 083 283 6190, ⓦwww .idelandwild.co.za. This mango farm in a lush valley on the banks of the Sabie River offers two thatched rondavels, a family unit and two honeymoon suites (with their own spa bath) in the lush garden, as well as two en-suite bedrooms in the main house. All have kitchenettes, and there's a Jacuzzi, sauna and swimming pool – and, for some adrenaline, quad-bike riding on the farm. ❸–❹

Rissington Inn 2km south of town, just off the R40 ☎013 737 7700, ⓦwww.rissington .co.za. A relaxed and informal place (kids are welcome), with fourteen rooms set in the gardens of a large thatched homestead. Best are the garden suites which have roofless outside showers, open to warm breezes and starry skies. You also get a swimming pool and excellent food and service into the bargain. To get here from Hazyview, take the R40 south and watch for the signposts. ❹–❻

Sabi River Sun 2km from Hazyview on the R536 on the banks of the Sabie River ☎013 737 7311, ⓦwww.southernsun.com. A luxury family resort along the Sabie River, landscaped around a large golf course. While it is primarily a time-share resort, there are hotel rooms, a restaurant and pub, and a children's playground with a laid-on activity programme during the school holidays. ❻

Thulamela 1km down White River Rd, off the R40 ☎013 737 7171, ⓦwww.thulamela.co.za. A romantic guesthouse with wine in the fridge and rose petals on the bed, run by a dietician who serves healthy breakfasts. Guests are put up in en-suite timber cottages, each with its own deck, Jacuzzi and bushveld views. No children under 16. ❺

Eating and drinking

There are a number of decent places to eat around Hazyview which, like the town's accommodation, are mostly dotted along the main roads connecting Hazyview with neighbouring towns. Perry's Bridge Centre, on the corner of the R40 and R356, is the best place to stop off, with a couple of good places to eat, plus coffees, beers and pizza. The cheapest all-day breakfasts are also at Perry's, at the Corner Shop, where you can also buy game and beef biltong from its biltong bar. For a delicious African meal, the best place is the evening feast and dancing at Shangana Cultural Village.

Kuka Perry's Bridge Centre ☎013 737 6957. Sophisticated Afro-chic restaurant and cocktail bar with colourful, modern decor and both indoor and outdoor seating. As well as game and meat dishes, there are good salads. Daily from 7am until late.
Perry's Bridge Perry's Bridge Centre ☎013 737 7767. The home-brewed lager and ale is worth a shot, accompanied by a menu of grills, with a reasonable selection for children. Daily from 11am until late.
Shangana 4km out of town on the R535 to Graskop ☎013 737 7000 or 013 737 8191. Delicious African dinners (R233) cooked in massive pots over an open fire by the chief's wives; the menu can include crocodile in spicy peanut sauce, beef and honey-glazed sweet potato, with tropical fruit on skewers for dessert. Vegetarians are well catered for, with plenty of vegetables and a bean dish. You eat in huts and are served very graciously by women from the household. Meals are the climax of a tour of the village and an energetic show of dancing, included in the price.
Summerfields Kitchen 4.5km out of town on the R536 Sabie Rd ☎013 737 6500. Lovely setting on a rose farm (though none for picking or sale). Lunches, served on a wooden deck under cream umbrellas, include mushroom and tarragon pie and home-made pizza, while dinners feature the likes of crispy salmon or peppered fillet. Prices are reasonable and there's a kids' menu and play area. Tues–Sat breakfast, lunch & dinner, Sun breakfast & lunch only.

Hazyview activities: Skyway Trails and the Elephant Sanctuary

There are a couple of really worthwhile activities around Hazyview, both of which can be booked independently, or at no extra charge through Big 5 Country Tourism (see opposite). The **aerial cable way** Skyway Trails (☎082 825 0209 or 013 737 8374, ⓦwww.skywaytrails.com) offers three-hour jaunts (R450) above the trees, on which you glide from platform to platform over the valley, securely clipped to a stout cable. Helmets and harnesses are provided and the guides are capable and fun. No skills are needed, other than a degree of calmness and a head for heights, and children aged 6–10 can ride with a guide. You meet at *Gecko Lodge*, 3km along on the R536, where you are kitted up and given a short lesson before being transported to the hilltop where the trail begins.

At the **Elephant Sanctuary** (☎079 624 9436, ⓦwww.elephantsanctuary .co.za) 5km from Hazyview on the R536 road to Sabie, you can touch and feed the three orphaned elephants rescued from a culling programme, now being rehabilitated into their own "patchwork" family at the sanctuary. A variety of programmes (R500 each) offers close encounters with the elephants – the "Brush Down" Programme, where you groom the animals and feel the texture of their skin and ears, combined with "Trunk in Hand" where you walk alongside them, lightly holding their trunks, are recommended. You can also go for a ride (R895).

If you'd prefer to ride horses, Mzuri Horse Trails, 5km from town along the R536 to Sabie (℡013 737 8191; prices from R125), offers trails of up to three hours through indigenous bush and fruit orchards.

Orpen Gate

After Hazyview, the R40 passes through irrigated farmlands and low hills dotted with bushveld trees. As you approach **Bosbokrand**, 28km to the north, the corridor between the Escarpment and big-game country changes, with the sudden appearance of shantytowns, busy roads, overgrazed lands and dense settlements interspersed with the odd papaya and banana tree. Bosbokrand is also known as **Bushbuck Ridge** (a direct translation from the Afrikaans), the name coming from the hilly finger extending east from the Escarpment – although any bushbucks that might once have wandered here have long since been displaced by the cattle and goats.

Despite the fact that maps indicate little or no habitation, the busy and sometimes hazardous road passes through the former Bantustan of **Lebowa**, where people live crammed at a density six times greater than the provincial average. **Klaserie**, 42km north of Bosbokrand in the middle of game farms, sits poised on the border between Mpumalanga and Limpopo Province. Forty-five kilometres east from here lies **Orpen Gate**. The pick of the places to stay in the vicinity is *Timbavati Safari Lodge* (℡015 793 0415 or 082 362 2922, Ⓦwww .timbavatisafarilodge.com; half board ❹), which has space for couples or larger groups in thatched Ndebele-styled huts, plus a pool, bar and pleasant outdoor dining with wholesome, hearty dinners under the stars. Walks on the property itself are safe, with the chance of sighting giraffe, zebra and buck. Worthwhile visits to the tribal villages across the road can easily be arranged and staff can organize game drives and adventure activities in the area. The *Lodge* is easily accessed, on the Orpen Gate Road, 13km from Klaserie and 20km from the gate to Kruger itself.

Hoedspruit

Lurking in the undulating lowveld, straight up the R40 from Klaserie, with the hazy blue mountains of the Escarpment visible on the distant horizon, is the small but growing service centre of **HOEDSPRUIT**. The town lies at the heart of a concentration of **private game reserves** and lodges, and is a good base for specialist activities, such as **horse-riding** and **rafting** on the Blyde River, visiting **animal rehabilitation centres** and lazy **hot-air ballooning** over the bush.

Hoedspruit is a significant arrival point for air travellers heading for Kruger, though it is not a place to base yourself for the park. Daily flights from Johannesburg and Cape Town arrive at **Eastgate airport** (℡015 793 3681), some 14km south of Hoedspruit. Avis has an office at the airport (℡015 793 2014), and rental outlets in Nelspruit can send cars up to Hoedspruit. For transfers to game lodges from here, contact Eastgate Safaris (℡015 793 3678 or 082 774 9544) though most lodges send vehicles to meet guests. Hoedspruit itself has a small centre, and you'll find everything you might need in the Kamogelo and Crossings Centre shopping malls on the R527 and R40 respectively, including an Internet café at the former and a well-stocked Pick 'n Pay supermarket and ATM at the latter.

There's a mix of **accommodation** available within striking distance of Hoedspruit; westwards towards the Blyde River Canyon are a couple of highly recommended stays, and, as you'd expect with its proximity to Kruger, there are several game activities in the area. To the east, on the fringes of Kruger itself, are some of South Africa's most luxurious safari camps in the **Manyeleti** and **Timbavati** reserves (see p.707).

Around Hoedspruit

The **Moholoholo Wildlife Rehabilitation Centre** lies on the R531 between the R40 and R527, about 3km from the tarred turn-off to the Blydepoort Dam (tours Mon–Sat 9.30am & 3pm, and during school holidays Sun at 3pm; R80; booking essential ☎015 795 5236, ⓦwww.moholoholo .co.za). Ex-ranger Brian Jones has embarked on an individual crusade to rescue and rehabilitate injured and abandoned animals, notably raptors, but also lions, leopards and others. Tours are most informative and you get to see a lot of endangered animals close up. The centre is part of a wider reserve and both night drives and early-morning walks are offered, and there is also accommodation (see p.688). For those interested in more than a visit, there are gap year and volunteer projects – details on the website.

Along similar lines, but not as good, is the **Hoedspruit Research and Breeding Centre for Endangered Species** (more commonly called the **Cheetah Project**; daily 8am–3pm; R100; ☎015 793 1633), 20km south of Hoedspruit on the R40. Open vehicles depart from here every hour on the hour, for a two-hour tour around pens and cages containing cheetah, wild dog, blue crane and other endangered species such as ground hornbills, all bred for restocking and research. A small restaurant on site serves tea, cake, sandwiches and hot dogs.

The **Nyani Shangaan Cultural Village** (☎083 512 4865; ❸), 4km along the Guernsey Road which turns east off the R40, 22km south of Hoedspruit, is a good option for lunch or overnighting, with dinner and a display of traditional dancing laid on. Unlike some of the more commercialized cultural villages, this is a genuine effort developed by Axon Khosa, a local Shangaan man, who asked his grandparents what the villages were like when they were children. He and his extended family take visitors on a tour of the village and offer a **meal**, which is usually a chicken dish with butternut or gem squash, served with wild spinach and groundnuts mixed into *mielie pap*. You can **stay overnight** (booking essential) in a hut with traditional dung floors and thatching that looks untidy by comparison with the safari lodges, but is authentically Shangaan. The walls are constructed with mud from termite mounds and are beautifully hand-decorated with white, orange and black motifs. There are fold-up mattresses, cold showers and flush toilets for guests.

Along the R527, near its junction with the R36, the **Monsoon Gallery** (daily 8.30am–4.30pm; ☎015 795 5114, ⓦwww.countryhouse.com), 29km west of Hoedspruit, makes a good place to pause on your journey. Its great African arts and crafts shop has an absorbing selection of authentic material, including ironwork and woodcarving from Zimbabwe, superb tapestries from the Karosswerkers factory near Tzaneen, Venda pots and jewellery, and African music CDs and books. Also part of the same outfit is a great **place to eat** – *Mad Dogz Café* (☎015 795 5425; daily 7.30am–4.30pm), where breakfasts, lunches and teas are served in a shady garden; service is slow, but the food is well priced and nicely presented. There's also some excellent **accommodation** here (see p.688).

Activities: horse-riding and hot-air ballooning

There are a couple of activities available around Hoedspruit, including **horse-riding** with Off-Beat Safaris, 13km north of town (☎015 793 2422 or

@082 494 1735, @www.offbeatsafaris.co.za; R200), a recommended way to view giraffe, kudu, zebra and wildebeest. Rides set off at 8.30am and 2pm daily, though you do need to book in advance. **Hot-air ballooning** is a fabulous way to appreciate the bushveld, and flights are offered by Wynand from *Otter's Den* (@015 795 5488; R2100). Conditions have to be perfect, and flights are generally very early in the morning when the weather is at its most stable. They leave from different locations depending on the weather – you'll be advised in good time where to meet your flight.

Accommodation around Hoedspruit

Blue Cottages Country House @015 795 5114, @www.countryhouse.co.za. Superbly comfortable suites in a farmhouse filled with African artefacts and fabrics, set in an enticingly cool and colourful tropical garden; more modest, but also beautiful, are the garden cottages. Breakfast is served at *Mad Dogz Café* and you can have a mid-priced dinner served in your garden by candlelight. ❸

Gwala Gwala 35km south of Hoedspruit, on the Guernsey road @015 793 3491 or @083 701 2490, @www.gwala.co.za. The place to go if you're looking for tranquillity, walking and birding. Accommodation is in luxury safari tents; the owners give you plenty of space and privacy, and there are no more than ten guests at a time. Big Five game drives into a neighbouring reserve are included in the rate and drives into Kruger can be arranged. ❽

Moholoholo Forest Camp 26km from Hoedspruit on the R531 @013 795 5236, @www.moholoholo.co.za. *Moholoholo* has three different accommodation options, the best – and most expensive – being *Forest Lodge*, in the foothills of the Drakensberg escarpment, an unshowy yet comfortable safari camp with meals thrown in and plenty of game, including rhino, on the property. For self-catering or B&B there is the more rustic *Mountain View*, off the R531. *Mountain View* ❸, *Forest Lodge* ❼

Otter's Den On the R531, not far from the junction with the R527 @015 795 5488 or 082 572 2223, @www.ottersden.co.za. A small and relaxing camp sleeping eight, on a bush-covered island in the Blyde River recommended for fishing and bird-watching. Arrival at the camp is dramatic: you leave your car and walk over the river on a wooden bridge, with snorting hippos below. The en-suite chalets are on stilts overlooking the river, and there's a river-fed rock swimming pool. Owner Wynand can accompany you on fascinating walks to identify trees and birds, and his passion is running hot-air ballooning trips. Half board ❻

Trackers On the R531 abutting the canyon's cliffs 25km from Hoedspruit @015 795 5033 or 082 494 4266, @www.trackers.co.za. A variety of accommodation – camping, a backpacker house with a dorm and six doubles, self-catering chalets – on a farm with indigenous bushveld vegetation, where you may see zebra and antelope. Half board is available, though do bring your own drinks. A botanist living on the farm runs recommended guided walks through the bush. ❶–❹

Zuleika Country House Signposted on the R531 @015 795 5064 or 082 823 0609, @www .zuleika.co.za. Though close to *Otter's Den*, in a citrus farming area, *Zuleika* doesn't have river frontage, though it has a pretty tropical garden and swimming pool. Its fifteen rooms are all decorated to a high standard, and vary in price depending on whether you self-cater or go for a luxury B&B room with a mountain-facing wooden deck. ❹–❻

Phalaborwa

The most northerly access to the central section of Kruger is at **PHALABORWA** ("pal-a-bore-wa"), 74km north of Hoedspruit. The name means "better than the south", a cheeky sobriquet coined as the town developed on the back of its extensive mineral wealth. During the 1960s, the borders of the park near Phalaborwa suddenly developed a kink, and large copper deposits were found, miraculously, just outside the protected national park area.

Phalaborwa is a 490-kilometre drive from Jo'burg, up the N1 to Polokwane, then the R71 via Tzaneen. The town is right at the gate to the park and is thus an extremely viable base, with some excellent activities on offer. Keen golfers shouldn't miss the chance of a round at the signposted **Hans Merensky Country Club** (☎015 781 3931, Ⓦwww.hansmerensky.co.za), where it's not unusual to see giraffes and elephants sauntering across the fairways. You can whet your appetite before heading into the park with a sundowner **boat trip** with Jumbo River Safaris (booking essential on ☎015 781 6168; R100), which sets out at 3pm down the Olifants River and frequently encounters game, including elephants. Kruger Park's own activities, run from **Phalaborwa Gate** (☎013 735 3547 or 3548), are definitely worth doing, and participants can be collected from their accommodation. Top of the list are the **bush braais** (R350), a combination of a night drive and a braai inside a *boma* at Sable Dam, where you experience all the night sounds of the bush while chomping on your *boerewors*. Bush breakfasts are organized at the same location, which is not open to the general public. The price includes entrance to Kruger Park, plus the food. **Walking safaris** and drives into the park are also bookable at the gate.

Mining began at Phalaborwa some time after 200AD, and the **Masorini Heritage Site**, close to Phalaborwa Gate, is a reconstruction of an iron-smelting village. It comprises a number of granaries and huts with pottery, grinding stones and mats, where the people of Masorini eked out a living from making and trading iron spears, hoes and other metal implements.

You may see dust-encrusted vehicles driving around town which have long aerials with small flags attached to the top of them – this is so that they can be seen from, and not squished by, the big trucks manoeuvring around the mines. Also unusual are the Beware of the Hippos road signs – particularly in the dry winter months, hippos wander about looking for nice gardens to eat up. A resident family of warthogs also wanders the streets.

Practicalities

Regular SA Airlink (☎015 781 5823) flights arrive from Johannesburg at Phalaborwa **airport**, five minutes' drive from Kruger's Phalaborwa Gate, off President Steyn Street. Unfortunately, this is one of the most expensive flights in the country. All Phalaborwa's **car rental** firms are represented at the airport: Avis (☎015 781 3169), Budget (☎015 781 5404) and Imperial (☎015 781 0376).

Two buses do the trip from Johannesburg: Translux (☎015 781 1037) goes via Polokwane, while City to City (same number) takes in Dullstroom, Lydenburg and Hoedspruit. **Phalaborwa Tourist Information**, at the corner of President Steyn and Van Eck Street (closed Sun; ☎015 781 3620, Ⓦwww.phalaborwa.co.za), dispenses the usual services. Phalaborwa has a good selection of **shops**, including the well-stocked *Link* pharmacy, open until 8pm, in the shopping mall in Nelson Mandela Avenue.

The closest Kruger restcamps from here are Letaba, 50km into the park (90-min drive minimum) and Shimuwini, 52km inside. Mad Safari (☎015 781 1200 or 072 418 7286, Ⓦwww.madsafari.co.za) offers transfers from the airport to game farms and lodges, as well as day-trips into Kruger and up the Escarpment.

Accommodation

Phalaborwa has plenty of **places to stay**, with some good options at the lower end.

Daan & Zena's 15 Birkenhead St ☎015 781 6049, Ⓦwww.daanzena.co.za. Brightly painted and friendly B&B (self-catering available) in en-suite rooms located in three neighbouring houses, with a/c and TV in each room, and three swimming pools to choose from. ❷–❸

Elephant Walk 30 Anna Scheepers St ☎015 781 5860 or 082 495 0575, Ⓦwww.elewalk.com. A small and friendly hostel with camping facilities and budget tours into Kruger, and booking service for Phalaborwa/Kruger activities. Besides dorms and twins, they have four en-suite garden rooms, with a swimming pool in the garden. **①**–**③**

Elmecon On the corner of Park and Selati sts ☎015 781 1110, This new B&B has four en-suite rooms with TV and a/c, a swimming pool and a braai. **⑤**

Matomani Lodge Essenhout St ☎015 781 5681. Self-catering apartments in a refurbished 1960s block, with breakfast optional. **④**

Sefapane Lodge Copper St, a 5min drive out of town towards Kruger Gate ☎015 780 6711, ⓦ www.sefapane.co.za. Relaxed and upmarket accommodation in neat beehive huts, with a restaurant, a nice pool and a poolside bar. **⑤**

Eating and drinking

Phalaborwa's selection of **places to eat** is mostly linked to accommodation establishments. The restaurant at *Sefapane Lodge* is pretty decent for lunch or dinner, and its sunken **bar** beside the swimming pool is convivial. You'll find the usual steaks and fresh salads at the *Yurok Spur* in the main shopping mall in Nelson Mandela Avenue, and steaks and pasta at *Buffalo Pub & Grill* (closed Sun) very visible on Hendrick van Eck, the main road out to Kruger. Worth visiting is *Marloe*, 31 Grosvenor Crescent (☎082 493 5403; open daily 10am–6pm), a bistro and tea garden (wheelchair-friendly) with an art gallery and organic herb nursery.

Kruger National Park

KRUGER NATIONAL PARK is arguably the emblem of South African tourism, the place that delivers best what most visitors to Africa want to see – scores of elephants, lions and a cast of thousands of other game roaming the

▲ Leopard and cub at Kruger National Park

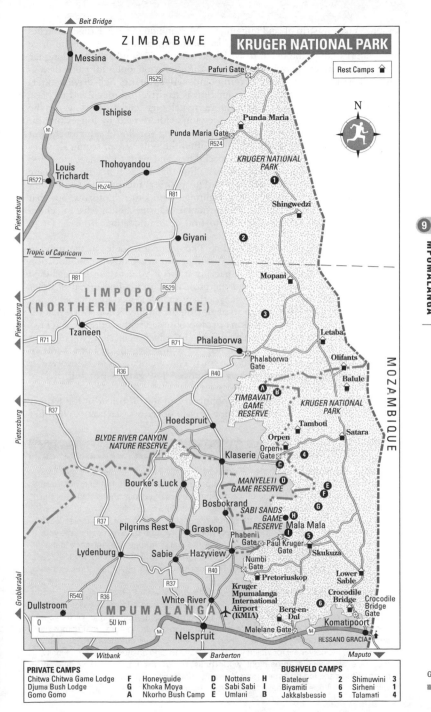

KRUGER NATIONAL PARK

ZIMBABWE

Rest Camps

N

▲ Beit Bridge

Messina

Pafuri Gate

R525

Tshipise

Punda Maria

Punda Maria Gate
R524

KRUGER NATIONAL PARK

Louis Trichardt
R522

Thohoyandou
H524

N1

R81

Shingwedzi

②

Giyani

Tropic of Capricorn

Mopani

R81

R529

LIMPOPO
(NORTHERN PROVINCE)

③

Tzaneen
R71

R71   Phalaborwa

Letaba

Phalaborwa Gate

Olifants

R36

R40

Balule

TIMBAVATI GAME RESERVE

Ⓐ Ⓑ

KRUGER NATIONAL PARK

Hoedspruit

BLYDE RIVER CANYON NATURE RESERVE

Tamboti

Orpen   Satara

Klaserie   Orpen Gate

R37

Ⓒ

④

Bourke's Luck

MANYELETI GAME RESERVE Ⓓ

Ⓔ
Ⓕ

Bosbokrand

SABI SANDS GAME RESERVE Ⓗ

Ⓖ

Pilgrims Rest   Graskop

Ⓘ

Mala Mala

Phabeni Gate

⑤

R37

Lydenburg   Sabie   Hazyview

Paul Kruger Gate

Skukuza

Numbi Gate

MOZAMBIQUE

R540   R36   R37   R40

White River

Pretoriuskop

Lower Sable

Kruger Mpumalanga International Airport (KMIA)

⑥

Crocodile Bridge

Dullstroom

Berg-en-Dal

Crocodile Bridge Gate

MPUMALANGA

Malelane Gate

Komatipoort

0   50 km

Nelspruit

RESSANO GRACIA

N4

▼ Witbank   ▼ Barberton   ▼ Maputo ▼

Pietersburg ◄   Pietersburg ◄   Pietersburg ◄   Grobleršdal ◄

9

MPUMALANGA

PRIVATE CAMPS				BUSHVELD CAMPS	
Chitwa Chitwa Game Lodge		Honeyguide	F	Nottens	H		Bateleur	2	Shimuwini	3
Djuma Bush Lodge		Khoka Moya	G	Sabi Sabi	C		Biyamiti	6	Sirheni	1
Gomo Gomo	A	Nkorho Bush Camp	E	Umlani	B		Jakkalsbessie	5	Talamati	4

savanna. A narrow strip of land hugging the Mozambique border, Kruger stretches across Limpopo Province and Mpumalanga, an astonishing 414-kilometre drive from Pafuri Gate in the north to Malelane Gate in the south, all of it along tar, with many well-kept gravel roads looping off to provide routes for game drives.

Kruger is designed for **self-driving** and **self-catering**. Self-driving offers complete flexibility, though the temptation is to drive too much and too fast, leading to fewer sightings. Furthermore, rental cars tend to be low off the ground and aren't as good for game viewing as those used by lodges or tour operators. However, you can hop in a car knowing you'll find supplies at most of the restcamps – indeed self-driving is often the only way of seeing Kruger's animals if you're travelling with young children and want to manage time and food your own way. Several lodges don't allow under-12s either, though many have started including children over 6. The park's popularity means that not only are you likely to share animal sightings with other motorists, but that **accommodation** is at a premium, particularly during South African school holidays, when you may not be able to find accommodation. Book as far in advance as possible.

Kruger comes pretty close to fulfilling *Out of Africa* fantasies in the **private game reserves** on its western flank – where you get luxury accommodation and food, but, more importantly (especially if this is your first safari), qualified rangers to show you the game and the bush with only a tiny group of other guests. The ideal is to do a bit of each, perhaps spending a couple of nights in a private lodge and a further two or so exploring the public section. But whatever you choose, be sure to relax and don't get too obsessed with seeing the Big Five. Remember that wildlife doesn't imitate TV documentaries: you're most unlikely to see lion-kills (you may not see a lion at all), or huge herds of wildebeest migrating across dusty savanna. The element of luck involved is exactly what makes game spotting so addictive. A few **game-spotting tips** are outlined in the box on p.699.

Walking in the wild is growing in popularity, so much so that in the Kruger Park all of the private reserves and some private operators (see box, p.696) offer

Walks and game drives

Whether you're staying in Kruger or not, you can still join one of the early morning, mid-morning, sunset or night **game drives** organized by the park. Not only are these drives, priced at R130–220, one of the cheapest ways of accessing the park, but the viewing is unsurpassed because of the height of the open vehicles. Drives in smaller, more comfortable vehicles are a little more expensive, but worth it. The drives leave from every camp in the park (book at reception, or even better when you make your reservation) and, for those staying outside the park, from these entrance gates: Crocodile Bridge (☎013 735 6012), Malelane (☎013 735 6152), Numbi (☎013 735 5133), Paul Kruger (☎013 735 5107), Phabeni (☎013 735 5890) and Phalaborwa (☎013 735 3547 or 3548).

For those staying inside the park, three-hour **game walks** (R245) are conducted every morning at dawn from every camp, and there are also afternoon walks (R195). Groups are restricted to eight people, so it's worth booking beforehand, or try your camp when you arrive. **Bush breakfasts and braais**, departing from most camps as well as the entry gates, combine a short drive with a meal outdoors. It's probably going to be the only meal for which you'll ever have to sign an indemnity form. Finally, there are also several three-night **wilderness trails** (see box, p.702) in different parts of the park, led by armed rangers – a fabulous way of getting in touch with the wilderness, but one you'll have to book months in advance.

escorted game walks. Note that Kruger National Park is **malarial**, for more on which, see p.71 .

Some history

It's highly questionable whether Kruger National Park can be considered "a pristine wilderness", as it's frequently called, given that people have been living in or around it for thousands of years. **San hunter–gatherers** have left their mark in the form of paintings and engravings at 150 sites so far discovered, and there's evidence of farming cultures at many places in the park. Around 1000–1300 AD, centrally organized states were building stone palaces and engaging in **trade** that brought Chinese porcelain, jewellery and cloth into the area.

But it was the arrival of white **fortune seekers** in the second half of the nineteenth century that made the greatest impact on the region. African farmers were kicked off their traditional lands in the early twentieth century to create the park, and there has been an ambivalent attitude to the hunters, criminals and poachers (like the notorious ivory hunter Cecil Barnard), who made their livelihoods here decimating game populations. Barnard's exploits are admiringly recounted in the *Ivory Trail* by T.V. Bulpin, while every other episode of the still-popular yarn, *Jock of the Bushveld*, set in the area, includes accounts of hunting.

Paul Kruger, former president of the South African Republic, is usually credited with having the foresight to set aside land for wildlife conservation. Kruger figures as a shrewd, larger-than-life figure in Afrikaner history, and it was **James Stevenson-Hamilton**, the first warden of the national park, who cunningly put forward Kruger's name in order to soften up Afrikaner opposition to the park's creation. In fact, Stevenson-Hamilton knew that Kruger was no conservationist and was actually an inveterate hunter; Kruger "never in his life thought of animals except as *biltong*", Stevenson-Hamilton wrote in a private letter. He also remarked that few people had any interest in wild animals unless they were dead. It was his tenacity which saved the animals which hadn't been shot out, rather than Kruger's. Times have changed a lot in the management of the park: the first black director, David Mabunda (currently head of SANParks), was appointed in 1998.

Kruger is going from strength to strength. The park has been extended into Mozambique with the establishment of the Great Limpopo Transfrontier Park, and two border posts linking Kruger to Mozambique have been created, one right at the north of the park at Pafuri near *Punda Maria Camp*, the other at Giriyondo, between *Letaba* and *Mopani* camps. In another recent development, SANParks has awarded concessions to private operators to open a handful of luxury lodges inside Kruger itself; for more details of these, check the commercially run website ⓦ www.krugerpark.co.za. Accommodation for all camps in the park can now be booked through SANparks central reservations (see box, p.697).

When to visit

Kruger is rewarding at any time of the year, though each season has its advantages and drawbacks. If you don't like the heat, avoid high **summer** (Dec–Feb), when on a bad day temperatures can nudge 45°C – though they're generally in the mid- to high thirties. Many of the camps have air conditioning or fans, and it's definitely worth considering renting an air-conditioned car. Throughout the summer the heat can be tempered by short thunder showers. At this time of the year, everything becomes greener, softer and prettier, and from early November you're likely to spot cute young animals.

Among the nearly 150 species of **mammals** seen in the park are cheetah, leopard, lion, spotted hyena, wild dog, black and white rhino, blue wildebeest, buffalo, Burchell's zebra, bushbuck, eland, elephant, giraffe, hippo, impala, kudu, mountain reedbuck, nyala, oribi, reedbuck, roan antelope, sable antelope, tsessebe, warthog and waterbuck.

The staggering 507 **bird species** include raptors, hefty-beaked hornbills, ostriches and countless colourful specimens. The **birders' "big six"** are saddle-billed stork, kori bustard, martial eagle, lappet-faced vulture, Pel's fishing owl and ground hornbill.

Keep your eyes open and you'll also see a variety of **reptiles, amphibians** and **insects** – most rewardingly in the grounds of the restcamps themselves: there's always something to see up the trees, in the bushes or even inside your rondavel. If you spot a miniature ET-like reptile crawling upside down on the ceiling, don't be tempted to kill it; it's an insect-eating gecko and is doing you a good turn. If, however, you have a horror of insects or frogs, stay away from Kruger in the rainy season (Nov–March).

Common among the three-hundred-plus **tree** species are the baobab, cluster fig, knobthorn, Natal mahogany, monkey orange, raisin bush, tamboti, coral tree, fever tree, jackalberry, leadwood, marula, mopane, lala palm and sausage tree.

There's little rain during the cooler **winter** months of April to August; the vegetation withers over this period, making it easier to spot game. Although daytime temperatures rise to the mid-twenties (days are invariably bright and sunny throughout winter), the nights and early mornings can be very cold, especially in June and July, when you'll definitely need warm clothes. Rondavels in the public restcamps have heaters in the bedrooms. A definite plus of winter is the virtual absence of mosquitoes and other insects.

Orientation

The public section of Kruger can be divided roughly into **three sections**, each with a distinct character and terrain. If your time is limited, it's best to choose just one or two areas to explore, but if you're staying for five days or more, consider driving the length of the park slowly, savouring the changes in landscape along the way.

The southern, central and northern sections are sometimes referred to as "the circus", "the zoo" and "the wilderness" – sobriquets that carry more than a germ of truth. The **southern section** has the greatest concentration of game, attracts the highest number of visitors and is the most easily accessible part of the park if you're coming from Johannesburg, 478km away on the N4. The park **headquarters** is here (at *Skukuza*), with an **airport**, car rental, a filling station, car repair workshop, car wash, bank, post office and doctor, as well as rondavels to accommodate a thousand people. The **central section** also offers good game viewing, as well as two of the most attractive camps in the park at **Olifants** and **Letaba**. The further north you go, the thinner both animal populations and visitors become, but it's the **northern section** that really conveys a sense of wilderness, reaching its zenith at the marvellously old-fashioned **Punda Maria** camp, which dates back to the 1930s. If you are keen on bird-watching, the far north of the park is a must. Make sure you take the S63 along the Pafuri River to **Crooks' Corner**, especially in summer when the area offers some of the best birding in South Africa.

Outside the public section, big-game country continues in several exclusive and expensive **private game reserves**, clustering on huge tracts of land to the west, often referred to as Greater Kruger. The three major private reserves are **Sabi Sands** to the south and **Timbavati** and **Manyeleti**, adjoining the central section of the national park. As far as animals are concerned, the private and public areas are joined in an enormous, seamless whole. The only real differences are that private reserves are not places you drive around yourself, and they offer a greater sense of being in the wilderness as there are no tarred roads or buildings away from the lodges. If you do arrive by car, you'll have to leave it at the lodge and you won't see the vehicle again until you leave. Finally, note that the private reserves don't allow day visits.

Getting to Kruger and the private reserves

It's possible to **fly** into Nelspruit (see p.677; for the southern section), Hoedspruit (see p.686; for the central and northern sections) or Phalaborwa (see p.688; for the northern section) and rent a car for the rest of the journey. SAA and SA Airlink fly **from Johannesburg** to Nelspruit and to Phalaborwa; SA Airlink also flies **from Durban** to Nelspruit and **from Cape Town** to Nelspruit and Hoedspruit. Nationwide is slightly less expensive, and flies **from Cape Town and Johannesburg** to Nelspruit. If you're staying in a private game lodge, you can arrange to be transferred from any of these airports. If money is no object, you can fly into Nelspruit and take one of the small planes which service the expensive lodges.

Unfortunately, flights to airports near Kruger are pricey and there are no special deals. If you're in Cape Town or Durban, you may find it cheaper to take a budget flight (with kulula.com, for example) to Johannesburg and rent a car at the airport for the easy, five-hour drive to the park; the airport is on the N4 motorway to Kruger.

Another option for Kruger is taking a **bus** to Nelspruit or Phalaborwa from Johannesburg and booking one of the many **tours** on offer at the backpacker lodges. The *Old Vic Inn*, *Funky Monkey* and *Elephant Walk* in Nelspruit and Phalaborwa respectively can both arrange tours; in **Hazyview** contact *Backpackers at Gecko Lodge* (see p.684). There are even tours from Johannesburg itself which make life really easy, especially if your international flights depart or arrive in Jo'burg, and you're on your own (see box, p.696).

Kruger entrance gates

There are nine **entrance gates** along the western and southern borders of Kruger. The N4 **from Johannesburg** brushes along Kruger's southern boundary en route to Mozambique and quickly gets you close to the **southern gates** of Malelane (☏013 735 6152), 411km away, and Crocodile Bridge (☏013 735 6012), another 57km further on. These are also the closest if you're coming **from KwaZulu-Natal**, either via Barberton or Swaziland. If you've been exploring the **Blyde River Canyon** area, access is off the R538/R40 between White River and Klaserie to the **western gates** (Phabeni ☏013 735 5890, Paul Kruger ☏013 735 5107, Orpen ☏013 735 6355, and Phalaborwa ☏013 735 3547 or 3548) leading into the southern and central sections of the park. The easiest way to get to the two **northern gates** on the west side is off the N1 from Johannesburg to Musina on South Africa's northern border, taking the R524 east at Makhado for Punda Maria Gate (☏013 735 6870), or the R525, 58km further north, to Pafuri Gate (☏013 735 5574; see p.737).

If you're trying to get from one part of the park to another, note that although it's far more fun driving inside, the **speed limit** (see box, p.697) makes it a slow journey – and you're bound to make frequent stops to watch animals.

There are an increasing number of tours to Kruger – your best bet for getting there if you're not driving. Most of these depart from Johannesburg. Prices given are per person unless otherwise noted. Most safari companies cover the conservation fees as part of their deal.

Bundu Bus Tours and Safaris ☏011 675 0767, ⊛www.bundusafaris.com. A range of safaris, all departing and returning to wherever you're staying in Johannesburg, Pretoria or Nelspruit. Most popular is a four-day trip, starting in the south (daily except Sun; R3600); after camping there for two nights (in tents with beds), you spending the third at *Bundu Safari Lodge*, 30km from Orpen Gate. Longer tours also taking in Swaziland, KwaZulu-Natal and Botswana are available.

Livingstone Trails ☏082 654 9478, ⊛www.livingstonetrails.co.za. Four-day trips from Johannesburg, taking in the spectacular Blyde River Canyon, and day and night drives in Kruger Park. You can choose camping (R3250) or bedded accommodation in private lodges (R3950). The price includes full board on the middle days, plus dinner on the first day and breakfast on the last.

The Machampane Wilderness Trails Camp ☏012 426 5111. Three-night/four-day walking-trail experience on the Lebombo plateau, with an experienced and armed game ranger, staying in eight-bed, en-suite tented and fully catered accommodation in a forested area at the source of the Machampane River (R2700).

Outlook Small Group Explorations ☏011 894 5406, ⊛www.outlook.co.za. Four-day trips in the southern section of Kruger, with three nights in National Parks accommodation. Groups are small (two to five), and you're collected and returned to your lodgings in Johannesburg. The price, R6050 per person, includes food, accommodation in chalets, game drives and guide hire.

Rhino Walking Safaris Bridget Bagley ☏011 467 1886, ⊛www.rws.co.za. Three- to four-night stays, with morning and afternoon walks, based either at the *Rhino Post Safari Lodge* on the pretty Mutlumuvi River (R2750), or at *Plains Camp*, on the Timitene Plain (R2250), where accommodation is in luxury tents; the price for the latter includes a hike to an overnight camp in the bush consisting of sleep-out decks among tree-tops in tents raised 10m off the ground.

Shingwedzi 4x4 Eco-Trail Johan Kriek ☏012 348 2708. Guided 4WD trail which departs from Punda Maria, entering Mozambique at Pafuri, and follows the Shingwedzi and Limpopo rivers, traversing the park from the east across Nwambiya Sandveld and back, to end at Massingir Dam. The cost is R3800 per vehicle per four-night trail (no vehicles provided; max 6 vehicles per trip).

Transfrontiers ☏083 382 5098 or 083 700 7987, ⊛www.transfrontiers.com. One of the best and most reputable options if you want to walk in Kruger. On its four-night/five-day safaris (R5300), which depart regularly from Jo'burg hostels, you spend two nights in the Timbavati Reserve, and two nights in Klaserie. Accommodation is in large tents with proper beds, duvets and pillows. The guides are knowledgeable and fun.

Wildlife Safaris ☏011 791 4238 or 011 792 2080, ⊛www.wildlifesaf.co.za. Three-night Kruger trips (R4540 or R3920 economy option), which include one night at a comfortable safari camp, and two inside the park using National Parks accommodation. Worth thinking about is its four-day trip from Johannesburg, taking in Hluhluwe-Imfolozi Park (see p.514) after Kruger, and ending in Durban (R5480 or R4860 economy).

Kruger restcamps and bushveld camps

At most of the fourteen main **restcamps** inside Kruger, the sounds of the African night tend to get drowned out by air conditioning and the merriment of braais and beer. It's not all bad news, though; at least you'll have all the facilities you could ever want on hand. Nearly all camps have electricity, public telephones, petrol stations, shops (though they don't stock much in the way of fruit or vegetables), restaurants, laundrettes and snack bars. Most now also have pools and offer game drives and game walks, while some do bush breakfasts and bush braais combined with night drives. These activities are very popular and worth booking when you make your initial reservation. The restcamps are very pleasant, with walks around the edges, labelled trees to help you identify what you see on drives, and plenty of birds and smaller creatures around the camps themselves. Several, including *Lower Sabie*, *Skukuza*, *Olifants* and *Letaba*, have views onto rivers where, from a distance, you can see game coming to drink.

Accommodation at all the Kruger camps has been upgraded and renovated. You'll find **thatched rondavels**, each with an outdoor eating area and facing communally towards each other rather than out towards the views. The best rondavels are on the camp perimeters or directly facing onto rivers. Just about all restcamps now have a **campsite** (with shared kitchen and washing facilities), which provide the park's cheapest accommodation (R40, children R20). Sites for **caravans** and **camper vans** are available wherever there's camping and often have a power point.

Most camps have **furnished safari tents** and **huts** (R185–500), in configurations usually sleeping two to four people. These are fully equipped, with shared communal kitchens and ablutions.

Kruger essentials: the public section

Kruger's restcamps and bushveld camps are administered by SANParks (☎012 428 9111, ⊛www.sanparks.org/parks/kruger) – the place to book accommodation in advance (though on the day you can book directly with the camps). The **conservation fee** at Kruger is, for most foreign visitors, R132 per day (children aged 2–15 pay R66). If you're planning on **staying** at the park over school holidays or weekends, book well ahead. Booking in writing opens thirteen months in advance; closer to the date, you can usually book somewhere, especially at off-peak times, if you're not too particular about where you stay in the park.

Every restcamp is fenced off and has a gate that's open at the times indicated below. You are required to return to your restcamp or leave the park prior to closing times. Except where specified, all times refer to both park and camp gates, and are strictly upheld.

Jan	4.30am–6.30pm (camp); 5.30am–6.30pm (park)	Sept	6am–6pm
		Oct	5.30am–6pm
Feb	5.30am–6.30pm	Nov & Dec	4.30am–6.30pm (camp); 5.30am–6.30pm (park)
March	5.30am–6pm		
April	6am–6pm		
May–July	6am–5.30pm		

The **receptions** at restcamps are open daily from 8am to 5.30pm, **shops** from 8am until half an hour after gate closing. **Restaurants** open between 7am and 9am for breakfast, between noon and 2pm for lunch and between 6pm and 9pm for dinner.

Driving

Only approved roads should be used; don't drive on unmarked roads and never drive off-road. Do buy a Kruger **map** showing all the marked roads. Roads have numbers rather than names. Some are tarred, some are dirt. **Speed limits** are 50kph on tar, 40kph on untarred roads and 20kph in restcamps; speed traps operate in some parts of the park. Never leave your car (it's illegal and dangerous), except at designated sites.

Bungalows, cottages and family cottages (R500–1005) sleep two to six people and come in several variations, with fully equipped kitchens and bathrooms.

Top of the range includes **guest cottages, guesthouses and bush lodges** (R985–1870) containing multiple bedroom units with en-suite bathrooms, kitchens, living rooms and exclusive views.

For a more rustic experience, head out to one of the handful of **bushveld camps** (R995 sleeping four) away from day-to-day trivialities and the tourist pack. The bushveld camps have accommodation of the same standard as the main restcamps, but accommodate fewer people, and are far smaller. They dispense with shops or restaurants, but are within reasonable reach of the restcamps – just in case you can't survive without a Coke.

Southern Kruger restcamps

The so-called "circus" is the busiest section of the Kruger, with its hub at **Skukuza**, the biggest of all the Kruger camps, and **Lower Sabie**, one of the most popular. Apart from containing some of the best places for seeing large quantities of game, southern Kruger is also easily reached from Johannesburg along the N4. At peak times of year, the area buzzes with vehicles jostling to get up close anywhere that big cats are sighted – events which always seem to induce bad human behaviour.

Berg-en-Dal

In the southwest corner of the park, 12km northwest of **Malelane Gate**, **Berg-en-Dal** (℡013 735 6106 or 6107) is set attractively among *koppies* in a shallow grassy basin (its Afrikaans name means "hill and dale"). Built in the 1980s, the camp overlooks the Matjulu stream and dam, and has modern, fully equipped chalets that break with the Kruger tradition of thatched rondavels. The chalets are landscaped among indigenous bushveld vegetation and are widely spaced to provide privacy. Facilities include a beautifully positioned swimming pool, a shop with a good range of food, a licensed restaurant reputed to give excellent service, snack bar, filling station and laundry.

The focus of the camp is the Rhino Trail along the perimeter fence (with Braille facilities), meandering under riverine trees along the Matjulu dam, where there are resident crocodiles and nesting fish eagles. Game includes white rhino, leopards and lions, and plenty of kudu. Sable and mountain reedbuck are among more unusual sightings. Some say this is the best camp from which to set out on a morning walk, because of the high likelihood of encountering white rhino, and the pretty scenery.

Crocodile Bridge

East of *Berg-en-Dal*, **Crocodile Bridge** (℡013 735 6012) is the least impressive of Kruger's restcamps, and its position at the very southern edge of the park, overlooking sugar-cane farms, does nothing to enhance your bush experience. However, old hands say this is a tremendously underrated camp as there is a high density of general game, and you have an excellent chance of seeing the Big Five.

Located at the **Crocodile Bridge Gate** on the north bank of the Crocodile River, the camp is reached via Komatipoort, 12km to the south on the Mozambique border. Accommodation includes camping, two-bed permanent tents and en-suite bungalows sleeping two to three, with cooking facilities. Amenities are limited to a laundry and filling station, and a shop selling basic supplies.

Game-viewing tips

For a general survey of South African fauna and habitats, see "Wildlife", pp.844–860. The excellent *Make the Most of Kruger*, available at most restcamps, is well worth investing in for the basic interpretation it provides of the park ecology and for filling in those empty moments. For an accessible and engrossing guide to the **behaviour** of African mammals, check out the widely available *Safari Companion* by Richard Estes (see "Books", p.881); even commonplace species such as impala become fascinating when you understand what they're doing and why, and this provides constant interest on days when, for instance, big cats stubbornly refuse to put in an appearance. Another winner is *Exploring Kruger,* a Prime Origins guide with a separate Kruger Park map, by Brett Hilton-Barber and Lee Berger, which details the best drives and locations to see particular animals and birds.

Here are some pointers to bear in mind both before and during your game-viewing excursion:

- The best times of day for game viewing are when it's cooler, during the early morning and late afternoon. Set out as soon as the camp gates open in the morning and go out again as the temperature starts dropping in the afternoon. Take a siesta during the midday heat, just as the animals do, when they head for deep shade where you're less likely to see them.

- It's worth investing in a detailed **map of Kruger** (available at virtually every restcamp) in order to choose a route which includes rivers or pans where you can stop and enjoy the scenery and birdlife while you wait for game to come down to drink, especially in the late afternoon.

- **Driving really slowly** pays off, particularly if you stop often, in which case switch off your engine, open your window and use your senses. Don't try consciously to spot animals – many are well disguised. Instead, watch for any movement or something that strikes you as a bit out of place. There are also the smells and sounds of the wilds; twigs breaking or the alarm calls of animals can hint at something afoot.

- Don't embark on overambitious drives from your restcamp. You'll see as much game sitting quietly in your car as you would frantically driving around all day. Other stopped cars are often a good indicator of a game sighting.

- **Binoculars** are a must for scanning the horizon.

- Take **food and drink** with you – you don't want to have to break off that terrific lion-sighting because you're starving. When you feel you've had your fill of game viewing, you could make for one of Kruger's designated **picnic sites**, where there's always boiling water available, tables and chairs to enjoy your picnic in the wild, and braai places powered with gas.

Try the tarred H4 north and dirt S25 east for elephant, rhino and buffalo. For cheetah, among the best places are the open plains along the S28 Nhola Road. If you're pushing north to *Lower Sabie*, it's worth taking the drive slowly, as this area, dotted with knobthorn and marula trees, is known for its herbivores, which include giraffe, kudu, steenbok, wildebeest, zebra, buffalo and waterbuck as well as ostrich, warthog and the magnificent black sable antelope. You should also keep your eyes peeled for predators such as lion, cheetah, hyena and jackal.

Lower Sabie

Some 35km north of *Crocodile Bridge*, often fully booked and very busy, ⚑ **Lower Sabie** (☎013 735 6056 or 6057) occupies game–rich country that places it among the top three restcamps in the Kruger for animal-spotting. The surrounding open savanna and the camp's position on the banks of the Sabie

River attract game to drink and graze, and the terrain around here is rated among the most beautiful in the southern Kruger. Within kilometres of the entrance gate to the camp, a number of waterholes and dams populated with crocodiles and hippos make good spots to park and watch for game coming to quench their thirst. In the thorn-thicket country hard by the west of the camp, you'll find promising terrain for catching sight of elephants moving between the trees as well as white rhino grazing on the sweet grasses, which also bring herds of buffalo and, in their wake, lions. Accommodation includes camping, safari tents, bungalows and guest cottages, some with river views. There's a restaurant, a cafeteria, a shop, a swimming pool, a filling station and a laundry.

Pretoriuskop

Due west of *Lower Sabie*, but not directly connected to it, **Pretoriuskop** is reached via **Numbi Gate** (℡013 735 5128 or 5132), 9km to its west. Set in an area of sourveld, characterized by granite outcrops, tall grass and sickle bush favoured by mountain reedbuck, sable and white rhino, the camp is in an area stalked by lions, wild dogs and side-striped jackals. However, given the dense bush, game viewing is disappointing, and all you're likely to spot are larger species such as kudus and giraffes. While this isn't the best camp for game, it's worth doing the Voortrekker Road (H2-2) from Numbi Gate to Crocodile Bridge and stopping off at the historical plaques along the way, commemorating various explorers and traders.

Accommodation consists of en-suite cottages and guesthouses, bungalows and cheaper huts and camping with shared ablution and cooking facilities. The camp has a restaurant, a snack bar, a shop, a laundry, a semi-natural rock swimming pool – one of the most beautiful in Kruger, with a surrounding garden and picnic area – and a filling station. Around the perimeter fence at night, you're almost certain to see patrolling hyenas, waiting for scraps from braais.

Skukuza

Kruger's largest restcamp, **Skukuza** (℡013 735 4152), accommodates over a thousand people, and lies at the centre of the best game-viewing area in the park. Its position is a mixed blessing; although you get large amounts of game, hordes of humans aren't far behind, and cars speeding at animal sightings can chase away the very animals they are trying to see.

Accommodation is in a range of en-suite guesthouses, cottages and bungalows, or more cheaply in huts, safari tents and camping, with shared ablutions and kitchens. The closest entry point is through **Paul Kruger Gate**, 12km to the west, which in turn is 42km east of Hazyview. *Skukuza* is the hub of Kruger, with its own airport and car-rental agency, and its sprawling collection of rondavels resembles a small town. There are two swimming pools, and a deli café with **Internet** facilities. Its garage can repair your vehicle, and there's also a post office, a bank, a filling station, two **restaurants**, a **cafeteria** and a really good **library** (Mon–Fri 8.30am–4pm & 7–9pm, Sat 8.30am–12.45pm, 1.45–4pm & 7–9pm, Sun 8.30am–12.45pm & 1.45–4pm), with a collection of natural-history books and exhibits. Another highlight of *Skukuza* is the **open-air cinema** showing wildlife videos every evening under the stars. **Golf** at Skukuza is also a draw: eighteen holes costs R210. Night drives and day drives in open vehicles can be arranged at the main complex – the night drives are excellent, since all the other vehicles are safely tucked up for the night, and you'll have the road to yourself.

Skukuza lies on the edge of the Sabie River, which is overlooked by a wide paved walkway furnished with park benches, from which you can see crocodiles floating by like driftwood on the brown water. Most people drive along the Sabie River to *Lower Sabie*, on the H4, one of the best places in the whole park to see game. The tangled riverine forest, flanked by acacia bush and mixed savanna, is the most fertile and varied in the park. Another great drive is northeast on the H1-2 to Tshokwane picnic site, stopping at Elephant, Jones, Leeupan and Siloweni waterholes.

Central Kruger restcamps

Game viewing can be extremely good in the "zoo", the rough triangle between *Orpen, Satara* and *Letaba,* which is reckoned to be one of the global hot spots for lions. At **Olifants** you'll find the Kruger's most dramatically located camp, with fantastic views into a river gorge, while **Satara** is one of the most popular – its placement is ideal for making sorties into fertile wildlife country. It is estimated that there are about sixty lion prides in this central area, but, even so, you may not be lucky enough to see one.

Orpen and Maroela
Like *Crocodile Bridge*, **Orpen** (☎013 735 6355) is located right by an entrance gate, 45km east of Klaserie, and is recommended mainly if you're arriving late and don't have time to get further into the park before the camp gates close. *Orpen* is very good for game viewing though, far preferable to its southern counterpart, because the substantial Timbavati Private Game Reserve lies to the west of Orpen, so you're already well into the wilderness once you get here.

The camp is small, peaceful and shaded by beautiful trees; it's a lovely drive from here along a river to get to *Satara*, the nearest big camp. Facilities include a filling station, a shop and a swimming pool, and accommodation is in bungalows and en-suite guest cottages, with communal kitchens. If you want to camp, you'll need to go to the small **Maroela** satellite camping area, overlooking the Timbavati River, approximately 4km from *Orpen*. You must report to *Orpen* reception to check in before going to the campsite, which has electricity.

Tamboti
Not far from Orpen Gate, Kruger's only tented camp, **Tamboti** (☎013 735 6355), is reached by turning left 2km after *Orpen* and continuing for 1km. You sleep in budget (R275) or semi luxury (R625) safari tents in a tranquil position on the banks of the frequently dry Timbavati River, set among apple leaf trees, sycamore figs and jackalberries. From the tents, elephants can often be seen just beyond the electrified fence, digging in the river bed for moisture, hence the camp's popularity (you'll have to book ahead to be sure of getting a place). The Timbavati River roads (S39 and S40) can be rewarding for game.

Each walk-in tent has its own deck overlooking the river, but best of all are numbers 21 and 22, which enjoy the deep shade of large riverine trees, something you'll appreciate in the midsummer heat. The tents have fridges and electric lighting, while all kitchen, washing and toilet facilities are in two shared central blocks (bring your own cooking and eating utensils).

Satara
Forty-six kilometres due east of Orpen Gate, **Satara** (☎013 735 6306 or 6307) ranks second only to *Skukuza* (92km to the south) in size and the excellence of its game viewing. Set in the middle of flat grasslands, the camp commands no great views, but is preferable to *Skukuza* because it avoids the feeling of suburban boxes on top of each other. Very busy in season, accommodation ranges from

Wilderness trails

Undertaken with the guidance of an experienced ranger, Kruger's three-night **wilderness trails**, listed below, pass through areas of notable beauty with diverse plant and animal life. However, they don't bring you closer to game than driving; they're really about getting closer to the vegetation and smaller creatures, though you have a good chance of encountering big game. Groups are limited to eight people staying in the same camp, comprising four rustic, two-bed huts, served by reed-walled showers and flush toilets; simple meals are provided. You walk for five hours in the morning, return to the camp for lunch and a siesta, and go walking again for an hour or two in the evening, returning to sit around a campfire.

The trails are heavily subscribed. You can **book** up to thirteen months in advance through SANParks (see p.697). The cost is around R2510 per person, including accommodation and meals.

•**Bushman Trail** covers the southwestern section of the park, near *Berg-en-Dal* restcamp. The trail camp is in a secluded valley, characterized by granite hills. San paintings in many of the hill shelters are an added feature.

•**Metsimetsi Trail** is midway between Skukuza and Satara, with the camp at the foot of a mountain and overlooking a small waterhole. Black rhino and large predators move through the undulating savanna and rocky gorges and ravines.

•**Napi Trail** sets out from a camp between *Skukuza* and *Pretoriuskop* into woodland bushveld. Undulating terrain and granite hills suit the area's resident population of white rhino, while black rhino, elephant, lion and buffalo are also often seen. Birdlife is prolific.

•**Nyalaland Trail** is based in the remote northern section of the park along the Madzaringwe Stream north of *Punda Maria*. The area is known for its fever-tree and baobab forests, prolific birdlife and spectacular views.

•**Olifants Trail** has its camp on the southern bank of the Olifants River, from which it offers a magnificent view of the river. Riverine bush and gorges characterize the terrain, and lion, buffalo and elephant are often seen.

•**Sweni Trail** overlooks the Sweni stream in the wilderness area near Nwanetsi, and provides a view of marula and knobthorn savanna. A resident pride of lions pads about here and is frequently seen.

•**Wolhuter Trail** lies in the vicinity of *Berg-en-Dal* and *Pretoriuskop* camps in the southern section of the park, where rhinos are relatively common, as is a wide variety of other game.

•**Olifants River** Backpack Trail is a new guided, three-night trail, catering for adventurous souls and following the course of the Olifants River. You are required to be self-sufficient – carrying your own food, bedding and so on – but this is more than compensated for by the spectacular scenery and exciting wildlife. Maximum group size is eight, and needs to be booked by one party.

camping, through bungalows and cottages arranged around lawned areas shaded by large trees, to secluded guesthouses; besides a shop, filling station, laundry and AA vehicle repair workshop, there's also a swimming pool, restaurant and cafeteria, where you can eat in a virtual blizzard of noisy birds.

About halfway along the tarred road between *Satara* and *Skukuza*, the area around Tshokwane picnic site can be good for lions, hence the number of motorists here. The area around *Satara* itself is usually good for sighting grazers such as buffalo, wildebeest, zebra, kudu, impala and elephant. Rewarding drives are the Timbavati River Road (S39) and the drive east of Satara along the S100, which snakes along the N'wanetsi River towards the Lebombo Mountains marking the border with Mozambique.

Balule

On the southern bank of the Olifants River, **Balule** (☎013 735 6306 or 6307) is 41km north of *Satara* and 87km from Phalaborwa Gate. A very basic satellite to *Olifants* (11km to the north), *Balule* is one of the few restcamps where two can stay for under R100 without resorting to camping.

Compact *Balule* has two sections, one consisting of six rustic three-bed rondavels and another of fifteen camping and caravan sites. Each section has its own communal ablution and cooking facilities. There are iron washstands with enamel bowls and no windows. You can forget about air conditioning; the only electricity is in the fence to keep out lions. Guests have to bring their own crockery, cutlery and utensils, and must report to *Satara* or *Olifants* at least half an hour before the gates close.

Olifants

With a terrific setting on cliffs overlooking the braided Olifants River, **Olifants** (☎013 735 6606 or 6607) has a charmingly old-fashioned feel and is reckoned by many to be the best restcamp in Kruger. It's possible to spend hours sitting on the benches on the covered look-out terrace, gazing into the valley whose airspace is crisscrossed by Bateleur eagles and yellow-billed kites cruising the thermals, while the rushing of the water below creates a hypnotic rhythm. Of the thatched, en-suite rondavels, numbers 1–24 boast superb views overlooking the valley; it's worth booking well in advance to get one of these. There are also more exclusive guesthouses. You can eat at the restaurant or the snack bar, and there's a shop and a laundry.

The river marks the division between rugged, rocky veld with ghostly fever trees growing along the riverbanks to the south, and, to the north, mopane woodland which attracts the large antelope such as eland, roan, sable and tsessebe. This is also promising country for spotting elephant, giraffe, lion, hyena and cheetah, and you should look out for the tiny klipspringer, a pretty antelope that inhabits rocky terrain which it nimbly negotiates by boulder-hopping. A highlight of the area is some of the dirt roads which loop along the Olifants River.

▲ Sunset at *Olifants*

Mountain biking is a new venture at Kruger, available only at *Olifants*. Only six people at a time, accompanied by armed field guides, can go on the trails (hence it's best to book in advance through *Olifants* directly or SANPark), and the scenery is wonderful. The morning or afternoon ride costs R300, while the full-day 24-kilometre Mozambique Border Trail (consisting of three different routes graded for difficulty and technicality) is R600.

Letaba

Letaba (☏013 735 6636 or 6637) is set in *mopane* shrubland along the Letaba River, 34km north of *Olifants*. Old and quite large, the camp is beautifully located on an oxbow curve, and though very few of the rondavels afford a view, the restaurant does have great vistas; you can spend a day just watching herds of buffalo mooching around, elephants drifting past and a host of other plains game. There is the full range of accommodation and the camp offers the usual shopping and laundry facilities, a swimming pool, a vehicle-repair workshop, and an interesting **museum** with exhibits on the life of elephants, including displays on bulls with inordinately large tusks.

Northern Kruger restcamps

You won't find edge-to-edge game in the northern "wilderness", the least visited of Kruger's regions, but you do get a much stronger feeling here of being in the wilds, particularly after you've crossed the Tropic of Capricorn north of **Mopani** camp and hit **Punda Maria** camp, which feels like a real old-time outpost in the bush.

Mopani

Some 42km north of *Letaba*, **Mopani** (☏013 735 6535 or 6536) is one of the newer camps in Kruger and overlooks the Pioneer Dam. The dam, one of the few water sources in the vicinity, attracts animals to drink and provides an outstanding lookout for a variety of wildlife, including elephant, buffalo and antelope.

A sprawling place in the middle of monotonous *mopane* scrub, the camp is designed more for driving than walking. There's modern en-suite accommodation built of rough-hewn stone and thatch – bungalows, cottages, guest cottages and houses, a restaurant – above average for Kruger – and a bar with a good view across to the dam. Other facilities include a shop, a laundry and filling station; the swimming pool provides cool relief after a long drive.

Shingwedzi

A fairly large camp featuring a campsite, square, brick huts and a few older, colonial-style whitewashed, thatched bungalows, one cottage and a guest-house, **Shingwedzi** (☏013 735 6806 or 6807), 63km north of *Mopani*, is sited in extensive grounds shaded by *pals* and *mopane* trees. The dining room has a terrace, frequented by starlings and cheeky hornbills jostling to pounce on your food. From the terrace you get a long view down across the usually dry Shingwedzi River. Look out for the weavers' nests with their long, tube-like entrances hanging from the eaves outside reception and the cafeteria. Facilities include a shop, a filling station and a swimming pool, and night drives are on offer.

Punda Maria and Pafuri

Kruger's northernmost camp, 🛖 **Punda Maria** (☏013 735 6873), 71km beyond *Shingwedzi*, is a relaxed, tropical outpost near the Zimbabwe border.

To aficionados, this is the real Kruger, the park's wildest and least visited camp, regarded as unpretentious and peaceful. There's less of a concentration of game up here, but this isn't to say you won't see wildlife (the Big Five all breeze through from time to time) – it's simply that you have to work that much harder at spotting game in the woodlands and dense *mopane* scrubland.

The real rewards of *Punda* are in its landscapes and stunningly varied vegetation, with a remarkable nine biomes all converging here, which also makes it a paradise for bird-watchers. The landscape around Punda has many craggy sandstone cliffs, the hilltops crowned with giant baobabs, some as old as 4000 years. Accommodation is camping, or in safari tents, with communal cooking and ablution areas, or en-suite fully equipped bungalows, two of them family bungalows. The camp has a very simple restaurant, a small shop and a filling station, a swimming pool and bird hide. From *Punda Maria* you can go on a guided visit to the spectacular historical and archeological site of **Thulamela** with its majestic location – overlooking the confluence of the Luvuvhu and Limpopo rivers. The stone ruins are reminiscent of Great Zimbabwe, and the inhabitants of Thulamela traded with those of Great Zimbabwe from the fifteenth to mid-seventeenth centuries.

Pafuri picnic site, 46km north of Punda, should on no account be missed, as it's here that you'll experience the true richness of northern Kruger. The site is a large area under the shade of massive thorn trees, leadwoods and jackalberry trees on the banks of the Luvuvhu River and is the ultimate place for lunch. An interpretation board gives a fascinating account of human history in the area. There are braai facilities, a constantly boiling kettle to make your own tea, and the attendant can sell you ice-cold canned drinks.

Bushveld camps

If you want to stay at a bushveld camp, book as early as possible, as demand for the bush experience they offer is pretty high. Note that the camps are out of bounds to anyone not booked in to stay. Most offer game drives during the day and at night.

Bateleur

About 40km southwest of *Shingwedzi* restcamp, ⚑ **Bateleur** (☎013 735 6843) is well off the beaten track, in the remote northern section of the park on the banks of the frequently dry Mashokwe stream. The camp has a timber viewing-deck, excellently placed for views of game coming to drink at a seasonally full waterhole. The nearby Silver Fish and Rooibosrand dams also attract game as well as birdlife in prodigious quantities. There are three six-bed cottages and four four-bed cottages; each has its own kitchenette and fridge, with electricity provided by solar panels.

Biyamiti

⚑ **Biyamiti** (☎013 735 6171) lies on the banks of the Mbiyamiti River, about 41km northeast of the Malelane Gate and 26km west of Crocodile Bridge Gate. Its proximity to the latter is one of the main advantages of this very southerly camp. Another plus point is that the terrain attracts large numbers of game including lion, elephant and rhinos. There are ten two-bed guest cottages and five one-bed cottages, all with fully equipped kitchens.

Boulders Bush Lodge

An exclusive bush lodge, **Boulders Bush Lodge** (book through and check in at *Mopani*; see p.704) must be reserved en bloc (max 12 people, R1870). The camp is embedded in rocky outcrops, a backdrop to cottages built on stilts, where wooden boardwalks connect bedrooms to the communal area and viewing deck. Bedrooms are all en suite and the communal living area consists of a kitchen, dining room, bar, lounge and braai area. There is only solar power here.

Sable and Shipandani overnight hides

Unique accommodation for intrepid visitors (R300 for 2 people, up to 6 accommodated), these are bird hides by day which transform into primitive overnight dwellings by night. The *Sable* hide, approximately 10km from Phalaborwa Gate, overlooks the Sable Dam where an abundance of animals gathers to drink. Contact Phalaborwa Gate (see p.688) for bookings. *Shipandani* is situated 3km south of *Mopani* on the Tzendze River, frequented by buffalo herds and many elephant bulls. Contact *Mopani* (see p.704) for bookings.

Shimuwini

Shimuwini (☎013 735 6683) lies on the upper reaches of the Shimuwini Dam, which is filled by the Letaba River, about 50km from the Phalaborwa Gate on the Mooiplaas Road. Situated in *mopane* and bushwillow country, with sycamore figs along the banks of the river, this peaceful camp is not known for its game but is a perennial favourite among bird-watchers. It's an excellent place for spotting riverine bird species, including fish eagles. Accommodation is in five two-bedroom cottages, nine more elite two-bedroom guest cottages, and one three-bedroom guest cottage.

Sirheni

Sirheni (☎ 013 735 6860) is on the bank of Sirheni Dam, roughly 54km south of *Punda Maria*. It's a fine spot for bird-watching, beautifully tucked into riverine forest, with some game also passing through the area. The big pull, however, is its remote bushveld atmosphere in an area that sees few visitors. There are five four-bedroom cottages and ten guest cottages, all en suite and equipped with kitchens, and the camp's two bird hides are a great pull.

Talamati

Lying on the banks of the usually dry Nwaswitsontso stream, about 31km south of Orpen Gate, the mixed bushwillow woodland setting of **Talamati** (☎013 735 6343) attracts giraffe, kudu, wildebeest, zebra and predators like lion, hyena and jackal, as well as rhino and sable. Two hides within the perimeter of the camp overlook a waterhole, where game viewing can be excellent. The camp has ten comfortable two-bedroom and four smaller one-bedroom cottages arranged in an L-shape along the river in a forest of leadwoods and russet bushwillows.

Tzendze Rustic Camp

The back-to-basics **Tzendze Rustic Camp** (☎013 735 6535 or 6536), opened in November 2006, caters for those who wish to escape the typical Kruger camp vibe. It is 7km south of *Mopani*, where the nearest shop is situated. There is no electricity here – the lighting in the ablutions is from a solar battery system and hot water in the outdoor showers is from gas geysers. There are thirty camping sites (sites 14, 15 and 16 are best), but as each is surrounded by trees and scrub the atmosphere is wild and rustic.

Private reserves – Greater Kruger

Kruger's western flank is comprised of private reserves, whose boundaries with Kruger are unfenced – the whole zone is often referred to as **Greater Kruger**. Within each reserve are a number of safari lodges, each on large tracts of land, and while there are neighbouring safari camps, there are no fences. Lodges with smaller properties often gain traversing rights on larger or better stocked areas, and rangers are in radio contact with other vehicles when big game is found, so that game sightings are shared. Rules are strict about the number of vehicles allowed at a sighting, so that, for example, if you are watching lions, there are only likely to be two vehicles present. While vehicles are allowed to drive all over the bush in Sabi Sands, which gives great viewing as you follow, for example, a leopard walking through a rocky river bed, there is much concern about off-road driving causing harm to the environment. Manyeleti and *Honey-guide Camp* get a big thumbs-up for obeying no off-road driving regulations, which certainly keeps vegetation and smaller creatures from harm.

The largest area of land is owned by *Mala Mala* in the Sabi Sands, with an extensive boundary with Kruger Park. Several tiny airstrips are in operation, with planes buzzing in and out from Nelspruit or Johannesburg, though you can drive in an ordinary car to all the lodges or camps. Some establishments have three different lodges on their properties, each one different in character, and with some price variations.

It's in these private reserves that you'll find utterly luxurious and romantic accommodation, fabulous food and classic safaris on Land Rovers, where you'll see plenty of big game, smaller animals and birds. All lodges follow the same basic formula: full board, with dawn and late-afternoon game drives conducted by a ranger, assisted by a tracker, in open vehicles. Afternoon outings usually turn into night drives following sundowners in the bush. In winter months you'll be given blankets on the vehicle and even hot water bottles in some places, to cope with the cold. Dinners are inevitably lamplit, around a fire, in the open. They all also offer bushwalks, usually after breakfast, and most overlook waterholes or plains, so that you can look out for animals during the time you're in camp, when you're not lazing around the pool or perusing their collection of animal books.

The **Sabi Sands reserve** (Ⓦ www.sabi.krugerpark.co.za) is one of the best places in the world for seeing leopards and lions. **Sabi Sands South** is the most exclusive of all the game-viewing areas in South Africa, not only because of the superb game, but because of its proximity to Nelspruit, and by car it's an easy one- to two-hour run to the lodges from Hazyview. **Sabi Sands North** is cheaper, and the game is good, but access is more difficult. From the R40 you turn east at Acornhoek, travelling along dirt roads through traditional African villages for a couple of hours to reach the lodges. The same goes for **Manyeleti** which is north of Sabi Sands. **Timbavati** is the most northerly reserve, accessed from the Orpen Gate road, but easier to reach, with far less travelling on dirt roads, than either Manyeleti or Sabi Sands North.

In terms of **wildlife**, if it's leopards you are after, Sabi Sands is best, especially in the south, where they have become quite blasé about people and vehicles. Timbavati is much quieter and wilder than Sabi Sands, and is known for its large herds of buffalo, with plenty of lions and elephants, though it's not good for viewing leopards and cheetah, with the one exception of *Gomo Gomo Lodge* where you could well see leopards. Timbavati's name is associated with the extraordinary phenomenon of **white lions**, and while you may see some prides carrying the recessive gene which makes them look a little paler, the last sighting of a full-on white lion was in 1993. Manyeleti has a good spread of all game, with some stirring landscapes of open grasslands and rocky outcrops, where it borders Kruger. During the apartheid days, Manyeleti was the only part of Kruger black people were allowed in, and consequently is far less developed than the other reserves, with little accommodation, which works to its advantage in that there are fewer vehicles about.

Prices are undeniably steep in the private reserves – you're paying for the African wilderness experience, and for rangers who are dedicated to showing you as much as possible. Prices quoted are per person per night sharing a room, and go from R2500 upwards, including all meals and all game activities. Winter rates are less, and some places offer winter specials. High season is between December and April. Several quote prices in US dollars, rather than in SA rands. You need to book ahead, and get driving instructions to your camp, as no pop-ins are allowed. All the lodges below come recommended and are all highly rated.

Manyeleti

Honeyguide 4km from Orpen Gate ☎ 011 341 0282, ⓦ www.honeyguidecamp.com. One of the more reasonably priced camps, and the only one to offer tented accommodation at each of its two locations, *Khoka Moya* which takes children and is contemporary in design, and *Mantobeni*, which has more of a traditional safari camp feel. With a lack of tended gardens, the camps maximize the bush feel, and although they don't have views of a river or a waterhole, they make up for it with attentive staff and superb rangers and trackers. Each tent is enormous and has its own bathroom with double showers and basins. Tea is brought to your tent early in the morning while you snuggle under duckdown duvets. The best thing about *Honeyguide* is that there is an imaginative children's programme, and great tolerance of children of all ages. Rangers will take your kids off your hands and make casts of animal tracks in the bush, teach them about wildlife and in the evenings sit them on cushions around the campfire. Meals are plated, and all beverages, including wine, are included in the price. Another plus is its location: just 4km down a dirt road from Orpen Gate. From R2600.

Timbavati

Gomo Gomo To the north, accessed from Orpen Rd ☎ 013 752 3954, ⓦ www.gomogomo.co.za *Gomo Gomo*'s draw is its position on a river which doesn't dry up, and good game viewing. The decor and thatched chalets are unexciting and it lacks the glamour and style of the upmarket lodges, but if your criteria is around spending less, this is an excellent choice. There are five chalets and four tents, some of them designed to take families. R1450.

Umlani Accessed from Orpen Rd, close to Orpen Gate ☎ 012 346 4028, ⓦ www.umlani.com. Eight reed-walled huts overlooking the dry Nhlaralumi River, each with an attached open-topped bush shower, heated by a wood boiler (there's no electricity). *Umlani* (the name means place of rest) isn't fenced off, the emphasis being very much on a bush experience, and windows are covered with flimsy blinds so that you get to hear all the sounds of the night. Showering in the outside shower and looking up at the stars is a highlight. The decor is simple, as is the food, though it's delicious and you don't end up overstuffed. Altogether, *Umlani* delivers a much more satisfying experience of the wilds than many other places, which are more like hotels in the bush. R2250.

Sabi Sands North

Chitwa Chitwa Game Lodge ☎ 011 883 1354, ⓦ www.chitwa.co.za. Beautifully set on the edge of the largest pan (lake) in the Sabi Sands, where you'll definitely see animals coming to drink as well as resident hippos and crocodiles. *Chitwa Chitwa* provides both luxury and the chance to spot big cats, but keeps its rates lower than high-profile neighbours to the south. It's the prettiest of the northern Sabi Sands lodges, and each sublimely comfy suite has a fireplace and a view of the water. The food is good and guests are occasionally treated to a sit-down breakfast out in the bush after their morning game drive. Two swimming pools allow kids to use one, and adults to enjoy lengths in the other. Rooms vary in price according to the level of luxury, from R2000 to R4000.

Djuma Game Reserve ☎013 735 5118, ⓦwww.djuma.com. Djuma's *Bush Lodge* is a relaxed place set in mixed woodland with eight, smallish A-frame thatched chalets decorated in simple but tastefully pared-back style. Service and guiding couldn't be better. For a hip, contemporary African feel with township art and funky fittings, Djuma's *Vuyatela* is one of the most imaginative of Kruger game lodges, each five-star suite also having its own plunge pool and mini-bar. Moreover, there is a library, gym and wellness centre for massages and beauty treatments. Good Internet access at both lodges, and children accepted at *Bush Lodge*.

Djuma is one of the more socially minded establishments, with traditional village trips organized during the day between game drives, and they support preschools in Dixi village. From R3870 at *Vuyatela* and R2750 at *Bush Lodge*.

Nkorho Bush Camp ☎013 735 5367, ⓦwww.nkorho.com. A small, family-operated outfit in thinly wooded grassland, *Nkorho* scores on affordability. The lack of pretence and the homely atmosphere give *Nkorho* the feeling of being on a friend's farm. There are six simple, comfortable, rectangular chalets with showers, catering to a maximum of sixteen guests. The communal areas comprise an open-air lounge area, a bar with a pool table and an African fantasy of a *boma* – constructed from gnarled tree trunks – where evening meals are served around a large open fire. The swimming pool overlooks a productive waterhole. From R1675.

Sabi Sands South

Mala Mala ☎011 268 2388, ⓦwww.malamala.com. The most fabled and exclusive game lodge in Southern Africa, which offers terrific game viewing, memorable food and great rangers – and rich and famous people in your vehicle. Nonetheless, the atmosphere is friendly and relaxed, *Main Camp* has thatched suites set along a river, a small gym and gracious gardens. Children are accepted and often a family is given its own Land Rover and guide. Guests get a certificate at the end for "capturing" the Big Five. *Main Camp* is the most affordable, while the other camps on the property, *Sable* and *Rattray's*, are more exclusive and consequently more expensive. *Main Camp* from R3895.

Nottens Bush Camp ☎013 735 5105, ⓦwww.nottens.com. Two decades old and still resisting the temptation to expand, this family-run outfit is one of the most popular and attractive small camps. Dinners are served at a communal table, with other meals either on a massive deck that acts as a viewing platform for the plain in front of the camp or, in winter, in the *boma* around a campfire. Accommodation is for a maximum of 18 (children over 8 welcome) in pleasant chalets lit by paraffin oil lamps, and with tin roofs. The lack of electricity is part of the camp's philosophy of bringing guests into contact with the bush. From R2900.

Sabi Sabi ☎011 447 7172, ⓦwww.sabisabi.com. *Sabi Sabi* has four different lodges, of which the largest, *Bush Lodge*, can't fail to please – the suites with indoor and outdoor showers, patios and gardens are fantastic, it's game rich, it's an easy drive from Hazyview, and the food buffets are extraordinary. *Bush Lodge*, though, has a hotel feel, with room for forty guests, television, mobile phone reception, Internet and a raft of Land Rovers waiting to take guests out on safari. But if you're just here to see game and don't actually want the wild, this is a perfect choice. Children are welcomed at *Bush Lodge* where they can also watch DVDs. For the very wealthy and childless, *Earth Lodge* is extraordinary, disguised, as you approach it, by bush and grass-covered hummocks. It's ultra-luxurious, contemporary eco-chic with a meditation garden, and an easel and paints in every suite, along with your very own butler to select something terrific from the large wine cellar. From R4500 at *Bush Lodge* to R6500 at *Earth Lodge*.

Travel details

Trains

Nelspruit to: Johannesburg (1 daily; 10hr); Pretoria (1 daily; 8hr).

Buses

Nelspruit to: Durban (weekly; 8hr); Johannesburg (3 daily; 5hr); Maputo (Mozambique; 2 daily; 4hr); Pretoria (3 daily; 4hr).

Baz Buses

Nelspruit to: Johannesburg (3 weekly; 4hr); Manzini (Swaziland; 3 weekly; 2hr 30min); Mbabane (Swaziland; 3 weekly; 3hr 30min); Pretoria (3 weekly; 5 hr).

Flights

Nelspruit KMIA to: Cape Town via Johannesburg (1 daily; 4hr); Durban (1 daily; 1hr 30min); Johannesburg (3–6 daily; 1hr 50min); Maputo (Mozambique; daily; 1hr 35min).
Hoedspruit to: Johannesburg (1 daily; 1hr).

Limpopo

CHAPTER 10

Highlights

✳ **Exploring the Letaba**
Experience this otherworldly area of forests, subtropical tea plantations, misty lakes and upmarket country-house guesthouses. See p.720

✳ **Horse-riding in the Waterberg** This mountain range offers some of South Africa's finest wilderness riding and horseback safaris. See p.725

✳ **Lapalala Wilderness** A wildlife conservation area at the heart of the Waterberg Biosphere, containing the world's only rhino museum. See p.727

✳ **Soutpansberg Mountains**
Spend the night in the mountains watching the magical display of stars above and let the soothing sound of the gushing waterfall gently lull you to sleep. See p.731

✳ **Venda crafts** Explore the remote, simple villages of the mystical Venda region and discover its skilful and distinctive art, pottery and wood carvings. See p.732

▲ Baobob

⑩

Limpopo

impopo province is South Africa's no-man's-land: a hot, thornbush-covered area caught between the dynamic heartland of Gauteng and, to the north, the Limpopo River, which acts as South Africa's border with Zimbabwe and, further west, Botswana. Running through the centre of this no-man's-land is the busy **N1** highway, here often called the **Great North Road**. The N1 links a series of towns established by the Voortrekker settlers; most of these are little more than service centres for the surrounding farmland, and there is no good reason to spend any time in any of them. The N1 is also South Africa's umbilical cord to the rest of Africa, and the importance of the N1 overshadows the rest of the province.

The eastern side of the province is game-rich lowveld, dominated by the seventy-kilometre-wide strip of Kruger National Park abutting the Mozambique border. This part of Limpopo is covered along with Kruger itself in the preceding chapter. The principal attractions of the rest of the province lie in its three wild and distinctive **mountain escarpments**. The most significant of these is the first rise of the **Drakensberg** Escarpment, on its long and often spectacular sweep through South Africa from north to south, marking the descent from highveld to lowveld. There's a lot to see in the mountains

Name changes in Limpopo

What was once known as South Africa's Northern Province was renamed **Limpopo** in 2002 and the capital, Pietersburg, was subsequently renamed **Polokwane**. A number of other towns with "colonial" names have also undergone official name changes, though some of these changes have been taken to court for various political and procedural reasons. Although the ruling in some instances has been found against the name change, this won't stop the same change being put forward again in the future. Whatever the outcome in each individual case, the old names won't fall out of use all that quickly, and the new failed names will also still be heard, especially as the amending of signage is proving a slow process. Examples of these that you are bound to come across while travelling in the province include:

Old name	New name
Ellisras	Lephalale
Louis Trichardt	Makhado
Messina	Musina
Naboomspruit	Mookgophong
Nylstroom	Modimolle
Potgietersrus	Mokopane
Warmbaths	Bela-Bela

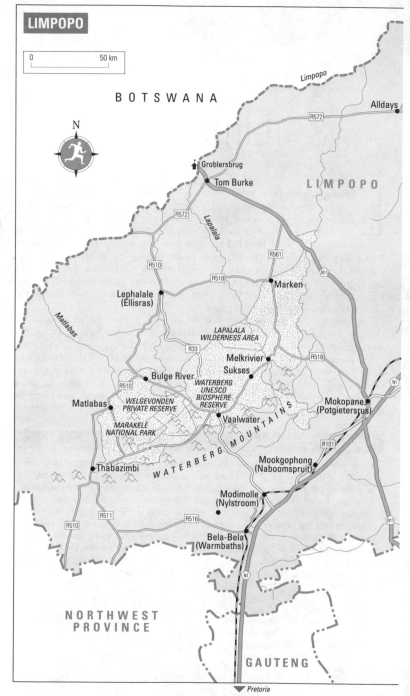

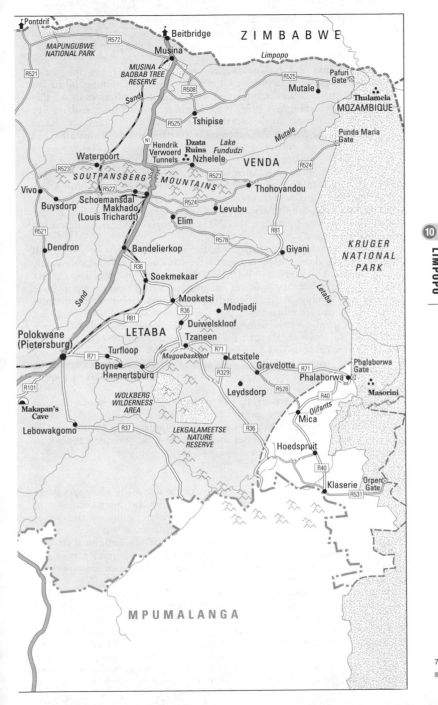

themselves, especially in the haunting, forested slopes of the **Letaba** area immediately to the east of **Polokwane**, the provincial capital. This region of lakes and waterfalls also provides some excellent walking and comfortable country guesthouses.

On the tranquil and remote western side of the N1 lies the sedate **Waterberg** massif. Once a domain of cattle farming and hunting, in the last two decades the area has transformed into a region dedicated to wildlife conservation, becoming a UNESCO Biosphere and offering malaria-free Big Five game viewing. In the north, lying parallel to the Limpopo River and bisected by the N1, are the subtropical **Soutpansberg Mountains**, and the intriguing and still very independently minded **Venda** region, a homeland during the apartheid era, to the east. North of the Soutpansberg are wide plains dominated by surreal baobab trees, much in evidence along the N1 as it leads to the only (very busy) border post between South Africa and Zimbabwe, at Beitbridge. The only viable alternative if you want to get to Zimbabwe from South Africa is the Groblersbrug/Martin's Drift border crossing (daily 8am–6pm) on the N11, although this means detouring through Botswana.

The N1 is, by South African standards, fast and easy, if often busy. It's a **toll road** with four toll stops along the way to the Mussina border, costing roughly R20 each time. The alternative R101 which runs roughly parallel to the N1 from Jo'burg to Polokwane is slower but free and worth considering if you're counting your pennies. As regards **public transport**, Greyhound, Intercape, SA Roadlink and Translux buses ply the N1 between Johannesburg and Beitbridge, stopping at Polokwane, Makhado and Musina; most services carry on to either Bulawayo and Victoria Falls or Harare in Zimbabwe. Translux runs buses between Tzaneen and Johannesburg via Polokwane. These and other routes are also covered by minibus taxis from any moderately sized town; the best way to find out where they're going and when they depart is to enquire at the taxi rank.

Parts of Limpopo are **malarial**; you will need to take prophylactics, and exercise caution against mosquitoes if you are travelling in the lowveld, including Kruger National Park, or north of the Soutpansberg Mountains. The Waterberg and Letaba areas were not affected at the time of writing, though it's worth double-checking the current situation before you go.

Some history

The first black Africans arrived in South Africa across the Limpopo River some time before 300 AD. The various movements and migrations, and of course trading, ensured a fluidity in the people who established themselves here, and the historical and cultural ties to the north are, as you might expect, stronger in this region than in other parts of South Africa. Traditional arts and crafts such as **pottery** and **woodcarving** are still an important part of life; legendary figures such as the **Rain Queen** (see p.724) retain great potency, and **witchcraft** is still encountered in many places.

The arrival of the **Voortrekker** ox-wagons in the early nineteenth century brought profound changes to the region. Their route roughly followed that of the N1 today, and brought about the founding of the towns now called Bela-Bela, Modimolle and Polokwane, among others. Led by men such as Louis Trichardt, Hermanus and Piet Potgieter, Andries Pretorius and Paul Kruger, the Voortrekkers who ventured this far north were determined people, and their conflicts with the local peoples were notoriously bitter. At **Makapan's Cave** (see box opposite) off the N1 near Mokopane, several thousand Ndebele were starved to death by an avenging Boer commando, while further to the north, Venda troops forced the Voortrekkers to abandon the settlement they had established at **Schoemansdal** in the Soutpansberg.

In the twentieth century, the **apartheid years** saw several large chunks of the province hived off as homeland areas, with Venda becoming notionally independent and Lebowa and Gazankulu self-governing. Today the contrasts between the old homelands and the white farming areas are manifest throughout the province. Indeed, in the 1999 elections the Northern Province produced the highest-percentage vote in the country for both the ANC and the right-wing Afrikaner Freedom Front – though in 2004 the province voted overwhelmingly in favour of the ANC.

The N1 to Polokwane

The core of Limpopo Province, at least in terms of density of settlement and land use, lies along the N1 which passes into Limpopo approximately 40km north of Pretoria. The generally flat bushveld, together with the dominance of farming here, however, means there is little by way of sights or diversions until you leave the highway and head for the mountains, either westward to the Waterberg (see p.725), or eastwards along the R71 from Polokwane into the otherworldly Letaba area (see p.720).

Polokwane

Lying almost dead central in the province of which it is the capital, **Polokwane** is the largest city on the Great North Road between Pretoria and the border, and is South Africa's fastest-growing city. It's mostly an administrative and industrial centre, and much of its energy derives from the large volume of traffic moving through the city on the N1. But it does have a couple of quirky attractions, including an excellent museum, and if you're heading towards the Letaba area, the lowveld or central Kruger National Park, Polokwane is the point to connect with the R71 to Tzaneen and Phalaborwa.

Makapan's Cave (Makapansgat)

About 180km north of Pretoria, and just northeast of the town of Mokopane, the network of limestone caves known as **Makapan's Cave** might be the repository of some of South Africa's most important paleontological finds, but to many locals it is better known for one of those incidents in South African history which is remembered in different ways by different sections of the population. In 1854, bent on revenge after a party of Voortrekkers had been ambushed, a Boer commando unit cornered the clan of Ndebele chief Makapan in the hills to the north of Mokopane. The Boers, led by Piet Potgieter, the nephew of Voortrekker leader Hermanus Potgieter who had been skinned alive not long before by kinsmen of Makapan, besieged the chief and an estimated three thousand of his followers inside the network of caves which ran through the hills. With little food and almost no water, the imprisoned Ndebele became increasingly desperate, and eventually seven hundred besieged men rushed out towards a nearby stream, only to be mown down by the patient Boers. When the siege was finally broken after four weeks, hundreds of rotting bodies were found inside the cave. The Boers lost only two men, one of them Potgieter, whose body was "heroically" retrieved by a young Paul Kruger.

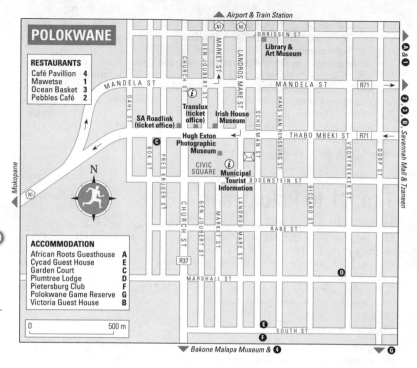

Airport & Train Station

POLOKWANE

RESTAURANTS
Café Pavillion 4
Mawetse 1
Ocean Basket 3
Pebbles Café 2

JORRISSEN ST

Library &
Art Museum

MANDELA ST

MANDELA ST R71

Translux
(ticket
office)

Irish House
Museum

SA Roadlink
(ticket office)

THABO MBEKI ST R71

Hugh Exton
Photographic
Museum

CIVIC
SQUARE

Municipal
Tourist
Information

BODENSTEIN ST

N

RABE ST

ACCOMMODATION
African Roots Guesthouse A
Cycad Guest House E
Garden Court C
Plumtree Lodge D
Pietersburg Club F
Polokwane Game Reserve G
Victoria Guest House B

R37

MARSHALL ST

0   500 m

SOUTH ST

Bakone Malapa Museum &

Arrival and information

The city's former airforce base now operates as **Gateway airport**, located on the N1 5km north of the city (☎015 288 0122 for information). The airport is served by both domestic flights (SA Airlink ☎015 288 0164 or 011 978 1111) and occasional international connections from neighbouring countries. All the city's **car-rental firms** are located here: Avis (☎015 288 0171), Budget (☎015 288 0169), Imperial (☎015 288 0097) and Tempest (☎015 288 0219), and **taxis** are also available (☎015 297 4493).

Daily trains to and from Musina stop at the **train station** (☎015 299 6202) on the northern edge of the city centre, just off the R521 (an extension of Market St). All the intercity **buses** pass through the centre of town: Translux and Greyhound stop in front of the Translux ticket office on Thabo Mbeki Street, a stone's throw from Civic Square. SA Roadlink buses stop at their ticket office also on Thabo Mbeki Street directly in front of the *Garden Court* hotel. City-to-city buses stop at a rank north of the centre off Nelson Mandela Drive.

There are two **tourist information** offices in Polokwane. One is the municipal tourist information service (Mon–Fri 8am–6pm, Sat 8am–1pm; ☎015 290 2010) at the Civil Square, which can help with information about the city's accommodation, attractions and transport. The other is the Limpopo Tourism and Parks Board, located on the corner of Mandela and Church streets (Mon–Fri 8am–4.30pm; ☎015 290 7300, ⓦwww.golimpopo.com), which runs a provincial service and stocks a wide array of glitzy brochures and maps. There is also a helpful budget travellers' tourist agent, SA Tours and Bookings (☎015 295 6162, ⓔsatours@mweb.co.za), at *Plumtree Lodge* (see opposite).

Accommodation

Polokwane seems to have a never-ending supply of places to stay, and there are signs for B&Bs and lodges on almost every street corner. We've listed some of the best options below. The Polokwane Game Reserve **campground** (☎015 290 2331) behind the golf course off Dorp Street has simple but adequate ablution facilities and some inexpensive chalets (❷). Although it's inside a game reserve there's little sense of it being surrounded by nature.

African Roots Guesthouse 58a Devenish St ☎015 297 0113, ⓦwww.africanroots .info. A relaxed, tasteful spot with immaculate and stylish rooms given character by local and foreign artefacts and works of art selected by the designer proprietors. Wi-Fi throughout. ❸

Cycad Guest House 2 Schoeman St on the corner of South St ☎015 291 2123, ⓦwww.sa-venues. com/np/cycad.htm. Within easy reach of the centre, *Cycad* offers 25 comfortable en-suite rooms in a characterless red-brick two-storey building. ❸

Garden Court On the corner of Thabo Mbeki and Bok sts ☎015 291 2030, ⓦwww.southernsun .com. Large, former Holiday Inn hotel complex, a couple of blocks from Civic Square, with predictable but decent rooms, a good restaurant and an outdoor pool. Breakfast not included. ❺

Plumtree Lodge 138 Marshall St ☎015 295 6153, ⓦwww.plumtree.co.za. Not far from the

centre, probably the smartest and most comfortable lodge in town, with a pool, a big garden and cheaper rates over the weekend. ❸

Pietersburg Club 122 South St ☎015 291 2900, ⓦwww.pcob.za/pburgclub. Within walking distance of the football stadium, this contemporary club house with a Victorian twist has comfortable en-suite rooms with garden-facing verandas ideal for sipping sundowners from the well-stocked cocktail bar. The club also encompasses an excellent restaurant. ❺

Victoria Guest House 32 Burger St ☎015 295 7599, ⓦwww.victoriaplace.co.za. As the name implies, a Victorian-style guesthouse consisting of eighteen individualistic en-suite rooms in three separate buildings and a self-catering section across the street. Known for its hearty breakfasts. ❸

The city and around

Polokwane has a busy, compact CBD set out on a grid pattern (which includes lots of one-way streets), with layers of industry and suburbia tightly packed around it. It may not be the most inspiring spot, but much of Limpopo's drive and enterprise emanates from its capital. At its heart, the **Civic Square**, a park area bounded on two sides by Landros Mare and Thabo Mbeki streets, has an incongruous but entertaining array of sculptures, statues and monuments, ranging from a family of giraffes to a fighter aircraft. In the middle of the park is a white church housing the small but absorbing **Hugh Exton Photographic Museum** (Mon–Fri 9am–3.30pm, Sun 3–5pm; free), which depicts the early years of the town through the work of a local commercial photographer; the portraits are excellent. Opposite the park, on the other side of Thabo Mbeki, is the old shop frontage of the decent **Irish House Museum** (Mon–Fri 8am–4pm; free), which includes displays on the city's past and natural history. For those inspired by the sculptures of the Civic Square, there's a small **art museum** (Mon–Fri 8am–4pm; free) above the library on Schoeman and Jorissen streets, together with an annexe of outdoor, industrial-type modern sculptures in a park on the left as you leave town on the N1 heading north.

The one sight in Polokwane really worth putting aside time to see is the open-air **Bakone Malapa Museum** (daily 8am–4.30pm; R6), 9km southeast of town on the R37. A simple but genuine project, it succeeds in conveying some of the old way of life of the local Bakone people – a grouping within the Northern Sotho – where many flashier examples have fallen short. A village of huts has been built in the traditional style, and fourteen people live permanently on site, working on crafts such as pottery and leatherworking through the day.

One of them also acts as a guide, and will explain the different activities you see, as well as the architecture, history and legends of the site.

Eating

True to its functional role, Polokwane has no shortage of chain **restaurants and takeaways**. The largest collection of these can be found at the Savannah Mall, on the fringes of the city along the Tzaneen road. Among the familiar names, look out on the lower level for *Ocean Basket*, part of a small chain of seafood restaurants. There are also a couple of locally owned places in town, including *Cafe Pavillion* (☎015 291 5359), serving quite classy meat and fish dishes, and delightful cakes in the tea garden, off Church Street, and *Pebbles Café* (☎015 295 6999) in the Tom Naude homestead at 39 Mandela St, which serves breakfasts, snacks, lunches and, through the week, evening meals. If you want to treat yourself to a special night out, the new *Mawetse* (☎015 297 4439, ⓦwww .mawetse.com), on the corner of Jorissen and Hoog streets and a stone's throw from *African Roots Guesthouse*, excels in fine dining, with separate champagne (only French) and cigar (only Cuban) lounges, and mouthwatering food served at a price (from R135 for Swiss chicken rolls).

Letaba

East of Polokwane, the **Letaba** is a forested, lush, mountainous area, contrasting very sharply with the hot lowveld immediately east and the wide, flat bushveld to the west, and marking the first dramatic rise of the Drakensberg Escarpment as it begins its sweep south through Mpumalanga. The forest begins around the mountain village of **Haenertsburg** and follows two very scenic parallel valleys to Limpopo's second-largest town, **Tzaneen**. The valleys are filled with lakes surrounded by dark pine forests, sparkling rivers, misty peaks and, towards Tzaneen, subtropical crops such as tea, macadamia nuts and avocados. With some very comfortable and beautifully located guesthouses, farm-stalls and tea rooms, hiking trails and trout fishing, the Letaba is in many ways an attractive, less well-known alternative to Mpumalanga's crowded highlands, although it is gradually making solid inroads onto the tourist route.

On the sixty-kilometre stretch between Polokwane and Haenertsburg are two huge, incongruous institutions, the **University of the North** at **Turfloop**, and **Zion City Moria** at **Boyne**, identified by a huge Star of David on the hill above it. At Easter, an incredible three million people gather here for the annual gathering of the Zion Christian Church, an independent, Africanized Christian Church. The symbols of followers of the church, a silver star or badge pinned to the chest, and sometimes a grey peaked cap, are worn right across the northern areas of South Africa. A certain amount of mystery and suspicion surrounds the movement, but there isn't really anything to see other than during the Easter gathering – which is the one time you want to stay well clear, as three million people can cause some mighty traffic jams.

Haenertsburg

Mellow **Haenertsburg** lies 60km from Polokwane, high on a hillside overlooking the R71 as the road winds down into the thickly wooded Magoebaskloof Valleys. Once an old gold-rush village, Haenertsburg has wonderful views over the area known as the Land of the Silver Mist. Not much more than a **main street**, it has

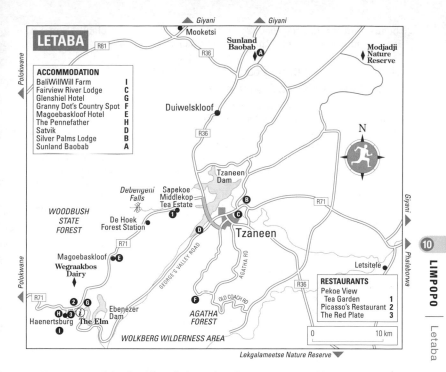

LETABA

ACCOMMODATION

BaliWillWill Farm	I
Fairview River Lodge	C
Glenshiel Hotel	G
Granny Dot's Country Spot	F
Magoebaskloof Hotel	E
The Pennefather	H
Satvik	D
Silver Palms Lodge	B
Sunland Baobab	A

Giyani
Giyani
Mooketsi
Sunland
Baobab
Modjadji
Nature
Reserve

Polokwane
R81
R36

Duiwelskloof
R36

N

Tzaneen
Dam

Debengeni
Falls
Sapekoe
Middlekop
Tea Estate
WOODBUSH
STATE
FOREST
De Hoek
Forest Station

R71
Tzaneen

Magoebaskloof
Wegraakbos
Dairy

Letsitele

R71
Ebenezer
Dam
Haenertsburg The Elm

GEORGE'S VALLEY ROAD
AGATHA RD
OLD COACH RD
AGATHA
FOREST

R36

RESTAURANTS

Pekoe View	
Tea Garden	1
Picasso's Restaurant	2
The Red Plate	3

WOLKBERG WILDERNESS AREA

0   10 km

Lekgalameetse Nature Reserve

Giyani
Phalaborwa

10

LIMPOPO | Letaba

at its eastern end the friendly gift shop, The Elms (Tues–Sun 8.30am–5pm), which also houses the useful **tourist office**, the Magoebaskloof Tourist Association (same hours; ☎015 276 4880, ⓦwww.magoebasklooftourism.co.za), where you can organize local accommodation or tours, or find out about good picnic spots and short walks in the area, including a tough one up to the **Iron Crown**, the peak above the village. *The Elms* is also the place to buy trout and ask about fly fishing. If you're planning to be in the area in May – a beautiful time with glorious autumnal colours in the valley – get details from them of the annual **music and cultural festival**, which sees national orchestras and choirs performing in unusual venues locally.

As for **accommodation**, *The Pennefather* (☎015 276 4885, ⓦwww .wheretostay.co.za-pennefather; ❸), conveniently located 300m down the road from The Elms and a stone's throw from the start of a hiking trail, has six new self-catering cottages built in the old mining style. There's also the *BaliWillWill Farm*, 2km into the hills from Haenertsburg past the police station (☎015 276 2212; ❸), with B&B rooms in the farmhouse or in a simple self-catering flat, and a shady area in the back for camping. On the R71, 2km east of Haenertsburg, the ⌘ *Glenshiel* (☎015 276 4335, ⓦwww .glenshiel.co.za; ❻) is one of the finer old country lodges in South Africa, with roaring fires, deep sofas, antiques and fine food, set in an old farmhouse surrounded by lush pine forests. Places to stay further along the two routes to Tzaneen are covered on p.722.

Good **food**, including pancakes and big breakfasts, can be had during the day at *Picasso's Restaurant* (Mon & Wed–Sun 8.30am–4.30pm) in a large wooden cabin beside the R71, and in the evenings at *The Red Plate* (Tues & Sun 10am–4pm, Wed–Sat 10am–10pm), on the main street beside *The Elms*. Also on the main street is the cosy *Iron Crown Pub and Grill* (Tues–Fri 11am–11pm, Sat 10am–11pm, Sun 9.30am–11pm), offering standard pub fare.

Georges Valley Road and the Magoebaskloof Valleys

Just east of Haenertsburg is a turning off the main R71 for the **Georges Valley Road**, which offers an alternative route to Tzaneen. There is, in fact, little to choose between the two options in terms of both distance and stunning scenery, and if you are spending any time in the area it's worth trying both. Along the Georges Valley Road lies a memorial to **John Buchan**, author of *The Thirty-Nine Steps*, who became captivated by the area when he visited not long after the Anglo-Boer War, calling it "a place enchanted and consecrated". There's also the tranquil **Ebeneezer Dam**, an atmospheric spot for swimming and picnicking. Some 4km from Tzaneen on the Georges Valley Road to the left, by a signboard, down a steep dirt track, ⚭ *Satvik* (☎015 307 3920 or 0845 562 414, ⓦwww.satvik.co.za; ❶) is an unusual and appealing backpacker lodge which makes use of a group of old whitewashed farmworkers' cottages set above the dam in a self-proclaimed wildlife preserve. Facilities, which include self-catering cottages sleeping four, en-suite doubles, and two twelve-bed dorms, are simple and rustic, but a lakeside bar and cooking area make it an atmospheric spot typical of Letaba, and one you could easily find yourself chilling out at for days on end, watching the area's rich birdlife and hiking along the dam's trails. To see the region from the air, the proprietor Louis also pilots microlight pleasure flights departing from the airfield just across the Georges Valley Road. A caravan campsite and bar-restaurant is planned for the future.

The R71 from Haenertsburg to Tzaneen

If, instead of turning down the Georges Valley Road, you stay on the **R71** east out of Haenertsburg for about 4km you'll reach the turning to the **Cheerio Gardens**, which holds an annual Cherry Blossom Festival at the end of September; the Magoebaskloof Tourist Association can provide details of various private show gardens in the area. Along this same turning is another wonderful piece of backwoods life, at the tiny **Wegraakbos Dairy** (☎015 276 1811), where cheese is made in traditional style over an open fire in a huge copper cauldron. A visit is thoroughly recommended; tours, which cost a few rand, are at 10am, but you can visit the dairy throughout the day, taste the cheese and walk around the farm and nearby woods.

A few kilometres beyond the turning, back on the R71, are the **Magoebaskloof Valleys**, named after the rogue chief Makgoba, who in 1895 had his head chopped off by native warriors serving under the Boer leader Abel Erasmus. There's accommodation here at the recently reopened *Magoebaskloof Hotel* (☎015 276 5400, ⓦwww.magoebaskloof.co.za; ❺), which was burnt almost to the ground in 2004. It boasts what is probably the most spectacular view in the area from its front deck, but the rest, including a pub with an old red postbox outside, is fairly uninspired.

The R71 twists and turns impressively as it crosses the Magoebaskloof pass, with dark forests and long views alternating on either side. A side road leads into the **Woodbush State Forest**, where there is a network of roads (not all passable), various multi-day hiking trails and the famous **Debegeni Falls**, an attractive series of waterfalls and natural pools. There are some braai sites by the river, and you can swim in various places if you're careful, but the smooth, slippery rock is very dangerous and a sign indicates that a few folk who tried the DIY waterslide didn't live to recommend it.

Between the turn-off to Debengeni and Tzaneen, the valley becomes broader, the rolling hillsides covered with huge stands of citrus, avocado and banana trees, as well as by the rich green texture of tea bushes. On the now sadly defunct **Sapekoe Middlekop** tea estate not far from the junction of the R71 and R36, a winding road leads up through the hugely overgrown tea bushes to the **Pekoe View tea garden** (daily 10am–5pm; free), with some of the best views in the whole valley. Tea and scones are always available, along with other snacks and drinks; packets of local tea (as long as stock lasts) and coffee can be bought in the shop. Depending on whether the estate gets going again (in 2007 the workers' salary packet, containing many millions of rand, mysteriously disappeared into the depths of someone's pocket), worthwhile factory tours may again be organized. On them you'll see tea being picked, learn about different grades of tea, and take a look at the production process in the factory.

Tzaneen and around

The dams and soaring gum forests surrounding **TZANEEN** are graceful and attractive. However, the town itself is fairly scruffy, worth avoiding as a place to stay though it is well endowed with shops. The one thing to see here is the **Tzaneen Museum** (Mon–Fri 9am–4pm, Sat 9am–noon; donation appreciated), situated in a tiny, four-roomed building in the grounds of the library at the top of Agatha Street. You'll need time: the dedicated curator and his assistants don't label any items, preferring to walk around with you and talk about the small but important collection, which includes sacred drums and other items associated with the Rain Queen (see p.724).

Translux and City Link **buses** connect Tzaneen with Polokwane and Johannesburg. The **Limpopo Tourism and Parks** office (Mon–Fri 8am–4pm; ☏015 307 3582, ⒲www.golimpopo.com), located on the north side of the R71 as you head out towards Phalaborwa, is a useful place to get general information about travelling in Limpopo, as well as pick up advice on travelling to spots such as Modjadji, the Magoebaskloof Valleys and Kruger National Park. For more detailed information about Tzaneen and **accommodation** in the area, the upgraded *Fairview River Lodge* (☏015 307 2679, ⒲www.fairviewlodge.co.za; ❹), on Old Gravelotte Road, now also runs a local tourist information service (☏015 307 6513, ⒲www.tzaneeninfo.co.za) in its reception. The lodge itself has plush self-catering chalets along the river next to its gold course as well as comfortable en-suite doubles. Other options in town itself aren't inspiring, especially in comparison with what is available in the surrounding countryside. Best of the bunch is the *Silver Palms Lodge* off Voortrekker Street (☏015 307 3092, ⒠mwjanalr@mweb.co.za; ❸), beside the Malaria Research Institute, which has some decent modern units around a pool. The road leading south out of town into the Wolkberg Mountains to Agatha has spectacular views out over the valleys and peaks of the escarpment, and some fairly predictable high-class country lodges. A more down-to-earth alternative in the Agatha area is *Granny Dot's Country Spot* (☏015 307 5149 or 083 760 0983, ⒲www.grannydots.co.za; ❸), about 10km from Tzaneen, along a dirt road (follow the signs). It's a small, cosy B&B with a few self-catering units with fabulous views of the mountainside, and close to the Rooikat Walking Trail, a circular marked forest trail on the Agatha ridge. There's also a backpackers' place on the Georges Valley Road (see opposite).

As for **food**, Tzaneen has a smattering of familiar takeaways and a few chain restaurants. The best in town is the *Tino's Pizzaria*, on the corner of Danie

Joubert and Lannie streets, while near the museum there's a pleasant French-style café, ⚜ *Ashley's Continental Corner*, set in an old Victorian garden at 30 Agatha St and dishing up fabulous breakfasts, salads, ice cream and cakes.

Modjadji Cycad Reserve

The area around the rather downbeat village of **MODJADJI**, 32km northeast of Tzaneen off the R36, is the home of the famous **Rain Queen**, the hereditary female monarch of the Lobedu people, whom legend maintains has the power to make rain – a useful talent in these often parched northern areas. Currently, for complicated political and emotional reasons there is no queen in post, so to speak, but her residence is a village up in the mists on a mountain where a

▲ Cycad at the Modjadji Cycad Reserve

special form of ancient cycad, or tree fern, flourishes. The **Modjadji Cycad Reserve** (daily 7.30am–6pm; R10) protects these plants in an area at the very top of the hill, and incorporates some fine views (often obscured by mist) and various short but pleasant, rather vaguely marked walking trails. There are a few facilities, including rondavels (self-catering ❷), a souvenir shop and information centre, which explains a bit more about the unique plants found here and, of course, the famous monarch.

Around 20km southeast of Modjadji (follow the signs) lies **Sunland Baobab** (☎015 309 9030, ⓦwww.bigbaobab.co.za; self-catering ❸), home to what is claimed to be the world's largest baobab tree. It's got a pub inside, whose owner will serve you draught beer while relating a few of the strange stories attached to his odd location. In front of the tree are five comfortable thatched A-frame tents and a pool, and there's a restaurant planned for the near future. If you're not staying overnight, you'll have to pay to get in (R10).

Letsitele

Thirty kilometres east of Tzaneen, **LETSITELE** is a small town whose main function is as a waypoint to a few places of interest in the area of lowveld abutting the escarpment. To the south are the large nature and wilderness areas of **Lekgalameetse** and **Wolkberg**, excellent places to explore on foot if you have a few days and a penchant for empty green landscapes. **Lekgalameetse Nature Reserve** (☎015 290 7300), reached from the R36, 44km south of Tzaneen, encompasses the transition between lowveld and escarpment and has accommodation in simple log cabins that are currently being refurbished (❷). **Wolkberg Wilderness Area** (☎015 276 1303) has a campsite at Serala Forest Station, which you get to from the Haenertsburg side (see p.720), but few other facilities – it's meant to be wild and untamed.

Near Letsitele itself is one of the most interesting handicraft projects in the province, **Kaross**, which produces intricate and striking embroidered Shangaan ethnic place mats, cushion covers, wall hangings and much more. You can arrange to see the workshops (ⓦwww.kaross.co.za; ☎015 345 1458), which employ over 150 locals, and buy their work at the excellent Kaross Studio on Giyani Road (R529) just north of Letsitele.

Waterberg

Even now, with the great gold-city belching its smoke almost within sight – even now, with invading civilization marching across the hills in seven-league boots, Waterberg still holds its charm.

Eugène Marais

Rising out of the plains to the west of the Great North Road, the **Waterberg** is one of the least known and most intriguing of South Africa's significant massifs. Once an area of lakes and swamps – hence its name – the elevated plateau can often seem as dry as its surrounding northern bushveld, yet it harbours a diversity of vegetation and topography that for years supported extensive farming and cattle-ranching. In recent times the majority of the old ranches have been converted into a multitude of private reserves catering either for the hugely lucrative hunting market (see p.728), or less profitable game viewing, with white rhino often heading the list, along with giraffe, large antelope and leopard. Today the entire area, some 14,500 square kilometres of both private and publicly owned land, is encompassed by one of the country's foremost conservation projects – the **Waterberg Savanna Biosphere Reserve**, designated by UNESCO in 2001. At the heart of the biosphere reserve is the highly regarded **Lapalala Wilderness Area** located north of **Vaalwater** – the only settlement of any size in the Waterberg. The biosphere reserve is founded on a close-knit association of landowners inspired by Lapala-la's example in combining wildlife conservation with the benefits of tourism.

As a game-viewing destination the Waterberg is an alternative to the lowveld areas around Kruger National Park, with the important advantage that malaria is not endemic to the Waterberg. However, it has impressive credentials as a vast area of true wilderness, and is certainly still less commercialized, the game here being less dense than around Kruger. West of Vaalwater, and also included within the biosphere reserve, are two large game reserves which hold the Big Five: **Marakele National Park** and the **Welgevonden** private reserve, the latter very much in the upmarket bracket.

Of all the private and public reserves in the Waterberg, the only one you can visit on day-trips is Marakele National Park; otherwise, to gain access, you'll almost always be expected to book into accommodation on the reserve, though such is the cooperative nature of many parts of the Waterberg that the owners of guesthouses located alongside a reserve have often negotiated access rights.

The area also offers some exciting **adventure activities**, including bush-hiking trails and some of the finest wilderness horse-riding in South Africa. Waterberg Transfers (℡082 320 6515, ⓦwww.waterbergtransfers.com) offers easy and efficient **long-distance taxi** links between places such as Johannesburg International Airport and the Waterberg (R1200).

Vaalwater

The small farming town of **Vaalwater** offers the visitor little more than a couple of useful places to stay and an orientation point on the R33, which connects the N1 at Modimolle with Lephalale. Vaalwater marks the junction between the R33 and the tarred road to Melkrivier and Marken. Around Vaalwater there are absorbing bush experiences on most levels, from luxury lodges to inexpensive self-catering cottages and wilderness campsites. The scenery in this part of the Waterberg is subtle rather than dramatic: the way to appreciate it is to stay for a few days.

In the easily missed centre of town is the Village Square, at the first T-junction as you approach from the east, where you'll find the **tourist office** (Mon–Fri

7am–7pm; ☎014 755 4567, ⓦwww.24-7info.net) which also houses an Internet café. If you need **accommodation** in town, the best option is the excellent ⚘ *Zeederberg Cottages* (☎014 755 3538, ⓦwww.zeederbergs.co.za; ❸), comprising a cluster of beautiful self-catering cottages and huts housing en-suite doubles and dorms (R150). Roughly 1km west of the Village Square along the R33 behind the Spar supermarket, the Zeederberg homestead was the town's first settlement and is today also a great base for organizing activities such as hiking or game viewing. Next to the supermarket is the excellent Black Mamba crafts gallery (Mon–Fri 8.30am–5pm, Sat 8.30am–1.30pm, Sun 9.30am–1pm), which in turn abuts the equally fabulous *Bush Stop Café* (Mon–Fri 8am–5pm, Sat 8am–1.30pm) which dishes up arguably the town's best breakfast and lunch menu. Next door, the Clive Walker Art Gallery – Maphoto Craft Art (Mon–Fri 8am–4.30pm, Sat 9am–1pm; free) displays works by Clive Walker (see below) alongside beadwork and other fine crafts made by disadvantaged women living within the Waterberg Biosphere. For **food and drink**, try the *Big Five Pub and Grill* (Mon–Sat 8am–9.30pm, Sun 9am–3pm) near the Village Square, which does full-on, hearty steaks and is the place to head to watch sports on TV. If you fancy **coffee and cake**, *La Fleur* (Mon–Fri 7.45am–5pm, Sat 7.45am–1pm), across the R33 by the Village Square, excels in both.

The Lapalala Wilderness Area and around

North of Vaalwater, turning left down a dirt road at the Melkrivier junction on the tarred Marken road, the **Lapalala Wilderness Area** (☎014 775 4071, ⓦwww.lapalala.com) is a 360-square-kilometre reserve established in 1981. Masterminded by the highly regarded South African conservationist and artist, Clive Walker, it provides sanctuary for endangered and rare animals, and has developed into one of the foremost conservation projects in the country. It was the first private game reserve in South Africa to obtain the highly endangered black rhino, five of which were acquired from Natal Parks Board for R2.2 million. In 1985 the Lapalala Wilderness School was established, and nowadays it introduces some 3000 children a year from all over Africa to the principles and practice of conservation, during week-long courses in the heart of the wilderness area.

There are three tented self-catering **bush camps** (all ❸) in different parts of Lapalala. Of these, *Lookout Camp* has a particularly atmospheric setting, its safari tents perched on the edge of a hillside overlooking the river valley.

An excellent introduction to some of the achievements of Lapalala, and the personalities involved, is at the world's only dedicated **Rhino Museum** (Tues–Sun 9am–5pm; R5), based in the old Melkrivier School, about 6km along the road to Lapalala off the Vaalwater to Marken tarred road. At 3pm you can see Lapalala's

---

Outdoor activities in the Waterberg

The Waterberg is an excellent place to come if you're interested in doing something a little more energetic along with game viewing. For **horse-riding safaris** ⚘ Horizon Horseback Adventures & Safaris (☎014 755 4003, ⓦwww.ridinginafrica.com; full board ❸) is a well-established and highly professional outfit based at *Triple B Ranch* which combines lovely chilled-out accommodation and delicious food with loads of fun for horse-lovers: as well as outrides, overnight rides and trips to game areas, activities include cattle-mustering, polocrosse and a cross-country course. For other activities, including **hiking** and **mountain biking**, *Lindani* (☎083 631 5579, ⓦwww.lindani.co.za; ❸) is a 35-square-kilometre farm between Vaalwater and Melkrivier, with various attractive thatched houses.

rhino **orphans** being fed, for R20. This includes the young black rhino Bwana, who lives in Clive and Conita Walker's back garden. Next door to the Rhino Museum is the equally worthwhile **Waterberg Museum** (same hours), which explores the origins of man in the Waterberg and looks at the various peoples and traditions which have held sway here over the centuries. Right next to the Rhino Museum, *Walker's Wayside Café* (☎014 755 4428; closed Mon) does great coffee and tasty lunch.

A short drive south of the Vaalwater to Melkrivier road, the **Triple B Ranch** has a stunning location overlooking vast plains, and the wide-open skies above, unpolluted by city or street lights, have an amazing display of stars most nights, something you can learn more about on one of the farm's absorbing two-hour **star tours**. As one of the oldest farms in the region and one of the few working farms still going strong, it is famous for its hardy, unusual-looking Bonsmara cattle. To find out more about them, and the farm's long history, you can join one of the fascinating **farm tours**. There's accommodation here too (see opposite).

Not far from the Triple B Ranch, the tiny stone **Saint John's church** at Twenty-Four Rivers on the southern edge of the ranch is worth a detour. It was designed by Sir Herbert Baker (see box, p.597) and commissioned by two maiden aunts, who expected that he would do it for free, since it was a place of worship; their assumption was, unsurprisingly, not shared by Baker. In the opposite direction, on the northern edge of the ranch near Horizon Horseback Adventure & Safaris (see p.727) the innovative new Beadle Crafts Workshop is a community outreach project where people from the local community with HIV/AIDS can work when they are well enough to do so. The resulting colourful and intricate beadwork on leather is well worth checking out, as is the tea room and shop (Mon–Sat 7.30am–5pm, Sun 9am–4pm; ⓦwww.beadle.co.za).

Accommodation

As well as the bush camps at Lapalala, there are a number of **self-catering chalets** and **cottages** in this part of the Waterberg, which, although not all located on game reserves, often make arrangements with larger farms or reserves

---

Hunting

To some it is barbaric blood lust, while to others it lies at the heart of conservation. **Hunting** presents an emotive issue which you'll hear vigorously debated in the Waterberg and in many rural areas of South Africa where it is regarded as an essential part of life in the bush. It is also a multi-million-rand industry and, although you don't necessarily read about them in the guidebooks, there are many more hunting reserves in South Africa than there are eco-friendly game reserves.

In **hunting reserves** the land is stocked with game specifically for the purpose of hunting, whereas in conservation-oriented game reserves the guiding principle is that tourists will pay simply to see the animals in their natural environment. However, wherever land has been fenced in (which is just about everywhere), the idea of a completely natural environment is inevitably compromised, and intervention is necessary to maintain a realistic balance and diversity of nature within that area. Such intervention – "management" is a common euphemism – takes place even in the most conservation-oriented reserves. More at issue is the extent to which this process is commercialized. Some reserves, knowing that they need to cull a certain number of animals, allow paying clients to hunt for that quota, providing a valuable source of income for the reserve and its conservation ideals. Inevitably, this leads to grey areas: how many animals need to be culled, for instance, when there is money at stake?

nearby for game walks or drives. As a result, they tend to be more affordable and flexible. Although self-catering in this price range is standard, most accommodation can provide food if it's ordered in advance. The best of these establishments includes *Le Thabo Pioneer Settlement* (℡014 755 4178 or 082 635 8967; self-catering ❸, full board ❺), a collection of small log cabins on the banks of the Melk River on the road to Lapalala. Pleasant self-catering accommodation is also available at *Windsong Cottages* (℡014 755 4425, ✉pcalcott@gmail.com; ❸), in five old farmhouse buildings on Triple B Ranch.

Marakele National Park

Southwest of Vaalwater, in the mountains to the northeast of the mining and hunting town of **Thabazimbi**, lies the 670-square-kilometre **Marakele National Park** (daily: May–Aug 8am–5pm; Sept–April 8am–6pm; ℡014 777 1745, ⓌWww.sanparks.org/parks/marakele), one of South Africa's newest national parks, reached via a twelve-kilometre tarred road from Thabazimbi. At its core are the **Kransberg**, a striking assortment of odd-shaped peaks, plateaus and cliffs. The diversity of land and altitude means that a variety of interesting plants, including ferns, orchids, and even proteas and cycads are found here, while the fauna includes tsessebe, roan and sable antelope, red hartebeest and eight hundred breeding pairs of the endangered Cape vulture. Larger game such as elephant, rhino and lion have also been introduced, many from Kruger National Park.

While the park has a great deal of potential, for the moment **day visitors** (R70) are restricted to a small area including Kransberg, with its inspiring views. There are two places to **stay** within the park. One is a self-catering tented camp (❹) situated on the banks of the Matlabas River, 17km from the main entrance, and there's also a well-equipped campsite 2km from the gate. Roads to these two places don't require a 4WD, though you'll need one to get around the rest of the reserve.

Welgevonden Reserve

Welgevonden, a reserve of 340 square kilometres to the west of Vaalwater and abutting Marakele, is in fact 61 private properties joined together as one big conservation area with a strict management plan that tightly regulates the number of lodges that can be built and the number of vehicles allowed in the reserve.

As many of the lodges in the Waterberg are small and relatively remote, it's advisable to prebook somewhere to stay, at least for your first couple of nights. Upmarket lodges usually offer full board and include early-morning and late-afternoon game drives or walks in their programmes, so it's worth arriving at a time when you can take full advantage of these. Check Ⓦwww.welgevonden .org for details of all the lodges.

Luxury accommodation

Within Welgevonden, the exclusive *Makweti Safari Lodge* (℡011 837 6776, Ⓦwww.makweti.com; ❾), with five stone-and-thatch suites built into the natural rock formations of the mountains, is both spectacular and luxurious, its sense of isolation complemented by the fact that game drives can range anywhere over the reserve. Nearby, also exclusive but otherwise quite different, is the tranquil *Ant's Nest* (℡014 755 4296, Ⓦwww.waterberg .net; ❾), a converted farmhouse set deep in the bush northeast of Vaalwater with white rhino, giraffe, gemsbok and blesbok in the private reserve, and drives, walks and, in particular, horse-riding offered. The sense of sheer escapism here is clinched by the fact that the owners only ever host one couple or party at a time.

The far north

The northernmost part of Limpopo Province is a hot, green, undeveloped rural region with as much in common with Zimbabwe as South Africa. The essential geographical features of the area are the **Limpopo River**, the border between South Africa and Zimbabwe (and, further west, Botswana), and the alluring **Soutpansberg mountain range**, aligned east–west just to the north of the area's main town, Makhado (or Louis Trichardt – the new name was recently contested again, and lost), which is otherwise unremarkable and not worth a stopover.

As a first impression of South Africa for visitors arriving from Zimbabwe, the far north cannot compete with the lure of attractions further south. Yet it is an area where the lack of sophistication and isolated history of the people and culture make absorbing contrasts to other parts of the country. Perhaps the most distinctive area is the **Venda** region, formerly an "independent" homeland under the apartheid regime; although economically impoverished, it remains rich in tradition, art and legend. East of the Venda lands is the northern tip of **Kruger National Park**, a less-visited but intriguing part of the park (see p.704); there are two entry gates to the park here, at **Punda Maria** and **Pafuri**.

Both the Limpopo River and the Soutpansberg mountain range lie in the path of the N1 highway, which crosses into Zimbabwe at **Beitbridge**. About 70km west of here the new **Mapungubwe National Park** encompasses a famous Iron-Age site – now also a UNESCO World Heritage Site – and for archeology buffs probably the area's most enticing attraction.

The Soutpansberg area

The **Soutpansberg Mountains** have an unusual claim to distinction, named as they are after a set of saltpans – one of the flatter natural features known to man. The name came about after Voortrekker pioneers, under the leadership of Louis Trichardt, established their first settlement by the pans on the northern side of the mountain range. While the settlement soon relocated to Schoemansdal, on the southern side, the moniker stuck.

An impressive range of hills, particularly when approached from the south, the Soutpansberg attract sufficient rainfall to create a subtropical climate, and spectacularly lush green farms along the southern slopes produce a range of exotic crops such as avocados, mangos, bananas and macadamia nuts. In other parts, the rocky *kloofs* and green hillsides offer some remote and unspoilt mountain retreats, shaded by up to 580 different species of tree, and the home of monkeys, small antelopes, foraging warthogs and some noble raptors. Not surprisingly, therefore, the uniqueness of the area has lead to a bid by local conservationists to designate it a UNESCO Biosphere Reserve with a similar protection and development status as the Waterberg Biosphere Reserve (see p.726), the hope being eventually to link the two up with Kruger National Park to form a so-called Golden Horseshoe.

The N1 highway bisects the range, passing through missable Makhado, situated in the southern shadow of the mountains, then climbing over a low pass and descending through a pair of tunnels on the northern side. Once over the escarpment, the highway runs north across mostly empty baobab plains to **Musina** and the **Limpopo River**.

The Soutpansberg Mountains

Lush, rounded mountains rising to a height of over 1700m and cut by some dramatic outcrops of pinky-orange rock, the **Soutpansberg** seem to form a final barrier of colourful relief before the long hot plains either side of the Limpopo River. Travelling north on the N1, you begin to climb immediately after leaving Makhado, up what becomes a narrow, winding road not easily negotiated by the heavy trucks plying the route.

Along this stretch of the **N1**, you'll pass a number of **hotels and guesthouses** that use the lush surroundings to create a mountain-resort-type atmosphere. The best of these includes the *Mountain View Hotel* (☎015 517 7031, ✉mountaininn@webmail.co.za; ④), 9km north of town, or, even better, *The Inn on Louis Trichardt* (☎015 517 7088, ⓦwww.inn-on-louistrichardt .co.za; ⑤), 12km north of town, which has various rooms set around pleasant gardens and a pool, as well as an attractive craft shop and tea garden in the grounds (daily 8am–5pm). Of the guesthouses hidden in the folds of the Soutpansberg, one of the nicest is 🏃 *Harnham House* (☎015 517 7260; ④), 6km westwards along the scenic Bluegumspoort road, which has rooms in the attractive main house as well as in a lovely remote cottage overlooking a dam. Backpacker beds and camping sites are also available here. Once over the low pass, on the much less dramatic northern slopes, you'll find the newly refurbished *Ingwe Ranch Motel* (☎015 517 7104; ④), offering a variety of rondavels and rooms, a coffee bar and one of the better restaurants in the area.

Accommodation away from the N1

Beyond the well-worn N1, you can get deeper into the more remote and wilder parts of the mountains if you have a couple of days to spare. Most of the accommodation options listed below are members of the Soutpansberg Conservancy (ⓦwww.soutpansberg.co.za), which promotes the natural heritage of the area as well as developing the tourism potential within the mountain range, the key elements of a current Biosphere Reserve bid still awaiting approval from UNESCO.

Bergpan Eco Resort On the north side of the mountains and east of Waterpoort along the R523 ☎015 593 0127, ✉bergpan@mweb.co.za. Tours of the saltpans that gave the mountains their name and a chance to experience salt-making are on offer, along with hiking and self-catering cottages. ②

🏃 **Lajuma Mountain Retreat** Along a turn-off on the R522, 46km west of Makhado ☎015 593 0352 or 083 308 7027, ⓦwww.lajuma.com. Situated by the top of Letjume, the highest point of the Soutpansberg, and an ideal spot from which to study the area's unique ecology, Lajuma attracts research students from all over the world. Two attractive self-catering thatched chalets perch on the mountainside overlooking a waterfall, and there's a romantic forest cottage tucked into the luxuriant tropical bush. The road up to the retreat can be dicey, at

best – if you don't have 4WD call in advance to be picked up at the gate. ②

Lesheba Wilderness 36km west of Makhado along the R522, located in a spectacular valley atop the mountain range ☎015 593 0076, ⓦwww .lesheba.co.za. A truly unique experience well worth the long uphill drive (safest in a 4WD): here the internationally acclaimed artist Noria Mabasa has used the ruins of old rondavels to create a replica Venda village alive with sculpted figures guests can admire when lounging at the pool or enjoying the fabulous individualistic accommodation. There are terrific opportunities to explore the area, with self-guided walks among the rhino and giraffe, and archeology trails are a speciality here. Full board ⑥, self-catering ④

Medike Mountain Reserve 29km west of Makhado off the R522 ☎015 516 0481,

Venda

To the east and north of Makhado lies the intriguing land of the **VhaVenda** people, a culturally and linguistically distinct African grouping known for their mystical legends, political independence and arts and crafts. **Venda** was demarcated as a homeland under the apartheid system in the 1950s, and became one of three notionally independent homelands in South Africa in the late 1970s. Of all the homelands, Venda was one of the least compromised, keeping both its geographic and cultural integrity, and largely being left to mind its own business during the dark years of apartheid. Its boundaries have regained their former fuzziness, within Limpopo, but the region has retained its strong, independent identity.

The best place to get **information** is from one of the established accommodation options such as the *Venda Sun* in the Venda capital, **Thohoyandou** (see opposite), which also has lists of tour guides offering trips round the area.

Aside from a sprinkling of accommodation in Thohoyandou, you'll find almost no tourist-oriented infrastructure whatsoever in Venda. However, it's

---

VhaVenda history and culture

The people who today call themselves **VhaVenda** are descended from a number of ancient groupings who migrated from the Great Lakes area in east-central Africa in the eleventh and twelfth centuries. Their identity gelled when a group under Chief Dimbanyika arrived at Dzata in the northern Soutpansberg, where a walled fort was later built. From here, they consolidated their power in the region, fending off attack from a number of different African groupings (including the Voortrekkers, whom they drove from their settlement at Schoemansdal in 1867). Although the VhaVenda suffered a reverse at the hands of the Boers in 1898, the onset of the Anglo-Boer War prevented that victory being consolidated. The British had little interest in such a remote region, and were content to allow their administration to be run by the local chiefs, a system of self-government which, in one contrived form or another, lasted through the apartheid years until 1994.

The **culture** of the VhaVenda is a fascinating one, steeped in mysticism and vivid legend. One pervading theme is water – always an important concern in hot, seasonal climates, but a resource in which Venda is unusually abundant. Lakes, rivers, waterfalls and lush forests all form sacred sites, while legends abound of *zwidutwane*, or water sprites, and snakes who live at the bottom of dark pools or lakes. You can still even find older people who hold a taboo against fish, partly because the animals live in water and partly because they believe that if you eat fish the crocodiles will go hungry and turn on other available food sources, such as humans.

Many VhaVenda **ceremonies** and **rituals** still hold great importance, with the most famous being the python, or *domba*, dance performed by young female initiates. Naked but for jewellery and a small piece of cloth around their waist, the teenage girls form a long chain, swaying and shuffling as the "snake" winds around a fire to the sound of a beating drum – another sacred object in Venda – often for hours on end. Your chances of seeing it performed are limited – although dancing can always be arranged (at a price, and with advance notice). The genuine thing is most common during spring; Heritage Day around the end of August or the beginning of September is a good time for celebrations.

a lot less dangerous to travel independently through Venda than many other places in South Africa, and the journey can be wonderfully rough, raw and rewarding.

Thohoyandou

THOHOYANDOU isn't a place you'll want to spend time in if you can help it, an ugly, dirty sprawl of broken concrete and undisciplined building, glamorized by a casino. It's reached from Makhado by following the R524 70km east, along the southern edge of the Soutpansberg; if you're heading on to Kruger, you'll be thankful that the road mercifully bypasses the centre of town altogether.

The highlight of the capital, at least according to the tourist authorities, is the **Tusk Venda Casino Hotel** (☎015 962 4600, ⓦwww.tusk-resorts.co.za /venda; ❻), a clone of the gambling dens tacitly encouraged in the homelands by the apartheid government and lapped up by South Africans denied such illicit entertainment in their own country. It is set in the heart of the downtown area, surrounded immediately by trees, but not far beyond the road and tatty shopping mall. To get to it, turn left off the R524 coming from Makhado at the service station, and right at the third set of traffic lights. The hotel has a pool, decent rooms and facilities, and an impressive record of supporting Venda arts and crafts, with useful maps and tours available. The only other reasonable place to stay in town is *Bougainvillea Lodge* (☎015 962 4064, ⓦwww .bougainvillalodge.com; ❸), just up the hill from the *Venda Sun*, a simple motel-like travellers' stop.

There isn't a wide choice of **places to eat** in Thohoyandou. In the middle of the shopping centre next to the *Venda Sun* there's the *African Traditional Buffet* serving inexpensive breakfast, lunch and dinner, plus a number of takeaway food shops. There's a pricier sit-down restaurant in the *Tusk Venda* itself. **Minibuses** for Makhado use the large, chaotic taxi rank in front of the shopping centre.

The R523 west from Thohoyandou

Along the northern side of the Soutpansberg, through a valley traced by the R523 road between the N1 and Thohoyandou, is the most appealing core of VhaVenda history and legend. This is where you'll find the lush forests, waterfalls and mountains which give Venda its mystical atmosphere.

Driving from Thohoyandou, climb out of town to the north and then west, leaving the suburbs to get among the elevated green scenery which lies enticingly ahead. You'll pass the **Vondo Dam**, created in the early 1990s and surrounded by pine forests, then climb over the **Thate Vondo Pass**. Over the summit, a small shack marks the entrance to a network of forest roads that take you into the area containing the most important lake in Venda, **Lake Fundudzi**, and the **Sacred Forest**, an area of dense indigenous forest which contains the burial ground of Venda chiefs. In the past you could only look at both from afar, as getting closer was a matter of deep sensitivity and you had to gain permission from the VhaVenda chief. Today access is unrestricted but there isn't a readily available map showing you the network of roads around the forest, and some of the roads require 4WD; you may be better off joining a **tour** (see opposite) or join forces with a local guide. Another option well worth considering is the **Mabudashango Hiking Trail**, a four-day, fifty-kilometre walk that takes you as close as any road to the main highlights of the area, including Lake Fundudzi and the Sacred Forest. The trail offers spectacular views and lush vegetation, and navigation isn't always easy, but at each of the camps along the way you'll find a shelter with water and toilet facilities; for details contact DWAF, the forestry department, on ☎015 516 0201.

Beyond the crest of the Thate Vondo Pass, the R523 follows the **Nzhelele River** down a valley of scattered but mostly unbroken settlement. Not far west of Mphephu, on the northern side of the road, are the **Dzata ruins**, the remains of the royal kraal of the kings of VhaVenda, dating from 1400. If you find the gate locked, you'll probably have to toot your horn to rouse the gateman, and even then you may find the place deserted.

Elim and around

Southeast of Makhado along the R578 lie some areas that used to form part of the self-governing homeland of **Gazankulu**, a Tsonga area. They feature the leftover scruffiness and vibrant roadside action typical of such rural areas – most notably at **ELIM**, a cluster of stalls, minibuses and hoardings on the site of a long-established Swiss mission hospital. A short way from here, along the road to Levubu, is the relaxing ⚘ *Shiluvari Lakeside Lodge* (☎015 556 3406, ⓦwww .shiluvari.com; ❹, full board ❺), with lawns running down to the edge of Albasini Dam and views over the water to the Soutpansberg.

Continuing on the R578 from Elim crossroads, towards the town of **Giyani**, you'll come upon a series of rural arts and crafts workshops (see box opposite). The traditions and skills in arts and crafts are not dissimilar to what you find in Venda, and most of the workshops and small factories have simple, rural roots, making the trip to see them a worthwhile adventure. *Shiluvari Lakeside Lodge* (see above) can help with guides to arts and crafts workshops in the area, and sells products from many of them in its exquisite and well-stocked crafts boutique.

▲ An elaborate woodcarving

The **Venda** and **Gazankulu** regions have established a strong reputation in **arts and crafts**. The best known of these are clay pots distinctively marked with angular designs in graphite silver and ochre. Also growing in status are woodcarvings, ranging from abstract to practical, though, while the best of these can be imaginative and bold, many are unfinished and overpriced. You'll also come across tapestries, fabrics, basketwork and painting. Finding your way to these craft villages can be quite an adventure, as they are widely scattered and the roads are poor, so the Ribolla Tourism Association, behind the Swiss mission hospital in Elim (Mon–Fri 8.30am–4.30pm; ☏015 556 4262, ✉ribollata@mweb.co.za), has set up a demarcated art route in the area, and hands out free maps of the route. It also has knowledgeable guides to take you around.

Gazankulu

The main route in the former homeland of Gazankulu is the R578 between **Elim** and **Giyani**. Travelling southeast from Elim crossroads, look out for a track leading up to the Rivoni workshop (opposite the turn to Waterval), where blind and other handicapped people make furniture and coffins – a line that evidently does a roaring trade. There isn't a great deal to see, but the place is industrious and there is a small shop. Back on the R578, turn left at the brow of the next hill, then up a right-hand fork to reach **Khomanani Paper**, where recycled paper and banana stems are used to make wonderfully textured paper, cards, books and frames.

The R578 then goes down a hill, at the bottom of which is a turning to **Mbhokota** village. Going along this, turn left at the T-junction and left again along a narrow track just past a small homestead with a busy garden, and you'll find a run-down collection of buildings where **Twananani** textiles are created using traditional Tsonga techniques – attractive, funky, hand-painted and batik garments with traditional African designs, made by around twenty people.

At the next junction off the R578, to Riverplaats, then along a right-hand fork, is the house and small workshop of Shangaan woodcarver **Jackson Thugwane**. He's an almost mystical figure, with pieces exhibited in major galleries around the country and in Europe. If he isn't there you won't find much to see; if he is, be prepared for a few absorbing hours of philosophy, theology, art and the state of the modern world. If you continue in the opposite direction down the road you came, straight past the T-junction, you'll find many of his works on display in the gallery of one of his students, the late John Baloyi Gallery. It's one of the biggest galleries in the area and contains works from a number of other, younger carvers nearby who have tried to emulate Jackson's success. If you take the left-hand fork after the Riverplaats sign, you will eventually come to a village called **Mashamba** where villagers make clay pots in the traditional way. This is, however, a trek deep into the rural areas of Gazankulu and road conditions are fairly unreliable.

Venda

In **Venda**, the craft villages are even more scattered and hard to find. There are a number of sites situated to the north of Thohoyandou, including **Mutale**, where traditional decorative drums are made. You can pick up a hand-drawn **arts and crafts map** of Venda at the *Tusk Venda* (see p.733).

North to the border

Once over the Soutpansberg, the N1 runs across hot, mostly featureless plains of dense bush and baobab trees for some 60km before reaching the town of **Musina**, the last settlement before the Zimbabwe border crossing at Beitbridge on the Limpopo River. Around 60km west of Musina, the new **Mapungubwe National Park** encompasses a famous Iron-Age site and is now also a UNESCO World Heritage Site.

Musina

Eighteen kilometres south of the border, **MUSINA** is above all a mining town, although it does attract a fair bit of the traffic passing through on the N1. The border at Beitbridge is open 24 hours a day, so there's no reason to linger. The one thing of note around Musina is the **Baobab Tree Reserve** encircling the town. According to legend, God planted baobab trees upside down with their roots in the air. The trees here aren't in great stands but rather dotted around the bushveld, each one with a plate nailed onto it displaying its protected status. Many are over 1000 years old, and the largest have been hollowed out inside and used as houses, bars, shops and even toilets. There are quite a number of fine examples by the roadside on the N1, although many of these are covered in graffiti. The entrance to the reserve, which doesn't have any facilities, is a couple of kilometres south of town.

Beitbridge

On the South African side of the Limpopo, there isn't much to **BEITBRIDGE** other than a tacky service station, a habitually long queue of trucks, some noisy minibus touts and the customs and immigration buildings (which include a duty-free shop). Two bridges cross the Limpopo (the river memorably described by Rudyard Kipling in *Just So Stories* as "great grey-green, greasy"), one for vehicles and one for pedestrians. The border is open 24 hours a day, but count yourself lucky if you get through without delay, hassle or hindrance.

Mapungubwe National Park

Sixty-eight kilometres west of Musina, situated by the confluence of the Limpopo and Shashi rivers, where South Africa, Zimbabwe and Botswana meet, **Mapungubwe National Park** (daily 6am–6pm; R70; ☎015 534 2014, ⓦwww.sanparks.org/parks/mapungubwe) is well worth a detour if you have even the faintest interest in the area's fascinating archeology. Known as Hill of the Jackals, this is one of South Africa's newest national

---

Mapungubwe and other archeological sites

As one of the early melting pots of southern Africa, Limpopo has a number of important **archeological sites** where excavations have helped piece together a picture of the different people who inhabited the land for thousands of years. Some of the most interesting sites are at places where iron was smelted, as the development from what was essentially a Stone-Age culture to an Iron-Age culture, with its associated improvement in tools for cultivation and war, was a vital part of the migration of black tribes into South Africa around 1500 years ago. The presence of slag and other wastes provides the strongest clues – the iron itself seldom survives the processes of erosion. Some of the most revealing excavations have taken place at **Thulamela**, inside Kruger National Park not far from the Punda Maria Gate, **Bakone Malapa** cultural village outside Polokwane, **Makapan's Cave** near Mokopane, **Masorini**, also in the Kruger park, not far from Phalaborwa, and the single most important site in Limpopo Province, **Mapungubwe** (Hill of the Jackals), west of Musina.

parks that came into being in 2004 primarily to protect a famous Iron Age site that led to its designation as a UNESCO World Heritage Site. The site was only discovered in 1933, when a local farmer climbed the dome-shaped granite hill and found remains of stone walls, iron tools, graves, pottery and jewellery, including a tiny rhinoceros and a bowl, both made out of gold. It is now thought that the years 1000–1300 AD were the heyday of a civilization centred at Mapungubwe, which later moved to the much more famous Great Zimbabwe. The long-term goal is eventually to develop the park into a tri-border park incorporating Mashatu Reserve in Botswana and the Tuli Circle in Zimbabwe.

There are a number of different accommodation options within the park (❸), from airy wooden cottages to a luxurious stone lodge and a fully equipped campsite, but no other facilities so you have to be fully self sufficient. An exhibition of the treasures of Mapungubwe can be seen at the University of Pretoria (see p.630).

Routes to the northern Kruger National Park

The R525 runs across the Musina plains towards **Pafuri Gate**, the most northerly of the Kruger entrances, past which is a border post to Mozambique, although there is little beyond unless you're well equipped for adventure. If you need a **place to stay** on your way to Kruger, there's *Pafuri Rivercamp* (☎082 785 0305, ⓦwww.pafuri.co.za; ❸), on the Mutale River just before you reach the Pafuri Gate. This incorporates a series of treetop tents and an open self-catering bush camp (meals can be arranged in advance, but there's no electricity), from where you can set off in pursuit of the profuse local plants and wildlife, or relax by the river or pool.

Travel details

Trains

One daily service (except Sat) as follows:
Musina to: Bela-Bela (10hr 45min); Johannesburg (14hr 30min); Makhado (2hr 30min); Mokopane (8hr 15min); Polokwane (6hr 15min); Pretoria (12hr 75min).

Buses

Beitbridge to: Johannesburg (4 daily; 8–10hr), Polokwane (4 daily; 4hr).

Polokwane to: Johannesburg (5 daily; 4–5hr); Tzaneen (daily; 1hr 45min).
Tzaneen to: Johannesburg (daily; 7hr 30min); Polokwane (daily; 1hr 45min).

Domestic flights

Polokwane to: Johannesburg (Mon–Fri 4 daily, Sat & Sun 1–2 daily; 50min).

Lesotho

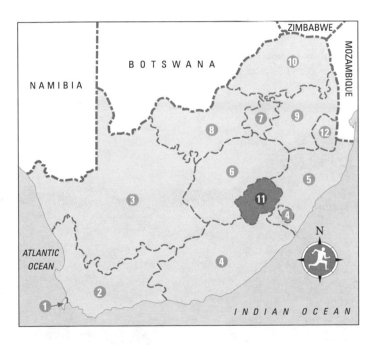

CHAPTER 11

Highlights

※ **Pony-trekking** The ideal way to see Lesotho, following paths from village to village through spectacular mountain scenery. See p.751

※ **Thaba Bosiu** The hilltop fortress from which Lesotho's greatest king, Moshoeshoe I, defended his kingdom against attackers. See p.758

※ **Maletsunyane Falls** A dramatic 200-metre waterfall plunging into a vast gorge deep in the remote highland region. See p.761

※ **"Roof of Africa" road** A winding road from Butha-Buthe to Sani Pass through dramatic mountain passes and valleys. See p.773

※ **Sehlabathebe National Park** A lonely mountain reserve with superb hiking. See p.782

▲ Riding in Lesotho

Lesotho

E ntirely surrounded by South Africa and sometimes mistaken for one of apartheid's ill-conceived semi-states, the aptly named "mountain kingdom" of **Lesotho** (pronounced "*Lee-su-tu*") is in fact proudly independent and very different in character from its dominant neighbour. Whereas the Rainbow Nation next door is, in many respects, distinctly European, laid-back Lesotho prides itself on its staunchly African heritage. Few people in the highlands of this fabulously beautiful and rugged land speak English or Afrikaans, though language isn't a barrier when the country's inhabitants – the **Basotho** – count among the most hospitable people in southern Africa. Another refreshing physical (and psychological) contrast is the almost total absence of fences, which means you can hike into the upland regions at will.

Travelling almost anywhere in Lesotho is an adventure: there are no motorways or slick city liner buses here (or, indeed, too many timetables), though the tarred **road network** is good, covered by rickety minibuses held together in some cases by little more than prayers. For the Basotho, **ponies** are the preferred method of transport, particularly in the highlands. You can do the same from pony-trekking lodges all over the country.

Lesotho is one of only a few countries to lie entirely above an altitude of 1000m, earning its nickname of "The Kingdom in the Sky". Even the sandstone **Lesotho lowlands** – which form a crescent along the country's western rim – would be highlands anywhere else. It's here that you'll find all the nation's major towns, including the busily practical capital of **Maseru**, with its very African mix of new glass buildings and dusty streets, which began life as tax-collection centres for the British administration. Lowland attractions include the weavers of **Teya-Teyaneng**, extraordinary caves near **Mateka**, rock paintings at **Liphofung**, and the mountain fortress at **Thaba Bosiu**, established by Lesotho's founder, King Moshoeshoe I.

At around 1400m above sea level sandstone gives way to basalt, which forms the bulk of the ruggedly beautiful **Lesotho highlands**. Once up the steep, twisting roads which lead into the mountains you can visit the engineering masterpieces of the **Katse** and **Mohale dams**, **ski** in the Maloti Mountains, fish from rivers everywhere and, above all, wander through the countryside, dividing your time between remote villages of simple stone-and-thatch huts and the peaceful solitude of the mountains. Three protected areas in particular are worth the effort of getting to: **Ts'ehlanyane National Park** and **Bokong Nature Reserve**, both in the Front Range of the Maloti Mountains and linked by a 39-kilometre hiking and horse-riding trail, and the exceedingly remote **Sehlabathebe National Park** in the east of the country, offering gloriously rugged hiking terrain.

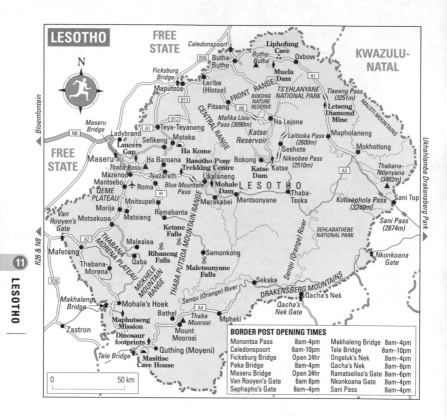

BORDER POST OPENING TIMES			
Monontsa Pass	8am–4pm	Makhaleng Bridge	8am–4pm
Caledonspoort	6am–10pm	Tele Bridge	8am–10pm
Ficksburg Bridge	Open 24hr	Ongeluk's Nek	8am–4pm
Peka Bridge	8am–4pm	Qacha's Nek	8am–8pm
Maseru Bridge	Open 24hr	Ramatseliso's Gate	8am–6pm
Van Rooyen's Gate	6am 8pm	Nkonkoana Gate	8am–4pm
Sephapho's Gate	8am–4pm	Sani Pass	8am–4pm

Some history

Lesotho exists because of the determined efforts of one man, **Moshoeshoe I** (1786–1870), to secure land for his people in the face of intense social upheaval and the insatiable land-hunger of others. Before the arrival of Moshoeshoe's ancestors, around 900 AD, the San inhabited Lesotho unchallenged. Today the San are gone, exterminated in 1873 by the last of many British campaigns against them. However, they left their mark in the country's rock paintings and elements of their tongue in the Sesotho language (including impossible buzzes and clicks), while traces of their vaguely oriental features and paler skin can still be discerned in some Basotho faces.

The Basotho first settled the fertile plains that today form the Lesotho lowlands and South Africa's Free State, before going on to colonize the mountains. They farmed these plains relatively peacefully for centuries, but by Moshoeshoe's time, tribes from elsewhere had forced thousands of Basotho off their land. Moshoeshoe proved his own marauding skills in 1809, when he rustled so many cattle from rival Chief Ramonaheng that he boasted, "I am the sharp shearer, the shaver . . . The blade that shaved off Ramonaheng's beard." After this feat he adopted the onomatopoeic name of Moshoeshoe, pronounced "Moshwehshweh", meaning the shearer (his real name was Leqopo). Moshoeshoe became chief in 1820 and established himself on top of a mountain near Butha-Buthe, where he became patron to many refugees in search of safety.

However, after a particularly vicious attack on Butha-Buthe in 1824, Moshoeshoe decided it was no longer safe and trekked south with his followers in search of a better mountain. He found one at Thaba Bosiu, which, though subsequently attacked repeatedly, was never taken. Moshoeshoe earned an almost mythical reputation for wisdom and generosity among ordinary Basotho that survives to this day.

Moshoeshoe had heard from travellers that **missionaries** brought peace, and so welcomed the arrival in 1833 of three from the Paris Evangelical Missionary Society, establishing them in Morija and taking an active interest in their work, though he never converted. The Paris missionaries established what is now the Lesotho Evangelical Church, second in size only to the Catholics, whose missionaries founded Roma in the 1860s (see p.760).

The kingdom was encroached upon by land-hungry Europeans from the 1840s onwards, and the **Orange Free State** government invaded in 1858, their soldiers destroying Morija and then launching a failed attack on Thaba Bosiu.

Some simple Sesotho

The Basotho language is **Sesotho**. It can be tricky to speak, as spellings rarely correspond with pronunciation, a legacy of the bizarre nineteenth-century transcription by French missionaries, in which locals take a perverse pride. For more information about Sesotho and tips on learning the language, see ⓦ www.sesotho.web.za.

Basics

Yes	*E* ("aye")
No	*E-e* ("ai-ai" as in the ai of hair)
Thank you	*Kea leboha* ("Kiya lee-bowa")
Today	*Kajeno* ("Ka-jen-noo")
Tomorrow	*Hosane* ("Ho-san-nee")
Yesterday	*Moobane* ("Mow-ban-nee")
Where is . . . ?	*E kae . . . ?* ("O kai ...")
Where can we stay?	*Nka lula hokae?* ("N-ka dula o kai")
Where are you going?	*U ea kae?* ("Oo ya kai")
Where are you from?	*U tsoa kae?* ("Oo tswa kai")
How much?	*Ke bokae?* ("Ke bo-kai")
I speak Sesotho a little	*Ke bua Sesotho ha nyane* ("Ke boo-a Sesotho han-yaney")

Greetings and responses

Hello (informal)	*Khotso* ("Khot-so" – literally "peace")
Hello (to one)	*Lumela* ("Do-mela")
...father (used to address any man)	*Ntate* ("N-dar-tay")
...mother (used to address any woman)	*Me* ("Mmeh")
...brother (used to address any boy)	*Abuti* ("A-boo-ti")
...sister (used to address any girl)	*Ausi* ("A-woo-si")
Hello (to many)	*Lumelang* ("Do-melang")
How are you?(formal)	*U phela jooang* ("O pela jwan")
I'm fine (formal)	*Ke phela hantle* ("Ke pela hank-le") with a clicked *k*
Goodbye (said by person leaving)	*Sala hantle* ("Sala hank-le" – literally "go well")
Goodbye (said by people remaining)	*Tsamaea hantle* ("Ts-my-ya hank-le" – literally "stay well")

They nonetheless captured plenty of farmland, whose acquisition was sanctioned by a British treaty in 1860. In 1865, the Orange Free State government cited Basotho cattle theft as the pretext for a new conflict, though few could deny Moshoeshoe's bitter assertion that "my great sin is that I possess a good and fertile country". The ensuing **Seqiti War** resulted in the destruction of Basotho crops, forcing Moshoeshoe into a humiliating treaty in 1866 which signed over most of his remaining good land. The war resumed in 1867, and was halted only by the British taking over what was left of the kingdom as the protectorate of **Basotholand** in 1868. The Treaty of Aliwal North in 1869 restored Moshoeshoe's land east of the Caledon but left the rest with the Free State, where it has remained to this day – a loss that still stings.

Moshoeshoe died in 1870 and the British handed Basotholand to the Cape administration a year later, which began taxing its new subjects, establishing a series of hut tax-collection points which have since grown into Lesotho's modest collection of small towns. Discontent turned to open rebellion in 1879, when the Cape government decided to confiscate all Basotho firearms. The result was the **Gun War**, one of few colonial-era conflicts in which the locals came out on top; the prize for the victorious Basotho was the resumption of direct rule from Britain in 1884.

Along with Bechuanaland and Swaziland, Basotholand rejected incorporation into the union of South Africa in 1910, with **King Letsie II** instead helping found the South African Native National Congress (later the ANC) in 1912. During the following years, the monarchy and chiefs' position declined, partly because British reforms forced their uneasy conversion into a junior arm of the colonial civil service, but also because social changes at work in the region, like migration, urbanization and rising education levels, proved too much for them to adapt to. In 1960, when **Moshoeshoe II** was crowned king, independence politics were in full swing, spearheaded by Pan-Africanist Ntsa Mokhele's Basotho Congress Party (BCP), and rivalled by the more conservative Basotho National Party (BNP). After narrowly winning the 1965 elections, the BNP led newly named Lesotho into **independence** on October 4, 1966. However, after losing the 1970 election, prime minister Leabua Jonathan annulled the result, declared a **state of emergency**, and carried on ruling until he was toppled in 1986 by a **military coup** led by Major General Metsing Lekhanya. Lekhanya ordered the **expulsion of the ANC** from Lesotho and signed an agreement that year with apartheid South Africa for the **Lesotho Highlands Water Project** (see box, p.769) – Africa's biggest engineering project to date, aiming to divert much of Lesotho's ample water resources to the thirsty South African province of Gauteng.

In 1990, Lekhanya sent Moshoeshoe II into exile and installed Moshoeshoe's son on the throne as **Letsie III**, but a year later Lekhanya was himself ousted by Major General Phisona, who then gave way to a **democratically elected government** led by Mokhele's BCP in 1993. Letsie stood down in favour of his father in 1995, but Moshoeshoe II died in a car crash the next year, and Letsie regained the throne.

In 1997, the BCP split with Mokhele and most of his cabinet, breaking away to form the Lesotho Congress for Democracy (LCD). The following year Mokhele's health deteriorated and he was forced to step down just before the **1998 elections**, where his successor Pakalitha Mosisili won by a landslide. Opposition parties cried foul amid widespread allegations of **vote-rigging**, and in July and August, crowds gathered outside the Royal Palace in Maseru demanding the results be overturned – these protests subsequently developed into a **mutiny** by Lesotho Defence Force soldiers. In September, under the flag of a Southern African Development Community (SADC) peacekeeping force,

South African troops crossed the border, and fierce fighting took place around military bases and at the strategically vital Katse Dam. Meanwhile, thousands of demonstrators protested at what they regarded as South Africa's heavy-handed intervention, and a large number of shops and offices across the country were looted and burned.

After the 1998 riots, Lesotho's electoral system was changed to combine majority voting and proportional representation: eighty parliamentary seats to be elected by the first-past-the-post system, forty through proportional representation. To everyone's relief, the **2002 elections** passed off without incident, with the LCD winning most of the seats, and the BNP leading the opposition. The peaceful nature of the vote was a hopeful sign of a more constructive political climate. However, October 2006 saw yet more political divisions, with the Minister of Communications, Tom Thabane, along with seventeen of his party colleagues, breaking away from the LCD government to form the All Basotho Convention (ABC) party. In response, the LCD government called an early election in February 2007, which was once again mired in controversy. Whilst the LCD party comfortably won the majority of the constituency seats, the allocation of the forty seats voted through proportional representation was contested by the opposition parties. SADC appointed the President of Botswana to mediate, who in turn requested electoral experts to examine the situation. Political tension came to a climax in June 2007 when gunshots were fired at the houses of several ministers and, in the following days, at the home of the leader of the ABC. As a result the government declared a state of emergency and an all-night curfew was imposed in Maseru. The situation calmed in the following months but the original dispute remains unresolved and the animosity between the two major political parties threatens to escalate once again.

Aside from politics, there are some promising economic opportunities for Lesotho. **Mining** is set to bring in significant revenue: since reopening in 2004, the diamond mine at Letseng has discovered three of the world's largest diamonds, and has the potential to provide up to twenty percent of Lesotho's GDP. The government has finalized its **Poverty Reduction Strategy** and continues to attract funding from international donors. And the royalties from the **Lesotho Highlands Water Project** are guaranteed for the foreseeable future.

However, a number of gargantuan challenges remain unanswered. **Poverty** remains entrenched, particularly in the rural areas of the country where the majority rely on small-scale agriculture. It was these areas which were pushed to the brink of emergency in 2007 when Lesotho suffered its worst **drought** in thirty years, resulting in a government appeal for food aid from the international community. **Environmental degradation** remains an issue too, ever visible in the numerous dongas across the country. And economically, Lesotho is still recovering from the massive losses in its textile exports after increased Chinese competition, and suffers very high levels of **unemployment**. Most devastating of all is the scourge of **HIV/AIDS**; the prevalence of the pandemic in Lesotho is one of the highest in the world, and life expectancy for the nation has plummeted to 35 years. The future prospects of the mountain kingdom rest upon whether it can overcome these challenges.

When to go

Lesotho's **winter** runs from May to July, when it often snows in the highlands and sometimes in the lowlands too. Although the days are usually clear and warm, it gets extremely cold at night and ice can make driving hazardous in the highlands, while snowfall blocks even tarred highways for days at a time. **Spring**

Accommodation

Accommodation **standards** are generally lower than in South Africa, and even mid-range places might have holes in bed linen leaky plumbing, or missing toilet seats. Places fall broadly into three categories: cheap and basic dorms in rural or religious training centres; bland, conventional urban hotels that get the bulk of their business from conferences and civil servants; and relaxed, well-run **tourist-oriented lodges**. The last, such as the *Malealea Lodge* (p.777), *Semonkong Lodge* (p.761), *Molumong Guest House* (p.773) and *Sani Top Chalets* (p.775), offer a range of accommodation from backpacker dorms to well-appointed rondavels; most also offer pony-trekking and hiking (see box, p.751).

Costs are slightly higher than in rural South Africa, with the cheapest doubles averaging M250–300, singles M200 and dorms around M100. Exceptions are the rural training centres, where you'll pay around M50 for a bunk.

Independent **camping** is possible all over rural Lesotho, while many lodges allow camping in their grounds. If you're camping rough, ask permission first, preferably from the village chief (*Morena oa motse*), who may ask you to pay a token fee of M20–30 per person. It's normally fine just to pitch your tent if there's no one around.

Airport tax

A **fee** of M50 is payable when departing Lesotho from Moshoeshoe I airport. This is usually included in the price of the plane ticket.

Books and maps

A useful supplement to the coverage in this chapter is the *Backpackers Guide to Lesotho* booklet, self-published every few years by Russell Suchet, who runs *Sani Lodge* over the border in KwaZulu-Natal (p.504); you can also buy copies at the Morija Museum and at some South African backpacker lodges. Some of these also stock a very good 1:250,000 **topographical map** of Lesotho which marks most trails; it's also available from the Department of Lands, Surveys and Physical Planning on Lerotholi Road, near the corner of Constitution Road, in Maseru (℡2232 2376; M50). This is also the only place where you can buy the really detailed 1:50,000 maps (M35), essential for serious hiking; plus 1:10,000 maps of Maseru and others. They also sell intriguing aerial shots of Lesotho from 1950 to the present day. For drivers, the 1:785,000 road map published by the Automobile Association of South Africa and sold at Maseru's tourist office (M10) is perfectly adequate, and contains detailed route descriptions on the back.

Costs, money and banks

Overall **costs** are marginally lower than in South Africa, though accommodation can be more expensive. **Credit cards** are of limited use; while hotels and lodges geared to foreign visitors accept them, as do a few Maseru restaurants, supermarkets and some of the craft shops in Teya-Teyaneng, you'll need cash for everything else.

Lesotho's currency is the **loti**, plural **maluti** (M), divided into 100 lisenti; the loti is tied to the South African rand (R1=M1). You can also use rand throughout Lesotho, but you cannot use or exchange maluti anywhere outside Lesotho (apart from in some South African border towns such as Ladybrand), so make sure you use them up or exchange them before leaving.

Banks are found in all Lesotho's towns, and while you can **change money** at some of them if you have enough patience, Maseru is the only place where it's relatively quick and painless. Banking hours are Monday to Friday 8.30am to 3.30pm, and Saturday 8am–noon; Saturdays are busy and best avoided, whilst queues can be huge at the end of the month when the majority of Basotho workers go to the bank to collect/cash their wages. Many banks have ATMs and most accept foreign cash cards. The larger hotels in Maseru and the lowland towns change money, but at ludicrously bad rates, making them very much a last resort.

Food and drink

The Basotho staple **food** is *papa,* maize meal which is boiled and stirred until it resembles stiff, white mashed potato. An alternative is *nyekoe*, brown beans mixed with sorghum and wheat. Both are fairly bland but filling and usually served with some kind of *nama* (meat) and *moroho* (leafy vegetable – usually spinach or cabbage). On the street, you'll find *dipapata*, delicious steamed bread, and a fried snack called *makoenya* or fat cakes.

For **drinks**, there's the usual array of sodas. The home-grown beer is *Maluti*, but most brands of South African beers, including *Hansa* and *Black Label*, can be found across the country. Traditional *joala* (beer) is brewed mostly in rural areas and is made from sorghum. It has a thick consistency and is an acquired taste, but if you're interested in trying some, look out for a yellow or white flag flying outside village huts, which signifies that *joala* is being brewed and sold.

Phone numbers

Lesotho's **country code** is ☎266, unless you're calling from South Africa, in which case it's ☎09266. There are no **area codes** (numbers given in the guide with area codes are in South Africa). To **phone abroad from Lesotho**, dial ☎00, followed by the country and area codes and subscriber number; for South Africa, dial ☎0027, then the area code omitting the initial "0", and the phone number. To call collect, dial the international operator on ☎109.

Public holidays

January 1 New Year's Day
March 11 Moshoeshoe Day
Good Friday
Easter Monday
May 1 Workers' Day
May 25 Heroes' Day
July 17 King's Birthday
Ascension Day (Thursday)
October 4 Independence Day
December 25 Christmas Day
December 26 Boxing Day

Red tape and embassies

Visas are not required for citizens of the EU, the Commonwealth (excepting India, Ghana, Nigeria and Pakistan) and the US. If you've travelled through a yellow fever zone, you'll need an International Certificate of Vaccination against yellow fever. The standard entry permit is for 14 or 28 days; should you need an extension, visit the Department of Immigration and Passport Services on Assisi Road in Maseru (☎2232 3771, ☎2231 0538). For details of Lesotho's embassies, see "Listings" on p.757.

Security

Overall, Lesotho is a safe country for travellers. Muggings and opportunistic theft are, however, a continuing problem in Maseru and some lowland border towns, particularly Maputsoe and Butha-Buthe; be careful wandering around back streets, and avoid walking around at night. In the highlands, however, most hikers and campers have little more to worry about than snarling dogs and persistent demands for sweets ("pompong" from the French *bon-bon*) from children. The practice of giving sweets

Contd...

to children originates with the early French missionaries and has encouraged begging throughout the country; if pestered for sweets simply smile and politely refuse. As ever, it's unwise to flaunt your wealth too visibly, and don't leave valuables like cameras lying around unattended.

Tour operators

Lesotho's tourist infrastructure remains sketchy in some areas, and arranging activities such as pony-trekking and visits to the natural parks can be time-consuming, especially without your own transport. If you're short on time, consider an **organized tour**. *Malealea Lodge* (p.777) in the southwest offers some innovative pony-trekking and 4WD combinations, whilst the *Trading Post Guest House* in Roma is probably the best source of information on 4WD trails. Coming from South Africa there are a few tour operators to choose from. Thaba Tours (☎+27 (0)33 701 2888, ⓦwww.thabatours.co.za) specializes in overland trips between Durban and Maseru via the Sani Pass and pony-trekking and hiking (6 days/5 nights full board R5500–6500). Maluti Treks (☎+27 (0)82 452 0633, ⓦwww.malutitreks.com) will also take you from Durban to Maseru every Tuesday and Friday (pick-ups at Clarens and Harrismith) and can arrange pony-trekking, hiking and visits to *Semonkong Lodge*.

Water

Tap water is sometimes safe to drink in the highlands, less so in the lowlands and particularly in Maseru. People with sensitive stomachs should stick to bottled. While Lesotho's rivers and streams are bilharzia-free, drinking from them is inadvisable unless you purify the water first.

Websites

ⓦ**www.lesotho.gov.ls** The Lesotho government's portal with national news and links to its ministries, including the Ministry of Tourism.

ⓦ**www.friendsoflesotho.org** Set up by former Peace Corps volunteers, it contains lots of background information about Lesotho, plenty of photos and some detailed topographical maps, plus the Peace Corp's manual to learning Sesotho.

ⓦ**www.seelesotho.com** Although somewhat out of date, this contains a wealth of information about the history, culture, flora and fauna of Lesotho, plus tips on where to visit and how to get there.

ⓦ**www.sesotho.web.za** The first stop if you are interested in learning Sesotho, with guidance in greetings and basic phrases in addition to references for Sesotho publications. There's an online dictionary too.

(Aug–Oct), when the snow melts, is a beautiful time, with new plants sprouting up everywhere. November to January is **summer**, when Lesotho gets most of its rain, often torrential, turning dirt roads into mudslides. Still, when it isn't raining the weather is usually sunny and the landscape is coloured in vivid shades of green. **Autumn** (Feb–April) is one of the best times to visit, as it doesn't usually rain too much and temperatures are moderate. Whatever the time of year, Lesotho can be very cold at night, particularly in the highlands, and prone to rapid weather changes, for which it's always wise to be prepared.

Getting to Lesotho

Lesotho is most comfortably reached by **plane** from Johannesburg (there are no flights from anywhere else). South African Airlink operates five flights a day to Moshoeshoe I International Airport from Monday to Friday and three on the weekends. Taxis and shuttle buses (M50) connect with Maseru, 18km to the northwest.

There are limited **bus** services from South African cities to Lesotho's main overland border at Maseru Bridge (2km from the capital). Intercape (see p.42) - runs a daily service from Cape Town and Durban, whilst Vaal Maseru (℡ +27 (0)18 462 1000, ⓦ www.vaalmaseru.co.za) has early-morning buses from Rustenburg and Klerksdorp in the North West Province daily (except Sun & Mon). There are frequent **minibus taxis** throughout the day from Johannesburg, Bloemfontein and Durban, and less frequently from a host of smaller towns in the Free State and North West Province to various border crossings in Lesotho's western lowlands – particularly Maseru Bridge, Ficksburg Bridge (next to Maputsoe) and Caledonspoort, close to Butha-Buthe, both to the north. All these places have plentiful onward transport connections within Lesotho. Much more awkward to reach, but infinitely more engaging an introduction to the country, is to enter via the Drakensberg, most spectacularly along the **Sani Pass**, into the country's remote eastern corner; see p.773 for details.

Drivers have a choice of fourteen border crossings. Distances to Maseru are 1150km from Cape Town, 550km from Durban, and 420km from Johannesburg. Easiest to reach are the western lowlands crossings, including Maseru Bridge, Ficksburg Bridge and Caledonspoort. For **border opening times**, see the map on p.742. If you've rented a car in South Africa, check the **insurance** covers you for Lesotho, especially in winter.

Getting around

Lesotho has a good tarred **road network**, though you can't avoid dirt (and often boulder-strewn) roads when heading to more out-of-the-way places. Wherever you travel, and especially when you make for the highlands, twisting roads, fast minibus taxis and frequent encounters with roadside pedestrians and livestock make **driving** tiring work. The main route through the **northern** part of the country is the continuous tarred road leading northeast from Maseru to Butha-Buthe and then southeast to Mokhotlong. While the onward section to Sani and into South Africa can be negotiated by an experienced driver in a saloon car in good weather, you should really only consider doing it in 4WD. Striking off the northern route, the **Katse dam road** from Leribe is tarred and of very high quality, though it involves some punishing gradients. On the **central route**, the tar extends for a way beyond Mohale Dam around Likalaneng but work is under way to continue it most of the way to Thaba-Tseka. The high-altitude route from here to Katse is 4WD only (although there are plans for tar by 2009). The **southern** route from Maseru is tarred as far as Mphaki, but is passable in an ordinary saloon up to Qacha's Nek. The road beyond Qacha's Nek to Sehlabathebe National Park is impassable without 4WD, though again minibus taxis and buses somehow manage it.

Car and 4WD rental is offered by Avis, Budget and Imperial Fleet in Maseru (see "Listings" on p.757). Depending on where you want to go, 4WD may be essential. **Fuel** costs roughly the same as in South Africa; unleaded is readily available in Maseru, but can be scarce elsewhere. The **speed limit** is 80kph, and 50kph in urban areas. **Hitching** is much safer than in South Africa and is a good way to get around. Some drivers expect payment, so negotiate this before you've travelled too far.

Public transport is chaotic and unregulated, but does at least go everywhere in the country. **Minibus taxis** are often the main form of transport, and run on

Hospitable and almost entirely fenceless, Lesotho is a **hiker's paradise**. It's possible to set off into the hills and walk for as long as you like, with no prospect of an angry farmer yelling at you to get off his land – quite a change from South Africa. In more remote areas, locals get around by pony, and **pony-trekking** – which can be arranged at most tourist-oriented lodges and two of the three national parks – is an undoubted highlight of any trip to the country.

Hiking

Always **prepare adequately** before setting out, and bring supplies for at least a day more than you think the hike will take. Be warned that in the highest reaches of the highlands there are very few villages; lovely as this is, it's also risky, so make sure someone knows where you've gone, and don't hike in remote areas on your own. Lesotho's weather is notoriously fickle – be prepared for all eventualities.

Bring enough cash (you can't count on rural banks changing money), a torch, plenty of food (there aren't many stores in remote rural areas), a water container, water-purifying tablets, an all-weather cooker with fuel (don't count on finding firewood), a genuinely waterproof tent, a sleeping mat and a very warm sleeping bag. A compass and map (see p.748) are also invaluable.

Pony-trekking

Ponies were introduced to Lesotho from the Cape in the nineteenth century, with one of the first given as a present to King Moshoeshoe I by chief Moorosi in 1829. By the time of Moshoeshoe's death in 1870, ponies were widespread throughout the kingdom and the Basotho had become expert riders.

Lesotho's ponies are famously hardy, capable of slogging away for hours and negotiating slippery rock passes. The Basotho rarely groom their mounts, so they usually look pretty dishevelled, but that doesn't affect their performance in the hills, where for many locals they are the only form of long-distance transport.

A number of lodges and other places offer **pony-trekking** (no previous equestrian experience needed) though only a few are well organized, the best being the *Malealea Lodge* (see p.777) and *Semonkong Lodge* (see p.761). Semonkong, Mokhotlong, Bokong, Ts'ehlanyane and the area around the Basotho Pony Trekking Centre (see p.762) are all high up; the others are lower down, with less variable weather conditions, though the terrain is harder on the ponies.

Costs vary according to group size, but tend to average M150–200 a day if you're on your own, or M120–150 per person in a couple; for overnights, count on an extra M100–200 per person, which can include a pack horse as well as accommodation. A full-day's ride typically involves six or seven hours (10–15km) in the saddle, so overnight trips can be quite strenuous. Children under 12 are not usually allowed on overnighters.

Wherever you go, make sure you bring a wide-brimmed sunhat, sun protection cream, waterproof gear, swimwear in summer, and a water bottle (and, if you're staying overnight, a sleeping bag and mat, torch and food, though cooking utensils and fuel should be provided).

major routes, at least until early afternoon. **Buses** are slower but safer than minibus taxis, and both are very inexpensive. The only **timetables** are for buses operated by Lesotho Freight and Bus Services; otherwise, the rule of thumb is to check the day before, and get to the bus or taxi rank early if you have a long way to go.

For **internal flights** you can charter planes out of Maseru Airport (not Moshoeshoe I; it's also known as "the old airport"), northeast of town, through the Mission Aviation Fellowship (p.757), which for example charges M2890 (one-way) to Mohotlong for a whole plane which can carry four to five people. These days, though, most well-heeled visitors use **helicopters** rented out by the Lesotho Defence Force (Private Bag A 166 Maseru ☎2231 2910, ask for Operations), which cost about the same price as planes (M3000 per hour).

Maseru and the central districts

The most convenient entry point from South Africa, and the country's most sophisticated urban centre by far, **Maseru** is a handy first stop for exploring Lesotho – the place to fill up on supplies, change money and organize onward transport. Apart from a few elegant colonial sandstone buildings, there's not a great deal to see here, and most visitors pass through fairly quickly. However, if you're in town for a few days there are plenty of excursions into the surrounding countryside, including to Lesotho's most famous mountain, **Thaba Bosiu**, the so-called "Mountain of the Night" where the founder of the nation, Moshoeshoe I, ruled for almost fifty years.

Further afield, **Roma** – 30km southeast of Maseru along the fast A3 – is the country's academic centre, surrounded by beautiful sandstone hills and with a historic Catholic mission. South of Roma, a road ascends into the **central highlands** along a series of mountain passes – one of the most striking drives in the country. At the end of the road, the village of **Semonkong** has a superb lodge, a spectacular waterfall nearby and a wide variety of outdoor activities on offer. Continuing along the A3 east of Roma, the highway heads up into Lesotho's **Central Range**, the tarmac ending shortly after the impressive Mohale Dam. Onward travel requires high clearance 2WD or 4WD. Though the final destination of **Thaba-Tseka** is unspectacular, the journey more than compensates, and from Thaba-Tseka it's possible to continue along a reasonably good dirt road to Katse and its massive dam (see p.767).

Maseru

Sprawling **MASERU**, the nation's capital and only big town, spills east from the Caledon River, which marks the border with South Africa. Maseru was established by the British in 1869 as the administrative centre for newly annexed Basotholand, but Britain put as little effort into developing Maseru as it did the rest of the country, no doubt expecting it to become just a minor South African town when Basotholand was incorporated into South Africa.

Surrounded by sprawling shantytown suburbs, the city has grown swiftly over recent years, poverty in Lesotho's rural areas having driven people to the capital in search of a better life. Few have found it yet, and the city has a high

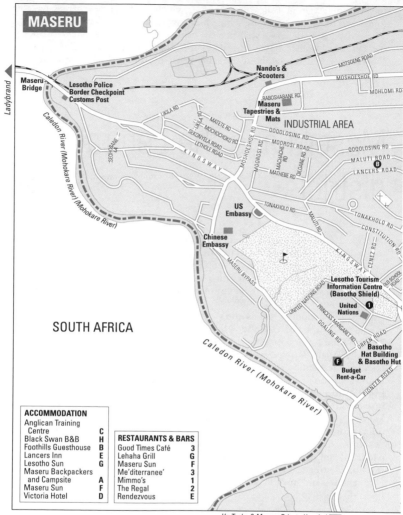

MASERU

Ladybrand

Caledon River (Mohokare River) (Mohokare River)

Maseru Bridge

Lesotho Police Border Checkpoint Customs Post

UKILA RD
MATETE RD
MOCHOCHOKO RD
SEKONYELA ROAD
LETHOLE ROAD
MOSHOESHOE RD
KINGSWAY

Nando's & Scooters

MOTSOENE ROAD
MOSHOESHOE RD.
MOHLOMI RD.
RABOSHABANE RD.

Maseru Tapestries & Mats

INDUSTRIAL AREA

QOQOLOSING RD.
MOOROSI ROAD
MACHACHE RD
CALOANE RD
MATHEBE RD
QOQOLOSING RD.
MALUTI ROAD
LANCERS ROAD

US Embassy

TONAKHOLO RD.
TONAKHOLO RD.
CONSTITUTION RD
MALUTI RD
CENEZ RD
CONSTITUTION RD

Chinese Embassy

MASERU BYPASS
KINGSWAY

SOUTH AFRICA

Caledon River (Mohokare River)

Lesotho Tourism Information Centre (Basotho Shield)

United Nations

UNITED NATIONS ROAD
PRINCESS MARGARET RD
DOALING RD
ORPEN ROAD
OLD SCHOOL ROAD

Basotho Hat Building & Basotho Hut

Budget Rent-a-Car

PIONEER ROAD

ACCOMMODATION

Anglican Training Centre	C
Black Swan B&B	H
Foothills Guesthouse	B
Lancers Inn	E
Lesotho Sun	G
Maseru Backpackers and Campsite	A
Maseru Sun	F
Victoria Hotel	D

RESTAURANTS & BARS

Good Times Café	3
Lehaha Grill	G
Maseru Sun	F
Me'diterranee'	3
Mimmo's	1
The Regal	2
Rendezvous	E

Ha Tseka & Maseru Private Hospital ▼

unemployment rate. Yet Maseru's compact centre has all the marks of an upwardly mobile African city, with slick fashions and mobile phones much in evidence.

Maseru's older buildings, as well as some stylish new ones, are built from well-crafted local **sandstone** – from which the city gets its name – though a number of ugly concrete box buildings diminish the effect and, unfortunately, dominate the skyline.

Most of the city's daytime action happens on or around **Kingsway**, the road which runs through town, becoming increasingly downmarket and lively as it heads east towards the cathedral. Compared to most towns and cities in South Africa, Maseru is relatively safe, and as long as you take the **safety precautions** you would in any other African city, you can walk around here comfortably by

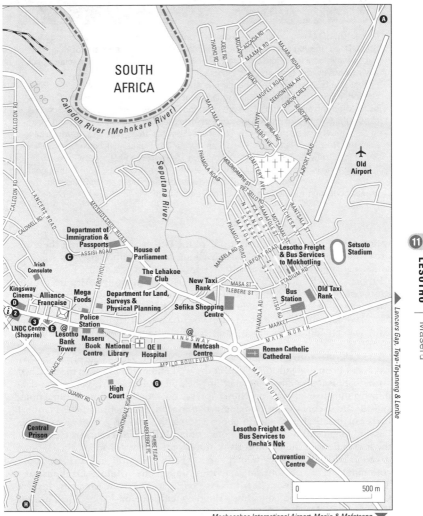

SOUTH AFRICA

Caledon River (Mohokare River)

Seputana River

Old Airport

Department of Immigration & Passports

House of Parliament

Irish Consulate

The Lehakoe Club

New Taxi Rank

Lesotho Freight & Bus Services to Mokhotling

Setsoto Stadium

Kingsway Cinema
Alliance Française

Mega Foods

Department for Land, Surveys & Physical Planning

Sefika Shopping Centre

Bus Station

Old Taxi Rank

LNDC Centre (Shoprite)

Lesotho Bank Tower

Police Station

Maseru Book Centre

National Library

QE II Hospital

Metcash Centre

Roman Catholic Cathedral

High Court

Central Prison

Lesotho Freight & Bus Services to Qacha's Nek

Convention Centre

0   500 m

Moshoeshoe International Airport, Morija & Mafetseng ▼

day. Walking around at night, however, is ill-advised, since the empty streets make wandering tourists fine targets for opportunistic muggers.

Arrival, information and transport

Buses and minibuses from South Africa terminate at the Maseru Bridge border crossing. Walk over the bridge and complete the formalities, then either walk or catch a minibus taxi or "4 plus 1" (saloon taxi - four passengers plus one driver) for the two-kilometre ride into town (both M3). **Minibus taxis** arriving from elsewhere in Lesotho will drop you at one of several chaotic ranks: see the box "Moving on from Maseru" on p.754 for details. **Buses** drop you in the calmer environment of Stadium Road (not at the bus station, which

Driving out of Maseru, orientation is easy, as both Main North Road (the A1) and Main South Road (the A2) start at the cathedral roundabout at the east end of Kingsway. Public transport leaves from a number of ranks and stations close to the roundabout – where exactly depends on the destination.

Most **buses** leave from the chaotic bus station between Market Street and Pitso Ground, northeast of the cathedral roundabout. Early morning long-distance **buses to Mokhotlong and Qacha's Nek** are operated by Lesotho Freight and Bus Services (☎ 2231 3535); for Mokhotlong they depart from Stadium Road next to Maseru Mart; to Qacha's Nek they depart from St James. **Minibus taxis heading south** depart from the New Taxi Rank (also known as Sefika Taxi Rank), just behind the Sefika Shopping Centre on Moshoeshoe Road. Urban taxis marked "Thetsane" pass by.

Minibus taxis heading east and north leave from the Old Taxi Rank, 200m east of the bus station – the easiest way to find it is to go up Main North Road from the roundabout then turn left up Motsamai Road; the rank is in the second block on the left.

is only for departures), on the east side of the city centre, from where there are urban minibus taxis and local taxis. Walking by day with luggage is safe, if a somewhat amusing sight for locals.

Flights touch down at Moshoeshoe I International Airport, 18km southeast of town off Main South Road (the A2 towards Mafeteng). South African Airlink operates a shuttle bus to and from Maseru (☎ 2235 0418; M50), which can pick you up or drop you at a hotel. Private taxis (see below) cost nearer M80. Alternatively, wait for an infrequent minibus taxi at the airport gate.

The **Lesotho tourist office** (Mon–Fri 8am–5pm, Sat 8.30am–1pm; ☎ 2231 2427, ℮ touristinfo@ltdc.org.ls) lies at the west end of Kingsway in the thatched Basotho Shield Building. The staff are helpful and can give you up-to-date information, a town map, brochures for various hotels and tourist attractions, and the latest contacts for booking accommodation at Sehlabathebe National Park. For practical information about visiting the various components of the Lesotho Highlands Water Project, contact the **LHDA Information Centre** on the fourth floor of the Lesotho Bank Tower on Kingsway (Mon–Fri 8am–5pm; ☎ & ℉ 2232 1934, ⓦ www.lhwp.org.ls). Lastly, practical information about community-run eco-tourism activities under the **Maloti–Drakensberg Transfrontier Project** (see box, p.765) can be had from its Project Coordinator, 7th floor, Post Office Building, entrance on Palace Road just off Kingsway (☎ 2231 2662, ⓦ www.maloti.org).

The city centre is compact and easy to **get around** on foot, though there are lots of **minibus taxis** running up and down Kingsway and into the suburbs, from just before dawn to around 8pm. At night, **private taxis** are the only option; operators include Luxury Telephone Taxis (☎ 2232 6211), Moonlite Taxis (☎ 2231 2605), Perfect Taxis (☎ 2232 5222) and Planet Taxis (☎ 2231 7777).

Accommodation

Maseru is the only place in the country where there's much choice of **accommodation**, offering everything from camping and grim dorms to luxury suites in plush hotels. The central options, on or near Kingsway, are the most practical if you don't have your own transport.

Anglican Training Centre Corner of Assisi and Lancers rds ☎ 2232 2046, ☏ 2231 4014. Large and fairly institutionalized place reasonably close to Kingsway offering spartan but adequate double rooms with communal showers and toilets. ❶

Black Swan B&B 770 Manong Rd, Hillsview ☎ 2232 5204, ⓦ www.blackswan.co.ls. In a quiet area of town, this new hotel has clean and attractive rooms and a small indoor pool set around a tidy compound. Breakfast is available in the dining room (M30). ❸

Foothills Guesthouse 121 Maluti Rd, Maseru West ☎ 5870 6566, ⓔ melvin@xsinet.co.za. This colonial-style, sandstone house offers homely accommodation in a quiet area of town, including six comfortable and spotless rooms and a couple of self-catering chalets. Self-catering ❷, B&B ❸

Lancers Inn Kingsway ☎ 2231 2114, ⓦ www .lancersinn.co.ls. Maseru's most charcterful and pleasant place to stay, set in a very central and attractive sandstone building which has been tastefully renovated since it was looted in the riots of 1998. There are well-priced and comfortable rondavels and chalets with en-suite bathrooms, a pool and a good beer garden and restaurant, all set in attractive gardens. ❹

Lesotho Sun off Nightingale Rd ☎ 2231 4300, ⓔ lesoresv@sunint.co.za. Maseru's largest and smartest accommodation option, this resort has comfortable (if smallish) rooms with TVs and good views over town, plus loads of sports facilities, health spa, pool, casino, cinema and several good restaurants. ❻

Maseru Backpackers and Campsite beyond the old airport on Airport Rd ☎ 2232 5166, ⓦ www .ldl.co.ls. The best camping option in Maseru, with clean shower blocks and a well-equipped kitchen, plus decent backpacker accommodation in small dormitories. The site overlooks the Maqalika Dam, and a range of outdoor activities can be arranged. ❶

Maseru Sun 12 Orpen Rd, Old Europa ☎ 2231 2434, ⓔ maseru@sunint.co.za. The second of the town's *Sun* hotels, with decent rooms in soothing, well-tended garden surroundings which are popular with locals in the evenings. There's also a good restaurant and a large, attractive swimming pool. ❻

Victoria Hotel Kingsway ☎ 2231 3687, ⓦ www .hotelvictoria.co.ls. This plain concrete high-rise is a prominent landmark in central Maseru, offering comfortable if unremarkable rooms, a bar and an adequate restaurant. ❸

The City

The city's most famous landmarks are a trio of imposing neo-traditional thatched buildings at the west end of Kingsway: the **Basotho Shield**, which houses the tourist office and which – viewed from above – does indeed resemble a shield; the **Basotho Hut** opposite, and the appropriately shaped **Basotho Hat Building**, housing the well-stocked Lesotho Cooperative

▲ The Basotho Hat Building, Maseru

The Basotho Hat Building is home to the impressive Lesotho Cooperative Handicrafts shop (☏2232 2523, ©lch@basothohat.co.ls; accepts credit cards). You'll find a few more crafts, mostly woven Basotho hats (*mokorotlo*), sold on the pavements around this end of town. Good handicraft outlets on the outskirts of town include Maseru Tapestries & Mats (☏2231 1773, ©maserutapestry@yahoo.com), signposted on Raboshabane Road, in the industrial area, which has handwoven tapestries and carpets; and the similar Seithati Weavers, 8km out along the Mafeteng road (☏2231 3975, ⓦwww.villageweavers.co.ls). See p.765 for more on Lesotho's craft industry.

Handicrafts shop (see box above). The main part of town lies east of here along Kingsway, though there's not much to see other than a handful of colonial-era buildings: the **Alliance Française** in the former library at the corner with Pioneer Road, the former **Anglican church** in a scruffy park facing *Lancers Inn* further up on the right, and the 1891 **Resident Commissioner's House** (now a government department), on the left beyond the towering **Post Office** building – evidence of Maseru's intention to create a thoroughly modern capital. Kingsway comes to an end at the traffic circle by the impressively large sandstone **Roman Catholic Cathedral**, where it splits into Main North Road and Main South Road.

Eating, drinking and nightlife

As you'd expect, Maseru has the best selection of **restaurants** in Lesotho. A couple of the familiar takeaway chains are here, including *KFC* on Kingsway and *Nando's* on Moshoeshoe Road in the industrial area. Next door to *Nando's*, *Scooters* does good takeaway pizzas (☏2231 4481). For more local fare, *Mega Foods*, behind the post office, is a popular lunch spot for Maseru's office workers. One place not to miss is the bakery beside *Lancers Inn*, where you can get delicious, freshly baked loaves, muffins and other treats.

With the exception of the *shebeens* down Kingsway, most of Maseru's **bars** are attached to hotels or restaurants. *Good Times Café* is perhaps the liveliest place in town and serves a range of cocktails and shooters, and has occasional live music on Friday and Saturday nights. The bars at the two *Sun* hotels (*Lesotho* and *Maseru*) also sometimes have music at the weekends, as does the *Lekakoe Club*, an impressive sports club and gym. Other than the cinema on Kingsway and the slot machines at the *Maseru* and *Lesotho Suns*, central Maseru is a dead loss in terms of **nightlife**.

Restaurants and bars

Good Times Café First floor of LNDC Shopping Centre ☏2231 7705. Trendy bar which serves a selection of European fare (although they don't always have everything on the menu), in addition to coffees and cakes. If you can stand the constant blaring of taxi horns, eat alfresco on the balcony.

Lehaha Grill At the *Lesotho Sun*, off Nightingale Rd. One of the poshest places in town, serving a delicious but somewhat pricey range of European-style dishes.

Maseru Sun 12 Orpen Rd. This hotel restaurant offers a choice of buffet or à la carte covering both African and international cuisine – the buffet is probably the better (and certainly the healthier) bet.

Me'diterranee' LNDC Shopping Centre. Across from Shoprite supermarket, this unpretentious pizzeria and coffee shop is popular with locals and tourists alike for its excellent-value pizza, pasta and burgers.

Mimmo's Across from UN House on UN Rd. Decent pizzas and filling pasta served in a pleasant setting. It's popular with the expats, particularly for lunch on the terrace.

The Regal Kingsway ☏2231 3930. On the first floor of the Basotho Hut, this stylish, "multi-cuisine" restaurant serves decent but pricey Indian, Chinese, Mexican and European dishes. Closed Sun.

Rendezvous *Lancers Inn*, Kingsway ☎2231 2114. Lesotho's classiest and arguably best restaurant, with an African- and French-themed menu and a candlelit atmosphere. The outdoor seating is popular at lunchtimes and early evening.

Listings

Airlines Lesotho Defence Force, Helicopter Section ☎2232 5425; Mission Aviation Fellowship ☎2231 4790; South African Airlink ☎2235 0418, ⓦwww .saairlink.co.za.

Airport information ☎2235 0777.

Banks The main branches of Standard Lesotho Bank, Nedbank and First National Bank are on Kingsway. The best place for foreign exchange is Standard Bank's international section on the ground floor of the Lesotho Bank Tower, Kingsway.

Books Maseru Book Centre on Kingsway, just past the Lesotho Bank, has a number of historical and cultural works published by Morija Museum; the craft shop in the Basotho Hat Building also has a selection.

Car rental Avis, Moshoeshoe I International Airport ☎2235 0328 and at the *Lesotho Sun* ☎2231 4325; Budget Rent-a-Car, *Maseru Sun* ☎2231 6344; Imperial Car Rental, Moshoeshoe I International Airport ☎2235 0292.

Cinema Kingsway Cinema on Kingsway Rd (☎2232 5964) and *Lesotho Sun* hotel show several Hollywood films daily.

Embassies and consulates Canada ☎2231 4187; China ☎2231 6521; Germany ☎2233 4198; Netherlands ☎2231 2114; Republic of Ireland ☎2231 4068; South Africa ☎2231 5758; UK ☎2231 3929; US ☎2231 2666.

Gym The Lehakoe Club, on the corner of Parliament and Moshoeshoe rds (☎ 2231 7640), offers everything from exercise classes, indoor and outdoor pools, squash, tennis and a well-equipped gym, all open to non-members.

Hospitals Queen Elizabeth II Hospital, Kingsway ☎2231 2501; Maseru Private Hospital, Thetsane Rd ☎2231 3260.

Internet access Newland Internet Cafe, on Kingsway across from the Post Office (daily 8am–7pm); SHA Computers Internet café, off Kingsway opposite the Metcash Centre (Mon–Fri 8.30am–5.30pm, Sat 8.30am–2.30pm).

Libraries State Library on Kingsway ☎2700 5917.

Pharmacy MHS Pharmacy, LNDC Shopping Centre, Kingsway ☎2232 5189.

Photography Foto First, LNDC Centre, Kingsway ☎2232 4478; Photo & Gift Galaxy, LNDC Centre, Kingsway ☎2232 1658.

Police Constitution Rd ☎2231 7262 or 7623.

Post office and couriers The post office is on Kingsway (Mon–Fri 8am–4.30pm, Sat 8am–noon). DHL, 1st floor, Options Building, Pioneer Rd ☎2231 1082; African Express, 83 Motsoene Rd, industrial area ☎2232 7910, ⓔinfo@af.ex.com.

Radio BBC World Service 90.2FM (24hr).

Swimming pool The pool at the *Maseru Sun* hotel is normally open to non-residents, as is the pool at the Lehakoe Club to non-members; expect to pay around M25.

Travel agents Flight ticketing and Intercape bus tickets are available through SAA City Centre Maseru Travel, next to the Maseru Book Centre, Kingsway (☎2231 4536, ⓔmampek .maserutravel@galileosa.co.za). Maluti Travel & Tours, next to First National Bank on Kingsway, (☎2232 7172), and Cosmo Travel, Metcash Complex, Kingsway (☎2231 3518, ⓔcosmotravel@leo.co.ls), also issues flight tickets. Intercape bus tickets are sold at the Shoprite supermarket in the LNDC Centre.

Around Maseru

Although you're unlikely to spend much of your time in Lesotho in Maseru itself, there are a number of rewarding places to visit within easy reach of the capital. A little oddly in a country dominated by towering mountains, it is two of the smaller hills, **Thaba Bosiu**, Moshoeshoe I's impregnable hilltop fortress, and nearby **Qiloane**, model for the Basotho hat (*mokorotlo*), which are the most famous, both ranking among the most important historical sites in the country. South of Maseru, the **Qeme Plateau** offers views over the city and surrounding countryside.

Thaba Bosiu

Thaba Bosiu is Lesotho's most important historical sight, a steep mountain with a large flat top about 20km east of Maseru that was the capital of the kingdom in the days of Moshoeshoe I. Declared a World Heritage Site by UNESCO, it is a place of great significance to the people of Lesotho, and the burial ground of the country's kings, and as such is well worth a visit.

Moshoeshoe I trekked with his followers from Butha-Buthe to Thaba Bosiu in July 1824 in a bid to settle somewhere far from the warrior clans then terrorizing the flat plains to the north and west, and somewhere that would be extremely hard for anyone to capture. Thaba Bosiu, with its crown of near-vertical cliffs, good grazing and seven or eight freshwater springs on top, fitted the bill perfectly, and despite numerous attacks, the mountain was never taken. The name means "Mountain of the Night", perhaps because, as legend has it, Moshoeshoe first arrived there in the evening, and immediate protective measures took all night to install. A more compelling reason, and the one most Basotho prefer, is that the mountain, which does not look particularly high or impressive by day, seems to grow inexorably as night falls, becoming huge and unconquerable.

Taking Thaba Bosiu

In 1828, the Ngwane were the first to attack Thaba Bosiu, but were decisively beaten, after which they never troubled Moshoeshoe again. **Mzilikhazi**, King of the Ndebele, who later conquered much of modern-day Zimbabwe, tried to take the mountain in 1831, but his men were defeated by a mass of great boulders flung down from the top by the Basotho; Moshoeshoe is reputed to have sent the Ndebele a large number of fat oxen after their defeat, an unprecedented move for a victorious chief – as if to say that he understood that their attack had been inspired by hunger and that he wanted to help them out.

There followed a twenty-year period of relative calm, during which time Moshoeshoe would receive visitors wearing a beautifully tailored dark-blue military uniform, complete with cloak, and offer them tea from a prized china tea service. He allowed the French missionary, Eugene Casalis, to establish a mission at the bottom of the mountain in 1837, and employed him as his secretary and interpreter. In 1852 a British punitive force led by the Cape governor, Sir George Cathcart, didn't even make it as far as the mountain, instead being attacked a short distance away by Moshoeshoe's well-armed troops, who forced their hasty withdrawal. Afrikaner forces fighting for the Orange Free State (OFS) made a brief attempt on Thaba Bosiu in 1858, but came back in 1865 in a more determined manner, armed with heavy artillery, and began steadily shelling the mountain, launching two simultaneous assaults a few days later. Eight men made it to the top, but were seriously wounded as soon as they did so, and speedily retreated back down. A week later, more Afrikaner troops and the OFS president turned up, and another assault was launched. General Wepener led his men right to the top of the Khubelu Pass, but he was shot at the top and mortally wounded. The Basotho then mounted a counterattack, and the Afrikaners withdrew. They continued the siege for a month, though, during which time most of the livestock on Thaba Bosiu died of hunger and the Basotho became so short of bullets that they melted down the shells being fired at them to make home-made ones.

Although they won this battle, the Basotho lost the war, and Moshoeshoe signed a humiliating treaty in 1866 which surrendered most of Lesotho's farmland to the OFS. Four years later the old king died and was buried on the top of Thaba Bosiu, and two years after that Lesotho was annexed to the Cape Colony.

There is a **visitor centre** (Mon–Fri 8am–5pm, Sat 8.30am–1pm; ☎22357207, ℮touristinfo@ltdc.org.ls; M10) at the foot of the mountain, with handicrafts, snacks and information leaflets on offer. An official guide will take you up the steep **Khubelu Pass** (or "Red Pass"), a cleft in the cliffs marked by two flagpoles, where the Afrikaner General Louw Wepener was killed trying to storm the mountain in 1865 (see box opposite), and on to the remains of Moshoeshoe's **European house**, built for him by a deserter from the 72nd Seaforth Highlanders, David F. Webber. From here, it's a short walk to the remains of Moshoeshoe's royal court and then to the **royal graveyard**, where the tombs of Moshoeshoe I and most of his successors are marked with simple stone cairns.

To the east of the mountain you get a great view of **Qiloane**, a strange cone-shaped mountain with a large nodule on the top, which was apparently the inspiration for the national headdress, the distinctive Basotho hat. Around the other side of the mountain is a kind of cave village where the royal household used to hide during attacks, and which were occupied and decorated with rock paintings by the San who lived there before them. The caves are about a six-kilometre drive from the Khubelu Pass, followed by a short walk.

Not far from the visitor's centre is the new Thaba Bosiu Cultural Village (☎2231 3034), nearly complete at the time of writing, which will offer a restaurant serving traditional Basotho food and drink, cultural performances and entertainment and various craft shops.

Practicalities

To get to Thaba Bosiu **by car**, take Main South Road, turning left at the sign for the National Heath Training Centre and just before the Shell petrol station. Follow this road for 10km, through a dip down into a riverbed where the road is temporarily untarred, and on to a T-junction. Turn left at the junction and Thaba Bosiu is about 3km further along on the right. During the day, frequent **minibus taxis** run here from Maseru's New Taxi Rank.

There's good **accommodation** next to the mountain within walking distance of the tourist office at *Mmelesi Lodge* (☎5886 1116, ℉2231 4033; ❷ with breakfast), one of the best-run Basotho-owned lodges in the country. Though often used for government conferences, it has a plush bar and a pleasant restaurant serving moderately priced meat and fish dishes, a braai area, and comfortable en-suite rondavels at the back.

Qeme Plateau

The large T-shaped **Qeme Plateau**, which measures over 25 square kilometres and provides superb vistas into the Free State and east into Lesotho, is only a short drive south of Maseru, near the South African border. To get here, take the Main South Road (the A2) as far as Ha Mantsebo, 25km from Maseru, and turn right at the signpost for Ha Tsolo. At the next crossroads turn right again and after 300m you'll see a sign for Tlametlu LEC; turn left there onto a dirt track and continue past the graveyard to Mantsebo football pitch. Leave your transport there and look out for a footpath climbing the plateau diagonally from left to right, which takes you to the top. The path is difficult to follow, so you may want to ask one of the villagers to guide you; there and back takes three or four hours. Once at the top, the boulders and grasslands make for an excellent stroll and picnic spot.

Roma to Semonkong

Southeast of Maseru, the historic Catholic mission and university town of **Roma** is worth a stop, while the road from here to **Semonkong** offers an epic drive through the stunning basalt peaks of the Thaba Putsoa range.

Roma

About 30km from Maseru along a good tar road, the mission town of **ROMA** has a beautiful location amid strangely sculpted sandstone foothills and is home to the **National University of Lesotho**, which began life in 1945 as Pius XII College, run by the Roman Catholic Church. Between 1964 and 1971 it was the university of all three of the former British southern African protectorates, now Lesotho, Botswana and Swaziland.

A kilometre or so further up the road is **Roma Mission**, most of which was built by French missionaries after 1862. Though grander than its counterpart in Morija, the mission is a little run-down these days, and there's not much reason to linger.

Practicalities

Several **buses** and many more **minibus taxis** travel daily between Maseru and Roma, making this one of the busiest public transport routes in the country. Minibus taxis leave Maseru from the New Taxi Rank by Sefika Shopping Centre (M10; 30–45min). The best **accommodation** is the ivy-festooned *Trading Post Guest House* (℡2234 0202, after 5.30pm ℡2234 0267, ⓦwww .tradingpost.co.za; doubles and rondavels ❷, backpacker rooms ❶). Built in 1903 as a trading store by John Thomas Thorn, and lived in by his family ever since, it offers luxury rondavels, en-suite doubles and backpacker twin rooms with shared bathrooms in the original sandstone house; plus a self-catering cottage (❷) and camping. Decent meals are available by prior arrangement, there's a small swimming pool, and the family can help arrange activities including pony-trekking in the surrounding hills and walks to nearby dinosaur footprints, San rock paintings and local weavers and crafters, plus 4WD trails. To get there, look for a sign on the right of the main road 2km before the centre of Roma marked "Trading Post", and head 200m up the dirt road.

There are a few bars near the university which serve cheap food, usually packed with students in term times. Opposite the main gate, *Kaycee's* is one of the most popular places in town, serving good-value fast food (for M15–25); its neighbour, the *Speak Easy Restaurant*, serves similar fare. Right next door to *Kaycee's* is the last place you can buy **fuel** before Semonkong.

Roma to Ramabanta

The road from Roma to Semonkong is one of the most spectacular in Lesotho, with superb views as you climb into the highlands. Where the tarred road turns to gravel at **Moitsupeli**, 18.5km beyond Roma, look ahead towards the twin summits of the appropriately named **Thabana-li-Mele** (Breast Mountains). After the next village of Ha Dinzulu, the road continues to climb, peaking at 2000m at Nkesi's Pass and then dropping down to the village of **RAMABANTA**, where the *Trading Post Adventures Guest House* (℡2234 0202, after 5.30pm ℡2234 0267, ⓦwww.tradingpost.co.za; dorm beds ❶, rooms ❸), sister establishment to the *Trading Post Guest House* in Roma, boasts seven lovely en-suite rooms in converted stables, three luxury rondavels sleeping four, backpacker accommodation in three-bed dorms and a campsite. Meals are available and, like the guesthouse in Roma, hikes and pony rides can be arranged, as can 4WD adventures (in your own car) with overnights in villages.

Semonkong and around

From Ramabanta, cross the Makhaleng River and then drive up to 3000m through the Thaba Putsoa mountain range, before descending gently to the curiously straggly town of **SEMONKONG**. The region was inhabited by the San until 1873, when – after a series of **genocidal campaigns** against them by the British – the last of Lesotho's San were finally exterminated by an expedition led by a certain Colonel Bowker. The town itself began life in the 1880s following the Gun War as a refuge for displaced Basotho from the lowlands. The town offers a few basic stores, plenty of **bars**, and even a post office and bank, though you can't rely on either. If you're here in winter, try to catch the local **horse races** on the last Saturday of every month.

From the lodge in Semonkong (see below), it's a day's walk or pony trek west (see box, p.762) into the pretty Thaba Putsoa mountains to the pristine 120-metre **Ketane Falls**. The falls are inaccessible by any other means of transport, and the pony trek is considered one of the best in the country. The falls can also be visited on a popular four-day pony trek from *Malealea Lodge* (see p.777).

Rather easier to reach are the **Maletsunyane Falls** (or Le Bihan Falls, after a French missionary), a pretty five-kilometre walk downriver. The dramatic falls, the highest single drop in southern Africa, plunge nearly 200m down a sheer and scary cliff into a swimmable pool, whose mist gives the falls their name: "Smoking Water". There's a steep path down to the bottom, where you can swim or camp. The pool usually freezes by June, but the waterfall keeps going all winter, spraying the surrounding rocks with ice, and forming an impressive ice cage over the pool.

Practicalities

The 120-kilometre **drive** from Maseru to Semonkong takes about three hours by private car; the road is tarred up to Moitsupeli, while the remaining 65km are decent gravel which is passable in all but the frailest 2WD. A couple of Lesotho Freight and Bus Services **buses** leave Maseru daily at 10am and 2pm, taking around six hours, and there are also at least a couple of minibuses. If you miss these, you can always get public transport to Roma and then a minibus taxi from there, though they stop running by mid-afternoon. *Semonkong Lodge* (see below) offers a free shuttle from Maseru's tourist information office on Tuesdays and Fridays, which usually leaves in the early afternoon – ring to book a place.

The ⚒ *Semonkong Lodge* is an excellent place to stay (☎2700 6037, ⓦwww .placeofsmoke.co.ls; dorms ❶, rooms ❸), 1km south of town beside the Maletsunyane River. One of the best lodges in Lesotho, this laid-back and well-run place offers en-suite doubles and a dormitory in cosy thatch-and-stone buildings, complete with electricity and hot showers, and with fireplaces in some rooms. There's also a campsite, a kitchen for self-caterers, a great bar with pool table, balcony and a decent selection of music, and delicious meals (including vegetarian). But the main reason for staying here is for the immense selection of **outdoor activities** on offer (see box, p.762). Unusually for lodges outside Maseru, it even accepts Mastercard and Visa credit cards. A cheaper alternative is the *Roman Catholic Lodge* (☎6315 5735; ❶) in the St Leonard Mission, which offers very basic accommodation with shared bathrooms. Meals cooked using ingredients grown in the mission are available by prior arrangement. The mission is signposted from the road into the town centre; alternatively, ask for directions and look out for the large cross on the bell tower.

The road to Thaba-Tseka

The central A3 runs over Lesotho's Central Range to the small district capital of **Thaba-Tseka**, 175km from Maseru. Beyond the turning for Roma, the first settlement of any size is **NAZARETH**. The *Molengoane Lodge*, on the left as you enter the village (ⓣ2234 7766, ⓦwww.molengoane-kapitseng.co.ls; ❷ including breakfast), offers clean and comfortable accommodation in rondavels and chalets, plus a bar and restaurant. Seven kilometres north of Nazareth at **Ha Baroana** are what were once some of the finest rock paintings in the country. They are still interesting, with discernible figures of animals, dancers and hunters, but they have been vandalized and washed away by child guides who throw water at them to make them more visible for tourists. The easiest way to get to the paintings is along a difficult dirt road, signposted off the main road just before the *Molengoane Lodge*. After 3.5km you'll reach the village of Ha Khotso; take the second turning on your right and then continue straight on for another 3km to Ha Baroana. The attractive new **visitors' centre** (daily 8am–5pm; M5) will offer you a guide to accompany you on the fifteen-minute walk down into the gorge.

After Nazareth, the highway ascends steeply into the mountains through the 2263-metre **Bushman's Pass**. Along the way you may see young boys desperately trying to sell lumps of quartzite and, more worryingly, Lesotho's national flower, the protected, rare and weirdly beautiful **spiral aloe**. Roughly 17km beyond Nazareth, at the top of the 2281-metre **Molimo Nthuse Pass** (which means "God Help Me"), is the **Basotho Pony Trekking Centre**. One of Lesotho's original trekking centres, it's the least expensive place to pony-trek in the country but has sadly gone downhill of late. A two-day/one-night trek costs just M125 per person plus M20 for accommodation in huts or M10 for camping; you'll need to bring all your supplies with you. **Reservations** are essential to

---

Walking and pony-trekking from Semonkong

Working in conjunction with the local community, *Semonkong Lodge* offers a bewildering choice of **outdoor activities**, ranging from short walks through town and along the river in search of bald ibis, to abseiling and adventurous pony-treks lasting several days and overnighting in basic huts. Advance bookings are required for overnight rides. Semonkong boasts the longest commercially run abseil in the world, a 204-metre descent down the Meletsunyane falls. It's an electrifying thirty-minute descent, just metres away from the crashing water. You'll be given half a day's training on a small cliff near the lodge before taking the challenge, and receive photos of the experience afterwards (M750 per person).

There are also a variety of **pony-treks**, from short jaunts visiting nearby sights to overnight expeditions. As ever, per person costs work out cheaper in larger groups; the maximum is fifteen people. Couples pay M180 per person for a full day's ride. Overnights, including the guide and pack horse, are around M650 per person in a couple for one night, M985 for two nights, and M2400 for six nights. For **walks**, pack horses are optional and recommended; again, in a couple expect to pay around M225 for a day and night (M500 with pack horse), or M835 (M1200 with pack horse) for six nights. For day-trips on foot, a guide costs M10 per hour.

ensure that someone's there when you arrive, thanks to the chaotic state of affairs at the Ministry of Agriculture's Livestock Services Department (☏ 2231 7284), which currently manages the place. Your best approach is to contact the tourist office in Maseru for the latest information about the centre.

The road carries on from here over the epic **Blue Mountain Pass** (2633m), with commanding vistas of the surrounding mountains, though the views are even better if you climb the hills on either side. From here, the tar road descends into the village of **LIKALANENG** and onto the nearby **Mohale Camp** which is full of Legoland-style prefab buildings erected for contractors working on the nearby **Mohale Dam**. The dam, about 9km beyond Mohale Camp and signposted off the A3, was completed in 2004 as Phase 1b of the Lesotho Highlands Water Project (see box, p.769). Unlike the astonishing engineering grace of Katse Dam (see p.768), Mohale is little more than an enormous pile of concrete-faced rubble, whose 145-metre-high barrier holds back almost a billion cubic metres of water. Nonetheless, a **visitor centre** (Mon–Fri 8am–5pm, Sat & Sun 10am–4pm; ☏ 2293 6217, ✉ levotm@lhda .org.ls), with a stunning location overlooking the dam, runs daily **tours** of the site (Mon–Fri 9am & 2pm, Sat & Sun 11am; M10). The visitor centre is difficult to reach without your own transport but is well signposted: continue 2km beyond Mohale Camp on the A3 and turn left. After 4km turn left again, through the LHDA security barrier (where you'll have to register) until you reach the centre. An alternative excursion in the area is a two-hour **boat cruise** up the Senqunyane and Bokong rivers (M65 per person; advance bookings essential on ☏ 5859 3797). The boats (either 9-person or 30-person) will only leave if they are full, but special cruises for fewer people can be arranged for a set fee of M600 for the smaller boat or M1600 for the larger one. The boats depart from Mohale Boating Office, 15km from the visitor centre and signposted off its approach road.

Back in Mohale Camp, there's decent **accommodation** at *Orion Mohale Lodge* (☏ 2293 6432, ✉ mohalelodge@orion-hotels.co.za; ❷–❸), a popular conference venue with comfortable rooms, tennis courts and a swimming pool. Buses and taxis from Maseru to Thaba-Tseka will drop you at the junction for Mohale Camp, from where it's a short walk to the hotel. Set to open soon, the *Thaba Chitja Island Chalets* will offer more luxurious, self-catering accommodation on a secluded island in Mohale reservoir; boats for the island will leave from Mohale Boating Office (contact the Lesotho Tourism Development Corporation in Maseru for more details on ☏ 2231 2238 or ⓦ www.ltdc.org.ls).

Thaba-Tseka

The rough road to **THABA-TSEKA** is a dramatic one, peaking in the heart of the Central Range at the 2860-metre **Mokhoabong Pass**, before descending to the town, which is over 2200m above sea level – although once here there's very little in this 1980s purpose-built administrative centre to detain you. If you need somewhere to **stay**, the friendly *Mountain Star Lodge* (☏ 2290 0415; ❷) has smallish en-suite rooms with TVs, good basic food in its restaurant, and a bar. If it's full, its nearby sister hotel, *Mohale Oa Masite* (☏ 2290 0980; ❷), offers very similar accommodation. Cheaper but more spartan accommodation in bunk beds is available at the self-catering *Farmers Training Centre* (☏ 2290 0231; ❶), a row of prefabricated building in the street above the post office and banks. The town's only **restaurant** is at the *Mountain Star Lodge*, though *Lilala Butchery and General Café* in the centre of town also serves hot and cold snacks.

Lesotho Freight and Bus Services operates three **buses** daily from Maseru, leaving the capital at 8.30am, 9am and 9.30am. These continue on to Bokong (next to Katse), Linakaneng and Sehong Hong (a good way along the A4 to Sehlabathebe) respectively, and are as far as you can travel by public transport on those routes. With your own vehicle you could tackle the spectacular road to Mokhotlong and the Sani Pass, but it's not one you should attempt in anything other than a 4WD. The road to Katse is much better and, although you still shouldn't attempt it in an ordinary saloon, there are a number of buses plying the route. From Katse there's a perfect tarred road to Leribe in the northwest (see p.767). There's no road southwest to Semonkong, though there are hikeable trails.

The northern districts

The route north from Maseru right the way round to **Sani Pass** takes in the best of both Lesotho's lowlands and highlands. The road is tarred all the way to Mokhotlong, and although it's breaking up in places, is fine for 2WD vehicles except in winter. The stretch from Mokhotlong to Sani Pass, and the dramatic winding road down the mighty Drakensberg into South Africa, is dirt, for which 4WD is strongly advised, even if it remains just about passable in a saloon car in good weather.

Maseru to Leribe

While most travellers speed through en route to the more spectacular highlands beyond, the lowland stretch between Maseru and Leribe offers a number of attractions. The Kome cave houses near **Mateka** are the most fascinating in Lesotho while the woven crafts in **Teya–Teyaneng** are of superb quality and design. The busy town of **Leribe** has less of interest, although it's close to one of the largest collections of dinosaur footprints in the country.

There are two good roads from Maseru to Teya-Teyaneng. The most commonly used is the scenic **Main North Road** (A1), which takes you through sandstone mountain-studded lowlands. A good alternative is the **Sefikeng Road**: follow Main North Road out of Maseru and turn right after 4km onto the B31, signposted to Kome Cave Village. This climbs up a steep series of hairpins to **Lancers Gap**, an extraordinary ridge with a great gap in the middle through which the road passes, so named because a Lancers regiment was allegedly ambushed and defeated in it during the Gun War.

Kome Cave Village

About 2km from the village of Mateka lies **Kome Cave Village**, once the country's best-kept architectural secret but now an increasingly popular tourist destination. The seven still-inhabited dwellings, sculpted out of mud under a huge rock overhang, look more like igloos or West African mud architecture than anything usually found in southern Africa.

The **Maloti–Drakensberg Transfrontier Project** focuses on Lesotho's highland areas bordering South Africa, from near Butha-Buthe in the north clockwise to beyond Qacha's Nek in the south. The project is a hopeful sign that the previously hapless management of the area's roads, tourist facilities and unique but fragile natural areas may soon be a thing of the past. Based on an integrated approach with South Africa, the project focuses on ecological issues and on the area's widespread poverty. The idea is to tackle both aspects by establishing **sustainable tourism** initiatives among local communities, with the emphasis on culture as much as on natural attractions. South African parks and reserves included in the project include Ukhahlamba Drakensberg Park, Royal Natal National Park, Golden Gate Highlands National Park and Ongelurksnek Nature Reserve. The project's first phase will be completed at the end of 2008, but a 20-year strategy has been developed. During this time, it's likely that some of these areas will become **transfrontier parks**.

For more information, including practical advice on community tourism projects initiated so far – which may include overnight stays in villages, walks to natural and cultural attractions, and meeting healers and craftspeople – contact the project coordinator on the 7th floor of the Post Office Building in Maseru (entrance on Palace Road, just off Kingsway; ☎2231 2662, ⓦwww.maloti.org).

Getting to the cave village by public transport is easiest via Teya-Teyaneng, where you can pick up fairly regular transport to Mateka. From here it's an easy thirty-minute walk down the hill to Kome and the **visitor centre**. If you're driving, take the bumpy, poorly signposted dirt track which starts behind the football field in Mateka. At the visitor centre (M10 for guided tour of the caves) you'll be offered a guide to accompany you on the ten-minute walk down to the caves. The centre currently has camping facilities and a craft shop, and there are plans to build a restaurant and accommodation as well.

Teya-Teyaneng and around

TEYA-TEYANENG (usually abbreviated to "T.Y.") means "place of shifting sands", after the way the nearby river changes its course from time to time. T.Y. is the **crafts capital** of Lesotho, specializing in all manner of weavings, from jerseys to elaborately designed wall hangings. There are four weaving outlets, all open daily from 8am to 5pm. The most central is **Setsoto Design** 300m from the *Blue Mountain Inn* (see p.766), where you can see tapestries being made. A good selection of woven products is sold in the adjacent shop: expect to pay around M200 for a bag and M1500 for a large tapestry. Three kilometres south of town, on the left as you come in from Maseru, look for signs to the small showroom of **Hatooa Mose Mosali** (☎2250 0772, ⓦwww.hatooamosemosali.co.ls), which translates as "women must stand up and work hard". There's a fairly limited range in stock but its catalogue displays some very special wall hangings, which you need to order as they take a week or two to make. A short distance further on, signposted to the right of the main road, the pleasant Anglican St Agnes Mission is home to **Helang Basali Handicrafts** (☎2250 1546), whose showroom has a limited selection of woven crafts. For the best choice of products, head to **Elelloang Basali Studio** (☎2250 1520), about 5km north of town on the road to Leribe (look for the red building on the main road constructed from recycled cans), where you'll find an extensive range of wall hangings, floor rugs, table mats and bags.

Practicalities

Teya-Teyaneng stretches either side of the main road but most of the shops, banks and post office are west of the highway. The **bus and taxi rank** is 100m east of the main highway on the road to Mapoteng. There's plenty of transport to and from Maseru and further north to Leribe and Butha-Buthe, and you rarely have to wait long. A couple of hundred metres past the post office and its transmitter is the *Blue Mountain Inn* (T & F 2250 0362, E skymountainhotels @ilesotho.com; ❷), the town's main **accommodation** option, a spacious and well-run hotel with dozens of small and old-fashioned but comfortable chalets, plus a new block with smarter, better-value rooms. It also has a **restaurant**, serving tasty meals (M30–70), plus a good selection of wines. There's also a pizzeria, three bars, a pool and a large lawn with shaded tables, and the manageress can help arrange trips to local sites including Kome cave village. Much more modest is *Ka Pitseng Guest House* (T 2250 1638; ❷ including breakfast), signposted from the main road as you approach the town from Maseru. This brand-new building lacks character but offers clean rooms and a decent restaurant (M50).

Maputsoe

A rough and chaotic manufacturing-based border town opposite the South African town of Ficksburg, **MAPUTSOE** is not a good place to stay long. Fortunately, the border is open 24 hours a day, and there's plenty of public transport to Maseru, Leribe and the north. The town's streets are filled with migrant workers commuting between Lesotho and South Africa, among them

---

Culture as fashion: the blanket and the hat

In a region of Africa where **traditional dress** has all but died out, Lesotho stands out as the exception. The **mokorotlo** (Basotho traditional hat) is not widely worn these days, admittedly, though you'll still occasionally see its distinctive cone and bobble in Lesotho, while in South Africa it's popular with Basotho migrant workers as a badge of ethnic distinction. Modelled on the shape of Qiloane Mountain near Thaba Bosiu, and made of woven straw, the *mokorotlo* has become the standard Basotho souvenir, sold in every craft shop, usually for M50 or less.

More prevalent than the *mokorotlo* is the Basotho **blanket**, still worn all over the country. When King Moshoeshoe was presented with a blanket by European traders in 1860, there were hardly any in his kingdom, the people wearing karosses made of animal hides instead. However, by 1872 traders were reporting insatiable demand for the blankets. Made from high-quality woven cloth, they were originally manufactured in Birmingham, England, and are today made in Port Elizabeth, South Africa. The ubiquitous Fraser's Stores, which you find all over the country, first established themselves by selling blankets, and still stock them today. Good ones (made of pure wool) cost about M400, a fortune by local standards – don't forget to buy an outsized safety pin to tie it with.

The blankets are very practical, keeping the body at an even temperature except when it's really hot outside (although the Basotho wear them whatever the weather). Blankets are also associated with fertility, which is why some carry the design of a maize cob, a Basotho symbol of fertility and prosperity. Young brides are supposed to wear a blanket around their hips until their first child is conceived, and boys wear different blankets before and after circumcision.

Although they have always been foreign imports, and are the commodities on which many European trader fortunes have been built, the blankets remain quintessentially Basotho, and a source of national pride.

---

an uncomfortable number of hustlers who can spot strangers a mile off. Many hustlers seem to congregate at Maputsoe's only **hotel**, the large *Sekekete* (☏2243 0789; ❷ including breakfast), on the main street 50m from the border. The hotel's plain but functional rooms are around the back, a short distance from the general commotion. You'll also find a reasonable **restaurant** here serving the usual chicken and steaks. There are a few takeaway options along the main street, and if you need a beer head for the locals' joint, the *Mohahlaula Public Bar* (opposite the LESCO food factory on the main road).

Leribe (Hlotse)

A dilapidated but still pleasant little shady town, **LERIBE** (officially called **Hlotse** but more commonly known by the name of the surrounding district) was founded in 1876 by an Anglican missionary, Reverend John Widdicombe, and suffered repeated sieges during the Gun War. There are one or two attractions in the area, including a set of **dinosaur footprints** a few kilometres south of town at the turn-of-the-twentieth-century **Tsikoane Mission** (right off Main North Road to Teya-Teyaneng). You'll need to climb up the rock overhang above the church, preferably with the help of a guide (ask at the mission), where you'll find over forty reasonably clear imprints. The **Leribe Craft Centre** (Mon–Fri 8am– 4.30pm, Sat 9.30am–1pm; ☏2240 0323), right by the major intersection on the main road, sells wonderful mohair scarves, blankets and table mats made by people with disabilities, plus a few books and a road map of Lesotho.

Practicalities

The highway from Maseru passes to the south of town, and between the Caltex and Excel petrol stations you'll find the main intersection. The road on the left leads up the hill to the town centre, passing *Kingdom Fried and Grilled Chicken* and the *Pelican Bar and Steakhouse*, both of which serve inexpensive big **meat dishes**. Further up the hill on the left is the town's only **accommodation** option, the poorly signed *Mountain View Hotel* (☏2240 0559; ❷) with a range of rondavels and rooms in lines of adjacent chalets overlooking a pleasant garden. At the time of writing, a major extension to the hotel was being constructed, as was a pool. The somewhat staid restaurant serves tasty meat and fish dishes, the occasional vegetarian pasta and light snacks (M35–60). There's also a lively **bar**, especialy busy with locals at weekends. Another good nightspot is the *Green Woodpecker Club* (open daily from noon) on the highway, 100m from the Caltex garage as you head for Maseru. There's a Standard Lesotho Bank in town with an ATM, plus a new Shoprite supermarket.

After the hotel take the first left to reach the **taxi rank**. There's plenty of **transport**, though if you're heading south, rather than waiting for a direct run, it's quicker to grab a seat on one of the frequent minibuses to Maputsoe and change there. The Lesotho Freight and Bus Services service to Mokhotlong doesn't enter town but stops 100m north of the Caltex garage by the Mount Royal Church; it passes by around 8am on its way to Mokhotlong and at around 1pm on its way back to Maseru.

The road to Katse Dam

To the east of Leribe rises the impressive Front Range of the Maloti Mountains. The region is at the heart of Phase 1a of the ambitious **Lesotho Highlands Water Project** (see box, p.769), whose centrepiece is the massive dam and reservoir at **Katse**. The 100-kilometre A8 highway built for the dam from Leribe is a remarkable journey almost worth doing for the drive alone. As part of the project, two new reserves were established: **Bokong Nature Reserve** just off the A8, and **Ts'ehlanyane National Park**, accessed along a dirt road off the A1 9km south of Butha-Buthe (see p.770).

Leribe to the Bokong Nature Reserve

The A8 begins at Leribe, from where it's a speedy, unexciting run through the lowlands to dreary **Pitseng**, notable only for the stylish 🍴 *Aloe's Guest House* (☎2700 5626; ❷). It has thatched bungalows set around a grassy compound with a small pool, self-catering facilities or food served upon request; it also has camping. Quadbikes, pony-trekking and guided hikes can be arranged. Follow the signs from the main road, where a 300-metre dirt track leads to the guesthouse.

From here the road climbs to 3090m at the **Mafika Lisiu Pass** in under 30km – a punishing journey for most cars. Be aware that at the time of writing there were problems with an armed security guard at the top of the pass, pestering cars for handouts or even claiming that visitors must pay a toll – politely refuse to pay.

Beyond Mafika Lisiu Pass the road weaves through the high-altitude hikers' paradise of **Bokong Nature Reserve**. The reserve's highlight is the dramatic **Lepaqoa Waterfall**, which freezes in winter to form a column of ice.

The reserve's **entrance** is next to the **visitors' centre**, signposted left off the highway 1km beyond the Mafika Lisiu Pass (daily 8am–5pm; M5, children M3). Perched dramatically on the edge of a 100-metre cliff overlooking the Lepaqoa valley, the visitor centre offers a 45-minute walk (M10 per group) along a poorly marked footpath to the top of the Lepaqoa Falls, as well as guides (M20 per day) and horses (M25 per hour, M50 for half day, M75 per day; minimum age 12) for hire. Particularly recommended is a possible two- to three-day hike along the alpine plateau to Ts'ehlanyane National Park to the north – bring your own camping gear and hire a guide from the visitor centre. **Camping** is possible throughout the reserve, and there are also two stone-and-thatch **rondavels** (❶) close to the falls (each with four single beds) with a shared kitchen and bathroom. They have gas and bedding, but you need to bring your own food. New accommodation is currently being built next to the visitor centre – five large self-contained chalets with fabulous views. There is a simple restaurant (M25) – with stunning panoramic views. Advance booking for the restaurant, accommodation and ponies is highly recommended; contact the Booking Officer, Lesotho Northern Parks, PO Box 333 Butha-Buthe 400 (☎2246 0723, ✉reception @datacom.co.ls). The reserve can be reached from Leribe on **minibuses** running roughly every two hours towards Katse. Minibuses returning to Leribe are often full, so go to Ha Lejone (see below) and pick up transport there.

Katse and the dam

After Bokong, the road descends to the northern shore of the massive **Katse Reservoir** and the small village of **HA LEJONE**. *Chocks Centre*, 1km down a gravel road, offers basic food, accommodation and camping (☎2233 2485; ❶). If you prefer cleanliness to character, there is a restaurant and tidy rooms in a neat compound at the new *Umbrella Guest House*, just along the dirt road (☎2700 7914; ❷).

From here, the road climbs once more, reaching 2600m at the **Laitsoka Pass**, before finally descending to pass below the dam wall and reach the now burgeoning town of Katse.

Lesotho's abundance of water but shortage of cash and Gauteng's monetary wealth and water poverty are the facts behind the stunningly ambitious **Lesotho Highlands Water Project** – Africa's largest engineering venture to date. The essence of the project is to dam Lesotho's major rivers, then divert the water through specially constructed tunnels, via a hydroelectric power station at 'Muela near Butha-Buthe, to South African rivers. For this, South Africa pays Lesotho royalties of around R24 million a month.

The treaty formalizing the project was signed in 1986, although without much popular consultation or assessment of the environmental impact. Various compensation arrangements have been put in place for villagers affected by flooding, though not unexpectedly there are grumbles that these promises have not been met. Meanwhile, the project marches inexorably forward, and it was no surprise that when South African peacekeeping forces entered Lesotho in 1998, one of their main priorities was to secure Katse Dam.

The project's first phase, which concluded in 2004, was split into two phases. **Phase 1a**, completed in 1997, saw the construction of the 185-metre-high Katse Dam, an underground hydroelectric plant at 'Muela, tunnels to South African rivers, and all the road infrastructure. Facilities were developed at Liphofung Cave as part of this phase, the idea being that local communities would benefit from tourism revenues. **Phase 1b** saw the construction of Mohale Dam on the Senqunyane River, linked to Katse reservoir by tunnel. In February 2007, following feasibility studies, the Lesotho Highlands Water Commission confirmed that the preferred site for phase 2 of the project is Polihali in Mokhotlong district, where a dam will be built and water transferred through a gravity tunnel to Katse reservoir.

Katse, Mohale and 'Muela each have visitor centres, though for guided tours of the installations it's best to book ahead at the **LHDA Information Centre** on the fourth floor of the Lesotho Bank Tower on Kingsway in Maseru (Mon–Fri 8am–5pm; ☎ & ℻2232 1934, ⓦwww.lhwp.org.ls). Tours for all of the sites cost R10.

KATSE town itself is drab and boring, with uniform box-like houses. But the massive dam, which holds back nearly two billion cubic metres of water, really is impressive, even if you aren't usually interested in engineering. To find out more, head for the **visitor centre**, with its bright blue roof (Mon–Fri 8am–noon & 1–4pm, Sat & Sun 8am–noon; ☎2291 0377), just before the town and dam. On weekdays aim to get there for 9am or 2pm to catch the daily hour-long **tours** of the facility; at weekends the tours start at 11am (M10). During initial excavations it was discovered that the bedrock was seismically unstable, so a moveable joint was incorporated into the dam's base, allowing it to flex. Even so, the rapid filling of the reservoir caused a series of minor **earth tremors**. This was all to be expected, said the engineers, but not by the inhabitants of Ha Mapaleng, where a tremor ripped a 30cm-wide, 1.5km-long gash through the village. The local prophetess explained that a huge **underground snake** had been disturbed by the dam's construction and that the entire village would be gobbled up. No one hung around to find out, and the village was eventually relocated 1km away.

Nearby attractions include a **botanical garden** (M10), something of a refuge camp for thousands of critically endangered spiral aloes rescued from the construction sites. A half-hour walk south of the visitor centre along the Thaba-Tseka road is the **Khohlo–Ntso Pony Trekking Association** (book in advance on ☎6318 6498), offering a range of horseback trips from two-hour jaunts to Chief Katse's erstwhile homestead (M140) to an adventurous two-night trip to Mount Manyofane and rock paintings at Khohlo–Ntso (M975).

LESOTHO

The road to Katse Dam

The only **place to stay** is the *Orion Katse Lodge* (☎2291 0202; ❸ including breakfast, self-contained houses sleeping 4–6 ❺–❻, dorm ❷). *Orion* took over in July 2007 with plans to give the entire place a facelift, and transform the currently drab rooms. The lodge offers fine views of the reservoir and its impressive birdlife, and a good restaurant serving a decent selection of meals. There are plans to start boat cruises, biking, pony-trekking and hiking. Camping is also possible at the visitor centre (toilets but no water – M40 per car). **Moving on**, public transport leaves from the taxi rank at the entrance to Katse village. There are daily buses to Maseru, leaving around 6am.

Butha-Buthe to Sani

The road from **Butha-Buthe** to the South African border at **Sani** is the most popular route into the Lesotho Highlands and travels through some of the most dramatic terrain in the country. Though there's not much to do in Butha-Buthe itself, there are several attractions nearby, including the beautiful **Ts'ehlanyane National Park**, fine **San rock art** at Liphofung Cave, and **'Muela Dam** with its underground hydroelectric power station. Further afield there's winter **skiing** near **Oxbow** and stunning mountain landscapes as you approach Sani Top.

Butha-Buthe and around

BUTHA-BUTHE (or Botha-Bothe, meaning "Lie Down") has a frontier feel – noisy, dirty and dusty – and offers little reason to stay, although it makes a good base for visiting nearby attractions. The town was founded in 1884 because the local chief refused to go to Leribe to pay taxes, necessitating a new tax centre nearer his residence. Butha-Buthe attracted traders from the outset, and is one of few towns in Lesotho with a sizeable Indian community.

Butha-Buthe Mountain, just east of town, is where Moshoeshoe I had his first stronghold before retreating to Thaba Bosiu in 1824. It's a stiff but not particularly difficult climb and the summit provides tremendous views. You can cut the hiking distance by catching a minibus as far as Ha Mopeli.

Practicalities

Probably the best **accommodation** in town is the *Likileng Lodge* (☎2246 0686, ✉fedicsles@leo.co.ls; ❷ including breakfast), which offers clean and functional en-suite rooms, a bar and a restaurant serving tasty meals. It's a couple of kilometres out of town on the left-hand side of the road heading to Oxbow, set in the large LHDA compound. The only central place to stay is the run-down *Crocodile Inn Hotel* (☎2246 0223, ✉crocodile-inn@ilesotho.com; ❷ including breakfast) next to the hospital, with shabby en-suite rooms and better (if smaller) rooms in rondavels. The hotel has two bars which attract dedicated drinkers until well into the morning, and an inexpensive restaurant. Alternatively food is served at the Total garage on the main road, next to the turning. More pleasant, but tricky to get to, is the self-catering *Butha-Buthe Youth Hostel* (☎2246 0027; ❷), also known as *Ha Thabo Ramakantane's*. This IYHF-accredited hostel is set in peaceful surroundings about 3.5km from town in the village of Ha Sechele. It's pretty basic and lacks running water or electricity (occasionally a generator is used for larger groups), but there's a kitchen for self-catering, the management is friendly and it's a great place to meet Basotho villagers and hike into the nearby hills. Unless you have a high-clearance vehicle, the only access is on foot: 50m before the Caledonspoort junction, turn right along a small dirt track which is signposted to St Paul's High School. Once past the school bear left and ask for directions; it's about an hour's walk from the town centre.

Moving on, there are frequent buses and minibuses to Maseru, Katse, and two or three a day to Mokhotlong.

Ts'ehlanyane National Park

A signposted turning 9km southeast of Butha-Buthe leads 32km southeast along good gravel into the western scarp of the Front Range, following a very picturesque valley. Covering 56 square kilometres of extremely rugged hiking terrain at the confluence of the Ts'ehlanyane and Holomo rivers, **Ts'ehlanyane National Park** (daily 8am–5pm; ☎2246 0723; M15, plus M5 per vehicle and M16 if staying overnight) is intended to protect several areas of ecological importance, particularly the indigenous *Leucosidea sericea* **woodland** known locally as *Ouhout* or *Che-che* – one of Lesotho's very few forested areas. Equally rare are stands of montane bamboo. **Mammals** present include mainly duikers, baboons, and serval cats; there's also the endangered *Metisella syrinx* butterfly, bearded vultures (lammergeiers) and ground woodpeckers. The **best time to visit** is spring, when the small yellow flowers along the river banks that give their unpronounceable name to the reserve are in flower. The highlight for hikers and pony-trekkers alike is a spectacular 39-kilometre trail linking the park with Bokong Nature Reserve to the south (see p.768), with swimming possible in streams along the way. Near to the park's reception, there's **accommodation** in a guesthouse which sleeps six people (M350 for the house) or in 3-bed dormitories (❷) An alternative is to stay at the park's "bush camp", where two self-catering rondavels, without electricity, offer a more rustic stay (❶, M200 minimum per rondavel). Horses are available for hire by prior arrangement (M25 per hour, M50 for half day, M75 per day; minimum age 12); book through the Lesotho Northern Parks office in Butha Buthe (☎2246 0723, ✉reception@datacom.co.ls).

'Muela and Liphofung Cave Cultural Historical Site

Heading northeast from Butha-Buthe, the road begins to climb into the Maloti Mountains. After 22km, you reach the small settlement of Khukhune where a good tar road on the right leads up to **'MUELA**, an integral part of the Lesotho Highlands Water Project (see box, p.769). Here the water flowing down the delivery tunnel from Katse Reservoir powers an underground hydroelectric station which supplies all of Lesotho with electricity, as well as a small surplus which is sold to South Africa. The real attraction lies underground, and there are **tours** of the power plant daily at 9am and 2pm from the **information centre** (☎ 2248 1211; M10) just beyond the *Muela Lodge*. The attractive **lodge** itself offers drinks and basic meals, although no accommodation.

Nine kilometres beyond the 'Muela turn-off is the signposted **Liphofung Cave Cultural Historical Site** (daily 8am–5pm; M15), actually a large sandstone overhang boasting a series of San **rock paintings**, from whose images it gets its name, "Place of the Eland". To avoid damaging the rock art you're obliged to take a tour with a guide. The site is also significant for the Basotho in its role as a hideout for the young Moshoeshoe I. The **visitor centre** has displays of Basotho culture in three traditional huts, and there's also a small craft shop. Ponies can be hired (M25 per hour, M75 per day) and cultural performances arranged. You can **stay** at the campsite, or in a couple of delightful rondavels (❶) sleeping four people each, or one of the new luxurious, two-storey versions which were nearly complete at the time of writing; homestays in the nearby village can also be arranged. Advance booking for the ponies and rondavels is recommended; contact the Booking Officer, Lesotho Northern Parks, PO Box 333, Butha-Buthe 400 (☎2246 0723, ✉reception@datacom .co.ls). Alternatively, signposted off the main road just before Liphofung, 2km down a tough dirt track, the *Mamohase B&B* (☎5805 8438) runs a homely set-up, offering local meals in the family dining room and a few beds in thatched rondavels next door with bucket showers and outdoor toilet (❸ half board).

Oxbow

The A1 from **Liphofung** into the highlands is one of the most dramatic roads in Lesotho, passing through some particularly striking sandstone cliffs before twisting tortuously up a chain of heart-stopping hairpins into the basalt. Some 20km beyond Liphofung, past **Moteng Pass** (2820m), you come to a string of unremarkable buildings in a narrow valley. The *New Oxbow Lodge* (☎+27 (0)51 933 2247, ⓦwww.oxbow.co.za; ❸) has seen better days but still has perfectly comfortable, warm rooms, plus camping facilities, a well-stocked bar, and a restaurant serving reasonably priced meals. There's good trout fishing on the Malibamatso River, and wonderful hiking in any direction. The lodge is also the last place you can buy petrol (although not diesel) before Mokhotlong.

A further 11km brings you to Mahlasela basin (3220m) and the incongruous *Afri-Ski Leisure Kingdom* (☎ +27 (0)11 888 8881, ⓦwww.afriski.net; double ❸; chalet ❺; backpackers ❷), a fledgling resort increasingly popular with South Africans. Between June and August, **skiing** is the main draw, down a one-kilometre run complete with ski lift and snow-making equipment if the weather doesn't oblige. Summer activities include trout- and fly-fishing, pony-trekking, 4WD trails and mountain biking. There's a well-stocked ski-shop with equipment for rent, plus a good restaurant and lively bar which pumps out music until the early hours. **Accommodation** ranges from bunks in the cramped backpackers' hostel, comfortable doubles in a couple of lodges, and luxurious four-bedroom chalets. There are ambitious plans for further expansion of the resort with hotels, shopping centre and golf course.

The road to Mokhotlong is often called "the Roof of Africa route", peaking at **Tlaeeng Pass** (3251m) and passing the ugly **Letseng diamond mine** en route. The road is fully tarred, although the extremes of temperature here have caused it to break in places and there are numerous potholes. Most transport stops at the small village of **Mapholaneng**, where there's a reasonable restaurant (*Thugela*) and a couple of well-stocked bars.

Mokhotlong

Perched on the banks of the scraggly Mokhotlong River, the wind-blown town of **MOKHOTLONG** ("Place of the Bald Ibis") lies at the end of the tarmac. Mokhotlong was once known as the "Loneliest Place in Africa", and it's easy to see why, since even with the tarmac road it still gets cut off from the rest of civilization for days or weeks at a time in winter. Mokhotlong began life as a remote police outpost in 1905, and gradually evolved into a trading centre for the region's highlanders, but remained isolated from the rest of Lesotho for years, with radio contact only established in 1947. An airstrip was constructed in 1948 and a rudimentary road link built in the 1950s, but Mokhotlong continued to get the bulk of its supplies by pony from Natal, via Sani, for a long time afterwards. Even today it feels remote, with locals usually riding into town for a shop and a drink on ponies, resplendent in their gumboots and blankets. However, it's the only town of any size in eastern Lesotho and a good place to stock up with supplies if you are using the Sani Top border post.

Practicalities

Getting to Mokhotlong is easiest on the daily 7am **bus from Maseru**, operated by Lesotho Freight and Bus Services. There are also up to three **minibus taxis** a day from Butha–Buthe. Local **taxi cabs** (M3 a ride) are handy for getting from the central bus and taxi stop to the hotels. There's a Standard Lesotho Bank in town with an ATM but it doesn't change money.

Onward transport from Mokhotlong is limited to roughly hourly minibuses to Ha Janteau, passing by the *Molumong Guest house* (see below), and a handful of minibuses to Underberg via Sani and the border whenever the road is passable, leaving around 5am. Heading back to the lowlands, the bus to Maseru leaves at 8am (except Sat), and there are three or four minibuses a day to Butha-Buthe between 7am and 2pm. There's nothing at all running to Thaba-Tseka, so hitching is the only option.

For such a remote place, there's a very good range of **accommodation** options in or around the town (see below). The **restaurant** at the *Mokhotlong Hotel* only offers a set menu (M50), but there is a good choice at the *Senqu Hotel*. The TV in the **public bar** at *Mokhotlong Hotel* makes it popular with hardy and definitely colourful locals, and there's also a private bar for guests only. There's a similar set-up at the *Senqu Hotel*, where the bar and pool table get busy at the weekends.

Accommodation

Farmers' Training Centre 2km north of town, signposted FTC. Basic and cheap accommodation with clean rooms but grubby shared bathrooms. The highlight is the pleasant location on the edge of town. No food available. ❶

Grow set back from the main road, on the left as you enter from the A1, 100m after Imperial Fleet Services ☎2292 0205. The office of an NGO working to tackle HIV/AIDS and improve the lives of the rural poor, it also offers simple and clean rooms and a self-catering kitchen in a pleasant little compound. ❶

Mokhotlong Hotel 1.5km north of town, opposite the hospital ☎2292 0212, ☏2292 0010. Rooms in the new wing are a slightly better bet, but both old and new wings offer simple rooms with no frills, the cheaper ones sharing bathrooms. ❷

Molumong Guest House 15km southwest of town along the dirt road to Thaba-Tseka, 8.5km off the Sani road ☎+27 (0)83 254 3323, ☏molumong @mweb.co.za. This is the remotest of Lesotho's

lodges, a rustic but characterful 1920s place with fantastic mountain views. The main house is self-catering, with very cosy doubles and dorms and a great lounge to relax in. There's also a bunkhouse plus a campsite. Only basic supplies are available in the village so come well stocked. The lodge also offers inexpensive pony-trekking, and is a good base for hiking. ❶–❷

St James Lodge In the grounds of St James Mission, 4km off the road to Sani ☎+27 (0)33 326 1601, ☏stjamesguestlodge@yahoo.com. This new self-catering lodge offers pleasant en-suite rooms, cheaper rondavels with separate bathrooms, and camping. Pony-trekking, cultural visits to the local village and a church tour are all available. A couple of minibuses run past the mission each day from Mohotlong. ❷

Senqu Hotel on the edge of town as you enter from the A1 ☎2292 0330, ☏www.safarinow.com /go/senquhotel. Very nice new rooms (request one with a balcony and good views), while the old rooms are still clean but looking a bit shabby. ❷

Sani and around

Branching off the Mokhotlong road 5km before the town, the rough gravel road to **SANI** twists its way in spectacular fashion for nearly 60km along the

Sehonkong River, peaking at **Kotisephola Pass** (3240m) before dropping to 2895m at **Sani Top**, a few kilometres from the South African border. If you wish to stop en route, your best bet is *No 10 Riverside* in Matsoaing village, 20km after Mohotlong, where the convivial Thabiso Nkune and his family offer local food, guided hikes, pony-trekking, cultural performances, and accommodation in a simple bunkhouse (❶). Bookings can be made via the Maloti Drakensburg Transfrontier Project office in Mohotlong (☎2231 2662, ✉info@maloti.org.ls).

At Sani Top there are plenty of rewarding hikes, including a stiff twelve-kilometre climb up **Thabana Ntlenyana**, at 3482m the highest point in southern Africa and walkable in a day if you start early. Also tough but stunningly beautiful is the forty-kilometre **Top-of-the-Berg** hike to Sehlabathebe National Park, which takes about four days.

Although the descent from Sani, down the dramatic, hairpin-bend-filled **Sani Pass** into South Africa, is just about possible in an ordinary car, you'd be much better off with a 4WD, while the ascent of the pass is definitely not recommended without one. In winter, the pass is frequently blocked by snow or ice.

Practicalities

Getting to Sani is only possible in good weather; if it's been snowing, you can forget it. For **public transport** to Sani on the Lesotho side see the Mokhotlong travel details on p.773. On the **South Africa** side minibuses run from Underberg to the border (see p.503). More comfortable would be to join a 4WD **tourist vehicle** up the Sani Pass. Sani Pass Carriers in Himeville (☎+27 (0)33 701 1017) can take you from Pietermaritzburg and Kokstad to Underburg (M125 per person). Here you can connect with either Sani Pass Tours (☎+27 (0)33 701 1064, ✉info@sanipasstours.com), Thaba Tours or Maluti Treks (see p.750); all three run daily at around 9am up to Sani Top (M300–400 per person) and return between 2.30pm and 4pm. Hitching shouldn't be too difficult, seeing as Mokhotlong's few stores tend to stock up in KwaZulu-Natal. The **border**, between *Sani Top Chalet* and Sani Pass, is open daily from 8am to 4pm; the Lesotho side stays open till 5pm to let vehicles through.

▲ The Sani Pass

There are several **accommodation** options on the South African side (see p.503). In Lesotho, the only place is the deservedly popular *Sani Top Chalet* (T&F +27 (0)33 702 1158, W www.sanitopchalet.co.za; dorms ❷, rooms ❹ half board, rondavels ❺ half board), which makes much of its claim to be the highest **pub** in Africa, at 2874m above sea level. The cliff-edge setting is superb, with awesome views into KwaZulu-Natal, and there's also hearty food on offer, while in the evenings you can drink in front of the fire or sit on the balcony and watch the sun set over the mountaintops. The rooms themselves – whether in the main building or the dorm – are simple and sometimes chilly, though nicely furnished – bathrooms are shared. The new rondavels are very attractive with open fireplaces, and there's also camping.

The southern districts

The country's **southern districts** can't match the mountains of north and central Lesotho for sheer scale, but they do hold some dramatic countryside which is relatively easy to visit – especially on horseback from the excellent tourist lodges at **Malealea** and **Semonkong**. The nineteenth-century mission town of **Morija** is perhaps the most historic in the country. Morija also has dinosaur footprints in the vicinity, as do **Mohale's Hoek** and, more accessibly, **Quthing**, further south. Moving on northeast past the town of **Qacha's Nek**, the isolated delights of **Sehlabathebe National Park** are so remote as to make visits here a true adventure.

Morija to Malealea

The main road south from Maseru, past the international airport and Qeme Plateau (see p.759), soon takes you to historic **Morija**, with its small cluster of mid-nineteenth-century buildings and museum. A further 45km away, along increasingly scenic roads, the lodge at **Malealea** is one of the most attractive – if busiest – in Lesotho. Set amid wonderful countryside, it's a perfect spot for hiking and well-organized pony-trekking in wind-carved sandstone hills.

Morija

Set at the foot of the Makhoarane Plateau 44km from Maseru, the pleasant little town of **MORIJA** houses the country's main museum and Lesotho's oldest building, church and printing press. The town was established in 1833 at Moshoeshoe I's behest as the country's first Christian mission, and granted to three missionaries of the Paris Evangelical Missionary Society (PEMS).

The large, red-brick **Lesotho Evangelical Church**, with its impressive teak-beamed roof, is almost always open. Begun in 1847, this is the third church built on the site, using the labour of Pedi economic migrants on their way to Cape Colony, though its tall steeple was only built in 1905. During the week you can visit the historic **printing works** nearby, which have produced

Basotho literature since the 1860s as well as the country's oldest newspaper, *Leselinyana la Lesotho* (Little Light of Lesotho), which has been in almost continual publication since 1863.

Most of Morija was razed to the ground by Afrikaner troops in 1858, and almost the only building left standing was **Maeder House**, in the printing press grounds, built in 1843. Today, this simple stone house contains a couple of small **craft shops** (both Mon–Sat 9am–5pm, Sun 2–5pm) Close by, just uphill, the bright-yellow **Morija Museum and Archives** (Mon–Sat 8am–5pm, Sun noon–5pm; ☎2236 0308, ⓦwww.morijafest.com; M6) is an excellent reason for coming to town, and also doubles as the town's tourist information centre. The exhibits are a stimulating combination of geological and fossil finds, ethnographic material and historic items connected with Moshoeshoe and his contemporaries. The museum also sells a range of books including the recommended *Guide to Morija* (M12).

In the first week of April the museum organizes the **Morija Arts and Cultural Festival** (ⓦwww.morijafest.com), the largest and most significant event of its kind in the country, where traditional music, dancing, horse races and crafts mix with theatre, cinema, sport and children's events. The museum also organizes the smaller **Morija Festival Cultural Competitions** during the first week of October, the culmination of countrywide school competitions in traditional dance, drama and poetry.

Practicalities

Getting to Morija is easy, with buses and minibuses running throughout the day from Maseru. There's no bus or taxi rank; most transport drops you outside the post office close to the museum, while buses heading on to Mafeteng and Mohale's Hoek will probably drop you on the highway 1km west of the centre.

Morija boasts one of Lesotho's most attractive **lodgings**, the delightful self-catering ⚵ *Morija Guest Houses and Tours* (also called *Ha Matela*; ☎2236 0306, ⓦwww.morijaguesthouses.com; ❷, half price if arriving by public transport), set in a dramatic spot right at the top of town on the way to the Makhoarane Plateau. The gloriously decorated thatched house contains several comfortable rooms, plus a fully equipped kitchen, lounge, and veranda with fantastic views over the surrounding area; it's best to reserve ahead to be sure of a room. Meals can be provided by prior arrangement. You can also stay in a couple of attractive self-catering Basotho cottages below the guesthouse (❷). The museum's tea shop (Mon–Sat 9am–4.30pm, Sun 2–4.30pm) offers cold drinks and simple Basotho **meals**. Alternatively, you can get excellent cheap meals for a very modest M15 in the snack bar attached to the grocer's opposite the post office. The guesthouse also offers full body or reflexology **massage** for M150 an hour.

Pony treks can be arranged through the *Morija Guest Houses* or museum, ranging from one-hour jaunts (M60, M120 with guide) to two-day trips (price negotiable). The best of various **walking trails** from Morija leads to an impressive sets of avian dinosaur footprints on one side of a large rock halfway up the Makhoarane Plateau, 45 minutes beyond the guesthouse. Guides are available for these walks; there are no fixed prices.

Malealea

A further 10km south of Morija you come to a dip in the road and the bustling minibus taxi stop at **Motsekuoa**, which marks the turning for the village of

Dongas and soil erosion in Lesotho

One thing you'll quickly notice about Lesotho is that the entire country is virtually treeless. Indeed, the country – once the grain basket of the region – is in deep ecological trouble, and acres of irreplaceable topsoil, loosened by decades of over-farming, are washed away down its rivers each year.

Yet during the nineteenth century the kingdom exported food to the neighbouring Orange Free State (OFS). The problems began with the expropriation of the best land by the OFS in the 1860s, which forced the Basotho to start farming hilly areas that had previously only been used for winter grazing. This process continues to this day, and you will even see crops being grown at over 2000m in districts like Semonkong and Mokhotlong. Mountains are no substitute for fertile plains, however, and Lesotho has been a net importer of food since the 1920s.

The ecological effect of the unrelenting cultivation of the Lesotho mountains has been devastating. The soil fertility has plummeted and, more seriously, huge quantities of topsoil are simply washed away in each summer's rains. In many places so much topsoil has gone that great ravines called **dongas** have opened up. Though they often look green enough, the remaining soil tends to lie close to the surface rock, making it useless for serious cultivation.

Efforts to slow this process have been under way for some time, most noticeably through the terracing of hillside fields. For one of the best examples of how simply dongas can be reclaimed, ask to be shown the way to the Musi family donga in the village beside the *Malealea Lodge* (see below) – reclamation of the donga began almost two decades ago by Fanuel Musi, and is now carried on by his grandson and wife; donations are appreciated. Ask at the lodge for a guide to take you there.

MALEALEA, one of the best-known places in Lesotho thanks to the hugely popular ⚹ *Malealea Lodge* (℡ +27 (0)82 552 4215, ⓦ www.malealea.com; forest huts ❶, Basotho huts and doubles ❷, rondavels ❸). Set in a spectacular spot in the foothills of the Thaba Putsoa range, the lodge was originally a trading store established by the British adventurer Mervyn Bosworth-Smith in 1905. It was Bosworth-Smith who wrote the words on the brass plaque at the top of the magnificent Gate of Paradise Pass, 6km before the lodge: "Wayfarer, pause and look upon a gateway of Paradise". The lodge has grown significantly from its trading-store origins, and is now a spacious compound with attractive twin-bedded houses and rondavels, plus basic backpackers' forest huts and camping. The owners actively encourage projects to support the local community, and have established the Malealea Development Trust to fund community development projects. The lodge has mapped out a series of hiking trails, but the main activity is **pony-trekking** (see box, p.778). The lodge is always a lively place; next to the dining room (set meals served at set times) is a great little bar and most evenings guests congregate around an open fire outside. Every night a local choir and band perform for guests, the latter bashing out tunes on home-made instruments. A games room and bumpy clay tennis court are also available. *Malealea*'s only downside is its popularity as a major stopover for package tours.

Getting to Malealea by **public transport** is fairly straightforward. From Maseru (85km), a daily minibus taxi leaves from the New Taxi Rank at around 11am direct to the gates of *Malealea Lodge*. If you miss it, jump on any of the frequent taxis to Mafeteng and change at Motsekuoa, where you'll find onward taxis to Malealea. From Mafeteng, simply take any bus heading along the A2 to Maseru and again change at Motsekuoa. If you're coming straight from South Africa, enquire with the lodge when you make your booking about transport from Bloemfontein via Wepener and Van Rooyens Gate border crossing.

Mafeteng, Mohale's Hoek and Quthing

There's little to detain you between **Mafeteng** and **Quthing** apart from a few good walks in the surrounding sandstone hills, including some leading to interesting sets of **dinosaur footprints**. **Mohale's Hoek** has probably the best accommodation in the area, and is a good point to explore the **Mokhele mountain range**.

Mafeteng and around

The bustling town of **MAFETENG**, 18km from Van Rooyenshek **border post** (daily 6am–10pm), will be the first place you come to in Lesotho if crossing from Wepener in the Free State. It means "the place of Lefeta's people", after the son of a French missionary Emile Rolland, who was the district's first magistrate and was nicknamed Lefeta, or "he who passes", by locals, who regarded him as virtually Basotho except for the fact that he skipped (or "passed by") initiation. Much of the town suffered in the 1998 riots, but the centre has now recovered. The only building of any interest is the District Administrator's **office** on the main street, worth a quick look for the carved animal heads studding its front wall.

There is a good nearby excursion, though you'll need your own transport. About 20km east of Mafeteng is the impressive **Thabana Morena Plateau**. Rising above the village of the same name, it rewards those who make the steep climb with good views of the Free State plains to the west and the Thaba Putsoa range to the east.

Practicalities

As befits a border town, Mafeteng has a very busy **bus station** where you can easily find transport north to Morija and Maseru, and southeast to Mohale's Hoek, Quthing and beyond. There are various small **places to eat** by the bus station and on the main street, but the best choice in town is *MS Kitchen* on the first floor of the building next to Nedbank. For **accommodation**, the anonymous-looking *Golden Hotel* (☏2270 0566; ❷), to the right of the highway from Maseru, just before you enter Mafeteng proper, offers functional en-suite rooms and a dining room serving pizzas and meat dishes. A better choice is the *Hotel Mafeteng* (☏2270 0236, ℻2270 0478; ❷), which looks like a 1960s airport control tower, but offers pleasant and spacious en-suite rooms, all with satellite TV, plus some cottages in a secluded garden and a good swimming pool. Its **restaurant** serves a range of moderately priced meat dishes and the owners can arrange pony rides in the vicinity. The hotel is on the south side of town; turn right off Main South Road 50m after the District Administrator's Office, just before the telecommunications tower and it's another 50m on your right-hand side.

Mafeteng's **nightlife** centres around the rather seedy, mirrored *Las Vegas* disco in the grounds of the *Hotel Mafeteng*, which blasts out soul and South African sounds until 4am on the last Friday and Saturday of the month. It's pretty quiet for the rest of the month, unless rented for private parties.

Mohale's Hoek

MOHALE'S HOEK, a short distance from the little-used Makhaleng Bridge **border post** (daily 8am–6pm), is a rather bedraggled little town, but it has a decent hotel and some interesting sites in the surrounding hills, including some well-preserved **dinosaur footprints**. Mohale was Moshoeshoe's younger brother, appointed to look after the area by the king as part of his bid to wrest control of the district from chief Moorosi. There are still quite a few of Moorosi's Baphuthi clan here, though, whose language is in some ways closer to Xhosa than Basotho.

You'll find Standard and Nedbank **banks**, both with ATMs, on the main street, which runs at right angles to the Mafeteng–Quthing road. Otherwise, there's nothing to see or do here apart from the excellent drive, walk or pony trek into the beautiful and little-visited **Mokhele Mountain Range** 10km east of town. Travel a few kilometres south on the main road to the little village of Mesitsaneng; turn left at the signpost for the primary school and head 11km east along a rough dirt track to the historic French **Maphutseng Mission**, in whose roof locals once hid from attacking Boers. When the road bends sharply to the left, branch right down a smaller track and you'll see a plateau a short walk away, where you'll find some **dinosaur footprints** and the remnants of an inscription recording their

---

Bog standard: the new VIP (ventilated pit latrine)

An unusual feature of the Lesotho landscape is the great number of **ventilated pit latrines** with white chimneys, which are easy to build and hygienic. Their main improvement on the old pit latrines, still in use in South Africa, is that they keep flies that have come into contact with human faeces away from food, thus helping prevent dysentery. The key to the design is the fact that, once the flies are in the pit, they never get out again. Typically, flies enter the latrine when someone opens the door, and then fly down through the latrine seat and into the pit itself. With the old design, they would then escape the way they came in, but with the new latrines they're attracted by the light at the top of the chimney, which is sealed with gauze. As long as people remember to close the lavatory seat and keep the latrine door shut this is pretty foolproof, keeping the flies buzzing harmlessly in the pit and chimney.

"discovery" in 1959. The Morija Museum (see p.776) plans to turn the beautiful sandstone mission into accommodation and to renovate the remains of the printing works.

Practicalities

Buses arrive at the busy station in the centre of Mohale's Hoek, while **minibus taxis** congregate on the main street near Shell – between them and the buses you should be able to find transport heading both north and south throughout the day. As usual, there are also plenty of inexpensive **places to eat** on the main street including a *Rooster's Golden Crispy Chicken*.

For **accommodation**, the *Hotel Mount Maluti* (☎2278 5224, Ⓔskymountainhotels@ilesotho.com; ❷) has comfortable rooms with TVs, plus a bar, tennis court and swimming pool. The hotel **restaurant** offers decent cuisine including superb pizzas fresh from the oven, or a set evening menu at M65.

Quthing and around

QUTHING, also known as **Moyeni** ("Place of the Wind"), is a curious split-level town established by the British after the Gun War in 1884. The town itself is messy, though it has an attractive setting beside a river gorge, with views of the surrounding hills improving as you climb to the upper part of town. During the day there are always plenty of **buses** and **minibus taxis** north towards Maseru, and much more infrequent services northeast towards Qacha's Nek (including a 10am Lesotho Freight and Bus Services bus from Maseru every other day of the week). You'll also find minibus taxis heading for the nearby Tele Bridge **border post** (daily 6am–10pm), where you can pick up transport to Sterkspruit in the Eastern Cape.

The **Masitise Cave House** (daily 8am–5pm; M10; Ⓔinfo@morijafest .com), a few kilometres west of Quthing, is well worth a visit. The extraordinary house was built into the side of a cave in 1866 by the missionary D.F. Ellenberger – whose *History of the Basuto: Ancient & Modern*, published in 1912, was the first study of its kind. The house has recently been converted into a **museum** and contains interesting displays about the history of the Quthing area, the Ellenbergers' fascinating home, and an explanation about the dinosaur footprint in the roof of one of the rooms in the house. Basic **accommodation** is available at the caretaker's house (☎5879 4167; ❶). Look for the sign on the main road to Masitise Primary School (not the high school), and continue along the dirt track for 1km past the school and church.

The most accessible **dinosaur footprints** in Lesotho are very near the lower section of Quthing. On the road to Mount Moorosi, about 400m from the junction to Quthing town centre, look out for the pink-thatched **visitor centre** (daily 8am–4pm; M5), beside the road on the left. There is a variety of clearly discernible footprints right next to the visitor centre, which also contains a limited range of handicrafts for sale.

Between Masitise and Quthing town centre is the pretty sandstone **Villa Maria Mission**, with its twin red spires. The *Villa Maria Guest House*, set in peaceful grounds behind the church (☎2275 0364; ❶), has inexpensive **accommodation**, with clean rooms and communal bathrooms. In town, about halfway between lower and upper Quthing, the *Fuleng Guest House* (☎2275 0260; ❷) offers excellent-value rooms in simple rondavels (although check as they vary in standard), or more luxurious and stylish rooms with TVs. About 100m down the dirt track just beyond *Fulung*, the intimate *Mountain Side Hotel* (☎2275 0257; ➋) has mostly adequate rooms (check the mattresses) – half overlook the street, while the others are more secluded and quiet. There's a cosy private bar, a friendly public one and a decent **restaurant** with a tasty fixed menu. An alternative option for cheap food is the *Mafikeng Restaurant* in lower Quthing, on the right as you climb the hill.

Mount Moorosi, Qacha's Nek and Sehlabathebe National Park

A far less used route into the highlands than the northern road to Mokhotlong, the mountain road from **Mount Moorosi to Sehlabathebe** is ruggedly beautiful. Highlights along the route include **Thaba Moorosi**, the mountain where the outlawed chief Moorosi made his last stand against the British in 1879, and the remote, pristine national park of **Sehlabathebe** – perfect for fishing, bird-watching and kilometre upon kilometre of isolated hiking.

Mount Moorosi and around

Just over 40km beyond Quthing, the small town of **MOUNT MOOROSI** was named after a chief who moved to the region in the 1850s. He was an ally of the San and had several San wives, but made an enemy of the British in the 1870s. British troops attacked his stronghold in 1879, but he held out for eight months until soldiers used scaling ladders on the steep cliffs and finally captured him, after which they cut off and publicly displayed his severed head. **Thaba Moorosi**, where the main battle took place, is 1km or so further along the main road on the right. The site is marked by some stone slabs in which British soldiers sent to catch the chief engraved their names. It's quite a tricky climb, though, so be sure to let someone in Mount Moorosi know where you are going. If you want to **stay** in the area, the *Moorosi Chalets* (☎ +27 (0)82 824 0883, ✉moorosi@mweb.co.za; ➋), a joint venture by the *Malealea Lodge*, the Quthing Wildlife Development Trust and the German charity DED, offer basic but attractive accommodation in en-suite rondavels or twin rooms with communal facilities. There's a kitchen for self-catering, or meals can be provided by prior arrangement. Activities available include pony-trekking, 4WD trips and village stays in Ha Thlaku, about two hours' hike away. To get there, continue for 5km from Mount Moorosi village on the road to Qacha's Nek, and look for the signboard for the chalets on the left, from where it's another 4km down a gravel road. shortly after rounding Thaba Moorosi, the main road leaves the Senqu River and heads swiftly into the highlands through the impressive **Quthing Gorge**, peaking after about 10km at the **Lebelonyane Pass** (2456m), with superb views. The road carries on through a series of attractive high-altitude valleys, before reaching the small village of **MPHAKI**, which has excellent accommodation at its *Farmers' Training Centre* (no phone; ➊), with well-equipped self-catering rondavels and a pleasant guesthouse.

Qacha's Nek

Some 34km east of Mphaki at **Sekake**, the road rejoins the southern banks of the Senqu, but deteriorates significantly in quality, though you can still make it with care in an ordinary vehicle. It's a beautiful, undulating drive, though once you reach the approach to **QACHA'S NEK** you'll see the depressingly familiar soil erosion and dongas. Named after chief Moorosi's son Ncatya, Qacha's Nek was an area famed for its banditry when the British founded the town in 1888 in an attempt to forestall the kind of trouble they'd experienced with chief Moorosi. Many of the "bandits" were in fact desperate San, hounded from their homes and having no means of survival; this left the British unmoved, and they hunted them to extermination throughout the 1860s and 1870s. Moorosi's Baphuthi people had started moving there in the 1850s, rapidly wiping out all the game, and turning the land over to grazing and cultivation instead. The area has unusually high rainfall, and the weather conditions favour conifers, including a few massive Canadian redwoods, giving Qacha's Nek an atmosphere completely different from most of virtually treeless Lesotho.

There's little to see in town, except the elegant **St Joseph's Church** at its eastern end, but the entire surrounding mountainous countryside is great for **hiking**. Qacha's Nek is also an important **border town** (daily 7am–8pm) and there's usually plenty of **public transport** heading southwest towards Quthing from the Shell garage in the centre of town. There's also a daily bus to and from Maseru operated by Lesotho Freight and Bus Services; it leaves Maseru at 7am, and Qacha's Nek at 8.30am, and takes over seven hours. You can hear **minibus taxis** a mile off, thanks to the cowbells tied to their fronts. On the other side of the border you'll find transport (roughly hourly) heading for the Eastern Cape town of Matatiele, from where it's easy to find buses and minibus taxis on to Kokstad and beyond.

The town's best **accommodation** is the *Letloepe Lodge* (☎2295 0383, ⓦwww.letloepelodge.co.ls; backpackers ❷, rondavels ❸), situated in an attractive setting at the bottom of the Letloepe cliff on the edge of town. The lodge offers comfortable en-suite rondavels with TVs, some with their own kitchenettes, and there is a restaurant if you don't want to self-cater. They also have cheaper backbacker accommodation in twin or triple rooms with shared bathrooms. Alternatively, the *Nthatuoa Hotel* (☎2295 0260; ❷) is the first building on the left as you enter Qacha's Nek from Maseru. The hotel has a variety of rooms, each more luxurious than the last; all are en suite, and you're also welcome to pitch a tent. All tariffs include a substantial breakfast from a restaurant which also serves lunch and dinner. Just past the hotel, near the *Farmers' Training Centre*, the friendly *Anna's B&B* (☎2295 0374, Ⓔannasb&b@leo.co.ls; ❶–❷) also offers a restaurant and choice of accommodation, either older rooms with shared bath or newer en-suite ones. Further out is the *Central Hotel* (☎2295 0488; ❷), a characterful place set in a sandstone building. It has nine en-suite rooms and is often full. Despite the name, it's over 1km out of town, next to the PEP department store. There are a few inexpensive **places to eat** in the centre of town, but for more substantial meals you're best off in one of the hotels.

Sehlabathebe National Park

The oldest nature reserve in the country, **Sehlabathebe National Park** (free entry – for now) is remote and almost inaccessible, but predictably peaceful and stunningly beautiful. Set on the border with South Africa in the southern reaches of the Drakensberg at an average altitude of 2400m, the park is best known for its prolific birdlife, excellent trout fishing, waterfalls, rock paintings and seemingly endless open spaces just perfect for hiking. There are also a few game animals: baboons, rhebok, eland and the secretive oribi antelope, mongoose, otters, wild cats and jackals. In good weather you probably won't be in any hurry to leave, but at any time of year mists and rain can emerge out of nowhere, even on the finest of days, so come prepared.

Practicalities

To get **to the park** from the Lesotho side of the border you'll need either a 4WD or to catch the daily Lesotho Freight and Bus Services bus from Qacha's Nek to Sehlabathebe village, just outside the park (departs at noon, returns at 5.30am), which takes four to five hours. The only other way into the park from the Lesotho side is to walk the forty-kilometre **Top-of-the-Berg hike** from Sani Top (see p.774). **From South Africa**, it's a day's walk to the park through the southern section of South Africa's Ukhahlamba Drakensberg Park along a dramatic path starting at Bushman's Nek, 38km from Underberg in KwaZulu-Natal.

Finding practical **information** is much easier now that the park has been incorporated into the **Maloti–Drakensberg Transfrontier Project** (see box, p.765) and put under the management of the Department of Parks at the Ministry of Tourism (℡2231 1767, ✉info@maloti.org.ls). Neither the Department of Parks nor the park office itself have any **maps**; if you want to do some serious hiking, go to the Department of Lands, Surveys and Physical Planning in Maseru (see box, p.748), where you should be able to pick up some detailed maps of the area.

Other than **camping**, which you can do anywhere provided you get a permit from the lodge, the park's only **accommodation** is the self-catering *Sehlabathebe Lodge* (℡2232 3600; ❶), around 10km from the main gate. The fourteen-bed lodge has an adequate kitchen for self-catering and provides bedding and has hot-water showers; it also has camping. To be sure of a room, book in advance. There are also plans to build a "mountain resort" nearby with fifteen more luxurious chalets, although no construction had started at the time of writing. **Outside the park** there are decent rooms at the beautiful *Range Management Guesthouse* (℡2295 0231; ❶) in Sehlabathebe village. Wherever you're staying, you'll need to be self-sufficient in food and bring spare fuel too.

Travel details

Buses

While there are lots of buses in Lesotho, only one company – the Lesotho Freight and Bus Services Corporation – keeps to a timetable (some of its routes operate in conjunction with other companies). Its services are as follows:

Maseru to: Bokong (daily at 8.30am; 7hr 30min); Linakaneng (daily at 9.30am; 8hr); Mokhotlong (alternating with Itumeleng Transport; daily at 7am; 7hr); Qacha's Nek (daily at 7am; 9hr 30min); Quthing (daily at 7am; 3hr 30min); Sehong Hong (daily at 9am; 8hr 30min); Semonkong (daily at 10am; 6hr).

Other buses simply leave when they're full, and as such operate just like minibus taxis (and are included in the section below).

Butha-Buthe to: Leribe (4 daily; 30min); Maputsoe (4 daily; 45min); Mokhotlong (2–3 daily; 7hr).

Leribe to: Butha-Buthe (4 daily; 30min); Maputsoe (5 daily; 30min); Maseru (8 daily; 2hr).

Mafeteng to: Maseru (5 daily; 1hr 30min); Mohale's Hoek (5 daily; 45min).

Maputsoe to: Butha-Buthe (4 daily; 45min); Leribe (5 daily; 30min); Maseru (8 daily; 2hr); Teya-Teyaneng (8 daily; 45min).

Maseru to: Leribe (8 daily; 2hr); Mafeteng (5 daily; 1hr 30min); Maputsoe (8 daily; 2hr); Morija (hourly;

50min); Qacha's Nek (1 daily; 10hr); Roma (4 daily; 1hr); Semonkong (2 daily; 5hr); Teya-Teyaneng (8 daily; 45min).
Mohale's Hoek to: Mafeteng (5 daily; 45min); Quthing (5 daily; 45min).
Mokhotlong to: Butha-Buthe (2–3 daily; 7hr); Sani (3 daily; 1hr 30min).
Qacha's Nek to: Maseru (1 daily; 10hr); Quthing (1 daily; 7hr).
Quthing to: Mohale's Hoek (5 daily; 45min); Qacha's Nek (1 daily; 7hr).

Roma to: Maseru (4 daily; 1hr); Semonkong (4 daily; 4hr).
Sani to: Mokhotlong (5 daily; 1hr 30min).
Semonkong to: Maseru (2 daily; 5hr); Roma (4 daily; 4hr).
Teya-Teyaneng to: Maputsoe (8 daily; 45min); Maseru (8 daily; 45min).

Flights

Maseru to: Johannesburg (Mon–Fri 5 daily, Sat & Sun 3 daily; 1hr 10min).

Swaziland

CHAPTER 12

Highlights

✶ **Royal festivals** The spectacular ceremonies of *Ncwala and Umhlanga* are colourful affirmations of Swazi national identity. See p.802

✶ **Malandela's Homestead** A collection of buildings bursting with creativity and enterprise, including the funky performance space House on Fire, and Gone Rural, one of the best of Swaziland's many attractive arts and crafts outlets. See p.805

✶ **Myxo's place, KaPhunga** Get a true taste of life in rural Swaziland – this enterprising project allows backpackers to live as part of a village for a few days. See p.807

✶ **Malolotja** A wild, rugged and breathtakingly beautiful reserve attracting hundreds of different bird species, with a network of trails perfect for hiking or horse-riding. See p.809

✶ **Whitewater rafting on the Great Usutu** As action-packed as anything south of the Zambezi – you can paddle a two-man croc raft down Swaziland's largest river. See p.815

✶ **Mkhaya Game Reserve** Swaziland's best wildlife experience, where you can walk with rhino and elephant before sleeping in the bush in open-sided cottages. See p.817

▲ Young women taking part in the Umhlanga ceremony

Swaziland

A tiny landlocked kingdom, **Swaziland** lies in the spanner-like grip of South Africa which surrounds it on three sides, with Mozambique providing its eastern border along the Lubombo Mountains. Although South Africa's influence predominates, Swaziland was a British protectorate from 1906 until its full independence in 1968, and today the country offers an intriguing mix of colonial heritage and homegrown confidence, giving the place a friendlier, more relaxed and often safer feeling than its larger neighbour.

Though Swaziland still feels a lot more commercialized than, say, Lesotho, its outstanding **scenery**, along with its commitment to **wildlife conservation**, makes it well worth a visit. With a car and a bit of time, you can explore some of the less trampled reserves, make overnight stops in unspoilt, out-of-the-way settlements and, if you time your visit well, take in something of Swaziland's well-preserved **cultural traditions**.

Swaziland is also something of a draw for **backpackers**, with useful transport links to different parts of South Africa as well as Mozambique, and some good backpacker lodges. The country also has plenty of adventure activities on offer – from mountain biking and horse-riding to whitewater rafting.

Swaziland has six **national parks**, between them exemplifying the country's geographical diversity, and all offering good-value accommodation. While not as efficiently run as South African national parks, the Swazi reserves are less officious, and many people warm to their easy-going nature. The best-known are those run by **Swazi Big Game Parks** (see p.804): Hlane Royal National Park in the lowveld, Mlilwane Wildlife Sanctuary near Mbabane, and the

Choosing the king

Swazi monarchs are always men of the **Dlamini** family, and over the course of their reign marry a number of women who are carefully selected from different clans to cement national unity. In theory, the king marries women from increasingly important families as he goes along, which means that the son of the last wife is always a strong contender for the succession. In practice, however, other wives with older sons are also in with a chance, resulting in unrest and power-struggles every time the king dies. After his death, the royal council, or *liqoqo*, selects the new **Queen Mother**, who rules as regent until her son is old enough to take charge. She usually has to work hard to ensure her position against ambitious uncles. The main advantage of this awkward process is that by the time the new king is old enough to rule, he and his mother have generally garnered enough support for him to do so effectively.

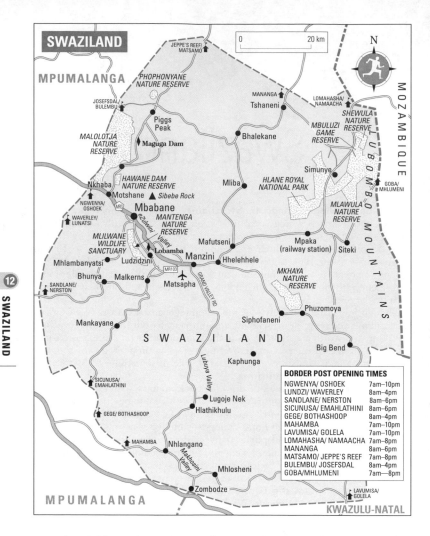

SWAZILAND

BORDER POST OPENING TIMES	
NGWENYA/ OSHOEK	7am–10pm
LUNDZI/ WAVERLEY	8am–4pm
SANDLANE/ NERSTON	8am–6pm
SICUNUSA/ EMAHLATHINI	8am–6pm
GEGE/ BOTHASHOOP	8am–6pm
MAHAMBA	7am–10pm
LAVUMISA/ GOLELA	7am–10pm
LOMAHASHA/ NAMAACHA	7am–8pm
MANANGA	8am–6pm
MATSAMO/ JEPPE'S REEF	7am–8pm
BULEMBU/ JOSEFSDAL	8am–4pm
GOBA/MHLUMENI	7am—8pm

upmarket Mkhaya Game Reserve between Manzini and Big Bend. The Swaziland National Trust Commission, based in Lobamba (Ⓦwww.sntc .org.za), manages Malolotja Nature Reserve in the northwest highveld, Mlawula Nature Reserve in the eastern lowveld and the tiny Mantenga Nature Reserve in the eZulwini Valley.

Despite encroaching political dissent, Swaziland remains one of the world's few absolute monarchies, and **King Mswati III**, educated at Britain's elite Sherbourne College, regularly appears in the country's sacred ceremonies, bedecked in the leopard skins of his office, participating in a ritual dance or assessing the year's crop of eligible maidens as they dance before him. He might even choose to add one to his collection of wives, carefully drawn from a wide selection of clans in order to knit the nation more closely together. If you can, plan to come to Swaziland for the **Ncwala** (around the end of Dec or the start of Jan) or **Umhlanga** (Aug or Sept) ceremonies, for more on which, see box, p.802.

Laid-back **Mbabane**, the country's tiny capital city, makes a useful base from which to explore the attractive central **eZulwini Valley**, home to the royal palace and the **Mlilwane Wildlife Sanctuary**. With your own transport, or a bit of determination and public transport, you can venture further afield, heading into the highveld of the northwest, and up to the fantastically beautiful **Malolotja Nature Reserve**, with its fabulous hiking country, soaring valleys and cliffs.

If you are trying to get between northern KwaZulu-Natal and the Kruger National Park in South Africa, Swaziland offers a good, fully tarred **through route** via the Matsamo border in the north and the Lavumisa and Mahamba borders in the south, passing by the Mkhaya Game Reserve and Big Bend. Approaching Kruger this way is a far more attractive option than skirting through the eastern parts of Mpumalanga.

Summers are hot, particularly in the eastern lowveld. **Winter** is usually sunny, but nights can be very chilly in the western highveld around the Malolotja Nature Reserve and Piggs Peak. In summer, rainfall is usually limited to short, drenching storms that play havoc with the smaller untarred roads. Note that Swaziland's eastern lowveld, including Hlane Royal National Park and Mkhaya Nature Reserve, is **malarial** during the summer months (Nov–May). For details on necessary precautions, see p.71.

Some history

The history of Swaziland dates back to the **Dlamini** clan and their king, **Ngwane**, who crossed the Lubombo Mountains from present-day Mozambique in around 1750. Pushed into southeast Swaziland by the Ndwandwe people of Zululand, the clan eventually settled at Mhlosheni and then Zombodze in the southwest, where Ngwane reigned precariously, under constant threat of Ndwandwe attack. His grandson, **Sobhuza I**, was forced to flee north from the Ndwandwe, but they in turn were defeated by the Zulu king Shaka in 1819. Sobhuza then established a new capital suitably far from Shaka in the eZulwini Valley, and made peace with the Ndwandwe by marrying the king's daughter.

Sobhuza's power grew as he brought more and more clans under his wing. His alliance with the newly arrived Afrikaners, forged out of mutual fear of the

siSwati phrases			
Basics			
Yes	*Yebo*	It's nice/tasty	*Kumnandzi*
(also a casual greeting)		Today	*Lamuhla*
No	*Cha*	Tomorrow	*Kusasa*
Thank you	*Ngiyabonga*	Yesterday	*Itolo*
Greetings and responses			
Hello (to one)	*Sawubona*	Goodbye (said by	*Sala kahle*
Hello (to many)	*Sanibona*	person leaving)	
How are you?	*Kunjani?*	Goodbye (said by	*Hamba kahle*
I'm fine	*Ngikhona*	person remaining)	
Travel			
Where is... ?	*Iphi I... ?*	Where are you	*U ya phi?*
Where can we	*Singahlala*	going?	
stay?	*kuphi?*	How much?	*Malini?*

Accommodation

Accommodation in the **mid- and upper range** is generally better value than in South Africa, although there isn't a wide choice, particularly in the guesthouse and B&B sector. **Backpacker** and **budget** places are on a par with South Africa. Camping in designated campsites is possible near almost every tourist attraction and in all the national parks except for Mkhaya.

Airport tax

A **fee** of E50 is payable when flying out of Matsapha Airport.

Books and maps

The Swazi Tourism Authority publishes a host of useful maps and brochures which can be picked up for free at tourist information offices and in the foyers of most hotels and guesthouses. Free detailed maps of hiking and riding trails are available at the six game parks and at nearby accommodation. For **books**, the well-stocked SNA newsagents (the Swazi equivalent of the South African CNA), found in Mbabane, Manzini and many larger malls, has a small selection of Swazi literature alongside more regional, especially South African, fiction and non-fiction.

Costs, money and banks

Costs are similar to those in South Africa, with food and fuel somewhat less expensive. Currency is the **lilangeni** – plural **emalangeni** (E) – which is tied to the South African rand (1 rand = 1 lilangeni). The rand is legal tender in Swaziland, so you won't have to change any money, but note that emalangeni are not convertible outside Swaziland. **Credit cards** such as Visa, Mastercard and American Express are widely accepted in hotels, restaurants and shops. The national parks and most hotels and hostels accept cards for payments such as accommodation and restaurant bills, but you'd be well advised to carry **cash** to pay for things such as guided walks and bike rental. **Banks** are omnipresent and easily found in most towns. Opening hours are generally Monday to Friday 8.30am to 3.30pm (Wed until 1pm), with some branches open on Saturday from 8.30am to 11.30am. There are ATMs outside practically all banks and most accept international cards.

Food and drink

Although Swazis will insist that there is a distinct Swazi cuisine which is based on *mealie* meal, various green leafy vegetables and beans, a range of meats – roasted or served in a stew – and a sort of yoghurty fermented milk called *Emasi*, it only tends to be prepared in the privacy of the home and you will seldom find it on offer in any restaurants. The fact that it, to the non-Swazi, tends to be rather bland may explain why there's not much demand. Ninety-nine percent of the food found in cafés and restaurants will be identical to that served in South Africa, indeed in many of the same chain restaurants.

Phone numbers

The **country code** for Swaziland is ☏268, followed by the destination number (there are no area codes). The code for phoning out from Swaziland is ☏00, followed by the country and area codes and finally the destination number. To **phone South Africa**, dial ☏07. To arrange a **collect call**, dial ☏94. Country codes are the same as those dialled from South Africa (see p.79). If you experience difficulties, call enquiries on ☏919490. Swaziland has its own mobile phone network – MTN – which works well in the eZulwini Valley but can be patchy elsewhere. International roaming is possible with certain phones and contracts. All Swazi mobile phone numbers are seven figures and begin with 6.

Public holidays

January 1	**July 22** (King Sobhuza II's birthday)
Good Friday	**August/September** (Umhlanga
Easter Monday	Dance Day)
April 19 (King Mswati III's birthday)	**September 6** (Independence Day)
April 25 (National Flag Day)	**December/January** (Ncwala Day)
May 1 Workers' Day	**December 25**
May 24 Ascension Day	**December 26**

Red tape and visas

Nationals of most Commonwealth countries (excluding Bangladesh, India, Pakistan and Sri Lanka), the US, Canada, South Africa, Australia and all EU countries do not require a visa if staying sixty days or less. For details of Swaziland's embassies see p.798.

Security

The **crime rate** in Swaziland is relatively low, especially compared to that in neighbouring South Africa, and you'll feel the difference almost immediately as you cross the border. That said, it's recommended to take normal precautions when walking in the centre of the two main towns – Manzini and Mbabane. They both die out after dark, at which times you're advised to use taxis.

Tour operators

The country's biggest and best **tour operator** is Swazi Trails (℡4162180, ⊛www .swazitrails.co.za), located in the Mantenga Craft Centre (see p.800). It runs tours to the Lobamba royal village, game parks, nature reserves, craft centres, local villages and even a local *sangoma*. It can also arrange horse-riding, hiking, mountain biking, caving and some great whitewater rafting trips (see p.815). There are also a handful of smaller local operations, including Inyatsi Tours and Safaris (℡6050224, ⊛michael1972@yahoo.com), which runs tours to different parts of Swaziland. The tourist office in Mbabane (see p.793) keeps information on other tour guides.

Water

Most tap water in Swaziland is potable although you may want to drink bottled water in game parks, where the water source is more uncertain, and as a general precaution if you have a dodgy stomach.

Websites

⊛**www.welcometoswaziland.com** Swaziland's official website is lively, colourful and packed with useful information, including hotel listings and alternative tours of Swaziland.

⊛**www.biggameparks.org** Provides information on three of the country's most visited reserves, the Hlane, Mlilwane and Mkhaya parks, with practical information about activities, and an accommodation booking site.

⊛**www.swazitravel-link.co.sz** Hosted by Swazi Trails, the most important tour operator in the country, with reams of information about accommodation, shopping and restaurants, and with details of a range of tours and activities around Swaziland, including cultural, wildlife and adventure options.

Zulu, was continued by his son **Mswati II** (after whom the Swazi people are named), who stretched his kingdom north to the Sabi River and sent raiding parties as far as the Limpopo River and east to the Indian Ocean.

Europeans arrived in greater numbers throughout the 1880s, after the discovery of gold in neighbouring Transvaal and at Piggs Peak and Forbes Reef in Swaziland. Mswati's son, **Mbandzeni**, granted large chunks of his territory in concessions to the new arrivals, emboldening Britain to ignore his claims to most of the rest, and by the time Swaziland became a protectorate of South Africa in 1894, there was precious little land left. After their victory in the Second Anglo–Boer War, Britain assumed control of the territory and retained it until 1968.

After World War II the British invested in their protectorate, establishing enormous **sugar plantations** in the northeast, and an **iron-ore mine** at Ngwenya in the highveld (today, the country's major export is sugar). Meanwhile, **Sobhuza II**, who had become king of the Swazis in 1921, concentrated on buying back his kingdom, and had acquired about half of it by the time independence came in 1968. The Swazi aristocracy managed the transition to independence skilfully, with its Imbokodvo party winning every parliamentary seat in the first elections. In 1973, a radical pan-Africanist party won three seats, prompting Sobhuza to **ban political parties** and declare a state of emergency which technically has been in place ever since. Political parties are generally viewed by most Swazis – a proud and relatively united people – as a source of division, creating factions and overcomplicating a simple political process. The parliament that governs Swaziland today is bicameral, with fifteen of the House of Assembly's 75 members appointed by the king, and the rest directly elected every five years. Of the Senate's thirty members, twenty are appointed by the king, and ten chosen by the House of Assembly. However, final authority always rests with the king, who continues to name the prime minister (who, by tradition, is always a Dlamini, and not necessarily an elected member of the House of Assembly) and approve or veto important legislation.

After Sobhuza's death in 1982, a period of intrigue ensued, with the Queen Mother Dzeliwe assuming the regency until deposed by Prince Bhekimpi, who ruled until 1985, purging all the opposition he could. The current king, **Mswati III**, the son of one of Sobhuza's seventy wives, was recalled from an English public school to become king in 1986, and parliamentary elections were held in 1987. New opposition began to emerge, most notably the **People's United Democratic Movement** (PUDEMO), which has strong support amongst Swazi workers, though in general Swazis are proud of their distinctive kingdom, and as a result calls for change are tempered by an unwillingness to show disloyalty to the king, or to expose Swaziland to what many see as the predatory ambitions of South Africa.

Thus the maintenance of tradition and appeals to broad nationalism have been key components of Swazi royalty's strategy to retain power. Relations with the current South African regime are uneasy: the ANC remembers the expulsion of its activists during the 1980s and wants speedy political change. Although Mswati III is sometimes said to favour reform, the authorities have worked hard to keep dissent bottled up, by means of sporadic police repression; opposition leaders have been prevented from speaking freely in the media, and poor turnouts marked the "elections" of 1993, 1998 and 2003. In 2006 a new constitution came into effect and introduced a Bill of Rights that includes freedom of association, but does not allow parliamentary candidates to stand for election of political parties. It also cements the king's executive role. Currently,

Swaziland is the only country in southern Africa not practising multiparty democracy. It seems only a matter of time before it is coerced by the other regional powers into doing so.

Getting there

Of the twelve border posts serving traffic from South Africa, the most popular is **Ngwenya/Oshoek** (7am–10pm), which is the closest one to Johannesburg and is the easiest route to Mbabane, only 20km to the east. A good alternative route is via the **Sandlane/Nerston** border post (8am–6pm), about 35km further south, and roughly 70km from the city. Although a longer journey, this road passes through some outstanding scenery and will take you past some excellent places to stay. Just past Sandlane, where there are some interesting San paintings (ask at the church for someone to show you the way), the road plunges deep into the vast and beautiful **Usutu Forest**, which covers over ten percent of Swaziland. After some steep climbs, you'll start a long descent to the factory town of **Bhunya**, whose hub is a belching pulp mill – reason enough not to linger. Press on for another 15km or so on the road to Mhlambanyatsi. Just before Mhlambanyatsi – and 27km from Mbabane – is a fine **hotel**, *The Forester's Arms* (☎4674377, @www.forestersarms .co.za; half board ❺), set in a picturesque clearing in the surrounding woodland, which can be explored by foot, or on horse or mountain bike, available at the hotel. The rooms are cosy with fireplaces and wonderful mountain views, and hearty meals are served (the flamboyant chef is likely to visit your table), making this a pleasant stop along the way; on Sundays, people from all over the country pour in to feast on the hotel's superb buffet lunch (E114) – you'll need to **book** ahead to be sure of a table.

Back on the road, **Mhlambanyatsi** itself has a small shopping centre and some filling stations, but little else. The road beyond it enters a beautiful, lush river valley dotted with traditional houses and eventually breaks through the hills to the plateau on which Mbabane stands, where you can connect with the main routes to the centre of the country.

Just off the N2 from Piet Retief in the southwest is the **Emahlathini /Sicunusa** (8am–6pm) border crossing, which leads to the wonderfully scenic and fast MR4. The northern crossing via **Bulembu** (8am–4pm) to Piggs Peak is perhaps the most spectacular in the country, but the bad road makes this journey hard going in an ordinary car. Crossing the border is usually very straightforward: you simply have to show your passport and pay E50 in **road tax**. Other border crossings include: **Jeppe's Reef/Matsamo** in the northwest (8am–8pm), handy if you're coming in from Kruger Park; **Mananga** in the northeast (8am–6pm); **Lavumisa/Golela** in the southeast (7am–10pm), close to the KwaZulu-Natal coast; and **Mahamba** in the south (7am–10pm). A new option is also the reopened eastern Goba/Mhlumeni border crossing from Mozambique (7am–8pm).

Buses and flights

The only timetabled **bus** company connecting South Africa and Swaziland is the Baz Bus (see p.42) which runs eastbound from Jo'burg to Durban via Mbabane and then Manzini on Monday, Wednesday and Saturday, departing for Durban the next morning; services from Durban for Swaziland leave on Monday, Wednesday and Friday and set off for Jo'burg the next morning. Small Kombi minibuses (see p.729) ply this route nonstop.

Swaziland has one **international airport**, Matsapha (often referred to as "Manzini"), between Mbabane and Manzini. Airlink Swaziland (☎5186155, www.flyswaziland.com), a partner of SAA, through whom it can be contacted in South Africa, flies four times daily to and from Johannesburg. Swazi Express Airways (☎5186840, ⒲www.swaziexpress.com;) flies in from Durban and Johannesburg daily Monday to Friday, and from Maputo and Vilanculos, both in Mozambique, three times weekly.

Getting around

Driving is the best way to see Swaziland; distances are small, all the main tourist sites are near good, tarred roads, and the major gravel roads are in decent condition. Most dirt roads are passable with an ordinary vehicle in dry months. Driving standards, however, leave a lot to be desired – highlighted by the fact that two of the last four ministers of transport have died in road accidents. The authorities permit a blood-alcohol level in drivers which is double that permitted in South Africa, which should make you think twice about long drives at night. Also, the general speed limit of 80kph outside towns is universally ignored and very rarely enforced. For Swazi car rental, see "Listings" on p.798.

Swaziland is crisscrossed by a network of so-called **Kombi** minibus routes that covers almost every corner of the country. The Kombis leave from bus stations in the main towns, when full, and ply the main routes linking the towns, calling at set stops along the way. This means that if for instance you want to get to Nyanza Farm in the Malkerns valley from Mbabane, you'll have to catch a Kombi to Malkerns, and then another from Malkerns towards Manzini, getting off at the Nyanza stop. Kombi travel is cheap – a ticket from Mbabane to Nyanza costs E10. Ask at the local bus station about the best route to get to your destination. The stations are organized by destination, so all Kombis to, say, Manzini will leave from one corner of the station, and to Piggs Peak from another. Although buses do tend to get quite packed, they are an efficient way of getting around, and a great way of meeting people.

Mbabane

Tucked in the jumble of granite peaks and valleys that make up the Dlangeni hills, Swaziland's administrative capital, **MBABANE** (pronounced "M-buh-ban"), is small, relaxed and unpretentious, with a population of only about 58,000. The city roughly marks the point where the mountainous southern African highveld descends briefly into middleveld, before bottoming out further east as dry lowveld.

There's not much to do in Mbabane, but many visitors find it more agreeable than hectic Manzini, especially if you need to get money (there is a multitude of working ATMs in the malls), find a comfortable bed or plan your trip ahead. This is a good base from which to start exploring Swaziland, especially if you're without your own transport: the Mlilwane Wildlife Sanctuary (see p.803) lies not far south, and the royal village of Lobamba (see p.801) makes an easy day-trip – vital if you're here when the *Umhlanga* or *Ncwala* ceremonies take place.

Arrival and information

Matsapha airport (☎5186192), 25km southeast of Mbabane, just west of Manzini, is Swaziland's only international airport. There's no public transport

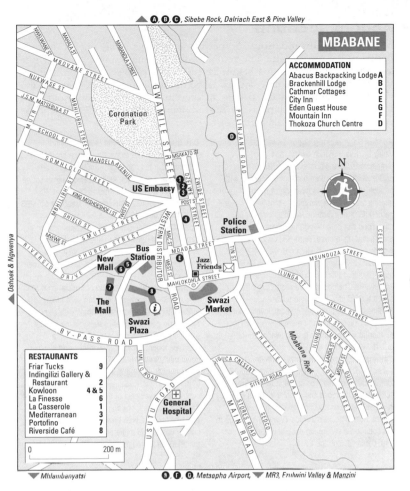

▲ Ⓐ, Ⓑ, Ⓒ, Sibebe Rock, Dalriach East & Pine Valley

MBABANE

ACCOMMODATION

Abacus Backpacking Lodge	A
Brackenhill Lodge	B
Cathmar Cottages	C
City Inn	E
Eden Guest House	G
Mountain Inn	F
Thokoza Church Centre	D

Coronation Park

US Embassy

Police Station

Bus Station

New Mall

Jazz Friends

The Mall

Swazi Plaza

Swazi Market

RESTAURANTS

Friar Tucks	9
Indingilizi Gallery &	
Restaurant	2
Kowloon	4 & 5
La Finesse	6
La Casserole	1
Mediterranean	3
Portofino	7
Riverside Café	8

General Hospital

0   200 m

12

SWAZILAND | Mbabane

◄ Oshoek & Ngwenya

▼ Mhlambanyatsi   Ⓐ, Ⓕ, Ⓖ, Matsapha Airport, ▼ MR3, Fzulwini Valley & Manzini

from here into Mbabane, so if you haven't arranged a pick-up with your hotel, you'll need to take a **taxi** or **rent a car** (see "Listings" on p.798). There's a foreign exchange bureau at the airport (daily 8am–5.30pm).

Buses and **minibuses** from South Africa stop at the main bus station off the Western Distributor Road, beside the Swazi Plaza mall. From here you can catch minibus **Kombis** to Manzini and Piggs Peak, and local buses within the Mbabane area. Kombis plying the Mbabane–Manzini route leave from the western side of the bus station – this is also where you can rent a **private taxi** for local travel.

Mbabane's **tourist office**, Swazi Plaza (Mon–Fri 8am–5pm, Sat 9am–1pm; ☏4042531 or 4090112), has a good supply of **maps**, brochures and the free monthly *What's On?* and *What's Happening in Swaziland?* guides.

Central Mbabane empties at night, and **muggings** are a risk for those wandering the streets alone. If you're going out after dark, arrange for a taxi to pick you up.

Accommodation

Mbabane's **accommodation** is somewhat limited, with only one worthwhile option in the town centre. The rest are a short minibus journey or taxi ride away. All of the places listed below have a free pick-up service from the bus station or airport, if you have booked accommodation in advance. There are also various guesthouses on the fringes of the city, and, if you have your own transport, most establishments in the eZulwini Valley (see p.798) are close enough to make viable alternatives.

Abacus Backpacking Lodge Luvivane St off Pine Valley Rd, East Dalriach ☎4047854, ℯabacusbackcomp@yahoo.co.uk. Brand-new backpackers' place 3km north of the centre, with an eight-bed dorm, and three smart doubles sharing facilities. You can pitch a tent in the large garden (E70) and rent mountain bikes (E50 per day). Food can be ordered throughout the day and there's dial-up Internet. Dorm ❶, double ❷

Brackenhill Lodge Mountain Drive ☎4042887, ℯbrackenhill@realnet.co.sz. Luxurious B&B on a quiet hillside 4.5km north of the city centre, off Fonteyn Rd. The comfortable rooms are often full so it's a good idea to book in advance. Facilities include a swimming pool, lovely hiking trails, dial-up Internet and a small breakfast restaurant where dinner is also available when ordered in advance. ❸

Cathmar Cottages 3km north of Mbabane on Pine Valley Rd ☎4043387 or 6021364, ℯtheresa .cathmar@africaonline.co.sz. Slightly run-down self-catering cottages and simpler wooden cabins in a lovely location north of town with views of Sibebe Rock. Facilities include TV and mini fridge in the cottages, a swimming pool, and breakfast for E40. Cabin ❷, cottage ❸

City Inn Gwamile St ☎4042406, ℯcityinn @realnet.co.sz. The oldest city-centre hotel, offering plain but spacious en-suite rooms, all carpeted and with TV. It incorporates a small coffee shop, and the *Pablo* diner facing the street. ❸

Eden Guest House 1km south of Mbabane off MR3 ☎4046317 or 6048962, ℴwww.kapola_eden .co.sz. Comfortable guesthouse accommodation in a large family home, in the southern outskirts of Mbabane. There are fifteen homely, well-equipped en-suite guest rooms, and a quiet, secluded garden with pool. ❸

Mountain Inn 4km southeast of Mbabane off MR3 ☎4042781, ℴwww.mountaininn.sz. A smart, efficiently run if slightly dated hotel, with sixty rooms and good facilities including a lovely pool and the *Friar Tuck* restaurant. Located on a spacious mountainside plot with wonderful views down eZulwini Valley. ❹

Thokoza Church Centre Polinjane Rd ☎4046681, ℯthokozaac@africaonline.co.sz. Church mission centre some way east of the city centre (turn left at the police station), offering drab but cheap two-or three-bed rooms, with breakfast. There is a 10pm curfew unless you make prior arrangements, and the area can be rough at night. ❷

The City

Mbabane's hilly **centre** is a pleasant jumble of office blocks, markets, malls and shacks that you can very easily explore on foot – which is just as well, as driving here can be stressful without a sound grasp of the street layout. **Gwamile Street** is the closest the city has to a main street; running south into the central business district (CBD), it's lined in parts by colonial administrative buildings which are attractive to look at, but can only be entered on official business. At the end of Gwamile Street, on the banks of the Mbabane River, lies the **Swazi Market**, with neat rows of curio stalls with a colourful selection of handicrafts, and, though prices aren't cheap, you can always haggle. It's just as interesting wandering further into the market, where fresh fruit and vegetable stalls make for a colourful scene (though prices here aren't negotiable).

The main focus of the city centre, however, is the sprawl of shopping malls down the hill from Gwamile Street. Most of Mbabane's main shops, banks and services are located in either the **Swazi Plaza** or the more upmarket **Mall** and **New Mall**. Alongside the Swazi Plaza is the busy bus and taxi rank.

Sibebe Rock

About 10km north of Mbabane along the Pine Valley road, Swaziland's most famous geological feature, a huge granite dome called **Sibebe Rock**, can be found among the Mbuluzi Mountains. Rising 300m above the Mbuluzi River Valley, the vast slabs of granite are very steep and dangerous in places, but among the scattered boulders at the summit are Bushman paintings indicating that the rock was inhabited by humans thousands of years ago. While the hard, coarse surface of the granite offers more grip than other types of rock, it can be very dangerous if you slip, so a guide is essential for any ascent. Swazi Trails (see p.795) offers a challenge they describe as "the steepest walk in the world", which ascends an impossible-looking path up the front face of the dome. Alternatively, the Sibebe Trust (☏4046070; E400 for a guide, E25 community fee), a local community initiative, organizes less adrenaline-fuelled walks along the top of the huge rock, arranged through the community office at the end of Pine Valley road. Swazi Trails also offers a **caving trip** in the same mountain range, which involves a lot of squeezing through narrow spaces and navigation by little more than a head torch and the encouraging words of your guide – it's a memorable adventure for those who don't mind enclosed spaces and a few bumps and scratches. Both the Sibebe Challenge and the caving trip are run as half-day trips, each costing around E500 including transport to and from various points in the eZulwini Valley and Mbabane, community fee, and drinks and snacks en route.

Eating, drinking and nightlife

You'll find the ubiquitous *Spur, Steers, Debonairs* (pizza) and *KFC* in Mbabane, but the town also has a smattering of very good **restaurants**, a selection of which is reviewed below. The city's liveliest **bar** is the *Plaza Bar*, in the Swazi Plaza complex. For live music there's the *Jazz Friends* club at the bottom of Gwamile Street, and at weekends you can usually catch a good local band at the *West End Girls* **nightclub**, above the *Yemfo* bar, reached down Western Distributor Road or West Street. For the best nightlife, however, most locals head out to happening spots along the eZulwini Valley or in Manzini. Check the daily *Times of Swaziland* for details. Women travellers on their own are likely to encounter some unwanted attention in bars and clubs, but the pestering probably won't be aggressive or persistent.

Restaurants

Friar Tucks At the *Mountain Inn*, 4km southeast of the city centre ☏4042781. Serves reliable buffet lunches and à la carte dinners, in an intimate, rather dark interior; there's also outdoor seating.

Indingilizi Gallery & Restaurant 112 Dzeliwe St ☏4046213. A very pleasant place to come for lunch. The restaurant is in the gallery's back garden, and serves light, wholesome dishes at reasonable prices. Mon–Fri 8am–5pm, Sat 8.30am–1pm.

Kowloon New Mall ☏4048637. A reliable Chinese restaurant and takeaway, known for its chicken satay (E40) and shrimp fried rice (E50). Mon–Sat 7.30am–8pm. There's also a branch on Gwamile St.

La Casserole Omni Centre, Gwamile St ☏4046426. Upmarket but good-value restaurant and takeaway, specializing in German dishes, with vegetarian selections, and excellent pizza. Daily 8am–10pm.

La Finesse New Mall ☏4045936. Fine dining in an excellent Portuguese/Mozambican seafood restaurant serving, among its specialities, a delightful fish curry for E65. Mon–Sat 10am–9.30pm.

Mediterranean Gwamile St ☏4043212. Despite the name, this is an Indian restaurant serving wonderful, moderately priced dishes in a dark, cavernous setting. Daily 11am–midnight.

Portofino Mall. Italian ice cream, good coffee, and well-prepared breakfasts and lunches, at very reasonable prices. Mon–Sat 8am–5.30pm, Sun 8.30am–2pm.

Riverside Café Swazi Plaza. On the first floor overlooking the river and the busy bus station, this café does delicious breakfasts, light lunches and salads as well as more substantial meals such as Mozambican *fejoada* (E39) and *peri-peri* baby chicken (E29). Very good value. Mon–Fri 8am–5pm, Sat 8am–2pm.

Listings

Airlines Airlink Swaziland ☎ 4043157, ⓦ www .flyswaziland.com; Swazi Express Airlines ☎ 5186840, ⓦ www.swaziexpress.com.
Banks Most banks are found in Gwamile St or in the Swazi Plaza. Branches include First National, Nedbank and Standard. Hours are generally Mon–Fri 9am–3.30pm (Wed 3pm), Sat 9–11.30am. The quietest time to bank is a weekday morning.
Bookshops Websters, at 120 Dzeliwe St and in the New Mall, has the best general selection. There is also an SNA newsagent (the Swazi equivalent of South Africa's CNA) in the Swazi Plaza.
Car rental Avis (☎ 5186222) and Imperial (☎ 5184393) are located at Matsapha airport, and there's another Imperial agent at the Engen service station at the junction of the By-Pass Rd and Main Rd (☎ 4041384). Affordable Car Hire (☎ 4049136 or 6020394) in the Swazi Plaza is cheaper.
Embassies Mozambique, Princess Drive ☎ 4043700; South Africa, New Mall ☎ 4044651;

UK Honorary Consulate, ☎ 4043469; US, Gwamile St ☎ 4046442. Note that the UK's representation in Swaziland is a Pretoria-based consul; for details, see ⓦ www.fco.gov.uk.
Emergencies Fire ☎ 933; Police ☎ 999.
Hospitals Mbabane Clinic Service (private), St Michael St ☎ 4042423; Government Hospital (public), Usutu Rd ☎ 4042111.
Internet access You can get online at Real Image at The Mall, or at the Swazi Post Internet café, upstairs in the Swazi Plaza.
Laundries Swaziland Steam Laundry & Dry, Gwamile St, and in the Swazi Plaza.
Pharmacy Mbabane Pharmacy, Gwamile St; Philani Pharmacy, in the Swazi Plaza; and Green Cross, in The Mall.
Post office The main post office is on Mahlokohla St (Mon–Fri 8.30am–4pm, Sat 8.30–11am), and there's a smaller one in the Swazi Plaza.
Taxi Take Me Home Taxis ☎ 6068120.

The eZulwini Valley

After passing through Mbabane, the smooth, four-lane **MR3** winds down the steep sides of Malagwane Hill in a series of sweeping curves, made hazardous by crawling lorries and reckless minibus taxis. The road then heads off southeast along the eZulwini Valley, but unless you're bound directly for Manzini and beyond, take the turning to the right not long after the foot of the hill onto the older and quieter **MR103**: this links most of the main sights of the scenic **eZulwini Valley** (Place of Heaven). In the 1960s, a succession of casinos, strip joints, hotels and caravan parks sprang up here, catering mainly for South African tourists. When gambling became legal in South Africa in the mid-1990s, however, the number of pleasure-seekers dropped; the tourist industry had to start looking beyond the noise of the slot machines and karaoke to the valley's cultural and natural assets, and in particular places such as the royal residences of **Lobamba** and **Ludzidzini**, the **Mantenga Nature Reserve** and **Mlilwane Wildlife Sanctuary**. The latter, in particular, is one of Swaziland's main attractions, with its range of accommodation from backpacker lodges to colonial guesthouses, as well as numerous activities, including hiking trails and game viewing from a mountain bike.

Malagwane Hill and along the eZulwini Valley Road

Soon after leaving Mbabane, the main Mbabane–Manzini road begins its giddy descent down **Malagwane Hill**. As the highway begins to level out at the bottom of the valley, the first main exit leads to the old eZulwini Valley road, the **MR103**, which runs parallel to the mountains on the southern side of the valley. A kilometre or so along the MR103, a right-hand turn leads to *Timbali Lodge* (☎ 4161156, ⓦ www.timbalilodge.co.sz), a former caravan park which has been transformed into a stylish guest lodge with shaded self-catering cottages sleeping five (E890), double chalets (④), a pool, bar and coffee shop serving breakfasts (included in chalet prices). It also houses *The Boma*, an outstanding new restaurant (same details) under an enormous, beautifully thatched roof which does fabulous international cuisine as well as mouthwatering Swazi-style spring rolls. A corner of the lodge's grounds remains open to caravans and tents (E60 per person). Next door to *Timbali* you'll find one of Swaziland's swankiest **restaurants**, the *Calabash* (☎4161187), which serves an excellent range of fresh seafood and specializes in German, Swiss and Austrian dishes.

Continuing along the MR103 valley road, you'll soon come to the Swazi Health and Beauty Studio, which incorporates the popular **Cuddle Puddle** (daily 6am–11pm; E10), a beautifully warm outdoor spa pool filled from a natural spring nearby and surrounded by tropical vegetation. Staff perform superb massages (10am–6pm; book on ☎4161164) and clients travel from as far afield as Cape Town for a relaxing treatment. Immediately beyond this lie three Sun **hotels** offering their usual blend of comfort and anonymity. The *Royal Swazi Sun* (☎4165000, ⓦwww.suninternational.com; ❽) is the smartest of the lot, with a fine swimming pool, a well-stocked bookstore, a golf course, wireless Internet, a good selection of restaurants and plenty of upmarket bars, as well as a swanky casino and a tatty adult cinema. The other Sun options offer slightly better value: the *Lugogo Sun* (☎4164500; ❼) provides a well-priced buffet that is particularly enticing at breakfast, and the *Ezulwini Sun* (☎4166500; ❻) has a beer garden open on Tuesday nights. All three have highly negotiable prices – and you'll get the best deals by booking through the Sun's Jo'burg headquarters (☎+27 (0)11 280 7444). Opposite the filling station, just past the Sun hotels, stands an extended line of **craft stalls**, commonly signposted by one or two tour buses drawn up alongside. This is a good place for mainstream Swazi crafts such as wood and soapstone carvings, though you have to haggle to get the prices down to sensible levels.

Also on this section of the eZulwini Valley road is the *Happy Valley Motel* (☎4161061, ⓦwww.happyvalley.co.sz; ❷), located 3km or so past the craft stalls. A remnant of Swaziland's days as a place of temptation for repressed white South Africans, the motel also houses the *If Not?* go-go bar and the *Why Not?* disco, a popular nightclub and venue for local and touring bands. The rooms in the motel are predictable but neat, with air conditioning and cable TV. Under the same roof is *Bella Vista Pizzeria* (Mon–Thurs & Sun 6.30am–midnight, Fri & Sat 6.30am–2am), which is popular with locals stopping for a drink, meal or takeaway.

Across the road is **Gables Shopping Centre**, which boasts an ATM, a large grocery store and *The Friendly Whistle* Internet café (Mon–Fri 8am–6pm, Sat 8am–3pm, Sun 10am–3pm). There are also several good **food** options in the shopping centre: *Linda's Coffee Shop* (Mon–Fri 8am–5pm, Sat & Sun 8am–3pm) does fabulous good-value breakfasts and light lunches, while, a few doors down from *Linda's*, *Kanimambo* (daily noon–2pm & 6.30–9pm) does delicious Mozambican fare. *The Great Taipei* (daily noon–2.30pm & 5.30–9pm) next door to *Kanimambo*, has a reliable range of Chinese food, while the friendly *Quartermaine's* (Tues–Fri 9am–10pm, Sat & Sun 8am–10pm) is a pub-restaurant dedicated to a character in *King Solomon's Mines*, serving standard steak-based pub grub from breakfast time onwards.

The Mantenga Valley

The Mantenga Valley follows the course of the Lusushwana (Little Usutu) River from the eZulwini Valley road, turning up into the hills to the west about 2km from the Sun hotels and 1km before reaching Gables Shopping Centre. Most prominent in the valley is the twin-peaked **Lugogo Mountain**, also known as "Sheba's Breasts", which featured in H. Rider Haggard's famous adventure novel *King Solomon's Mines*. Further along, on the western horizon, *Execution Rock* is a stark reminder of the days when murderers and thieves were punished by being forced to jump off the rock to their certain death below.

Apart from a series of good **craft centres**, the valley is dominated by the **Mantenga Nature Reserve**, home of the **Swazi Cultural Village** and **Swazi River Café**. There's a fair amount of new development by the side of the eZulwini Valley road in this area, so the road layout is subject to change, but by following signs to the *Mantenga Lodge* (see below) you should get onto the correct road.

Along the Mantenga road

The **Mantenga Craft Centre**, less than 1km from the turn-off from the eZulwini Valley road, consists of an attractive purpose-built village of craft shops. These specialize in more exclusive and individual crafts than are found in many other parts of Swaziland, including fabrics, artworks and better carvings. There's also a **tourist office** run by the main booking office for **Swazi Trails** (daily 8am–5pm; ☎4162180 or 6020261 after hours, ⓦwww.swazitravel-link.co.sz), the country's leading tour operator, where you can organize a wide range of cultural and adventure trips including a half-day arts and crafts trail, whitewater rafting (see p.815) and caving. Across from the Craft Centre is the rather run-down but friendly and tidy *Legends Backpacker Lodge* (☎4161870, ⒺQlegends @realnet.co.sz; ❶) with a few doubles ❶, a yard for camping, Internet access, communal kitchen and the popular *Shebeen* bar. It's a great place to base yourself if you're on a tight budget and want easy access to all that the valley has to offer. In between the Centre and the lodge is a short dirt road that will bring you to the beautifully located, family-run 🌴 *Mantenga Lodge* (☎4161049, ⓦwww .mantengalodge.com; ❸), an excellent choice for mid-priced **accommodation** in the eZulwini Valley. The lodge has 36 en-suite rooms, some in cosy chalets

▲ Swazi crafts

sleeping two nestled on the valley side, as well as a pool, terrace bar and top-of-the-range **restaurant** with especially good views. Turning left off the dirt road, immediately before *Mantenga Lodge*, another dirt road down the valley leads to a long, terracotta-painted building with large morning glories adorning the tin roof. This is the Guava Gallery (Tues–Sat 9am–5pm, Sun 10am–5pm) with more crafts worth checking out. Inside, the Jewellery Studio to the right sells jewellery hand-crafted in the eZulwini corridor, out of gold, silver, semi-precious stones and even elephant and giraffe hair, while the gallery, to the left, sells some highly original local arts and crafts, including paintings, sculptures and woven mats. In between the two, *Bellman's Bistro* (same hours) is renowned for its outstanding breakfasts and home-cooked meals.

Mantenga Nature Reserve

Not far past the Guava Gallery is the entrance gate to the **Mantenga Nature Reserve** (daily 6.30am–6pm; E45), now also the National Trust Commission's booking office (℡4161151, Ⓦ www.sntc.org.sz) for the Malolotja and Mlawula nature reserves (see p.809 & p.812). Mantenga Nature Reserve incorporates **Ligugu lemaSwati** (meaning "the pride of the Swazi people"), Swaziland's most authentic cultural village. This open-air living museum replicates a nineteenth-century Swazi homestead with sixteen beehive huts, all built in traditional style using wooden frames joined by leather strips, reed thatch, cow dung and termite-hill earth. Cattle and goats wander about, and there are often demonstrations of traditional activities and crafts. Twice daily (11.15am & 3.15pm) an enchanting thirty-minute traditional music and dance performance takes place in a small open-air arena, telling a story of Swazi soldiers in the Boer war, and the love and witchcraft they encounter when they return home. Informative and enthusiastic guides will take you round on free tours, and you can even **stay** in one of three beehive huts if you're prepared to rough it, as there's no bedding, no electricity, and you cook on a campfire (℡4161151; ❶). Rather more comfortable accommodation is available a little further up river in twenty luxury tents sleeping two, each located on a sturdy wooden platform and equipped with an en-suite toilet and hot shower (❸). All the platforms incorporate a deck in front of the tent – it's worth asking if tents no. 5 or 6 are free, as these have the best view of the pretty 95-metre **Mantenga Falls**. The tents are grouped around the thatched *Swazi River Café* (daily for breakfast, lunch and dinner), a restaurant serving "Swazi fusion cuisine" which can include spicy chicken livers and locally grown vegetables. The café, which also serves teas and coffees, is open to everyone, and has established a good reputation both with locals and those staying elsewhere in the eZulwini Valley.

Although the café and the cultural village are the main attractions, the rest of the reserve shouldn't be ignored, as there are some stunning **hikes** (free maps available at the entrance gate) and a beautiful **picnic** and **swimming** spot with views of the Mantenga Falls, a fifteen-minute walk from the café.

Lobamba and Ludzidzini

Some 20km south of Mbabane (and 5km past the Mantenga turning) at the heart of the eZulwini Valley, **LOBAMBA** was originally built in 1830 for King Sobhuza I, and became the royal kraal of Sobhuza II. The Houses of Parliament are situated here, and must be one of the few in the world to have cattle grazing undisturbed in surrounding fields. A paved road to the left leads down to the **National Museum** (Mon–Fri 8am–4.30pm, Sat & Sun 10am–4pm; E20, E25 for joint ticket with Memorial Park – see p.802) which provides a helpful potted history of the country, with displays of cultural artefacts and a mishmash of old photographs of Swazi people and royalty, of Manzini and Mbabane when they were one-horse towns, of sweaty British administrators in full colonial regalia attending functions of the Swazi royal house, and much more. The new natural history wing has as its only really interesting item a replica of a sixteenth-century head of Krishna discovered nearby. It was all that was found of what was a full-bodied statuette and the find has been interpreted as an indication of the high level of trade with the East at the time.

Outside the museum stands a life-size re-creation of a traditional Swazi homestead. Remarkably, given their size, these huts are actually portable. Across the road is **King Sobhuza II Memorial Park** (same hours as the National Museum), a peaceful open space dedicated to the much-loved late king. The park is encircled by three structures: to the right is the park's royal entrance, which is a no-go area for non-blue bloods; straight ahead is King Shebhuza II's mausoleum with his coffin inside and also no-go – it's guarded; and, to the left, a beautifully presented new Cultural Museum which has a host of old photos of the former king lining the wall, with outtakes of his various speeches on

Ncwala and Umhlanga

The most sacred of Swaziland's ceremonies, **Ncwala** celebrates kingship, national unity and the first fruits of the new year. Its timing is determined by royal astrologers; coinciding with the new moon in November, a group of selected men journey east to the ancestral home of the Ngwane on the shores of the Indian Ocean to collect foam from the waves. While they are there, the *Ncwala* ceremony begins, with songs and rituals performed until the afternoon of the full moon in December/early January, when the six days of the full *Ncwala* begin. Young Swazi men meet at **Lobamba** and are then sent away to gather branches of the *lusekwane* tree, from which they build a bower for the king. Warriors gather and sing songs that can only be sung at this time, while the king dances with them and eats the first fruits of the harvest. On the sixth day, objects representing the previous year are burnt on a massive bonfire, and prayers are offered to Swazi ancestors, asking them to put out the fire with rain. The ceremony ends amidst raucous singing, dancing and feasting. Visitors are allowed to attend most of *Ncwala*, but photography is prohibited during certain times (a free permit is also required; contact the Government Information Service, PO Box 338, Mbabane), so be sure to ask first to avoid having your camera smashed.

The **Umhlanga** is a **fertility** or **reed dance** which gets its name from the large reeds gathered by young women and brought to the residence of the Queen Mother to repair her kraal, usually in late August or early September. The sixth and seventh days are the most spectacular, when you can watch up to 25,000 young women, dressed in elaborate and carefully coded costumes, sing and dance before the king and Queen Mother at Lobamba, giving the king an opportunity to pick a **new wife**. The former king, Sobhuza II, invariably plucked a new mate from the bevy of young beauties and racked up a total of seventy wives during his lifetime. His successor, Mswati III, now in his early forties, has proved a little more restrained with only thirteen wives so far. In 2001 he caused some controversy by insisting that the young maidens parading in front of him at *Umhlanga* should continue to wear the *umcwasho*, a traditional regalia indicating that they were still virgins, for five years after the ceremony marking their passage from childhood to maidenhood. With HIV/AIDS spreading alarmingly in Swaziland, the king's pronouncement was seen as a fairly futile attempt to check the disease. He further angered the HIV/AIDS campaigners by first declaring that teenage girls should wait until their post-teens before they got married (read: become sexually active) only to then choose a girl of 17 at the reed dance as a new wife for himself.

posters standing in the middle of the room; especially touching is his heartfelt Independence Day speech to the nation. Nearby, Lobamba's **Somhlolo stadium** is the country's venue for major events and football matches, which are usually highly entertaining. For a few emalangeni on a Sunday afternoon, you can treat yourself to violence-free games of occasional great skill, with a good-humoured and vociferous crowd. Consult the local *Times of Swaziland* for details, or ask almost any male Swazi.

On the other side of the MR103 from Lobamba, the village of **LUDZIDZINI** is the kraal of the present king, Mswati III, and the Queen Mother. Unlike Lobamba, Ludzidzini cannot be visited or even photographed at all except during *Ncwala* (around New Year) and *Umhlanga* (end Aug/early Sept), when permission must be obtained (see box opposite).

Mlilwane Wildlife Sanctuary

For many visitors to Swaziland, the highlight of the eZulwini Valley is **Mlilwane Wildlife Sanctuary** (daily 24hr; E25), with its relaxed atmosphere and attractive, game-filled plains. The name Mlilwane refers to the "little fire" that sometimes appears when lightning strikes the granite mountains. As well as offering good game viewing and activities, Mlilwane is an easy alternative to staying in Mbabane or on the eZulwini strip. Given its popularity, it's wise to book ahead if you intend to stay overnight. If you arrive after 6pm, booking is essential for all accommodation except for *Sondzela* backpackers (see p.804).

The reserve holds a special place in the history of wildlife conservation in Swaziland; it was here that Ted Reilly (see box, p.804) first realized his dream of a sanctuary for Swaziland's fast-disappearing **wildlife**. Mlilwane's animals are mainly herbivorous, and include giraffe, zebra, bountiful numbers of antelope and the sanctuary's emblem, the warthog. There's also the occasional crocodile and hippopotamus, which means you still need to be cautious if viewing the game on foot, bike or horseback.

Over 40km of road enables you to drive through the park to view game. Alternatively, guided walks and drives are available through the park office at the main restcamp; the best of the self-guided **walking trails** is the Macobane Hill Trail, a gentle, four-hour hike through the mountains. The more adventurous can climb to the top of Nyonyane, the "Execution Rock", which rises so prominently in the north of the reserve. The office can supply laminated maps for all these for a E20 deposit. Whichever route you choose to take, it's important you tell a ranger of your plans before heading out. They keep track of who's out on their own and come out to find you if you're not back by dusk. There are also guided **mountain-bike tours** (E95 per hour) and **horseback trails** (from E100 per hour), both fairly relaxed ways of taking in the park's attractions. For those with a little more horseback experience, various overnight trails involve camping in caves and rustic trail camps in the more remote parts of the reserve; for the really committed, the Chubeka "Go Forward" Horse Trails, organized by Swaziland Big Game Parks, offer a four-night cross-country expedition taking in Mlilwane, Mkhaya Game Reserve and remote rural homesteads. For details, contact Big Game Parks Central Reservations (see p.804). If you're feeling less energetic, you can pass the time watching **hippos** wallowing in the hippo pool, overlooked by the *Hippo Haunt* restaurant at the main restcamp. The hippos are fed every day at 3pm.

Practicalities

To get to Mlilwane, take the turning from the eZulwini Valley road, signposted off the MR103 about 1km beyond the turn-off to Ludzidzini.

Swaziland owes the creation and survival of three of its major wildlife sanctuaries – Mlilwane, Mkhaya and Hlane – to **Ted Reilly**, who was born in Mlilwane in 1938, the son of a British Anglo-Boer War soldier who had stayed on. As Reilly was growing up, Swazi wildlife and its natural habitats were coming under serious threat from poachers and commercial farmers. In 1959, Reilly lobbied the colonial government to set aside land for parks, but was defeated by farmers who wanted the land for commercial agriculture. Undeterred, he turned his Mlilwane estate into a park anyway, and set about cultivating a relationship with **King Sobhuza II**, who was having trouble himself with poachers at the royal estate in Hlane. After Swazi independence, Sobhuza became much more powerful, and Reilly's relationship with him lent weight to his nature conservation efforts.

Despite rickety finances, the **Mlilwane Wildlife Sanctuary** opened in 1963, and the restocking and reintroduction of species has continued ever since (the reserve today is ten times the size of the original sanctuary). Meanwhile, Sobhuza asked Reilly to help stamp out poaching at Hlane. Reilly's tough approach resulted in shootouts with the poachers, earning him the praise of some, but the enmity of many. Matters came to a head in 1992 when, with the help of the South African Police Endangered Species Protection Unit, Reilly tracked down a poaching unit that had been operating in Mkhaya. In the ensuing gunfight one poacher was killed and another paralyzed, and criticism of Reilly's tactics intensified.

Reilly's dependence on royal connections has also generated controversy: critics claim it has prevented the development of a single parks board and a participatory, grass-roots involvement in conservation that is the key to long-term success. Some also assert that Reilly subordinates wildlife management principles to the needs of the tourist industry. Reilly's answer to his critics is simply to point to the three game parks his company runs. It's a powerful argument – without Reilly, the parks would not exist, and Swaziland and its visitors would be much the poorer for it. Ted Reilly still lives at Mlilwane and remains active in Swazi conservation. Both his son and daughter have followed in his footsteps and work in Mkhaya (p.817) and Mlilwane respectively.

From here, it's 3.5km along a dirt road to the entrance gate, where you pay your E25 entrance fee – if arriving after 6pm entry fees are paid at the main restcamp the following morning. Note that you'll need to show both your entry and accommodation receipts in order to leave the sanctuary again, or they may charge you twice. The reserve offers a wide variety of **accommodation** which should be booked through Swaziland Big Game Parks Central Reservations (℡5283944, ⊛www.biggameparks.org), though *Sondzela* (see below) can also be booked directly. In the **main restcamp**, about 3.5km from the gate, there's a host of different accommodation options including a campsite (E50), traditional beehive huts (❸) and two-person huts (❸), plus a swimming pool. Situated in the southern part of the sanctuary is *Sondzela* **backpacker lodge** (bookings ℡5283117), a friendly place now firmly established on the backpacking circuit, where you can stay in dorms (❶), doubles (❷) or comfortable adobe huts overlooking the valley with communal ablution facilities (❷), and relax in the lush garden by a large swimming pool. At the other end of the scale is *Reilly's Rock Hilltop Lodge* (full board; ❻), a lovely colonial home full of antiques and hardwood furniture situated on a hilltop surrounded by woodland and prolific birdlife. With only six rooms, it's more upmarket than a guesthouse but more rustic than a game lodge, and guests here can enjoy fantastic views from the balcony over the Mdzimba Mountains, wander round the gardens which surround the house, and take part in any of the activities offered elsewhere in the reserve. The only **restaurant** at Mlilwane is the *Hippo Haunt*, at the main restcamp, where there's also a bar. Inexpensive breakfast and dinner are available at *Sondzela*, served in front of the campfire.

For those who don't have their own **transport**, it's a fifteen-minute walk from *Sondzela* to the main restcamp, and there are regular **shuttle buses** (departing 7.30am) running between *Sondzela* and *Malandela's Homestead* (see below), where pick-ups for the **Baz Bus** are made.

Through the Malkerns Valley

Continuing on the MR103 towards Manzini, a turn to the southwest at Mahlanya, roughly 5km beyond the road to Mlilwane (beside a row of shops), takes you to the scenic, pineapple-growing **Malkerns Valley**. About 1km along this road, look out on the right-hand side for **Malandela's Homestead**, a fascinating collection of buildings where you can find craft shops, a pub and restaurant, a gallery and theatre, and an Internet café. Situated under a large thatched roof, *Malandela's Restaurant* (T5283115; daily 9.30am–9pm) has a European-style menu with good-quality à la carte **meals** including stews, game and fresh fish dishes. The restaurant's outdoor dining area provides excellent views of the adjoining fields and distant mountains, while the adjoining **pub** (Mon 11am–11pm, Tues–Sun 10am–11pm) has Guinness on tap and is a popular spot for locals to watch big rugby and soccer games on cable TV. Next door is *Malandela's B&B* (T5283448, E malandelas@africaonline.co.sz; ❷), with stylishly decorated rooms in colour themes. It tends to be full when there's a concert happening next door (see below), in which case advanced booking is essential.

On the other side of Malandela's pub, *Ziggy's* (Mon–Fri 8am–6pm, Sat & Sun 10am–5pm; T5283423) has wireless Internet access and a good array of tourist information leaflets. Next to it, ↗ Gone Rural (Mon–Sat 8am–5pm, Sun 9am–5pm; T5504936, W www.goneruralswaziland.co.sz) is one of the most successful and creative **local handicrafts projects** in Swaziland; the colourful and well-designed woven mats and baskets on sale here are made by a huge network of women working from villages all over the country. Further along, the funky House on Fire is a gallery and amphitheatre-like performance space (T5282110, W www.house-on-fire.com), worth checking out for contemporary African crafts and the exuberant imagination which has gone into designing the place. A big new **music festival**, Bush Fire (W www.bushfire.co.sz), was launched here in 2007, with Hugh Masekela headlining. Hugely successful, it is to become an annual event, held during the last weekend of September on a small field in front of the homestead.

A little further on, several more **craft shops** line the Malkerns–Manzini road: Swazi Candles (daily 8am–5pm) sells a bewildering array of brightly patterned wax candles; Baobab Batik, 2km further along, sells all manner of colourful batiks. Beside this is ↗ *Nyanza Cottage* (T5283090 or 6085779, W www.nyanza.co.sz; ❶–❷), an appealingly cluttered working farm roamed by dogs, cats, geese, turkeys, peacocks, horses and Jersey cows, with self-catering accommodation in a backpacker lodge which includes a few en-suite double rooms, and two spacious, rustic, and floorboard-creaking cottages sleeping six at the bottom of a farm track. The idyllic farm also runs the Nyanza Horse Trails, which offers cross-country and mountain rides lasting from half an hour to a whole day.

Manzini

MANZINI is Swaziland's largest city and its commercial hub. Almost all the country's industrial and commercial sector is based in or around here, and the city is dominated by office blocks and malls obscuring its few attractive edifices. With a rising crime rate and an atmosphere far less relaxed than Mbabane, Manzini would be an eminently missable place were it not for its outstanding **market** on the corner of Mhlakuvane and Mancishane streets (daily except Sun).

Much of Manzini's market is devoted to fruit and vegetables, household goods and traditional medicines, while an upper section that spills onto the steps below sells **crafts** and **fabrics**. The crafts selection is bigger, more varied and much better value than any other market in Swaziland, while the fabrics – from Zimbabwe, Congo and Mozambique – are hard to find elsewhere in the country.

North of the market, on Ngwane Street, stands **The Bhunu**, one of Manzini's shopping malls. **The Hub**, south of the market, on Mhlakuvane Street, is smarter and has a good supermarket, an ATM and a restaurant and takeaway. Manzini's only other point of interest is its original **Catholic mission**, an elegant stone building (not open to casual visitors) opposite the new cathedral on Sandlane Street (parallel to Mhlakuvane St).

Practicalities

Buses from all over the country and South Africa pull in at Manzini's busy main bus station at the end of Louw Street, just north of Ngwane Street. **Matsapha airport** (℡5186192) lies 8km west of the city centre; if you're arriving here, you'll need to take a **taxi** into central Manzini. The centre itself is small enough to walk around.

Manzini has a fair selection of **places to stay**. At the top of the range, at the northern end of Ngwane Street, *Tum's George Hotel* (℡5052260, Ⓦwww.tgh.sz; ④) has luxurious, spacious en-suite doubles with plush soft carpets, a pool, three

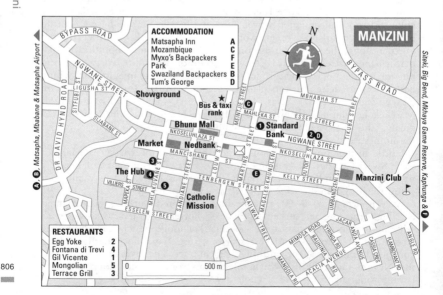

restaurants, a bar, and a beauty salon and spa. At the other end of the scale, near the bus station, on the corner of Meintjies and Mahleka streets, the *Mozambique Hotel* (☎5052489, ℗5056430; ❷) offers tiny overpriced rooms with paper-thin walls and no breakfast, but has a friendly, prostitute-filled bar. Slightly better value is the equally inexpensive but grandly named *Park Hotel* (☎5057423, ℮expo @swazi.net; ❷) on Mancishane Street, with somewhat worn en-suite doubles spread over three floors. Even better value but outside the centre on the old Mbabane road (the MR103) shortly before the turning towards Matsapha airport – when coming from Mbabane – is the modern, motel-like *Matsapha Inn* (☎5187482 or 5186888; ❷), with smart en-suite doubles lining a long corridor, and a bar-restaurant.

For **backpackers**, there's nothing in Manzini itself but two good options on its outskirts. Nine kilometres west of the city on the MR103, past the *Matsapha Inn*, at the junction to the Malkerns Valley, is the recently relocated *Swaziland Backpackers* (☎5282038, ⓦwww.swazilandbackpackers.co.za) with tidy six- and eight-bed dorms (❶), four decent doubles (❷) and some pleasant areas outside for camping. Inexpensive breakfasts and dinners are available, and there's also a pool with a pleasant poolside bar. It's the overnight stop for the **Baz Bus** and consequently attracts a fair number of passing travellers. Trips to various attractions, including the game reserves, and activities such as whitewater rafting can be organized, with pick-ups from here. *Myxo's Backpackers* (☎5058363 or 6044102, ⓦwww.myxosswaziland .com; ❶), about 6km east of Manzini on the Big Bend road, has quickly established itself as a relaxed spot with a very different feel to most white-run lodges in South Africa. Run by a young Swazi, Mxolisi Mdluli (or Myxo for short), it has dorms and doubles, and space for camping. Myxo also runs an ambitious community tourism project based in the **KaPhunga** village area, about 55km into the mountains southeast of Manzini. The village is the second-highest settlement in Swaziland after Piggs Peak and spreads over the top of a mountain rise with absolutely breathtaking views of the valley below – sugar-cane fields galore and the Lebombo Mountains in the distance. Here Myxo has built a mini homestead with authentic huts, separate from the main village, so that a certain amount of privacy is allowed both visitors and villagers. You're encouraged to sleep in the traditional Swazi way with a mattress on the hut floor, and facilities are fairly basic, but the gorgeous and real setting makes this absolutely adequate. During the day, visitors can join in whatever is going on in the village, such as building projects, farming work, brewing beer or teaching at the local school. Two-day trips (one night) to KaPhunga, including transport from Manzini and contributions to the village, cost around E520 per person including full board. Extra nights can be arranged.

For the town's best coffee, head to the *Egg Yoke* (daily 8am–11pm), next to *Tum's George,* which is also a fine **place to eat**, selling food prepared at the hotel's posh restaurant at half the price. Other good places in town include *Gil Vicente*, in the Ilanga Centre, Martins Street (Tues–Sun 8am to midnight), which serves tasty Portuguese dishes; the *Mongolian*, Villiers Street, where you'll find the best Chinese food in town; the *Terrace Grill*, Tenbergen Street (Mon–Sat 8am–midnight, Sun 10am–midnight), which doubles as a sports bar and serves well-prepared Spanish and Portuguese food; and the *Fontana di Trevi Pizzeria* (Mon–Sat 8.30am–9pm, Sun 10.30am–6.30pm), in The Hub on Mhlakuvane Street, which also does takeaways. For fast **Internet** the best place is the café on the first floor of the central post office building on Nkoseluhlaza Street.

Piggs Peak and the northwest

The highveld of **Piggs Peak** and the **northwest** is unquestionably the most beautiful region of Swaziland, with rolling hills perfect for hiking, countless sparkling streams, a sprinkling of waterfalls and some wonderful accommodation.

Most visitors to the northwest enter Swaziland after going through the Kruger National Park (see p.690), but Piggs Peak is only 64km north of Mbabane and easily reached from there, too. The most spectacular – and rugged – entrance into the country is via the Bulembu road from Barberton in Mpumalanga (see p.681), which passes through Bulembu village on the way to Piggs Peak.

From Jeppe's Reef/Matsamo border

From the **Jeppe's Reef/Matsamo border** (7am–8pm), the road on the Swazi side is good all the way to Ngwenya where it meets the fast MR3. Some 25km south of the border, the *Orion Piggs Peak Hotel & Casino* (℡4371104, Ⓦwww .oriongroup.co.za; ⑥) offers swish **accommodation** in a modern luxury hotel set in thousands of acres of mountainous pine forest. Despite the monolithic appearance of the hotel's exterior, the rooms have fabulous views, and there's an inviting swimming pool with a bar in the middle, plus a good buffet **restaurant**. In the lobby you can buy beautiful handmade Tintsaba crafts from the Tintsaba rural development project (Ⓦwww.tintsaba.com) based in Piggs Peak. However, the main focus of the place is the casino and slot machines.

For somewhere completely different in style and atmosphere, and altogether more relaxing, continue south for another few kilometres until signs on the right indicate the private ⚘ **Phophonyane Nature Reserve** (daily 10am– 5pm; E30 for day visits, E20 if you're staying overnight ℡4371429, Ⓦwww .phophonyane.co.sz), which is five slow kilometres away from the road. The five -square-kilometre reserve's carefully laid-out **trails** ensure there's plenty to see, including the Phophonyane Waterfall on its northwestern side. The vegetation is subtropical and attracts hundreds of colourful **bird species**. Animals include mongooses, bushbabies, otters and numerous snakes, but all are hard to spot. The **lodge** in the reserve is one of the most beautiful places to stay in Swaziland, offering five secluded two-person safari tents (⑤) next to the Phophonyane River, with private bathroom facilities in separate huts a few steps up from the tents; two of the tents have access to a communal kitchen. There are also family cottages sleeping up to five, with private kitchens and gardens (E650), and two new gorgeously romantic beehive huts (⑥). If you can't afford to stay, it's still worth stopping here for a short hike in the reserve and a mid-priced **meal** at the *Driftwood Restaurant*, a beautiful thatched former farmhouse. The reserve has two pools; one with salt water next to the restaurant, the other blended cleverly into the rocks beside the tumbling river and with a stunning location, looking out onto endless mountains and surrounded by luxuriant vegetation, but this one is very chilly.

Seven kilometres south of Phophonyane, 1km north of Piggs Peak, the turn-off to Kuthuleni is the start of a scenic fifty-kilometre drive along a new paved road to **Bhalekane**. There isn't much in Bhalekane (except a prison), but you can proceed from here to Tshaneni and the **northeast** (see p.811), or head south through fairly remote territory to Mafutseni and then Manzini.

From Bulembu

The road from Barberton in Mpumalanga, to Piggs Peak via **Bulembu border post** (8am–4pm), is briefly tarred out of Barberton, but soon deteriorates as it passes through some of the most rugged country imaginable, with the road near the border crossing in particularly poor shape. Looking up, you can see the Barberton–Havelock cableway, which used to carry asbestos from the now defunct Havelock mine to South Africa. Once in Swaziland, the road soon passes through Bulembu, with Piggs Peak a further 20km away.

Piggs Peak

PIGGS PEAK, a small, straggling forestry town along the main road, was named after a French prospector called William Pigg, who discovered gold nearby in 1884, where it was mined until the site was exhausted in 1954. Apart from the attractive surrounding countryside, there's nothing much to see here, but if you're heading to Malolotja Nature Reserve this is a good place to stock up on supplies.

The town's **bus station** and **market** are near the Total garage at the northern end of town, where there is also a shopping mall and a few **supermarkets**. For money, there are a couple of **banks** in the centre with ATMs at the front. The town's two good **places to stay** are both south of the centre. *Jabula Guest House* (☎4371052, ⓦwww.jabulabnb.com; ❸) in the residential area, east of the Mbabane Road – follow the signs – has three comfortable en-suite doubles and a newly done-up self-contained apartment sleeping four (E720). The recently renovated *Highland Inn* (☎4371144; ❷) on the outskirts of town, on the left-hand side of the Mbabane road, offers comfortable en-suite rooms with beautiful parquet flooring, in a pleasant colonial building. Next door, the *Woodcutter's Den* **restaurant** serves steaks and other meat dishes at fairly reasonable prices.

On to Malolotja Nature Reserve

Driving south, you soon leave the pine plantations behind and pass into rolling highveld grassland, peppered with rural dwellings. A few kilometres outside Pigs Peak a road loops off to the left past the new **Maguga Dam** on the scenic Komati River. Before reaching the dam a dirt road turns off to the left, and, after about 7km, arrives at the starting point for a thirty-minute hike into the mountains, to the breathtaking **Nsangwini Rock Art** (☎6373767; E45), so-called bushman paintings estimated to be around 4000 years old. Painted on a rock shelter perched dramatically over the Komati River, the views from the site are stunning. Visits to the site are organized by the Nsangwini community, who plough the profits back into the community. Back on the tarred road, the Maguga Dam sits snugly in a lowveld dip, surrounded on all four sides by the often mist-covered mountains. Next to it, the new *Maguga Lodge* (☎4373970, ⓦwww.magugalodge.com; ❺) has 33 comfortable en-suite rondavels and an outstanding restaurant which overlooks the dam from a large thatched balcony. The Sunday buffet lunch here comes especially recommended (E110), with hordes arriving in from South Africa and Mbabane. The Maguga loop hits the Piggs Peak–Mbabane road again just north of Nkhaba. Continue south for a few kilometres, and you'll reach the entrance to the Malolotja Nature Reserve. The main road continues south from here to join the Ngwenya–Mbabane road at Motshane (see p.811), 15km further on.

Malolotja Nature Reserve

Swaziland's least touristy park, the easy-going **Malolotja Nature Reserve** (daily 6am–6pm; E25; ☎4161151), offers awesome scenery and some of the finest hiking in southern Africa. This is a place to come for rugged, wild nature and tranquillity, rather than for game spotting. The mountains here, among the oldest in the world (3.6 billion years old), are covered in grassland and graced by myriad streams and waterfalls, including the 95-metre-high **Malolotja Falls**.

Nearly three hundred species of **birds** are found in Malolotja, with an impressive colony of the rare bald ibis just by the waterfalls. You'll have to look harder for **game**, although wildebeest, blesbok and zebra are often visible, and there are leopards and elephants lurking somewhere in the gaping tracts of mountain and valley. Malolotja's small network of roads passes some fine viewpoints and picnic sites, but to really savour this park's rugged wilderness and see its waterfalls you'll need to hike, or go by horseback (see opposite). A variety of **trails** is laid out in the reserve, from easy half-day excursions to seven-day marathons, with accommodation available en route (see below).

Malolotja also boasts **Ngwenya Mine** (daily 6am–6pm; E25, joint ticket with Malolotja), the world's most ancient at 43,000 years old. The Stone-Age workers here once dug for specularite and haematite, which were used as cosmetics and for religious rituals. To visit you must access the reserve from the southern gate near the Ngwenya Glass factory (see opposite) where guides will be waiting to take you to the mine site and the new visitor centre; note that to reach the mine from within the reserve you'll need to hike for two to three days. The **Forbes Reef Gold Mine**, a few kilometres south of the reserve's main entrance on the main tarred road, can be visited alone, but take care on the slippery banks; you can find it using the map you get on arrival at the main entrance.

Practicalities

Brochures and **maps** are available from the reserve's **office**, just inside the entrance gate. The office also issues permits for Hawane Dam Nature Reserve (see below), as well as the useful free *Hiking and Backpacking Guide*. **Minibus** Kombis between Mbabane and Piggs Peak stop at the main gate.

Accommodation should be booked in advance through the National Trust Commission booking office at Mantenga Nature Reserve (see p.801). The main restcamp has fifteen tent sites with hot water in a communal bath area and braai areas, but not much wind shelter. There is also an A-frame **chalet** (❷), which sleeps two, and thirteen well-located log **cabins** (❸), which can also house up to six people each. A small shop at the entrance sells basic **provisions**, but it's wiser to stock up in Piggs Peak or Mbabane. Twenty **campsites** without facilities are scattered around the reserve for those attempting longer hikes: you'll need to bring all your own equipment, including a cooker, as no fires are permitted.

If you're on a long hike during the summer, be prepared for hot days; however, temperatures drop dramatically in winter, when the nights can be freezing.

Hawane Dam and Resort

Technically part of the Malolotja Nature Reserve, but some 12km south of the main gate on the Mbabane road is the **Hawane Dam Nature Reserve** (daily: 6am–6pm; E25, joint ticket with Malolotja). Here lies a small area around the northern end of the Hawane Dam, designed to protect part of the Black Mbuluzi River wetlands. Hawane's main attraction is its wealth of **birdlife**, and there's an excellent trail for bird-watching.

A little further on, on the opposite side of the main road to the dam, is **Hawane Resort** (☎4424744, ⊛www.hawane.com; ❹), signposted down a one-kilometre track, with excellent accommodation in quirky triangular adobe chalets (one of the architect owners seems to have been let loose here) sleeping two, and backpacker accommodation in a nearby converted barn (❶). This is the place to head if you fancy exploring the attractive surrounding countryside – and Malolotja in particular – on horseback, as the resort has a range of ponies and horses for trails lasting anything between a couple of hours and a week. It also has an outstanding restaurant, ⚲ *Taste of Africa*, with delicious buffets and an à la carte menu that's difficult to better.

Ngwenya

The road from Piggs Peak meets the new fast MR3 between the Ngwenya/Oshoek border post and Mbabane at the small settlement of **Motshane**. A kilometre west of Motshane along the old highway is the Ngwenya Glass factory (daily 9am–4pm; ⓦ www.ngwenyaglass.co.sz), where one of Swaziland's best-known exports, **Ngwenya glass**, is made. Their products, which range from attractive wine glasses to endless trinkets in the shape of rotund animals, are made from recycled glass and are produced by highly skilled workers, and it's well worth stopping here just to see them blowing and crafting the glass from the viewing balcony above the roaring furnaces. The adjoining gift shop and **café** are usually swamped by coach-loads of tourists, who can further satisfy their craving for crafts a few hundred metres from the factory up the hill at **Endlotane Studios** (Mon–Fri 8am–4.30pm, Sat–Sun 9am–5pm; ⓦ www.endlotane.net), where large and colourful tapestries are painstakingly woven from mohair wool spun on the premises. Further up the hill there is an entrance to Malolotja Nature Reserve, allowing access to **Ngwenya Mine** (see opposite).

The northeast

Northeast Swaziland is dominated by sugar plantations stretching into the distance, shimmering from the constant water spray, wreaking havoc with the water table – and leaving many locals without – but earning the country valuable foreign exchange. Three large tracts of bush – **Hlane**, **Mlawula** and **Mbuluzi** – have been preserved as wildlife and nature reserves, and these are the main attractions for visitors to this region. Together with **Shewula Nature Reserve**, these form part of the **Lubombo Conservancy**, a grouping of protected land in the **Lubombo Mountains** that runs along Swaziland's eastern border and provides fantastic views of both Swaziland and the western fringes of Mozambique.

The most direct and obvious route to the reserves from Mbabane is to follow the signposted and tarred **Siteki road** for 100km. The **northern route** is a little over twice as long, but makes for a far more spectacular journey. Travel north to **Piggs Peak** from Mbabane, and turn right at the **Bhalekane** turn-off, roughly 1km later.

Tshaneni

The road from Piggs Peak passes through some fabulous scenery before eventually winding up at the sugar town of **TSHANENI**. The one **hotel** here, the *Impala Arms* (☎32322431; ❷), has plain but comfortable rooms; the bar has a pool table, and is filled with exuberant Swazi at weekends. If you need supplies, Tshaneni's Score **supermarket** will come in handy, and there is an ATM and a **garage** nearby for fuel.

The **Mananga border post** (8am–6pm) lies 5km north of here, from where the road leads to Komatipoort (see p.676). Heading south, however, the next town you'll meet is bougainvillea-festooned **Mhlume**. Twenty kilometres further on is a junction at Maphiveni: a left turn to the north takes you to the **Lomahasha/Namaacha border post** with Mozambique (7am–8pm), another 20km away past the dirt road leading to the Shewula Mountain Camp (see below) while a right turn followed almost immediately by a signposted left takes you first to Mbuluzi Game Reserve and then on to Mlawula Nature Reserve.

Shewula Mountain Camp

Ten kilometres north of the Maphiveni junction, a dirt roads to the right leads into the mountains and the **Shewula Mountain Camp** (booking essential ℡6051160, ⓦwww.shewulamountaincamp.info; ❶), run by the local Shewula community. Although it's isolated and time-consuming to reach, the camp has a spectacular site at one end of the plateau, with views west across northeast Swaziland and even, on a clear day, to the skyscrapers of Maputo to the east. It also offers an interesting insight into rural life in Swaziland. Accommodation is in four rondavels (which sleep up to six people), with bunks or doubles around communal ablution and dining areas, but there's no electricity and cooking is done on gas. Activities include hiking through Shewula Nature Reserve and a visit to the nearby village. If you don't want to self-cater, meals can be arranged in advance.

Mbuluzi Game Reserve

Privately owned and little known, **Mbuluzi** (daily 6am–6pm; E25 per person, E25 per vehicle staying overnight; ⓦwww.swaziplace.com/mbuluzi) is about 1km off the Manzini–Lomahasha road, and straddles the road to Mlawula. Set in classic lowveld bush, it's filled with thorn trees and hot in the summer. Currently the park is being restocked with game, including hippo and giraffe, which you can view in your own vehicle. The absence of predators in Mbuluzi's southern portion means that you can walk along a network of **trails** in this section.

Mbuluzi's self-catering **accommodation** (❾ for the whole lodge, which sleeps up to eight people) is its finest feature: three large and comfortable air-conditioned lodges with verandas overlook the Mlawula stream, whose luxuriant vegetation attracts birds and animals which you can watch from the verandas. There is also a campsite (E50) in the northern section of the reserve close to the Mbuluzi River with an ablution block with hot showers, if you remember to light the fire under the boiler two hours in advance.

Minibus Kombis from Manzini and Simunye to the Lomahasha border stop at the Maphiveni junction, from where it's a fifteen-minute hike to the gate.

Mlawula Nature Reserve

The largest single protected area in the Lubombo Mountains is the 165-square-kilometre **Mlawula Nature Reserve** (daily 6am–6pm; E25), south of the Mbuluzi River. The best reason to come to Mlawula is to stay at *Sara Bush Camp* (see opposite), but you can spend some time exploring a network of self-guided hiking **trails**. As well as climbing into the mountains and onto the plateau at the top of the Lubombo range where unique species of ironwood trees and cycads grow, the trails wend their way around the river heading for caves, a waterfall and a hyena pool, and vary in length from two to eight hours. The bush throughout the reserve is quite dense, however, which largely prevents you from seeing much game. Guides are available to lead you on the hiking trails.

The Mlawula stream and more substantial Mbuluzi River both flow through some spectacular valleys in this reserve, and Stone-Age tools over one million years old have been found along their beds. **Antelope**, **zebra** and **wildebeest** congregate near the water, but so do **crocodiles**, so resist the temptation to swim.

Practicalities

Minibus Kombis from Manzini and Simunye to the Lomahasha border stop at the Maphiveni junction, from where it's a four-kilometre hike to the main Mlawula Nature Reserve gate. To get here by **car**, continue past the Mbuluzi Reserve for a few kilometres until you see a sign pointing to the Mlawula Reserve on your right. With the opening of the Mhlumeni/Goba border crossing from Mozambique, a new gate into the reserve has opened at the eastern side of the reserve, on the main road from Siteki to the border. Kombis linking the border to Siteki stop outside the gate. You can pick up various leaflets at the park gate, but no supplies, so stock up beforehand.

Accommodation should be booked in advance through the National Trust Commission booking office at Mantenga Nature Reserve (see p.801). Overnight **camping** on the trails has not been permitted since the camping hut was burnt down, apparently by Mozambican border-hoppers, but there is a shaded campsite in the Siphiso River Valley. Much more appealing is the self-catering *Sara Bush Camp* (❷ per double tent), which has four large safari tents on wooden decks perched on the very edge of a cliff. Surrounded by bush, each tent also has its own bathing area, consisting of a tiny perch amongst the rocks on the cliff edge with a paraffin-boiler shower and galvanized iron washtub, allowing you to bathe outside with a stunning view west over the reserve and beyond, making it perfectly positioned for sunset. Each tent has a braai site and there's a communal lounge and kitchen area. Finally, a cluster of twenty stunning en-suite **chalets**, encompassing a pool and restaurant, has recently been completed near the new gate by the reopened Mozambican border post. However, due to problems with the water supply they have not yet opened for business. Check with the booking office for the latest details.

Hlane Royal National Park

Some 67km northeast of Manzini is **Hlane Royal National Park** (daily 6am–6pm; E25), the largest of Swaziland's parks. Formerly a private royal hunting ground, the main attraction here is the presence of big game, including **elephant**, **rhino**, **lion**, **leopard** and **cheetah**. Hlane is also one of the best parks in southern Africa to view elephants and rhino **on foot** – an unforgettable experience – in the company of a guide (E75 for 2hr 30min). These two species are in the northern area of the park, which you can also visit in your own vehicle, and rhino-sighting is virtually guaranteed. Other animals in this section include giraffe, zebra and waterbuck.

Various **southern enclosures** contain lion, cheetah and leopard, along with some more elephant and rhino; walking here is out of the question, but you can drive with a guide in your own car. If you don't have your own transport you can join a guided tour in one of the park's Land Rovers (E145 for 2hr 30min), with sunrise (5.30am) and sunset (4.30pm) tours (E155 for 2hr 30min); the sunrise and sunset tours are the most magical, with most sightings. Although the enclosures guarantee lion sightings, the animals are well habituated to vehicles and look completely disinterested in the whole experience – a pity, as the presence of lions in the country is meant to be the source of great pride to the Swazis, not least because they are the royal symbol.

Practicalities

The **entrance** to Hlane is roughly 7km south of Simunye, off the Manzini–Lomahasha road. **Kombis** between Manzini and Simunye stop 300m from the park gate.

Hlane has three **accommodation** options, all of which must be **booked** through Big Game Parks Central Reservations (T 5283944, W www .biggameparks.org). The main *Ndlovu* camp (●), situated near the gate, offers large self-catering thatched cottages sleeping up to eight people, but no electricity (paraffin lamps and gas cooker are provided). Nearby there's an open camping area and fourteen brand-new rondavels sleeping two (●) in the so-called *Wisteria* section but, again, without electricity. There's also a newly refurbished thatched restaurant and lounge area, with a wide deck overlooking a large nearby watering hole area which houses rhino, and attracts elephant and giraffe. Unless there's a large group staying, this area is fairly relaxed, with plenty of trees and shady spots to sit. The self-catering *Bhubesi* camp (●), with its six comfortable stone cottages overlooking a dry river, is 11km from *Ndlovu* along a dirt track, and feels much more remote, though the cottages here have electricity.

Siteki

Perched spectacularly on a hillside and gateway to the busy **Mhlumeni /Goba border post** with Mozambique (7am–8pm), **SITEKI**, just over 30km south of Mlawula Nature Reserve, is a fairly lively regional centre, with a **bus station** that operates Kombi services to Manzini and the border, a colourful **market**, and a number of lively restaurants along the main street. Down the road from the *Siteki* hotel, off the main road on the way out of town, is the headquarters of Litiko Letinyanga (T 3434512), a traditional healing organization, run by Dr Nhlavana Maseko, which seeks to improve the credibility of traditional healing with Western medical institutions. You may be able to arrange a session with a traditional healer, but you'll have to phone beforehand.

There are two good and very different **places to stay** in Siteki. The peach-coloured and newly refurbished *Siteki* (T 3436373, E sitekihotel @swazi.net; ●), at the town's main junction, has pleasant en-suite, air-conditioned rooms, with those on the top floor boasting lovely views of the valley. Downstairs, the hotel **restaurant** serves steaks and other meat dishes, and there's a great bar and weekend disco attached, which is popular with locals and gets very lively at weekends. The second option, *Mabuda Farm B&B* (T 3434124, W www.mabuda.co.za; ●), is a collection of cottages at the outskirts of town; follow signs to Mabuda from the main junction. The quaint old immaculate cottages are packed with character – creaking floorboards and wonky walls – and all have great views of the valley; some are self-catering, and others B&B. There's also a backpacking section with dorms (●), and a campsite planned for the near future.

At the beginning of the road ascending to the town, you'll pass through a foot-and-mouth disease control **checkpoint**; the guards only check you on the way out, to confiscate any meat products that you might have tucked away.

The south

Approaching Swaziland from one of its border crossings in the south is an excellent idea if you're travelling from northern KwaZulu-Natal through to the Kruger National Park or Mpumulanga. The scenery, particularly along the drive from **Mahamba** to Manzini through the **Grand Valley**, is really superb, and the road passes near most of the historical sites of the Swazi royal house. The south is also home to the **Mkhaya Nature Reserve**, Swaziland's most upmarket reserve and a sanctuary for the rare black rhino.

One of the most exhilarating things you can do in southern Swaziland is to **whitewater raft** on the beautiful Great Usutu River, located in the east of the country near the Mkhaya Nature Reserve. One of the best whitewater rivers in southern Africa, it's also one of the few where you can take a trip in a two-man "croc" raft. The route runs for 15km in summer (a bit less in winter), and crosses over rapids classed in grades two to four. The scenery en route is stunning, but hard to appreciate once you hit the rapids, which leave you paddling like crazy and doing your best not to fall in the water. Most people do capsize, but careful supervision ensures that everyone lives to tell the tale. Trips include pick-ups from various points in the eZulwini Valley and en route to the river, and cost around E650 a person, including a picnic lunch and evening sundowners (E550 for half a day). Contact Swazi Trails (☎4162180 or 6020261 after 5pm, ⓦwww.swazitravel-link.co.sz) for bookings and further information.

From Mahamba to Manzini

The **Mahamba border crossing** (7am–10pm) is the fastest link to Piet Retief in South Africa. Mahamba means "the runaways", which refers to nineteenth-century pretenders to the royal throne who fled here twice to escape retribution. The nearest major town is **NHLANGANO**, only 16km from the border. Nhlangano (the name means "meeting place", commemorating the meeting of the British and Swazi monarchs George V and Sobhuza II in 1947) is a good place to catch **buses** to Manzini.

▲ Whitewater rafting on the Great Usutu River

Following a disastrous fire in 2007 that razed the plush *Nhlangano Sun* casino hotel to the ground, the only **place to stay** around here is the homely *Phumula Farm Guest House* (T2079099, Wwww.swaziplace.com/phumula; ❸), about 5km from the border down a dirt road (follow the signs) with en-suite doubles and a pleasant garden with a braai area.

The **Makhosini Valley**, 8km **east of Nhlangano** on the Mhlosheni road, is the site of the main **royal burial grounds**, guarded and tended by the Mduli clan. To avoid disturbing their rulers' eternal rest, the Mduli never cut the grass; consequently, the grounds now stand out as islands of forest in a sea of cultivated land. The Mduli also grind the king's medicines and snuff, and have the interesting task of preventing any part of his body (including his faeces, semen and toenail clippings) from being used for magical purposes.

A little further on is a turn to the south to **Zombodze**, King Ngwane I's first royal residence in modern-day Swaziland. It's badly signposted, so follow signs for the nearby Ngwane High School.

Another 28km **north of Nhlangano**, along a good road, is the settlement of **HLATHIKHULU**, perched impressively on a hill and providing cool relief after the murderous heat below. Ngwane's grandson **Sobhuza I** fled near here from the attacks of the mighty Ndwandwe king Zwide, to a place called kaPhungalegazi ("place of the smell of blood"), though nothing is now left of the kraal he erected here. Sadly for the town, the main road steams right by it, leaving it forlorn on a diversion to the right.

The Ngwane clan fought a murderous but inconclusive battle with the Zulus under King Dingane in the nearby **Lubuya Valley** in 1839. This quiet valley is barely populated and, though there's nothing to remind you of the battle that once raged here, it's a good place for a picnic and a stroll. To get to the valley from Hlathikhulu, take the first turning right after heading north towards Manzini, towards Lugoje Nek, and a left turn at the fork here brings you to the valley. The battle left Dingane's army much reduced, making him an easy target for his brother Mpande the following year.

From Hlathikhulu, Manzini is 74km away, with the bulk of the drive passing along the **Grand Valley**, through which flows the sometimes mighty Mkhondvo River. The valley is hot, overgrazed and almost barren, but offers stunning hiking possibilities and stupendous views.

From Lavumisa to Manzini

Travelling north from KwaZulu-Natal, you'll come to the **Lavumisa/Golela border post** (7am–10pm). The border is named after one of the wives of Sobhuza I, whose son Malambule tried to overthrow Sobhuza's successor, Mswati II. Golela, on the South African side, means "many animals", and indeed this area was once predominantly a hunting ground. Today the animals have all but gone, though there are plans for an ambitious tri-border nature reserve, **Royal Jozini**, which will restock the area with the Big Five and provide new luxury accommodation. The reserve is still in the planning stages but you can check progress on Wwww.royaljozini.com. Until it becomes a reality, there's little reason to linger here, unless you're tempted by the prospect of a close encounter with one of the lions at a small game reserve, **Nisela Safaris** (daily 6am–6pm; E25; T3030318, Wwww.niselasafaris.co.za), across the Ingwavuma River, 35km north of the border and just north of the town of Nsoko. The reserve's animals, including giraffe, kudu, zebra and warthog, are for understandable reasons of preservation kept apart from the lions, who prowl their own separate enclosure. Accommodation is offered in traditional Swazi beehive huts sleeping two (●), thatched cabins (●), each sleeping four, a colonial-style guesthouse (●), and a fully kitted campsite; there's also a pool and restaurant. At the entrance to the reserve, a coffee shop and curio stall provide a rest stop for drivers making their way to or from the border.

The road north from Nsoko runs parallel to the **Lubombo Mountains**. A few kilometres before Big Bend, you'll pass **The Riverside**, a truck stop on the main road housing a functional **hotel** (☎ 3636910, ⓦ www.riversidehotel .co.sz; ●) with fabulous views from the sparkling en-suite rooms in a new first-floor section, and a good Portuguese restaurant; downstairs, Emoya Handicrafts offers a small selection of good-value pieces. A kilometre further on is an outstanding **restaurant**, *Lubombo Lobster* (☎ 3636380), which serves a wonderful seafood curry.

Big Bend itself, dominated by a huge sugar mill, is only worth visiting for its **hotel**, the *Bend Inn* (☎ 3636855; ●), on a hill at the far end of town beyond the golf course. A slightly run-down colonial establishment with superb views of the valley and well-positioned bars, the 23-bedroom motel-like place is a lively Swazi haunt on weekends, when major parties take place. The rooms are spartan but air-conditioned and comfortable, and the hotel **restaurant** serves good-value food.

From the centre of Big Bend, Kombi **buses** travel to Manzini and north to Siteki (see p.814).

Mkhaya Game Reserve

Roughly 30km north of Big Bend lies **Mkhaya Game Reserve**, situated along a turn-off from the wonderfully named village of **Phuzumoya** ("drink the wind") in classic lowveld scrubland, filled with acacia and thorn trees. A sanctuary for the rare **black rhino**, Mkhaya also accommodates **white rhino**, **elephant** and numerous antelopes such as nyala, sable and eland. As well as a tourist attraction, Mkhaya also operates as a refuge where endangered species such **roan antelope** and **tsessebe** are bred. Rubbing shoulders with them, in the reserve section closest to the road, are herds of **Nguni cattle** (see box below).

Day visits and overnight stays at Mkhaya must be booked in advance (see p.818), and you can't tour Mkhaya in your own vehicle, but must arrange to be met at the gate (10am or 4pm) from where you'll drive in convoy to the reserve's ranger base and the starting point of the first game drives. Kombi buses from Manzini to Big Bend stop at the gate; ask for the Phuzamoya shop drop.

Nguni cattle and Mkhaya

The long horned **Nguni cattle**, herded by the African clans when Europeans encountered them in the nineteenth century, were descendants of the early Iron Age herds. Although they are hardy, disease-resistant and well-adapted to their environment, white beef-farmers regarded them as too puny and unproductive for their industry, and replaced them with imported stock. By the 1970s, pure strains of long-horned cattle had virtually disappeared from Swaziland, and **Ted Reilly** initially purchased Mkhaya (see above) to save them. The sharp increase in the price of cattle feed in the late 1970s made the long-horns increasingly attractive commercially, enabling Reilly to sell them as pure-bred breeding stock, using the money to fund the game acquisition programme at Mkhaya. Today, the cattle graze here, in the section of the reserve closest to the road, alongside zebra, wildebeest and antelope, just as they always used to.

Day visitors are taken on a game drive from the ranger's base, and you'll have a high chance of encountering much of the big game. A generous **lunch** at the main camp is included in the price. For overnighters, morning and evening game drives are included in the accommodation price. Unlike game reserves in South Africa, Mkhaya's experienced Swazi rangers have few qualms about stopping in the middle of a game drive and inviting visitors to get out of the vehicle and walk quite close to white rhino and elephant. If you're staying overnight, early-morning game walks can also be organized.

You'll need to **book** your visit to Mkhaya through Swazi Big Game Parks Central Reservations (☎5283944, ⓦwww.biggameparks.org). Day visits cost E440, including lunch. The reserve's main camp, *Stone Camp*, makes up for the lack of elevation in the reserve with an atmospheric bush setting beside the dry Ngwenyane river bed. Full-board **accommodation** (including game drives ➑) is offered in seductively luxurious open-plan and open-sided thatched stone huts with en-suite toilets and showers, which give you a wonderful sense of sleeping right in the bush. All of these are secluded but secure and lit by paraffin lamps. Beautifully prepared three-course meals are served around a large campfire in the main part of the camp under the shade of a massive sausage tree (its seed pods look like sausages), and staff have been known to treat guests to traditional dancing.

Travel details

Buses

Minibus Kombis depart when they're full so there's no real way of saying how often they leave.
Big Bend to: Manzini (1hr 30min); Siteki (1hr 30min).
Manzini to: Big Bend (1hr 30min); Hlatsi (1hr 30min); Lavumisa (5hr); Mbabane (45min); Nhlangano (3hr 15min); Siteki (1hr 30min).
Mbabane to: Manzini (45min); Nhlangano (4hr); Piggs Peak (1hr).
Nhlangano to: Manzini (3hr 15min); Mbabane (4hr).
Piggs Peak to: Mbabane (1hr).
Siteki to: Big Bend (1hr 30min); Manzini (1hr 30min).

Baz Bus

There are three services a week on each of the two Baz Bus routes from Manzini, namely south to Durban and west to Jo'burg/Pretoria.

Manzini to: Ballito (9hr 15min); Durban (9hr 45min); Eshowe (7hr 45min); Gingindlovu (8hr 15min); Johannesburg (9hr); Malkerns Valley (15min); Mbabane (1hr); Mtubatuba (5hr 45min); Nelspruit (4hr); Pretoria (11hr 30min); St Lucia (5hr 15min).

Flights

Manzini to: Durban (daily Mon–Fri; 1hr); Johannesburg (4–5 daily; 1hr); Maputo (Mozambique; 1 daily Tues & Thurs; 30min); Vilanculos (Mozambique; 1 daily Mon, Wed & Fri; 1hr 30min).

Contexts

Contexts

History

Human history – or prehistory – probably began in South Africa. That, at least, is the story told by recent fossil finds, which show that *Homo sapiens* existed along Africa's southern coast over 50,000 years ago. The descendants of these nomadic Stone-Age people – ochre-skinned San hunter-gatherers and Khoikhoi herders – still inhabited the Western Cape when the first European seafarers arrived in the fifteenth century. By the time of the first Dutch settlement at the Cape in the mid-seventeenth century, tall, dark-skinned people, who had begun crossing the Limpopo around the time of Christ's birth, had occupied much of the eastern half of the country.

The stage was now set for the complex drama of South Africa's modern history, which in crude terms was a battle for the control of scarce resources between the various indigenous people, African states and the European colonizers. The twentieth century saw the temporary victory of colonialism, the unification of South Africa and the attempts by whites to keep at bay black demands for civil rights, culminating in the implementation of South Africa's most notorious social invention – **apartheid**. Ultimately, it was multiracialism that was victorious and, despite numerous problems, South Africa celebrated ten years of democracy in 2004 in a mood of high optimism.

Prehistory

When our ancestors climbed down from the trees, it is quite likely they did it in South Africa. In 1924, the world's **oldest hominid remains** and the first-ever evidence of human-like creatures to be discovered in Africa were dug up in the Northern Cape and identified as a "fossilized monkey skull". After a stint as a humble paperweight, the fossil came to the attention of Professor Raymond Dart at Johannesburg's University of the Witwatersrand, who identified the earthshaking find as an intermediate species between apes and humans, with a small brain but an upright posture. Still a little unsteady on its feet, our ancestor trod the plains of eastern and southern Africa, perhaps three million years ago. Dart called it *Australopithecus africanus*: **Africa's southern ape**. After the emergence of *A. africanus*, hominids spent the next couple of million years or so perfecting bipedal walking, tool-making and speech, and got big-headed (a huge expansion in brain size took place) until they finally strode forth as *Homo sapiens*: the modern humans. Another first for South Africa was the unearthing of the oldest fossil evidence of *Homo sapiens* in a cave at the Klasies River Mouth in the Eastern Cape, reckoned to be between 50,000 and 100,000 years old.

The first South Africans

Rock art provides evidence of human culture in the subcontinent dating back nearly 30,000 years and represents southern Africa's oldest and most enduring artistic tradition. The artists were hunter-gatherers, sometimes called Bushmen but more commonly **San**. This is a relatively modern term from the Nama language with roots in the concept of "inhabiting or dwelling", to reflect the fact these were South Africa's aboriginals. The most direct descendants of the late Stone Age, San people have survived in tiny pockets, mostly in Namibia and Botswana, making theirs the longest-spanning culture in the subcontinent. At one time they probably spread throughout sub-Saharan Africa, having pretty well perfected their **nomadic lifestyle**, which involved an enviable twenty-hour working week spent by the men hunting and the women gathering. This left considerable time for artistic and religious pursuits. People lived in small, loosely connected bands comprising family units and were free to leave and join up with other groups. In this egalitarian society the concept of private property had scant meaning because everything required for survival could be obtained from the environment.

About two thousand years ago, this changed when some groups in northern Botswana laid their hands on fat-tailed **sheep and cattle** from northern Africa, thus transforming themselves into **herding communities**. The introduction of livestock had a revolutionary effect on social organization, creating the idea of ownership and accumulation. Social divisions developed, and political units became larger and centred around a chief, who had important powers, such as the allocation of pasturage.

These were the first South Africans encountered by Portuguese mariners, who landed along the Cape coast in the fifteenth century. Known as **Khoikhoi** (meaning "men of men"), they were not ethnically distinct from the San, as many anthropologists once believed, but simply represented a distinct social organization. According to current thinking it was possible for Khoi who lost their livestock to revert to being San, and for San to lay their hands on animals to become Khoi, giving rise to the collective term "**Khoisan**". This dynamic view of history is significant because it throws out the nineteenth-century idea that race was an absolute determinant of history and culture – a concept that found great popularity among apartheid apologists.

Farms and crafts

Around two thousand years ago, tall, dark-skinned people who practised mixed farming – raising both crops and livestock – crossed the Limpopo River into what is today South Africa. San paintings from some time in the intervening period depict small ochre people and larger black ones in a variety of hostile and harmonious relationships, indicating contact between the two groups. These **Bantu-speaking** farmers were the ancestors of South Africa's majority African population, who gradually drifted south, to occupy the entire eastern half of the subcontinent as far as the Eastern Cape, where they were first encountered by Europeans in the sixteenth century.

Today there are four main **Bantu language groups** in South Africa. **Nguni** (comprising Zulu, Swazi and Xhosa) and **Sotho** (Sotho and Tswana) are by far the largest; the other two are **Venda** and **Tsonga**. Apart from having highly developed farming know-how and a far more sedentary life than the Khoisan, the early Bantu speakers were skilled craftworkers and knew about mining and smelting metals, including gold, copper and iron, which became an important factor in the extensive network of **trade** that developed.

The picture painted of them by the British, as bloodthirsty Africans engaged in endemic internecine conflicts, probably said more about the white colonizers than the Bantu speakers themselves. The nineteenth-century traveller Ludwig Alberti underlined this fact when he observed that the Xhosa of the Eastern Cape "cannot be regarded as a warlike people; a predominant inclination to pursue a quiet cattle-raising life is much more in evidence amongst them".

The Cape goes Dutch

In the fifteenth century, Portuguese mariners under the command of **Bartholomeu Dias** became the first Europeans to set foot in South Africa. Marking their progress, they left an unpleasant set of calling cards all along the coast – African men and women they had captured in West Africa and had cast ashore to trumpet the power and glory of Portugal to the locals. Little wonder that their first encounter with the Khoi along the Garden Route coast was not a happy one. It began with a group of Khoi stoning the Portuguese for taking water from a spring without asking permission and ended with a Khoi man lying dead with a crossbow bolt through his chest.

It was another 170 years before any European settlement was established in South Africa. In 1652, a group of white employees of the **Dutch East India Company**, which was engaged in trade between the Netherlands and the East Indies, pulled into Table Bay to set up a refreshment station to revictual company ships trading between Europe and the East. There was no thought at the time of setting up a colony; on the contrary, the Cape was a rather bum posting, given to the station commander **Jan van Riebeeck** because he had been caught with his hand in the till by the company bosses. Van Riebeeck dreamed up a number of schemes to isolate the Cape Peninsula from the rest of Africa, including a plan to build a canal that would cut it adrift. In the end, he had to satisfy himself with planting a **bitter almond hedge** (still growing in Cape Town's Kirstenbosch Gardens) to keep the natives at bay, symbolically representing an ambivalence about being European in Africa, which still haunts many white South Africans.

Despite Van Riebeeck's view that the **Khoi**, who were already living at the Cape, were "a savage set, living without conscience", from the start the Dutch were dependent on them to provide livestock, which was traded for trinkets. As the settlement developed, Van Riebeeck needed more **labour** to keep the show going, and bemoaned the fact that he was unsuccessful in persuading the Khoi to discard their herding life for the toil of ploughing furrows for him. Much to his annoyance, the bosses back in Holland had forbidden Van Riebeeck from enslaving the locals, and refused his request for slaves from elsewhere in the company's empire.

This led to the inexorable process of **colonization** of the lands around the fort, when a number of Dutch men were released in 1657 from their contracts to farm as **free burghers** on land granted by the company. The idea was that they would have to sell their produce to the company at a fixed price, thereby overcoming the labour shortage. The only snag with this was that the land didn't belong to the company in the first place, and the move sparked the first of a series of **Khoikhoi-Dutch wars**. Although the first campaign ended in stalemate, the Khoikhoi were ultimately no match for the Dutch, who had the tactical mobility of horses and the superior killing power of firearms. Campaigns continued through the 1660s and 1670s and proved rather profitable for Dutch raiders, who on one outing in 1674 rounded up eight hundred Khoi cattle and four thousand sheep.

Meanwhile, in 1658, van Riebeeck had managed successfully to purloin a shipload of **slaves** from West Africa, whetting an insatiable appetite for this form of labour. The Dutch East India Company itself became the biggest slave owner at the Cape and continued importing slaves, mostly from the East Indies, at such a pace that by 1711 there were more slaves than burghers in the colony. By the end of the eighteenth century there were almost fifteen thousand slaves and just under fourteen thousand burghers at the Cape. With the help of this ready workforce, the embryonic Cape Colony expanded outwards and trampled the Peninsula Khoikhoi, who by 1713 had lost everything. Most of their livestock (nearly fifty thousand animals) and most of their land west of the Hottentots Holland Mountains (the peaks 90km southeast of present-day Cape Town) had been gobbled up by the Dutch East India Company. Dispossession and diseases like smallpox, previously unknown in South Africa, decimated their numbers and shattered their social system. By the middle of the eighteenth century, those who remained had been reduced to a condition of miserable servitude to the colonists.

Impoverished whites living at the fringes of colonial society also had few options, but these included the possibility of dropping out of its grindingly class-conscious constraints. Many just packed up their waggons and rolled out into the interior, where they lived by the gun, either hunting game or taking cattle from the Khoi by force. Beyond the control of the Dutch East India Company, these nomadic **trekboers** began to assume a pastoral niche previously occupied by the Khoi. By the turn of the nineteenth century, *trekboers* had penetrated well into the Eastern Cape, pushing back the Khoi and San in the process. Not that the indigenous people gave up without a fight. As their lives became disrupted and living by traditional means became impossible, the Khoisan began to prey on the cattle and sheep of the *trekboers*. The *trekboers* responded by hunting down the San as vermin, killing the men and often taking women and children as slaves, bringing them to virtual extinction in South Africa.

After the **British occupation of the Cape** in 1795, the *trekboer* migration from the Cape accelerated. Britain was now the world's dominant naval power. In the ferment that followed the French Revolution, Britain feared for the security of the Cape sea route to the East and therefore sent a few war sloops into Table Bay, informing the Dutch officials there that they were no longer in charge.

Rise of the Zulus

While in the west of the country *trekboers* were migrating from the Cape Colony, in the east equally significant movements were under way. Throughout the seventeenth and eighteenth centuries, descendants of the first **Bantu speakers** to penetrate into South Africa had been swelling their numbers and had expanded right across the eastern half of the country, where the rainfall was high enough for their mixed farming economy. By the turn of the nineteenth century, the territory was brimming with people and cattle who were fast grazing it out, the limits of expansion having been reached. Exacerbating this was a sustained period of drought.

Nowhere was this more marked than in **KwaZulu-Natal**, where chiefdoms survived by subduing and absorbing their neighbours to gain control of pasturage, thus creating larger and more powerful groupings. By the early part of the nineteenth century, two chiefdoms, the **Ndwandwe** and the **Mthethwa**, dominated the eastern section of South Africa around the Tugela River. During the late 1810s a major confrontation between them ended in the defeat of the Mthethwa.

Out of their ruins emerged the **Zulus**, who were to become one of the most powerful polities in southern Africa. Prior to the defeat of the Mthethwa, the Zulus had been a minor clan under their domination. Around 1816, **Shaka** assumed the chieftaincy of the Zulus, whose fighting tactics he quickly transformed, supplementing the Nguni's traditional long javelin with the **assegai**, a short spear suitable for close combat. The throwing spear rendered a warrior unarmed once he had thrown it and was relatively easily deflected by a cowhide shield, but with a stabbing spear he could keep on fighting as long as he could stand. Shaka also introduced the tactic known as the "horns of the bull", by which the enemy were outflanked by highly disciplined formations spreading out to engulf them by means of two wings. The manoeuvre was used to devastating effect against the British at the Battle of Isandlwana in 1879.

By 1820, the Zulus had incorporated the fragments of the Mthethwa and defeated the Ndwandwe. By the middle of the decade they had formed a **centralized military state** with a forty-thousand-strong standing army. The nature of war in the east changed from the almost symbolic skirmishes that characterized Nguni raids up to the end of the eighteenth century, to decisive battles in which massacres of women and children weren't unknown. Nevertheless, the real strength of the system lay in its ability to absorb the survivors, who became members of the expanding Zulu state. Throughout the 1820s, Shaka sent out his armies to attack his neighbours and take their cattle. But in 1828, in a palace coup, he was stabbed to death by a servant and two of the king's half-brothers, one of whom, **Dingane**, succeeded him. Dingane continued with his brother's ruthless policies and tactics.

The rise of the Zulu state reverberated right across southern Africa and led to the creation of a series of **centralized Nguni states** as well as paving the way for Boer expansion into the interior. In a movement known as the **mfecane**, or forced migrations, huge areas of the country were laid waste and people across eastern South Africa were driven off their lands. They attempted to survive either in small groups or by banding together to form larger political organizations. To the north of the Zulu kingdom another Nguni group with strong cultural and linguistic affinities with the Zulus came together under Sobhuza I and his son Mswati II, after whom their new state **Swaziland** took its name. In North West Province, a few hundred Zulus under the leadership of **Mzilikazi** took refuge after rebelling against Shaka. By 1829 their numbers had swelled to around seventy thousand, but in 1838 they were routed by encroaching Voortrekkers, against whose firearms they proved no match. They relocated to southwestern Zimbabwe, where they re-established themselves as the **Matabele** (or **Ndebele**) kingdom. In the Drakensberg, on the west flank of KwaZulu-Natal, **Moshoeshoe I**, another chief with humble origins, used diplomacy and cunning to build up his state from the ruins of the *mfecane*. By providing a haven to refugees, he was able to build up a substantial state from disparate Sotho groupings. Believing that "peace is like the rain which makes the grass grow", he kept no standing army, relying instead on opportunism and good-neighbourliness to survive, which he did. His territory became the modern state of **Lesotho**.

The Great Trek

Back in the Cape, many Afrikaners were becoming fed up with British rule. Their principal grievance was the way in which the colonial authorities were tampering with labour relations and destroying what they saw as a divine distinction between blacks and whites. In 1828 the **Cape Ordinance 50** gave Khoi residents and free blacks equality with whites before the law. The **abolition of slavery** in 1834 was the last straw. One Voortrekker wrote: "it's not so much their freedom that drove us to such lengths, as their being placed on an equal footing with Christians, contrary to the laws of God and the natural distinction of race".

In this spirit, fifteen thousand Afrikaners (one out of ten living in the colony) set out to leave the Cape and once and for all shake off the meddlesome British. When they arrived in the eastern half of the country, they were delighted to find vast tracts of apparently unoccupied land. In fact, they were merely stumbling into the eye of the *mfecane* storm – areas that had been temporarily cleared either by war parties or by fearful people hiding out to escape detection. As they fanned out further they encountered the Nguni states and a series of battles followed. By the middle of the nineteenth century, the Voortrekkers had consolidated control and established the two Boer states of the **South African Republic** (now Mpumalanga, North West and Limpopo provinces) and the **Orange Free State** (now Free State), the independence of both of which was recognized by Britain in the 1850s.

Gold and diamonds

Britain wasn't too concerned about the interior of South Africa. Its strategic position apart, South Africa was a chaotic and undeveloped backwater at the butt-end of the empire. At this time, the United States, which was first settled by Britons a mere thirty years before the Dutch hit South Africa, had a population of over thirty million people of European extraction and 80,000km of railways, compared with South Africa's 250,000 whites and 120km of railways. Things changed in the 1860s, with the discovery of **diamonds** (the world's largest deposit) around modern-day Kimberley, and even more significantly in the 1880s, with the discovery of **gold** on the Witwatersrand (now Gauteng). Together, these finds were the catalyst that transformed South Africa from a down-at-heel rural society into an urbanized industrial one. In the process great fortunes were made by capitalists like **Cecil Rhodes**, traditional African society was crushed and the independence of the Boer republics ended.

Although the **Gauteng goldfields** were exceptionally well endowed with ore, they were also particularly difficult to mine, requiring the sinking of deep shafts. Exploiting the mines required costly equipment and cheap labour to operate it. Capital quickly flowed in from Western investors eager for profit: even today the West retains strong links with the South African mines, and South Africa remains the world's largest producer of gold.

The Anglo-Boer War

Despite the benefits it brought, the discovery of gold was also one of the principal causes of the Anglo-Boer War. Gold-mining had shifted the economic centre of South Africa from the British-controlled Cape to a Boer republic, while at the same time, Britain's European rival, Germany, was beginning to make political and economic inroads in the Boer republics. Britain feared losing its strategic Cape naval base, but perhaps even more important were questions of international finance and the substantial British investment in the mines. London was at the heart of world trade and was eager to see a flourishing gold-mining industry in South Africa, but the Boers seemed rather sluggish about modernizing their infrastructure to assist the exploitation of the mines.

In any case, a number of Britons had for some time seen the unification of South Africa as the key to securing **British interests** in the subcontinent. To this end, under a wafer-thin pretext, the British empire had declared war and subdued the last of the independent African kingdoms by means of the **Zulu War** of 1879. This secured KwaZulu-Natal and meant that all the coastal territories of South Africa were under British control. To control the entire subcontinent south of the Limpopo, all that remained was to bring the two Boer republics under the Union Jack.

During the closing years of the nineteenth century, Britain demanded that the South African Republic grant voting rights to British miners living there – a demand that, if met, would have meant the end of Boer political control over their own state, since they were outnumbered by the foreigners. The Boers turned down the request and war broke out in October 1899. The British command, which had been used to fighting colonial wars against enemies armed with spears, believed they were looking at a walkover; in the words of Lord Kitchener, "a teatime war" that would get the troops home in time to open their Christmas presents.

In fact, the battle turned into Britain's most expensive campaign since the Napoleonic Wars. During the early phase of the war, the Boers took the imperial power by surprise and penetrated into British-controlled KwaZulu-Natal and the Northern Cape, inflicting a series of humiliating defeats. By June a reinforced British army was pushing the Boers back and once again the high command was talking about being home in time for their Christmas pudding. But the Boers fought on for another two years of protracted guerrilla war. **Lord Kitchener** responded ruthlessly with a scorched-earth policy that left the countryside a smouldering wasteland and thousands of women and children homeless. To house these thousands of dispossessed, the British introduced the **concentration camp**, in which 26,370 Boer women and children died. For some Afrikaners, this episode remains a major source of bitterness against the British even today. Less widely publicized were the **African concentration camps** which took 14,000 lives. By 1902, the Boers were demoralized and split between those who couldn't face another winter of near starvation (the so-called "hands-uppers") and those who wanted to fight on ("the bitter-enders"). In May that year, the Boer republics signed a treaty surrendering their independence in exchange for British promises of reconstruction. By the end of the so-called "teatime war", Britain had committed nearly half a million men to the field and lost 22,000 of them. Of the 88,000 Boers who fought, 7000 died in combat. With the two Boer republics and the two British colonies under imperial control, the way was clear for the federation of the **Union of South Africa** in 1910.

Migrant labour and the Bambatha Rebellion

Between the conclusion of the Anglo–Boer War and the unification of South Africa, the mines suffered a shortage of **unskilled labour**. Most Africans still lived by agriculture, either as tenant farmers on white farms or in reserves created by the colonial government. They had no need to desert their traditional farming way of life for a thankless existence in shantytowns far away from home. To counter this, the government took measures to compel them to supply their labour. One method was the imposition of **taxes** that had to be paid in coin, thus forcing Africans from subsistence farming and into the cash economy. Responding to one such tax, a group of Zulus protested in 1906 and refused to pay up. The authorities declared martial law and dealt mercilessly with the protesters, burning their huts and seizing all their possessions. This provoked a full-blown rebellion led by Chief Bambatha, which was ruthlessly put down by the colonial authorities, with four thousand rebels dying in the process. This marked an end to armed resistance by Africans for over half a century. After the defeat of the **Bambatha Rebellion**, the number of African men from Zululand working in the Gauteng mines shot up by sixty percent. By 1909, eighty percent of adult males in the territory were absent from their homes and working as migrant labourers. **Migrant labour**, with its shattering effects on family life, became one of the foundations of South Africa's economic and social system, and was a basic cornerstone of apartheid.

Kick-starting Afrikanerdom

In a parallel development, large numbers of **Afrikaners** were forced to leave rural areas in the early part of the twentieth century. This was partly due to the aftermath of British scorched-earth tactics during the Anglo-Boer War, but also a result of overcrowding, drought and pestilence. Many Afrikaners joined the ranks of a swelling poor **white working class** that felt itself caught in a vice: victimized and despised on the one hand by the English-speaking capitalists who commanded the economy, and on the other under pressure from lower-paid Africans competing for their jobs.

In 1918 (the year Nelson Mandela was born) a group of Afrikaners formed the **Broederbond** ("the brotherhood"), a secret society to promote the interest of Afrikaners and to forge an Afrikaner republic in South Africa. It aimed to uplift impoverished members of the *volk* ("people") and to develop a sense of pride in their language, religion and culture. Ultimately, the Broederbond was to dominate every aspect of the way the country was run for close on half a century.

During the 1930s, a number of young Afrikaner intellectuals travelled to Europe, where they were inspired by the jackbooted march of **fascism** in Portugal, Spain, Italy and Germany. This extreme manifestation of nationalism appeared to hold the key to realizing Afrikaner nationhood. It was around this time that Afrikaner intellectuals began using the term **apartheid** (pronounced "apart-hate", not "apart-hide"). Among the leading lights of apartheid who could be found kicking their heels in Germany in the 1930s were **Nico Diederichs**, who became one of the ministers of finance while the Afrikaner nationalist National Party was in power; **Hendrik Frensch Verwoerd**, apartheid's leading theorist and prime minister from 1958 to 1966; and **Piet Meyer**, controller of the state broadcasting service, who named his son Izan ("Nazi" spelled backwards – he later claimed this was sheer coincidence).

In 1939, the Broederbond kicked into action with a scheme that launched ten thousand Afrikaner businesses in the space of a decade. Some of these are still among the leading players in South Africa's economy.

Africans' claims

Despite having relied on African cooperation for their victory in the Anglo-Boer War and having hinted at enhanced rights for blacks after the war, the British excluded blacks from the cosy deal between Afrikaners and Britain that resulted in the unification of South Africa. It wasn't long, in fact, before the white Union government began eroding African rights. In response, a group of middle-class mission-educated Africans formed the **South African Native National Congress** (later to become the ANC) in 1912. The founders weren't interested in overthrowing the white government; they simply wanted recognition by white society. Middle-class blacks already enjoyed the vote in the Cape Province (now the Western, Northern and Eastern Capes) on the basis of a **qualified franchise** according to education and property ownership, and the early African leaders wanted this extended to the rest of the country. Taking as their model the evolutionary growth of democracy in Britain, they hoped that this would eventually lead to universal suffrage.

In 1914, the leaders set off as a deputation for London, to protest against the 1913 **Natives' Land Act**, which severely restricted property ownership by blacks and provided for the division of South Africa into distinct African and white areas, with blacks – despite constituting the overriding majority of the population – confined to less than ten percent of the land surface. The trip was unsuccessful, and the Land Act would be the legal foundation for the formalization of apartheid some 35 years later.

Through the early half of the twentieth century, the ANC remained a conservative organization, unwilling to engage in active protest. This led to accusations that its leaders were "good boys tied to the apron strings of the white liberals". In response, a number of alternative mass organizations arose. Among the largest was the **Industrial and Commercial Union**, an African trade union founded in 1919, which at its peak in 1928 had gathered an impressive 150,000 members. But in the 1930s it ran out of steam. The first political movement in the country not organized along ethnic lines was the **South African Communist Party**, founded in 1921 with a multiracial executive. While it never itself gained widespread membership, it became an important force inside the ANC.

Throughout the 1930s, the ANC plodded on with speeches, petitions and pleas, which proved completely fruitless. They suffered a major setback in 1936 with the **termination of the African franchise** in the Cape Province. This left the ANC crippled and hobbling impotently into the 1940s.

World War II split Afrikanerdom. There were those like Prime Minister **Jan Smuts** who stood firmly in favour of joining the war alongside Britain. But for others, like **John Vorster** (who later became Prime Minister), Britain was the old enemy, so they supported Germany, some signing up with the **Ossewa Brandwag** (the "Ox Wagon Torch Commando"), which carried out sabotage against the government. After the war there were hopes of reform from Smuts, who at the time was playing a leading role in the formation of the **United Nations**. Smuts even had a part in penning the Preamble to the Charter on Human Rights, but while his work for abstract "human rights" earned him a statue next to Winston Churchill outside Britain's parliament, he was in no hurry to grant such rights to the majority of South Africans. Even conservative African leaders were losing patience: one, Councillor Paul Mosaka, complained that "we have been asked to cooperate with a toy telephone. We have been speaking into an apparatus which cannot transmit sound."

Young Turks and striking miners

In 1944, a young hothead called **Nelson Mandela** got together with his friends **Oliver Tambo** and **Walter Sisulu** under the leadership of **Anton Lembede** to form the **ANC Youth League**. Strict Africanists, they refused to work with any other organizations – such as the Indian Congress. The League's founding manifesto criticized the ANC leadership as a group who regarded themselves as "gentlemen with clean hands". Lembede's radical brand of politics was based on his idea that "Africa is the black man's country". He continued: "We have inhabited Africa, our motherland, from time immemorial. Africa belongs to us."

The 1945 annual conference of the ANC adopted a document called "**Africans' Claims in South Africa**", which reflected an emerging politicization resulting from the experiences of the war and especially the defeat of fascism. The document demanded **universal franchise** and an end to the **colour bar**, which reserved most skilled jobs for whites.

In 1946 the African Mineworkers' Union launched one of the biggest strikes in the country's history in protest against falling living standards. Virtually the entire Gauteng gold-mining region came to a standstill as 100,000 workers downed tools. Smuts sent in police who forced the workers back down the shafts at gunpoint.

The following year, the ANC Youth League was thrown into confusion when Lembede died suddenly. He was succeeded by **A.P. Mda**, and **Nelson Mandela** took his first step into public life when he was elected general secretary of the organization.

Winds of change

For years, the white government had been hinting at easing up on segregation, and even Smuts himself, who was no soft liberal, had reckoned that it was untenable and would have to end at some point. His deputy, **J.H. Hofmeyr**, had thrown caution to the winds and committed himself to scrapping job reservation, which excluded blacks from skilled jobs. "I take my stand on the ultimate removal of the colour bar", he went on record as saying.

At the same time, **European decolonization** was beginning in earnest, with Britain withdrawing from India in the same year. This seemed to have implications for political rights for black South Africans. But more important still was the movement of people, with the relentless influx of Africans into the urban areas breaking the stereotype of them as rural tribespeople. Playing for time, the government appointed the **Fagan Commission** to look into the question of the **pass laws**, which controlled the movement of Africans and sought to keep them out of the white cities unless they had a job. The laws led to millions of black South Africans being condemned to a ghetto existence in the rural areas, where there were no jobs, poverty reigned and infant mortality was high.

When the Fagan Commission reported its findings in 1948, it concluded that "the trend to urbanization is irreversible and the pass laws should be eased". While some blacks may have felt heartened by this hint of reform, this was the last thing many whites wanted to hear. For Afrikaners, it raised all sorts of fears about losing their identity, while Afrikaner farmers were alarmed by the idea of a labour shortage caused by Africans leaving the rural areas for better prospects in the cities. To white workers in general, the threat of losing their jobs to lower-paid African workers was a real one.

The National Party comes to power

Against this background of black aspiration and white fears, the Smuts government called a **general election**. The opposition **National Party**, which promoted Afrikaner nationalism, campaigned on a *swart gevaar* or "black peril" ticket, playing on white insecurity and fear. With an eye on the vote of Afrikaner workers and farmers, they promised to reverse the tide of Africans coming into the cities and send them all back to the reserves. For white business they made the conflicting promise to bring black workers into the cities as a cheap and plentiful supply of labour.

On Friday May 28, 1948, South Africa awoke to a National Party victory at the (whites-only) polls. Party leader **D.F. Malan** was summoned to Pretoria by the governor general to form a cabinet. On arriving by train at Pretoria station he told a group of ecstatic supporters: "For the first time, South Africa is our own. May God grant that it always remains our own. We Afrikaners are not a work of Man, but a creation of God. It is to us that millions of barbarous blacks look for guidance, justice and the Christian way of life."

Meanwhile, the ANC was riven by its own power struggle. Fed up with the ineffectiveness of the old guard, and faced with the rabid D.F. Malan, the Youth League staged a putsch, voted in their own leadership with Nelson Mandela on the executive and adopted the League's radical **Programme of Action**, with an arsenal of tactics that Mandela explained would include "the new weapons of boycott, strike, civil disobedience and non-cooperation".

The 1950s: peaceful protest

During the 1950s, the National Party began putting in place a barrage of laws that would eventually constitute the structure of apartheid. Some early onslaughts on black civil rights included the **Coloured Voters Act**, which stripped coloureds of the vote; the **Bantu Authorities Act**, which set up puppet authorities to govern Africans in the reserves; the **Population Registration Act**, which classified every South African at birth as "white, native or coloured"; the **Group Areas Act**, which divided South Africa into ethnically distinct areas; and the **Suppression of Communism Act**, which made any anti-apartheid opposition (Communist or not) a criminal offence.

The ANC responded in 1952 with the **Defiance Campaign**, which kicked off with a letter to the government demanding the same civil rights for blacks that whites enjoyed. During the campaign, eight thousand volunteers deliberately broke the apartheid laws above, and were jailed. The campaign rolled on through 1952 until the police provoked violence in October by firing on a prayer meeting in East London. A riot followed in which two white people were killed, thus appearing to discredit claims that the campaign was non-violent. The government used this as an excuse to swoop on the homes of the ANC leadership, resulting in the detention and then **banning** of over one hundred ANC organizers. Bannings were designed to restrict a person's movement and political activities: a banned person was prohibited from seeing more than one person at a time or talking

- The people shall govern.
- All national groups shall have equal rights.
- The people shall share the nation's wealth.
- The land shall be shared by those who work it.
- All shall be equal before the law.
- All shall enjoy equal human rights.
- There shall be work and security for all.
- The doors of learning and culture shall be opened.
- There shall be houses, security and comfort.
- There shall be peace and friendship.

to any other banned person; prohibited from entering certain buildings; kept under surveillance; required to report regularly to the police; and could not be quoted or published.

The most far-reaching event of the decade was the **Congress of the People**, held near Johannesburg in 1955. At a mass meeting of nearly three thousand delegates, four organizations, representing Africans, coloureds, whites and Indians, formed a strategic partnership called the **Congress Alliance**. Explaining the historic significance of the meeting, ANC leader Chief **Albert Luthuli** commented that "for the first time in the history of our multiracial nation its people will meet as equals, irrespective of race, colour and creed to formulate a freedom charter for all the people of our country". Adopted at the Congress of the People, the **Freedom Charter** (see box above) became the principal document defining ANC policy.

The government found the breadth of the movement and its principles of freedom and equality too much to stomach and they sent in the police to round up 156 opposition leaders, who were charged with treason. Evidence at the **Treason Trial** was based on the Freedom Charter, which was described as a "blueprint for violent Communist revolution". Although all the defendants were acquitted, the four-year trial disrupted the ANC and splits began to emerge. From within the organization a group of Africanists criticized the Freedom Charter because it promoted cooperation with white activists. At the 1958 ANC national conference they attempted to hijack the leadership, but when they failed they walked out and formed the **Pan Africanist Congress** (PAC) under the leadership of the charismatic **Robert Mangaliso Sobukwe**. Upstaging the ANC, the PAC launched an anti-pass campaign ten days before a similar one planned by the ANC.

Sharpeville

On March 21, 1960, Sobukwe and thousands of followers left home to present themselves without passes to police stations. Sobukwe gave strict instructions to keep the demonstrations peaceful and not to be provoked by anyone. Across Gauteng and the Western Cape there were demonstrations which in due course dispersed, but at **Sharpeville** police station, south of Johannesburg, the crowd refused to leave, despite being buzzed by low-flying Sabre jets. A scuffle broke out, the police panicked and opened fire, killing 69 and injuring nearly 200. Most were shot in the back.

In a rapid sequence of events, demonstrations swept the country on **March 27**, and ANC activist Oliver Tambo (later to become the ANC leader in exile until the release of Mandela) illegally left the country. The following day, Africans staged a **total stay-away** from work and thousands followed Nelson Mandela and Albert Luthuli in a public pass-burning demonstration. The day after that, the government declared a **state of emergency** and rounded up 22,000 people. One day later, a United Nations Security Council resolution called for the government to abandon apartheid, to which it reacted swiftly with bans on the ANC and PAC. It was now illegal to be a member of either organization. Among white South Africans there was near hysteria as the value of the rand slipped and shares slumped. Some feared an imminent and bloody revolution.

Later that month, Prime Minister **Hendrik Verwoerd** was shot twice in the head by a half-crazed white farmer. Many people hoped that if he died, this would provide a speedy retreat from apartheid. But Dr Verwoerd survived, with his prestige enhanced and his appetite for apartheid stronger than ever. More than anyone else, Verwoerd made apartheid his own and formulated it into a coherent system based around the idea of **notionally independent bantustans**, in which Africans were to exercise their political rights away from the white areas. The underlying aim was to divide Africans into distinct ethnic groups, thereby dismantling the black majority into several separate "tribal" minorities, none of which on its own could outnumber whites.

After the banning of opposition in 1960, Dr Verwoerd pressed ahead with his cherished dream of an all-white **Afrikaner republic**, which he succeeded in achieving in March 1961 through a referendum. For his pains, the Commonwealth Prime Ministers' Conference in London kicked the republic out of the British Commonwealth and Mandela called for a national convention "to determine a non-racial democratic constitution". Instead, Verwoerd appointed one-time neo Nazi **John Vorster** to the post of justice minister. A trained lawyer, Vorster eagerly set about passing a succession of repressive laws that circumvented normal legal procedures and flouted all principles of natural justice.

Some in the ANC realized that the rules of the game had changed irrevocably. "The time comes in the life of any nation when there remain only two choices: submit or fight. That time has now come to South Africa. We shall not submit," Mandela told the world, before going underground as commander in chief of **Umkhonto we Sizwe** (Spear of the Nation, aka MK), a newly formed armed wing involving ANC and Communist Party leaders. The organization was dedicated to economic and symbolic acts of sabotage and was under strict orders not to kill or injure people. Mandela operated clandestinely for a year, travelling in disguise, leaving the country illegally and popping up unexpectedly at meetings – all of which earned him the nickname, the "Black Pimpernel". In August 1962 he was finally arrested, tried and imprisoned. He was let out again briefly in 1963 to defend himself against charges of treason at the **Rivonia Trial**. Mandela and nine other ANC leaders were all found guilty and handed life sentences.

Apartheid: the dark days

With the leadership of the liberation movement behind bars, the Rivonia Trial marked the beginning of the decade in which everything seemed to be going the white government's way. Resistance was stifled, the state grew more powerful, and for white South Africans, businessmen and foreign investors life seemed perfect. The panic caused by the Sharpeville massacre soon became a dim memory and confidence returned. For black South Africans, poverty deepened – a state of affairs enforced by apartheid legislation.

There was a minor setback in 1966 when Dr Verwoerd was stabbed to death in parliament by a messenger, who was declared insane. The breach was filled by **John Vorster**, whose approach was more pragmatic than that of Verwoerd. Not averse to travelling in Africa to shake hands with tame black leaders like Hastings Banda of Malawi in the interests of detente, his approach to black South Africans was rather less chummy. His premiership was characterized by an increased use of the police as an instrument of repression, while bannings, detentions without trial, house arrests and deaths of political prisoners in detention became commonplace.

The ANC was impotent, and resistance by its armed wing MK was virtually nonexistent. This was partly because up to the mid-1970s South Africa was surrounded by sympathetic white regimes – in neighbouring Rhodesia and Mozambique – making it close to impossible to infiltrate combatants into the country. But as South Africa swung into the 1970s, the uneasy peace began to fray, prompted at first by deteriorating black living standards, which reawakened industrial action. **Trade unions** came to fill the vacuum left by the ANC and neither Vorster nor any of his National Party successors proved able to stem the escalation of strikes, despite all the repressive resources at their disposal.

The **Soweto uprising** of June 16, 1976, signalled the transfer of protest from the workplace to the townships, as black youths took to the streets in protest against the imposition of Afrikaans as a medium of instruction in their schools. The protest spread across the country after police opened fire and killed 13-year-old Hector Petersen during one march. By the following February, 575 people (nearly a quarter of them children) had been killed in the rolling series of revolts that followed.

The government was forced to rely increasingly on armed police to impose order. Even this was unable to stop the mushrooming of new liberation organizations, many of them part of the broadly based **Black Consciousness Movement**. As the unrest rumbled on into 1977, the Vorster government responded by banning all the new black organizations and detaining their leadership. In September 1977, **Steve Biko** (one of the detained) became the forty-sixth political prisoner to meet his end in jail at the hands of the security police.

In place of the banned organizations, a fresh crop had sprung up by the end of the 1970s. The government never again successfully put the lid on opposition, which escalated through the 1980s. There were rent, bus and school boycotts, strikes and campaigns against removals. By the end of the decade, business was complaining that apartheid wasn't working any more, and even the government was starting to agree. The growth of the black population was outstripping that of whites; from a peak of 21 percent of the population in 1910, whites now made up only 16 percent. This proportion was set to fall to 10 percent by the end of the century. The sums just didn't add up.

Total strategy

It was becoming clear that Vorster's deployment of the police couldn't solve South Africa's problems, and in 1978 he was deposed by his defence minister **Pieter Willem (P.W.) Botha** in a palace coup. Under Vorster's premiership,

Botha had turned the **South African Defence Force** into the most awesome military machine on the African continent and it became central to his strategy for maintaining white power. Botha realized that the days of old-style apartheid were over, and he adopted a two-handed strategy, of reform accompanied by unprecedented repression. Believing there was a total onslaught on South Africa from both inside and outside the country, he devised his so-called **Total Strategy**, which aimed to draw every facet of white society into the fight against the opponents of apartheid. This included "Youth Preparedness" military training programmes in white schools, propaganda campaigns, the extension of conscription, and political reforms aimed at co-opting Indians and coloureds.

The 1980s saw the growing use of **sabotage** against the apartheid state. In June 1980, MK, the ANC's armed wing, successfully attacked the heavily guarded strategic oil refinery at **Sasolburg**, taking the government by surprise. During 1981, there were over ninety MK armed actions against police stations, railway lines, power plants, military bases and army recruiting offices.

Botha began thinking about reforms and moved **Nelson Mandela** and other imprisoned ANC leaders from Robben Island to Pollsmoor Prison in mainland Cape Town. At the same time, he poured ever-increasing numbers of troops into African townships to stop unrest, while using economic incentives to attempt to draw neighbouring countries into a "**constellation of Southern African states**" under South Africa's leadership. Between 1981 and 1983, the army was used to enforce compliance on every one of the country's neighbours. An undeclared war against **Angola** reduced a potentially oil-rich country to war-ravaged ruins, while a South African-sponsored conflict in **Mozambique** brought a poverty-stricken country to its knees. Nor was Botha averse to sending commando units across the borders into **Botswana, Zimbabwe, Swaziland** and **Lesotho** to attack and bomb South African refugees.

Botha hoped that by making a few reforms that tinkered with apartheid, and by creating a black middle class as a buffer against the ANC, he could get the world off his back and stem internal unrest. On both counts he was wrong. Unrest continued, detentions and executions – in contravention of the Geneva Convention – of political activists increased, and heavy sentences were handed down in political trials. Used to maintaining control through the barrel of a gun, Botha was lost for any real political initiatives. Nevertheless, in 1983 he concocted what he believed was a master plan for a so-called **New Constitution** in which coloureds and Indians would be granted the vote. But before anyone got too excited, he qualified this with the revelation that each group would be represented in separate chambers, which would have no executive power. Meanwhile, for Africans, apartheid would continue as usual.

Botha hoped for a tactical alliance between whites, coloureds and Indians in opposition to Africans. The scheme was a dismal failure that only served to alienate right-wingers, who saw it as selling out white privilege. As Botha was punting this ramshackle scheme, 15,000 anti-apartheid delegates met at Mitchell's Plain in Cape Town, the biggest opposition gathering since the Congress of the People in 1955. They formed the **United Democratic Front** (UDF), a multiracial umbrella for 575 organizations, under a leadership that included ANC veterans. The UDF endorsed the Freedom Charter and became a proxy for the ANC. Two years of strikes, protest and boycotts followed.

In the face of intensifying protest, the government looked for ways to respond, and between March and December 1983 it offered five times to **release Mandela**, provided he agreed to banishment to the Transkei Bantustan. Five times he refused and this cat-and-mouse game continued right through the 1980s as the pressure mounted and South Africa's townships became ungovernable. Towards the end of the decade, the world watched as apartheid troops and police were regularly shown on TV beating up and shooting unarmed Africans. The Commonwealth, despite the concerted efforts of British Prime Minister Margaret Thatcher to stop them, condemned the apartheid government. The United States and Australia **severed air links** and the US Congress defied President Reagan, passing the comprehensive Anti-Apartheid Act which promoted **disinvestment**. In 1985, the **Chase Manhattan Bank** announced that it would no longer be prepared to roll over its loan to South Africa. Over the next two years, ninety US firms closed down their South African operations. An increasingly desperate Botha now modified his conditions for releasing Mandela, offering to "release Mandela if he renounces violence".

Mandela issued a moving reply, read by his daughter Zinzi to a crowd at Jabulani Stadium, in Soweto: "I am surprised by the conditions the government wants to impose on me. I am not a violent man. It was only when all other forms of resistance were no longer open to us that we turned to armed struggle. Let Botha show that he is different to Malan, Strijdom and Verwoerd. Let him renounce violence. I cherish my own freedom dearly but I care even more for yours."

As events unfolded, a subtle shift became increasingly apparent: Botha was the prisoner and he desperately needed Mandela to release him. On the one hand black resistance wasn't abating, while on the other Botha was facing a white **right-wing backlash**. At every by-election the ultra-right-wing Conservative Party had been eroding government majorities, while by the late 1980s the neo-Nazi **Afrikaner Weerstand Beweging** (Afrikaner Resistance Movement, aka AWB) broke up National Party meetings and threatened civil war.

Crisis

In 1986, Botha declared yet another **state of emergency** and unleashed a last-ditch storm of tyranny. Bannings of people and meetings followed, and shootings by the police were carried out with impunity. There were mass arrests, detentions, treason trials and torture. Sinister hit squads were deployed to assassinate the UDF leadership. Alarmed by the spiral of violence that was engulfing the country, a group of South African businessmen, mostly Afrikaners, flew to Senegal in 1987 to meet an ANC delegation headed by **Thabo Mbeki**. A joint statement pressed for unequivocal support for a negotiated settlement.

Weeks after the world celebrated **Mandela's seventieth birthday** in July 1988 with a huge bash at London's Wembley Stadium, Mandela was rushed off to Tygerberg Hospital, suffering from tuberculosis. Although he was better by October, the government announced that he wouldn't be returning to Pollsmoor Prison. Instead he was moved to a warder's cottage at Victor Verster (now Groot Drakenstein) Prison just outside Paarl. Outside the prison walls, Botha's policies had hit the buffers and even the army top brass were pushing for change. They told Botha that there could be no decisive military victory over the anti-apartheid opposition and the undeclared war in Angola was bleeding the treasury dry.

At the beginning of 1989, Mandela wrote to Botha from Victor Verster calling for negotiations. "I am disturbed by the spectre of a South Africa split into two hostile camps – blacks on one side, whites on the other," he wrote. An intransigent character, Botha found himself with little room to manoeuvre. When he suffered a stroke, his party colleagues moved swiftly to oust him and replaced him with **Frederik Willem (F.W.) De Klerk**.

Drawn from the conservative wing of the National Party, De Klerk made it clear from the start that he was totally opposed to majority rule. But he inherited a massive pile of problems that could no longer be ignored: the economy was in trouble and the cost of maintaining apartheid prohibitive; the illegal influx of Africans from the country to the city had become an unstoppable flood; blacks hadn't been taken in by Botha's constitutional reforms, and even South Africa's friends were beginning to lose patience. In September 1989, US President **George Bush** (the elder) let De Klerk know that if there wasn't progress on releasing Mandela within six months, he would extend US sanctions against South Africa.

De Klerk gambled on his own party's five-decade track record in gerrymandering and on his own ability to outmanoeuvre the ANC. In February 1990, De Klerk announced the **unbanning** of the ANC, the PAC, the Communist Party and 33 other organizations, as well as the **release of Mandela**. On Sunday February 11, at around 4pm, Mandela stepped out of Victor Verster

▲ First picture of Nelson Mandela after his release from prison

Prison and was driven to City Hall in Cape Town, from where he spoke publicly for the first time in three decades. He told his supporters that the factors which necessitated armed struggle still existed, but that he believed that "a climate conducive to a negotiated settlement will exist soon".

That May, Mandela and De Klerk signed an **agreement** in which the government undertook to repeal repressive laws and release political prisoners, while Mandela persuaded the ANC to suspend the armed struggle. As events moved slowly towards full-blown negotiations it became clear that De Klerk still clung to race-based notions for a settlement: "Majority rule is not suitable for South Africa," he said, "because it will lead to the domination of minorities."

Negotiations

The **negotiating** process which took place between 1990 and 1994 was fragile, and at many points a descent into chaos looked likely. Obstacles included ongoing violence linked to a sinister "**Third Force**" – elements in the apartheid security forces who were working behind the scenes to destabilize the ANC; **threats of civil war** from heavily armed right-wingers; and a low-key war of attrition in KwaZulu-Natal between Zulu nationalists of the **Inkatha Freedom Party** and ANC supporters, which had already claimed three thousand lives between 1987 and 1990.

In April 1993 it looked as if the whole process was going to unravel with the **assassination of Chris Hani**, the most popular ANC leader after Mandela. Hani's slaying by a right-wing gunman touched deep fears among all South Africans. A descent into civil war loomed and for three consecutive nights the nation watched as Mandela appeared on prime-time television appealing for calm. This marked the decisive turning point as it became apparent that the ANC president was able to hold the country together, while De Klerk kept his head down. Pushing his strategic advantage, Mandela swiftly called for the immediate setting of an **election date**. On June 3, 1993, the poll was proposed for April 27, 1994, and Mandela was able to tell his followers that "the countdown to democracy has begun".

The 1994 election

Despite a last attempt by right-wingers to disrupt the poll by bombing Johannesburg International airport, the **election** of April 27, 1994, passed peacefully. At the age of 76, Nelson Mandela, along with millions of his fellow citizens, voted for the first time in his life in his country's elections. On May 2, De Klerk conceded defeat after an ANC landslide, in which they took 62.7 percent of the vote. Of the remaining significant parties, the National Party fared best with 20.4 percent, followed by the Inkatha Freedom Party with 10.5 percent. The ANC was dominant in all but two of the provinces, the National Party taking the **Western Cape** decisively and Inkatha achieving a tight 50.3 percent majority in its **KwaZulu-Natal** heartland. One of the disappointments for the ANC was its inability to appeal broadly to non-Africans; ironically, the National Party won an overwhelming proportion of Indian, coloured and white support.

For the ANC, the real struggle was only beginning. It inherited a country of 38 million people. Of these it was estimated that six million were unemployed, nine million were destitute, ten million had no access to running water, and twenty million had no electricity. Among adult blacks, sixty percent were illiterate and fewer than fifty percent of black children under 14 went to school. Infant mortality ran at eighty deaths per thousand among Africans, compared with just seven among whites.

The Mandela presidency

Few people in recorded history have been the subject of such high expectations; still fewer have matched them; Mandela has exceeded them. We knew of his fortitude before he left jail; we have since experienced his extraordinary reserves of goodwill, his sense of fun and the depth of his maturity. As others' prisoner, he very nearly decided the date of his own release; as president, he has wisely chosen the moment of his going. Any other nation would consider itself privileged to have his equal as its leader. His last full year in power provides us with an occasion again to consider his achievement in bringing and holding our fractious land together.

Mail & Guardian, December 24, 1998

South Africa's first five years of democracy are inextricably linked to the towering figure of **Nelson Mandela**. On the one hand, he had to temper the impatience of a black majority that, having finally achieved civil rights, found it hard to understand why economic advancement wasn't following quickly. And on the other, he had to mollify the fears of many whites who, having seen their political privileges stripped away, imagined an imminent collapse of their lifestyle. The achievements of the government, however, were more uneven than those of its leader.

Soon after taking power, Mandela announced the **Reconstruction and Development Plan** (RDP), which set health, housing, education and economic growth as its priorities. This was to be realized in the electrifying of 350,000 homes in the ensuing year, the provision of decent education for all children, and in the building of 2.5 million houses by the end of the decade. But in August 1994, Mandela's keynote address, outlining the government's progress in its first hundred days of office, was greeted by industrial action protests at the slow pace of change. By the end of 1997, only 350,000 new houses had been built, though the introduction of clean, piped water and electricity to over a million homes was a significant success.

In response to the impression that whites weren't doing enough to redress imbalances and that many officials had forgotten about liberation and were simply riding the gravy train – or just plain corrupt – Mandela called for a **"new patriotism"** and attacked the "culture of rapacity" that appeared to underlie many of these problems.

The overriding theme of the Mandela presidency was that of **reconciliation**. Perhaps the highlight of this policy was in May and June 1995, when the rugby union **World Cup** was staged in South Africa. The Springboks – for many years international pariahs due to their whites–only membership – won, watched by Mandela, sporting Springbok colours. The most significant sideshow of the period was the **Truth and Reconciliation Commission**, set up to examine gross human rights abuses in South Africa between 1960 and 1993 (see box on pp.840–841).

C

The **New Constitution**, approved in May 1996, ensured that South Africa would remain a parliamentary democracy with an executive president. One of the most progressive constitutions in the world, it incorporated an extensive bill of rights. The main points were the outlawing of discrimination on the grounds of race, gender, pregnancy, ethnic or social origin, sexual orientation, disability, religion, belief, culture or language; protection of freedom of religion, belief, movement, association, expression and artistic creativity; prohibition of slavery, servitude, forced labour, torture, detention without trial, violence or cruel punishment; guarantee of the right to life (banning capital punishment but permitting abortion); and the appointment of a public protector to defend individuals against maladministration.

Despite the victory of liberal democratic principles, South Africa still displayed a singular lack of the trappings associated with civil society. **Crime**, sensationalized daily in the media, continued to dog the country. In the closing

The Truth and Reconciliation Commission

As you type, you don't know you are crying until you feel and see the tears on your hands.

Chief typist of the transcripts of the TRC hearings, as told to Archbishop Tutu

By the time South Africa achieved democracy in 1994, it was internationally accepted that **apartheid** was, in the words of a UN resolution, "a crime against humanity", and that atrocities had been committed in its name. But no one could have imagined how systematic and horrific these atrocities had been. This was only to emerge at the hearings of the **Truth and Reconciliation Commission** (TRC), set up to investigate gross abuses of human rights under apartheid. Under the chairmanship of Nobel Peace laureate, Archbishop **Desmond Tutu**, the commission was mandated to examine acts committed between March 1960, the date of the Sharpeville massacre, and May 10, 1994, the day of Mandela's inauguration as president.

The objective of the TRC was to discover the secret history of apartheid and to gain "as complete a picture as possible of the nature, causes and extent of human rights violations". The main means of achieving this was through evidence given by victims and perpetrators. To facilitate this, there was provision for **amnesty** to be granted in exchange for "full disclosure of all the relevant facts relating to acts associated with a political objective committed in the course of the conflicts of the past".

The commission began sitting in April 1996 and completed its hearings in July 1998 (with investigations continuing until 2000). Unique among the truth commissions of the late twentieth century, including those in Latin America, the South African TRC operated **in public**, allowing all South Africans to share a knowledge of what had actually happened. Among the deeply moving **testimonies** given by over 21,000 people were individual stories from parents, siblings and friends of those who had disappeared. Others gave gruesome accounts of torture, bombings and murders on an extensive scale. In his foreword to the TRC report, Tutu recalls "how at one of our hearings a mother cried out plaintively: 'Please cannot you bring back even just a bone of my child so that I can bury him?'"

Leading members of the former government and the ANC appeared before the TRC, among them former president **F.W. De Klerk**. In May 1996, he told the commission that he had not been aware of any atrocities committed under apartheid – a statement Archbishop Tutu said he found difficult to believe, especially given the avalanche of information available to De Klerk as president. Further evidence of a systematic and brutal campaign of repression by the apartheid government came to light during a trial (incidental to the TRC) in September 1996 of former police colonel, **Eugene De Kock**, who was pleading in mitigation after being convicted on 89

stages of the ANC's first five years, the police were reporting an average of 52 murders a day, a rape every half hour (including a frightening rise in child rape), and one car theft every nine minutes.

The rise and fall of Thabo Mbeki

In 1997 **Thabo Mbeki** succeeded Mandela as the leader of the ANC and after the 1999 general election, which the ANC won by a landslide, he became president of South Africa.

Despite his intellect – possibly because of it – Mbeki was initially respected but has failed to endear himself to South Africa's citizens. He certainly lacks Mandela's common touch and most South Africans find him remote, an impression

charges of murder, gun-running and fraud. He revealed that his activities were not the work of a rogue unit, but part of a well-coordinated campaign by the security forces, carried out with the full knowledge of the government, including presidents Botha and De Klerk.

After two-and-a-half years of hearings across the country, the TRC released its 3500-page **report** on October 29, 1998. Unsurprisingly, the commission found that "the South African government was in the period 1960–94 the primary perpetrator of gross human rights abuses in South Africa, and from 1974, in Southern Africa". The TRC heard overwhelming evidence that from the 1970s to the 1990s the state had been involved in criminal activities including "extra-judicial killings of political opponents". Among the violations it listed were torture, abduction, sexual abuse, incursions across South Africa's borders to kill opponents in exile, and the deployment of hit squads. It also found that the ANC (and a number of other organizations, including the PAC and Inkatha) was guilty of human-rights violations, though on nowhere near the scale of the government. The report acknowledged that the ANC had been waging a just war against apartheid but drew "a distinction between a 'just war' and 'just means'".

There was considerable **criticism of the TRC** from all quarters. Many people felt that justice would have been better served by a Nuremberg style trial of those guilty of gross violations, but Tutu argued that this would have been impossible in South Africa, given that neither side had won a military victory. Defending the amnesty provisions, he pointed out that "members of the security establishment would have scuppered the negotiated settlement had they thought they were going to run a gauntlet of trials for their involvement in past violations".

The South African media has tended to give the impression that the Truth and Reconciliation Commission led to a deterioration of race relations in South Africa (as if that were possible). However, a market research survey carried out for *Business Day* in August 1998 found that attitudes to the TRC split along racial lines. Eighty percent of black respondents believed that "the people in South Africa will now be able to live together more easily", while ninety percent of whites felt that the commission would not bring the races closer.

Responding to the lack of support for the TRC, and sometimes even active obstructionism from white leaders, Tutu remarked: "I have been saddened by a mean-spiritedness in some of the leadership of the white community. They should be saying: 'How fortunate we are that these people do not want to treat us how we treated them. How fortunate that things have remained much the same for us except for the loss of some political power.'"

reinforced by the feeling that he jets around the world promoting Third World issues, rather than dealing with South Africa's domestic problems.

And no domestic problem has proved more divisive than Mbeki's stance on **AIDS**, the country's biggest killer. For a long time Mbeki rejected the provision of anti-retrovirals in state hospitals, persuaded by denialists that ARVs were toxic. Only in November 2003 did the ANC government bow to pressure and agree to provide anti-AIDS drugs to all South Africans infected with HIV.

Mbeki's administration has been markedly more successful at achieving economic stability and winning investor confidence in South Africa. The implementation of a neo-Thatcherite **economic policy** by the highly competent finance minister, **Trevor Manuel**, has won applause internationally and at home from most centrist and centre-right economists. However, it has also drawn a predictable barrage of fire from South Africa's left for a policy that they see as quite inappropriate to a country beset by one of the world's most inequitable distributions of wealth and by growing unemployment. Even the **Black Economic Empowerment** (BEE) project, enacted in legislation in 2004, which encouraged white-owned companies to employ Africans, coloureds and Indians in preference to whites, and sought to bring a large proportion of big business under black control, has failed to redress economic imbalances, creating instead a relatively small oligarchy of rich black entrepreneurs. Certainly, there has been a noticeable growth of a **black middle class**, most evident in Johannesburg, where blacks are moving into the former whites-only suburbs and a growing cohort of newly affluent bourgeois blacks drive to upmarket malls in their BMWs (dubbed Black Man's Wish in the townships) – the car of choice for status-conscious South Africans of all races. But for those at the bottom of the pile – working-class township dwellers and rural peasants – BEE has had no discernible impact. For the most part, the poor are still poor – and predominantly black.

This has exposed tensions in the alliance involving the ANC and two junior partners, the South African Communist Party and the Congress of South African Trade Unions. Although there are frequent rumblings about a split and the formation of a left-wing opposition party, this seems unlikely since, despite the yawning ideological divide, the three are painfully aware that they will probably have to sink or swim together.

Given this, the unseating of Thabo Mbeki as leader of the ANC at the party's national congress in December 2007 should perhaps have come as no surprise. What *was* surprising was the identity of his replacement: the controversial erstwhile Deputy President, **Jacob Zuma**. At the time of his election as party leader, Zuma faced probable corruption charges for having allegedly taken bribes from French company Thint in connection with South Africa's arms procurement programme. He had also recently shaken off a rape charge brought against him by the daughter of a family friend. Although acquitted of having committed the sexual offence, the ANC president demonstrated his lack of judgement when he was forced to admit in court that he had had unprotected sex with his accuser, whom he knew to be HIV-positive. Zuma told the court that as a precaution against contracting the virus, following intercourse he had taken a shower, leading South Africa's top political cartoonist, Zapiro (see "Books", p.880), to henceforward routinely depict him with a shower grafted onto his head.

Either of the two criminal charges might have been sufficient to sink most politicians, but Zuma proved his grit as a political streetfighter by turning events to his advantage. A supreme populist, he portrayed himself as a man of the people fighting off a conspiracy by an elite. At the 2007 ANC conference he humiliated Mbeki with a landslide victory, helped by support from the influential ANC Youth League, the ANC Women's League, and the Congress of SA Trade Unions, which hoped to buy influence and move the party to the left. Although Mbeki will remain President of South Africa for two more years, the real power has shifted to Zuma, who as party leader would under normal circumstances become South Africa's next president following the 2009 general election.

But circumstances rarely turn out to be normal in South Africa, and during the closing days of 2007 Zuma was charged (again) with bribery, fraud, racketeering, money laundering and tax evasion. Despite the strong *prima facie* case against him, Zuma's popularity was undiminished and he showed no intention of standing down. This should make the years leading up to South Africa's hosting of the soccer World Cup in 2010 interesting, if nail-biting, ones, with the ANC Youth League and others threatening political action if the Zuma trial goes ahead.

Whether Zuma gets a fair trial – indeed, whether he gets a trial at all – will be a critical test of the Constitution and the independence of the judiciary. In round one of what looks set to be a protracted battle between the populists and the judiciary, Deputy Chief Justice Dikgang Moseneke commented in early 2008: "I chose this job very carefully. I have another ten to twelve years on the bench and I want to use my energy to help create an equal society. It's not what the ANC wants or what the [2007 conference] delegates want; it is about what is good for our people."

Perhaps the biggest question facing the nation now is whether the Constitution can withstand the populist forces represented by Zuma and indeed whether Zuma himself can contain the forces he has unleashed.

Wildlife

Apart from Kruger, Kgalagadi Transfrontier, Hluhluwe-Imfolozi, Addo Elephant, the Pilanesberg and a number of private parks, where you'll see the **Big Five** (lion, leopard, buffalo, elephant and rhino), over a hundred other reserves offer numerous smaller predators and dozens of herbivores, including endangered species, in invariably beautiful settings. Besides offering thrilling experiences, the major South African reserves are islands of living archeology, hinting at the teeming life that moved across the subcontinent as far south as present-day Cape Town, before European settlers with firearms swept it to the margins of the country.

This account supplements the wildlife guide in the colour section at the start of the book (to which bracketed page numbers refer). The aim is to inspire you to go beyond checklists, to appreciate the interactions of the bush and help you get more out of your safari. Beyond the scope of this account are the hundreds of colourful bird species that are an inseparable part of the South African landscape and whose calls are a constant element of its soundtrack. Some outstanding field guides are listed on pp.881–882.

Primates

Southern Africa has the lowest diversity of **primates** on the continent, a mere five species (compared with Kenya's twelve) excluding *Homo sapiens*. They include two varieties of bushbaby, two monkeys and one species of baboon – the largest and most formidable of the lot. Great apes such as gorillas and chimpanzees aren't found in the wild in southern Africa.

Chacma baboons

Chacma baboons, *Papio ursinus* (also called *cynocephalus*; see p.21), the local subspecies of common savanna monkeys, are the primates most widely found in South Africa. Males can be somewhat intimidating in size and manner and are frequently bold enough to raid vehicles or accommodation in search of food, undeterred by the close presence of people.

Baboons are highly gregarious and are invariably found in troops, which can number as few as fifteen to as many as a hundred, though around forty is common. Social relations are complex, revolving around jockeying to climb the social ladder and avoiding being toppled from its upper rungs. Rank, gender, precedence, physical strength and family ties determine an individual's position in the troop, which is led by a dominant male. Males are unreconstructed chauvinists, every adult male enjoying dominance over every female.

Days are dominated by the need to forage and hunt for food; baboons are highly opportunistic omnivores who will as happily tuck into a scorpion or a newborn antelope in the bushveld as they will clean up the entire crop from an orange tree on a Garden Route citrus farm. **Grooming** is a fundamental part of the social glue during times of relaxation. When baboons and other monkeys perform this massage-like activity on each other, the specks which they pop into their mouths are sometimes parasites – notably ticks – and sometimes flecks of skin.

Vervet monkeys

Another widespread primate you're likely to see in the eastern half of the country, and along the coastal belt as far west as Mossel Bay, are **vervet monkeys**, *Cercopithecus aethiops* (see p.21). Although happy foraging in grasslands, they rarely venture far from woodland, particularly along river courses. You can see them outside reserves, living around nearby farms and even on suburban fringes, where opportunities for scavenging are promising. In the Eastern Cape, KwaZulu-Natal and along the Garden Route you might see them hanging about along the verges of the coastal roads, risking their lives "playing chicken" with the traffic. Vervets are principally vegetarians but they are not averse to eating invertebrates, small lizards, nestlings and eggs, as well as processed foods like biscuits and sweets – when they can snatch them from visitors.

Vervet society is made up of family groups of females and young, defended by associate males, and is highly caste-ridden. A mother's rank determines that of her daughter from infancy, and lower-ranking adult females risk being castigated if they fail to show due respect to these "upper crust" youngsters.

Samango monkeys

In striking contrast with the cheekier, upfront disposition of vervets, the rarer **samango monkeys**, *Cercopithecus mitis* (see p.21), are shy animals that may only give themselves away through their loud explosive call or the breaking of branches as they go about their business. Found only in isolated pockets of KwaZulu-Natal, the Eastern Cape and Mpumalanga, they tend to hang out in the higher reaches of gallery forest, though on occasion they venture into the open to forage.

Although they bear a passing resemblance to vervets, samangos are larger and have long cheek hair that gives the passing appearance of Darth Vader. Like vervets, they're highly social and live in troops of females under the proprietorship of a dominant male, but unlike their relatives they are more inclined to fan out when looking for food.

Bushbabies

With their large, soft, fluffy pelts, huge, saucer-like eyes, large, rounded ears and superficially cat-like appearance, **bushbabies** are the ultimate in cute, cuddly-looking primates. Of the half-dozen or so species endemic to Africa, only the thick-tailed bushbaby, *Otolemur crassicaudatus,* and, about half the size, the lesser bushbaby, *Galago moholi,* see p.21 are found south of the Limpopo. The former is restricted to the eastern fringes of the subcontinent, while the latter overlaps its range in the northeast and extends across the north of the country into North West Province. Unlike other bushbabies, including the lesser, which leap with ease and speed, *O. crassicaudatus* is a slow mover that hops or walks along branches, often with considerable stealth.

If you're staying at any of the KwaZulu-Natal reserves, you stand a fair chance of seeing a bushbaby after dark as they emerge from the dense forest canopy, where they rest in small groups, for spells of lone foraging for tree gum and fruit. Even if you don't see one, you're bound to hear their piercing scream cut through the sounds of the night. Bushbabies habituate easily to humans and will sometimes come into lodge dining rooms, scavenging for titbits.

South Africa's **ecological zones** encompass a range of climate, topography and vegetation supporting a rich diversity of animal life. There are thornveld deserts, pockets of forest, tangles of subtropical vegetation, grassy savannas, mountainous peaks and several distinct coastal habitats. Geographically, South Africa is divided in two by successive mountain ranges that run in a huge arc from the Cape Peninsula to Mpumalanga, approximately parallel to the coast. This Great Escarpment divides the vast, drier interior plateau from the wetter marginal zone merging with the coastal belt. The plateau and coastal margin can each be divided into a series of ecological zones, or biomes, which share a climate and similar vegetation.

The lowveld

The **lowveld**, or bushveld, is the stereotypical African landscape of great plains, forming a backdrop for thousands of animals. It stretches down across a third of Africa, from Malawi into South Africa; here it forms a large, crescent-shaped swath running parallel to the Limpopo River, then sweeps down between the Drakensberg and the subtropical coastal strip that runs from the northern KwaZulu-Natal coast into the Eastern Cape as far as Port Elizabeth. Typical vegetation consists of mixed **savanna** and **dry woodlands** and includes deciduous broad-leaved trees such as **marulas**, whose fruit is highly sought-after by elephants. The moister subtropical lowveld, along the Mpumalanga and northern KwaZulu-Natal borders, contains thorny **acacias**, green-barked **fever trees** and thick-set **baobabs**, with **palm** trees thriving in the river valleys. In the drier transitional zones to the west, bordering the arid zone, succulent species such as **aloes** (with flowers like those of kniphofia, the red-hot poker) and massive candelabra-tree **euphorbias** dominate.

Subtropical lowland

South of the Mozambique border, to the Great Fish River in the Eastern Cape, lies the narrow **coastal plain**, at below 400m. This was once thickly forested, though the indigenous woodland has been replaced by cane fields, particularly in KwaZulu-Natal. One of the wildest environments in the country survives in the northernmost part of coastal Kwazulu-Natal, where extensive **dunes** and **wetlands** constitute a transitional zone between the Mozambique tropics and the subtropical part of the province. Some 21 ecosystems have been identified here. With the notable exception of lions, a terrific array of wildlife can be seen, including aquatic and semi-aquatic species such as crocodile, hippo, terrapin, clawless otter, reedbuck and water monitor lizard. Giant forests on the protected west flank of its dunes are home to red duiker, bushpig, and vervet and samango monkeys.

From southern KwaZulu-Natal into the Wild Coast of the Eastern Cape, dozens of major river courses have etched deep valleys that protect the remnants of dwindling forests. Nowhere is it more dramatic, though, than at Oribi Gorge Nature Reserve, near Port Shepstone, where a twenty-four-kilometre-long and five-kilometre-wide gorge is part of an environment descending from **clifftop grasslands**, down **sandstone cliffs**, to dense **riverine forests**. Here you'll find leopards, bushbuck, vervets, samango monkeys and two species of the small duiker antelope.

The fynbos region

A **heathland** system, *fynbos* (pronounced "fayn-boss") grows on the back of the Cape fold mountains that cut off the coastal belt from the semi-arid Karoo interior, extending in an arc from the Olifants River in the north to Port Elizabeth in the east, and including the Cape Peninsula. Despite its diversity, *fynbos* is extremely poor in nutrients and is unable to support large animals in great quantities. Although a reasonable cross section of mammals, including lion and elephant, inhabited the zone when the first settlers arrived, they were soon wiped out in the localized area. One, the blue antelope, a large species related to the sable, was totally extinguished.

Most exciting of its mammals today are the fairly numerous but infrequently seen Cape mountain leopards. The same species as those elsewhere in the country, they're smaller here – an adaptation to the scarcity of nutrients. Other predators include caracals, African wild cats and jackals. The Cape of Good Hope section of Table Mountain National Park is one of the best places to get an idea of *fynbos*, and is inhabited by baboons, Cape mountain zebras and the endangered bontebok. For more on *fynbos*, see p.153.

The western arid zone

Permanent surface water is almost totally absent throughout the **western arid zone** – the Orange River is its only perennial watercourse. This vast zone includes the entire Kalahari ecological zone entering the Northern Cape from Botswana, as well as the succulent Karoo zone along the west coast and the Nama Karoo zone in the extensive interior. The South African Kalahari is a lonely region of **red sandveld** punctuated with **camelthorn acacia** trees; the Karoo coastal zone contains **succulents** which explode into swaths of colourful flowers in August and September after the winter rains; and the Nama Karoo consists mainly of wiry **dwarf shrubs** in flat country fringed with low hills.

The Karoo once hosted great herds of migrating antelope including springbok and bontebok. Now they're only seen behind fences, raised for their meat alongside millions of sheep. However, some species that once roamed the Karoo, including gemsbok, hartebeest and black wildebeest, have been reintroduced into Kgalagadi Transfrontier Park, the zone's most notable game reserve, which some rate as a rival to Kruger because of its wilder ambience and excellent wildlife. Besides the above mammals, here you might also encounter lion, cheetah, jackal and bat-eared foxes, baboon, reedbuck, klipspringer and caracal. Only elephant and buffalo are notably absent.

The highveld

The high-lying central plateau (generally 1200–1829m up) of South Africa, known as the **highveld**, takes in the territory south of Johannesburg, including the Free State east of Bloemfontein, and is defined in the south and east by the Great Escarpment. This zone varies from flat, grassy, treeless **plains** to the rugged peaks of the **Drakensberg**, where you'll find **alpine-type vegetation** above an altitude of 3000m. Most of the region is now covered by **semi-desert** scrub and **maize fields**, with indigenous vegetation surviving only around the peaks and in the rugged valleys. Of the mammals that once thrived here, only smaller species, such as caracal, mongoose and hare, have survived the massive agricultural onslaught. However, at Suikerbosrand Nature Reserve, just south of Jo'burg, you can see once-endangered species such as blesbok, as well as cheetah, springbok, hartebeest, oribi, zebra, mountain reedbuck, rhebok, duiker, steenbok, kudu and brown hyena. One bird you could well see among cultivated fields is the blue crane – South Africa's national bird – which feeds on the seeds of standing crops. In the reserves of the Drakensberg, mountain-adapted antelope, such as klipspringer and mountain reedbuck, and baboon, porcupine and jackal all thrive.

Afro-montane forest

South Africa is one of the least forested countries in the world, a tiny fraction of one percent of its surface carrying indigenous woodland. **Afro-montane forest**, which requires high annual rainfall, exists only in isolated pockets, most famous of which is the Knysna Forest on the southern slopes of the Western Cape's Outeniqua Mountains. Best known for its **giant trees**, including yellowwood, stinkwood and ironwood, it also has leopard, bushpig, bushbuck, caracals and mongoose. Similar forest survives in the Eastern Cape in the Katberg-Hogsback area, where baboon, vervet and samango monkeys, duiker, bushbuck and porcupine are common.

Carnivores

Almost three dozen species of **carnivore** are found in South Africa, ranging from mongooses and weasels to dog-relatives, hyenas and seven species of cat.

Dog-relatives

South Africa's five **dog-relatives**, the Canidae, consist of two foxes, two jackals and the wild dog. The member of the Canidae you're most likely to see is the **black-backed jackal**, *Canis mesomelas* (see p.23), found especially in the country's reserves. It bears a strong resemblance to a small, skinny German Shepherd, but with muzzle more like that of a fox, and is distinguished from the grey **side-striped jackal**, *Canis adjustus*, by the white-flecked black saddle on its back, to which it owes its name. In South Africa, the side-striped jackal is found only in and around Kruger and the extreme north of KwaZulu-Natal, the latter being the only region where any confusion can arise. The fact that the black-backed jackal seeks a drier habitat, in contrast to the side-striped's preference for well-watered woodland, is an additional identification pointer. Both are omnivorous, with diets that take in carrion, small animals, reptiles, birds and insects, as well as wild fruit and berries; and both are most commonly spotted alone or in pairs, though family groups are occasionally sighted.

The **bat-eared fox**, *Otocyon megalotis* (see p.22), is found throughout the western half of the country and along the Limpopo strip. It can easily be distinguished from the jackals by its outsized ears, its shorter, pointier muzzle and its considerably smaller size. The bat-eared fox's black Zorro mask helps distinguish it from the similar sized **Cape fox**, *Vulpes chama*, which inhabitats an overlapping range. Like other dogs, the bat-eared fox is an omnivore, but it favours termites and larvae, which is where its large radar-like ears come in handy. With these it can triangulate the precise position of dung-beetle larvae up to 30cm underground and dig them out. Bat-eared foxes tend to live in pairs or family groups, an arrangement that affords mutual protection.

Once widely distributed hunters of the African plains, **wild dogs**, *Lycaon pictus* (see p.23), have been brought to the edge of extinction. For many years they were shot on sight, having gained an unjustified reputation as cruel and wanton killers of cattle and sheep. More recent scientific evidence reveals them to be economical and efficient hunters – and more successful at it than any other African species. They have only survived in the Kruger, and have been reintroduced into Hluhluwe-Imfolozi, though you'd be extremely lucky to see a pack trotting along for a hunt. Capable of sustaining high speeds (up to 50kph) over long distances, wild dogs lunge at their prey en masse, tearing it to pieces – a gruesome finish, but no more grisly than the suffocating muzzle-bite of a lion. The entire pack of ten to fifteen animals participates in looking after the pups, bringing back food and regurgitating it for them.

Hyenas

The largest carnivores after lions are **hyenas**, and apart from the lion, the **spotted hyena**, *Crocuta crocuta* (see p.24), is the meat-eater you will most often see; they occur in Kruger, Hluhluwe-Imfolozi and Kgalagadi parks. Although considered a scavenger *par excellence*, the spotted hyena is a formidable hunter, most often found where antelopes and zebras are present. Exceptionally efficient consumers, with immensely strong teeth and jaws, spotted hyenas eat virtually every part of their prey, including bones and hide and, where habituated to humans, often steal shoes, unwashed pans and refuse from tents. Although they can be seen by day, they are most active at night – when they issue their unnerving whooping cries. Clans of twenty or so animals are dominated by females, who are larger than the males and compete with each other for rank. Curiously, female hyenas' genitalia are hard to distinguish from males', leading to a popular misconception that they are hermaphroditic.

The **brown hyena**, *Hyaena brunnea*, is restricted to parts of Namibia, Botswana, Zimbabwe and South Africa, where it's generally seen only in the northernmost regions. That it's usually seen singly also distinguishes this hyena from its less shaggy and slightly smaller spotted cousin.

The hyena-like **aardwolf**, *Proteles cristatus,* is smaller than the spotted hyena and far lighter (about two-thirds the height at the shoulder and roughly a tenth of its weight), as well as being less shaggy, with vertical dark stripes along its tawny body. It is further distinguished from hyenas by its insectivorous diet and its particular preference for harvester termites, which it laps up en masse (up to 200,000 in one night) with its broad sticky tongue. Far more widely distributed in South Africa than the hyenas, this nocturnal animal is sometimes active in the cooler hours just before dusk or after dawn. Although they aren't often seen, keep an eye open at the Cape of Good Hope, Karoo, Mountain Zebra, Pilanesberg, Kruger, Hluhluwe-Imfolozi and Kgagaladi reserves.

Cats

Apart from lions, which notably live in social groups, **cats** are solitary carnivores. With the exception of the cheetah, which is anatomically distinct from the other cats, the remaining members of the family are so similar that, as Richard Estes comments in *The Safari Companion*, big cats are just "jumbo versions" of the domestic cat, "distinguished mainly by a modification of the larynx that enables them to roar".

Perhaps it's just a question of size, but the most compelling of the *Felidae* for most people on safari are **lions**, *Panthera leo* (see p.25), the largest cats, and indeed the most massive predators in Africa. It's fortunate then that, despite having the most limited distribution of any cat in South Africa, lions are the ones you're most likely to see. Of the public reserves, the Kruger and Kgalagadi parks have healthy populations, and prides have been reintroduced into Hluhluwe-Imfolozi and Addo Elephant National Park, in both of which numbers are relatively limited.

Lazy, gregarious and sizeable, lions rarely attempt to hide, making them relatively easy to find, especially if someone else has already spotted them – a gathering of stationary vehicles frequently signals lions. Seeing them hunt is another matter, and you're less likely to see David Attenborough-esque enactments of the chase. In fact, their fabled reputation as cold, efficient hunters is ill-founded, as lions are only successful around thirty percent of the time, and only then if operating as a group. Males don't hunt at all if they can help it and will happily enjoy a free lunch courtesy of the females of the pride.

The lion may be king, but most successful and arguably most beautiful of the large cats is the **leopard**, *Panthera pardus* (see p.25), which survives from the southern coastal strip of Africa all the way to China. Highly adaptable, they can subsist in extremes of aridity or cold, as well as in proximity to human habitation, where they happily prey on domestic animals – which accounts for their absence in the sheep-farming regions of central South Africa, due to extermination by farmers. They're present in the rugged, mountainous southern areas of the Western Cape, but you are most unlikely to encounter these secretive, solitary animals here. Your best chance of a sighting is at the private lodges in **Sabi Sands**, abutting Kruger, which trade on their leopards being highly habituated to people. You'll need greater luck and sharper eyes to see them in the public reserves they inhabit, including the Kruger, Kgalagadi, Hluhluwe-Imfolozi and Mkhuze. Powerfully built, they can bring down prey twice their weight and drag an impala their own weight up a tree. The chase is not part of the leopard's tactical repertoire; they hunt by stealth, getting to within 2m of their target before pouncing.

In the flesh, the **cheetah**, *Acionyx jubatus* (see p.25), is so different from the leopard that it's hard to see how there could ever be any confusion. Cheetahs are the greyhounds of the big-cat world, with small heads, very long legs and an exterior decor of fine spots. Unlike leopards, cheetahs never climb trees, being designed rather for activity on the open plains. They live alone, or sometimes briefly form a pair during mating. Hunting is normally a solitary activity, down to eyesight and an incredible burst of speed that can take the animal up to 100kph for a few seconds. Because they're lighter than lions and less powerful than leopards, cheetahs can't rely on strength to bring down their prey. Instead they resort to tripping or knocking the victim off balance by striking its hindquarters, and then pounce. Once widespread across South Africa, now they're only seen in a few reserves, including Kruger, Kgalagadi and Hluhluwe-Imfolozi.

The other *Felidae* are usually classified as small cats, although the **caracal**, *Caracal caracal* (see p.24), is a substantial animal. An unmistakeable and awesome hunter, with great climbing agility, it's able to take prey, such as adult impala and sheep, which far exceed its own weight of eight to eighteen kilos. More commonly it will feed on birds, which it pounces on, sometimes while still in flight, as well as smaller mammals, including dassies. Found across most of South Africa, excluding KwaZulu-Natal, but not often seen, caracals live in the Mountain Zebra National Park (one of the best places to see them), plus Kruger, Giant's Castle, the Cape Peninsula, Karoo and Kgalagadi.

Long-legged and spotted, **servals** (see p.25), are higher at the shoulder but lighter than caracals, and are equally rarely seen, although they are present in the Kruger, Hluhluwe-Imfolozi and Giant's Castle parks. Efficient hunters, servals use their large rounded ears to pinpoint prey (usually small rodents, birds or reptiles), which they pounce on with both front paws after performing impressive athletic leaps.

Of the genuinely small cats, the **African wild cat**, *Felis lybica*, is distributed throughout South Africa and is easily mistaken for a domestic tabby, although its legs are longer and it has reddish ears. First domesticated six thousand years ago by the Egyptians, wild cats are so closely related to the domestic version that the two are able to interbreed freely. You're unlikely to encounter the compact small **spotted cat**, *Felis nigripes* (also known as the black-footed cat), a beautifully spotted fluffy animal, which is so rarely seen that little is known about its behaviour in the wild.

Smaller carnivores

Among the smaller predators is the unusual **honey badger**, *Mellivora capensis* (see p.23), related to the European badger and with a reputation for defending itself extremely fiercely. Primarily an omnivorous forager, it will tear open bees' nests (to which it is led by a small bird, the honey guide), its thick, loose hide rendering it impervious to stings.

Small-spotted (or common) **genets**, *Genetta genetta* (see p.24), are reminiscent of slender elongated cats, and were once domesticated around the Mediterranean (but cats turned out to be better mouse hunters). In fact, they are viverrids, related to mongooses, and are frequently seen after dark around national-park lodges, where they live a semi-domesticated existence. Found throughout the country, apart from KwaZulu-Natal, they're difficult to distinguish from the **large-spotted genet**, *Genetta tigrina*, which has bigger spots and a black (instead of white) tip to its tail. These are found in northeastern parts of the country, KwaZulu-Natal and along the coastal margin as far west as the Cape Peninsula.

Most species of **mongoose** (see p.24), of which there are nearly a dozen in South Africa, are also tolerant of humans and, even when disturbed, can usually be observed for some time before disappearing. Their snake-fighting reputation is greatly overplayed: in practice they are mostly social foragers, fanning out through the bush like beaters on a shoot, rooting for anything edible – mostly invertebrates, eggs, lizards and frogs.

One of the best places to see Cape **clawless otters**, *Aonyx capensis*, a large, heavily built species, is in the Tsitsikamma National Park, where it feeds on crabs, fishes and octopuses and will commonly forage on cliff faces and in tidal pools. They are also common in the KwaZulu-Natal reserves and the Kruger.

The **civet** (or African civet), *civettictis civetta* (see p.23), is a stocky animal resembling a large, terrestrial genet. It was formerly kept in captivity for its musk (once an ingredient in perfume), which is secreted from glands near the tail. Civets aren't often seen, but they're predictable creatures, wending their way along the same path at the same time, night after night.

Antelope

South Africa has roughly a third of all antelope species in Africa, and antelope are the most regularly seen family of animals in the country's game reserves. You'll even spot some on farmland along the extensive open stretches that separate interior towns. South African antelope are subdivided into a number of **tribes**, and like buffalo, giraffe and domestic cattle, they are **ruminants** – animals that have four stomachs and chew the cud.

Bushbuck tribe

Bushbuck are the only non-territorial African antelope, and you'll see them in the shadows of thickets and bush cover, which they use for defence against predators. Among the bushbuck, it's generally only males that have horns, which are curved and spiralled. The exception is the largest of the tribe, indeed the largest living antelope, the **eland**, *Taurotragus oryx* (see p.31), in which both sexes have straight horns (but still marked by distinctive spiralling). The eland is built like an ox and moves with the slow deliberation of one, though it's a great jumper. Once widely found, herds survive around the Kruger, Kgalagadi and a tiny enclave in the northern KwaZulu-Natal Drakensberg, plus they've been reintroduced to a number of other reserves throughout the country.

The magnificent **kudu**, *Tragelaphus strepsiceros* (see p.31), is more elegantly built, and males are adorned with sensational spiralled horns that can easily reach 1.5m in length – it's these that you'll often see mounted in old-fashioned country hotels. Female groups usually include three or more members and will sometimes combine temporarily to form larger herds; males form similarly sized but more transient groupings, although it's not uncommon to encounter lone bulls.

Despite a distinct family resemblance, you could never confuse a kudu with a **bushbuck**, *Tragelaphus scriptus* (see p.30), which is considerably shorter and has a single twist to its horns, in contrast to the kudu's two or three turns. They also differ in being the only solitary members of the tribe, one reason you're less likely to spot them. Apart from the major reserves, they're found in Addo Elephant and Greater St Lucia parks.

Nyalas, *Tragelaphus angasi* (see p.30), are midway in size between the kudu and bushbuck, with which they could be confused at first glance. Telling pointers are their size, the sharp vertical white stripes on the side of the nyala (up to fourteen on the male, eighteen on the female) and, in the males, a short stiff mane from neck to shoulder. Females tend to group with their two last offspring and gather with other females in small herds, rarely exceeding ten. Males become more solitary the older they get. You'll tend to see males and females separately, as they only deliberately congregate for mating.

Horse antelope

Restricted mainly to the Kruger, the **sable**, *Hippotragus niger* (see p.32), is easily as magnificent as the kudu. A sleek, black upper body set in sharp counterpoint to its white underparts and facial markings, as well as its massive backwardly curving horns, make this the thoroughbred of the ruminants, particularly when galloping majestically across the savanna (though they prefer woodland). Highly hierarchical female herds number between one and three dozen, while territorial bulls frequently keep their distance, remaining under cover where you could easily miss them.

The **roan**, *Hippotragus equinus* (see p.31), looks very similar, but is larger than a sable (it's Africa's second-largest antelope), with less impressive horns and lighter colouring. You're more likely to see them in open savanna than sables.

Geographically more restricted, **gemsbok** (also known as the oryx), *Oryx gazella* (see p.31), are only seen in South Africa in Kgalagadi, the southernmost part of their range, which stretches down from the deserts of Namibia and Botswana. If you encounter a herd of these highly gregarious grazers, you should be left in no doubt as to what they are. Like the roan and sable, they have thick-set bodies and superficially similar facial markings, but their greyish-fawn colouring, black and white underbody markings and long, slender, almost straight backward-pointing horns make them unmistakeable. Gemsbok are highly adapted for survival in the arid country they inhabit, able to go for long periods without water, relying instead on melons and vegetation for moisture. They tolerate temperatures above 40°C by raising their normal body temperature of 35°C above that of the surrounding air, losing heat by conduction and radiation; their brains are kept cool by a supply of blood from their noses.

Hartebeests

With their bracket-shaped, relatively short horns and ungainly appearance, **hartebeest** look vaguely like elongated cows – particularly in their faces. All hartebeest are gregarious, but the exemplar of this is the **blue wildebeest**, *Connochaetes taurinus* (see p.28), which, in East Africa, gather in hundreds of thousands for their annual migration. You won't see these numbers in South Africa, but you'll see smaller herds if you go to any of the reserves in the northern half of the country or KwaZulu-Natal, as well as a number in the southern half, where they've been reintroduced. A particularly photogenic sight is wildebeest mingling with zebras, a habit said to be for mutual defence, though it may simply reflect the fact that they are both grazers and therefore hang around similar terrain. You're less likely to see **black wildebeest**, *Connochaetes gnou*, which were brought to the edge of extinction in the nineteenth century and now number around three thousand in South Africa, though you may find them in the Karoo and Mountain Zebra parks as well as Giant's Castle. You can tell them apart from their blue cousins by their darker colour (brown rather than the black suggested by their name) and long white tail.

Rather inelegant, like the wildebeests, the **red hartebeest**, *Alcelaphus buselaphus* (see p.28), the extremely rare **Lichtenstein's hartebeest**, *Sigmocerus lichtensteinii*, and the **tsessebe**, *Damaliscus lunatus* (see p.29), are all highly similar in appearance, but confusion is only likely to arise at the Kruger, the one place Lichtenstein's are found in the same range as tsessebes. The key distinction is in the horns, which in the hartebeest curve round almost to touch each other, while the tsessebe's are more splayed. Parks where you can see red hartebeests include Mountain Zebra, Karoo, Addo and Kgalagadi.

The **blesbok**, *Damaliscus dorcas phillipsi*, and **bontebok**, *Damaliscus dorcas dorcas*, are near identical subspecies of the same animal and resemble darker, better-looking versions of the tsessebe. The largest bontebok population is at De Hoop Nature Reserve, with other members of the subspecies at the Cape of Good Hope section of Table Mountain National Park. Good places to see blesbok include Mountain Zebra National Park and Suikerbosrand Nature Reserve. After springboks, blesboks are the most important game-farm species in the country, and you may see them on Karoo farms.

Duiker and dwarf antelope

Duiker and the dwarf tribe are non-herding antelope that are either solitary or live in pairs. Despite their size, or perhaps because of it, males tend to be highly aggressive and are able to use their straight, stiletto-sharp horns to deadly effect.

The smallest South African antelope, the **blue duiker**, *Philantomba monticola*, weighs in at around 4kg, has an arched back and stands 35cm at the shoulder (roughly the height of a cat). Extremely shy, it is seldom seen in the southern and eastern coastal forests (as well as Ndumo Game Reserve) where it lives. The slightly larger **red duiker**, *Cephalophus natalensis*, is three times heavier, and enjoys a similar environment to the blue, but inhabits only the woodlands and forest of KwaZulu-Natal.

You're more likely to see the **common duiker** (sometimes called the grey duiker, reflecting its colouring), *Sylvicapra grimmia* (see p.30), which occurs all over South Africa and is among the antelopes most tolerant of human habitation. When under threat it freezes in the undergrowth, but if chased will dart off in an erratic zigzagging run designed to throw pursuers off balance.

This type of fast darting movement is also characteristic of **dwarf antelope**, particularly the **Cape grysbok**, *Raphicerus melanotis*, and **Sharpe's grysbok**, *Raphicerus sharpii*, which bear a close resemblance to each other, but can't be confused because their ranges don't overlap. The Cape grysbok lives in the Western Cape *fynbos* belt (including Cape of Good Hope reserve and Addo), while Sharpe's occur in the northeastern corner of the country around the Kruger. Both are nocturnal and so are not often sighted.

A relative of the grysbok, the **steenbok**, *Raphicerus campestris* (see p.32), is by far the most commonly sighted of all the dwarf antelope, and you can spot them by day or night all over the country (except parts of KwaZulu-Natal). Its large, dark eyes, massive ears and delicate frame give this elegant half-metre-high antelope an engaging Bambi-like appearance.

Another dwarf antelope you could well see is the **klipspringer**, *Oreotragus oreotragus* (see p.32), whose Afrikaans name (meaning "rock jumper") reflects its goat-like adaptation to living on *koppies* and cliffs – the only antelope to do so, making it unmistakeable. It's also the only one to walk on the tips of its hooves. Keep your eyes peeled at Kruger or Mountain Zebra parks (and other wilderness areas where there are rocky outcrops) for their large, bounding movements to scale steep inclines, or their hopping from rock to rock.

The largest of the dwarves is the **oribi**, *Ourebia ourebi* (see p.32), which could be taken for an outsized steenbok or a small gazelle, as its movements are more akin to theirs, faster and smoother than those of other dwarves. Only found in small pockets of KwaZulu-Natal, oribis live in small parties of a ram and several ewes. You may hear their short sharp warning whistle as you approach, before you see them. After they flee a little way, they will frequently stop to look back at you.

Gazelle

Springbok, *Antidorcas marsupalis* (see p.29), are the symbol of the national cricket and rugby teams. South Africa's only gazelle, they are the most populous members of this tribe. They're tolerant of a wide range of open country, from deserts to wetter savanna.

These medium-sized antelope are said to have once migrated in their millions across the drylands of South Africa, but today their numbers are greatly reduced and the network of fences segmenting the country has ended such mass movements. They can be seen in reserves in the western arid zone of the country, in which region they're also raised on farms for venison and hides. Their characteristic horns and dark horizontal patch on their sides, separating their reddish tawny upper body from their white underparts, are definitive identifiers. Springbok are recorded as having reached nearly 90kph and are noted for "pronking", a movement in which they arch their backs and straighten their legs as they leap into the air.

Impala

Larger and heavier than springbok, which they superficially resemble, **impala**, *Aepyceros melampus* (see p.29), are antelope in a tribe of their own. Elegant and athletic, they are prodigious jumpers that have been recorded leaping distances of 11m and heights of 3m. Only the males carry the distinctive lyre-shaped pair of horns. They are so common in the reserves of the northeast and of KwaZulu-Natal that some jaded rangers look on them as the goats of the savanna – a perception that carries more than a germ of truth, as these flexible feeders are both browsers and grazers.

Ewes and lambs form tight herds that can number over a hundred, moving about in a home range that may overlap the territory of several rams. During the rut, which takes place during the first five months of each year, these males will cut out harem herds of around twenty and expend considerable amounts of effort herding them and driving off any potential rivals.

Near-aquatic antelope

All species of the near-aquatic Kob tribe live close to water. Largest of the tribe, **waterbuck**, *Kobus ellipsiprymnus* (see p.30), are sturdy antelope – 1.3m at the shoulder – with shaggy reddish-brown coats and a white horseshoe marking on their rumps. Only the males have horns. Sociable animals, they usually gather in small herds of up to ten, and occasionally up to thirty. They're found sporadically in the northeastern reserves, close to woodland and permanent water.

Two closely related species, the **common reedbuck**, *Redunca arundinum* (see p.29), and the slightly smaller **mountain reedbuck**, *Redunca fulvorufula*, both roughly two-thirds the height of waterbuck, are tan-coloured antelope. The common reedbuck favours a habitat of tall grass or reedbeds for refuge, while the mountain reedbuck inhabits hilly country with trees or grassy slopes.

All three species can be seen in suitable habitat in the Kruger, while the waterbuck and common reedbuck will also be sighted in the wetland reserves of KwaZulu-Natal, and the mountain reedbuck in the Mountain Zebra, Giant's Castle and Pilanesberg parks.

Other hoofed ruminants

Alongside cattle, sheep, goats and antelope, buffalo and giraffe are also **hoofed ruminants**. Bacteria in their digestive systems process plant matter into carbohydrates, while the dead bacteria are absorbed as protein – a highly efficient arrangement that makes them economical consumers, far more so than non-ruminants such as elephants, which pass vast quantities of what they eat as unutilized fibre. Species that concentrate on grasses are grazers; those eating leaves are browsers.

Buffalo

You won't have to be in the Kruger or most of the other reserves in South Africa for long to see **buffalo**, *Syncerus caffer* (see p.28), a common safari animal that, as one of the Big Five, appears on every hunter's shopping list. Don't let their resemblance to domestic cattle or water buffalo (to which they are not at all closely related) or apparent docility lull you into complacency; lone bulls, in particular, are noted and feared even by hardened hunters as dangerous and relentless killers. In other words, don't assume that the absence of carnivores in some reserves means it's safe to go walking without a guide.

Buffalo are non-territorial and highly gregarious, gathering in hundreds or even sometimes thousands. Herds under one or more dominant bulls consist of clans of a dozen or so related females under a leading cow. You'll be able to spot such distinct units within the group: at rest, clan members often cuddle up close to each other. There are separate pecking orders among females and males, the latter being forced to leave the herd during adolescence (at about three years) or once they're over the hill, to form bachelor herds, which you can recognize by their small numbers. Evicted old bulls (sometimes called "*daga* boys" – *daga* meaning mud – on account of their penchant for mud baths), stripped of their social position and sex lives, understandably become resentful and embittered loners and are to be avoided at all costs. To distinguish males (as shown in the colour guide) from females, look for their heavier horns bisected by a distinct boss, or furrow.

Giraffe

Giraffe, *Giraffa camelopardalis* (see p.27), are among the easiest animals to spot because their long necks make them visible above the low scrub. The tallest mammals on earth, they spend their daylight hours browsing on the leaves of trees too high up for other species; combretum and acacias are favourites. Their highly flexible lips and prehensile tongues give them almost hand-like agility and enable them to select the most nutritious leaves while avoiding deadly-sharp acacia thorns. At night they lie down and spend the evening ruminating. Non-territorial, they gather in loose, leaderless herds; if you encounter a bachelor herd, look out for young males testing their strength with neck wrestling. When the female comes into oestrus, which can happen at any time of year, the dominant male mates with her. She will give birth after a gestation period of approximately fourteen months. Over half of all young, however, fall prey to lions or hyenas in their early years. Kruger, Pilanesberg and the KwaZulu-Natal parks are all good places to see them.

Non-ruminants

Non-ruminating mammals have more primitive digestive systems than animals that chew the cud. Although both have bacteria in their gut that convert vegetable matter into carbohydrates, the less efficient system of the non-ruminants means they have to consume more raw material and to process it faster. The upside is they can handle food that's far more fibrous.

Elephants

Elephants, *Loxodonta africana* (see p.26), were once found throughout South Africa. Now you'll only see them in a handful of reserves, notably the Kruger, Pilanesberg, Hluhluwe-Imfolozi, Tembe and Addo, the last of which protects the only population to survive naturally in the southern two-thirds of the country. Otherwise, one or two elephants may still survive in the Knysna Forest, but their days are numbered and they are rarely, if ever, seen. When encountered in the flesh, elephants seem even bigger than you would imagine. You'll need little persuasion from those flapping warning ears to back off if you're too close, but they are at the same time amazingly graceful. In a matter of moments a large herd can merge into the trees and disappear, silent on their padded, carefully placed feet, their presence betrayed only by the noisy cracking of branches as they strip trees and uproot saplings.

Elephants are the most engaging of animals to watch, perhaps because their interactions, behaviour patterns and personality have so many human parallels. Like people, they lead complex, interdependent social lives, growing from helpless infancy through self-conscious adolescence to adulthood. Babies are born with other cows in close attendance, after a 22-month gestation. Calves suckle for two to three years. Basic family units are composed of a group of related females, tightly protecting their young and led by a venerable matriarch. It's the matriarch that's most likely to bluff a charge – though occasionally she may get carried away and tusk a vehicle or person.

Bush mythology has it that elephants become embarrassed and ashamed after killing a human, covering the body with sticks and grass. They certainly pay much attention to the disposal of their own dead relatives, often dispersing the bones and spending time near the remains. Old animals die in their 70s or 80s, when their last set of teeth wears out and they can no longer feed.

Dassies (hyraxes)

Dassies look like they ought to be rodents but, amazingly, despite being fluffy and rabbit-sized, their closest relatives (from some way back) are elephants. Their name (pronounced like "dusty" without the "t") is the Afrikaans version of *dasje*, meaning "little badger", given to them by the first Dutch settlers.

Tree dassies, *Dendrohyrax arboreus*, a rarely seen, solitary species, live along the Eastern Cape and southern KwaZulu-Natal coastal plains, where they take refuge in forest and thick bush. In contrast, **rock dassies**, *Procavia capensis* (see p.26), are widely distributed, having thrived with the elimination of predators. They hang out in suitably rocky habitat all over the country apart from north of the Orange River in the western half of the country and in the east along the northern KwaZulu-Natal coast, and in the Western Cape. One of the most dramatic places you'll see them is sunning themselves along the rocky shore of the Tsitsikamma National Park, as breakers crash down ahead.

Like reptiles, hyraxes have poor body control systems and rely on shelter against both the cold and hot sunlight. They wake up sluggish and seek out rocks to catch the early morning sun – this is one of the best times to look out for them. One adult stands sentry against predators and issues a low-pitched warning cry in response to a threat. Dassies live in colonies of a dominant male and eight or more related females and their offspring.

Rhinos

Two species of rhinoceros are found in Africa: the hook-lipped or **black rhino**, *Diceros bicornis* (see p.26), and the much heavier square-lipped or **white rhino**, *Ceratotherium simum* (see p.26). Both have come close to extinction in the African wild and have all but disappeared. Happily, South Africa has bucked this continental trend and, due to timely conservation measures (especially in KwaZulu-Natal), it's the best place in the world to see both. Spend a day or two at Ithala, Hluhluwe-Imfolozi or Mkhuze reserves and you're bound to see one species or the other. Elsewhere, look for white rhinos at Addo and both varieties at Kruger and Pilanesberg.

"Hook-lipped" and "square-lipped" are technically more accurate terms for the two rhinos. "Black" and "white" are based on a linguistic misunderstanding – somewhere along the line, the German *weid,* which refers to the square-lipped's wide mouth, was misheard as "white". The term has stuck, despite both rhinos being a greyish muddy colour.

The shape of their lips is highly significant as it indicates their respective diets and consequently their favoured habitat. The cantankerous and smaller black rhino has the narrow prehensile lips of a browser, suited to picking leaves off trees and bushes, while the wide, flatter mouth of the twice-as-heavy white rhino is well suited to chomping away at grasses like a lawnmower. Diet and habitat also account for the greater sociability of the white rhino, which relies on safety in numbers under the exposure of open grassland; the solitary black rhino relies on the camouflage of dense thickets, which is why you'll find them so much more difficult to see.

Rhinos give birth to a single calf after a gestation period of fifteen to eighteen months, and the baby is not weaned until it is at a least a year old, sometimes two. Their population grows slowly compared with most animals, another factor contributing to their predicament.

Hippos

Hippopotamuses, *Hippopotamus amphibius* (see p.27), are highly adaptable animals that once inhabited South African waterways from the Limpopo in the north to the marshes of the Cape Peninsula in the south. Today they're restricted to the northeastern corner of the country, with the most southerly indigenous population living in KwaZulu-Natal. You will find them elsewhere, in places where they've been reintroduced, such as the Double Drift Reserve in the Eastern Cape.

Hippos need fresh water deep enough to submerge themselves in, with a surrounding of suitable grazing grass. By day, they need to spend most of their time in water to protect their thin, hairless skin. After dark, hippos leave the water to spend the whole night grazing, often walking up to 10km in one session. Their grunting and jostling in the water may give the impression of loveable buffoons, but throughout Africa they are feared, and rightly so, as they are reckoned to be responsible for more human deaths on the continent than any other animal. When disturbed, lone bulls and cows with calves can become extremely aggressive. Their fearsomely long incisors can slash through a canoe with ease; on land they can charge at speeds up to 30kph, with a tight turning circle.

Zebras

Zebras are closely related to horses and, together with them, donkeys and wild asses, form the equid family. Of the three species of zebra, two live in South Africa.

The Burchell's or **plains zebra**, *Equus burchelli* (see p.27), has small ears and thick, black stripes, with lighter "shadows"; it survives in Mpumalanga, KwaZulu-Natal and along the Limpopo. Elsewhere it has been widely introduced and you'll see plains zebra in many reserves across the country.

The **Cape mountain zebra**, *Equus zebra zebra*, only narrowly escaped extinction, but now survives in healthy if limited numbers in the Mountain Zebra National Park in the Eastern Cape, and in other reserves in the southwest, wherever there is suitably mountainous terrain. Distinguishing characteristics of the mountain zebra are the dewlap on its lower neck, the absence of shadow stripes, its larger ears, and stripes that go all the way down to its hooves – in contrast to the Burchell's, whose stripes fade out as they progress down its legs.

Zebras congregate in family herds of a breeding stallion and two mares (or more) and their foals. Unattached males will often form bachelor herds. Among plains zebras, offspring leave the family group after between one and two years, while mountain zebras are far more tolerant in allowing adolescents to remain in the family.

Pigs

Two **wild pigs** are found in South Africa. If you're visiting the Kruger, Pilanesberg or the KwaZulu-Natal parks, families of **warthogs**, *Phacochoerus aethiopicus* (see p.27), will become a familiar sight, trotting across the savanna with their tails erect like communications antennae. Family groups usually consist of a mother and her litter of two to four piglets, or occasionally two or three females and their young. Boars join the group only to mate; they're distinguished from sows by their prominent face warts, which are thought to be defensive pads protecting their heads during often violent fights. Warthogs shelter in holes in the ground, usually porcupine or aardvark burrows, although they are quite capable of making their own – in fact, they are supreme diggers who routinely dig up nutritious bulbs.

Bushpigs, *Potamochoerus porcus*, are slightly more widely distributed than warthogs in South Africa, but because they're nocturnal forest dwellers, they aren't seen as often. Their northerly range overlaps with that of the hogs, but they also extend along the southern coastal woodlands of the Eastern Cape as far west as Mossel Bay. Much like hairier versions of domestic pigs, they live in harems called "sounders", consisting of a boar with several females and their piglets. Fathers drive out male offspring when they approach adolescence.

Other mammals

Despite their common taste for ants and termites, their nocturnal foraging and their outlandish appearance, aardvarks and pangolins are quite unrelated. The **aardvark**, *Orycteropus afer* (see p.22), is one of Africa's – indeed the world's – strangest animals, a solitary mammal weighing up to 70kg. Its name, Afrikaans for "earth pig", is an apt description, as it holes up during the day in large burrows that are excavated with remarkable speed and energy. It emerges at night to visit termite mounds within a radius of up to 5km, digging for its main diet. It's most likely to be common in bush country that's well scattered with termite mounds. Holes dug into the base of these are a tell-tale sign of the presence of aardvarks.

Pangolins, *Manis temminckii*, are equally unusual – scale-covered mammals, resembling armadillos and feeding on ants and termites. Under attack they roll themselves into a ball. Pangolins occur widely in South Africa, north of the Orange River.

▲ A pangolin

A number of species of rabbits and hares bounce about the South African landscape, but the **scrub hare**, *Lepus saxatilis*, distinguished by its exceptionally long ears, is the commonest and one you'll undoubtedly see in scrubby, wooded country throughout the region. Wherever there's rocky terrain south of the Orange River and in KwaZulu-Natal, keep an eye open for **rock rabbits**, which look just like brown- and white-speckled domestic bunnies.

If you go on a night drive you'd be most unlucky not to see the glinting eyes of **spring hares**, *Pedetes capensis* (see p.22), which, despite their resemblance to rabbit-sized kangaroos, are in fact true rodents. In the western arid zone **ground squirrels**, *Xerus inauris*, can be spotted scurrying about during the day looking for roots, seeds and bulbs, while in the northeast, **tree squirrels**, *Paraxerus cepapi*, enjoy a similar diet. The most singular and largest of the African rodents is the **porcupine**, *Hystrix africae-australis* (see p.22), which is quite unmistakeable with its coat of many quills. Porcupines are widespread and present in most reserves but, because they're nocturnal, you may only see shed quills lying along the path or in front of their burrows.

Scores of different **bats**, either fruit- or insect-eaters, leave their roosts each night and take off into the South African night, but all you're likely to see of them is some erratic flying against a moonlit sky. The foxy-faced **Egyptian fruit bat**, *Rousettus aegyptiacus*, is virtually single-handedly responsible for pollinating baobab trees, thus keeping them from extinction. And while **rats and mice** are probably not what brought you on safari, it's worth noting that over forty different species are found in South Africa.

Music

M usic from South Africa has a deserved following. The country has some of Africa's most diverse recorded music output and its music industry is among the continent's most developed. It doesn't take much effort for an interested listener to encounter anything from indigenous African sounds that have remained largely unchanged for the last two hundred years, to a variety of white pop styles that would not be out of place anywhere in the Western world.

Compilations of South African music released abroad usually concentrate on the country's African genres and furthermore tend to ignore newer styles, so Western fans can be forgiven for thinking that the **iscathamiya** vocalizing of Ladysmith Black Mambazo, or the **mbaqanga** ("township jive") made famous by Paul Simon's *Graceland* album and artists such as Mahlathini and the Mahotella Queens, remains at the cutting edge locally. In fact, *iscathamiya* has now all but retreated to the Zulu worker hostels whence it originated, while *mbaqanga* is popular but old-fashioned – a safe bet for a DJ at an African wedding, but not the thing to play to an urban party crowd.

Far and away the most popular music in the country, at least in terms of consistently racking up the largest sales figures, is African **gospel**. Among urban black youth, much the biggest sound is **kwaito** and local **hip-hop**, while more mature urban Africans often prefer **jazz**. Attracting both black and white fans is **Afropop**, a skilful blend of various older African styles with Western pop influences.

South Africa's **English-speaking whites** tend to favour international pop. **Afrikaans speakers** have a weakness for home-grown pop balladeers, and older or rural Afrikaners often prefer listening and dancing to *boeremusiek*, a so-called "traditional" mixture of Germanic and Dutch elements and US country music. Both English- and Afrikaans-speakers also support a wide range of local musicians representing virtually every modern pop variant, from boy bands to hard rock; electronic dance music has a following among many white 20-somethings from both sides of the linguistic divide, as well as their peers of Indian origin.

Among Zulus, **maskanda**, a guitar-and-vocal neo-traditional style, remains firmly entrenched, while the largely coloured-supported ballroom dancing circuit regularly features a network of small dance bands, although these aren't well represented by commercial recordings. Tourists in Cape Town over the Christmas/New Year holidays should not miss the musicians at the coloured "Coon Carnival" (see p.57), whose roots can be traced back 150 years to visiting African American minstrels, and to the Malay choirs, who are additionally influenced by music brought from the Indonesian archipelago in the eighteenth century.

Paradoxically, judging by what one often hears pumping from the nation's radios, clubs and car stereos, more of the population than anywhere else on the continent listens to American sounds. African American music in particular has been popular with black South Africans for over a hundred years, and has been critical in the development of local sounds. Concern over imported music smothering South African sounds has led to **radio quotas** whereby, depending on the profile of the station, a quarter to forty percent of airtime must be devoted to local music. The policy has arguably had the greatest impact in the realm of black urban youth music, which commercially is in its healthiest state in decades. The prospects for its white equivalent, notwithstanding some

▲ Johannesburg musician

world-class material, are not so good: given the relatively small size of the white population, white South African pop musicians are often presented with a stark choice: stagnate or emigrate.

Gospel

Choral harmony and melody are perhaps black South Africa's greatest musical gifts to the world, and nowhere are they better manifested than in its **churches**. In the mainstream Catholic, Anglican and Methodist denominations a tradition of choral singing has evolved that has taken the style of European classical composers and loosened it up, added rhythm and, as always, some great dance routines. This type of choral singing is immensely popular, with regular competitions involving amazingly attired choirs – some of which are over one hundred strong. If you can't make it to a competition, you can watch the choirs every Sunday on TV (SABC 1).

In the **Pentecostal** churches, the music is more American-influenced, yet the harmonies and melodies remain uniquely South African and intensely moving. Pentecostal gospel music is the main recorded style; look out for groups like **Lord Comforters**, **Joyous Celebration**, **Pure Magic**, **Lusanda Spiritual Group** and the powerful **Rebecca Malope** (see box, opposite).

Also worth seeking out is the music of the **Zionist churches**, which have more members than any other denomination in the country. Their devotees are required to donate ten percent of their income to the church, live an ultra-clean life and attend all the services and conventions, in distinctive long robes, often adorned with sashes. Zionist gospel is an extraordinary mix of mournfulness and fervour, with a tonality all of its own, rendering it perfect for the moving night vigils that precede funerals, as well as regular church services. Services are held outside, often in parks, where you are welcome to watch as long as you do

Diminutive **Rebecca Malope** is South Africa's biggest-selling music star, enjoying years at the top of the gospel scene, with only stadia able to hold her fans, every album going gold or platinum, popular magazines full of her photos, views and story, and everyone knowing the lyrics of her songs. Well, nearly everyone that is, for Rebecca Malope is virtually unknown outside Africa.

The daughter of a Sotho father and Swazi mother, Rebecca was born in Nelspruit, Mpumalanga, in 1969, and soon began singing in the local Assemblies of God church, where her grandfather was a pastor. Her initial recordings were mostly forgettable bubblegum pop. She was spotted in Jo'burg by **Sizwe Zako**, who would become her lynchpin keyboard player. Under his tutelage, and so she says, because of letters from fans pleading that she sing God's songs, Rebecca returned to gospel in 1990, where she has been amply rewarded. Rebecca denies that she is apolitical, saying she sometimes sings at rallies, but selects songs that tell the politicians what she believes they need to hear.

Rebecca's musical formula, engineered by Zako, who also produces, rarely varies. The songs are anthems characterized by swirling keyboards and excellent backing singers, and are delivered in her tremendous, soaring and sometimes husky voice, accompanied by dramatic gestures.

so respectfully. Zionist gospel cassettes and CDs are easily spotted, as their covers invariably feature the substantial performing choir in full robes, often with the preacher out in front in some suitably religious pose.

Kwaito and hip-hop

South Africa's definitive youth sound, **kwaito**, has been around for over a decade. Apparently, DJs importing dance music in the early 1990s found that white clubs were unresponsive to Chicago house and so tried it in black nightclubs instead. Here DJs found that people preferred it when they slowed the records from 45 to 33rpm. Innovative producers soon began to try out their own versions and to experiment, incorporating South African melodies and DJs singing doggerel verses incorporating the latest, wickedest phrases of *tsotsi taal* – ghetto rude-boy slang.

In an accurate reflection of the depressed and nihilistic mood of township youth culture, *kwaito*'s vibe tends to be downbeat, and the music frequently carries a strong association with gangsterism and explicit sexuality. This is often condemned by older and God-fearing South Africans, which matters "niks" (nothing) to its young township fans, to whom *kwaito* embodies the style and groove of the new South Africa.

The popularity of many *kwaito* performers is often fairly short-lived. For example, **Arthur**, one of the pioneers of the genre, now produces newer hopefuls. Some artists worth looking out for include **Tokollo** (ex-**TKZee**), **Mzekezeke** (who always performs with his trademark mask), **Kabelo**, the hard-rock-influenced **Mandoza**, and the matchstick-chewing, gangster-styled **Zola**. Zola starred in the hit South African drama series *Yizo Yizo* about the interplay between a township school and local young gangsters, and the two soundtrack CDs from the programme are a virtual who's who of the *kwaito* scene. Kalawa Jazmee, a record label run by Oscar Mdlongwa, aka **DJ Oskido**,

Kwaito killed the careers of many of the 1980s pop stars, but the late **Brenda Fassie** managed not only to survive the new music, but to thrive on it. Brenda was South Africa's true pop queen and the one local artist whose music is still pretty much guaranteed to get things going on the dance floor, wherever you are in the country.

Brenda began her career in the early 1980s as the lead singer for **Brenda and the Big Dudes**, enjoying a string of bubblegum hits, including the classic "Weekend Special", which for years was a South African disco anthem. Her sound mixed *kwaito*, *mbaqanga*, gospel and her own extraordinary persona, earning massive and deserved success with tunes like "Vul'Ndlela" and "Nomakanjani". Although never one for politics, she skilfully caught the mood of the time in the tense year of 1989 with a moving song about police brutality, "Good Black Woman", on the album *Too Late for Mama*.

During the 1990s, while contemporaries like her one-time arch rival **Yvonne Chaka Chaka** produced comfortable material aimed more at middle-class and middle-aged audiences, Brenda made a point of hanging out with the youth in Soweto and in Hillbrow, Johannesburg's fastest-paced inner-city patch. The result was a lesbian love affair that thrilled the tabloids, a bad crack habit, a tendency to lose the plot completely on stage – and the best music she had ever produced.

Tragically, if not inevitably, her many demons eventually caught up with her, and after falling into a two-week-long coma, which even saw President Thabo Mbeki coming to her hospital bedside, she died in 2004. Her funeral was a massive media event that witnessed an outpouring of grief exceeding that attending the deaths of most "struggle" veterans, and a few months later, when a television programme solicited telephone votes for the all-time greatest South Africans, Brenda came in comfortably at number seventeen, the highest placing of any musician.

has been responsible for several successful *kwaito* groups including **Trompies**, **Bongo Maffin** and the self-consciously retro **Mafikizolo**. The label's production values are generally a cut above the rest and with each release they seem to have added more actual singing and melody to the mix. **Malaika**, the sensational *kwaito*-turned-Afro-pop trio, have adopted this formula, to great commercial – but dubious artistic – effect.

Local **hip-hop** artists are more likely than their *kwaito* counterparts to use English instead of an African language, and tend to come from middle-class backgrounds instead of the townships – as a result of which they can afford to spend more on production. Among the hip-hop names making a splash are **Skwatta Kamp**, **Optical Illusion**, **Cashless Society**, **Zubz** and **H20**. Although the supporters of local hip-hop eagerly proclaim that it is now replacing *kwaito*, the reality is more nuanced, and the difference between the two styles isn't always clear cut. Among the hip-hop artists rated by purists are Cape Town's **Parliament**, **Wildlife Society**, **Fifth Floor**, and **Lions of Zion** (who, as their name suggests, blend hip-hop and reggae), along with **Basement Platform** from Johannesburg.

House, rap and reggae

DJ-mixed South African **house** attracts practitioners and fans from all parts of the country's racial and cultural divisions, but it is black DJs such as **DJ Fresh**, **Glen Lewis**, **DJ Mbuso** and **Oskido** who garner by far the most attention from the local media. The recordings they mix with are almost exclusively from either the UK or France.

South African **rap** has enjoyed sustained popularity since the early 1990s, but has remained almost completely ghettoized within the coloured community of the Western Cape. Heavily influenced by African American rappers such as Public Enemy, the performers often exude a palpable sense of being "Americans trapped in Africa". Pioneers of the style were the heavily politicized **Prophets of Da City**, several members of which made names for themselves as solo artists after the group's break-up, most notably **Rahim**, **Junior Solela** and **Ishmael**. Other performers who have since come up are **Brasse Van Die Kaap** (who rap in Afrikaans), **Reddy D** and **Godessa**, while a new Cape Town-based record and production company, African Dope, has also enjoyed recent success with **Teba**, **Funny Carp** and crossover jazz-Latin-hip-hop-funksters **Moodphase5ive**, among others.

What is unusual as regards the place of **Lucky Dube** (who died tragically in 2007 in a botched hijacking) in the local **reggae** scene is the total lack of successful emulators. An energetic, disciplined and talented live performer, Dube could also deliver a falsetto like Smokey Robinson's, which added a distinct twist to his otherwise familiar roots reggae sound.

Neo-traditional music

As with *kwaito*, the instrumentation in **neo-traditional music** is really just a backdrop to the lyrics and the dance routines. One of its major stars is the Shangaan singer **Thomas Chauke**, perhaps the single bestselling artist in any neo-traditional genre. Hailing from Limpopo Province, he makes heavy use of a drum machine and an electronic keyboard and often picks out some intricate lead-guitar work to complement his vocals.

Sotho neo-traditional music has declined commercially in recent years, largely because of a lack of support from SABC Radio Sotho, who no longer need to maintain the ethnic exclusivity of the apartheid era. Nevertheless, the bass lines are good, the shouting is definitely first-class and the accordions can take on an almost Cajun tinge. **Tau Oa Matshela** and **Tau Oa Linare** are some of the groups to look out for.

Xhosa and Tswana neo-traditional music rarely makes it to the national scene, but **Zulu music** is more pervasive, both in its a cappella form, known as **iscathamiya**, and as a vocal/guitar-based style called **maskanda**. A unique guitar-picking style (*ukupika*) is central to the instrumental sound, though these days it may be overshadowed by a hammily played electronic keyboard. Each song starts with the *izihlabo* (an instrumental flourish), followed by the main melody, which is interrupted by the lead singer's *ukubonga*, a fast-spoken declamation, usually in deep rural Zulu, that always used to be some kind of praise poem, but could just as well in modern songs be a denunciation of a woman's cooking pot. For particularly fine examples of the art, look out for **Phuzekhemisi**, **Shiyani Ncgobo** and the late, great **Mfaz'Omnyama**. Another star of the neo-traditional scene is the queen of Ndebele music, **Nothembi Mkhwebane**. As well as being a talented and veteran performer, Nothembi, who sings and plays electric guitar, is also known for her sensational outfits, decorated with typical intricate Ndebele bead and metalwork.

Ladysmith Black Mambazo and the iscathamiya sound

The best known of South Africa's many neo-traditional musical genres is Zulu **iscathamiya** (or **mbube**), the distinctive male a cappella choral style made internationally famous by Ladysmith Black Mambazo. The style originated among Zulu rural migrants in urban hostels following World War I, and by 1939 the first commercial hit, "Mbube" by Solomon Linda and His Original Evening Birds, had been recorded, eventually selling 100,000 copies. The song was later reworked as "The Lion Sleeps Tonight", which became a number one hit in both the US and UK and was featured in the Walt Disney movie and musical, *The Lion King*.

Although it enjoyed pan-ethnic popularity in the 1940s and 1950s, by the 1960s *iscathamiya* had reverted to its role as the defining sound of Zulu men's hostels. The music was cleverly used by apartheid-era SABC Radio Zulu to promote rigid ethnic identity, with songs dwelling on Zuluness and the need to leave the cities and return to the rural areas.

In 1973, after recording for the SABC for several years, **Ladysmith Black Mambazo** made their first commercial release, *Amabutho*, for the Gallo label. It quickly sold over 25,000 copies (gold-disc status in South Africa) and since that time the group has recorded about forty others, most of which have also gone gold. Following their collaboration with him on *Graceland*, Paul Simon produced their *Shaka Zulu* album, which sold 100,000 copies around the world and took *iscathamiya* to the international stage. In 1997, Ladysmith Black Mambazo extended its Afropop credentials with *Heavenly*, an album that featured collaborations with, among other international artists, Dolly Parton. Following the exposure of their song "Inkanyezi Nezazi" in a British TV advertisement for Heinz baked beans, the group went on to sell over a million units in the UK, an all-time record for a South African act.

Having briefly flirted with the Zulu nationalist politics of the Inkhatha Freedom Party in the late 1980s, Ladysmith Black Mambazo now prefer to dwell on religious matters, and restrict their politics to calls for peace. Though non-Zulu speakers can appreciate the group's smooth dance steps, immaculate singing and vocal arrangements, the true glory of their music for Zulus is the beauty of the lyrics, written by the group's gentle lead singer **Joseph Shabalala**, who is surely one of South Africa's greatest living poets.

Jazz

Jazz has been widely popular in South Africa for many decades, and you can almost always find performances in Johannesburg, Pretoria or Cape Town on virtually any weekend, and sometimes midweek too. It was **South African jazz** that was the music most associated with the struggle against apartheid, especially after the music's main exponents went into self-imposed exile in the 1960s.

Jazz's roots in the country are much older than this, harking back to the emergence of *marabi* music in Johannesburg's African slums some time after World War I. *Marabi* was at first played on pianos in Jo'burg's illegal *shebeens*; always revolving around a simple three-chord structure, and combining elements of indigenous African styles with various Western musical influences, it continued to develop in the 1930s, with guitars, banjos and concertinas added to the line-up. During World War II, American swing became popular in South Africa, following which swing and *marabi* were fused into a new style usually referred to as **African jazz**. This remained predominant throughout the 1940s and 1950s, and produced the first South African musical exiles in vocalists **Miriam Makeba** and the **Manhattan Brothers**.

The next development was a move in the direction of the American avant-garde, as personified by Thelonious Monk and John Coltrane. The two early, prime exponents of this in South Africa were the **Jazz Epistles**, featuring Hugh Masekela, Jonas Gwangwa, Abdullah Ibrahim (then called Dollar Brand) and the great Kippie Moeketsi; and the **Blue Notes**, who included in their line-up Chris McGregor and Dudu Pukwana. Legislation prohibiting mixed-race public performances caused most of the Epistles to individually leave South Africa in the early 1960s, while the Blue Notes departed en masse in 1964. Some exiled South African jazzers detached themselves from their roots, while others such as **Hugh Masekela** reinterpreted their township influences. Back home, old-style African jazz as performed by the **Elite Swingsters** and **Ntemi Piliso's Alexandra All Stars** remained popular.

In the 1970s and 1980s, various South African strains were fused with funk, soul and rock influences to produce a more accessible, populist brand of jazz, from bands such as **Sakile**, **The Drive** and the **Jazz Ministers**. In the last decade, following the end of apartheid, the surviving exiles began to trickle back and a new, younger generation of jazz musicians yet again married old local traditions with contemporary international trends.

Today, almost all of the old African jazz artists are gone, while most exiled artists, including Miriam Makeba, Hugh Masekela and **Jonas Gwangwa**, are back home and receiving the domestic recognition they have long deserved. A few of the original avant-garde veterans like Abdullah Ibrahim, **Mankunku** and **Bheki Mseleku** continue to perform fairly regularly, but there are remarkably few players remaining from even the relatively recent fusion days. In their place, a large group of new jazz names have emerged that includes vocalists (**Gloria Bosman**, **Judith Sephuma**, **Sibongile Kumalo**), saxophonists (**McCoy Mrubata**, **Zim Ngqawana**), keyboard players (**Paul Hamner**, **Themba Mkhize**), guitarists (**Jimmy Dludlu**, **Selaelo Selota**) and the odd trumpeter (**Prince Lengoasa**, **Marcus Wyatt**). Although many of the stars of this new generation emulate the smooth style of the Earl Klugh school, there are other players whose tastes are considerably more muscular.

Political music

Political songs were once performed during marches, demonstrations, rallies and most of all at the funerals of slain activists, though their heyday has passed with the collapse of apartheid. The lyrics sang the praises of Umkhonto we Sizwe (the ANC's armed wing), or stated bluntly that "*uMama uyajabula uma ngibulala iBhunu*" ("My mother is happy when I kill a Boer"). Performances were usually accompanied by the *toyi-toyi*, a combination of a march and a dance; still widely used, it's performed on the spot or on the move, with knees brought high.

In the 1980s, **Mzwakhe Mbuli** made his name as "the people's poet", performing his articulate and angry political poetry at countless rallies around the country. His house was firebombed by the authorities, and Mzwakhe himself was harassed and detained, but his poetry remained defiant, with titles like *Unbroken Spirit* and *Now is the Time*. In 1989, Mzwakhe correctly discerned the signs of the times, proclaiming in one poem that "the bull is dying at last, kicking at random", and in the following year, while celebrating Mandela's release, he urged prophetically: "When you vote and get elected, think of those who died."

After the 1994 elections, Mzwakhe was for a time a contented man, asking disillusioned compatriots, "if this is not the time for happiness, when is?", while also using his poetry to urge an end to social ills like criminality and drug addiction. Controversially, however, he served several years in a maximum-security prison in the company of apartheid mass murderers like Eugene de Kock, after being convicted of armed robbery (Mzwakhe says he was framed because he was aware of drug-smuggling involving officialdom).

Afropop

Afropop is to some degree a catch-all category, yet it's arguably where many contemporary South African artists sit most comfortably. Afropop is characterized by a knack for combining various local African styles with Western popular influences, the ability to attract a multiracial audience, and the eschewing of computer-generated backing in favour of actual instruments.

The beginnings of Afropop go back to Miriam Makeba's first American recordings in the early 1960s. More contemporary examples would include Paul Simon's 1987 *Gracelands*, a collaboration with Ladysmith Black Mambazo and other local African artists; and the music of **Juluka** and **Savuka**, two bands led in the 1980s and 1990s by Johnny Clegg, whose melding of mainstream pop harmonies with Zulu dance routines and a touch of *mbaqanga* gained great popularity both in South Africa and in France. The music of bubblegum-pop queen **Yvonne Chaka Chaka** from the 1980s and 1990s could also be deemed Afropop. Artists who have subsequently adopted similar formulas include **Jabu Khanyile** (sometimes billed with a band as **Bayete** – his music might be described as Zulu-pop), **Vusi Mahlasela**, **Ringo** (influenced by African jazz and Xhosa traditional music) and **Busi Mhlongo** (influenced by African jazz and Zulu *maskanda*).

A recent Afropop star is the much acclaimed **Thandiswa Mazwai**. Although she has consciously incorporated quite a few different styles, both American and local, into her first album, her live persona tends to emphasize her Xhosa roots, and she is already being widely referred to as the new Makeba.

White pop and rock

English-speaking South Africans have successfully replicated virtually every popular Western musical style going back to the late nineteenth century, and some have found fame in the outside world. A list of the country's most successful musical émigrés would include rockers **Manfred Mann** in the 1960s and more recently **Dave Matthews**. At the time of writing, several successful local rock/punk bands have recently relocated overseas, including **Seether**, **Just Jinger** and **Wonderboom**.

Thanks to TV coverage, including the local version of *Pop Idols*, the action is not restricted to rock but extends to virtually every variety of contemporary pop. Young male vocal sensations, for example, include **Danny K**, whose slick R&B is particularly popular among teenagers, and **Heinz Winkler**, where smooth pop meets "adult contemporary".

Afrikaans music

Like South African jazz, *Afrikaansmusiek* is another world unto itself, with a multitude of sub-categories and a long list of heroes and heroines. Its development can be traced back to the seventeenth century with the mixing of German–Dutch and French music, while from the late 1920s until the 1960s American country was the greatest outside influence. This was also the period that saw the first truly "populist" recordings being released, frequently covers of American hits, sung in Afrikaans. A somewhat more rugged and largely instrumental variant called **boeremusiek** ("farmer music") has the concertina as a lead instrument, backed originally with acoustic string instrumentation, and subsequently with drums, electric bass and electronic keyboards.

By the early 1970s, the influence of country was starting to decline. In its stead came the lighter end of foreign pop music and in particular, Eurodisco. A long line of bouncy Afrikaans pop stars ensued, while a more sober side was represented by the light operatic style of **Gé Korsten**, probably the single most popular Afrikaans artist of the period.

Following the end of apartheid, a general concern about the future of the Afrikaans language and culture spurred a revival of interest in Afrikaans music. There is undoubtedly more stylistic variety now than ever before: witness the house/disco of **Juanita**, the heavy rock of **Karen Zoid** and **Jackhammer**, the modernized *boeremusiek* of the **Klipwerf Orkes**, and the Neil Diamond-esque songs of **Steve Hofmeyer** (the bestselling Afrikaans music artist).

Discography

In the reviews below, items marked with an asterisk are international releases. Other items are South African releases, issued either by local labels or by the South African operations of international labels.

Cross-genre compilations

Various Artists *The Rough Guide to the Music of South Africa (2nd ed)* (World Music Network★). Excellent cross section of sounds combining big names like Lucky Dube, Yvonne Chaka Chaka and Miriam Makeba with some interesting less-known musicians.

Various Artists *Mzansi Music: Young Urban South Africa* (Trikont★). Fifteen-track collection that captures the city beat of Mzansi's (South Africa's) youth.

Mbaqanga

Mahlathini and the Mahotella Queens *The Best of Mahlathini and the Mahotella Queens* (Gallo). Perfect introduction to the sound of this most stomping of *mbaqanga* outfits.

Soul Brothers *Igobondela*, *The Best of The Soul Brothers* and *The Early Years* (Gallo). If *The Best of* whets your appetite, investigate *The Early Years*, a series comprising the classic first twelve albums by these *mbaqanga* stalwarts, recorded in the 1970s and early 1980s. *Igobondela* (2004) is the band's first album to combine studio and live tracks and demonstrates how they're still capable of delivering the goods.

Various Artists *From Marabi to Disco* (Gallo). A mini-encyclopedia of the development of township musical style from the late 1930s to the early 1980s, with informative sleeve notes.

Various Artists *The Indestructible Beat of Soweto Volumes 1–6* (Earthworks★). Superb compilation, mainly featuring 1980s *mbaqanga*, along with a few more traditional samples. As compiler Trevor Herman writes, "best heard loud and standing up".

Gospel

Amadodana Ase Wesile *Morena U Ba Elele* (Gallo). A representative offering of spiritual anthems from this popular Methodist male choir, who wear blazers and red waistcoats, keep time by thumping a Bible, and can make huge congregations sway and sing as one.

Imvuselelo Yase Natali *Izigi* (BMG). One of the most extraordinary gospel acts in South Africa, fronted by the charismatic – and at times plain bizarre – Reverend Makitaza. If you ever get the chance to see this group, don't miss them.

IPCC *Ummeli Wethu* (Gallo). An excellent offering from one of South Africa's most popular gospel choirs, replete with charisma and stunning melodies.

Lusanda Spiritual Group *Abanye Bayawela* (Gallo). The biggest-selling album from a gospel music sensation. Lusanda Mcinga's innovation has been to add guitar and keyboard backing to African Methodist hymns formerly rendered a cappella.

Rebecca Malope *Shwele Baba* (CCP). One of Rebecca's finest albums, with the title track a strong contender for her best-ever song and the rest of the cuts all pretty good too.

Solly Moholo *Abanye Bayawela Motlhang ke Kolobetswa "Die poppe sal dans"* (CCP). A beautiful release from the country's finest Sotho gospel artist.

Pure Magic *Greatest Hits* (EMI). Simply wonderful melodic gospel-pop from this group featuring the silky lead vocals of Vuyo Mokoena and produced by Sizwe Zako (of Rebecca Malope fame).

Various Artists *Choirs of South Africa* (Roi Music). Stirring gospel anthems delivered by mass choirs with exuberance and power. All that's missing is the visual spectacle of their members dressed in flowing garments and swaying to the mighty sounds.

Various Artists *Gospel Spirit of Africa* (Gallo). An excellent compilation of most of South Africa's top current gospel acts, including the Holy Cross Choir and the Holy Brothers, and Ladysmith Black Mambazo in gospel mode.

Various Artists *Rough Guide to South African Gospel* (Rough Guides★). A comprehensive survey of South African gospel going back to the 1950s.

Various *Joyous Celebration Volumes 1–8* (Sony, SA). Eight albums of classic gospel from some of South Africa's finest gospel artists, taken from their seemingly endless roadshow around the country, where they play to packed audiences.

Kwaito and hip-hop

Alaska *Most Wanted* (Sony Music). Well-produced, ultra-stylish *kwaito* from this well-dressed foursome, featuring great beats and some particularly impenetrable ghetto lyrics.

Bongo Maffin *Bongolution* (Sony Music). A fine release from a popular group which combines Jamaican-style ragga lyrics with *kwaito* beats, and includes the catchy hit "The Way Kungakhona".

Brenda Fassie *African Princess of Pop* and *Memeza* (CCP). The former is a posthumous survey covering the entire career of South Africa's very own Madonna; the latter, featuring the massive hit "Vul'Ndlela", was Brenda's most commercially successful effort and holds the all-time sales record (600,000 plus and still rising) for a locally produced album.

H20 *Amanzi'mtoti* (Outrageous Records). Debut album that launched hip-hop duo Siphiwe Norten and Menzi Dludla into Africa and features their biggest hit, "It's Wonderful".

Kabelo *And the Beat Goes On* (Universal). A monster hit from one of the biggest *kwaito* stars.

Mafikizolo *Sibongile* (Sony Music). Solid melodies, well sung and harmonized (the trio's female vocalist, Sibongile Nkosi, is outstanding).

Makhendlas *Jammer* (CCP). Features two massive hits, "Emenwe" and "Ayeye Aho", from the brother of *kwaito* pioneer Arthur. Makhendlas tragically shot himself immediately after killing a troublesome fan after a gig in late 1998.

Malaika *Malaika* (Sony Music). Hugely successful, this is very much in the style pioneered by Mafikizolo but features even more contemporary African-American influences.

Mandoza *Nakalakala* (CCP). Not only was this album massively popular with African urban youth, the title track has been one of very few *kwaito* recordings to truly cross over into the white pop arena.

M'Du *No Pas No Special* (Sony Music). A popular though somewhat downbeat album from one of *kwaito's* most enduring stars.

Skwatta Kamp *Khut En Joyn* (Nkuli). A fairly relentless first offering from the *enfants terrible* of the local hip-hop scene. The track "Politics" certainly gives a somewhat different take on the state of South Africa's democratic governance.

TKZee *Halloween* (BMG). Complete with trademark catchy anthems and R&B-based sounds, this is a solid early (1998) offering from these popular *kwaito* artists. The track "Magesh" is considered a classic.

Trompies *Boostin' Kabelz* (Sony Music). Kicking sounds from one of the coolest *kwaito* acts on the circuit, including the irresistible "Di Potsotso".

Zola *Mdlwembe* (EMI). The first solo album of "Mr Ghetto Fabulous", full of menacing rhythms and including the surprise gospel hit "Mzione".

Various Artists *Cape of Good Dope* (African Dope Records). Eclectic mix showcasing the label's performers, including Lions of Zion, Godessa, Moodphase5ive and Kalahari Surfers.

Various Artists *Yizo Yizo Volumes 1 & 2* (CCP). The soundtrack to South Africa's hippest TV drama, with cuts from virtually every major *kwaito* artist.

Rap and reggae

Lucky Dube *Prisoner* (Gallo). Originally a township jive singer, the late Dube made a switch to reggae that was both artistically and commercially inspired. *Prisoner* was South Africa's second bestselling album ever, full of stirring Peter Tosh-style roots tunes.

Prophets of Da City *Ghetto Code* (Universal). South Africa's rap supremos' finest release, full of tough but articulate rhymes and some seriously funky backing tracks, all in true Cape Flats style.

Neo-traditional

Amampondo *Drums for Tomorrow* (Melt 2000). South Africa's most famous marimba band deliver a fine and well-produced set here, full of their distinctive Xhosa melodies and powerful polyrhythms.

Ladysmith Black Mambazo *Favourites* (Gallo). A fine greatest hits selection from the group's first decade in the Seventies and early Eighties. Contains the wonderful "Nomathemba" and "Hello My Baby", among others.

Ladysmith Black Mambazo *Congratulations South Africa: The Ultimate Collection* (Wrasse★). This double CD is a mixed bag of Afropop and 1990s *iscathamiya*, including "Inkanyezi Nezazi", which gained the group plenty of new fans after being used in a Heinz baked-beans advert.

DZM Madosini *Power to the Women* (Melt 2000). A magnificent exposition of traditional Xhosa vocal harmonies, accompanied by the indigenous mouthbow, that is considerably enhanced by the impeccable (and expensive) production.

Mfaz'Omnyama *Ngisebenzile Mama* (Gallo). The title means "I have been working, Mum", and is amply justified by this superb set, featuring some of the best *maskanda* ever recorded.

Nothembi Mkhwebane *Akanamandl' Usathana* (Gallo). Beautiful guitar-driven sounds from the Ndebele music queen, with a cover showing Nothembi in one of her impressive traditional outfits.

Shiyani Ncgobo *Introducing* (Sheer Sound). A very fine *maskanda* album aimed largely at a foreign audience, and thus with far more variety than a domestic offering would feature.

Phuzekhemisi *Ngo 49* (Gallo). Every album recorded by this reigning *maskanda* champion features stunning guitar work, great vocals and murderous bass lines, but *Ngo 49* is perhaps his finest release, thanks to some exceptional production work by the late West Nkosi.

Women of Mambazo *Mamizolo* (Gallo). Beautiful *iscathamiya* melodies and harmonizations, not rendered by the usual male line-up but by a female group led by Nellie Shabalala, the late wife of Ladysmith Black Mambazo leader Joseph Shabalala.

Various Artists *Singing in an Open Space* (Rounder★). A survey of Zulu guitar recordings from 1962 to 1982, when the style was still referred to as "Zulu Traditional".

Jazz

Jimmy Dludlu *Essence of Rhythm* (Universal). Dludlu is the essence of
smooth jazz, and is arguably the single most popular representative of

what is in turn the most commercially successful jazz style in South Africa today.

Elite Swingsters *Siya Gida* (Universal). A final flowering from these African jazz stalwarts. Lots of great danceable music as well as some fine vocals by the late great Dolly Rathebe.

Paul Hamner *Trains to Taung* (Sheer Sound). This album is constructed around Hamner's dreamy, acoustic piano-based compositions. Now considered a classic and one of the first expositions of the new jazz of the post-apartheid era.

Abdullah Ibrahim (Dollar Brand) *Mannenberg – Is Where It's Happening* (The Sun/EMI, SA). Most of Ibrahim's catalogue veers towards the esoteric, but *Mannenberg* (1975) is the master's most accessible work by far, and also his biggest commercial success.

Sibongile Khumalo *Ancient Evenings* (Sony Music). Though a classically trained opera singer, Khumalo takes on both jazz and a variety of traditional melodies on this wonderful album, demonstrating why she is currently one of South Africa's best-loved singers.

Miriam Makeba and the Skylarks *Miriam Makeba and the Skylarks* (Teal) and *Welela* (Universal★). *Welela,* from 1989, is probably Makeba's finest album – great songs, wonderfully performed and totally lacking the ham-fisted production that encumbers so many of her American recordings. The Teal release contains 32 great recordings from the 1950s.

Manhattan Brothers *The Very Best of The Manhattan Brothers* (Gallo). A collection of classic recordings cut between 1948 and 1959 by this seminal vocal quartet, who crossed African-American secular harmonies with indigenous influences.

Mankunku *Yakal' Inkomo* (Universal). A successful blend of Coltrane influences with some classic township melodies.

Hugh Masekela *Still Grazing* (Universal) and *Black to the Future* (Sony Music). *Still Grazing* is the best available compilation of Masekela's work in the 1960s and 1970s, released to coincide with his autobiography of the same name. It includes his biggest-ever hit, "Grazing in the Grass". In the late 1990s Masekela scored a deserved hit with *Black to the Future*, featuring the excellent "Chileshe", an impassioned plea to his countrymen to discard their intense xenophobia towards African immigrants.

Moses Taiwa Molelekwa *Genes and Spirits* (Melt 2000). Fascinating jazz /drum 'n' bass fusion by a talented young pianist, who died tragically in 2001.

Zim Ngqawana *Vadzimu* (Sheer Sound). Ngqawana is one of the most revered figures in local jazz, despite also being the very antithesis of the smooth style that currently dominates. This is a typically adventurous exposition incorporating a variety of influences from hard bop to traditional African.

Sakile *Sakile* (Sony Music). A prime example of the jazz fusion popular in the 1980s, Sakile spawned two major figures in saxophonist Khaya Mahlangu and bass player Sipho Gumede.

Philip Tabane and Malombo *Unh!* (Elektra★) and *Ke a Bereka* (Tusk). The masterful guitarist, with a sound and a style entirely his own, does his take on Afro-jazz. The second release veers in a more traditional direction, but is still unmistakeably Tabane.

Various Artists *African Connection Parts I–IV* (Sheer Sound). This series of double-CD compilations from the country's premier independent label provides an accessible survey of current South African jazz.

Political

Mzwakhe Mbuli *Resistance is Defence* (Earthworks★). Great sample of the militant lyricism of the people's poet, including a moving ode to Mandela's release.

Various Artists *Freedom Songs* (Making Music Productions). Superb double-CD set documenting the "struggle music" that helped power anti-apartheid resistance.

Afropop

Bayete *Umkhaya-Lo* (Polygram). A seminal fusion of South African sounds with laid-back soul and funk, blended by lead singer Jabu Khany-ile's unique mixing talent and spiced with his beautifully soothing vocals.

Yvonne Chaka Chaka *Bombani* (Teal) and *The Best of Yvonne Chaka Chaka* (Teal, SA). *Bombani* bombed, yet is Yvonne's most intricate and interesting release, mixing a range of traditional styles and featuring wonderful melodies. *The Best of* is pretty much all the 1980s disco-style Yvonne you need, including her biggest hit "Umqombothi".

Johnny Clegg *Best of Juluka/Savuka* (Universal). Born in England, the prolific Clegg mixes white pop harmonies and township rhythms, gaining him a multiracial following in South Africa.

Ladysmith Black Mambazo *Heavenly* (Gallo/Spectrum★). An inspired and commercially successful foray into Afropop, featuring solo versions of various pop classics as well as vocal collaborations with Dolly Parton and Lou Rawls.

Vusi Mahlasela *Silang Mabele* (BMG). Lush harmonies and lilting melodies from this sweet-voiced township balladeer.

Thandiswa Mazwai *Zabalaza* (Gallo). Although somewhat over-produced in its attempt to cover too many musical bases, this album by the ex-singer with *kwaito* outfit Bongo Maffin is more than redeemed by the very powerful title track.

Busi Mhlongo *Urbanzulu* (Melt 2000). An immaculately and expensively produced Zulu *maskanda*-pop classic from this powerful jazz vocalist and *sangoma*.

Ringo *Sondelani* (CCP). A superb modern reworking of traditional Xhosa sounds by this bald Capetonian heart-throb, including the hit track *Sondela*, which has become one of South Africa's most popular love songs.

White pop and rock

Danny K *J23* (Gallo) and *Same Difference* (CCP). The first is an elaborately produced melange of R&B and hip-hop from a vocalist massively popular with the country's white-teenyboppers and 20-somethings, while the second, a collaboration with *kwaito* star Mandoza, won the "best album" title at the 2007 SA Music Awards.

Freedom's Children *Astra* (Fresh). Recorded in 1970, *Astra* is considered by an older generation of local rock connoisseurs to be the single-finest product of the country's "underground music" movement.

Just Jinger *All Comes Around* (BMG). Unexpectedly racking up sales of over 50,000 copies, this classic 1997 release demonstrated that local English rock was far from dead.

Mango Groove *The Best of Mango Groove* (Gallo). Mango Groove's mixture of white pop leavened with a touch of pennywhistle/township jive was briefly – from the late 1980s up to the dawn of democracy – the most commercially successful sound in South African music.

Springbok Nude Girls *Afterlife Satisfaction* (Sony Music). One of South Africa's most popular white bands before they disbanded, here delivering a powerful, if not particularly original, belting rock set.

Watershed *In the Meantime* (EMI). Highly melodic, well-produced pop rock; lead singer Craig Hinds' voice has a particularly appealing warm quality.

Various Artists *The Best of SA Pop Vols 1–3* (Gallo). Three double CDs covering all the biggest radio hits of the local English pop scene from the 1960s through to the early 1980s.

Afrikaans

Chris Blignaut *Die Juweel Jare* (Gallo). Classic vocal material from the 1950s and early 1960s by the first Afrikaans recording star.

Anton Goosen *Bushrock* (Gallo). Goosen is one of South Africa's finest songwriters and performers. His style might best be described as Afrikaans folk rock, and his recordings are always well produced. *Bushrock* is a good place to start checking him out; it's his one English-language album.

Steve Hofmeyr *Toeka* (EMI). A smooth pop vocalist, Hofmeyer is currently the most commercially successful artist in Afrikaans music. In *Toeka* he trots through a bunch of classic songs from the past three decades.

Johannes Kerkorrel *Ge-Trans-To-Meer* (Gallo-Tusk). The late Kerkorrel was the leading light of the Afrikaans alternative scene of the 1990s, his brand of angst-laden pop also popular in Holland and Belgium.

Klipwerf Orkes *Hantam Deurnag* (Universal). Rollicking instrumental music for dancing that at times sounds almost Cajun, from the hugely popular exponents of modern *boeremusiek*.

With contributions by Rob Allingham

Books

For a country with such a low proportion of its population literate and reading regularly, South Africa generates a good amount of literature, particularly about subjects the literate feel guilty about – namely, politics and history. Titles marked ⚥ are particularly recommended.

History, society and anthropology

William Beinart *Twentieth-Century South Africa*. A useful and concise account of South African history, with an emphasis on economic history that manages to emphasize the essential without descending into tedium. His predictions for the future seem wobbly now, but there's nothing unusual about that.

Terry Bell and Dumisa Ntsebeza *Unfinished Business: South Africa, Apartheid and Truth*. A critical account from the left of the failings of the Truth and Reconciliation Commission, which argues that many features of apartheid remain intact and asks how long South Africa's "miracle" can survive.

Axel-Ivar Berglund *Zulu Thought Patterns and Symbolism*. A sensitive and knowledgeable account of rural Zulu world views, as told to the author, with the minimum of interpretation. He does, however, set the scene well, and make thought-provoking connections between the various views expressed, while bending over backwards to avoid tedious judgementalism.

Ian Berry *Living Apart*. Superbly evocative and moving photographs spanning the 1950s to 1990s, which chart a compelling vision of the politics of the nation, but at the level of the individual.

Philip Bonner *Kings, Commoners and Concessionaries*. The definitive history (so far) of nineteenth-century Swaziland, by a skilled historian with a gratifying grasp of the source material and mostly reliable judgement. Its one weakness is a lack of oral historical research.

Emile Boonzaier, Candy Malherbe, Andy Smith and Penny Berens *The Cape Herders: A History of the Khoikhoi of Southern Africa*. This accessible account of the Khoikhoi successfully explodes the many prejudices and myths that surround them and explores their way of life, their interaction with Europeans, and what remains of them today.

Richard Calland *Anatomy of South Africa: Who Holds the Power*. An incisive dissection of politics and power in South Africa today, from one of the country's most respected commentators.

Jane Carruthers *The Kruger National Park: A Social and Political History*. Examining the scientific and ideological forces that gave rise to the creation of Kruger National Park, this fascinating book asks important questions about our notions of nature and conservation.

Clive Chipkin *Johannesburg Style*. Perhaps the title is a contradiction in terms, but this is an intriguing study of architecture – and society – in the South African city.

J. Christopher *The Atlas of Apartheid.* Detailed but accessible study of the policy and implementation of urban and regional planning that gave South African towns and cities their current form.

Paul Faber *Group Portraits South Africa: Nine Family Histories.* Fascinating account revealing the complexities of South Africa past and present, of the histories of nine South African families of different races, backgrounds and aspirations. One of the families featured is that of writer Sol Plaatje. Includes photos and illustrations.

Hermann Giliomee and Bernard Mbenga *A New History of South Africa.* A comprehensive, reliable and entertaining account of South Africa's history, published in 2007, making it the first new major work on the topic in a decade.

Stephen Gill *A Short History of Lesotho.* The best single volume you'll find on Lesotho's history, a thoughtful and well-informed account by the chief archivist at the Morija Museum. Gill clearly loves Lesotho and has little sympathy for its many invaders, but is a little over-generous in his account of Lesotho's missionaries.

Barbara Hutton *Robben Island: Symbol of Resistance.* A straightforward, illustrated account of Robben Island from prehistoric times to the present, with a good overview of prison conditions in the apartheid years.

Antjie Krog *Country of My Skull.* A deeply personal and gripping account of the hearings of the Truth and Reconciliation Commission. Krog, an Afrikaner former-SABC radio journalist and poet, reveals the complexity of horrors committed by apartheid, and also paints an admiring picture of Commission head Desmond Tutu.

Hilda Kuper *The Swazi, A South African Kingdom.* A combination of anthropology and history, written in the 1960s. The theoretical perspectives seem pretty dated now, though Kuper's observations still sound sharp. Her political insight was often astute too, though she was too fond of the Dlamini royal house to provide much of a critical perspective on them.

J.D. Lewis-Williams *Discovering Southern African Rock Art* and *Images of Power: Understanding Bushman Rock Art.* Concise books written by an expert in the field, full of drawings and photos. The author concludes that most of the paintings depict images perceived while in a state of shamanic trance, and reflect a San world-view in which the spiritual and material were both a part of everyday life. Also worth investigating are the same author's *San Spirituality, Roots, Expression and Social Consequences* and *Stories that Float from Afar: Ancestral Folklore of the San of Southern Africa.*

Hein Marais *South Africa: Limits to Change? The Political Economy of Transition.* A readable assessment of why the privileged classes remain just that, and why the new government has followed relatively conservative economic policies.

Noel Mostert *Frontiers: The Epic of South Africa's Creation and the Tragedy of the Xhosa People.* An academically solid, brilliantly written history of the Xhosa of the Eastern Cape, and their tragic fate in the frontier wars against the British.

Alan Mountain *An Unsung Heritage: Perspectives on Slavery.* An account of the nature of slavery in the Cape, and the contribution imported slaves made to the fabric of the area today. Best of all is the guide to slave heritage sites in the Cape Peninsula, Winelands and West Coast, and along the Garden Route, with attractive photos and illustrations.

Mike Nicol *Sea-Mountain, Fire City: Living in Cape Town*. Basing his narrative on the apparently prosaic business of moving house from one part of the city to another, Nicol maps many of the fissures that make Cape Town such a divided city.

Dougie Oakes (ed) *Illustrated History of South Africa*. Although now over a decade old, this physically weighty but lightly written and beautifully illustated volume is essential for anyone seriously interested in the rise of apartheid and the country's turbulent passage to democracy.

Thomas Pakenham *The Boer War*. The definitive liberal history of the Anglo-Boer War that reads grippingly like a novel, managing to maintain a panoramic sweep of events while homing in on the quirks and foibles of the individuals involved.

Jeff Peires *The Dead Will Arise* and *The House of Phalo*. The leading historian of the Xhosa tells in beautifully readable prose the stories of the Eastern Cape before the arrival of whites, as well as the impact of colonialism on their lives and society.

Allister Sparks *Beyond the Miracle: Inside the New South Africa*. An examination by a veteran journalist of the prospects for South Africa, after ten years of democracy, looking beyond the initial buoyancy following the end of apartheid to emerging patterns in its government.

Desmond Tutu *No Future Without Forgiveness*. The Truth and Reconciliation Commission as described by its chairman. There are better accounts of the hearings, but the book offers essential insight into one of South Africa's most unlikely heroes.

Nigel Worden, Elizabeth van Heyningen and Vivian Bickford-Smith *Cape Town: The Making of a City*. The definitive and highly readable illustrated account of the social and political development of South Africa's first city from 1620 to 1899, written by three leading historians based at the University of Cape Town. A companion volume covers the twentieth century.

Autobiography and biography

Breyten Breytenbach *The True Confessions of an Albino Terrorist*. In vividly poetic language, the exiled Afrikaner poet tells the entertaining story of how he returned to South Africa in 1975 – only to be arrested and jailed for seven years.

Luli Callinicos *Oliver Tambo: Beyond the Engeli Mountains*. The life story of the man who was once president of the ANC in exile, leading the fight against apartheid while Mandela languished in jail. The only ANC leader who could hold a candle to Mandela, Tambo did not live to see the fruits of his struggle – he died in 1993, on the eve of liberation.

J.M. Coetzee *Boyhood* and *Youth*. Two riveting and disquieting accounts of growing up in a provincial town, and the author subsequently finding his way in the world, both in South Africa and London. Notable especially for the candour with which Coetzee, who won the 2003 Nobel prize for literature, writes about relationships with his mother and father.

Robin Denniston *Trevor Huddleston, A Life*. An inspiring biography of the

English churchman who worked among Johannesburg's urban blacks in the 1950s and later founded the Anti-Apartheid Movement.

Mark Gevisser *Portraits of Power: Profiles of a Changing South Africa.* Although now over a decade old, this collection of forty mini-biographies cutting through a cross section of South African society still offers acute insights into a number of the country's significant players, placing them in their social context.

Nelson Mandela *Long Walk to Freedom.* The superb bestselling autobiography of the South African president. Mandela's generosity of spirit and tremendous understanding of the delicate balance between principle and tactics come through very strongly, and the book is wonderfully evocative of his early years and intensely moving about his long years in prison. However, when it comes to his love life, the byzantine intricacies of ANC politics during its long years as an illegal organization, and the story behind the negotiated settlement, Mandela is more diplomatic than candid.

Greg Marinovich and Joao Silva *The Bang Bang Club: Snapshots from a Hidden War.* The compelling story of four news photographers who snapped the country's most violent townships in the late 1980s and early 1990s. Two survived to tell the tale; Ken Oosterbroek was killed in crossfire days before the 1994 elections and Ken Carter committed suicide not long afterwards.

Benjamin Pogrund *How Can Man Die Better? The Life of Robert Sobukwe.* Long-overdue story of one of the most important anti-apartheid liberation heroes, the late leader of the Pan Africanist Congress and a contemporary of Nelson Mandela, feared so much by the white government that they passed a special law – The Sobukwe Clause – to keep him in solitary confinement on Robben Island after he'd served his sentence.

Albie Sachs *The Soft Vengeance of a Freedom Fighter.* ANC veteran Sachs here relates the story of how, in exile in Mozambique, he was almost killed by a South African security police bomb. The book vividly traces his recovery and the mental difficulties he went through to emerge with a new vision of the struggle. Today Sachs is a judge in the South African Constitutional Court.

Anthony Sampson *Mandela, The Authorised Biography.* Released to coincide with Mandela's retirement from the presidency in 1999, Sampson's authoritative volume competes with *A Long Walk to Freedom* in both interest and sheer poundage. Firmly grounded in the author's long association with his subject, as well as exhaustive research and interviews, it offers a broader perspective and sharper analysis than the autobiography.

Chris van Wyk *Shirley, Goodness and Mercy: A Childhood Memoir.* A memoir of growing up in a working-class coloured family in Johannesburg during the apartheid era, with humorous and poignant touches.

The arts

David Coplan *In Township Tonight: South Africa's Black City Music and Theatre.* Newly updated classic that traces local music from its indigenous roots through slave orchestras and

looks at its humanizing influence in the harsh environment of the apartheid townships.

S. Francis and Rico *Madam and Eve.* Various volumes of telling and witty cartoons conveying the daily struggle between an African domestic worker and her white madam in the northern suburbs of Johannesburg, these cartoons say more about post-apartheid society than countless academic tomes.

Z.B. Molefe and Mike Mzileni *A Common Hunger to Sing*. Large-format, well-illustrated tribute to the country's black women singers and the obstacles they have overcome.

Paul Weinberg *Then & Now*. Collection by eight photographers, tracing the changes in their subjects and approaches as South Africa moved from apartheid into the present democratic era.

Sue Williamson *Resistance Art in South Africa* and *Art in South Africa: The Future Present*. Taken together, these two volumes map the course of South African art from the early 1980s to the present day, accompanied by a commentary that's both thoughtful and concise enough to let the artworks speak for themselves.

Zapiro *Da Zuma Code*. In a country where satire is in notoriously short supply, Zapiro is the leading cartoonist, consistently exposing what needs to be exposed. This book is number eleven in a series, containing work originally published in a number of dailies as well as the *Mail & Guardian* and *Sunday Times*.

Travel writing

Richard Dobson and Ruben Mowszowski *Karoo Moons: A Photographic Journey*. If you need encouragement to explore the desert interior of South Africa, these enticing images should do the trick.

Sihle Khumalo *Dark Continent, My Black Arse*. Insightful and witty account by a black South African who quit his well-paid job to realize a dream of travelling from the Cape to Cairo by public transport.

Ben Maclennan *The Wind Makes Dust: Four Centuries of Travel in South Africa*. A remarkable anthology of fascinating travel pieces, meticulously unearthed and researched.

Dervla Murphy *South from the Limpopo: Travels Through South Africa*. A fascinating and intrepid journey – by bicycle – through the new South Africa. The author isn't afraid to explore the complexities and paradoxes of this country.

Paul Theroux *Dark Star Safari*. Theroux's powerful account of his overland trip from Cairo to Cape Town, with a couple of chapters on South Africa, including an account of meeting writer Nadine Gordimer.

Specialist guides

G.M. Branch *Two Oceans*. Don't be fooled by the coffee-table format; this is a comprehensive guide to southern Africa's marine life.

David Bristow *Best Hikes in Southern Africa* and *Best Hikes of the Drakensberg*. The South Africa book is a well-written and reliable guide that does your homework for you, selecting the best trails from a confusingly extensive lot. The Drakensberg paperback is indispensable for anyone exploring the massif, with detailed route instructions and informative background about natural history.

Brett Hilton-Barber and Lee Berger *A Guide to the Cradle of Mankind.* Full of photographs and illustrations, this indispensible guide takes you around the world heritage sites of the Cradle of Humankind near Jo'burg – Sterkfontein, Swartkrans and Kromdraai.

Jaynee Levy *The Complete Guide to Walks & Trails in Southern Africa.* Although now somewhat dated, this encyclopedic tome is still a hiker's bible, covering over five hundred trails suitable for all abilities, with practical information about what to take and where to book. One to invest in if you're a keen trailist spending time in the country, but definitely not light reading to take on a walk.

Mike Lundy *Best Walks in the Cape Peninsula.* Handy, solidly researched guide to some of the peninsula's many walks, and small enough to fit comfortably in a backpack.

Willie and Sandra Olivier *Hiking Trails of Southern Africa.* Covers less ground than Levy, but in its revised 2007 edition is far more up to date and is written up with greater depth, including excellent natural history commentary on each trail.

Colin Paterson-Jones *Best Walks of the Garden Route.* Handy for accessing some of South Africa's premier coastline and forests, away from the ribbon of development along the Garden Route.

Steve Pike *Surfing South Africa.* Classic guide, updated in 2007, to everything to do with swells, surf spots and waves by a veteran journalist and surfing aficionado.

Birds

Hugh Chittenden (ed) *Robert's Bird Guide.* The definitive reference work on the subcontinent's entire avifauna population: if it's not in Robert's, it doesn't exist. Alas, the weight of this makes it more of a book to consult in a library than on a trip.

Ian Sinclair *Sasol Birds of Southern Africa.* Comprehensive volume full of photos geared to the field, with useful pointers to aid quick identification.

Mammals

Richard D. Estes *Safari Companion.* Although this can occasionally sound like a manual on how to treat your porters, it's basically a vital guide on how to understand African wildlife, with interesting and readable information on the behaviour and social structures of the major species.

Chris and Tilde Stuart *Field Guide to the Mammals of Southern Africa.* One of the best books on this subject, providing excellent background and clear illustrations to help you recognize a species.

Flora

Richard Cowling and Shirley Pierce *Namaqualand: A Succulent Desert*. Botanists Cowling and Pierce explain how Namaqualand's flowers can survive in such harsh desert conditions, with some good photography supporting the text.

L. McMahon and M. Fraser *A Fynbos Year*. Exquisitely illustrated and well-written book about South Africa's unique floral kingdom.

Keith and Meg Coates Palgrave *Trees of Southern Africa*. The authoritative book on the subject, but too big to carry around.

Freeman Patterson *Namaqualand: Garden of the Gods*. In this classic coffee-table book, Canadian photographer Freeman Patterson succeeds admirably in conveying the beauty and wonder of Namaqualand's flowers.

Braam and Piet van Wyk *Field Guide to the Trees of Southern Africa*. Covering Southern Africa's 900 species, this fully comprehensive guide is more practical to carry than Coates Palgrave.

Wine

🏃 **Philip van Zyl (ed)** *John Platter South African Wines*. Annually updated pocket guide to South Africa's current output, with ratings by the country's top wine writers.

Elmari Swart and Izak Smit *The Essential Guide to South African Wines: Terroir & Travel*. Detailed field guide to South Africa's wine regions breaking them down into "pockets" with their own endemic *terroir*, with maps and coordinates (useful if you're travelling with a GPS) for getting to specific wineries.

Fiction

Tatamkhulu Afrika *The Innocents*. Set in the struggle years, this novel examines the moral and ethical issues of the time from a Muslim perspective.

🏃 **Herman Charles Bosman** *Unto Dust*. A superb collection of short stories from South Africa's master of the genre, all set in the tiny Afrikaner farming district of Groot Marico in the 1930s. The tales share a narrator who, with delicious irony, reveals the passions and foibles of his community.

André Brink *A Chain of Voices*. This superbly evocative tale of Cape eighteenth-century life explores the impact of slavery on one farming family, culminating in a dramatic and murderous end.

🏃 **Michael Chapman** *Omnibus of a Century of South African Short Stories*. The most comprehensive ever collection of South African tale-telling, starting with San oral stories and working up to twenty-first-century writing, including work by Olive Schreiner, Alan Paton, Es'kia Mphahlele and Ivan Vladislavic.

Imraan Coovadia *Green Eyed Thieves*. Story shortlisted for the M-Net Award for English fiction, in which the location straddles Johannesburg and New York. The cast of characters includes twins in a family of thieves, various other crooks and lawyers, George Bush, a Pakistani brigadier and Mohammed Atta (pilot of one of the planes that flew into the World Trade Center on 9/11).

J.M. Coetzee *Age of Iron* and *Disgrace*. In a *Mail & Guardian* poll of writers, *Age of Iron* emerged as the finest South African novel of the 1990s. The book depicts a white female classics professor dying from cancer during the political craziness of the 1980s. She is joined by a tramp who sets up home in her garden, and thus evolves a curious and fascinating relationship that transforms her. But even better is *Disgrace*, a disturbing story of a university professor's fall from grace, set in the Eastern Cape. No writer better portrays the ever-present undercurrents of violence and unease in South Africa.

Achmat Dangor *Bitter Fruit*. From one of the best Cape Town writers, *Bitter Fruit* is the story of the son of two anti-apartheid activists, and of an act of violence and injustice threading two generations, which is resurrected by the Truth and Reconciliation Commission. The book portrays a brittle family, a dysfunctional society, and how we address – or fail to address – the past's deepest wounds.

Nadine Gordimer *July's People*. A liberal white family is rescued by its gardener July from revolution, and taken to his home village for safety, where Gordimer teases out the power dynamics of this fraught situation with customary insight and eloquence.

Dan Jacobson *The Trap* and *A Dance in the Sun*. Taut novellas written in the 1950s and published in one volume, skilfully portraying the developing tensions and nuances of the white-versus-black lives of the era.

Shaun Johnson *The Native Commissioner*. Eloquent account of a government official unable to come to terms with the white man's place in Africa. It won its author the 2006 M-Net Award for English fiction.

Alex La Guma *A Walk in the Night and Other Stories*. An evocative collection of short stories by this talented political activist/author, set in District Six, the ethnically mixed quarter of Cape Town razed by the apartheid government.

Anne Landsman *The Devil's Chimney*. A stylish and entertaining piece of magic realism about the Karoo town of Oudtshoorn in the days of the ostrich-feather boom.

Zakes Mda *Ways of Dying*, *His Madonna of Excelsior* and *The Heart of Redness*. The first is a brilliant tale of a professional mourner, full of sly insights into the culture of black South Africa; *Madonna* focuses on a family at the heart of the scandalous case in the Free State, in which nineteen people from the small town of Excelsior were charged with breaking the Immorality Act, which forbade sex between races; while *Heart*, which won the *Sunday Times* Fiction Prize, weaves the historical story of the Eastern Cape cattle killings with a contemporary narrative.

Niq Mhlongo *Dog Eat Dog*. One of the irreverent exponents of post-apartheid literature, Mhlongo has been described as "the voice of the *kwaito* [hip-hop] generation". This novel looks at the life of a student who spends his time bunking classes, picking up girls and playing the system.

Thomas Mofolo *Chaka*. Lesotho's first great fiction writer, Mofolo penned this epic tale in Sotho in 1909. The book centres on the Zulu king Shaka, here portrayed as a man fatally controlled by his strong passions. The original English translation gave the text a misleadingly biblical slant, which has been corrected in this newer translation by Daniel Kunene.

Isaac Mogotsi *Alexandra Tales.* Delightful tales of family life in the run-down, lively homes of Johannesburg's Alexandra township, all with a clever and provocative twist in the tail.

Phaswane Mpe *Welcome to Our Hillbrow.* A young black man from the rural areas hits the fleshpots of present-day Hillbrow, where xenophobia, violence and AIDS (from which the author subsequently died) reign, in an exploration of the clash between economic reality and traditional beliefs.

Es'kia Mphahlele *Down Second Avenue.* A classic autobiographical novel set in the 1940s in the impoverished township of Alexandra, where Mphahlele grew up as part of a large extended family battling daily to survive the problems and injustices of the age.

Alan Paton *Cry, The Beloved Country.* Classic 1948 novel encapsulating the deep injustices of the country, by one of South Africa's great liberals. With tremendous lyricism, the book describes the journey of a black pastor from rural Natal to Johannesburg (which is depicted as a veritable Sodom and Gomorrah) to rescue his missing son from its clutches.

Kathy Perkins *Black South African Women – An Anthology of Plays.* Groundbreaking collection of ten plays by a wide range of known and unknown playwrights such as Gcina Mhlope, Sindiwe Nagona, Muthal Naidoo and Lueen Conning.

Sol Plaatje *Mhudi.* The first English novel by a South African writer, *Mhudi* is set in the 1830s, at a time when the Afrikaner Great Trek had just begun. It's the epic tale of a young rural woman who saves her future husband from the raids of the Ndebele, who were then a powerful state in the Marico region. The author was a political activist and one of the founder members of the ANC.

Linda Rode *Crossing Over.* Collection of 26 stories by new and emerging South African writers on the experiences of adolescence and early adulthood in a period of political transition.

Olive Schreiner *Story of an African Farm.* The first-ever South African novel, written in 1883 (when the author used a male pseudonym). Though subject to the ideologies of the era, the book nonetheless explores with a genuinely open vision the tale of two female cousins living on a remote Karoo farm, when their young lives are disrupted by an Irish traveller.

Mongane Wally Serote *To Every Birth Its Blood.* Serote's only novel is a powerfully turbulent affair that traces how a township man who is interested only in jazz, drinking and sex gains a political consciousness through the humiliations he is subjected to by authority.

Ivan Vladislavic *The Restless Supermarket, The Exploded View* and *Portrait with Keys: Joburg and What-What.* *The Restless Supermarket* is a dark and intricate urban satire from South Africa's most exciting contemporary writer, about Johannesburg's notorious Hillbrow district during the last days of apartheid. *The Exploded View* is a collection of four interlinked pieces, a great follow-up from a writer who's unrivalled at evoking the contradictions and fascinations of Jo'burg, while *Portrait* is not so much a novel as an account, in a series of numbered texts, of the city that inspires Vladislavic's imagination.

Poetry

Guy Butler (ed) *A Book of South African Verse*; **Jack Cope and Uys Krige (eds)** *The Penguin Book of South African Verse*. Early anthologies that, for better or for worse, "mapped" South African poetry. Butler's comment in his introduction – "Most of our poets have tried to belong to Africa and, finding her savage, shallow and uncooperative, have been forced to give their allegiance, not to any other country, but to certain basic conceptions" (read Europe) – remains controversial.

Roy Campbell *Selected Poems*. Very much a figure from a period of South Africa's literary colonialism, Roy Campbell, despite his sometimes politically repellent views, remains a major figure, and one of the most lyrically gifted and satirically sharp poets that South Africa has ever produced.

Tim Couzens and Essop Patel (eds) *Return of the Amasi Bird: Black South African Poetry 1891–1981*. Comprehensive collection of black South African poetry, which stretches right back to the early colonial era and extends to the cries of liberation and beyond.

Jeremy Cronin *Inside* and *Out*. Written by a leading member of the South African Communist Party, *Inside*, first published in 1983, is probably the most inventive work of South African prison poetry. *Out* charts Cronin's reaction to post-apartheid South Africa, and continuing resistance to the many forms of betrayal of South Africa's larger populace.

Ingrid de Kok *Transfer, Terrestrial Things* and *Seasonal Fires*. Probably the most intelligent of South Africa's feminist poets, technically adroit and always moving.

Denis Hirson (ed) *The Lava of this Land: South African Poetry 1960–1996*. This comprehensive anthology of South African poetry includes work from the oral period, as well as translations from Afrikaans and other languages. The most useful introduction to date.

Ingrid Jonker *Selected Poems*. One of the few Afrikaans-language poets to whom English translation does justice. The poems display a remarkable rawness in depicting the outrage of 1960s apartheid, as well as a grief-stricken lyricism from a poet who drowned herself in 1965 off Sea Point.

Mongane Wally Serote *Selected Poems*. The leading light among South Africa's many protest poets, with a work that ranges from early rage to incantations of freedom, leavened with humour and startling imagery.

Stephen Watson *The Other City*. No one better evokes Cape Town's changeable beauty, though Watson also writes of the heart and the great universal themes that make him a first-rate poet of the world, rather than just of his native city.

Language

Language

Language

S outh Africa has eleven official languages, all of which have equal status under the law. In practice, however, **English** is the *lingua franca* that dominates politics, commerce and the media. If you're staying in the main cities and national parks you'll rarely, if ever, need to use any other language. **Afrikaans**, although a language you seldom need to speak, nevertheless remains very much in evidence and you will certainly encounter it on official forms and countless signs, particularly on the road; for this reason we give a comprehensive list of written Afrikaans terms you could come across.

Unless you're planning on staying a very long time, there's little point trying to get to grips with the whole gamut of indigenous African languages, of which there are nine official ones and several unofficial ones. Having said that, it's always useful to know a few phrases of the local indigenous language, especially greetings – the use of which will always be appreciated even if you aren't able to carry your foray through to a proper conversation. For basic greetings in Afrikaans, and five of the most commonly used indigenous African languages, see the box on p.894.

The nine official African languages are split into four groups: **Nguni**, which consists of Zulu, Xhosa, siSwati and Ndebele; **Sotho**, which comprises Northern Sotho, Southern Sotho (or Sesotho) and Tswana; and **Venda** and **Tsonga**. Most black people speak languages in the first two groups. In common with all indigenous southern African languages, these operate under very different principles to European languages in that their sentences are dominated by the noun, with which the other words, such as verbs and adjectives, must agree in person, gender, number or case. Known as concordal agreement, this is achieved by supplementing word stems – the basic element of each word – with prefixes or suffixes to change meaning.

The Nguni group, and Southern Sotho, both contain a few **clicks** adopted from San languages, which are difficult for speakers of European languages. In practice, most English-speaking South Africans sidestep the issue altogether and pronounce African names in ways that are often only approximations. To get to grips with the Zulu phrases we've listed, it's worth investing in one of the Zulu-language cassettes available in bookshops in KwaZulu-Natal. Tapes for other languages can be more difficult to come by, but it's always worth checking out bookshops.

English

South African English is a mixed bag, one language with many variants. Forty percent of whites are mother-tongue English speakers, many of whom believe that they are (or at least should be) speaking standard British English. In fact, South African English has its own distinct character, and is as different from the Queen's English as is Australian. Its most notable characteristic is its huge and rich vocabulary, with unique words and usages, some drawn from Afrikaans and the indigenous African languages. The hefty *Oxford Dictionary of South African English* makes an interesting browse.

As a language used widely by non-native speakers, there is great **variation in pronunciation** and usage – largely a result of mother-tongue interference from other languages. Take, for example, the sentence "The bad bird sat on the bed", which speakers of some African languages (which don't distinguish between some of the vowel sounds of English) might pronounce as "The bed bed set on the bed". While some English-speaking whites feel that their language is being mangled and misused, linguists argue that it is simply being transformed.

Afrikaans

Broadly speaking, Afrikaans is a dialect of **Dutch**, which became modified on the Cape frontier through its encounter with French, German and English settlers, and is peppered with words and phrases from indigenous tongues as well as languages used by slaves. Some historians argue, very plausibly, that Afrikaans was first written in Arabic script in the early nineteenth century by Cape Muslims.

Despite this heritage, the language was used by Afrikaners from the late nineteenth century onwards as a key element in the construction of their racially exclusive ethnic identity. The attempt, in 1976, by the apartheid government to make Afrikaans the medium of instruction in black schools, which led to the Soweto uprising, confirmed the hated status of the language for many urban Africans, which persists to this day.

Contrary to popular belief outside South Africa, the majority of Afrikaans-speakers are not white but coloured, and the language, far from dying out, is in fact understood by more South Africans than any other language. It's the predominant tongue in the Western and Northern Cape provinces, and in the Free State is the language of the media.

Afrikaans signs

Bed en Ontbyt	Bed and breakfast	**Links**	Left
Derde	Third	**Lughawe**	Airport
Dankie	Thank you	**Mans**	Men
Doeane	Customs	**Mark**	Market
Drankwinkel	Liquor shop	**Ompad**	Detour
Droe vrugte	Dry fruit	**Pad**	Road
Eerste	First	**Padwerke voor**	Roadworks ahead
Vrugte	Fruit	**Pastorie**	Parsonage
Geen ingang	No entry	**Perron**	Platform (train station)
Gevaar	Danger	**Plaas**	Farm
Grens	Border	**Poskantoor**	Post office
Hoof	Main	**Regs**	Right
Hoog	High	**Ry**	Go
Ingang	Entry	**Sentrum**	Centre
Inligting	Information	**Singel**	Crescent
Kantoor	Office	**Slaghuis**	Butcher
Kerk	Church	**Stadig**	Slow
Kort	Short	**Stad**	City

Stad sentrum	City/town centre		Verbode	Prohibited
Stasie	Station		Verkeer	Traffic
Straat	Street		Versigtig	Carefully
Strand	Beach		Vierde	Fourth
Swembad	Swimming pool		Vrouens	Women
Toegang	Admission		Vyfde	Fifth
Tweede	Second			

The Nguni group

Zulu (or isiZulu), the most widely spoken black African language in South Africa, is understood by around twelve million people. It's the mother tongue of residents of the southeastern parts of the country, including the whole of KwaZulu-Natal, the eastern Free State, southern Mpumalanga and Gauteng. Some linguists believe that Zulu's broad reach could make it an alternative to English as a South African *lingua franca*. Don't confuse Zulu with **Fanakalo**, which is a pidgin Zulu mixed with other languages. Still sometimes spoken on the mines, it is not popular with most Zulu speakers, though many white South Africans tend to believe it is.

For all practical purposes, **siSwati**, the language spoken in Swaziland, is almost identical to Zulu, but for historical reasons has developed its own identity. The same applies to **Ndebele**, which shares around 95 percent in common with Zulu. It broke off from Zulu (around the same time as siSwati) when a group of Zulu-speakers fled north to escape the expansionism of Shaka. Ndebele is now spoken in pockets of Gauteng and North West provinces as well as throughout southern Zimbabwe.

Xhosa (an example of a word beginning with a click sound) is Nelson Mandela's mother tongue, which he shares with seven million other South Africans, predominantly in the Eastern Cape. The language is also spoken by Africans in the Western Cape, most of whom are concentrated in Cape Town.

The Sotho group

Northern Sotho dialects, which are numerous and diverse, are spoken by around 2.5 million people in a huge arc of South Africa that takes in the country around the Kruger National Park, around to the Botswana border and south from there to Pretoria. **Southern Sotho**, one of the first African languages to be written, is spoken in the Free State, parts of Gauteng, as well as Lesotho and the areas of the Eastern Cape bordering it.

Tswana, also characterized by a great diversity of dialects, is geographically the most widespread language in southern Africa, and is the principal language of Botswana. In South Africa its dialects are dispersed through the Northern Cape, the Free State and North West provinces.

As with the Nguni languages, the distinctions between the languages in the Sotho group owe more to history, politics and geography than to pure linguistic factors; speakers of some Northern Sotho dialects can understand some dialects of Tswana more readily than they can other Northern Sotho dialects.

Pronouncing place names

The largest number of unfamiliar place names that visitors are likely to encounter in South Africa are of Afrikaans origin, followed by names with origins in the Nguni group of languages. **Afrikaans** and English names are found across the country, while African names tend to be more localized, according to the predominant language in that area. **Nguni group** pronunciations generally apply in the Eastern Cape, KwaZulu-Natal, parts of Mpumalanga and Swaziland, while **Sotho group** names will be found in North West Province, Limpopo, the Northern Cape, Free State and parts of Gauteng. Sometimes you'll encounter names with **Khoisan** derivations, such as "Tsitsikamma" (in which the *ts* is pronounced as in "tsunami"). The pronunciation tips below are intended as a guide and are neither comprehensive nor definitive.

Afrikaans

In common with other Germanic languages, Afrikaans has a number of consonants that are **guttural**. Apart from these, most consonant sounds will be unproblematic for English-speakers. However Afrikaans has numerous vowels and diphthongs, which have rough English equivalents but which are frequently spelled in an unfamiliar way – take, for example, the variation in the pronunciation of the letter "e" in the list below.

Vowels and diphthongs

a as in Kakamas	u as in pup
aa as in Braamfontein	a as in car
ae as in Haenertsburg	a as in car but slightly lengthened
aai as in Smitswinkelbaai	y as in dry
au as in Augrabies	o as in blow
ar as in Garies	u as in burrow
e as in Bontebok	er as in rubber, but clipped
e as in Clarens	e as in angel
e as in Hemel-en-Aarde	ee as in beer
ee as in Riebeek	ee as in beer
ei as in Bloemfontein	ai as in pain
eu as in Keurboomstrand	u as in cure
i as in Calitzdorp	e as in angel
ie as in Diepwalle	i as in pick
o as in Bontebok	o as in cork, but clipped
oe as in Bloemfontein	oo as in book
oo as in Kloof	oo as in boor
ou as in Oudrif	o as in wrote
u as in Wuppertaal	i as in pick
ui as in Nelspruit	a as in gate
uu as in Suurbraak	o as in wrote
y as in Vanrhynsdorp	ai as in pain

Consonants

d as in Suikerbosrand	t as in runt
g as in Magersfontein	guttural ch as in the Scottish loch
tj as in Matjiesfontein	k as in key
v as in Nyslvlei	f as in fig
w as in Waterkant	v as in vase

Nguni group

The clicks in Nguni languages are the most unfamiliar and difficult sounds for English-speakers to pronounce. The three basic clicks – which, as it happens, occur in the names of three places featured in the Wild Coast section of chapter 4 – are: the **dental click** (transliterated using "c", as in the Cwebe Nature Reserve) made by pulling the tongue away from the front teeth as one would when expressing disapproval in "tsk tsk"; the **palatal click** (transliterated "q", as in Qholorha Mouth) made by pulling the tongue away from the palate as you would when trying to replicate the sound of a bubbly cork being popped; and the **lateral click** (transliterated "x", as in Nxaxo Mouth), made by pulling away the tongue from the side teeth. To complicate matters, each click can be pronounced in one of three ways (aspirated, nasalized or delayed) and may change when spoken in combination with other consonants.

Vowels

a as in KwaZulu	a as in father
e as in Cwebe	e as in bend
i as in Kwambonambi	ee as in flee
o as in Umkomaas	a as in tall
u as in Hluhluwe	u as in put

Consonants

dl as in Dlinza	aspirated ll as in the Welsh Llewellyn
g as in Haga-Haga	hard g as in hug

hl as in Hluhluwe	aspirated ll as in the Welsh Llewellyn (though often pronounced like the shl in shlemiel by English-speakers)
ph as in Mphephu	p as in pass followed followed by a rapid rush of air
r as in Qholorha	guttural ch as in the Scottish loch
ty as in Idutywa	approximately the initial sound in tube

Sotho group

Vowels

a as in Thaba	a as in father
e as in Motsekuoa	e as in he
o as in Mantsebo	o as in bore, but curtailed
u as in Butha	u as in full

Consonants

j as in Ha-Lejone	y as in yes
hl as in Hlotse	aspirated ll as in the Welsh Llewellyn (often pronounced like the shl in shlemiel by English-speakers)
ph as in Maphutseng	p as in pool
th as in Thaba	t as in tar

Basic greetings and farewells

ENGLISH	AFRIKAANS	NORTHERN SOTHO	SESOTHO	TSWANA	XHOSA	ZULU
Yes	Ja	Ee	E!	Ee	Ewe	Yebo
No	Nee	Aowa	Tjhe	Nnyaa	Hayi	Cha
Please	Asseblief	Hle.../...hle	(Ka kopo) hle	Tsweetswee	Nceda	Uxolo
Thank you	Dankie	Ke a leboga	Ke a leboha	Ke a leboga	Enkosi	Ngiyabonga
Excuse me	Verskoon my	Tshwarelo	Ntshwaerele	Intshwarele	Uxolo	Uxolo
Good morning	Goiemore	Thobela/dumela	Dumela (ng)	Dumela	Molo/bhota	Sawubona
Good afternoon	Goeiemiddag	Thobela/dumela	Dumela (ng)	Dumela	Molo/bhoto	Sawubona
Good evening	Goeinaand	Thobela/dumela	Fonaneng	Dumela	Molo/bhota	Sawubona
Goodbye	Totsiens	Sala gabotse/	Sala(ng) hantle	Sala sentle	Nisale kakuhle sepele gabotse	Sala kahle
See you later	Sien jou later	Re tla bonana	Re tla bonana	Ke tla go bona	Sobe sibonane	Sizobanana
Until we meet again	Totsiens	Go fihla re kopana gape	ho fihlela re bonana	Go fitlhelela re bonana gape	De sibonane kwakhona	Size sibonane
How do you do?	Aangename kennis?	Ke leboga go le tseba	Ke thabela ho o tseba	O tsogile jang?	Kunjani	Ninjani?
How are you?	Hoe gaan dit?	Le kae?	O/le sa phela?	O tsogile jang?	Kunjani?	Ninjani?
I'm fine, thanks	Goed dankie	Re gona	Ke phela hantle	Ke tsogile sentle enkosi	Ndiphilile,	Ngisaphila

Glossary

Words whose spelling makes it hard to guess how to render them have their approximate pronunciation given in italics. Where *gh* occurs in the pronunciation, it denotes the **ch** sound in the Scottish word lo**ch**. Sometimes we've used the letter "r" in the pronunciation even though the word in question doesn't contain this letter; for example, we've given the pronunciation of "Egoli" as "*air-gaw-lee*". In these instances the syllable containing the "r" is meant to represent a familiar word or sound from English; the "r" itself shouldn't be pronounced.

African In the context of South Africa, an indigenous South African

Aloe Family of spiky indigenous succulents, often with dramatic orange flowers

Apartheid (*apart-hate*) Term used from the 1940s for the National Party's official policy of "racial separation"

Arvie Afternoon

Assegai (*assa-guy*) Short stabbing spear introduced by Shaka to the Zulu armies

Baai Afrikaans word meaning "bay"; also a common suffix in place names eg Stilbaai

Bakkie (*bucky*) Light truck or van

Bantu (*bun-two*) Unscientific apartheid term for indigenous black people; in linguistics, a group of indigenous Southern African languages

Bantustan Term used under apartheid for the territories such as Transkei, reserved for Africans

Bergie A vagrant living on the slopes of Table Mountain in Cape Town

Black Imprecise term that sometimes refers collectively to Africans, Indians and coloureds, but more usually is used to mean Africans (see above)

Boer (*boor*) Literally "farmer", but also refers to early Dutch colonists at the Cape and Afrikaners

Boland (*boor-lunt*) Southern part of the Western Cape

Boma An enclosure or palisade

Boy Offensive term used to refer to an adult African man who is a servant

Bundu (approximately *boon-doo*, but with the vowels shortened) Wilderness or back country

Burgher Literally a citizen, but more specifically members of the Dutch community at the Cape in the seventeenth and eighteenth centuries

Bush See *bundu*

Bushman Southern Africa's earliest, but now almost extinct, inhabitants who lived by hunting and gathering

Bushveld Country composed largely of thorny bush

Cape Dutch Nineteenth-century, whitewashed, gabled style of architecture

Ciskei (*sis-kye*) Eastern Cape region west of the Kei River, declared a "self-governing territory" for Xhosa speakers in 1972, and now reincorporated into South Africa

Cocopan Small tip truck on rails used to transport gold ore

Coloured Mulattos or people of mixed race

Commandos Burgher military units during the Frontier and Boer wars

Dagga (*dugh-a*) Marijuana

Dagha (*dah-ga*) Mud used in indigenous construction

Dassie (*dussy*) Hyrax

Disa (*die-za*) One of twenty species of beautiful indigenous orchids, most famous of which is the red disa or "Pride of Table Mountain"

Dominee (*dour-min-ee*) Reverend (abbreviated to DS)

Donga Dry, eroded ditch

Dorp Country town or village (derived from Afrikaans)

Drift Fording point in a river (derived from Afrikaans)

Drostdy (*dross-tea*) Historically, the building of the *landdrost* or magistrate

Egoli (*air-gaw-lee*) Zulu name for Johannesburg (literally "city of gold")

Fanakalo or **fanagalo** (*fun-a-galaw*) Pidgin mixture of English, Zulu and Afrikaans used to facilitate communication between white foremen and African workers on the mines or farms

Fundi Expert

Fynbos (*fayn-boss*) Term for vast range of fine-leafed species that predominate in the southern part of the Western Cape (see p.846)

Girl Offensive term used to refer to an African woman who is a servant

Gogga (*gho-gha*) Creepy-crawly or insect

Griqua Person of mixed white, Bushman and Hottentot descent

Group Areas Act Now-defunct law passed in 1950 that provided for the establishment of separate areas for each "racial group"

Highveld High-lying areas of Gauteng and Mpumalanga

Homeland See Bantustan

Hottentot Now unfashionable term for indigenous Khoisan herders encountered by the first settlers at the Cape

Impi Zulu regiment

Indaba Zulu term meaning a group discussion and now used in South African English for any meeting or conference

Inkatha (*in-ka-ta*) Fiercely nationalist Zulu political party, formed in 1928 as a cultural organization

Is it? Really?

Jislaaik! (*yis-like*) Exclamation equivalent to "Geez!" or "Crikey!"

Joeys Affectionate abbreviation for Johannesburg

Jol Party, celebration

Just now In a while

Kaffir Highly objectionable term of abuse for Africans

Karoo Arid plateau that occupies a large proportion of the South African interior

Khoikhoi (*ghoy-ghoy*) Self-styled name of South Africa's original herding inhabitants

Kloof (*klo-ef*; rhymes with "boor") Ravine or gorge

Knobkerrie Wooden club

Kokerboom (both the first and last syllable rhyme with "boor") Quiver tree – a type of aloe found in the Northern Cape

Kopje Dutch spelling of *koppie*

Koppie Hillock

Kraal Enclosure of huts for farm animals or collection of traditional huts occupied by an extended family

Kramat (*crum-mutt*) Shrine of a Muslim holy man

Krans (*crunce*) Sheer cliff face

Laager (*lager*) A circular encampment of ox wagons, used as fortification by Voortrekkers

Lapa Courtyard of group of Ndebele houses; also used to describe an enclosed area at safari camps, where braais are held

Lebowa (*lab-o-a*) Now-defunct homeland for North Sotho speakers

Lekker Nice

Lobola (*la-ball-a*) Bride price, paid by an African man to his wife's parents

Location Old-fashioned term for segregated African area on the outskirts of a town or farm

Lowveld Low-lying subtropical region of Mpumalanga and Limpopo provinces

Malay Misnomer for Cape Muslims of Asian descent

Matjieshuis (*mikeys-hace*) Reed hut

Mbaqanga (*m-ba-kung-a*) A genre of music that originated in Soweto in the 1960s

Mbira (*m-beer-a*) African thumb piano, often made with a gourd

MK Umkhonto we Sizwe (Spear of the Nation), the armed wing of the ANC, now incorporated into the national army

Mlungu (*m-loon-goo*) African term for a white person, equivalent to honkie

Moffie (*mawf-ee*) Gay person

Muti (*moo-tee*) See *umuthi*

Nek Saddle between two mountains

Nguni (*n-goo-nee*) Group of southeastern Bantu-speaking people comprising Zulu, Xhosa and Swazi

Nkosi Sikelel 'i Afrika "God Bless Africa", anthem of the ANC and now of South Africa

Nyanga (*nyun-ga*) Traditional healer

Outspan A place set aside for animals to rest; can also mean to unharness oxen from a wagon

Pass Document that Africans used to have to carry at all times, which essentially rendered them aliens in their own country

Pastorie (*puss-tour-ee*) Parsonage

Platteland (*plutta-lunt*) Country districts

Poort Narrow pass through mountains along river course

Pronk (*prawnk*) Characteristic jump of springbok or impala

Protea National flower of South Africa

Qwaqwa Now-defunct homeland for South Sotho speakers

Raadsaal (the "d" is pronounced "t") Council or parliament building

Restcamp Accommodation for visitors to national parks

Robot Traffic light

Rondavel (*ron-daa-vil*, with the stress on the middle syllable) Circular building based on traditional African huts

SABC South African Broadcasting Authority

Sangoma (*sun-gom-a*) Traditional spirit medium and healer

Shebeen (*sha-bean*) Unlicensed tavern

Shell Ultra City Clean, bright stops along major national roads, with a filling station, restaurant, shop and sometimes a hotel.

Sjambok (*sham-bok*) Rawhide whip

Southeaster Prevailing wind in the Western Cape

Spaza shops (*spa-za*) Small stall or kiosk

Strandloper Name given by the Dutch to the indigenous people of the Cape; literally beachcomber

Stoep Veranda

Tackie Sneakers or plimsolls

Township Areas set aside under apartheid for Africans

Transkei (*trans-kye*) Now-defunct homeland for Xhosa speakers

Trekboer (*trek-boor*) Nomadic Afrikaner farmers, usually in the eighteenth and nineteenth century

Umuthi (*oo-moo-tee*) Traditional herbal medicine

Velskoen (*fel-scoon*) Rough suede shoes

Vlei (*flay*) Swamp

VOC Verenigde Oostindische Compagnie, the Dutch East India Company

Voortrekker (the first syllable rhymes with "boor") Dutch burghers who migrated inland in their ox wagons in the nineteenth century to escape British colonialism

ZAR Zuid Afrikaansche Republiek; an independent Boer republic that included present-day Gauteng, Mpumalanga and Limpopo provinces and which was Britain's main opponent in the Anglo-Boer War

Food and drink

Amarula Liqueur made from the berries of the marula tree

Begrafnisrys (*ba-ghruff-niss-race*) Literally "funeral rice"; traditional Cape Muslim dish of yellow rice cooked with raisins

Biltong Sun-dried salted strip of meat, chewed as a snack

Blatjang (*blutt-young*) Cape Muslim chutney that has become a standard condiment on South African dinner tables

Bobotie (*ba-boor-tea*) Traditional Cape curried mince topped with a savoury custard and often cooked with apricots and almonds

Boerekos (*boor-a-coss*) Farm food, usually consisting of loads of meat and vegetables cooked using butter and sugar

Boerewors (*boor-a-vorce*) Spicy lengths of sausage that are *de rigueur* at braais

Bokkoms Dried fish, much like salt fish

Braai or **braaivleis** (*bry-flace*) Barbecue

Bredie Cape vegetable and meat stew

Bunny chow Originally a curried takeaway served in a scooped-out half loaf of bread, but now often wrapped in a roti; a KwaZulu-Natal staple

Cane or cane spirit A potent vodka-like spirit distilled from sugar cane and generally mixed with a soft drink such as Coke

Cap Classique Sparkling wine fermented in the bottle in exactly the same way as Champagne; also called Méthode Cap Classic

Cape gooseberry Fruit of the physalis; a sweet yellow berry

Cape salmon or geelbek (*ghear-l-beck*) Delicious firm-fleshed sea fish (unrelated to Northern-hemisphere salmon).

Cape Velvet A sweet liqueur-and-cream dessert beverage that resembles Irish Cream liqueur

Denningvleis (*den-ning-flace*) Spicy traditional Cape lamb stew

Frikkadel Fried onion and meat balls

Geelbek See Cape salmon

Hanepoort (*harner-poort*) Delicious sweet dessert grape

Kabeljou (*cobble-yo*) Common South African marine fish, also called *kob*

Kerrievis (*kerry-fiss*) See Pickled fish

Kingklip Highly prized deepwater fish caught along the Atlantic and Indian ocean coasts

Kob See *kabeljou*

Koeksister (*cook-sister*) Deep-fried plaited doughnut, dripping with syrup

Maas or amasi or amaas Traditional African beverage consisting of naturally soured milk, available as a packaged dairy product in supermarkets

Maaskaas Cottage cheese made from *maas*

Mageu or mahewu or maheu (*ma-gh-weh*) Traditional African beer made from maize meal and water, now packaged and commercially available

Malva Very rich and very sweet traditional baked Cape dessert

Mampoer (*mum-poor*) Moonshine; home-distilled spirit made from soft fruit, commonly peaches

Mealie See *mielie*

Melktert (*melk-tairt*) Traditional Cape custard pie

Mielie Maize

Mielie pap (*mealy pup*) Maize porridge, varying from a thin mixture to a stiff one that can resemble polenta

Mopani worm (*ma-parny*) Black spotted caterpillar that is a delicacy among Africans in some parts of the country

Mqomboti (*m-qom-booty*) Traditional African beer made from fermented sorghum

Musselcracker Large-headed fish with powerful jaws and firm, white flesh

Naartjie (*nar-chee*) Tangerine or mandarin

Pap (*pup*) Porridge

Peri-peri Delicious hottish spice of Portuguese origin commonly used with grilled chicken

Perlemoen (*pear-la-moon*) Abalone

Pickled fish Traditional Cape dish of fish preserved with onions, vinegar and curry; available tinned in supermarkets

Pinotage A uniquely South African cultivar hybridized from Pinot Noir and Hermitage grapes and from which a wine of the same name is made

Potjiekos or potjie (*poy-key-kos*) Food cooked slowly over embers in a three-legged cast-iron pot

Putu (*poo-too*) Traditional African *mielie pap* (see above) prepared until it forms dry crumbs

Rooibos (*roy-boss*) tea Indigenous herbal tea; see p.307

Roti A chapati; called *rooti* in the Western Cape

Rusks Tasty biscuits made from sweetened bread that has been slow-cooked

Salmon trout Freshwater fish that is often smoked to create a cheaper and pretty good imitation of smoked salmon

Salomie Cape version of a roti; unleavened bread

Sambals (*sam-bills*) Accompaniments, such as chopped bananas, green peppers, desiccated coconut and chutney, served with Cape curries

Samp Traditional African dish of broken maize kernels, frequently cooked with beans

Skokiaan (*skok-ee-yan*) Potent home-brew

Smoorsnoek (*smore-snook*) Smoked *snoek*

Snoek (*snook*) Large fish that features in many traditional Cape recipes

Sosatie (*so-sah-ti*) Spicy skewered mince

Spanspek (*spon-speck*) A sweet melon

Steenbras (*ste-en-bruss*) A delicious white-fleshed fish

Van der Hum South African *naartjie*-flavoured liqueur

Vetkoek (*fet-cook*) Deep-fried doughnut-like cake

Waterblommetjiebredie (*vata-blom-a-key-bree-dee*) Cape meat stew made with waterlily rhizomes

Witblits (*vit-blitz*) Moonshine

Yellowtail Delicious darkish-fleshed marine fish

Travel store

UK & Ireland
Britain
Devon & Cornwall
Dublin **D**
Edinburgh **D**
England
Ireland
The Lake District
London
London **D**
London Mini Guide
Scotland
Scottish Highlands
& Islands
Wales

Europe
Algarve **D**
Amsterdam
Amsterdam **D**
Andalucía
Athens **D**
Austria
Baltic States
Barcelona
Barcelona **D**
Belgium &
Luxembourg
Berlin
Brittany & Normandy
Bruges **D**
Brussels
Budapest
Bulgaria
Copenhagen
Corfu
Corsica
Costa Brava **D**
Crete
Croatia
Cyprus
Czech & Slovak
Republics
Denmark
Dodecanese & East
Aegean Islands
Dordogne & The Lot
Europe
Florence & Siena
Florence **D**
France
Germany
Gran Canaria **D**
Greece
Greek Islands

Hungary
Ibiza & Formentera **D**
Iceland
Ionian Islands
Italy
The Italian Lakes
Languedoc &
Roussillon
Lanzarote &
Fuerteventura **D**
Lisbon **D**
The Loire Valley
Madeira **D**
Madrid **D**
Mallorca **D**
Mallorca & Menorca
Malta & Gozo **D**
Menorca
Moscow
The Netherlands
Norway
Paris
Paris **D**
Paris Mini Guide
Poland
Portugal
Prague
Prague **D**
Provence
& the Côte D'Azur
Pyrenees
Romania
Rome
Rome **D**
Sardinia
Scandinavia
Sicily
Slovenia
Spain
St Petersburg
Sweden
Switzerland
Tenerife &
La Gomera **D**
Turkey
Tuscany & Umbria
Venice & The Veneto
Venice **D**
Vienna

Asia
Bali & Lombok
Bangkok
Beijing

Cambodia
China
Goa
Hong Kong & Macau
Hong Kong
& Macau **D**
India
Indonesia
Japan
Kerala
Laos
Malaysia, Singapore
& Brunei
Nepal
The Philippines
Rajasthan, Dehli
& Agra
Singapore
Singapore **D**
South India
Southeast Asia
Sri Lanka
Taiwan
Thailand
Thailand's Beaches
& Islands
Tokyo
Vietnam

Australasia
Australia
Melbourne
New Zealand
Sydney

North America
Alaska
Baja California
Boston
California
Canada
Chicago
Colorado
Florida
The Grand Canyon
Hawaii
Honolulu **D**
Las Vegas **D**
Los Angeles
Maui **D**
Miami & South Florida
Montréal
New England
New Orleans **D**
New York City

New York City **D**
New York City Mini
Guide
Orlando & Walt
Disney World® **D**
Pacific Northwest
San Francisco
San Francisco **D**
Seattle
Southwest USA
Toronto
USA
Vancouver
Washington DC
Washington DC **D**
Yellowstone & The
Grand Tetons
Yosemite

Caribbean
& Latin America
Antigua & Barbuda **D**
Argentina
Bahamas
Barbados **D**
Belize
Bolivia
Brazil
Cancùn & Cozumel **D**
Caribbean
Central America
Chile
Costa Rica
Cuba
Dominican Republic
Dominican Republic **D**
Ecuador
Guatemala
Jamaica
Mexico
Peru
St Lucia **D**
South America
Trinidad & Tobago
Yúcatan

Africa & Middle East
Cape Town & the
Garden Route
Dubai **D**
Egypt
Gambia
Jordan

D: Rough Guide
DIRECTIONS for
short breaks

Available from all good bookstores

For more information go to www.roughguides.com

ROUGH GUIDES

Visit us online
www.roughguides.com

Information on over 25,000 destinations around the world

- **Read** Rough Guides' trusted travel info
- **Access** exclusive articles from Rough Guides authors
- **Update** yourself on new books, maps, CDs and other products
- **Enter** our competitions and win travel prizes
- **Share** ideas, journals, photos & travel advice with other users
- **Earn** points every time you contribute to the Rough Guide
  community and get rewards

BROADEN YOUR HORIZONS

"The most accurate maps in the world"

San Jose Mercury News

AFRICA

IT'S CLOSER THAN YOU THINK

THE AFRICA
CHANNEL

WHERE AFRICA COMES ALIVE!

An All New, All-English, 24/7 Destination Channel For
The World Traveler In You.

www.theafricachannel.com

Small print and

Index

A Rough Guide to Rough Guides

Published in 1982, the first Rough Guide – to Greece – was a student scheme that became a publishing phenomenon. Mark Ellingham, a recent graduate in English from Bristol University, had been travelling in Greece the previous summer and couldn't find the right guidebook. With a small group of friends he wrote his own guide, combining a highly contemporary, journalistic style with a thoroughly practical approach to travellers' needs.

The immediate success of the book spawned a series that rapidly covered dozens of destinations. And, in addition to impecunious backpackers, Rough Guides soon acquired a much broader and older readership that relished the guides' wit and inquisitiveness as much as their enthusiastic, critical approach and value-for-money ethos.

These days, Rough Guides include recommendations from shoestring to luxury and cover more than 200 destinations around the globe, including almost every country in the Americas and Europe, more than half of Africa and most of Asia and Australasia. Our ever-growing team of authors and photographers is spread all over the world, particularly in Europe, the USA and Australia.

In the early 1990s, Rough Guides branched out of travel, with the publication of Rough Guides to World Music, Classical Music and the Internet. All three have become benchmark titles in their fields, spearheading the publication of a wide range of books under the Rough Guide name.

Including the travel series, Rough Guides now number more than 350 titles, covering: phrasebooks, waterproof maps, music guides from Opera to Heavy Metal, reference works as diverse as Conspiracy Theories and Shakespeare, and popular culture books from iPods to Poker. Rough Guides also produce a series of more than 120 World Music CDs in partnership with World Music Network.

Visit www.roughguides.com to see our latest publications.

Rough Guide travel images are available for commercial licensing at www.roughguidespictures.com

Rough Guide credits

Text editor: Ann-Marie Shaw
Layout: Ankur Guha
Cartography: Rajesh Mishra
Picture editor: Emily Taylor
Production: Vicky Baldwin
Proofreader: Jan McCann
Cover design: Chloë Roberts
Editorial: London Ruth Blackmore, Alison Murchie, Karoline Thomas, Andy Turner, Keith Drew, Edward Aves, Alice Park, Lucy White, Jo Kirby, James Smart, Natasha Foges, Róisín Cameron, Emma Traynor, Emma Gibbs, Kathryn Lane, Christina Valhouli, Monica Woods, James Rice, Mani Ramaswamy, Joe Staines, Peter Buckley, Matthew Milton, Tracy Hopkins, Ruth Tidball; **New York** Andrew Rosenberg, Steven Horak, AnneLise Sorensen, April Isaacs, Ella Steim, Anna Owens, Sean Mahoney, Paula Neudorf, Courtney Miller; **Delhi** Madhavi Singh, Karen D'Souza
Design & Pictures: London Scott Stickland, Dan May, Diana Jarvis, Mark Thomas, Chloë Roberts, Nicole Newman, Sarah Cummins; **Delhi** Umesh Aggarwal, Ajay Verma, Jessica Subramanian, Pradeep Thapliyal, Sachin Tanwar, Anita Singh, Nikhil Agarwal
Production: Rebecca Short
Cartography: London Maxine Repath, Ed Wright, Katie Lloyd-Jones; **Delhi** Jai Prakash Mishra, Rajesh Chhibber, Ashutosh Bharti, Animesh Pathak, Jasbir Sandhu, Karobi Gogoi, Amod Singh, Alakananda Bhattacharya, Swati Handoo
Online: Narender Kumar, Rakesh Kumar, Amit Verma, Rahul Kumar, Ganesh Sharma, Debojit Borah, Saurabh Sati, Ravi Yadav
Marketing & Publicity: London Liz Statham, Niki Hanmer, Louise Maher, Jess Carter, Vanessa Godden, Vivienne Watton, Anna Paynton, Rachel Sprackett, Libby Jellie; **New York** Geoff Colquitt, Katy Ball, Nancy Lambert; **Delhi** Ragini Govind
Manager India: Punita Singh
Reference Director: Andrew Lockett
Operations Manager: Helen Phillips
PA to Publishing Director: Nicola Henderson
Publishing Director: Martin Dunford
Commercial Manager: Gino Magnotta
Managing Director: John Duhigg

Publishing information

This fifth edition published July 2008 by
Rough Guides Ltd,
80 Strand, London WC2R 0RL
345 Hudson St, 4th Floor,
New York, NY 10014, USA
14 Local Shopping Centre, Panchsheel Park,
New Delhi 110017, India
Distributed by the Penguin Group
Penguin Books Ltd,
80 Strand, London WC2R 0RL
Penguin Group (USA)
375 Hudson Street, NY 10014, USA
Penguin Group (Australia)
250 Camberwell Road, Camberwell,
Victoria 3124, Australia
Penguin Books Canada Ltd,
10 Alcorn Avenue, Toronto, Ontario,
Canada M4V 1E4
Penguin Group (NZ)
67 Apollo Drive, Mairangi Bay, Auckland 1310,
New Zealand
Cover concept by Peter Dyer.

Typeset in Bembo and Helvetica to an original design by Henry Iles.

Printed and bound in China

© Tony Pinchuck, Barbara McCrea, Donald Reid, Greg Mthembu-Salter 2008

No part of this book may be reproduced in any form without permission from the publisher except for the quotation of brief passages in reviews.

928pp includes index

A catalogue record for this book is available from the British Library

ISBN: 987-1-85828-449-1

The publishers and authors have done their best to ensure the accuracy and currency of all the information in **The Rough Guide to South Africa**, however, they can accept no responsibility for any loss, injury, or inconvenience sustained by any traveller as a result of information or advice contained in the guide.

1   3   5   7   9   8   6   4   2

Help us update

We've gone to a lot of effort to ensure that the fifth edition of **The Rough Guide to South Africa** is accurate and up to date. However, things change – places get "discovered", opening hours are notoriously fickle, restaurants and rooms raise prices or lower standards. If you feel we've got it wrong or left something out, we'd like to know, and if you can remember the address, the price, the hours, the phone number, so much the better.

Please send your comments with the subject line **"Rough Guide South Africa Update"** to ® mail@roughguides.com. We'll credit all contributions and send a copy of the next edition (or any other Rough Guide if you prefer) for the very best emails.

Have your questions answered and tell others about your trip at
⑨ community.roughguides.com

Acknowledgements

Tony would like to thank our brilliant editor Annie Shaw for her sure-footedness and light touch in leading the authors (while attending to children) across sometimes rough terrain, and for keeping her head on days that I felt like I'd lost mine. Also thanks to our picture editor Emily Taylor for digging up imaginative and evocative images that truly sparkle. To Nicci Joubert-van Doesburgh: thanks for putting in hard work and late nights; and to Barbara McCrea for her huge contribution to the book. A very big thanks to Gabriel Pinchuck (10) and his African penguin Mumble for operating the GPS on our research trips together and for being the best travelling companion in the world (well, in the Western Cape at least).

Barbara would like to thank our editor Annie Shaw for her steady hand and for being a pleasure to work with, Tony Pinchuck for his ability to be on track and finish projects; the overworked contributors and researchers Nicky Joubert-Van Doesburgh, Carolyn Howell, Liz Mackenzie and Christine Morling; my brother Robert McCrea for driving us around the Kruger area; Stanley Singer for Cape Town restaurant tips; Vanessa Berger for Grahamstown student hang-outs; my mother Pat McCrea for Eastern Cape back-up; the many unmentioned and generous people who gave us information, meals and help along the way; my travelling partner Hillel Braude who made all the research trips worthwhile; and finally my lively son Gabriel Pinchuck who has been doing Rough Guide research since he was born and especially liked the buffalos at Kruger. Thanks also to the following people and fabulous accommodation establishments who hosted or helped us: Beneta Bester at *Karukareb* and horse-riding in the spring flowers; *High Hopes* and *Acorns on Oak*, Greyton; *Moonstuck* on Pringle Bay; John at *Old Mill Lodge*, McGregor; *De Oude Herberg*, Tulbagh; Heather Dugmore at Sutherland; *Seven Church Street*, Montagu; *De Oue Werf*, Oudtshoorn; *Kleinplaas Holiday Resort*; elephant stroking at Buffelsdrift, Oudtshoorn; *Eight Bells Inn*, Robinson Pass; Leon at *Tradouw Guest House*, Barrydale; *Sanbona Game Lodge*, Grant and Marie at the *Retreat at Groenfontein*, Calitzdorp; Lisa at *Onse Rus*, Prince Albert; Dr Judy Maguire's archelogical walk to rock paintings on her Prince Albert farm; *Klippe Rivier Homestead*, Swellendam; *Two Feathers Horse Trails* Swellendam; *Pebble Beach B&B*, Algulhas; *Arniston Hotel*; *Buchu Bush Camp*, De Hoop; *Verfheuwel Guestfarm*, De Hoop; David Bellamy at the *Art Hotel*, Riebeek Kasteel; *Pampoenfontein Farm Cottages*, Porterville; *Dunes Guest House*, Paternoster; Bill and Janine at *Oudrif*; *Peterfield Farm Cottages*, Citrusdal; *De Pakhuys* and the memorable Land Rover trip to Wuppertal; Fish River Horse Safaris, Port Alfred; Bella at *Villa de Mer*, Port Alfred; *Cavers Farm*, Bedford; *Oribi Haven*, Kasouga; *Sabi River Sun*; *Eva at Big 5 Country*, Hazyview; *Canopy tour*, Hazyview; *Elephant Sanctuary*; Shangana Cultural Village; *Moholoholo Animal Rehab*; *Timbavati Safari Lodge*; Tina Bohm of *Malachite Transfers*; and to the dreamy Kruger safari lodges *Umlani*, *Honeyguide*, *Sabi Sabi*, *Chitwa Chitwa* and *Djuma*.

Carlos would like to thank Hildur Amato and Ben Amato.

Lone would like to thank her three faithful travel companions, Nana Muschenheim, Sylvia Smith and Paul West, who took it in turn to humour her on her various impossible whims. She would also like to express her gratitude to all the many helpful people she met en route – you know who you are. You made travelling in South Africa and especially Swaziland a doddle.

Ross would like to thank the following people for their help and, in some cases, friendship and warm hospitality: Elaine and Brian Agar, Jane and Jonathan Chennells, Hettie and Derick Holman, Pet Trümpelmann, Ruth Walker, Elize Mcallister, Richard Chennells, Patrick Moroney, Yael Duncan, Herbert Howe, Lee and Bill McGaw, Dallas Reed, Normaine and Dave Short, Debbi Pretorius, Michelle and Micky Brooks, Herliane Portenschlager, Perry Winkel, Melissa Klurman, Gabriele Klink, Ian Duncan, Maria and Doddy, Peter Koen, Kian Barker, Meg Van Maasdyk, Graham Chennells, Sharon Lewis, Des and Monique James, Shelley Klomfass and Jeremy Robertson.

In Lesotho, **Adam** and **Katrine** would like to thank the two Adams in Maseru; Sean, Paula and Craig in Semonkong; Juliet in Leribe plus the other development workers and staff from Skillshare International and AVI who gave us their tips. Much appreciation goes to the ever-cheerful ladies at the tourism office in Maseru; Lesotho Tourism Development Corporation; and our patient colleagues Berry, Mapitsoe and Mokome who never complained at our long list of questions! Finally, thanks to the staff from all the places where we rested our weary heads, including *Malealea Lodge*, *Sani Top Chalets* and *Orion Mohale Lodge*, who usually went out of their way to help our research.

Finally, **the editor** would like to thank the authors and contributors for being so easy to work with, Ankur Guha for flexible and patient typesetting, Emily Taylor for inspired pictures and many convivial phone conferences, Rajesh Mishra (and Katie Lloyd-Jones) for delivering great maps to impossible deadlines, Jan McCann for eagle-eyed proofreading, and Jo Kirby for her support and guidance.

Readers' letters

Thanks to all the readers who have taken the time to write in with comments and suggestions (and apologies if we've inadvertently omitted or misspelt anyone's name):

Renee Ambito, Skye Aspden, Pieter Badenhorst, Lucy Barker and Philip Normington, Irene and Rienzi Beckett, Keith Beelders, Liza Botha, Jo Brink, Bertus and Juliet Britz, David Broadbent, Dick Butler, Barbara Clark, Kathleen Clay, Anthony Crawford Brunt, Elliot Cahn, Mike Cavanagh,

Emily Charles and Alex Hatch, Mike and Eileen Christie, Robin Christie, Jill Clark, Fiona Cole, David Cooknell, Erin Conradie, Aidan and Heather Corr, Meg Cowper-Lewis, Marianne Crane, Erika Cule, Carisa Cunningham, David and Tina Davies, Ruth Denton, Herbert Drewniok, Dave and Melanie Dudley, Moira Dunworth, Jannie du Toit, Audrey and Melvyn du Valle, Christine Duxbury, Laurence Elton, Simon Eriksen, Huw Evans, Jill Foster, Chris Frean, Tanja Gehren, Barbara Giacomin, Heather Giannandrea, Kathy Gie, Tony Gloster, Meg Goodare, Hana Hall, Carol Hamilton, Cathy Harris, Haley Harvey, Gavin Heath, Niels and Margret Hendriks, Rod Hirst, Nigel Hollington, Jane Holman, Clive Hooper, Simon Hoten, David Hoult, Joy Hull, Bob Hyde, Ran Jan, Decima Jones, Laurence Jones, R. A. Kastell, Carole and Alan Kenyon, Uli Kress, J.R.W Kronfield, David Land, Annie Lavery, Eddy le Couvreur, Robby Letsholo, Grant Lindsay, Yolande Lombard, Rodney Lord, Kim McConkey and Chandra Ramarao, Peter and Lois McDonald, Stella and John Macdougall, John Major, Linda Mannheim, Genevieve Marshall, Shelley Mason, John Miller, Jo Moskon, Darragh Morgan, Dr David Murphy, Dwight Newman, Alex Nikolic, Stuart and Sue Nuttal, Jarl Olsen, Alan Palmer, David Pearson, Barbara Pellow, Lloyd Perry, Joyce Plotnikoff and Richard Woolfson, Tessa and Harry Rajak, Stephen and Mary Rea, John Read, Dallas Reed, Laurent Ribes, Neil Richmond, Carolyn and Julia Rigg, Hazel Rofe, Su Roxburgh and Steve Parkes, Joanne Rushby, Edmund Salomons, Noam Schimmel, Nicholas M Schmidt, Amanda Sebestyen, Nick Sebley, Dave Short, Daan and Zena Smit, Xolile Speelman, Angela Speight, Mike Tayler-Smith, June Taylor, Chris and Jenny Tily, Amiene van der Merwe, Adrie and Adrie van Doorn, Helen & Martin Vegoda, Hans Verstrate, Marie Verwey, Dominique and Brigitte Vigliotti, Angela Warren, Nigel Watson, Helmut and Christian Wilderer, Richard and Ying Wiseman, Thomas Wiser, Judge R.H. Zulman.

Photo credits

All photos © Rough Guides except the following:

Cover
Front cover: Landscape with tree and mountain, near Capetown © Getty
Back cover: African elephant profile © Steve Bloom/Getty
Inside back cover: Rural Xhosa children playing outdoors © visualsafari.com/Alamy

Title page
Ndebele woman's headband and necklaces © Martin Harvey

Full page
Baby elephant with mother © Martin Harvey

Introduction
Aloe plant in Kruger National Park © Bill Bachmann/Danita Delimont Agency/Digital Railroad
Rock art in Cederberg Wilderness © Friedrich von Horsten/Alamy
King Protea blooms © Frans Lanting/Corbis
Cape Town, City Hall © PCL/Alamy
Johannesburg skyline © Dennis Cox/Alamy
Roofs of beach huts, St James, Cape Town © Charles O'Rear/Corbis
A pair of African penguins on Boulders Beach near Simon's Town © Jon Hicks/Alamy
Clifton Beach in Bantry Bay © Rainer Jahns Photography/Digital Railroad

Things not to miss
01 Drakensberg mountains rising above clouds © Roger De La Harpe/Gallo Images/Corbis
02 Halfmens – Richtersveld © Lanz Von Hörsten/ Courtesy of South African Tourism
03 A Hindu couple partake in a ritual ceremony at their wedding, Durban © Rajesh Jantilal/ epa/Corbis
04 Namaqualand daisies, Goegap Nature Reserve © Gerhard Dreyer/Courtesy of South African Tourism
05 Cape Point © Courtesy of South African Tourism
06 White sand dunes with blue sky, De Hoop Nature Reserve © Friedrich von Horsten/ Alamy
07 Humpback whale, Western Cape © Rod Haestier/ Courtesy of South African Tourism
08 Sani Pass © Richard Crampton/Rex Features
09 Nelson Mandela's prison cell © Jean Miele/ Corbis
10 Madikwe Game Reserve © www.seasonsinafrica.com
11 Bulungula Lodge © Courtesy of Bulungula Lodge
12 Kliptown, Soweto © Jon Hrusa/epa/Corbis
13 Donkeys crossing Black Umfolozi River, Hluhluwe © Roger De La Harpe/photolibrary
14 Basotho Cultural Village © Walter Knirr/ Courtesy of South African Tourism
15 Addo Elephant National Park © Martin Harvey
17 Swartberg Nature Reserve, Gamkas © Walter Knirr/Courtesy of South African Tourism
18 Pony trekking © Suzanne Porter
19 The Wild Coast © Courtesy of South African Tourism
20 The Wine routes © Courtesy of South African Tourism
21 Whitewater rafting © Ariadne Van Zandbergen/ photolibrary
22 Don Laka, South Africa © Eric Miller/iAfrika Photos

ROUGH GUIDES

SMALL PRINT

Index

Map entries are in colour.

INDEX

H

INDEX

INDEX

Q

R

S

INDEX

Map symbols

maps are listed in the full index using coloured text

----	International boundary	⚐	Campsite
---	Chapter division boundary	🛆	Picnic site
-- ··	Provincial boundary	🏛	Monument
N2	National road	⚑	Border crossing post
R62	Regional road	ⓘ	Information centre
M8	Metropolitan road	◆	Place of interest
	Minor road	⚔	Battlefield
	Pedestrianized street	∴	Ruins
	Untarred road		Hide
=====	Dirt track	♜	Castle
—○—	Railway line and station	⌒	Cave
•—•	Cable car	🛆	Lighthouse
---	Tram line	♣	Vineyard
-----	Path	✉	Post office
⟋	River and dam	⊞	Hospital
⏑	Bridge		Fuel station
■ ■ ■	Wall	P	Parking
⊠	Gate	⚑	Golf course
\\\|//	Hill shading		Swimming pool
⌃⌃	Mountain range	⚑	Public gardens
▲	Peak	✡	Synagogue
⫽	Mountain pass		Mosque
⚎	Waterfall		Church (town maps)
⸕	Swamp		Building
⚘	Viewpoint	⬭	Stadium
★	Bus stop	+++	Christian cemetery
✈	Airport		Park/National park
◉	Accommodation		Beach
▣	Restaurant		Forest/nature reserve
⌂	Rest camp